CIVIL PROCEDURE IN CALIFORNIA

STATE AND FEDERAL

2026 Edition

Supplemental Materials for Use with All Civil Procedure Casebooks

■ ■ ■

David I. Levine
Hon. Raymond L. Sullivan Professor of Law
University of California
College of the Law, San Francisco

AMERICAN CASEBOOK SERIES®

WEST ACADEMIC

860 Blue Gentian Road, Suite 350
Eagan, MN 55121
1-877-888-1330

Published in the United States of America

ISBN: 979-8-31770-422-3

PREFACE TO THE 2026 EDITION

In learning Civil Procedure, it is often quite useful to compare how different judicial systems handle certain problems. Indeed, in many places, a lawyer cannot practice without familiarity with at least two systems of procedure, one for the state courts and one for federal court. Some states, notably California, have not simply adopted the Federal Rules of Civil Procedure for use in their own courts. For these reasons, it seemed useful to compile a rule book and case supplement that would enable professors of Civil Procedure, particularly those teaching in California law schools, to use a comparative perspective. The book is designed to be used in conjunction with any of the existing casebooks in Civil Procedure.

This edition includes: a complete version of the Federal Rules of Civil Procedure with selected Advisory Committee Notes, as well as selected Federal Rules of Appellate Procedure; selected federal statutes on the judiciary; a substantial selection of provisions from the California Code of Civil Procedure; selected federal and California constitutional provisions; selected California Rules of Court; a comparative table of rules; and edited cases from California appellate courts. The cases were chosen because they are illustrative of important areas in which California procedure differs from its federal counterpart. In editing the judicial opinions and the notes of the Advisory Committee on the Federal Rules of Civil Procedure, case and statute citations, as well as footnotes, have been omitted without specifying. Numbered footnotes retain the original numbering; lettered footnotes have been added by the editor.

Finally, I thank the late Mary Kay Kane for her many years of work on this project. She helped to develop the first edition of this supplement. She continued to lend her excellent judgment and keen eye through many of the subsequent editions. All remaining errors, alas, are mine alone.

DIL

San Francisco, California
April 2026

TABLE OF CONTENTS

Comparative Table

Fed.R.Civ.P.	Cal.Code Civ.Proc.
2	§ 307*
3	§§ 350*, 411.10
4	§§ 412.20, 412.30–417.30, 485.010, 485.210–.240, 492.010
4(m)	§§ 583.210, 583.250
5	§§ 465*, 1011–13a
6(b)	§§ 12–13(b)
7	§§ 422.10, 1010
8	§§ 425.10–.12, 431.10–.30
8(c)	§ 360.5
9	§§ 456–57*
10	§§ 422.30–.40*
11	§§ 128.5, 128.7, 177.5, 178, 446
12	§§ 418.10, 430.10–.80, 472a–472c, 1014
12(c)	§ 597
12(f)	§§ 435–37
13	§§ 426.10–.60, 428.20, 428.50, 428.80
14	§§ 428.10, 428.70
15	§§ 469–70, 471.5–472, 473
15(b)	§ 309
15(d)	§ 464
17(a)	§§ 367, 369*, 374*
18	§§ 427.10, 428.30
19	§ 389
20(a)	§§ 378–79, 382
22	§§ 386–386.6
24	§ 387
26	§§ 2016.090, 2017.010–2019.210, 2024.010–.060, 2034.010–.730
27	§§ 2035.010–2036.050
30	§§ 2016.030, 2020.010–.510, 2025.010–.340
31	§§ 2028.010–.080

* Not included due to similarity to Fed.R.Civ.P.

Fed.R.Civ.P.	Cal.Code Civ.Proc.
33	§§ 2030.010–.410
34	§§ 2031.010–.510
35	§§ 2032.010–.650
36	§§ 2033.010–.740
37	§§ 1991–1992, 2023.010–.040
38	§§ 592, 631
40	§§ 629–30
41	§§ 581, 583.310, 583.330, 583.360, 583.410, 583.420
41(b)	§ 583.130
42	§ 1048
45	§§ 1987–87, 1989
48	§§ 193, 194, 197, 198, 203, 204, 205, 613, 618
49	§§ 624–25
50	§ 581c
51	§ 607a
52	§§ 632, 909
54	§§ 1032, 1033.5
54(d)	§§ 1021, 1021.5–.7
55	§§ 473.5, 474, 585, 587
56	§§ 437c, 2015.5
57	§ 106c*
59	§§ 657, 659, 659a, 662, 662.5, 663
60(b)	§ 473
65	§§ 527, 529
66	§ 564
68	§ 998

F.R.A.P.	Cal.Code Civ.Proc.
38	§§ 907, 916, 917.1

* Not included due to similarity to Fed.R.Civ.P.

Civil Procedure in California

State and Federal

2026 Edition

Supplemental Materials for Use with All Civil Procedure Casebooks

FEDERAL RULES OF CIVIL PROCEDURE FOR THE UNITED STATES DISTRICT COURTS

■ ■ ■

As Amended to December 1, 2025

Table of Rules

Title I. Scope of Rules; Form of Action

Title II. Commencing an Action; Service of Process, Pleadings, Motions, and Orders

Title III. Pleadings and Motions

Title VII. Judgment

Title VIII. Provisional and Final Remedies

Title IX. Special Proceedings

Title X. District Courts and Clerks: Conducting Business; Issuing Orders

Title XI. General Provisions

TITLE I. SCOPE OF RULES; FORM OF ACTION

Rule 1. Scope and Purpose

These rules govern the procedure in all civil actions and proceedings in the United States district courts, except as stated in Rule 81. They should be construed, administered, and employed by the court and the parties to secure the just, speedy, and inexpensive determination of every action and proceeding.

(As amended Dec. 29, 1948, eff. Oct. 20, 1949; Feb. 28, 1966, eff. July 1, 1966; Apr. 22, 1993, eff. Dec. 1, 1993; Apr. 30, 2007, eff. Dec. 1, 2007; Apr. 29, 2015, eff. Dec. 1, 2015.)

NOTES OF ADVISORY COMMITTEE ON RULES

2007 AMENDMENT

The language of Rule 1 has been amended as part of the general restyling of the Civil Rules to make them more easily understood and to make style and terminology consistent throughout the rules. These changes are intended to be stylistic only.

The merger of law, equity, and admiralty practice is complete. There is no need to carry forward the phrases that initially accomplished the merger.

The former reference to "suits of a civil nature" is changed to the more modern "civil actions and proceedings." This change does not affect such questions as whether the Civil Rules apply to summary proceedings created by statute.

* * *

5. *Other Changes*

The style changes to the rules are intended to make no changes in substantive meaning. A very small number of minor technical amendments that arguably do change meaning were approved separately from the restyled rules, but become effective at the same time. An example is adding "e-mail address" to the information that must be included in pleadings. * * *

2015 AMENDMENT

Rule 1 is amended to emphasize that just as the court should construe and administer these rules to secure the just, speedy, and inexpensive determination of every action, so the parties share the responsibility to employ the rules in the same way. Most lawyers and parties cooperate to achieve these ends. But discussions of ways to improve the administration of civil justice regularly include pleas to discourage over-use, misuse, and abuse of procedural tools that increase cost and result in delay. Effective advocacy is consistent with—and indeed depends upon—cooperative and proportional use of procedure.

This amendment does not create a new or independent source of sanctions. Neither does it abridge the scope of any other of these rules.

Rule 2. One Form of Action

There is one form of action—the civil action.

(As amended Apr. 30, 2007, eff. Dec. 1, 2007.)

TITLE II. COMMENCING AN ACTION; SERVICE OF PROCESS, PLEADINGS, MOTIONS, AND ORDERS

Rule 3. Commencing an Action

A civil action is commenced by filing a complaint with the court.

(As amended Apr. 30, 2007, eff. Dec. 1, 2007.)

Rule 4. Summons

(a) Contents; Amendments.

(1) ***Contents.*** A summons must:

(A) name the court and the parties;

(B) be directed to the defendant;

(C) state the name and address of the plaintiff's attorney or—if unrepresented—of the plaintiff;

(D) state the time within which the defendant must appear and defend;

(E) notify the defendant that a failure to appear and defend will result in a default judgment against the defendant for the relief demanded in the complaint;

(F) be signed by the clerk; and

(G) bear the court's seal.

(2) ***Amendments.*** The court may permit a summons to be amended.

(b) Issuance. On or after filing the complaint, the plaintiff may present a summons to the clerk for signature and seal. If the summons is properly completed, the clerk must sign, seal, and issue it to the plaintiff for service on the defendant. A summons—or a copy of a summons that is addressed to multiple defendants—must be issued for each defendant to be served.

(c) Service.

(1) ***In General.*** A summons must be served with a copy of the complaint. The plaintiff is responsible for having the summons and complaint served within the time allowed by Rule 4(m) and must furnish the necessary copies to the person who makes service.

(2) ***By Whom.*** Any person who is at least 18 years old and not a party may serve a summons and complaint.

(3) ***By a Marshal or Someone Specially Appointed.*** At the plaintiff's request, the court may order that service be made by a United States marshal or deputy marshal or by a person specially appointed by the court. The court must so order if the plaintiff is authorized to proceed in forma pauperis under 28 U.S.C. § 1915 or as a seaman under 28 U.S.C. § 1916.

(d) Waiving Service.

(1) ***Requesting a Waiver.*** An individual, corporation, or association that is subject to service under Rule 4(e), (f), or (h) has a duty to avoid unnecessary expenses of serving the summons. The plaintiff may notify such a defendant that an action has been commenced and request that the defendant waive service of a summons. The notice and request must:

(A) be in writing and be addressed:

(i) to the individual defendant; or

(ii) for a defendant subject to service under Rule 4(h), to an officer, a managing or general agent, or any other agent authorized by appointment or by law to receive service of process;

(B) name the court where the complaint was filed;

(C) be accompanied by a copy of the complaint, 2 copies of the waiver form appended to this Rule 4, and a prepaid means for returning the form;

(D) inform the defendant, using the form appended to this Rule 4, of the consequences of waiving and not waiving service;

(E) state the date when the request is sent;

(F) give the defendant a reasonable time of at least 30 days after the request was sent—or at least 60 days if sent to the defendant outside any judicial district of the United States—to return the waiver; and

(G) be sent by first-class mail or other reliable means.

(2) ***Failure to Waive.*** If a defendant located within the United States fails, without good cause, to sign and return a waiver requested by a plaintiff located within the United States, the court must impose on the defendant:

(A) the expenses later incurred in making service; and

(B) the reasonable expenses, including attorney's fees, of any motion required to collect those service expenses.

(3) ***Time to Answer After a Waiver.*** A defendant who, before being served with process, timely returns a waiver need not serve an answer to the complaint until 60 days after the request was sent—or until 90 days after it was sent to the defendant outside any judicial district of the United States.

(4) ***Results of Filing a Waiver.*** When the plaintiff files a waiver, proof of service is not required and these rules apply as if a summons and complaint had been served at the time of filing the waiver.

(5) ***Jurisdiction and Venue Not Waived.*** Waiving service of a summons does not waive any objection to personal jurisdiction or to venue.

(e) **Serving an Individual Within a Judicial District of the United States.** Unless federal law provides otherwise, an individual—other than a minor, an incompetent person, or a person whose waiver has been filed—may be served in a judicial district of the United States by:

(1) following state law for serving a summons in an action brought in courts of general jurisdiction in the state where the district court is located or where service is made; or

(2) doing any of the following:

(A) delivering a copy of the summons and of the complaint to the individual personally;

(B) leaving a copy of each at the individual's dwelling or usual place of abode with someone of suitable age and discretion who resides there; or

(C) delivering a copy of each to an agent authorized by appointment or by law to receive service of process.

(f) **Serving an Individual in a Foreign Country.** Unless federal law provides otherwise, an individual—other than a minor, an incompetent person, or a person whose waiver has been filed—may be served at a place not within any judicial district of the United States:

(1) by any internationally agreed means of service that is reasonably calculated to give notice, such as those authorized by the Hague Convention on the Service Abroad of Judicial and Extrajudicial Documents;

(2) if there is no internationally agreed means, or if an international agreement allows but does not specify other means, by a method that is reasonably calculated to give notice:

(A) as prescribed by the foreign country's law for service in that country in an action in its courts of general jurisdiction;

(B) as the foreign authority directs in response to a letter rogatory or letter of request; or

(C) unless prohibited by the foreign country's law, by:

(i) delivering a copy of the summons and of the complaint to the individual personally; or

(ii) using any form of mail that the clerk addresses and sends to the individual and that requires a signed receipt; or

(3) by other means not prohibited by international agreement, as the court orders.

(g) Serving a Minor or an Incompetent Person. A minor or an incompetent person in a judicial district of the United States must be served by following state law for serving a summons or like process on such a defendant in an action brought in the courts of general jurisdiction of the state where service is made. A minor or an incompetent person who is not within any judicial district of the United States must be served in the manner prescribed by Rule 4(f)(2)(A), (f)(2)(B), or (f)(3).

(h) Serving a Corporation, Partnership, or Association. Unless federal law provides otherwise or the defendant's waiver has been filed, a domestic or foreign corporation, or a partnership or other unincorporated association that is subject to suit under a common name, must be served:

(1) in a judicial district of the United States:

(A) in the manner prescribed by Rule 4(e)(1) for serving an individual; or

(B) by delivering a copy of the summons and of the complaint to an officer, a managing or general agent, or any other agent authorized by appointment or by law to receive service of process and—if the agent is one authorized by statute and the statute so requires—by also mailing a copy of each to the defendant; or

(2) at a place not within any judicial district of the United States, in any manner prescribed by Rule 4(f) for serving an individual, except personal delivery under (f)(2)(C)(i).

(i) Serving the United States and Its Agencies, Corporations, Officers, or Employees.

(1) ***United States.*** To serve the United States, a party must:

(A)(i) deliver a copy of the summons and of the complaint to the United States attorney for the district where the action is brought—or to an assistant United States attorney or clerical employee whom the United States attorney designates in a writing filed with the court clerk—or

(ii) end a copy of each by registered or certified mail to the civil-process clerk at the United States attorney's office;

(B) send a copy of each by registered or certified mail to the Attorney General of the United States at Washington, D.C.; and

(C) if the action challenges an order of a nonparty agency or officer of the United States, send a copy of each by registered or certified mail to the agency or officer.

(2) ***Agency; Corporation; Officer or Employee Sued in an Official Capacity.*** To serve a United States agency or corporation, or a United States officer or employee sued only in an official capacity, a party must serve the United States and also send a copy of the summons and of the complaint by registered or certified mail to the agency, corporation, officer, or employee.

(3) ***Officer or Employee Sued Individually.*** To serve a United States officer or employee sued in an individual capacity for an act or omission occurring in connection with duties performed on the United States' behalf (whether or not the officer or employee is also sued in an official capacity), a party must serve the United States and also serve the officer or employee under Rule 4(e), (f), or (g).

(4) ***Extending Time.*** The court must allow a party a reasonable time to cure its failure to:

(A) serve a person required to be served under Rule 4(i)(2), if the party has served either the United States attorney or the Attorney General of the United States; or

(B) serve the United States under Rule 4(i)(3), if the party has served the United States officer or employee.

(j) Serving a Foreign, State, or Local Government.

(1) ***Foreign State.*** A foreign state or its political subdivision, agency, or instrumentality must be served in accordance with 28 U.S.C. § 1608.

(2) ***State or Local Government.*** A state, a municipal corporation, or any other state-created governmental organization that is subject to suit must be served by:

(A) delivering a copy of the summons and of the complaint to its chief executive officer; or

(B) serving a copy of each in the manner prescribed by that state's law for serving a summons or like process on such a defendant.

(k) Territorial Limits of Effective Service.

(1) ***In General.*** Serving a summons or filing a waiver of service establishes personal jurisdiction over a defendant:

(A) who is subject to the jurisdiction of a court of general jurisdiction in the state where the district court is located;

(B) who is a party joined under Rule 14 or 19 and is served within a judicial district of the United States and not more than 100 miles from where the summons was issued;

(C) when authorized by a federal statute.

(2) ***Federal Claim Outside State-Court Jurisdiction.*** For a claim that arises under federal law, serving a summons or filing a waiver of service establishes personal jurisdiction over a defendant if:

(A) the defendant is not subject to jurisdiction in any state's courts of general jurisdiction; and

(B) exercising jurisdiction is consistent with the United States Constitution and laws.

(*l*) Proving Service.

(1) ***Affidavit Required.*** Unless service is waived, proof of service must be made to the court. Except for service by a United States marshal or deputy marshal, proof must be by the server's affidavit.

(2) ***Service Outside the United States.*** Service not within any judicial district of the United States must be proved as follows:

(A) if made under Rule 4(f)(1), as provided in the applicable treaty or convention; or

(B) if made under Rule 4(f)(2) or (f)(3), by a receipt signed by the addressee, or by other evidence satisfying the court that the summons and complaint were delivered to the addressee.

(3) ***Validity of Service; Amending Proof.*** Failure to prove service does not affect the validity of service. The court may permit proof of service to be amended.

(m) Time Limit for Service. If a defendant is not served within 90 days after the complaint is filed, the court—on motion or on its own after notice to the plaintiff—must dismiss the action without prejudice against that defendant or order that service be made within a specified time. But if the plaintiff shows good cause for the failure, the court must extend the time for service for an appropriate period. This subdivision (m) does not apply to service in a foreign country under Rule 4(f), 4(h)(2), or 4(j)(1), or to service of a notice under Rule 71.1(d)(3)(A).

(n) Asserting Jurisdiction over Property or Assets.

(1) ***Federal Law.*** The court may assert jurisdiction over property if authorized by a federal statute. Notice to claimants of the property must be given as provided in the statute or by serving a summons under this rule.

(2) ***State Law.*** On a showing that personal jurisdiction over a defendant cannot be obtained in the district where the action is brought by reasonable efforts to serve a summons under this rule, the court may assert jurisdiction over the defendant's assets found in the district. Jurisdiction is acquired by seizing the assets under the circumstances and in the manner provided by state law in that district.

Rule 4. Notice of a Lawsuit and Request to Waive Service of Summons.

(Caption)

To (*name the defendant or—if the defendant is a corporation, partnership, or association—name an officer or agent authorized to receive service*):

Why are you getting this?

A lawsuit has been filed against you, or the entity you represent, in this court under the number shown above. A copy of the complaint is attached.

This is not a summons, or an official notice from the court. It is a request that, to avoid expenses, you waive formal service of a summons by signing and returning the enclosed waiver. To avoid these expenses, you must return the signed waiver within (*give at least 30 days or at least 60 days if the defendant is outside any judicial district of the United States*) from the date shown below, which is the date this notice was sent. Two copies of the waiver form are enclosed, along with a stamped, self-addressed envelope or other prepaid means for returning one copy. You may keep the other copy.

What happens next?

If you return the signed waiver, I will file it with the court. The action will then proceed as if you had been served on the date the waiver is filed, but no summons will be served on you and you will have 60 days from the date this notice is sent (see the date below) to answer the complaint (or 90 days if this notice is sent to you outside any judicial district of the United States).

If you do not return the signed waiver within the time indicated, I will arrange to have the summons and complaint served on you. And I will ask the court to require you, or the entity you represent, to pay the expenses of making service.

Please read the enclosed statement about the duty to avoid unnecessary expenses.

I certify that this request is being sent to you on the date below.

Date: ______________

____

(Signature of the attorney or unrepresented party)

____

(Printed name)

____

(Address)

____

(E-mail address)

____

(Telephone number)

Rule 4. Waiver of the Service of Summons.

(Caption)

To (*name the plaintiff's attorney or the unrepresented plaintiff*):

I have received your request to waive service of a summons in this action along with a copy of the complaint, two copies of this waiver form, and a prepaid means of returning one signed copy of the form to you.

I, or the entity I represent, agree to save the expense of serving a summons and complaint in this case.

I understand that I, or the entity I represent, will keep all defenses or objections to the lawsuit, the court's jurisdiction, and the venue of the action, but that I waive any objections to the absence of a summons or of service.

I also understand that I, or the entity I represent, must file and serve an answer or a motion under Rule 12 within 60 days from __________, the date when this request was sent (or 90 days if it was sent outside the United States). If I fail to do so, a default judgment will be entered against me or the entity I represent.

Date: ______________

____

(Signature of the attorney or unrepresented party)

____

(Printed name)

____

(Address)

____

(E-mail address)

____

(Telephone number)

(Attach the following)

Duty to Avoid Unnecessary Expenses of Serving a Summons

Rule 4 of the Federal Rules of Civil Procedure requires certain defendants to cooperate in saving unnecessary expenses of serving a summons and complaint. A defendant who is located in the United States and who fails to return a signed waiver of service requested by a plaintiff located in the United States will be required to pay the expenses of service, unless the defendant shows good cause for the failure.

"Good cause" does not include a belief that the lawsuit is groundless, or that it has been brought in an improper venue, or that the court has no jurisdiction over this matter or over the defendant or the defendant's property.

If the waiver is signed and returned, you can still make these and all other defenses and objections, but you cannot object to the absence of a summons or of service.

If you waive service, then you must, within the time specified on the waiver form, serve an answer or a motion under Rule 12 on the plaintiff and file a copy with the court. By signing and returning the waiver form, you are allowed more time to respond than if a summons had been served.

(As amended Jan. 21, 1963, eff. July 1, 1963; Feb. 28, 1966, eff. July 1, 1966; Apr. 29, 1980, eff. Aug. 1, 1980; Pub.L. 97–462, § 2, Jan. 12, 1983, 96 Stat. 2527; Mar. 2, 1987, eff. Aug. 1, 1987; Apr. 22, 1993, eff. Dec. 1, 1993; Apr. 17, 2000, eff. Dec. 1, 2000; Apr. 30, 2007, eff. Dec. 1, 2007; Apr. 29, 2015, eff. Dec. 1, 2015; Apr. 28, 2016, eff. Dec. 1, 2016; Apr. 27, 2017, effective Dec. 1, 2017.)

NOTES OF ADVISORY COMMITTEE ON RULES

2015 AMENDMENT

Subdivision (d). Abrogation of Rule 84 and the other official forms requires that former Forms 5 and 6 be directly incorporated into Rule 4.

Rule 4.1. Serving Other Process

(a) In General. Process—other than a summons under Rule 4 or a subpoena under Rule 45—must be served by a United States marshal or deputy marshal or by a person specially appointed for that purpose. It may be served anywhere within the territorial limits of the state where the district court is located and, if authorized by a federal statute, beyond those limits. Proof of service must be made under Rule 4(*l*).

(b) Enforcing Orders: Committing for Civil Contempt. An order committing a person for civil contempt of a decree or injunction issued to enforce federal law may be served and enforced in any district. Any other order in a civil-contempt proceeding may be served only in the state where the issuing court is located or elsewhere in the United States within 100 miles from where the order was issued.

(Added Apr. 22, 1993; eff. Dec. 1, 1993. As amended Apr. 30, 2007, eff. Dec. 1, 2007.)

Rule 5. Serving and Filing Pleadings and Other Papers

(a) Service: When Required.

(1) ***In General.*** Unless these rules provide otherwise, each of the following papers must be served on every party:

(A) an order stating that service is required;

(B) a pleading filed after the original complaint, unless the court orders otherwise under Rule 5(c) because there are numerous defendants;

(C) a discovery paper required to be served on a party, unless the court orders otherwise;

(D) a written motion, except one that may be heard ex parte; and

(E) a written notice, appearance, demand, or offer of judgment, or any similar paper.

(2) ***If a Party Fails to Appear.*** No service is required on a party who is in default for failing to appear. But a pleading that asserts a new claim for relief against such a party must be served on that party under Rule 4.

(3) ***Seizing Property.*** If an action is begun by seizing property and no person is or need be named as a defendant, any service required before the filing of an appearance, answer, or claim must be made on the person who had custody or possession of the property when it was seized.

(b) Service: How Made.

(1) ***Serving an Attorney.*** If a party is represented by an attorney, service under this rule must be made on the attorney unless the court orders service on the party.

(2) ***Service in General.*** A paper is served under this rule by:

(A) handing it to the person;

(B) leaving it:

(i) at the person's office with a clerk or other person in charge or, if no one is in charge, in a conspicuous place in the office; or

(ii) if the person has no office or the office is closed, at the person's dwelling or usual place of abode with someone of suitable age and discretion who resides there;

(C) mailing it to the person's last known address—in which event service is complete upon mailing;

(D) leaving it with the court clerk if the person has no known address;

(E) sending it to a registered user by filing it with the court's electronic-filing system or sending it by other electronic means that the person consented to in writing—in either of which events service is complete upon filing or sending, but is not effective if the filer or sender learns that it did not reach the person to be served; or

(F) delivering it by any other means that the person consented to in writing—in which event service is complete when the person making service delivers it to the agency designated to make delivery.

(3) ***Using Court Facilities.*** [Abrogated (Apr. 26, 2018, eff. Dec. 1, 2018.)]

(c) Serving Numerous Defendants.

(1) ***In General.*** If an action involves an unusually large number of defendants, the court may, on motion or on its own, order that:

(A) defendants' pleadings and replies to them need not be served on other defendants;

(B) any crossclaim, counterclaim, avoidance, or affirmative defense in those pleadings and replies to them will be treated as denied or avoided by all other parties; and

(C) filing any such pleading and serving it on the plaintiff constitutes notice of the pleading to all parties.

(2) ***Notifying Parties.*** A copy of every such order must be served on the parties as the court directs.

(d) Filing.

(1) ***Required Filings; Certificate of Service.***

(A) Papers after the Complaint. Any paper after the complaint that is required to be served must be filed no later than a reasonable time after service. But disclosures under Rule 26(a)(1) or (2) and the following discovery requests and responses must not be filed until they are used in the proceeding or the court orders filing: depositions, interrogatories, requests for documents or tangible things or to permit entry onto land, and requests for admission.

(B) Certificate of Service. No certificate of service is required when a paper is served by filing it with the court's electronic-filing system. When a paper that is required to be served is served by other means:

(i) if the paper is filed, a certificate of service must be filed with it or within a reasonable time after service; and

(ii) if the paper is not filed, a certificate of service need not be filed unless filing is required by court order or by local rule.

(2) ***Nonelectronic Filing.*** A paper not filed electronically is filed by delivering it:

(A) to the clerk; or

(B) to a judge who agrees to accept it for filing, and who must then note the filing date on the paper and promptly send it to the clerk.

(3) ***Electronic Filing and Signing.***

(A) By a Represented Person—Generally Required; Exceptions. A person represented by an attorney must file electronically, unless nonelectronic filing is allowed by the court for good cause or is allowed or required by local rule.

(B) By an Unrepresented Person—When Allowed or Required. A person not represented by an attorney:

(i) may file electronically only if allowed by court order or by local rule; and

(ii) may be required to file electronically only by court order, or by a local rule that includes reasonable exceptions.

(C) Signing. A filing made through a person's electronic-filing account and authorized by that person, together with that person's name on a signature block, constitutes the person's signature.

(D) Same as a Written Paper. A paper filed electronically is a written paper for purposes of these rules.

(4) ***Acceptance by the Clerk.*** The clerk must not refuse to file a paper solely because it is not in the form prescribed by these rules or by a local rule or practice.

(As amended Jan. 21, 1963, eff. July 1, 1963; Mar. 30, 1970, eff. July 1, 1970; Apr. 29, 1980, eff. Aug. 1, 1980; Mar. 2, 1987, eff. Aug. 1, 1987; Apr. 30, 1991, eff. Dec. 1, 1991; Apr. 22, 1993, eff. Dec. 1, 1993; Apr. 23, 1996, eff. Dec. 1, 1996; Apr. 17, 2000, eff. Dec. 1, 2000; Apr. 23, 2001, eff. Dec. 1, 2001; Apr. 12, 2006, eff. Dec. 1, 2006; Apr. 30, 2007, eff. Dec. 1, 2007; Apr. 26, 2018, eff. Dec. 1, 2018.)

Rule 5.1. Constitutional Challenge to a Statute—Notice, Certification, and Intervention

(a) Notice by a Party. A party that files a pleading, written motion, or other paper drawing into question the constitutionality of a federal or state statute must promptly:

(1) file a notice of constitutional question stating the question and identifying the paper that raises it, if:

(A) a federal statute is questioned and the parties do not include the United States, one of its agencies, or one of its officers or employees in an official capacity; or

(B) a state statute is questioned and the parties do not include the state, one of its agencies, or one of its officers or employees in an official capacity; and

(2) serve the notice and paper on the Attorney General of the United States if a federal statute is questioned—or on the state attorney general if a state statute is questioned—either by certified or registered mail or by sending it to an electronic address designated by the attorney general for this purpose.

(b) Certification by the Court. The court must, under 28 U.S.C. § 2403, certify to the appropriate attorney general that a statute has been questioned.

(c) Intervention; Final Decision on the Merits. Unless the court sets a later time, the attorney general may intervene within 60 days after the notice is filed or after the court certifies the challenge, whichever is earlier. Before the time to intervene expires, the court may reject the constitutional challenge, but may not enter a final judgment holding the statute unconstitutional.

(d) No Forfeiture. A party's failure to file and serve the notice, or the court's failure to certify, does not forfeit a constitutional claim or defense that is otherwise timely asserted.

(Added Apr. 12, 2006, eff. Dec. 1, 2006. As amended, Apr. 30, 2007, eff. Dec. 1, 2007.)

Rule 5.2. Privacy Protection for Filings Made With the Court

(a) Redacted Filings. Unless the court orders otherwise, in an electronic or paper filing with the court that contains an individual's social-security number, taxpayer-identification number, or birth date, the name of an individual known to be a minor, or a financial-account number, a party or nonparty making the filing may include only:

(1) the last four digits of the social-security number and taxpayer-identification number;

(2) the year of the individual's birth;

(3) the minor's initials; and

(4) the last four digits of the financial-account number.

(b) Exemptions from the Redaction Requirement. The redaction requirement does not apply to the following:

(1) a financial-account number that identifies the property allegedly subject to forfeiture in a forfeiture proceeding;

(2) the record of an administrative or agency proceeding;

(3) the official record of a state-court proceeding;

(4) the record of a court or tribunal, if that record was not subject to the redaction requirement when originally filed;

(5) a filing covered by Rule 5.2(c) or (d); and

(6) a pro se filing in an action brought under 28 U.S.C. §§ 2241, 2254, or 2255.

(c) Limitations on Remote Access to Electronic Files; Social-Security Appeals and Immigration Cases. Unless the court orders otherwise, in an action for benefits under the Social Security Act, and in an action or proceeding relating to an order of removal, to relief from removal, or to immigration benefits or detention, access to an electronic file is authorized as follows:

(1) the parties and their attorneys may have remote electronic access to any part of the case file, including the administrative record;

(2) any other person may have electronic access to the full record at the courthouse, but may have remote electronic access only to:

(A) the docket maintained by the court; and

(B) an opinion, order, judgment, or other disposition of the court, but not any other part of the case file or the administrative record.

(d) Filings Made Under Seal. The court may order that a filing be made under seal without redaction. The court may later unseal the filing or order the person who made the filing to file a redacted version for the public record.

(e) Protective Orders. For good cause, the court may by order in a case:

(1) require redaction of additional information; or

(2) limit or prohibit a nonparty's remote electronic access to a document filed with the court.

(f) Option for Additional Unredacted Filing Under Seal. A person making a redacted filing may also file an unredacted copy under seal. The court must retain the unredacted copy as part of the record.

(g) Option for Filing a Reference List. A filing that contains redacted information may be filed together with a reference list that identifies each item of redacted information and specifies an appropriate identifier that uniquely corresponds to each item listed. The list must be filed under seal and may be amended as of right. Any reference in the case to a listed identifier will be construed to refer to the corresponding item of information.

(h) Waiver of Protection of Identifiers. A person waives the protection of Rule 5.2(a) as to the person's own information by filing it without redaction and not under seal.

(Added Apr. 30, 2007, eff. Dec. 1, 2007.)

Rule 6. Computing and Extending Time; Time for Motion Papers

(a) Computing Time. The following rules apply in computing any time period specified in these rules, in any local rule or court order, or in any statute that does not specify a method of computing time.

(1) ***Period Stated in Days or a Longer Unit.*** When the period is stated in days or a longer unit of time:

(A) exclude the day of the event that triggers the period;

(B) count every day, including intermediate Saturdays, Sundays, and legal holidays; and

(C) include the last day of the period, but if the last day is a Saturday, Sunday, or legal holiday, the period continues to run until the end of the next day that is not a Saturday, Sunday, or legal holiday.

(2) ***Period Stated in Hours.*** When the period is stated in hours:

(A) begin counting immediately on the occurrence of the event that triggers the period;

(B) count every hour, including hours during intermediate Saturdays, Sundays, and legal holidays; and

(C) if the period would end on a Saturday, Sunday, or legal holiday, the period continues to run until the same time on the next day that is not a Saturday, Sunday, or legal holiday.

(3) ***Inaccessibility of the Clerk's Office.*** Unless the court orders otherwise, if the clerk's office is inaccessible:

(A) on the last day for filing under Rule 6(a)(1), then the time for filing is extended to the first accessible day that is not a Saturday, Sunday, or legal holiday; or

(B) during the last hour for filing under Rule 6(a)(2), then the time for filing is extended to the same time on the first accessible day that is not a Saturday, Sunday, or legal holiday.

(4) ***"Last Day" Defined.*** Unless a different time is set by a statute, local rule, or court order, the last day ends:

(A) for electronic filing, at midnight in the court's time zone; and

(B) for filing by other means, when the clerk's office is scheduled to close.

(5) ***"Next Day" Defined.*** The "next day" is determined by continuing to count forward when the period is measured after an event and backward when measured before an event.

(6) ***"Legal Holiday" Defined.*** "Legal holiday" means:

(A) the day set aside by statute for observing New Year's Day, Martin Luther King Jr.'s Birthday, Washington's Birthday, Memorial Day, Juneteenth National Independence Day, Independence Day, Labor Day, Columbus Day, Veterans' Day, Thanksgiving Day, or Christmas Day;

(B) any day declared a holiday by the President or Congress; and

(C) for periods that are measured after an event, any other day declared a holiday by the state where the district court is located.

(b) Extending Time.

(1) ***In General.*** When an act may or must be done within a specified time, the court may, for good cause, extend the time:

(A) with or without motion or notice if the court acts, or if a request is made, before the original time or its extension expires; or

(B) on motion made after the time has expired if the party failed to act because of excusable neglect.

(2) ***Exceptions.*** A court must not extend the time to act under Rules 50(b) and (d), 52(b), 59(b), (d), and (e), and 60(b).

(c) Motions, Notices of Hearing, and Affidavits.

(1) ***In General.*** A written motion and notice of the hearing must be served at least 14 days before the time specified for the hearing, with the following exceptions:

(A) when the motion may be heard ex parte;

(B) when these rules set a different time; or

(C) when a court order—which a party may, for good cause, apply for ex parte—sets a different time.

(2) ***Supporting Affidavit.*** Any affidavit supporting a motion must be served with the motion. Except as Rule 59(c) provides otherwise, any opposing affidavit must be served at least 7 days before the hearing, unless the court permits service at another time.

(d) Additional Time After Certain Kinds of Service. When a party may or must act within a specified time after service and service is made under Rule 5(b)(2)(C) (mail), (D) (leaving with the clerk), or (F) (other means consented to), 3 days are added after the period would otherwise expire under Rule 6(a).

(As amended Dec. 27, 1946, eff. Mar. 19, 1948; Jan. 21, 1963, eff. July 1, 1963; Feb. 28, 1966, eff. July 1, 1966; Dec. 4, 1967, eff. July 1, 1968; Mar. 1, 1971, eff. July 1, 1971; Apr. 28, 1983, eff. Aug. 1, 1983; Apr. 29, 1985, eff. Aug. 1, 1985; Mar. 2, 1987, eff. Aug. 1, 1987; Apr. 26, 1999, eff. Dec. 1, 1999; Apr. 23, 2001, eff. Dec. 1, 2001; Apr. 25, 2005, eff. Dec. 1, 2005; Apr. 30, 2007, eff. Dec. 1, 2007; Mar. 26, 2009, eff. Dec. 1, 2009; Apr. 28, 2016, eff. Dec. 1, 2016; Apr. 24, 2023, eff. Dec. 1, 2023.)

TITLE III. PLEADINGS AND MOTIONS

Rule 7. Pleadings Allowed; Form of Motions and Other Papers

(a) Pleadings. Only these pleadings are allowed:

(1) a complaint;

(2) an answer to a complaint;

(3) an answer to a counterclaim designated as a counterclaim;

(4) an answer to a crossclaim;

(5) a third-party complaint;

(6) an answer to a third-party complaint; and

(7) if the court orders one, a reply to an answer.

(b) Motions and Other Papers.

(1) ***In General.*** A request for a court order must be made by motion. The motion must:

(A) be in writing unless made during a hearing or trial;

(B) state with particularity the grounds for seeking the order; and

(C) state the relief sought.

(2) ***Form.*** The rules governing captions and other matters of form in pleadings apply to motions and other papers.

(As amended Dec. 27, 1946, eff. Mar. 19, 1948; Jan. 21, 1963, eff. July 1, 1963; Apr. 28, 1983, eff. Aug. 1, 1983; Apr. 30, 2007, eff. Dec. 1, 2007.)

Rule 7.1. Disclosure Statement

(a) Who Must File; Contents.

(1) ***Nongovernmental Corporations.*** A nongovernmental corporate party or a nongovernmental corporation that seeks to intervene must file a statement that:

(A) identifies any parent corporation and any publicly held corporation owning 10% or more of its stock; or

(B) states that there is no such corporation.

(2) ***Parties or Intervenors in a Diversity Case.*** In an action in which jurisdiction is based on diversity under 28 U.S.C. § 1332(a), a party or intervenor must, unless the court orders otherwise, file a disclosure statement. The statement must name—and identify the citizenship of—every individual or entity whose citizenship is attributed to that party or intervenor:

(A) when the action is filed in or removed to federal court, and

(B) when any later event occurs that could affect the court's jurisdiction under § 1332(a).

(b) Time to File; Supplemental Filing. A party, intervenor, or proposed intervenor must:

(1) file the disclosure statement with its first appearance, pleading, petition, motion, response, or other request addressed to the court; and

(2) promptly file a supplemental statement if any required information changes.

(Added Apr. 29, 2002, eff. Dec. 1, 2002. As amended Apr. 30, 2007, eff. Dec. 1, 2007; Apr. 11, 2022, eff. Dec. 1, 2022.)

NOTES OF ADVISORY COMMITTEE ON RULES

2002 ADOPTION

* * * The information required by Rule 7.1(a) reflects the "financial interest" standard of Canon 3C(1)(c) of the Code of Conduct for United States Judges. This information will support properly informed disqualification decisions in situations that call for automatic disqualification under Canon 3C(1)(c). It does not cover all of the circumstances that may call for disqualification under the financial interest standard, and does not deal at all with other circumstances that may call for disqualification.

Although the disclosures required by Rule 7.1(a) may seem limited, they are calculated to reach a majority of the circumstances that are likely to call for disqualification on the basis of financial information that a judge may not know or recollect. Framing a rule that calls for more detailed disclosure will be difficult. Unnecessary disclosure requirements place a burden on the parties and on courts. Unnecessary disclosure of volumes of information may create a risk that a judge will overlook the one bit of information that might require disqualification, and also may create a risk that unnecessary disqualifications will be made rather than attempt to unravel a potentially difficult question. It has not been feasible to dictate more detailed disclosure requirements in Rule 7.1(a).

Rule 7.1 does not prohibit local rules that require disclosures in addition to those required by Rule 7.1. * * *

Rule 8. General Rules of Pleading

(a) Claim for Relief. A pleading that states a claim for relief must contain:

(1) a short and plain statement of the grounds for the court's jurisdiction, unless the court already has jurisdiction and the claim needs no new jurisdictional support;

(2) a short and plain statement of the claim showing that the pleader is entitled to relief; and

(3) a demand for the relief sought, which may include relief in the alternative or different types of relief.

(b) Defenses; Admissions and Denials.

(1) ***In General.*** In responding to a pleading, a party must:

(A) state in short and plain terms its defenses to each claim asserted against it; and

(B) admit or deny the allegations asserted against it by an opposing party.

(2) ***Denials—Responding to the Substance.*** A denial must fairly respond to the substance of the allegation.

(3) ***General and Specific Denials.*** A party that intends in good faith to deny all the allegations of a pleading—including the jurisdictional grounds—may do so by a general denial. A party that does not intend to deny all the allegations must either specifically deny designated allegations or generally deny all except those specifically admitted.

(4) ***Denying Part of an Allegation.*** A party that intends in good faith to deny only part of an allegation must admit the part that is true and deny the rest.

(5) ***Lacking Knowledge or Information.*** A party that lacks knowledge or information sufficient to form a belief about the truth of an allegation must so state, and the statement has the effect of a denial.

(6) ***Effect of Failing to Deny.*** An allegation—other than one relating to the amount of damages—is admitted if a responsive pleading is required and the allegation is not denied. If a responsive pleading is not required, an allegation is considered denied or avoided.

(c) Affirmative Defenses.

(1) ***In General.*** In responding to a pleading, a party must affirmatively state any avoidance or affirmative defense, including:

- accord and satisfaction;
- arbitration and award;
- assumption of risk;
- contributory negligence;
- duress;
- estoppel;
- failure of consideration;
- fraud;
- illegality;
- injury by fellow servant;
- laches;
- license;
- payment;
- release;
- res judicata;
- statute of frauds;
- statute of limitations; and
- waiver.

(2) ***Mistaken Designation.*** If a party mistakenly designates a defense as a counterclaim, or a counterclaim as a defense, the court must, if justice requires, treat the pleading as though it were correctly designated, and may impose terms for doing so.

(d) Pleading to Be Concise and Direct; Alternative Statements; Inconsistency.

(1) ***In General.*** Each allegation must be simple, concise, and direct. No technical form is required.

(2) ***Alternative Statements of a Claim or Defense.*** A party may set out two or more statements of a claim or defense alternatively or hypothetically, either in a single count or defense or in separate ones. If a party makes alternative statements, the pleading is sufficient if any one of them is sufficient.

(3) ***Inconsistent Claims or Defenses.*** A party may state as many separate claims or defenses as it has, regardless of consistency.

(e) Construing Pleadings. Pleadings must be construed so as to do justice.

(As amended Feb. 28, 1966, eff. July 1, 1966; Mar. 2, 1987, eff. Aug. 1, 1987; Apr. 30, 2007, eff. Dec. 1, 2007; Apr. 28, 2010, eff. Dec. 1, 2010.)

Rule 9. Pleading Special Matters

(a) Capacity or Authority to Sue; Legal Existence.

(1) ***In General.*** Except when required to show that the court has jurisdiction, a pleading need not allege:

(A) a party's capacity to sue or be sued;

(B) a party's authority to sue or be sued in a representative capacity; or

(C) the legal existence of an organized association of persons that is made a party.

(2) ***Raising Those Issues.*** To raise any of those issues, a party must do so by a specific denial, which must state any supporting facts that are peculiarly within the party's knowledge.

(b) Fraud or Mistake; Conditions of Mind. In alleging fraud or mistake, a party must state with particularity the circumstances constituting fraud or mistake. Malice, intent, knowledge, and other conditions of a person's mind may be alleged generally.

(c) Conditions Precedent. In pleading conditions precedent, it suffices to allege generally that all conditions precedent have occurred or been performed. But when denying that a condition precedent has occurred or been performed, a party must do so with particularity.

(d) Official Document or Act. In pleading an official document or official act, it suffices to allege that the document was legally issued or the act legally done.

(e) Judgment. In pleading a judgment or decision of a domestic or foreign court, a judicial or quasi-judicial tribunal, or a board or officer, it suffices to plead the judgment or decision without showing jurisdiction to render it.

(f) Time and Place. An allegation of time or place is material when testing the sufficiency of a pleading.

(g) Special Damages. If an item of special damage is claimed, it must be specifically stated.

(h) Admiralty or Maritime Claim.

(1) ***How Designated.*** If a claim for relief is within the admiralty or maritime jurisdiction and also within the court's subject-matter jurisdiction on some other ground, the pleading may designate the claim as an admiralty or maritime claim for purposes of Rules 14(c), 38(e), and 82 and the Supplemental Rules for Admiralty or Maritime Claims and Asset Forfeiture Actions. A claim cognizable only in the admiralty or maritime jurisdiction is an admiralty or maritime claim for those purposes, whether or not so designated.

(2) ***Designation for Appeal.*** A case that includes an admiralty or maritime claim within this subdivision (h) is an admiralty case within 28 U.S.C. § 1292(a)(3).

(As amended Feb. 28, 1966, eff. July 1, 1966; Dec. 4, 1967, eff. July 1, 1968; Mar. 30, 1970, eff. July 1, 1970; Mar. 2, 1987, eff. Aug. 1, 1987; Apr. 11, 1997, eff. Dec. 1, 1997; Apr. 12, 2006, eff. Dec. 1, 2006; Apr. 30, 2007, eff. Dec. 1, 2007.)

Rule 10. Form of Pleadings

(a) Caption; Names of Parties. Every pleading must have a caption with the court's name, a title, a file number, and a Rule 7(a) designation. The title of the complaint must name all the parties; the title of other pleadings, after naming the first party on each side, may refer generally to other parties.

(b) Paragraphs; Separate Statements. A party must state its claims or defenses in numbered paragraphs, each limited as far as practicable to a single set of circumstances. A later pleading may refer by number to a paragraph in an earlier pleading. If doing so would promote clarity, each claim founded on a separate transaction or occurrence—and each defense other than a denial—must be stated in a separate count or defense.

(c) Adoption by Reference; Exhibits. A statement in a pleading may be adopted by reference elsewhere in the same pleading or in any other pleading or motion. A copy of a written instrument that is an exhibit to a pleading is a part of the pleading for all purposes.

(As amended Apr. 30, 2007, eff. Dec. 1, 2007.)

Rule 11. Signing Pleadings, Motions, and Other Papers; Representations to the Court; Sanctions

(a) Signature. Every pleading, written motion, and other paper must be signed by at least one attorney of record in the attorney's name—or by a party personally if the party is unrepresented. The paper must state the signer's address, e-mail address, and telephone number. Unless a rule or statute specifically states otherwise, a pleading need not be verified or accompanied by an affidavit. The court must strike an unsigned paper unless the omission is promptly corrected after being called to the attorney's or party's attention.

(b) Representations to the Court. By presenting to the court a pleading, written motion, or other paper—whether by signing, filing, submitting, or later advocating it—an attorney or unrepresented party certifies that to the best of the person's knowledge, information, and belief, formed after an inquiry reasonable under the circumstances:

(1) it is not being presented for any improper purpose, such as to harass, cause unnecessary delay, or needlessly increase the cost of litigation;

(2) the claims, defenses, and other legal contentions are warranted by existing law or by a nonfrivolous argument for extending, modifying, or reversing existing law or for establishing new law;

(3) the factual contentions have evidentiary support or, if specifically so identified, will likely have evidentiary support after a reasonable opportunity for further investigation or discovery; and

(4) the denials of factual contentions are warranted on the evidence or, if specifically so identified, are reasonably based on belief or a lack of information.

(c) Sanctions.

(1) ***In General.*** If, after notice and a reasonable opportunity to respond, the court determines that Rule 11(b) has been violated, the court may impose an appropriate sanction on any attorney, law firm, or party that violated the rule or is responsible for the violation. Absent exceptional circumstances, a law firm must be held jointly responsible for a violation committed by its partner, associate, or employee.

(2) ***Motion for Sanctions.*** A motion for sanctions must be made separately from any other motion and must describe the specific conduct that allegedly violates Rule 11(b). The motion must be served under Rule 5, but it must not be filed or be presented to the court if the challenged paper, claim, defense, contention, or denial is withdrawn or appropriately corrected within 21 days after service or within another time the court sets. If warranted, the court may award to the prevailing party the reasonable expenses, including attorney's fees, incurred for the motion.

(3) ***On the Court's Initiative.*** On its own, the court may order an attorney, law firm, or party to show cause why conduct specifically described in the order has not violated Rule 11(b).

(4) ***Nature of a Sanction.*** A sanction imposed under this rule must be limited to what suffices to deter repetition of the conduct or comparable conduct by others similarly situated. The sanction may include nonmonetary directives; an order to pay a penalty into court; or, if imposed on motion and warranted for effective deterrence, an order directing payment to the movant of part or all of the reasonable attorney's fees and other expenses directly resulting from the violation.

(5) ***Limitations on Monetary Sanctions.*** The court must not impose a monetary sanction:

(A) against a represented party for violating Rule 11(b)(2); or

(B) on its own, unless it issued the show-cause order under Rule 11(c)(3) before voluntary dismissal or settlement of the claims made by or against the party that is, or whose attorneys are, to be sanctioned.

(6) ***Requirements for an Order.*** An order imposing a sanction must describe the sanctioned conduct and explain the basis for the sanction.

(d) Inapplicability to Discovery. This rule does not apply to disclosures and discovery requests, responses, objections, and motions under Rules 26 through 37.

(As amended Apr. 28, 1983, eff. Aug. 1, 1983; Mar. 2, 1987, eff. Aug. 1, 1987; Apr. 22, 1993, eff. Dec. 1, 1993; Apr. 30, 2007, eff. Dec. 1, 2007.)

NOTES OF ADVISORY COMMITTEE ON RULES

1993 AMENDMENT

Purpose of revision. This revision is intended to remedy problems that have arisen in the interpretation and application of the 1983 revision of the rule. * * *

The rule retains the principle that attorneys and pro se litigants have an obligation to the court to refrain from conduct that frustrates the aims of Rule 1. The revision broadens the scope of this obligation, but places greater constraints on the imposition of sanctions and should reduce the number of motions for sanctions presented to the court.

* * *

Subdivisions (b) and (c). These subdivisions restate the provisions requiring attorneys and pro se litigants to conduct a reasonable inquiry into the law and facts before signing pleadings, written motions, and other documents, and prescribing sanctions for violation of these obligations. The revision in part expands the responsibilities of litigants to the court, while providing greater constraints and flexibility in dealing with infractions of the rule. The rule continues to require litigants to "stop-and-think" before initially making legal or factual contentions. It also, however, emphasizes the duty of candor by subjecting litigants to potential sanctions for insisting upon a position after it is no longer tenable and by generally providing protection against sanctions if they withdraw or correct contentions after a potential violation is called to their attention.

The rule applies only to assertions contained in papers filed with or submitted to the court. It does not cover matters arising for the first time during oral presentations to the court, when counsel may make statements that would not have been made if there had been more time for study and reflection. However, a litigant's obligations with respect to the contents of these papers are not measured solely as of the time they are filed with or submitted to the court, but include reaffirming to the court and advocating positions contained in those pleadings and motions after learning that they cease to have any merit. For example, an attorney who during a pretrial conference insists on a claim or defense should be viewed as "presenting to the court" that contention and would be subject to the obligations of subdivision (b) measured as of that time. Similarly, if after a notice of removal is filed, a party urges in federal court the allegations of a pleading filed in state court (whether as claims, defenses, or in disputes regarding removal or remand), it would be viewed as "presenting"—and hence certifying to the district court under Rule 11—those allegations.

The certification with respect to allegations and other factual contentions is revised in recognition that sometimes a litigant may have good reason to believe that a fact is true or false but may need discovery, formal or informal, from opposing parties or third persons to gather and confirm the evidentiary basis for the allegation. Tolerance of factual contentions in initial pleadings by plaintiffs or defendants when specifically identified as made on information and belief does not relieve litigants from the obligation to conduct an appropriate investigation into the facts that is reasonable under the circumstances; it is not a license to join parties, make claims, or present defenses without any factual basis or justification. Moreover, if evidentiary support is not obtained after a reasonable opportunity for further investigation or discovery, the party has a duty under the rule not to persist with that contention. Subdivision (b) does not require a formal amendment to pleadings for which evidentiary support is not obtained, but rather calls upon a litigant not thereafter to advocate such claims or defenses.

The certification is that there is (or likely will be) "evidentiary support" for the allegation, not that the party will prevail with respect to its contention regarding the fact. That summary judgment is rendered against a party does not necessarily mean, for purposes of this certification, that it had no evidentiary support for its position. On the other hand, if a party has evidence with respect to a contention that would suffice to defeat a motion for summary judgment based thereon, it would have sufficient "evidentiary support" for purposes of Rule 11.

Denials of factual contentions involve somewhat different considerations. Often, of course, a denial is premised upon the existence of evidence contradicting the alleged fact. At other times a denial is permissible because, after an appropriate investigation, a party has no information concerning the matter or, indeed, has a reasonable basis for doubting the credibility of the only evidence relevant to the matter. A party should not deny an allegation it knows to be true; but it is not required, simply because it lacks contradictory evidence, to admit an allegation that it believes is not true.

* * *

Arguments for extensions, modifications, or reversals of existing law or for creation of new law do not violate subdivision (b)(2) provided they are "nonfrivolous." This establishes an objective standard, intended to eliminate any "empty-head pure-heart" justification for patently frivolous arguments. However, the extent to which a litigant has researched the issues and found some support for its theories even in minority opinions, in law review articles, or through consultation with other attorneys should certainly be taken into account in determining whether paragraph (2) has been violated. Although arguments for a change of law are not required to be specifically so identified, a contention that is so identified should be viewed with greater tolerance under the rule.

The court has available a variety of possible sanctions to impose for violations, such as striking the offending paper; issuing an admonition, reprimand, or censure; requiring participation in seminars or other educational programs; ordering a fine payable to the court; referring the matter to disciplinary authorities (or, in the case of government attorneys, to the Attorney General, Inspector General, or agency head), etc. * * * Whether the improper conduct was willful, or negligent; whether it was part of a pattern of activity, or an isolated event; whether it infected the entire pleading, or only one particular count or defense; whether the person has engaged in similar conduct in other litigation; whether it was intended to injure; what effect it had on the litigation process in time or expense; whether the responsible person is trained in the law; what amount, given the financial resources of the responsible person, is needed to deter that person from repetition in the same case; what amount is needed to deter similar activity by other litigants: all of these may in a particular case be proper considerations. The court has significant discretion in determining what sanctions, if any, should be imposed for a violation, subject to the principle that the sanctions should not be more severe than reasonably necessary to deter repetition of the conduct by the offending person or comparable conduct by similarly situated persons.

* * *

The sanction should be imposed on the persons—whether attorneys, law firms, or parties—who have violated the rule or who may be determined to be responsible for the violation. The person signing, filing, submitting, or advocating a document has a nondelegable responsibility to the court, and in most situations is the person to be sanctioned for a violation. Absent exceptional circumstances, a law firm is to be held also responsible when, as a result of a motion under subdivision (c)(1)(A), one of its partners, associates, or employees is determined to have violated the rule. Since such a motion may be filed only if the offending paper is not withdrawn or corrected within 21 days after service of the motion, it is appropriate that the law firm ordinarily be viewed as jointly responsible under established principles of agency. This provision is designed to remove the restrictions of the former rule. *Cf. Pavelic & LeFlore v. Marvel Entertainment Group*, 493 U.S. 120 (1989)(1983 version of Rule 11 does not permit sanctions against law firm of attorney signing groundless complaint).

The revision permits the court to consider whether other attorneys in the firm, co-counsel, other law firms, or the party itself should be held accountable for their part in causing a violation. * * *

Sanctions that involve monetary awards (such as a fine or an award of attorney's fees) may not be imposed on a represented party for causing a violation of subdivision (b)(2), involving frivolous contentions of law. Monetary responsibility for such violations is more properly placed solely on the party's attorneys. With this limitation, the rule should not be subject to attack under the Rules Enabling Act. *See Willy v. Coastal Corp.*, 503 U.S. 131 (1992); *Business Guides, Inc. v. Chromatic Communications Enter. Inc.*, 498 U.S. 533 (1991). This restriction does not limit the court's power to impose sanctions or remedial orders that may have collateral financial consequences upon a party, such as dismissal of a claim, preclusion of a defense, or preparation of amended pleadings.

* * *

The rule provides that requests for sanctions must be made as a separate motion, *i.e.*, not simply included as an additional prayer for relief contained in another motion. The motion for sanctions is not, however, to be filed until at least 21 days (or such other period as the court may set) after being served. If, during this period, the alleged violation is corrected, as by withdrawing (whether formally or informally) some allegation or contention, the motion should not be filed with the court. These provisions are intended to provide a type of "safe harbor" against motions under Rule 11 in that a party will not be subject to sanctions on the basis of another party's motion unless, after receiving the motion, it refuses to withdraw that position or to acknowledge candidly that it does not currently have evidence to support a specified allegation. Under the former rule, parties were sometimes reluctant to abandon a questionable contention lest that be viewed as evidence of a violation of Rule 11; under the revision, the timely withdrawal of a contention will protect a party against a motion for sanctions.

To stress the seriousness of a motion for sanctions and to define precisely the conduct claimed to violate the rule, the revision provides that the "safe harbor" period begins to run only upon service of the motion. In most cases, however, counsel should be expected to give informal notice to the other party, whether in person or by a telephone call or letter, of a potential violation before proceeding to prepare and serve a Rule 11 motion.

As under former Rule 11, the filing of a motion for sanctions is itself subject to the requirements of the rule and can lead to sanctions. However, service of a cross motion under Rule 11 should rarely be needed since under the revision the court may award to the person who prevails on a motion under Rule 11—whether the movant or the target of the motion—reasonable expenses, including attorney's fees, incurred in presenting or opposing the motion.

The power of the court to act on its own initiative is retained, but with the condition that this be done through a show cause order. This procedure provides the person with notice and an opportunity to respond. The revision provides that a monetary sanction imposed after a court-initiated show cause order be limited to a penalty payable to the court and that it be imposed only if the show cause order is issued before any voluntary dismissal or an agreement of the parties to settle the claims made by or against the litigant. Parties settling a case should not be subsequently faced with an unexpected order from the court leading to monetary sanctions that might have affected their willingness to settle or voluntarily dismiss a case. Since show cause orders will ordinarily be issued only in situations that are akin to a contempt of court, the rule does not provide a "safe harbor" to a litigant for withdrawing a claim, defense, etc., after a show cause order has been issued on the court's own initiative. Such corrective action, however, should be taken into account in deciding what—if any—sanction to impose if, after consideration of the litigant's response, the court concludes that a violation has occurred.

Subdivision (d). Rules 26(g) and 37 establish certification standards and sanctions that apply to discovery disclosures, requests, responses, objections, and motions. It is appropriate that Rules 26 through 37, which are specially designed for the discovery process, govern such documents and conduct rather than the more general provisions of Rule 11. Subdivision (d) has been added to accomplish this result.

Rule 11 is not the exclusive source for control of improper presentations of claims, defenses, or contentions. It does not supplant statutes permitting awards of attorney's fees to prevailing parties or alter the principles governing such awards. It does not inhibit the court in punishing for contempt, in exercising its inherent powers, or in imposing sanctions, awarding expenses, or directing remedial action authorized under other rules or under 28 U.S.C. § 1927. *See Chambers v. NASCO*, 501 U.S. 32 (1991). *Chambers* cautions, however, against reliance upon inherent powers if appropriate sanctions can be imposed under provisions such as Rule 11, and the procedures specified in Rule 11—notice, opportunity to respond, and findings—should ordinarily be employed when imposing a sanction under the court's inherent powers. Finally, it should be noted that Rule 11 does not preclude a party from initiating an independent action for malicious prosecution or abuse of process.

Rule 12. Defenses and Objections: When and How Presented; Motion for Judgment on the Pleadings; Consolidating Motions; Waiving Defenses; Pretrial Hearing

(a) Time to Serve a Responsive Pleading. Unless another time is specified by a federal statute, the time for serving a responsive pleading is as follows:

(1) ***In General.***

(A) A defendant must serve an answer:

(i) within 21 days after being served with the summons and complaint; or

(ii) if it has timely waived service under Rule 4(d), within 60 days after the request for a waiver was sent, or within 90 days after it was sent to the defendant outside any judicial district of the United States.

(B) A party must serve an answer to a counterclaim or crossclaim within 21 days after being served with the pleading that states the counterclaim or crossclaim.

(C) A party must serve a reply to an answer within 21 days after being served with an order to reply, unless the order specifies a different time.

(2) ***United States and Its Agencies, Officers, or Employees Sued in an Official Capacity.*** The United States, a United States agency, or a United States officer or employee sued only in an official capacity must serve an answer to a complaint, counterclaim, or crossclaim within 60 days after service on the United States attorney.

(3) ***United States Officers or Employees Sued in an Individual Capacity.*** A United States officer or employee sued in an individual capacity for an act or omission occurring in connection with duties performed on the United States' behalf must serve an answer to a complaint, counterclaim, or crossclaim within 60 days after service on the officer or employee or service on the United States attorney, whichever is later.

(4) ***Effect of a Motion.*** Unless the court sets a different time, serving a motion under this rule alters these periods as follows:

(A) if the court denies the motion or postpones its disposition until trial, the responsive pleading must be served within 14 days after notice of the court's action; or

(B) if the court grants a motion for a more definite statement, the responsive pleading must be served within 14 days after the more definite statement is served.

(b) How to Present Defenses. Every defense to a claim for relief in any pleading must be asserted in the responsive pleading if one is required. But a party may assert the following defenses by motion:

(1) lack of subject-matter jurisdiction;

(2) lack of personal jurisdiction;

(3) improper venue;

(4) insufficient process;

(5) insufficient service of process;

(6) failure to state a claim upon which relief can be granted; and

(7) failure to join a party under Rule 19.

A motion asserting any of these defenses must be made before pleading if a responsive pleading is allowed. If a pleading sets out a claim for relief that does not require a responsive pleading, an opposing party may assert at trial any defense to that claim. No defense or objection is waived by joining it with one or more other defenses or objections in a responsive pleading or in a motion.

(c) Motion for Judgment on the Pleadings. After the pleadings are closed—but early enough not to delay trial—a party may move for judgment on the pleadings.

(d) Result of Presenting Matters Outside the Pleadings. If, on a motion under Rule 12(b)(6) or 12(c), matters outside the pleadings are presented to and not excluded by the court, the motion must be treated as one for summary judgment under Rule 56. All parties must be given a reasonable opportunity to present all the material that is pertinent to the motion.

(e) Motion for a More Definite Statement. A party may move for a more definite statement of a pleading to which a responsive pleading is allowed but which is so vague or ambiguous that the party cannot reasonably prepare a response. The motion must be made before filing a responsive pleading and must point out the defects complained of and the details desired. If the court orders a more definite statement and the order is not obeyed within 14 days after notice of the order or within the time the court sets, the court may strike the pleading or issue any other appropriate order.

(f) Motion to Strike. The court may strike from a pleading an insufficient defense or any redundant, immaterial, impertinent, or scandalous matter. The court may act:

(1) on its own; or

(2) on motion made by a party either before responding to the pleading or, if a response is not allowed, within 21 days after being served with the pleading.

(g) Joining Motions.

(1) ***Right to Join.*** A motion under this rule may be joined with any other motion allowed by this rule.

(2) ***Limitation on Further Motions.*** Except as provided in Rule 12(h)(2) or (3), a party that makes a motion under this rule must not make another motion under this rule raising a defense or objection that was available to the party but omitted from its earlier motion.

(h) Waiving and Preserving Certain Defenses.

(1) ***When Some Are Waived.*** A party waives any defense listed in Rule 12(b)(2)–(5) by:

(A) omitting it from a motion in the circumstances described in Rule 12(g)(2); or

(B) failing to either:

(i) make it by motion under this rule; or

(ii) include it in a responsive pleading or in an amendment allowed by Rule 15(a)(1) as a matter of course.

(2) ***When to Raise Others.*** Failure to state a claim upon which relief can be granted, to join a person required by Rule 19(b), or to state a legal defense to a claim may be raised:

(A) in any pleading allowed or ordered under Rule 7(a);

(B) by a motion under Rule 12(c); or

(C) at trial.

(3) ***Lack of Subject-Matter Jurisdiction.*** If the court determines at any time that it lacks subject-matter jurisdiction, the court must dismiss the action.

(i) Hearing Before Trial. If a party so moves, any defense listed in Rule 12(b)(1)–(7)—whether made in a pleading or by motion—and a motion under Rule 12(c) must be heard and decided before trial unless the court orders a deferral until trial.

(As amended Dec. 27, 1946, eff. Mar. 19, 1948; Jan. 21, 1963, eff. July 1, 1963; Feb. 28, 1966, eff. July 1, 1966; Mar. 2, 1987, eff. Aug. 1, 1987; Apr. 22, 1993, eff. Dec. 1, 1993; Apr. 17, 2000, eff. Dec. 1, 2000; Apr. 30, 2007, eff. Dec. 1, 2007; Mar. 26, 2009, eff. Dec. 1, 2009; Apr. 2, 2024, eff. Dec. 1, 2024.)

NOTES OF ADVISORY COMMITTEE ON RULES

1946 AMENDMENT

* * *

Subdivision (b). * * *

Rule 12(b)(6), permitting a motion to dismiss for failure of the complaint to state a claim on which relief can be granted, is substantially the same as the old demurrer for failure of a pleading to state a cause of action. Some courts have held that as the rule by its terms refers to statements in the complaint, extraneous matter on affidavits, depositions or otherwise, may not be introduced in support of the motion, or to resist it. On the other hand, in many cases the district courts have permitted the introduction of such material. * * * In dealing with such situations the Second Circuit has made the sound suggestion that whatever its label or original basis, the motion may be treated as a motion for summary judgment and disposed of as such.

It has also been suggested that this practice could be justified on the ground that the federal rules permit "speaking" motions. The Committee entertains the view that on motion under Rule 12(b)(6) to dismiss for failure of the complaint to state a good claim, the trial court should have authority to permit the introduction of extraneous matter, such as may be offered on a motion for summary judgment, and if it does not exclude such matter the motion should then be treated as a motion for summary judgment and disposed of in the manner and on the conditions stated in Rule 56 relating to summary judgments, and, of course, in such a situation, when the case reaches the circuit court of appeals, that court should treat the motion in the same way. The Committee believes that such practice, however, should be tied to the summary judgment rule. The term "speaking motion" is not mentioned in the rules, and if there is such a thing its limitations are undefined. Where extraneous matter is received, by tying further proceedings to the summary judgment rule the courts have a definite basis in the rules for disposing of the motion.

* * *

Rule 13. Counterclaim and Crossclaim

(a) Compulsory Counterclaim.

(1) ***In General.*** A pleading must state as a counterclaim any claim that—at the time of its service—the pleader has against an opposing party if the claim:

(A) arises out of the transaction or occurrence that is the subject matter of the opposing party's claim; and

(B) does not require adding another party over whom the court cannot acquire jurisdiction.

(2) ***Exceptions.*** The pleader need not state the claim if:

(A) when the action was commenced, the claim was the subject of another pending action; or

(B) the opposing party sued on its claim by attachment or other process that did not establish personal jurisdiction over the pleader on that claim, and the pleader does not assert any counterclaim under this rule.

(b) **Permissive Counterclaim.** A pleading may state as a counterclaim against an opposing party any claim that is not compulsory.

(c) **Relief Sought in a Counterclaim.** A counterclaim need not diminish or defeat the recovery sought by the opposing party. It may request relief that exceeds in amount or differs in kind from the relief sought by the opposing party.

(d) **Counterclaim Against the United States.** These rules do not expand the right to assert a counterclaim—or to claim a credit—against the United States or a United States officer or agency.

(e) **Counterclaim Maturing or Acquired After Pleading.** The court may permit a party to file a supplemental pleading asserting a counterclaim that matured or was acquired by the party after serving an earlier pleading.

(f) **[Abrogated]**

(g) **Crossclaim Against a Coparty.** A pleading may state as a crossclaim any claim by one party against a coparty if the claim arises out of the transaction or occurrence that is the subject matter of the original action or of a counterclaim, or if the claim relates to any property that is the subject matter of the original action. The crossclaim may include a claim that the coparty is or may be liable to the crossclaimant for all or part of a claim asserted in the action against the crossclaimant.

(h) **Joining Additional Parties.** Rules 19 and 20 govern the addition of a person as a party to a counterclaim or crossclaim.

(i) **Separate Trials; Separate Judgments.** If the court orders separate trials under Rule 42(b), it may enter judgment on a counterclaim or crossclaim under Rule 54(b) when it has jurisdiction to do so, even if the opposing party's claims have been dismissed or otherwise resolved.

(As amended Dec. 27, 1946, eff. Mar. 19, 1948; Jan. 21, 1963, eff. July 1, 1963; Feb. 28, 1966, eff. July 1, 1966; Mar. 2, 1987, eff. Aug. 1, 1987; Apr. 30, 2007, eff. Dec. 1, 2007; Mar. 26, 2009, eff. Dec. 1, 2009.)

Rule 14. Third-Party Practice

(a) When a Defending Party May Bring in a Third Party.

(1) ***Timing of the Summons and Complaint.*** A defending party may, as third-party plaintiff, serve a summons and complaint on a nonparty who is or may be liable to it for all or part of the claim against it. But the third-party plaintiff must, by motion, obtain the court's leave if it files the third-party complaint more than 14 days after serving its original answer.

(2) ***Third-Party Defendant's Claims and Defenses.*** The person served with the summons and third-party complaint—the "third-party defendant":

(A) must assert any defense against the third-party plaintiff's claim under Rule 12;

(B) must assert any counterclaim against the third-party plaintiff under Rule 13(a), and may assert any counterclaim against the third-party plaintiff under Rule 13(b) or any crossclaim against another third-party defendant under Rule 13(g);

(C) may assert against the plaintiff any defense that the third-party plaintiff has to the plaintiff's claim; and

(D) may also assert against the plaintiff any claim arising out of the transaction or occurrence that is the subject matter of the plaintiff's claim against the third-party plaintiff.

(3) ***Plaintiff's Claims Against a Third-Party Defendant.*** The plaintiff may assert against the third-party defendant any claim arising out of the transaction or occurrence that is the subject matter of the plaintiff's claim against the third-party plaintiff. The third-party defendant must then assert any defense under Rule 12 and any counterclaim under Rule 13(a), and may assert any counterclaim under Rule 13(b) or any crossclaim under Rule 13(g).

(4) ***Motion to Strike, Sever, or Try Separately.*** Any party may move to strike the third-party claim, to sever it, or to try it separately.

(5) ***Third-Party Defendant's Claim Against a Nonparty.*** A third-party defendant may proceed under this rule against a nonparty who is or may be liable to the third-party defendant for all or part of any claim against it.

(6) ***Third-Party Complaint In Rem.*** If it is within the admiralty or maritime jurisdiction, a third-party complaint may be in rem. In that event, a reference in this rule to the "summons" includes the

warrant of arrest, and a reference to the defendant or third-party plaintiff includes, when appropriate, a person who asserts a right under Supplemental Rule C(6)(a)(i) in the property arrested.

(b) When a Plaintiff May Bring in a Third Party. When a claim is asserted against a plaintiff, the plaintiff may bring in a third party if this rule would allow a defendant to do so.

(c) Admiralty or Maritime Claim.

(1) ***Scope of Impleader.*** If a plaintiff asserts an admiralty or maritime claim under Rule 9(h), the defendant or a person who asserts a right under Supplemental Rule C(6)(a)(i) may, as a third-party plaintiff, bring in a third-party defendant who may be wholly or partly liable—either to the plaintiff or to the third-party plaintiff—for remedy over, contribution, or otherwise on account of the same transaction, occurrence, or series of transactions or occurrences.

(2) ***Defending Against a Demand for Judgment for the Plaintiff.*** The third-party plaintiff may demand judgment in the plaintiff's favor against the third-party defendant. In that event, the third-party defendant must defend under Rule 12 against the plaintiff's claim as well as the third-party plaintiff's claim; and the action proceeds as if the plaintiff had sued both the third-party defendant and the third-party plaintiff.

(As amended Dec. 27, 1946, eff. Mar. 19, 1948; Jan. 21, 1963, eff. July 1, 1963; Feb. 28, 1966, eff. July 1, 1966; Mar. 2, 1987, eff. Aug. 1, 1987; Apr. 17, 2000, eff. Dec. 1, 2000; Apr. 12, 2006, eff. Dec. 1, 2006; Apr. 30, 2007, eff. Dec. 1, 2007; Mar. 26, 2009, eff. Dec. 1, 2009.)

NOTES OF ADVISORY COMMITTEE ON RULES

2007 AMENDMENT

* * *

Former Rule 14 twice refers to counterclaims under Rule 13. In each case, the operation of Rule 13(a) depends on the state of the action at the time the pleading is filed. If plaintiff and third-party defendant have become opposing parties because one has made a claim for relief against the other, Rule 13(a) requires assertion of any counterclaim that grows out of the transaction or occurrence that is the subject matter of that claim. Rules 14(a)(2)(B) and (a)(3) reflect the distinction between compulsory and permissive counterclaims.

Rule 15. Amended and Supplemental Pleadings

(a) Amendments Before Trial.

(1) ***Amending as a Matter of Course.*** A party may amend its pleading once as a matter of course no later than:

(A) 21 days after serving it, or

(B) if the pleading is one to which a responsive pleading is required, 21 days after service of a responsive pleading or 21 days after service of a motion under Rule 12(b), (e), or (f), whichever is earlier.

(2) ***Other Amendments.*** In all other cases, a party may amend its pleading only with the opposing party's written consent or the court's leave. The court should freely give leave when justice so requires.

(3) ***Time to Respond.*** Unless the court orders otherwise, any required response to an amended pleading must be made within the time remaining to respond to the original pleading or within 14 days after service of the amended pleading, whichever is later.

(b) Amendments During and After Trial.

(1) ***Based on an Objection at Trial.*** If, at trial, a party objects that evidence is not within the issues raised in the pleadings, the court may permit the pleadings to be amended. The court should freely permit an amendment when doing so will aid in presenting the merits and the objecting party fails to satisfy the court that the evidence would prejudice that party's action or defense on the merits. The court may grant a continuance to enable the objecting party to meet the evidence.

(2) ***For Issues Tried by Consent.*** When an issue not raised by the pleadings is tried by the parties' express or implied consent, it must be treated in all respects as if raised in the pleadings. A party may move—at any time, even after judgment—to amend the pleadings to conform them to the evidence and to raise an unpleaded issue. But failure to amend does not affect the result of the trial of that issue.

(c) Relation Back of Amendments.

(1) ***When an Amendment Relates Back.*** An amendment to a pleading relates back to the date of the original pleading when:

(A) the law that provides the applicable statute of limitations allows relation back;

(B) the amendment asserts a claim or defense that arose out of the conduct, transaction, or occurrence set out—or attempted to be set out—in the original pleading; or

(C) the amendment changes the party or the naming of the party against whom a claim is asserted, if Rule 15(c)(1)(B) is satisfied and if, within the period provided by Rule 4(m) for serving the summons and complaint, the party to be brought in by amendment:

(i) received such notice of the action that it will not be prejudiced in defending on the merits; and

(ii) knew or should have known that the action would have been brought against it, but for a mistake concerning the proper party's identity.

(2) ***Notice to the United States.*** When the United States or a United States officer or agency is added as a defendant by amendment, the notice requirements of Rule 15(c)(1)(C)(i) and (ii) are satisfied if, during the stated period, process was delivered or mailed to the United States attorney or the United States attorney's designee, to the Attorney General of the United States, or to the officer or agency.

(d) Supplemental Pleadings. On motion and reasonable notice, the court may, on just terms, permit a party to serve a supplemental pleading setting out any transaction, occurrence, or event that happened after the date of the pleading to be supplemented. The court may permit supplementation even though the original pleading is defective in stating a claim or defense. The court may order that the opposing party plead to the supplemental pleading within a specified time.

(As amended Jan. 21, 1963, eff. July 1, 1963; Feb. 28, 1966, eff. July 1, 1966; Mar. 2, 1987, eff. Aug. 1, 1987; Apr. 30, 1991, eff. Dec. 1, 1991; Act of Dec. 9, 1991, Pub.L. 102–198, 105 Stat. 1623; Apr. 22, 1993, eff. Dec. 1, 1993; Apr. 30, 2007, eff. Dec. 1, 2007; Mar. 26, 2009, eff. Dec. 1, 2009; Apr. 24, 2023, eff. Dec. 1, 2023.)

NOTES OF ADVISORY COMMITTEE ON RULES

1991 AMENDMENT

The rule has been revised to prevent parties against whom claims are made from taking unjust advantage of otherwise inconsequential pleading errors to sustain a limitations defense.

Paragraph (c)(1). This provision is new. It is intended to make it clear that the rule does not apply to preclude any relation back that may be permitted under the applicable limitations law. * * * Whatever may be the controlling body of limitations law, if that law affords a more forgiving principle of relation back than the one provided in this rule, it should be available to save the claim. If *Schiavone v. Fortune*, 477 U.S. 21 (1986) implies the contrary, this paragraph is intended to make a material change in the rule.

Paragraph (c)(3). This paragraph has been revised to change the result in *Schiavone v. Fortune, supra,* with respect to the problem of a misnamed defendant. An intended defendant who is notified of an action within the period allowed by Rule 4[(m)] for service of a summons and complaint may not under the revised rule defeat the action on account of a defect in the pleading with respect to the defendant's name, provided that the requirements of clauses (A) and (B) have been met. If the notice requirement is met within the Rule 4[(m)] period, a complaint may be amended at any time to correct a formal defect such as a misnomer or misidentification. On the basis of the text of the former rule, the Court reached a result in *Schiavone v. Fortune* that was inconsistent with the liberal pleading practices secured by Rule 8. * * *

In allowing a name-correcting amendment within the time allowed by Rule 4[(m)], this rule allows not only the 120 days specified in that rule, but also any additional time resulting from any extension ordered by the court pursuant to that rule, as may be granted, for example, if the defendant is a fugitive from service of the summons.

* * *

Rule 16. Pretrial Conferences; Scheduling; Management

(a) Purposes of a Pretrial Conference. In any action, the court may order the attorneys and any unrepresented parties to appear for one or more pretrial conferences for such purposes as:

(1) expediting disposition of the action;

(2) establishing early and continuing control so that the case will not be protracted because of lack of management;

(3) discouraging wasteful pretrial activities;

(4) improving the quality of the trial through more thorough preparation; and

(5) facilitating settlement.

(b) Scheduling and Management.

(1) ***Scheduling Order.*** Except in categories of actions exempted by local rule, the district judge—or a magistrate judge when authorized by local rule—must issue a scheduling order:

(A) after receiving the parties' report under Rule 26(f); or

(B) after consulting with the parties' attorneys and any unrepresented parties at a scheduling conference.

(2) ***Time to Issue.*** The judge must issue the scheduling order as soon as practicable, but unless the judge finds good cause for delay, the judge must issue it within the earlier of 90 days after any defendant has been served with the complaint or 60 days after any defendant has appeared.

(3) ***Contents of the Order.***

(A) *Required Contents.* The scheduling order must limit the time to join other parties, amend the pleadings, complete discovery, and file motions.

(B) *Permitted Contents.* The scheduling order may:

(i) modify the timing of disclosures under Rules 26(a) and 26(e)(1);

(ii) modify the extent of discovery;

(iii) provide for disclosure, discovery, or preservation of electronically stored information;

(iv) include the timing and method for complying with Rule 26(b)(5)(A) and any agreements the parties reach for asserting claims of privilege or of protection as trial-preparation material after information is produced, including agreements reached under Federal Rule of Evidence 502;

(v) direct that before moving for an order relating to discovery, the movant must request a conference with the court;

(vi) set dates for pretrial conferences and for trial; and

(vii) include other appropriate matters.

(4) ***Modifying a Schedule.*** A schedule may be modified only for good cause and with the judge's consent.

(c) **Attendance and Matters for Consideration at a Pretrial Conference.**

(1) ***Attendance.*** A represented party must authorize at least one of its attorneys to make stipulations and admissions about all matters that can reasonably be anticipated for discussion at a pretrial conference. If appropriate, the court may require that a party or its representative be present or reasonably available by other means to consider possible settlement.

(2) ***Matters for Consideration.*** At any pretrial conference, the court may consider and take appropriate action on the following matters:

(A) formulating and simplifying the issues, and eliminating frivolous claims or defenses;

(B) amending the pleadings if necessary or desirable;

(C) obtaining admissions and stipulations about facts and documents to avoid unnecessary proof, and ruling in advance on the admissibility of evidence;

(D) avoiding unnecessary proof and cumulative evidence, and limiting the use of testimony under Federal Rule of Evidence 702;

(E) determining the appropriateness and timing of summary adjudication under Rule 56;

(F) controlling and scheduling discovery, including orders affecting disclosures and discovery under Rule 26 and Rules 29 through 37;

(G) identifying witnesses and documents, scheduling the filing and exchange of any pretrial briefs, and setting dates for further conferences and for trial;

(H) referring matters to a magistrate judge or a master;

(I) settling the case and using special procedures to assist in resolving the dispute when authorized by statute or local rule;

(J) determining the form and content of the pretrial order;

(K) disposing of pending motions;

(L) adopting special procedures for managing potentially difficult or protracted actions that may involve complex issues, multiple parties, difficult legal questions, or unusual proof problems;

(M) ordering a separate trial under Rule 42(b) of a claim, counterclaim, crossclaim, third-party claim, or particular issue;

(N) ordering the presentation of evidence early in the trial on a manageable issue that might, on the evidence, be the basis for a judgment as a matter of law under Rule 50(a) or a judgment on partial findings under Rule 52(c);

(O) establishing a reasonable limit on the time allowed to present evidence; and

(P) facilitating in other ways the just, speedy, and inexpensive disposition of the action.

(d) Pretrial Orders. After any conference under this rule, the court should issue an order reciting the action taken. This order controls the course of the action unless the court modifies it.

(e) Final Pretrial Conference and Orders. The court may hold a final pretrial conference to formulate a trial plan, including a plan to facilitate the admission of evidence. The conference must be held as close to the start of trial as is reasonable, and must be attended by at least one attorney who will conduct the trial for each party and by any unrepresented party. The court may modify the order issued after a final pretrial conference only to prevent manifest injustice.

(f) Sanctions.

(1) ***In General.*** On motion or on its own, the court may issue any just orders, including those authorized by Rule 37(b)(2)(A)(ii)–(vii), if a party or its attorney:

(A) fails to appear at a scheduling or other pretrial conference;

(B) is substantially unprepared to participate—or does not participate in good faith—in the conference; or

(C) fails to obey a scheduling or other pretrial order.

(2) ***Imposing Fees and Costs.*** Instead of or in addition to any other sanction, the court must order the party, its attorney, or both to pay the reasonable expenses—including attorney's fees—incurred because of any noncompliance with this rule, unless the noncompliance was substantially justified or other circumstances make an award of expenses unjust.

(As amended Apr. 28, 1983, eff. Aug. 1, 1983; Mar. 2, 1987, eff. Aug. 1, 1987; Apr. 22, 1993, eff. Dec. 1, 1993; Apr. 12, 2006, eff. Dec. 1, 2006; Apr. 30, 2007, eff. Dec. 1, 2007; Apr. 29, 2015, eff. Dec. 1, 2015; Apr. 23, 2025, eff. Dec. 1, 2025.)

NOTES OF ADVISORY COMMITTEE ON RULES

1983 AMENDMENT

Introduction

* * *

Given the significant changes in federal civil litigation since 1938 that are not reflected in Rule 16, it has been extensively rewritten and expanded to meet the challenges of modern litigation. Empirical studies reveal that when a trial judge intervenes personally at an early stage to assume judicial control over a case and to schedule dates for completion by the parties of the principal pretrial steps, the case is disposed of by settlement or trial more efficiently and with less cost and delay than when the parties are left to their own devices. Flanders, *Case Management and Court Management in United States District Courts* 17, Federal Judicial Center (1977). Thus, the rule mandates a pretrial scheduling order. However, although scheduling and pretrial conferences are encouraged in appropriate cases, they are not mandated.

Discussion

* * *

Subdivision (b): Scheduling and Planning. The most significant change in Rule 16 is the mandatory scheduling order described in Rule 16(b), which is based in part on Wisconsin Civil Procedure Rule 802.10. The idea of scheduling orders is not new. It has been used by many federal courts.

Although a mandatory scheduling order encourages the court to become involved in case management early in the litigation, it represents a degree of judicial involvement that is not warranted in many cases. Thus, subdivision (b) permits each district court to promulgate a local rule under Rule 83 exempting certain categories of cases in which the burdens of scheduling orders exceed the administrative efficiencies that would be gained. Logical candidates for this treatment include social security disability matters, habeas corpus petitions, forfeitures, and reviews of certain administrative actions.

* * *

Subdivision (c): Subjects to Be Discussed at Pretrial Conferences. This subdivision expands upon the list of things that may be discussed at a pretrial conference that appeared in original Rule 16. The intention is to encourage better planning and management of litigation. Increased judicial control during the pretrial process accelerates the processing and termination of cases.

* * *

Counsel bear a substantial responsibility for assisting the court in identifying the factual issues worthy of trial. If counsel fail to identify an issue for the court, the right to have the issue tried is waived. Although an order specifying the issues is intended to be binding, it may be amended at trial to avoid manifest injustice. See Rule 16(e). However, the rule's effectiveness depends on the court employing its discretion sparingly.

* * *

Subdivision (d): Final Pretrial Conference. This provision has been added to make it clear that the time between any final pretrial conference (which in a simple case may be the only pretrial conference) and trial should be as short as possible to be certain that the litigants make substantial progress with the case and avoid the inefficiency of having that preparation repeated when there is a delay between the last pretrial conference and trial. * * * the timing has been left to the court's discretion.

At least one of the attorneys who will conduct the trial for each party must be present at the final pretrial conference. At this late date there should be no doubt as to which attorney or attorneys this will be. Since the agreements and stipulations made at this final conference will control the trial, the presence of lawyers who will be involved in it is especially useful to assist the judge in structuring the case, and to lead to a more effective trial.

Subdivision (e): Pretrial Orders.

* * *

Once formulated, pretrial orders should not be changed lightly; but total inflexibility is undesirable. See, *e.g., Clark v. Pennsylvania R.R. Co.*, 328 F.2d 591 (2d Cir.1964). The exact words used to describe the standard for amending the pretrial order probably are less important than the meaning given them in practice. By not imposing any limitation on the ability to modify a pretrial order, the rule reflects the reality that in any process of continuous management what is done at one conference may have to be altered at the next. In the case of the final pretrial order, however, a more stringent standard is called for and the words "to prevent manifest injustice," which appeared in the original rule, have been retained. They have the virtue of familiarity and adequately describe the restraint the trial judge should exercise.

* * *

Subdivision (f): Sanctions. Original Rule 16 did not mention the sanctions that might be imposed for failing to comply with the rule. However, courts have not hesitated to enforce it by appropriate measures. * * *

To reflect that existing practice, and to obviate dependence upon Rule 41(b) or the court's inherent power to regulate litigation, *cf. Societe Internationale Pour Participations Industrielles Et Commerciales, S.A. v. Rogers*, 357 U.S. 197 (1958), Rule 16(f) expressly provides for imposing sanctions on disobedient or recalcitrant parties, their attorneys, or both in four types of situations. Rodes, Ripple & Mooney, *Sanctions Imposable for Violations of the Federal Rules of Civil Procedure* 65–67, 80–84, Federal Judicial Center (1981). Furthermore, explicit reference to sanctions reenforces the rule's intention to encourage forceful judicial management.

Rule 16(f) incorporates portions of Rule 37(b)(2), which prescribes sanctions for failing to make discovery. This should facilitate application of Rule 16(f), since courts and lawyers already are familiar with the Rule 37 standards. Among the sanctions authorized by the new subdivision are: preclusion order, striking a pleading, staying the proceeding, default judgment, contempt, and charging a party, his attorney, or both with the expenses, including attorney's fees, caused by noncompliance. The contempt sanction, however, is only available for a violation of a court order. The references in Rule 16(f) are not exhaustive.

* * *

2015 AMENDMENT

The provision for consulting at a scheduling conference by "telephone, mail, or other means" is deleted. A scheduling conference is more effective if the court and parties engage in direct simultaneous communication. The conference may be held in person, by telephone, or by more sophisticated electronic means.

The time to issue the scheduling order is reduced to the earlier of 90 days (not 120 days) after any defendant has been served, or 60 days (not 90 days) after any defendant has appeared. This change, together with the shortened time for making service under Rule 4(m), will reduce delay at the beginning of litigation. At the same time, a new provision recognizes that the court may find good cause to extend the time to issue the scheduling order. In some cases it may be that the parties cannot prepare adequately for a meaningful Rule 26(f) conference and then a scheduling conference in the time allowed. Litigation involving complex issues, multiple parties, and large organizations, public or private, may be more likely to need extra time to establish meaningful collaboration between counsel and the people who can supply the information needed to participate in a useful way.

* * *

Rule 16.1. Multidistrict Litigation

(a) Initial Management Conference. After the Judicial Panel on Multidistrict Litigation transfers actions, the transferee court should schedule an initial management conference to develop an initial plan for orderly pretrial activity in the MDL proceedings.

(b) Report for the Conference.

(1) ***Submitting a Report.*** The transferee court should order the parties to meet and to submit a report to the court before the conference.

(2) ***Required Content: the Parties' Views on Leadership Counsel and Other Matters.*** The report must address any matter the court designates—which may include any matter in Rule 16—and, unless the court orders otherwise, the parties' views on:

(A) whether leadership counsel should be appointed and, if so:

(i) the timing of the appointments;

(ii) the structure of leadership counsel;

(iii) the procedure for selecting leadership and whether the appointments should be reviewed periodically;

(iv) their responsibilities and authority in conducting pretrial activities and any role in facilitating resolution of the MDL proceedings;

(v) the proposed methods for regularly communicating with and reporting to the court and nonleadership counsel;

(vi) any limits on activity by nonleadership counsel; and

(vii) whether and when to establish a means for compensating leadership counsel;

(B) any previously entered scheduling or other orders that should be vacated or modified;

(C) a schedule for additional management conferences with the court;

(D) how to manage the direct filing of new actions in the MDL proceedings; and

(E) whether related actions have been—or are expected to be—filed in other courts, and whether to adopt methods for coordinating with them.

(3) ***Additional Required Content: the Parties' Initial Views on Various Matters.*** Unless the court orders otherwise, the report also must address the parties' initial views on:

(A) whether consolidated pleadings should be prepared;

(B) how and when the parties will exchange information about the factual bases for their claims and defenses;

(C) discovery, including any difficult issues that may arise;

(D) any likely pretrial motions;

(E) whether the court should consider any measures to facilitate resolving some or all actions before the court;

(F) whether any matters should be referred to a magistrate judge or a master; and

(G) the principal factual and legal issues likely to be presented.

(4) ***Permitted Content.*** The report may include any other matter that the parties wish to bring to the court's attention.

(c) Initial Management Order. After the conference, the court should enter an initial management order addressing the matters in Rule 16.1(b) and, in the court's discretion, any other matters. This order controls the course of the proceedings unless the court modifies it.

(Added Apr. 23, 2025, eff. Dec. 1, 2025.)

NOTES OF ADVISORY COMMITTEE ON RULES

2025 ADOPTION

The Multidistrict Litigation Act, 28 U.S.C. § 1407, was adopted in 1968. It empowers the Judicial Panel on Multidistrict Litigation to transfer one or more actions for coordinated or consolidated pretrial proceedings to promote the just and efficient conduct of such actions. The number of civil actions subject to transfer orders from the Panel has increased since the statute was enacted but has leveled off in recent years. These actions have accounted for a substantial portion of the federal civil docket. There has been no reference to multidistrict litigation (MDL proceedings) in the Civil Rules. The addition of

Rule 16.1 is designed to provide a framework for the initial management of MDL proceedings.

Not all MDL proceedings present the management challenges this rule addresses, and, thus, it is important to maintain flexibility in managing MDL proceedings. Of course, other multiparty litigation that did not result from a Judicial Panel transfer order may present similar management challenges. For example, multiple actions in a single district (sometimes called related cases and assigned by local rule to a single judge) may exhibit characteristics similar to MDL proceedings. In such situations, courts may find it useful to employ procedures similar to those Rule 16.1 identifies in handling those multiparty proceedings. In both MDL proceedings and other multiparty litigation, the Manual for Complex Litigation also may be a source of guidance.

* * *

TITLE IV. PARTIES

Rule 17. Plaintiff and Defendant; Capacity; Public Officers

(a) Real Party in Interest.

(1) ***Designation in General.*** An action must be prosecuted in the name of the real party in interest. The following may sue in their own names without joining the person for whose benefit the action is brought:

(A) an executor;

(B) an administrator;

(C) a guardian;

(D) a bailee;

(E) a trustee of an express trust;

(F) a party with whom or in whose name a contract has been made for another's benefit; and

(G) a party authorized by statute.

(2) ***Action in the Name of the United States for Another's Use or Benefit.*** When a federal statute so provides, an action for another's use or benefit must be brought in the name of the United States.

(3) ***Joinder of the Real Party in Interest.*** The court may not dismiss an action for failure to prosecute in the name of the real party in interest until, after an objection, a reasonable time has been allowed for the real party in interest to ratify, join, or be substituted into the action. After ratification, joinder, or substitution, the action proceeds as if it had been originally commenced by the real party in interest.

(b) Capacity to Sue or Be Sued. Capacity to sue or be sued is determined as follows:

(1) for an individual who is not acting in a representative capacity, by the law of the individual's domicile;

(2) for a corporation, by the law under which it was organized; and

(3) for all other parties, by the law of the state where the court is located, except that:

(A) a partnership or other unincorporated association with no such capacity under that state's law may sue or be sued in its common name to enforce a substantive right existing under the United States Constitution or laws; and

(B) 28 U.S.C. §§ 754 and 959(a) govern the capacity of a receiver appointed by a United States court to sue or be sued in a United States court.

(c) Minor or Incompetent Person.

(1) ***With a Representative.*** The following representatives may sue or defend on behalf of a minor or an incompetent person:

(A) a general guardian;

(B) a committee;

(C) a conservator; or

(D) a like fiduciary.

(2) ***Without a Representative.*** A minor or an incompetent person who does not have a duly appointed representative may sue by a next friend or by a guardian ad litem. The court must appoint a guardian ad litem—or issue another appropriate order—to protect a minor or incompetent person who is unrepresented in an action.

(d) Public Officer's Title and Name. A public officer who sues or is sued in an official capacity may be designated by official title rather than by name, but the court may order that the officer's name be added.

(As amended Dec. 27, 1946, eff. Mar. 19, 1948; Dec. 29, 1948, eff. Oct. 20, 1949; Feb. 28, 1966, eff. July 1, 1966; Mar. 2, 1987, eff. Aug. 1, 1987; Apr. 25, 1988, eff. Aug. 1, 1988; Nov. 18, 1988, Pub.L. 100–690, § 7049, 102 Stat. 4401; Apr. 30, 2007, eff. Dec. 1, 2007.)

Rule 18. Joinder of Claims

(a) In General. A party asserting a claim, counterclaim, crossclaim, or third-party claim may join, as independent or alternative claims, as many claims as it has against an opposing party.

(b) Joinder of Contingent Claims. A party may join two claims even though one of them is contingent on the disposition of the other; but the court may grant relief only in accordance with the parties' relative substantive rights. In particular, a plaintiff may state a claim for money and a claim to set aside a conveyance that is fraudulent as to that plaintiff, without first obtaining a judgment for the money.

(As amended Feb. 28, 1966, eff. July 1, 1966; Mar. 2, 1987, eff. Aug. 1, 1987; Apr. 30, 2007, eff. Dec. 1, 2007.)

Rule 19. Required Joinder of Parties

(a) Persons Required to Be Joined if Feasible.

(1) ***Required Party.*** A person who is subject to service of process and whose joinder will not deprive the court of subject-matter jurisdiction must be joined as a party if:

(A) in that person's absence, the court cannot accord complete relief among existing parties; or

(B) that person claims an interest relating to the subject of the action and is so situated that disposing of the action in the person's absence may:

(i) as a practical matter impair or impede the person's ability to protect the interest; or

(ii) leave an existing party subject to a substantial risk of incurring double, multiple, or otherwise inconsistent obligations because of the interest.

(2) ***Joinder by Court Order.*** If a person has not been joined as required, the court must order that the person be made a party. A person who refuses to join as a plaintiff may be made either a defendant or, in a proper case, an involuntary plaintiff.

(3) ***Venue.*** If a joined party objects to venue and the joinder would make venue improper, the court must dismiss that party.

(b) When Joinder Is Not Feasible. If a person who is required to be joined if feasible cannot be joined, the court must determine whether, in equity and good conscience, the action should proceed among the existing parties or should be dismissed. The factors for the court to consider include:

(1) the extent to which a judgment rendered in the person's absence might prejudice that person or the existing parties;

(2) the extent to which any prejudice could be lessened or avoided by:

(A) protective provisions in the judgment;

(B) shaping the relief; or

(C) other measures;

(3) whether a judgment rendered in the person's absence would be adequate; and

(4) whether the plaintiff would have an adequate remedy if the action were dismissed for nonjoinder.

(c) **Pleading the Reasons for Nonjoinder.** When asserting a claim for relief, a party must state:

(1) the name, if known, of any person who is required to be joined if feasible but is not joined; and

(2) the reasons for not joining that person.

(d) **Exception for Class Actions.** This rule is subject to Rule 23.

(As amended Feb. 28, 1966, eff. July 1, 1966; Mar. 2, 1987, eff. Aug. 1, 1987; Apr. 30, 2007, eff. Dec. 1, 2007.)

NOTES OF ADVISORY COMMITTEE ON RULES

1966 AMENDMENT

* * *

The subdivision (a) definition of persons to be joined is not couched in terms of the abstract nature of their interests—"joint," "united," "separable," or the like.

* * *

Subdivision (b).—When a person as described in subdivision (a)(1)–(2) cannot be made a party, the court is to determine whether in equity and good conscience the action should proceed among the parties already before it, or should be dismissed. * * * The subdivision sets out four relevant considerations drawn from the experience revealed in the decided cases. The factors are to a certain extent overlapping, and they are not intended to exclude other considerations which may be applicable in particular situations.

The first factor brings in a consideration of what a judgment in the action would mean to the absentee. Would the absentee be adversely affected in a practical sense, and if so, would the prejudice be immediate and serious, or remote and minor? The possible collateral consequences of the judgment upon the parties already joined are also to be appraised. Would any party be exposed to a fresh action by the absentee, and if so, how serious is the threat? * * *

The second factor calls attention to the measures by which prejudice may be averted or lessened. The "shaping of relief" is a familiar expedient to this end. See, e.g., the award of money damages in lieu of specific relief where the latter might affect an absentee adversely. * * *

Sometimes the party is himself able to take measures to avoid prejudice. Thus a defendant faced with a prospect of a second suit by an absentee may be in a position to bring the latter into the action by defensive interpleader. * * * So also the absentee may sometimes be able to avert prejudice to himself by voluntarily appearing in the action or intervening on an ancillary basis. * * * The court should consider whether this, in turn, would impose undue hardship on the absentee. * * *

The third factor—whether an "adequate" judgment can be rendered in the absence of a given person—calls attention to the extent of the relief that can be accorded among the parties joined. It meshes with the other factors, especially the "shaping of relief" mentioned under the second factor.

The fourth factor, looking to the practical effects of a dismissal, indicates that the court should consider whether there is any assurance that the plaintiff, if dismissed, could sue effectively in another forum where better joinder would be possible. * * *

The subdivision uses the word "indispensable" only in a conclusory sense, that is, a person is "regarded as indispensable" when he cannot be made a party and, upon consideration of the factors above mentioned, it is determined that in his absence it would be preferable to dismiss the action, rather than to retain it.

* * *

Rule 20. Permissive Joinder of Parties

(a) Persons Who May Join or Be Joined.

(1) ***Plaintiffs.*** Persons may join in one action as plaintiffs if:

(A) they assert any right to relief jointly, severally, or in the alternative with respect to or arising out of the same transaction, occurrence, or series of transactions or occurrences; and

(B) any question of law or fact common to all plaintiffs will arise in the action.

(2) ***Defendants.*** Persons—as well as a vessel, cargo, or other property subject to admiralty process in rem—may be joined in one action as defendants if:

(A) any right to relief is asserted against them jointly, severally, or in the alternative with respect to or arising out of the same transaction, occurrence, or series of transactions or occurrences; and

(B) any question of law or fact common to all defendants will arise in the action.

(3) ***Extent of Relief.*** Neither a plaintiff nor a defendant need be interested in obtaining or defending against all the relief demanded. The court may grant judgment to one or more plaintiffs according to their rights, and against one or more defendants according to their liabilities.

(b) Protective Measures. The court may issue orders—including an order for separate trials—to protect a party against embarrassment, delay, expense, or other prejudice that arises from including a person against whom the party asserts no claim and who asserts no claim against the party.

(As amended Feb. 28, 1966, eff. July 1, 1966; Mar. 2, 1987, eff. Aug. 1, 1987; Apr. 30, 2007, eff. Dec. 1, 2007.)

Rule 21. Misjoinder and Nonjoinder of Parties

Misjoinder of parties is not a ground for dismissing an action. On motion or on its own, the court may at any time, on just terms, add or drop a party. The court may also sever any claim against a party.

(As amended Apr. 30, 2007, eff. Dec. 1, 2007.)

Rule 22. Interpleader

(a) Grounds.

(1) ***By a Plaintiff.*** Persons with claims that may expose a plaintiff to double or multiple liability may be joined as defendants and required to interplead. Joinder for interpleader is proper even though:

(A) the claims of the several claimants, or the titles on which their claims depend, lack a common origin or are adverse and independent rather than identical; or

(B) the plaintiff denies liability in whole or in part to any or all of the claimants.

(2) ***By a Defendant.*** A defendant exposed to similar liability may seek interpleader through a crossclaim or counterclaim.

(b) Relation to Other Rules and Statutes. This rule supplements—and does not limit—the joinder of parties allowed by Rule 20. The remedy this rule provides is in addition to—and does not supersede or limit—the remedy provided by 28 U.S.C. §§ 1335, 1397, and 2361. An action under those statutes must be conducted under these rules.

(As amended Dec. 29, 1948, eff. Oct. 20, 1949; Mar. 2, 1987, eff. Aug. 1, 1987; Apr. 30, 2007, eff. Dec. 1, 2007.)

Rule 23. Class Actions

(a) Prerequisites. One or more members of a class may sue or be sued as representative parties on behalf of all members only if:

(1) the class is so numerous that joinder of all members is impracticable;

(2) there are questions of law or fact common to the class;

(3) the claims or defenses of the representative parties are typical of the claims or defenses of the class; and

(4) the representative parties will fairly and adequately protect the interests of the class.

(b) Types of Class Actions. A class action may be maintained if Rule 23(a) is satisfied and if:

(1) prosecuting separate actions by or against individual class members would create a risk of:

(A) inconsistent or varying adjudications with respect to individual class members that would establish incompatible standards of conduct for the party opposing the class; or

(B) adjudications with respect to individual class members that, as a practical matter, would be dispositive of the interests of the other members not parties to the individual adjudications or would substantially impair or impede their ability to protect their interests;

(2) the party opposing the class has acted or refused to act on grounds that apply generally to the class, so that final injunctive relief or corresponding declaratory relief is appropriate respecting the class as a whole; or

(3) the court finds that the questions of law or fact common to class members predominate over any questions affecting only individual members, and that a class action is superior to other available methods for fairly and efficiently adjudicating the controversy. The matters pertinent to these findings include:

(A) the class members' interests in individually controlling the prosecution or defense of separate actions;

(B) the extent and nature of any litigation concerning the controversy already begun by or against class members;

(C) the desirability or undesirability of concentrating the litigation of the claims in the particular forum; and

(D) the likely difficulties in managing a class action.

(c) Certification Order; Notice to Class Members; Judgment; Issues Classes; Subclasses.

(1) ***Certification Order.***

(A) *Time to Issue.* At an early practicable time after a person sues or is sued as a class representative, the court must determine by order whether to certify the action as a class action.

(B) *Defining the Class; Appointing Class Counsel.* An order that certifies a class action must define the class and the class claims, issues, or defenses, and must appoint class counsel under Rule 23(g).

(C) *Altering or Amending the Order.* An order that grants or denies class certification may be altered or amended before final judgment.

(2) ***Notice.***

(A) *For (b)(1) or (b)(2) Classes.* For any class certified under Rule 23(b)(1) or (b)(2), the court may direct appropriate notice to the class.

(B) *For (b)(3) Classes.* For any class certified under Rule 23(b)(3)—or upon ordering notice under Rule 23(e)(1) to a class proposed to be certified for purposes of settlement under Rule 23(b)(3)—the court must direct to class members the best notice that is practicable under the circumstances, including individual notice to all members who can be identified through reasonable effort. The notice may be by one or more of the following: United States mail, electronic means, or other appropriate means. The notice must clearly and concisely state in plain, easily understood language:

(i) the nature of the action;

(ii) the definition of the class certified;

(iii) the class claims, issues, or defenses;

(iv) that a class member may enter an appearance through an attorney if the member so desires;

(v) that the court will exclude from the class any member who requests exclusion;

(vi) the time and manner for requesting exclusion; and

(vii) the binding effect of a class judgment on members under Rule 23(c)(3).

(3) ***Judgment.*** Whether or not favorable to the class, the judgment in a class action must:

(A) for any class certified under Rule 23(b)(1) or (b)(2), include and describe those whom the court finds to be class members; and

(B) for any class certified under Rule 23(b)(3), include and specify or describe those to whom the Rule 23(c)(2) notice was directed, who have not requested exclusion, and whom the court finds to be class members.

(4) ***Particular Issues.*** When appropriate, an action may be brought or maintained as a class action with respect to particular issues.

(5) ***Subclasses.*** When appropriate, a class may be divided into subclasses that are each treated as a class under this rule.

(d) Conducting the Action.

(1) ***In General.*** In conducting an action under this rule, the court may issue orders that:

(A) determine the course of proceedings or prescribe measures to prevent undue repetition or complication in presenting evidence or argument;

(B) require—to protect class members and fairly conduct the action—giving appropriate notice to some or all class members of:

(i) any step in the action;

(ii) the proposed extent of the judgment; or

(iii) the members' opportunity to signify whether they consider the representation fair and adequate, to intervene and present claims or defenses, or to otherwise come into the action;

(C) impose conditions on the representative parties or on intervenors;

(D) require that the pleadings be amended to eliminate allegations about representation of absent persons and that the action proceed accordingly; or

(E) deal with similar procedural matters.

(2) ***Combining and Amending Orders.*** An order under Rule 23(d)(1) may be altered or amended from time to time and may be combined with an order under Rule 16.

(e) Settlement, Voluntary Dismissal, or Compromise. The claims, issues, or defenses of a certified class—or a class proposed to be certified for purposes of settlement—may be settled, voluntarily dismissed, or compromised only with the court's approval. The following procedures apply to a proposed settlement, voluntary dismissal, or compromise:

(1) ***Notice to the Class.***

(A) Information That Parties Must Provide to the Court. The parties must provide the court with information sufficient to enable it to determine whether to give notice of the proposal to the class.

(B) Grounds for a Decision to Give Notice. The court must direct notice in a reasonable manner to all class members who would be bound by the proposal if giving notice is justified by the parties' showing that the court will likely be able to:

(i) approve the proposal under Rule 23(e)(2); and

(ii) certify the class for purposes of judgment on the proposal.

(2) ***Approval of the Proposal.*** If the proposal would bind class members, the court may approve it only after a hearing and only on finding that it is fair, reasonable, and adequate after considering whether:

(A) the class representatives and class counsel have adequately represented the class;

(B) the proposal was negotiated at arm's length;

(C) the relief provided for the class is adequate, taking into account:

(i) the costs, risks, and delay of trial and appeal;

(ii) the effectiveness of any proposed method of distributing relief to the class, including the method of processing class-member claims;

(iii) the terms of any proposed award of attorney's fees, including timing of payment; and

(iv) any agreement required to be identified under Rule 23(e)(3); and

(D) the proposal treats class members equitably relative to each other.

(3) ***Identifying Agreements.*** The parties seeking approval must file a statement identifying any agreement made in connection with the proposal.

(4) ***New Opportunity to be Excluded.*** If the class action was previously certified under Rule 23(b)(3), the court may refuse to approve a settlement unless it affords a new opportunity to request exclusion to individual class members who had an earlier opportunity to request exclusion but did not do so.

(5) ***Class-Member Objections.***

(A) *In General.* Any class member may object to the proposal if it requires court approval under this subdivision (e). The objection must state whether it applies only to the objector, to a specific subset of the class, or to the entire class, and also state with specificity the grounds for the objection.

(B) *Court Approval Required for Payment in Connection with an Objection.* Unless approved by the court after a hearing, no payment or other consideration may be provided in connection with:

(i) forgoing or withdrawing an objection, or

(ii) forgoing, dismissing, or abandoning an appeal from a judgment approving the proposal.

(C) *Procedure for Approval After an Appeal.* If approval under Rule 23(e)(5)(B) has not been obtained before an appeal is docketed in the court of appeals, the procedure of Rule 62.1 applies while the appeal remains pending.

(f) **Appeals.** A court of appeals may permit an appeal from an order granting or denying class-action certification under this rule, but not from an order under Rule 23(e)(1). A party must file a petition for permission to appeal with the circuit clerk within 14 days after the order is entered, or within 45 days after the order is entered if any party is the United States, a United States agency, or a United States officer or employee sued for an act or omission occurring in connection with duties performed on the United States' behalf. An appeal does not stay proceedings in the district court unless the district judge or the court of appeals so orders.

(g) **Class Counsel.**

(1) ***Appointing Class Counsel.*** Unless a statute provides otherwise, a court that certifies a class must appoint class counsel. In appointing class counsel, the court:

(A) must consider:

(i) the work counsel has done in identifying or investigating potential claims in the action;

(ii) counsel's experience in handling class actions, other complex litigation, and the types of claims asserted in the action;

(iii) counsel's knowledge of the applicable law; and

(iv) the resources that counsel will commit to representing the class;

(B) may consider any other matter pertinent to counsel's ability to fairly and adequately represent the interests of the class;

(C) may order potential class counsel to provide information on any subject pertinent to the appointment and to propose terms for attorney's fees and nontaxable costs;

(D) may include in the appointing order provisions about the award of attorney's fees or nontaxable costs under Rule 23(h); and

(E) may make further orders in connection with the appointment.

(2) ***Standard for Appointing Class Counsel.*** When one applicant seeks appointment as class counsel, the court may appoint that applicant only if the applicant is adequate under Rule 23(g)(1) and (4). If more than one adequate applicant seeks appointment, the court must appoint the applicant best able to represent the interests of the class.

(3) ***Interim Counsel.*** The court may designate interim counsel to act on behalf of a putative class before determining whether to certify the action as a class action.

(4) ***Duty of Class Counsel.*** Class counsel must fairly and adequately represent the interests of the class.

(h) Attorney's Fees and Nontaxable Costs. In a certified class action, the court may award reasonable attorney's fees and nontaxable costs that are authorized by law or by the parties' agreement. The following procedures apply:

(1) A claim for an award must be made by motion under Rule 54(d)(2), subject to the provisions of this subdivision (h), at a time the court sets. Notice of the motion must be served on all parties and, for motions by class counsel, directed to class members in a reasonable manner.

(2) A class member, or a party from whom payment is sought, may object to the motion.

(3) The court may hold a hearing and must find the facts and state its legal conclusions under Rule 52(a).

(4) The court may refer issues related to the amount of the award to a special master or a magistrate judge, as provided in Rule 54(d)(2)(D).

(As amended Feb. 28, 1966, eff. July 1, 1966; Mar. 2, 1987, eff. Aug. 1, 1987; Apr. 24, 1998, eff. Dec. 1, 1998; Mar. 27, 2003, eff. Dec. 1, 2003; Apr. 30, 2007, eff. Dec. 1, 2007; Mar. 26, 2009, eff. Dec. 1, 2009; Apr. 26, 2018, eff. Dec. 1, 2018.)

NOTES OF ADVISORY COMMITTEE ON RULES

1966 AMENDMENT

Difficulties with the original rule. The categories of class actions in the original rule were defined in terms of the abstract nature of the rights involved: the so-called "true" category was defined as involving "joint, common, or secondary rights"; the "hybrid" category, as involving "several" rights related to "specific property"; the "spurious" category, as involving "several" rights affected by a common question and related to common relief. It was thought that the definitions accurately described the situations amenable to the class-suit device, and also would indicate the proper extent of the judgment in each category, which would in turn help to determine the res judicata effect of the judgment if questioned in a later action. Thus the judgments in "true" and "hybrid" class actions would extend to the class (although in somewhat different ways); the judgment in a "spurious" class action would extend only to the parties including intervenors. See Moore, Federal Rules of Civil Procedure: Some Problems Raised by the Preliminary Draft, 25 Geo.L.J. 551, 570–76 (1937).

In practice the terms "joint," "common," etc., which were used as the basis of the Rule 23 classification proved obscure and uncertain. * * *

The "spurious" action envisaged by original Rule 23 was in any event an anomaly because, although denominated a "class" action and pleaded as such, it was supposed not to adjudicate the rights or liabilities of any person not a party. It was believed to be an advantage of the "spurious" category that it would invite decisions that a member of the "class" could, like a member of the class in a "true" or "hybrid" action, intervene on an ancillary basis without being required to show an independent basis of Federal jurisdiction, and have the benefit of the date of the commencement of the action for purposes of the statute of limitations. See 3 Moore's Federal Practice, pars. 23.10[1], 23.12 (2d ed. 1963). These results were attained in some instances but not in others. * * *

Finally, the original rule did not squarely address itself to the question of the measures that might be taken during the course of the action to assure procedural fairness, particularly giving notice to members of the class, which may in turn be related in some instances to the extension of the judgment to the class. * * *

The amended rule describes in more practical terms the occasions for maintaining class actions; provides that all class actions maintained to the end as such will result in judgments including those whom the court finds to be members of the class, whether or not the judgment is favorable to the class; and refers to the measures which can be taken to assure the fair conduct of these actions.

Subdivision (a) states the prerequisites for maintaining any class action * * *. These are necessary but not sufficient conditions for a class action. * * * Subdivision (b) describes the additional elements which in varying situations justify the use of a class action.

Subdivision (b)(1). The difficulties which would be likely to arise if resort were had to separate actions by or against the individual members of the class here furnish the reasons for, and the principal key to, the propriety and value of utilizing the class-action device. The considerations stated under clauses (A) and (B) are comparable to certain of the elements which define the persons whose joinder in an action is desirable as stated in Rule 19(a), as amended. * * *

Clause (A): One person may have rights against, or be under duties toward, numerous persons constituting a class, and be so positioned that conflicting or varying adjudications in lawsuits with individual members of the class might establish incompatible standards to govern his conduct. The class action device can be used effectively to obviate the actual or virtual dilemma which would thus confront the party opposing the class. * * * To illustrate: Separate actions by individuals against a municipality to declare a bond issue invalid or condition or limit it, to prevent or limit the making of a particular appropriation or to compel or invalidate an assessment, might create a risk of inconsistent or varying determinations. In the same way, individual litigations of the rights and duties of riparian owners, or of landowners' rights and duties respecting a claimed nuisance, could create a possibility of incompatible adjudications. Actions by or against a class provide a ready and fair means of achieving unitary adjudication. * * *

Clause (B): This clause takes in situations where the judgment in a nonclass action by or against an individual member of the class, while not technically concluding the other members, might do so as a practical matter. The vice of an individual action would lie in the fact that the other members of the class, thus practically concluded, would have had no representation in the lawsuit. In an action by policy holders against a fraternal benefit association attacking a financial reorganization of the society, it would hardly have been practical, if indeed it would have been possible, to confine the effects of a validation of the reorganization to the individual plaintiffs. * * * The same reasoning applies to an action which charges a breach of trust by an indenture trustee or other fiduciary similarly affecting the members of a larger class of security holders or other beneficiaries, and which requires an accounting or like measures to restore the subject of the trust. * * *.

In various situations an adjudication as to one or more members of the class will necessarily or probably have an adverse practical effect on the interests of other members who should therefore be represented in the lawsuit. This is plainly the case when claims are made by numerous persons against a fund insufficient to satisfy all claims. A class action by or against representative members to settle the validity of the claims as a whole, or in groups, followed by separate proof of the amount of each valid claim and proportionate distribution of the fund, meets the problem. * * * The same reasoning applies to an action by a creditor to set aside a fraudulent conveyance by the debtor and to appropriate the property to his claim, when the debtor's assets are insufficient to pay all creditors' claims. * * *. Similar problems, however, can arise in the absence of a fund either present or potential. A negative or mandatory injunction secured by one of a numerous class may disable the opposing party from performing claimed duties toward the other members of the class or materially affect his ability to do so. An adjudication as to movie "clearances and runs" nominally affecting only one exhibitor would often have practical effects on all the exhibitors in the same territorial area. Cf. *United States v. Paramount Pictures, Inc.*, 66 F.Supp. 323, 341–46 (S.D.N.Y.1946); 334 U.S. 131, 144–48 (1948). Assuming a sufficiently numerous class of exhibitors, a class action would be advisable. (Here representation of subclasses of exhibitors could become necessary; see subdivision (c)(3)(B).)

Subdivision (b)(2). This subdivision is intended to reach situations where a party has taken action or refused to take action with respect to a class, and final relief of an injunctive nature or of a corresponding declaratory nature, settling the legality of the behavior with respect to the class as a whole, is appropriate. Declaratory relief "corresponds" to injunctive relief when as a practical matter it affords injunctive relief or serves as a basis for later injunctive relief. The subdivision does not extend to cases in which the appropriate final relief relates exclusively or predominantly to money damages. Action or inaction is directed to a class within the meaning of this subdivision even if it has taken effect or is threatened only as to one or a few members of the class, provided it is based on grounds which have general application to the class.

* * *

Subdivision (b)(3). In the situations to which this subdivision relates, class-action treatment is not as clearly called for as in those described above, but it may nevertheless be convenient and desirable depending upon the particular facts. Subdivision (b)(3) encompasses those cases in which a class action would achieve economies of time, effort, and expense, and promote uniformity of decision as to persons similarly situated, without sacrificing procedural fairness or bringing about other undesirable results. * * *.

The court is required to find, as a condition of holding that a class action may be maintained under this subdivision, that the questions common to the class predominate over the questions affecting individual members. It is only where this predominance exists that economies can be achieved by means of the class-action device. In this view, a fraud perpetrated on numerous persons by the use of similar misrepresentations may be an appealing situation for a class action, and it may remain so despite the need, if liability is found, for separate determination of the damages suffered by individuals within the class. On the other hand, although having some common core, a fraud case may be unsuited for treatment as a class action if there was material variation in the representations made or in the kinds or degrees of reliance by the persons to whom they were addressed. * * * A "mass accident" resulting in injuries to numerous persons is ordinarily not appropriate for a class action because of the likelihood that significant questions, not only of damages but of liability and defenses of liability, would be present, affecting the individuals in different ways. * * *

That common questions predominate is not itself sufficient to justify a class action under subdivision (b)(3), for another method of handling the litigious situation may be available which has greater practical advantages. Thus one or more actions agreed to by the parties as test or model actions may be preferable to a class action; or it may prove feasible and preferable to consolidate actions. * * * Even when a number of separate actions are proceeding simultaneously, experience shows that the burdens on the parties and the courts can sometimes be reduced by arrangements for avoiding repetitious discovery or the like. * * *

Factors (A)–(D) are listed, non-exhaustively, as pertinent to the findings. The court is to consider the interests of individual members of the class in controlling their own litigations and carrying them on as they see fit. * * *

In this connection the court should inform itself of any litigation actually pending by or against the individuals. The interests of individuals in conducting separate lawsuits may be so strong as to call for denial of a class action. On the other hand, these interests may be theoretic rather than practical; the class may have a high degree of cohesion and prosecution of the action through representatives would be quite unobjectionable, or the amounts at stake for individuals may be so small that separate suits would be impracticable. The burden that separate suits would impose on the party opposing the class, or upon the court calendars, may also fairly be considered. (See the discussion, under subdivision (c)(2) below, of the right of members to be excluded from the class upon their request.)

Also pertinent is the question of the desirability of concentrating the trial of the claims in the particular forum by means of a class action, in contrast to allowing the claims to be litigated separately in forums to which they would ordinarily be brought. Finally, the court should consider the problems of management which are likely to arise in the conduct of a class action.

* * *

2018 AMENDMENT

Rule 23 is amended mainly to address issues related to settlement, and also to take account of issues that have emerged since the rule was last amended in 2003.

Subdivision (c)(2). As amended, Rule 23(e)(1) provides that the court must direct notice to the class regarding a proposed class-action settlement only after determining that the prospect of class certification and approval of the proposed settlement justifies giving notice. This decision has been called "preliminary approval" of the proposed class certification in Rule 23(b)(3) actions. It is common to send notice to the class simultaneously under both Rule 23(e)(1) and Rule 23(c)(2)(B), including a provision for class members to decide by a certain date whether to opt out. This amendment recognizes the propriety of this combined notice practice.

Subdivision (c)(2) is also amended to recognize contemporary methods of giving notice to class members. Since *Eisen v. Carlisle & Jacquelin*, 417 U.S. 156 (1974), interpreted the individual notice requirement for class members in Rule 23(b)(3) class actions, many courts have read the rule to require notice by first class mail in every case. But technological change since 1974 has introduced other means of communication that may sometimes provide a reliable additional or alternative method for giving notice. Although first class mail may often be the preferred primary method of giving notice, courts and counsel have begun to employ new technology to make notice more effective. Because there is no reason to expect that technological change will cease, when selecting a method or methods of giving notice courts should consider the capacity and limits of current technology, including class members' likely access to such technology.

Rule 23(c)(2)(B) is amended to take account of these changes. The rule continues to call for giving class members "the best notice that is practicable." It does not specify any particular means as preferred. Although it may sometimes be true that electronic methods of notice, for example email, are the most promising, it is important to keep in mind that a significant portion of class members in certain cases may have limited or no access to email or the Internet.

Instead of preferring any one means of notice, therefore, the amended rule relies on courts and counsel to focus on the means or combination of means most likely to be effective in the case before the court. The court should exercise its discretion to select appropriate means of giving notice. In providing the court with sufficient information to enable it to decide whether to give notice to the class of a proposed class-action settlement under Rule 23(e)(1), it would ordinarily be important to include details about the proposed method of giving notice and to provide the court with a copy of each notice the parties propose to use.

* * *

Subdivision (e). The introductory paragraph of Rule 23(e) is amended to make explicit that its procedural requirements apply in instances in which the court has not certified a class at the time that a proposed settlement is presented to the court. The notice required under Rule 23(e)(1) then should also satisfy the notice requirements of amended Rule 23(c)(2)(B) for a class to be certified under Rule 23(b)(3), and trigger the class members' time to request exclusion. Information about the opt-out rate could then be available to the court when it considers final approval of the proposed settlement.

Subdivision (e)(1). The decision to give notice of a proposed settlement to the class is an important event. It should be based on a solid record supporting the conclusion that the proposed settlement will likely earn final approval after notice and an opportunity to object. The parties must provide the court with information sufficient to determine whether notice should be sent. At the time they seek notice to the class, the proponents of the settlement should ordinarily provide the court with all available materials they intend to submit to support approval under Rule 23(e)(2) and that they intend to make available to class members. The amended rule also specifies the standard the court should use in deciding whether to send notice—that it likely will be able both to approve the settlement proposal under Rule 23(e)(2) and, if it has not previously certified a class, to certify the class for purposes of judgment on the proposal.

* * *

Subdivision (e)(2). The central concern in reviewing a proposed class-action settlement is that it be fair, reasonable, and adequate. Courts have generated lists of factors to shed light on this concern. Overall, these factors focus on comparable considerations, but each circuit has developed its own vocabulary for expressing these concerns. In some circuits, these lists have remained essentially unchanged for thirty or forty years. The goal of this amendment is not to displace any factor, but rather to focus the court and the lawyers on the core concerns of procedure and substance that should guide the decision whether to approve the proposal.

* * *

This amendment therefore directs the parties to present the settlement to the court in terms of a shorter list of core concerns, by focusing on the primary procedural considerations and substantive qualities that should always matter to the decision whether to approve the proposal.

Approval under Rule 23(e)(2) is required only when class members would be bound under Rule 23(c)(3). Accordingly, in addition to evaluating the proposal itself, the court must determine whether it can certify the class under the standards of Rule 23(a) and (b) for purposes of judgment based on the proposal.

Paragraphs (A) and (B). These paragraphs identify matters that might be described as "procedural" concerns, looking to the conduct of the litigation and of the negotiations leading up to the proposed settlement. Attention to these matters is an important foundation for scrutinizing the substance of the proposed settlement. If the court has appointed class counsel or interim class counsel, it will have made an initial evaluation of counsel's capacities and experience. But the focus at this point is on the actual performance of counsel acting on behalf of the class.

* * *

Paragraphs (C) and (D). These paragraphs focus on what might be called a "substantive" review of the terms of the proposed settlement. The relief that the settlement is expected to provide to class members is a central concern. Measuring the proposed relief may require evaluation of any proposed claims process; directing that the parties report back to the court about actual claims experience may be important. The contents of any agreement identified under Rule 23(e)(3) may also bear on the adequacy of the proposed relief, particularly regarding the equitable treatment of all members of the class.

Another central concern will relate to the cost and risk involved in pursuing a litigated outcome. Often, courts may need to forecast the likely range of possible classwide recoveries and the likelihood of success in obtaining such results. That forecast cannot be done with arithmetic accuracy, but it can provide a benchmark for comparison with the settlement figure.

If the class has not yet been certified for trial, the court may consider whether certification for litigation would be granted were the settlement not approved.

Examination of the attorney-fee provisions may also be valuable in assessing the fairness of the proposed settlement. Ultimately, any award of attorney's fees must be evaluated under Rule 23(h), and no rigid limits exist for such awards. Nonetheless, the relief actually delivered to the class can be a significant factor in determining the appropriate fee award.

Often it will be important for the court to scrutinize the method of claims processing to ensure that it facilitates filing legitimate claims. A claims processing method should deter or defeat unjustified claims, but the court should be alert to whether the claims process is unduly demanding.

Paragraph (D) calls attention to a concern that may apply to some class action settlements—inequitable treatment of some class members vis-a-vis others. Matters of concern could include whether the apportionment of relief among class members takes appropriate account of differences among their claims, and whether the scope of the release may affect class members in different ways that bear on the apportionment of relief.

* * *

Subdivision (e)(5). The submissions required by Rule 23(e)(1) may provide information critical to decisions whether to object or opt out. Objections by class members can provide the court with important information bearing on its determination under Rule 23(e)(2) whether to approve the proposal.

Subdivision (e)(5)(A). The rule is amended to remove the requirement of court approval for every withdrawal of an objection. An objector should be free to withdraw on concluding that an objection is not justified. But Rule 23(e)(5)(B)(i) requires court approval of any payment or other consideration in connection with withdrawing the objection.

The rule is also amended to clarify that objections must provide sufficient specifics to enable the parties to respond to them and the court to evaluate them. One feature required of objections is specification whether the objection asserts interests of only the objector, or of some subset of the class, or of all class members. Beyond that, the rule directs that the objection state its grounds "with specificity." Failure to provide needed specificity may be a basis for rejecting an objection. Courts should take care, however, to avoid unduly burdening class members who wish to object, and to recognize that a class member who is not represented by counsel may present objections that do not adhere to technical legal standards.

Subdivision (e)(5)(B). Good-faith objections can assist the court in evaluating a proposal under Rule 23(e)(2). It is legitimate for an objector to seek payment for providing such assistance under Rule 23(h).

But some objectors may be seeking only personal gain, and using objections to obtain benefits for themselves rather than assisting in the settlement-review process. At least in some instances, it seems that objectors—or their counsel—have sought to obtain consideration for withdrawing their objections or dismissing appeals from judgments approving class settlements. And class counsel sometimes may feel that avoiding the delay produced by an appeal justifies providing payment or other consideration to these objectors. Although the payment may advance class interests in a particular case, allowing payment perpetuates a system that can encourage objections advanced for improper purposes.

The court-approval requirement currently in Rule 23(e)(5) partly addresses this concern. Because the concern only applies when consideration is given in connection with withdrawal of an objection, however, the amendment requires approval under Rule 23(e)(5)(B)(i) only when consideration is involved. Although such payment is usually made to objectors or their counsel, the rule also requires court approval if a payment in connection with forgoing or withdrawing an objection or appeal is instead to another recipient. The term "consideration" should be broadly interpreted, particularly when the withdrawal includes some arrangements beneficial to objector counsel. If the consideration involves a payment to counsel for an objector, the proper procedure is by motion under Rule 23(h) for an award of fees.

* * *

Subdivision (f). As amended, Rule 23(e)(1) provides that the court must direct notice to the class regarding a proposed class-action settlement only after determining that the prospect of eventual class certification justifies giving notice. But this decision does not grant or deny class certification, and review under Rule 23(f) would be premature. This amendment makes it clear that an appeal under this rule is not permitted until the district court decides whether to certify the class.

* * *

Rule 23.1. Derivative Actions

(a) Prerequisites. This rule applies when one or more shareholders or members of a corporation or an unincorporated association bring a derivative action to enforce a right that the corporation or association may properly assert but has failed to enforce. The derivative action may not be maintained if it appears that the plaintiff does not fairly and adequately represent the interests of shareholders or members who are similarly situated in enforcing the right of the corporation or association.

(b) Pleading Requirements. The complaint must be verified and must:

(1) allege that the plaintiff was a shareholder or member at the time of the transaction complained of, or that the plaintiff's share or membership later devolved on it by operation of law;

(2) allege that the action is not a collusive one to confer jurisdiction that the court would otherwise lack; and

(3) state with particularity:

(A) any effort by the plaintiff to obtain the desired action from the directors or comparable authority and, if necessary, from the shareholders or members; and

(B) the reasons for not obtaining the action or not making the effort.

(c) Settlement, Dismissal, and Compromise. A derivative action may be settled, voluntarily dismissed, or compromised only with the court's approval. Notice of a proposed settlement, voluntary dismissal, or compromise must be given to shareholders or members in the manner that the court orders.

(Added Feb. 28, 1966, eff. July 1, 1966, and amended Mar. 2, 1987, eff. Aug. 1, 1987; Apr. 30, 2007, eff. Dec. 1, 2007.)

Rule 23.2. Actions Relating to Unincorporated Associations

This rule applies to an action brought by or against the members of an unincorporated association as a class by naming certain members as representative parties. The action may be maintained only if it appears that those parties will fairly and adequately protect the interests of the association and its members. In conducting the action, the court may issue any appropriate orders corresponding with those in Rule 23(d), and the procedure for settlement, voluntary dismissal, or compromise must correspond with the procedure in Rule 23(e).

(Added Feb. 28, 1966, eff. July 1, 1966, and amended Apr. 30, 2007, eff. Dec. 1, 2007.)

Rule 24. Intervention

(a) Intervention of Right. On timely motion, the court must permit anyone to intervene who:

(1) is given an unconditional right to intervene by a federal statute; or

(2) claims an interest relating to the property or transaction that is the subject of the action, and is so situated that disposing of the action may as a practical matter impair or impede the movant's ability to protect its interest, unless existing parties adequately represent that interest.

(b) Permissive Intervention.

(1) ***In General.*** On timely motion, the court may permit anyone to intervene who:

(A) is given a conditional right to intervene by a federal statute; or

(B) has a claim or defense that shares with the main action a common question of law or fact.

(2) ***By a Government Officer or Agency.*** On timely motion, the court may permit a federal or state governmental officer or agency to intervene if a party's claim or defense is based on:

(A) a statute or executive order administered by the officer or agency; or

(B) any regulation, order, requirement, or agreement issued or made under the statute or executive order.

(3) ***Delay or Prejudice.*** In exercising its discretion, the court must consider whether the intervention will unduly delay or prejudice the adjudication of the original parties' rights.

(c) Notice and Pleading Required. A motion to intervene must be served on the parties as provided in Rule 5. The motion must state the grounds for intervention and be accompanied by a pleading that sets out the claim or defense for which intervention is sought.

(As amended Dec. 27, 1946, eff. Mar. 19, 1948; Dec. 29, 1948, eff. Oct. 20, 1949; Jan. 21, 1963, eff. July 1, 1963; Feb. 28, 1966, eff. July 1, 1966; Mar. 2, 1987, eff. Aug. 1, 1987; Apr. 30, 1991, eff. Dec. 1, 1991; Apr. 12, 2006, eff. Dec. 1, 2006; Apr. 30, 2007, eff. Dec. 1, 2007.)

NOTES OF ADVISORY COMMITTEE ON RULES

1966 AMENDMENT

In attempting to overcome certain difficulties which have arisen in the application of present Rule 24(a)(2) and (3), this amendment draws upon the revision of the related Rules 19 (joinder of persons needed for just adjudication) and 23 (class actions), and the reasoning underlying that revision.

* * *

Original Rule 24(a)(2) * * * made it a condition of intervention that "the applicant is or may be bound by a judgment in the action," and this created difficulties with intervention in class actions. If the "bound" language was read literally in the sense of res judicata, it could defeat intervention in some meritorious cases. A member of a class to whom a judgment in a class action extended by its terms (see Rule 23(c)(3), as amended) might be entitled to show in a later action, when the judgment in the class action was claimed to operate as res judicata against him, that the "representative" in the class action had not in fact adequately represented him. If he could make this showing, the class-action judgment might be held not to bind him. See *Hansberry v. Lee*, 311 U.S. 32 (1940). If a class member sought to intervene in the class action proper, while it was still pending, on grounds of inadequacy of representation, he could be met with the argument: if the representation was in fact inadequate, he would not be "bound" by the judgment when it was subsequently asserted against him as res judicata, hence he was not entitled to intervene; if the representation was in fact adequate, there was no occasion or ground for intervention. See *Sam Fox Publishing Co. v. United States*, 366 U.S. 683 (1961); cf. *Sutphen Estates, Inc. v. United States*, 342 U.S. 19 (1951). This reasoning might be linguistically justified by original Rule 24(a)(2); but it could lead to poor results. * * *

The amendment provides that an applicant is entitled to intervene in an action when his position is comparable to that of a person under Rule 19(a)(2)(i), as amended, unless his interest is already adequately represented in the action by existing parties. The Rule 19(a)(2)(i) criterion imports practical considerations, and the deletion of the "bound" language similarly frees the rule from undue preoccupation with strict considerations of res judicata.

The representation whose adequacy comes into question under the amended rule is not confined to formal representation like that provided by a trustee for his beneficiary or a representative party in a class action for a member of the class. A party to an action may provide practical representation to the absentee seeking intervention although no such formal relationship exists between them, and the adequacy of this practical representation will then have to be weighed. * * *

An intervention of right under the amended rule may be subject to appropriate conditions or restrictions responsive among other things to the requirements of efficient conduct of the proceedings.

Rule 25. Substitution of Parties

(a) Death.

(1) ***Substitution if the Claim Is Not Extinguished.*** If a party dies and the claim is not extinguished, the court may order substitution of the proper party. A motion for substitution may be made by any party or by the decedent's successor or representative. If the motion is not made within 90 days after service of a statement noting the death, the action by or against the decedent must be dismissed.

(2) ***Continuation Among the Remaining Parties.*** After a party's death, if the right sought to be enforced survives only to or against the remaining parties, the action does not abate, but proceeds in favor of or against the remaining parties. The death should be noted on the record.

(3) ***Service.*** A motion to substitute, together with a notice of hearing, must be served on the parties as provided in Rule 5 and on nonparties as provided in Rule 4. A statement noting death must be served in the same manner. Service may be made in any judicial district.

(b) Incompetency. If a party becomes incompetent, the court may, on motion, permit the action to be continued by or against the party's representative. The motion must be served as provided in Rule 25(a)(3).

(c) Transfer of Interest. If an interest is transferred, the action may be continued by or against the original party unless the court, on motion, orders the transferee to be substituted in the action or joined with the original party. The motion must be served as provided in Rule 25(a)(3).

(d) Public Officers; Death or Separation from Office. An action does not abate when a public officer who is a party in an official capacity dies, resigns, or otherwise ceases to hold office while the action is pending. The officer's successor is automatically substituted as a party. Later proceedings should be in the substituted party's name, but any misnomer not affecting the parties' substantial rights must be disregarded. The court may order substitution at any time, but the absence of such an order does not affect the substitution.

(As amended Dec. 29, 1948, eff. Oct. 20, 1949; Apr. 17, 1961, eff. July 19, 1961; Jan. 21, 1963, eff. July 1, 1963; Mar. 2, 1987, eff. Aug. 1, 1987; Apr. 30, 2007, eff. Dec. 1, 2007.)

TITLE V. DISCLOSURES AND DISCOVERY

Rule 26. Duty to Disclose; General Provisions Governing Discovery

(a) Required Disclosures.

(1) ***Initial Disclosure.***

(A) *In General.* Except as exempted by Rule 26(a)(1)(B) or as otherwise stipulated or ordered by the court, a party must, without awaiting a discovery request, provide to the other parties:

(i) the name and, if known, the address and telephone number of each individual likely to have discoverable information—along with the subjects of that information—that the disclosing party may use to support its claims or defenses, unless the use would be solely for impeachment;

(ii) a copy—or a description by category and location—of all documents, electronically stored information, and tangible things that the disclosing party has in its possession, custody, or control and may use to support its claims or defenses, unless the use would be solely for impeachment;

(iii) a computation of each category of damages claimed by the disclosing party—who must also make available for inspection and copying as under Rule 34 the documents or other evidentiary material, unless privileged or protected from disclosure, on which each computation is based, including materials bearing on the nature and extent of injuries suffered; and

(iv) for inspection and copying as under Rule 34, any insurance agreement under which an insurance business may be liable to satisfy all or part of a possible judgment in the action or to indemnify or reimburse for payments made to satisfy the judgment.

(B) *Proceedings Exempt from Initial Disclosure.* The following proceedings are exempt from initial disclosure:

(i) an action for review on an administrative record;

(ii) a petition for habeas corpus or any other proceeding to challenge a criminal conviction or sentence;

(iii) an action brought without an attorney by a person in the custody of the United States, a state, or a state subdivision;

(iv) an action to enforce or quash an administrative summons or subpoena;

(v) an action by the United States to recover benefit payments;

(vi) an action by the United States to collect on a student loan guaranteed by the United States;

(vii) a proceeding ancillary to a proceeding in another court; and

(viii) an action to enforce an arbitration award.

(C) *Time for Initial Disclosures—In General.* A party must make the initial disclosures at or within 14 days after the parties' Rule 26(f) conference unless a different time is set by stipulation or court order, or unless a party objects during the conference that initial disclosures are not appropriate in this action and states the objection in the proposed discovery plan. In ruling on the objection, the court must determine what disclosures, if any, are to be made and must set the time for disclosure.

(D) *Time for Initial Disclosures—For Parties Served or Joined Later.* A party that is first served or otherwise joined after the Rule 26(f) conference must make the initial disclosures within 30 days after being served or joined, unless a different time is set by stipulation or court order.

(E) *Basis for Initial Disclosure; Unacceptable Excuses.* A party must make its initial disclosures based on the information then reasonably available to it. A party is not excused from making its disclosures because it has not fully investigated the case or because it challenges the sufficiency of another party's disclosures or because another party has not made its disclosures.

(2) ***Disclosure of Expert Testimony.***

(A) *In General.* In addition to the disclosures required by Rule 26(a)(1), a party must disclose to the other parties the identity of any witness it may use at trial to present evidence under Federal Rule of Evidence 702, 703, or 705.

(B) *Witnesses Who Must Provide a Written Report.* Unless otherwise stipulated or ordered by the court, this disclosure must be accompanied by a written report—prepared and signed by the witness—if the witness is one retained or specially employed to provide expert testimony in the case or one whose duties as the party's employee regularly involve giving expert testimony. The report must contain:

(i) a complete statement of all opinions the witness will express and the basis and reasons for them;

(ii) the facts or data considered by the witness in forming them;

(iii) any exhibits that will be used to summarize or support them;

(iv) the witness's qualifications, including a list of all publications authored in the previous 10 years;

(v) a list of all other cases in which, during the previous 4 years, the witness testified as an expert at trial or by deposition; and

(vi) a statement of the compensation to be paid for the study and testimony in the case.

(C) *Witnesses Who Do Not Provide a Written Report.* Unless otherwise stipulated or ordered by the court, if the witness is not required to provide a written report, this disclosure must state:

(i) the subject matter on which the witness is expected to present evidence under Federal Rule of Evidence 702, 703, or 705; and

(ii) a summary of the facts and opinions to which the witness is expected to testify.

(D) *Time to Disclose Expert Testimony.* A party must make these disclosures at the times and in the sequence that the court orders. Absent a stipulation or a court order, the disclosures must be made:

(i) at least 90 days before the date set for trial or for the case to be ready for trial; or

(ii) if the evidence is intended solely to contradict or rebut evidence on the same subject matter identified by another party under Rule 26(a)(2)(B) or (C), within 30 days after the other party's disclosure.

(E) *Supplementing the Disclosure.* The parties must supplement these disclosures when required under Rule 26(e).

(3) ***Pretrial Disclosures.***

(A) *In General.* In addition to the disclosures required by Rule 26(a)(1) and (2), a party must provide to the other parties and promptly file the following information about the evidence that it may present at trial other than solely for impeachment:

(i) the name and, if not previously provided, the address and telephone number of each witness—separately identifying those the party expects to present and those it may call if the need arises;

(ii) the designation of those witnesses whose testimony the party expects to present by deposition and, if not taken stenographically, a transcript of the pertinent parts of the deposition; and

(iii) an identification of each document or other exhibit, including summaries of other evidence—separately identifying those items the party expects to offer and those it may offer if the need arises.

(B) *Time for Pretrial Disclosures; Objections.* Unless the court orders otherwise, these disclosures must be made at least 30 days before trial. Within 14 days after they are made, unless the court sets a different time, a party may serve and promptly file a list of the following objections: any objections to the use under Rule 32(a) of a deposition designated by another party under Rule 26(a)(3)(A)(ii); and any objection, together with the grounds for it, that may be made to the admissibility of materials identified under Rule 26(a)(3)(A)(iii). An objection not so made—except for one under Federal Rule of Evidence 402 or 403—is waived unless excused by the court for good cause.

(4) ***Form of Disclosures.*** Unless the court orders otherwise, all disclosures under Rule 26(a) must be in writing, signed, and served.

(b) Discovery Scope and Limits.

(1) ***Scope in General.*** Unless otherwise limited by court order, the scope of discovery is as follows: Parties may obtain discovery regarding any nonprivileged matter that is relevant to any party's claim or defense and proportional to the needs of the case, considering the importance of the issues at stake in the action, the amount in controversy, the parties' relative access to relevant information, the parties' resources, the importance of the discovery in resolving the issues, and whether the burden or expense of the proposed discovery outweighs its likely benefit. Information within this scope of discovery need not be admissible in evidence to be discoverable.

(2) ***Limitations on Frequency and Extent.***

(A) *When Permitted.* By order, the court may alter the limits in these rules on the number of depositions and interrogatories or on the length of depositions under Rule 30. By order or local rule, the court may also limit the number of requests under Rule 36.

(B) *Specific Limitations on Electronically Stored Information.* A party need not provide discovery of electronically stored information from sources that the party identifies as not reasonably accessible because of undue burden or cost. On motion to compel discovery or for a protective order, the party from whom discovery is sought must show that the information is not reasonably accessible because of undue burden or cost. If that showing is made, the court may nonetheless order discovery from such sources if the requesting party shows good cause, considering the limitations of Rule 26(b)(2)(C). The court may specify conditions for the discovery.

(C) *When Required.* On motion or on its own, the court must limit the frequency or extent of discovery otherwise allowed by these rules or by local rule if it determines that:

(i) the discovery sought is unreasonably cumulative or duplicative, or can be obtained from some other source that is more convenient, less burdensome, or less expensive;

(ii) the party seeking discovery has had ample opportunity to obtain the information by discovery in the action; or

(iii) the proposed discovery is outside the scope permitted by Rule 26(b)(1).

(3) ***Trial Preparation: Materials.***

(A) *Documents and Tangible Things.* Ordinarily, a party may not discover documents and tangible things that are prepared in anticipation of litigation or for trial by or for another party or its representative (including the other party's attorney, consultant, surety, indemnitor, insurer, or agent). But, subject to Rule 26(b)(4), those materials may be discovered if:

(i) they are otherwise discoverable under Rule 26(b)(1); and

(ii) the party shows that it has substantial need for the materials to prepare its case and cannot, without undue hardship, obtain their substantial equivalent by other means.

(B) *Protection Against Disclosure.* If the court orders discovery of those materials, it must protect against disclosure of the mental impressions, conclusions, opinions, or legal theories of a party's attorney or other representative concerning the litigation.

(C) *Previous Statement.* Any party or other person may, on request and without the required showing, obtain the person's own previous statement about the action or its subject matter. If the request is refused, the person may move for a court order, and Rule 37(a)(5) applies to the award of expenses. A previous statement is either:

(i) a written statement that the person has signed or otherwise adopted or approved; or

(ii) a contemporaneous stenographic, mechanical, electrical, or other recording—or a transcription of it—that recites substantially verbatim the person's oral statement.

(4) ***Trial Preparation: Experts.***

(A) *Deposition of an Expert Who May Testify.* A party may depose any person who has been identified as an expert whose opinions may be presented at trial. If Rule 26(a)(2)(B) requires a report from the expert, the deposition may be conducted only after the report is provided.

(B) *Trial-Preparation Protection for Draft Reports or Disclosures.* Rules 26(b)(3)(A) and (B) protect drafts of any report or disclosure required under Rule 26(a)(2), regardless of the form in which the draft is recorded.

(C) *Trial-Preparation Protection for Communications Between a Party's Attorney and Expert Witnesses.* Rules 26(b)(3)(A) and (B) protect communications between the party's attorney and any witness required to provide a report under Rule 26(a)(2)(B), regardless of the form of the communications, except to the extent that the communications:

(i) relate to compensation for the expert's study or testimony;

(ii) identify facts or data that the party's attorney provided and that the expert considered in forming the opinions to be expressed; or

(iii) identify assumptions that the party's attorney provided and that the expert relied on in forming the opinions to be expressed.

(D) *Expert Employed Only for Trial Preparation.* Ordinarily, a party may not, by interrogatories or deposition, discover facts known or opinions held by an expert who has been retained or specially employed by another party in anticipation of litigation or to prepare for trial and who is not expected to be called as a witness at trial. But a party may do so only:

(i) as provided in Rule 35(b); or

(ii) on showing exceptional circumstances under which it is impracticable for the party to obtain facts or opinions on the same subject by other means.

(E) *Payment.* Unless manifest injustice would result, the court must require that the party seeking discovery:

(i) pay the expert a reasonable fee for time spent in responding to discovery under Rule 26(b)(4)(A) or (D); and

(ii) for discovery under (D), also pay the other party a fair portion of the fees and expenses it reasonably incurred in obtaining the expert's facts and opinions.

(5) ***Claiming Privilege or Protecting Trial-Preparation Materials.***

(A) *Information Withheld.* When a party withholds information otherwise discoverable by claiming that the information is privileged or subject to protection as trial-preparation material, the party must:

(i) expressly make the claim; and

(ii) describe the nature of the documents, communications, or tangible things not produced or disclosed—and do so in a manner that, without revealing information itself privileged or protected, will enable other parties to assess the claim.

(B) *Information Produced.* If information produced in discovery is subject to a claim of privilege or of protection as trial-preparation material, the party making the claim may notify any party that received the information of the claim and the basis for it. After being notified, a party must promptly return, sequester, or destroy the specified information and any copies it has; must not use or disclose the information until the claim is resolved; must take reasonable steps to retrieve the information if the party disclosed it before being notified; and may promptly present the information to the court under seal for a determination of the claim. The producing party must preserve the information until the claim is resolved.

(c) Protective Orders.

(1) ***In General.*** A party or any person from whom discovery is sought may move for a protective order in the court where the action is pending—or as an alternative on matters relating to a deposition, in the court for the district where the deposition will be taken. The motion must include a certification that the movant has in good faith conferred or attempted to confer with other affected parties in an effort to resolve the dispute without court action. The court may, for good cause, issue an order to protect a party or person from annoyance, embarrassment, oppression, or undue burden or expense, including one or more of the following:

(A) forbidding the disclosure or discovery;

(B) specifying terms, including time and place or the allocation of expenses, for the disclosure or discovery;

(C) prescribing a discovery method other than the one selected by the party seeking discovery;

(D) forbidding inquiry into certain matters, or limiting the scope of disclosure or discovery to certain matters;

(E) designating the persons who may be present while the discovery is conducted;

(F) requiring that a deposition be sealed and opened only on court order;

(G) requiring that a trade secret or other confidential research, development, or commercial information not be revealed or be revealed only in a specified way; and

(H) requiring that the parties simultaneously file specified documents or information in sealed envelopes, to be opened as the court directs.

(2) ***Ordering Discovery.*** If a motion for a protective order is wholly or partly denied, the court may, on just terms, order that any party or person provide or permit discovery.

(3) ***Awarding Expenses.*** Rule 37(a)(5) applies to the award of expenses.

(d) Timing and Sequence of Discovery.

(1) ***Timing.*** A party may not seek discovery from any source before the parties have conferred as required by Rule 26(f), except in a proceeding exempted from initial disclosure under Rule 26(a)(1)(B), or when authorized by these rules, by stipulation, or by court order.

(2) ***Early Rule 34 Requests.***

(A) *Time to Deliver.* More than 21 days after the summons and complaint are served on a party, a request under Rule 34 may be delivered:

(i) to that party by any other party, and

(ii) by that party to any plaintiff or to any other party that has been served.

(B) *When Considered Served.* The request is considered to have been served at the first Rule 26(f) conference.

(3) ***Sequence.*** Unless the parties stipulate or the court orders otherwise for the parties' and witnesses' convenience and in the interests of justice:

(A) methods of discovery may be used in any sequence; and

(B) discovery by one party does not require any other party to delay its discovery.

(e) Supplementing Disclosures and Responses.

(1) ***In General.*** A party who has made a disclosure under Rule 26(a)—or who has responded to an interrogatory, request for production, or request for admission—must supplement or correct its disclosure or response:

(A) in a timely manner if the party learns that in some material respect the disclosure or response is incomplete or incorrect, and if the additional or corrective information has not otherwise been made known to the other parties during the discovery process or in writing; or

(B) as ordered by the court.

(2) ***Expert Witness.*** For an expert whose report must be disclosed under Rule 26(a)(2)(B), the party's duty to supplement extends both to information included in the report and to information given during the expert's deposition. Any additions or changes to this information must be disclosed by the time the party's pretrial disclosures under Rule 26(a)(3) are due.

(f) Conference of the Parties; Planning for Discovery.

(1) ***Conference Timing.*** Except in a proceeding exempted from initial disclosure under Rule 26(a)(1)(B) or when the court orders otherwise, the parties must confer as soon as practicable—and in any event at least 21 days before a scheduling conference is to be held or a scheduling order is due under Rule 16(b).

(2) ***Conference Content; Parties' Responsibilities.*** In conferring, the parties must consider the nature and basis of their claims and defenses and the possibilities for promptly settling or resolving the case; make or arrange for the disclosures required by Rule 26(a)(1); discuss any issues about preserving discoverable information; and develop a proposed discovery plan. The attorneys of record and all unrepresented parties that have appeared in the case are jointly responsible for arranging the conference, for attempting in good faith to agree on the proposed discovery plan, and for submitting to the court within 14 days after the conference a written report outlining the plan. The court may order the parties or attorneys to attend the conference in person.

(3) ***Discovery Plan.*** A discovery plan must state the parties' views and proposals on:

(A) what changes should be made in the timing, form, or requirement for disclosures under Rule 26(a), including a statement of when initial disclosures were made or will be made;

(B) the subjects on which discovery may be needed, when discovery should be completed, and whether discovery should be conducted in phases or be limited to or focused on particular issues;

(C) any issues about disclosure, discovery, or preservation of electronically stored information, including the form or forms in which it should be produced;

(D) any issues about claims of privilege or of protection as trial-preparation materials, including the timing and method for complying with Rule 26(b)(5)(A) and—if the parties agree on a procedure to assert these claims after production—whether to ask the court to include their agreement in an order under Federal Rule of Evidence 502;

(E) what changes should be made in the limitations on discovery imposed under these rules or by local rule, and what other limitations should be imposed; and

(F) any other orders that the court should issue under Rule 26(c) or under Rule 16(b) and (c).

(4) ***Expedited Schedule.*** If necessary to comply with its expedited schedule for Rule 16(b) conferences, a court may by local rule:

(A) require the parties' conference to occur less than 21 days before the scheduling conference is held or a scheduling order is due under Rule 16(b); and

(B) require the written report outlining the discovery plan to be filed less than 14 days after the parties' conference, or excuse the parties from submitting a written report and permit them to report orally on their discovery plan at the Rule 16(b) conference.

(g) Signing Disclosures and Discovery Requests, Responses, and Objections.

(1) ***Signature Required; Effect of Signature.*** Every disclosure under Rule 26(a)(1) or (a)(3) and every discovery request, response, or objection must be signed by at least one attorney of record in the attorney's own name—or by the party personally, if unrepresented—and must state the signer's address, e-mail address, and telephone number. By signing, an attorney or party certifies that to the best of the person's knowledge, information, and belief formed after a reasonable inquiry:

(A) with respect to a disclosure, it is complete and correct as of the time it is made; and

(B) with respect to a discovery request, response, or objection, it is:

(i) consistent with these rules and warranted by existing law or by a nonfrivolous argument for extending, modifying, or reversing existing law, or for establishing new law;

(ii) not interposed for any improper purpose, such as to harass, cause unnecessary delay, or needlessly increase the cost of litigation; and

(iii) neither unreasonable nor unduly burdensome or expensive, considering the needs of the case, prior discovery in the case, the amount in controversy, and the importance of the issues at stake in the action.

(2) ***Failure to Sign.*** Other parties have no duty to act on an unsigned disclosure, request, response, or objection until it is signed, and the court must strike it unless a signature is promptly supplied after the omission is called to the attorney's or party's attention.

(3) ***Sanction for Improper Certification.*** If a certification violates this rule without substantial justification, the court, on motion or on its own, must impose an appropriate sanction on the signer, the party on whose behalf the signer was acting, or both. The sanction may include an order to pay the reasonable expenses, including attorney's fees, caused by the violation.

(As amended Dec. 27, 1946, eff. Mar. 19, 1948; Jan. 21, 1963, eff. July 1, 1963; Feb. 28, 1966, eff. July 1, 1966; Mar. 30, 1970, eff. July 1, 1970; Apr. 29, 1980, eff. Aug. 1, 1980; Apr. 28, 1983, eff. Aug. 1, 1983; Mar. 2, 1987, eff. Aug. 1, 1987; Apr. 22, 1993, Dec. 1, 1993; Apr. 17, 2000, eff. Dec. 1, 2000; Apr. 12, 2006, eff. Dec. 1, 2006; Apr. 30, 2007, eff. Dec. 1, 2007; Apr. 28, 2010, eff. Dec. 1, 2010; Apr. 29, 2015, eff. Dec. 1, 2015; Apr. 23, 2025, eff. Dec. 1, 2025.)

NOTES OF ADVISORY COMMITTEE ON RULES

1970 AMENDMENT

* * *

Subdivision (b)(3)—Trial Preparation: Materials. Some of the most controversial and vexing problems to emerge from the discovery rules have arisen out of requests for the production of documents or things prepared in anticipation of litigation or for trial. The existing rules make no explicit provision for such materials. Yet, two verbally distinct doctrines have developed, each conferring a qualified immunity on these materials—the "good cause" requirement in Rule 34 (now generally held applicable to discovery of documents via deposition under Rule 45 and interrogatories under Rule 33) and the work-product doctrine of *Hickman v. Taylor*, 329 U.S. 495 (1947). Both demand a showing of justification before production can be had, the one of "good cause" and the other variously described in the *Hickman* case: "necessity or justification," "denial * * * would unduly prejudice the preparation of petitioner's case," or "cause hardship or injustice". 329 U.S. at 509–510.

* * *

Basic Standard.—

* * *

The Rules are amended by eliminating the general requirement of "good cause" from Rule 34 but retaining a requirement of a special showing for trial preparation materials in this subdivision. The required showing is expressed, not in terms of "good cause" whose generality has tended to encourage confusion and controversy, but in terms of the elements of the special showing to be made: substantial need of the materials in the preparation of the case and inability without undue hardship to obtain the substantial equivalent of the materials by other means.

These changes conform to the holdings of the cases, when viewed in light of their facts. Apart from trial preparation, the fact that the materials sought are documentary does not in and of itself require a special showing beyond relevance and absence of privilege. The protective provisions are of course available, and if the party from whom production is sought raises a special issue of privacy (as with respect to income tax returns or grand jury minutes) or points to evidence primarily impeaching, or can show serious burden or expense, the court will exercise its traditional power to decide whether to issue a protective order. On the other hand, the requirement of a special showing for discovery of trial preparation materials reflects the view that each side's informal evaluation of its case should be protected, that each side should be encouraged to prepare independently, and that one side should not automatically have the benefit of the detailed preparatory work of the other side. * * *

Elimination of a "good cause" requirement from Rule 34 and the establishment of a requirement of a special showing in this subdivision will eliminate the confusion caused by having two verbally distinct requirements of justification that the courts have been unable to distinguish clearly. Moreover, the language of the subdivision suggests the factors which the courts should consider in determining whether the requisite showing has been made. The importance of the materials sought to the party seeking them in preparation of his case and the difficulty he will have obtaining them by other means are factors noted in the *Hickman* case. The courts should also consider the likelihood that the party, even if he obtains the information by independent means, will not have the substantial equivalent of the documents the production of which he seeks.

Consideration of these factors may well lead the court to distinguish between witness statements taken by an investigator, on the one hand, and other parts of the investigative file, on the other. * * * The witness may have given a fresh and contemporaneous account in a written statement while he is available to the party seeking discovery only a substantial time thereafter. * * * Or he may be reluctant or hostile. * * * Or he may have a lapse of memory. * * * Or he may probably be deviating from his prior statement. * * * On the other hand, a much stronger showing is needed to obtain evaluative materials in an investigator's reports. * * *

Materials assembled in the ordinary course of business, or pursuant to public requirements unrelated to litigation, or for other nonlitigation purposes are not under the qualified immunity provided by this subdivision. * * * No change is made in the existing doctrine, noted in the *Hickman* case, that one party may discover relevant facts known or available to the other party, even though such facts are contained in a document which is not itself discoverable.

Treatment of Lawyers; Special Protection of Mental Impressions, Conclusions, Opinions, and Legal Theories Concerning the Litigation.—

* * *

Subdivision (b)(3) reflects the trend of the cases by requiring a special showing, not merely as to materials prepared by an attorney, but also as to materials prepared in anticipation of litigation or preparation for trial by or for a party or any representative acting on his behalf. The subdivision then goes on to protect against disclosure the mental impressions, conclusions, opinions, or legal theories concerning the litigation of an attorney or other representative of a party. The *Hickman* opinion drew special attention to the need for protecting an attorney against discovery of memoranda prepared from recollection of oral interviews. The courts have steadfastly safeguarded against disclosure of lawyers' mental impressions and legal theories, as well as mental impressions and subjective evaluations of investigators and claim-agents. In enforcing this provision of the subdivision, the courts will sometimes find it necessary to order disclosure of a document but with portions deleted.

Rules 33 and 36 have been revised in order to permit discovery calling for opinions, contentions, and admissions relating not only to fact but also to the application of law to fact. Under those rules, a party and his attorney or other representative may be required to disclose, to some extent, mental impressions, opinions, or conclusions. But documents or parts of documents containing these matters are protected against discovery by this subdivision. Even though a party may ultimately have to disclose in response to interrogatories or requests to admit, he is entitled to keep confidential documents containing such matters prepared for internal use.

Party's Right to Own Statement.—An exception to the requirement of this subdivision enables a party to secure production of his own statement without any special showing. The cases are divided. * * *

Courts which treat a party's statement as though it were that of any witness overlook the fact that the party's statement is, without more, admissible in evidence. Ordinarily, a party gives a statement without insisting on a copy because he does not yet have a lawyer and does not understand the legal consequences of his actions. Thus, the statement is given at a time when he functions at a disadvantage. Discrepancies between his trial testimony and earlier statement may result from lapse of memory or ordinary inaccuracy; a written statement produced for the first time at trial may give such discrepancies a prominence which they do not deserve. In appropriate cases the court may order a party to be deposed before his statement is produced.

* * *

Witness' Right to Own Statement.—A second exception to the requirement of this subdivision permits a non-party witness to obtain a copy of his own statement without any special showing. Many, though not all, of the considerations supporting a party's right to obtain his statement apply also to the non-party witness. Insurance companies are increasingly recognizing that a witness is entitled to a copy of his statement and are modifying their regular practice accordingly.

* * *

1993 AMENDMENT

Subdivision (a). Through the addition of paragraphs (1)–(4), this subdivision imposes on parties a duty to disclose, without awaiting formal discovery requests, certain basic information that is needed in most cases to prepare for trial or make an informed decision about settlement. The rule requires all parties (1) early in the case to exchange information regarding potential witnesses, documentary evidence, damages, and insurance, (2) at an appropriate time during the discovery period to identify expert witnesses and provide a detailed written statement of the testimony that may be offered at trial through specially retained experts, and (3) as the trial date approaches to identify the particular evidence that may be offered at trial. The enumeration in Rule 26(a) of items to be disclosed does not prevent a court from requiring by order or local rule that the parties disclose additional information without a discovery request. Nor are parties precluded from using traditional discovery methods to obtain further information regarding these matters, as for example asking an expert during a deposition about testimony given in other litigation beyond the four-year period specified in Rule 26(a)(2)(B).

A major purpose of the revision is to accelerate the exchange of basic information about the case and to eliminate the paper work involved in requesting such information, and the rule should be applied in a manner to achieve those objectives. The concepts of imposing a duty of disclosure were set forth in Brazil, *The Adversary Character of Civil Discovery: A Critique and*

Proposals for Change, 31 *Vand.L.Rev.* 1348 (1978), and Schwarzer, *The Federal Rules, the Adversary Process, and Discovery Reform,* 50 *U.Pitt.L.Rev.* 703, 721–23 (1989).

* * *

Subdivision (b). * * * The information explosion of recent decades has greatly increased both the potential cost of wide-ranging discovery and the potential for discovery to be used as an instrument for delay or oppression. Amendments to Rules 30, 31, and 33 place presumptive limits on the number of depositions and interrogatories, subject to leave of court to pursue additional discovery. The revisions in Rule 26(b)(2) are intended to provide the court with broader discretion to impose additional restrictions on the scope and extent of discovery and to authorize courts that develop case tracking systems based on the complexity of cases to increase or decrease by local rule the presumptive number of depositions and interrogatories allowed in particular types or classifications of cases. The revision also dispels any doubt as to the power of the court to impose limitations on the length of depositions under Rule 30 or on the number of requests for admission under Rule 36.

* * *

Paragraph (5) is a new provision. A party must notify other parties if it is withholding materials otherwise subject to disclosure under the rule or pursuant to a discovery request because it is asserting a claim of privilege or work product protection. To withhold materials without such notice is contrary to the rule, subjects the party to sanctions under Rule 37(b)(2), and may be viewed as a waiver of the privilege or protection.

The party must also provide sufficient information to enable other parties to evaluate the applicability of the claimed privilege or protection. Although the person from whom the discovery is sought decides whether to claim a privilege or protection, the court ultimately decides whether, if this claim is challenged, the privilege or protection applies. Providing information pertinent to the applicability of the privilege or protection should reduce the need for in camera examination of the documents.

* * *

The obligation to provide pertinent information concerning withheld privileged materials applies only to items "otherwise discoverable." If a broad discovery request is made—for example, for all documents of a particular type during a twenty year period—and the responding party believes in good faith that production of documents for more than the past three years would be unduly burdensome, it should make its objection to the breadth of the request and, with respect to the documents generated in that three year period, produce the unprivileged documents and describe those withheld under the claim of privilege. If the court later rules that documents for a seven year period are properly discoverable, the documents for the additional four years should then be either produced (if not privileged) or described (if claimed to be privileged).

* * *

Subdivision (d). This subdivision is revised to provide that formal discovery—as distinguished from interviews of potential witnesses and other informal discovery—not commence until the parties have met and conferred as required by subdivision (f). Discovery can begin earlier if authorized under Rule 30(a)(2)(C) (deposition of person about to leave the country) or by local rule, order, or stipulation. This will be appropriate in some cases, such as those involving requests for a preliminary injunction or motions challenging personal jurisdiction. * * *

Subdivision (e). This subdivision is revised to provide that the requirement for supplementation applies to all disclosures required by subdivisions (a)(1)–(3). Like the former rule, the duty, while imposed on a "party," applies whether the corrective information is learned by the client or by the attorney. Supplementations need not be made as each new item of information is learned but should be made at appropriate intervals during the discovery period, and with special promptness as the trial date approaches. It may be useful for the scheduling order to specify the time or times when supplementations should be made.

* * *

The obligation to supplement disclosures and discovery responses applies whenever a party learns that its prior disclosures or responses are in some material respect incomplete or incorrect. There is, however, no obligation to provide supplemental or corrective information that has been otherwise made known to the parties in writing or during the discovery process, as when a witness not previously disclosed is identified during the taking of a deposition or when an expert during a deposition corrects information contained in an earlier report.

Subdivision (f).

* * *

[F]ormer subdivision (f) envisioned the development of proposed discovery plans as an optional procedure to be used in relatively few cases. The revised rule directs that in all cases not exempted by local rule or special order the litigants must meet in person and plan for discovery. Following this meeting, the parties submit to the court their proposals for a discovery plan and can begin formal discovery. Their report will assist the court in seeing that the timing and scope of disclosures under revised Rule 26(a) and the limitations on the extent of discovery under these rules and local rules are tailored to the circumstances of the particular case.

* * *

The report is to be submitted to the court within 10 days after the meeting and should not be difficult to prepare. In most cases counsel should be able to agree that one of them will be responsible for its preparation and submission to the court. Form 35 has been added in the Appendix to the Rules, both to illustrate the type of report that is contemplated and to serve as a checklist for the meeting.

The litigants are expected to attempt in good faith to agree on the contents of the proposed discovery plan. If they cannot agree on all aspects of the plan, their report to the court should indicate the competing proposals of the parties on those items, as well as the matters on which they agree. Unfortunately, there may be cases in which, because of disagreements about time or place or for other reasons, the meeting is not attended by all parties or, indeed, no meeting takes place. In such situations, the report—or reports—should describe the circumstances and the court may need to consider sanctions under Rule 37(g).

* * *

2000 AMENDMENT

Purposes of amendments. The Rule 26(a)(1) initial disclosure provisions are amended to establish a nationally uniform practice. The scope of the disclosure obligation is narrowed to cover only information that the disclosing party may use to support its position. In addition, the rule exempts specified categories of proceedings from initial disclosure, and permits a party who contends that disclosure is not appropriate in the circumstances of the case to present its objections to the court, which must then determine whether disclosure should be made. * * *

The initial disclosure requirements added by the 1993 amendments permitted local rules directing that disclosure would not be required or altering its operation. The inclusion of the "opt out" provision reflected the strong opposition to initial disclosure felt in some districts, and permitted experimentation with differing disclosure rules in those districts that were favorable to disclosure.

* * *

The Committee has discerned widespread support for national uniformity. Many lawyers have experienced difficulty in coping with divergent disclosure and other practices as they move from one district to another. Lawyers surveyed by the Federal Judicial Center ranked adoption of a uniform national disclosure rule second among proposed rule changes (behind increased availability of judges to resolve discovery disputes) as a means to reduce litigation expenses without interfering with fair outcomes. National uniformity is also a central purpose of the Rules Enabling Act of 1934, as amended, 28 U.S.C. §§ 2072–2077.

* * *

Subdivision (a)(1). The amendments remove the authority to alter or opt out of the national disclosure requirements by local rule, invalidating not only formal local rules but also informal "standing" orders of an individual judge or court that purport to create exemptions from—or limit or expand—the disclosure provided under the national rule. Case-specific orders remain proper, however, and are expressly required if a party objects that initial disclosure is not appropriate in the circumstances of the action. Specified categories of proceedings are excluded from initial disclosure under subdivision (a)(1)(E). In addition, the parties can stipulate to forgo disclosure, as was true before. But even in a case excluded by subdivision (a)(1)(E) or in which the parties stipulate to bypass disclosure, the court can order exchange of similar information in managing the action under Rule 16.

The initial disclosure obligation of subdivisions (a)(1)(A) and (B) has been narrowed to identification of witnesses and documents that the disclosing party may use to support its claims or defenses. "Use" includes any use at a pretrial conference, to support a motion, or at trial. The disclosure obligation is also triggered by intended use in discovery, apart from use to respond to a discovery request; use of a document to question a witness during a deposition is a common example. The disclosure obligation attaches both to witnesses and documents a party intends to use and also to witnesses and to documents the party intends to use if—in the language of Rule 26(a)(3)—"the need arises."

A party is no longer obligated to disclose witnesses or documents, whether favorable or unfavorable, that it does not intend to use. The obligation to disclose information the party may use connects directly to the exclusion sanction of Rule 37(c)(1). Because the disclosure obligation is limited to material that the party may use, it is no longer tied to particularized allegations in the pleadings. Subdivision (e)(1), which is unchanged, requires supplementation if information later acquired would have been subject to the disclosure requirement. As case preparation continues, a party must supplement its disclosures when it determines that it may use a witness or document that it did not previously intend to use.

The disclosure obligation applies to "claims and defenses," and therefore requires a party to disclose information it may use to support its denial or rebuttal of the allegations, claim, or defense of another party. It thereby bolsters the requirements of Rule 11(b)(4), which authorizes denials "warranted on the evidence," and disclosure should include the identity of any witness or document that the disclosing party may use to support such denials.

* * *

Subdivision (b)(1). In 1978, the Committee published for comment a proposed amendment, suggested by the Section of Litigation of the American Bar Association, to refine the scope of discovery by deleting the "subject matter" language. This proposal was withdrawn, and the Committee has since then made other changes in the discovery rules to address concerns about overbroad discovery. Concerns about costs and delay of discovery have persisted nonetheless, and other bar groups have repeatedly renewed similar proposals for amendment to this subdivision to delete the "subject matter" language. Nearly one-third of the lawyers surveyed in 1997 by the Federal Judicial Center endorsed narrowing the scope of discovery as a means of reducing litigation expense without interfering with fair case resolutions. The Committee has heard that in some instances, particularly cases involving large quantities of discovery, parties seek to justify discovery requests that sweep far beyond the claims and defenses of the parties on the ground that they nevertheless have a bearing on the "subject matter" involved in the action.

The amendments proposed for subdivision (b)(1) include one element of these earlier proposals but also differ from these proposals in significant ways. The similarity is that the amendments describe the scope of party-controlled discovery in terms of matter relevant to the claim or defense of any party. The court, however, retains authority to order discovery of any matter relevant to the subject matter involved in the action for good cause. The amendment is designed to involve the court more actively in regulating the breadth of sweeping or contentious discovery. The Committee has been informed repeatedly by lawyers that involvement of the court in managing discovery is an important method of controlling problems of inappropriately broad discovery. Increasing the availability of judicial officers to resolve discovery disputes and increasing court management of discovery were both strongly endorsed by the attorneys surveyed by the Federal Judicial Center. Under the amended provisions, if there is an objection that discovery goes beyond material relevant to the parties' claims or defenses, the court would become involved to determine whether the discovery is relevant to the claims or defenses and, if not, whether good cause exists for authorizing it so long as it is relevant to the subject matter of the action. The good-cause standard warranting broader discovery is meant to be flexible.

The Committee intends that the parties and the court focus on the actual claims and defenses involved in the action. The dividing line between information relevant to the claims and defenses and that relevant only to the subject matter of the action cannot be defined with precision. A variety of types of information not directly pertinent to the incident in suit could be relevant to the claims or defenses raised in a given action. For example, other incidents of the same type, or involving the same product, could be properly discoverable under the revised standard. Information about organizational arrangements or filing systems of a party could be discoverable if likely to yield or lead to the discovery of admissible information. Similarly, information that could be used to impeach a likely witness, although not otherwise relevant to the claims or defenses, might be properly discoverable. In each instance, the determination whether such information is discoverable because it is relevant to the claims or defenses depends on the circumstances of the pending action.

The rule change signals to the court that it has the authority to confine discovery to the claims and defenses asserted in the pleadings, and signals to the parties that they have no entitlement to discovery to develop new claims or defenses that are not already identified in the pleadings. In general, it is hoped that reasonable lawyers can cooperate to manage discovery without the need for judicial intervention. When judicial intervention is invoked, the actual scope of discovery should be determined according to the reasonable needs of the action. The court may permit broader discovery in a particular case depending on the circumstances of the case, the nature of the claims and defenses, and the scope of the discovery requested.

The amendments also modify the provision regarding discovery of information not admissible in evidence. As added in 1946, this sentence was designed to make clear that otherwise relevant material could not be withheld because it was hearsay or otherwise inadmissible. The Committee was concerned that the "reasonably calculated to lead to the discovery of admissible evidence" standard set forth in this sentence might swallow any other limitation on the scope of discovery. Accordingly, this sentence has been amended to clarify that information must be relevant to be discoverable, even though inadmissible, and that discovery of such material is permitted if reasonably calculated to lead to the discovery of admissible evidence. As used here, "relevant" means within the scope of discovery as defined in this subdivision, and it would include information relevant to the subject matter involved in the action if the court has ordered discovery to that limit based on a showing of good cause.

* * *

2006 AMENDMENT

Subdivision (a). Rule 26(a)(1)(B) is amended to parallel Rule 34(a) by recognizing that a party must disclose electronically stored information as well as documents that it may use to support its claims or defenses. * * *

Subdivision (b)(2). The amendment to Rule 26(b)(2) is designed to address issues raised by difficulties in locating, retrieving, and providing discovery of some electronically stored information. Electronic storage systems often make it easier to locate and retrieve information. These advantages are properly taken into account in determining the reasonable scope of discovery in a particular case. But some sources of electronically stored information can be accessed only with substantial burden and cost. In a particular case, these burdens and costs may make the information on such sources not reasonably accessible.

* * *

If the parties cannot agree whether, or on what terms, sources identified as not reasonably accessible should be searched and discoverable information produced, the issue may be raised either by a motion to compel discovery or by a motion for a protective order. The parties must confer before bringing either motion. If the parties do not resolve the issue and the court must decide, the responding party must show that the identified sources of information are not reasonably accessible because of undue burden or cost. The requesting party may need discovery to test this assertion. Such discovery might take the form of requiring the responding party to conduct a sampling of information contained on the sources identified as not reasonably accessible; allowing some form of inspection of such sources; or taking depositions of witnesses knowledgeable about the responding party's information systems.

Once it is shown that a source of electronically stored information is not reasonably accessible, the requesting party may still obtain discovery by showing good cause, considering the limitations of Rule 26(b)(2)(C) that balance the costs and potential benefits of discovery. The decision whether to require a responding party to search for and produce information that is not reasonably accessible depends not only on the burdens and costs of doing so, but also on whether those burdens and costs can be justified in the circumstances of the case. Appropriate considerations may include: (1) the specificity of the discovery request; (2) the quantity of information available from other and more easily accessed sources; (3) the failure to produce relevant information that seems likely to have existed but is no longer available on more easily accessed sources; (4) the likelihood of finding relevant, responsive information that cannot be obtained from other, more easily accessed sources; (5) predictions as to the importance and usefulness of the further information; (6) the importance of the issues at stake in the litigation; and (7) the parties' resources.

The responding party has the burden as to one aspect of the inquiry—whether the identified sources are not reasonably accessible in light of the burdens and costs required to search for, retrieve, and produce whatever responsive information may be found. The requesting party has the burden of showing that its need for the discovery outweighs the burdens and costs of locating, retrieving, and producing the information.

* * *

Subdivision (b)(5). The Committee has repeatedly been advised that the risk of privilege waiver, and the work necessary to avoid it, add to the costs and delay of discovery. When the review is of electronically stored information, the risk of waiver, and the time and effort required to avoid it, can increase substantially because of the volume of electronically stored information and the difficulty in ensuring that all information to be produced has in fact been reviewed. Rule 26(b)(5)(A) provides a procedure for a party that has withheld information on the basis of privilege or protection as trial-preparation material to make the claim so that the requesting party can decide whether to contest the claim and the court can resolve the dispute. Rule 26(b)(5)(B) is added to provide a procedure for a party to assert a claim of privilege or trial-preparation material protection after information is produced in discovery in the action and, if the claim is contested, permit any party that received the information to present the matter to the court for resolution.

Rule 26(b)(5)(B) does not address whether the privilege or protection that is asserted after production was waived by the production. The courts have developed principles to determine whether, and under what circumstances, waiver results from inadvertent production of privileged or protected information. Rule 26(b)(5)(B) provides a procedure for presenting and addressing these issues. * * *

A party asserting a claim of privilege or protection after production must give notice to the receiving party. That notice should be in writing unless the circumstances preclude it. Such circumstances could include the assertion of the claim during a deposition. The notice should be as specific as possible in identifying the information and stating the basis for the claim. Because the receiving party must decide whether to challenge the claim and may sequester the information and submit it to the court for a ruling on whether the claimed privilege or protection applies and whether it has been waived, the notice should be sufficiently detailed so as to enable the receiving party and the court to understand the basis for the claim and to determine whether waiver has occurred. Courts will continue to examine whether a claim of privilege or protection was made at a reasonable time when delay is part of the waiver determination under the governing law.

After receiving notice, each party that received the information must promptly return, sequester, or destroy the information and any copies it has. The option of sequestering or destroying the information is included in part because the receiving party may have incorporated the information in protected trial-preparation materials. No receiving party may use or disclose the information pending resolution of the privilege claim. The receiving party may present to the court the questions whether the information is privileged or protected as trial-preparation material, and whether the privilege or protection has been waived. If it does so, it must provide the court with the grounds for the privilege or protection specified in the producing party's notice, and serve all parties. In presenting the question, the party may use the content of the information only to the extent permitted by the applicable law of privilege, protection for trial-preparation material, and professional responsibility.

If a party disclosed the information to nonparties before receiving notice of a claim of privilege or protection as trial-preparation material, it must take reasonable steps to retrieve the information and to return it, sequester it until the claim is resolved, or destroy it.

Whether the information is returned or not, the producing party must preserve the information pending the court's ruling on whether the claim of privilege or of protection is properly asserted and whether it was waived. As with claims made under Rule 26(b)(5)(A), there may be no ruling if the other parties do not contest the claim.

Subdivision (f). Rule 26(f) is amended to direct the parties to discuss discovery of electronically stored information during their discovery-planning conference.

* * *

Rule 26(f) is also amended to provide that the parties should discuss any issues relating to assertions of privilege or of protection as trial-preparation materials, including whether the parties can facilitate discovery by agreeing on procedures for asserting claims of privilege or protection after production and whether to ask the court to enter an order that includes any agreement the parties reach. The Committee has repeatedly been advised about the discovery difficulties that can result from efforts to guard against waiver of privilege and work-product protection. Frequently parties find it necessary to spend large amounts of time reviewing materials requested through discovery to avoid waiving privilege. These efforts are necessary because materials subject to a claim of privilege or protection are often difficult to identify. A failure to withhold even one such item may result in an argument that there has been a waiver of privilege as to all other privileged materials on that subject matter. Efforts to avoid the risk of waiver can impose substantial costs on the party producing the material and the time required for the privilege review can substantially delay access for the party seeking discovery.

These problems often become more acute when discovery of electronically stored information is sought. The volume of such data, and the informality that attends use of e-mail and some other types of electronically stored information, may make privilege determinations more difficult, and privilege review correspondingly more expensive and time consuming. Other aspects of electronically stored information pose particular difficulties for privilege review. For example, production may be sought of information automatically included in electronic files but not apparent to the creator or to readers. Computer programs may retain draft language, editorial comments, and other deleted matter (sometimes referred to as "embedded data" or "embedded edits") in an electronic file but not make them apparent to the reader. Information describing the history, tracking, or management of an electronic file (sometimes called "metadata") is usually not apparent to the reader viewing a hard copy or a screen image. Whether this information should be produced may be among the topics discussed in the Rule 26(f) conference. If it is, it may need to be reviewed to ensure that no privileged information is included, further complicating the task of privilege review.

Parties may attempt to minimize these costs and delays by agreeing to protocols that minimize the risk of waiver. They may agree that the responding party will provide certain requested materials for initial examination without waiving any privilege or protection—sometimes known as a "quick peek." The requesting party then designates the documents it wishes to have actually produced. This designation is the Rule 34 request. The responding party then responds in the usual course, screening only those documents actually requested for formal production and asserting privilege claims as provided in Rule 26(b)(5)(A). On other occasions, parties enter agreements—sometimes called "clawback agreements"—that production without intent to waive privilege or protection should not be a waiver so long as the responding party identifies the documents mistakenly produced, and that the documents should be returned under those circumstances. Other voluntary arrangements may be appropriate depending on the circumstances of each litigation. In most circumstances, a party who receives information under such an arrangement cannot assert that production of the information waived a claim of privilege or of protection as trial-preparation material.

* * *

2010 AMENDMENT

* * *

Subdivision (b)(4). Rule 26(b)(4)(B) is added to provide work-product protection under Rule 26(b)(3)(A) and (B) for drafts of expert reports or disclosures. This protection applies to all witnesses identified under Rule 26(a)(2)(A), whether they are required to provide reports under Rule 26(a)(2)(B) or are the subject of disclosure under Rule 26(a)(2)(C). It applies regardless of the form in which the draft is recorded, whether written, electronic, or otherwise. It also applies to drafts of any supplementation under Rule 26(e); see Rule 26(a)(2)(E).

Rule 26(b)(4)(C) is added to provide work-product protection for attorney-expert communications regardless of the form of the communications, whether oral, written, electronic, or otherwise. The addition of Rule 26(b)(4)(C) is designed to protect counsel's work product and ensure that lawyers may interact with retained experts without fear of exposing those communications to searching discovery. The protection is limited to communications between an expert witness required to provide a report under Rule 26(a)(2)(B) and the attorney for the party on whose behalf the witness will be testifying, including any "preliminary" expert opinions. Protected "communications" include those between the party's attorney and assistants of the expert witness. The rule does not itself protect communications between counsel and other expert witnesses, such as those for whom disclosure is required under Rule 26(a)(2)(C). The rule does not exclude protection under other doctrines, such as privilege or independent development of the work-product doctrine.

The most frequent method for discovering the work of expert witnesses is by deposition, but Rules 26(b)(4)(B) and (C) apply to all forms of discovery.

Rules 26(b)(4)(B) and (C) do not impede discovery about the opinions to be offered by the expert or the development, foundation, or basis of those opinions. For example, the expert's testing of material involved in litigation, and notes of any such testing, would not be exempted from discovery by this rule. Similarly, inquiry about communications the expert had with anyone other than the party's counsel about the opinions expressed is unaffected by the rule.

* * *

2015 AMENDMENT

Rule 26(b)(1) is changed in several ways.

Information is discoverable under revised Rule 26(b)(1) if it is relevant to any party's claim or defense and is proportional to the needs of the case. The considerations that bear on proportionality are moved from present Rule 26(b)(2)(C)(iii), slightly rearranged and with one addition.

Most of what now appears in Rule 26(b)(2)(C)(iii) was first adopted in 1983. * * *

The 1983 Committee Note stated that the new provisions were added "to deal with the problem of over-discovery. The objective is to guard against redundant or disproportionate discovery by giving the court authority to reduce the amount of discovery that may be directed to matters that are otherwise proper subjects of inquiry. The new sentence is intended to encourage judges to be more aggressive in identifying and discouraging discovery overuse. The grounds mentioned in the amended rule for limiting discovery reflect the existing practice of many courts in issuing protective orders under Rule 26(c). . . . On the whole, however, district judges have been reluctant to limit the use of the discovery devices."

The clear focus of the 1983 provisions may have been softened, although inadvertently, by the amendments made in 1993.

* * *

The present amendment restores the proportionality factors to their original place in defining the scope of discovery. This change reinforces the Rule 26(g) obligation of the parties to consider these factors in making discovery requests, responses, or objections.

Restoring the proportionality calculation to Rule 26(b)(1) does not change the existing responsibilities of the court and the parties to consider proportionality, and the change does not place on the party seeking discovery the burden of addressing all proportionality considerations.

Nor is the change intended to permit the opposing party to refuse discovery simply by making a boilerplate objection that it is not proportional. The parties and the court have a collective responsibility to consider the proportionality of all discovery and consider it in resolving discovery disputes.

The parties may begin discovery without a full appreciation of the factors that bear on proportionality. A party requesting discovery, for example, may have little information about the burden or expense of responding. A party requested to provide discovery may have little information about the importance of the discovery in resolving the issues as understood by the requesting party. Many of these uncertainties should be addressed and reduced in the parties' Rule 26(f) conference and in scheduling and pretrial conferences with the court. But if the parties continue to disagree, the discovery dispute could be brought before the court and the parties' responsibilities would remain as they have been since 1983. A party claiming undue burden or expense ordinarily has far better information—perhaps the only information—with respect to that part of the determination. A party claiming that a request is important to resolve the issues should be able to explain the ways in which the underlying information bears on the issues as that party understands them. The court's responsibility, using all the information provided by the parties, is to consider these and all the other factors in reaching a case-specific determination of the appropriate scope of discovery.

The direction to consider the parties' relative access to relevant information adds new text to provide explicit focus on considerations already implicit in present Rule 26(b)(2)(C)(iii). Some cases involve what often is called "information asymmetry." One party—often an individual plaintiff—may have very little discoverable information. The other party may have vast amounts of information, including information that can be readily retrieved and information that is more difficult to retrieve. In practice these circumstances often mean that the burden of responding to discovery lies heavier on the party who has more information, and properly so.

Restoring proportionality as an express component of the scope of discovery warrants repetition of parts of the 1983 and 1993 Committee Notes that must not be lost from sight. The 1983 Committee Note explained that "[t]he rule contemplates greater judicial involvement in the discovery process and thus acknowledges the reality that it cannot always operate on a self-regulating basis." The 1993 Committee Note further observed that "[t]he information explosion of recent decades has greatly increased both the potential cost of wide-ranging discovery and the potential for discovery to be used as an instrument for delay or oppression." What seemed an explosion in 1993 has been exacerbated by the advent of e-discovery. The present amendment again reflects the need for continuing and close judicial involvement in the cases that do not yield readily to the ideal of effective party management. It is expected that discovery will be effectively managed by the parties in many cases. But there will be important occasions for judicial management, both when the parties are legitimately unable to resolve important differences and when the parties fall short of effective, cooperative management on their own.

It also is important to repeat the caution that the monetary stakes are only one factor, to be balanced against other factors. The 1983 Committee Note recognized "the significance of the substantive issues, as measured in philosophic, social, or institutional terms. Thus the rule recognizes that many cases in public policy spheres, such as employment practices, free speech, and other matters, may have importance far beyond the monetary amount involved." Many other substantive areas also may involve litigation that seeks relatively small amounts of money, or no money at all, but that seeks to vindicate vitally important personal or public values.

So too, consideration of the parties' resources does not foreclose discovery requests addressed to an impecunious party, nor justify unlimited discovery requests addressed to a wealthy party. The 1983 Committee Note cautioned that "[t]he court must apply the standards in an even-handed manner that will prevent use of discovery to wage a war of attrition or as a device to coerce a party, whether financially weak or affluent."

The burden or expense of proposed discovery should be determined in a realistic way. This includes the burden or expense of producing electronically stored information. Computer-based methods of searching such information continue to develop, particularly for cases involving large volumes of electronically stored information. Courts and parties should be willing to consider the opportunities for reducing the burden or expense of discovery as reliable means of searching electronically stored information become available.

* * *

The amendment deletes the former provision authorizing the court, for good cause, to order discovery of any matter relevant to the subject matter involved in the action. The Committee has been informed that this language is rarely invoked. Proportional discovery relevant to any party's claim or defense suffices, given a proper understanding of what is relevant to a claim or defense. The distinction between matter relevant to a claim or defense and matter relevant to the subject matter was introduced in 2000. The 2000 Note offered three examples of information that, suitably focused, would be relevant to the parties' claims or defenses. The examples were "other incidents of the same type, or involving the same product"; "information about organizational arrangements or filing systems"; and "information that could be used to impeach a likely witness." Such discovery is not foreclosed by the amendments. Discovery that is relevant to the parties' claims or defenses may also support amendment of the pleadings to add a new claim or defense that affects the scope of discovery.

The former provision for discovery of relevant but inadmissible information that appears "reasonably calculated to lead to the discovery of admissible evidence" is also deleted. The phrase has been used by some, incorrectly, to define the scope of discovery. * * * It is replaced by the direct statement that "Information within this scope of discovery need not be admissible in evidence to be discoverable." Discovery of nonprivileged information not admissible in evidence remains available so long as it is otherwise within the scope of discovery.

* * *

Rule 26(c)(1)(B) is amended to include an express recognition of protective orders that allocate expenses for disclosure or discovery. Authority to enter such orders is included in the present rule, and courts already exercise this authority. Explicit recognition will forestall the temptation some parties may feel to contest this authority. Recognizing the authority does not imply that cost-shifting should become a common practice. Courts and parties should continue to assume that a responding party ordinarily bears the costs of responding.

Rule 26(d)(2) is added to allow a party to deliver Rule 34 requests to another party more than 21 days after that party has been served even though the parties have not yet had a required Rule 26(f) conference. Delivery may be made by any party to the party that has been served, and by that party to any plaintiff and any other party that has been served. Delivery does not count as service; the requests are considered to be served at the first Rule 26(f) conference. Under Rule 34(b)(2)(A) the time to respond runs from service. This relaxation of the discovery moratorium is designed to facilitate focused discussion during the Rule 26(f) conference. Discussion at the conference may produce changes in the requests. The opportunity for advance scrutiny of requests delivered before the Rule 26(f) conference should not affect a decision whether to allow additional time to respond.

* * *

Rule 27. Depositions to Perpetuate Testimony

(a) Before an Action Is Filed.

(1) ***Petition.*** A person who wants to perpetuate testimony about any matter cognizable in a United States court may file a verified petition in the district court for the district where any expected adverse party resides. The petition must ask for an order authorizing the petitioner to depose the named persons in order to perpetuate their testimony. The petition must be titled in the petitioner's name and must show:

(A) that the petitioner expects to be a party to an action cognizable in a United States court but cannot presently bring it or cause it to be brought;

(B) the subject matter of the expected action and the petitioner's interest;

(C) the facts that the petitioner wants to establish by the proposed testimony and the reasons to perpetuate it;

(D) the names or a description of the persons whom the petitioner expects to be adverse parties and their addresses, so far as known; and

(E) the name, address, and expected substance of the testimony of each deponent.

(2) ***Notice and Service.*** At least 21 days before the hearing date, the petitioner must serve each expected adverse party with a copy of the petition and a notice stating the time and place of the hearing. The notice may be served either inside or outside the district or state in the manner provided in Rule 4. If that service cannot be made with reasonable diligence on an expected adverse party, the court may order service by publication or otherwise. The court must appoint an attorney to represent persons not served in the manner provided in Rule 4 and to cross-examine the deponent if an unserved person is not otherwise represented. If any expected adverse party is a minor or is incompetent, Rule 17(c) applies.

(3) ***Order and Examination.*** If satisfied that perpetuating the testimony may prevent a failure or delay of justice, the court must issue an order that designates or describes the persons whose depositions may be taken, specifies the subject matter of the examinations, and states whether the depositions will be taken orally or by written interrogatories. The depositions may then be taken under these rules, and the court may issue orders like those authorized by Rules 34 and 35. A reference in these rules to the court where an action is pending means, for purposes of this rule, the court where the petition for the deposition was filed.

(4) ***Using the Deposition.*** A deposition to perpetuate testimony may be used under Rule 32(a) in any later-filed district-court action involving the same subject matter if the deposition either was taken under these rules or, although not so taken, would be admissible in evidence in the courts of the state where it was taken.

(b) Pending Appeal.

(1) ***In General.*** The court where a judgment has been rendered may, if an appeal has been taken or may still be taken, permit a party to depose witnesses to perpetuate their testimony for use in the event of further proceedings in that court.

(2) ***Motion.*** The party who wants to perpetuate testimony may move for leave to take the depositions, on the same notice and service as if the action were pending in the district court. The motion must show:

(A) the name, address, and expected substance of the testimony of each deponent; and

(B) the reasons for perpetuating the testimony.

(3) ***Court Order.*** If the court finds that perpetuating the testimony may prevent a failure or delay of justice, the court may permit the depositions to be taken and may issue orders like those authorized by Rules 34 and 35. The depositions may be taken and used as any other deposition taken in a pending district-court action.

(c) Perpetuation by an Action. This rule does not limit a court's power to entertain an action to perpetuate testimony.

(As amended Dec. 27, 1946, eff. Mar. 19, 1948; Dec. 29, 1948, eff. Oct. 20, 1949; Mar. 1, 1971, eff. July 1, 1971; Mar. 2, 1987, eff. Aug. 1, 1987; Apr. 25, 2005, eff. Dec. 1, 2005; Apr. 30, 2007, eff. Dec. 1, 2007; Mar. 26, 2009, eff. Dec. 1, 2009.)

Rule 28. Persons Before Whom Depositions May Be Taken

(a) Within the United States.

(1) ***In General.*** Within the United States or a territory or insular possession subject to United States jurisdiction, a deposition must be taken before:

(A) an officer authorized to administer oaths either by federal law or by the law in the place of examination; or

(B) a person appointed by the court where the action is pending to administer oaths and take testimony.

(2) ***Definition of "Officer."*** The term "officer" in Rules 30, 31, and 32 includes a person appointed by the court under this rule or designated by the parties under Rule 29(a).

(b) **In a Foreign Country.**

(1) ***In General.*** A deposition may be taken in a foreign country:

(A) under an applicable treaty or convention;

(B) under a letter of request, whether or not captioned a "letter rogatory";

(C) on notice, before a person authorized to administer oaths either by federal law or by the law in the place of examination; or

(D) before a person commissioned by the court to administer any necessary oath and take testimony.

(2) ***Issuing a Letter of Request or a Commission.*** A letter of request, a commission, or both may be issued:

(A) on appropriate terms after an application and notice of it; and

(B) without a showing that taking the deposition in another manner is impracticable or inconvenient.

(3) ***Form of a Request, Notice, or Commission.*** When a letter of request or any other device is used according to a treaty or convention, it must be captioned in the form prescribed by that treaty or convention. A letter of request may be addressed "To the Appropriate Authority in [name of country]." A deposition notice or a commission must designate by name or descriptive title the person before whom the deposition is to be taken.

(4) ***Letter of Request—Admitting Evidence.*** Evidence obtained in response to a letter of request need not be excluded merely because it is not a verbatim transcript, because the testimony was not taken under oath, or because of any similar departure from the requirements for depositions taken within the United States.

(c) **Disqualification.** A deposition must not be taken before a person who is any party's relative, employee, or attorney; who is related to or employed by any party's attorney; or who is financially interested in the action.

(As amended Dec. 27, 1946, eff. Mar. 19, 1948; Jan. 21, 1963, eff. July 1, 1963; Apr. 29, 1980, eff. Aug. 1, 1980; Mar. 2, 1987, eff. Aug. 1, 1987; Apr. 22, 1993, eff. Dec. 1, 1993; Apr. 30, 2007, eff. Dec. 1, 2007.)

Rule 29. Stipulations About Discovery Procedure

Unless the court orders otherwise, the parties may stipulate that:

(a) a deposition may be taken before any person, at any time or place, on any notice, and in the manner specified—in which event it may be used in the same way as any other deposition; and

(b) other procedures governing or limiting discovery be modified—but a stipulation extending the time for any form of discovery must have court approval if it would interfere with the time set for completing discovery, for hearing a motion, or for trial.

(As amended Mar. 30, 1970, eff. July 1, 1970; Apr. 22, 1993, eff. Dec. 1, 1993; Apr. 30, 2007, eff. Dec. 1, 2007.)

Rule 30. Depositions by Oral Examination

(a) When a Deposition May Be Taken.

(1) ***Without Leave.*** A party may, by oral questions, depose any person, including a party, without leave of court except as provided in Rule 30(a)(2). The deponent's attendance may be compelled by subpoena under Rule 45.

(2) ***With Leave.*** A party must obtain leave of court, and the court must grant leave to the extent consistent with Rule 26(b)(1) and (2):

(A) if the parties have not stipulated to the deposition and:

(i) the deposition would result in more than 10 depositions being taken under this rule or Rule 31 by the plaintiffs, or by the defendants, or by the third-party defendants;

(ii) the deponent has already been deposed in the case; or

(iii) the party seeks to take the deposition before the time specified in Rule 26(d), unless the party certifies in the notice, with supporting facts, that the deponent is expected to leave the United States and be unavailable for examination in this country after that time; or

(B) if the deponent is confined in prison.

(b) Notice of the Deposition; Other Formal Requirements.

(1) ***Notice in General.*** A party who wants to depose a person by oral questions must give reasonable written notice to every other party. The notice must state the time and place of the deposition and, if known, the deponent's name and address. If the name is unknown, the notice must provide a general description sufficient to identify the person or the particular class or group to which the person belongs.

(2) ***Producing Documents.*** If a subpoena duces tecum is to be served on the deponent, the materials designated for production, as set out in the subpoena, must be listed in the notice or in an attachment. The notice to a party deponent may be accompanied by a request under Rule 34 to produce documents and tangible things at the deposition.

(3) ***Method of Recording.***

(A) *Method Stated in the Notice.* The party who notices the deposition must state in the notice the method for recording the testimony. Unless the court orders otherwise, testimony may be recorded by audio, audiovisual, or stenographic means. The noticing party bears the recording costs. Any party may arrange to transcribe a deposition.

(B) *Additional Method.* With prior notice to the deponent and other parties, any party may designate another method for recording the testimony in addition to that specified in the original notice. That party bears the expense of the additional record or transcript unless the court orders otherwise.

(4) ***By Remote Means.*** The parties may stipulate—or the court may on motion order—that a deposition be taken by telephone or other remote means. For the purpose of this rule and Rules 28(a), 37(a)(2), and 37(b)(1), the deposition takes place where the deponent answers the questions.

(5) ***Officer's Duties.***

(A) *Before the Deposition.* Unless the parties stipulate otherwise, a deposition must be conducted before an officer appointed or designated under Rule 28. The officer must begin the deposition with an on-the-record statement that includes:

(i) the officer's name and business address;

(ii) the date, time, and place of the deposition;

(iii) the deponent's name;

(iv) the officer's administration of the oath or affirmation to the deponent; and

(v) the identity of all persons present.

(B) *Conducting the Deposition; Avoiding Distortion.* If the deposition is recorded nonstenographically, the officer must repeat the items in Rule 30(b)(5)(A)(i)–(iii) at the beginning of each unit of the recording medium. The deponent's and attorneys' appearance or demeanor must not be distorted through recording techniques.

(C) *After the Deposition.* At the end of a deposition, the officer must state on the record that the deposition is complete and must set out any stipulations made by the attorneys about custody of the transcript or recording and of the exhibits, or about any other pertinent matters.

(6) ***Notice or Subpoena Directed to an Organization.*** In its notice or subpoena, a party may name as the deponent a public or private corporation, a partnership, an association, a governmental agency, or other entity and must describe with reasonable particularity the matters for examination. The named organization must designate one or more officers, directors, or managing agents, or designate other persons who consent to testify on its behalf; and it may set out the matters on which each person designated will testify. Before or promptly after the notice or subpoena is served, the serving party and the organization must confer in good faith about the matters for examination. A subpoena must advise a nonparty organization of its duty to confer with the serving party and to designate each person who will testify. The persons designated must testify about information known or reasonably available to the organization. This paragraph (6) does not preclude a deposition by any other procedure allowed by these rules.

(c) Examination and Cross-Examination; Record of the Examination; Objections; Written Questions.

(1) ***Examination and Cross-Examination.*** The examination and cross-examination of a deponent proceed as they would at trial under the Federal Rules of Evidence, except Rules 103 and 615. After putting the deponent under oath or affirmation, the officer must record the testimony by the method designated under Rule 30(b)(3)(A). The testimony must be recorded by the officer personally or by a person acting in the presence and under the direction of the officer.

(2) ***Objections.*** An objection at the time of the examination—whether to evidence, to a party's conduct, to the officer's qualifications, to the manner of taking the deposition, or to any other aspect of the deposition—must be noted on the record, but the examination still proceeds; the testimony is taken subject to any objection. An objection must be stated concisely in a nonargumentative and nonsuggestive manner. A person may instruct a deponent not to answer only when necessary to preserve a privilege, to enforce a limitation ordered by the court, or to present a motion under Rule 30(d)(3).

(3) ***Participating Through Written Questions.*** Instead of participating in the oral examination, a party may serve written questions in a sealed envelope on the party noticing the deposition, who must deliver them to the officer. The officer must ask the deponent those questions and record the answers verbatim.

(d) Duration; Sanction; Motion to Terminate or Limit.

(1) ***Duration.*** Unless otherwise stipulated or ordered by the court, a deposition is limited to 1 day of 7 hours. The court must allow additional time consistent with Rule 26(b)(1) and (2) if needed to fairly examine the deponent or if the deponent, another person, or any other circumstance impedes or delays the examination.

(2) ***Sanction.*** The court may impose an appropriate sanction—including the reasonable expenses and attorney's fees incurred by any party—on a person who impedes, delays, or frustrates the fair examination of the deponent.

(3) ***Motion to Terminate or Limit.***

(A) *Grounds.* At any time during a deposition, the deponent or a party may move to terminate or limit it on the ground that it is being conducted in bad faith or in a manner that unreasonably annoys, embarrasses, or oppresses the deponent or party. The motion may be filed in the court where the action is pending or the deposition is being taken. If the objecting deponent or party so demands, the deposition must be suspended for the time necessary to obtain an order.

(B) *Order.* The court may order that the deposition be terminated or may limit its scope and manner as provided in Rule 26(c). If terminated, the deposition may be resumed only by order of the court where the action is pending.

(C) *Award of Expenses.* Rule 37(a)(5) applies to the award of expenses.

(e) Review by the Witness; Changes.

(1) ***Review; Statement of Changes.*** On request by the deponent or a party before the deposition is completed, the deponent must be allowed 30 days after being notified by the officer that the transcript or recording is available in which:

(A) to review the transcript or recording; and

(B) if there are changes in form or substance, to sign a statement listing the changes and the reasons for making them.

(2) ***Changes Indicated in the Officer's Certificate.*** The officer must note in the certificate prescribed by Rule 30(f)(1) whether a review was requested and, if so, must attach any changes the deponent makes during the 30-day period.

(f) Certification and Delivery; Exhibits; Copies of the Transcript or Recording; Filing.

(1) ***Certification and Delivery.*** The officer must certify in writing that the witness was duly sworn and that the deposition accurately records the witness's testimony. The certificate must accompany the record of the deposition. Unless the court orders otherwise, the officer must seal the deposition in an envelope or package bearing the title of the action and marked "Deposition of [witness's name]" and must promptly send it to the attorney who arranged for the transcript or recording. The attorney must store it under conditions that will protect it against loss, destruction, tampering, or deterioration.

(2) ***Documents and Tangible Things.***

(A) *Originals and Copies.* Documents and tangible things produced for inspection during a deposition must, on a party's request, be marked for identification and attached to the deposition. Any party may inspect and copy them. But if the person who produced them wants to keep the originals, the person may:

(i) offer copies to be marked, attached to the deposition, and then used as originals—after giving all parties a fair opportunity to verify the copies by comparing them with the originals; or

(ii) give all parties a fair opportunity to inspect and copy the originals after they are marked—in which event the originals may be used as if attached to the deposition.

(B) *Order Regarding the Originals.* Any party may move for an order that the originals be attached to the deposition pending final disposition of the case.

(3) ***Copies of the Transcript or Recording.*** Unless otherwise stipulated or ordered by the court, the officer must retain the stenographic notes of a deposition taken stenographically or a copy of the recording of a deposition taken by another method. When paid reasonable charges, the officer must furnish a copy of the transcript or recording to any party or the deponent.

(4) ***Notice of Filing.*** A party who files the deposition must promptly notify all other parties of the filing.

(g) Failure to Attend a Deposition or Serve a Subpoena; Expenses. A party who, expecting a deposition to be taken, attends in person or by an attorney may recover reasonable expenses for attending, including attorney's fees, if the noticing party failed to:

(1) attend and proceed with the deposition; or

(2) serve a subpoena on a nonparty deponent, who consequently did not attend.

(As amended Jan. 21, 1963, eff. July 1, 1963; Mar. 30, 1970, eff. July 1, 1970; Mar. 1, 1971, eff. July 1, 1971; Nov. 20, 1972, eff. July 1, 1975; Apr. 29, 1980, eff. Aug. 1, 1980; Mar. 2, 1987, eff. Aug. 1, 1987; Apr. 22, 1993, eff. Dec. 1, 1993; Apr. 17, 2000; eff. Dec. 1, 2000; Apr. 30, 2007, eff. Dec. 1, 2007; Apr. 29, 2015, eff. Dec. 1, 2015; Apr. 27, 2020, eff. Dec. 1, 2020.)

NOTES OF ADVISORY COMMITTEE ON RULES

1993 AMENDMENT

Subdivision (a). * * *

Paragraph (2)(A) is new. It provides a limit on the number of depositions the parties may take, absent leave of court or stipulation with the other parties. One aim of this revision is to assure judicial review under the standards stated in Rule 26(b)(2) before any side will be allowed to take more than ten depositions in a case without agreement of the other parties. A second objective is to emphasize that counsel have a professional obligation to develop a mutual cost-effective plan for discovery in the case. Leave to take additional depositions should be granted when consistent with the principles of Rule 26(b)(2), and in some cases the ten-per-side limit should be reduced in accordance with those same principles. Consideration should ordinarily be given at the planning meeting of the parties under Rule 26(f) and at the time of a scheduling conference under Rule 16(b) as to enlargements or reductions in the number of depositions, eliminating the need for special motions.

A deposition under Rule 30(b)(6) should, for purposes of this limit, be treated as a single deposition even though more than one person may be designated to testify.

In multi-party cases, the parties on any side are expected to confer and agree as to which depositions are most needed, given the presumptive limit on the number of depositions they can take without leave of court. If these disputes cannot be amicably resolved, the court can be requested to resolve the dispute or permit additional depositions.

Paragraph (2)(B) is new. It requires leave of court if any witness is to be deposed in the action more than once. This requirement does not apply when a deposition is temporarily recessed for convenience of counsel or the deponent or to enable additional materials to be gathered before resuming the deposition. If significant travel costs would be incurred to resume the deposition, the parties should consider the feasibility of conducting the balance of the examination by telephonic means.

Paragraph (2)(C) revises the second sentence of the former subdivision (a) as to when depositions may be taken. Consistent with the changes made in Rule 26(d), providing that formal discovery ordinarily not commence until after the litigants have met and conferred as directed in revised Rule 26(f), the rule requires leave of court or agreement of the parties if a deposition is to be taken before that time (except when a witness is about to leave the country).

Subdivision (b). The primary change in subdivision (b) is that parties will be authorized to record deposition testimony by nonstenographic means without first having to obtain permission of the court or agreement from other counsel.

* * *

New paragraph (2) confers on the party taking the deposition the choice of the method of recording, without the need to obtain prior court approval for one taken other than stenographically. A party choosing to record a deposition only by videotape or audiotape should understand that a transcript will be required by Rule 26(a)(3)(B) and Rule 32(c) if the deposition is later to be offered as evidence at trial or on a dispositive motion under Rule 56. Objections to the nonstenographic recording of a deposition, when warranted by the circumstances, can be presented to the court under Rule 26(c).

Paragraph (3) provides that other parties may arrange, at their own expense, for the recording of a deposition by a means (stenographic, visual, or sound) in addition to the method designated by the person noticing the deposition.

* * *

Paragraph (7) is revised to authorize the taking of a deposition not only by telephone but also by other remote electronic means, such as satellite television, when agreed to by the parties or authorized by the court.

Subdivision (c). * * * [T]he revision addresses a recurring problem as to whether other potential deponents can attend a deposition. Courts have disagreed, some holding that witnesses should be excluded through invocation of Rule 615 of the evidence rules, and others holding that witnesses may attend unless excluded by an order under Rule 26(c)(5). The revision provides that other witnesses are not automatically excluded from a deposition simply by the request of a party. Exclusion, however, can be ordered under Rule 26(c)(5) when appropriate; and, if exclusion is ordered, consideration should be given as to whether the excluded witnesses likewise should be precluded from reading, or being otherwise informed about, the testimony given in the earlier depositions. The revision addresses only the matter of attendance by potential deponents, and does not attempt to resolve issues concerning attendance by others, such as members of the public or press.

Subdivision (d). The first sentence of new paragraph (1) provides that any objections during a deposition must be made concisely and in a non-argumentative and non-suggestive manner. Depositions frequently have been unduly prolonged, if not unfairly frustrated, by lengthy objections and colloquy, often suggesting how the deponent should respond. While objections may, under the revised rule, be made during a deposition, they ordinarily should be limited to those that under Rule 32(d)(3) might be waived if not made at that time, i.e., objections on grounds that might be immediately obviated, removed, or cured, such as to the form of a question or the responsiveness of an answer. Under Rule 32(b), other objections can, even without the so-called "usual stipulation" preserving objections, be raised for the first time at trial and therefore should be kept to a minimum during a deposition.

Directions to a deponent not to answer a question can be even more disruptive than objections. The second sentence of new paragraph (1) prohibits such directions except in the three circumstances indicated: to claim a privilege or protection against disclosure (e.g., as work product), to enforce a court directive limiting the scope or length of permissible discovery, or to suspend a deposition to enable presentation of a motion under paragraph (3).

* * *

Paragraph (3) authorizes appropriate sanctions not only when a deposition is unreasonably prolonged, but also when an attorney engages in other practices that improperly frustrate the fair examination of the deponent, such as making improper objections or giving directions not to answer prohibited by paragraph (1). In general, counsel should not engage in any conduct during a deposition that would not be allowed in the presence of a judicial officer. The making of an excessive number of unnecessary objections may itself constitute sanctionable conduct, as may the refusal of an attorney to agree with other counsel on a fair apportionment of the time allowed for examination of a deponent or a refusal to agree to a reasonable request for some additional time to complete a deposition, when that is permitted by the local rule or order.

* * *

2000 AMENDMENT

Subdivision (d). Paragraph (1) has been amended to clarify the terms regarding behavior during depositions. The references to objections "to evidence" and limitations "on evidence" have been removed to avoid disputes about what is "evidence" and whether an objection is to, or a limitation is on, discovery instead. It is intended that the rule apply to any objection to a question or other issue arising during a deposition, and to any limitation imposed by the court in connection with a deposition, which might relate to duration or other matters.

* * *

Paragraph (2) imposes a presumptive durational limitation of one day of seven hours for any deposition. The Committee has been informed that overlong depositions can result in undue costs and delays in some circumstances. This limitation contemplates that there will be reasonable breaks during the day for lunch and other reasons, and that the only time to be counted is the time occupied by the actual deposition. For purposes of this durational limit, the deposition of each person designated under Rule 30(b)(6) should be considered a separate deposition. The presumptive duration may be extended, or otherwise altered, by agreement. Absent agreement, a court order is needed. The party seeking a court order to extend the examination, or otherwise alter the limitations, is expected to show good cause to justify such an order.

Parties considering extending the time for a deposition—and courts asked to order an extension—might consider a variety of factors. For example, if the witness needs an interpreter, that may prolong the examination. If the examination will cover events occurring over a long period of time, that may justify allowing additional time. In cases in which the witness will be questioned about numerous or lengthy documents, it is often desirable for the interrogating party to send copies of the documents to the witness sufficiently in advance of the deposition so that the witness can become familiar with them. Should the witness nevertheless not read the documents in advance, thereby prolonging the deposition, a court could consider that a reason for extending the time limit. If the examination reveals that documents have been requested but not produced, that may justify further examination once production has occurred. In multi-party cases, the need for each party to examine the witness may warrant additional time, although duplicative questioning should be avoided and parties with similar interests should strive to designate one lawyer to question about areas of common interest. Similarly, should the lawyer for the witness want to examine the witness, that may require additional time. Finally, with regard to expert witnesses, there may more often be a need for additional time—even after the submission of the report required by Rule 26(a)(2)—for full exploration of the theories upon which the witness relies.

* * *

The rule directs the court to allow additional time where consistent with Rule 26(b)(2) if needed for a fair examination of the deponent. In addition, if the deponent or another person impedes or delays the examination, the court must authorize extra time. The amendment makes clear that additional time should also be allowed where the examination is impeded by an "other circumstance," which might include a power outage, a health emergency, or other event.

* * *

2015 AMENDMENT

Rule 30 is amended in parallel with Rules 31 and 33 to reflect the recognition of proportionality in Rule 26(b)(1).

Rule 31. Depositions by Written Questions

(a) When a Deposition May Be Taken.

(1) ***Without Leave.*** A party may, by written questions, depose any person, including a party, without leave of court except as provided in Rule 31(a)(2). The deponent's attendance may be compelled by subpoena under Rule 45.

(2) ***With Leave.*** A party must obtain leave of court, and the court must grant leave to the extent consistent with Rule 26(b)(1) and (2):

(A) if the parties have not stipulated to the deposition and:

(i) the deposition would result in more than 10 depositions being taken under this rule or Rule 30 by the plaintiffs, or by the defendants, or by the third-party defendants;

(ii) the deponent has already been deposed in the case; or

(iii) the party seeks to take a deposition before the time specified in Rule 26(d); or

(B) if the deponent is confined in prison.

(3) ***Service; Required Notice.*** A party who wants to depose a person by written questions must serve them on every other party, with a notice stating, if known, the deponent's name and address. If the name is unknown, the notice must provide a general description sufficient to identify the person or the particular class or group to which the person belongs. The notice must also state the name or descriptive title and the address of the officer before whom the deposition will be taken.

(4) ***Questions Directed to an Organization.*** A public or private corporation, a partnership, an association, or a governmental agency may be deposed by written questions in accordance with Rule 30(b)(6).

(5) ***Questions from Other Parties.*** Any questions to the deponent from other parties must be served on all parties as follows: cross-questions, within 14 days after being served with the notice and direct questions; redirect questions, within 7 days after being served with cross-questions; and recross-questions, within 7 days after being served with redirect questions. The court may, for good cause, extend or shorten these times.

(b) Delivery to the Officer; Officer's Duties. The party who noticed the deposition must deliver to the officer a copy of all the questions served and of the notice. The officer must promptly proceed in the manner provided in Rule 30(c), (e), and (f) to:

(1) take the deponent's testimony in response to the questions;

(2) prepare and certify the deposition; and

(3) send it to the party, attaching a copy of the questions and of the notice.

(c) Notice of Completion or Filing.

(1) ***Completion.*** The party who noticed the deposition must notify all other parties when it is completed.

(2) ***Filing.*** A party who files the deposition must promptly notify all other parties of the filing.

(As amended Mar. 30, 1970, eff. July 1, 1970; Mar. 2, 1987, eff. Aug. 1, 1987; Apr. 22, 1993, eff. Dec. 1, 1993; Apr. 30, 2007, eff. Dec. 1, 2007; Apr. 29, 2015, eff. Dec. 1, 2015.)

NOTES OF ADVISORY COMMITTEE ON RULES

2015 AMENDMENT

Rule 31 is amended in parallel with Rules 30 and 33 to reflect the recognition of proportionality in Rule 26(b)(1).

Rule 32. Using Depositions in Court Proceedings

(a) Using Depositions.

(1) ***In General.*** At a hearing or trial, all or part of a deposition may be used against a party on these conditions:

(A) the party was present or represented at the taking of the deposition or had reasonable notice of it;

(B) it is used to the extent it would be admissible under the Federal Rules of Evidence if the deponent were present and testifying; and

(C) the use is allowed by Rule 32(a)(2) through (8).

(2) ***Impeachment and Other Uses.*** Any party may use a deposition to contradict or impeach the testimony given by the deponent as a witness, or for any other purpose allowed by the Federal Rules of Evidence.

(3) ***Deposition of Party, Agent, or Designee.*** An adverse party may use for any purpose the deposition of a party or anyone who, when deposed, was the party's officer, director, managing agent, or designee under Rule 30(b)(6) or 31(a)(4).

(4) ***Unavailable Witness.*** A party may use for any purpose the deposition of a witness, whether or not a party, if the court finds:

(A) that the witness is dead;

(B) that the witness is more than 100 miles from the place of hearing or trial or is outside the United States, unless it appears that the witness's absence was procured by the party offering the deposition;

(C) that the witness cannot attend or testify because of age, illness, infirmity, or imprisonment;

(D) that the party offering the deposition could not procure the witness's attendance by subpoena; or

(E) on motion and notice, that exceptional circumstances make it desirable—in the interest of justice and with due regard to the importance of live testimony in open court—to permit the deposition to be used.

(5) ***Limitations on Use.***

(A) *Deposition Taken on Short Notice.* A deposition must not be used against a party who, having received less than 14 days' notice of the deposition, promptly moved for a protective order under Rule 26(c)(1)(B) requesting that it not be taken or be taken at a different time or place—and this motion was still pending when the deposition was taken.

(B) *Unavailable Deponent; Party Could Not Obtain an Attorney.* A deposition taken without leave of court under the unavailability provision of Rule 30(a)(2)(A)(iii) must not be used against a party who shows that, when served with the notice, it could not, despite diligent efforts, obtain an attorney to represent it at the deposition.

(6) ***Using Part of a Deposition.*** If a party offers in evidence only part of a deposition, an adverse party may require the offeror to introduce other parts that in fairness should be considered with the part introduced, and any party may itself introduce any other parts.

(7) ***Substituting a Party.*** Substituting a party under Rule 25 does not affect the right to use a deposition previously taken.

(8) ***Deposition Taken in an Earlier Action.*** A deposition lawfully taken and, if required, filed in any federal- or state-court action may be used in a later action involving the same subject matter between the same parties, or their representatives or successors in interest, to the same extent as if taken in the later action. A

deposition previously taken may also be used as allowed by the Federal Rules of Evidence.

(b) Objections to Admissibility. Subject to Rules 28(b) and 32(d)(3), an objection may be made at a hearing or trial to the admission of any deposition testimony that would be inadmissible if the witness were present and testifying.

(c) Form of Presentation. Unless the court orders otherwise, a party must provide a transcript of any deposition testimony the party offers, but may provide the court with the testimony in nontranscript form as well. On any party's request, deposition testimony offered in a jury trial for any purpose other than impeachment must be presented in nontranscript form, if available, unless the court for good cause orders otherwise.

(d) Waiver of Objections.

(1) ***To the Notice.*** An objection to an error or irregularity in a deposition notice is waived unless promptly served in writing on the party giving the notice.

(2) ***To the Officer's Qualification.*** An objection based on disqualification of the officer before whom a deposition is to be taken is waived if not made:

(A) before the deposition begins; or

(B) promptly after the basis for disqualification becomes known or, with reasonable diligence, could have been known.

(3) ***To the Taking of the Deposition.***

(A) *Objection to Competence, Relevance, or Materiality.* An objection to a deponent's competence—or to the competence, relevance, or materiality of testimony—is not waived by a failure to make the objection before or during the deposition, unless the ground for it might have been corrected at that time.

(B) *Objection to an Error or Irregularity.* An objection to an error or irregularity at an oral examination is waived if:

(i) it relates to the manner of taking the deposition, the form of a question or answer, the oath or affirmation, a party's conduct, or other matters that might have been corrected at that time; and

(ii) it is not timely made during the deposition.

(C) *Objection to a Written Question.* An objection to the form of a written question under Rule 31 is waived if not served in writing on the party submitting the question within the time for serving responsive questions or, if the question is a recross-question, within 7 days after being served with it.

(4) ***To Completing and Returning the Deposition.*** An objection to how the officer transcribed the testimony—or prepared, signed, certified, sealed, endorsed, sent, or otherwise dealt with the deposition—is waived unless a motion to suppress is made promptly after the error or irregularity becomes known or, with reasonable diligence, could have been known.

(As amended Mar. 30, 1970, eff. July 1, 1970; Nov. 20, 1972, eff. July 1, 1975; Apr. 29, 1980, eff. Aug. 1, 1980; Mar. 2, 1987, eff. Aug. 1, 1987; Apr. 22, 1993, eff. Dec. 1, 1993; Apr. 30, 2007, eff. Dec. 1, 2007; Mar. 26, 2009, eff. Dec. 1, 2009.)

Rule 33. Interrogatories to Parties

(a) In General.

(1) ***Number.*** Unless otherwise stipulated or ordered by the court, a party may serve on any other party no more than 25 written interrogatories, including all discrete subparts. Leave to serve additional interrogatories may be granted to the extent consistent with Rule 26(b)(1) and (2).

(2) ***Scope.*** An interrogatory may relate to any matter that may be inquired into under Rule 26(b). An interrogatory is not objectionable merely because it asks for an opinion or contention that relates to fact or the application of law to fact, but the court may order that the interrogatory need not be answered until designated discovery is complete, or until a pretrial conference or some other time.

(b) Answers and Objections.

(1) ***Responding Party.*** The interrogatories must be answered:

(A) by the party to whom they are directed; or

(B) if that party is a public or private corporation, a partnership, an association, or a governmental agency, by any officer or agent, who must furnish the information available to the party.

(2) ***Time to Respond.*** The responding party must serve its answers and any objections within 30 days after being served with the interrogatories. A shorter or longer time may be stipulated to under Rule 29 or be ordered by the court.

(3) ***Answering Each Interrogatory.*** Each interrogatory must, to the extent it is not objected to, be answered separately and fully in writing under oath.

(4) ***Objections.*** The grounds for objecting to an interrogatory must be stated with specificity. Any ground not stated in a timely objection is waived unless the court, for good cause, excuses the failure.

(5) ***Signature.*** The person who makes the answers must sign them, and the attorney who objects must sign any objections.

(c) Use. An answer to an interrogatory may be used to the extent allowed by the Federal Rules of Evidence.

(d) Option to Produce Business Records. If the answer to an interrogatory may be determined by examining, auditing, compiling, abstracting, or summarizing a party's business records (including electronically stored information), and if the burden of deriving or ascertaining the answer will be substantially the same for either party, the responding party may answer by:

(1) specifying the records that must be reviewed, in sufficient detail to enable the interrogating party to locate and identify them as readily as the responding party could; and

(2) giving the interrogating party a reasonable opportunity to examine and audit the records and to make copies, compilations, abstracts, or summaries.

(As amended Dec. 27, 1946, eff. Mar. 19, 1948; Mar. 30, 1970, eff. July 1, 1970; Apr. 29, 1980, eff. Aug. 1, 1980; Apr. 22, 1993, eff. Dec. 1, 1993; Apr. 12, 2006, eff. Dec. 1, 2006; Apr. 30, 2007, eff. Dec. 1, 2007; Apr. 29, 2015, eff. Dec. 1, 2015.)

NOTES OF ADVISORY COMMITTEE ON RULES

1970 AMENDMENT

* * *

Subdivision [(c)]. * * *

Rule 33 is amended to provide that an interrogatory is not objectionable merely because it calls for an opinion or contention that relates to fact or the application of law to fact. Efforts to draw sharp lines between facts and opinions have invariably been unsuccessful, and the clear trend of the cases is to permit "factual" opinions. As to requests for opinions or contentions that call for the application of law to fact, they can be most useful in narrowing and sharpening the issues, which is a major purpose of discovery. * * * On the other hand, under the new language interrogatories may not extend to issues of "pure law," *i.e.,* legal issues unrelated to the facts of the case.

Since interrogatories involving mixed questions of law and fact may create disputes between the parties which are best resolved after much or all of the other discovery has been completed, the court is expressly authorized to defer an answer. Likewise, the court may delay determination until pretrial conference, if it believes that the dispute is best resolved in the presence of the judge.

The principal question raised with respect to the cases permitting such interrogatories is whether they reintroduce undesirable aspects of the prior pleading practice, whereby parties were chained to misconceived contentions or theories, and ultimate determination on the merits was frustrated. * * * But there are few if any instances in the recorded cases demonstrating that such frustration has occurred. The general rule governing the use of answers to interrogatories is that under ordinary circumstances they do not limit proof. * * * Although in exceptional circumstances reliance on an answer may cause such prejudice that the court will hold the answering party bound to his answer, *e.g., Zielinski v. Philadelphia Piers, Inc.*, 139 F.Supp. 408 (E.D.Pa.1956), the interrogating party will ordinarily not be entitled to rely on the unchanging character of the answers he receives and cannot base prejudice on such reliance. The rule does not affect the power of a court to permit withdrawal or amendment of answers to interrogatories.

The use of answers to interrogatories at trial is made subject to the rules of evidence. The provisions governing use of depositions, to which Rule 33 presently refers, are not entirely apposite to answers to interrogatories, since deposition practice contemplates that all parties will ordinarily participate through cross-examination.

1980 AMENDMENT

Subdivision [(d)]. The Committee is advised that parties upon whom interrogatories are served have occasionally responded by directing the interrogating party to a mass of business records or by offering to make all of their records available, justifying the response by the option provided by this subdivision. Such practices are an abuse of the option. A party who is permitted by the terms of this subdivision to offer records for inspection in lieu of answering an interrogatory should offer them in a manner that permits the same direct and economical access that is available to the party. If the information sought exists in the form of compilations, abstracts or summaries then available to the responding party, those should be made available to the interrogating party. The final sentence is added to make it clear that a responding party has the duty to specify, by category and location, the records from which answers to interrogatories can be derived.

1993 AMENDMENT

* * *

Subdivision (a). Revision of this subdivision limits interrogatory practice. Because Rule 26(a)(1)(3) requires disclosure of much of the information previously obtained by this form of discovery, there should be less occasion to use it. Experience in over half of the district courts has confirmed that limitations on the number of interrogatories are useful and manageable. Moreover, because the device can be costly and may be used as a means of harassment, it is desirable to subject its use to the control of the court form—or if no form was specified in the request—the party must state the form or forms it intends to use.

(E) *Producing the Documents or Electronically Stored Information.* Unless otherwise stipulated or ordered by the court, these procedures apply to producing documents or electronically stored information:

(i) A party must produce documents as they are kept in the usual course of business or must organize and label them to correspond to the categories in the request;

(ii) If a request does not specify a form for producing electronically stored information, a party must produce it in a form or forms in which it is ordinarily maintained or in a reasonably usable form or forms; and

(iii) A party need not produce the same electronically stored information in more than one form.

(c) Nonparties. As provided in Rule 45, a nonparty may be compelled to produce documents and tangible things or to permit an inspection.

(As amended Dec. 27, 1946, eff. Mar. 19, 1948; Mar. 30, 1970, eff. July 1, 1970; Apr. 29, 1980, eff. Aug. 1, 1980; Mar. 2, 1987, eff. Aug. 1, 1987; Apr. 30, 1991, eff. Dec. 1, 1991; Apr. 22, 1993, eff. Dec. 1, 1993; Apr. 12, 2006, eff. Dec. 1, 2006; Apr. 30, 2007, eff. Dec. 1, 2007; Apr. 29, 2015, eff. Dec. 1, 2015.)

NOTES OF ADVISORY COMMITTEE ON RULES

2015 AMENDMENT

Several amendments are made in Rule 34, aimed at reducing the potential to impose unreasonable burdens by objections to requests to produce.

Rule 34(b)(2)(A) is amended to fit with new Rule 26(d)(2). The time to respond to a Rule 34 request delivered before the parties' Rule 26(f) conference is 30 days after the first Rule 26(f) conference.

Rule 34(b)(2)(B) is amended to require that objections to Rule 34 requests be stated with specificity. This provision adopts the language of Rule 33(b)(4), eliminating any doubt that less specific objections might be suitable under Rule 34. The specificity of the objection ties to the new provision in Rule 34(b)(2)(C) directing that an objection must state whether any responsive materials are being withheld on the basis of that objection. An objection may state that a request is overbroad, but if the objection recognizes that some part of the request is appropriate the objection should state the scope that is not overbroad. Examples would be a statement that the responding party will limit the search to documents or electronically stored information created within a given period of time prior to the events in suit, or to specified sources. When there is such an objection, the statement of what has been withheld can properly identify as matters "withheld" anything beyond the scope of the search specified in the objection.

Rule 34(b)(2)(B) is further amended to reflect the common practice of producing copies of documents or electronically stored information rather than simply permitting inspection. The response to the request must state that copies will be produced. The production must be completed either by the time for inspection specified in the request or by another reasonable time specifically identified in the response. When it is necessary to make the production in stages the response should specify the beginning and end dates of the production.

Rule 34(b)(2)(C) is amended to provide that an objection to a Rule 34 request must state whether anything is being withheld on the basis of the objection. This amendment should end the confusion that frequently arises when a producing party states several objections and still produces information, leaving the requesting party uncertain whether any relevant and responsive information has been withheld on the basis of the objections. The producing party does not need to provide a detailed description or log of all documents withheld, but does need to alert other parties to the fact that documents have been withheld and thereby facilitate an informed discussion of the objection. An objection that states the limits that have controlled the search for responsive and relevant materials qualifies as a statement that the materials have been "withheld."

Rule 35. Physical and Mental Examinations

(a) Order for an Examination.

(1) ***In General.*** The court where the action is pending may order a party whose mental or physical condition—including blood group—is in controversy to submit to a physical or mental examination by a suitably licensed or certified examiner. The court has the same authority to order a party to produce for examination a person who is in its custody or under its legal control.

(2) ***Motion and Notice; Contents of the Order.*** The order:

(A) may be made only on motion for good cause and on notice to all parties and the person to be examined; and

(B) must specify the time, place, manner, conditions, and scope of the examination, as well as the person or persons who will perform it.

(b) Examiner's Report.

(1) ***Request by the Party or Person Examined.*** The party who moved for the examination must, on request, deliver to the requester a copy of the examiner's report, together with like reports of all earlier examinations of the same condition. The request may be made by the party against whom the examination order was issued or by the person examined.

(2) ***Contents.*** The examiner's report must be in writing and must set out in detail the examiner's findings, including diagnoses, conclusions, and the results of any tests.

(3) ***Request by the Moving Party.*** After delivering the reports, the party who moved for the examination may request—and is entitled to receive—from the party against whom the examination order was issued like reports of all earlier or later examinations of the same condition. But those reports need not be delivered by the party with custody or control of the person examined if the party shows that it could not obtain them.

(4) ***Waiver of Privilege.*** By requesting and obtaining the examiner's report, or by deposing the examiner, the party examined waives any privilege it may have—in that action or any other action involving the same controversy—concerning testimony about all examinations of the same condition.

(5) ***Failure to Deliver a Report.*** The court on motion may order—on just terms—that a party deliver the report of an examination. If the report is not provided, the court may exclude the examiner's testimony at trial.

(6) ***Scope.*** This subdivision (b) applies also to an examination made by the parties' agreement, unless the agreement states otherwise. This subdivision does not preclude obtaining an examiner's report or deposing an examiner under other rules.

(As amended Mar. 30, 1970, eff. July 1, 1970; Mar. 2, 1987, eff. Aug. 1, 1987; Act of Nov. 18, 1988, § 7047(b), Pub.L. 100–690, 102 Stat. 4181; Apr. 30, 1991, eff. Dec. 1, 1991; Apr. 30, 2007, eff. Dec. 1, 2007.)

NOTES OF ADVISORY COMMITTEE ON RULES

1970 AMENDMENT

Subdivision (a). Rule 35(a) has hitherto provided only for an order requiring a party to submit to an examination. It is desirable to extend the rule to provide for an order against the party for examination of a person in his custody or under his legal control. As appears from the provisions of amended Rule 37(b)(2) and the comment under that rule, an order to "produce" the third person imposes only an obligation to use good faith efforts to produce the person.

The amendment will settle beyond doubt that a parent or guardian suing to recover for injuries to a minor may be ordered to produce the minor for examination. Further, the amendment expressly includes blood examination within the kinds of examinations that can be ordered under the rule. Provisions similar to the amendment have been adopted in at least 10 States; Calif.Code Civ.Proc. § 2032 * * *.

The amendment makes no change in the requirements of Rule 35 that, before a court order may issue the relevant physical or mental condition must be shown to be "in controversy" and "good cause" must be shown for the examination. Thus, the amendment has no effect on the recent decision of the Supreme Court in *Schlagenhauf v. Holder*, 379 U.S. 104 (1964), stressing the importance of these requirements and applying them to the facts of the case. The amendment makes no reference to employees of a party. Provisions relating to employees in the State statutes and rules cited above appear to have been virtually unused.

* * *

Subdivision (b)(3). This new subdivision removes any possible doubt that reports of examination may be obtained although no order for examination has been made under Rule 35(a). Examinations are very frequently made by agreement, and sometimes before the party examined has an attorney. * * *

The subdivision also makes clear that reports of examining physicians are discoverable not only under Rule 35(b), but under other rules as well. To be sure, if the report is privileged, then discovery is not permissible under any rule other than Rule 35(b) and it is permissible under Rule 35(b) only if the party requests a copy of the report of examination made by the other party's doctor. But if the report is unprivileged and is subject to discovery under the provisions of rules other than Rule 35(b)—such as Rules 34 or 26(b)(3) or (4)—discovery should not depend upon whether the person examined demands a copy of the report. * * *

1991 AMENDMENT

* * *

The requirement that the examiner be *suitably* licensed or certified is a new requirement. The court is thus expressly authorized to assess the credentials of the examiner to assure that no person is subjected to a court-ordered examination by an examiner whose testimony would be of such limited value that it would be unjust to require the person to undergo the invasion of privacy associated with the examination. This authority is not wholly new, for under the former rule, the court retained discretion to refuse to order an examination, or to restrict an examination. The revision is intended to encourage the exercise of this discretion, especially with respect to examinations by persons having narrow qualifications.

The court's responsibility to determine the suitability of the examiner's qualifications applies even to a proposed examination by a physician. If the proposed examination and testimony calls for an expertise that the proposed examiner does not have, it should not be ordered, even if the proposed examiner is a physician. The rule does not, however, require that the license or certificate be conferred by the jurisdiction in which the examination is conducted.

Rule 36. Requests for Admission

(a) Scope and Procedure.

(1) ***Scope.*** A party may serve on any other party a written request to admit, for purposes of the pending action only, the truth of any matters within the scope of Rule 26(b)(1) relating to:

(A) facts, the application of law to fact, or opinions about either; and

(B) the genuineness of any described documents.

(2) ***Form; Copy of a Document.*** Each matter must be separately stated. A request to admit the genuineness of a document must be accompanied by a copy of the document unless it is, or has been, otherwise furnished or made available for inspection and copying.

(3) ***Time to Respond; Effect of Not Responding.*** A matter is admitted unless, within 30 days after being served, the party to whom the request is directed serves on the requesting party a written answer or objection addressed to the matter and signed by the party or its attorney. A shorter or longer time for responding may be stipulated to under Rule 29 or be ordered by the court.

(4) ***Answer.*** If a matter is not admitted, the answer must specifically deny it or state in detail why the answering party cannot truthfully admit or deny it. A denial must fairly respond to the substance of the matter; and when good faith requires that a party qualify an answer or deny only a part of a matter, the answer must specify the part admitted and qualify or deny the rest. The answering party may assert lack of knowledge or information as a reason for failing to admit or deny only if the party states that it has made reasonable inquiry and that the information it knows or can readily obtain is insufficient to enable it to admit or deny.

(5) ***Objections.*** The grounds for objecting to a request must be stated. A party must not object solely on the ground that the request presents a genuine issue for trial.

(6) ***Motion Regarding the Sufficiency of an Answer or Objection.*** The requesting party may move to determine the sufficiency of an answer or objection. Unless the court finds an objection justified, it must order that an answer be served. On finding that an answer does not comply with this rule, the court may order either that the matter is admitted or that an amended answer be served. The court may defer its final decision until a pretrial conference or a specified time before trial. Rule 37(a)(5) applies to an award of expenses.

(b) Effect of an Admission; Withdrawing or Amending It. A matter admitted under this rule is conclusively established unless the court, on motion, permits the admission to be withdrawn or amended. Subject to Rule 16(e), the court may permit withdrawal or amendment if it would promote the presentation of the merits of the action and if the court is not persuaded that it would prejudice the requesting party in maintaining or defending the action on the merits. An admission under this rule is not an admission for any other purpose and cannot be used against the party in any other proceeding.

(As amended Dec. 27, 1946, eff. Mar. 19, 1948; Mar. 30, 1970, eff. July 1, 1970; Mar. 2, 1987, eff. Aug. 1, 1987; Apr. 30, 2007, eff. Dec. 1, 2007.)

NOTES OF ADVISORY COMMITTEE ON RULES

1970 AMENDMENT

Rule 36 serves two vital purposes, both of which are designed to reduce trial time. Admissions are sought, first to facilitate proof with respect to issues that cannot be eliminated from the case, and secondly, to narrow the issues by eliminating those that can be. The changes made in the rule are designed to serve these purposes more effectively. * * *

Subdivision (a). As revised, the subdivision provides that a request may be made to admit any matters within the scope of Rule 26(b) that relate to statements or opinions of fact or of the application of law to fact. It thereby eliminates the requirement that the matters be "of fact." * * *

Not only is it difficult as a practical matter to separate "fact" from "opinion," * * * but an admission on a matter of opinion may facilitate proof or narrow the issues or both. An admission of a matter involving the application of law to fact may, in a given case, even more clearly narrow the issues. For example, an admission that an employee acted in the scope of his employment may remove a major issue from the trial. * * * The amended provision does not authorize requests for admissions of law unrelated to the facts of the case.

Requests for admission involving the application of law to fact may create disputes between the parties which are best resolved in the presence of the judge after much or all of the other discovery has been completed. Power is therefore expressly conferred upon the court to defer decision until a pretrial conference is held or until a designated time prior to trial. On the other hand, the court should not automatically defer decision; in many instances, the importance of the admission lies in enabling the requesting party to avoid the burdensome accumulation of proof prior to the pretrial conference.

Courts have also divided on whether an answering party may properly object to requests for admission as to matters which that party regards as "in dispute." * * * The proper response in such cases is an answer. The very purpose of the request is to ascertain whether the answering party is prepared to admit or regards the matter as presenting a genuine issue for trial. In his answer, the party may deny, or he may give as his reason for inability to admit or deny the existence of a genuine issue. The party runs no risk of sanctions if the matter is genuinely in issue since Rule 37(c) provides a sanction of costs only when there are no good reasons for a failure to admit.

On the other hand, requests to admit may be so voluminous and so framed that the answering party finds the task of identifying what is in dispute and what is not unduly burdensome. If so, the responding party may obtain a protective order under Rule 26(c). * * *

Another sharp split of authority exists on the question whether a party may base his answer on lack of information or knowledge without seeking out additional information. * * *

The revised rule requires only that the answering party make reasonable inquiry and secure such knowledge and information as are readily obtainable by him. In most instances, the investigation will be necessary either to his own case or to preparation for rebuttal. Even when it is not, the information may be close enough at hand to be "readily obtainable." Rule 36 requires only that the party state that he has taken these steps. The sanction for failure of a party to inform himself before he answers lies in the award of costs after trial, as provided in Rule 37(c).

* * *

A problem peculiar to Rule 36 arises if the responding party serves answers that are not in conformity with the requirements of the rule—for example, a denial is not "specific," or the explanation of inability to admit or deny is not "in detail." Rule 36 now makes no provision for court scrutiny of such answers before trial, and it seems to contemplate that defective answers bring about admissions just as effectively as if no answer had been served. Some cases have so held. * * *

Giving a defective answer the automatic effect of an admission may cause unfair surprise. A responding party who purported to deny or to be unable to admit or deny will for the first time at trial confront the contention that he has made a binding admission. Since it is not always easy to know whether a denial is "specific" or an explanation is "in detail," neither party can know how the court will rule at trial and whether proof must be prepared. Some courts, therefore, have entertained motions to rule on defective answers. They have at times ordered that amended answers be served, when the defects were technical, and at other times have declared that the matter was admitted. * * * The rule as revised conforms to the latter practice.

Subdivision (b). * * *

The new provisions give an admission a conclusively binding effect, for purposes only of the pending action, unless the admission is withdrawn or amended. In form and substance a Rule 36 admission is comparable to an admission in pleadings or a stipulation drafted by counsel for use at trial, rather than to an evidentiary admission of a party. Unless the party securing an admission can depend on its binding effect, he cannot safely avoid the expense of preparing to prove the very matters on which he has secured the admission, and the purpose of the rule is defeated.

Provision is made for withdrawal or amendment of an admission. This provision emphasizes the importance of having the action resolved on the merits, while at the same time assuring each party that justified reliance on an admission in preparation for trial will not operate to his prejudice.

Rule 37. Failure to Make Disclosures or to Cooperate in Discovery; Sanctions

(a) Motion for an Order Compelling Disclosure or Discovery.

(1) ***In General.*** On notice to other parties and all affected persons, a party may move for an order compelling disclosure or discovery. The motion must include a certification that the movant has in good faith conferred or attempted to confer with the person or party failing to make disclosure or discovery in an effort to obtain it without court action.

(2) ***Appropriate Court.*** A motion for an order to a party must be made in the court where the action is pending. A motion for an order to a nonparty must be made in the court where the discovery is or will be taken.

(3) ***Specific Motions.***

(A) *To Compel Disclosure.* If a party fails to make a disclosure required by Rule 26(a), any other party may move to compel disclosure and for appropriate sanctions.

(B) *To Compel a Discovery Response.* A party seeking discovery may move for an order compelling an answer, designation, production, or inspection. This motion may be made if:

(i) a deponent fails to answer a question asked under Rule 30 or 31;

(ii) a corporation or other entity fails to make a designation under Rule 30(b)(6) or 31(a)(4);

(iii) a party fails to answer an interrogatory submitted under Rule 33; or

(iv) a party fails to produce documents or fails to respond that inspection will be permitted—or fails to permit inspection—as requested under Rule 34.

(C) *Related to a Deposition.* When taking an oral deposition, the party asking a question may complete or adjourn the examination before moving for an order.

(4) ***Evasive or Incomplete Disclosure, Answer, or Response.*** For purposes of this subdivision (a), an evasive or incomplete disclosure, answer, or response must be treated as a failure to disclose, answer, or respond.

(5) ***Payment of Expenses; Protective Orders.***

(A) *If the Motion Is Granted (or Disclosure or Discovery Is Provided After Filing).* If the motion is granted—or if the disclosure or requested discovery is provided after the motion was filed—the court must, after giving an opportunity to be heard, require the party or deponent whose conduct necessitated the motion, the party or attorney advising that conduct, or both to pay the movant's reasonable expenses incurred in making the motion, including attorney's fees. But the court must not order this payment if:

(i) the movant filed the motion before attempting in good faith to obtain the disclosure or discovery without court action;

(ii) the opposing party's nondisclosure, response, or objection was substantially justified; or

(iii) other circumstances make an award of expenses unjust.

(B) *If the Motion Is Denied.* If the motion is denied, the court may issue any protective order authorized under Rule 26(c) and must, after giving an opportunity to be heard, require the movant, the attorney filing the motion, or both to pay the party or deponent who opposed the motion its reasonable expenses incurred in opposing the motion, including attorney's fees. But the court must not order this payment if the motion was substantially justified or other circumstances make an award of expenses unjust.

(C) *If the Motion Is Granted in Part and Denied in Part.* If the motion is granted in part and denied in part, the court may issue any protective order authorized under Rule 26(c) and may, after giving an opportunity to be heard, apportion the reasonable expenses for the motion.

(b) Failure to Comply with a Court Order.

(1) ***Sanctions Sought in the District Where the Deposition Is Taken.*** If the court where the discovery is taken orders a deponent to be sworn or to answer a question and the deponent fails to obey, the failure may be treated as contempt of court. If a deposition-related motion is transferred to the court where the action is pending, and that court orders a deponent to be sworn or

to answer a question and the deponent fails to obey, the failure may be treated as contempt of either the court where the discovery is taken or the court where the action is pending.

(2) ***Sanctions Sought in the District Where the Action Is Pending.***

(A) *For Not Obeying a Discovery Order.* If a party or a party's officer, director, or managing agent—or a witness designated under Rule 30(b)(6) or 31(a)(4)—fails to obey an order to provide or permit discovery, including an order under Rule 26(f), 35, or 37(a), the court where the action is pending may issue further just orders. They may include the following:

(i) directing that the matters embraced in the order or other designated facts be taken as established for purposes of the action, as the prevailing party claims;

(ii) prohibiting the disobedient party from supporting or opposing designated claims or defenses, or from introducing designated matters in evidence;

(iii) striking pleadings in whole or in part;

(iv) staying further proceedings until the order is obeyed;

(v) dismissing the action or proceeding in whole or in part;

(vi) rendering a default judgment against the disobedient party; or

(vii) treating as contempt of court the failure to obey any order except an order to submit to a physical or mental examination.

(B) *For Not Producing a Person for Examination.* If a party fails to comply with an order under Rule 35(a) requiring it to produce another person for examination, the court may issue any of the orders listed in Rule 37(b)(2)(A)(i)–(vi), unless the disobedient party shows that it cannot produce the other person.

(C) *Payment of Expenses.* Instead of or in addition to the orders above, the court must order the disobedient party, the attorney advising that party, or both to pay the reasonable expenses, including attorney's fees, caused by the failure, unless the failure was substantially justified or other circumstances make an award of expenses unjust.

(c) Failure to Disclose, to Supplement an Earlier Response, or to Admit.

(1) ***Failure to Disclose or Supplement.*** If a party fails to provide information or identify a witness as required by Rule 26(a) or (e), the party is not allowed to use that information or witness to supply evidence on a motion, at a hearing, or at a trial, unless the failure was substantially justified or is harmless. In addition to or instead of this sanction, the court, on motion and after giving an opportunity to be heard:

(A) may order payment of the reasonable expenses, including attorney's fees, caused by the failure;

(B) may inform the jury of the party's failure; and

(C) may impose other appropriate sanctions, including any of the orders listed in Rule 37(b)(2)(A)(i)–(vi).

(2) ***Failure to Admit.*** If a party fails to admit what is requested under Rule 36 and if the requesting party later proves a document to be genuine or the matter true, the requesting party may move that the party who failed to admit pay the reasonable expenses, including attorney's fees, incurred in making that proof. The court must so order unless:

(A) the request was held objectionable under Rule 36(a);

(B) the admission sought was of no substantial importance;

(C) the party failing to admit had a reasonable ground to believe that it might prevail on the matter; or

(D) there was other good reason for the failure to admit.

(d) Party's Failure to Attend Its Own Deposition, Serve Answers to Interrogatories, or Respond to a Request for Inspection.

(1) ***In General.***

(A) *Motion; Grounds for Sanctions.* The court where the action is pending may, on motion, order sanctions if:

(i) a party or a party's officer, director, or managing agent—or a person designated under Rule 30(b)(6) or 31(a)(4)—fails, after being served with proper notice, to appear for that person's deposition; or

(ii) a party, after being properly served with interrogatories under Rule 33 or a request for inspection under Rule 34, fails to serve its answers, objections, or written response.

(B) *Certification.* A motion for sanctions for failing to answer or respond must include a certification that the movant has in good faith conferred or attempted to confer with the party failing to act in an effort to obtain the answer or response without court action.

(2) ***Unacceptable Excuse for Failing to Act.*** A failure described in Rule 37(d)(1)(A) is not excused on the ground that the discovery sought was objectionable, unless the party failing to act has a pending motion for a protective order under Rule 26(c).

(3) ***Types of Sanctions.*** Sanctions may include any of the orders listed in Rule 37(b)(2)(A)(i)–(vi). Instead of or in addition to these sanctions, the court must require the party failing to act, the attorney advising that party, or both to pay the reasonable expenses, including attorney's fees, caused by the failure, unless the failure was substantially justified or other circumstances make an award of expenses unjust.

(e) Failure to Preserve Electronically Stored Information. If electronically stored information that should have been preserved in the anticipation or conduct of litigation is lost because a party failed to take reasonable steps to preserve it, and it cannot be restored or replaced through additional discovery, the court:

(1) upon finding prejudice to another party from loss of the information, may order measures no greater than necessary to cure the prejudice; or

(2) only upon finding that the party acted with the intent to deprive another party of the information's use in the litigation may:

(A) presume that the lost information was unfavorable to the party;

(B) instruct the jury that it may or must presume the information was unfavorable to the party; or

(C) dismiss the action or enter a default judgment.

(f) Failure to Participate in Framing a Discovery Plan. If a party or its attorney fails to participate in good faith in developing and submitting a proposed discovery plan as required by Rule 26(f), the court may, after giving an opportunity to be heard, require that party or attorney to pay to any other party the reasonable expenses, including attorney's fees, caused by the failure.

(As amended Dec. 29, 1948, eff. Oct. 20, 1949; Mar. 30, 1970, eff. July 1, 1970; Apr. 29, 1980, eff. Aug. 1, 1980; Pub.L. 96–481, Title II, § 205(a), Oct. 21, 1980, 94 Stat. 2330; Mar. 2, 1987, eff. Aug. 1, 1987; Apr. 22, 1993, eff. Dec. 1, 1993; Apr. 17, 2000, eff. Dec. 1, 2000; Apr. 12, 2006, eff. Dec. 1, 2006; Apr. 30, 2007, eff. Dec. 1, 2007; Apr. 16, 2013, eff. Dec. 1, 2013; Apr. 29, 2015, eff. Dec. 1, 2015.)

NOTES OF ADVISORY COMMITTEE ON RULES

1993 AMENDMENT

Subdivision (a). This subdivision is revised to reflect the revision of Rule 26(a), requiring disclosure of matters without a discovery request.

Pursuant to new subdivision (a)(2)(A), a party dissatisfied with the disclosure made by an opposing party may under this rule move for an order to compel disclosure. In providing for such a motion, the revised rule parallels the provisions of the former rule dealing with failures to answer particular interrogatories. Such a motion may be needed when the information to be disclosed might be helpful to the party seeking the disclosure but not to the party required to make the disclosure. If the party required to make the disclosure would need the material to support its own contentions, the more effective enforcement of the disclosure requirement will be to exclude the evidence not disclosed, as provided in subdivision (c)(1) of this revised rule.

Language is included in the new paragraph and added to the subparagraph (B) that requires litigants to seek to resolve discovery disputes by informal means before filing a motion with the court. This requirement is based on successful experience with similar local rules of court promulgated pursuant to Rule 83.

* * *

Under revised paragraph (3), evasive or incomplete disclosures and responses to interrogatories and production requests are treated as failures to disclose or respond. Interrogatories and requests for production should not be read or interpreted in an artificially restrictive or hypertechnical manner to avoid disclosure of information fairly covered by the discovery request, and to do so is subject to appropriate sanctions under subdivision (a).

* * *

Subdivision (c). The revision provides a self-executing sanction for failure to make a disclosure required by Rule 26(a), without need for a motion under subdivision (a)(2)(A).

Paragraph (1) prevents a party from using as evidence any witnesses or information that, without substantial justification, has not been disclosed as required by Rules 26(a) and 26(e)(1). This automatic sanction provides a strong inducement for disclosure of material that the disclosing party would expect to use as evidence, whether at a trial, at a hearing, or on a motion, such as one under Rule 56. As disclosure of evidence offered solely for impeachment purposes is not required under those rules, this preclusion sanction likewise does not apply to that evidence.

Limiting the automatic sanction to violations "without substantial justification," coupled with the exception for violations that are "harmless," is needed to avoid unduly harsh penalties in a variety of situations: e.g., the inadvertent omission from a Rule 26(a)(1)(A) disclosure of the name of a potential witness known to all parties; the failure to list as a trial witness a person so listed by another party; or the lack of knowledge of a pro se litigant of the requirement to make disclosures. In the latter situation, however, exclusion would be proper if the requirement for disclosure had been called to the litigant's attention by either the court or another party.

Preclusion of evidence is not an effective incentive to compel disclosure of information that, being supportive of the position of the opposing party, might advantageously be concealed by the disclosing party. However, the rule provides the court with a wide range of other sanctions—such as declaring specified facts to be established, preventing contradictory evidence, or, like spoliation of evidence, allowing the jury to be informed of the fact of nondisclosure—that, though not self-executing, can be imposed when found to be warranted after a hearing. The failure to identify a witness or document in a disclosure statement would be admissible under the Federal Rules of Evidence under the same principles that allow a party's interrogatory answers to be offered against it.

Subdivision (d). This subdivision is revised to require that, where a party fails to file any response to interrogatories or a Rule 34 request, the discovering party should informally seek to obtain such responses before filing a motion for sanctions.

The last sentence of this subdivision is revised to clarify that it is the pendency of a motion for protective order that may be urged as an excuse for a violation of subdivision (d). If a party's motion has been denied, the party cannot argue that its subsequent failure to comply would be justified. In this connection, it should be noted that the filing of a motion under Rule 26(c) is not self-executing—the relief authorized under that rule depends on obtaining the court's order to that effect.

* * *

2015 AMENDMENT

* * *

Subdivision (e). Present Rule 37(e), adopted in 2006, provides: "Absent exceptional circumstances, a court may not impose sanctions under these rules on a party for failing to provide electronically stored information lost as a result of the routine, good-faith operation of an electronic information system." This limited rule has not adequately addressed the serious problems resulting from the continued exponential growth in the volume of such information. Federal circuits have established significantly different standards for imposing sanctions or curative measures on parties who fail to preserve electronically stored information. These developments have caused litigants to expend excessive effort and money on preservation in order to avoid the risk of severe sanctions if a court finds they did not do enough.

New Rule 37(e) replaces the 2006 rule. It authorizes and specifies measures a court may employ if information that should have been preserved is lost, and specifies the findings necessary to justify these measures. It therefore forecloses reliance on inherent authority or state law to determine when certain measures should be used. The rule does not affect the validity of an independent tort claim for spoliation if state law applies in a case and authorizes the claim.

The new rule applies only to electronically stored information, also the focus of the 2006 rule. It applies only when such information is lost. Because electronically stored information often exists in multiple locations, loss from one source may often be harmless when substitute information can be found elsewhere.

The new rule applies only if the lost information should have been preserved in the anticipation or conduct of litigation and the party failed to take reasonable steps to preserve it. Many court decisions hold that potential litigants have a duty to preserve relevant information when litigation is reasonably foreseeable. Rule 37(e) is based on this common-law duty; it does not attempt to create a new duty to preserve. The rule does not apply when information is lost before a duty to preserve arises.

In applying the rule, a court may need to decide whether and when a duty to preserve arose. Courts should consider the extent to which a party was on notice that litigation was likely and that the information would be relevant. A variety of events may alert a party to the prospect of litigation. Often these events provide only limited information about that prospective litigation, however, so that the scope of information that should be preserved may remain uncertain. It is important not to be blinded to this reality by hindsight arising from familiarity with an action as it is actually filed.

Although the rule focuses on the common-law obligation to preserve in the anticipation or conduct of litigation, courts may sometimes consider whether there was an independent requirement that the lost information be preserved. Such requirements arise from many sources—statutes, administrative regulations, an order in another case, or a party's own information-retention protocols. The court should be sensitive, however, to the fact that such independent preservation requirements may be addressed to a wide variety of concerns unrelated to the current litigation. The fact that a party had an independent obligation to preserve information does not necessarily mean that it had such a duty with respect to the litigation, and the fact that the party failed to observe some other preservation obligation does not itself prove that its efforts to preserve were not reasonable with respect to a particular case.

The duty to preserve may in some instances be triggered or clarified by a court order in the case. Preservation orders may become more common, in part because Rules 16(b)(3)(B)(iii) and 26(f)(3)(C) are amended to encourage discovery plans and orders that address preservation. Once litigation has commenced, if the parties cannot reach agreement about preservation issues, promptly seeking judicial guidance about the extent of reasonable preservation may be important.

The rule applies only if the information was lost because the party failed to take reasonable steps to preserve the information. Due to the ever-increasing volume of electronically stored information and the multitude of devices that generate such information, perfection in preserving all relevant electronically stored information is often impossible. As under the current rule, the routine, good-faith operation of an electronic information system would be a relevant factor for the court to consider in evaluating whether a party failed to take reasonable steps to preserve lost information, although the prospect of litigation may call for reasonable steps to preserve information by intervening in that routine operation. This rule recognizes that "reasonable steps" to preserve suffice; it does not call for perfection. The court should be sensitive to the party's sophistication with regard to litigation in evaluating preservation efforts; some litigants, particularly individual litigants, may be less familiar with preservation obligations than others who have considerable experience in litigation.

Because the rule calls only for reasonable steps to preserve, it is inapplicable when the loss of information occurs despite the party's reasonable steps to preserve. For example, the information may not be in the party's control. Or information the party has preserved may be destroyed by events outside the party's control—the computer room may be flooded, a "cloud" service may fail, a malign software attack may disrupt a storage system, and so on. Courts may, however, need to assess the extent to which a party knew of and protected against such risks.

Another factor in evaluating the reasonableness of preservation efforts is proportionality. The court should be sensitive to party resources; aggressive preservation efforts can be extremely costly, and parties (including governmental parties) may have limited staff and resources to devote to those efforts. A party may act reasonably by choosing a less costly form of information preservation, if it is substantially as effective as more costly forms. It is important that counsel become familiar with their clients' information systems and digital data—including social media—to address these issues. A party urging that preservation requests are disproportionate may need to provide specifics about these matters in order to enable meaningful discussion of the appropriate preservation regime.

When a party fails to take reasonable steps to preserve electronically stored information that should have been preserved in the anticipation or conduct of litigation, and the information is lost as a result, Rule 37(e) directs that the initial focus should be on whether the lost information can be restored or replaced through additional discovery. Nothing in the rule limits the court's powers under Rules 16 and 26 to authorize additional discovery. Orders under Rule 26(b)(2)(B) regarding discovery from sources that would ordinarily be considered inaccessible or under Rule 26(c)(1)(B) on allocation of expenses may be pertinent to solving such problems. If the information is restored or replaced, no further measures should be taken. At the same time, it is important to emphasize that efforts to restore or replace lost information through discovery should be proportional to the apparent importance of the lost information to claims or defenses in the litigation. For example, substantial measures should not be employed to restore or replace information that is marginally relevant or duplicative.

* * *

TITLE VI. TRIALS

Rule 38. Right to a Jury Trial; Demand

(a) Right Preserved. The right of trial by jury as declared by the Seventh Amendment to the Constitution—or as provided by a federal statute—is preserved to the parties inviolate.

(b) Demand. On any issue triable of right by a jury, a party may demand a jury trial by:

(1) serving the other parties with a written demand—which may be included in a pleading—no later than 14 days after the last pleading directed to the issue is served; and

(2) filing the demand in accordance with Rule 5(d).

(c) Specifying Issues. In its demand, a party may specify the issues that it wishes to have tried by a jury; otherwise, it is considered to have demanded a jury trial on all the issues so triable. If the party has demanded a jury trial on only some issues, any other party may—within 14 days after being served with the demand or within a shorter time ordered by the court—serve a demand for a jury trial on any other or all factual issues triable by jury.

(d) Waiver; Withdrawal. A party waives a jury trial unless its demand is properly served and filed. A proper demand may be withdrawn only if the parties consent.

(e) Admiralty and Maritime Claims. These rules do not create a right to a jury trial on issues in a claim that is ban admiralty or maritime claim under Rule 9(h).

(As amended Feb. 28, 1966, eff. July 1, 1966; Mar. 2, 1987, eff. Aug. 1, 1987; Apr. 22, 1993, eff. Dec. 1, 1993; Apr. 30, 2007, eff. Dec. 1, 2007; Mar. 26, 2009, eff. Dec. 1, 2009.)

Rule 39. Trial by Jury or by the Court

(a) When a Demand Is Made. When a jury trial has been demanded under Rule 38, the action must be designated on the docket as a jury action. The trial on all issues so demanded must be by jury unless:

(1) the parties or their attorneys file a stipulation to a nonjury trial or so stipulate on the record; or

(2) the court, on motion or on its own, finds that on some or all of those issues there is no federal right to a jury trial.

(b) When No Demand Is Made. Issues on which a jury trial is not properly demanded are to be tried by the court. But the court may, on motion, order a jury trial on any issue for which a jury might have been demanded.

(c) Advisory Jury; Jury Trial by Consent. In an action not triable of right by a jury, the court, on motion or on its own:

(1) may try any issue with an advisory jury; or

(2) may, with the parties' consent, try any issue by a jury whose verdict has the same effect as if a jury trial had been a matter of right, unless the action is against the United States and a federal statute provides for a nonjury trial.

(As amended Apr. 30, 2007, eff. Dec. 1, 2007.)

Rule 40. Scheduling Cases for Trial

Each court must provide by rule for scheduling trials. The court must give priority to actions entitled to priority by a federal statute.

(As amended Apr. 30, 2007, eff. Dec. 1, 2007.)

Rule 41. Dismissal of Actions

(a) Voluntary Dismissal.

(1) ***By the Plaintiff.***

(A) *Without a Court Order.* Subject to Rules 23(e), 23.1(c), 23.2, and 66 and any applicable federal statute, the plaintiff may dismiss an action without a court order by filing:

(i) a notice of dismissal before the opposing party serves either an answer or a motion for summary judgment; or

(ii) a stipulation of dismissal signed by all parties who have appeared.

(B) *Effect.* Unless the notice or stipulation states otherwise, the dismissal is without prejudice. But if the plaintiff previously dismissed any federal- or state-court action based on or including the same claim, a notice of dismissal operates as an adjudication on the merits.

(2) ***By Court Order; Effect.*** Except as provided in Rule 41(a)(1), an action may be dismissed at the plaintiff's request only by court order, on terms that the court considers proper. If a defendant has pleaded a counterclaim before being served with the plaintiff's motion to dismiss, the action may be dismissed over the defendant's objection only if the counterclaim can remain pending for independent adjudication. Unless the order states otherwise, a dismissal under this paragraph (2) is without prejudice.

(b) Involuntary Dismissal; Effect. If the plaintiff fails to prosecute or to comply with these rules or a court order, a defendant may move to dismiss the action or any claim against it. Unless the dismissal order states otherwise, a dismissal under this subdivision (b) and any dismissal not under this rule—except one for lack of jurisdiction, improper venue, or failure to join a party under Rule 19—operates as an adjudication on the merits.

(c) Dismissing a Counterclaim, Crossclaim, or Third-Party Claim. This rule applies to a dismissal of any counterclaim, crossclaim, or third-party claim. A claimant's voluntary dismissal under Rule 41(a)(1)(A)(i) must be made:

(1) before a responsive pleading is served; or

(2) if there is no responsive pleading, before evidence is introduced at a hearing or trial.

(d) Costs of a Previously Dismissed Action. If a plaintiff who previously dismissed an action in any court files an action based on or including the same claim against the same defendant, the court:

(1) may order the plaintiff to pay all or part of the costs of that previous action; and

(2) may stay the proceedings until the plaintiff has complied.

(As amended Dec. 27, 1946, eff. Mar. 19, 1948; Jan. 21, 1963, eff. July 1, 1963; Feb. 28, 1966, eff. July 1, 1966; Dec. 4, 1967, eff. July 1, 1968; Mar. 2, 1987, eff. Aug. 1, 1987; Apr. 30, 1991, eff. Dec. 1, 1991; Apr. 30, 2007, eff. Dec. 1, 2007.)

Rule 42. Consolidation; Separate Trials

(a) Consolidation. If actions before the court involve a common question of law or fact, the court may:

(1) join for hearing or trial any or all matters at issue in the actions;

(2) consolidate the actions; or

(3) issue any other orders to avoid unnecessary cost or delay.

(b) Separate Trials. For convenience, to avoid prejudice, or to expedite and economize, the court may order a separate trial of one or more separate issues, claims, crossclaims, counterclaims, or third-party claims. When ordering a separate trial, the court must preserve any federal right to a jury trial.

(As amended Feb. 28, 1966, eff. July 1, 1966; Apr. 30, 2007, eff. Dec. 1, 2007.)

Rule 43. Taking Testimony

(a) In Open Court. At trial, the witnesses' testimony must be taken in open court unless a federal statute, the Federal Rules of Evidence, these rules, or other rules adopted by the Supreme Court provide otherwise. For good cause in compelling circumstances and with appropriate safeguards, the court may permit testimony in open court by contemporaneous transmission from a different location.

(b) Affirmation Instead of an Oath. When these rules require an oath, a solemn affirmation suffices.

(c) Evidence on a Motion. When a motion relies on facts outside the record, the court may hear the matter on affidavits or may hear it wholly or partly on oral testimony or on depositions.

(d) Interpreter. The court may appoint an interpreter of its choosing; fix reasonable compensation to be paid from funds provided by law or by one or more parties; and tax the compensation as costs.

(As amended Feb. 28, 1966, eff. July 1, 1966; Nov. 20, 1972, eff. July 1, 1975; Dec. 18, 1972, eff. July 1, 1975; Mar. 2, 1987, eff. Aug. 1, 1987; Apr. 23, 1996, eff. Dec. 1, 1996; Apr. 30, 2007, eff. Dec. 1, 2007.)

Rule 44. Proving an Official Record

(a) Means of Proving.

(1) ***Domestic Record.*** Each of the following evidences an official record—or an entry in it—that is otherwise admissible and is kept within the United States, any state, district, or commonwealth, or any territory subject to the administrative or judicial jurisdiction of the United States:

(A) an official publication of the record; or

(B) a copy attested by the officer with legal custody of the record—or by the officer's deputy—and accompanied by a certificate that the officer has custody. The certificate must be made under seal:

(i) by a judge of a court of record in the district or political subdivision where the record is kept; or

(ii) by any public officer with a seal of office and with official duties in the district or political subdivision where the record is kept.

(2) ***Foreign Record.***

(A) *In General.* Each of the following evidences a foreign official record—or an entry in it—that is otherwise admissible:

(i) an official publication of the record; or

(ii) the record—or a copy—that is attested by an authorized person and is accompanied either by a final certification of genuineness or by a certification under a treaty or convention to which the United States and the country where the record is located are parties.

(B) *Final Certification of Genuineness.* A final certification must certify the genuineness of the signature and official position of the attester or of any foreign official whose certificate of genuineness relates to the attestation or is in a chain of certificates of genuineness relating to the attestation. A final certification may be made by a secretary of a United States embassy or legation; by a consul general, vice consul, or consular agent of the United States; or by a diplomatic or consular official of the foreign country assigned or accredited to the United States.

(C) *Other Means of Proof.* If all parties have had a reasonable opportunity to investigate a foreign record's authenticity and accuracy, the court may, for good cause, either:

(i) admit an attested copy without final certification; or

(ii) permit the record to be evidenced by an attested summary with or without a final certification.

(b) Lack of a Record. A written statement that a diligent search of designated records revealed no record or entry of a specified tenor is admissible as evidence that the records contain no such record or entry. For domestic records, the statement must be authenticated under Rule 44(a)(1). For foreign records, the statement must comply with (a)(2)(C)(ii).

(c) Other Proof. A party may prove an official record—or an entry or lack of an entry in it—by any other method authorized by law.

(As amended Feb. 28, 1966, eff. July 1, 1966; Mar. 2, 1987, eff. Aug. 1, 1987; Apr. 30, 1991, eff. Dec. 1, 1991; Apr. 30, 2007, eff. Dec. 1, 2007.)

Rule 44.1. Determining Foreign Law

A party who intends to raise an issue about a foreign country's law must give notice by a pleading or other writing. In determining foreign law, the court may consider any relevant material or source, including testimony, whether or not submitted by a party or admissible under the Federal Rules of Evidence. The court's determination must be treated as a ruling on a question of law.

(Added Feb. 28, 1966, eff. July 1, 1966, and amended Nov. 20, 1972, eff. July 1, 1975; Mar. 2, 1987, eff. Aug. 1, 1987; Apr. 30, 2007, eff. Dec. 1, 2007.)

Rule 45. Subpoena

(a) In General.

(1) ***Form and Contents.***

(A) *Requirements—In General.* Every subpoena must:

(i) state the court from which it issued;

(ii) state the title of the action and its civil-action number;

(iii) command each person to whom it is directed to do the following at a specified time and place: attend and testify; produce designated documents, electronically stored information, or tangible things in that person's possession, custody, or control; or permit the inspection of premises; and

(iv) set out the text of Rule 45(d) and (e).

(B) *Command to Attend a Deposition—Notice of the Recording Method.* A subpoena commanding attendance at a deposition must state the method for recording the testimony.

(C) *Combining or Separating a Command to Produce or to Permit Inspection; Specifying the Form for Electronically Stored Information.* A command to produce documents, electronically stored information, or tangible things or to permit the inspection of premises may be included in a subpoena commanding attendance at a deposition, hearing, or trial, or may be set out in a separate subpoena. A subpoena may specify the form or forms in which electronically stored information is to be produced.

(D) *Command to Produce; Included Obligations.* A command in a subpoena to produce documents, electronically stored information, or tangible things requires the responding party to permit inspection, copying, testing, or sampling of the materials.

(2) ***Issuing Court.*** A subpoena must issue from the court where the action is pending.

(3) ***Issued by Whom.*** The clerk must issue a subpoena, signed but otherwise in blank, to a party who requests it. That party must complete it before service. An attorney also may issue and sign a subpoena if the attorney is authorized to practice in the issuing court.

(4) ***Notice to Other Parties Before Service.*** If the subpoena commands the production of documents, electronically stored information, or tangible things or the inspection of premises before trial, then before it is served on the person to whom it is directed, a notice and a copy of the subpoena must be served on each party.

(b) Service.

(1) ***By Whom and How; Tendering Fees.*** Any person who is at least 18 years old and not a party may serve a subpoena. Serving a subpoena requires delivering a copy to the named person and, if the subpoena requires that person's attendance, tendering the fees for 1 day's attendance and the mileage allowed by law. Fees and mileage need not be tendered when the subpoena issues on behalf of the United States or any of its officers or agencies.

(2) ***Service in the United States.*** A subpoena may be served at any place within the United States.

(3) ***Service in a Foreign Country.*** 28 U.S.C. § 1783 governs issuing and serving a subpoena directed to a United States national or resident who is in a foreign country.

(4) ***Proof of Service.*** Proving service, when necessary, requires filing with the issuing court a statement showing the date and manner of service and the names of the persons served. The statement must be certified by the server.

(c) Place of Compliance.

(1) ***For a Trial, Hearing, or Deposition.*** A subpoena may command a person to attend a trial, hearing, or deposition only as follows:

(A) within 100 miles of where the person resides, is employed, or regularly transacts business in person; or

(B) within the state where the person resides, is employed, or regularly transacts business in person, if the person

(i) is a party or a party's officer; or

(ii) is commanded to attend a trial and would not incur substantial expense.

(2) ***For Other Discovery.*** A subpoena may command:

(A) production of documents, electronically stored information, or tangible things at a place within 100 miles of where the person resides, is employed, or regularly transacts business in person; and

(B) inspection of premises at the premises to be inspected.

(d) Protecting a Person Subject to a Subpoena; Enforcement.

(1) ***Avoiding Undue Burden or Expense; Sanctions.*** A party or attorney responsible for issuing and serving a subpoena must take reasonable steps to avoid imposing undue burden or expense on a person subject to the subpoena. The court for the district where compliance is required must enforce this duty and impose an appropriate sanction—which may include lost earnings and reasonable attorney's fees—on a party or attorney who fails to comply.

(2) ***Command to Produce Materials or Permit Inspection.***

(A) *Appearance Not Required.* A person commanded to produce documents, electronically stored information, or tangible things, or to permit the inspection of premises, need not appear in person at the place of production or inspection unless also commanded to appear for a deposition, hearing, or trial.

(B) *Objections.* A person commanded to produce documents or tangible things or to permit inspection may serve on the party or attorney designated in the subpoena a written objection to inspecting, copying, testing or sampling any or all of the materials or to inspecting the premises—or to producing electronically stored information in the form or forms requested. The objection must be served before the earlier of the time specified for compliance or 14 days after the subpoena is served. If an objection is made, the following rules apply:

(i) At any time, on notice to the commanded person, the serving party may move the court for the district where compliance is required for an order compelling production or inspection.

(ii) These acts may be required only as directed in the order, and the order must protect a person who is neither a party nor a party's officer from significant expense resulting from compliance.

(3) ***Quashing or Modifying a Subpoena.***

(A) *When Required.* On timely motion, the court for the district where compliance is required must quash or modify a subpoena that:

(i) fails to allow a reasonable time to comply;

(ii) requires a person to comply beyond the geographical limits specified in Rule 45(c);

(iii) requires disclosure of privileged or other protected matter, if no exception or waiver applies; or

(iv) subjects a person to undue burden.

(B) *When Permitted.* To protect a person subject to or affected by a subpoena, the court for the district where compliance is required may, on motion, quash or modify the subpoena if it requires:

(i) disclosing a trade secret or other confidential research, development, or commercial information; or

(ii) disclosing an unretained expert's opinion or information that does not describe specific occurrences in dispute and results from the expert's study that was not requested by a party.

(C) *Specifying Conditions as an Alternative.* In the circumstances described in Rule 45(c)(3)(B), the court may, instead of quashing or modifying a subpoena, order appearance or production under specified conditions if the serving party:

(i) shows a substantial need for the testimony or material that cannot be otherwise met without undue hardship; and

(ii) ensures that the subpoenaed person will be reasonably compensated.

(e) Duties in Responding to a Subpoena.

(1) ***Producing Documents or Electronically Stored Information.*** These procedures apply to producing documents or electronically stored information:

(A) *Documents.* A person responding to a subpoena to produce documents must produce them as they are kept in the ordinary course of business or must organize and label them to correspond to the categories in the demand.

(B) *Form for Producing Electronically Stored Information Not Specified.* If a subpoena does not specify a form for producing electronically stored information, the person responding must produce it in a form or forms in which it is ordinarily maintained or in a reasonably usable form or forms.

(C) *Electronically Stored Information Produced in Only One Form.* The person responding need not produce the same electronically stored information in more than one form.

(D) *Inaccessible Electronically Stored Information.* The person responding need not provide discovery of electronically stored information from sources that the person identifies as not reasonably accessible because of undue burden or cost. On motion to compel discovery or for a protective order, the person responding must show that the information is not reasonably accessible because of undue burden or cost. If that showing is made, the court may nonetheless order discovery from such sources if the requesting party shows good cause, considering the limitations of Rule 26(b)(2)(C). The court may specify conditions for the discovery.

(2) ***Claiming Privilege or Protection.***

(A) *Information Withheld.* A person withholding subpoenaed information under a claim that it is privileged or subject to protection as trial-preparation material must:

(i) expressly make the claim; and

(ii) describe the nature of the withheld documents, communications, or tangible things in a manner that, without revealing information itself privileged or protected, will enable the parties to assess the claim.

(B) *Information Produced.* If information produced in response to a subpoena is subject to a claim of privilege or of protection as trial-preparation material, the person making the claim may notify any party that received the information of the claim and the basis for it. After being notified, a party must promptly return, sequester, or destroy the specified information and any copies it has; must not use or disclose the information until the claim is resolved; must take reasonable steps to retrieve the information if the party disclosed it before being notified; and may promptly present the information under seal to the court for the district where compliance is required for a determination of the claim. The person who produced the information must preserve the information until the claim is resolved.

(f) **Transferring a Subpoena-Related Motion.** When the court where compliance is required did not issue the subpoena, it may transfer a motion under this rule to the issuing court if the person subject to the subpoena consents or if the court finds exceptional circumstances. Then, if the attorney for a person subject to a subpoena is authorized to practice in the court where the motion was made, the attorney may file papers and appear on the motion as an officer of the issuing court. To enforce its order, the issuing court may transfer the order to the court where the motion was made.

(g) Contempt. The court for the district where compliance is required—and also, after a motion is transferred, the issuing court—may hold in contempt a person who, having been served, fails without adequate excuse to obey the subpoena or an order related to it.

(As amended Dec. 27, 1946, eff. Mar. 19, 1948; Dec. 29, 1948, eff. Oct. 20, 1949; Mar. 30, 1970, eff. July 1, 1970; Apr. 29, 1980, eff. Aug. 1, 1980; Apr. 29, 1985, eff. Aug. 1, 1985; Mar. 2, 1987, eff. Aug. 1, 1987; Apr. 30, 1991, eff. Dec. 1, 1991; Apr. 25, 2005, eff. Dec. 1, 2005; Apr. 12, 2006, eff. Dec. 1, 2006; Apr. 30, 2007, eff. Dec. 1, 2007; Apr. 16, 2013, eff. Dec. 1, 2013.)

NOTES OF ADVISORY COMMITTEE ON RULES

* * *

2013 AMENDMENT

Rule 45 was extensively amended in 1991. The goal of the present amendments is to clarify and simplify the rule. The amendments recognize the court where the action is pending as the issuing court, permit nationwide service of a subpoena, and collect in a new subdivision (c) the previously scattered provisions regarding place of compliance. These changes resolve a conflict that arose after the 1991 amendment about a court's authority to compel a party or party officer to travel long distances to testify at trial; such testimony may now be required only as specified in new Rule 45(c). In addition, the amendments introduce authority in new Rule 45(f) for the court where compliance is required to transfer a subpoena-related motion to the court where the action is pending on consent of the person subject to the subpoena or in exceptional circumstances.

* * *

Rule 46. Objecting to a Ruling or Order

A formal exception to a ruling or order is unnecessary. When the ruling or order is requested or made, a party need only state the action that it wants the court to take or objects to, along with the grounds for the request or objection. Failing to object does not prejudice a party who had no opportunity to do so when the ruling or order was made.

(As amended Mar. 2, 1987, eff. Aug. 1, 1987; Apr. 30, 2007, eff. Dec. 1, 2007.)

Rule 47. Selecting Jurors

(a) Examining Jurors. The court may permit the parties or their attorneys to examine prospective jurors or may itself do so. If the court examines the jurors, it must permit the parties or their attorneys to make any further inquiry it considers proper, or must itself ask any of their additional questions it considers proper.

(b) Peremptory Challenges. The court must allow the number of peremptory challenges provided by 28 U.S.C. § 1870.

(c) Excusing a Juror. During trial or deliberation, the court may excuse a juror for good cause.

(As amended Feb. 28, 1966, eff. July 1, 1966; Apr. 30, 1991, eff. Dec. 1, 1991; Apr. 30, 2007, eff. Dec. 1, 2007.)

Rule 48. Number of Jurors; Verdict; Polling

(a) Number of Jurors. A jury must begin with at least 6 and no more than 12 members, and each juror must participate in the verdict unless excused under Rule 47(c).

(b) Verdict. Unless the parties stipulate otherwise, the verdict must be unanimous and must be returned by a jury of at least 6 members.

(c) Polling. After a verdict is returned but before the jury is discharged, the court must on a party's request, or may on its own, poll the jurors individually. If the poll reveals a lack of unanimity or lack of assent by the number of jurors that the parties stipulated to, the court may direct the jury to deliberate further or may order a new trial.

(As amended, Apr. 30, 1991, eff. Dec. 1, 1991; Apr. 30, 2007, eff. Dec. 1, 2007; Mar. 26, 2009, eff. Dec. 1, 2009.)

Rule 49. Special Verdict; General Verdict and Questions

(a) Special Verdict.

(1) ***In General.*** The court may require a jury to return only a special verdict in the form of a special written finding on each issue of fact. The court may do so by:

(A) submitting written questions susceptible of a categorical or other brief answer;

(B) submitting written forms of the special findings that might properly be made under the pleadings and evidence; or

(C) using any other method that the court considers appropriate.

(2) ***Instructions.*** The court must give the instructions and explanations necessary to enable the jury to make its findings on each submitted issue.

(3) ***Issues Not Submitted.*** A party waives the right to a jury trial on any issue of fact raised by the pleadings or evidence but not submitted to the jury unless, before the jury retires, the party demands its submission to the jury. If the party does not demand submission, the court may make a finding on the issue. If the court makes no finding, it is considered to have made a finding consistent with its judgment on the special verdict.

(b) General Verdict with Answers to Written Questions.

(1) ***In General.*** The court may submit to the jury forms for a general verdict, together with written questions on one or more issues of fact that the jury must decide. The court must give the instructions and explanations necessary to enable the jury to render a general verdict and answer the questions in writing, and must direct the jury to do both.

(2) ***Verdict and Answers Consistent.*** When the general verdict and the answers are consistent, the court must approve, for entry under Rule 58, an appropriate judgment on the verdict and answers.

(3) ***Answers Inconsistent with the Verdict.*** When the answers are consistent with each other but one or more is inconsistent with the general verdict, the court may:

(A) approve, for entry under Rule 58, an appropriate judgment according to the answers, notwithstanding the general verdict;

(B) direct the jury to further consider its answers and verdict; or

(C) order a new trial.

(4) ***Answers Inconsistent with Each Other and the Verdict.*** When the answers are inconsistent with each other and one or more is also inconsistent with the general verdict, judgment must not be entered; instead, the court must direct the jury to further consider its answers and verdict, or must order a new trial.

(As amended Jan. 21, 1963, eff. July 1, 1963; Mar. 2, 1987, eff. Aug. 1, 1987; Apr. 30, 2007, eff. Dec. 1, 2007.)

Rule 50. Judgment as a Matter of Law in a Jury Trial; Related Motion for a New Trial; Conditional Ruling

(a) Judgment as a Matter of Law.

(1) ***In General.*** If a party has been fully heard on an issue during a jury trial and the court finds that a reasonable jury would not have a legally sufficient evidentiary basis to find for the party on that issue, the court may:

(A) resolve the issue against the party; and

(B) grant a motion for judgment as a matter of law against the party on a claim or defense that, under the controlling law, can be maintained or defeated only with a favorable finding on that issue.

(2) ***Motion.*** A motion for judgment as a matter of law may be made at any time before the case is submitted to the jury. The motion must specify the judgment sought and the law and facts that entitle the movant to the judgment.

(b) **Renewing the Motion After Trial; Alternative Motion for a New Trial.** If the court does not grant a motion for judgment as a matter of law made under Rule 50(a), the court is considered to have submitted the action to the jury subject to the court's later deciding the legal questions raised by the motion. No later than 28 days after the entry of judgment—or if the motion addresses a jury issue not decided by a verdict, no later than 28 days after the jury was discharged—the movant may file a renewed motion for judgment as a matter of law and may include an alternative or joint request for a new trial under Rule 59. In ruling on the renewed motion, the court may:

(1) allow judgment on the verdict, if the jury returned a verdict;

(2) order a new trial; or

(3) direct the entry of judgment as a matter of law.

(c) **Granting the Renewed Motion; Conditional Ruling on a Motion for a New Trial.**

(1) ***In General.*** If the court grants a renewed motion for judgment as a matter of law, it must also conditionally rule on any motion for a new trial by determining whether a new trial should be granted if the judgment is later vacated or reversed. The court must state the grounds for conditionally granting or denying the motion for a new trial.

(2) ***Effect of a Conditional Ruling.*** Conditionally granting the motion for a new trial does not affect the judgment's finality; if the judgment is reversed, the new trial must proceed unless the appellate court orders otherwise. If the motion for a new trial is conditionally denied, the appellee may assert error in that denial; if the judgment is reversed, the case must proceed as the appellate court orders.

(d) **Time for a Losing Party's New-Trial Motion.** Any motion for a new trial under Rule 59 by a party against whom judgment as a matter of law is rendered must be filed no later than 28 days after the entry of the judgment.

(e) **Denying the Motion for Judgment as a Matter of Law; Reversal on Appeal.** If the court denies the motion for judgment as a matter of law, the prevailing party may, as appellee, assert grounds entitling it to a new trial should the appellate court conclude that the trial court erred in denying the motion. If the appellate court reverses the judgment, it may order a new trial, direct the trial court to determine whether a new trial should be granted, or direct the entry of judgment.

(As amended Jan. 21, 1963, eff. July 1, 1963; Mar. 2, 1987, eff. Aug. 1, 1987; Apr. 30, 1991, eff. Dec. 1, 1991; Apr. 22, 1993, eff. Dec. 1, 1993; Apr. 27, 1994, eff. Dec. 1, 1994; Apr. 27, 1995, eff. Dec. 1, 1995; Apr. 12, 2006, eff. Dec. 1, 2006; Apr. 30, 2007, eff. Dec. 1, 2007; Mar. 26, 2009, eff. Dec. 1, 2009.)

1991 AMENDMENT

* * *

The revision abandons the familiar terminology of *direction of verdict* for several reasons. The term is misleading as a description of the relationship between judge and jury. It is also freighted with anachronisms some of which are the subject of the text of former subdivision (a) of this rule that is deleted in this revision. Thus, it should not be necessary to state in the text of this rule that a motion made pursuant to it is not a waiver of the right to jury trial, and only the antiquities of directed verdict practice suggest that it might have been. The term "judgment as a matter of law" is an almost equally familiar term and appears in the text of Rule 56; its use in Rule 50 calls attention to the relationship between the two rules. Finally, the change enables the rule to refer to pre-verdict and post-verdict motions with a terminology that does not conceal the common identity of two motions made at different times in the proceeding.

* * *

Paragraph (a)(1) articulates the standard for the granting of a motion for judgment as a matter of law. It effects no change in the existing standard. That existing standard was not expressed in the former rule, but was articulated in long-standing case law. The expressed standard makes clear that action taken under the rule is a performance of the court's duty to assure enforcement of the controlling law and is not an intrusion on any responsibility for factual determinations conferred on the jury by the Seventh Amendment or any other provision of federal law. Because this standard is also used as a reference point for entry of summary judgment under 56(a), it serves to link the two related provisions.

The revision authorizes the court to perform its duty to enter judgment as a matter of law at any time during the trial, as soon as it is apparent that either party is unable to carry a burden of proof that is essential to that party's case. Thus, the second sentence of paragraph (a)(1) authorizes the court to consider a motion for judgment as a matter of law as soon as a party has completed a presentation on a fact essential to that party's case. Such early action is appropriate when economy and expedition will be served. In no event, however, should the court enter judgment against a party who has not been apprised of the materiality of the dispositive fact and been afforded an opportunity to present any available evidence bearing on that fact. * * *

Paragraph (a)(2) retains the requirement that a motion for judgment be made prior to the close of the trial, subject to renewal after a jury verdict has been rendered. The purpose of this requirement is to assure the responding party an opportunity to cure any deficiency in that party's proof that may have been overlooked until called to the party's attention by a late motion for judgment.

* * *

Subdivision (b). This provision retains the concept of the former rule that the post-verdict motion is a renewal of an earlier motion made at the close of the evidence. One purpose of this concept was to avoid any question arising under the Seventh Amendment. It remains useful as a means of defining the appropriate issue posed by the post-verdict motion. A post-trial motion for judgment can be granted only on grounds advanced in the pre-verdict motion.

Often it appears to the court or to the moving party that a motion for judgment as a matter of law made at the close of the evidence should be reserved for a post-verdict decision. This is so because a jury verdict for the moving party moots the issue and because a pre-verdict ruling gambles that a reversal may result in a new trial that might have been avoided. For these reasons, the court may often wisely decline to rule on a motion for judgment as a matter of law made at the close of the evidence, and it is not inappropriate for the moving party to suggest such a postponement of the ruling until after the verdict has been rendered.

2007 AMENDMENT

* * *

Amended Rule 50(e) identifies the appellate court's authority to direct the entry of judgment. This authority was not described in former Rule 50(d), but was recognized in *Weisgram v. Marley Co.*, 528 U.S. 440 (2000), and in *Neely v. Martin K. Eby Construction Company*, 386 U.S. 317 (1967). When Rule 50(d) was drafted in 1963, the Committee Note stated that "[s]ubdivision (d) does not attempt a regulation of all aspects of the procedure where the motion for judgment n.o.v. and any accompanying motion for a new trial are denied. . . ." Express recognition of the authority to direct entry of judgment does not otherwise supersede this caution.

Rule 51. Instructions to the Jury; Objections; Preserving a Claim of Error

(a) Requests.

(1) ***Before or at the Close of the Evidence.*** At the close of the evidence or at any earlier reasonable time that the court orders, a party may file and furnish to every other party written requests for the jury instructions it wants the court to give.

(2) ***After the Close of the Evidence.*** After the close of the evidence, a party may:

(A) file requests for instructions on issues that could not reasonably have been anticipated by an earlier time that the court set for requests; and

(B) with the court's permission, file untimely requests for instructions on any issue.

(b) Instructions. The court:

(1) must inform the parties of its proposed instructions and proposed action on the requests before instructing the jury and before final jury arguments;

(2) must give the parties an opportunity to object on the record and out of the jury's hearing before the instructions and arguments are delivered; and

(3) may instruct the jury at any time before the jury is discharged.

(c) Objections.

(1) ***How to Make.*** A party who objects to an instruction or the failure to give an instruction must do so on the record, stating distinctly the matter objected to and the grounds for the objection.

(2) ***When to Make.*** An objection is timely if:

(A) a party objects at the opportunity provided under Rule 51(b)(2); or

(B) a party was not informed of an instruction or action on a request before that opportunity to object, and the party objects promptly after learning that the instruction or request will be, or has been, given or refused.

(d) Assigning Error; Plain Error.

(1) ***Assigning Error.*** A party may assign as error:

(A) an error in an instruction actually given, if that party properly objected; or

(B) a failure to give an instruction, if that party properly requested it and—unless the court rejected the request in a definitive ruling on the record—also properly objected.

(2) ***Plain Error.*** A court may consider a plain error in the instructions that has not been preserved as required by Rule 51(d)(1) if the error affects substantial rights.

(As amended Mar. 2, 1987, eff. Aug. 1, 1987; Mar. 27, 2003, eff. Dec. 1, 2003; Apr. 30, 2007, eff. Dec. 1, 2007.)

Rule 52. Findings and Conclusions by the Court; Judgment on Partial Findings

(a) Findings and Conclusions.

(1) ***In General.*** In an action tried on the facts without a jury or with an advisory jury, the court must find the facts specially and state its conclusions of law separately. The findings and conclusions may be stated on the record after the close of the evidence or may appear in an opinion or a memorandum of decision filed by the court. Judgment must be entered under Rule 58.

(2) ***For an Interlocutory Injunction.*** In granting or refusing an interlocutory injunction, the court must similarly state the findings and conclusions that support its action.

(3) ***For a Motion.*** The court is not required to state findings or conclusions when ruling on a motion under Rule 12 or 56 or, unless these rules provide otherwise, on any other motion.

(4) ***Effect of a Master's Findings.*** A master's findings, to the extent adopted by the court, must be considered the court's findings.

(5) ***Questioning the Evidentiary Support.*** A party may later question the sufficiency of the evidence supporting the findings, whether or not the party requested findings, objected to them, moved to amend them, or moved for partial findings.

(6) ***Setting Aside the Findings.*** Findings of fact, whether based on oral or other evidence, must not be set aside unless clearly erroneous, and the reviewing court must give due regard to the trial court's opportunity to judge the witnesses' credibility.

(b) Amended or Additional Findings. On a party's motion filed no later than 28 days after the entry of judgment, the court may amend its findings—or make additional findings—and may amend the judgment accordingly. The motion may accompany a motion for a new trial under Rule 59.

(c) Judgment on Partial Findings. If a party has been fully heard on an issue during a nonjury trial and the court finds against the party on that issue, the court may enter judgment against the party on a claim or defense that, under the controlling law, can be maintained or defeated only with a favorable finding on that issue. The court may, however, decline to render any judgment until the close of the evidence. A judgment on partial findings must be supported by findings of fact and conclusions of law as required by Rule 52(a).

(As amended Dec. 27, 1946, eff. Mar. 19, 1948; Jan. 21, 1963, eff. July 1, 1963; Apr. 28, 1983, eff. Aug. 1, 1983; Apr. 29, 1985, eff. Aug. 1, 1985; Apr. 30, 1991, eff. Dec. 1, 1991; Apr. 22, 1993, eff. Dec. 1, 1993; Apr. 27, 1995, eff. Dec. 1, 1995; Apr. 30, 2007, eff. Dec. 1, 2007; Mar. 26, 2009, eff. Dec. 1, 2009.)

NOTES OF ADVISORY COMMITTEE ON RULES

1985 AMENDMENT

Rule 52(a) has been amended (1) to avoid continued confusion and conflicts among the circuits as to the standard of appellate review of findings of fact by the court, (2) to eliminate the disparity between the standard of review as literally stated in Rule 52(a) and the practice of some courts of appeals, and (3) to promote nationwide uniformity.

Some courts of appeal have stated that when a trial court's findings do not rest on demeanor evidence and evaluation of a witness' credibility, there is no reason to defer to the trial court's findings and the appellate court more readily can find them to be clearly erroneous. * * * Others go further, holding that appellate review may be had without application of the "clearly erroneous" test since the appellate court is in as good a position as the trial court to review a purely documentary record. * * *

A third group has adopted the view that the "clearly erroneous" rule applies in all nonjury cases even when findings are based solely on documentary evidence or on inferences from undisputed facts.

* * *

The principal argument advanced in favor of a more searching appellate review of findings by the district court based solely on documentary evidence is that the rationale of Rule 52(a) does not apply when the findings do not rest on the trial court's assessment of credibility of the witnesses but on an evaluation of documentary proof and the drawing of inferences from it, thus eliminating the need for any special deference to the trial court's findings. These considerations are outweighed by the public interest in the stability and judicial economy that would be promoted by recognizing that the trial court, not the appellate tribunal, should be the finder of the facts. To permit courts of appeals to share more actively in the fact-finding function would tend to undermine the legitimacy of the district courts in the eyes of litigants, multiply appeals by encouraging appellate retrial of some factual issues, and needlessly reallocate judicial authority.

Rule 53. Masters

(a) Appointment.

(1) ***Scope.*** Unless a statute provides otherwise, a court may appoint a master only to:

(A) perform duties consented to by the parties;

(B) hold trial proceedings and make or recommend findings of fact on issues to be decided without a jury if appointment is warranted by:

(i) some exceptional condition; or

(ii) the need to perform an accounting or resolve a difficult computation of damages; or

(C) address pretrial and posttrial matters that cannot be effectively and timely addressed by an available district judge or magistrate judge of the district.

(2) ***Disqualification.*** A master must not have a relationship to the parties, attorneys, action, or court that would require disqualification of a judge under 28 U.S.C. § 455, unless the parties, with the court's approval, consent to the appointment after the master discloses any potential grounds for disqualification.

(3) ***Possible Expense or Delay.*** In appointing a master, the court must consider the fairness of imposing the likely expenses on the parties and must protect against unreasonable expense or delay.

(b) Order Appointing a Master.

(1) ***Notice.*** Before appointing a master, the court must give the parties notice and an opportunity to be heard. Any party may suggest candidates for appointment.

(2) ***Contents.*** The appointing order must direct the master to proceed with all reasonable diligence and must state:

(A) the master's duties, including any investigation or enforcement duties, and any limits on the master's authority under Rule 53(c);

(B) the circumstances, if any, in which the master may communicate ex parte with the court or a party;

(C) the nature of the materials to be preserved and filed as the record of the master's activities;

(D) the time limits, method of filing the record, other procedures, and standards for reviewing the master's orders, findings, and recommendations; and

(E) the basis, terms, and procedure for fixing the master's compensation under Rule 53(g).

(3) ***Issuing.*** The court may issue the order only after:

(A) the master files an affidavit disclosing whether there is any ground for disqualification under 28 U.S.C. § 455; and

(B) if a ground is disclosed, the parties, with the court's approval, waive the disqualification.

(4) ***Amending.*** The order may be amended at any time after notice to the parties and an opportunity to be heard.

(c) Master's Authority.

(1) ***In General.*** Unless the appointing order directs otherwise, a master may:

(A) regulate all proceedings;

(B) take all appropriate measures to perform the assigned duties fairly and efficiently; and

(C) if conducting an evidentiary hearing, exercise the appointing court's power to compel, take, and record evidence.

(2) ***Sanctions.*** The master may by order impose on a party any noncontempt sanction provided by Rule 37 or 45, and may recommend a contempt sanction against a party and sanctions against a nonparty.

(d) Master's Orders. A master who issues an order must file it and promptly serve a copy on each party. The clerk must enter the order on the docket.

(e) Master's Reports. A master must report to the court as required by the appointing order. The master must file the report and promptly serve a copy on each party, unless the court orders otherwise.

(f) Action on the Master's Order, Report, or Recommendations.

(1) ***Opportunity for a Hearing; Action in General.*** In acting on a master's order, report, or recommendations, the court must give the parties notice and an opportunity to be heard; may receive evidence; and may adopt or affirm, modify, wholly or partly reject or reverse, or resubmit to the master with instructions.

(2) ***Time to Object or Move to Adopt or Modify.*** A party may file objections to—or a motion to adopt or modify—the master's order, report, or recommendations no later than 21 days after a copy is served, unless the court sets a different time.

(3) ***Reviewing Factual Findings.*** The court must decide de novo all objections to findings of fact made or recommended by a master, unless the parties, with the court's approval, stipulate that:

(A) the findings will be reviewed for clear error; or

(B) the findings of a master appointed under Rule 53(a)(1)(A) or (C) will be final.

(4) ***Reviewing Legal Conclusions.*** The court must decide de novo all objections to conclusions of law made or recommended by a master.

(5) ***Reviewing Procedural Matters.*** Unless the appointing order establishes a different standard of review, the court may set aside

a master's ruling on a procedural matter only for an abuse of discretion.

(g) Compensation.

(1) ***Fixing Compensation.*** Before or after judgment, the court must fix the master's compensation on the basis and terms stated in the appointing order, but the court may set a new basis and terms after giving notice and an opportunity to be heard.

(2) ***Payment.*** The compensation must be paid either:

(A) by a party or parties; or

(B) from a fund or subject matter of the action within the court's control.

(3) ***Allocating Payment.*** The court must allocate payment among the parties after considering the nature and amount of the controversy, the parties' means, and the extent to which any party is more responsible than other parties for the reference to a master. An interim allocation may be amended to reflect a decision on the merits.

(h) Appointing a Magistrate Judge. A magistrate judge is subject to this rule only when the order referring a matter to the magistrate judge states that the reference is made under this rule.

(As amended Feb. 28, 1966, eff. July 1, 1966; Apr. 28, 1983, eff. Aug. 1, 1983; Mar. 2, 1987, eff. Aug. 1, 1987; Apr. 30, 1991, eff. Dec. 1, 1991; Apr. 22, 1993, eff. Dec. 1, 1993; Mar. 27, 2003, eff. Dec. 1, 2003; Apr. 30, 2007, eff. Dec. 1, 2007; Mar. 26, 2009, eff. Dec. 1, 2009.)

TITLE VII. JUDGMENT

Rule 54. Judgment; Costs

(a) Definition; Form. "Judgment" as used in these rules includes a decree and any order from which an appeal lies. A judgment should not include recitals of pleadings, a master's report, or a record of prior proceedings.

(b) Judgment on Multiple Claims or Involving Multiple Parties. When an action presents more than one claim for relief—whether as a claim, counterclaim, crossclaim, or third-party claim—or when multiple parties are involved, the court may direct entry of a final judgment as to one or more, but fewer than all, claims or parties only if the court expressly determines that there is no just reason for delay. Otherwise, any order or other decision, however designated, that adjudicates fewer than all the claims or the rights and liabilities of fewer than all the parties does not end the action as to any of the claims or parties and may be revised at any time before the entry of a judgment adjudicating all the claims and all the parties' rights and liabilities.

(c) Demand for Judgment; Relief to Be Granted. A default judgment must not differ in kind from, or exceed in amount, what is demanded in the pleadings. Every other final judgment should grant the relief to which each party is entitled, even if the party has not demanded that relief in its pleadings.

(d) Costs; Attorney's Fees.

(1) ***Costs Other Than Attorney's Fees.*** Unless a federal statute, these rules, or a court order provides otherwise, costs—other than attorney's fees—should be allowed to the prevailing party. But costs against the United States, its officers, and its agencies may be imposed only to the extent allowed by law. The clerk may tax costs on 14 days' notice. On motion served within the next 7 days, the court may review the clerk's action.

(2) ***Attorney's Fees.***

(A) *Claim to Be by Motion.* A claim for attorney's fees and related nontaxable expenses must be made by motion unless the substantive law requires those fees to be proved at trial as an element of damages.

(B) *Timing and Contents of the Motion.* Unless a statute or a court order provides otherwise, the motion must:

(i) be filed no later than 14 days after the entry of judgment;

(ii) specify the judgment and the statute, rule, or other grounds entitling the movant to the award;

(iii) state the amount sought or provide a fair estimate of it; and

(iv) disclose, if the court so orders, the terms of any agreement about fees for the services for which the claim is made.

(C) *Proceedings.* Subject to Rule 23(h), the court must, on a party's request, give an opportunity for adversary submissions on the motion in accordance with Rule 43(c) or 78. The court may decide issues of liability for fees before receiving submissions on the value of services. The court must find the facts and state its conclusions of law as provided in Rule 52(a).

(D) *Special Procedures by Local Rule; Reference to a Master or a Magistrate Judge.* By local rule, the court may establish special procedures to resolve fee-related issues without extensive evidentiary hearings. Also, the court may refer issues concerning the value of services to a special master under Rule 53 without regard to the limitations of Rule 53(a)(1), and may refer a motion for attorney's fees to a magistrate judge under Rule 72(b) as if it were a dispositive pretrial matter.

(E) *Exceptions.* Subparagraphs (A)–(D) do not apply to claims for fees and expenses as sanctions for violating these rules or as sanctions under 28 U.S.C. § 1927.

(As amended Dec. 27, 1946, eff. Mar. 19, 1948; Apr. 17, 1961, eff. July 19, 1961; Mar. 2, 1987, eff. Aug. 1, 1987; Apr. 22, 1993, eff. Dec. 1, 1993; Apr. 29, 2002, eff. Dec. 1, 2002; Mar. 27, 2003, eff. Dec. 1, 2003; Apr. 30, 2007, eff. Dec. 1, 2007; Mar. 26, 2009, eff. Dec. 1, 2009.)

Rule 55. Default; Default Judgment

(a) Entering a Default. When a party against whom a judgment for affirmative relief is sought has failed to plead or otherwise defend, and that failure is shown by affidavit or otherwise, the clerk must enter the party's default.

(b) Entering a Default Judgment.

(1) ***By the Clerk.*** If the plaintiff's claim is for a sum certain or a sum that can be made certain by computation, the clerk—on the plaintiff's request, with an affidavit showing the amount due—must enter judgment for that amount and costs against a defendant who has been defaulted for not appearing and who is neither a minor nor an incompetent person.

(2) ***By the Court.*** In all other cases, the party must apply to the court for a default judgment. A default judgment may be entered against a minor or incompetent person only if represented by a general guardian, conservator, or other like fiduciary who has appeared. If the party against whom a default judgment is sought has appeared personally or by a representative, that party or its representative must be served with written notice of the application at least 7 days before the hearing. The court may conduct hearings or make referrals—preserving any federal statutory right to a jury trial—when, to enter or effectuate judgment, it needs to:

(A) conduct an accounting;

(B) determine the amount of damages;

(C) establish the truth of any allegation by evidence; or

(D) investigate any other matter.

(c) Setting Aside a Default or a Default Judgment. The court may set aside an entry of default for good cause, and it may set aside a final default judgment under Rule 60(b).

(d) Judgment Against the United States. A default judgment may be entered against the United States, its officers, or its agencies only if the claimant establishes a claim or right to relief by evidence that satisfies the court.

(As amended Mar. 2, 1987, eff. Aug. 1, 1987; Apr. 30, 2007, eff. Dec. 1, 2007; Mar. 26, 2009, eff. Dec. 1, 2009; Apr. 29, 2015, eff. Dec. 1, 2015.)

NOTES OF ADVISORY COMMITTEE ON RULES

2007 AMENDMENT

* * *

Former Rule 55(a) directed the clerk to enter a default when a party failed to plead or otherwise defend "as provided by these rules." The implication from the reference to defending "as provided by these rules" seemed to be that the clerk should enter a default even if a party did something showing an intent to defend, but that act was not specifically described by the rules. Courts in fact have rejected that implication. Acts that show an intent to defend have frequently prevented a default even though not connected to any particular rule. "[A]s provided by these rules" is deleted to reflect Rule 55(a)'s actual meaning.

* * *

Rule 56. Summary Judgment

(a) Motion for Summary Judgment or Partial Summary Judgment. A party may move for summary judgment, identifying each claim or defense—or the part of each claim or defense—on which summary judgment is sought. The court shall grant summary judgment if the movant shows that there is no genuine dispute as to any material fact and the movant is entitled to judgment as a matter of law. The court should state on the record the reasons for granting or denying the motion.

(b) Time to File a Motion. Unless a different time is set by local rule or the court orders otherwise, a party may file a motion for summary judgment at any time until 30 days after the close of all discovery.

(c) Procedures.

(1) ***Supporting Factual Positions.*** A party asserting that a fact cannot be or is genuinely disputed must support the assertion by:

(A) citing to particular parts of materials in the record, including depositions, documents, electronically stored information, affidavits or declarations, stipulations (including those made for purposes of the motion only), admissions, interrogatory answers, or other materials; or

(B) showing that the materials cited do not establish the absence or presence of a genuine dispute, or that an adverse party cannot produce admissible evidence to support the fact.

(2) ***Objection That a Fact Is Not Supported by Admissible Evidence.*** A party may object that the material cited to support or dispute a fact cannot be presented in a form that would be admissible in evidence.

(3) ***Materials Not Cited.*** The court need consider only the cited materials, but it may consider other materials in the record.

(4) ***Affidavits or Declarations.*** An affidavit or declaration used to support or oppose a motion must be made on personal knowledge, set out facts that would be admissible in evidence, and show that the affiant or declarant is competent to testify on the matters stated.

(d) **When Facts Are Unavailable to the Nonmovant.** If a nonmovant shows by affidavit or declaration that, for specified reasons, it cannot present facts essential to justify its opposition, the court may:

(1) defer considering the motion or deny it;

(2) allow time to obtain affidavits or declarations or to take discovery; or

(3) issue any other appropriate order.

(e) **Failing to Properly Support or Address a Fact.** If a party fails to properly support an assertion of fact or fails to properly address another party's assertion of fact as required by Rule 56(c), the court may:

(1) give an opportunity to properly support or address the fact;

(2) consider the fact undisputed for purposes of the motion;

(3) grant summary judgment if the motion and supporting materials—including the facts considered undisputed—show that the movant is entitled to it; or

(4) issue any other appropriate order.

(f) **Judgment Independent of the Motion.** After giving notice and a reasonable time to respond, the court may:

(1) grant summary judgment for a nonmovant;

(2) grant the motion on grounds not raised by a party; or

(3) consider summary judgment on its own after identifying for the parties material facts that may not be genuinely in dispute.

(g) **Failing to Grant All the Requested Relief.** If the court does not grant all the relief requested by the motion, it may enter an order stating any material fact—including an item of damages or other relief—that is not genuinely in dispute and treating the fact as established in the case.

(h) **Affidavit or Declaration Submitted in Bad Faith.** If satisfied that an affidavit or declaration under this rule is submitted in bad faith or solely for delay, the court—after notice and a reasonable time to respond—may order the submitting party to pay the other party the reasonable expenses, including attorney's fees, it incurred as a result. An offending party or attorney may also be held in contempt or subjected to other appropriate sanctions.

(As amended Dec. 27, 1946, eff. Mar. 19, 1948; Jan. 21, 1963, eff. July 1, 1963; Mar. 2, 1987, eff. Aug. 1, 1987; Apr. 30, 2007, eff. Dec. 1, 2007; Mar. 26, 2009, eff. Dec. 1, 2009; Apr. 28, 2010, eff. Dec. 1, 2010.)

NOTES OF ADVISORY COMMITTEE ON RULES

2010 AMENDMENT

* * *

Subdivision (a). Subdivision (a) carries forward the summary-judgment standard expressed in former subdivision (c), changing only one word—genuine "issue" becomes genuine "dispute." "Dispute" better reflects the focus of a summary-judgment determination.

* * *

Subdivision (c). Subdivision (c) is new. It establishes a common procedure for several aspects of summary-judgment motions synthesized from similar elements developed in the cases or found in many local rules.

Subdivision (c)(1) addresses the ways to support an assertion that a fact can or cannot be genuinely disputed. It does not address the form for providing the required support. Different courts and judges have adopted different forms including, for example, directions that the support be included in the motion, made part of a separate statement of facts, interpolated in the body of a brief or memorandum, or provided in a separate statement of facts included in a brief or memorandum.

Subdivision (c)(1)(A) describes the familiar record materials commonly relied upon and requires that the movant cite the particular parts of the materials that support its fact positions. Materials that are not yet in the record—including materials referred to in an affidavit or declaration—must be placed in the record. Once materials are in the record, the court may, by order in the case, direct that the materials be gathered in an appendix, a party may voluntarily submit an appendix, or the parties may submit a joint appendix.

The appendix procedure also may be established by local rule. Pointing to a specific location in an appendix satisfies the citation requirement. So too it may be convenient to direct that a party assist the court in locating materials buried in a voluminous record.

Subdivision (c)(1)(B) recognizes that a party need not always point to specific record materials. One party, without citing any other materials, may respond or reply that materials cited to dispute or support a fact do not establish the absence or presence of a genuine dispute. And a party who does not have the trial burden of production may rely on a showing that a party who does have the trial burden cannot produce admissible evidence to carry its burden as to the fact.

Subdivision (c)(2) provides that a party may object that material cited to support or dispute a fact cannot be presented in a form that would be admissible in evidence. The objection functions much as an objection at trial, adjusted for the pretrial setting. The burden is on the proponent to show that the material is admissible as presented or to explain the admissible form that is anticipated. There is no need to make a separate motion to strike. If the case goes to trial, failure to challenge admissibility at the summary-judgment stage does not forfeit the right to challenge admissibility at trial.

Subdivision (c)(3) reflects judicial opinions and local rules provisions stating that the court may decide a motion for summary judgment without undertaking an independent search of the record. Nonetheless, the rule also recognizes that a court may consider record materials not called to its attention by the parties.

Subdivision (c)(4) carries forward some of the provisions of former subdivision (e)(1). Other provisions are relocated or omitted. The requirement that a sworn or certified copy of a paper referred to in an affidavit or declaration be attached to the affidavit or declaration is omitted as unnecessary given the requirement in subdivision (c)(1)(A) that a statement or dispute of fact be supported by materials in the record.

* * *

Rule 57. Declaratory Judgment

These rules govern the procedure for obtaining a declaratory judgment under 28 U.S.C. § 2201. Rules 38 and 39 govern a demand for a jury trial. The existence of another adequate remedy does not preclude a declaratory judgment that is otherwise appropriate. The court may order a speedy hearing of a declaratory-judgment action.

(As amended Dec. 29, 1948, eff. Oct. 20, 1949; Apr. 30, 2007, eff. Dec. 1, 2007.)

Rule 58. Entering Judgment

(a) Separate Document. Every judgment and amended judgment must be set out in a separate document, but a separate document is not required for an order disposing of a motion:

(1) for judgment under Rule 50(b);

(2) to amend or make additional findings under Rule 52(b);

(3) for attorney's fees under Rule 54;

(4) for a new trial, or to alter or amend the judgment, under Rule 59; or

(5) for relief under Rule 60.

(b) Entering Judgment.

(1) ***Without the Court's Direction.*** Subject to Rule 54(b) and unless the court orders otherwise, the clerk must, without awaiting the court's direction, promptly prepare, sign, and enter the judgment when:

(A) the jury returns a general verdict;

(B) the court awards only costs or a sum certain; or

(C) the court denies all relief.

(2) ***Court's Approval Required.*** Subject to Rule 54(b), the court must promptly approve the form of the judgment, which the clerk must promptly enter, when:

(A) the jury returns a special verdict or a general verdict with answers to written questions; or

(B) the court grants other relief not described in this subdivision (b).

(c) Time of Entry. For purposes of these rules, judgment is entered at the following times:

(1) if a separate document is not required, when the judgment is entered in the civil docket under Rule 79(a); or

(2) if a separate document is required, when the judgment is entered in the civil docket under Rule 79(a) and the earlier of these events occurs:

(A) it is set out in a separate document; or

(B) 150 days have run from the entry in the civil docket.

(d) Request for Entry. A party may request that judgment be set out in a separate document as required by Rule 58(a).

(e) Cost or Fee Awards. Ordinarily, the entry of judgment may not be delayed, nor the time for appeal extended, in order to tax costs or award fees. But if a timely motion for attorney's fees is made under Rule 54(d)(2), the court may act before a notice of appeal has been filed and become effective to order that the motion have the same effect under Federal Rule of Appellate Procedure 4(a)(4) as a timely motion under Rule 59.

(As amended Dec. 27, 1946, eff. Mar. 19, 1948; Jan. 21, 1963, eff. July 1, 1963; Apr. 22, 1993, eff. Dec. 1, 1993; Apr. 29, 2002, eff. Dec. 1, 2002; Apr. 30, 2007, eff. Dec. 1, 2007.)

NOTES OF ADVISORY COMMITTEE ON RULES

2002 AMENDMENT

Rule 58 has provided that a judgment is effective only when set forth on a separate document and entered as provided in Rule 79(a). * * *

Rule 58(a) preserves the core of the present separate document requirement, both for the initial judgment and for any amended judgment. * * *

Rule 58 is amended, however, to address a problem that arises under Appellate Rule 4(a). Some courts treat such orders as those that deny a motion for new trial as a "judgment," so that appeal time does not start to run until the order is entered on a separate document. Without attempting to address the question whether such orders are appealable, and thus judgments as defined by Rule 54(a), the amendment provides that entry on a separate document is not required for an order disposing of the motions listed in Appellate Rule 4(a). * * *

Rule 58(b) discards the attempt to define the time when a judgment becomes "effective." * * * Rule 58(b) replaces the definition of effectiveness with a new provision that defines the time when judgment is entered. If judgment is promptly set forth on a separate document, as should be done when required by Rule 58(a)(1), the new provision will not change the effect of Rule 58. But in the cases in which court and clerk fail to comply with this simple requirement, the motion time periods set by Rules 50, 52, 54, 59, and 60 begin to run after expiration of 150 days from entry of the judgment in the civil docket as required by Rule 79(a).

* * *

Rule 59. New Trial; Altering or Amending a Judgment

(a) In General.

(1) ***Grounds for New Trial.*** The court may, on motion, grant a new trial on all or some of the issues—and to any party—as follows:

(A) after a jury trial, for any reason for which a new trial has heretofore been granted in an action at law in federal court; or

(B) after a nonjury trial, for any reason for which a rehearing has heretofore been granted in a suit in equity in federal court.

(2) ***Further Action After a Nonjury Trial.*** After a nonjury trial, the court may, on motion for a new trial, open the judgment if one has been entered, take additional testimony, amend findings of fact and conclusions of law or make new ones, and direct the entry of a new judgment.

(b) Time to File a Motion for a New Trial. A motion for a new trial must be filed no later than 28 days after the entry of judgment.

(c) Time to Serve Affidavits. When a motion for a new trial is based on affidavits, they must be filed with the motion. The opposing party has 14 days after being served to file opposing affidavits. The court may permit reply affidavits.

(d) New Trial on the Court's Initiative or for Reasons Not in the Motion. No later than 28 days after the entry of judgment, the court, on its own, may order a new trial for any reason that would justify granting one on a party's motion. After giving the parties notice and an opportunity to be heard, the court may grant a timely motion for a new trial for a reason not stated in the motion. In either event, the court must specify the reasons in its order.

(e) Motion to Alter or Amend a Judgment. A motion to alter or amend a judgment must be filed no later than 28 days after the entry of the judgment.

(As amended Dec. 27, 1946, eff. Mar. 19, 1948; Feb. 28, 1966, eff. July 1, 1966; Apr. 27, 1994, eff. Dec. 1, 1994; Apr. 27, 1995, eff. Dec. 1, 1995; Apr. 30, 2007, eff. Dec. 1, 2007; Mar. 26, 2009, eff. Dec. 1, 2009.)

Rule 60. Relief from a Judgment or Order

(a) Corrections Based on Clerical Mistakes; Oversights and Omissions. The court may correct a clerical mistake or a mistake arising from oversight or omission whenever one is found in a judgment, order, or other part of the record. The court may do so on motion or on its own, with or without notice. But after an appeal has been docketed in the appellate court and while it is pending, such a mistake may be corrected only with the appellate court's leave.

(b) Grounds for Relief from a Final Judgment, Order, or Proceeding. On motion and just terms, the court may relieve a party or its legal representative from a final judgment, order, or proceeding for the following reasons:

(1) mistake, inadvertence, surprise, or excusable neglect;

(2) newly discovered evidence that, with reasonable diligence, could not have been discovered in time to move for a new trial under Rule 59(b);

(3) fraud (whether previously called intrinsic or extrinsic), misrepresentation, or misconduct by an opposing party;

(4) the judgment is void;

(5) the judgment has been satisfied, released or discharged; it is based on an earlier judgment that has been reversed or vacated; or applying it prospectively is no longer equitable; or

(6) any other reason that justifies relief.

(c) Timing and Effect of the Motion.

(1) ***Timing.*** A motion under Rule 60(b) must be made within a reasonable time—and for reasons (1), (2), and (3) no more than a year after the entry of the judgment or order or the date of the proceeding.

(2) ***Effect on Finality.*** The motion does not affect the judgment's finality or suspend its operation.

(d) Other Powers to Grant Relief. This rule does not limit a court's power to:

(1) entertain an independent action to relieve a party from a judgment, order, or proceeding;

(2) grant relief under 28 U.S.C. § 1655 to a defendant who was not personally notified of the action; or

(3) set aside a judgment for fraud on the court.

(e) Bills and Writs Abolished. The following are abolished: bills of review, bills in the nature of bills of review, and writs of coram nobis, coram vobis, and audita querela.

(As amended Dec. 27, 1946, eff. Mar. 19, 1948; Dec. 29, 1948, eff. Oct. 20, 1949; Mar. 2, 1987, eff. Aug. 1, 1987; Apr. 30, 2007, eff. Dec. 1, 2007.)

Rule 61. Harmless Error

Unless justice requires otherwise, no error in admitting or excluding evidence—or any other error by the court or a party—is ground for granting a new trial, for setting aside a verdict, or for vacating, modifying, or otherwise disturbing a judgment or order. At every stage of the proceeding, the court must disregard all errors and defects that do not affect any party's substantial rights.

(As amended Apr. 30, 2007, eff. Dec. 1, 2007.)

Rule 62. Stay of Proceedings to Enforce a Judgment

(a) Automatic Stay. Except as provided in Rule 62(c) and (d), execution on a judgment and proceedings to enforce it are stayed for 30 days after its entry, unless the court orders otherwise.

(b) Stay by Bond or Other Security. At any time after judgment is entered, a party may obtain a stay by providing a bond or other security. The stay takes effect when the court approves the bond or other security and remains in effect for the time specified in the bond or other security.

(c) Stay of an Injunction, Receivership, or Patent Accounting Order. Unless the court orders otherwise, the following are not stayed after being entered, even if an appeal is taken:

(1) an interlocutory or final judgment in an action for an injunction or receivership; or

(2) a judgment or order that directs an accounting in an action for patent infringement.

(d) Injunction Pending an Appeal. While an appeal is pending from an interlocutory order or final judgment that grants, continues, modifies, refuses, dissolves, or refuses to dissolve or modify an injunction, the court may suspend, modify, restore, or grant an injunction on terms for bond or other terms that secure the opposing party's rights. If the judgment appealed from is rendered by a statutory three-judge district court, the order must be made either:

(1) by that court sitting in open session; or

(2) by the assent of all its judges, as evidenced by their signatures.

(e) Stay Without Bond on an Appeal by the United States, Its Officers, or Its Agencies. The court must not require a bond, obligation, or other security from the appellant when granting a stay on an appeal by the United States, its officers, or its agencies or on an appeal directed by a department of the federal government.

(f) Stay in Favor of a Judgment Debtor Under State Law. If a judgment is a lien on the judgment debtor's property under the law of the state where the court is located, the judgment debtor is entitled to the same stay of execution the state court would give.

(g) Appellate Court's Power Not Limited. This rule does not limit the power of the appellate court or one of its judges or justices:

(1) to stay proceedings—or suspend, modify, restore, or grant an injunction—while an appeal is pending; or

(2) to issue an order to preserve the status quo or the effectiveness of the judgment to be entered.

(h) Stay with Multiple Claims or Parties. A court may stay the enforcement of a final judgment entered under Rule 54(b) until it enters a later judgment or judgments, and may prescribe terms necessary to secure the benefit of the stayed judgment for the party in whose favor it was entered.

(As amended Dec. 27, 1946, eff. Mar. 19, 1948; Dec. 29, 1948, eff. Oct. 20, 1949; Apr. 17, 1961, eff. July 19, 1961; Mar. 2, 1987, eff. Aug. 1, 1987; Apr. 30, 2007, eff. Dec. 1, 2007; Mar. 26, 2009, eff. Dec. 1, 2009; Apr. 26, 2018, eff. Dec. 1, 2018.)

Rule 62.1. Indicative Ruling on a Motion for Relief That is Barred by a Pending Appeal

(a) Relief Pending Appeal. If a timely motion is made for relief that the court lacks authority to grant because of an appeal that has been docketed and is pending, the court may:

(1) defer considering the motion;

(2) deny the motion; or

(3) state either that it would grant the motion if the court of appeals remands for that purpose or that the motion raises a substantial issue.

(b) Notice to the Court of Appeals. The movant must promptly notify the circuit clerk under Federal Rule of Appellate Procedure 12.1 if the district court states that it would grant the motion or that the motion raises a substantial issue.

(c) Remand. The district court may decide the motion if the court of appeals remands for that purpose.

(Added Mar. 26, 2009, eff. Dec. 1, 2009.)

Rule 63. Judge's Inability to Proceed

If a judge conducting a hearing or trial is unable to proceed, any other judge may proceed upon certifying familiarity with the record and determining that the case may be completed without prejudice to the parties. In a hearing or a nonjury trial, the successor judge must, at a party's request, recall any witness whose testimony is material and disputed and who is available to testify again without undue burden. The successor judge may also recall any other witness.

(As amended Mar. 2, 1987, eff. Aug. 1, 1987; Apr. 30, 1991, eff. Dec. 1, 1991; Apr. 30, 2007, eff. Dec. 1, 2007.)

TITLE VIII. PROVISIONAL AND FINAL REMEDIES

Rule 64. Seizing a Person or Property

(a) Remedies Under State Law—In General. At the commencement of and throughout an action, every remedy is available that, under the law of the state where the court is located, provides for seizing a person or property to secure satisfaction of the potential judgment. But a federal statute governs to the extent it applies.

(b) Specific Kinds of Remedies. The remedies available under this rule include the following—however designated and regardless of whether state procedure requires an independent action:

- arrest;

- attachment;
- garnishment;
- replevin;
- sequestration; and
- other corresponding or equivalent remedies.

(As amended Apr. 30, 2007, eff. Dec. 1, 2007.)

Rule 65. Injunctions and Restraining Orders

(a) Preliminary Injunction.

(1) ***Notice.*** The court may issue a preliminary injunction only on notice to the adverse party.

(2) ***Consolidating the Hearing with the Trial on the Merits.*** Before or after beginning the hearing on a motion for a preliminary injunction, the court may advance the trial on the merits and consolidate it with the hearing. Even when consolidation is not ordered, evidence that is received on the motion and that would be admissible at trial becomes part of the trial record and need not be repeated at trial. But the court must preserve any party's right to a jury trial.

(b) Temporary Restraining Order.

(1) ***Issuing Without Notice.*** The court may issue a temporary restraining order without written or oral notice to the adverse party or its attorney only if:

(A) specific facts in an affidavit or a verified complaint clearly show that immediate and irreparable injury, loss, or damage will result to the movant before the adverse party can be heard in opposition; and

(B) the movant's attorney certifies in writing any efforts made to give notice and the reasons why it should not be required.

(2) ***Contents; Expiration.*** Every temporary restraining order issued without notice must state the date and hour it was issued; describe the injury and state why it is irreparable; state why the order was issued without notice; and be promptly filed in the clerk's office and entered in the record. The order expires at the time after entry—not to exceed 14 days—that the court sets, unless before that time the court, for good cause, extends it for a like period or the adverse party consents to a longer extension. The reasons for an extension must be entered in the record.

(3) ***Expediting the Preliminary-Injunction Hearing.*** If the order is issued without notice, the motion for a preliminary injunction must be set for hearing at the earliest possible time, taking precedence over all other matters except hearings on older matters of the same character. At the hearing, the party who obtained the order must proceed with the motion; if the party does not, the court must dissolve the order.

(4) ***Motion to Dissolve.*** On 2 days' notice to the party who obtained the order without notice—or on shorter notice set by the court—the adverse party may appear and move to dissolve or modify the order. The court must then hear and decide the motion as promptly as justice requires.

(c) **Security.** The court may issue a preliminary injunction or a temporary restraining order only if the movant gives security in an amount that the court considers proper to pay the costs and damages sustained by any party found to have been wrongfully enjoined or restrained. The United States, its officers, and its agencies are not required to give security.

(d) **Contents and Scope of Every Injunction and Restraining Order.**

(1) ***Contents.*** Every order granting an injunction and every restraining order must:

(A) state the reasons why it issued;

(B) state its terms specifically; and

(C) describe in reasonable detail—and not by referring to the complaint or other document—the act or acts restrained or required.

(2) ***Persons Bound.*** The order binds only the following who receive actual notice of it by personal service or otherwise:

(A) the parties;

(B) the parties' officers, agents, servants, employees, and attorneys; and

(C) other persons who are in active concert or participation with anyone described in Rule 65(d)(2)(A) or (B).

(e) **Other Laws Not Modified.** These rules do not modify the following:

(1) any federal statute relating to temporary restraining orders or preliminary injunctions in actions affecting employer and employee;

(2) 28 U.S.C. § 2361, which relates to preliminary injunctions in actions of interpleader or in the nature of interpleader; or

(3) 28 U.S.C. § 2284, which relates to actions that must be heard and decided by a three-judge district court.

(f) **Copyright Impoundment.** This rule applies to copyright-impoundment proceedings.

(As amended Dec. 27, 1946, eff. Mar. 19, 1948; Dec. 29, 1948, eff. Oct. 20, 1949; Feb. 28, 1966, eff. July 1, 1966; Mar. 2, 1987, eff. Aug. 1, 1987; Apr. 23, 2001, eff. Dec. 1, 2001; Apr. 30, 2007, eff. Dec. 1, 2007; Mar. 26, 2009, eff. Dec. 1, 2009.)

Rule 65.1. Proceedings Against a Security Provider

Whenever these rules (including the Supplemental Rules for Admiralty or Maritime Claims and Asset Forfeiture Actions) require or allow a party to give security, and security is given with one or more security providers, each provider submits to the court's jurisdiction and irrevocably appoints the court clerk as its agent for receiving service of any papers that affect its liability on the security. The security provider's liability may be enforced on motion without an independent action. The motion and any notice that the court orders may be served on the court clerk, who must promptly send a copy of each to every security provider whose address is known.

(Added Feb. 28, 1966, eff. July 1, 1966, and amended Mar. 2, 1987, eff. Aug. 1, 1987; Apr. 12, 2006, eff. Dec. 1, 2006; Apr. 30, 2007, eff. Dec. 1, 2007; Apr. 26, 2018, eff. Dec. 1, 2018.)

Rule 66. Receivers

These rules govern an action in which the appointment of a receiver is sought or a receiver sues or is sued. But the practice in administering an estate by a receiver or a similar court-appointed officer must accord with the historical practice in federal courts or with a local rule. An action in which a receiver has been appointed may be dismissed only by court order.

(As amended Dec. 27, 1946, eff. Mar. 19, 1948; Dec. 29, 1948, eff. Oct. 20, 1949; Apr. 30, 2007, eff. Dec. 1, 2007.)

Rule 67. Deposit into Court

(a) **Depositing Property.** If any part of the relief sought is a money judgment or the disposition of a sum of money or some other deliverable thing, a party—on notice to every other party and by leave of court—may deposit with the court all or part of the money or thing, whether or not that party claims any of it. The depositing party must deliver to the clerk a copy of the order permitting deposit.

(b) **Investing and Withdrawing Funds.** Money paid into court under this rule must be deposited and withdrawn in accordance with 28 U.S.C. §§ 2041 and 2042 and any like statute. The money must be deposited in an interest-bearing account or invested in a court-approved, interest-bearing instrument.

(As amended Dec. 29, 1948, eff. Oct. 20, 1949; Apr. 28, 1983, eff. Aug. 1, 1983; Apr. 30, 2007, eff. Dec. 1, 2007.)

Rule 68. Offer of Judgment

(a) Making an Offer; Judgment on an Accepted Offer. At least 14 days before the date set for trial, a party defending against a claim may serve on an opposing party an offer to allow judgment on specified terms, with the costs then accrued. If, within 14 days after being served, the opposing party serves written notice accepting the offer, either party may then file the offer and notice of acceptance, plus proof of service. The clerk must then enter judgment.

(b) Unaccepted Offer. An unaccepted offer is considered withdrawn, but it does not preclude a later offer. Evidence of an unaccepted offer is not admissible except in a proceeding to determine costs.

(c) Offer After Liability Is Determined. When one party's liability to another has been determined but the extent of liability remains to be determined by further proceedings, the party held liable may make an offer of judgment. It must be served within a reasonable time—but at least 14 days—before the date set for a hearing to determine the extent of liability.

(d) Paying Costs After an Unaccepted Offer. If the judgment that the offeree finally obtains is not more favorable than the unaccepted offer, the offeree must pay the costs incurred after the offer was made.

(As amended Dec. 27, 1946, eff. Mar. 19, 1948; Feb. 28, 1966, eff. July 1, 1966; Mar. 2, 1987, eff. Aug. 1, 1987; Apr. 30, 2007, eff. Dec. 1, 2007; Mar. 26, 2009, eff. Dec. 1, 2009.)

Rule 69. Execution

(a) In General.

(1) ***Money Judgment; Applicable Procedure.*** A money judgment is enforced by a writ of execution, unless the court directs otherwise. The procedure on execution—and in proceedings supplementary to and in aid of judgment or execution—must accord with the procedure of the state where the court is located, but a federal statute governs to the extent it applies.

(2) ***Obtaining Discovery.*** In aid of the judgment or execution, the judgment creditor or a successor in interest whose interest appears of record may obtain discovery from any person—including the judgment debtor—as provided in these rules or by the procedure of the state where the court is located.

(b) Against Certain Public Officers. When a judgment has been entered against a revenue officer in the circumstances stated in 28 U.S.C. § 2006, or against an officer of Congress in the circumstances describe the property sufficiently to identify it, but need not describe any property other than that to be taken from the named defendant. The notice must also state:

(i) that the action is to condemn property;

(ii) the interest to be taken;

(iii) the authority for the taking;

(iv) the uses for which the property is to be taken;

(v) that the defendant may serve an answer on the plaintiff's attorney within 21 days after being served with the notice;

(vi) that the failure to so serve an answer constitutes consent to the taking and to the court's authority to proceed with the action and fix the compensation; and

(vii) that a defendant who does not serve an answer may file a notice of appearance.

(B) *Conclusion.* The notice must conclude with the name, telephone number, and e-mail address of the plaintiff's attorney and an address within the district in which the action is brought where the attorney may be served.

(3) ***Serving the Notice.***

(A) *Personal Service.* When a defendant whose address is known resides within the United States or a territory subject to the administrative or judicial jurisdiction of the United States, personal service of the notice (without a copy of the complaint) must be made in accordance with Rule 4.

(B) *Service by Publication.*

(i) A defendant may be served by publication only when the plaintiff's attorney files a certificate stating that the attorney believes the defendant cannot be personally served, because after diligent inquiry within the state where the complaint is filed, the defendant's place of residence is still unknown or, if known, that it is beyond the territorial limits of personal service. Service is then made by publishing the notice—once a week for at least three successive weeks—in a newspaper published in the county where the property is located or, if there is no such newspaper, in a newspaper with general circulation where the property is located. Before the last publication, a copy of the notice must also be mailed to every defendant who cannot be personally served but whose place of residence is then known. Unknown owners may be served by publication in the same manner by a notice addressed to "Unknown Owners."

(ii) Service by publication is complete on the date of the last publication. The plaintiff's attorney must prove publication and mailing by a certificate, attach a printed copy of the published notice, and mark on the copy the newspaper's name and the dates of publication.

(4) ***Effect of Delivery and Service.*** Delivering the notice to the clerk and serving it have the same effect as serving a summons under Rule 4.

(5) ***Proof of Service; Amending the Proof or Notice.*** Rule 4(*l*) governs proof of service. The court may permit the proof or the notice to be amended.

(e) Appearance or Answer.

(1) ***Notice of Appearance.*** A defendant that has no objection or defense to the taking of its property may serve a notice of appearance designating the property in which it claims an interest. The defendant must then be given notice of all later proceedings affecting the defendant.

(2) ***Answer.*** A defendant that has an objection or defense to the taking must serve an answer within 21 days after being served with the notice. The answer must:

(A) identify the property in which the defendant claims an interest;

(B) state the nature and extent of the interest; and

(C) state all the defendant's objections and defenses to the taking.

(3) ***Waiver of Other Objections and Defenses; Evidence on Compensation.*** A defendant waives all objections and defenses not stated in its answer. No other pleading or motion asserting an additional objection or defense is allowed. But at the trial on compensation, a defendant—whether or not it has previously appeared or answered—may present evidence on the amount of compensation to be paid and may share in the award.

(f) Amending Pleadings. Without leave of court, the plaintiff may—as often as it wants—amend the complaint at any time before the trial on compensation. But no amendment may be made if it would result in a dismissal inconsistent with Rule 71.1(i)(1) or (2). The plaintiff need not serve a copy of an amendment, but must serve notice of the filing, as provided in Rule 5(b), on every affected party who has appeared and, as provided in Rule 71.1(d), on every affected party who has not appeared. In addition, the plaintiff must give the clerk at least one copy of each amendment for the defendants' use, and additional copies at the request of the clerk or a defendant. A defendant may appear or answer in the time and manner and with the same effect as provided in Rule 71.1(e).

(g) Substituting Parties. If a defendant dies, becomes incompetent, or transfers an interest after being joined, the court may, on motion and notice of hearing, order that the proper party be substituted. Service of the motion and notice on a nonparty must be made as provided in Rule 71.1(d)(3).

(h) Trial of the Issues.

(1) ***Issues Other Than Compensation; Compensation.*** In an action involving eminent domain under federal law, the court tries all issues, including compensation, except when compensation must be determined:

(A) by any tribunal specially constituted by a federal statute to determine compensation; or

(B) if there is no such tribunal, by a jury when a party demands one within the time to answer or within any additional time the court sets, unless the court appoints a commission.

(2) ***Appointing a Commission; Commission's Powers and Report.***

(A) *Reasons for Appointing.* If a party has demanded a jury, the court may instead appoint a three-person commission to determine compensation because of the character, location, or quantity of the property to be condemned or for other just reasons.

(B) *Alternate Commissioners.* The court may appoint up to two additional persons to serve as alternate commissioners to hear the case and replace commissioners who, before a decision is filed, the court finds unable or disqualified to perform their duties. Once the commission renders its final decision, the court must discharge any alternate who has not replaced a commissioner.

(C) *Examining the Prospective Commissioners.* Before making its appointments, the court must advise the parties of the identity and qualifications of each prospective commissioner and alternate, and may permit the parties to examine them. The parties may not suggest appointees, but for good cause may object to a prospective commissioner or alternate.

(D) *Commission's Powers and Report.* A commission has the powers of a master under Rule 53(c). Its action and report are determined by a majority. Rule 53(d), (e), and (f) apply to its action and report.

(i) **Dismissal of the Action or a Defendant.**

(1) ***Dismissing the Action.***

(A) *By the Plaintiff.* If no compensation hearing on a piece of property has begun, and if the plaintiff has not acquired title or a lesser interest or taken possession, the plaintiff may, without a court order, dismiss the action as to that property by filing a notice of dismissal briefly describing the property.

(B) *By Stipulation.* Before a judgment is entered vesting the plaintiff with title or a lesser interest in or possession of property, the plaintiff and affected defendants may, without a court order, dismiss the action in whole or in part by filing a stipulation of dismissal. And if the parties so stipulate, the court may vacate a judgment already entered.

(C) *By Court Order.* At any time before compensation has been determined and paid, the court may, after a motion and hearing, dismiss the action as to a piece of property. But if the plaintiff has already taken title, a lesser interest, or possession as to any part of it, the court must award compensation for the title, lesser interest, or possession taken.

(2) ***Dismissing a Defendant.*** The court may at any time dismiss a defendant who was unnecessarily or improperly joined.

(3) ***Effect.*** A dismissal is without prejudice unless otherwise stated in the notice, stipulation, or court order.

(j) **Deposit and Its Distribution.**

(1) ***Deposit.*** The plaintiff must deposit with the court any money required by law as a condition to the exercise of eminent domain and may make a deposit when allowed by statute.

(2) ***Distribution; Adjusting Distribution.*** After a deposit, the court and attorneys must expedite the proceedings so as to distribute the deposit and to determine and pay compensation. If the compensation finally awarded to a defendant exceeds the amount distributed to that defendant, the court must enter judgment against the plaintiff for the deficiency. If the compensation awarded to a defendant is less than the amount distributed to that defendant, the court must enter judgment against that defendant for the overpayment.

(k) Condemnation Under a State's Power of Eminent Domain. This rule governs an action involving eminent domain under state law. But if state law provides for trying an issue by jury—or for trying the issue of compensation by jury or commission or both—that law governs.

(*l*) Costs. Costs are not subject to Rule 54(d).

(Added Apr. 30, 1951, eff. Aug. 1, 1951, and amended Jan. 21, 1963, eff. July 1, 1963; Apr. 29, 1985, eff. Aug. 1, 1985; Mar. 2, 1987, eff. Aug. 1, 1987; Apr. 25, 1988, eff. Aug. 1, 1988; Nov. 18, 1988, Pub.L. 100–690, § 7050, 102 Stat. 4401; Apr. 22, 1993, eff. Dec. 1, 1993; Mar. 27, 2003, eff. Dec. 1, 2003; Apr. 30, 2007, eff. Dec. 1, 2007; Mar. 26, 2009, eff. Dec. 1, 2009.)

Rule 72. Magistrate Judges: Pretrial Order

(a) Nondispositive Matters. When a pretrial matter not dispositive of a party's claim or defense is referred to a magistrate judge to hear and decide, the magistrate judge must promptly conduct the required proceedings and, when appropriate, issue a written order stating the decision. A party may serve and file objections to the order within 14 days after being served with a copy. A party may not assign as error a defect in the order not timely objected to. The district judge in the case must consider timely objections and modify or set aside any part of the order that is clearly erroneous or is contrary to law.

(b) Dispositive Motions and Prisoner Petitions.

(1) ***Findings and Recommendations.*** A magistrate judge must promptly conduct the required proceedings when assigned, without the parties' consent, to hear a pretrial matter dispositive of a claim or defense or a prisoner petition challenging the conditions of confinement. A record must be made of all evidentiary proceedings and may, at the magistrate judge's discretion, be made of any other proceedings. The magistrate judge must enter a recommended disposition, including, if appropriate, proposed findings of fact. The clerk must immediately serve a copy on each party as provided in Rule 5(b).

(2) ***Objections.*** Within 14 days after being served with a copy of the recommended disposition, a party may serve and file specific written objections to the proposed findings and recommendations. A party may respond to another party's objections within 14 days after being served with a copy. Unless the district judge orders otherwise, the objecting party must promptly arrange for transcribing the record, or whatever portions of it the parties agree to or the magistrate judge considers sufficient.

(3) ***Resolving Objections.*** The district judge must determine de novo any part of the magistrate judge's disposition that has been properly objected to. The district judge may accept, reject, or modify the recommended disposition; receive further evidence; or return the matter to the magistrate judge with instructions.

(Added Apr. 28, 1983, eff. Aug. 1, 1983, and amended Apr. 30, 1991, eff. Dec. 1, 1991; Apr. 22, 1993, eff. Dec. 1, 1993; Apr. 30, 2007, eff. Dec. 1, 2007; Mar. 26, 2009, eff. Dec. 1, 2009; Apr. 24, 2023, eff. Dec. 1, 2023.)

Rule 73. Magistrate Judges: Trial by Consent; Appeal

(a) Trial by Consent. When authorized under 28 U.S.C. § 636(c), a magistrate judge may, if all parties consent, conduct a civil action or proceeding, including a jury or nonjury trial. A record must be made in accordance with 28 U.S.C. § 636(c)(5).

(b) Consent Procedure.

(1) ***In General.*** When a magistrate judge has been designated to conduct civil actions or proceedings, the clerk must give the parties written notice of their opportunity to consent under 28 U.S.C. § 636(c). To signify their consent, the parties must jointly or separately file a statement consenting to the referral. A district judge or magistrate judge may be informed of a party's response to the clerk's notice only if all parties have consented to the referral.

(2) ***Reminding the Parties About Consenting.*** A district judge, magistrate judge, or other court official may remind the parties of the magistrate judge's availability, but must also advise them that they are free to withhold consent without adverse substantive consequences.

(3) ***Vacating a Referral.*** On its own for good cause—or when a party shows extraordinary circumstances—the district judge may vacate a referral to a magistrate judge under this rule.

(c) Appealing a Judgment. In accordance with 28 U.S.C. § 636(c)(3), an appeal from a judgment entered at a magistrate judge's direction may be taken to the court of appeals as would any other appeal from a district-court judgment.

(Added Apr. 28, 1983, eff. Aug. 1, 1983, and amended Mar. 2, 1987, eff. Aug. 1, 1987; Apr. 22, 1993, eff. Dec. 1, 1993; Apr. 11, 1997, eff. Dec. 1, 1997; Apr. 30, 2007, eff. Dec. 1, 2007.)

Rule 74. [Abrogated.]

Rule 75. [Abrogated.]

Rule 76. [Abrogated.]

TITLE X. DISTRICT COURTS AND CLERKS: CONDUCTING BUSINESS; ISSUING ORDERS

Rule 77. Conducting Business; Clerk's Authority; Notice of an Order or Judgment

(a) When Court Is Open. Every district court is considered always open for filing any paper, issuing and returning process, making a motion, or entering an order.

(b) Place for Trial and Other Proceedings. Every trial on the merits must be conducted in open court and, so far as convenient, in a regular courtroom. Any other act or proceeding may be done or conducted by a judge in chambers, without the attendance of the clerk or other court official, and anywhere inside or outside the district. But no hearing—other than one ex parte—may be conducted outside the district unless all the affected parties consent.

(c) Clerk's Office Hours; Clerk's Orders.

(1) ***Hours.*** The clerk's office—with a clerk or deputy on duty—must be open during business hours every day except Saturdays, Sundays, and legal holidays. But a court may, by local rule or order, require that the office be open for specified hours on Saturday or a particular legal holiday other than one listed in Rule 6(a)(6)(A).

(2) ***Orders.*** Subject to the court's power to suspend, alter, or rescind the clerk's action for good cause, the clerk may:

(A) issue process;

(B) enter a default;

(C) enter a default judgment under Rule 55(b)(1); and

(D) act on any other matter that does not require the court's action.

(d) Serving Notice of an Order or Judgment.

(1) ***Service.*** Immediately after entering an order or judgment, the clerk must serve notice of the entry, as provided in Rule 5(b), on each party who is not in default for failing to appear. The clerk must record the service on the docket. A party also may serve notice of the entry as provided in Rule 5(b).

(2) ***Time to Appeal Not Affected by Lack of Notice.*** Lack of notice of the entry does not affect the time for appeal or relieve—or authorize the court to relieve—a party for failing to appeal within the time allowed, except as allowed by Federal Rule of Appellate Procedure (4)(a).

(As amended Dec. 27, 1946, eff. Mar. 19, 1948; Jan. 21, 1963, eff. July 1, 1963; Dec. 4, 1967, eff. July 1, 1968; Mar. 1, 1971, eff. July 1, 1971; Mar. 2, 1987, eff. Aug. 1, 1987; Apr. 30, 1991, eff. Dec. 1, 1991; Apr. 23, 2001, eff. Dec. 1, 2001; Apr. 30, 2007, eff. Dec. 1, 2007; Apr. 25, 2014, eff. Dec. 1, 2014.)

Rule 78. Hearing Motions; Submission on Briefs

(a) Providing a Regular Schedule for Oral Hearings. A court may establish regular times and places for oral hearings on motions.

(b) Providing for Submission on Briefs. By rule or order, the court may provide for submitting and determining motions on briefs, without oral hearings.

(As amended Mar. 2, 1987, eff. Aug. 1, 1987; Apr. 30, 2007, eff. Dec. 1, 2007.)

Rule 79. Records Kept by the Clerk

(a) Civil Docket.

(1) ***In General.*** The clerk must keep a record known as the "civil docket" in the form and manner prescribed by the Director of the Administrative Office of the United States Courts with the approval of the Judicial Conference of the United States. The clerk must enter each civil action in the docket. Actions must be assigned consecutive file numbers, which must be noted in the docket where the first entry of the action is made.

(2) ***Items to be Entered.*** The following items must be marked with the file number and entered chronologically in the docket:

(A) papers filed with the clerk;

(B) process issued, and proofs of service or other returns showing execution; and

(C) appearances, orders, verdicts, and judgments.

(3) ***Contents of Entries; Jury Trial Demanded.*** Each entry must briefly show the nature of the paper filed or writ issued, the substance of each proof of service or other return, and the substance and date of entry of each order and judgment. When a jury trial has been properly demanded or ordered, the clerk must enter the word "jury" in the docket.

(b) Civil Judgments and Orders. The clerk must keep a copy of every final judgment and appealable order; of every order affecting title to or a lien on real or personal property; and of any other order that the court directs to be kept. The clerk must keep these in the form and manner prescribed by the Director of the Administrative Office of the United States Courts with the approval of the Judicial Conference of the United States.

(c) Indexes; Calendars. Under the court's direction, the clerk must:

(1) keep indexes of the docket and of the judgments and orders described in Rule 79(b); and

(2) prepare calendars of all actions ready for trial, distinguishing jury trials from nonjury trials.

(d) Other Records. The clerk must keep any other records required by the Director of the Administrative Office of the United States Courts with the approval of the Judicial Conference of the United States.

(As amended Dec. 27, 1946, eff. Mar. 19, 1948; Dec. 29, 1948, eff. Oct. 20, 1949; Jan. 21, 1963, eff. July 1, 1963; Apr. 30, 2007, eff. Dec. 1, 2007.)

Rule 80. Stenographic Transcript as Evidence

If stenographically reported testimony at a hearing or trial is admissible in evidence at a later trial, the testimony may be proved by a transcript certified by the person who reported it.

(As amended Dec. 27, 1946, eff. Mar. 19, 1948; Apr. 30, 2007, eff. Dec. 1, 2007.)

TITLE XI. GENERAL PROVISIONS

Rule 81. Applicability of the Rules in General; Removed Actions

(a) Applicability to Particular Proceedings.

(1) ***Prize Proceedings.*** These rules do not apply to prize proceedings in admiralty governed by 10 U.S.C. §§ 7651–7681.

(2) ***Bankruptcy.*** These rules apply to bankruptcy proceedings to the extent provided by the Federal Rules of Bankruptcy Procedure.

(3) ***Citizenship.*** These rules apply to proceedings for admission to citizenship to the extent that the practice in those proceedings is not specified in federal statutes and has previously conformed to the practice in civil actions. The provisions of 8 U.S.C. § 1451 for service by publication and for answer apply in proceedings to cancel citizenship certificates.

(4) ***Special Writs.*** These rules apply to proceedings for habeas corpus and for quo warranto to the extent that the practice in those proceedings:

(A) is not specified in a federal statute, the Rules Governing Section 2254 Cases, or the Rules Governing Section 2255 Cases; and

(B) has previously conformed to the practice in civil actions.

(5) ***Proceedings Involving a Subpoena.*** These rules apply to proceedings to compel testimony or the production of documents through a subpoena issued by a United States officer or agency under a federal statute, except as otherwise provided by statute, by local rule, or by court order in the proceedings.

(6) ***Other Proceedings.*** These rules, to the extent applicable, govern proceedings under the following laws, except as these laws provide other procedures:

(A) 7 U.S.C. §§ 292, 499g(c), for reviewing an order of the Secretary of Agriculture;

(B) 9 U.S.C., relating to arbitration;

(C) 15 U.S.C. § 522, for reviewing an order of the Secretary of the Interior;

(D) 15 U.S.C. § 715d(c), for reviewing an order denying a certificate of clearance;

(E) 29 U.S.C. §§ 159, 160, for enforcing an order of the National Labor Relations Board;

(F) 33 U.S.C. §§ 918, 921, for enforcing or reviewing a compensation order under the Longshore and Harbor Workers' Compensation Act; and

(G) 45 U.S.C. § 159, for reviewing an arbitration award in a railway-labor dispute.

(b) Scire Facias and Mandamus. The writs of scire facias and mandamus are abolished. Relief previously available through them may be obtained by appropriate action or motion under these rules.

(c) Removed Actions.

(1) ***Applicability.*** These rules apply to a civil action after it is removed from a state court.

(2) ***Further Pleading.*** After removal, repleading is unnecessary unless the court orders it. A defendant who did not answer before removal must answer or present other defenses or objections under these rules within the longest of these periods:

(A) 21 days after receiving—through service or otherwise—a copy of the initial pleading stating the claim for relief;

(B) 21 days after being served with the summons for an initial pleading on file at the time of service; or

(C) 7 days after the notice of removal is filed.

(3) ***Demand for a Jury Trial.***

(A) *As Affected by State Law.* A party who, before removal, expressly demanded a jury trial in accordance with state law need not renew the demand after removal. If the state law did not require an express demand for a jury trial, a party need not make one after removal unless the court orders the parties to do so within a specified time. The court must so order at a party's request and may so order on its own. A party who fails to make a demand when so ordered waives a jury trial.

(B) *Under Rule 38.* If all necessary pleadings have been served at the time of removal, a party entitled to a jury trial under Rule 38 must be given one if the party serves a demand within 14 days after:

(i) it files a notice of removal; or

(ii) it is served with a notice of removal filed by another party.

(d) Law Applicable.

(1) ***"State Law" Defined.*** When these rules refer to state law, the term "law" includes the state's statutes and the state's judicial decisions.

(2) ***"State" Defined.*** The term "state" includes, where appropriate, the District of Columbia and any United States commonwealth or territory.

(3) ***"Federal Statute" Defined in the District of Columbia.*** In the United States District Court for the District of Columbia, the term "federal statute" includes any Act of Congress that applies locally to the District.

(As amended Dec. 27, 1946, eff. Mar. 19, 1948; Dec. 29, 1948, eff. Oct. 20, 1949; Apr. 30, 1951, eff. Aug. 1, 1951; Jan. 21, 1963, eff. July 1, 1963; Feb. 28, 1966, eff. July 1, 1966; Dec. 4, 1967, eff. July 1, 1968; Mar. 1, 1971, eff. July 1, 1971; Mar. 2, 1987, eff. Aug. 1, 1987; Apr. 23, 2001, eff. Dec. 1, 2001; Apr. 29, 2002, eff. Dec. 1, 2002; Apr. 30, 2007, eff. Dec. 1, 2007; Mar. 26, 2009, eff. Dec. 1, 2009.)

Rule 82. Jurisdiction and Venue Unaffected

These rules do not extend or limit the jurisdiction of the district courts or the venue of actions in those courts. An admiralty or maritime claim under Rule 9(h) is governed by 28 U.S.C. § 1390.

(As amended Dec. 29, 1948, eff. Oct. 20, 1949; Feb. 28, 1966, eff. July 1, 1966; Apr. 23, 2001, eff. Dec. 1, 2001; Apr. 30, 2007, eff. Dec. 1, 2007; Apr. 28, 2016, eff. Dec. 1, 2016.)

Rule 83. Rules by District Courts; Judge's Directives

(a) Local Rules.

(1) ***In General.*** After giving public notice and an opportunity for comment, a district court, acting by a majority of its district judges, may adopt and amend rules governing its practice. A local rule must be consistent with—but not duplicate—federal statutes and rules adopted under 28 U.S.C. §§ 2072 and 2075, and must conform to any uniform numbering system prescribed by the Judicial Conference of the United States. A local rule takes effect on the date specified by the district court and remains in effect unless amended by the court or abrogated by the judicial council of the circuit. Copies of rules and amendments must, on their adoption, be furnished to the judicial council and the Administrative Office of the United States Courts and be made available to the public.

(2) ***Requirement of Form.*** A local rule imposing a requirement of form must not be enforced in a way that causes a party to lose any right because of a nonwillful failure to comply.

(b) Procedure When There Is No Controlling Law. A judge may regulate practice in any manner consistent with federal law, rules adopted under 28 U.S.C. §§ 2072 and 2075, and the district's local rules. No sanction or other disadvantage may be imposed for noncompliance with any requirement not in federal law, federal rules, or the local rules unless the alleged violator has been furnished in the particular case with actual notice of the requirement.

(As amended Apr. 29, 1985, eff. Aug. 1, 1985; Apr. 27, 1994, eff. Dec. 1, 1994; Apr. 27, 1995, eff. Dec. 1, 1995; Apr. 30, 2007, eff. Dec. 1, 2007.)

Rule 84. Forms [Abrogated.]

NOTES OF ADVISORY COMMITTEE ON RULES

2015 AMENDMENT

Rule 84 was adopted when the Civil Rules were established in 1938 "to indicate, subject to the provisions of these rules, the simplicity and brevity of statement which the rules contemplate." The purpose of providing illustrations for the rules, although useful when the rules were adopted, has been fulfilled. Accordingly, recognizing that there are many alternative sources for forms, including the website of the Administrative Office of the United States Courts, the websites of many district courts, and local law libraries that contain many commercially published forms, Rule 84 and the Appendix of Forms are no longer necessary and have been abrogated. The abrogation of Rule 84 does not alter existing pleading standards or otherwise change the requirements of Civil Rule 8.

Rule 85. Title

These rules may be cited as the Federal Rules of Civil Procedure.

(As amended Apr. 30, 2007, eff. Dec. 1, 2007.)

Rule 86. Effective Dates

(a) In General. These rules and any amendments take effect at the time specified by the Supreme Court, subject to 28 U.S.C. § 2074. They govern:

(1) proceedings in an action commenced after their effective date; and

(2) proceedings after that date in an action then pending unless:

(A) the Supreme Court specifies otherwise; or

(B) the court determines that applying them in a particular action would be infeasible or work an injustice.

(b) December 1, 2007 Amendments. If any provision in Rules 1–5.1, 6–73, or 77–86 conflicts with another law, priority in time for the purpose of 28 U.S.C. § 2072(b) is not affected by the amendments taking effect on December 1, 2007.

(As amended Dec. 27, 1946, eff. Mar. 19, 1948; Dec. 29, 1948, eff. Oct. 20, 1949; Apr. 17, 1961, eff. July 19, 1961; Jan. 21, 1963, and Mar. 18, 1963, eff. July 1, 1963; Apr. 30, 2007, eff. Dec. 1, 2007.)

NOTES OF ADVISORY COMMITTEE ON RULES

2007 AMENDMENT

* * *

Rule 86(b) is added to clarify the relationship of amendments taking effect on December 1, 2007, to other laws for the purpose of applying the "supersession" clause in 28 U.S.C. § 2072(b). Section 2072(b) provides that a law in conflict with an Enabling Act Rule "shall be of no further force or effect after such rule[ ] ha[s] taken effect." The amendments that take effect on December 1, 2007, result from the general restyling of the Civil Rules and from a small number of technical revisions adopted on a parallel track. None of these amendments is intended to affect resolution of any conflict that might arise between a rule and another law. Rule 86(b) makes this intent explicit. Any conflict that arises should be resolved by looking to the date the specific conflicting rule provision first became effective.

Rule 87. Civil Rules Emergency

(a) Conditions for an Emergency. The Judicial Conference of the United States may declare a Civil Rules emergency if it determines that extraordinary circumstances relating to public health or safety, or affecting physical or electronic access to a court, substantially impair the court's ability to perform its functions in compliance with these rules.

(b) Declaring an Emergency.

(1) ***Content.*** The declaration:

(A) must designate the court or courts affected;

(B) adopts all the emergency rules in Rule 87(c) unless it excepts one or more of them; and

(C) must be limited to a stated period of no more than 90 days.

(2) ***Early Termination.*** The Judicial Conference may terminate a declaration for one or more courts before the termination date.

(3) ***Additional Declarations.*** The Judicial Conference may issue additional declarations under this rule.

(c) Emergency Rules.

(1) ***Emergency Rules 4(e), (h)(1), (i), and (j)(2), and for serving a minor or incompetent person.*** The court may by order authorize service on a defendant described in Rule 4(e), (h)(1), (i), or (j)(2)—or on a minor or incompetent person in a judicial district of the United States—by a method that is reasonably calculated to give notice. A method of service may be completed under the order after the declaration ends unless the court, after notice and an opportunity to be heard, modifies or rescinds this order.

(2) ***Emergency Rule 6(b)(2).***

(A) *Extension of Time to File Certain Motions.* A court may, by order, apply Rule 6(b)(1)(A) to extend for a period of no more than 30 days after entry of the order the time to act under Rules 50(b) and (d), 52(b), 59(b), (d), and (e), and 60(b).

(B) *Effect on Time to Appeal.* Unless the time to appeal would otherwise be longer:

(i) if the court denies an extension, the time to file an appeal runs for all parties from the date the order denying the motion to extend is entered;

(ii) if the court grants an extension, a motion authorized by the court and filed within the extended period is, for purposes of Appellate Rule 4(a)(4)(A), filed "within the time allowed by" the Federal Rules of Civil Procedure; and

(iii) if the court grants an extension and no motion authorized by the court is made within the extended period, the time to file an appeal runs for all parties from the expiration of the extended period.

(C) *Declaration Ends.* An act authorized by an order under this emergency rule may be completed under the order after the emergency declaration ends.

(Added Apr. 24, 2023, eff. Dec. 1, 2023.)

Selected Federal Rules of Appellate Procedure

■ ■ ■

As Amended to December 1, 2025

Table of Rules

TITLE I. APPLICABILITY OF RULES

Rule 1. Scope of Rules; Definition; Title

(a) Scope of Rules.

(1) These rules govern procedure in the United States courts of appeals.

(2) When these rules provide for filing a motion or other document in the district court, the procedure must comply with the practice of the district court.

(b) Definition. In these rules, 'state' includes the District of Columbia and any United States commonwealth or territory.

(c) Title. These rules are to be known as the Federal Rules of Appellate Procedure.

(As amended Apr. 30, 1979, eff. Aug. 1, 1997; Apr. 25, 1989, eff. Dec. 1, 1989; Apr. 29, 1994, eff. Dec. 1, 1994; Apr. 24, 1998, eff. Dec. 1, 1998; Apr. 29, 2002, eff. Dec. 1, 2002; Apr. 28, 2010, eff. Dec. 1, 2010.)

Rule 2. Suspension of Rules

(a) In a Particular Case. On its own or party's motion, a court of appeals may—to expedite its decision or for other good cause—suspend any provision of these rules in a particular case and order proceedings as it directs, except as otherwise provided in Rule 26(b).

(b) In an Appellate Rules Emergency.

(1) Conditions for an Emergency. The Judicial Conference of the United States may declare an Appellate Rules emergency if it determines that extraordinary circumstances relating to public health or safety, or affecting physical or electronic access to a court, substantially impair the court's ability to perform its functions in compliance with these rules.

(2) Content. The declaration must:

(A) designate the circuit or circuits affected; and

(B) be limited to a stated period of no more than 90 days.

(3) Early Termination. The Judicial Conference may terminate a declaration for one or more circuits before the termination date.

(4) Additional Declarations. The Judicial Conference may issue additional declarations under this rule.

(5) Proceedings in a Rules Emergency. When a rules emergency is declared, the court may:

(A) suspend in all or part of that circuit any provision of these rules, other than time limits imposed by statute and described in Rule 26(b)(1)–(2); and

(B) order proceedings as it directs.

(As amended Apr. 24, 1998, eff. Dec. 1, 1998; Apr. 24, 2023, eff. Dec. 1, 2023.)

TITLE II. APPEAL FROM A JUDGMENT OR ORDER OF A DISTRICT COURT

Rule 3. Appeal as of Right—How Taken

(a) Filing the Notice of Appeal.

(1) An appeal permitted by law as of right from a district court to a court of appeals may be taken only by filing a notice of appeal with the district clerk within the time allowed by Rule 4. At the time of filing, the appellant must furnish the clerk with enough copies of the notice to enable the clerk to comply with Rule 3(d).

(2) An appellant's failure to take any step other than the timely filing of a notice of appeal does not affect the validity of the appeal, but is ground only for the court of appeals to act as it considers appropriate, including dismissing the appeal.

(3) An appeal from a judgment by a magistrate judge in a civil case is taken in the same way as an appeal from any other district court judgment.

(4) An appeal by permission under 28 U.S.C. § 1292(b) or an appeal in a bankruptcy case may be taken only in the manner prescribed by Rule 5 and Rule 6, respectively.

(b) Joint or Consolidated Appeals.

(1) When two or more parties are entitled to appeal from a district-court judgment or order, and their interests make joinder practicable, they may file a joint notice of appeal. They may then proceed on appeal as a single appellant.

(2) When the parties have filed separate timely notices of appeal, the appeals may be joined or consolidated by the court of appeals.

(c) Contents of the Notice of Appeal.

(1) A notice of appeal must:

(A) specify the party or parties taking the appeal by naming each one in the caption or body of the notice, but an attorney representing more than one party may describe those parties with such terms as "all plaintiffs," "the defendants," "the plaintiffs A, B, et al.," or "all defendants except X";

(B) designate the judgment, order, or part thereof being appealed; and

(C) name the court to which the appeal is taken.

(2) A pro se notice of appeal is considered filed on behalf of the signer and the signer's spouse and minor children (if they are parties), unless the notice clearly indicates otherwise.

(3) In a class action, whether or not the class has been certified, the notice of appeal is sufficient if it names one person qualified to bring the appeal as representative of the class.

(4) The notice of appeal encompasses all orders that, for purposes of appeal, merge into the designated judgment or appealable order. It is not necessary to designate those orders in the notice of appeal.

(5) In a civil case, a notice of appeal encompasses the final judgment, whether or not that judgment is set out in a separate document under Federal Rule of Civil Procedure 58, if the notice designates:

(A) an order that adjudicates all remaining claims and the rights and liabilities of all remaining parties; or

(B) an order described in Rule 4(a)(4)(A).

(6) An appellant may designate only part of a judgment or appealable order by expressly stating that the notice of appeal is so limited. Without such an express statement, specific designations do not limit the scope of the notice of appeal.

(7) An appeal must not be dismissed for informality of form or title of the notice of appeal, for failure to name a party whose intent to appeal is otherwise clear from the notice, or for failure to properly designate the judgment if the notice of appeal was filed after entry of the judgment and designates an order that merged into that judgment.

(8) Forms 1A and 1B in the Appendix of Forms are suggested forms of notices of appeal.

(d) Serving the Notice of Appeal.

(1) The district clerk must serve notice of the filing of a notice of appeal by sending a copy to each party's counsel of record—excluding the appellant's—or, if a party is proceeding pro se, to the party's last known address. When a defendant in a criminal case appeals, the clerk must also serve a copy of the notice of appeal on the defendant. The clerk must promptly send a copy of the notice of appeal and of the docket entries—and any later docket entries—to the clerk of the court of appeals named in the notice. The district clerk must note, on each copy, the date when the notice of appeal was filed.

(2) If an inmate confined in an institution files a notice of appeal in the manner provided by Rule 4(c), the district clerk must also note the date when the clerk docketed the notice.

(3) The district clerk's failure to serve notice does not affect the validity of the appeal. The clerk must note on the docket the names of the parties to whom the clerk sends copies, with the date of sending. Service is sufficient despite the death of a party or the party's counsel.

(e) Payment of Fees. Upon filing a notice of appeal, the appellant must pay the district clerk all required fees. The district clerk receives the appellate docket fee on behalf of the court of appeals.

(As amended Apr. 30, 1979, eff. Aug. 1, 1979; Mar. 10, 1986, eff. July 1, 1986; Apr. 25, 1989, eff. Dec. 1, 1989; Apr. 22, 1993, eff. Dec. 1, 1993; Apr. 29, 1994, eff. Dec. 1, 1994; Apr. 24, 1998, eff. Dec. 1, 1998; Apr. 25, 2019, eff. Dec. 1, 2019; Apr. 14, 2021, eff. Dec. 1, 2021.)

Rule 4. Appeal as of Right—When Taken

(a) Appeal in a Civil Case.

(1) Time for Filing a Notice of Appeal.

(A) In a civil case, except as provided in Rules 4(a)(1)(B), 4(a)(4), and 4(c), the notice of appeal required by Rule 3 must be filed with the district clerk within 30 days after the judgment or order appealed from is entered.

(B) The notice of appeal may be filed by any party within 60 days after entry of the judgment or order appealed from if one of the parties is:

(i) the United States;

(ii) a United States agency;

(iii) a United States officer or employee sued in an official capacity; or

(iv) a current or former United States officer or employee sued in an individual capacity for an act or omission occurring in connection with duties performed on the United States' behalf—including all instances in which the United States represents that person when the judgment or order is entered or files the appeal for that person.

(C) An appeal from an order granting or denying an application for a writ of error coram nobis is an appeal in a civil case for purposes of Rule 4(a).

(2) Filing Before Entry of Judgment. A notice of appeal filed after the court announces a decision or order—but before the entry of the judgment or offer—is treated as filed on the date of and after the entry.

(3) Multiple Appeals. If one party timely files a notice of appeal, any other party may file a notice of appeal within 14 days after the date when the first notice was filed, or within the time otherwise prescribed by this Rule 4(a), whichever period ends later.

(4) Effect of a Motion on a Notice of Appeal.

(A) If a party files in the district court any of the following motions under the Federal Rules of Civil Procedure—and does so within the time allowed by those rules—the time to file an appeal runs for all parties from the entry of the order disposing of the last such remaining motion:

(i) for judgment under Rule 50(b)

(ii) to amend or make additional factual findings under Rule 52(b), whether or not granting the motion would alter the judgment;

(iii) for attorney's fees under Rule 54 if the district court extends the time to appeal under Rule 58;

(iv) to alter or amend the judgment under Rule 59;

(v) for a new trial under Rule 59; or

(vi) for relief under Rule 60 if the motion is filed within the time allowed for filing a motion under Rule 59.

(B)(i) If a party files a notice of appeal after the court announces or enters a judgment—but before it disposes of any motion listed in Rule 4(a)(4)(A)—the notice becomes effective to appeal a judgment or order, in whole or in part, when the order disposing of the last such remaining motion is entered.

(ii) A party intending to challenge an order disposing of any motion listed in Rule 4(a)(4)(A), or a judgment's alteration or amendment upon such a motion, must file a notice of appeal, or an amended notice of appeal—in compliance with Rule 3(c)—within the time prescribed by this Rule measured from the entry of the order disposing of the last such remaining motion.

(iii) No additional fee is required to file an amended notice.

(5) Motion for Extension of Time.

(A) The district court may extend the time to file a notice of appeal if:

(i) a party so moves no later than 30 days after the time prescribed by this Rule 4(a) expires; and

(ii) regardless of whether its motion is filed before or during the 30 days after the time prescribed by this Rule 4(a) expires, that party shows excusable neglect or good cause.

(B) A motion filed before the expiration of the time prescribed in Rule 4(a)(1) or (3) may be ex parte unless the court requires otherwise. If the motion is filed after the expiration of the prescribed time, notice must be given to the other parties in accordance with local rules.

(C) No extension under this Rule 4(a)(5) may exceed 30 days after the prescribed time or 14 days after the date when the order granting the motion is entered, whichever is later.

(6) Reopening the Time to File an Appeal. The district court may reopen the time to file an appeal for a period of 14 days after the date when its order to reopen is entered, but only if all the following conditions are satisfied:

(A) the court finds that the moving party did not receive notice under Federal Rule of Civil Procedure 77(d) of the entry of the judgment or order sought to be appealed within 21 days after entry;

(B) the motion is filed within 180 days after the judgment or order is entered or within 14 days after the moving party receives notice under Federal Rule of Civil Procedure 77(d) of the entry, whichever is earlier; and

(C) the court finds that no party would be prejudiced.

(7) Entry Defined.

(A) A judgment or order is entered for purposes of this Rule 4(a):

(i) if Federal Rule of Civil Procedure 58(a) does not require a separate document, when the judgment or order is entered in the civil docket under Federal Rules of Civil Procedure 79(a); or

(ii) if Federal Rule of Civil Procedure 58(a) requires a separate document, when the judgment or order is entered in the civil docket under Federal Rule of Civil Procedure 79(a) and when the earlier of these events occurs:

- the judgment or order is set forth on a separate document, or
- 150 days have run from entry of the judgment or order in the civil docket under Federal Rule of Civil Procedure 79(a).

(B) A failure to set forth a judgment or order on a separate document when required by Federal Rule of Civil Procedure 58(a) does not affect the validity of an appeal from that judgment or order.

* * *

(c) Appeal by an Inmate Confined in an Institution.

(1) If an institution has a system designed for legal mail, an inmate confined there must use that system to receive the benefit of this Rule 4(c)(1). If an inmate files a notice of appeal in either a civil or a criminal case, the notice is timely if it is deposited in the institution's internal mail system on or before the last day for filing and:

(A) it is accompanied by:

(i) a declaration in compliance with 28 U.S.C. § 1746—or a notarized statement—setting out the date of deposit and stating that first-class postage is being prepaid; or

(ii) evidence (such as a postmark or date stamp) showing that the notice was so deposited and that postage was prepaid; or

(B) the court of appeals exercises its discretion to permit the later filing of a declaration or notarized statement that satisfies Rule 4(c)(1)(A)(i).

(2) If an inmate files the first notice of appeal in a civil case under this Rule 4(c), the 14-day period provided in paragraph (4)(a)(3) for another party to file a notice of appeal runs from the date when the district court dockets the first notice.

(3) When a defendant in a criminal case files a notice of appeal under this Rule 4(c), the 30-day period for the government to file its notice of appeal runs from the entry of the judgment or order appealed from or from the district court's docketing of the defendant's notice of appeal, whichever is later.

(d) Mistaken Filing in the Court of Appeals. If a notice of appeal in either a civil or a criminal case is mistakenly filed in the court of appeals, the clerk of that court must note on the notice the date when it was received and send it to the district clerk. The notice is then considered filed in the district court on the date so noted.

(As amended Apr. 30, 1979, eff. Aug. 1, 1979; Nov. 18, 1988; Apr. 30, 1991, eff. Dec. 1, 1991; Apr. 22, 1993, eff. Dec. 1, 1993; Apr. 27, 1995, eff. Dec. 1, 1995; Apr. 24, 1998, eff. Dec. 1, 1998; Apr. 29, 2002, eff. Dec. 1, 2002; Apr. 25, 2005, eff. Dec. 1, 2005; Mar. 26, 2009, eff. Dec. 1, 2009; Apr. 28, 2010, eff. Dec. 1, 2010; Apr. 26, 2011, eff. Dec. 1, 2011; Apr. 28, 2016, eff. Dec. 1, 2016; Apr. 27, 2017, eff. Dec. 1, 2017; Apr. 24, 2023, eff. Dec. 1, 2023.)

Rule 5. Appeal by Permission

(a) Petition for Permission to Appeal.

(1) To request permission to appeal when an appeal is within the court of appeals' discretion, a party must file a petition with the circuit clerk and serve it on all other parties to the district-court action.

(2) The petition must be filed within the time specified by the statute or rule authorizing the appeal or, if no such time is specified, within the time provided by Rule 4(a) for filing a notice of appeal.

(3) If a party cannot petition for appeal unless the district court first enters an order granting permission to do so or stating that the necessary conditions are met, the district court may amend its order, either on its own or in response to a party's motion, to include the required permission or statement. In that event, the time to petition runs from entry of the amended order.

(b) Contents of the Petition; Answer or Cross-Petition; Oral Argument.

(1) The petition must include the following:

(A) the facts necessary to understand the question presented;

(B) the question itself;

(C) the relief sought;

(D) the reasons why the appeal should be allowed and is authorized by a statute or rule; and

(E) an attached copy of:

(i) the order, decree, or judgment complained of and any related opinion or memorandum, and

(ii) any order stating the district court's permission to appeal or finding that the necessary conditions are met.

(2) A party may file an answer in opposition or cross-petition within 10 days after the petition is served.

(3) The petition and answer will be submitted without oral argument unless the court of appeals orders otherwise.

(c) Form of Papers; Number of Copies; Length Limits. All papers must conform to Rule 32(c)(2). An original and 3 copies must be filed unless the court requires a different number by local rule or by order in a particular case. Except by the court's permission, and excluding the accompanying documents required by Rule 5(b)(1)(E):

(1) a paper produced using a computer must not exceed 5,200 words; and

(2) a handwritten or typewritten paper must not exceed 20 pages.

(d) Grant of Permission; Fees; Cost Bond; Filing the Record.

(1) Within 14 days after the entry of the order granting permission to appeal, the appellant must:

(A) pay to the district clerk all required fees; and

(B) file a cost bond if required under Rule 7.

(2) A notice of appeal need not be filed. The date when the order granting permission to appeal is entered serves as the date of the notice of appeal for calculating time under these rules.

(3) The district clerk must notify the circuit clerk once the petitioner has paid the fees. Upon receiving this notice, the circuit clerk must enter the appeal on the docket. The record must be forwarded and filed in accordance with Rules 11 and 12(c).

(As amended Apr. 30, 1979, eff. Aug. 1, 1979; Apr. 29, 1994, eff. Dec. 1, 1994; Apr. 24, 1998, eff. Dec. 1, 1998; Apr. 29, 2002, eff. Dec. 1, 2002; Mar. 26, 2009, eff. Dec. 1, 2009; Apr. 28, 2016, eff. Dec. 1, 2016; Apr. 25, 2019, eff. Dec. 1, 2019.)

Rule 7. Bond for Costs on Appeal in a Civil Case

In a civil case, the district court may require an appellant to file a bond or provide other security in any form and amount necessary to ensure payment of costs on appeal. Rule 8(b) applies to a surety on a bond given under this rule.

(As amended Apr. 30, 1979, eff. Aug. 1, 1979; Apr. 24, 1998, eff. Dec. 1, 1998.)

Rule 8. Stay or Injunction Pending Appeal

(a) Motion for Stay.

(1) Initial Motion in the District Court. A party must ordinarily move first in the district court for the following relief:

(A) a stay of the judgment or order of a district court pending appeal;

(B) approval of a bond or other security provided to obtain a stay of judgment; or

(C) an order suspending, modifying, restoring, or granting an injunction while an appeal is pending.

(2) Motion in the Court of Appeals; Conditions on Relief. A motion for the relief mentioned in Rule 8(a)(1) may be made to the court of appeals or to one of its judges.

(A) The motion must:

(i) show that moving first in the district court would be impracticable; or

(ii) state that, a motion having been made, the district court denied the motion or failed to afford the relief requested and state any reasons given by the district court for its action.

(B) The motion must also include:

(i) the reasons for granting the relief requested and the facts relied on;

(ii) originals or copies of affidavits or other sworn statements supporting facts subject to dispute; and

(iii) relevant parts of the record.

(C) The moving party must give reasonable notice of the motion to all parties.

(D) A motion under this Rule 8(a)(2) must be filed with the circuit clerk and normally will be considered by a panel of the court. But in an exceptional case in which time requirements make that procedure impracticable, the motion may be made to and considered by a single judge.

(E) The court may condition relief on a party's filing a bond or other security in the district court.

(b) Proceeding Against a Security Provider. If a party gives security with one or more security providers, each provider submits to the jurisdiction of the district court and irrevocably appoints the district clerk as its agent on whom any papers affecting its liability on the security may be served. On motion, a security provider's liability may be enforced in the district court without the necessity of an independent action. The motion and any notice that the district court prescribes may be served on the district clerk, who must promptly send a copy to each security provider whose address is known.

(c) Stay in a Criminal Case. Rule 38 of the Federal Rules of Criminal Procedure governs a stay in a criminal case.

(As amended Mar. 10, 1986, eff. July 1, 1986; Apr. 27, 1995, eff. Dec. 1, 1995; Apr. 24, 1998, eff. Dec. 1, 1998; Apr. 26, 2018, eff. Dec. 1, 2018.)

TITLE V. EXTRAORDINARY WRITS

Rule 21. Writs of Mandamus and Prohibition, and Other Extraordinary Writs

(a) Mandamus or Prohibition to a Court: Petition, Filing, Service, and Docketing.

(1) A party petitioning for a writ of mandamus or prohibition directed to a court must file the petition with the circuit clerk and serve it on all parties to the proceeding in the trial court. The party must also provide a copy to the trial-court judge. All parties to the proceeding in the trial court other than the petitioner are respondents for all purposes.

(2)(A) The petition must be titled "In re [name of petitioner]."

(B) The petition must state:

(i) the relief sought;

(ii) the issues presented;

(iii) the facts necessary to understand the issues presented by the petition; and

(iv) the reasons why the writ should issue.

(C) The petition must include a copy of any order or opinion or parts of the record that may be essential to understand the matters set forth in the petition.

(3) Upon receiving the prescribed docket fee, the clerk must docket the petition and submit it to the court.

(b) Denial; Order Directing Answer; Briefs; Precedence.

(1) The court may deny the petition without an answer. Otherwise, it must order the respondent, if any, to answer within a fixed time.

(2) The clerk must serve the order to respond on all persons directed to respond.

(3) Two or more respondents may answer jointly.

(4) The court of appeals may invite or order the trial-court judge to address the petition or may invite an amicus curiae to do so. The trial-court judge may request permission to address the petition but may not do so unless invited or ordered to do so by the court of appeals.

(5) If briefing or oral argument is required, the clerk must advise the parties, and when appropriate, the trial-court judge or amicus curiae.

(6) The proceeding must be given preference over ordinary civil cases.

(7) The circuit clerk must send a copy of the final disposition to the trial-court judge.

(c) Other Extraordinary Writs. An application for an extraordinary writ other than one provided for in Rule 21(a) must be made by filing a petition with the circuit clerk and serving it on the respondents. Proceedings on the application must conform, so far as is practicable, to the procedures prescribed in Rule 21(a) and (b).

(d) Form of Papers; Number of Copies; Length Limits. All papers must conform to Rule 32(c)(2). An original and 3 copies must be filed unless the court requires the filing of a different number by local rule or by order in a particular case. Except by the court's permission, and excluding the accompanying documents required by Rule 21(a)(2)(C):

(1) a paper produced using a computer must not exceed 7,800 words; and

(2) a handwritten or typewritten paper must not exceed 30 pages.

(As amended Apr. 29, 1994, eff. Dec. 1, 1994; Apr. 23, 1996, eff. Dec. 1, 1996; Apr. 24, 1998, eff. Dec. 1, 1998; Apr. 29, 2002, eff. Dec. 1, 2002; Apr. 28, 2016, eff. Dec. 1, 2016; Apr. 25, 2019, eff. Dec. 1, 2019.)

TITLE VII. GENERAL PROVISIONS

Rule 25. Filing and Service

(a) Filing.

(1) Filing with the Clerk. A paper required or permitted to be filed in a court of appeals must be filed with the clerk.

(2) Filing: Method and Timeliness.

(A) Nonelectronic Filing.

(i) In General. For a paper not filed electronically, filing may be accomplished by mail addressed to the clerk, but filing is not timely unless the clerk receives the papers within the time fixed for filing.

(ii) A Brief or Appendix. A brief or appendix not filed electronically is timely filed, however, if on or before the last day for filing, it is:

- mailed to the clerk by first-class mail, or other class of mail that is at least as expeditious, postage prepaid; or

- dispatched to a third-party commercial carrier for delivery to the clerk within 3 days.

(iii) Inmate Filing. If an institution has a system designed for legal mail, an inmate confined there must use that system to receive the benefit of this Rule 25(a)(2)(A)(iii). A paper not filed electronically by an inmate is timely if it is deposited in the institution's internal mail system on or before the last day for filing and:

- it is accompanied by: a declaration in compliance with 28 U.S.C. § 1746—or a notarized statement—setting out the date of deposit and stating that first-class postage is being prepaid; or evidence (such as a postmark or date stamp) showing that the paper was so deposited and that postage was prepaid; or
- the court of appeals exercises its discretion to permit the later filing of a declaration or notarized statement that satisfies Rule 25(a)(2)(A)(iii).

(B) Electronic Filing and Signing.

(i) By a Represented Person—Generally Required; Exceptions. A person represented by an attorney must file electronically, unless nonelectronic filing is allowed by the court for good cause or is allowed or required by local rule.

(ii) By an Unrepresented Person—When Allowed or Required. A person not represented by an attorney:

- may file electronically only if allowed by court order or by local rule; and
- may be required to file electronically only by court order, or by a local rule that includes reasonable exceptions.

(iii) Signing. A filing made through a person's electronic-filing account and authorized by that person, together with that person's name on a signature block, constitutes the person's signature.

(iv) Same as a Written Paper. A paper filed electronically is a written paper for purposes of these rules.

(3) Filing a Motion with a Judge. If a motion requests relief that may be granted by a single judge, the judge may permit the motion to be filed with the judge; the judge must note the filing date on the motion and give it to the clerk.

(4) Clerk's Refusal of Documents. The clerk must not refuse to accept for filing any paper presented for that purpose solely because it is not presented in proper form as required by these rules or by any local rule or practice.

(5) Privacy Protection. An appeal in a case whose privacy protection was governed by Federal Rule of Bankruptcy Procedure 9037, Federal Rule of Civil Procedure 5.2, or Federal Rule of Criminal Procedure 49.1 is governed by the same rule on appeal. In all other proceedings, privacy protection is governed by Federal Rule of Civil Procedure 5.2, except that Federal Rule of Criminal Procedure 49.1 governs when an extraordinary writ is sought in a criminal case. The provisions on remote electronic access in Federal Rule of Civil Procedure 5.2(c)(1) and (2) apply in a petition for review of a benefits decision of the Railroad Retirement Board under the Railroad Retirement Act.

(b) Service of All Papers Required. Unless a rule requires service by the clerk, a party must, at or before the time of filing a paper, serve a copy on the other parties to the appeal or review. Service on a party represented by counsel must be made on the party's counsel.

(c) Manner of Service.

(1) Nonelectronic service may be any of the following:

(A) personal, including delivery to a responsible person at the office of counsel;

(B) by mail; or

(C) by third-party commercial carrier for delivery within 3 days.

(2) Electronic service of a paper may be made (A) by sending it to a registered user by filing it with the court's electronic-filing system or (B) by sending it by other electronic means that the person to be served consented to in writing.

(3) When reasonable considering such factors as the immediacy of the relief sought, distance, and cost, service on a party must be by a manner at least as expeditious as the manner used to file the paper with the court.

(4) Service by mail or by commercial carrier is complete on mailing or delivery to the carrier. Service by electronic means is complete on filing or sending, unless the party making service is notified that the paper was not received by the party served.

(d) Proof of Service.

(1) A paper presented for filing shall contain either of the following if it was served other than through the court's electronic-filing system:

(A) an acknowledgment of service by the person served; or

(B) proof of service consisting of a statement by the person who made service certifying:

(i) the date and manner of service;

(ii) the names of the persons served; and

(iii) their mail or electronic addresses, facsimile numbers, or the addresses of the places of delivery, as appropriate for the manner of service.

(2) When a brief or appendix is filed by mailing or dispatch in accordance with Rule 25(a)(2)(A)(ii), the proof of service must also state the date and manner by which the document was mailed or dispatched to the clerk.

(3) Proof of service may appear on or be affixed to the papers filed.

(e) Number of Copies. When these rules require the filing or furnishing of a number of copies, a court may require a different number by local rule or by order in a particular case.

(As amended Mar. 10, 1986, eff. July 1, 1986; Apr. 30, 1991, eff. Dec. 1, 1991; Apr. 22, 1993, eff. Dec. 1, 1993; Apr. 29, 1994, eff. Dec. 1, 1994; Apr. 23, 1996, eff. Dec. 1, 1996; Apr. 24, 1998, eff. Dec. 1, 1998; Apr. 29, 2002, eff. Dec. 1, 2002; Apr. 12, 2006, eff. Dec. 1, 2006; Apr. 30, 2007, eff. Dec. 1, 2007; Mar. 26, 2009, eff. Dec. 1, 2009; Apr. 28, 2016, eff. Dec. 1, 2016; Apr. 26, 2018, eff. Dec. 1, 2018; Apr. 25, 2019, eff. Dec. 1, 2019; Apr. 11, 2022, eff. Dec. 1, 2022.)

Rule 26. Computing and Extending Time

(a) Computing Time. The following rules apply in computing any time period specified in these rules, in any local rule or court order, or in any statute that does not specify a method of computing time.

(1) Period Stated in Days or a Longer Unit. When the period is stated in days or a longer unit of time:

(A) exclude the day of the event that triggers the period;

(B) count every day, including intermediate Saturdays, Sundays, and legal holidays; and

(C) include the last day of the period, but if the last day is a Saturday, Sunday, or legal holiday, the period continues to run until the end of the next day that is not a Saturday, Sunday, or legal holiday.

(2) Period Stated in Hours. When the period is stated in hours:

(A) begin counting immediately on the occurrence of the event that triggers the period;

(B) count every hour, including hours during intermediate Saturdays, Sundays, and legal holidays; and

(C) if the period would end on a Saturday, Sunday, or legal holiday, the period continues to run until the same time on the next day that is not a Saturday, Sunday, or legal holiday.

(3) Inaccessibility of the Clerk's Office. Unless the court orders otherwise, if the clerk's office is inaccessible:

(A) on the last day for filing under Rule 26(a)(1), then the time for filing is extended to the first accessible day that is not a Saturday, Sunday, or legal holiday; or

(B) during the last hour for filing under Rule 26(a)(2), then the time for filing is extended to the same time on the first accessible day that is not a Saturday, Sunday, or legal holiday.

(4) "Last Day" Defined. Unless a different time is set by a statute, local rule, or court order, the last day ends:

(A) for electronic filing in the district court, at midnight in the court's time zone;

(B) for electronic filing in the court of appeals, at midnight in the time zone of the circuit clerk's principal office;

(C) for filing under Rules 4(c)(1), 25(a)(2)(A)(ii), and 25(a)(2)(A)(iii)—and filing by mail under Rule 13(a)(2)—at the latest time for the method chosen for delivery to the post office, third-party commercial carrier, or prison mailing system; and

(D) for filing by other means, when the clerk's office is scheduled to close.

(5) "Next Day" Defined. The "next day" is determined by continuing to count forward when the period is measured after an event and backward when measured before an event.

(6) "Legal Holiday" Defined. "Legal holiday" means:

(A) the day set aside by statute for observing New Year's Day, Martin Luther King Jr.'s Birthday, Washington's Birthday, Memorial Day, Juneteenth National Independence Day,

Independence Day, Labor Day, Columbus Day, Veterans' Day, Thanksgiving Day, or Christmas Day;

(B) any day declared a holiday by the President or Congress; and

(C) for periods that are measured after an event, any other day declared a holiday by the state where either of the following is located: the district court that rendered the challenged judgment or order, or the circuit clerk's principal office.

(b) Extending Time. For good cause, the court may extend the time prescribed by these rules or by its order to perform any act, or may permit an act to be done after that time expires. But the court may not extend the time to file:

(1) a notice of appeal (except as authorized in Rule 4) or a petition for permission to appeal; or

(2) a notice of appeal from or a petition to enjoin, set aside, suspend, modify, enforce, or otherwise review an order of an administrative agency, board, commission, or officer of the United States, unless specifically authorized by law.

(c) Additional Time after Certain Kinds of Service. When a party may or must act within a specified time after being served, and the paper is not served electronically on the party or delivered to the party on the date stated in the proof of service, 3 days are added after the period would otherwise expire under Rule 26(a).

(As amended Mar. 1, 1971, eff. July 1, 1971; Mar. 10, 1986, eff. July 1, 1986; Apr. 25, 1989, eff. Dec. 1, 1989; Apr. 30, 1991, eff. Dec. 1, 1991; Apr. 23, 1996, eff. Dec. 1, 1996; Apr. 24, 1998, eff. Dec. 1, 1998; Apr. 29, 2002, eff. Dec. 1, 2002; Apr. 25, 2005, eff. Dec. 1, 2005; Mar. 26, 2009, eff. Dec. 1, 2009; Apr. 28, 2016, eff. Dec. 1, 2016; Apr. 26, 2018, eff. Dec. 1, 2018; Apr. 25, 2019, eff. Dec. 1, 2019; Apr. 24, 2023, eff. Dec. 1, 2023.)

Rule 32.1. Citing Judicial Dispositions

(a) Citation Permitted. A court may not prohibit or restrict the citation of federal judicial opinions, orders, judgments, or other written dispositions that have been:

(i) designated as "unpublished," "not for publication," "non-precedential," "not precedent," or the like; and

(ii) issued on or after January 1, 2007.

(b) Copies Required. If a party cites a federal judicial opinion, order, judgment, or other written disposition that is not available in a publicly accessible electronic database, the party must file and serve a copy of that opinion, order, judgment, or disposition with the brief or other paper in which it is cited.

(Added Apr. 12, 2006, eff. Dec. 1, 2006.)

Rule 38. Frivolous Appeal—Damages and Costs

If a court of appeals determines that an appeal is frivolous, it may, after a separately filed motion or notice from the court and reasonable opportunity to respond, award just damages and single or double costs to the appellee.

(As amended Apr. 29, 1994, eff. Dec. 1, 1994; Apr. 24, 1998, eff. Dec. 1, 1998.)

Rule 39. Costs

(a) Allocating Costs Among the Parties. The following rules apply to allocating taxable costs among the parties unless the law provides, the parties agree, or the court orders otherwise:

(1) if an appeal is dismissed, costs are allocated against the appellant;

(2) if a judgment is affirmed, costs are allocated against the appellant;

(3) if a judgment is reversed, costs are allocated against the appellee;

(4) if a judgment is affirmed in part, reversed in part, modified, or vacated, each party bears its own costs.

(b) Reconsideration. Once the allocation of costs is established by the entry of judgment, a party may seek reconsideration of that allocation by filing a motion in the court of appeals within 14 days after the entry of judgment. But issuance of the mandate under Rule 41 must not be delayed awaiting a determination of the motion. The court of appeals retains jurisdiction to decide the motion after the mandate issues.

(c) Costs Governed by Allocation Determination. The allocation of costs applies both to costs taxable in the court of appeals under Rule 39(e) and to costs taxable in district court under Rule 39(f).

(d) Costs For and Against the United States. Costs for or against the United States, its agency, or officer will be allocated under Rule 39(a) only if authorized by law.

(e) Costs on Appeal Taxable in the Court of Appeals.

(1) Costs Taxable. The following costs on appeal are taxable in the court of appeals for the benefit of the party entitled to costs:

(A) the production of necessary copies of a brief or appendix, or copies of records authorized by Rule 30(f);

(B) the docketing fee; and

(C) a filing fee paid in the court of appeals.

(2) Costs of Copies. Each court of appeals must, by local rule, set the maximum rate for taxing the cost of producing necessary copies of a brief or appendix, or copies of records authorized by Rule 30(f). The rate must not exceed that generally charged for such work in the area where the clerk's office is located and should encourage economical methods of copying.

(3) Bill of Costs: Objections; Insertion in Mandate.

(A) A party who wants costs taxed in the court of appeals must—within 14 days after judgment is entered—file with the circuit clerk and serve an itemized and verified bill of those costs.

(B) Objections must be filed within 14 days after the bill of costs is served, unless the court extends the time.

(C) The clerk must prepare and certify an itemized statement of costs for insertion in the mandate, but issuance of the mandate must not be delayed for taxing costs. If the mandate issues before costs are finally determined, the district clerk must—upon the circuit clerk's request—add the statement of costs, or any amendment of it, to the mandate.

(f) Costs on Appeal Taxable in the District Court. The following costs on appeal are taxable in the district court for the benefit of the party entitled to costs:

(1) the preparation and transmission of the record;

(2) the reporter's transcript, if needed to determine the appeal;

(3) premiums paid for a bond or other security to preserve rights pending appeal; and

(4) the fee for filing the notice of appeal.

(As amended Apr. 30, 1979, eff. Aug. 1, 1979; Mar. 10, 1986, eff. July 1, 1986; Apr. 24, 1998, eff. Dec. 1, 1998; Mar. 26, 2009, eff. Dec. 1, 2009; Apr. 26, 2018, eff. Dec. 1, 2018; Apr. 25, 2019, eff. Dec. 1, 2019; Apr. 23, 2025, eff. Dec. 1, 2025.)

Rule 40. Panel Rehearing; En Banc Determination

(a) A Party's Options. A party may seek rehearing of a decision through a petition for panel rehearing, a petition for rehearing en banc, or both. Unless a local rule provides otherwise, a party seeking both forms of rehearing must file the petitions as a single document. Panel rehearing is the ordinary means of reconsidering a panel decision; rehearing en banc is not favored.

(b) Content of a Petition.

(1) Petition for Panel Rehearing. A petition for panel rehearing must:

(A) state with particularity each point of law or fact that the petitioner believes the court has overlooked or misapprehended; and

(B) argue in support of the petition.

(2) Petition for Rehearing En Banc. A petition for rehearing en banc must begin with a statement that:

(A) the panel decision conflicts with a decision of the court to which the petition is addressed (with citation to the conflicting case or cases) and the full court's consideration is therefore necessary to secure or maintain uniformity of the court's decisions;

(B) the panel decision conflicts with a decision of the United States Supreme Court (with citation to the conflicting case or cases);

(C) the panel decision conflicts with an authoritative decision of another United States court of appeals (with citation to the conflicting case or cases); or

(D) the proceeding involves one or more questions of exceptional importance, each concisely stated.

(c) When Rehearing En Banc May Be Ordered. On their own or in response to a party's petition, a majority of the circuit judges who are in regular active service and who are not disqualified may order that an appeal or other proceeding be reheard en banc. Unless a judge calls for a vote, a vote need not be taken to determine whether the case will be so reheard. Rehearing en banc is not favored and ordinarily will be allowed only if one of the criteria in Rule 40(b)(2)(A)–(D) is met.

(d) Time to File; Form; Length; Response; Oral Argument.

(1) Time. Unless the time is shortened or extended by order or local rule, any petition for panel rehearing or rehearing en banc must be filed within 14 days after judgment is entered—or, if the panel later amends its decision (on rehearing or otherwise), within 14 days after the amended decision is entered. But in a civil case, unless an order shortens or extends the time, the petition may be filed by any party within 45 days after entry of judgment or of an amended decision if one of the parties is:

(A) the United States;

(B) a United States agency;

(C) a United States officer or employee sued in an official capacity; or

(D) a current or former United States officer or employee sued in an individual capacity for an act or omission occurring in connection with duties performed on the United States' behalf—including all instances in which the United States represents that person when the court of appeals' judgment is entered or files that person's petition.

(2) Form of the Petition. The petition must comply in form with Rule 32. Copies must be filed and served as Rule 31 prescribes, except that the number of filed copies may be prescribed by local rule or altered by order in a particular case.

(3) Length. Unless the court or a local rule allows otherwise, the petition (or a single document containing a petition for panel rehearing and a petition for rehearing en banc) must not exceed:

(A) 3,900 words if produced using a computer; or

(B) 15 pages if handwritten or typewritten.

(4) Response. Unless the court so requests, no response to the petition is permitted. Ordinarily, the petition will not be granted without such a request. If a response is requested, the requirements of Rule 40(d)(2)–(3) apply to the response.

(5) Oral Argument. Oral argument on whether to grant the petition is not permitted.

(e) If a Petition Is Granted. If a petition for panel rehearing or rehearing en banc is granted, the court may:

(1) dispose of the case without further briefing or argument;

(2) order additional briefing or argument; or

(3) issue any other appropriate order.

(f) Panel's Authority After a Petition for Rehearing En Banc. The filing of a petition for rehearing en banc does not limit the panel's authority to take action described in Rule 40(e).

(g) Initial Hearing En Banc. On its own or in response to a party's petition, a court may hear an appeal or other proceeding initially en banc. A party's petition must be filed no later than the date when its principal brief is due. The provisions of Rule 40(b)(2), (c), and (d)(2)–(5) apply to an initial hearing en banc. But initial hearing en banc is not favored and ordinarily will not be ordered.

(As amended Apr. 30, 1979, eff. Aug. 1, 1979; Apr. 29, 1994, eff. Dec. 1, 1994; Apr. 24, 1998, eff. Dec. 1, 1998; Apr. 26, 2011, eff. Dec. 1, 2011; Apr. 28, 2016, eff. Dec. 1, 2016; Apr. 27, 2020, eff. Dec. 1, 2020; Apr. 2, 2024, eff. Dec. 1, 2024.)

Rule 48. Masters

(a) Appointment; Powers. A court of appeals may appoint a special master to hold hearings, if necessary, and to recommend factual findings and disposition in matters ancillary to proceedings in the court. Unless the order referring a matter to a master specifies or limits the master's powers, those powers include, but are not limited to, the following:

(1) regulating all aspects of a hearing;

(2) taking all appropriate action for the efficient performance of the master's duties under the order;

(3) requiring the production of evidence upon all matters embraced in the reference; and

(4) administering oaths and examining witnesses and parties.

(b) If the master is not a judge or court employee, the court must determine the master's compensation and whether the cost is to be charged to any party.

(As amended Apr. 29, 1994, eff. Dec. 1, 1994; Apr. 24, 1998, eff. Dec. 1, 1998.)

SELECTED PROVISIONS OF THE CONSTITUTION OF THE UNITED STATES

■ ■ ■

Table of Contents

PREAMBLE

We the People of the United States, in Order to form a more perfect Union, establish Justice, insure domestic Tranquility, provide for the common defense, promote the general Welfare, and secure the Blessings of Liberty to ourselves and our Posterity, do ordain and establish this Constitution for the United States of America.

ARTICLE I.

* * *

Section 8. The Congress shall have Power To lay and collect Taxes, Duties, Imposts and Excises, to pay the Debts and provide for the common Defense and general Welfare of the United States; but all Duties, Imposts and Excises shall be uniform throughout the United States;

To borrow Money on the credit of the United States;

To regulate Commerce with foreign Nations, and among the several States, and with the Indian Tribes;

To establish an uniform Rule of Naturalization, and uniform Laws on the subject of Bankruptcies throughout the United States;

To coin Money, regulate the Value thereof, and of foreign Coin, and fix the Standard of Weights and Measures;

To provide for the Punishment of counterfeiting the Securities and current Coin of the United States;

To establish Post Offices and post Roads;

To promote the Progress of Science and useful Arts, by securing for limited Times to Authors and Inventors the exclusive Right to their respective Writings and Discoveries;

To constitute Tribunals inferior to the supreme Court;

To define and punish Piracies and Felonies committed on the high Seas, and Offences against the Law of Nations;

To declare War, grant Letters of Marque and Reprisal, and make Rules concerning Captures on Land and Water;

To raise and support Armies, but no Appropriation of Money to that Use shall be for a longer Term than two Years;

To provide and maintain a Navy;

To make Rules for the Government and Regulation of the land and naval Forces;

To provide for calling forth the Militia to execute the Laws of the Union, suppress Insurrections and repel Invasions;

To provide for organizing, arming, and disciplining, the Militia, and for governing such Part of them as may be employed in the Service of the United States, reserving to the States respectively, the Appointment of the Officers, and the Authority of training the Militia according to the discipline prescribed by Congress;

To exercise exclusive Legislation in all Cases whatsoever, over such District (not exceeding ten Miles square) as may, by Cession of particular States, and the Acceptance of Congress, become the Seat of the Government of the United States, and to exercise like Authority over all Places purchased by the Consent of the Legislature of the State in which the same shall be, for the Erection of Forts, Magazines, Arsenals, dock-Yards, and other needful Buildings;—And

To make all Laws which shall be necessary and proper for carrying into Execution the foregoing Powers, and all other Powers vested by this Constitution in the Government of the United States, or in any Department or Officer thereof.

* * *

ARTICLE III.

Section 1. The judicial Power of the United States, shall be vested in one supreme Court, and in such inferior Courts as the Congress may from time to time ordain and establish. The Judges, both of the supreme and inferior Courts, shall hold their Offices during good Behavior, and shall, at stated Times, receive for their Services, a Compensation, which shall not be diminished during their Continuance in Office.

Section 2. The judicial Power shall extend to all Cases, in Law and Equity, arising under this Constitution, the Laws of the United States, and Treaties made, or which shall be made, under their Authority;—to all Cases affecting Ambassadors, other public Ministers and Consuls;—to all Cases of admiralty and maritime Jurisdiction;—to Controversies to which the United States shall be a Party;—to Controversies between two or more States;—between a State and Citizens of another State;—between Citizens of different States;—between Citizens of the same State claiming Lands under Grants of different States, and between a State, or the Citizens thereof, and foreign States, Citizens or Subjects.

In all Cases affecting Ambassadors, other public Ministers and Consuls, and those in which a State shall be Party, the supreme Court shall have original Jurisdiction. In all the other Cases before mentioned, the supreme Court shall have appellate Jurisdiction, both as to Law and Fact, with such Exceptions, and under such Regulations as the Congress shall make.

The Trial of all Crimes, except in Cases of Impeachment, shall be by Jury; and such Trial shall be held in the State where the said Crimes shall have been committed; but when not committed within any State, the Trial shall be at such Place or Places as the Congress may by Law have directed.

* * *

ARTICLE IV.

Section 1. Full Faith and Credit shall be given in each State to the public Acts, Records, and judicial Proceedings of every other State. And the Congress may by general Laws prescribe the Manner in which such Acts, Records and Proceedings shall be proved, and the Effect thereof.

Section 2. The Citizens of each State shall be entitled to all Privileges and Immunities of Citizens in the several States.

* * *

ARTICLE VI.

* * *

This Constitution, and the Laws of the United States which shall be made in Pursuance thereof; and all Treaties made, or which shall be made, under the Authority of the United States, shall be the supreme Law of the Land; and the Judges in every State shall be bound thereby, any Thing in the Constitution or Laws of any State to the Contrary notwithstanding.

* * *

AMENDMENT I. [1791]

Congress shall make no law respecting an establishment of religion, or prohibiting the free exercise thereof; or abridging the freedom of speech, or of the press; or the right of the people peaceably to assemble, and to petition the Government for a redress of grievances.

* * *

AMENDMENT IV. [1791]

The right of the people to be secure in their persons, houses, papers, and effects, against unreasonable searches and seizures, shall not be violated, and no Warrants shall issue, but upon probable cause, supported by Oath or affirmation, and particularly describing the place to be searched, and the persons or things to be seized.

AMENDMENT V. [1791]

No person shall be held to answer for a capital, or otherwise infamous crime, unless on a presentment or indictment of a Grand Jury, except in cases arising in the land or naval forces, or in the Militia, when in actual service in time of War or public danger; nor shall any person be subject for the same offence to be twice put in jeopardy of life or limb; nor shall be compelled in any criminal case to be a witness against himself, nor be deprived of life, liberty, or property, without due process of law; nor shall private property be taken for public use, without just compensation.

AMENDMENT VI. [1791]

In all criminal prosecutions, the accused shall enjoy the right to a speedy and public trial, by an impartial jury of the State and district wherein the crime shall have been committed, which district shall have been previously ascertained by law, and to be informed of the nature and cause of the accusation; to be confronted with the witnesses against him; to have compulsory process for obtaining witnesses in his favor, and to have the Assistance of Counsel for his defense.

AMENDMENT VII. [1791]

In Suits at common law, where the value in controversy shall exceed twenty dollars, the right of trial by jury shall be preserved, and no fact tried by a jury, shall be otherwise re-examined in any Court of the United States, than according to the rules of the common law.

AMENDMENT VIII. [1791]

Excessive bail shall not be required, nor excessive fines imposed, nor cruel and unusual punishments inflicted.

AMENDMENT IX. [1791]

The enumeration in the Constitution, of certain rights, shall not be construed to deny or disparage others retained by the people.

The powers not delegated to the United States by the Constitution, nor prohibited by it to the States, are reserved to the States respectively, or to the people.

AMENDMENT X. [1791]

The powers not delegated to the United States by the Constitution, nor prohibited by it to the States, are reserved to the States respectively, or to the people.

AMENDMENT XI. [1798]

The Judicial power of the United States shall not be construed to extend to any suit in law or equity, commenced or prosecuted against one of the United States by Citizens of another State, or by Citizens or Subjects of any Foreign State.

* * *

AMENDMENT XIV. [1868]

Section 1. All persons born or naturalized in the United States, and subject to the jurisdiction thereof, are citizens of the United States and of the State wherein they reside. No State shall make or enforce any law which shall abridge the privileges or immunities of citizens of the United States; nor shall any State deprive any person of life, liberty, or property, without due process of law; nor deny to any person within its jurisdiction the equal protection of the laws.

* * *

Section 5. The Congress shall have power to enforce, by appropriate legislation, the provisions of this article.

Selected Provisions of Title 28, United States Code—Judiciary and Judicial Procedure

■ ■ ■

As Amended to January 1, 2026

§ 41. Number and Composition of Circuits

The thirteen judicial circuits of the United States are constituted as follows:

Circuits	Composition
District of Columbia	District of Columbia.
First	Maine, Massachusetts, New Hampshire, Puerto Rico, Rhode Island.
Second	Connecticut, New York, Vermont.
Third	Delaware, New Jersey, Pennsylvania, Virgin Islands.
Fourth	Maryland, North Carolina, South Carolina, Virginia, West Virginia.
Fifth	District of the Canal Zone, Louisiana, Mississippi, Texas.
Sixth	Kentucky, Michigan, Ohio, Tennessee.
Seventh	Illinois, Indiana, Wisconsin.
Eighth	Arkansas, Iowa, Minnesota, Missouri, Nebraska, North Dakota, South Dakota.
Ninth	Alaska, Arizona, California, Idaho, Montana, Nevada, Oregon, Washington, Guam, Hawaii.
Tenth	Colorado, Kansas, New Mexico, Oklahoma, Utah, Wyoming.
Eleventh	Alabama, Florida, Georgia.
Federal	All Federal judicial districts.

(As amended Oct. 31, 1951, c. 655, § 34, 65 Stat. 723; Oct. 14, 1980, Pub.L. 96–452, § 2, 94 Stat. 1994; Apr. 2, 1982, Pub.L. 97–164, Title I, § 101, 96 Stat. 25.)

§ 133. Appointment and Number of District Judges

(a) The President shall appoint, by and with the advice and consent of the Senate, district judges for the several judicial districts, as follows:

Districts	Judges
Alabama:	
Northern	7
Middle	3

Districts	Judges
Southern	3
Alaska	3
Arizona	8
Arkansas:	
Eastern	5
Western	3
California:	
Northern	14
Eastern	6
Central	27
Southern	13
Colorado	7
Connecticut	8
Delaware	4
District of Columbia	15
Florida:	
Northern	4
Middle	15
Southern	17
Georgia:	
Northern	11
Middle	4
Southern	3
Hawaii	3
Idaho	2
Illinois:	
Northern	22
Central	4
Southern	4
Indiana:	
Northern	5
Southern	5
Iowa:	
Northern	2
Southern	3

Districts	Judges
Kansas	5
Kentucky:	
Eastern	5
Western	4
Eastern and Western	1
Louisiana:	
Eastern	12
Middle	3
Western	7
Maine	3
Maryland	10
Massachusetts	13
Michigan:	
Eastern	15
Western	4
Minnesota	7
Mississippi:	
Northern	3
Southern	6
Missouri:	
Eastern	6
Western	5
Eastern and Western	2
Montana	3
Nebraska	3
Nevada	7
New Hampshire	3
New Jersey	17
New Mexico	6
New York:	
Northern	5
Southern	28
Eastern	15
Western	4

Districts	Judges
North Carolina:	
Eastern	4
Middle	4
Western	4
North Dakota	2
Ohio:	
Northern	11
Southern	8
Oklahoma:	
Northern	3
Eastern	1
Western	6
Northern, Eastern, and Western	1
Oregon	6
Pennsylvania:	
Eastern	22
Middle	6
Western	10
Puerto Rico	7
Rhode Island	3
South Carolina	10
South Dakota	3
Tennessee:	
Eastern	5
Middle	4
Western	5
Texas:	
Northern	12
Southern	19
Eastern	7
Western	13
Utah	5
Vermont	2

Districts	Judges
Virginia:	
Eastern	11
Western	4
Washington:	
Eastern	4
Western	7
West Virginia:	
Northern	3
Southern	5
Wisconsin:	
Eastern	5
Western	2
Wyoming	3

(b)(1) In any case in which a judge of the United States (other than a senior judge) assumes the duties of a full-time office of Federal judicial administration, the President shall appoint, by and with the advice and consent of the Senate, an additional judge for the court of which such judge serves. If the judge who assumes the duties of such full-time office leaves that office and resumes the duties as an active judge of the court, then the President shall not appoint a judge to fill the first vacancy which occurs thereafter in that court.

(2) For purposes of paragraph (1), the term "office of Federal judicial administration" means a position as Director of the Federal Judicial Center, Director of the Administrative Office of the United States Courts, or Counselor to the Chief Justice.

(As amended Aug. 3, 1949, c. 387, § 2(a), 63 Stat. 493; Aug. 14, 1950, c. 708, 64 Stat. 443; Aug. 29, 1950, c. 819, § 1, 64 Stat. 562; Sept. 5, 1950, c. 848, § 1, 64 Stat. 578; Feb. 10, 1954, c. 6, § 2(a)(3), 68 Stat. 9; Sept. 7, 1957, Pub.L. 85–310, 71 Stat. 631; July 7, 1958, Pub.L. 85–508, § 12(c), 72 Stat. 348; Mar. 18, 1959, Pub.L. 86–3, § 9(b), 73 Stat. 8; May 19, 1961, Pub.L. 87–36, § 2(d), 75 Stat. 81; July 30, 1962, Pub.L. 87–562, § 3, 76 Stat. 248; Oct. 7, 1965, Pub.L. 89–242, § 1(c), 79 Stat. 951; Mar. 18, 1966, Pub.L. 89–372, § 4, 80 Stat. 77; June 2, 1970, Pub.L. 91–272, § 1(c), (d), 84 Stat. 294, 295; Dec. 18, 1971, Pub.L. 92–208, § 3(d), 85 Stat. 742; Oct. 2, 1978, Pub.L. 95–408, § 4(b)(2), 92 Stat. 885; Oct. 20, 1978, Pub.L. 95–486, § 1(c), 92 Stat. 1630; Jan. 14, 1983, Pub.L. 97–471, § 3, 96 Stat. 2601; July 10, 1984, Pub.L. 98–353, Title II, § 202(e), 98 Stat. 348; Dec. 1, 1990, Pub.L. 101–650, § 203(d), 104 Stat. 5089; Oct. 6, 1997, Pub.L. 102–53, § 4, 111 Stat. 1174; Nov. 29, 1999, Pub.L. 106–113, Div. B, § 1000(a)(1), 113 Stat. 1535, 1501A–37; Dec. 21, 2000, Pub.L. 106–553, § 1(a)(2), 114 Stat. 2762, 2762A–85; Nov. 2, 2002, Pub.L. 107–273, § 312(a)(2), 116 Stat. 1787, 1788; Oct. 13, 2008, Pub.L. 110–402, § 1(b)(1), 122 Stat. 4254.)

§ 455. Disqualification of Justice, Judge, or Magistrate Judge

(a) Any justice, judge, or magistrate judge of the United States shall disqualify himself in any proceeding in which his impartiality might reasonably be questioned.

(b) He shall also disqualify himself in the following circumstances:

(1) Where he has a personal bias or prejudice concerning a party, or personal knowledge of disputed evidentiary facts concerning the proceeding;

(2) Where in private practice he served as lawyer in the matter in controversy, or a lawyer with whom he previously practiced law served during such association as a lawyer concerning the matter, or the judge or such lawyer has been a material witness concerning it;

(3) Where he has served in governmental employment and in such capacity participated as counsel, adviser or material witness concerning the proceeding or expressed an opinion concerning the merits of the particular case in controversy;

(4) He knows that he, individually or as a fiduciary, or his spouse or minor child residing in his household, has a financial interest in the subject matter in controversy or in a party to the proceeding, or any other interest that could be substantially affected by the outcome of the proceeding;

(5) He or his spouse, or a person within the third degree of relationship to either of them, or the spouse of such a person:

> **(i)** Is a party to the proceeding, or an officer, director, or trustee of a party;
>
> **(ii)** Is acting as a lawyer in the proceeding;
>
> **(iii)** Is known by the judge to have an interest that could be substantially affected by the outcome of the proceeding;
>
> **(iv)** Is to the judge's knowledge likely to be a material witness in the proceeding.

(c) A judge should inform himself about his personal and fiduciary financial interests, and make a reasonable effort to inform himself about the personal financial interests of his spouse and minor children residing in his household.

(d) For the purposes of this section the following words or phrases shall have the meaning indicated:

(1) "proceeding" includes pretrial, trial, appellate review, or other stages of litigation;

(2) the degree of relationship is calculated according to the civil law system;

(3) "fiduciary" includes such relationships as executor, administrator, trustee, and guardian;

(4) "financial interest" means ownership of a legal or equitable interest, however small, or a relationship as director, adviser, or other active participant in the affairs of a party, except that:

(i) Ownership in a mutual or common investment fund that holds securities is not a "financial interest" in such securities unless the judge participates in the management of the fund;

(ii) An office in an educational, religious, charitable, fraternal, or civic organization is not a "financial interest" in securities held by the organization;

(iii) The proprietary interest of a policyholder in a mutual insurance company, of a depositor in a mutual savings association, or a similar proprietary interest, is a "financial interest" in the organization only if the outcome of the proceeding could substantially affect the value of the interest;

(iv) Ownership of government securities is a "financial interest" in the issuer only if the outcome of the proceeding could substantially affect the value of the securities.

(e) No justice, judge, or magistrate judge shall accept from the parties to the proceeding a waiver of any ground for disqualification enumerated in subsection (b). Where the ground for disqualification arises only under subsection (a), waiver may be accepted provided it is preceded by a full disclosure on the record of the basis for disqualification.

(f) Notwithstanding the preceding provisions of this section, if any justice, judge, magistrate judge, or bankruptcy judge to whom a matter has been assigned would be disqualified, after substantial judicial time has been devoted to the matter, because of the appearance or discovery, after the matter was assigned to him or her, that he or she individually or as a fiduciary, or his or her spouse or minor child residing in his or her household, has a financial interest in a party (other than an interest that could be substantially affected by the outcome), disqualification is not required if the justice, judge, magistrate judge, bankruptcy judge, spouse or minor child, as the case may be, divests himself or herself of the interest that provides the grounds for the disqualification.

(As amended, Dec. 5, 1974, Pub.L. 93–512, § 1, 88 Stat. 1609; Nov. 6, 1978, Pub.L. 95–598, § 214(a), (b), 92 Stat. 2661; Nov. 19, 1988, Pub.L. 100–702, § 1007, 102 Stat. 4667; Dec. 1, 1990, Pub.L. 101–650, § 321, 104 Stat. 5117.)

§ 636. Jurisdiction, Powers, and Temporary Assignment

(a) Each United States magistrate judge serving under this chapter shall have within the district in which sessions are held by the court that appointed the magistrate judge, at other places where that court may function, and elsewhere as authorized by law—

(1) all powers and duties conferred or imposed upon United States commissioners by law or by the Rules of Criminal Procedure for the United States District Courts;

(2) the power to administer oaths and affirmations, issue orders pursuant to section 3142 of title 18 concerning release or detention of persons pending trial, and take acknowledgments, affidavits, and depositions;

(3) the power to conduct trials under section 3401, title 18, United States Code, in conformity with and subject to the limitations of that section;

(4) the power to enter a sentence for a petty offense; and

(5) the power to enter a sentence for a class A misdemeanor in a case in which the parties have consented.

(b)(1) Notwithstanding any provision of law to the contrary—

(A) a judge may designate a magistrate judge to hear and determine any pretrial matter pending before the court, except a motion for injunctive relief, for judgment on the pleadings, for summary judgment, to dismiss or quash an indictment or information made by the defendant, to suppress evidence in a criminal case, to dismiss or to permit maintenance of a class action, to dismiss for failure to state a claim upon which relief can be granted, and to involuntarily dismiss an action. A judge of the court may reconsider any pretrial matter under this subparagraph (A) where it has been shown that the magistrate judge's order is clearly erroneous or contrary to law.

(B) a judge may also designate a magistrate judge to conduct hearings, including evidentiary hearings, and to submit to a judge of the court proposed findings of fact and recommendations for the disposition, by a judge of the court, of any motion excepted in subparagraph (A), of applications for posttrial relief made by individuals convicted of criminal offenses and of prisoner petitions challenging conditions of confinement.

(C) the magistrate judge shall file his proposed findings and recommendations under subparagraph (B) with the court and a copy shall forthwith be mailed to all parties.

Within fourteen days after being served with a copy, any party may serve and file written objections to such proposed findings and recommendations as provided by rules of court. A judge of the court shall make a de novo determination of those portions of the report or specified proposed findings or recommendations to which objection is made. A judge of the court may accept, reject, or modify, in whole or in part, the findings or recommendations made by the magistrate judge. The judge may also receive further evidence or recommit the matter to the magistrate judge with instructions.

(2) A judge may designate a magistrate judge to serve as a special master pursuant to the applicable provisions of this title and the Federal Rules of Civil Procedure for the United States district courts. A judge may designate a magistrate judge to serve as a special master in any civil case, upon consent of the parties, without regard to the provisions of rule 53(b) of the Federal Rules of Civil Procedure for the United States district courts.

(3) A magistrate judge may be assigned such additional duties as are not inconsistent with the Constitution and laws of the United States.

(4) Each district court shall establish rules pursuant to which the magistrate judges shall discharge their duties.

(c) Notwithstanding any provision of law to the contrary—

(1) Upon the consent of the parties, a full-time United States magistrate judge or a part-time United States magistrate judge who serves as a full-time judicial officer may conduct any or all proceedings in a jury or nonjury civil matter and order the entry of judgment in the case, when specially designated to exercise such jurisdiction by the district court or courts he serves. Upon the consent of the parties, pursuant to their specific written request, any other part-time magistrate judge may exercise such jurisdiction, if such magistrate judge meets the bar membership requirements set forth in section 631(b)(1) and the chief judge of the district court certifies that a full-time magistrate judge is not reasonably available in accordance with guidelines established by the judicial council of the circuit. When there is more than one judge of a district court, designation under this paragraph shall be by the concurrence of a majority of all the judges of such district court, and when there is no such concurrence, then by the chief judge.

(2) If a magistrate judge is designated to exercise civil jurisdiction under paragraph (1) of this subsection, the clerk of court shall, at the time the action is filed, notify the parties of the availability of a magistrate judge to exercise such jurisdiction. The decision of the parties shall be communicated to the clerk of court. Thereafter, either the district court judge or the magistrate judge may again advise the parties of the availability of the magistrate judge, but in so doing, shall also advise the parties that they are free to withhold consent without adverse substantive consequences. Rules of court for the reference of civil matters to magistrate judges shall include procedures to protect the voluntariness of the parties' consent.

(3) Upon entry of judgment in any case referred under paragraph (1) of this subsection, an aggrieved party may appeal directly to the appropriate United States court of appeals from the judgment of the magistrate judge in the same manner as an appeal from any other judgment of a district court. The consent of the parties allows a magistrate judge designated to exercise civil jurisdiction under paragraph (1) of this subsection to direct the entry of a judgment of the district court in accordance with the Federal Rules of Civil Procedure. Nothing in this paragraph shall be construed as a limitation of any party's right to seek review by the Supreme Court of the United States.

(4) The court may, for good cause shown on its own motion, or under extraordinary circumstances shown by any party, vacate a reference of a civil matter to a magistrate judge under this subsection.

(5) The magistrate judge shall, subject to guidelines of the Judicial Conference, determine whether the record taken pursuant to this section shall be taken by electronic sound recording, by a court reporter, or by other means.

(d) The practice and procedure for the trial of cases before officers serving under this chapter shall conform to rules promulgated by the Supreme Court pursuant to section 2072 of this title.

(e) Contempt authority.—

(1) In general.—A United States magistrate judge serving under this chapter shall have within the territorial jurisdiction prescribed by the appointment of such magistrate judge the power to exercise contempt authority as set forth in this subsection.

(2) Summary criminal contempt authority.—A magistrate judge shall have the power to punish summarily by fine or imprisonment, or both, such contempt of the authority of such magistrate judge constituting misbehavior of any person in the magistrate judge's presence so as to obstruct the administration of justice. The order of contempt shall be issued under the Federal Rules of Criminal Procedure.

(3) Additional criminal contempt authority in civil consent and misdemeanor cases.—In any case in which a United States magistrate judge presides with the consent of the parties under subsection (c) of this section, and in any misdemeanor case proceeding before a magistrate judge under section 3401 of title 18, the magistrate judge shall have the power to punish, by fine or imprisonment, or both, criminal contempt constituting disobedience or resistance to the magistrate judge's lawful writ, process, order, rule, decree, or command. Disposition of such contempt shall be conducted upon notice and hearing under the Federal Rules of Criminal Procedure.

(4) Civil contempt authority in civil consent and misdemeanor cases.—In any case in which a United States magistrate judge presides with the consent of the parties under subsection (c) of this section, and in any misdemeanor case proceeding before a magistrate judge under section 3401 of title 18, the magistrate judge may exercise the civil contempt authority of the district court. This paragraph shall not be construed to limit the authority of a magistrate judge to order sanctions under any other statute, the Federal Rules of Civil Procedure, or the Federal Rules of Criminal Procedure.

(5) Criminal contempt penalties.—The sentence imposed by a magistrate judge for any criminal contempt provided for in paragraphs (2) and (3) shall not exceed the penalties for a Class C misdemeanor as set forth in sections 3581(b)(8) and 3571(b)(6) of title 18.

(6) Certification of other contempts to the district court.—Upon the commission of any such act—

(A) in any case in which a United States magistrate judge presides with the consent of the parties under subsection (c) of this section, or in any misdemeanor case proceeding before a magistrate judge under section 3401 of title 18, that may, in the opinion of the magistrate judge, constitute a serious criminal contempt punishable by penalties exceeding those set forth in paragraph (5) of this subsection, or

(B) in any other case or proceeding under subsection (a) or (b) of this section, or any other statute, where—

(i) the act committed in the magistrate judge's presence may, in the opinion of the magistrate judge, constitute a serious criminal contempt punishable by penalties exceeding those set forth in paragraph (5) of this subsection,

(ii) the act that constitutes a criminal contempt occurs outside the presence of the magistrate judge, or

(iii) the act constitutes a civil contempt, the magistrate judge shall forthwith certify the facts to a district judge and may serve or cause to be served, upon any person whose behavior is brought into question under this paragraph, an order requiring such person to appear before a district judge upon a day certain to show cause why that person should not be adjudged in contempt by reason of the facts so certified. The district judge shall thereupon hear the evidence as to the act or conduct complained of and, if it is such as to warrant punishment, punish such person in the same manner and to the same extent as for a contempt committed before a district judge.

(7) Appeals of magistrate judge contempt orders.—The appeal of an order of contempt under this subsection shall be made to the court of appeals in cases proceeding under subsection (c) of this section. The appeal of any other order of contempt issued under this section shall be made to the district court.

(f) In an emergency and upon the concurrence of the chief judges of the districts involved, a United States magistrate judge may be temporarily assigned to perform any of the duties specified in subsection (a), (b), or (c) of this section in a judicial district other than the judicial district for which he has been appointed. No magistrate judge shall perform any of such duties in a district to which he has been temporarily assigned until an order has been issued by the chief judge of such district specifying (1) the emergency by reason of which he has been transferred, (2) the duration of his assignment, and (3) the duties which he is authorized to perform. A magistrate judge so assigned shall not be entitled to additional compensation but shall be reimbursed for actual and necessary expenses incurred in the performance of his duties in accordance with section 635.

(g) A United States magistrate judge may perform the verification function required by section 4107 of title 18, United States Code. A magistrate judge may be assigned by a judge of any United States district court to perform the verification required by section 4108 and the appointment of counsel authorized by section 4109 of title 18, United States Code, and may perform such functions beyond the territorial limits of the United States. A magistrate judge assigned such functions shall have no authority to perform any other function within the territory of a foreign country.

(h) A United States magistrate judge who has retired may, upon the consent of the chief judge of the district involved, be recalled to serve as a magistrate judge in any judicial district by the judicial council of the circuit within which such district is located. Upon recall, a magistrate judge may receive a salary for such service in accordance with regulations promulgated by the Judicial Conference, subject to the restrictions on the payment of an annuity set forth in section 377 of this title or in subchapter III of chapter 83, and chapter 84, of title 5 which are applicable to such magistrate judge. The requirements set forth in subsections (a), (b)(3), and (d) of section 631, and paragraph (1) of subsection (b) of such section to the extent such paragraph requires membership of the bar of the location in which an individual is to serve as a magistrate judge, shall not apply to the recall of a retired magistrate judge under this subsection or section 375 of this title. Any other requirement set forth in section 631(b) shall apply to the recall of a retired magistrate judge under this subsection or section 375 of this title unless such retired magistrate judge met such requirement upon appointment or reappointment as a magistrate judge under section 361.

(As amended Oct. 17, 1968, Pub.L. 90–578, Title I, § 101, 82 Stat. 1113; Mar. 1, 1972, Pub.L. 92–239, §§ 1, 2, 86 Stat. 47; Oct. 21, 1976, Pub.L. 94–577, § 1, 90 Stat. 2729; Oct. 28, 1977, Pub.L. 95–144, § 2, 91 Stat. 1220; Oct. 10, 1979, Pub.L. 96–82, § 2, 93 Stat. 643; Oct. 12, 1984, Pub.L. 98–473, Title II, § 208, 98 Stat. 1986; Nov. 8, 1984, Pub.L. 98–620, Title IV, § 402(29)(B), 98 Stat. 3359; Nov. 14, 1986, Pub.L. 99–651, Title II, § 201(a)(2), 100 Stat. 3647; Nov. 15, 1988, Pub.L. 100–659, § 4(c), 102 Stat. 3918; Nov. 18, 1988, Pub.L. 100–690, Title VII, § 7322, 102 Stat. 4467; Nov. 19, 1988, Pub.L. 100–702, Title IV, § 404(b)(1), Title X, § 1014, 102 Stat. 4651, 4669; Dec. 1, 1990, Pub.L. 101–650, Title III, § 308, 104 Stat. 5089; Oct. 19, 1996, Pub.L. 104–317, Title II, §§ 201, 202(b), 207, 110 Stat. 3848, 3849, 3851; Nov. 13, 2000, Pub.L. 106–518, Title II, §§ 202, 203(b), 114 Stat. 2412, 2414; Nov. 2, 2002, Pub.L. 107–273, Title III, § 3002(b), 116 Stat. 1805; Sept. 9, 2005, Pub.L. 109–63, § 2(d), 119 Stat. 1995; May 7, 2009, Pub.L. 111–16, § 6(1), 123 Stat. 1608, 1609.)

§ 1251. Original Jurisdiction

(a) The Supreme Court shall have original and exclusive jurisdiction of all controversies between two or more States.

(b) The Supreme Court shall have original but not exclusive jurisdiction of:

(1) All actions or proceedings to which ambassadors, other public ministers, consuls, or vice consuls of foreign states are parties;

(2) All controversies between the United States and a State;

(3) All actions or proceedings by a State against the citizens of another State or against aliens.

(As amended Sept. 30, 1978, Pub.L. 95–393, § 8(b), 92 Stat. 810.)

§ 1253. Direct Appeals From Decisions of Three-Judge Courts

Except as otherwise provided by law, any party may appeal to the Supreme Court from an order granting or denying, after notice and hearing, an interlocutory or permanent injunction in any civil action, suit or proceeding required by any Act of Congress to be heard and determined by a district court of three judges.

§ 1254. Courts of Appeals; Certiorari; Certified Questions

Cases in the courts of appeals may be reviewed by the Supreme Court by the following methods:

(1) By writ of certiorari granted upon the petition of any party to any civil or criminal case, before or after rendition of judgment or decree;

(2) By certification at any time by a court of appeals of any question of law in any civil or criminal case as to which instructions are desired, and upon such certification the Supreme Court may give binding instructions or require the entire record to be sent up for decision of the entire matter in controversy.

(As amended June 27, 1988, Pub.L. 100–352, §§ 2(a), (b), 7, 102 Stat. 662, 664.)

§ 1257. State Courts; Certiorari

(a) Final judgments or decrees rendered by the highest court of a State in which a decision could be had, may be reviewed by the Supreme Court by writ of certiorari where the validity of a treaty or statute of the United States is drawn in question or where the validity of a statute of any State is drawn in question on the ground of its being repugnant to the Constitution, treaties or laws of the United States, or where any title, right, privilege or immunity is specially set up or claimed under the Constitution or the treaties or statutes of, or commission held or authority exercised under, the United States.

(b) For the purposes of this section, the term "highest court of a State" includes the District of Columbia Court of Appeals.

(As amended July 29, 1970, Pub.L. 91–358, Title I, § 172(a)(1), 84 Stat. 590; June 27, 1988, Pub.L. 100–352, §§ 3, 7, 102 Stat. 662, 664.)

§ 1291. Final Decisions of District Courts

The courts of appeals (other than the United States Court of Appeals for the Federal Circuit) shall have jurisdiction of appeals from all final decisions of the district courts of the United States, the United States District Court for the District of the Canal Zone, the District Court of Guam, and the District Court of the Virgin Islands, except where a direct review may be had in the Supreme Court. The jurisdiction of the United States Court of Appeals for the Federal Circuit shall be limited to the jurisdiction described in sections 1292(c) and (d) and 1295 of this title.

(As amended Oct. 31, 1951, c. 655, § 48, 65 Stat. 726; July 7, 1958, Pub.L. 85–508, § 12(e), 72 Stat. 348; Apr. 2, 1982, Pub.L. 97–164, Title I, § 124, 96 Stat. 36.)

§ 1292. Interlocutory Decisions

(a) Except as provided in subsections (c) and (d) of this section, the courts of appeals shall have jurisdiction of appeals from:

(1) Interlocutory orders of the district courts of the United States, the United States District Court for the District of the Canal Zone, the District Court of Guam, and the District Court of the Virgin Islands, or of the judges thereof, granting, continuing, modifying, refusing or dissolving injunctions, or refusing to dissolve or modify injunctions, except where a direct review may be had in the Supreme Court;

(2) Interlocutory orders appointing receivers, or refusing orders to wind up receiverships or to take steps to accomplish the purposes thereof, such as directing sales or other disposals of property;

(3) Interlocutory decrees of such district courts or the judges thereof determining the rights and liabilities of the parties to admiralty cases in which appeals from final decrees are allowed.

(b) When a district judge, in making in a civil action an order not otherwise appealable under this section, shall be of the opinion that such order involves a controlling question of law as to which there is substantial ground for difference of opinion and that an immediate appeal from the order may materially advance the ultimate termination of the litigation, he shall so state in writing in such order. The Court of Appeals which would have jurisdiction of an appeal of such action may thereupon, in its discretion, permit an appeal to be taken from such order, if application is made to it within ten days after the entry of the order: *Provided, however,* That application for an appeal hereunder shall not stay proceedings in the district court unless the district judge or the Court of Appeals or a judge thereof shall so order.

(c) The United States Court of Appeals for the Federal Circuit shall have exclusive jurisdiction—

(1) of an appeal from an interlocutory order or decree described in subsection (a) or (b) of this section in any case over which the court would have jurisdiction of an appeal under section 1295 of this title; and

(2) of an appeal from a judgment in a civil action for patent infringement which would otherwise be appealable to the United States Court of Appeals for the Federal Circuit and is final except for an accounting.

(d)(1) When the chief judge of the Court of International Trade issues an order under the provisions of section 256(b) of this title, or when any judge of the Court of International Trade, in issuing any other interlocutory order, includes in the order a statement that a controlling question of law is involved with respect to which there is a substantial ground for difference of opinion and that an immediate appeal from that order may materially advance the ultimate termination of the litigation, the United States Court of Appeals for the Federal Circuit may, in its discretion, permit an appeal to be taken from such order, if application is made to that Court within ten days after the entry of such order.

(2) When the chief judge of the United States Court of Federal Claims issues an order under section 798(b) of this title, or when any judge of the United States Court of Federal Claims, in issuing an interlocutory order, includes in the order a statement that a controlling question of law is involved with respect to which there is a substantial ground for difference of opinion and that an immediate appeal from that order may materially advance the ultimate termination of the litigation, the United States Court of Appeals for the Federal Circuit may, in its discretion, permit an appeal to be taken from such order, if application is made to that Court within ten days after the entry of such order.

(3) Neither the application for nor the granting of an appeal under this subsection shall stay proceedings in the Court of International Trade or in the Court of Federal Claims, as the case may be, unless a stay is ordered by a judge of the Court of International Trade or of the Court of Federal Claims or by the United States Court of Appeals for the Federal Circuit or a judge of that court.

(4)(A) The United States Court of Appeals for the Federal Circuit shall have exclusive jurisdiction of an appeal from an interlocutory order of a district court of the United States, the District Court of Guam, the District Court of the Virgin Islands, or the District Court for the Northern Mariana Islands, granting or denying, in whole or in part, a motion to transfer an action to the United States Court of Federal Claims under section 1631 of this title.

(B) When a motion to transfer an action to the Court of Federal Claims is filed in a district court, no further proceedings shall be taken in the district court until 60 days after the court has ruled upon the motion. If an appeal is taken from the district court's grant or denial of the motion, proceedings shall be further stayed until the appeal has been decided by the Court of Appeals for the Federal Circuit. The stay of proceedings in the district court shall not bar the granting of preliminary or injunctive relief, where appropriate and where expedition is reasonably necessary. However, during the period in which proceedings are stayed as provided in this subparagraph, no transfer to the Court of Federal Claims pursuant to the motion shall be carried out.

(e) The Supreme Court may prescribe rules, in accordance with section 2072 of this title, to provide for an appeal of an interlocutory decision to the courts of appeals that is not otherwise provided for under subsection (a), (b), (c), or (d).

(As amended Oct. 31, 1951, c. 655, § 49, 65 Stat. 726; July 7, 1958, Pub.L. 85–508, § 12(e), 72 Stat. 348; Sept. 2, 1958, Pub.L. 85–919, 72 Stat. 1770; Apr. 2, 1982, Pub.L. 97–164, Title I, § 125, 96 Stat. 36; Nov. 8, 1984, Pub.L. 98–620, Title IV, § 412, 98 Stat. 3362; Nov. 19, 1988, Pub.L. 100–702, Title V, § 501, 102 Stat. 4652; Oct. 29, 1992, Pub.L. 102–572, Title I, § 101, Title IX, § 906(c), 106 Stat. 4506, 4518.)

§ 1330. Actions Against Foreign States

(a) The district courts shall have original jurisdiction without regard to amount in controversy of any nonjury civil action against a foreign state as defined in section 1603(a) of this title as to any claim for relief in personam with respect to which the foreign state is not entitled to immunity either under sections 1605–1607 of this title or under any applicable international agreement.

(b) Personal jurisdiction over a foreign state shall exist as to every claim for relief over which the district courts have jurisdiction under subsection (a) where service has been made under section 1608 of this title.

(c) For purposes of subsection (b), an appearance by a foreign state does not confer personal jurisdiction with respect to any claim for relief not arising out of any transaction or occurrence enumerated in sections 1605–1607 of this title.

(Added Oct. 21, 1976, Pub.L. 94–583, § 2(a), 90 Stat. 2891.)

§ 1331. Federal Question

The district courts shall have original jurisdiction of all civil actions arising under the Constitution, laws, or treaties of the United States.

(As amended July 25, 1958, Pub.L. 85–554, § 1, 72 Stat. 415; Oct. 21, 1976, Pub.L. 94–574, § 2, 90 Stat. 2721; Dec. 1, 1980, Pub.L. 96–486, § 2(a), 94 Stat. 2369.)

§ 1332. Diversity of Citizenship; Amount in Controversy; Costs

(a) The district courts shall have original jurisdiction of all civil actions where the matter in controversy exceeds the sum or value of $75,000, exclusive of interest and costs, and is between—

(1) citizens of different States;

(2) citizens of a State and citizens or subjects of a foreign state, except that the district courts shall not have original jurisdiction under this subsection of an action between citizens of a State and citizens or subjects of a foreign state who are lawfully admitted for permanent residence in the United States and are domiciled in the same State.

(3) citizens of different States and in which citizens or subjects of a foreign state are additional parties; and

(4) a foreign state, defined in section 1603(a) of this title, as plaintiff and citizens of a State or of different States.

(b) Except when express provision therefor is otherwise made in a statute of the United States, where the plaintiff who files the case originally in the Federal courts is finally adjudged to be entitled to recover less than the sum or value of $75,000, computed without regard to any setoff or counterclaim to which the defendant may be adjudged to be entitled, and exclusive of interest and costs, the district court may deny costs to the plaintiff and, in addition, may impose costs on the plaintiff.

(c) For the purposes of this section and section 1441 of this title—

(1) a corporation shall be deemed to be a citizen of every State and foreign state by which it has been incorporated and of the State or foreign state where it has its principal place of business, except that in any direct action against the insurer of a policy or contract of liability insurance, whether incorporated or unincorporated, to which action the insured is not joined as a party-defendant, such insurer shall be deemed a citizen of—

(A) every State and foreign state of which the insured is a citizen;

(B) every State and foreign state by which the insurer has been incorporated; and

(C) the State or foreign state where the insurer has its principal place of business; and

(2) the legal representative of the estate of a decedent shall be deemed to be a citizen only of the same State as the decedent, and the legal representative of an infant or incompetent shall be deemed to be a citizen only of the same State as the infant or incompetent.

(d)(1) In this subsection—

(A) the term 'class' means all of the class members in a class action;

(B) the term 'class action' means any civil action filed under rule 23 of the Federal Rules of Civil Procedure or similar State statute or rule of judicial procedure authorizing an action to be brought by 1 or more representative persons as a class action;

(C) the term 'class certification order' means an order issued by a court approving the treatment of some or all aspects of a civil action as a class action; and

(D) the term 'class members' means the persons (named or unnamed) who fall within the definition of the proposed or certified class in a class action.

(2) The district courts shall have original jurisdiction of any civil action in which the matter in controversy exceeds the sum or value of $5,000,000, exclusive of interest and costs, and is a class action in which—

(A) any member of a class of plaintiffs is a citizen of a State different from any defendant;

(B) any member of a class of plaintiffs is a foreign state or a citizen or subject of a foreign state and any defendant is a citizen of a State; or

(C) any member of a class of plaintiffs is a citizen of a State and any defendant is a foreign state or a citizen or subject of a foreign state.

(3) A district court may, in the interests of justice and looking at the totality of the circumstances, decline to exercise jurisdiction under paragraph (2) over a class action in which greater than one-third but less than two-thirds of the members of all proposed plaintiff classes in the aggregate and the primary defendants are citizens of the State in which the action was originally filed based on consideration of—

(A) whether the claims asserted involve matters of national or interstate interest;

(B) whether the claims asserted will be governed by laws of the State in which the action was originally filed or by the laws of other States;

(C) whether the class action has been pleaded in a manner that seeks to avoid Federal jurisdiction;

(D) whether the action was brought in a forum with a distinct nexus with the class members, the alleged harm, or the defendants;

(E) whether the number of citizens of the State in which the action was originally filed in all proposed plaintiff classes in the aggregate is substantially larger than the number of citizens from any other State, and the citizenship of the other members of the proposed class is dispersed among a substantial number of States; and

(F) whether, during the 3-year period preceding the filing of that class action, 1 or more other class actions asserting the same or similar claims on behalf of the same or other persons have been filed.

(4) A district court shall decline to exercise jurisdiction under paragraph (2)—

(A)(i) over a class action in which—

(I) greater than two-thirds of the members of all proposed plaintiff classes in the aggregate are citizens of the State in which the action was originally filed;

(II) at least 1 defendant is a defendant—

(aa) from whom significant relief is sought by members of the plaintiff class;

(bb) whose alleged conduct forms a significant basis for the claims asserted by the proposed plaintiff class; and

(cc) who is a citizen of the State in which the action was originally filed; and

(III) principal injuries resulting from the alleged conduct or any related conduct of each defendant were incurred in the State in which the action was originally filed; and

(ii) during the 3-year period preceding the filing of that class action, no other class action has been filed asserting the same or similar factual allegations against any of the defendants on behalf of the same or other persons; or

(B) two-thirds or more of the members of all proposed plaintiff classes in the aggregate, and the primary defendants, are citizens of the State in which the action was originally filed.

(5) Paragraphs (2) through (4) shall not apply to any class action in which—

(A) the primary defendants are States, State officials, or other governmental entities against whom the district court may be foreclosed from ordering relief; or

(B) the number of members of all proposed plaintiff classes in the aggregate is less than 100.

(6) In any class action, the claims of the individual class members shall be aggregated to determine whether the matter in controversy exceeds the sum or value of $5,000,000, exclusive of interest and costs.

(7) Citizenship of the members of the proposed plaintiff classes shall be determined for purposes of paragraphs (2) through (6) as of the date of filing of the complaint or amended complaint, or, if the case stated by the initial pleading is not subject to Federal jurisdiction, as of the date of service by plaintiffs of an amended pleading, motion, or other paper, indicating the existence of Federal jurisdiction.

(8) This subsection shall apply to any class action before or after the entry of a class certification order by the court with respect to that action.

(9) Paragraph (2) shall not apply to any class action that solely involves a claim—

(A) concerning a covered security as defined under 16(f)(3) of the Securities Act of 1933 (15 U.S.C. 78p(f)(3)) and section 28(f)(5)(E) of the Securities Exchange Act of 1934 (15 U.S.C. 78bb(f)(5)(E));

(B) that relates to the internal affairs or governance of a corporation or other form of business enterprise and that arises under or by virtue of the laws of the State in which such corporation or business enterprise is incorporated or organized; or

(C) that relates to the rights, duties (including fiduciary duties), and obligations relating to or created by or pursuant to any security (as defined under section 2(a)(1) of the Securities Act of 1933 (15 U.S.C. 77b(a)(1)) and the regulations issued thereunder).

(10) For purposes of this subsection and section 1453, an unincorporated association shall be deemed to be a citizen of the State where it has its principal place of business and the State under whose laws it is organized.

(11)(A) For purposes of this subsection and section 1453, a mass action shall be deemed to be a class action removable under paragraphs (2) through (10) if it otherwise meets the provisions of those paragraphs.

(B)(i) As used in subparagraph (A), the term "mass action" means any civil action (except a civil action within the scope of section

1711(2)) in which monetary relief claims of 100 or more persons are proposed to be tried jointly on the ground that the plaintiffs' claims involve common questions of law or fact, except that jurisdiction shall exist only over those plaintiffs whose claims in a mass action satisfy the jurisdictional amount requirements under subsection (a).

(ii) As used in subparagraph (A), the term "mass action" shall not include any civil action in which—

(I) all of the claims in the action arise from an event or occurrence in the State in which the action was filed, and that allegedly resulted in injuries in that State or in States contiguous to that State;

(II) the claims are joined upon motion of a defendant;

(III) all of the claims in the action are asserted on behalf of the general public (and not on behalf of individual claimants or members of a purported class) pursuant to a State statute specifically authorizing such action; or

(IV) the claims have been consolidated or coordinated solely for pretrial proceedings.

(C)(i) Any action(s) removed to Federal court pursuant to this subsection shall not thereafter be transferred to any other court pursuant to section 1407, or the rules promulgated thereunder, unless a majority of the plaintiffs in the action request transfer pursuant to section 1407.

(ii) This subparagraph will not apply—

(I) to cases certified pursuant to rule 23 of the Federal Rules of Civil Procedure; or

(II) if plaintiffs propose that the action proceed as a class action pursuant to rule 23 of the Federal Rules of Civil Procedure.

(D) The limitations periods on any claims asserted in a mass action that is removed to Federal court pursuant to this subsection shall be deemed tolled during the period that the action is pending in Federal court.

(e) The word "States", as used in this section, includes the Territories, the District of Columbia, and the Commonwealth of Puerto Rico.

(As amended July 26, 1956, c. 740, 70 Stat. 658; July 25, 1958, Pub.L. 85–554, § 2, 72 Stat. 415; Aug. 14, 1964, Pub.L. 88–439, § 1, 78 Stat. 445; Oct. 21, 1976, Pub.L. 94–583, § 3, 90 Stat. 2891; Nov. 19, 1988, Pub.L. 100–702, § 201, 102 Stat. 4642; Oct. 19, 1996, Pub.L. 104–317, Title II, § 205(a), 110 Stat. 3850; Feb. 18, 2005, Pub.L. 109–002, § 4(a), 119 Stat. 9; Dec. 7, 2011, Pub.L. 112–63, § 101, 125 Stat. 758.)

§ 1335. Interpleader

(a) The district courts shall have original jurisdiction of any civil action of interpleader or in the nature of interpleader filed by any person, firm, or corporation, association, or society having in his or its custody or possession money or property of the value of $500 or more, or having issued a note, bond, certificate, policy of insurance, or other instrument of value or amount of $500 or more, or providing for the delivery or payment or the loan of money or property of such amount or value, or being under any obligation written or unwritten to the amount of $500 or more, if

(1) Two or more adverse claimants, of diverse citizenship as defined in subsection (a) or (d) of section 1332 of this title, are claiming or may claim to be entitled to such money or property, or to any one or more of the benefits arising by virtue of any note, bond, certificate, policy or other instrument, or arising by virtue of any such obligations; and if

(2) the plaintiff has deposited such money or property or has paid the amount of or the loan or other value of such instrument or the amount due under such obligation into the registry of the court, there to abide the judgment of the court, or has given bond payable to the clerk of the court in such amount and with such surety as the court or judge may deem proper, conditioned upon the compliance by the plaintiff with the future order or judgment of the court with respect to the subject matter of the controversy.

(b) Such an action may be entertained although the titles or claims of the conflicting claimants do not have a common origin, or are not identical, but are adverse to and independent of one another.

(As amended Feb. 18, 2005, Pub.L. 109–002, § 4(b), 119 Stat. 12).

§ 1337. Commerce and Antitrust Regulations; Amount in Controversy, Costs

(a) The district courts shall have original jurisdiction of any civil action or proceeding arising under any Act of Congress regulating commerce or protecting trade and commerce against restraints and monopolies: *Provided, however,* That the district courts shall have original jurisdiction of an action brought under section 11706 or 14706 of title 49, only if the matter in controversy for each receipt or bill of lading exceeds $10,000, exclusive of interest and costs.

(b) Except when express provision therefor is otherwise made in a statute of the United States, where a plaintiff who files the case under section 11706 or 14706 of title 49, originally in the Federal courts is finally adjudged to be entitled to recover less than the sum or value of $10,000, computed without regard to any setoff or counterclaim to which the defendant may be adjudged to be entitled, and exclusive of any interest and costs, the district court may deny costs to the plaintiff and, in addition, may impose costs on the plaintiff.

(c) The district courts shall not have jurisdiction under this section of any matter within the exclusive jurisdiction of the Court of International Trade under chapter 95 of this title.

(As amended Oct. 20, 1978, Pub.L. 95–486, § 9(a), 92 Stat. 1633; Oct. 10, 1980, Pub.L. 96–417, Title V, § 505, 94 Stat. 1743; Jan. 12, 1983, Pub.L. 97–449, § 5(f), 96 Stat. 2442; Dec. 29, 1995, Pub.L. 104–88, Title III, § 305(a)(3), 109 Stat. 944.)

§ 1338. Patents, Plant Variety Protection, Copyrights, Mask Works, Designs, Trade-Marks, and Unfair Competition

(a) The district courts shall have original jurisdiction of any civil action arising under any Act of Congress relating to patents, plant variety protection, copyrights and trademarks. No State court shall have jurisdiction over any claim for relief arising under any Act of Congress relating to patents, plant variety protection, or copyrights. For purposes of this subsection, the term "State" includes any State of the United States, the District of Columbia, the Commonwealth of Puerto Rico, the United States Virgin Islands, American Samoa, Guam, and the Northern Mariana Islands.

(b) The district courts shall have original jurisdiction of any civil action asserting a claim of unfair competition when joined with a substantial and related claim under the copyright, patent, plant variety protection or trademark laws.

(c) Subsections (a) and (b) apply to exclusive rights in mask works under chapter 9 of title 17, and to exclusive rights in designs under Chapter 13 of title 17, to the same extent as such subsections apply to copyrights.

(As amended Dec. 24, 1970, Pub.L. 91–577, Title III, § 143(b), 84 Stat. 1559; Nov. 19, 1988, Pub.L. 100–702, § 1020, 102 Stat. 4642; Oct. 28, 1998, Pub.L. 105–304, Title V, § 503(b)(1), (2)(A), 112 Stat. 2917; Nov. 29, 1999, Pub.L. 106–113, Div. B, § 1000(a)(9), 113 Stat. 1536, 1501A–551; Sept. 16, 2011, Pub.L. 112–29, § 19(a), 125 Stat. 331.)

§ 1343. Civil Rights and Elective Franchise

(a) The district courts shall have original jurisdiction of any civil action authorized by law to be commenced by any person:

(1) To recover damages for injury to his person or property, or because of the deprivation of any right or privilege of a citizen of the United States, by any act done in furtherance of any conspiracy mentioned in section 1985 of Title 42;

(2) To recover damages from any person who fails to prevent or to aid in preventing any wrongs mentioned in section 1985 of Title 42 which he had knowledge were about to occur and power to prevent;

(3) To redress the deprivation, under color of any State law, statute, ordinance, regulation, custom or usage, of any right, privilege or immunity secured by the Constitution of the United States or by any Act of Congress providing for equal rights of citizens or of all persons within the jurisdiction of the United States;

(4) To recover damages or to secure equitable or other relief under any Act of Congress providing for the protection of civil rights, including the right to vote.

(b) For purposes of this section—

(1) the District of Columbia shall be considered to be a State; and

(2) any Act of Congress applicable exclusively to the District of Columbia shall be considered to be a statute of the District of Columbia.

(As amended Sept. 3, 1954, c. 1263, § 42, 68 Stat. 1241; Sept. 9, 1957, Pub.L. 85–315, Part III, § 121, 71 Stat. 637; Dec. 29, 1979, Pub.L. 96–170, § 2, 93 Stat. 1284.)

§ 1359. Parties Collusively Joined or Made

A district court shall not have jurisdiction of a civil action in which any party, by assignment or otherwise, has been improperly or collusively made or joined to invoke the jurisdiction of such court.

§ 1367. Supplemental Jurisdiction

(a) Except as provided in subsections (b) and (c) or as expressly provided otherwise by Federal statute, in any civil action of which the district courts have original jurisdiction, the district courts shall have supplemental jurisdiction over all other claims that are so related to claims in the action within such original jurisdiction that they form part of the same case or controversy under Article III of the United States Constitution. Such supplemental jurisdiction shall include claims that involve the joinder or intervention of additional parties.

(b) In any civil action of which the district courts have original jurisdiction founded solely on section 1332 of this title, the district courts shall not have supplemental jurisdiction under subsection (a) over claims by plaintiffs against persons made parties under Rule 14, 19, 20, or 24 of the Federal Rules of Civil Procedure, or over claims by persons proposed to be joined as plaintiffs under Rule 19 of such rules, or seeking to intervene as plaintiffs under Rule 24 of such rules, when exercising supplemental jurisdiction over such claims would be inconsistent with the jurisdictional requirements of section 1332.

(c) The district courts may decline to exercise supplemental jurisdiction over a claim under subsection (a) if—

(1) the claim raises a novel or complex issue of State law,

(2) the claim substantially predominates over the claim or claims over which the district court has original jurisdiction,

(3) the district court has dismissed all claims over which it has original jurisdiction, or

(4) in exceptional circumstances, there are other compelling reasons for declining jurisdiction.

(d) The period of limitations for any claim asserted under subsection (a), and for any other claim in the same action that is voluntarily dismissed at the same time as or after the dismissal of the claim under subsection (a), shall be tolled while the claim is pending and for a period of 30 days after it is dismissed unless State law provides for a longer tolling period.

(e) As used in this section, the term 'State' includes the District of Columbia, the Commonwealth of Puerto Rico, and any territory or possession of the United States.

(Added Dec. 1, 1990, Pub.L. 101–650, § 310(a), 104 Stat. 5113.)

§ 1369. Multiparty, Multiforum Jurisdiction

(a) The district courts shall have original jurisdiction of any civil action involving minimal diversity between adverse parties that arises from a single accident, where at least 75 natural persons have died in the accident at a discrete location, if—

(1) a defendant resides in a State and a substantial part of the accident took place in another State or other location, regardless of whether that defendant is also a resident of the State where a substantial part of the accident took place;

(2) any two defendants reside in different States, regardless of whether such defendants are also residents of the same State or States; or

(3) substantial parts of the accident took place in different States.

(b) The district court shall abstain from hearing any civil action described in subsection (a) in which—

the substantial majority of all plaintiffs are citizens of a single State of which the primary defendants are also citizens; and

the claims asserted will be governed primarily by the laws of that State.

(c) For purposes of this section—

(1) minimal diversity exists between adverse parties if any party is a citizen of a State and any adverse party is a citizen of another State, a citizen or subject of a foreign state, or a foreign state as defined in section 1603(a) of this title;

(2) a corporation is deemed to be a citizen of any State, and a citizen or subject of any foreign state, in which it is incorporated or has its principal place of business, and is deemed to be a resident of any State in which it is incorporated or licensed to do business or is doing business;

(3) the term "injury" means—

(A) physical harm to a natural person; and

(B) physical damage to or destruction of tangible property, but only if physical harm described in subparagraph (A) exists;

(4) the term "accident" means a sudden accident, or a natural event culminating in an accident, that results in death incurred at a discrete location by at least 75 natural persons; and

(5) the term "State" includes the District of Columbia, the Commonwealth of Puerto Rico, and any territory or possession of the United States.

(d) In any action in a district court which is or could have been brought, in whole or in part, under this section, any person with a claim arising from the accident described in subsection (a) shall be permitted to intervene as a party plaintiff in the action, even if that person could not have brought an action in a district court as an original matter.

(e) A district court in which an action under this section is pending shall promptly notify the judicial panel on multidistrict litigation of the pendency of the action.

(Added Nov. 2, 2002, Pub.L. 107–273, § 11020(b)(1)(A), 116 Stat. 1826.)

§ 1390. Scope

(a) Venue Defined.—As used in this chapter, the term "venue" refers to the geographic specification of the proper court or courts for the litigation of a civil action that is within the subject-matter jurisdiction of the district courts in general, and does not refer to any grant or restriction of subject-matter jurisdiction providing for a civil action to be adjudicated only by the district court for a particular district or districts.

(b) Exclusion of Certain Cases.—Except as otherwise provided by law, this chapter shall not govern the venue of a civil action in which the district court exercises the jurisdiction conferred by section 1333, except that such civil actions may be transferred between district courts as provided in this chapter.

(c) Clarification Regarding Cases Removed From State Courts.—This chapter shall not determine the district court to which a civil action pending in a State court may be removed, but shall govern the transfer of an action so removed as between districts and divisions of the United States district courts.

(Added Dec. 7, 2011, Pub.L. 112–63, § 201(a), 125 Stat. 762.)

§ 1391. Venue Generally

(a) Applicability of Section.—Except as otherwise provided by law—

(1) this section shall govern the venue of all civil actions brought in district courts of the United States; and

(2) the proper venue for a civil action shall be determined without regard to whether the action is local or transitory in nature.

(b) Venue in General.—A civil action may be brought in—

(1) a judicial district in which any defendant resides, if all defendants are residents of the State in which the district is located;

(2) a judicial district in which a substantial part of the events or omissions giving rise to the claim occurred, or a substantial part of property that is the subject of the action is situated; or

(3) if there is no district in which an action may otherwise be brought as provided in this section, any judicial district in which any defendant is subject to the court's personal jurisdiction with respect to such action.

(c) Residency.—For all venue purposes—

(1) a natural person, including an alien lawfully admitted for permanent residence in the United States, shall be deemed to reside in the judicial district in which that person is domiciled;

(2) an entity with the capacity to sue and be sued in its common name under applicable law, whether or not incorporated, shall be deemed to reside, if a defendant, in any judicial district in which such defendant is subject to the court's personal jurisdiction with respect to the civil action in question and, if a plaintiff, only in the judicial district in which it maintains its principal place of business; and

(3) a defendant not resident in the United States may be sued in any judicial district, and the joinder of such a defendant shall be disregarded in determining where the action may be brought with respect to other defendants.

(d) Residency of Corporations in States with Multiple Districts.—For purposes of venue under this chapter, in a State which has more than one judicial district and in which a defendant that is a corporation is subject to personal jurisdiction at the time an action is commenced, such corporation shall be deemed to reside in any district in that State within which its contacts would be sufficient to subject it to personal jurisdiction if that district were a separate State, and, if there is no such district, the corporation shall be deemed to reside in the district within which it has the most significant contacts.

(e) Actions Where Defendant is Officer or Employee of the United States.—

(1) In General.—A civil action in which a defendant is an officer or employee of the United States or any agency thereof acting in his official capacity or under color of legal authority, or an agency of the United States, or the United States, may, except as otherwise provided by law, be brought in any judicial district in which (A) a defendant in the action resides, (B) a substantial part of the events or omissions giving rise to the claim occurred, or a substantial part of property that is the subject of the action is situated, or (C) the plaintiff resides if no real property is involved in the action. Additional persons may be joined as parties to any such action in accordance with the Federal Rules of Civil Procedure and with such other venue requirements as would be applicable if the United States or one of its officers, employees, or agencies were not a party.

(2) Service.—The summons and complaint in such an action shall be served as provided by the Federal Rules of Civil Procedure except that the delivery of the summons and complaint to the officer or agency as required by the rules may be made by certified mail beyond the territorial limits of the district in which the action is brought.

(f) Civil Actions Against a Foreign State.—A civil action against a foreign state as defined in section 1603(a) of this title may be brought—

(1) in any judicial district in which a substantial part of the events or omissions giving rise to the claim occurred, or a substantial part of property that is the subject of the action is situated;

(2) in any judicial district in which the vessel or cargo of a foreign state is situated, if the claim is asserted under section 1605(b) of this title;

(3) in any judicial district in which the agency or instrumentality is licensed to do business or is doing business, if the action is brought against an agency or instrumentality of a foreign state as defined in section 1603(b) of this title; or

(4) in the United States District Court for the District of Columbia if the action is brought against a foreign state or political subdivision thereof.

(g) Multiparty, Multiforum Litigation.—A civil action in which jurisdiction of the district court is based upon section 1369 of this title may be brought in any district in which any defendant resides or in which a substantial part of the accident giving rise to the action took place.

(As amended Oct. 5, 1962, Pub.L. 87–748, § 2, 76 Stat. 744; Dec. 23, 1963, Pub.L. 88–234, 77 Stat. 473; Nov. 2, 1966, Pub.L. 89–714, §§ 1, 2, 80 Stat. 1111; Oct. 21, 1976, Pub.L. 94–574, § 3, 90 Stat. 2721; Oct. 21, 1976, Pub.L. 94–583, § 5, 90 Stat. 2897; Nov. 19, 1988, Pub.L. 100–702, § 1013, 102 Stat. 4642; Dec. 1, 1990, Pub.L. 101–650, § 311, 104 Stat. 5089; Dec. 9, 1991, Pub.L. 102–198, § 3, 105 Stat. 1623; Oct. 29, 1992, Pub.L. 102–572, Title V, § 504, 106 Stat. 4513; Oct. 3, 1995, Pub.L. 104–34, § 532, 109 Stat. 293; Nov. 2, 2002, Pub.L. 107–273, § 11020(b)(2), 116 Stat. 1827; Dec. 7, 2011, Pub.L. 112–63, § 202, 125 Stat. 763.)

§ 1397. Interpleader

Any civil action of interpleader or in the nature of interpleader under section 1335 of this title may be brought in the judicial district in which one or more of the claimants reside.

§ 1400. Patents and Copyrights, Mask Works, and Designs

(a) Civil actions, suits, or proceedings arising under any Act of Congress relating to copyrights or exclusive rights in mask works or designs may be instituted in the district in which the defendant or his agent resides or may be found.

(b) Any civil action for patent infringement may be brought in the judicial district where the defendant resides, or where the defendant has committed acts of infringement and has a regular and established place of business.

(As amended Nov. 19, 1988, Pub.L. 100–702, § 1020, 102 Stat. 4642; Oct. 28, 1998, Pub.L. 105–304, Title V, § 503(c)(1), (2), 112 Stat. 2917; Aug. 5, 1999, Pub.L. 106–44, § 2(a), 113 Stat. 223.)

§ 1401. Stockholder's Derivative Action

Any civil action by a stockholder on behalf of his corporation may be prosecuted in any judicial district where the corporation might have sued the same defendants.

§ 1404. Change of Venue

(a) For the convenience of parties and witnesses, in the interest of justice, a district court may transfer any civil action to any other district or division where it might have been brought or to any district or division to which all parties have consented.

(b) Upon motion, consent or stipulation of all parties, any action, suit or proceeding of a civil nature or any motion or hearing thereof, may be transferred, in the discretion of the court, from the division in which pending to any other division in the same district. Transfer of proceedings in rem brought by or on behalf of the United States may be transferred under this section without the consent of the United States where all other parties request transfer.

(c) A district court may order any civil action to be tried at any place within the division in which it is pending.

(d) Transfers from a district court of the United States to the District Court of Guam, the District Court for the Northern Mariana Islands, or the District Court of the Virgin Islands shall not be permitted under this section. As otherwise used in this section, the term "district court" includes the District Court of Guam, the District Court for the Northern Mariana

Islands, and the District Court of the Virgin Islands, and the term "district" includes the territorial jurisdiction of each such court.

(As amended Oct. 18, 1962, Pub.L. 87–845, § 9, 76A Stat. 699; Oct. 19, 1996, Pub.L. 104–317, Title VI, § 610(a), 110 Stat. 3860; Dec. 7, 2011, Pub.L. 112–63, § 204, 125 Stat. 764.)

§ 1406. Cure or Waiver of Defects

(a) The district court of a district in which is filed a case laying venue in the wrong division or district shall dismiss, or if it be in the interest of justice, transfer such case to any district or division in which it could have been brought.

(b) Nothing in this chapter shall impair the jurisdiction of a district court of any matter involving a party who does not interpose timely and sufficient objection to the venue.

(c) As used in this section, the term "district court" includes the District Court of Guam, the District Court for the Northern Mariana Islands, and the District Court of the Virgin Islands, and the term "district" includes the territorial jurisdiction of each such court.

(As amended May 24, 1949, c. 139, § 81, 63 Stat. 101; Sept. 13, 1960, Pub.L. 86–770, § 1, 74 Stat. 912; Oct. 18, 1962, Pub.L. 87–845, § 10, 76A Stat. 699; Apr. 2, 1982, Pub.L. 97–164, Title I, § 132, 96 Stat. 39; Oct. 19, 1996, Pub.L. 104–317, Title VI, § 610(b), 110 Stat. 3860.)

§ 1407. Multidistrict Litigation

(a) When civil actions involving one or more common questions of fact are pending in different districts, such actions may be transferred to any district for coordinated or consolidated pretrial proceedings. Such transfers shall be made by the judicial panel on multidistrict litigation authorized by this section upon its determination that transfers for such proceedings will be for the convenience of parties and witnesses and will promote the just and efficient conduct of such actions. Each action so transferred shall be remanded by the panel at or before the conclusion of such pretrial proceedings to the district from which it was transferred unless it shall have been previously terminated: *Provided, however,* That the panel may separate any claim, cross-claim, counter-claim, or third-party claim and remand any of such claims before the remainder of the action is remanded.

(b) Such coordinated or consolidated pretrial proceedings shall be conducted by a judge or judges to whom such actions are assigned by the judicial panel on multidistrict litigation. For this purpose, upon request of the panel, a circuit judge or a district judge may be designated and assigned temporarily for service in the transferee district by the Chief Justice of the United States or the chief judge of the circuit, as may be required, in accordance with the provisions of chapter 13 of this title. With the consent of the transferee district court, such actions may be assigned by the panel to a judge or judges of such district. The judge or judges to whom such actions are assigned, the members of the judicial panel on multidistrict litigation, and other circuit and district judges designated when needed by the panel may exercise the powers of a district judge in any district for the purpose of conducting pretrial depositions in such coordinated or consolidated pretrial proceedings.

(c) Proceedings for the transfer of an action under this section may be initiated by—

(i) the judicial panel on multidistrict litigation upon its own initiative, or

(ii) motion filed with the panel by a party in any action in which transfer for coordinated or consolidated pretrial proceedings under this section may be appropriate. A copy of such motion shall be filed in the district court in which the moving party's action is pending.

The panel shall give notice to the parties in all actions in which transfers for coordinated or consolidated pretrial proceedings are contemplated, and such notice shall specify the time and place of any hearing to determine whether such transfer shall be made. Orders of the panel to set a hearing and other orders of the panel issued prior to the order either directing or denying transfer shall be filed in the office of the clerk of the district court in which a transfer hearing is to be or has been held. The panel's order of transfer shall be based upon a record of such hearing at which material evidence may be offered by any party to an action pending in any district that would be affected by the proceedings under this section, and shall be supported by findings of fact and conclusions of law based upon such record. Orders of transfer and such other orders as the panel may make thereafter shall be filed in the office of the clerk of the district court of the transferee district and shall be effective when thus filed. The clerk of the transferee district court shall forthwith transmit a certified copy of the panel's order to transfer to the clerk of the district court from which the action is being transferred. An order denying transfer shall be filed in each district wherein there is a case pending in which the motion for transfer has been made.

(d) The judicial panel on multidistrict litigation shall consist of seven circuit and district judges designated from time to time by the Chief Justice of the United States, no two of whom shall be from the same circuit. The concurrence of four members shall be necessary to any action by the panel.

(e) No proceedings for review of any order of the panel may be permitted except by extraordinary writ pursuant to the provisions of title 28, section 1651, United States Code. Petitions for an extraordinary writ to review an order of the panel to set a transfer hearing and other orders of the panel issued prior to the order either directing or denying transfer shall be filed only in the court of appeals having jurisdiction over the district in which a hearing is to be or has been held. Petitions for an extraordinary writ to review an order to transfer or orders subsequent to transfer shall be filed only in the court of appeals having jurisdiction over the transferee district. There shall be no appeal or review of an order of the panel denying a motion to transfer for consolidated or coordinated proceedings.

(f) The panel may prescribe rules for the conduct of its business not inconsistent with Acts of Congress and the Federal Rules of Civil Procedure.

(g) Nothing in this section shall apply to any action in which the United States or a State is a complainant arising under the antitrust laws. "Antitrust laws" as used herein include those acts referred to in the Act of October 15, 1914, as amended (38 Stat. 730; 15 U.S.C. 12), and also include the Act of June 19, 1936 (49 Stat. 1526; 15 U.S.C. 13, 13a, and 13b) and the Act of September 26, 1914, as added March 21, 1938 (52 Stat. 116, 117; 15 U.S.C. 56).

(Added Apr. 29, 1968, Pub.L. 90–296, § 1, 82 Stat. 109, and amended Sept. 30, 1976, Pub.L. 94–435, Title III, § 303, 90 Stat. 1396; Dec. 29, 2022, Pub.L. 117–328, Title III, § 301, 136 Stat. 4459.)

§ 1441. Removal of Civil Actions

(a) Generally.—Except as otherwise expressly provided by Act of Congress, any civil action brought in a State court of which the district courts of the United States have original jurisdiction, may be removed by the defendant or the defendants, to the district court of the United States for the district and division embracing the place where such action is pending.

(b) Removal Based on Diversity of Citizenship.—

(1) In determining whether a civil action is removable on the basis of the jurisdiction under section 1332(a) of this title, the citizenship of defendants sued under fictitious names shall be disregarded.

(2) A civil action otherwise removable solely on the basis of the jurisdiction under section 1332(a) of this title may not be removed if any of the parties in interest properly joined and served as defendants is a citizen of the State in which such action is brought.

(c) Joinder of Federal Law Claims and State Law Claims.—

(1) If a civil action includes—

(A) a claim arising under the Constitution, laws, or treaties of the United States (within the meaning of section 1331 of this title), and

(B) a claim not within the original or supplemental jurisdiction of the district court or a claim that has been made nonremovable by statute, the entire action may be removed if the action would be removable without the inclusion of the claim described in subparagraph (B).

(2) Upon removal of an action described in paragraph (1), the district court shall sever from the action all claims described in paragraph (1)(B) and shall remand the severed claims to the State court from which the action was removed. Only defendants against whom a claim described in paragraph (1)(A) has been asserted are required to join in or consent to the removal under paragraph (1).

(d) Actions Against Foreign States.—

Any civil action brought in a State court against a foreign state as defined in section 1603(a) of this title may be removed by the foreign state to the district court of the United States for the district and division embracing the place where such action is pending. Upon removal the action shall be tried by the court without jury. Where removal is based upon this subsection, the time limitations of section 1446(b) of this chapter may be enlarged at any time for cause shown.

(e) Multiparty, Multiforum Jurisdiction.—

(1) Notwithstanding the provisions of subsection (b) of this section, a defendant in a civil action in a State court may remove the action to the district court of the United States for the district and division embracing the place where the action is pending if—

(A) the action could have been brought in a United States district court under section 1369 of this title; or

(B) the defendant is a party to an action which is or could have been brought, in whole or in part, under section 1369 in a United States district court and arises from the same accident as the action in State court, even if the action to be removed could not have been brought in a district court as an original matter.

The removal of an action under this subsection shall be made in accordance with section 1446 of this title, except that a notice of removal may also be filed before trial of the action in State court within 30 days after the date on which the defendant first becomes a party to an action under section 1369 in a United States district court that arises from the same accident as the action in State court, or at a later time with leave of the district court.

(2) Whenever an action is removed under this subsection and the district court to which it is removed or transferred under section 1407(j) has made a liability determination requiring further proceedings as to damages, the district court shall remand the action to the State court from which it had been removed for the determination of damages, unless the court finds that, for the convenience of parties and witnesses and in the interest of justice, the action should be retained for the determination of damages.

(3) Any remand under paragraph (2) shall not be effective until 60 days after the district court has issued an order determining liability and has certified its intention to remand the removed action for the determination of damages. An appeal with respect to the liability determination of the district court may be taken during that 60-day period to the court of appeals with appellate jurisdiction over the district court. In the event a party files such an appeal, the remand shall not be effective until the appeal has been finally disposed of. Once the remand has become effective, the liability determination shall not be subject to further review by appeal or otherwise.

(4) Any decision under this subsection concerning remand for the determination of damages shall not be reviewable by appeal or otherwise.

(5) An action removed under this subsection shall be deemed to be an action under section 1369 and an action in which jurisdiction is based on section 1369 of this title for purposes of this section and sections 1407, 1697, and 1785 of this title.

(6) Nothing in this subsection shall restrict the authority of the district court to transfer or dismiss an action on the ground of inconvenient forum.

(f) Derivative Removal Jurisdiction.—The court to which a civil action is removed under this section is not precluded from hearing and determining any claim in such civil action because the State court from which such civil action is removed did not have jurisdiction over that claim.

(As amended Oct. 21, 1976, Pub.L. 94–583, § 6, 90 Stat. 2898; June 19, 1986, Pub.L. 99–336, § 3(a), 100 Stat. 637; Nov. 19, 1988, Pub.L. 100–702, § 1016, 102 Stat. 4642; Dec. 1, 1990, Pub.L. 101–650, § 312, 104 Stat. 5089; Dec. 9, 1991, Pub.L. 102–198, § 4, 105 Stat. 1623; Nov. 2, 2002, Pub.L. 107–273, § 11020(b)(3), 116 Stat. 1827; Dec. 7, 2011, Pub.L. 112–63, § 103(a), 125 Stat. 759.)

§ 1443. Civil Rights Cases

Any of the following civil actions or criminal prosecutions, commenced in a State court may be removed by the defendant to the district court of the United States for the district and division embracing the place wherein it is pending:

(1) Against any person who is denied or cannot enforce in the courts of such State a right under any law providing for the equal civil rights of citizens of the United States, or of all persons within the jurisdiction thereof;

(2) For any act under color of authority derived from any law providing for equal rights, or for refusing to do any act on the ground that it would be inconsistent with such law.

§ 1446. Procedure for Removal of Civil Actions

(a) Generally.—A defendant or defendants desiring to remove any civil action or criminal prosecution from a State court shall file in the district court of the United States for the district and division within which such action is pending a notice of removal signed pursuant to Rule 11 of the Federal Rules of Civil Procedure and containing a short and plain statement of the grounds for removal, together with a copy of all process, pleadings, and orders served upon such defendant or defendants in such action.

(b) Requirements; Generally.—

(1) The notice of removal of a civil action or proceeding shall be filed within 30 days after the receipt by the defendant, through service or otherwise, of a copy of the initial pleading setting forth the claim for relief upon which such action or proceeding is based, or within 30 days after the service of summons upon the defendant if such initial pleading has then been filed in court and is not required to be served on the defendant, whichever period is shorter.

(2)(A) When a civil action is removed solely under section 1441(a), all defendants who have been properly joined and served must join in or consent to the removal of the action.

(B) Each defendant shall have 30 days after receipt by or service on that defendant of the initial pleading or summons described in paragraph (1) to file the notice of removal.

(C) If defendants are served at different times, and a later-served defendant files a notice of removal, any earlier-served defendant may consent to the removal even though that earlier-served defendant did not previously initiate or consent to removal.

(3) Except as provided in subsection (c), if the case stated by the initial pleading is not removable, a notice of removal may be filed within 30 days after receipt by the defendant, through service or otherwise, of a copy of an amended pleading, motion, order or other paper from which it may first be ascertained that the case is one which is or has become removable.

(c) Requirements; Removal Based on Diversity of Citizenship.—

(1) A case may not be removed under subsection (b)(3) on the basis of jurisdiction conferred by section 1332 more than 1 year after commencement of the action, unless the district court finds that the plaintiff has acted in bad faith in order to prevent a defendant from removing the action.

(2) If removal of a civil action is sought on the basis of the jurisdiction conferred by section 1332(a), the sum demanded in good faith in the initial pleading shall be deemed to be the amount in controversy, except that—

(A) the notice of removal may assert the amount in controversy if the initial pleading seeks—

(i) nonmonetary relief; or

(ii) a money judgment, but the State practice either does not permit demand for a specific sum or permits recovery of damages in excess of the amount demanded; and

(B) removal of the action is proper on the basis of an amount in controversy asserted under subparagraph (A) if the district court finds, by the preponderance of the evidence, that the amount in controversy exceeds the amount specified in section 1332(a).

(3)(A) If the case stated by the initial pleading is not removable solely because the amount in controversy does not exceed the amount specified in section 1332(a), information relating to the amount in controversy in the record of the State proceeding, or in responses to discovery, shall be treated as an "other paper" under subsection (b)(3).

(B) If the notice of removal is filed more than 1 year after commencement of the action and the district court finds that the plaintiff deliberately failed to disclose the actual amount in controversy to prevent removal, that finding shall be deemed bad faith under paragraph (1).

(d) Notice to Adverse Parties and State Court.—Promptly after the filing of such petition for removal of a civil action the defendant or defendants shall give written notice thereof to all adverse parties and shall file a copy of the notice with the clerk of such State court, which shall effect the removal and the State court shall proceed no further unless and until the case is remanded.

(e) Counterclaim in 337 Proceeding.—With respect to any counterclaim removed to a district court pursuant to section 337(c) of the Tariff Act of 1930, the district court shall resolve such counterclaim in the same manner as an original complaint under the Federal Rules of Civil Procedure, except that the payment of a filing fee shall not be required in such cases and the counterclaim shall relate back to the date of the original complaint in the proceeding before the International Trade Commission under section 337 of that Act.

[**(f)** Redesignated **(e)**]

(g) Where the civil action or criminal prosecution that is removable under section 1442(a) is a proceeding in which a judicial order for testimony or documents is sought or issued or sought to be enforced, the 30-day requirement of subsection (b) of this section and paragraph (1) of section 1455(b) is satisfied if the person or entity desiring to remove the proceeding files the notice of removal not later than 30 days after receiving, through service, notice of any such proceeding.

(As amended May 24, 1949, c. 139, § 83, 63 Stat. 101; Sept. 29, 1965, Pub.L. 89–215, 79 Stat. 887; July 30, 1977, Pub.L. 95–78, § 3, 91 Stat. 321; Nov. 19, 1988, Pub.L. 100–702, § 1016(b), 102 Stat. 4669; Dec. 9, 1991, Pub.L. 102–198, § 10a, 105 Stat. 1623; Dec. 8, 1994, Pub L. 103–465, Title III, § 321(b)(2), 108 Stat. 4946; Oct. 19, 1996, Pub.L. 104–317, Title VI, § 603, 110 Stat. 3857; Nov. 9, 2011, Pub.L. 112–51, § 2(c), 125 Stat. 545; Dec. 7, 2011, Pub.L. 112–63, §§ 103(b), 104, 125 Stat. 760, 762.)

§ 1447. Procedure After Removal Generally

(a) In any case removed from a State court, the district court may issue all necessary orders and process to bring before it all proper parties whether served by process issued by the State court or otherwise.

(b) It may require the removing party to file with its clerk copies of all records and proceedings in such State court or may cause the same to be brought before it by writ of certiorari issued to such State court.

(c) A motion to remand the case on the basis of any defect other than lack of subject matter jurisdiction must be made within 30 days after the filing of the notice of removal under section 1446(a). If at any time before final judgment it appears that the district court lacks subject matter jurisdiction, the case shall be remanded. An order remanding the case may require payment of just costs and any actual expenses, including attorney fees, incurred as a result of the removal. A certified copy of the order of remand shall be mailed by the clerk to the clerk of the State court. The State court may thereupon proceed with such case.

(d) An order remanding a case to the State court from which it was removed is not reviewable on appeal or otherwise, except that an order remanding a case to the State court from which it was removed pursuant to section 1442 or 1443 of this title shall be reviewable by appeal or otherwise.

(e) If after removal the plaintiff seeks to join additional defendants whose joinder would destroy subject matter jurisdiction, the court may deny joinder, or permit joinder and remand the action to the State court.

(As amended May 24, 1949, c. 139, § 84, 63 Stat. 102; July 2, 1964, Pub.L. 88–352, Title IX, § 901, 78 Stat. 266; Nov. 19, 1988, Pub.L. 100–702, § 1016, 102 Stat. 4670; Dec. 9, 1991, Pub.L. 102–198, § 10(b), 105 Stat. 1626; Oct. 1, 1996, Pub.L. 104–219, § 1, 110 Stat. 3022; Nov. 9, 2011, Pub.L. 112–51, § 2(d), 125 Stat. 546.)

§ 1448. Process After Removal

In all cases removed from any State court to any district court of the United States in which any one or more of the defendants has not been served with process or in which the service has not been perfected prior to removal, or in which process served proves to be defective, such process or service may be completed or new process issued in the same manner as in cases originally filed in such district court.

This section shall not deprive any defendant upon whom process is served after removal of his right to move to remand the case.

§ 1453. Removal of Class Actions

(a) In this section, the terms "class", "class action", "class certification order", and "class member" shall have the meanings given such terms under section 1332(d)(1).

(b) A class action may be removed to a district court of the United States in accordance with section 1446 (except that the 1-year limitation under section 1446(c)(1) shall not apply), without regard to whether any defendant is a citizen of the State in which the action is brought, except that such action may be removed by any defendant without the consent of all defendants.

(c)(1) Section 1447 shall apply to any removal of a case under this section, except that notwithstanding section 1447(d), a court of appeals may accept an appeal from an order of a district court granting or denying a motion to remand a class action to the State court from which it was removed if application is made to the court of appeals not more than 10 days after entry of the order.

(2) If the court of appeals accepts an appeal under paragraph (1), the court shall complete all action on such appeal, including rendering judgment, not later than 60 days after the date on which such appeal was filed, unless an extension is granted under paragraph (3).

(3) The court of appeals may grant an extension of the 60-day period described in paragraph (2) if—

(A) all parties to the proceeding agree to such extension, for any period of time; or

(B) such extension is for good cause shown and in the interests of justice, for a period not to exceed 10 days.

(4) If a final judgment on the appeal under paragraph (1) is not issued before the end of the period described in paragraph (2), including any extension under paragraph (3), the appeal shall be denied.

(d) This section shall not apply to any class action that solely involves—

(1) a claim concerning a covered security as defined under section 16(f)(3) of the Securities Act of 1933 (15 U.S.C. 78p(f)(3)) and section 28(f)(5)(E) of the Securities Exchange Act of 1934 (15 U.S.C. 78bb(f)(5)(E));

(2) a claim that relates to the internal affairs or governance of a corporation or other form of business enterprise and arises under or by virtue of the laws of the State in which such corporation or business enterprise is incorporated or organized; or

(3) a claim that relates to the rights, duties (including fiduciary duties), and obligations relating to or created by or pursuant to any security (as defined under section 2(a)(1) of the Securities Act of 1933 (15 U.S.C. 77b(a)(1)) and the regulations issued thereunder).

(Added Feb. 18, 2005, Pub.L. 109–002, § 5(a), 119 Stat. 12. As amended May 7, 2009, Pub.L. 111–16, § 6(2), 123 Stat. 1608, 1609; Dec. 7, 2011, Pub.L. 112–63, § 103(d)(2), 125 Stat. 762.)

§ 1631. Transfer to Cure Want of Jurisdiction

Whenever a civil action is filed in a court as defined in section 610 of this title or an appeal, including a petition for review of administrative action, is noticed for or filed with such a court and that court finds that there is a want of jurisdiction, the court shall, if it is in the interest of justice, transfer such action or appeal to any other such court in which the action or appeal could have been brought at the time it was filed or noticed, and the action or appeal shall proceed as if it had been filed in or noticed for the court to which it is transferred on the date upon which it was actually filed in or noticed for the court from which it is transferred.

(Added Pub.L. 97–164, Title III, § 301(a), Apr. 2, 1982, 96 Stat. 55.)

§ 1651. Writs

(a) The Supreme Court and all courts established by Act of Congress may issue all writs necessary or appropriate in aid of their respective jurisdictions and agreeable to the usages and principles of law.

(b) An alternative writ or rule nisi may be issued by a justice or judge of a court which has jurisdiction.

(As amended May 24, 1949, c. 139, § 90, 63 Stat. 102.)

§ 1652. State Laws as Rules of Decision

The laws of the several states, except where the Constitution or treaties of the United States or Acts of Congress otherwise require or provide, shall be regarded as rules of decision in civil actions in the courts of the United States, in cases where they apply.

§ 1653. Amendment of Pleadings to Show Jurisdiction

Defective allegations of jurisdiction may be amended, upon terms, in the trial or appellate courts.

§ 1658. Time Limitations on the Commencement of Civil Actions Arising Under Acts of Congress

(a) Except as otherwise provided by law, a civil action arising under an Act of Congress enacted after the date of the enactment of this section may not be commenced later than 4 years after the cause of action accrues.

(b) Notwithstanding subsection (a), a private right of action that involves a claim of fraud, deceit, manipulation, or contrivance in contravention of a regulatory requirement concerning the securities laws, as defined in section 3(a)(47) of the Securities Exchange Act of 1934 (15 U.S.C. 78c(a)(47)), may be brought not later than the earlier of—

(1) 2 years after the discovery of the facts constituting the violation; or

(2) 5 years after such violation.

(Added Dec. 1, 1990, Pub.L. 101–650, § 313, 104 Stat. 5089. Amended July 30, 2002, Pub.L. 107–204, § 804(a), 116 Stat. 801.)

§ 1738. State and Territorial Statutes and Judicial Proceedings; Full Faith and Credit

The Acts of the legislature of any State, Territory, or Possession of the United States, or copies thereof, shall be authenticated by affixing the seal of such State, Territory or Possession thereto.

The records and judicial proceedings of any court of any such State, Territory or Possession, or copies thereof, shall be proved or admitted in other courts within the United States and its Territories and Possessions by the attestation of the clerk and seal of the court annexed, if a seal exists, together with a certificate of a judge of the court that the said attestation is in proper form.

Such Acts, records and judicial proceedings or copies thereof, so authenticated, shall have the same full faith and credit in every court within the United States and its Territories and Possessions as they have by law or usage in the courts of such State, Territory or Possession from which they are taken.

§ 1738A. Full Faith and Credit Given to Child Custody Determinations

(a) The appropriate authorities of every State shall enforce according to its terms, and shall not modify except as provided in subsection (f), (g), and (h) of this section, any custody determination or visitation determination made consistently with the provisions of this section by a court of another State.

(b) As used in this section, the term—

(1) "child" means a person under the age of eighteen;

(2) "contestant" means a person, including a parent or grandparent, who claims a right to custody or visitation of a child;

(3) "custody determination" means a judgment, decree, or other order of a court providing for the custody or visitation of a child, and includes permanent and temporary orders, and initial orders and modifications;

(4) "home State" means the State in which, immediately preceding the time involved, the child lived with his parents, a parent, or a person acting as parent, for at least six consecutive months, and in the case of a child less than six months old, the State in which the child lived from birth with any of such persons. Periods of temporary absence of any of such persons are counted as part of the six-month or other period;

(5) "modification" and "modify" refer to a custody or visitation determination which modifies, replaces, supersedes, or otherwise is made subsequent to, a prior custody or visitation determination concerning the same child, whether made by the same court or not;

(6) "person acting as a parent" means a person, other than a parent, who has physical custody of a child and who has either been awarded custody by a court or claims a right to custody;

(7) "physical custody" means actual possession and control of a child;

(8) "State" means a State of the United States, the District of Columbia, the Commonwealth of Puerto Rico, or a territory or possession of the United States; and

(9) "visitation determination" means a judgment, decree, or other order of a court providing for the visitation of a child and includes permanent and temporary orders and initial orders and modifications.

(c) A child custody or visitation determination made by a court of a State is consistent with the provisions of this section only if—

(1) such court has jurisdiction under the law of such State; and

(2) one of the following conditions is met:

(A) such State (i) is the home State of the child on the date of the commencement of the proceeding, or (ii) had been the child's home State within six months before the date of the commencement of the proceeding and the child is absent from such State because of his removal or retention by a contestant or for other reasons, and a contestant continues to live in such State;

(B)(i) it appears that no other State would have jurisdiction under subparagraph (A), and **(ii)** it is in the best interest of the child that a court of such State assume jurisdiction because (I) the child and his parents, or the child and at least one contestant, have a significant connection with such State other than mere physical presence in such

State, and (II) there is available in such State substantial evidence concerning the child's present or future care, protection, training, and personal relationships;

(C) the child is physically present in such State and (i) the child has been abandoned, or (ii) it is necessary in an emergency to protect the child because the child, a sibling, or parent of the child has been subjected to or threatened with mistreatment or abuse;

(D)(i) it appears that no other State would have jurisdiction under subparagraph (A), (B), (C), or (E), or another State has declined to exercise jurisdiction on the ground that the State whose jurisdiction is in issue is the more appropriate forum to determine the custody of the child, and **(ii)** it is in the best interest of the child that such court assume jurisdiction; or

(E) the court has continuing jurisdiction pursuant to subsection (d) of this section.

(d) The jurisdiction of a court of a State which has made a child custody or visitation determination consistently with the provisions of this section continues as long as the requirement of subsection (c)(1) of this section continues to be met and such State remains the residence of the child or of any contestant.

(e) Before a child custody or visitation determination is made, reasonable notice and opportunity to be heard shall be given to the contestants, any parent whose parental rights have not been previously terminated and any person who has physical custody of a child.

(f) A court of a State may modify a determination of the custody of the same child made by a court of another State, if—

(1) it has jurisdiction to make such a child custody determination; and

(2) the court of the other State no longer has jurisdiction, or it has declined to exercise such jurisdiction to modify such determination.

(g) A court of a State shall not exercise jurisdiction in any proceeding for a custody or visitation determination commenced during the pendency of a proceeding in a court of another State where such court of that other State is exercising jurisdiction consistently with the provisions of this section to make a custody or visitation determination.

(Added Dec. 28, 1980, Pub.L. 96–611, § 8(a), 94 Stat. 3569. As amended, Nov. 12, 1998, Pub.L. 105–374, § 1, 112 Stat. 3383; Oct. 28, 2000, Pub.L. 106–386, Div. B, 1303(d), 114 Stat. 1512.)

§ 1746. Unsworn Declarations Under Penalty of Perjury

Wherever, under any law of the United States or under any rule, regulation, order, or requirement made pursuant to law, any matter is required or permitted to be supported, evidenced, established, or proved by the sworn declaration, verification, certificate, statement, oath, or affidavit, in writing of the person making the same (other than a deposition, or an oath of office, or an oath required to be taken before a specified official other than a notary public), such matter may, with like force and effect, be supported, evidenced, established, or proved by the unsworn declaration, certificate, verification, or statement, in writing of such person which is subscribed by him, as true under penalty of perjury, and dated, in substantially the following form:

(1) If executed without the United States: "I declare (or certify, verify, or state) under penalty of perjury under the laws of the United States of America that the foregoing is true and correct. Executed on (date).

(Signature)".

(2) If executed within the United States, its territories, possessions, or commonwealths: "I declare (or certify, verify, or state) under penalty of perjury that the foregoing is true and correct. Executed on (date).

(Signature)".

(Added Pub.L. 94–550, § 1(a), Oct. 18, 1976, 90 Stat. 2534.)

§ 1861. Declaration of Policy

It is the policy of the United States that all litigants in Federal courts entitled to trial by jury shall have the right to grand and petit juries selected at random from a fair cross section of the community in the district or division wherein the court convenes. It is further the policy of the United States that all citizens shall have the opportunity to be considered for service on grand and petit juries in the district courts of the United States, and shall have an obligation to serve as jurors when summoned for that purpose.

(As amended Sept. 9, 1957, Pub.L. 85–315, Part V, § 152, 71 Stat. 638; Mar. 27, 1968, Pub.L. 90–274, § 101, 82 Stat. 54.)

§ 1862. Discrimination Prohibited

No citizen shall be excluded from service as a grand or petit juror in the district courts of the United States or in the Court of International Trade on account of race, color, religion, sex, national origin, or economic status.

(As amended Mar. 27, 1968, Pub.L. 90–274, § 101, 82 Stat. 54; Oct. 10, 1980, Pub.L. 96–417, Title III, § 302(c), 94 Stat. 1739.)

§ 1863. Plan for Random Jury Selection

(a) Each United States district court shall devise and place into operation a written plan for random selection of grand and petit jurors that shall be designed to achieve the objectives of sections 1861 and 1862 of this title, and that shall otherwise comply with the provisions of this title. The plan shall be placed into operation after approval by a reviewing panel consisting of the members of the judicial council of the circuit and either the chief judge of the district whose plan is being reviewed or such other active district judge of that district as the chief judge of the district may designate. The panel shall examine the plan to ascertain that it complies with the provisions of this title. If the reviewing panel finds that the plan does not comply, the panel shall state the particulars in which the plan fails to comply and direct the district court to present within a reasonable time an alternative plan remedying the defect or defects. Separate plans may be adopted for each division or combination of divisions within a judicial district. The district court may modify a plan at any time and it shall modify the plan when so directed by the reviewing panel. The district court shall promptly notify the panel, the Administrative office of the United States Courts, and the Attorney General of the United States, of the initial adoption and future modifications of the plan by filing copies therewith. Modifications of the plan made at the instance of the district court shall become effective after approval by the panel. Each district court shall submit a report on the jury selection process within its jurisdiction to the Administrative office of the United States Courts in such form and at such times as the Judicial Conference of the United States may specify. The Judicial Conference of the United States may, from time to time, adopt rules and regulations governing the provisions and the operation of the plans formulated under this title.

(b) Among other things, such plan shall—

(1) either establish a jury commission, or authorize the clerk of the court, to manage the jury selection process. If the plan establishes a jury commission, the district court shall appoint one citizen to serve with the clerk of the court as the jury commission: *Provided, however,* That the plan for the District of Columbia may establish a jury commission consisting of three citizens. The citizen jury commissioner shall not belong to the same political party as the clerk serving with him. The clerk or the jury commission, as the case may be, shall act under the supervision and control of the chief judge of the district court or such other judge of the district court as the plan may provide. Each jury commissioner shall, during his tenure in office, reside in the judicial district or division for which he is appointed. Each citizen jury commissioner shall receive compensation to be fixed by the district court plan at a rate not to exceed $50 per day for each day necessarily employed in the performance of his duties, plus reimbursement for travel, subsistence, and other necessary expenses incurred by him in the performance of such duties. The Judicial Conference of the United States may establish standards for allowance of travel, subsistence, and other necessary expenses incurred by jury commissioners.

(2) specify whether the names of prospective jurors shall be selected from the voter registration lists or the lists of actual voters of the political subdivisions within the district or division. The plan shall prescribe some other source or sources of names in addition to voter lists where necessary to foster the policy and protect the rights secured by sections 1861 and 1862 of this title. The plan for the District of Columbia may require the names of prospective jurors to be selected from the city directory rather than from voter lists. The plans for the districts of Puerto Rico and the Canal Zone may prescribe some other source or sources of names of prospective jurors in lieu of voter lists, the use of which shall be consistent with the policies declared and rights secured by sections 1861 and 1862 of this title. The plan for the district of Massachusetts may require the names of prospective jurors to be selected from the resident list provided for in Chapter 234A, Massachusetts General Laws, or comparable authority, rather than from voter lists.

(3) specify detailed procedures to be followed by the jury commission or clerk in selecting names from the sources specified in paragraph (2) of this subsection. These procedures shall be designed to ensure the random selection of a fair cross section of the persons residing in the community in the district or division wherein the court convenes. They shall ensure that names of persons residing in each of the counties, parishes, or similar political subdivisions within the judicial district or division are placed in a master jury wheel; and shall ensure that each county, parish, or similar political subdivision within the district or division is substantially proportionally represented in the master jury wheel for that judicial district, division, or combination of divisions. For the purposes of determining proportional representation in the master jury wheel, either the number of actual voters at the last general election in each county, parish, or similar political subdivision, or the number of registered voters if registration of voters is uniformly required throughout the district or division, may be used.

(4) provide for a master jury wheel (or a device similar in purpose and function) into which the names of those randomly selected shall be placed. The plan shall fix a minimum number of names to be placed initially in the master jury wheel, which shall be at least one-half of 1 per centum of the total number of persons on the lists used as a source of names for the district or division; but if this number of names is believed to be cumbersome and unnecessary, the plan may fix a smaller number of names to be placed in the master wheel, but in no event less than one thousand. The chief judge of the district court, or such other district court judge as the plan may provide, may order additional names to be placed in the master jury wheel from time to time as necessary. The plan shall provide for periodic emptying and refilling of the master jury wheel at specified times, the interval for which shall not exceed four years.

(5)(A) except as provided in subparagraph (B), specify those groups of persons or occupational classes whose members shall, on individual request therefore, be excused from jury service. Such groups or classes shall be excused only if the district court finds, and the plan states, that jury service by such class or group would entail undue hardship or extreme inconvenience to the members thereof, and excuse of members thereof would not be inconsistent with sections 1861 and 1862 of this title.

(B) specify that volunteer safety personnel, upon individual request, shall be excused from jury service. For purposes of this subparagraph, the term 'volunteer safety personnel' means individuals serving a public agency (As defined in section 1203(6) of title I of the Omnibus Crime Control and Safe Streets Act of 1968) in an official capacity, without compensation, as firefighters or members of a rescue squad or ambulance crew.

(6) specify that the following persons are barred from jury service on the ground that they are exempt: (A) members in active service in the Armed Forces of the United States; (B) members of the fire or police departments of any State, the District of Columbia, any territory or possession of the United States, or any subdivision of a State, the District of Columbia, or such territory or possession; (C) public officers in the executive, legislative, or judicial branches of the Government of the United States, or of any State, the District of Columbia, any territory or possession of the United States, or any subdivision of a State, the District of Columbia, or such territory or possession, who are actively engaged in the performance of official duties.

(7) fix the time when the names drawn from the qualified jury wheel shall be disclosed to parties and to the public. If the plan permits these names to be made public, it may nevertheless permit the chief judge of the district court, or such other district court judge as the plan may provide, to keep these names confidential in any case where the interests of justice so require.

(8) specify the procedures to be followed by the clerk or jury commission in assigning persons whose names have been drawn from the qualified jury wheel to grand and petit jury panels.

(c) The initial plan shall be devised by each district court and transmitted to the reviewing panel specified in subsection (a) of this section within one hundred and twenty days of the date of enactment of the Jury Selection and Service Act of 1968. The panel shall approve or direct the modification of each plan so submitted within sixty days thereafter. Each plan or modification made at the direction of the panel shall become effective after approval at such time thereafter as the panel directs, in no event to exceed ninety days from the date of approval. Modifications made at the instance of the district court under subsection (a) of this section shall be effective at such time thereafter as the panel directs, in no event to exceed ninety days from the date of modification.

(d) State, local, and Federal officials having custody, possession, or control of voter registration lists, lists of actual voters, or other appropriate records shall make such lists and records available to the jury commission or clerks for inspection, reproduction, and copying at all reasonable times as the commission or clerk may deem necessary and proper for the performance of duties under this title. The district courts shall have jurisdiction upon application by the Attorney General of the United States to compel compliance with this subsection by appropriate process.

(As amended Mar. 27, 1968, Pub.L. 90–274, § 101, 82 Stat. 54; Apr. 6, 1972, Pub.L. 92–269, § 2, 86 Stat. 117; Nov. 2, 1978, Pub.L. 95–572, § 2(a), 92 Stat. 2453; Nov. 19, 1988, Pub.L. 100–702, Title VIII, § 802(b), (c), 102 Stat. 4657, 4658; Oct. 29, 1992, Pub.L. 102–572, Title IV, § 401, 106 Stat. 4511.)

§ 1864. Drawing of Names From the Master Jury Wheel; Completion of Juror Qualification Form

(a) From time to time as directed by the district court, the clerk or a district judge shall draw at random from the master jury wheel the names of as many persons as may be required for jury service. The clerk or jury commission shall post a general notice for public review in the clerk's office and on the court's website explaining the process by which names are periodically and randomly drawn. The clerk or jury commission may, upon order of the court, prepare an alphabetical list of the names drawn from the master jury wheel. Any list so prepared shall not be disclosed to any person except pursuant to the district court plan or pursuant to section 1867 or 1868 of this title. The clerk or jury commission shall mail to every person whose name is drawn from the master wheel a juror qualification form accompanied by instructions to fill out and return the form, duly signed and sworn, to the clerk or jury commission by mail within ten days. If the person is unable to fill out the form, another shall do it for him, and shall indicate that he has done so and the reason therefor. In any case in which it appears that there is an omission, ambiguity, or error in a form, the clerk or jury commission shall return the form with instructions to the person to make such additions or corrections as may be necessary and to return the form to the clerk or jury commission within ten days. Any person who fails to return a completed juror qualification form as instructed may be summoned by the clerk or jury commission forthwith to appear before the clerk or jury commission to fill out a juror qualification form. A person summoned to appear because of failure to return a juror qualification form as instructed who personally appears and executes a juror qualification form before the clerk or jury commission may, at the discretion of the district court, except where his prior failure to execute and mail such form was willful, be entitled to receive for such appearance the same fees and travel allowances paid to jurors under section 1871 of this title. At the time of his appearance for jury service, any person may be required to fill out another juror qualification form in the presence of the jury commission or the clerk or the court, at which time, in such cases as it appears warranted, the person may be questioned, but only with regard to his responses to questions contained on the form. Any information thus acquired by the clerk or jury commission may be noted on the juror qualification form and transmitted to the chief judge or such district court judge as the plan may provide.

(b) Any person summoned pursuant to subsection (a) of this section who fails to appear as directed shall be ordered by the district court forthwith to appear and show cause for his failure to comply with the summons. Any person who fails to appear pursuant to such order or who fails to show good cause for noncompliance with the summons may be fined not more than $1,000, imprisoned not more than three days, ordered to perform community service, or any combination thereof. Any person who willfully misrepresents a material fact on a juror qualification form for the purpose of avoiding or securing service as a juror may be fined not more than $1,000, imprisoned not more than three days, ordered to perform community service, or any combination thereof.

(As amended Mar. 27, 1968, Pub.L. 90–274, § 101, 82 Stat. 57; Nov. 19, 1988, Pub.L. 100–702, § 803(a), 102 Stat. 4658; Oct. 13, 2008, Pub.L. 110–406, §§ 5(a), 17(a), 122 Stat. 4292, 4295.)

§ 1865. Qualifications for Jury Service

(a) The chief judge of the district court, or such other district court judge as the plan may provide, on his initiative or upon recommendation of the clerk or jury commission, or the clerk under supervision of the court if the court's jury selection plan so authorizes, shall determine solely on the basis of information provided on the juror qualification form and other competent evidence whether a person is unqualified for, or exempt, or to be excused from jury service. The clerk shall enter such determination in the space provided on the juror qualification form and in any alphabetical list of names drawn from the master jury wheel. If a person did not appear in response to a summons, such fact shall be noted on said list.

(b) In making such determination the chief judge of the district court, or such other district court judge as the plan may provide, or the clerk if the court's jury selection plan so provides, shall deem any person qualified to serve on grand and petit juries in the district court unless he—

(1) is not a citizen of the United States eighteen years old who has resided for a period of one year within the judicial district;

(2) is unable to read, write, and understand the English language with a degree of proficiency sufficient to fill out satisfactorily the juror qualification form;

(3) is unable to speak the English language;

(4) is incapable, by reason of mental or physical infirmity, to render satisfactory jury service; or

(5) has a charge pending against him for the commission of, or has been convicted in a State or Federal court of record of, a crime punishable by imprisonment for more than one year and his civil rights have not been restored.

(As amended Mar. 27, 1968, Pub.L. 90–274, § 101, 82 Stat. 58; Apr. 6, 1972, Pub.L. 92–269, § 1, 86 Stat. 117; Nov. 2, 1978, Pub.L. 95–572, § 3(a), 92 Stat. 2453; Nov. 19, 1988, Pub.L. 100–702, § 803, 102 Stat. 4642; Nov. 13, 2000, Pub.L. 106–518, 114 Stat. 2418.)

§ 1866. Selection and Summoning of Jury Panels

(a) The jury commission, or in the absence thereof the clerk, shall maintain a qualified jury wheel and shall place in such wheel names of all persons drawn from the master jury wheel who are determined to be qualified as jurors and not exempt or excused pursuant to the district court plan. From time to time, the jury commission or the clerk shall draw at random from the qualified jury wheel such number of names of persons as may be required for assignment to grand and petit jury panels. The clerk or jury commission shall post a general notice for public review in the clerk's office and on the court's website explaining the process by which names are periodically and randomly drawn. The jury commission or the clerk shall prepare a separate list of names of persons assigned to each grand and petit jury panel.

(b) When the court orders a grand or petit jury to be drawn, the clerk or jury commission or their duly designated deputies shall issue summonses for the required number of jurors.

Each person drawn for jury service may be served personally, or by registered, certified, or first-class mail addressed to such person at his usual residence or business address.

If such service is made personally, the summons shall be delivered by the clerk or the jury commission or their duly designated deputies to the marshal who shall make such service.

If such service is made by mail, the summons may be served by the marshal or by the clerk, the jury commission or their duly designated deputies, who shall make affidavit of service and shall attach thereto any receipt from the addressee for a registered or certified summons.

(c) Except as provided in section 1865 of this title or in any jury selection plan provision adopted pursuant to paragraph (5) or (6) of section 1863(b) of this title, no person or class of persons shall be disqualified, excluded, excused, or exempt from service as jurors: *Provided,* That any person summoned for jury service may be (1) excused by the court, or by the clerk under supervision of the court if the court's jury selection plan so authorizes, upon a showing of undue hardship or extreme inconvenience, for such period as the court deems necessary, at the conclusion of which such person either shall be summoned again for jury service under subsections (b) and (c) of this section or, if the court's jury selection plan so provides, the name of such person shall be reinserted into the qualified jury wheel for selection pursuant to subsection (a) of this section, or (2) excluded by the court on the ground that such person may be unable to render impartial jury service or that his service as a juror would be likely to disrupt the proceedings, or (3) excluded upon peremptory challenge as provided by law, or (4) excluded pursuant to the procedure specified by law upon a challenge by any party for good cause shown, or (5) excluded upon determination by the court that his service as a juror would be likely to threaten the secrecy of the proceedings, or otherwise adversely affect the integrity of jury deliberations. No person shall be excluded under clause (5) of this subsection unless the judge, in open court, determines that such is warranted and that exclusion of the person will not be inconsistent with sections 1861 and 1862 of this title. The number of persons excluded under clause (5) of this subsection shall not exceed one per centum of the number of persons who return executed jury qualification forms during the period, specified in the plan, between two consecutive fillings of the master jury wheel. The names of persons excluded under clause (5) of this subsection, together with detailed explanations for the exclusions, shall be forwarded immediately to the judicial council of the circuit, which shall have the power to make any appropriate order, prospective or retroactive, to redress any misapplication of clause (5) of this subsection, but otherwise exclusions effectuated under such clause shall not be subject to challenge under the provisions of this title. Any person excluded from a particular jury under clause (2), (3), or (4) of this subsection shall be eligible to sit on another jury if the basis for his initial exclusion would not be relevant to his ability to serve on such other jury.

(d) Whenever a person is disqualified, excused, exempt, or excluded from jury service, the jury commission or clerk shall note in the space provided on his juror qualification form or on the juror's card drawn from the qualified jury wheel the specific reason therefor.

(e) In any two-year period, no person shall be required to (1) serve or attend court for prospective service as a petit juror for a total of more than thirty days, except when necessary to complete service in a particular case, or (2) serve on more than one grand jury, or (3) serve as both a grand and petit juror.

(f) When there is an unanticipated shortage of available petit jurors drawn from the qualified jury wheel, the court may require the marshal to summon a sufficient number of petit jurors selected at random from the voter registration lists, lists of actual voters, or other lists specified in the plan, in a manner ordered by the court consistent with sections 1861 and 1862 of this title.

(g) Any person summoned for jury service who fails to appear as directed may be ordered by the district court to appear forthwith and show cause for failure to comply with the summons. Any person who fails to show good cause for noncompliance with a summons may be fined not more than $1,000, imprisoned not more than three days, ordered to perform community service, or any combination thereof.

(As amended May 24, 1949, c. 139, § 96, 63 Stat. 103; Mar. 27, 1968, Pub.L. 90–274, § 101, 82 Stat. 58; Dec. 11, 1970, Pub.L. 91–543, 84 Stat. 1408; Nov. 2, 1978, Pub.L. 95–572, § 2(b), 92 Stat. 2453; Jan. 12, 1983, Pub.L. 97–463, § 2, 96 Stat. 2531; Nov. 19, 1988, Pub.L. 100–702, § 801, 102 Stat. 4657; Oct. 13, 2008, Pub.L. 110–406, §§ 4, 5(b), 17(b), 122 Stat. 4292, 4295.)

§ 1867. Challenging Compliance With Selection Procedures

(a) In criminal cases, before the voir dire examination begins, or within seven days after the defendant discovered or could have discovered, by the exercise of diligence, the grounds therefor, whichever is earlier, the defendant may move to dismiss the indictment or stay the proceedings against him on the ground of substantial failure to comply with the provisions of this title in selecting the grand or petit jury.

(b) In criminal cases, before the voir dire examination begins, or within seven days after the Attorney General of the United States discovered or could have discovered, by the exercise of diligence, the grounds therefor, whichever is earlier, the Attorney General may move to dismiss the indictment or stay the proceedings on the ground of substantial failure to comply with the provisions of this title in selecting the grand or petit jury.

(c) In civil cases, before the voir dire examination begins, or within seven days after the party discovered or could have discovered, by the exercise of diligence, the grounds therefor, whichever is earlier, any party may move to stay the proceedings on the ground of substantial failure to comply with the provisions of this title in selecting the petit jury.

(d) Upon motion filed under subsection (a), (b), or (c) of this section, containing a sworn statement of facts which, if true, would constitute a substantial failure to comply with the provisions of this title, the moving party shall be entitled to present in support of such motion the testimony of the jury commission or clerk, if available, any relevant records and papers not public or otherwise available used by the jury commissioner or clerk, and any other relevant evidence. If the court determines that there has been a substantial failure to comply with the provisions of this title in selecting the grand jury, the court shall stay the proceedings pending the selection of a grand jury in conformity with this title or dismiss the indictment, whichever is appropriate. If the court determines that there has been a substantial failure to comply with the provisions of this title in selecting the petit jury, the court shall stay the proceedings pending the selection of a petit jury in conformity with this title.

(e) The procedures prescribed by this section shall be the exclusive means by which a person accused of a Federal crime, the Attorney General of the United States or a party in a civil case may challenge any jury on the ground that such jury was not selected in conformity with the provisions of this title. Nothing in this section shall preclude any person or the United States from pursuing any other remedy, civil or criminal, which may be available for the vindication or enforcement of any law prohibiting discrimination on account of race, color, religion, sex, national origin or economic status in the selection of persons for service on grand or petit juries.

(f) The contents of records or papers used by the jury commission or clerk in connection with the jury selection process shall not be disclosed, except pursuant to the district court plan or as may be necessary in the preparation or presentation of a motion under subsection (a), (b), or (c) of this section, until after the master jury wheel has been emptied and refilled pursuant to section 1863(b)(4) of this title and all persons selected to serve as jurors before the master wheel was emptied have completed such service. The parties in a case shall be allowed to inspect, reproduce, and copy such records or papers at all reasonable times during the preparation and pendency of such a motion. Any person who discloses the contents of any record or paper in violation of this subsection may be fined not more than $1,000 or imprisoned not more than one year, or both.

(As amended Sept. 2, 1957, Pub.L. 85–259, 71 Stat. 583; Mar. 27, 1968, Pub.L. 90–274, § 101, 82 Stat. 59.)

§ 1870. Challenges

In civil cases, each party shall be entitled to three peremptory challenges. Several defendants or several plaintiffs may be considered as a single party for the purposes of making challenges, or the court may allow additional peremptory challenges and permit them to be exercised separately or jointly.

All challenges for cause or favor, whether to the array or panel or to individual jurors, shall be determined by the court.

(As amended Sept. 16, 1959, Pub.L. 86–282, 73 Stat. 565.)

§ 1915. Proceedings in Forma Pauperis

(a)(1) Subject to subsection (b), any court of the United States may authorize the commencement, prosecution or defense of any suit, action or proceeding, civil or criminal, or appeal therein, without prepayment of fees or security therefor, by a person who submits an affidavit that includes a statement of all assets such prisoner possesses that the person is unable to pay such fees or give security therefor. Such affidavit shall state the nature of the action, defense or appeal and affiant's belief that the person is entitled to redress.

(2) A prisoner seeking to bring a civil action or appeal a judgment in a civil action or proceeding without prepayment of fees or security therefor, in addition to filing the affidavit filed under paragraph (1), shall submit a certified copy of the trust fund account statement (or institutional equivalent) for the prisoner for the 6-month period immediately preceding the filing of the complaint or notice of appeal, obtained from the appropriate official at each prison at which the prisoner is or was confined.

(3) An appeal may not be taken in forma pauperis if the trial court certifies in writing that it is not taken in good faith.

(b)(1) Notwithstanding subsection (a), if a prisoner brings a civil action or files an appeal in forma pauperis, the prisoner shall be required to pay the full amount of a filing fee. The court shall assess and, when funds exist, collect, as a partial payment of any court fees required by law, an initial partial filing fee of 20 percent of the greater of—

(A) the average monthly deposits to the prisoner's account; or

(B) the average monthly balance in the prisoner's account for the 6-month period immediately preceding the filing of the complaint or notice of appeal.

(2) After payment of the initial partial filing fee, the prisoner shall be required to make monthly payments of 20 percent of the preceding month's income credited to the prisoner's account. The agency having custody of the prisoner shall forward payments from the prisoner's account to the clerk of the court each time the amount in the account exceeds $10 until the filing fees are paid.

(3) In no event shall the filing fee collected exceed the amount of fees permitted by statute for the commencement of a civil action or an appeal of a civil action or criminal judgment.

(4) In no event shall a prisoner be prohibited from bringing a civil action or appealing a civil or criminal judgment for the reason that the prisoner has no assets and no means by which to pay the initial partial filing fee.

(c) Upon the filing of an affidavit in accordance with subsections (a) and (b) and the prepayment of any partial filing fee as may be required under subsection (b), the court may direct payment by the United States of the expenses of (1) printing the record on appeal in any civil or criminal case, if such printing is required by the appellate court; (2) preparing a transcript of proceedings before a United States magistrate in any civil or criminal case, if such transcript is required by the district court, in the case of proceedings conducted under section 636(b) of this title or under section 3401(b) of title 18, United States Code; and (3) printing the record on appeal if such printing is required by the appellate court, in the case of proceedings conducted pursuant to section 636(c) of this title. Such expenses shall be paid when authorized by the Director of the Administrative office of the United States Courts.

(d) The officers of the court shall issue and serve all process, and perform all duties in such cases. Witnesses shall attend as in other cases, and the same remedies shall be available as are provided for by law in other cases.

(e)(1) The court may request an attorney to represent any person unable to afford counsel.

(2) Notwithstanding any filing fee, or any portion thereof, that may have been paid, the court shall dismiss the case at any time if the court determines that—

(A) the allegation of poverty is untrue; or

(B) the action or appeal—

(i) is frivolous or malicious;

(ii) fails to state a claim on which relief may be granted; or

(iii) seeks monetary relief against a defendant who is immune from such relief.

(f)(1) Judgment may be rendered for costs at the conclusion of the suit or action as in other proceedings, but the United States shall not be liable for any of the costs thus incurred. If the United States has paid the cost of a stenographic transcript or printed record for the prevailing party, the same shall be taxed in favor of the United States.

(2)(A) If the judgment against a prisoner includes the payment of costs under this subsection, the prisoner shall be required to pay the full amount of the costs ordered.

(B) The prisoner shall be required to make payments for costs under this subsection in the same manner as is provided for filing fees under subsection (a)(2).

(C) In no event shall the costs collected exceed the amount of the costs ordered by the court.

(g) In no event shall a prisoner bring a civil action or appeal a judgment in a civil action or proceeding under this section if the prisoner has, on 3 or more prior occasions, while incarcerated or detained in any facility, brought an action or appeal in a court of the United States that was dismissed on the grounds that it is frivolous, malicious, or fails to state a claim upon which relief may be granted, unless the prisoner is under imminent danger of serious physical injury.

(h) As used in this section, the term "prisoner" means any person incarcerated or detained in any facility who is accused of, convicted of, sentenced for, or adjudicated delinquent for, violations of criminal law or the terms and conditions of parole, probation, pretrial release, or diversionary program.

(As amended May 24, 1949, c. 139, § 98, 63 Stat. 104; Oct. 31, 1951, c. 655, § 51(b, c), 65 Stat. 727; Sept. 21, 1959, Pub.L. 86–320, 73 Stat. 590; Oct. 10, 1979, Pub.L. 96–82, § 6, 93 Stat. 645; Apr. 26, 1996, Pub.L. 104–134, Title I, § 101[(a)][Title VIII, § 804(a), (c) to (e)], 110 Stat. 1321–73, 1321–74; renumbered Title I, May 2, 1996, Pub.L. 104–140, § 1(a), 110 Stat. 1327.)

§ 1920. Taxation of Costs

A judge or clerk of any court of the United States may tax as costs the following:

(1) Fees of the clerk and marshal;

(2) Fees for printed or electronically recorded transcripts necessarily obtained for use in the case;

(3) Fees and disbursements for printing and witnesses;

(4) Fees for exemplification and the costs of making copies of any materials where the copies are necessarily obtained for use in the case;

(5) Docket fees under section 1923 of this title;

(6) Compensation of court appointed experts, compensation of interpreters, and salaries, fees, expenses, and costs of special interpretation services under section 1828 of this title.

A bill of costs shall be filed in the case and, upon allowance, included in the judgment or decree.

(As amended Oct. 28, 1978, Pub.L. 95–539, § 7, 92 Stat. 2044; Oct. 13, 2008, Pub.L. 110–406, § 6, 122 Stat. 4292.)

§ 1927. Counsel's Liability for Excessive Costs

Any attorney or other person admitted to conduct cases in any court of the United States or any Territory thereof who so multiplies the proceedings in any case unreasonably and vexatiously may be required by the court to satisfy personally the excess costs, expenses, and attorneys' fees reasonably incurred because of such conduct.

(As amended Sept. 12, 1980, Pub.L. 96–349, § 3, 94 Stat. 1156.)

§ 1961. Interest

(a) Interest shall be allowed on any money judgment in a civil case recovered in a district court. Execution therefor may be levied by the marshal, in any case where, by the law of the State in which such court is held, execution may be levied for interest on judgments recovered in the courts of the State. Such interest shall be calculated from the date of the entry of the judgment, at a rate equal to the weekly average 1-year constant maturity Treasury yield, as published by the Board of Governors of the Federal Reserve System, for the calendar week preceding the date of the judgment. The Director of the Administrative Office of the United States Courts shall distribute notice of that rate and any changes in it to all Federal judges.

(b) Interest shall be computed daily to the date of payment except as provided in section 2516(b) of this title and section 1304(b) of title 31, and shall be compounded annually.

(c)(1) This section shall not apply in any judgment of any court with respect to any internal revenue tax case. Interest shall be allowed in such cases at the underpayment rate or overpayment rate (whichever is appropriate) established under section 6621 of the Internal Revenue Code of 1954.

(2) Except as otherwise provided in paragraph (1) of this subsection, interest shall be allowed on all final judgments against the United States in the United States Court of Appeals for the Federal circuit, at the rate provided in subsection (a) and as provided in subsection (b).

(3) Interest shall be allowed, computed, and paid on judgments of the United States Court of Federal Claims only as provided in paragraph (1) of this subsection or in any other provision of law.

(4) This section shall not be construed to affect the interest on any judgment of any court not specified in this section.

(As amended Apr. 2, 1982, Pub.L. 97–164, Title III, § 302(a), 96 Stat. 55; Sept. 13, 1982, Pub.L. 97–258, § 2(m)(1), 96 Stat. 1062; Jan. 12, 1983, Pub.L. 97–452, § 2(d)(1), 96 Stat. 2478; Oct. 22, 1986, Pub.L. 99–514, Title XV, § 1511(c)(17), 100 Stat. 2745; Oct. 29, 1992, Pub.L. 102–572, Title IX, § 902(b)(1), 106 Stat. 4516; Dec. 21, 2000, Pub.L. 106–554, § 1(a)(7), 114 Stat. 2763, 2763A–636.)

§ 2071. Rule-Making Power Generally

(a) The Supreme Court and all courts established by Act of Congress may from time to time prescribe rules for the conduct of their business.

Such rules shall be consistent with Acts of Congress and rules of practice and procedure prescribed under section 2072 of this title.

(b) Any rule prescribed by a court, other than the Supreme Court, under subsection (a) shall be prescribed only after giving appropriate public notice and an opportunity for comment. Such rule shall take effect upon the date specified by the prescribing court and shall have such effect on pending proceedings as the prescribing court may order.

(c)(1) A rule of a district court prescribed under subsection (a) shall remain in effect unless modified or abrogated by the judicial council of the relevant circuit.

(2) Any other rule prescribed by a court other than the Supreme Court under subsection (a) shall remain in effect unless modified or abrogated by the Judicial Conference.

(d) Copies of rules prescribed under subsection (a) by a district court shall be furnished to the judicial council, and copies of all rules prescribed by a court other than the Supreme Court under subsection (a) shall be furnished to the Director of the Administrative office of the United States Courts and made available to the public.

(e) If the prescribing court determines that there is an immediate need for a rule, such court may proceed under this section without public notice and opportunity for comment, but such court shall promptly thereafter afford such notice and opportunity for comment.

(f) No rule may be prescribed by a district court other than under this section.

(As amended May 24, 1949, c. 139, § 102, 63 Stat. 104; Nov. 19, 1988, Pub.L. 100–702, § 403(a)(1), 102 Stat. 4650.)

§ 2072. Rules of Procedure and Evidence; Power to Prescribe

(a) The Supreme Court shall have the power to prescribe general rules of practice and procedure and rules of evidence for cases in the United States district courts (including proceedings before magistrates thereof) and courts of appeals.

(b) Such rules shall not abridge, enlarge or modify any substantive right. All laws in conflict with such rules shall be of no further force or effect after such rules have taken effect.

(c) Such rules may define when a ruling of a district court is final for the purposes of appeal under section 1291 of this title.

(Added Nov. 19, 1988, Pub.L. 100–702, § 401(a), 102 Stat. 4648. As amended Dec. 1, 1990, Pub.L. 101–650, § 315, 104 Stat. 5115, 5117.)

§ 2073. Rules of Procedure and Evidence; Method of Prescribing

(a)(1) The Judicial Conference shall prescribe and publish the procedures for the consideration of proposed rules under this section.

(2) The Judicial Conference may authorize the appointment of committees to assist the Conference by recommending rules to be prescribed under sections 2072 and 2075 of this title. Each such committee shall consist of members of the bench and the professional bar, and trial and appellate judges.

(b) The Judicial Conference shall authorize the appointment of a standing committee on rules of practice, procedure, and evidence under subsection (a) of this section. Such standing committee shall review each recommendation of any other committees so appointed and recommend to the Judicial Conference rules of practice, procedure, and evidence and such changes in rules proposed by a committee appointed under subsection (a)(2) of this section as may be necessary to maintain consistency and otherwise promote the interest of justice.

(c)(1) Each meeting for the transaction of business under this chapter by any committee appointed under this section shall be open to the public, except when the committee so meeting, in open session and with a majority present, determines that it is in the public interest that all or part of the remainder of the meeting on that day shall be closed to the public, and states the reason for so closing the meeting. Minutes of each meeting for the transaction of business under this chapter shall be maintained by the committee and made available to the public, except that any portion of such minutes, relating to a closed meeting and made available to the public, may contain such deletions as may be necessary to avoid frustrating the purposes of closing the meeting.

(2) Any meeting for the transaction of business under this chapter, by a committee appointed under this section, shall be preceded by sufficient notice to enable all interested persons to attend.

(d) In making a recommendation under this section or under section 2072 or 2075, the body making that recommendation shall provide a proposed rule, an explanatory note on the rule, and a written report explaining the body's action, including any minority or other separate views.

(e) Failure to comply with this section does not invalidate a rule prescribed under section 2072 or 2075 of this title.

(Added Nov. 19, 1988, Pub.L. 100–702, § 401(a), 102 Stat. 4648. As Amended, Oct. 22, 1994, Pub.L. 103–394, § 104(e), 108 Stat. 4110.)

§ 2074. Rules of Procedure and Evidence; Submission to Congress; Effective Date

(a) The Supreme Court shall transmit to the Congress not later than May 1 of the year in which a rule prescribed under section 2072 is to become effective a copy of the proposed rule. Such rule shall take effect no earlier than December 1 of the year in which such rule is so transmitted unless otherwise provided by law. The Supreme Court may fix the extent such rule shall apply to proceedings then pending, except that the Supreme Court shall not require the application of such rule to further proceedings then pending to the extent that, in the opinion of the court in which such proceedings are pending, the application of such rule in such proceedings would not be feasible or would work injustice, in which event the former rule applies.

(b) Any such rule creating, abolishing, or modifying an evidentiary privilege shall have no force or effect unless approved by Act of Congress.

(As amended May 24, 1949, c. 139, § 103, 63 Stat. 104; July 18, 1949, c. 343, § 2, 63 Stat. 446; May 10, 1950, c. 174, § 2, 64 Stat. 158; July 7, 1958, Pub.L. 85–508, § 12(m), 72 Stat. 348; Nov. 6, 1966, Pub.L. 89–773, § 1, 80 Stat. 1323; Nov. 19, 1988, Pub.L. 100–702, § 401, 102 Stat. 4649.)

§ 2106. Determination

The Supreme Court or any other court of appellate jurisdiction may affirm, modify, vacate, set aside or reverse any judgment, decree, or order of a court lawfully brought before it for review, and may remand the cause and direct the entry of such appropriate judgment, decree, or order, or require such further proceedings to be had as may be just under the circumstances.

§ 2111. Harmless Error

On the hearing of any appeal or writ of certiorari in any case, the court shall give judgment after an examination of the record without regard to errors or defects which do not affect the substantial rights of the parties.

(Added May 24, 1949, c. 139, § 110, 63 Stat. 105.)

§ 2201. Creation of Remedy

(a) In a case of actual controversy within its jurisdiction, except with respect to Federal taxes other than actions brought under section 7428 of the Internal Revenue Code of 1986, a proceeding under section 505 or 1146 of title 11, or in any civil action involving an antidumping or countervailing duty proceeding regarding a class or kind of merchandise of a free trade area country (as defined in section 516A(f)(9) of the Tariff Act of 1930), as determined by the administering authority, any court of the United States, upon the filing of an appropriate pleading, may declare the rights and other legal relations of any interested party seeking such declaration, whether or not further relief is or could be sought. Any such declaration shall have the force and effect of a final judgment or decree and shall be reviewable as such.

(b) For limitations on actions brought with respect to drug patents see section 505 or 512 of the Federal Food, Drug, and Cosmetic Act, or section 351 of the Public Health Service Act.

(As amended May 24, 1949, c. 139, § 111, 63 Stat. 105; Aug. 28, 1954, c. 1033, 68 Stat. 890; July 7, 1958, Pub.L. 85–508, § 12(p), 72 Stat. 349; Oct. 4, 1976, Pub.L. 94–455, Title XIII, § 1306(b)(8), 90 Stat. 1719; Nov. 6, 1978, Pub.L. 95–598, Title II, § 249, 92 Stat. 2672; Sept. 24, 1984, Pub.L. 98–417, Title I, § 106, 98 Stat. 1597; Sept. 28, 1988, Pub.L. 100–449, Title IV, § 402(c), 102 Stat. 1884; Nov. 16, 1988, Pub.L. 100–670, Title I, § 107(b), 102 Stat. 3984; Dec. 8, 1993, Pub.L. 103–182, § 414(B), 107 Stat. 2147; Mar. 23, 2010, Pub.L. 111–148, Title VII, § 7002(c)(2), 124 Stat. 816; Jan. 29, 2020, Pub.L. 116–113, Title IV, § 423(b), 134 Stat. 11.)

§ 2202. Further Relief

Further necessary or proper relief based on a declaratory judgment or decree may be granted, after reasonable notice and hearing, against any adverse party whose rights have been determined by such judgment.

§ 2283. Stay of State Court Proceedings

A court of the United States may not grant an injunction to stay proceedings in a State court except as expressly authorized by Act of Congress, or where necessary in aid of its jurisdiction, or to protect or effectuate its judgments.

§ 2361. Process and Procedure

In any civil action of interpleader or in the nature of interpleader under section 1335 of this title, a district court may issue its process for all claimants and enter its order restraining them from instituting or prosecuting any proceeding in any State or United States court affecting the property, instrument or obligation involved in the interpleader action until further order of the court. Such process and order shall be returnable at such time as the court or judge thereof directs, and shall be addressed to and served by the United States marshals for the respective districts where the claimants reside or may be found.

Such district court shall hear and determine the case, and may discharge the plaintiff from further liability, make the injunction permanent, and make all appropriate orders to enforce its judgment.

(As amended May 24, 1949, c. 139, § 117, 63 Stat. 105.)

§ 2402. Jury Trial in Actions Against United States

Subject to chapter 179 of this title, any action against the United States under section 1346 shall be tried by the court without a jury, except that any action against the United States under section 1346(a)(1) shall, at the request of either party to such action, be tried by the court with a jury.

(As amended July 30, 1954, c. 648, § 2(a), 68 Stat. 589; Oct. 26, 1996, Pub.L. 104–331, § 3(b)(3), (d), 110 Stat. 4069, 4071.)

§ 2403. Intervention by United States or a State; Constitutional Question

(a) In any action, suit or proceeding in a court of the United States to which the United States or any agency, officer or employee thereof is not a party, wherein the constitutionality of any Act of Congress affecting the public interest is drawn in question, the court shall certify such fact to the Attorney General, and shall permit the United States to intervene for presentation of evidence, if evidence is otherwise admissible in the case, and for argument on the question of constitutionality. The United States shall, subject to the applicable provisions of law, have all the rights of a party and be subject to all liabilities of a party as to court costs to the extent necessary for a proper presentation of the facts and law relating to the question of constitutionality.

(b) In any action, suit, or proceeding in a court of the United States to which a State or any agency, officer, or employee thereof is not a party, wherein the constitutionality of any statute of that State affecting the public interest is drawn in question, the court shall certify such fact to the attorney general of the State, and shall permit the State to intervene for presentation of evidence, if evidence is otherwise admissible in the case, and for argument on the question of constitutionality. The State shall, subject to the applicable provisions of law, have all the rights of a party and be subject to all liabilities of a party as to court costs to the extent necessary for a proper presentation of the facts and law relating to the question of constitutionality.

(As amended Aug. 12, 1976, Pub.L. 94–381, § 5, 90 Stat. 1120.)

§ 2412. Costs and Fees

(a)(1) Except as otherwise specifically provided by statute, a judgment for costs, as enumerated in section 1920 of this title, but not including the fees and expenses of attorneys, may be awarded to the prevailing party in any civil action brought by or against the United States or any agency or any official of the United States acting in his or her official capacity in any court having jurisdiction of such action. A judgment for costs when taxed against the United States shall, in an amount established by statute, court rule, or order, be limited to reimbursing in whole or in part the prevailing party for the costs incurred by such party in the litigation.

(2) A judgment for costs, when awarded in favor of the United States in an action brought by the United States, may include an amount equal to the filing fee prescribed under section 1914(a) of this title. The preceding sentence shall not be construed as requiring the United States to pay any filing fee.

(b) Unless expressly prohibited by statute, a court may award reasonable fees and expenses of attorneys, in addition to the costs which may be awarded pursuant to subsection (a), to the prevailing party in any civil action brought by or against the United States or any agency or any official of the United States acting in his or her official capacity in any court having jurisdiction of such action. The United States shall be liable for such fees and expenses to the same extent that any other party would be liable under the common law or under the terms of any statute which specifically provides for such an award.

(c)(1) Any judgment against the United States or any agency and any official of the United States acting in his or her official capacity for costs pursuant to subsection (a) shall be paid as provided in sections 2414 and 2517 of this title and shall be in addition to any relief provided in the judgment.

(2) Any judgment against the United States or any agency and any official of the United States acting in his or her official capacity for fees and expenses of attorneys pursuant to subsection (b) shall be paid as provided in sections 2414 and 2517 of this title, except that if the basis for the award is a finding that the United States acted in bad faith, then the award shall be paid by any agency found to have acted in bad faith and shall be in addition to any relief provided in the judgment.

(d)(1)(A) Except as otherwise specifically provided by statute, a court shall award to a prevailing party other than the United States fees and other expenses, in addition to any costs awarded pursuant to subsection (a), incurred by that party in any civil action (other than cases sounding in tort), including proceedings for judicial review of agency action, brought by or against the United States in any court having jurisdiction of that action, unless the court finds that the position of the United States was substantially justified or that special circumstances make an award unjust.

(B) A party seeking an award of fees and other expenses shall, within thirty days of final judgment in the action, submit to the court an application for fees and other expenses which shows that the party is a prevailing party and is eligible to receive an award under this subsection, and the amount sought, including an itemized statement from any attorney or expert witness representing or appearing in behalf of the party stating the actual time expended and the rate at which fees and other expenses are computed. The party shall also allege that the position of the United States was not substantially justified. Whether or not the position of the United States was substantially justified shall be determined on the basis of the record (including the record with respect to the action or failure to act by the agency upon which the civil action is based) which is made in the civil action for which fees and other expenses are sought.

(C) The court, in its discretion, may reduce the amount to be awarded pursuant to this subsection, or deny an award, to the extent that the prevailing party during the course of the proceedings engaged in conduct which unduly and unreasonably protracted the final resolution of the matter in controversy.

(D) If, in a civil action brought by the United States or a proceeding for judicial review of an adversary adjudication described in section 504(a)(4) of title 5, the demand by the United States is substantially in excess of the judgment finally obtained by the United States and is unreasonable when compared with such judgment, under the facts and circumstances of the case, the court shall award to the party the fees and other expenses related to defending against the excessive demand, unless the party has committed a willful violation of law or otherwise acted in bad faith, or special circumstances make an award unjust. Fees and expenses awarded under this subparagraph shall be paid only as a consequence of appropriations provided in advance.

(2) For the purposes of this subsection—

(A) "fees and other expenses" includes the reasonable expenses of expert witnesses, the reasonable cost of any study, analysis, engineering report, test, or project which is found by the court to be necessary for the preparation of the party's case, and reasonable attorney fees (The amount of fees awarded under this subsection shall be based upon prevailing market rates for the kind and quality of the services furnished, except that (i) no expert witness shall be compensated at a rate in excess of the highest rate of compensation for expert witnesses paid by the United States; and (ii) attorney fees shall not be awarded in excess of $125 per hour unless the court determines that an increase in the cost of living or a special factor, such as the limited availability of qualified attorneys for the proceedings involved, justifies a higher fee.);

(B) "party" means (i) an individual whose net worth did not exceed $2,000,000 at the time the civil action was filed, or (ii) any owner of an unincorporated business, or any partnership, corporation, association, unit of local government, or organization, the net worth of which did not exceed $7,000,000 at the time the civil action was filed, and which had not more than 500 employees at the time the civil action was filed; except that an organization described in section 501(c)(3) of the Internal Revenue Code of 1986 (26 U.S.C. 501(c)(3)) exempt from taxation under section 501(a) of such Code, or a cooperative association as defined in section 15(a) of the Agricultural Marketing Act (12 U.S.C.

1141j(a)), may be a party regardless of the net worth of such organization or cooperative association or for purposes of subsection (d)(1)(D), a small entity as defined in section 601 of Title 5;

(C) "United States" includes any agency and any official of the United States acting in his or her official capacity;

(D) "position of the United States" means, in addition to the position taken by the United States in the civil action, the action or failure to act by the agency upon which the civil action is based; except that fees and expenses may not be awarded to a party for any portion of the litigation in which the party has unreasonably protracted the proceedings;

(E) "civil action brought by or against the United States" includes an appeal by a party, other than the United States, from a decision of a contracting officer rendered pursuant to a disputes clause in a contract with the Government or pursuant to the Contract Disputes Act of 1978;

(F) "court" includes the United States Court of Federal Claims and the United States Court of Appeals for Veterans Claims;

(G) "final judgment" means a judgment that is final and not appealable, and includes an order of settlement;

(H) "prevailing party", in the case of eminent domain proceedings, means a party who obtains a final judgment (other than by settlement), exclusive of interest, the amount of which is at least as close to the highest valuation of the property involved that is attested to at trial on behalf of the property owner as it is to the highest valuation of the property involved that is attested to at trial on behalf of the Government; and

(I) "demand" means the express demand of the United States which led to the adversary adjudication, but shall not include a recitation of the maximum statutory penalty (i) in the complaint, or (ii) elsewhere when accompanied by an express demand for a lesser amount.

(3) In awarding fees and other expenses under this subsection to a prevailing party in any action for judicial review of an adversary adjudication, as defined in subsection (b)(1)(C) of section 504 of title 5, or an adversary adjudication subject to chapter 71 of title 41, the court shall include in that award fees and other expenses to the same extent authorized in subsection (a) of such section, unless the court finds that during such adversary adjudication the position of the United States was substantially justified, or that special circumstances make an award unjust.

(4) Fees and other expenses awarded under this subsection to a party shall be paid by any agency over which the party prevails from any funds made available to the agency by appropriation or otherwise.

(5)(A) Not later than March 31 of the first fiscal year beginning after the date of enactment of the John D. Dingell, Jr. Conservation, Management, and Recreation Act, and every fiscal year thereafter, the Chairman of the Administrative Conference of the United States shall submit to Congress and make publicly available online a report on the amount of fees and other expenses awarded during the preceding fiscal year pursuant to this subsection.

(B) Each report under subparagraph (A) shall describe the number, nature, and amount of the awards, the claims involved in the controversy, and any other relevant information that may aid Congress in evaluating the scope and impact of such awards.

(C)(i) Each report under subparagraph (A) shall account for all payments of fees and other expenses awarded under this subsection that are made pursuant to a settlement agreement, regardless of whether the settlement agreement is sealed or otherwise subject to a nondisclosure provision.

(ii) The disclosure of fees and other expenses required under clause (i) shall not affect any other information that is subject to a nondisclosure provision in a settlement agreement.

(D) The Chairman of the Administrative Conference of the United States shall include and clearly identify in each annual report under subparagraph (A), for each case in which an award of fees and other expenses is included in the report—

(i) any amounts paid under section 1304 of title 31 for a judgment in the case;

(ii) the amount of the award of fees and other expenses; and

(iii) the statute under which the plaintiff filed suit.

(6) As soon as practicable, and in any event not later than the date on which the first report under paragraph (5)(A) is required to be submitted, the Chairman of the Administrative Conference of the United States shall create and maintain online a searchable database containing, with respect to each award of fees and other expenses under this subsection made on or after the date of enactment of the John D. Dingell, Jr. Conservation, Management, and Recreation Act, the following information:

(A) The case name and number, hyperlinked to the case, if available.

(B) The name of the agency involved in the case.

(C) The name of each party to whom the award was made as such party is identified in the order or other court document making the award.

(D) A description of the claims in the case.

(E) The amount of the award.

(F) The basis for the finding that the position of the agency concerned was not substantially justified.

(7) The online searchable database described in paragraph (6) may not reveal any information the disclosure of which is prohibited by law or a court order.

(8) The head of each agency (including the Attorney General of the United States) shall provide to the Chairman of the Administrative Conference of the United States in a timely manner all information requested by the Chairman to comply with the requirements of paragraphs (5), (6), and (7).

(e) The provisions of this section shall not apply to any costs, fees, and other expenses in connection with any proceeding to which section 7430 of the Internal Revenue Code of 1954 applies (determined without regard to subsections (b) and (f) of such section). Nothing in the preceding sentence shall prevent the awarding under subsection (a) of this section, of costs enumerated in section 1920 of this title (as in effect on October 1, 1981).

(f) If the United States appeals an award of costs or fees and other expenses made against the United States under this section and the award is affirmed in whole or in part, interest shall be paid on the amount of the award as affirmed. Such interest shall be computed at the rate determined under section 1961(a) of this title, and shall run from the date of the award through the day before the date of the mandate of affirmance.

(As amended July 18, 1966, Pub.L. 89–507, § 1, 80 Stat. 308; Oct. 21, 1980, Pub.L. 96–481, Title II, § 204(a), (c), 94 Stat. 2327, 2329; Sept. 3, 1982, Pub.L. 97–248, Title II, § 292(c), 96 Stat. 574; Aug. 5, 1985, Pub.L. 99–80, §§ 2, 6, 99 Stat. 184, 186; Oct. 29, 1992, Pub.L. 102–572, Title III, § 301(a), Title V, §§ 502(b), 506(a), 106 Stat. 4511–4513, 4516; Dec. 21, 1995, Pub.L. 104–66, Title I, § 1091(b), 109 Stat. 722; Mar. 29, 1996, Pub.L. 104–121, Title II, § 232, 110 Stat. 863; Nov. 11, 1998, Pub.L. 105–368, Title V, § 512(b)(1)(B), 112 Stat. 3342; Jan. 4, 2011, Pub.L. 111–350, § 5(g)(9), 124 Stat. 3848; Mar. 12, 2019, Pub.L. 116–9, Title IV, § 4201(a)(2), (3), 133 Stat. 763.)

SELECTED PROVISIONS OF THE CONSTITUTION OF CALIFORNIA

■ ■ ■

Article I, §§ 1, 16.
Article VI, §§ 1–4, 6–13.

ARTICLE I

[*Inalienable Rights*]

Sec. 1. All people are by nature free and independent and have inalienable rights. Among these are enjoying and defending life and liberty, acquiring, possessing, and protecting property, and pursuing and obtaining safety, happiness, and privacy.

(Added Nov. 5, 1974.)

[*Trial by Jury*]

Sec. 16. Trial by jury is an inviolate right and shall be secured to all, but in a civil cause three-fourths of the jury may render a verdict. A jury may be waived in a criminal cause by the consent of both parties expressed in open court by the defendant and the defendant's counsel. In a civil cause a jury may be waived by the consent of the parties expressed as prescribed by statute.

[*Number of Jurors in Civil Trials*]

In civil causes the jury shall consist of 12 persons or a lesser number agreed on by the parties in open court. In civil causes other than causes within the appellate jurisdiction of the court of appeal the Legislature may provide that the jury shall consist of eight persons or a lesser number agreed on by the parties in open court.

[*Number of Jurors in Criminal Trials*]

In criminal actions in which a felony is charged, the jury shall consist of 12 persons. In criminal actions in which a misdemeanor is charged, the jury shall consist of 12 persons or a lesser number agreed on by the parties in open court.

(As amended November 4, 1980; Stats.1996, Res. ch. 36, (Prop. 220, approved June 2, 1998, eff. June 3, 1998).)

ARTICLE VI

Judicial

[*Judicial Power Vested in Courts*]

Sec. 1. The judicial power of this State is vested in the Supreme Court, courts of appeal, and superior courts, all of which are courts of record.

(New section adopted November 8, 1966; Amended Nov. 8, 1988; Stats.1994, Res. ch. 113 (Prop. 191, approved Nov. 8, 1994, operative Jan. 1, 1995); Stats.1996, Res. ch. 36, (Prop. 220, approved June 2, 1998, operative June 3, 1998); Stats.2002, res. ch. 88 (Prop. 48, approved Nov. 5, 2002, operative Nov. 6, 2002).)

[*Supreme Court*]

Sec. 2. The Supreme Court consists of the Chief Justice of California and 6 associate justices. The Chief Justice may convene the court at any time. Concurrence of 4 judges present at the argument is necessary for a judgment.

An acting Chief Justice shall perform all functions of the Chief Justice when the Chief Justice is absent or unable to act. The Chief Justice or, if the Chief Justice fails to do so, the court shall select an associate justice as acting Chief Justice.

(As amended November 5, 1974.)

[*Judicial Districts—Courts of Appeal*]

Sec. 3. The Legislature shall divide the State into districts each containing a court of appeal with one or more divisions. Each division consists of a presiding justice and 2 or more associate justices. It has the power of a court of appeal and shall conduct itself as a 3-judge court. Concurrence of 2 judges present at the argument is necessary for a judgment.

An acting presiding justice shall perform all functions of the presiding justice when the presiding justice is absent or unable to act. The presiding justice or, if the presiding justice fails to do so, the Chief Justice shall select an associate justice of that division as acting presiding justice.

(As amended November 5, 1974.)

[*Superior Courts*]

Sec. 4. In each county there is a superior court of one or more judges. The Legislature shall prescribe the number of judges and provide for the officers and employees of each superior court. If the governing body of each affected county concurs, the Legislature may provide that one or more judges serve more than one superior court.

In each superior court there is an appellate division. The Chief Justice shall assign judges to the appellate division for specified terms pursuant to rules, not inconsistent with statute, adopted by the Judicial Council to promote the independence of the appellate division.

(As amended November 5, 1974; Stats.1996, Res. ch. 36, (Prop. 220, approved June 2, 1998, operative June 3, 1998).)

[*Judicial Council—Membership and Powers*]

Sec. 6. (a) The Judicial Council consists of the Chief Justice and one other judge of the Supreme Court, 3 judges of courts of appeal, 10 judges of superior courts, two nonvoting court administrators, and any other nonvoting members as determined by the voting membership of the council, each appointed by the Chief Justice for a three-year term pursuant to procedures established by the council; four members of the State Bar appointed by its governing body for three-year terms; and one member of each house of the Legislature appointed as provided by the house.

(b) Council membership terminates if a member ceases to hold the position that qualified the member for appointment. A vacancy shall be filled by the appointing power for the remainder of the term.

(c) The council may appoint an Administrative Director of the Courts, who serves at its pleasure and performs functions delegated by the council or the Chief Justice, other than adopting rules of court administration, practice and procedure.

(d) To improve the administration of justice the council shall survey judicial business and make recommendations to the courts, make recommendations annually to the Governor and Legislature, adopt rules for court administration, practice and procedure, and perform other functions prescribed by statute. The rules adopted shall not be inconsistent with statute.

(e) The Chief Justice shall seek to expedite judicial business and to equalize the work of judges. The Chief Justice may provide for the assignment of any judge to another court but only with the judge's consent if the court is of lower jurisdiction. A retired judge who consents may be assigned to any court.

(f) Judges shall report to the council as the Chief Justice directs concerning the condition of judicial business in their courts. They shall cooperate with the council and hold court as assigned.

(As amended November 5, 1974; Stats.1994, Res. ch. 113 (Prop. 191, approved Nov. 8, 1994, operative Jan. 1, 1995); Stats.1996, Res. ch. 36, (Prop. 220, approved June 2, 1998, operative June 3, 1998); Stats.2002, Res. ch. 88 (Prop. 48, approved Nov. 5, 2002, operative Nov. 6, 2002).)

[*Commission on Judicial Appointments—Membership*]

Sec. 7. The Commission on Judicial Appointments consists of the Chief Justice, the Attorney General, and the presiding justice of the court of appeal of the affected district or, if there are 2 or more presiding justices, the one who has presided longest or, when a nomination or appointment to the Supreme Court is to be considered, the presiding justice who has presided longest on any court of appeal.

(New section adopted November 8, 1966.)

[*Commission On Judicial Performance*]

Sec. 8. (a) The Commission on Judicial Performance consists of one judge of a court of appeal and two judges of superior courts, and each appointed by the Supreme Court; 2 members of the State Bar who have practiced law in this State for 10 years, each appointed by the Governor; and 6 citizens who are not judges, retired judges, or members of the State Bar of California, 2 of whom shall be appointed by the Governor, 2 by the Senate Committee on Rules, and 2 by the Speaker of the Assembly. Except as provided in subdivisions (b) and (c), all terms are for 4 years. No member shall serve more than 2 4-year terms, or for more than a total of 10 years if appointed to fill a vacancy.

(b) Commission membership terminates if a member ceases to hold the position that qualified the member for appointment. A vacancy shall be filled by the appointing power for the remainder of the term. A member whose term has expired may continue to serve until the vacancy has been filled by the appointing power. Appointing powers may appoint members who are already serving on the commission prior to March 1, 1995, to a single 2-year term, but may not appoint them to an additional term thereafter.

(c) To create staggered terms among the members of the Commission on Judicial Performance, the following members shall be appointed, as follows:

(1) Two members appointed by the Supreme Court to a term commencing March 1, 1995, shall each serve a term of 2 years and may be reappointed to one full term.

(2) One attorney appointed by the Governor to a term commencing March 1, 1995, shall serve a term of 2 years and may be reappointed to one full term.

(3) One citizen member appointed by the Governor to a term commencing March 1, 1995, shall serve a term of 2 years and may be reappointed to one full term.

(4) One member appointed by the Senate Committee on Rules to a term commencing March 1, 1995, shall serve a term of 2 years and may be reappointed to one full term.

(5) One member appointed by the Speaker of the Assembly to a term commencing March 1, 1995, shall serve a term of 2 years and may be reappointed to one full term.

(6) All other members shall be appointed to full 4-year terms commencing March 1, 1995.

(As amended November 5, 1974; November 2, 1976; November 8, 1988; Stats.1994, Res. ch. 111 (Prop. 191, approved Nov. 8, 1994, operative Jan. 1, 1995); Stats.1996, Res. ch. 36, (Prop. 220, approved June 2, 1998, operative June 3, 1998); Stats.2002, Res. ch. 88 (Prop. 48, approved Nov. 5, 2002, operative Nov. 6, 2002).)

[*State Bar*]

Sec. 9. The State Bar of California is a public corporation. Every person admitted and licensed to practice law in this State is and shall be a member of the State Bar except while holding office as a judge of a court of record.

(New section adopted November 8, 1966.)

[*Jurisdiction—Original*]

Sec. 10. The Supreme Court, courts of appeal, superior courts, and their judges have original jurisdiction in habeas corpus proceedings. Those courts also have original jurisdiction in proceedings for extraordinary relief in the nature of mandamus, certiorari, and prohibition. The appellate division of the superior court has original jurisdiction in proceedings for extraordinary relief in the nature of mandamus, certiorari, and prohibition directed to the superior court in causes subject to its appellate jurisdiction.

Superior courts have original jurisdiction in all other causes.

The court may make such comment on the evidence and the testimony and credibility of any witness as in its opinion is necessary for the proper determination of the cause.

(New section adopted November 8, 1966; Amended by Stats.1996, Res. ch. 36, (Prop. 220, approved June 2, 1998, operative June 3, 1998); Stats.2002, Res. ch. 88 (Prop. 48, approved Nov. 5, 2002, operative Nov. 6, 2002).)

[*Jurisdiction—Appellate*]

Sec. 11. (a) The Supreme Court has appellate jurisdiction when judgment of death has been pronounced. With that exception courts of appeal have appellate jurisdiction when superior courts have original jurisdiction in causes of a type within the appellate jurisdiction of the courts of appeal on June 30, 1995, and in other causes prescribed by statute. When appellate jurisdiction in civil causes is determined by the amount in controversy, the Legislature may change the appellate jurisdiction of the courts of appeal by changing the jurisdictional amount in controversy.

(b) Except as provided in subdivision (a), the appellate division of the superior court has appellate jurisdiction in causes prescribed by statute.

(c) The Legislature may permit courts exercising appellate jurisdiction to take evidence and make findings of fact when jury trial is waived or not a matter of right.

(New section adopted November 8, 1966. Amended by Stats.1994, Res. ch. 113 (Prop. 191, approved Nov. 8, 1994, operative Jan. 1, 1995); Stats.1996, Res. ch. 36, (Prop. 220, approved June 2, 1998, operative June 3, 1998).)

[*Transfer of Causes—Jurisdiction—Review of Decisions*]

Sec. 12. (a) The Supreme Court may, before decision, transfer to itself a cause in a court of appeal. It may, before decision, transfer a cause from itself to a court of appeal or from one court of appeal or division to another. The court to which a cause is transferred has jurisdiction.

(b) The Supreme Court may review the decision of a court of appeal in any cause.

(c) The Judicial Council shall provide, by rules of court, for the time and procedure for transfer and for review, including, among other things, provisions for the time and procedure for transfer with instructions, for review of all or part of a decision, and for remand as improvidently granted.

(d) This section shall not apply to an appeal involving a judgment of death.

(As amended November 6, 1984. Operative May 6, 1985.)

[*Judgment—When Set Aside*]

Sec. 13. No judgment shall be set aside, or new trial granted, in any cause, on the ground of misdirection of the jury, or of the improper admission or rejection of evidence, or for any error as to any matter of pleading, or for any error as to any matter of procedure, unless, after an examination of the entire cause, including the evidence, the court shall be of the opinion that the error complained of has resulted in a miscarriage of justice.

(New section adopted November 8, 1966.)

SELECTED PROVISIONS OF CALIFORNIA CODE OF CIVIL PROCEDURE

■ ■ ■

Current with legislation through the 2025 Portion of the 2025–2026 Regular Session

Summary Table of Contents

TITLE 7A. PRETRIAL CONFERENCES §§ 575–576

TITLE 8. OF THE TRIAL AND JUDGMENT IN CIVIL ACTIONS

1. Judgment in General §§ 577, 580–581c
1.5 Dismissal for Delay in Prosecution §§ 583.130, 583.150, 583.210–583.220, 583.240–583.250, 583.310, 583.330–583.360, 583.410–583.420
2. Judgment Upon Failure to Answer §§ 585–586
3. Issues—The Mode of Trial and Postponements §§ 588, 592, 598
4. Trial by Jury §§ 607–608, 613, 618, 624–625, 629–630
4.5 Voluntary Expedited Jury Trials §§ 630.01–630.11
4.6 Mandatory Expedited Jury Trials in Limited Civil Cases §§ 630.20–630.29
5. Trial by Court §§ 631–631.3, 631.8
6. Of References and Trials by Referees §§ 638–639
7. Provisions Relating to Trials in General §§ 657, 659–660, 662–663
8. The Manner of Giving and Entering Judgment § 664.6

TITLE 9. ENFORCEMENT OF JUDGMENTS

3. Period for Enforcement and Renewal of Judgments §§ 683.010–683.180

TITLE 11. CONTRIBUTION AMONG JOINT JUDGMENT DEBTORS

1. Releases from and Contribution Among Joint Tortfeasors §§ 877–877.6

TITLE 13. APPEALS IN CIVIL ACTIONS

1. Appeals in General §§ 901–902, 904.1, 906–907, 909

TITLE 14. MISCELLANEOUS PROVISIONS

2. Bonds and Undertakings § 996.440
3. Offers by a Party to Compromise § 998
3.5 Confidential Settlement Agreements §§ 1001–1002
4. Motions and Orders §§ 1003, 1005, 1008
5. Notices, and Filing and Service of Papers §§ 1010–1011, 1014
6. Of Costs §§ 1021–1021.5, 1032, 1033.5
7. General Provisions §§ 1048–1049
8. Declaratory Relief § 1060

PART 3. OF SPECIAL PROCEEDINGS OF A CIVIL NATURE

TITLE 3. OF SUMMARY PROCEEDINGS

2.5 Judicial Arbitration §§ 1141.10–1141.12, 1141.17, 1141.20–1141.21

PART 1. OF COURTS OF JUSTICE

TITLE 1. ORGANIZATION AND JURISDICTION

Chapter 1. Courts of Justice in General

§ 32.5. Jurisdictional Classification

The "jurisdictional classification" of a case means its classification as a limited civil case or an unlimited civil case. *(Added by Stats.1998, c. 931, § 19, eff. Sept. 28, 1998. Amended by Stats.2002, c. 784, § 22.)*

§ 36. Motion for Preference; Party Over 70 Years of Age; Party Under 14 Years of Age; Medical Reasons; Interests of Justice; Time of Trial

(a) A party to a civil action who is over 70 years of age may petition the court for a preference, which the court shall grant if the court makes both of the following findings:

(1) The party has a substantial interest in the action as a whole.

(2) The health of the party is such that a preference is necessary to prevent prejudicing the party's interest in the litigation.

(b) A civil action to recover damages for wrongful death or personal injury shall be entitled to preference upon the motion of any party to the action who is under 14 years of age unless the court finds that the party does not have a substantial interest in the case as a whole. A civil action subject to subdivision (a) shall be given preference over a case subject to this subdivision.

(c) Unless the court otherwise orders:

(1) A party may file and serve a motion for preference supported by a declaration of the moving party that all essential parties have been served with process or have appeared.

(2) At any time during the pendency of the action, a party who reaches 70 years of age may file and serve a motion for preference.

(d) In its discretion, the court may also grant a motion for preference that is accompanied by clear and convincing medical documentation that concludes that one of the parties suffers from an illness or condition raising substantial medical doubt of survival of that party beyond six months, and that satisfies the court that the interests of justice will be served by granting the preference.

(e) Notwithstanding any other provision of law, the court may in its discretion grant a motion for preference that is supported by a showing that satisfies the court that the interests of justice will be served by granting this preference.

(f) Upon the granting of such a motion for preference, the court shall set the matter for trial not more than 120 days from that date and there shall be no continuance beyond 120 days from the granting of the motion for preference except for physical disability of a party or a party's attorney, or upon a showing of good cause stated in the record. Any continuance shall be for no more than 15 days and no more than one continuance for physical disability may be granted to any party.

(g) Upon the granting of a motion for preference pursuant to subdivision (b), a party in an action based upon a health provider's alleged professional negligence, as defined in Section 364, shall receive a trial date not sooner than six months and not later than nine months from the date that the motion is granted. *(Added by Stats.1979, c. 151, § 2. Amended by Stats.1981, c. 215, § 1; Stats.1988, c. 1237, § 1; Stats.1989, c. 913, § 1; Stats.1990, c. 428, § 1; Stats.2008, c. 218, § 1.)*

Chapter 4. Superior Courts

§ 77. Appellate Department of Superior Court; Composition; Designated Judges; Decisions; Transaction of Business; Jurisdiction and Powers; Procedure

(a) In every county, there is an appellate division of the superior court consisting of three judges or, when the Chief Justice finds it necessary, four judges.

The Chief Justice shall assign judges to the appellate division for specified terms pursuant to rules, not inconsistent with statute, adopted by the Judicial Council to promote the independence and quality of each appellate division. Each judge assigned to the appellate division of a superior court shall be a judge of that court, a judge of the superior court of another county, or a judge retired from the superior court or a court of higher jurisdiction in this state.

The Chief Justice shall designate one of the judges of each appellate division as the presiding judge of the division.

(b) In an appellate division, no more than three judges shall participate in a hearing or decision. The presiding judge of the division shall designate the three judges who shall participate.

(c) In addition to their other duties, the judges designated as members of the appellate division of the superior court shall serve for the period specified in the order of designation. Whenever a judge is designated to serve in the appellate division of the superior court of a county other than the county in which that judge was elected or appointed as a superior court judge, or if the judge is retired, in a county other than the county in which the judge resides, the judge shall receive expenses for travel, board, and lodging. If the judge is out of the judge's county overnight or longer, by reason of the designation, that judge shall be paid a per diem allowance in lieu of expenses for board and lodging in the same amounts as are payable for those purposes to justices of the Supreme Court under the rules of the Department of General Services. In addition, a retired judge shall receive for the time so served, amounts equal to that which the judge would have received if the judge had been assigned to the superior court of the county.

(d) The concurrence of two judges of the appellate division of the superior court shall be necessary to render the decision in every case in, and to transact any other business except business that may be done at chambers by the presiding judge of, the division. A judgment of the appellate division in an appeal shall contain a brief statement of the reasons for the judgment. A judgment stating only "affirmed" or "reversed" is insufficient. The presiding judge shall convene the appellate division when necessary. The presiding judge shall also supervise its business and transact any business that may be done at chambers.

(e) The appellate division of the superior court has jurisdiction on appeal in all cases in which an appeal may be taken to the superior court or the appellate division of the superior court as provided by law, except where the appeal is a retrial in the superior court.

(f) The powers of each appellate division shall be the same as are now or may hereafter be provided by law or rule of the Judicial Council relating to appeals to the appellate division of the superior courts.

(g) The Judicial Council shall promulgate rules, not inconsistent with law, to promote the independence of, and govern the practice and procedure and the disposition of the business of, the appellate division.

(h) Notwithstanding subdivisions (b) and (d), appeals from convictions of traffic infractions may be heard and decided by one judge of the appellate division of the superior court. *(Added by Stats.1955, c. 527, § 1. Amended by Stats.1961, c. 937, § 1; Stats.1976, c. 1288, § 1; Stats.1984, c. 704, § 1; Stats.1998, c. 931, § 21; Stats.1998, c. 932, § 11.5; Stats.1999, c. 344, § 2; Stats.1999, c. 853, § 1.5; Stats.2002, c. 784, § 26; Stats.2006, c. 538, § 60; Stats.2014, c. 58, § 1; Stats.2016, c. 31, § 10; Stats.2018, c. 92, § 40.)*

Chapter 5.1 Limited Civil Cases

Article 1. Jurisdiction in Limited Civil Cases

§ 85. Actions Treated as Limited Civil Case; Conditions

Notwithstanding any law, including, but not limited to, a law that classified an action or special proceeding as a limited civil case, an action or special proceeding shall be treated as a limited civil case only if all of the following conditions are satisfied:

(a) The amount in controversy does not exceed thirty-five thousand dollars ($35,000). As used in this section, "amount in controversy" means the amount of the demand, or the recovery sought, or the value of the property, or the amount of the lien, that is in controversy in the action, exclusive of attorneys' fees, interest, and costs.

(b) The relief sought is a type that may be granted in a limited civil case.

(c) The relief sought, whether in the complaint, a cross-complaint, or otherwise, is exclusively of a type described in one or more laws that classify an action or special proceeding as a limited civil case or that provide that an action or special proceeding is within the original jurisdiction of the superior court * * *. *(Added by Stats.1998, c. 931, § 28. Amended by Stats.2012, c. 99, § 3; Stats.2015, c. 176, § 3; Stats.2023, c. 861, § 2.)*

§ 86. Jurisdiction

(a) The following civil cases and proceedings are limited civil cases:

(1) A case at law if the demand, exclusive of interest, or the value of the property in controversy amounts to thirty-five thousand dollars ($35,000) or less. This paragraph does not apply to a case that involves the legality of any tax, impost, assessment, toll, or municipal fine, except an action to enforce payment of delinquent unsecured personal property taxes if the legality of the tax is not contested by the defendant.

(2) An action for dissolution of partnership if the total assets of the partnership do not exceed thirty-five thousand dollars ($35,000) or an action of interpleader if the amount of money or the value of the property involved does not exceed thirty-five thousand dollars ($35,000).

(3) An action to cancel or rescind a contract if the relief is sought in connection with an action to recover money not exceeding thirty-five

thousand dollars ($35,000) or property of a value not exceeding thirty-five thousand dollars ($35,000), paid or delivered under, or in consideration of, the contract; an action to revise a contract where the relief is sought in an action upon the contract if the action otherwise is a limited civil case.

(4) A proceeding in forcible entry or forcible or unlawful detainer if the whole amount of damages claimed is thirty-five thousand dollars ($35,000) or less.

(5) An action to enforce and foreclose a lien on personal property if the amount of the lien is thirty-five thousand dollars ($35,000) or less.

(6) An action to enforce and foreclose, or a petition to release, a lien arising under Chapter 4 (commencing with Section 8400) of Title 2 of Part 6 of Division 4 of the Civil Code, or to enforce and foreclose an assessment lien on a common interest development as defined in Section 4100 or 6534 of the Civil Code, if the amount of the liens is thirty-five thousand dollars ($35,000) or less. However, if an action to enforce the lien affects property that is also affected by a similar pending action that is not a limited civil case, or if the total amount of liens sought to be foreclosed against the same property aggregates an amount in excess of thirty-five thousand dollars ($35,000), the action is not a limited civil case.

(7) An action for declaratory relief if brought pursuant to either of the following:

(A) By way of cross-complaint as to a right of indemnity with respect to the relief demanded in the complaint or a cross-complaint in an action or proceeding that is otherwise a limited civil case.

(B) To conduct a trial after a nonbinding fee arbitration between an attorney and client, pursuant to Article 13 (commencing with Section 6200) of Chapter 4 of Division 3 of the Business and Professions Code, if the amount in controversy is thirty-five thousand dollars ($35,000) or less.

(8) An action to issue a temporary restraining order or preliminary injunction; to take an account, if necessary to preserve the property or rights of any party to a limited civil case; to make any order or perform any act, pursuant to Title 9 (commencing with Section 680.010) of Part 2 (enforcement of judgments) in a limited civil case; to appoint a receiver pursuant to Section 564 in a limited civil case; or to determine title to personal property seized in a limited civil case.

(9) An action under Article 3 (commencing with Section 708.210) of Chapter 6 of Division 2 of Title 9 of Part 2 for the recovery of an interest in personal property or to enforce the liability of the debtor of a judgment debtor if the interest claimed adversely is of a value not exceeding thirty-five thousand dollars ($35,000) or the debt denied does not exceed thirty-five thousand dollars ($35,000).

(10) An arbitration-related petition filed pursuant to either of the following:

(A) Article 2 (commencing with Section 1292) of Chapter 5 of Title 9 of Part 3, except for uninsured motorist arbitration proceedings in accordance with Section 11580.2 of the Insurance Code, if the petition is filed before the arbitration award becomes final and the matter to be resolved by arbitration is a limited civil case under paragraphs (1) to (9), inclusive, of subdivision (a) or if the petition is filed after the arbitration award becomes final and the amount of the award and all other rulings, pronouncements, and decisions made in the award are within paragraphs (1) to (9), inclusive, of subdivision (a).

(B) To confirm, correct, or vacate a fee arbitration award between an attorney and client that is binding or has become binding, pursuant to Article 13 (commencing with Section 6200) of Chapter 4 of Division 3 of the Business and Professions Code, if the arbitration award is thirty-five thousand dollars ($35,000) or less.

(b) The following cases in equity are limited civil cases:

(1) A case to try title to personal property when the amount involved is not more than thirty-five thousand dollars ($35,000).

(2) A case when equity is pleaded as a defensive matter in any case that is otherwise a limited civil case.

(3) A case to vacate a judgment or order of the court obtained in a limited civil case through extrinsic fraud, mistake, inadvertence, or excusable neglect. *(Added by Stats.1976, c. 1288, § 5. Amended by Stats.1978, c. 146, § 1; Stats.1979, c. 958, § 1; Stats.1981, c. 714, § 57; Stats.1982, c. 466, § 14; Stats.1982, c. 497, § 25; Stats.1984, c. 538, § 1; Stats.1984, c. 1719, § 1.1; Stats.1985, c. 879, § 1; Stats.1985, c. 1383, § 1; Stats.1986, c. 88, § 1; Stats.1986, c. 953, § 1; Stats.1987, c. 104, § 1; Stats.1988, c. 463, § 1; Stats.1993, c. 1261, § 1; Stats.1993, c. 1262, § 4.5; Stats.1997, c. 527, § 2; Stats.1998, c. 931, § 29; Stats.2001, c. 44, § 1; Stats.2010, c. 697, § 21, operative July 1, 2012; Stats.2012, c. 181, § 42; Stats.2013, c. 605, § 22; Stats.2023, c. 861, § 3.)*

§ 88. Unlimited Civil Case; Reference

A civil action or proceeding other than a limited civil case may be referred to as an unlimited civil case. *(Added by Stats.1999, c. 344, § 4.)*

Article 2. Economic Litigation for Limited Civil Cases

§ 90. Application of Law Applicable to Civil Actions

Except where changed by the provisions of this article, all provisions of law applicable to civil actions generally apply to actions subject to this article. *(Added by Stats.1982, c. 1581, § 1. Amended by Stats.2003, c. 149, § 3.)*

§ 91. Application of Article Provisions; Withdrawal of Action From Application

(a) Except as otherwise provided in this section, the provisions of this article apply to every limited civil case.

(b) The provisions of this article do not apply to any action under Chapter 5.5 (commencing with Section 116.110) or any proceeding under Chapter 4 (commencing with Section 1159) of Title 3 of Part 3.

(c) Any action may, upon noticed motion, be withdrawn from the provisions of this article, upon a showing that it is impractical to prosecute or defend the action within the limitations of these provisions. *(Added by Stats.1982, c. 1581, § 1. Amended by Stats.1983, c. 102, § 1; Stats.1985, c. 1383, § 2; Stats.1998, c. 931, § 36.)*

§ 92. Pleadings; Answer; Motions

(a) The pleadings allowed are complaints, answers, cross-complaints, answers to cross-complaints and general demurrers.

(b) The answer need not be verified, even if the complaint or cross-complaint is verified.

(c) Special demurrers are not allowed.

(d) Motions to strike are allowed only on the ground that the damages or relief sought are not supported by the allegations of the complaint.

(e) Except as limited by this section, all other motions are permitted. *(Added by Stats.1982, c. 1581, § 1. Amended by Stats.1983, c. 102, § 2.)*

§ 93. Questionnaires

(a) The plaintiff has the option to serve case questionnaires with the complaint, using forms approved by the Judicial Council. The questionnaires served shall include a completed copy of the plaintiff's completed case questionnaire, and a blank copy of the defendant's questionnaire.

(b) Any defendant upon whom a case questionnaire is served shall serve a completed defendant's case questionnaire upon the requesting plaintiff with the answer.

(c) The case questionnaire shall be designed to elicit fundamental information about each party's case, including names and addresses of all witnesses with knowledge of any relevant facts, a list of all documents relevant to the case, a statement of the nature and amount of damages, and information covering insurance coverages, injuries and treating physicians. The Judicial Council shall design and develop forms for case questionnaires.

(d) Approved forms shall be made available by the clerk of the court.

(e) If a party on whom a case questionnaire has been served under subdivision (a) or (b) fails to serve a timely or a complete response to that questionnaire, the party serving the questionnaire may move for an order compelling a response or a further response and for a monetary sanction under Chapter 7 (commencing with Section 2023.010) of Title 4 of Part 4. If a party then fails to obey an order compelling a response or a further response, the court may make those orders that are just, including the imposition of an issue sanction, an evidence sanction, or a terminating sanction under Chapter 7 (commencing with Section 2023.010) of Title 4 of Part 4. In lieu of or in addition to that sanction, the court may impose a monetary sanction under Chapter 7 (commencing with Section 2023.010) of Title 4 of Part 4. *(Added by Stats.1982, c. 1581, § 1. Amended by Stats.1987, c. 86, § 1; Stats.2004, c. 182, § 5, operative July 1, 2005.)*

§ 94. Discovery

Discovery is permitted only to the extent provided by this section and Section 95. This discovery shall comply with the notice and format requirements of the particular method of discovery, as provided in Title 4 (commencing with Section 2016.010) of Part 4. As to each adverse party, a party may use the following forms of discovery:

(a) Any combination of 35 of the following:

(1) Interrogatories (with no subparts) under Chapter 13 (commencing with Section 2030.010) of Title 4 of Part 4.

(2) Demands to produce documents or things under Chapter 14 (commencing with Section 2031.010) of Title 4 of Part 4.

(3) Requests for admission (with no subparts) under Chapter 16 (commencing with Section 2033.010) of Title 4 of Part 4.

(b) One oral or written deposition under Chapter 9 (commencing with Section 2025.010), Chapter 10 (commencing with Section 2026.010), or Chapter 11 (commencing with Section 2028.010) of Title 4 of Part 4. For purposes of this subdivision, a deposition of an organization shall be treated as a single deposition even though more than one person may be designated or required to testify pursuant to Section 2025.230.

(c) Any party may serve on any person a deposition subpoena duces tecum requiring the person served to mail copies of documents, books, or records to the party's counsel at a specified address, along with an affidavit complying with Section 1561 of the Evidence Code.

The party who issued the deposition subpoena shall mail a copy of the response to any other party who tenders the reasonable cost of copying it.

(d) Physical and mental examinations under Chapter 15 (commencing with Section 2032.010) of Title 4 of Part 4.

(e) The identity of expert witnesses under Chapter 18 (commencing with Section 2034.010) of Title 4 of Part 4. *(Added by Stats.1982, c. 1581, p. 6227, § 1. Amended by Stats.1987, c. 86, § 1.3; Stats.2004, c. 182, § 6, operative July 1, 2005; Stats.2005, c. 294, § 2; Stats.2006, c. 538, § 61.)*

§ 95. Additional Discovery

(a) The court may, on noticed motion and subject to such terms and conditions as are just, authorize a party to conduct additional discovery, but only upon a showing that the moving party will be unable to prosecute or defend the action effectively without the additional discovery. In making a determination under this section, the court shall take into account whether the moving party has used all applicable discovery in good faith, and whether the party has attempted to secure the additional discovery by stipulation or by means other than formal discovery.

(b) The parties may stipulate to additional discovery. *(Added by Stats.1982, c. 1581, § 1.)*

Chapter 5.5 Small Claims Court

§ 116.210. Small Claims Division

In each superior court there shall be a small claims division. The small claims division may be known as the small claims court. *(Added by Stats.1990, c. 1305, § 3. Amended by Stats.1998, c. 931, § 38; Stats.2002, c. 784, § 30.)*

§ 116.220. Jurisdiction

(a) The small claims court has jurisdiction in the following actions:

(1) Except as provided in subdivisions (c), (e), and (f), for recovery of money, if the amount of the demand does not exceed six thousand two hundred fifty dollars ($6,250).

(2) Except as provided in subdivisions (c), (e) and (f), to enforce payment of delinquent unsecured personal property taxes in an amount not to exceed six thousand two hundred fifty dollars ($6,250), if the legality of the tax is not contested by the defendant.

(3) To issue the writ of possession authorized by Sections 1861.5 and 1861.10 of the Civil Code if the amount of the demand does not exceed six thousand two hundred fifty dollars ($6,250).

(4) To confirm, correct, or vacate a fee arbitration award not exceeding six thousand two hundred fifty dollars ($6,250) between an attorney and client that is binding or has become binding, or to conduct a hearing de novo between an attorney and client after nonbinding arbitration of a fee dispute involving no more than six thousand two hundred fifty dollars ($6,250) in controversy, pursuant to Article 13

(commencing with Section 6200) of Chapter 4 of Division 3 of the Business and Professions Code.

(5) For an injunction or other equitable relief only when a statute expressly authorizes a small claims court to award that relief.

(b) In any action seeking relief authorized by paragraphs (1) to (4), inclusive, of subdivision (a), the court may grant equitable relief in the form of rescission, restitution, reformation, and specific performance, in lieu of, or in addition to, money damages. The court may issue a conditional judgment. The court shall retain jurisdiction until full payment and performance of any judgment or order.

(c) Notwithstanding subdivision (a), the small claims court has jurisdiction over a defendant guarantor as follows:

(1) For any action brought by a natural person against the Registrar of the Contractors State License Board as the defendant guarantor, the small claims jurisdictional limit stated in Section 116.221 shall apply.

(2) For any action against a defendant guarantor that does not charge a fee for its guarantor or surety services, if the amount of the demand does not exceed three thousand one hundred twenty-five dollars ($3,125).

(3) For any action brought by a natural person against a defendant guarantor that charges a fee for its guarantor or surety services, if the amount of the demand does not exceed eight thousand one hundred twenty-five dollars ($8,125).

(4) For any action brought by an entity other than a natural person against a defendant guarantor that charges a fee for its guarantor or surety services or against the Registrar of the Contractors State License Board as the defendant guarantor, if the amount of the demand does not exceed five thousand dollars ($5,000).

(d) In any case in which the lack of jurisdiction is due solely to an excess in the amount of the demand, the excess may be waived, but any waiver shall not become operative until judgment.

(e) Notwithstanding subdivision (a), in any action filed by a plaintiff incarcerated in a Department of Corrections and Rehabilitation facility, the small claims court has jurisdiction over a defendant only if the plaintiff has alleged in the complaint that the plaintiff has exhausted the plaintiff's administrative remedies against that department, including compliance with Sections 905.2 and 905.4 of the Government Code. The final administrative adjudication or determination of the plaintiff's administrative claim by the department may be attached to the complaint at the time of filing in lieu of that allegation.

(f) In any action governed by subdivision (e), if the plaintiff fails to provide proof of compliance with the requirements of subdivision (e) at the time of trial, the judicial officer shall, at the plaintiff's discretion, either dismiss the action or continue the action to give the plaintiff an opportunity to provide that proof.

(g) For purposes of this section, "department" includes an employee of a department against whom a claim has been filed under this chapter arising out of an employee's duties as an employee of that department. *(Added by Stats.1990, c. 1305, § 3. Amended by Stats.1990, c. 1683, § 3; Stats.1991, c. 133, § 1; Stats.1991, c. 915, § 3; Stats.1992, c. 8, § 1, eff. Feb. 19, 1992; Stats.1992, c. 142, § 2; Stats.1993, c. 1262, § 5; Stats.1993, c. 1264, § 95; Stats.1994, c. 479, § 10; Stats.1995, c. 366, § 1; Stats.1998, c. 240, § 2; Stats.1999, c. 982, § 6; Stats.2006, c. 150, § 1; Stats.2008, c. 157, § 4; Stats.2009, c. 468, § 1; Stats.2023, c. 861, § 5.)*

§ 116.221. Additional Jurisdiction

In addition to the jurisdiction conferred by Section 116.220, the small claims court has jurisdiction in an action brought by a natural person, if the amount of the demand does not exceed twelve thousand five hundred dollars ($12,500), except as otherwise prohibited by subdivision (c) of Section 116.220 or subdivision (a) of Section 116.231. *(Added by Stats.2005, c. 600, c. 618, § 2. Amended by Stats.2011, c. 64, § 1; Stats.2018, c. 92, § 41; Stats.2023, c. 861, § 6.)*

Chapter 6. General Provisions Respecting Courts of Justice

Article 2. Incidental Powers and Duties of Courts

§ 128. Powers of Courts; Contempt Orders; Execution of Sentence; Stay Pending Appeal; Orders Affecting County Government

(a) Every court shall have the power to do all of the following:

(1) To preserve and enforce order in its immediate presence.

(2) To enforce order in the proceedings before it, or before a person or persons empowered to conduct a judicial investigation under its authority.

(3) To provide for the orderly conduct of proceedings before it, or its officers.

(4) To compel obedience to its judgments, orders, and process, and to the orders of a judge out of court, in an action or proceeding pending therein.

(5) To control in furtherance of justice, the conduct of its ministerial officers, and of all other persons in any manner connected with a judicial proceeding before it, in every matter pertaining thereto.

(6) To compel the attendance of persons to testify in an action or proceeding pending therein, in the cases and manner provided in this code.

(7) To administer oaths in an action or proceeding pending therein, and in all other cases where it may be necessary in the exercise of its powers and duties.

(8) To amend and control its process and orders so as to make them conform to law and justice. An appellate court shall not reverse or vacate a duly entered judgment upon an agreement or stipulation of the parties unless the court finds both of the following:

(A) There is no reasonable possibility that the interests of nonparties or the public will be adversely affected by the reversal.

(B) The reasons of the parties for requesting reversal outweigh the erosion of public trust that may result from the nullification of a judgment and the risk that the availability of stipulated reversal will reduce the incentive for pretrial settlement.

(b) Notwithstanding Section 1211 or any other law, if an order of contempt is made affecting an attorney, his or her agent, investigator, or any person acting under the attorney's direction, in the preparation and conduct of any action or proceeding, the execution of any sentence shall be stayed pending the filing within three judicial days of a petition for extraordinary relief testing the lawfulness of the court's order, the violation of which is the basis of the contempt except for the conduct as may be proscribed by subdivision (b) of Section 6068 of the Business and Professions Code, relating to an attorney's duty to maintain respect due to the courts and judicial officers.

(c) Notwithstanding Section 1211 or any other law, if an order of contempt is made affecting a public safety employee acting within the scope of employment for reason of the employee's failure to comply with a duly issued subpoena or subpoena duces tecum, the execution of any sentence shall be stayed pending the filing within three judicial days of a petition for extraordinary relief testing the lawfulness of the court's order, a violation of which is the basis for the contempt.

As used in this subdivision, "public safety employee" includes any peace officer, firefighter, paramedic, or any other employee of a public law enforcement agency whose duty is either to maintain official records or to analyze or present evidence for investigative or prosecutorial purposes.

(d) Notwithstanding Section 1211 or any other law, if an order of contempt is made affecting the victim of a sexual assault, where the contempt consists of refusing to testify concerning that sexual assault, the execution of any sentence shall be stayed pending the filing within three judicial days of a petition for extraordinary relief testing the lawfulness of the court's order, a violation of which is the basis for the contempt.

As used in this subdivision, "sexual assault" means any act made punishable by Section 261, 262, 264.1, 285, 286, 287, 288, or 289 of, or former Section 288a of, the Penal Code.

(e) Notwithstanding Section 1211 or any other law, if an order of contempt is made affecting the victim of domestic violence, where the contempt consists of refusing to testify concerning that domestic violence, the execution of any sentence shall be stayed pending the filing within three judicial days of a petition for extraordinary relief testing the lawfulness of the court's order, a violation of which is the basis for the contempt.

As used in this subdivision, the term "domestic violence" means "domestic violence" as defined in Section 6211 of the Family Code.

(f) Notwithstanding Section 1211 or any other provision of law, no order of contempt shall be made affecting a county government or any member of its governing body acting pursuant to its constitutional or statutory authority unless the court finds, based on a review of evidence presented at a hearing conducted for this purpose, that either of the following conditions exist:

(1) That the county has the resources necessary to comply with the order of the court.

(2) That the county has the authority, without recourse to voter approval or without incurring additional indebtedness, to generate the additional resources necessary to comply with the order of the court, that compliance with the order of the court will not expose the county, any member of its governing body, or any other county officer to liability for failure to perform other constitutional or statutory duties, and that compliance with the order of the court will not deprive the county of resources necessary for its reasonable support and maintenance. *(Added by Stats.1987, c. 3, § 2, eff. March 11, 1987, operative March 11, 1989. Amended by Stats.1991, c. 866, § 1; Stats.1992, c. 163, § 13; Stats.1992, c. 697, § 2; Stats.1993, c. 219, § 63.3; Stats.1999, c. 508, § 1; Stats.2018, c. 423, § 7.)*

§ 128.5. Frivolous Actions or Delaying Tactics; Order for Payment of Expenses; Punitive Damages; Sanctions

(a) A trial court may order a party, the party's attorney, or both, to pay the reasonable expenses, including attorney's fees, incurred by another party as a result of actions or tactics, made in bad faith, that are frivolous or solely intended to cause unnecessary delay. This section also applies to judicial arbitration proceedings under Chapter 2.5 (commencing with Section 1141.10) of Title 3 of Part 3.

(b) For purposes of this section:

(1) "Actions or tactics" include, but are not limited to, the making or opposing of motions or the filing and service of a complaint, cross-complaint, answer, or other responsive pleading. The mere filing of a complaint without service thereof on an opposing party does not constitute "actions or tactics" for purposes of this section.

(2) "Frivolous" means totally and completely without merit or for the sole purpose of harassing an opposing party.

(c) Expenses pursuant to this section shall not be imposed except on notice contained in a party's moving or responding papers or, on the court's own motion, after notice and opportunity to be heard. An order imposing expenses shall be in writing and shall recite in detail the action or tactic or circumstances justifying the order.

(d) In addition to any award pursuant to this section for an action or tactic described in subdivision (a), the court may assess punitive damages against the plaintiff on a determination by the court that the plaintiff's action was an action maintained by a person convicted of a felony against the person's victim, or the victim's heirs, relatives, estate, or personal representative, for injuries arising from the acts for which the person was convicted of a felony, and that the plaintiff is guilty of fraud, oppression, or malice in maintaining the action.

(e) This section shall not apply to disclosures and discovery requests, responses, objections, and motions.

(f) Sanctions ordered pursuant to this section shall be ordered pursuant to the following conditions and procedures:

(1) If, after notice and a reasonable opportunity to respond, the court issues an order pursuant to subdivision (a), the court may, subject to the conditions stated below, impose an appropriate sanction upon the party, the party's attorneys, or both, for an action or tactic described in subdivision (a). In determining what sanctions, if any, should be ordered, the court shall consider whether a party seeking sanctions has exercised due diligence.

(A) A motion for sanctions under this section shall be made separately from other motions or requests and shall describe the specific alleged action or tactic, made in bad faith, that is frivolous or solely intended to cause unnecessary delay.

(B) If the alleged action or tactic is the making or opposing of a written motion or the filing and service of a complaint, cross-complaint, answer, or other responsive pleading that can be withdrawn or appropriately corrected, a notice of motion shall be served as provided in Section 1010, but shall not be filed with or presented to the court, unless 21 days after service of the motion or any other period as the court may prescribe, the challenged action or tactic is not withdrawn or appropriately corrected.

(C) If warranted, the court may award to the party prevailing on the motion the reasonable expenses and attorney's fees incurred in presenting or opposing the motion. Absent exceptional circumstances, a law firm shall be held jointly responsible for violations committed by its partners, associates, and employees.

(D) If the alleged action or tactic is the making or opposing of a written motion or the filing and service of a complaint, cross-complaint, answer, or other responsive pleading that can be withdrawn or appropriately corrected, the court on its own motion may enter an order describing the specific action or tactic, made in bad faith, that is frivolous or solely intended to cause unnecessary delay, and direct an attorney, law firm, or party to show cause why it has made an action or tactic as defined in subdivision (b), unless, within 21 days of service of the order to show cause, the challenged action or tactic is withdrawn or appropriately corrected.

(2) An order for sanctions pursuant to this section shall be limited to what is sufficient to deter repetition of the action or tactic or comparable action or tactic by others similarly situated. Subject to the limitations in subparagraphs (A) and (B), the sanction may consist of, or include, directives of a nonmonetary nature, an order to pay a penalty into court, or, if imposed on motion and warranted for effective deterrence, an order directing payment to the movant of some or all of the reasonable attorney's fees and other expenses incurred as a direct result of the action or tactic described in subdivision (a).

(A) Monetary sanctions may not be awarded against a represented party for a violation of presenting a claim, defense, and other legal contentions that are warranted by existing law or by a nonfrivolous argument for the extension, modification, or reversal of existing law or the establishment of new law.

(B) Monetary sanctions may not be awarded on the court's motion unless the court issues its order to show cause before a voluntary dismissal or settlement of the claims made by or against the party that is, or whose attorneys are, to be sanctioned.

(g) A motion for sanctions brought by a party or a party's attorney primarily for an improper purpose, such as to harass or to cause unnecessary delay or needless increase in the cost of litigation, shall itself be subject to a motion for sanctions. It is the intent of the Legislature that courts shall vigorously use its sanction authority to deter the improper actions or tactics or comparable actions or tactics of others similarly situated.

(h) The liability imposed by this section is in addition to any other liability imposed by law for acts or omissions within the purview of this section.

(i) This section applies to actions or tactics that were part of a civil case filed on or after January 1, 2015. *(Added by Stats.1981, c. 762, § 1. Amended by Stats.1984, c. 355, § 1; Stats.1985, c. 296, § 1; Stats.1990, c. 887, § 1; Stats.1994, c. 1062, § 1; Stats.2014, c. 425, § 1; Stats.2017, c. 169, § 1, eff. Aug. 7, 2017.)*

§ 128.7. Signature Requirement for Court Papers; Certification That Specified Conditions Met; Violations; Sanctions; Punitive Damages

(a) Every pleading, petition, written notice of motion, or other similar paper shall be signed by at least one attorney of record in the attorney's individual name, or, if the party is not represented by an attorney, shall be signed by the party. Each paper shall state the signer's address and telephone number, if any. Except when otherwise provided by law, pleadings need not be verified or accompanied by affidavit. An unsigned paper shall be stricken unless omission of the signature is corrected promptly after being called to the attention of the attorney or party.

(b) By presenting to the court, whether by signing, filing, submitting, or later advocating, a pleading, petition, written notice of motion, or other similar paper, an attorney or unrepresented party is certifying that to the best of the person's knowledge, information, and belief, formed after an inquiry reasonable under the circumstances, all of the following conditions are met:

(1) It is not being presented primarily for an improper purpose, such as to harass or to cause unnecessary delay or needless increase in the cost of litigation.

(2) The claims, defenses, and other legal contentions therein are warranted by existing law or by a nonfrivolous argument for the extension, modification, or reversal of existing law or the establishment of new law.

(3) The allegations and other factual contentions have evidentiary support or, if specifically so identified, are likely to have evidentiary support after a reasonable opportunity for further investigation or discovery.

(4) The denials of factual contentions are warranted on the evidence or, if specifically so identified, are reasonably based on a lack of information or belief.

(c) If, after notice and a reasonable opportunity to respond, the court determines that subdivision (b) has been violated, the court may, subject to the conditions stated below, impose an appropriate sanction upon the attorneys, law firms, or parties that have violated subdivision (b) or are responsible for the violation. In determining what sanctions, if any, should be ordered, the court shall consider whether a party seeking sanctions has exercised due diligence.

(1) A motion for sanctions under this section shall be made separately from other motions or requests and shall describe the specific conduct alleged to violate subdivision (b). Notice of motion shall be served as provided in Section 1010, but shall not be filed with or presented to the court unless, within 21 days after service of the motion, or any other period as the court may prescribe, the challenged paper, claim, defense, contention, allegation, or denial is not withdrawn or appropriately corrected. If warranted, the court may award to the party prevailing on the motion the reasonable expenses and attorney's fees incurred in presenting or opposing the motion. Absent exceptional circumstances, a law firm shall be held jointly responsible for violations committed by its partners, associates, and employees.

(2) On its own motion, the court may enter an order describing the specific conduct that appears to violate subdivision (b) and directing an attorney, law firm, or party to show cause why it has not violated subdivision (b), unless, within 21 days of service of the order to show cause, the challenged paper, claim, defense, contention, allegation, or denial is withdrawn or appropriately corrected.

(d) A sanction imposed for violation of subdivision (b) shall be limited to what is sufficient to deter repetition of this conduct or comparable conduct by others similarly situated. Subject to the limitations in paragraphs (1) and (2), the sanction may consist of, or include, directives of a nonmonetary nature, an order to pay a penalty into court, or, if imposed on motion and warranted for effective deterrence, an order directing payment to the movant of some or all of the reasonable attorney's fees and other expenses incurred as a direct result of the violation.

(1) Monetary sanctions may not be awarded against a represented party for a violation of paragraph (2) of subdivision (b).

(2) Monetary sanctions may not be awarded on the court's motion unless the court issues its order to show cause before a voluntary dismissal or settlement of the claims made by or against the party that is, or whose attorneys are, to be sanctioned.

(e) When imposing sanctions, the court shall describe the conduct determined to constitute a violation of this section and explain the basis for the sanction imposed.

(f) In addition to any award pursuant to this section for conduct described in subdivision (b), the court may assess punitive damages against the plaintiff upon a determination by the court that the plaintiff's action was an action maintained by a person convicted of a felony against the person's victim, or the victim's heirs, relatives, estate, or personal representative, for injuries arising from the acts for which the person was convicted of a felony, and that the plaintiff is guilty of fraud, oppression, or malice in maintaining the action.

(g) This section shall not apply to disclosures and discovery requests, responses, objections, and motions.

(h) A motion for sanctions brought by a party or a party's attorney primarily for an improper purpose, such as to harass or to cause unnecessary delay or needless increase in the cost of litigation, shall itself be subject to a motion for sanctions. It is the intent of the Legislature that courts shall vigorously use its sanctions authority to deter that improper conduct or comparable conduct by others similarly situated.

(i) This section shall apply to a complaint or petition filed on or after January 1, 1995, and any other pleading, written notice of motion, or other similar paper filed in that matter. *(Added by Stats.1994, c. 1062, § 3. Amended by Stats.1998, c. 121, § 2; Stats.2002, c. 491, § 1; Stats.2005, c. 706, § 9.)*

TITLE 2. JUDICIAL OFFICERS

Chapter 2. Power of Judges at Chambers

§ 166.1. Controlling Question of Law Involving Substantial Grounds for Difference of Opinion and Appellate Resolution of Which May Materially Advance Conclusion of Litigation; Indication by Judge in Interlocutory Order

Upon the written request of any party or his or her counsel, or at the judge's discretion, a judge may indicate in any interlocutory order a belief that there is a controlling question of law as to which there are substantial grounds for difference of opinion, appellate resolution of which may materially advance the conclusion of the litigation. Neither the denial of a request for, nor the objection of another party or counsel to, such a commentary in the interlocutory order, may be grounds for a writ or appeal. *(Added by Stats.2002, c. 705, § 1.)*

Chapter 4. Incidental Powers and Duties of Judicial Officers

§ 177. Conduct of Proceedings

A judicial officer shall have power:

(a) To preserve and enforce order in the officer's immediate presence, and in proceedings before the officer, when the officer is engaged in the performance of official duty.

(b) To compel obedience to the officer's lawful orders as provided in this code.

(c) To compel the attendance of persons to testify in a proceeding before the officer, in the cases and manner provided in this code.

(d) To administer oaths to persons in a proceeding pending before the officer, and in all other cases where it may be necessary in the exercise of the officer's powers and duties.

(e) To prohibit activities that threaten access to state courthouses and court proceedings, and to prohibit interruption of judicial administration, including protecting the privilege from civil arrest at courthouses and court proceedings. *(Enacted 1872. Amended by Code Am.1880, c. 35, § 1; Stats.2019, c. 787, § 3.)*

§ 177.5. Money Sanctions

A judicial officer shall have the power to impose reasonable money sanctions, not to exceed fifteen hundred dollars ($1,500), notwithstanding any other provision of law, payable to the court, for any violation of a lawful court order by a person, done without good cause or substantial justification. This power shall not apply to advocacy of counsel before the court. For the purposes of this section, the term "person" includes a witness, a party, a party's attorney, or both.

Sanctions pursuant to this section shall not be imposed except on notice contained in a party's moving or responding papers; or on the court's own motion, after notice and opportunity to be heard. An order imposing sanctions shall be in writing and shall recite in detail the conduct or circumstances justifying the order. *(Added by Stats.1982, c. 1564, § 1. Amended by Stats.2005, c. 75, § 27, eff. July 19, 2005, operative Jan. 1, 2006.)*

Chapter 5. Miscellaneous Provisions Respecting Courts of Justice

§ 187. Jurisdiction; Means to Carry Into Effect; Mode of Proceeding

When jurisdiction is, by the Constitution or this Code, or by any other statute, conferred on a Court or judicial officer, all the means necessary to carry it into effect are also given; and in the exercise of this jurisdiction, if the course of proceeding be not specifically pointed out by this Code or the statute, any suitable process or mode of proceeding may be adopted which may appear most conformable to the spirit of this Code. *(Enacted 1872. Amended by Code Am.1880, c. 35, § 1.)*

TITLE 3. PERSONS SPECIALLY INVESTED WITH POWERS OF A JUDICIAL NATURE

Chapter 1. Trial Jury Selection and Management Act

§ 191. State Policy; Random Selection; Opportunity and Obligation to Serve

The Legislature recognizes that trial by jury is a cherished constitutional right, and that jury service is an obligation of citizenship.

It is the policy of the State of California that all persons selected for jury service shall be selected at random from the population of the area served by the court; that all qualified persons have an equal opportunity, in accordance with this chapter, to be considered for jury service in the state and an obligation to serve as jurors when summoned for that purpose; and that it is the responsibility of jury commissioners to manage all jury systems in an efficient, equitable, and cost-effective manner, in accordance with this chapter. *(Added by Stats.1988, c. 1245, § 2.)*

§ 193. Kinds of Juries

Juries are of three kinds:

(a) Grand juries established pursuant to Title 4 (commencing with Section 888) of Part 2 of the Penal Code.

(b) Trial juries.

(c) Juries of inquest. *(Added by Stats.1988, c. 1245, § 2.)*

§ 194. Definitions

The following definitions govern the construction of this chapter:

(a) "County" means any county or any coterminous city and county.

(b) "Court" means a superior court of this state, and includes, when the context requires, any judge of the court.

(c) "Deferred jurors" are those prospective jurors whose request to reschedule their service to a more convenient time is granted by the jury commissioner.

(d) "Excused jurors" are those prospective jurors who are excused from service by the jury commissioner for valid reasons based on statute, state or local court rules, and policies.

(e) "Juror pool" means the group of prospective qualified jurors appearing for assignment to trial jury panels.

(f) "Jury of inquest" is a body of persons summoned from the citizens before the sheriff, coroner, or other ministerial officers, to inquire of particular facts.

(g) "Master list" means a list of names randomly selected from the source lists.

(h) "Potential juror" means any person whose name appears on a source list.

(i) "Prospective juror" means a juror whose name appears on the master list.

(j) "Qualified juror" means a person who meets the statutory qualifications for jury service.

(k) "Qualified juror list" means a list of qualified jurors.

(*l*) "Random" means that which occurs by mere chance indicating an unplanned sequence of selection where each juror's name has substantially equal probability of being selected.

(m) "Source list" means a list used as a source of potential jurors.

(n) "Summons list" means a list of prospective or qualified jurors who are summoned to appear or to be available for jury service.

(*o*) "Trial jurors" are those jurors sworn to try and determine by verdict a question of fact.

(p) "Trial jury" means a body of persons selected from the citizens of the area served by the court and sworn to try and determine by verdict a question of fact.

(q) "Trial jury panel" means a group of prospective jurors assigned to a courtroom for the purpose of voir dire. *(Added by Stats.1988, c. 1245, § 2. Amended by Stats.1998, c. 931, § 50; Stats.2002, c. 784, § 39.)*

§ 197. Source Lists of Jurors; Contents; Data From Department of Motor Vehicles; Confidentiality

(a) All persons selected for jury service shall be selected at random, from a source or sources inclusive of a representative cross section of the population of the area served by the court. Sources may include, in addition to other lists, customer mailing lists, telephone directories, or utility company lists.

(b)(1) The list of registered voters and the Department of Motor Vehicles' list of licensed drivers and identification cardholders resident within the area served by the court, are appropriate source lists for selection of jurors. Until January 1, 2022, only these two source lists, when substantially purged of duplicate names, shall be considered inclusive of a representative cross section of the population, within the meaning of subdivision (a).

(2) The list of resident state tax filers is an appropriate source list for selection of jurors. Beginning on January 1, 2022, the list of resident state

tax filers, the list of registered voters, and the Department of Motor Vehicles' list of licensed drivers and identification cardholders resident within the area served by the court, when substantially purged of duplicate names, shall be considered inclusive of a representative cross section of the population, within the meaning of subdivision (a).

(c) The Department of Motor Vehicles shall furnish the jury commissioner of each county with the current list of the names, addresses, and other identifying information of persons residing in the county who are age 18 years or older and who are holders of a current driver's license or identification card issued pursuant to Article 3 (commencing with Section 12800) of, or Article 5 (commencing with Section 13000) of, Chapter 1 of Division 6 of the Vehicle Code. The conditions under which these lists shall be compiled semiannually shall be determined by the director, consistent with any rules which may be adopted by the Judicial Council. This service shall be provided by the Department of Motor Vehicles pursuant to Section 1812 of the Vehicle Code. The jury commissioner shall not disclose the information furnished by the Department of Motor Vehicles pursuant to this section to any person, organization, or agency.

(d)(1) The Franchise Tax Board shall annually furnish the jury commissioner of each county with a list of resident state tax filers for their county in consultation with the Judicial Council.

(2) The list of resident state tax filers shall be submitted to the jury commissioner of each county by November 1, 2021, and each November 1 thereafter.

(3)(A) For purposes of this section, "list of resident state tax filers" means a list that includes the name, date of birth, principal residence address, and county of principal residence, of persons who are 18 years of age or older and have filed a California resident income tax return for the preceding taxable year.

(B) For purposes of this paragraph, "county of principal residence" means the county in which the taxpayer has their principal residence on the date that the taxpayer filed their California resident income tax return.

(C) For the purposes of this paragraph, "principal residence" is used in the same manner it is used in Section 121 of the Internal Revenue Code. *(Added by Stats.1988, c. 1245, § 2. Amended by Stats.2020, c. 230, § 1.)*

§ 198. Master and Qualified Juror Lists; Random Selection; Use of Lists

(a) Random selection shall be utilized in creating master and qualified juror lists, commencing with selection from source lists, and continuing through selection of prospective jurors for voir dire.

(b) The jury commissioner shall, at least once in each 12-month period, randomly select names of prospective trial jurors from the source list or lists, to create a master list.

(c) The master jury list shall be used by the jury commissioner, as provided by statute and state and local court rules, for the purpose of (1) mailing juror questionnaires and subsequent creation of a qualified juror list, and (2) summoning prospective jurors to respond or appear for qualification and service. *(Added by Stats.1988, c. 1245, § 2.)*

§ 203. Persons Qualified to Be Trial Jurors; Exceptions

(a) All persons are eligible and qualified to be prospective trial jurors, except the following:

(1) Persons who are not citizens of the United States.

(2) Persons who are less than 18 years of age.

(3) Persons who are not domiciliaries of the State of California, as determined pursuant to Article 2 (commencing with Section 2020) of Chapter 1 of Division 2 of the Elections Code.

(4) Persons who are not residents of the jurisdiction wherein they are summoned to serve.

(5) Persons who have been convicted of malfeasance in office and whose civil rights have not been restored.

(6) Persons who are not possessed of sufficient knowledge of the English language, provided that no person shall be deemed incompetent solely because of the loss of sight or hearing in any degree or other disability which impedes the person's ability to communicate or which impairs or interferes with the person's mobility.

(7) Persons who are serving as grand or trial jurors in any court of this state.

(8) Persons who are the subject of conservatorship.

(9) Persons while they are incarcerated in any prison or jail.

(10) Persons who have been convicted of a felony and are currently on parole, postrelease community supervision, felony probation, or mandated supervision for the conviction of a felony.

(11) Persons who are currently required to register as a sex offender pursuant to Section 290 of the Penal Code based on a felony conviction.

(b) No person shall be excluded from eligibility for jury service in the State of California, for any reason other than those reasons provided by this section.

(c) The provisions of this section are severable. If any provision of this section or its application is held invalid, that invalidity shall not affect other provisions or applications that can be given effect without the invalid provision or application. *(Added by Stats.1988, c. 1245, § 2. Amended by Stats.1994, c. 923, § 1; Stats.2019, c. 591, § 1.)*

§ 204. Exemptions and Excuses From Jury Service

(a) No eligible person shall be exempt from service as a trial juror by reason of occupation, economic status, or any characteristic listed or defined in Section 11135 of the Government Code, or for any other reason. No person shall be excused from service as a trial juror except as specified in subdivision (b).

(b) An eligible person may be excused from jury service only for undue hardship, upon themselves or upon the public, as defined by the Judicial Council. *(Added by Stats.1988, c. 1245, § 5. Amended by Stats.2000, c. 43, § 2; Stats.2007, c. 568, § 15.)*

§ 205. Juror Questionnaires; Contents; Use; Additional Questionnaires; Inclusivity Standard

(a) If a jury commissioner requires a person to complete a questionnaire, the questionnaire shall ask only questions related to juror identification, qualification, and ability to serve as a prospective juror.

(b) Except as ordered by the court, the questionnaire referred to in subdivision (a) shall be used solely for qualifying prospective jurors, and for management of the jury system, and not for assisting in the courtroom voir dire process of selecting trial jurors for specific cases.

(c) The court may require a prospective juror to complete such additional questionnaires as may be deemed relevant and necessary for assisting in the voir dire process or to ascertain whether a fair cross section of the population is represented as required by law, if such procedures are established by local court rule.

(d) The trial judge may direct a prospective juror to complete additional questionnaires as proposed by counsel in a particular case to assist the voir dire process.

(e) The Judicial Council shall adopt a standard of judicial administration to ensure that juror identification and any juror questionnaire is inclusive, including allowing a juror the ability to express their gender identity or gender expression, if applicable.

(f) This section shall become operative on January 1, 2026. *(Added by Stats.1988, c. 1245, § 5. Amended by Stats.2024, c. 812, §§ 11 & 12.)*

§ 220. Number of Jurors

A trial jury shall consist of 12 persons, except that in civil actions and cases of misdemeanor, it may consist of 12 or any number less than 12, upon which the parties may agree. *(Added by Stats.1988, c. 1245, § 5.)*

§ 222.5. Prospective Jurors; Examination; Opening Statements; Questionnaires

(a) To select a fair and impartial jury in a civil jury trial, the trial judge shall conduct an initial examination of prospective jurors. At the final status conference or at the first practical opportunity prior to voir dire, whichever comes first, the trial judge shall consider and discuss with counsel the form and subject matter of voir dire questions. Before voir dire by the trial judge, the parties may submit questions to the trial judge. The trial judge may include additional questions requested by the parties as the trial judge deems proper.

(b)(1) Upon completion of the trial judge's initial examination, counsel for each party shall have the right to examine, by oral and direct questioning, any of the prospective jurors in order to enable counsel to intelligently exercise both peremptory challenges and challenges for cause. The scope of the examination conducted by counsel shall be within reasonable limits prescribed by the trial judge in the judge's sound discretion subject to the provisions of this chapter. During any examination conducted by counsel for the parties, the trial judge shall permit liberal and probing examination calculated to discover bias or prejudice with regard to the circumstances of the particular case before the court. The fact that a topic has been included in the trial judge's examination shall not preclude appropriate follow up questioning in the same area by counsel. The trial judge shall permit counsel to conduct voir dire examination without requiring prior submission of the questions unless a particular counsel engages in improper questioning.

(2) The trial judge shall not impose specific unreasonable or arbitrary time limits or establish an inflexible time limit policy for voir dire.

(3) For purposes of this section, an "improper question" is any question that, as its dominant purpose, attempts to precondition the prospective jurors to a particular result, indoctrinate the jury, or question the prospective jurors concerning the pleadings or the applicable law.

(c)(1) In exercising the judge's sound discretion, the trial judge shall give due consideration to all of the following:

(A) The amount of time requested by trial counsel.

(B) Any unique or complex elements, legal or factual, in the case.

(C) Length of the trial.

(D) Number of parties.

(E) Number of witnesses.

(F) Whether the case is designated as a complex or long cause.

(2) As voir dire proceeds, the judge shall permit supplemental time for questioning based on any of the following:

(A) Individual responses or conduct of jurors that may evince attitudes inconsistent with suitability to serve as a fair and impartial juror in the particular case.

(B) Composition of the jury panel.

(C) An unusual number of for cause challenges.

(d) Upon the request of a party, the trial judge shall allow a brief opening statement by counsel for each party prior to the commencement of the oral questioning phase of the voir dire process.

(e) In civil cases, the trial judge may, upon stipulation by counsel for all the parties appearing in the action, permit counsel to examine the prospective jurors outside a judge's presence.

(f) A trial judge shall not arbitrarily or unreasonably refuse to submit reasonable written questionnaires, the contents of which are determined by the court in its sound discretion, when requested by counsel. If a questionnaire is utilized, the parties shall be given reasonable time to evaluate the responses to the questionnaires before oral questioning commences.

(g) To help facilitate the jury selection process, at the earliest practical time, the judge in a civil trial shall provide the parties with both the alphabetical list and the list of prospective jurors in the order in which they will be called. *(Added by Stats.1990, c. 1232, § 1.5 Amended by Stats.2011, c. 409, § 1; Stats.2017, c. 337, § 1.)*

§ 224. Disabled Jurors; Presence of Service Providers; Instructions; Appointment

(a) If a party does not cause the removal by challenge of an individual juror who is deaf, hard of hearing, blind, visually impaired, or speech impaired and who requires auxiliary services to facilitate communication, the party shall stipulate to the presence of a service provider in the jury room during jury deliberations, and prepare and deliver to the court proposed jury instructions to the service provider.

(b) As used in this section, "service provider" includes, but is not limited to, a person who is a sign language interpreter, oral interpreter, deaf-blind interpreter, reader, or speech interpreter. If auxiliary services are required during the course of jury deliberations, the court shall instruct the jury and the service provider that the service provider for the juror with a disability is not to participate in the jury's deliberations in any manner except to facilitate communication between the juror with a disability and other jurors.

(c) The court shall appoint a service provider whose services are needed by a juror with a disability to facilitate communication or participation. A sign language interpreter, oral interpreter, or deaf-blind interpreter appointed pursuant to this section shall be a qualified interpreter, as defined in subdivision (f) of Section 754 of the Evidence Code. Service providers appointed by the court under this subdivision shall be compensated in the same manner as provided in subdivision (i) of Section 754 of the Evidence Code. *(Added by Stats.1988, c. 1245, § 2. Amended by Stats.1992, c. 913, § 9; Stats.1993, c. 1214, § 3; Stats.2016, c. 94, § 3.)*

§ 225. Challenges; Definition; Classes and Types

A challenge is an objection made to the trial jurors that may be taken by any party to the action, and is of the following classes and types:

(a) A challenge to the trial jury panel for cause.

(1) A challenge to the panel may only be taken before a trial jury is sworn. The challenge shall be reduced to writing, and shall plainly and distinctly state the facts constituting the ground of challenge.

(2) Reasonable notice of the challenge to the jury panel shall be given to all parties and to the jury commissioner, by service of a copy thereof.

(3) The jury commissioner shall be permitted the services of legal counsel in connection with challenges to the jury panel.

(b) A challenge to a prospective juror by either:

(1) A challenge for cause, for one of the following reasons:

(A) General disqualification—that the juror is disqualified from serving in the action on trial.

(B) Implied bias—as, when the existence of the facts as ascertained, in judgment of law disqualifies the juror.

(C) Actual bias—the existence of a state of mind on the part of the juror in reference to the case, or to any of the parties, which will prevent the juror from acting with entire impartiality, and without prejudice to the substantial rights of any party.

(2) A peremptory challenge to a prospective juror. *(Added by Stats.1988, c. 1245, § 5.)*

§ 226. Challenges to Individual Jurors; Time; Form; Exclusion on Peremptory Challenge

(a) A challenge to an individual juror may only be made before the jury is sworn.

(b) A challenge to an individual juror may be taken orally or may be made in writing, but no reason need be given for a peremptory challenge, and the court shall exclude any juror challenged peremptorily.

(c) All challenges for cause shall be exercised before any peremptory challenges may be exercised.

(d) All challenges to an individual juror, except a peremptory challenge, shall be taken, first by the defendants, and then by the people or plaintiffs. *(Added by Stats.1988, c. 1245, § 2.)*

§ 227. Challenges for Cause; Time; Order

The challenges of either party for cause need not all be taken at once, but they may be taken separately, in the following order, including in each challenge all the causes of challenge belonging to the same class and type:

(a) To the panel.

(b) To an individual juror, for a general disqualification.

(c) To an individual juror, for an implied bias.

(d) To an individual juror, for an actual bias. *(Added by Stats.1988, c. 1245, § 2.)*

§ 228. Challenges for General Disqualification; Grounds

Challenges for general disqualification may be taken on one or both of the following grounds, and for no other:

(a) A want of any of the qualifications prescribed by this code to render a person competent as a juror.

(b) The existence of any incapacity which satisfies the court that the challenged person is incapable of performing the duties of a juror in the particular action without prejudice to the substantial rights of the challenging party. *(Added by Stats.1988, c. 1245, § 5. Amended by Stats.2002, c. 1008, § 1.)*

§ 229. Challenges for Implied Bias; Causes

A challenge for implied bias may be taken for one or more of the following causes, and for no other:

(a) Consanguinity or affinity within the fourth degree to any party, to an officer of a corporation which is a party, or to any alleged witness or victim in the case at bar.

(b) Standing in the relation of, or being the parent, spouse, or child of one who stands in the relation of, guardian and ward, conservator and conservatee, master and servant, employer and clerk, landlord and tenant, principal and agent, or debtor and creditor, to either party or to an officer of a corporation which is a party, or being a member of the family of either party; or a partner in business with either party; or surety on any bond or obligation for either party, or being the holder of bonds or shares of capital stock of a corporation which is a party; or having stood within one year previous to the filing of the complaint in the action in the relation of attorney and client with either party or with the attorney for either party. A depositor of a bank or a holder of a savings account in a savings and loan association shall not be deemed a creditor of that bank or savings and loan association for the purpose of this paragraph solely by reason of his or her being a depositor or account holder.

(c) Having served as a trial or grand juror or on a jury of inquest in a civil or criminal action or been a witness on a previous or pending trial between the same parties, or involving the same specific offense or cause of action; or having served as a trial or grand juror or on a jury within one year previously in any criminal or civil action or proceeding in which either party was the plaintiff or defendant or in a criminal action where either party was the defendant.

(d) Interest on the part of the juror in the event of the action, or in the main question involved in the action, except his or her interest as a member or citizen or taxpayer of a county, city and county, incorporated city or town, or other political subdivision of a county, or municipal water district.

(e) Having an unqualified opinion or belief as to the merits of the action founded upon knowledge of its material facts or of some of them.

(f) The existence of a state of mind in the juror evincing enmity against, or bias towards, either party.

(g) That the juror is party to an action pending in the court for which he or she is drawn and which action is set for trial before the panel of which the juror is a member.

(h) If the offense charged is punishable with death, the entertaining of such conscientious opinions as would preclude the juror finding the defendant guilty; in which case the juror may neither be permitted nor compelled to serve. *(Added by Stats.1988, c. 1245, § 2.)*

§ 230. Challenges for Cause; Trial; Witnesses

Challenges for cause shall be tried by the court. The juror challenged and any other person may be examined as a witness in the trial of the challenge, and shall truthfully answer all questions propounded to them. *(Added by Stats.1988, c. 1245, § 2.)*

§ 231. Peremptory Challenges; Joint Defendants; Passing Peremptory Challenges

(a) In criminal cases, if the offense charged is punishable with death, or with imprisonment in the state prison for life, the defendant is entitled to 20 and the people to 20 peremptory challenges. Except as provided in subdivision (b), in a trial for any other offense, the defendant is entitled to 10 and the state to 10 peremptory challenges. When two or more defendants are jointly tried, their challenges shall be exercised jointly, but each defendant shall also be entitled to five additional challenges which may be exercised separately, and the people shall also be entitled to additional challenges equal to the number of all the additional separate challenges allowed the defendants.

(b) If the offense charged is punishable with a maximum term of imprisonment of one year or less, the defendant is entitled to six and the state to six peremptory challenges. When two or more defendants are jointly tried, their challenges shall be exercised jointly, but each defendant shall also be entitled to four additional challenges which may be exercised separately, and the state shall also be entitled to additional challenges equal to the number of all the additional separate challenges allowed the defendants.

(c) In civil cases, each party shall be entitled to six peremptory challenges. If there are more than two parties, the court shall, for the purpose of allotting peremptory challenges, divide the parties into two or more sides according to their respective interests in the issues. Each side shall be entitled to eight peremptory challenges. If there are several parties on a side, the court shall divide the challenges among them as nearly equally as possible. If there are more than two sides, the court shall grant such additional peremptory challenges to a side as the interests of justice may require, provided that the peremptory challenges of one side shall not exceed the aggregate number of peremptory challenges of all other sides. If any party on a side does not use his or her full share of peremptory challenges, the unused challenges may be used by the other party or parties on the same side.

(d) Peremptory challenges shall be taken or passed by the sides alternately, commencing with the plaintiff or people, and each party shall be entitled to have the panel full before exercising any peremptory challenge. When each side passes consecutively, the jury shall then be sworn, unless the court, for good cause, shall otherwise order. The number of peremptory challenges remaining with a side shall not be diminished by any passing of a peremptory challenge.

(e) If all the parties on both sides pass consecutively, the jury shall then be sworn, unless the court, for good cause, shall otherwise order. The number of peremptory challenges remaining with a side shall not be diminished by any passing of a peremptory challenge.

(f) This section shall become operative on January 1, 2021. *(Added by Stats.1988, c. 1245, § 5. Amended by Stats.1989, c. 1416, § 9; Stats.2016, c. 33, § 2; Stats.2016, c. 33, § 3, operative Jan. 1, 2021.)*

§ 231.5. Peremptory Challenges to Remove Prospective Jurors; Bias

A party shall not use a peremptory challenge to remove a prospective juror on the basis of an assumption that the prospective juror is biased merely because of a characteristic listed or defined in Section 11135 of the Government Code, or similar grounds. *(Added by Stats.2000, c. 43, § 3. Amended by Stats.2015, c. 115, § 1.)**

§ 231.7. Prohibition of Peremptory Challenge on the Basis of Race, Ethnicity, Gender, Gender Identity, Sexual Orientation, National Origin, or Religious Affiliation; Actual or Perceived Membership in Any Group; Motion

(a) A party shall not use a peremptory challenge to remove a prospective juror on the basis of the prospective juror's race, ethnicity, gender, gender identity, sexual orientation, national origin, or religious affiliation, or the perceived membership of the prospective juror in any of those groups.

(b) A party, or the trial court on its own motion, may object to the improper use of a peremptory challenge under subdivision (a). After the objection is made, any further discussion shall be conducted outside the presence of the panel. The objection shall be made before the jury is impaneled, unless information becomes known that could not have reasonably been known before the jury was impaneled.

(c) Notwithstanding Section 226, upon objection to the exercise of a peremptory challenge pursuant to this section, the party exercising the peremptory challenge shall state the reasons the peremptory challenge has been exercised.

(d)(1) The court shall evaluate the reasons given to justify the peremptory challenge in light of the totality of the circumstances. The court shall consider only the reasons actually given and shall not speculate on, or assume the existence of, other possible justifications for the use of the peremptory challenge. If the court determines there is a substantial likelihood that an objectively reasonable person would view race, ethnicity, gender, gender identity, sexual orientation, national origin, or religious affiliation, or perceived membership in any of those groups, as a factor in the use of the peremptory challenge, then the objection shall be sustained. The court need not find purposeful discrimination to sustain the objection. The court shall explain the reasons for its ruling on the record. A motion brought under this section shall also be deemed a sufficient presentation

---

* [Ed.] Gov't Code § 11135(a) prohibits discrimination on the basis of "race, national origin, ethnic group identification, religion, age, sex, sexual orientation, color, genetic information, or disability." Subsection (f) "includes a perception that a person has any of those characteristics or that the person is associated with a person who has, or is perceived to have, any of those characteristics."

of claims asserting the discriminatory exclusion of jurors in violation of the United States and California Constitutions.

(2)(A) For purposes of this section, an objectively reasonable person is aware that unconscious bias, in addition to purposeful discrimination, have resulted in the unfair exclusion of potential jurors in the State of California.

(B) For purposes of this section, a "substantial likelihood" means more than a mere possibility but less than a standard of more likely than not.

(C) For purposes of this section, "unconscious bias" includes implicit and institutional biases.

(3) In making its determination, the circumstances the court may consider include, but are not limited to, any of the following:

(A) Whether any of the following circumstances exist:

(i) The objecting party is a member of the same perceived cognizable group as the challenged juror.

(ii) The alleged victim is not a member of that perceived cognizable group.

(iii) Witnesses or the parties are not members of that perceived cognizable group.

(B) Whether race, ethnicity, gender, gender identity, sexual orientation, national origin, or religious affiliation, or perceived membership in any of those groups, bear on the facts of the case to be tried.

(C) The number and types of questions posed to the prospective juror, including, but not limited to, any of the following:

(i) Consideration of whether the party exercising the peremptory challenge failed to question the prospective juror about the concerns later stated by the party as the reason for the peremptory challenge pursuant to subdivision (c).

(ii) Whether the party exercising the peremptory challenge engaged in cursory questioning of the challenged potential juror.

(iii) Whether the party exercising the peremptory challenge asked different questions of the potential juror against whom the peremptory challenge was used in contrast to questions asked of other jurors from different perceived cognizable groups about the same topic or whether the party phrased those questions differently.

(D) Whether other prospective jurors, who are not members of the same cognizable group as the challenged prospective juror, provided similar, but not necessarily identical, answers but were not the subject of a peremptory challenge by that party.

(E) Whether a reason might be disproportionately associated with a race, ethnicity, gender, gender identity, sexual orientation, national origin, or religious affiliation, or perceived membership in any of those groups.

(F) Whether the reason given by the party exercising the peremptory challenge was contrary to or unsupported by the record.

(G) Whether counsel or counsel's office, if it is a public entity, exercising the challenge has used peremptory challenges disproportionately against a given race, ethnicity, gender, gender identity, sexual orientation, national origin, or religious affiliation, or perceived membership in any of those groups, in the present case or in past cases, including whether the counsel or counsel's office, if it is a public entity, who made the challenge has a history of prior violations under Batson v. Kentucky (1986) 476 U.S. 79, People v. Wheeler (1978) 22 Cal.3d 258, Section 231.5, or this section.

(e) A peremptory challenge for any of the following reasons is presumed to be invalid unless the party exercising the peremptory challenge can show by clear and convincing evidence that an objectively reasonable person would view the rationale as unrelated to a prospective juror's race, ethnicity, gender, gender identity, sexual orientation, national origin, or religious affiliation, or perceived membership in any of those groups, and that the reasons articulated bear on the prospective juror's ability to be fair and impartial in the case:

(1) Expressing a distrust of or having a negative experience with law enforcement or the criminal legal system.

(2) Expressing a belief that law enforcement officers engage in racial profiling or that criminal laws have been enforced in a discriminatory manner.

(3) Having a close relationship with people who have been stopped, arrested, or convicted of a crime.

(4) A prospective juror's neighborhood.

(5) Having a child outside of marriage.

(6) Receiving state benefits.

(7) Not being a native English speaker.

(8) The ability to speak another language.

(9) Dress, attire, or personal appearance.

(10) Employment in a field that is disproportionately occupied by members listed in subdivision (a) or that serves a population disproportionately comprised of members of a group or groups listed in subdivision (a).

(11) Lack of employment or underemployment of the prospective juror or prospective juror's family member.

(12) A prospective juror's apparent friendliness with another prospective juror of the same group as listed in subdivision (a).

(13) Any justification that is similarly applicable to a questioned prospective juror or jurors, who are not members of the same cognizable group as the challenged prospective juror, but were not the subject of a peremptory challenge by that party. The unchallenged prospective juror or jurors need not share any other characteristics with the challenged prospective juror for peremptory challenge relying on this justification to be considered presumptively invalid.

(f) For purposes of subdivision (e), the term "clear and convincing" refers to the degree of certainty the factfinder must have in determining whether the reasons given for the exercise of a peremptory challenge are unrelated to the prospective juror's cognizable group membership, bearing in mind conscious and unconscious bias. To determine that a presumption of invalidity has been overcome, the factfinder shall determine that it is highly probable that the reasons given for the exercise of a peremptory challenge are unrelated to conscious or unconscious bias and are instead specific to the juror and bear on that juror's ability to be fair and impartial in the case.

(g)(1) The following reasons for peremptory challenges have historically been associated with improper discrimination in jury selection:

(A) The prospective juror was inattentive, or staring or failing to make eye contact.

(B) The prospective juror exhibited either a lack of rapport or problematic attitude, body language, or demeanor.

(C) The prospective juror provided unintelligent or confused answers.

(2) The reasons set forth in paragraph (1) are presumptively invalid unless the trial court is able to confirm that the asserted behavior occurred, based on the court's own observations or the observations of counsel for the objecting party. Even with that confirmation, the counsel offering the reason shall explain why the asserted demeanor, behavior, or manner in which the prospective juror answered questions matters to the case to be tried.

(h) Upon a court granting an objection to the improper exercise of a peremptory challenge, the court shall do one or more of the following:

(1) Quash the jury venire and start jury selection anew. This remedy shall be provided if requested by the objecting party.

(2) If the motion is granted after the jury has been impaneled, declare a mistrial and select a new jury if requested by the defendant.

(3) Seat the challenged juror.

(4) Provide the objecting party additional challenges.

(5) Provide another remedy as the court deems appropriate.

(i) This section applies in all jury trials in which jury selection begins on or after January 1, 2022.

(j) The denial of an objection made under this section shall be reviewed by the appellate court de novo, with the trial court's express factual findings reviewed for substantial evidence. The appellate court shall not impute to the trial court any findings, including findings of a prospective juror's demeanor, that the trial court did not expressly state on the record. The reviewing court shall consider only reasons actually given under subdivision (c) and shall not speculate as to or consider reasons that were not given to explain either the party's use of the peremptory challenge or the party's failure to challenge similarly situated jurors who are not members of the same cognizable group as the challenged juror, regardless of whether the moving party made a comparative analysis argument in the trial court. Should the appellate court determine that the objection was erroneously denied, that error shall be deemed prejudicial, the judgment shall be reversed, and the case remanded for a new trial.

(k)(1) Except as specified in paragraph (2), this section shall not apply to civil cases.

(2) This section shall apply in the following civil cases:

(A) Civil cases involving a civil rights violation, including the following:

(i) Actions alleging a violation against a protected class enumerated in subdivision (a).

(ii) Actions alleging a violation of the Tom Bane Civil Rights Act (Section 52.1 of the Civil Code) or the Unruh Civil Rights Act (Section 51 of the Civil Code).

(iii) Actions alleging a violation pursuant to Section 1983 of Title 42 of the United States Code.

(iv) Actions alleging a violation of Title VI of the federal Civil Rights Act of 1964 (42 U.S.C. Sec. 2000d, et seq.), the federal

Voting Rights Act of 1965 (52 U.S.C. Sec. 10301 et seq.), or the federal Fair Housing Act (42 U.S.C. Sec. 3601 et seq.).

(v) Actions alleging a violation of the California Fair Employment and Housing Act (Part 2.8 (commencing with Section 12900) of Division 3 of Title 2 of the Government Code), including, but not limited to, actions alleging discrimination, harassment, or retaliation.

(B) Actions for the civil commitment of a person, including a person who is determined to be a sexually violent predator pursuant to Article 4 (commencing with Section 6600) of Chapter 2 of Part 2 of Division 6 of the Welfare and Institutions Code.

(C) Civil cases for damages arising from a hate crime.

(*l*) For civil cases governed under paragraph (2) of subdivision (k), the party bringing the claim described in paragraph (2) of subdivision (k) shall notify the court and the other party or parties, after the final status conference, or, if no final status conference is held, at least 15 calendar days before the date of the trial, that the procedures under this section apply.

(m) It is the intent of the Legislature that enactment of this section shall not, in purpose or effect, lower the standard for judging challenges for cause or expand use of challenges for cause.

(n) The provisions of this section are severable. If any provision of this section or its application is held invalid, that invalidity shall not affect other provisions or applications that can be given effect without the invalid provision or application. *(Added by Stats.2020, c. 318, § 2. Amended by Stats.2025, c. 656, § 1.)*

§ 232. Perjury acknowledgement and agreement

(a) Prior to the examination of prospective trial jurors in the panel assigned for voir dire, the following perjury acknowledgment and agreement shall be obtained from the panel, which shall be acknowledged by the prospective jurors with the statement "I do":

"Do you understand and agree, under penalty of perjury, that you will accurately and truthfully answer all questions about your qualifications and ability to serve as a juror in this case, and that failure to do so may result in criminal prosecution?"

(b) As soon as the selection of the trial jury is completed, the following acknowledgment and agreement shall be obtained from the trial jurors, which shall be acknowledged by the statement "I do":

"Do you understand and agree that you will carefully consider the case being heard in this court, and that you will reach a verdict based only on the evidence presented to you and the instructions on the law given by the court?" *(Added by Stats.1988, c. 1245, § 2. Amended by Stats.1989, c. 1416, § 10; Stats.2025, c. 29, § 1.)*

PART 2. OF CIVIL ACTIONS

TITLE 2. OF THE TIME OF COMMENCING CIVIL ACTIONS

Chapter 3. The Time of Commencing Actions Other Than for the Recovery of Real Property

§ 335. Periods of Limitation

The periods prescribed for the commencement of actions other than for the recovery of real property, are as follows: *(Enacted 1872.)*

§ 335.1. Two Years

Within two years: An action for assault, battery, or injury to, or for the death of, an individual caused by the wrongful act or neglect of another. *(Added by Stats.2002, c. 448, § 2.)*

§ 340. One Year

Within one year:

(a) Statutory penalty or forfeiture to individual and state. An action upon a statute for a penalty or forfeiture, if the action is given to an individual, or to an individual and the state, except if the statute imposing it prescribes a different limitation.

(b) Statutory forfeiture or penalty to state. An action upon a statute for a forfeiture or penalty to the people of this state.

(c) Libel, slander, false imprisonment, seduction, forged or raised checks, injury to animals by feeder or veterinarian. An action for libel, slander, false imprisonment, seduction of a person below the age of legal consent, or by a depositor against a bank for the payment of a forged or raised check, or a check that bears a forged or unauthorized endorsement, or against any person who boards or feeds an animal or fowl or who engages in the practice of veterinary medicine as defined in Section 4826 of the Business and Professions Code, for that person's neglect resulting in injury or death to an animal or fowl in the course of boarding or feeding the animal or fowl or in the course of the practice of veterinary medicine on that animal or fowl.

(d) Damages for seizure. An action against an officer to recover damages for the seizure of any property for a statutory forfeiture to the state, or for the detention of, or injury to property so seized, or for damages done to any person in making that seizure.

(e) Action by good faith improver. An action by a good faith improver for relief under Chapter 10 (commencing with Section 871.1) of

Title 10 of Part 2. The time begins to run from the date upon which the good faith improver discovers that the good faith improver is not the owner of the land upon which the improvements have been made. *(Enacted 1872. Amended by Code Am.1873–74, c. 383, § 34; Code Am.1875–76, c. 29, § 1; Stats.1905, c. 258, § 2; Stats.1929, c. 518, § 1; Stats.1939, c. 1103, § 1; Stats.1949, c. 863, § 1; Stats.1953, c. 1382, § 1; Stats.1963, c. 1681, § 2; Stats.1968, c. 150, § 1; Stats.1973, c. 20, § 1; Stats.1982, c. 517, § 97; Stats.2002, c. 448, § 3.)*

§ 340.1. Childhood Sexual Assault; Certificates of Merit Executed by Attorney; Violations; Failure to File; Name Designation of Defendant; Periods of Limitation; Legislative Intent

(a) There is no time limit for the commencement of any of the following actions for recovery of damages suffered as a result of childhood sexual assault:

(1) An action against any person for committing an act of childhood sexual assault.

(2) An action for liability against any person or entity who owed a duty of care to the plaintiff, if a wrongful or negligent act by that person or entity was a legal cause of the childhood sexual assault that resulted in the injury to the plaintiff.

(3) An action for liability against any person or entity if an intentional act by that person or entity was a legal cause of the childhood sexual assault that resulted in the injury to the plaintiff.

(b)(1) In an action described in subdivision (a), a person who is sexually assaulted and proves it was as the result of a cover up may recover up to treble damages against a defendant who is found to have covered up the sexual assault of a minor, unless prohibited by another law.

(2) For purposes of this subdivision, a "cover up" is a concerted effort to hide evidence relating to childhood sexual assault.

(c) "Childhood sexual assault" as used in this section includes any act committed against the plaintiff that occurred when the plaintiff was under the age of 18 years and that would have been proscribed by Section 266j of the Penal Code; Section 285 of the Penal Code; paragraph (1) or (2) of subdivision (b), or of subdivision (c), of Section 286 of the Penal Code; subdivision (a) or (b) of Section 288 of the Penal Code; paragraph (1) or (2) of subdivision (b), or of subdivision (c), of Section 287 or of former Section 288a of the Penal Code; subdivision (h), (i), or (j) of Section 289 of the Penal Code; any sexual conduct as defined in paragraph (1) of subdivision (d) of Section 311.4 of the Penal Code; Section 647.6 of the Penal Code; or any prior laws of this state of similar effect at the time the act was committed. This subdivision does not limit the availability of causes of action permitted under subdivision (a), including causes of action against persons or entities other than the alleged perpetrator of the abuse.

(d) This section shall not be construed to alter the otherwise applicable burden of proof, as defined in Section 115 of the Evidence Code, that a plaintiff has in a civil action subject to this section.

(e) Every plaintiff 40 years of age or older at the time the action is filed shall file certificates of merit as specified in subdivision (f).

(f) Certificates of merit setting forth the facts that support the declaration shall be executed by the attorney for the plaintiff and by a licensed mental health practitioner selected by the plaintiff declaring, respectively, as follows:

(1) That the attorney has reviewed the facts of the case, consulted with at least one mental health practitioner who the attorney reasonably believes is knowledgeable of the relevant facts and issues involved in the particular action, and concluded on the basis of that review and consultation that there is reasonable and meritorious cause for the filing of the action.

(2) That the mental health practitioner consulted is licensed to practice and practices in this state and is not a party to the action, that the practitioner is not treating and has not treated the plaintiff, and that the practitioner has interviewed the plaintiff and is knowledgeable of the relevant facts and issues involved in the particular action, and has concluded, on the basis of the practitioner's knowledge of the facts and issues, that in the practitioner's professional opinion there is a reasonable basis to believe that the plaintiff had been subject to childhood sexual abuse.

(g) If certificates are required pursuant to subdivision (e), the attorney for the plaintiff shall execute a separate certificate of merit for each defendant named in the complaint.

(h) In any action subject to subdivision (e), a defendant shall not be served, and the duty to serve a defendant with process does not attach, until the court has reviewed the certificates of merit filed pursuant to subdivision (f) with respect to that defendant, and has found, in camera, based solely on those certificates of merit, that there is reasonable and meritorious cause for the filing of the action against that defendant. At that time, the duty to serve that defendant with process shall attach.

(i) A violation of this section may constitute unprofessional conduct and may be the grounds for discipline against the attorney.

(j) The failure to file certificates in accordance with this section shall be grounds for a demurrer pursuant to Section 430.10 or a motion to strike pursuant to Section 435.

(k) In any action subject to subdivision (e), a defendant shall be named by "Doe" designation in any pleadings or papers filed in the action until there has been a showing of corroborative fact as to the charging allegations against that defendant.

(*l*) At any time after the action is filed, the plaintiff may apply to the court for permission to amend the complaint to substitute the name of the defendant or defendants for the fictitious designation, as follows:

(1) The application shall be accompanied by a certificate of corroborative fact executed by the attorney for the plaintiff. The certificate shall declare that the attorney has discovered one or more facts corroborative of one or more of the charging allegations against a defendant or defendants, and shall set forth in clear and concise terms the nature and substance of the corroborative fact. If the corroborative fact is evidenced by the statement of a witness or the contents of a document, the certificate shall declare that the attorney has personal knowledge of the statement of the witness or of the contents of the document, and the identity and location of the witness or document shall be included in the certificate. For purposes of this section, a fact is corroborative of an allegation if it confirms or supports the allegation. The opinion of any mental health practitioner concerning the plaintiff shall not constitute a corroborative fact for purposes of this section.

(2) If the application to name a defendant is made before that defendant's appearance in the action, neither the application nor the certificate of corroborative fact by the attorney shall be served on the defendant or defendants, nor on any other party or their counsel of record.

(3) If the application to name a defendant is made after that defendant's appearance in the action, the application shall be served on all parties and proof of service provided to the court, but the certificate of corroborative fact by the attorney shall not be served on any party or their counsel of record.

(m) The court shall review the application and the certificate of corroborative fact in camera and, based solely on the certificate and any reasonable inferences to be drawn from the certificate, shall, if one or more facts corroborative of one or more of the charging allegations against a defendant has been shown, order that the complaint may be amended to substitute the name of the defendant or defendants.

(n) The court shall keep under seal and confidential from the public and all parties to the litigation, other than the plaintiff, any and all certificates of corroborative fact filed pursuant to subdivision (*l*).

(*o*) Upon the favorable conclusion of the litigation with respect to any defendant for whom a certificate of merit was filed or for whom a certificate of merit should have been filed pursuant to this section, the court may, upon the motion of a party or upon the court's own motion, verify compliance with this section by requiring the attorney for the plaintiff who was required by subdivision (f) to execute the certificate to reveal the name, address, and telephone number of the person or persons consulted with pursuant to subdivision (f) that were relied upon by the attorney in preparation of the certificate of merit. The name, address, and telephone number shall be disclosed to the trial judge in camera and in the absence of the moving party. If the court finds there has been a failure to comply with this section, the court may order a party, a party's attorney, or both, to pay any reasonable expenses, including attorney's fees, incurred by the defendant for whom a certificate of merit should have been filed.

(p) This section applies to any claim in which the childhood sexual assault occurred on and after January 1, 2024. Notwithstanding any other law, a claim for damages based on conduct described in paragraphs (1) through (3), inclusive, of subdivision (a), in which the childhood sexual assault occurred on or before December 31, 2023 may only be commenced pursuant to the applicable statute of limitations set forth in existing law as it read on December 31, 2023.

(q) Notwithstanding any other law, including Chapter 1 of Part 3 of Division 3.6 of Title 1 of the Government Code (commencing with Section 900) and Chapter 2 of Part 3 of Division 3.6 of Title 1 of the Government Code (commencing with Section 910), a claim for damages described in paragraphs (1) through (3), inclusive, of subdivision (a), is not required to be presented to any government entity prior to the commencement of an action. *(Added by Stats.1986, c. 914, § 1. Amended by Stats.1990, c. 1578, § 1; Stats.1994, c. 288, § 1; Stats.1998, c. 1032, § 1; Stats.1999, c. 120, § 1; Stats.2002, c. 149, § 1; Stats.2018, c. 423, § 8; Stats.2019, c. 861, § 1; Stats.2022, c. 444, § 1; Stats.2023, c. 655, § 1.)*

§ 340.5. Action Against Health Care Provider; Three Years From Injury or One Year from Discovery; Exceptions; Minors

In an action for injury or death against a health care provider based upon such person's alleged professional negligence, the time for the commencement of action shall be three years after the date of injury or one year after the plaintiff discovers, or through the use of reasonable diligence should have discovered, the injury, whichever occurs first. In no event shall the time for commencement of legal action exceed three years unless tolled for any of the following: (1) upon proof of fraud, (2) intentional concealment, or (3) the presence of a foreign body, which has no therapeutic or diagnostic purpose or effect, in the person of the injured person. Actions by a minor shall be commenced within three years from the date of the alleged wrongful act except that actions by a minor under the full age of six years shall be commenced within three years or prior to his eighth birthday whichever provides a longer period. Such time limitation shall be tolled for minors for any period during which parent or guardian and defendant's insurer or health care provider have committed fraud or collusion in the failure to bring an action on behalf of the injured minor for professional negligence.

For the purposes of this section:

(1) "Health care provider" means any person licensed or certified pursuant to Division 2 (commencing with Section 500) of the Business and Professions Code, or licensed pursuant to the Osteopathic Initiative Act, or the Chiropractic Initiative Act, or licensed pursuant to Chapter 2.5 (commencing with Section 1440) of Division 2 of the Health and Safety Code; and any clinic, health dispensary, or health facility, licensed pursuant to Division 2 (commencing with Section 1200) of the Health and Safety Code. "Health care provider" includes the legal representatives of a health care provider;

(2) "Professional negligence" means a negligent act or omission to act by a health care provider in the rendering of professional services, which act or omission is the proximate cause of a personal injury or wrongful death, provided that such services are within the scope of services for which the provider is licensed and which are not within any restriction imposed by the licensing agency or licensed hospital. *(Added by Stats.1970, c. 360, § 1. Amended by Stats.1975, c. 1, § 25; Stats.1975, c. 2, § 1.192.)*

§ 340.6. Attorneys; Wrongful Professional Act or Omission; Tolling of Period

(a) An action against an attorney for a wrongful act or omission, other than for actual fraud, arising in the performance of professional services shall be commenced within one year after the plaintiff discovers, or through the use of reasonable diligence should have discovered, the facts constituting the wrongful act or omission, or four years from the date of the wrongful act or omission, whichever occurs first. If the plaintiff is required to establish the plaintiff's factual innocence for an underlying criminal charge as an element of the plaintiff's claim, the action shall be commenced within two years after the plaintiff achieves postconviction exoneration in the form of a final judicial disposition of the criminal case. Except for a claim for which the plaintiff is required to establish the plaintiff's factual innocence, the time for commencement of legal action shall not exceed four years except that the period shall be tolled during the time that any of the following exist:

(1) The plaintiff has not sustained actual injury.

(2) The attorney continues to represent the plaintiff regarding the specific subject matter in which the alleged wrongful act or omission occurred.

(3) The attorney willfully conceals the facts constituting the wrongful act or omission when those facts are known to the attorney, except that this subdivision shall toll only the four-year limitation.

(4) The plaintiff is under a legal or physical disability that restricts the plaintiff's ability to commence legal action.

(5) A dispute between the lawyer and client concerning fees, costs, or both is pending resolution under Article 13 (commencing with Section 6200) of Chapter 4 of Division 3 of the Business and Professions Code. As used in this paragraph, "pending" means from the date a request for arbitration is filed until 30 days after receipt of notice of the award of the arbitrators, or receipt of notice that the arbitration is otherwise terminated, whichever occurs first.

(b) In an action based upon an instrument in writing, the effective date of which depends upon some act or event of the future, the period of limitations provided for by this section shall commence to run upon the occurrence of that act or event. *(Added by Stats.1977, c. 863, § 1. Amended by Stats.2009, c. 432, § 2; Stats.2019, c. 13, § 2.)*

Chapter 5. The Commencement of Actions Based upon Professional Negligence

§ 364. Notice of Intention; Time; Law Governing; Fictitious Name; Effect of Failure to Comply

(a) No action based upon the health care provider's professional negligence may be commenced unless the defendant has been given at least 90 days' prior notice of the intention to commence the action.

(b) No particular form of notice is required, but it shall notify the defendant of the legal basis of the claim and the type of loss sustained, including with specificity the nature of the injuries suffered.

(c) The notice may be served in the manner prescribed in Chapter 5 (commencing with Section 1010) of Title 14 of Part 2.

(d) If the notice is served within 90 days of the expiration of the applicable statute of limitations, the time for the commencement of the action shall be extended 90 days from the service of the notice.

(e) The provisions of this section shall not be applicable with respect to any defendant whose name is unknown to the plaintiff at the time of filing the complaint and who is identified therein by a fictitious name, as provided in Section 474.

(f) For the purposes of this section:

(1) "Health care provider" means any person licensed or certified pursuant to Division 2 (commencing with Section 500) of the Business and Professions Code, or licensed pursuant to the Osteopathic Initiative Act, or

the Chiropractic Initiative Act, or licensed pursuant to Chapter 2.5 (commencing with Section 1440) of Division 2 of the Health and Safety Code; and any clinic, health dispensary, or health facility, licensed pursuant to Division 2 (commencing with Section 1200) of the Health and Safety Code. "Health care provider" includes the legal representatives of a health care provider;

(2) "Professional negligence" means negligent act or omission to act by a health care provider in the rendering of professional services, which act or omission is the proximate cause of a personal injury or wrongful death, provided that such services are within the scope of services for which the provider is licensed and which are not within any restriction imposed by the licensing agency or licensed hospital. *(Added by Stats.1975, 2nd Ex.Sess., c. 1, p. 3970, § 25.5. Amended by Stats.1975, 2nd Ex.Sess., c. 2, § 1.193, eff. Sept. 24, 1975, operative Dec. 15, 1975.)*

TITLE 3. OF THE PARTIES TO CIVIL ACTIONS

Chapter 5. Permissive Joinder

§ 378. Plaintiffs; Joinder; Relief Granted

(a) All persons may join in one action as plaintiffs if:

(1) They assert any right to relief jointly, severally, or in the alternative, in respect of or arising out of the same transaction, occurrence, or series of transactions or occurrences and if any question of law or fact common to all these persons will arise in the action; or

(2) They have a claim, right, or interest adverse to the defendant in the property or controversy which is the subject of the action.

(b) It is not necessary that each plaintiff be interested as to every cause of action or as to all relief prayed for. Judgment may be given for one or more of the plaintiffs according to their respective right to relief. *(Enacted 1872. Amended by Stats.1927, c. 386, § 1; Stats.1971, c. 244, § 4.)*

§ 379. Defendants; Joinder

(a) All persons may be joined in one action as defendants if there is asserted against them:

(1) Any right to relief jointly, severally, or in the alternative, in respect of or arising out of the same transaction, occurrence, or series of transactions or occurrences and if any question of law or fact common to all these persons will arise in the action; or

(2) A claim, right, or interest adverse to them in the property or controversy which is the subject of the action.

(b) It is not necessary that each defendant be interested as to every cause of action or as to all relief prayed for. Judgment may be given against one or more of the defendants according to their respective liabilities.

(c) Where the plaintiff is in doubt as to the person from whom he or she is entitled to redress, he or she may join two or more defendants, with the intent that the question as to which, if any, of the defendants is liable, and to what extent, may be determined between the parties. *(Enacted 1872. Amended by Stats.1971, c. 244, § 5; Stats.1971, c. 950, § 1 Stats.1975, c. 1241, § 6.)*

§ 382. Nonconsent to Joinder as Plaintiff; Representative Actions

If the consent of any one who should have been joined as plaintiff cannot be obtained, he may be made a defendant, the reason thereof being stated in the complaint; and when the question is one of a common or general interest, of many persons, or when the parties are numerous, and it is impracticable to bring them all before the court, one or more may sue or defend for the benefit of all. *(Enacted 1872. Amended by Stats.1971, c. 244, § 12.)*

Chapter 6. Interpleader

§ 386. Interpleader

(a) Defendant in action on contract or for specific personal property; substitution of third party claimant or cross-complaint; deposit in court or delivery; discharge from liability; action against conflicting claimants. A defendant, against whom an action is pending upon a contract, or for specific personal property, may, at any time before answer, upon affidavit that a person not a party to the action makes against him, and without any collusion with him, a demand upon such contract, or for such property, upon notice to such person and the adverse party, apply to the court for an order to substitute such person in his place, and discharge him from liability to either party, on his depositing in court the amount claimed on the contract, or delivering the property or its value to such person as the court may direct; and the court may, in its discretion, make the order; or such defendant may file a verified cross-complaint in interpleader, admitting that he has no interest in such amount or such property claimed, or in a portion of such amount or such property and alleging that all or such portion of the amount or property is demanded by parties to such action or cross-action and apply to the court upon notice to such parties for an order to deliver such property or portion thereof or its value to such person as the court shall direct. And whenever conflicting claims are or may be made upon a person for or relating to personal property, or the performance of an obligation, or any portion thereof, such person may bring an action against the conflicting claimants to compel them to interplead and litigate their several claims. The order of substitution may be made and the action of interpleader may be maintained, and the applicant or interpleading party be discharged from liability to all or any of the conflicting claimants, although their titles or claims have not a common origin, or are not identical but are adverse to and independent of one another.

(b) Entity or person subject to multiple claims which give rise to multiple liability; action against claimants to compel interpleader and litigation of claims. Any person, firm, corporation, association or other entity against whom double or multiple claims are made, or may be made, by two or more persons which are such that they may give rise to double or multiple liability, may bring an action against the claimants to compel them to interplead and litigate their several claims.

When the person, firm, corporation, association or other entity against whom such claims are made, or may be made, is a defendant in an action brought upon one or more of such claims, it may either file a verified cross-complaint in interpleader, admitting that it has no interest in the money or property claimed, or in only a portion thereof, and alleging that all or such portion is demanded by parties to such action, and apply to the court upon notice to such parties for an order to deliver such money or property or such portion thereof to such person as the court shall direct; or may bring a separate action against the claimants to compel them to interplead and litigate their several claims. The action of interpleader may be maintained although the claims have not a common origin, are not identical but are adverse to and independent of one another, or the claims are unliquidated and no liability on the part of the party bringing the action or filing the cross-complaint has arisen. The applicant or interpleading party may deny liability in whole or in part to any or all of the claimants. The applicant or interpleading party may join as a defendant in such action any other party against whom claims are made by one or more of the claimants or such other party may interplead by cross-complaint; provided, however, that such claims arise out of the same transaction or occurrence.

(c) Deposit of amount payable in court; stoppage of interest and damages for detention of property. Any amount which a plaintiff or cross-complainant admits to be payable may be deposited by him with the clerk of the court at the time of the filing of the complaint or cross-complaint in interpleader without first obtaining an order of the court therefor. Any interest on amounts deposited and any right to damages for detention of property so delivered, or its value, shall cease to accrue after the date of such deposit or delivery.

(d) Answer by defendant; allegation of ownership or interest. A defendant named in a complaint to compel conflicting claimants to interplead and litigate their claims, or a defendant named in a cross-complaint in interpleader, may, in lieu of or in addition to any other pleading, file an answer to the complaint or cross-complaint which shall be served upon all other parties to the action and which shall contain allegations of fact as to his ownership of or other interest in the amount or property and any affirmative defenses and the relief requested. The allegations in such answer shall be deemed denied by all other parties to the action, unless otherwise admitted in the pleadings.

(e) Conflicting claims to property on deposit; issue triable by court; deficiency; trial of claim. Except in cases where by the law a right to a jury trial is now given, conflicting claims to funds or property or the value thereof so deposited or delivered shall be deemed issues triable by the court, and such issues may be first tried. In the event the amount deposited shall be less than the amount claimed to be due by one or more of the conflicting claimants thereto, or in the event the property or the value thereof delivered is less than all of the property or the value thereof claimed by one or more of such conflicting claimants, any issues of fact involved in determining whether there is a deficiency in such deposit or delivery shall be tried by the court or a jury as provided in Title 8 (commencing with Section 577) of Part 2 of this code.

(f) Other proceedings; restraining order. After any such complaint or cross-complaint in interpleader has been filed, the court in which it is filed may enter its order restraining all parties to the action from instituting or further prosecuting any other proceeding in any court in this state affecting the rights and obligations as between the parties to the interpleader until further order of the court. *(Enacted 1872. Amended by Stats.1881, c. 23, § 1; Stats.1951, c. 1142, § 1; Stats.1970, c. 563, § 1; Stats.1975, c. 670, § 1.)*

§ 386.1. Investment of Deposits; Allocation of Interest

Where a deposit has been made pursuant to Section 386, the court shall, upon the application of any party to the action, order such deposit to be invested in an insured interest-bearing account. Interest on such amount shall be allocated to the parties in the same proportion as the original funds are allocated. *(Added by Stats.1972, c. 553, § 1. Amended by Stats.1979, c. 173, § 1.)*

§ 386.5. Stakeholder; Dismissal From Action on Deposit With Clerk

Where the only relief sought against one of the defendants is the payment of a stated amount of money alleged to be wrongfully withheld, such defendant may, upon affidavit that he is a mere stakeholder with no interest in the amount or any portion thereof and that conflicting demands have been made upon him for the amount by parties to the action, upon notice to such parties, apply to the court for an order discharging him from liability and dismissing him from the action on his depositing with the clerk of the court the amount in dispute and the court may, in its discretion, make such order. *(Added by Stats.1953, c. 328, § 1.)*

§ 386.6. Costs and Attorney Fees; Attorney Pro Se

(a) A party to an action who follows the procedure set forth in Section 386 or 386.5 may insert in his motion, petition, complaint, or cross complaint a request for allowance of his costs and reasonable attorney fees incurred in such action. In ordering the discharge of such party, the court may, in its discretion, award such party his costs and reasonable attorney fees from the amount in dispute which has been deposited with the court. At the time of final judgment in the action the court may make such further provision for assumption of such costs and attorney fees by one or more of the adverse claimants as may appear proper.

(b) A party shall not be denied the attorney fees authorized by subdivision (a) for the reason that he is himself an attorney, appeared in pro se, and performed his own legal services. *(Added by Stats.1955, c. 951, § 1. Amended by Stats.1974, c. 273, § 1.)*

Chapter 7. Intervention

§ 387. Intervention; Procedure

(a) For purposes of this section:

(1) "Defendant" includes a cross-defendant.

(2) "Plaintiff" includes a cross-complainant.

(b) An intervention takes place when a nonparty, deemed an intervenor, becomes a party to an action or proceeding between other persons by doing any of the following:

(1) Joining a plaintiff in claiming what is sought by the complaint.

(2) Uniting with a defendant in resisting the claims of a plaintiff.

(3) Demanding anything adverse to both a plaintiff and a defendant.

(c) A nonparty shall petition the court for leave to intervene by noticed motion or ex parte application. The petition shall include a copy of the proposed complaint in intervention or answer in intervention and set forth the grounds upon which intervention rests.

(d)(1) The court shall, upon timely application, permit a nonparty to intervene in the action or proceeding if either of the following conditions is satisfied:

(A) A provision of law confers an unconditional right to intervene.

(B) The person seeking intervention claims an interest relating to the property or transaction that is the subject of the action and that person is so situated that the disposition of the action may impair or impede that person's ability to protect that interest, unless that person's interest is adequately represented by one or more of the existing parties.

(2) The court may, upon timely application, permit a nonparty to intervene in the action or proceeding if the person has an interest in the matter in litigation, or in the success of either of the parties, or an interest against both.

(e) If leave to intervene is granted by the court, the intervenor shall do both of the following:

(1) Separately file the complaint in intervention, answer in intervention, or both.

(2) Serve a copy of the order, or notice of the court's decision or order, granting leave to intervene and the pleadings in intervention as follows:

(A) A party to the action or proceeding who has not yet appeared shall be served in the same manner for service of summons pursuant to Article 3 (commencing with Section 415.10) of Chapter 4 of Title 5 of Part 2.

(B) A party who has appeared in the action or proceeding, whether represented by an attorney or not represented by an attorney, shall be served in the same manner for service of summons pursuant to Article 3 (commencing with Section 415.10) of Chapter 4 of Title 5 of Part 2, or in the manner provided by Chapter 5 (commencing with Section 1010) of Title 14 of Part 2.

(f) Within 30 days after service of a complaint in intervention or answer in intervention, a party may move, demur, or otherwise plead to the complaint in intervention or answer in intervention in the same manner as to an original complaint or answer. *(Enacted in 1872. Amended by Code Am.1873–74, c. 383, p. 296, § 44; Stats.1907, c. 371, p. 703, § 1; Stats.1969, c. 1611, p. 3379, § 5, operative July 1, 1970; Stats.1970, c. 484, p. 961, § 1; Stats.1977, c. 450, p. 1486, § 1; Stats.2017, c. 131, § 1.)*

Chapter 8. Compulsory Joinder

§ 389. Joinder as Party; Conditions; Indispensable Person, Factors; Statement of Reasons for Nonjoinder; Class Actions

(a) A person who is subject to service of process and whose joinder will not deprive the court of jurisdiction over the subject matter of the action shall be joined as a party in the action if (1) in his absence complete relief cannot be accorded among those already parties or (2) he claims an interest relating to the subject of the action and is so situated that the disposition of the action in his absence may (i) as a practical matter impair or impede his ability to protect that interest or (ii) leave any of the persons already parties subject to a substantial risk of incurring double, multiple, or otherwise inconsistent obligations by reason of his claimed interest. If he has not been so joined, the court shall order that he be made a party.

(b) If a person as described in paragraph (1) or (2) of subdivision (a) cannot be made a party, the court shall determine whether in equity and good conscience the action should proceed among the parties before it, or should be dismissed without prejudice, the absent person being thus regarded as indispensable. The factors to be considered by the court include: (1) to what extent a judgment rendered in the person's absence might be prejudicial to him or those already parties; (2) the extent to which, by protective provisions in the judgment, by the shaping of relief, or other measures, the prejudice can be lessened or avoided; (3) whether a judgment rendered in the person's absence will be adequate; (4) whether the plaintiff or cross-complainant will have an adequate remedy if the action is dismissed for nonjoinder.

(c) A complaint or crosscomplaint shall state the names, if known to the pleader, of any persons as described in paragraph (1) or (2) of subdivision (a) who are not joined, and the reasons why they are not joined.

(d) Nothing in this section affects the law applicable to class actions. *(Enacted 1872. Amended by 1897, c. 12, § 1; Stats.1907, c. 371, § 3; Stats.1957, c. 1498, § 2; Stats.1971, c. 244, § 15.)*

TITLE 4. OF THE PLACE OF TRIAL, RECLASSIFICATION, AND COORDINATION OF CIVIL ACTIONS

Chapter 1. Place of Trial

§ 392. Real Property Actions; Proper Court

(a) Subject to the power of the court to transfer actions and proceedings as provided in this title, the superior court in the county where the real property that is the subject of the action, or some part thereof, is situated, is the proper court for the trial of the following actions:

(1) For the recovery of real property, or of an estate or interest therein, or for the determination in any form, of that right or interest, and for injuries to real property.

(2) For the foreclosure of all liens and mortgages on real property.

(b) In the court designated as the proper court in subdivision (a), the proper court location for trial of a proceeding for an unlawful detainer, as defined in Section 1161, is the location where the court tries that type of proceeding that is nearest or most accessible to where the real property that is the subject of the action, or some part thereof, is situated. Otherwise any location of the superior court designated as the proper court in subdivision (a) is a proper court location for the trial. The court may specify by local rule the nearest or most accessible court location where the court tries that type of case. *(Amended by Stats.1976, c. 73, § 3; Stats.1998, c. 931, § 60; Stats.2002, c. 806, § 7.)*

§ 394. Actions by or Against a City, County, City and County or Local Agency; Transfer of Cases; Proper Court

(a) An action or proceeding against a county, or city and county, a city, or local agency, may be tried in the county, or city and county, or the county in which the city or local agency is situated, unless the action or proceeding is brought by a county, or city and county, a city, or local agency, in which case it may be tried in any county, or city and county, not a party thereto and in which the city or local agency is not situated. Except for actions initiated by the local child support agency pursuant to Section 17400, 17402, 17404, or 17416 of the Family Code, any action or proceeding brought by a county, city and county, city, or local agency within a certain county, or city and county, against a resident of another county, city and county, or city, or a corporation doing business in the latter, shall be, on motion of either party, transferred for trial to a county, or city and county, other than the plaintiff, if the plaintiff is a county, or city and county, and other than that in which the plaintiff is situated, if the plaintiff is a city, or a local agency, and other than that in which the defendant resides, or is doing business, or is situated. Whenever an action or proceeding is brought against a county, city and county, city, or local agency, in any county, or city and county, other than the defendant, if the defendant is a county, or city and county, or, if the defendant is a city, or local agency, other than that in which the defendant is situated, the action or proceeding must be, on motion of that defendant, transferred for trial to a county, or city and county, other than that in which the plaintiff, or any of the plaintiffs, resides, or is doing business, or is situated, and other than the plaintiff county, or city and county, or county in which that plaintiff city or local agency is situated, and other than the defendant county, or city and county, or county in which the defendant city or local agency is situated; provided, however, that any action or proceeding against the city, county, city and county, or local agency for injury occurring within the city, county, or city and county, or within the county in which the local agency is situated, to person or property or person and property caused by the negligence or alleged negligence of the city, county, city and county, local agency, or its agents or employees, shall be tried in that county, or city and county, or if a city is a defendant, in the city or in the county in which the city is situated, or if a local agency is a defendant, in the county in which the local agency is situated. In that action or proceeding, the parties thereto may, by stipulation in writing, or made in open court, and entered in the minutes, agree upon any county, or city and county, for the place of trial thereof. When the action or proceeding is one in which a jury is not of right, or in case a jury is waived, then in lieu of transferring the cause, the court in the original county may request the chairperson of the Judicial Council to assign a disinterested judge from a neutral county to hear that cause and all proceedings in connection therewith. When the action or proceeding is transferred to another county for trial, a witness required to respond to a subpoena for a hearing within the original county shall be compelled to attend hearings in the county to which the cause is transferred. If the demand for transfer is made by one party and the opposing party does not consent thereto, the additional costs of the nonconsenting party occasioned by the transfer of the cause, including living and traveling expenses of the nonconsenting party and material witnesses, found by the court to be material, and called by the nonconsenting party, not to exceed five dollars ($5) per day each in excess of witness fees and mileage otherwise allowed by law, shall be assessed by the court hearing the cause against the party requesting the transfer. To the extent of that excess, those costs shall be awarded to the nonconsenting party regardless of the outcome of the trial. This section shall apply to actions or proceedings now pending or hereafter brought.

(b) For the purposes of this section, "local agency" shall mean any governmental district, board, or agency, or any other local governmental body or corporation, but shall not include the State of California or any of its agencies, departments, commissions, or boards. *(Enacted 1872. Amended by Stats.1881, c. 30, § 1; Stats.1891, c. 61, § 1; Stats.1907, c. 369, § 2; Stats.1915, c. 434, § 1; Stats.1921, c. 382, § 1; Stats.1929, c. 112, § 1; Stats.1931, c. 942, § 1; Stats.1933, c. 744, § 5; Stats.1970, c. 604, § 1; Stats.1971, c. 957, § 1; Stats.1994, c. 1269, § 2.2; Stats.2002, c. 784, § 52; Stats.2002, c. 927, § 1.)*

§ 395. Actions Generally; Proper Court; Waiver by Agreement

(a) Except as otherwise provided by law and subject to the power of the court to transfer actions or proceedings as provided in this title, the superior court in the county where the defendants or some of them reside at the commencement of the action is the proper court for the trial of the action. If the action is for injury to person or personal property or for death from wrongful act or negligence, the superior court in either the county where the injury occurs or the injury causing death occurs or the county where the defendants, or some of them reside at the commencement of the action, is a proper court for the trial of the action. In a proceeding for dissolution of marriage, the superior court in the county where either the petitioner or respondent has been a resident for three months next preceding the commencement of the proceeding is the proper court for the trial of the proceeding. In a proceeding for nullity of marriage or legal separation of the parties, the superior court in the county where either the petitioner or the respondent resides at the commencement of the proceeding is the proper court for the trial of the proceeding. In a proceeding to enforce an obligation of support under Section 3900 of the Family Code, the superior court in the county where the child resides is the proper court for the trial of the action. In a proceeding to establish and enforce a foreign judgment or court order for the support of a minor child, the superior court in the county where the child resides is the proper court for the trial of the action. Subject to subdivision (b), if a defendant has contracted to perform an obligation in a particular county, the superior court in the county where the obligation is to be performed, where the contract in fact was entered into, or where the defendant or any defendant resides at the commencement of the action is a proper court for the trial of an action founded on that obligation, and the county where the obligation is incurred is the county where it is to be performed, unless there is a special contract in writing to the contrary. If none of the defendants reside in the state or if they reside in the state and the county where they reside is unknown to the plaintiff, the action may be tried in the superior court in any county that the plaintiff may designate in his or her complaint, and, if the defendant is about to depart from the state, the action may be tried in the superior court in any county where either of the parties reside or service is made. If any person is improperly joined as a defendant or has been made a defendant solely for the purpose of having the action tried in the superior court in the county where he or she resides, his or her residence shall not be considered in determining the proper place for the trial of the action.

(b) Subject to the power of the court to transfer actions or proceedings as provided in this title, in an action arising from an offer or provision of goods, services, loans or extensions of credit intended primarily for personal, family or household use, other than an obligation described in Section 1812.10 or Section 2984.4 of the Civil Code, or an action arising from a transaction consummated as a proximate result of either an unsolicited telephone call made by a seller engaged in the business of consummating transactions of that kind or a telephone call or electronic transmission made by the buyer or lessee in response to a solicitation by the seller, the superior court in the county where the buyer or lessee in fact signed the contract, where the buyer or lessee resided at the time the contract was entered into, or where the buyer or lessee resides at the commencement of the action is the proper court for the trial of the action. In the superior court designated in this subdivision as the proper court, the proper court location for trial of a case is the location where the court tries that type of case that is nearest or most accessible to where the buyer or lessee resides, where the buyer or lessee in fact signed the contract, where the buyer or lessee resided at the time the contract was entered into, or where the buyer or lessee resides at the commencement of the action. Otherwise, any location of the superior court designated as the proper court in this subdivision is a proper court location for the trial. The court may specify by local rule the nearest or most accessible court location where the court tries that type of case.

(c) Any provision of an obligation described in subdivision (b) waiving that subdivision is void and unenforceable. *(Enacted 1872. Amended by Stats.1907, c. 369, § 3; Stats.1911, c. 421, § 1; Stats.1933, c. 744, § 6; Stats.1939, c. 981, § 1; Stats.1951, c. 869, § 3; Stats.1955, c. 832, § 1;*

Stats.1969, c. 1608, § 11; Stats.1970, c. 75, § 1; Stats.1971, c. 1640, § 1; Stats.1972, c. 1117, § 1; Stats.1972, c. 1118, § 3; Stats.1972, c. 1119, § 3; Stats.1976, c. 610, § 1; Stats.1991, c. 228, § 3; Stats.1992, c. 163, § 17; Stats.1994, c. 1269, § 2.4; Stats.1998, c. 473, § 1; Stats.1998, c. 931, § 62; Stats.1998, c. 931, § 62.5; Stats.2002, c. 806, § 8.)

§ 395.1. Executor, Administrator, Guardian, Conservator or Trustee in Official or Representative Capacity

Except as otherwise provided in Section 17005 of the Probate Code pertaining to trustees, when a defendant is sued in an official or representative capacity as executor, administrator, guardian, conservator, or trustee on a claim for the payment of money or for the recovery of personal property, the county which has jurisdiction of the estate which the defendant represents shall be the proper county for the trial of the action. *(Added by Stats.1943, c. 1043, § 1. Amended by Stats.1979, c. 730, § 20; Stats.1986, c. 820, § 16.)*

§ 395.2. Unincorporated Associations

If an unincorporated association has filed a statement with the Secretary of State pursuant to statute, designating its principal office in this state, the proper county for the trial of an action against the unincorporated association is the same as it would be if the unincorporated association were a corporation and, for the purpose of determining the proper county, the principal place of business of the unincorporated association shall be deemed to be the principal office in this state listed in the statement. *(Added by Stats.1967, c. 1324, § 2. Amended by Stats.2004, c. 178, § 2.)*

§ 395.5. Actions Against Corporations or Associations; Place of Trial

A corporation or association may be sued in the county where the contract is made or is to be performed, or where the obligation or liability arises, or the breach occurs; or in the county where the principal place of business of such corporation is situated, subject to the power of the court to change the place of trial as in other cases. *(Added by Stats.1972, c. 118, § 1.)*

§ 396. Superior Court Lacking Jurisdiction of Appeal or Petition; Transfer to Court Having Jurisdiction

(a) No appeal or petition filed in the superior court shall be dismissed solely because the appeal or petition was not filed in the proper state court.

(b) If the superior court lacks jurisdiction of an appeal or petition, and a court of appeal or the Supreme Court would have jurisdiction, the appeal or petition shall be transferred to the court having jurisdiction upon terms as to costs or otherwise as may be just, and proceeded with as if regularly filed in the court having jurisdiction. *(Added by Stats.2008, c. 56, § 2.)*

§ 396b. Trial in Court Having Jurisdiction of Subject Matter But Not Proper Court; Transfer; Domestic Relations Cases; Retention of Cause for Convenience of Witnesses; Time to File Response Upon Denial of Motion for Transfer

(a) Except as otherwise provided in Section 396a, if an action or proceeding is commenced in a court having jurisdiction of the subject matter thereof, other than the court designated as the proper court for the trial thereof, under this title, the action may, notwithstanding, be tried in the court where commenced, unless the defendant, at the time he or she answers, demurs, or moves to strike, or, at his or her option, without answering, demurring, or moving to strike and within the time otherwise allowed to respond to the complaint, files with the clerk, a notice of motion for an order transferring the action or proceeding to the proper court, together with proof of service, upon the adverse party, of a copy of those papers. Upon the hearing of the motion the court shall, if it appears that the action or proceeding was not commenced in the proper court, order the action or proceeding transferred to the proper court.

(b) In its discretion, the court may order the payment to the prevailing party of reasonable expenses and attorney's fees incurred in making or resisting the motion to transfer whether or not that party is otherwise entitled to recover his or her costs of action. In determining whether that order for expenses and fees shall be made, the court shall take into consideration (1) whether an offer to stipulate to change of venue was reasonably made and rejected, and (2) whether the motion or selection of venue was made in good faith given the facts and law the party making the motion or selecting the venue knew or should have known. As between the party and his or her attorney, those expenses and fees shall be the personal liability of the attorney not chargeable to the party. Sanctions shall not be imposed pursuant to this subdivision except on notice contained in a party's papers, or on the court's own noticed motion, and after opportunity to be heard.

(c) The court in a proceeding for dissolution of marriage or legal separation or under the Uniform Parentage Act (Part 3 (commencing with Section 7600) of Division 12 of the Family Code) may, prior to the determination of the motion to transfer, consider and determine motions for allowance of temporary spousal support, support of children, and counsel fees and costs, and motions to determine custody of and visitation with children, and may make all necessary and proper orders in connection therewith.

(d) In any case, if an answer is filed, the court may consider opposition to the motion to transfer, if any, and may retain the action in the county where commenced if it appears that the convenience of the witnesses or the ends of justice will thereby be promoted.

(e) If the motion to transfer is denied, the court shall allow the defendant time to move to strike, demur, or otherwise plead if the defendant has not previously filed a response. *(Added by Stats.1933, c. 744, § 8a. Amended by Stats.1939, c. 149, § 1; Stats.1951, c. 869, § 6; Stats.1969, c. 345, § 1; Stats.1969, c. 1608, § 12; Stats.1969, c. 1609, § 28; Stats.1974, c. 1369, § 2; Stats.1981, c. 122, § 1; Stats.1982, c. 704, § 1; Stats.1983, c. 1167, § 1; Stats.1989, c. 1416, § 11; Stats.1989, c. 1417, § 3.5; Stats.1992, c. 163, § 18; Stats.2005, c. 706, § 10.)*

§ 397. Change of Place of Trial; Grounds

The court may, on motion, change the place of trial in the following cases:

(a) When the court designated in the complaint is not the proper court.

(b) When there is reason to believe that an impartial trial cannot be had therein.

(c) When the convenience of witnesses and the ends of justice would be promoted by the change.

(d) When from any cause there is no judge of the court qualified to act.

(e) When a proceeding for dissolution of marriage has been filed in the county in which the petitioner has been a resident for three months next preceding the commencement of the proceeding, and the respondent at the time of the commencement of the proceeding is a resident of another county in this state, to the county of the respondent's residence when the ends of justice would be promoted by the change. If a motion to change the place of trial is made pursuant to this paragraph, the court may, prior to the determination of such motion, consider and determine motions for allowance of temporary spousal support, support of children, temporary restraining orders, attorneys' fees, and costs, and make all necessary and proper orders in connection therewith. *(Enacted 1872. Amended by Stats.1907, c. 369, § 5; Stats.1933, c. 744, § 9; Stats.1955, c. 832, § 2; Stats.1969, c. 1608, § 13; Stats.1992, c. 163, § 19.)*

§ 398. Transfer; Proper Court Having Jurisdiction

(a) If a court orders the transfer of an action or proceeding for a cause specified in subdivisions (b), (c), and (d) of Section 397, the action or proceeding shall be transferred to a court having jurisdiction of the subject matter of the action upon agreement of the parties by stipulation in writing, or in open court and entered in the minutes or docket. If the parties do not so agree, the action or proceeding shall be transferred to the nearest or most accessible court where the like objection or cause for making the order does not exist.

(b) If an action or proceeding is commenced in a court other than one designated as a proper court for the trial thereof by the provisions of this title, and the same is ordered transferred for that reason, the action or proceeding shall be transferred to a proper court upon agreement of the parties by stipulation in writing, or in open court and entered in the minutes or docket. If the parties do not so agree, the action or proceeding shall be transferred to a proper court in the county in which the action or proceeding was commenced which the defendant may designate or, if there is no proper court in that county, to a proper court, in a proper county, designated by the defendant. If the defendant does not designate the court as herein provided, or if the court orders the transfer of an action on its own motion as provided in this title, the action or proceeding shall be transferred to the proper court as determined by the court in which the action or proceeding is pending.

(c) The designation of the court by the defendant as provided for in subdivision (b), may be made in the notice of motion for change of venue or in open court and entered in the minutes or docket at the time the order for transfer is made. *(Enacted 1872. Amended by Stats.1881, c. 30, § 2; Stats.1897, c. 124, § 1; Stats.1925, c. 438, § 1; Stats.1927, c. 744, § 2; Stats.1933, c. 744, § 10; Stats.2015, c. 303, § 39.)*

Chapter 2. Reclassification of Civil Actions and Proceedings

§ 403.010. Expansion or Limitations with Respect to this Chapter

Nothing in this chapter expands or limits the law on whether a plaintiff, cross-complainant, or petitioner may file an amended complaint or other amended initial pleading. Nothing in this chapter expands or limits the law on whether, and to what extent, an amendment relates back to the date of filing the original complaint or other initial pleading. *(Added by Stats.1999, c. 344, § 11, eff. Sept. 7, 1999. Amended by Stats.2002, c. 784, § 56.)*

§ 403.020. Amended Complaint or Other Initial Pleading; Changed Jurisdictional Classification; Reclassification

(a) If a plaintiff, cross-complainant, or petitioner files an amended complaint or other amended initial pleading that changes the jurisdictional classification from limited to unlimited, the party at the time of filing the pleading shall pay the reclassification fee provided in Section 403.060, and the clerk shall promptly reclassify the case. If the amendment changes the jurisdictional classification from unlimited to limited, no reclassification fee is required, and the clerk shall promptly reclassify the case.

(b) For purposes of this chapter, an amendment to an initial pleading shall be treated in the same manner as an amended initial pleading.

(Added by Stats.1999, c. 344, § 11. Amended by Stats.2001, c. 159, § 38; Stats.2001, c. 824, § 2.)

§ 403.030. Limited Civil Cases; Cross-Complainant; Caption Change; Reclassification

If a party in a limited civil case files a cross-complaint that causes the action or proceeding to exceed the maximum amount in controversy for a limited civil case or otherwise fail to satisfy the requirements for a limited civil case as prescribed by Section 85, the caption of the cross-complaint shall state that the action or proceeding is a limited civil case to be reclassified by cross-complaint, or words to that effect. The party at the time of filing the cross-complaint shall pay the reclassification fees provided in Section 403.060, and the clerk shall promptly reclassify the case. *(Added by Stats.1999, c. 344, § 11, eff. Sept. 7, 1999. Amended by Stats.2001, c. 824, § 3.)*

§ 403.040. Motion for Reclassification

(a) The plaintiff, cross-complainant, or petitioner may file a motion for reclassification within the time allowed for that party to amend the initial pleading. The defendant or cross-defendant may file a motion for reclassification within the time allowed for that party to respond to the initial pleading. The court, on its own motion, may reclassify a case at any time. A motion for reclassification does not extend the moving party's time to amend or answer or otherwise respond. The court shall grant the motion and enter an order for reclassification, regardless of any fault or lack of fault, if the case has been classified in an incorrect jurisdictional classification.

(b) If a party files a motion for reclassification after the time for that party to amend that party's initial pleading or to respond to a complaint, cross-complaint, or other initial pleading, the court shall grant the motion and enter an order for reclassification only if both of the following conditions are satisfied:

(1) The case is incorrectly classified.

(2) The moving party shows good cause for not seeking reclassification earlier.

(c) If the court grants a motion for reclassification, the payment of the reclassification fee shall be determined, unless the court orders otherwise, as follows:

(1) If a case is reclassified as an unlimited civil case, the party whose pleading causes the action or proceeding to exceed the maximum amount in controversy for a limited civil case or otherwise fails to satisfy the requirements of a limited civil case under Section 85 shall pay the reclassification fee provided in Section 403.060.

(2) If a case is reclassified as a limited civil case, no reclassification fee is required.

(d) If the court grants an order for reclassification of an action or proceeding pursuant to this section, the reclassification shall proceed as follows:

(1) If the required reclassification fee is paid pursuant to Section 403.060 or no reclassification fee is required, the clerk shall promptly reclassify the case.

(2) An action that has been reclassified pursuant to this section shall not be further prosecuted in any court until the required reclassification fee is paid. If the required reclassification fee has not been paid within five days after service of notice of the order for reclassification, any party interested in the case, regardless of whether that party is named in the complaint, may pay the fee, and the clerk shall promptly reclassify the case as if the fee had been paid as provided in Section 403.060. The fee shall then be a proper item of costs of the party paying it, recoverable if that party prevails in the action or proceeding. Otherwise, the fee shall be offset against and deducted from the amount, if any, awarded to the party responsible for the fee, if that party prevails in the action or proceeding.

(3) If the fee is not paid within 30 days after service of notice of an order of reclassification, the court on its own motion or the motion of any party may order the case to proceed as a limited civil case, dismiss the action or cross-action without prejudice on the condition that no other action or proceeding on the same matters may be commenced in any other court until the reclassification fee is paid, or take such other action as the court may deem appropriate.

(e) Nothing in this section shall be construed to require the superior court to reclassify an action or proceeding because the judgment to be rendered, as determined at the trial or hearing, is one that might have been rendered in a limited civil case.

(f) In any case where the misclassification is due solely to an excess in the amount of the demand, the excess may be remitted and the action may continue as a limited civil case. *(Added by Stats.1999, c. 344, § 11, eff. Sept. 7, 1999. Amended by Stats.2001, c. 824, § 4.)*

§ 403.050. Stipulation as to Reclassification

(a) The parties to the action or proceeding may stipulate to reclassification of the case within the time allowed to respond to the initial pleading.

(b) If the stipulation for reclassification changes the jurisdictional classification of the case from limited to unlimited, the reclassification fee provided in Section 403.060 shall be paid at the time the stipulation is filed.

(c) Upon filing of the stipulation and, if required under subdivision (b), the payment of the reclassification fee provided in Section 403.060, the clerk shall promptly reclassify the case. *(Added by Stats.2001, c. 824, § 6.)*

§ 403.060. Reclassification Fees

(a) For reclassification of a case from a limited civil case to an unlimited civil case, a fee shall be charged as provided in Section 70619 of the Government Code. This reclassification fee shall be in addition to any other fee due for that appearance or filing in a limited civil case. No additional amounts shall be charged for appearance or filing fees paid prior to reclassification. After reclassification, the fees ordinarily charged in an unlimited case shall be charged.

(b) If a reclassification fee is required and is not paid at the time an amended complaint or other initial pleading, a cross-complaint, or a stipulation for reclassification is filed under Section 403.020, 403.030, or 403.050, the clerk shall not reclassify the case and the case shall remain and proceed as a limited civil case.

(c) No fee shall be charged for reclassification of a case from an unlimited civil case to a limited civil case. The fees ordinarily required for filing or appearing in a limited civil case shall be charged at the time of filing a pleading that reclassifies the case. Parties are not entitled to a refund of the difference between any fees previously paid for appearance or filing in an unlimited civil case and the fees due in a limited civil case. After reclassification, the fees ordinarily charged in a limited civil case shall be charged. *(Added by Stats.2001, c. 824, § 8. Amended by Stats.2005, c. 75, § 29, eff. July 19, 2005, operative Jan. 1, 2006.)*

§ 403.070. Commencement of Action; Court Authority

(a) An action or proceeding that is reclassified shall be deemed to have been commenced at the time the complaint or petition was initially filed, not at the time of reclassification.

(b) The court shall have and exercise over the reclassified action or proceeding the same authority as if the action or proceeding had been originally commenced as reclassified, all prior proceedings being saved. The court may allow or require whatever amendment of the pleadings, filing and service of amended, additional, or supplemental pleadings, or giving of notice, or other appropriate action, as may be necessary for the proper presentation and determination of the action or proceeding as reclassified. *(Added by Stats.1999, c. 344, § 11, eff. Sept. 7, 1999.)*

TITLE 5. JURISDICTION AND SERVICE OF PROCESS

Chapter 1. Jurisdiction and Forum

§ 410.10. Basis

A court of this state may exercise jurisdiction on any basis not inconsistent with the Constitution of this state or of the United States. *(Added by Stats.1969, c. 1610, § 3.)*

§ 410.30. Stay or Dismissal of Action; General Appearance

(a) When a court upon motion of a party or its own motion finds that in the interest of substantial justice an action should be heard in a forum outside this state, the court shall stay or dismiss the action in whole or in part on any conditions that may be just.

(b) The provisions of Section 418.10 do not apply to a motion to stay or dismiss the action by a defendant who has made a general appearance. *(Added by Stats.1969, c. 1610, § 3. Amended by Stats.1972, c. 601, § 1; Stats.1986, c. 968, § 4.)*

§ 410.50. Time of Acquisition; General Appearance as Equivalent to Personal Service of Summons

(a) Except as otherwise provided by statute, the court in which an action is pending has jurisdiction over a party from the time summons is served on him as provided by Chapter 4 (commencing with Section 413.10). A general appearance by a party is equivalent to personal service of summons on such party.

(b) Jurisdiction of the court over the parties and the subject matter of an action continues throughout subsequent proceedings in the action. *(Added by Stats.1969, c. 1610, § 3.)*

Chapter 2. Commencing Civil Actions

§ 411.10. Complaint

A civil action is commenced by filing a complaint with the court. *(Added by Stats.1969, c. 1610, § 3, operative July 1, 1970.)*

Chapter 3. Summons

§ 412.20. Summons; Formalities; Contents

(a) Except as otherwise required by statute, a summons shall be directed to the defendant, signed by the clerk and issued under the seal of the court in which the action is pending, and it shall contain:

(1) The title of the court in which the action is pending.

(2) The names of the parties to the action.

(3) A direction that the defendant file with the court a written pleading in response to the complaint within 30 days after summons is served on the defendant.

(4) A notice that, unless the defendant so responds, their default will be entered upon application by the plaintiff, and the plaintiff may apply to the court for the relief demanded in the complaint, which could result in garnishment of wages, taking of money or property, or other relief.

(5) The following statement in boldface type: "You may seek the advice of an attorney in any matter connected with the complaint or this summons. Such attorney should be consulted promptly so that your pleading may be filed or entered within the time required by this summons."

(6) The following introductory legend at the top of the summons above all other matter, in boldface type, in English and Spanish:

"Notice! You have been sued. The court may decide against you without your being heard unless you respond within 30 days. Read information below."

(b) Each county may, by ordinance, require that the legend contained in paragraph (6) of subdivision (a) be set forth in every summons issued out of the courts of that county in any additional foreign language, if the legend in the additional foreign language is set forth in the summons in the same manner as required in that paragraph.

(c) A summons in a form approved by the Judicial Council is deemed to comply with this section.

(d) For actions regarding residential property brought pursuant to Section 1161, the Judicial Council shall, by January 1, 2027, create for mandatory use a single summons form that includes the information described in paragraphs (3) to (6), inclusive, of subdivision (a) in English, Spanish, Chinese, Tagalog, Vietnamese, and Korean. The Judicial Council shall publish this form on its internet website. *(Added by Stats.1969, c. 1610, § 3. Amended by Stats.1974, c. 363, § 1; Stats.1989, c. 79, § 1; Stats.1989, c. 1105, § 6; Stats.2025, c. 344, § 1.)*

§ 412.30. Action Against Corporation or Unincorporated Association; Notice; Contents; Default Judgment

In an action against a corporation or an unincorporated association (including a partnership), the copy of the summons that is served shall contain a notice stating in substance: "To the person served: You are hereby served in the within action (or special proceeding) on behalf of (here state the name of the corporation or the unincorporated association) as a person upon whom a copy of the summons and of the complaint may be delivered to effect service on said party under the provisions of (here state appropriate provisions of Chapter 4 (commencing with Section 413.10) of the Code of Civil Procedure)." If service is also made on such person as an individual, the notice shall also indicate that service is being made on such person as an individual as well as on behalf of the corporation or the unincorporated association.

If such notice does not appear on the copy of the summons served, no default may be taken against such corporation or unincorporated association or against such person individually, as the case may be. *(Added by Stats.1969, c. 1610, § 3.)*

Chapter 4. Service of Summons

§ 413.10. Law Governing Service

Except as otherwise provided by statute, a summons shall be served on a person:

(a) Within this state, as provided in this chapter.

(b) Outside this state but within the United States, as provided in this chapter or as prescribed by the law of the place where the person is served.

(c) Outside the United States, as provided in this chapter or as directed by the court in which the action is pending, or, if the court before or after service finds that the service is reasonably calculated to give actual notice, as prescribed by the law of the place where the person is served or as directed by the foreign authority in response to a letter rogatory. These rules are subject to the provisions of the Convention on the "Service Abroad of Judicial and Extrajudicial Documents" in Civil or Commercial Matters (Hague Service Convention). *(Added by Stats.1969, c. 1610, § 3. Amended by Stats.1984, c. 191, § 1.)*

§ 413.30. Procedure When No Provision Made for Service; Proof of Service

(a)(1) If no provision is made in this chapter or other law for the service of summons, or if a plaintiff, despite exercising reasonable diligence, has been unable to effect service of the summons by any of the methods authorized under this chapter, the court in which the action is pending may, upon motion, direct that summons be served in a manner that is reasonably calculated to give actual notice to the party to be served, including by electronic mail or other electronic technology, and that proof of such service be made as prescribed by the court.

(2) A plaintiff seeking to establish reasonable diligence under this section shall set forth facts detailing all attempts to serve the defendant by each of the methods prescribed by statute, including facts demonstrating why each method was unsuccessful at every address or location where the defendant is likely to be found.

(b) This section does not apply in an action against a governmental entity or an agent or employee of the governmental entity who has been sued in an official or individual capacity. *(Added by Stats.1969, c. 1610, § 3. Amended by Stats.2025, c. 403, § 1.)*

§ 414.10. Authorized Persons

A summons may be served by any person who is at least 18 years of age and not a party to the action. *(Added by Stats.1969, c. 1610, § 3.)*

§ 415.10. Personal Delivery of Copy of Summons and Complaint; Date

A summons may be served by personal delivery of a copy of the summons and of the complaint to the person to be served. Service of a summons in this manner is deemed complete at the time of such delivery.

The date upon which personal delivery is made shall be entered on or affixed to the face of the copy of the summons at the time of its delivery. However, service of a summons without such date shall be valid and effective. *(Added by Stats.1969, c. 1610, § 3. Amended by Stats.1976, c. 789, § 1.)*

§ 415.20. Leaving Copy of Summons and Complaint at Office, Dwelling House, Usual Place of Abode or Business, or Usual Mailing Address; Mailing Copy; Private Mailboxes

(a) In lieu of personal delivery of a copy of the summons and complaint to the person to be served as specified in Section 416.10, 416.20, 416.30, 416.40, or 416.50, a summons may be served by leaving a copy of the summons and complaint during usual office hours in the person's office or, if no physical address is known, at the person's usual mailing address, other than a United States Postal Service post office box, with the person who is apparently in charge thereof, and by thereafter mailing a copy of the summons and complaint by first-class mail, postage prepaid to the person to be served at the place where a copy of the summons and complaint were left. When service is effected by leaving a copy of the summons and complaint at a mailing address, it shall be left with a person at least 18 years of age, who shall be informed of the contents thereof. Service of a summons in this manner is deemed complete on the 10th day after the mailing.

(b) If a copy of the summons and complaint cannot with reasonable diligence be personally delivered to the person to be served, as specified in Section 416.60, 416.70, 416.80, or 416.90, a summons may be served by leaving a copy of the summons and complaint at the person's dwelling house, usual place of abode, usual place of business, or usual mailing address other than a United States Postal Service post office box, in the presence of a competent member of the household or a person apparently in charge of their office, place of business, or usual mailing address other than a United States Postal Service post office box, at least 18 years of age, who shall be informed of the contents thereof, and by thereafter mailing a copy of the summons and of the complaint by first-class mail, postage prepaid to the person to be served at the place where a copy of the summons and complaint were left. Service of a summons in this manner is deemed complete on the 10th day after the mailing.

(c) Notwithstanding subdivision (b), if the only address reasonably known for the person to be served is a private mailbox obtained through a commercial mail receiving agency, service of process may be effected on the first delivery attempt by leaving a copy of the summons and complaint with the commercial mail receiving agency in the manner described in subdivision (d) of Section 17538.5 of the Business and Professions Code.

(d) This section shall remain in effect only until January 1, 2027, and as of that date is repealed. *(Added by Stats.1969, c. 1610, § 3, operative July 1, 1970. Amended by Stats.1989, c. 1416, § 15; Stats.2003, c. 128, § 1; Stats.2017, c. 129, § 1; Stats.2025, c. 563, § 4.)*

§ 415.21. Access to Gated Communities; Identification

(a) Notwithstanding any other law, any person shall be granted access to a gated community or a covered multifamily dwelling for a reasonable period of time for the sole purpose of performing lawful service of process or service of a subpoena upon displaying a current driver's license or other identification, and one of the following:

(1) A badge or other confirmation that the individual is acting in the individual's as a representative of a county sheriff or marshal, or as an investigator employed by an office of the Attorney General, a county counsel, a city attorney, a district attorney, or a public defender.

(2) Evidence of current registration as a process server pursuant to Chapter 16 (commencing with Section 22350) of Division 8 of the Business and Professions Code or of licensure as a private investigator pursuant to Chapter 11.3 (commencing with Section 7512) of Division 3 of the Business and Professions Code.

(b) This section shall only apply to a gated community or a covered multifamily dwelling that is staffed at the time service of process is attempted by a guard or other security personnel assigned to control access to the community or dwelling.

(c) For purposes of this section, "covered multifamily dwelling" means either of the following:

(1) An apartment building, including a timeshare apartment building not considered a place of public accommodation or transient lodging, with three or more dwelling units.

(2) A condominium, including a timeshare condominium not considered a place of public accommodation or transient lodging, with four

or more dwelling units. *(Added by Stats.1994, c. 691, § 1. Amended by Stats.2005, c. 706, § 11; Stats.2012, c. 113, § 1; Stats.2014, c. 470, § 2; Stats.2016, c. 88, § 1; Stats.2019, c. 12, § 1.)*

§ 415.30. Service by Mail

(a) A summons may be served by mail as provided in this section. A copy of the summons and of the complaint shall be mailed (by first-class mail or airmail, postage prepaid) to the person to be served, together with two copies of the notice and acknowledgment provided for in subdivision (b) and a return envelope, postage prepaid, addressed to the sender.

(b) The notice specified in subdivision (a) shall be in substantially the following form:

(Title of court and cause, with action number, to be inserted by the sender prior to mailing)

NOTICE

To: (Here state the name of the person to be served.)

This summons is served pursuant to Section 415.30 of the California Code of Civil Procedure. Failure to complete this form and return it to the sender within 20 days may subject you (or the party on whose behalf you are being served) to liability for the payment of any expenses incurred in serving a summons upon you in any other manner permitted by law. If you are served on behalf of a corporation, unincorporated association (including a partnership), or other entity, this form must be signed in the name of such entity by you or by a person authorized to receive service of process on behalf of such entity. In all other cases, this form must be signed by you personally or by a person authorized by you to acknowledge receipt of summons. Section 415.30 provides that this summons is deemed served on the date of execution of an acknowledgment of receipt of summons.

____

Signature of Sender

ACKNOWLEDGMENT OF RECEIPT OF SUMMONS

This acknowledges receipt on (insert date) of a copy of the summons and of the complaint at (insert address).

Date: _______

(Date this acknowledgment is executed)

____

Signature of person acknowledging receipt, with title if acknowledgment is made on behalf of another person.

(c) Service of a summons pursuant to this section is deemed complete on the date a written acknowledgment of receipt of summons is executed, if such acknowledgment thereafter is returned to the sender.

(d) If the person to whom a copy of the summons and of the complaint are mailed pursuant to this section fails to complete and return the acknowledgment form set forth in subdivision (b) within 20 days from the date of such mailing, the party to whom the summons was mailed shall be liable for reasonable expenses thereafter incurred in serving or attempting to serve the party by another method permitted by this chapter, and, except for good cause shown, the court in which the action is pending, upon motion, with or without notice, shall award the party such expenses whether or not he is otherwise entitled to recover his costs in the action.

(e) A notice or acknowledgment of receipt in form approved by the Judicial Council is deemed to comply with this section. *(Added by Stats.1969, c. 1610, § 3.)*

§ 415.40. Service on Person Outside State

A summons may be served on a person outside this state in any manner provided by this article or by sending a copy of the summons and of the complaint to the person to be served by first-class mail, postage prepaid, requiring a return receipt. Service of a summons by this form of mail is deemed complete on the 10th day after such mailing. *(Added by Stats.1969, c. 1610, § 3. Amended by Stats.1982, c. 249, § 1.)*

§ 415.50. Service by Publication

(a) A summons may be served by publication if upon affidavit it appears to the satisfaction of the court in which the action is pending that the party to be served cannot with reasonable diligence be served in another manner specified in this article and that either:

(1) A cause of action exists against the party upon whom service is to be made or he or she is a necessary or proper party to the action.

(2) The party to be served has or claims an interest in real or personal property in this state that is subject to the jurisdiction of the court or the relief demanded in the action consists wholly or in part in excluding the party from any interest in the property.

(b) The court shall order the summons to be published in a named newspaper, published in this state, that is most likely to give actual notice to the party to be served. If the party to be served resides or is located out of this state, the court may also order the summons to be published in a named newspaper outside this state that is most likely to give actual notice to that party. The order shall direct that a copy of the summons, the complaint, and the order for publication be forthwith mailed to the party if his or her address is ascertained before expiration of the time prescribed for publication of the summons. Except as otherwise provided by statute, the publication shall be made as provided by Section 6064 of the Government Code unless the court, in its discretion, orders publication for a longer period.

(c) Service of a summons in this manner is deemed complete as provided in Section 6064 of the Government Code.

(d) Notwithstanding an order for publication of the summons, a summons may be served in another manner authorized by this chapter, in which event the service shall supersede any published summons.

(e) As a condition of establishing that the party to be served cannot with reasonable diligence be served in another manner specified in this article, the court may not require that a search be conducted of public databases where access by a registered process server to residential addresses is prohibited by law or by published policy of the agency providing the database, including, but not limited to, voter registration rolls and records of the Department of Motor Vehicles. *(Added by Stats.1969, c. 1610, § 3. Amended by Stats.1972, c. 601, § 2; Stats.1984, c. 352, § 1; Stats.2002, c. 197, § 2; Stats.2003, c. 449, § 8.)*

§ 416.10. Corporations Generally

A summons may be served on a corporation by delivering a copy of the summons and the complaint by any of the following methods:

(a) To the person designated as agent for service of process as provided by any provision in Section 202, 1502, 2105, or 2107 of the Corporations Code (or Sections 3301 to 3303, inclusive, or Sections 6500 to 6504, inclusive, of the Corporations Code, as in effect on December 31, 1976, with respect to corporations to which they remain applicable).

(b) To the president, chief executive officer, or other head of the corporation, a vice president, a secretary or assistant secretary, a treasurer or assistant treasurer, a controller or chief financial officer, a general manager, or a person authorized by the corporation to receive service of process.

(c) If the corporation is a bank, to a cashier or assistant cashier or to a person specified in subdivision (a) or (b).

(d) If authorized by any provision in Section 1701, 1702, 2110, or 2111 of the Corporations Code (or Sections 3301 to 3303, inclusive, or Sections 6500 to 6504, inclusive, of the Corporations Code, as in effect on December 31, 1976, with respect to corporations to which they remain applicable), as provided by that provision. *(Added by Stats.1969, c. 1610, § 3. Amended by Stats.1975, c. 682, § 3; Stats.1976, c. 641, § 1.1; Stats.2006, c. 567, § 7.)*

§ 416.50. Public Entity

(a) A summons may be served on a public entity by delivering a copy of the summons and of the complaint to the clerk, secretary, president, presiding officer, or other head of its governing body.

(b) As used in this section, "public entity" includes the state and any office, department, division, bureau, board, commission, or agency of the state, the Regents of the University of California, a county, city, district, public authority, public agency, and any other political subdivision or public corporation in this state. *(Added by Stats.1969, c. 1610, § 3.)*

§ 416.90. Persons Not Otherwise Specified

A summons may be served on a person not otherwise specified in this article by delivering a copy of the summons and of the complaint to such person or to a person authorized by him to receive service of process. *(Added by Stats.1969, c. 1610, § 3.)*

§ 417.10. Service Within State; Manner

Proof that a summons was served on a person within this state shall be made:

(a) If served under Section 415.10, 415.20, or 415.30, by the affidavit of the person making the service showing the time, place, and manner of the service and facts showing that such service was made in accordance with this chapter. The affidavit shall recite or in other manner show the name of the person to whom a copy of the summons and of the complaint were delivered, and, if appropriate, the person's title or the capacity in which the person is served, and that the notice required by Section 412.30 appeared on the copy of the summons served, if in fact it did appear.

If service is made by mail pursuant to Section 415.30, proof of service shall include the acknowledgment of receipt of summons in the form provided by that section or other written acknowledgment of receipt of summons satisfactory to the court.

(b) If served by publication pursuant to Section 415.50, by the affidavit of the publisher or printer, or the publisher's or the printer's foreperson or principal clerk, showing the time and place of publication, and an affidavit showing the time and place a copy of the summons and of the complaint were mailed to the party to be served, if in fact mailed.

(c) If served pursuant to another law of this state, in the manner prescribed by that law, if no manner is prescribed, in the manner prescribed by this section for proof of a similar manner of service.

(d) By the written admission of the party.

(e) If served by posting pursuant to Section 415.45, by the affidavit of the person who posted the premises, showing the time and place of posting, and an affidavit showing the time and place copies of the summons and of the complaint were mailed to the party to be served, if in fact mailed.

(f) All proof of personal service shall be made on a form adopted by the Judicial Council.

(g) This section shall remain in effect only until January 1, 2027, and as of that date is repealed. *(Added by Stats.1969, c. 1610, § 3. Amended by Stats.1972, c. 719, § 2; Stats.1980, c. 676, § 65; Stats.1986, c. 953, § 2; Stats.2006, c. 538, § 63; Stats.2025, c. 563, § 8.)*

§ 417.20. Service Outside State; Manner

Proof that a summons was served on a person outside this state shall be made:

(a) If served in a manner specified in a statute of this state, as prescribed by Section 417.10, and if service is made by mail pursuant to Section 415.40, proof of service shall include evidence satisfactory to the court establishing actual delivery to the person to be served, by a signed return receipt or other evidence;

(b) In the manner prescribed by the court order pursuant to which the service is made;

(c) Subject to any additional requirements that may be imposed by the court in which the action is pending, in the manner prescribed by the law of the place where the person is served for proof of service in an action in its courts of general jurisdiction; or

(d) By the written admission of the party.

(e) If served by posting pursuant to Section 415.45, by the affidavit of the person who posted the premises, showing the time and place of posting, and an affidavit showing the time and place copies of the summons and of the complaint were mailed to the party to be served, if in fact mailed. *(Added by Stats.1969, c. 1610, p. 3363, § 3. Amended by Stats.1972, c. 719, § 3.)*

§ 417.40. Proof of Service Signed by Registered Process Server; Additional Contents

(a) Any proof of service which is signed by a person registered under Chapter 16 (commencing with Section 22350) of Division 8 of the Business and Professions Code or the person's employee or independent contractor shall indicate the county in which the person is registered and the number assigned to the person pursuant to Section 22355 of the Business and Professions Code.

(b) This section shall remain in effect only until January 1, 2027, and as of that date is repealed. *(Added by Stats.1971, c. 1661, § 3. Amended by Stats.2025, c. 563, § 10.)*

Chapter 5. Objection to Jurisdiction

§ 418.10. Motion to Quash Service of Summons or to Stay or Dismiss Action; Procedure

(a) A defendant, on or before the last day of his or her time to plead or within any further time that the court may for good cause allow, may serve and file a notice of motion for one or more of the following purposes:

(1) To quash service of summons on the ground of lack of jurisdiction of the court over him or her.

(2) To stay or dismiss the action on the ground of inconvenient forum.

(3) To dismiss the action pursuant to the applicable provisions of Chapter 1.5 (commencing with Section 583.110) of Title 8.

(b) The notice shall designate, as the time for making the motion, a date not more than 30 days after filing of the notice. The notice shall be served in the same manner, and at the same times, prescribed by subdivision (b) of Section 1005. The service and filing of the notice shall extend the defendant's time to plead until 15 days after service upon him or her of a written notice of entry of an order denying his motion, except that for good cause shown the court may extend the defendant's time to plead for an additional period not exceeding 20 days.

(c) If the motion is denied by the trial court, the defendant, within 10 days after service upon him or her of a written notice of entry of an order of the court denying his or her motion, or within any further time not exceeding 20 days that the trial court may for good cause allow, and before pleading, may petition an appropriate reviewing court for a writ of mandate to require the trial court to enter its order quashing the service of summons or staying or dismissing the action. The defendant shall file or enter his or her responsive pleading in the trial court within the time prescribed by subdivision (b) unless, on or before the last day of the defendant's time to plead, he or she serves upon the adverse party and files with the trial court a notice that he or she has petitioned for a writ of mandate. The service and filing of the notice shall extend the defendant's time to plead until 10 days after service upon him or her of a written notice of the final judgment in the mandate proceeding. The time to plead may for good cause shown be extended by the trial court for an additional period not exceeding 20 days.

(d) No default may be entered against the defendant before expiration of his or her time to plead, and no motion under this section, or under Section 473 or 473.5 when joined with a motion under this section, or application to the court or stipulation of the parties for an extension of the time to plead, shall be deemed a general appearance by the defendant.

(e) A defendant or cross-defendant may make a motion under this section and simultaneously answer, demur, or move to strike the complaint or cross-complaint.

(1) Notwithstanding Section 1014, no act by a party who makes a motion under this section, including filing an answer, demurrer, or motion to strike constitutes an appearance, unless the court denies the motion made under this section. If the court denies the motion made under this section, the defendant or cross-defendant is not deemed to have generally appeared until entry of the order denying the motion.

(2) If the motion made under this section is denied and the defendant or cross-defendant petitions for a writ of mandate pursuant to subdivision (c), the defendant or cross-defendant is not deemed to have generally appeared until the proceedings on the writ petition have finally concluded.

(3) Failure to make a motion under this section at the time of filing a demurrer or motion to strike constitutes a waiver of the issues of lack of personal jurisdiction, inadequacy of process, inadequacy of service of process, inconvenient forum, and delay in prosecution. *(Added by Stats.1969, c. 1610, § 3. Amended by Stats.1989, c. 693, § 1; Stats.1993, c. 456, § 1; Stats.2002, c. 69, § 1.)**

TITLE 6. OF THE PLEADINGS IN CIVIL ACTIONS

Chapter 1. The Pleadings in General

§ 422.10. Allowable Pleadings

The pleadings allowed in civil actions are complaints, demurrers, answers, and cross-complaints. *(Added by Stats.1971, c. 244, § 18.)*

§ 422.30. Caption; Contents

(a) Every pleading shall contain a caption setting forth:

(1) The name of the court and county in which the action is brought.

(2) The title of the action.

(b) In a limited civil case, the caption shall state that the case is a limited civil case, and the clerk shall classify the case accordingly. *(Added by Stats.1971, c. 244, p. 378, § 20, operative July 1, 1972. Amended by Stats.1998, c. 931, § 71, eff. Sept. 28, 1998; Stats.1999, c. 344, § 13, eff. Sept. 7, 1999; Stats.2002, c. 784, § 60.)*

Chapter 2. Pleadings Demanding Relief

§ 425.10. Statement of Facts; Demand for Judgment

A complaint or cross complaint shall contain both of the following:

---

* [Ed.] Section 2 of the 2002 amending statute notes, "It is the intent of the Legislature in enacting this act to conform California practice with respect to challenging personal jurisdiction to the practice under Rule 12(b) of the Federal Rules of Civil Procedure."

(a)(1) A statement of the facts constituting the cause of action, in ordinary and concise language.

(2) A demand for judgment for the relief to which the pleader claims to be entitled. If the recovery of money or damages is demanded, the amount demanded shall be stated.

(b) Notwithstanding subdivision (a), where an action is brought to recover actual or punitive damages for personal injury or wrongful death, the amount demanded shall not be stated, but the complaint shall comply with Section 422.30 and, in a limited civil case, with subdivision (b) of Section 70613 of the Government Code. *(Added by Stats.1971, c. 244, § 23. Amended by Stats.1974, c. 1481, § 1; Stats.1979, c. 778, § 2; Stats.1998, c. 931, § 72, eff. Sept. 28, 1998; Stats.2001, c. 812, § 1; Stats.2005, c. 75, § 32, eff. July 19, 2005, operative Jan. 1, 2006.)*

§ 425.11. Personal Injury or Wrongful Death Actions; Statement of Nature and Amount of Damages; Service of Statement

(a) As used in this section:

(1) "Complaint" includes a cross-complaint.

(2) "Plaintiff" includes a cross-complainant.

(3) "Defendant" includes a cross-defendant.

(b) When a complaint is filed in an action to recover damages for personal injury or wrongful death, the defendant may at any time request a statement setting forth the nature and amount of damages being sought. The request shall be served upon the plaintiff, who shall serve a responsive statement as to the damages within 15 days. In the event that a response is not served, the defendant, on notice to the plaintiff, may petition the court in which the action is pending to order the plaintiff to serve a responsive statement.

(c) If no request is made for the statement referred to in subdivision (b), the plaintiff shall serve the statement on the defendant before a default may be taken.

(d) The statement referred to in subdivision (b) shall be served in the following manner:

(1) If a party has not appeared in the action, the statement shall be served in the same manner as a summons.

(2) If a party has appeared in the action, the statement shall be served upon the party's attorney, or upon the party if the party has appeared without an attorney, in the manner provided for service of a summons or in the manner provided by Chapter 5 (commencing with Section 1010) of Title 14 of Part 2.

(e) The statement referred to in subdivision (b) may be combined with the statement described in Section 425.115. *(Added by Stats.1974, c. 1481, § 2. Amended by Stats.1993, c. 456, § 2; Stats.1995, c. 796, § 2; Stats.1998, c. 931, § 73; Stats.2001, c. 812, § 2; Stats.2006, c. 538, § 63.5.)*

§ 425.115. Punitive Damages; Service of Statement; Form

(a) As used in this section:

(1) "Complaint" includes a cross-complaint.

(2) "Plaintiff" includes a cross-complainant.

(3) "Defendant" includes a cross-defendant.

(b) The plaintiff preserves the right to seek punitive damages pursuant to Section 3294 of the Civil Code on a default judgment by serving upon the defendant the following statement, or its substantial equivalent:

NOTICE TO ______________________. ______________
(Insert name of defendant or cross-defendant) *(Insert name of plaintiff*

______________ reserves the right to seek $ ____________ in punitive
or cross-complainant) *(Insert dollar amount)*

damages when ______________________ seeks a judgment
(Insert name of plaintiff or cross-complainant)

in the suit filed against you.

______________________ ______________
(Insert name of attorney or party appearing in propria persona) *(Date)*

(c) If the plaintiff seeks punitive damages pursuant to Section 3294 of the Civil Code, and if the defendant appears in the action, the plaintiff shall not be limited to the amount set forth in the statement served on the defendant pursuant to this section.

(d) A plaintiff who serves a statement upon the defendant pursuant to this section shall be deemed to have complied with Sections 425.10 and 580 of this code and Section 3295 of the Civil Code.

(e) The plaintiff may serve a statement upon the defendant pursuant to this section, and may serve the statement as part of the statement required by Section 425.11.

(f) The plaintiff shall serve the statement upon the defendant pursuant to this section before a default may be taken, if the motion for default judgment includes a request for punitive damages.

(g) The statement referred to in subdivision (b) shall be served by one of the following methods:

(1) If the party has not appeared in the action, the statement shall be served in the same manner as a summons pursuant to Article 3 (commencing with Section 415.10) of Chapter 4 of Title 5 of Part 2 of the Code of Civil Procedure.

(2) If the party has appeared in the action, the statement shall be served upon his or her attorney, or upon the party if he or she has appeared without an attorney, either in the same manner as a summons pursuant to Article 3 (commencing with Section 415.10) of Chapter 4 or in the manner provided by Chapter 5 (commencing with Section 1010) of Title 14. *(Added by Stats.1995, c. 796, § 3. Amended by Stats.2005, c. 706, § 12.)*

§ 425.12. Official Forms for Use in Trial Court; Development and Approval; Consultation with Advisory Committee

(a) The Judicial Council shall develop and approve official forms for use in trial courts of this state for any complaint, crosscomplaint or answer in any action based upon personal injury, property damage, wrongful death, unlawful detainer, breach of contract or fraud.

(b) The Judicial Council shall develop and approve an official form for use as a statement of damages pursuant to Sections 425.11 and 425.115.

(c) In developing the forms required by this section, the Judicial Council shall consult with a representative advisory committee which shall include, but not be limited to, representatives of the plaintiff's bar, the defense bar, the public interest bar, court administrators and the public. The forms shall be drafted in nontechnical language and shall be made available through the office of the clerk of the appropriate trial court. *(Added by Stats.1979, c. 843, § 1. Amended by Stats.1982, c. 272, § 1; Stats.1984, c. 354, § 1; Stats.1995, c. 796, § 4.)*

§ 425.13. Negligence Actions Against Health Care Providers; Claims for Punitive Damages; Amended Pleadings

(a) In any action for damages arising out of the professional negligence of a health care provider, no claim for punitive damages shall be included in a complaint or other pleading unless the court enters an order allowing an amended pleading that includes a claim for punitive damages to be filed. The court may allow the filing of an amended pleading claiming punitive damages on a motion by the party seeking the amended pleading and on the basis of the supporting and opposing affidavits presented that the plaintiff has established that there is a substantial probability that the plaintiff will prevail on the claim pursuant to Section 3294 of the Civil Code. The court shall not grant a motion allowing the filing of an amended pleading that includes a claim for punitive damages if the motion for such an order is not filed within two years after the complaint or initial pleading is filed or not less than nine months before the date the matter is first set for trial, whichever is earlier.

(b) For the purposes of this section, "health care provider" means any person licensed or certified pursuant to Division 2 (commencing with Section 500) of the Business and Professions Code, or licensed pursuant to the Osteopathic Initiative Act, or the Chiropractic Initiative Act, or licensed pursuant to Chapter 2.5 (commencing with Section 1440) of Division 2 of the Health and Safety Code; and any clinic, health dispensary, or health facility, licensed pursuant to Division 2 (commencing with Section 1200) of the Health and Safety Code. "Health care provider" includes the legal representatives of a health care provider. *(Added by Stats.1987, c. 1498, § 7. Amended by Stats.1988, c. 1204, § 1; Stats.1988, c. 1205, § 1.)*

§ 425.16. Anti-SLAPP Actions; Motion to Strike; Discovery; Remedies

(a) The Legislature finds and declares that there has been a disturbing increase in lawsuits brought primarily to chill the valid exercise of the constitutional rights of freedom of speech and petition for the redress of grievances. The Legislature finds and declares that it is in the public interest to encourage continued participation in matters of public significance, and that this participation should not be chilled through abuse of the judicial process. To this end, this section shall be construed broadly.

(b)(1) A cause of action against a person arising from any act of that person in furtherance of the person's right of petition or free speech under the United States Constitution or the California Constitution in connection with a public issue shall be subject to a special motion to strike, unless the court determines that the plaintiff has established that there is a probability that the plaintiff will prevail on the claim.

(2) In making its determination, the court shall consider the pleadings, and supporting and opposing affidavits stating the facts upon which the liability or defense is based.

(3) If the court determines that the plaintiff has established a probability that the plaintiff will prevail on the claim, neither that determination nor the fact of that determination shall be admissible in evidence at any later stage of the case, or in any subsequent action, and no burden of proof or degree of proof otherwise applicable shall be affected by that determination in any later stage of the case or in any subsequent proceeding.

(c)(1) Except as provided in paragraph (2), in any action subject to subdivision (b), a prevailing defendant on a special motion to strike shall be entitled to recover that defendant's attorney's fees and costs. If the court finds that a special motion to strike is frivolous or is solely intended to cause unnecessary delay, the court shall award costs and reasonable attorney's fees to a plaintiff prevailing on the motion, pursuant to Section 128.5.

(2) A defendant who prevails on a special motion to strike in an action subject to paragraph (1) shall not be entitled to attorney's fees and costs if that cause of action is brought pursuant to Section 11130, 11130.3, 54960, or 54960.1 of the Government Code, or pursuant to Chapter 2 (commencing with Section 7923.100) of Part 4 of Division 10 of Title 1 of the Government Code. Nothing in this paragraph shall be construed to prevent a prevailing defendant from recovering attorney's fees and costs pursuant to Section 7923.115, 11130.5, or 54960.5 of the Government Code.

(d) This section shall not apply to any enforcement action brought in the name of the people of the State of California by the Attorney General, Insurance Commissioner, district attorney, or city attorney, acting as a public prosecutor.

(e) As used in this section, "act in furtherance of a person's right of petition or free speech under the United States or California Constitution in connection with a public issue" includes: (1) any written or oral statement or writing made before a legislative, executive, or judicial proceeding, or any other official proceeding authorized by law, (2) any written or oral statement or writing made in connection with an issue under consideration or review by a legislative, executive, or judicial body, or any other official proceeding authorized by law, (3) any written or oral statement or writing made in a place open to the public or a public forum in connection with an issue of public interest, or (4) any other conduct in furtherance of the exercise of the constitutional right of petition or the constitutional right of free speech in connection with a public issue or an issue of public interest.

(f) The special motion may be filed within 60 days of the service of the complaint or, in the court's discretion, at any later time upon terms it deems proper. The motion shall be scheduled by the clerk of the court for a hearing not more than 30 days after the service of the motion unless the docket conditions of the court require a later hearing.

(g) All discovery proceedings in the action shall be stayed upon the filing of a notice of motion made pursuant to this section. The stay of discovery shall remain in effect until notice of entry of the order ruling on the motion. The court, on noticed motion and for good cause shown, may order that specified discovery be conducted notwithstanding this subdivision.

(h) For purposes of this section, "complaint" includes "cross-complaint" and "petition," "plaintiff" includes "cross-complainant" and "petitioner," and "defendant" includes "cross-defendant" and "respondent."

(i) An order granting or denying a special motion to strike shall be appealable under Section 904.1.

(j)(1) Any party who files a special motion to strike pursuant to this section, and any party who files an opposition to a special motion to strike, shall, promptly upon so filing, transmit to the Judicial Council, by email or facsimile, a copy of the endorsed, filed caption page of the motion or opposition, a copy of any related notice of appeal or petition for a writ, and a conformed copy of any order issued pursuant to this section, including any order granting or denying a special motion to strike, discovery, or fees.

(2) The Judicial Council shall maintain a public record of information transmitted pursuant to this subdivision for at least three years, and may store the information on microfilm or other appropriate electronic media. *(Added by Stats.1992, c. 726, § 2. Amended by Stats.1993, c. 1239, § 1; Stats.1997, c. 271, § 1; Stats.1999, c. 960, § 1, eff. Oct. 10, 1999; Stats.2005, c. 535, § 1, eff. Oct. 5, 2005; Stats.2009, c. 65, § 1; Stats.2010, c. 328, § 34; Stats.2021, c. 615, § 56; Stats.2024, c. 444, § 1.)*

§ 425.17. Legislative Findings and Declarations Regarding California Anti-SLAPP Law; Application of § 425.16

(a) The Legislature finds and declares that there has been a disturbing abuse of Section 425.16, the California Anti-SLAPP Law, which has undermined the exercise of the constitutional rights of freedom of speech and petition for the redress of grievances, contrary to the purpose and intent of Section 425.16. The Legislature finds and declares that it is in the public interest to encourage continued participation in matters of public significance, and that this participation should not be chilled through abuse of the judicial process or Section 425.16.

(b) Section 425.16 does not apply to any action brought solely in the public interest or on behalf of the general public if all of the following conditions exist:

(1) The plaintiff does not seek any relief greater than or different from the relief sought for the general public or a class of which the plaintiff is a member. A claim for attorney's fees, costs, or penalties does not constitute greater or different relief for purposes of this subdivision.

(2) The action, if successful, would enforce an important right affecting the public interest, and would confer a significant benefit, whether pecuniary or nonpecuniary, on the general public or a large class of persons.

(3) Private enforcement is necessary and places a disproportionate financial burden on the plaintiff in relation to the plaintiff's stake in the matter.

(c) Section 425.16 does not apply to any cause of action brought against a person primarily engaged in the business of selling or leasing goods or services, including, but not limited to, insurance, securities, or financial instruments, arising from any statement or conduct by that person if both of the following conditions exist:

(1) The statement or conduct consists of representations of fact about that person's or a business competitor's business operations, goods, or services, that is made for the purpose of obtaining approval for, promoting, or securing sales or leases of, or commercial transactions in, the person's goods or services, or the statement or conduct was made in the course of delivering the person's goods or services.

(2) The intended audience is an actual or potential buyer or customer, or a person likely to repeat the statement to, or otherwise influence, an actual or potential buyer or customer, or the statement or conduct arose out of or within the context of a regulatory approval process, proceeding, or investigation, except where the statement or conduct was made by a telephone corporation in the course of a proceeding before the California Public Utilities Commission and is the subject of a lawsuit brought by a competitor, notwithstanding that the conduct or statement concerns an important public issue.

(d) Subdivisions (b) and (c) do not apply to any of the following:

(1) Any person enumerated in subdivision (b) of Section 2 of Article I of the California Constitution or Section 1070 of the Evidence Code, or any person engaged in the dissemination of ideas or expression in any book or academic journal, while engaged in the gathering, receiving, or processing of information for communication to the public.

(2) Any action against any person or entity based upon the creation, dissemination, exhibition, advertisement, or other similar promotion of any dramatic, literary, musical, political, or artistic work, including, but not limited to, a motion picture or television program, or an article published in a newspaper or magazine of general circulation.

(3) Any nonprofit organization that receives more than 50 percent of its annual revenues from federal, state, or local government grants, awards, programs, or reimbursements for services rendered.

(e) If any trial court denies a special motion to strike on the grounds that the action or cause of action is exempt pursuant to this section, the appeal provisions in subdivision (i) of Section 425.16 and paragraph (13) of subdivision (a) of Section 904.1 do not apply to that action or cause of action. *(Added by Stats.2003, c. 338, § 1. Amended by Stats.2011, c. 296, § 36.5.)*

§ 425.18. SLAPPback Actions; Motion to Strike; Limitations Periods; Discovery; Remedies

(a) The Legislature finds and declares that a SLAPPback is distinguishable in character and origin from the ordinary malicious prosecution action. The Legislature further finds and declares that a SLAPPback cause of action should be treated differently, as provided in this section, from an ordinary malicious prosecution action because a SLAPPback is consistent with the Legislature's intent to protect the valid exercise of the constitutional rights of free speech and petition by its deterrent effect on SLAPP (strategic lawsuit against public participation) litigation and by its restoration of public confidence in participatory democracy.

(b) For purposes of this section, the following terms have the following meanings:

(1) "SLAPPback" means any cause of action for malicious prosecution or abuse of process arising from the filing or maintenance of a prior cause of action that has been dismissed pursuant to a special motion to strike under Section 425.16.

(2) "Special motion to strike" means a motion made pursuant to Section 425.16.

(c) The provisions of subdivisions (c), (f), (g), and (i) of Section 425.16, and paragraph (13) of subdivision (a) of Section 904.1, shall not apply to a special motion to strike a SLAPPback.

(d)(1) A special motion to strike a SLAPPback shall be filed within any one of the following periods of time, as follows:

(A) Within 120 days of the service of the complaint.

(B) At the court's discretion, within six months of the service of the complaint.

(C) At the court's discretion, at any later time in extraordinary cases due to no fault of the defendant and upon written findings of the court stating the extraordinary case and circumstance.

(2) The motion shall be scheduled by the clerk of the court for a hearing not more than 30 days after the service of the motion unless the docket conditions of the court require a later hearing.

(e) A party opposing a special motion to strike a SLAPPback may file an ex parte application for a continuance to obtain necessary discovery. If it appears that facts essential to justify opposition to that motion may exist, but cannot then be presented, the court shall grant a reasonable continuance to permit the party to obtain affidavits or conduct discovery or may make any other order as may be just.

(f) If the court finds that a special motion to strike a SLAPPback is frivolous or solely intended to cause unnecessary delay, the court shall award costs and reasonable attorney's fees to a plaintiff prevailing on the motion, pursuant to Section 128.5.

(g) Upon entry of an order denying a special motion to strike a SLAPPback claim, or granting the special motion to strike as to some but less than all causes of action alleged in a complaint containing a SLAPPback claim, an aggrieved party may, within 20 days after service of a written notice of the entry of the order, petition an appropriate reviewing court for a peremptory writ.

(h) A special motion to strike may not be filed against a SLAPPback by a party whose filing or maintenance of the prior cause of action from which the SLAPPback arises was illegal as a matter of law.

(i) This section does not apply to a SLAPPback filed by a public entity. *(Added by Stats.2005, c. 535, § 2, eff. Oct. 5, 2005.)*

§ 425.50. Allegation of Construction-related Accessibility Claim; Statement of Facts in Complaint; Verification by Plaintiff; Amendment of Complaint

(a) An allegation of a construction-related accessibility claim in a complaint, as defined in subdivision (a) of Section 55.52 of the Civil Code, shall state facts sufficient to allow a reasonable person to identify the basis of the violation or violations supporting the claim, including all of the following:

(1) A plain language explanation of the specific access barrier or barriers the individual encountered, or by which the individual alleges he or she was deterred, with sufficient information about the location of the alleged barrier to enable a reasonable person to identify the access barrier.

(2) The way in which the barrier denied the individual full and equal use or access, or in which it deterred the individual, on each particular occasion.

(3) The date or dates of each particular occasion on which the claimant encountered the specific access barrier, or on which he or she was deterred.

(4)(A) Except in complaints that allege physical injury or damage to property, a complaint filed by or on behalf of a high-frequency litigant shall also state all of the following:

(i) Whether the complaint is filed by, or on behalf of, a high-frequency litigant.

(ii) In the case of a high-frequency litigant who is a plaintiff, the number of complaints alleging a construction-related accessibility claim that the high-frequency litigant has filed during the 12 months prior to filing the complaint.

(iii) In the case of a high-frequency litigant who is a plaintiff, the reason the individual was in the geographic area of the defendant's business.

(iv) In the case of a high-frequency litigant who is a plaintiff, the reason why the individual desired to access the defendant's business, including the specific commercial, business, personal, social, leisure, recreational, or other purpose.

(B) As used in this section "high-frequency litigant" has the same meaning as set forth in subdivision (b) of Section 425.55.

(b)(1) A complaint alleging a construction-related accessibility claim, as those terms are defined in subdivision (a) of Section 55.3 of the Civil Code, shall be verified by the plaintiff. A complaint filed without verification shall be subject to a motion to strike.

(2) A complaint alleging a construction-related accessibility claim filed by, or on behalf of, a high-frequency litigant shall state in the caption "ACTION SUBJECT TO THE SUPPLEMENTAL FEE IN GOVERNMENT CODE SECTION 70616.5."

(c) A complaint alleging a construction-related accessibility claim shall be signed by at least one attorney of record in the attorney's individual name, or, if the party is not represented by an attorney, shall be signed by the party. By signing the complaint, the attorney or unrepresented party is certifying that, to the best of the person's knowledge, information, and belief, formed after an inquiry reasonable under the circumstances, all of the following conditions are met:

(1) It is not being presented primarily for an improper purpose, such as to harass or to cause unnecessary delay or needless increase in the cost of litigation.

(2) The claims, defenses, and other legal contentions therein are warranted by existing law or by a nonfrivolous argument for the extension, modification, or reversal of existing law or the establishment of new law.

(3) The allegations and other factual contentions have evidentiary support or, if specifically so identified, are likely to have evidentiary support after a reasonable opportunity for further investigation or discovery.

(4) The denials of factual contentions are warranted on the evidence or, if specifically so identified, are reasonably based on a lack of information or belief.

(d) A court may, after notice and a reasonable opportunity to respond, determine whether subdivision (c) has been violated and, if so, impose sanctions as provided in Section 128.7 for violations of subdivision (b) of Section 128.7.

(e) Nothing in this section shall limit the right of a plaintiff to amend a complaint under Section 472, or with leave of the court under Section 473. However, an amended pleading alleging a construction-related accessibility claim shall be pled as required by subdivision (a).

(f) The determination whether an attorney is a high-frequency litigant shall be made solely on the basis of the verified complaint and any other publicly available documents. Notwithstanding any other law, no party to the proceeding may conduct discovery with respect to whether an attorney is a high-frequency litigant.

(g) This section shall become operative on January 1, 2013. *(Added by Stats.2012, c. 383, § 13. Amended by Stats.2013, c. 76, § 22; Stats.2015, c. 755, § 5, eff. Oct. 10, 2015.)*

§ 425.55. Legislative Findings and Declarations Regarding the Protection of the Civil Rights of Persons with Disabilities; "High-frequency Litigant" Defined

(a) The Legislature finds and declares all of the following:

(1) Protection of the civil rights of persons with disabilities is of the utmost importance to this state, and private enforcement is the essential means of achieving that goal, as the law has been designed.

(2) According to information from the California Commission on Disability Access, more than one-half, or 54 percent, of all construction-related accessibility complaints filed between 2012 and 2014 were filed by two law firms. Forty-six percent of all complaints were filed by a total of 14 parties. Therefore, a very small number of plaintiffs have filed a disproportionately large number of the construction-related accessibility claims in the state, from 70 to 300 lawsuits each year. Moreover, these lawsuits are frequently filed against small businesses on the basis of boilerplate complaints, apparently seeking quick cash settlements rather than correction of the accessibility violation. This practice unfairly taints the reputation of other innocent disabled consumers who are merely trying to go about their daily lives accessing public accommodations as they are entitled to have full and equal access under the state's Unruh Civil Rights Act (Section 51 of the Civil Code) and the federal Americans with Disability Act of 1990 (Public Law 101–336).

(3) Therefore, given these special and unique circumstances, the provisions of this section are warranted for this limited group of plaintiffs.

(b) For the purposes of this article, "high-frequency litigant" means a person, except as specified in paragraph (3), who utilizes court resources in actions arising from alleged construction-related access violations at such a high level that it is appropriate that additional safeguards apply so as to ensure that the claims are warranted. A "high-frequency litigant" means one or more of the following:

(1) A plaintiff who has filed 10 or more complaints alleging a construction-related accessibility violation within the 12-month period immediately preceding the filing of the current complaint alleging a construction-related accessibility violation.

(2) An attorney who has represented as attorney of record 10 or more high-frequency litigant plaintiffs in actions that were resolved within the 12-month period immediately preceding the filing of the current complaint alleging a construction-related accessibility violation, excluding all of the following actions:

(A) An action in which an early evaluation conference was held pursuant to Section 55.54 of the Civil Code.

(B) An action in which judgment was entered in favor of the plaintiff.

(C) An action in which the construction-related accessibility violations alleged in the complaint were remedied in whole or in part, or a favorable result was achieved, after the plaintiff filed a complaint or provided a demand letter, as defined in Section 55.3 of the Civil Code.

(3) This section does not apply to an attorney employed or retained by a qualified legal services project or a qualified support center, as defined in Section 6213 of the Business and Professions Code, when acting within the scope of employment to represent a client in asserting a construction-related accessibility claim, or the client in such a case. *(Added by Stats.2015, c. 755, § 6, eff. Oct. 10, 2015.)*

§ 426.10. Definitions

As used in this article:

(a) "Complaint" means a complaint or cross-complaint.

(b) "Plaintiff" means a person who files a complaint or cross-complaint.

(c) "Related cause of action" means a cause of action which arises out of the same transaction, occurrence, or series of transactions or occurrences as the cause of action which the plaintiff alleges in his complaint. *(Added by Stats.1971, c. 244, § 23.)*

§ 426.30. Waiver of Related Cause of Action; Exceptions

(a) Except as otherwise provided by statute, if a party against whom a complaint has been filed and served fails to allege in a cross-complaint any related cause of action which (at the time of serving his answer to the complaint) he has against the plaintiff, such party may not thereafter in any other action assert against the plaintiff the related cause of action not pleaded.

(b) This section does not apply if either of the following are established:

(1) The court in which the action is pending does not have jurisdiction to render a personal judgment against the person who failed to plead the related cause of action.

(2) The person who failed to plead the related cause of action did not file an answer to the complaint against him. *(Added by Stats.1971, c. 244, § 23.)*

§ 426.40. Application

This article does not apply if any of the following are established:

(a) The cause of action not pleaded requires for its adjudication the presence of additional parties over whom the court cannot acquire jurisdiction.

(b) Both the court in which the action is pending and any other court to which the action is transferrable pursuant to Section 396 are prohibited by the federal or state constitution or by a statute from entertaining the cause of action not pleaded.

(c) At the time the action was commenced, the cause of action not pleaded was the subject of another pending action. *(Added by Stats.1971, c. 244, § 23.)*

§ 426.50. Failure to Plead Cause of Action; Notice; Amendment

A party who fails to plead a cause of action subject to the requirements of this article, whether through oversight, inadvertence, mistake, neglect, or other cause, may apply to the court for leave to amend his pleading, or to file a cross-complaint, to assert such cause at any time during the course of the action. The court, after notice to the adverse party, shall grant, upon such terms as may be just to the parties, leave to amend the pleading, or to file the cross-complaint, to assert such cause if the party who failed to plead the cause acted in good faith. This subdivision shall be liberally construed to avoid forfeiture of causes of action. *(Added by Stats.1971, c. 244, § 23.)*

§ 426.60. Application to Civil Actions; Exceptions

(a) This article applies only to civil actions and does not apply to special proceedings.

(b) This article does not apply to actions in the small claims court.

(c) This article does not apply where the only relief sought is a declaration of the rights and duties of the respective parties in an action for declaratory relief under Chapter 8 (commencing with Section 1060) of Title 14 of this part. *(Added by Stats.1971, c. 244, § 23.)*

§ 427.10. Joinder of Other Causes of Action by Plaintiff

(a) A plaintiff who in a complaint, alone or with coplaintiffs, alleges a cause of action against one or more defendants may unite with such cause any other causes which he has either alone or with any coplaintiffs against any of such defendants.

(b) Causes of action may be joined in a crosscomplaint in accordance with Sections 428.10 and 428.30. *(Added by Stats.1971, c. 244, § 23.)*

§ 428.10. Filing of Cross-Complaint; Causes of Action

A party against whom a cause of action has been asserted in a complaint or cross-complaint may file a cross-complaint setting forth either or both of the following:

(a) Any cause of action he has against any of the parties who filed the complaint or cross-complaint against him. Nothing in this subdivision authorizes the filing of a cross-complaint against the plaintiff in an action commenced under Title 7 (commencing with Section 1230.010) of Part 3.

(b) Any cause of action he has against a person alleged to be liable thereon, whether or not such person is already a party to the action, if the cause of action asserted in his cross-complaint (1) arises out of the same transaction, occurrence, or series of transactions or occurrences as the cause brought against him or (2) asserts a claim, right, or interest in the property or controversy which is the subject of the cause brought against him. *(Added by Stats.1971, c. 244, § 23. Amended by Stats.1975, c. 1240, § 4.)*

§ 428.20. Joinder of Person as Cross-Party

When a person files a cross-complaint as authorized by Section 428.10, he may join any person as a cross-complainant or cross-defendant, whether or not such person is already a party to the action, if, had the cross-complaint been filed as an independent action, the joinder of that party would have been permitted by the statutes governing joinder of parties. *(Added by Stats.1971, c. 244, § 23.)*

§ 428.30. Joinder of Other Causes of Action by Cross-Complainant

Where a person files a cross-complaint as authorized by Section 428.10, he may unite with the cause of action asserted in the cross-complaint any other causes of action he has against any of the cross-defendants, other than the plaintiff in an eminent domain proceeding, whether or not such cross-defendant is already a party to the action. *(Added by Stats.1971, c. 244, § 23.)*

§ 428.40. Separate Document

The cross-complaint shall be a separate document. *(Added by Stats.1971, c. 244, § 23.)*

§ 428.50. Filing of Cross-Complaint; Leave of Court

(a) A party shall file a cross-complaint against any of the parties who filed the complaint or cross-complaint against him or her before or at the same time as the answer to the complaint or cross-complaint.

(b) Any other cross-complaint may be filed at any time before the court has set a date for trial.

(c) A party shall obtain leave of court to file any cross-complaint except one filed within the time specified in subdivision (a) or (b). Leave may be granted in the interest of justice at any time during the course of the action. *(Added by Stats.1971, c. 244, § 23. Amended by Stats.1983, c. 176, § 1.)*

§ 428.60. Service; Appearance

A cross-complaint shall be served on each of the parties in an action in the following manner:

(1) If a party has not appeared in the action, a summons upon the cross-complaint shall be issued and served upon him in the same manner as upon commencement of an original action.

(2) If a party has appeared in the action, the cross-complaint shall be served upon his attorney, or upon the party if he has appeared without an attorney, in the manner provided for service of summons or in the manner provided by Chapter 5 (commencing with Section 1010) of Title 14 of Part 2 of this code. *(Added by Stats.1971, c. 244, § 23. Amended by Stats.1974, c. 429, § 1.)*

§ 428.70. Definitions

(a) As used in this section:

(1) "Third-party plaintiff" means a person against whom a cause of action has been asserted in a complaint or cross-complaint, who claims the right to recover all or part of any amounts for which he may be held liable on such cause of action from a third person, and who files a cross-complaint stating such claim as a cause of action against the third person.

(2) "Third-party defendant" means the person who is alleged in a cross-complaint filed by a third-party plaintiff to be liable to the third-party plaintiff if the third-party plaintiff is held liable on the claim against him.

(b) In addition to the other rights and duties a third-party defendant has under this article, he may, at the time he files his answer to the cross-complaint, file as a separate document a special answer alleging against the person who asserted the cause of action against the third-party plaintiff any defenses which the third-party plaintiff has to such cause of action. The special answer shall be served on the third-party plaintiff and on the person who asserted the cause of action against the third-party plaintiff. *(Added by Stats.1971, c. 244, § 23.)*

§ 428.80. Abolition of Counterclaim

The counterclaim is abolished. Any cause of action that formerly was asserted by a counterclaim shall be asserted by a cross-complaint. Where any statute refers to asserting a cause of action as a counterclaim, such cause shall be asserted as a cross-complaint. The erroneous designation of a pleading as a counterclaim shall not affect its validity, but such pleading shall be deemed to be a cross-complaint. *(Added by Stats.1971, c. 244, § 23.)*

Chapter 3. Objections to Pleadings; Denials and Defenses

§ 430.10. Objections by Defendant; Grounds

The party against whom a complaint or cross-complaint has been filed may object, by demurrer or answer as provided in Section 430.30, to the pleading on any one or more of the following grounds:

(a) The court has no jurisdiction of the subject of the cause of action alleged in the pleading.

(b) The person who filed the pleading does not have the legal capacity to sue.

(c) There is another action pending between the same parties on the same cause of action.

(d) There is a defect or misjoinder of parties.

(e) The pleading does not state facts sufficient to constitute a cause of action.

(f) The pleading is uncertain. As used in this subdivision, "uncertain" includes ambiguous and unintelligible.

(g) In an action founded upon a contract, it cannot be ascertained from the pleading whether the contract is written, is oral, or is implied by conduct.

(h) No certificate was filed as required by Section 411.35. *(Added by Stats.1971, c. 244, § 29. Amended by Stats.1973, c. 828, § 2; Stats.1979, c. 973, § 2; Stats.1979, c. 988, § 2; Stats.1980, c. 163, § 2; Stats.1980, c. 500, § 1; Stats.1990, c. 216, § 8; Stats.1993, c. 456, § 3; Stats.2020, c. 370, § 35.)*

§ 430.20. Objections by Plaintiff; Grounds

A party against whom an answer has been filed may object, by demurrer as provided in Section 430.30, to the answer upon any one or more of the following grounds:

(a) The answer does not state facts sufficient to constitute a defense.

(b) The answer is uncertain. As used in this subdivision, "uncertain" includes ambiguous and unintelligible.

(c) Where the answer pleads a contract, it cannot be ascertained from the answer whether the contract is written or oral. *(Added by Stats.1971, c. 244, § 29.)*

§ 430.30. Objections by Demurrer and Answer

(a) When any ground for objection to a complaint, cross-complaint, or answer appears on the face thereof, or from any matter of which the court is required to or may take judicial notice, the objection on that ground may be taken by a demurrer to the pleading.

(b) When any ground for objection to a complaint or cross-complaint does not appear on the face of the pleading, the objection may be taken by answer.

(c) A party objecting to a complaint or cross-complaint may demur and answer at the same time. *(Added by Stats.1971, c. 244, § 29.)*

§ 430.40. Demurrer; Time

(a) A person against whom a complaint or cross-complaint has been filed may, within 30 days after service of the complaint or cross-complaint, demur to the complaint or cross-complaint.

(b) A party who has filed a complaint or cross-complaint may, within 10 days after service of the answer to his pleading, demur to the answer. *(Added by Stats.1971, c. 244, § 29.)*

§ 430.41. Meet and Confer Prior to Filing Demurrer; Conference of Parties Where Leave to Amend Granted; Limit on Number of Amendments; Actions Excepted; Appeal Rights

(a) Before filing a demurrer pursuant to this chapter, the demurring party shall meet and confer in person, by telephone, or by video conference with the party who filed the pleading that is subject to demurrer for the purpose of determining whether an agreement can be reached that would resolve the objections to be raised in the demurrer. If an amended complaint, cross-complaint, or answer is filed, the responding party shall meet and confer again with the party who filed the amended pleading before filing a demurrer to the amended pleading.

(1) As part of the meet and confer process, the demurring party shall identify all of the specific causes of action that it believes are subject to demurrer and identify with legal support the basis of the deficiencies. The party who filed the complaint, cross-complaint, or answer shall provide legal support for its position that the pleading is legally sufficient or, in the

alternative, how the complaint, cross-complaint, or answer could be amended to cure any legal insufficiency.

(2) The parties shall meet and confer at least 5 days before the date the responsive pleading is due. If the parties are not able to meet and confer at least 5 days before to the date the responsive pleading is due, the demurring party shall be granted an automatic 30-day extension of time within which to file a responsive pleading, by filing and serving, on or before the date on which a demurrer would be due, a declaration stating under penalty of perjury that a good faith attempt to meet and confer was made and explaining the reasons why the parties could not meet and confer. The 30-day extension shall commence from the date the responsive pleading was previously due, and the demurring party shall not be subject to default during the period of the extension. Any further extensions shall be obtained by court order upon a showing of good cause.

(3) The demurring party shall file and serve with the demurrer a declaration stating either of the following:

(A) The means by which the demurring party met and conferred with the party who filed the pleading subject to demurrer, and that the parties did not reach an agreement resolving the objections raised in the demurrer.

(B) That the party who filed the pleading subject to demurrer failed to respond to the meet and confer request of the demurring party or otherwise failed to meet and confer in good faith.

(4) Any determination by the court that the meet and confer process was insufficient shall not be grounds to overrule or sustain a demurrer.

(b) A party demurring to a pleading that has been amended after a demurrer to an earlier version of the pleading was sustained shall not demur to any portion of the amended complaint, cross-complaint, or answer on grounds that could have been raised by demurrer to the earlier version of the complaint, cross-complaint, or answer.

(c) If a court sustains a demurrer to one or more causes of action and grants leave to amend, the court may order a conference of the parties before an amended complaint or cross-complaint or a demurrer to an amended complaint or cross-complaint, may be filed. If a conference is held, the court shall not preclude a party from filing a demurrer and the time to file a demurrer shall not begin until after the conference has concluded. This section does not prohibit the court from ordering a conference on its own motion at any time or prevent a party from requesting that the court order a conference to be held.

(d) This section does not apply to the following civil actions:

(1) An action in which a party not represented by counsel is incarcerated in a local, state, or federal correctional institution.

(2) A proceeding in forcible entry, forcible detainer, or unlawful detainer.

(e)(1) In response to a demurrer and prior to the case being at issue, a complaint or cross-complaint shall not be amended more than three times, absent an offer to the trial court as to such additional facts to be pleaded that there is a reasonable possibility the defect can be cured to state a cause of action. The three-amendment limit shall not include an amendment made without leave of the court pursuant to Section 472, provided the amendment is made before a demurrer to the original complaint or cross-complaint is filed.

(2) Nothing in this section affects the rights of a party to amend its pleading or respond to an amended pleading after the case is at issue.

(f) Nothing in this section affects appellate review or the rights of a party pursuant to Section 430.80.

(g) If a demurrer is overruled as to a cause of action and that cause of action is not further amended, the demurring party preserves its right to appeal after final judgment without filing a further demurrer. *(Added by Stats.2015, c. 418, § 1. Amended by Stats.2020, c. 36, § 15; Stats.2023, c. 478, § 9.)*

§ 430.50. Demurrer to All or Part of Pleadings

(a) A demurrer to a complaint or cross-complaint may be taken to the whole complaint or cross-complaint or to any of the causes of action stated therein.

(b) A demurrer to an answer may be taken to the whole answer or to any one or more of the several defenses set up in the answer. *(Added by Stats.1971, c. 244, § 29.)*

§ 430.60. Specification of Grounds

A demurrer shall distinctly specify the grounds upon which any of the objections to the complaint, cross-complaint, or answer are taken. Unless it does so, it may be disregarded. *(Added by Stats.1971, c. 244, § 29.)*

§ 430.70. Demurrer Based on Matter of Which Court May Take Judicial Notice; Specification

When the ground of demurrer is based on a matter of which the court may take judicial notice pursuant to Section 452 or 453 of the Evidence Code, such matter shall be specified in the demurrer, or in the supporting points and authorities for the purpose of invoking such notice, except as the court may otherwise permit. *(Added by Stats.1971, c. 244, § 29.)*

§ 430.80. Failure to Object by Demurrer or Answer; Waiver; Exceptions

(a) If the party against whom a complaint or cross-complaint has been filed fails to object to the pleading, either by demurrer or answer, that party is deemed to have waived the objection unless it is an objection that the court has no jurisdiction of the subject of the cause of action alleged in the pleading or an objection that the pleading does not state facts sufficient to constitute a cause of action.

(b) If the party against whom an answer has been filed fails to demur thereto, that party is deemed to have waived the objection unless it is an objection that the answer does not state facts sufficient to constitute a defense. *(Added by Stats.1971, c. 244, § 29. Amended by Stats.1983, c. 1167, § 2.)*

§ 430.90. Removal of Civil Action to Federal Court; Filing Response; Time

(a) Where the defendant has removed a civil action to federal court without filing a response in the original court and the case is later remanded for improper removal, the time to respond shall be as follows:

(1) If the defendant has not generally appeared in either the original or federal court, then 30 days from the day the original court receives the case on remand to move to dismiss the action pursuant to Section 583.250 or to move to quash service of summons or to stay or dismiss the action pursuant to Section 418.10, if the court has not ruled on a similar motion filed by the defendant prior to the removal of the action to federal court.

(2) If the defendant has not filed an answer in the original court, then 30 days from the day the original court receives the case on remand to do any of the following:

(A) Answer the complaint.

(B) Demur or move to strike all or a portion of the complaint if: (i) an answer was not filed in the federal court, and (ii) a demurrer or motion to strike raising the same or similar issues was not filed and ruled upon by the original court prior to the removal of the action to federal court or was not filed and ruled upon in federal court prior to the remand. If the demurrer or motion to strike is denied by the court, the defendant shall have 30 days to answer the complaint unless an answer was filed with the demurrer or motion to strike.

(b) For the purposes of this section, time shall be calculated from the date of the original court's receipt of the order of remand. *(Added by Stats.1995, c. 796, § 5.)*

§ 431.10. Material and Immaterial Allegations, Defined

(a) A material allegation in a pleading is one essential to the claim or defense and which could not be stricken from the pleading without leaving it insufficient as to that claim or defense.

(b) An immaterial allegation in a pleading is any of the following:

(1) An allegation that is not essential to the statement of a claim or defense.

(2) An allegation that is neither pertinent to nor supported by an otherwise sufficient claim or defense.

(3) A demand for judgment requesting relief not supported by the allegations of the complaint or cross-complaint.

(c) An "immaterial allegation" means "irrelevant matter" as that term is used in Section 436. *(Added by Stats.1971, c. 244, § 29. Amended by Stats.1982, c. 704, § 2; Stats.1983, c. 1167, § 3; Stats.1986, c. 540, § 2.)*

§ 431.20. Uncontroverted Allegations Deemed True; New Matter in Answer Deemed Controverted

(a) Every material allegation of the complaint or cross-complaint, not controverted by the answer, shall, for the purposes of the action, be taken as true.

(b) The statement of any new matter in the answer, in avoidance or constituting a defense, shall, on the trial, be deemed controverted by the opposite party. *(Added by Stats.1971, c. 244, § 29.)*

§ 431.30. Answer; Contents; Information and Belief; Denials; Defenses

(a) As used in this section:

(1) "Complaint" includes a cross-complaint.

(2) "Defendant" includes a person filing an answer to a cross-complaint.

(b) The answer to a complaint shall contain:

(1) The general or specific denial of the material allegations of the complaint controverted by the defendant.

(2) A statement of any new matter constituting a defense.

(c) Affirmative relief may not be claimed in the answer.

(d) If the complaint is subject to Article 2 (commencing with Section 90) of Chapter 5.1 of Title 1 of Part 1 or is not verified, a general denial is sufficient but only puts in issue the material allegations of the complaint. If the complaint is verified, unless the complaint is subject to Article 2 (commencing with Section 90) of Chapter 5.1 of Title 1 of Part 1, the denial of the allegations shall be made positively or according to the information and belief of the defendant. However, if the cause of action is a claim assigned to a third party for collection and the complaint is verified, the denial of the allegations shall be made positively or according to the information and belief of the defendant, even if the complaint is subject to Article 2 (commencing with Section 90) of Chapter 5.1 of Title 1 of Part 1.

(e) If the defendant has no information or belief upon the subject sufficient to enable him or her to answer an allegation of the complaint, he or she may so state in his or her answer and place his or her denial on that ground.

(f) The denials of the allegations controverted may be stated by reference to specific paragraphs or parts of the complaint; or by express admission of certain allegations of the complaint with a general denial of all of the allegations not so admitted; or by denial of certain allegations upon information and belief, or for lack of sufficient information or belief, with a general denial of all allegations not so denied or expressly admitted.

(g) The defenses shall be separately stated, and the several defenses shall refer to the causes of action which they are intended to answer, in a manner by which they may be intelligibly distinguished. *(Added by Stats.1971, c. 244, § 29. Amended by Stats.1979, c. 212, § 2; Stats.1985, c. 621, § 1; Stats.1986, c. 281, § 1; Stats.2003, c. 149, § 8.)*

§ 432.10. Motion, Demurrer or Other Plea; Time

A party served with a cross-complaint may within 30 days after the service move, demur, or otherwise plead to the cross-complaint in the same manner as to an original complaint. *(Added by Stats.1971, c. 244, § 29.)*

Chapter 4. Motion to Strike

§ 435. Notice of Motion to Strike Whole or Part of Complaint

(a) As used in this section:

(1) The term "complaint" includes a cross-complaint.

(2) The term "pleading" means a demurrer, answer, complaint, or cross-complaint.

(b)(1) Any party, within the time allowed to respond to a pleading may serve and file a notice of motion to strike the whole or any part thereof, but this time limitation shall not apply to motions specified in subdivision (e).

(2) A notice of motion to strike the answer or the complaint, or a portion thereof, shall specify a hearing date set in accordance with Section 1005.

(3) A notice of motion to strike a demurrer, or a portion thereof, shall set the hearing thereon concurrently with the hearing on the demurrer.

(c) If a party serves and files a notice of motion to strike without demurring to the complaint, the time to answer is extended and no default may be entered against that defendant, except as provided in Sections 585 and 586.

(d) The filing of a notice of motion to strike an answer or complaint, or portion thereof, shall not extend the time within which to demur.

(e) A motion to strike, as specified in this section, may be made as part of a motion pursuant to subparagraph (A) of paragraph (1) of subdivision (i) of Section 438. *(Added by Stats.1955, c. 1452, § 3a. Amended by Stats.1971, c. 244, § 33 Stats.1982, c. 704, § 3; Stats.1993, c. 456, § 3.5.)*

§ 435.5. Meeting Prior to Filing Motion to Strike; Resolution of Objections; Amended Pleadings

(a) Before filing a motion to strike pursuant to this chapter, the moving party shall meet and confer in person, by telephone, or by video conference with the party who filed the pleading that is subject to the motion to strike for the purpose of determining if an agreement can be reached that resolves the objections to be raised in the motion to strike. If an amended pleading is filed, the responding party shall meet and confer again with the party who filed the amended pleading before filing a motion to strike the amended pleading.

(1) As part of the meet and confer process, the moving party shall identify all of the specific allegations that it believes are subject to being stricken and identify with legal support the basis of the deficiencies. The party who filed the pleading shall provide legal support for its position that the pleading is legally sufficient, or, in the alternative, how the pleading could be amended to cure any legal insufficiency.

(2) The parties shall meet and confer at least 5 days before the date a motion to strike must be filed. If the parties are unable to meet and confer at least 5 days before the date the motion to strike must be filed, the moving party shall be granted an automatic 30-day extension of time within which to file a motion to strike, by filing and serving, on or before the date a motion to strike must be filed, a declaration stating under penalty of perjury that a good faith attempt to meet and confer was made and explaining the reasons why the parties could not meet and confer. The 30-day extension shall commence from the date the motion to strike was previously due, and the moving party shall not be subject to default during the period of the extension. Any further extensions shall be obtained by court order upon a showing of good cause.

(3) The moving party shall file and serve with the motion to strike a declaration stating either of the following:

(A) The means by which the moving party met and conferred with the party who filed the pleading subject to the motion to strike, and that the parties did not reach an agreement resolving the objections raised by the motion to strike.

(B) That the party who filed the pleading subject to the motion to strike failed to respond to the meet and confer request of the moving party or otherwise failed to meet and confer in good faith.

(4) A determination by the court that the meet and confer process was insufficient is shall not be grounds to grant or deny the motion to strike.

(b) A party moving to strike a pleading that has been amended after a motion to strike an earlier version of the pleading was granted shall not move to strike any portion of the pleadings on grounds that could have been raised by a motion to strike as to the earlier version of the pleading.

(c)(1) If a court grants a motion to strike and grants leave to amend, the court may order a conference of the parties before an amended pleading, or a motion to strike an amended pleading, may be filed. If the conference is held, the court shall not preclude a party from filing a motion to strike and the time to file a motion to strike shall not begin until after the conference has concluded.

(2) This section does not prohibit the court from ordering a conference on its own motion at any time or prevent a party from requesting that the court order that a conference be held.

(d) This section does not apply to any of the following:

(1) An action in which a party not represented by counsel is incarcerated in a local, state, or federal correctional institution.

(2) A proceeding in forcible entry, forcible detainer, or unlawful detainer.

(3) A special motion brought pursuant to Section 425.16.

(4) A motion brought less than 30 days before trial.

(e)(1) In response to a motion to strike and before the case is at issue, a pleading shall not be amended more than three times, absent an offer to the trial court of additional facts to be pleaded that, if pleaded, would result in a reasonable possibility that the defect can be cured. The three-amendment limit does not include an amendment made without leave of the court pursuant to Section 472, if the amendment is made before a motion to strike as to the original pleading is filed.

(2) This section does not affect the rights of a party to amend its pleading or respond to an amended pleading after the case is at issue.

(f) This section does not affect appellate review or the rights of a party pursuant to Section 430.80.

(g) If a motion to strike is denied and the pleading is not further amended, the moving party preserves its right to appeal after final judgment without filing a further motion to strike. *(Added by Stats.2017, c. 273, § 1. Amended by Stats.2020, c. 36, § 16; Stats.2023, c. 478, § 10.)*

§ 436. Discretion of Court to Strike Pleadings or Portions of Pleadings

The court may, upon a motion made pursuant to Section 435, or at any time in its discretion, and upon terms it deems proper:

(a) Strike out any irrelevant, false, or improper matter inserted in any pleading.

(b) Strike out all or any part of any pleading not drawn or filed in conformity with the laws of this state, a court rule, or an order of the court. *(Added by Stats.1982, c. 704, § 3.5. Amended by Stats.1983, c. 1167, § 4.)*

§ 437. Grounds for Motion to Strike; Judicial Notice; Specification

(a) The grounds for a motion to strike shall appear on the face of the challenged pleading or from any matter of which the court is required to take judicial notice.

(b) Where the motion to strike is based on matter of which the court may take judicial notice pursuant to Section 452 or 453 of the Evidence Code, such matter shall be specified in the notice of motion, or in the supporting points and authorities, except as the court may otherwise permit. *(Added by Stats.1982, c. 704, § 4.)*

Chapter 5. Summary Judgments and Motions for Judgment on the Pleadings

§ 437c. Grounds for and Effect of Summary Judgment; Procedure on Motion

(a)(1) A party may move for summary judgment in an action or proceeding if it is contended that the action has no merit or that there is no defense to the action or proceeding. The motion may be made at any time after 60 days have elapsed since the general appearance in the action or proceeding of each party against whom the motion is directed or at any earlier time after the general appearance that the court, with or without notice and upon good cause shown, may direct.

(2) Notice of the motion and supporting papers shall be served on all other parties to the action at least 81 days before the time appointed for hearing. If the notice is served by mail, the required 81-day period of notice shall be increased by 5 days if the place of address is within the State of California, 10 days if the place of address is outside the State of California but within the United States, and 20 days if the place of address is outside the United States. If the notice is served by facsimile transmission, express

mail, or another method of delivery providing for overnight delivery, the required 81-day period of notice shall be increased by two court days.

(3) The motion shall be heard no later than 30 days before the date of trial, unless the court for good cause orders otherwise. The filing of the motion shall not extend the time within which a party must otherwise file a responsive pleading.

(4) A party shall not bring more than one motion for summary judgment against an adverse party to the action or proceeding. This limitation does not apply to motions for summary adjudication.

(5) Notwithstanding any other provision of this section, on motion or application of any party and a showing of good cause, the court may grant leave for the moving party to bring an additional motion for summary judgment. The moving party shall serve the notice and supporting papers for any such additional motion in accordance with paragraph (2) of subdivision (a).

(b)(1) The motion shall be supported by affidavits, declarations, admissions, answers to interrogatories, depositions, and matters of which judicial notice shall or may be taken. The supporting papers shall include a separate statement setting forth plainly and concisely all material facts that the moving party contends are undisputed. Each of the material facts stated shall be followed by a reference to the supporting evidence. The failure to comply with this requirement of a separate statement may in the court's discretion constitute a sufficient ground for denying the motion.

(2) An opposition to the motion shall be served and filed not less than 20 days preceding the noticed or continued date of hearing, unless the court for good cause orders otherwise. The opposition, where appropriate, shall consist of affidavits, declarations, admissions, answers to interrogatories, depositions, and matters of which judicial notice shall or may be taken.

(3) The opposition papers shall include a separate statement that responds to each of the material facts contended by the moving party to be undisputed, indicating if the opposing party agrees or disagrees that those facts are undisputed. The statement also shall set forth plainly and concisely any other material facts the opposing party contends are disputed. Each material fact contended by the opposing party to be disputed shall be followed by a reference to the supporting evidence. Failure to comply with this requirement of a separate statement may constitute a sufficient ground, in the court's discretion, for granting the motion.

(4) A reply to the opposition shall be served and filed by the moving party not less than 11 days preceding the noticed or continued date of hearing, unless the court for good cause orders otherwise. The reply shall not include any new evidentiary matter, additional material facts, or

separate statement submitted with the reply and not presented in the moving papers or opposing papers.

(5) Evidentiary objections not made at the hearing shall be deemed waived.

(6) Except for subdivision (c) of Section 1005 relating to the method of service of opposition and reply papers, Sections 1005 and 1013, extending the time within which a right may be exercised or an act may be done, do not apply to this section.

(7) An incorporation by reference of a matter in the court's file shall set forth with specificity the exact matter to which reference is being made and shall not incorporate the entire file.

(c) The motion for summary judgment shall be granted if all the papers submitted show that there is no triable issue as to any material fact and that the moving party is entitled to a judgment as a matter of law. In determining if the papers show that there is no triable issue as to any material fact the court shall consider all of the evidence set forth in the papers, except the evidence to which objections have been made and sustained by the court, and all inferences reasonably deducible from the evidence, except summary judgment shall not be granted by the court based on inferences reasonably deducible from the evidence if contradicted by other inferences or evidence that raise a triable issue as to any material fact.

(d) Supporting and opposing affidavits or declarations shall be made by a person on personal knowledge, shall set forth admissible evidence, and shall show affirmatively that the affiant is competent to testify to the matters stated in the affidavits or declarations. An objection based on the failure to comply with the requirements of this subdivision, if not made at the hearing, shall be deemed waived.

(e) If a party is otherwise entitled to summary judgment pursuant to this section, summary judgment shall not be denied on grounds of credibility or for want of cross-examination of witnesses furnishing affidavits or declarations in support of the summary judgment, except that summary judgment may be denied in the discretion of the court if the only proof of a material fact offered in support of the summary judgment is an affidavit or declaration made by an individual who was the sole witness to that fact; or if a material fact is an individual's state of mind, or lack thereof, and that fact is sought to be established solely by the individual's affirmation thereof.

(f)(1) A party may move for summary adjudication as to one or more causes of action within an action, one or more affirmative defenses, one or more claims for damages, or one or more issues of duty, if the party contends that the cause of action has no merit, that there is no affirmative defense to the cause of action, that there is no merit to an affirmative defense as to any cause of action, that there is no merit to a claim for damages, as specified in Section 3294 of the Civil Code, or that one or more defendants either owed or did not owe a duty to the plaintiff or plaintiffs. A motion for summary adjudication shall be granted only if it completely disposes of a cause of action, an affirmative defense, a claim for damages, or an issue of duty.

(2) A motion for summary adjudication may be made by itself or as an alternative to a motion for summary judgment and shall proceed in all procedural respects as a motion for summary judgment. A party shall not move for summary judgment based on issues asserted in a prior motion for summary adjudication and denied by the court unless that party establishes, to the satisfaction of the court, newly discovered facts or circumstances or a change of law supporting the issues reasserted in the summary judgment motion.

(g) Upon the denial of a motion for summary judgment on the ground that there is a triable issue as to one or more material facts, the court shall, by written or oral order, specify one or more material facts raised by the motion that the court has determined there exists a triable controversy. This determination shall specifically refer to the evidence proffered in support of and in opposition to the motion that indicates that a triable controversy exists. Upon the grant of a motion for summary judgment on the ground that there is no triable issue of material fact, the court shall, by written or oral order, specify the reasons for its determination. The order shall specifically refer to the evidence proffered in support of and, if applicable, in opposition to the motion that indicates no triable issue exists. The court shall also state its reasons for any other determination. The court shall record its determination by court reporter or written order.

(h) If it appears from the affidavits submitted in opposition to a motion for summary judgment or summary adjudication or both that facts essential to justify opposition may exist but cannot, for reasons stated, be presented, the court shall deny the motion, order a continuance to permit affidavits to be obtained or discovery to be had, or make any other order as may be just. The application to continue the motion to obtain necessary discovery may also be made by ex parte motion at any time on or before the date the opposition response to the motion is due.

(i) If, after granting a continuance to allow specified additional discovery, the court determines that the party seeking summary judgment has unreasonably failed to allow the discovery to be conducted, the court shall grant a continuance to permit the discovery to go forward or deny the motion for summary judgment or summary adjudication. This section does not affect or limit the ability of a party to compel discovery under the Civil Discovery Act (Title 4 (commencing with Section 2016.010) of Part 4).

(j) If the court determines at any time that an affidavit was presented in bad faith or solely for the purpose of delay, the court shall order the party who presented the affidavit to pay the other party the amount of the reasonable expenses the filing of the affidavit caused the other party to incur. Sanctions shall not be imposed pursuant to this subdivision except on notice contained in a party's papers or on the court's own noticed motion, and after an opportunity to be heard.

(k) Unless a separate judgment may properly be awarded in the action, a final judgment shall not be entered on a motion for summary judgment before the termination of the action, but the final judgment shall, in addition to any matters determined in the action, award judgment as established by the summary proceeding provided for in this section.

(*l*) In an action arising out of an injury to the person or to property, if a motion for summary judgment is granted on the basis that the defendant was without fault, no other defendant during trial, over plaintiff's objection, may attempt to attribute fault to or comment on the absence or involvement of the defendant who was granted the motion.

(m)(1) A summary judgment entered under this section is an appealable judgment as in other cases. Upon entry of an order pursuant to this section, except the entry of summary judgment, a party may, within 20 days after service upon the party of a written notice of entry of the order, petition an appropriate reviewing court for a peremptory writ. If the notice is served by mail, the initial period within which to file the petition shall be increased by five days if the place of address is within the State of California, 10 days if the place of address is outside the State of California but within the United States, and 20 days if the place of address is outside the United States. If the notice is served by facsimile transmission, express mail or another method of delivery providing for overnight delivery, the initial period within which to file the petition shall be increased by two court days. The superior court may, for good cause, and before the expiration of the initial period, extend the time for one additional period not to exceed 10 days.

(2) Before a reviewing court affirms an order granting summary judgment or summary adjudication on a ground not relied upon by the trial court, the reviewing court shall afford the parties an opportunity to present their views on the issue by submitting supplemental briefs. The supplemental briefs may include an argument that additional evidence relating to that ground exists, but the party has not had an adequate opportunity to present the evidence or to conduct discovery on the issue. The court may reverse or remand based upon the supplemental briefs to allow the parties to present additional evidence or to conduct discovery on the issue. If the court fails to allow supplemental briefs, a rehearing shall be ordered upon timely petition of a party.

(n)(1) If a motion for summary adjudication is granted, at the trial of the action, the cause or causes of action within the action, affirmative defense or defenses, claim for damages, or issue or issues of duty as to the motion that has been granted shall be deemed to be established and the action shall proceed as to the cause or causes of action, affirmative defense or defenses, claim for damages, or issue or issues of duty remaining.

(2) In the trial of the action, the fact that a motion for summary adjudication is granted as to one or more causes of action, affirmative defenses, claims for damages, or issues of duty within the action shall not bar any cause of action, affirmative defense, claim for damages, or issue of duty as to which summary adjudication was either not sought or denied.

(3) In the trial of an action, neither a party, a witness, nor the court shall comment to a jury upon the grant or denial of a motion for summary adjudication.

(*o*) A cause of action has no merit if either of the following exists:

(1) One or more of the elements of the cause of action cannot be separately established, even if that element is separately pleaded.

(2) A defendant establishes an affirmative defense to that cause of action.

(p) For purposes of motions for summary judgment and summary adjudication:

(1) A plaintiff or cross-complainant has met that party's burden of showing that there is no defense to a cause of action if that party has proved each element of the cause of action entitling the party to judgment on the cause of action. Once the plaintiff or cross-complainant has met that burden, the burden shifts to the defendant or cross-defendant to show that a triable issue of one or more material facts exists as to the cause of action or a defense thereto. The defendant or cross-defendant shall not rely upon the allegations or denials of its pleadings to show that a triable issue of material fact exists but, instead, shall set forth the specific facts showing that a triable issue of material fact exists as to the cause of action or a defense thereto.

(2) A defendant or cross-defendant has met that party's burden of showing that a cause of action has no merit if the party has shown that one or more elements of the cause of action, even if not separately pleaded, cannot be established, or that there is a complete defense to the cause of action. Once the defendant or cross-defendant has met that burden, the burden shifts to the plaintiff or cross-complainant to show that a triable issue of one or more material facts exists as to the cause of action or a defense thereto. The plaintiff or cross-complainant shall not rely upon the allegations or denials of its pleadings to show that a triable issue of material fact exists but, instead, shall set forth the specific facts showing

that a triable issue of material fact exists as to the cause of action or a defense thereto.

(q) In granting or denying a motion for summary judgment or summary adjudication, the court need rule only on those objections to evidence that it deems material to its disposition of the motion. Objections to evidence that are not ruled on for purposes of the motion shall be preserved for appellate review.

(r) This section does not extend the period for trial provided by Section 1170.5.

(s) Subdivisions (a) and (b) do not apply to actions brought pursuant to Chapter 4 (commencing with Section 1159) of Title 3 of Part 3.

(t) Notwithstanding subdivision (f), a party may move for summary adjudication of a legal issue or a claim for damages other than punitive damages that does not completely dispose of a cause of action, affirmative defense, or issue of duty pursuant to this subdivision.

(1)(A) Before filing a motion pursuant to this subdivision, the parties whose claims or defenses are put at issue by the motion shall submit to the court both of the following:

(i) A joint stipulation stating the issue or issues to be adjudicated.

(ii) A declaration from each stipulating party that the motion will further the interest of judicial economy by decreasing trial time or significantly increasing the likelihood of settlement.

(B) The joint stipulation shall be served on any party to the civil action who is not also a party to the motion.

(2) Within 15 days of receipt of the stipulation and declarations, unless the court has good cause for extending the time, the court shall notify the stipulating parties if the motion may be filed. In making this determination, the court may consider objections by a nonstipulating party made within 10 days of the submission of the stipulation and declarations.

(3) If the court elects not to allow the filing of the motion, the stipulating parties may request, and upon request the court shall conduct, an informal conference with the stipulating parties to permit further evaluation of the proposed stipulation. The stipulating parties shall not file additional papers in support of the motion.

(4)(A) A motion for summary adjudication made pursuant to this subdivision shall contain a statement in the notice of motion that reads substantially similar to the following: "This motion is made pursuant to subdivision (t) of Section 437c of the Code of Civil Procedure. The parties to this motion stipulate that the court shall hear this motion and that the resolution of this motion will further the interest of judicial economy by decreasing trial time or significantly increasing the likelihood of settlement."

(B) The notice of motion shall be signed by counsel for all parties, and by those parties in propria persona, to the motion.

(5) A motion filed pursuant to this subdivision may be made by itself or as an alternative to a motion for summary judgment and shall proceed in all procedural respects as a motion for summary judgment.

(u) For purposes of this section, a change in law does not include a later enacted statute without retroactive application. *(Added by Stats.2011, c. 419, § 4, operative Jan. 1, 2015. Amended by Stats.2015, c. 161, § 1; Stats.2015, c. 345, § 1.5; Stats.2016, c. 86, § 22; Stats.2024, c. 99, § 1.)*

§ 438. Judgment on the Pleadings; Grounds; Motions; Conditions for Motions; Amended Complaint or Answer

(a) As used in this section:

(1) "Complaint" includes a cross-complaint.

(2) "Plaintiff" includes a cross-complainant.

(3) "Defendant" includes a cross-defendant.

(b)(1) A party may move for judgment on the pleadings.

(2) The court may upon its own motion grant a motion for judgment on the pleadings.

(c)(1) The motion provided for in this section may only be made on one of the following grounds:

(A) If the moving party is a plaintiff, that the complaint states facts sufficient to constitute a cause or causes of action against the defendant and the answer does not state facts sufficient to constitute a defense to the complaint.

(B) If the moving party is a defendant, that either of the following conditions exist:

(i) The court has no jurisdiction of the subject of the cause of action alleged in the complaint.

(ii) The complaint does not state facts sufficient to constitute a cause of action against that defendant.

(2) The motion provided for in this section may be made as to either of the following:

(A) The entire complaint or cross-complaint or as to any of the causes of action stated therein.

(B) The entire answer or one or more of the affirmative defenses set forth in the answer.

(3) If the court on its own motion grants the motion for judgment on the pleadings, it shall be on one of the following bases:

(A) If the motion is granted in favor of the plaintiff, it shall be based on the grounds that the complaint states facts sufficient to constitute a cause or causes of action against the defendant and the answer does not state facts sufficient to constitute a defense to the complaint.

(B) If the motion is granted in favor of the defendant, that either of the following conditions exist:

(i) The court has no jurisdiction of the subject of the cause of action alleged in the complaint.

(ii) The complaint does not state facts sufficient to constitute a cause of action against that defendant.

(d) The grounds for motion provided for in this section shall appear on the face of the challenged pleading or from any matter of which the court is required to take judicial notice. Where the motion is based on a matter of which the court may take judicial notice pursuant to Section 452 or 453 of the Evidence Code, the matter shall be specified in the notice of motion, or in the supporting points and authorities, except as the court may otherwise permit.

(e) No motion may be made pursuant to this section if a pretrial conference order has been entered pursuant to Section 575, or within 30 days of the date the action is initially set for trial, whichever is later, unless the court otherwise permits.

(f) The motion provided for in this section may be made only after one of the following conditions has occurred:

(1) If the moving party is a plaintiff, and the defendant has already filed his or her answer to the complaint and the time for the plaintiff to demur to the answer has expired.

(2) If the moving party is a defendant, and the defendant has already filed his or her answer to the complaint and the time for the defendant to demur to the complaint has expired.

(g) The motion provided for in this section may be made even though either of the following conditions exist:

(1) The moving party has already demurred to the complaint or answer, as the case may be, on the same grounds as is the basis for the motion provided for in this section and the demurrer has been overruled,

provided that there has been a material change in applicable case law or statute since the ruling on the demurrer.

(2) The moving party did not demur to the complaint or answer, as the case may be, on the same grounds as is the basis for the motion provided for in this section.

(h)(1) The motion provided for in this section may be granted with or without leave to file an amended complaint or answer, as the case may be.

(2) Where a motion is granted pursuant to this section with leave to file an amended complaint or answer, as the case may be, then the court shall grant 30 days to the party against whom the motion was granted to file an amended complaint or answer, as the case may be.

(3) If the motion is granted with respect to the entire complaint or answer without leave to file an amended complaint or answer, as the case may be, then judgment shall be entered forthwith in accordance with the motion granting judgment to the moving party.

(4) If the motion is granted with leave to file an amended complaint or answer, as the case may be, then the following procedures shall be followed:

(A) If an amended complaint is filed after the time to file an amended complaint has expired, then the court may strike the complaint pursuant to Section 436 and enter judgment in favor of that defendant against that plaintiff or a plaintiff.

(B) If an amended answer is filed after the time to file an amended answer has expired, then the court may strike the answer pursuant to Section 436 and proceed to enter judgment in favor of that plaintiff and against that defendant or a defendant.

(C) Except where subparagraphs (A) and (B) apply, if the motion is granted with respect to the entire complaint or answer with leave to file an amended complaint or answer, as the case may be, but an amended complaint or answer is not filed, then after the time to file an amended complaint or answer, as the case may be, has expired, judgment shall be entered forthwith in favor of the moving party.

(i)(1) Where a motion for judgment on the pleadings is granted with leave to amend, the court shall not enter a judgment in favor of a party until the following proceedings are had:

(A) If an amended pleading is filed and the moving party contends that pleading is filed after the time to file an amended pleading has expired or that the pleading is in violation of the court's prior ruling on the motion, then that party shall move to strike the pleading and enter judgment in its favor.

(B) If no amended pleading is filed, then the party shall move for entry of judgment in its favor.

(2) All motions made pursuant to this subdivision shall be made pursuant to Section 1010.

(3) At the hearing on the motion provided for in this subdivision, the court shall determine whether to enter judgment in favor of a particular party. *(Added by Stats.1993, c. 456, § 5. Amended by Stats.1994, c. 493, § 2, eff. Sept. 12, 1994.)*

§ 439. Meeting Prior to Filing Motion for Judgment on the Pleadings; Resolution of Claims; Amended Pleadings

(a) Before filing a motion for judgment on the pleadings pursuant to this chapter, the moving party shall meet and confer in person, by telephone, or by video conference with the party who filed the pleading that is subject to the motion for judgment on the pleadings for the purpose of determining if an agreement can be reached that resolves the claims to be raised in the motion for judgment on the pleadings. If an amended pleading is filed, the responding party shall meet and confer again with the party who filed the amended pleading before filing a motion for judgment on the pleadings against the amended pleading.

(1) As part of the meet and confer process, the moving party shall identify all of the specific allegations that it believes are subject to judgment and identify with legal support the basis of the claims. The party who filed the pleading shall provide legal support for its position that the pleading is not subject to judgment, or, in the alternative, how the pleading could be amended to cure any claims it is subject to judgment.

(2) The parties shall meet and confer at least 5 days before the date a motion for judgment on the pleadings is filed. If the parties are unable to meet and confer by that time, the moving party shall be granted an automatic 30-day extension of time within which to file a motion for judgment on the pleadings, by filing and serving, on or before the date a motion for judgment on the pleadings must be filed, a declaration stating under penalty of perjury that a good faith attempt to meet and confer was made and explaining the reasons why the parties could not meet and confer. The 30-day extension shall commence from the date the motion for judgment on the pleadings was previously filed, and the moving party shall not be subject to default during the period of the extension. Any further extensions shall be obtained by court order upon a showing of good cause.

(3) The moving party shall file and serve with the motion for judgment on the pleadings a declaration stating either of the following:

(A) The means by which the moving party met and conferred with the party who filed the pleading subject to the motion for judgment on the pleadings, and that the parties did not reach an agreement resolving the claims raised by the motion for judgment on the pleadings.

(B) That the party who filed the pleading subject to the motion for judgment on the pleadings failed to respond to the meet and confer request of the moving party or otherwise failed to meet and confer in good faith.

(4) A determination by the court that the meet and confer process was insufficient is shall not be grounds to grant or deny the motion for judgment on the pleadings.

(b) A party moving for judgment on a pleading that has been amended after a motion for judgment on the pleadings on an earlier version of the pleading was granted shall not move for judgment on any portion of the pleadings on grounds that could have been raised by a motion for judgment on the pleadings as to the earlier version of the pleading.

(c)(1) If a court grants a motion for judgment on the pleadings and grants leave to amend, the court may order a conference of the parties before an amended pleading, or a motion for judgment on an amended pleading, may be filed. If the conference is held, the court shall not preclude a party from filing a motion for judgment on the pleadings and the time to file a motion for judgment on the pleadings shall not begin until after the conference has concluded.

(2) This section does not prohibit the court from ordering a conference on its own motion at any time or prevent a party from requesting that the court order that a conference be held.

(d) This section does not apply to any of the following:

(1) An action in which a party not represented by counsel is incarcerated in a local, state, or federal correctional institution.

(2) A proceeding in forcible entry, forcible detainer, or unlawful detainer.

(3) A special motion brought pursuant to Section 425.16.

(4) A motion brought less than 30 days before trial.

(e)(1) In response to a motion for judgment on the pleadings and before the case is at issue, a pleading shall not be amended more than three times, absent an offer to the trial court of additional facts to be pleaded that, if pleaded, would result in a reasonable possibility that the defect can be cured. The three-amendment limit does not include an amendment made without leave of the court pursuant to Section 472, if the amendment is made before a motion for judgments on the pleadings as to the original pleading is filed.

(2) This section does not affect the rights of a party to amend its pleading or respond to an amended pleading after the case is at issue.

(f) This section does not affect appellate review or the rights of a party pursuant to Section 430.80.

(g) If a motion for judgment on the pleadings is denied and the pleading is not further amended, the moving party preserves its right to appeal after final judgment without filing a further motion for judgment on the pleadings. *(Added by Stats.2017, c. 273, § 2. Amended by Stats.2020, c. 36, § 17; Stats.2023, c. 478, § 11.)*

Chapter 6. Verification of Pleadings

§ 446. Subscription of Pleadings; Necessity of Verification; Affidavit of Party; Who May Verify; Verification by Attorney or by Officer of Corporation or Agency; Affidavit; Assertion of Truth Under Penalty of Perjury

(a) Every pleading shall be subscribed by the party or his or her attorney. When the state, any county thereof, city, school district, district, public agency, or public corporation, or any officer of the state, or of any county thereof, city, school district, district, public agency, or public corporation, in his or her official capacity, is plaintiff, the answer shall be verified, unless an admission of the truth of the complaint might subject the party to a criminal prosecution, or, unless a county thereof, city, school district, district, public agency, or public corporation, or an officer of the state, or of any county, city, school district, district, public agency, or public corporation, in his or her official capacity, is defendant. When the complaint is verified, the answer shall be verified. In all cases of a verification of a pleading, the affidavit of the party shall state that the same is true of his own knowledge, except as to the matters which are therein stated on his or her information or belief, and as to those matters that he or she believes it to be true; and where a pleading is verified, it shall be by the affidavit of a party, unless the parties are absent from the county where the attorney has his or her office, or from some cause unable to verify it, or the facts are within the knowledge of his or her attorney or other person verifying the same. When the pleading is verified by the attorney, or any other person except one of the parties, he or she shall set forth in the affidavit the reasons why it is not made by one of the parties.

When a corporation is a party, the verification may be made by any officer thereof. When the state, any county thereof, city, school district, district, public agency, or public corporation, or an officer of the state, or of any county thereof, city, school district, district, public agency, or public corporation, in his or her official capacity is plaintiff, the complaint need not be verified; and if the state, any county thereof, city, school district, district, public agency, or public corporation, or an officer of such state, county, city, school district, district, public agency, or public corporation, in his or her official capacity is defendant, its or his or her answer need not be verified.

When the verification is made by the attorney for the reason that the parties are absent from the county where he or she has his or her office, or from some other cause are unable to verify it, or when the verification is made on behalf of a corporation or public agency by any officer thereof, the attorney's or officer's affidavit shall state that he or she has read the pleading and that he or she is informed and believes the matters therein to be true and on that ground alleges that the matters stated therein are true. However, in those cases the pleadings shall not otherwise be considered as an affidavit or declaration establishing the facts therein alleged.

A person verifying a pleading need not swear to the truth or his or her belief in the truth of the matters stated therein but may, instead, assert the truth or his or her belief in the truth of those matters "under penalty of perjury."

(b) This section shall become operative on January 1, 1999, unless a statute that becomes effective on or before this date extends or deletes the repeal date of Section 446, as amended by Assembly Bill 3594 of the 1993–94 Regular Session. *(Added by Stats.1994, c. 1062, § 5, operative Jan. 1, 1999.)*

Chapter 7. General Rules of Pleading

§ 452. Liberal Construction

In the construction of a pleading, for the purpose of determining its effect, its allegations must be liberally construed, with a view to substantial justice between the parties. *(Enacted 1872.)*

§ 458. Statute of Limitations; Pleading and Proof

In pleading the Statute of Limitations it is not necessary to state the facts showing the defense, but it may be stated generally that the cause of action is barred by the provisions of Section ____ (giving the number of the section and subdivision thereof, if it is so divided, relied upon) of the Code of Civil Procedure; and if such allegation be controverted, the party pleading must establish, on the trial, the facts showing that the cause of action is so barred. *(Enacted 1872.)*

Chapter 8. Variance—Mistakes in Pleadings and Amendments

§ 472. Amendment Without Leave of Court

(a) A party may amend its pleading once without leave of the court at any time before the answer, demurrer, or motion to strike is filed, or after a demurrer or motion to strike is filed but before the demurrer or motion to strike is heard if the amended pleading is filed and served no later than the date for filing an opposition to the demurrer or motion to strike. A party may amend the pleading after the date for filing an opposition to the demurrer or motion to strike, upon stipulation by the parties. The time for responding to an amended pleading shall be computed from the date of service of the amended pleading.

(b) This section shall not apply to a special motion brought pursuant to Section 425.16. *(Enacted 1872. Amended by Code Am.1873–74, c. 383, § 59; Stats.1933, c. 744, § 31; Stats.1951, c. 1737, § 56, operative Jan. 1, 1952; Stats.1972, c. 73, § 3; Stats.1977, c. 1257, § 13, eff. Jan. 3, 1977; Stats.1983, c. 142, § 4; Stats.2015, c. 418, § 2; Stats.2017, c. 273, § 3; Stats.2020, c. 36, § 19.)*

§ 472a. Demurrers; Motion to Strike; Motion to Dismiss Relating to Service of Summons

(a) A demurrer is not waived by an answer filed at the same time.

(b) Except as otherwise provided by rule adopted by the Judicial Council, if a demurrer to a complaint or to a cross-complaint is overruled and there is no answer filed, the court shall allow an answer to be filed upon such terms as may be just. If a demurrer to the answer is overruled, the action shall proceed as if no demurrer had been interposed, and the facts alleged in the answer shall be considered as denied to the extent mentioned in Section 431.20.

(c) Subject to the limitations imposed by subdivision (e) of Section 430.41, if a demurrer is sustained, the court may grant leave to amend the pleading upon any terms as may be just and shall fix the time within which the amendment or amended pleading shall be filed. If a demurrer is stricken pursuant to Section 436 and there is no answer filed, the court shall allow an answer to be filed on terms that are just.

(d) If a motion to strike is granted pursuant to Section 436, the court may order that an amendment or amended pleading be filed upon terms it deems proper. If a motion to strike a complaint or cross-complaint, or portion thereof, is denied, the court shall allow the party filing the motion to strike to file an answer.

(e) If a motion to dismiss an action pursuant to Article 2 (commencing with Section 583.210) of Chapter 1.5 of Title 8 is denied, the court shall allow a pleading to be filed. *(Added by Stats.1933, c. 744, § 32. Amended by Stats.1951, c. 1737, § 57; Stats.1971, c. 1475, § 1; Stats.1982, c. 704, § 6; Stats.1983, c. 142, § 5; Stats.1983, c. 1167, § 5; Stats.1984, c. 572, § 2; Stats.1989, c. 1416, § 17; Stats.1993, c. 456, § 6; Stats.2015, c. 418, § 4; Stats.2020, c. 36, § 20.)*

§ 473. Amendments Permitted by Court; Enlargement of Time to Answer or Demur; Continuance, Costs; Relief from Judgment, etc., Taken by Mistake, Inadvertence, Surprise, or Excusable Neglect; Vacating Default Judgment; Compensatory Costs and Legal Fees; Penalties; Clerical Mistakes in Judgment or Order; Relief

(a)(1) The court may, in furtherance of justice, and on any terms as may be proper, allow a party to amend any pleading or proceeding by adding or striking out the name of any party, or by correcting a mistake in the name of a party, or a mistake in any other respect; and may, upon like terms, enlarge the time for answer or demurrer. The court may likewise, in its discretion, after notice to the adverse party, allow, upon any terms as may be just, an amendment to any pleading or proceeding in other particulars; and may upon like terms allow an answer to be made after the time limited by this code.

(2) When it appears to the satisfaction of the court that the amendment renders it necessary, the court may postpone the trial, and may, when the postponement will by the amendment be rendered necessary, require, as a condition to the amendment, the payment to the adverse party of any costs as may be just.

(b) The court may, upon any terms as may be just, relieve a party or the party's legal representative from a judgment, dismissal, order, or other proceeding taken against the party through the party's mistake, inadvertence, surprise, or excusable neglect. Application for this relief shall be accompanied by a copy of the answer or other pleading proposed to be filed therein, otherwise the application shall not be granted, and shall be made within a reasonable time, in no case exceeding six months, after the judgment, dismissal, order or proceeding was taken. However, in the case of a judgment, dismissal, order or other proceeding determining the ownership or right to possession of real or personal property, without extending the six-month period, when a notice in writing is personally served within the State of California both upon the party against whom the judgment, dismissal, order or other proceeding has been taken, and upon the party's attorney of record, if any, notifying that party and the party's attorney of record, if any, that the order, judgment, dismissal, or other proceeding was taken against the party and that any rights the party has to apply for relief under the provisions of Section 473 of the Code of Civil Procedure shall expire 90 days after service of the notice, then the application shall be made within 90 days after service of the notice upon the defaulting party or the party's attorney of record, if any, whichever service shall be later. No affidavit or declaration of merits shall be required of the moving party. Notwithstanding any other requirements of this section, the court shall, whenever an application for relief is made no more than six months after entry of judgment, is in proper form, and is accompanied by an attorney's sworn affidavit attesting to the attorney's mistake, inadvertence, surprise or neglect, vacate any (1) resulting default entered by the clerk against the attorney's client, and which will result in entry of a default judgment, or (2) resulting default judgment or dismissal entered against the attorney's client unless the court find that the default or dismissal was not in fact caused by the attorney's mistake, inadvertence, surprise, or neglect. The court shall, whenever relief is granted based on an attorney's affidavit of fault, direct the attorney to pay reasonable compensatory legal fees and costs to opposing counsel or parties. However, this section shall not lengthen the time within which an action shall be brought to trial pursuant to Section 583.310.

(c)(1) Whenever the court grants relief from a default, default judgment, or dismissal based on any of the provisions of this section, the court may do any of the following:

(A) Impose a penalty of no greater than one thousand dollars ($1,000) upon an offending attorney or party.

(B) Direct that an offending attorney pay an amount no greater than one thousand dollars ($1,000) to the State Bar Client Security Fund.

(C) Grant other relief as is appropriate.

(2) However, where the court grants relief from a default or default judgment pursuant to this section based upon the affidavit of the defaulting party's attorney attesting to the attorney's mistake, inadvertence, surprise, or neglect, the relief shall not be made conditional upon the attorney's payment of compensatory legal fees or costs or monetary penalties imposed by the court or upon compliance with other sanctions ordered by the court.

(d) The court may, upon motion of the injured party, or its own motion, correct clerical mistakes in its judgment or orders as entered, so as to conform to the judgment or order directed, and may, on motion of either party after notice to the other party, set aside any void judgment or order.

(e) This section shall remain in effect only until January 1, 2027, and as of that date is repealed. *(Enacted 1872. Amended by Code Am.1873–74, c. 383, § 60; Code Am.1880, c. 14, § 3; Stats.1917, c. 159, § 1; Stats.1933, c. 744, § 34; Stats.1961, c. 722, § 1; Stats.1981, c. 122, § 2; Stats.1988, c. 1131, § 1; Stats.1991, c. 1003, § 1; Stats.1992, c. 427, § 16; Stats.1992, c. 876, § 4; Stats.1996, c. 60, § 1; Stats.2025, c. 563, § 12.)*

§ 473.2. Motion to Set Aside Default [eff. Jan. 1, 2027]

(a) A party that was not served with a summons and complaint in accordance with this chapter may file and serve a motion to set aside or vacate the default or default judgment and for leave to defend the action or to move for dismissal.

(b)(1) A party moving to set aside or vacate a default or a default judgment pursuant to subdivision (a) shall proffer evidence, through a sworn affidavit or otherwise, that service was not lawfully effected. Proffering evidence that service was not lawfully effected rebuts a presumption of the facts stated in the process server's return.

(2) If a process server files their return before the operative date of this section, the absence of the photograph required by Section 417.10 shall not by itself render the proof of service unlawful or insufficient.

(c) In responding to a motion that is filed pursuant to this section and that complies with subdivision (b), the party seeking a default or default judgment has the burden of proving by a preponderance of the evidence that service of the summons and complaint was lawful.

(d) In deciding a motion filed pursuant to subdivision (a), the court shall take evidence as to the lawfulness of the service of process and shall not deny a reasonable request by either party to conduct a hearing and permit oral testimony.

(e) This section does not limit any other remedies available under law.

(f) This section shall become operative on January 1, 2027. *(Added by Stats.2025, c. 563, § 14.)*

§ 473.5. Motion to Set Aside Default and for Leave to Defend Action

(a) When service of a summons has not resulted in actual notice to a party in time to defend the action and a default or default judgment has been entered against the party in the action, the party may serve and file a notice of motion to set aside the default or default judgment and for leave to defend the action. The notice of motion shall be served and filed within a reasonable time, but in no event exceeding the earlier of: (i) two years after entry of a default judgment against the party; or (ii) 180 days after service on the party of a written notice that the default or default judgment has been entered.

(b) A notice of motion to set aside a default or default judgment and for leave to defend the action shall designate as the time for making the motion a date prescribed by subdivision (b) of Section 1005, and it shall be accompanied by an affidavit showing under oath that the party's lack of actual notice in time to defend the action was not caused by the party's avoidance of service or inexcusable neglect. The party shall serve and file with the notice a copy of the answer, motion, or other pleading proposed to be filed in the action.

(c) Upon a finding by the court that the motion was made within the period permitted by subdivision (a) and that the party's lack of actual notice in time to defend the action was not caused by the party's avoidance of service or inexcusable neglect, it may set aside the default or default judgment on whatever terms as may be just and allow the party to defend the action.

(d) This section shall remain in effect only until January 1, 2027, and as of that date is repealed. *(Added by Stats.1969, c. 1610, § 23. Amended by Stats.1990, c. 1491, § 5; Stats.2025, c. 563, § 15.)*

§ 474. Defendant Designated by Fictitious Name; Amendment; Requirements for Default Judgment; Notice to Person Served

When the plaintiff is ignorant of the name of a defendant, he must state that fact in the complaint, or the affidavit if the action is commenced by affidavit, and such defendant may be designated in any pleading or proceeding by any name, and when his true name is discovered, the pleading or proceeding must be amended accordingly; provided, that no default or default judgment shall be entered against a defendant so designated, unless it appears that the copy of the summons or other process, or, if there be no summons or process, the copy of the first pleading or notice served upon such defendant bore on the face thereof a notice stating in substance: "To the person served: You are hereby served in the within action (or proceedings) as (or on behalf of) the person sued under the fictitious name of (designating it)." The certificate or affidavit of service must state the fictitious name under which such defendant was served and the fact that notice of identity was given by endorsement upon the document served as required by this section. The foregoing requirements for entry of a default or default judgment shall be applicable only as to fictitious names designated pursuant to this section and not in the event the plaintiff has sued the defendant by an erroneous name and shall not be applicable to entry of a default or default judgment based upon service, in the manner otherwise provided by law, of an amended pleading, process or notice designating defendant by his true name. *(Enacted 1872. Amended by Stats.1953, c. 1244, § 1; Stats.1955, c. 886, § 1.)*

TITLE 6.5 ATTACHMENT

Chapter 3. Actions in Which Attachment Authorized

§ 483.01. Claims Subject to Attachment; Minimum Amount; Secured Claims; Claims Against Natural Persons; Other Relief

(a) Except as otherwise provided by statute, an attachment may be issued only in an action on a claim or claims for money, each of which is based upon a contract, express or implied, where the total amount of the claim or claims is a fixed or readily ascertainable amount not less than five hundred dollars ($500) exclusive of costs, interest, and attorney's fees.

(b) An attachment may not be issued on a claim which is secured by any interest in real or personal property arising from agreement, statute, or other rule of law (including any mortgage or deed of trust of realty, any security interest subject to Division 9 (commencing with Section 9101) of the Commercial Code, and any statutory, common law, or equitable lien). However, an attachment may be issued where the claim was originally so secured but, without any act of the plaintiff or the person to whom the security was given, the security has become valueless or has decreased in value to less than the amount then owing on the claim, in which event the amount for which the attachment may issue shall not exceed the lesser of the amount of the decrease or the difference between the value of the security and the amount then owing on the claim.

(c) If the action is against a defendant who is a natural person, an attachment may be issued only on a claim which arises out of the conduct by the defendant of a trade, business, or profession. An attachment may not be issued on a claim against a defendant who is a natural person if the claim is based on the sale or lease of property, a license to use property, the furnishing of services, or the loan of money where the property sold or leased, or licensed for use, the services furnished, or the money loaned was used by the defendant primarily for personal, family, or household purposes.

(d) An attachment may be issued pursuant to this section whether or not other forms of relief are demanded. *(Amended by Stats.1982, c. 1198, § 27, operative July 1, 1983; Stats.1990, c. 943, § 1; Stats.1993, c. 589, § 26; Stats.1995, c. 591, § 1, Stats.1997, c. 222, § 1.)*

Chapter 7. Property Subject to Attachment

§ 487.010. Subject Property

The following property of the defendant is subject to attachment:

(a) Where the defendant is a corporation, all corporate property for which a method of levy is provided by Article 2 (commencing with Section 488.300) of Chapter 8.

(b) Where the defendant is a partnership or other unincorporated association, all partnership or association property for which a method of levy is provided by Article 2 (commencing with Section 488.300) of Chapter 8.

(c) Where the defendant is a natural person, all of the following property:

(1) Interests in real property except leasehold estates with unexpired terms of less than one year.

(2) Accounts receivable, chattel paper, and general intangibles arising out of the conduct by the defendant of a trade, business, or profession, except any such individual claim with a principal balance of less than one hundred fifty dollars ($150).

(3) Equipment.

(4) Farm products.

(5) Inventory.

(6) Final money judgments arising out of the conduct by the defendant of a trade, business, or profession.

(7) Money on the premises where a trade, business, or profession is conducted by the defendant and, except for the first one thousand dollars ($1,000), money located elsewhere than on such premises and deposit accounts, but, if the defendant has more than one deposit account or has at least one deposit account and money located elsewhere than on the premises where a trade, business, or profession is conducted by the defendant, the court, upon application of the plaintiff, may order that the writ of attachment be levied so that an aggregate amount of one thousand dollars ($1,000) in the form of such money and in such accounts remains free of levy.

(8) Negotiable documents of title.

(9) Instruments.

(10) Securities.

(11) Minerals or the like (including oil and gas) to be extracted.

(d) In the case of a defendant described in subdivision (c), community property of a type described in subdivision (c) is subject to attachment if the community property would be subject to enforcement of the judgment obtained in the action in which the attachment is sought. Unless the provision or context otherwise requires, if community property that is subject to attachment is sought to be attached:

(1) Any provision of this title that applies to the property of the defendant or to obligations owed to the defendant also applies to the community property interest of the spouse of the defendant and to obligations owed to either spouse that are community property.

(2) Any provision of this title that applies to property in the possession or under the control of the defendant also applies to community property in the possession or under the control of the spouse of the defendant. *(Added by Stats.1974, c. 1516, § 9. Amended by Stats.1976, c. 437, § 24; Stats.1982, c. 1198, § 46.)*

§ 487.020. Exempt Property

Except as provided in paragraph (2) of subdivision (a) of Section 3439.07 of the Civil Code, the following property is exempt from attachment:

(a) All property exempt from enforcement of a money judgment.

(b) Property which is necessary for the support of a defendant who is a natural person or the family of such defendant supported in whole or in part by the defendant.

(c) "Earnings" as defined by Section 706.011.

(d) All property not subject to attachment pursuant to Section 487.010. *(Added by Stats.1974, c. 1516, § 9. Amended by Stats.1976, c. 437, § 25; Stats.1982, c. 1198, § 47; Stats.1986, c. 383, § 7.)*

Chapter 9. Undertakings

§ 489.210. Undertaking Prerequisite to Attachment or Order

Before issuance of a writ of attachment, a temporary protective order, or an order under subdivision (b) of Section 491.415, the plaintiff shall file an undertaking to pay the defendant any amount the defendant may recover for any wrongful attachment by the plaintiff in the action. *(Added by Stats.1974, c. 1516, § 9. Amended by Stats.1976, c. 437, § 37.5; Stats.1984, c. 538, § 7.)*

§ 489.220. Amount of Undertaking

(a) Except as provided in subdivision (b), the amount of an undertaking filed pursuant to this article shall be ten thousand dollars ($10,000).

(b) If, upon objection to the undertaking, the court determines that the probable recovery for wrongful attachment exceeds the amount of the undertaking, it shall order the amount of the undertaking increased to the amount it determines to be the probable recovery for wrongful attachment if it is ultimately determined that the attachment was wrongful. *(Added by Stats.1974, c. 1516, § 9. Amended by Stats.1976, c. 437, § 38; Stats.1977, c. 1257, § 14; Stats.1998, c. 931, § 74, eff. Sept. 28, 1998; Stats.2001, c. 812, § 3.)*

TITLE 7. OTHER PROVISIONAL REMEDIES IN CIVIL ACTIONS

Chapter 1. General Provisions

§ 501. Imprisonment for Debt or Tort Prohibited

A person may not be imprisoned in a civil action for debt or tort, whether before or after judgment. Nothing in this section affects any power a court may have to imprison a person who violates a court order. *(Added by Stats.1974, c. 1516, § 11.)*

Chapter 3. Injunction

§ 525. Definition; Grant; Enforcement

An injunction is a writ or order requiring a person to refrain from a particular act. It may be granted by the court in which the action is brought, or by a judge thereof; and when granted by a judge, it may be enforced as an order of the court. *(Enacted 1872. Amended by Code Am.1880, c. 15, § 3; Stats.1907, c. 272, § 1.)*

§ 526. Cases in Which Authorized; Restrictions on Grant

(a) An injunction may be granted in the following cases:

(1) When it appears by the complaint that the plaintiff is entitled to the relief demanded, and the relief, or any part thereof, consists in restraining the commission or continuance of the act complained of, either for a limited period or perpetually.

(2) When it appears by the complaint or affidavits that the commission or continuance of some act during the litigation would produce waste, or great or irreparable injury, to a party to the action.

(3) When it appears, during the litigation, that a party to the action is doing, or threatens, or is about to do, or is procuring or suffering to be done, some act in violation of the rights of another party to the action respecting the subject of the action, and tending to render the judgment ineffectual.

(4) When pecuniary compensation would not afford adequate relief.

(5) Where it would be extremely difficult to ascertain the amount of compensation which would afford adequate relief.

(6) Where the restraint is necessary to prevent a multiplicity of judicial proceedings.

(7) Where the obligation arises from a trust.

(b) An injunction cannot be granted in the following cases:

(1) To stay a judicial proceeding pending at the commencement of the action in which the injunction is demanded, unless such restraint is necessary to prevent a multiplicity of proceedings.

(2) To stay proceedings in a court of the United States.

(3) To stay proceedings in another state upon a judgment of a court of that state.

(4) To prevent the execution of a public statute by officers of the law for the public benefit.

(5) To prevent the breach of a contract the performance of which would not be specifically enforced, other than a contract in writing for the rendition of personal services from one to another where the promised service is of a special, unique, unusual, extraordinary, or intellectual character, which gives it peculiar value, the loss of which cannot be reasonably or adequately compensated in damages in an action at law, and where the compensation for the personal services is as follows:

(A) As to contracts entered into on or before December 31, 1993, the minimum compensation provided in the contract for the personal services shall be at the rate of six thousand dollars ($6,000) per annum.

(B) As to contracts entered into on or after January 1, 1994, the criteria of clause (i) or (ii), as follows, are satisfied:

(i) The compensation is as follows:

(I) The minimum compensation provided in the contract shall be at the rate of nine thousand dollars ($9,000) per annum for the first year of the contract, twelve thousand dollars ($12,000) per annum for the second year of the contract, and fifteen thousand dollars ($15,000) per annum for the third to seventh years, inclusive, of the contract.

(II) In addition, after the third year of the contract, there shall actually have been paid for the services through and including the contract year during which the injunctive relief is sought, over and above the minimum contractual compensation specified in subclause (I), the amount of fifteen thousand dollars ($15,000) per annum during the fourth and fifth years of the contract, and thirty thousand dollars ($30,000) per annum during the sixth and seventh years of the contract. As a condition to petitioning for an injunction, amounts payable under this clause may be paid at any time prior to seeking injunctive relief.

(ii) The aggregate compensation actually received for the services provided under a contract that does not meet the criteria of subparagraph (A), is at least 10 times the applicable aggregate minimum amount specified in subclauses (I) and (II) of clause (i) through and including the contract year during which the injunctive relief is sought. As a condition to petitioning for an injunction, amounts payable under this subparagraph may be paid at any time prior to seeking injunctive relief.

(C) Compensation paid in any contract year in excess of the minimums specified in clauses (i) and (ii) of subparagraph (B) shall apply to reduce the compensation otherwise required to be paid under those provisions in any subsequent contract years. However, an injunction may be granted to prevent the breach of a contract entered into between any nonprofit cooperative corporation or association and a member or stockholder thereof, in respect to any provision regarding the sale or delivery to the corporation or association of the products produced or acquired by the member or stockholder.

(6) To prevent the exercise of a public or private office, in a lawful manner, by the person in possession.

(7) To prevent a legislative act by a municipal corporation. *(Enacted 1872. Amended by Stats.1907, c. 272, § 2; Stats.1919, c. 224, § 1; Stats.1925, c. 408, § 1; Stats.1992, c. 177, § 2; Stats.1993, c. 836, § 2.)*

§ 527. Grants Before Judgment Upon Verified Complaint or Affidavits; Service; Notice; Procedures; Application; Fees

(a) A preliminary injunction may be granted at any time before judgment upon a verified complaint, or upon affidavits if the complaint in the one case, or the affidavits in the other, show satisfactorily that sufficient grounds exist therefor. No preliminary injunction shall be granted without notice to the opposing party.

(b) A temporary restraining order or a preliminary injunction, or both, may be granted in a class action, in which one or more of the parties sues or defends for the benefit of numerous parties upon the same grounds as in other actions, whether or not the class has been certified.

(c) No temporary restraining order shall be granted without notice to the opposing party, unless both of the following requirements are satisfied:

(1) It appears from facts shown by affidavit or by the verified complaint that great or irreparable injury would result to the applicant before the matter can be heard on notice.

(2) The applicant or the applicant's attorney certifies one of the following to the court under oath:

(A) That within a reasonable time prior to the application he or she informed the opposing party or his or her attorney at what time and where the application would be made.

(B) That the applicant in good faith attempted but was unable to inform the opposing party and the opposing party's attorney, specifying the efforts made to contact them.

(C) That for reasons specified the applicant should not be required to so inform the opposing party or the opposing party's attorney.

(d) In case a temporary restraining order shall be granted without notice in the contingency specified in subdivision (c):

(1) The matter shall be made returnable on an order requiring cause to be shown why the injunction should not be granted, on the earliest day that the business of the court will admit of, but not later than 15 days or, if good cause appears to the court, 22 days from the date the restraining order is issued.

(2) The party who obtained the temporary restraining order shall, within five days from the date the temporary restraining order is issued or two days prior to the hearing, whichever is earlier, serve on the opposing party a copy of the complaint if not previously served, the order to show cause stating the date, time, and place of the hearing, any affidavits to be used in the application, and a copy of the points and authorities in support of the application. The court may for good cause, on motion of the applicant or on its own motion, shorten the time required by this paragraph for the service on the opposing party.

(3) When the matter first comes up for hearing, if the party who obtained the temporary restraining order is not ready to proceed, or if the party failed to effect service as required by paragraph (2), the court shall resolve the temporary restraining order.

(4) The opposing party is entitled to one continuance for a reasonable period of not less than 15 days or any shorter period requested by the opposing party, to enable the opposing party to meet the application for a preliminary injunction. If the opposing party obtains a continuance under this paragraph, the temporary restraining order shall remain in effect until the date of the continued hearing.

(5) Upon the filing of an affidavit by the applicant that the opposing party could not be served within the time required by paragraph (2), the court may reissue any temporary restraining order previously issued. The reissued order shall be made returnable as provided by paragraph (1), with the time for hearing measured from the dates of reissuance. No fee shall be charged for reissuing the order.

(e) The opposing party may, in response to an order to show cause, present affidavits relating to the granting of the preliminary injunction, and if the affidavits are served on the applicant at least two days prior to the hearing, the applicant shall not be entitled to any continuance on account thereof. On the day the order is made returnable, the hearing shall take precedence over all other matters on the calendar of the day, except older matters of the same character, and matters to which special precedence may be given by law. When the cause is at issue it shall be set for trial at the earliest possible date and shall take precedence over all other cases, except older matters of the same character, and matters to which special precedence may be given by law.

(f) Notwithstanding failure to satisfy the time requirements of this section, the court may nonetheless hear the order to show cause why a preliminary injunction should not be granted if the moving and supporting papers are served within the time required by Section 1005 and one of the following conditions is satisfied:

(1) The order to show cause is issued without a temporary restraining order.

(2) The order to show cause is issued with a temporary restraining order, but is either not set for hearing within the time required by paragraph (1) of subdivision (d), or the party who obtained the temporary restraining order fails to effect service within the time required by paragraph (2) of subdivision (d).

(g) This section does not apply to an order issued under the Family Code.

(h) As used in this section:

(1) "Complaint" means a complaint or cross-complaint.

(2) "Court" means the court in which the action is pending. *(Enacted 1872. Amended by Stats.1895, c. 49, § 1; Stats.1907, c. 272, § 3; Stats.1911, c. 42, § 1; Stats.1963, c. 878, § 2; Stats.1970, c. 488, § 1; Stats.1977, c. 720, § 1; Stats.1978, c. 346, § 1; Stats.1979, c. 129, § 1; Stats.1979, c. 795, § 7; Stats.1981, c. 182, § 1; Stats.1982, c. 812, § 1; Stats.1992, c. 163, § 23; Stats.1993, c. 583, § 1; Stats.1994, c. 587, § 5; Stats.1995, c. 796, § 6; Stats.2000, c. 688, § 4.)*

§ 529. Undertaking; Objection; Insufficiency; Dissolution of Injunction; Exceptions

(a) On granting an injunction, the court or judge must require an undertaking on the part of the applicant to the effect that the applicant will pay to the party enjoined any damages, not exceeding an amount to be specified, the party may sustain by reason of the injunction, if the court finally decides that the applicant was not entitled to the injunction. Within five days after the service of the injunction, the person enjoined may object to the undertaking. If the court determines that the applicant's undertaking is insufficient and a sufficient undertaking is not filed within the time required by statute, the order granting the injunction must be dissolved.

(b) This section does not apply to any of the following persons:

(1) Either spouse against the other in a proceeding for legal separation or dissolution of marriage.

(2) The applicant for an order described in Division 10 (commencing with Section 6200 of the Family Code).

(3) A public entity or officer described in Section 995.220.

(4) An applicant requesting an injunction under subdivision (d) of Section 1708.85 of the Civil Code.

(5) An applicant requesting an injunction under subdivision (d) of Section 1708.89 of the Civil Code. *(Enacted 1872. Amended by Code Am.1873–74, c. 624, § 1; Code Am.1880, c. 64, § 1; Stats.1907, c. 272, § 4; Stats.1931, c. 140, § 1; Stats.1933, c. 744, § 66; Stats.1979, c. 795, § 9;*

Stats.1982, c. 517, § 123; Stats.1992, c. 163, § 25; Stats.1993, c. 219, § 63.7; Stats.2021, c. 518, § 2; Stats.2024, c. 557, § 3.)

Chapter 5. Receivers

§ 564. Appointment; Cases in Which Authorized; Definitions

(a) A receiver may be appointed, in the manner provided in this chapter, by the court in which an action or proceeding is pending in any case in which the court is empowered by law to appoint a receiver.

(b) A receiver may be appointed by the court in which an action or proceeding is pending, or by a judge of that court, in the following cases:

(1) In an action by a vendor to vacate a fraudulent purchase of property, or by a creditor to subject any property or fund to the creditor's claim, or between partners or others jointly owning or interested in any property or fund, on the application of the plaintiff, or of any party whose right to or interest in the property or fund, or the proceeds of the property or fund, is probable, and where it is shown that the property or fund is in danger of being lost, removed, or materially injured.

(2) In an action by a secured lender for the foreclosure of a deed of trust or mortgage and sale of property upon which there is a lien under a deed of trust or mortgage, where it appears that the property is in danger of being lost, removed, or materially injured, or that the condition of the deed of trust or mortgage has not been performed, and that the property is probably insufficient to discharge the deed of trust or mortgage debt.

(3) After judgment, to carry the judgment into effect.

(4) After judgment, to dispose of the property according to the judgment, or to preserve it during the pendency of an appeal, or pursuant to the Enforcement of Judgments Law (Title 9 (commencing with Section 680.010)), or after sale of real property pursuant to a decree of foreclosure, during the redemption period, to collect, expend, and disburse rents as directed by the court or otherwise provided by law.

(5) Where a corporation has been dissolved, as provided in Section 565.

(6) Where a corporation is insolvent, or in imminent danger of insolvency, or has forfeited its corporate rights.

(7) In an action of unlawful detainer.

(8) At the request of the Public Utilities Commission pursuant to Section 1825 or 1826 of the Public Utilities Code.

(9) In all other cases where necessary to preserve the property or rights of any party.

(10) At the request of the Office of Statewide Health Planning and Development, or the Attorney General, pursuant to Section 129173 of the Health and Safety Code.

(11) In an action by a secured lender for specific performance of an assignment of rents provision in a deed of trust, mortgage, or separate assignment document. The appointment may be continued after entry of a judgment for specific performance if appropriate to protect, operate, or maintain real property encumbered by a deed of trust or mortgage or to collect rents therefrom while a pending nonjudicial foreclosure under power of sale in a deed of trust or mortgage is being completed.

(12) In a case brought by an assignee under an assignment of leases, rents, issues, or profits pursuant to subdivision (g) of Section 2938 of the Civil Code.

(c) A receiver may be appointed, in the manner provided in this chapter, including, but not limited to, Section 566, by the superior court in an action brought by a secured lender to enforce the rights provided in Section 2929.5 of the Civil Code, to enable the secured lender to enter and inspect the real property security for the purpose of determining the existence, location, nature, and magnitude of any past or present release or threatened release of any hazardous substance into, onto, beneath, or from the real property security. The secured lender shall not abuse the right of entry and inspection or use it to harass the borrower or tenant of the property. Except in case of an emergency, when the borrower or tenant of the property has abandoned the premises, or if it is impracticable to do so, the secured lender shall give the borrower or tenant of the property reasonable notice of the secured lender's intent to enter and shall enter only during the borrower's or tenant's normal business hours. Twenty-four hours' notice shall be presumed to be reasonable notice in the absence of evidence to the contrary.

(d) Any action by a secured lender to appoint a receiver pursuant to this section shall not constitute an action within the meaning of subdivision (a) of Section 726.

(e) For purposes of this section:

(1) "Borrower" means the trustor under a deed of trust, or a mortgagor under a mortgage, where the deed of trust or mortgage encumbers real property security and secures the performance of the trustor or mortgagor under a loan, extension of credit, guaranty, or other obligation. The term includes any successor in interest of the trustor or mortgagor to the real property security before the deed of trust or mortgage has been discharged, reconveyed, or foreclosed upon.

(2) "Hazardous substance" means any of the following:

(A) Any "hazardous substance" as defined in subdivision (h) of Section 25281 of the Health and Safety Code.

(B) Any "waste" as defined in subdivision (d) of Section 13050 of the Water Code.

(C) Petroleum including crude oil or any fraction thereof, natural gas, natural gas liquids, liquefied natural gas, or synthetic gas usable for fuel, or any mixture thereof.

(3) "Real property security" means any real property and improvements, other than a separate interest and any related interest in the common area of a residential common interest development, as the terms "separate interest," "common area," and "common interest development" are defined in Sections 4095, 4100, and 4185 of the Civil Code, or real property consisting of one acre or less that contains 1 to 15 dwelling units.

(4) "Release" means any spilling, leaking, pumping, pouring, emitting, emptying, discharging, injecting, escaping, leaching, dumping, or disposing into the environment, including continuing migration, of hazardous substances into, onto, or through soil, surface water, or groundwater.

(5) "Secured lender" means the beneficiary under a deed of trust against the real property security, or the mortgagee under a mortgage against the real property security, and any successor in interest of the beneficiary or mortgagee to the deed of trust or mortgage. *(Enacted 1872. Amended by Stats.1919, c. 166, § 1; Stats.1933, c. 744, § 85a; Stats.1941, c. 444, § 1; Stats.1980, c. 1078, § 1; Stats.1982, c. 497, § 34; Stats.1991, c. 1167, § 2; Stats.1992, c. 167, § 2; Stats.1994, c. 414, § 2; Stats.1995, c. 384, § 1; Stats.1996, c. 1023, § 29; Stats.1996, c. 49, § 4; Stats.1996, c. 1154, § 2; Stats.1996, c. 1154, § 2.1; Stats.1998, c. 931, § 75; Stats.2001, c. 44, § 4; Stats.2002, c. 999, § 3; Stats.2012, c. 181, § 44; Stats.2020, c. 27, § 1.)*

Chapter 6. Deposit In Court

§ 572. Order for Deposit; When Authorized

When it is admitted by the pleadings, or shown upon the examination of a party to the action, that he or she has in his or her possession, or under his or her control, any money or other thing capable of delivery, which, being the subject of litigation, is held by him or her as trustee for another party, or which belongs or which is due to another party or which should, under the circumstances of the case be held by the court pending final disposition of the action, the court may order the same, upon motion, to be deposited in court or delivered to such party, upon those conditions that may be just, subject to the further direction of the court. *(Enacted 1872. Amended by Stats.1907, c. 375, p. 710, § 1; Stats.1986, c. 540, § 6.)*

TITLE 7A. PRETRIAL CONFERENCES

§ 575. Promulgation of Rules by Judicial Council

The Judicial Council may promulgate rules governing pretrial conferences, and the time, manner and nature thereof, in civil cases at issue, or in one or more classes thereof, in the superior courts. *(Added by Stats.1955, c. 632, § 1. Amended by Stats.1977, c. 1257, § 17; Stats.1998, c. 931, § 76; Stats.2002, c. 784, § 61.)*

§ 575.1. Local Rules; Scope; Purpose; Promulgation

(a) The presiding judge of each superior court may prepare with the assistance of appropriate committees of the court, proposed local rules designed to expedite and facilitate the business of the court. The rules need not be limited to those actions on the civil active list, but may provide for the supervision and judicial management of actions from the date they are filed. Rules prepared pursuant to this section shall be submitted for consideration to the judges of the court and, upon approval by a majority of the judges, the judges shall have the proposed rules published and submitted to the local bar for consideration and recommendations.

(b) After a majority of the judges have officially adopted the rules, they shall be filed with the Judicial Council as required by Section 68071 of the Government Code and as specified in rules adopted by the Judicial Council. The Judicial Council shall prescribe rules to ensure that a complete current set of local rules and amendments, for each county in the state, is made available for public examination in each county. The local rules shall also be published for general distribution in accordance with rules adopted by the Judicial Council. Each court shall make its local rules available for inspection and copying in every location of the court that generally accepts filing of papers. The court may impose a reasonable charge for copying the rules and may impose a reasonable page limit on copying. The rules shall be accompanied by a notice indicating where a full set of the rules may be purchased.

(c) If a judge of a court adopts a rule that applies solely to cases in that judge's courtroom, or a particular branch or district of a court adopts a rule that applies solely to cases in that particular branch or district of a court, the court shall publish these rules as part of the general publication of rules required by the California Rules of Court. The court shall organize the rules so that rules on a common subject, whether individual, branch, district, or courtwide appear sequentially. Individual judges' rules and branch and district rules are local rules of court for purposes of this section and for purposes of the adoption, publication, comment, and filing requirements set forth in the Judicial Council rules applicable to local court rules. *(Added by Stats.1982, c. 1402, § 1. Amended by Stats.1989, c. 1416, § 19; Stats.1993, c. 925, § 1; Stats.1993, c. 926, § 3.5; Stats.1998, c. 931, § 77; Stats.2003, c. 149, § 9.)*

§ 575.2. Noncompliance With Local Rules; Effects

(a) Local rules promulgated pursuant to Section 575.1 may provide that if any counsel, a party represented by counsel, or a party if in pro se, fails to comply with any of the requirements thereof, the court on motion of a party or on its own motion may strike out all or any part of any pleading of that party, or, dismiss the action or proceeding or any part thereof, or enter a judgment by default against that party, or impose other penalties of a lesser nature as otherwise provided by law, and may order that party or his or her counsel to pay to the moving party the reasonable expenses in making the motion, including reasonable attorney fees. No penalty may be imposed under this section without prior notice to, and an opportunity to be heard by, the party against whom the penalty is sought to be imposed.

(b) It is the intent of the Legislature that if a failure to comply with these rules is the responsibility of counsel and not of the party, any penalty shall be imposed on counsel and shall not adversely affect the party's cause of action or defense thereto. *(Added by Stats.1982, c. 1402, § 2. Amended by Stats.2002, c. 806, § 14.)*

§ 576. Amendment of Pleadings or Pretrial Conference Order

Any judge, at any time before or after commencement of trial, in the furtherance of justice, and upon such terms as may be proper, may allow the amendment of any pleading or pretrial conference order. *(Added by Stats.1963, c. 882, § 1.)*

TITLE 8. OF THE TRIAL AND JUDGMENT IN CIVIL ACTIONS

Chapter 1. Judgment in General

§ 577. Judgment Defined

A judgment is the final determination of the rights of the parties in an action or proceeding. *(Enacted 1872.)*

§ 580. Relief Granted; No Answer; Limited Civil Case

(a) The relief granted to the plaintiff, if there is no answer, cannot exceed that demanded in the complaint, or in the statement required by Section 425.11, or in the statement provided for by Section 425.115; but in any other case, the court may grant the plaintiff any relief consistent with the case made by the complaint and embraced within the issue. The court may impose liability, regardless of whether the theory upon which liability is sought to be imposed involves legal or equitable principles.

(b) Notwithstanding subdivision (a), the following types of relief may not be granted in a limited civil case:

(1) Relief exceeding the maximum amount in controversy for a limited civil case as provided in Section 85, exclusive of attorney's fees, interest, and costs.

(2) A permanent injunction, except as otherwise authorized by statute.

(3) A determination of title to real property.

(4) Declaratory relief, except as authorized by Section 86. (*Enacted 1872. Amended by Stats.1993, c. 456, § 8; Stats.1995, c. 796, § 9; Stats.1998, c. 931, § 78; Stats.2006, c. 86, § 1; Stats.2007, c. 43, § 5.*)

§ 581. Dismissal; Definitions

(a) As used in this section:

(1) "Action" means any civil action or special proceeding.

(2) "Complaint" means a complaint and a cross-complaint.

(3) "Court" means the court in which the action is pending.

(4) "Defendant" includes a cross-defendant.

(5) "Plaintiff" includes a cross-complainant.

(6) "Trial." A trial shall be deemed to actually commence at the beginning of the opening statement or argument of any party or his or her counsel, or if there is no opening statement, then at the time of the administering of the oath or affirmation to the first witness, or the introduction of any evidence.

(b) An action may be dismissed in any of the following instances:

(1) With or without prejudice, upon written request of the plaintiff to the clerk, filed with papers in the case, or by oral or written request to the court at any time before the actual commencement of trial, upon payment of the costs, if any.

(2) With or without prejudice, by any party upon the written consent of all other parties.

(3) By the court, without prejudice, when no party appears for trial following 30 days' notice of time and place of trial.

(4) By the court, without prejudice, when dismissal is made pursuant to the applicable provisions of Chapter 1.5 (commencing with Section 583.110).

(5) By the court, without prejudice, when either party fails to appear on the trial and the other party appears and asks for dismissal.

(c) A plaintiff may dismiss his or her complaint, or any cause of action asserted in it, in its entirety, or as to any defendant or defendants, with or without prejudice prior to the actual commencement of trial.

(d) Except as otherwise provided in subdivision (e), the court shall dismiss the complaint, or any cause of action asserted in it, in its entirety or as to any defendant, with prejudice, when upon the trial and before the final submission of the case, the plaintiff abandons it.

(e) After the actual commencement of trial, the court shall dismiss the complaint, or any causes of action asserted in it, in its entirety or as to any defendants, with prejudice, if the plaintiff requests a dismissal, unless all affected parties to the trial consent to dismissal without prejudice or by order of the court dismissing the same without prejudice on a showing of good cause.

(f) The court may dismiss the complaint as to that defendant when:

(1) Except where Section 597 applies, after a demurrer to the complaint is sustained without leave to amend and either party moves for dismissal.

(2) Except where Section 597 applies, after a demurrer to the complaint is sustained with leave to amend, the plaintiff fails to amend it within the time allowed by the court and either party moves for dismissal.

(3) After a motion to strike the whole of a complaint is granted without leave to amend and either party moves for dismissal.

(4) After a motion to strike the whole of a complaint or portion thereof is granted with leave to amend the plaintiff fails to amend it within the time allowed by the court and either party moves for dismissal.

(g) The court may dismiss without prejudice the complaint in whole, or as to that defendant, when dismissal is made under the applicable provisions of Chapter 1.5 (commencing with Section 583.110).

(h) The court may dismiss without prejudice the complaint in whole, or as to that defendant, when dismissal is made pursuant to Section 418.10.

(i) No dismissal of an action may be made or entered, or both, under paragraph (1) of subdivision (b) where affirmative relief has been sought by the cross-complaint of a defendant or if there is a motion pending for an order transferring the action to another court under the provisions of Section 396b.

(j) No dismissal may be made or entered, or both, under paragraph (1) or (2) of subdivision (b) except upon the written consent of the attorney for the party or parties applying therefor, or if consent of the attorney is not obtained, upon order of dismissal by the court after notice to the attorney.

(k) No action may be dismissed which has been determined to be a class action under the provisions of this code unless and until notice that the court deems adequate has been given and the court orders the dismissal.

(*l*) The court may dismiss, without prejudice, the complaint in whole, or as to that defendant when either party fails to appear at the trial and the other party appears and asks for the dismissal.

(m) The provisions of this section shall not be deemed to be an exclusive enumeration of the court's power to dismiss an action or dismiss a complaint as to a defendant. *(Added by Stats.1986, c. 540, § 8. Amended by Stats.1987, c. 1080, § 3; Stats.1993, c. 456, § 9.)*

§ 581c. Nonsuit; Partial Grant of Motion; Effect

(a) Only after, and not before, the plaintiff has completed his or her opening statement, or after the presentation of his or her evidence in a trial by jury, the defendant, without waiving his or her right to offer evidence in the event the motion is not granted, may move for a judgment of nonsuit.

(b) If it appears that the evidence presented, or to be presented, supports the granting of the motion as to some but not all of the issues involved in the action, the court shall grant the motion as to those issues and the action shall proceed as to the issues remaining. Despite the granting of the motion, no final judgment shall be entered prior to the termination of the action, but the final judgment in the action shall, in addition to any matters determined in the trial, award judgment as determined by the motion herein provided for.

(c) If the motion is granted, unless the court in its order for judgment otherwise specifies, the judgment of nonsuit operates as an adjudication upon the merits.

(d) In actions which arise out of an injury to the person or to property, when a motion for judgment of nonsuit was granted on the basis that the defendant was without fault, no other defendant during trial, over plaintiff's objection, may attempt to attribute fault to or comment on the absence or involvement of the defendant who was granted the motion. *(Added by Stats.1947, c. 990, § 2. Amended by Stats.1961, c. 692, § 1; Stats.1980, c. 187, § 1; Stats.1982, c. 1510, § 2; Stats.1998, c. 200, § 1.)*

Chapter 1.5 Dismissal for Delay in Prosecution

§ 583.130. Plaintiff to Proceed With Reasonable Diligence; Stipulations and Disposition of Action on Merits Favored

It is the policy of the state that a plaintiff shall proceed with reasonable diligence in the prosecution of an action but that all parties shall cooperate in bringing the action to trial or other disposition. Except as otherwise provided by statute or by rule of court adopted pursuant to statute, the policy favoring the right of parties to make stipulations in their own interests and the policy favoring trial or other disposition of an action on the merits are generally to be preferred over the policy that requires dismissal for failure to proceed with reasonable diligence in the prosecution of an action in construing the provisions of this chapter. *(Added by Stats.1984, c. 1705, § 5.)*

§ 583.150. Dismissal or Sanction Imposed Under Rule

This chapter does not limit or affect the authority of a court to dismiss an action or impose other sanctions under a rule adopted by the court pursuant to Section 575.1 or by the Judicial Council pursuant to statute, or otherwise under inherent authority of the court. *(Added by Stats.1984, c. 1705, § 5.)*

§ 583.210. Time of Service of Summons and Complaint; Time for Filing Proof of Service

(a) The summons and complaint shall be served upon a defendant within three years after the action is commenced against the defendant. For the purpose of this subdivision, an action is commenced at the time the complaint is filed.

(b) Proof of service of the summons shall be filed within 60 days after the time the summons and complaint must be served upon a defendant. *(Added by Stats.1984, c. 1705, § 5. Amended by Stats.2005, c. 300, § 4.)*

§ 583.220. Exceptions; Written Stipulation; General Appearance

The time within which service must be made pursuant to this article does not apply if the defendant enters into a stipulation in writing or does another act that constitutes a general appearance in the action. For the purpose of this section none of the following constitutes a general appearance in the action:

(a) A stipulation pursuant to Section 583.230 extending the time within which service must be made.

(b) A motion to dismiss made pursuant to this chapter, whether joined with a motion to quash service or a motion to set aside a default judgment, or otherwise.

(c) An extension of time to plead after a motion to dismiss made pursuant to this chapter. *(Added by Stats.1984, c. 1705, § 5.)*

§ 583.240. Computation of Time

In computing the time within which service must be made pursuant to this article, there shall be excluded the time during which any of the following conditions existed:

(a) The defendant was not amenable to the process of the court.

(b) The prosecution of the action or proceedings in the action was stayed and the stay affected service.

(c) The validity of service was the subject of litigation by the parties.

(d) Service, for any other reason, was impossible, impracticable, or futile due to causes beyond the plaintiff's control. Failure to discover relevant facts or evidence is not a cause beyond the plaintiff's control for the purpose of this subdivision. *(Added by Stats.1984, c. 1705, § 5.)*

§ 583.250. Failure to Make Timely Service; Mandatory Nature of Article

(a) If service is not made in an action within the time prescribed in this article:

(1) The action shall not be further prosecuted and no further proceedings shall be held in the action.

(2) The action shall be dismissed by the court on its own motion or on motion of any person interested in the action, whether named as a party or not, after notice to the parties.

(b) The requirements of this article are mandatory and are not subject to extension, excuse, or exception except as expressly provided by statute. *(Added by Stats.1984, c. 1705, § 5.)*

§ 583.310. Time to Bring Action to Trial

An action shall be brought to trial within five years after the action is commenced against the defendant. *(Added by Stats.1984, c. 1705, § 5.)*

§ 583.330. Extension of Time

The parties may extend the time within which an action must be brought to trial pursuant to this article by the following means:

(a) By written stipulation. The stipulation need not be filed but, if it is not filed, the stipulation shall be brought to the attention of the court if relevant to a motion for dismissal.

(b) By oral agreement made in open court, if entered in the minutes of the court or a transcript is made. *(Added by Stats.1984, c. 1705, § 5.)*

§ 583.340. Computation of Time

In computing the time within which an action must be brought to trial pursuant to this article, there shall be excluded the time during which any of the following conditions existed:

(a) The jurisdiction of the court to try the action was suspended.

(b) Prosecution or trial of the action was stayed or enjoined.

(c) Bringing the action to trial, for any other reason, was impossible, impracticable, or futile. *(Added by Stats.1984, c. 1705, § 5.)*

§ 583.350. Tolling or Extension of Time Resulting in Less Than Six Months to Bring Action

If the time within which an action must be brought to trial pursuant to this article is tolled or otherwise extended pursuant to statute with the result that at the end of the period of tolling or extension less than six months remains within which the action must be brought to trial, the action shall not be dismissed pursuant to this article if the action is brought to trial within six months after the end of the period of tolling or extension. *(Added by Stats.1984, c. 1705, § 5.)*

§ 583.360. Dismissal on Motion of Court or Defendant; Mandatory Nature of Article

(a) An action shall be dismissed by the court on its own motion or on motion of the defendant, after notice to the parties, if the action is not brought to trial within the time prescribed in this article.

(b) The requirements of this article are mandatory and are not subject to extension, excuse, or exception except as expressly provided by statute. *(Added by Stats.1984, c. 1705, § 5.)*

§ 583.410. Discretion to Dismiss Under Appropriate Circumstances; Procedure

(a) The court may in its discretion dismiss an action for delay in prosecution pursuant to this article on its own motion or on motion of the defendant if to do so appears to the court appropriate under the circumstances of the case.

(b) Dismissal shall be pursuant to the procedure and in accordance with the criteria prescribed by rules adopted by the Judicial Council. *(Added by Stats.1984, c. 1705, § 5.)*

§ 583.420. Grounds for Dismissal; Computation of Time

(a) The court may not dismiss an action pursuant to this article for delay in prosecution except after one of the following conditions has occurred:

(1) Service is not made within two years after the action is commenced against the defendant.

(2) The action is not brought to trial within the following times:

(A) Three years after the action is commenced against the defendant unless otherwise prescribed by rule under subparagraph (B).

(B) Two years after the action is commenced against the defendant if the Judicial Council by rule adopted pursuant to Section 583.410 so prescribed for the court because of the condition of the court calendar or for other reasons affecting the conduct of litigation or the administration of justice.

(3) A new trial is granted and the action is not again brought to trial within the following times:

(A) If a trial is commenced but no judgment is entered because of a mistrial or because a jury is unable to reach a decision, within two years after the order of the court declaring the mistrial or the disagreement of the jury is entered.

(B) If after judgment a new trial is granted and no appeal is taken, within two years after the order granting the new trial is entered.

(C) If on appeal an order granting a new trial is affirmed or a judgment is reversed and the action remanded for a new trial, within two years after the remittitur is filed by the clerk of the trial court.

(b) The times provided in subdivision (a) shall be computed in the manner provided for computation of the comparable times under Articles 2 (commencing with Section 583.210) and 3 (commencing with Section 583.310). *(Added by Stats.1984, c. 1705, § 5.)*

Chapter 2. Judgment Upon Failure to Answer

§ 585. Judgment on Default

Judgment may be had, if the defendant fails to answer the complaint, as follows:

(a) In an action arising upon contract or judgment for the recovery of money or damages only, if the defendant has, or if more than one defendant, if any of the defendants have, been served, other than by publication, and no answer, demurrer, notice of motion to strike of the character specified in subdivision (f), notice of motion to transfer pursuant to Section 396b, notice of motion to dismiss pursuant to Article 2 (commencing with Section 583.210) of Chapter 1.5 of Title 8, notice of motion to quash service of summons or to stay or dismiss the action pursuant to Section 418.10, or notice of the filing of a petition for writ of mandate as provided in Section 418.10 has been filed with the clerk of the court within the time specified in the summons, or within further time as may be allowed, the clerk, upon written application of the plaintiff, and proof of the service of summons, shall enter the default of the defendant or defendants, so served, and immediately thereafter enter judgment for the principal amount demanded in the complaint, in the statement required by Section 425.11, or in the statement provided for in Section 425.115, or a lesser amount if credit has been acknowledged, together with interest allowed by law or in accordance with the terms of the contract, and the costs against the defendant, or defendants, or against one or more of the defendants. If, by rule of court, a schedule of attorneys' fees to be allowed has been adopted, the clerk may include in the judgment attorneys' fees in accordance with the schedule (1) if the contract provides that attorneys' fees shall be allowed in the event of an action thereon, or (2) if the action is one in which the plaintiff is entitled by statute to recover attorneys' fees in addition to money or damages. The plaintiff shall file a written request at the time of application for entry of the default of the defendant or defendants, to have attorneys' fees fixed by the court, whereupon, after the entry of the default, the court shall hear the application for determination of the attorneys' fees and shall render judgment for the attorneys' fees and for the other relief demanded in the complaint, in the statement required by Section 425.11, or in the statement provided for in Section 425.115, or a lesser amount if credit has been acknowledged, and the costs against the defendant, or defendants, or against one or more of the defendants.

(b) In other actions, if the defendant has been served, other than by publication, and no answer, demurrer, notice of motion to strike of the character specified in subdivision (f), notice of motion to transfer pursuant to Section 396b, notice of motion to dismiss pursuant to Article 2 (commencing with Section 583.210) of Chapter 1.5 of Title 8, notice of motion to quash service of summons or to stay or dismiss the action pursuant to Section 418.10 or notice of the filing of a petition for writ of mandate as provided in Section 418.10 has been filed with the clerk of the court within the time specified in the summons, or within further time as may be allowed, the clerk, upon written application of the plaintiff, shall enter the default of the defendant. The plaintiff thereafter may apply to the court for the relief demanded in the complaint. The court shall hear the evidence offered by the plaintiff, and shall render judgment in the plaintiff's favor for that relief, not exceeding the amount stated in the complaint, in the statement required by Section 425.11, or in the statement provided for by Section 425.115, as appears by the evidence to be just. If the taking of an account, or the proof of any fact, is necessary to enable the court to give judgment or to carry the judgment into effect, the court may take the account or hear the proof, or may, in its discretion, order a reference for that purpose. If the action is for the recovery of damages, in whole or in part, the court may order the damages to be assessed by a jury; or if, to determine the amount of damages, the examination of a long account is involved, by a reference as above provided.

(c) In all actions where the service of the summons was by publication, upon the expiration of the time for answering, and upon proof of the publication and that no answer, demurrer, notice of motion to strike of the character specified in subdivision (f), notice of motion to transfer pursuant to Section 396b, notice of motion to dismiss pursuant to Article 2 (commencing with Section 583.210) of Chapter 1.5 of Title 8, notice of motion to quash service of summons or to stay or dismiss the action pursuant to Section 418.10, or notice of the filing of a petition for writ of mandate as provided in Section 418.10 has been filed, the clerk, upon written application of the plaintiff, shall enter the default of the defendant. The plaintiff thereafter may apply to the court for the relief demanded in the complaint; and the court shall hear the evidence offered by the plaintiff, and shall render judgment in the plaintiff's favor for that relief, not exceeding the amount stated in the complaint, in the statement required by Section 425.11, or in the statement provided for in Section 425.115, as appears by the evidence to be just. If the defendant is not a resident of the state, the court shall require the plaintiff, or the plaintiff's agent, to be examined, on oath, respecting any payments that have been made to the plaintiff, or to anyone for the plaintiff's use, on account of any demand mentioned in the complaint, in the statement required by Section 425.11, or in the statement provided for in Section 425.115, and may render judgment for the amount that the plaintiff is entitled to recover. In all cases affecting the title to or possession of real property, where the service of the summons was by publication and the defendant has failed to answer, no judgment shall be rendered upon proof of mere occupancy, unless the occupancy has continued for the time and has been of the character necessary to confer title by prescription. In all cases where the plaintiff bases a claim upon a paper title, the court shall require evidence establishing the plaintiff's equitable right to judgment before rendering judgment. In actions involving only the possession of real property where the complaint is verified and shows by proper allegations that no party to the action claims title to the real property involved, either by prescription, accession, transfer, will, or succession, but only the possession thereof, the court may render judgment upon proof of occupancy by plaintiff and ouster by defendant.

(d) In the cases referred to in subdivisions (b) and (c), or upon an application to have attorneys' fees fixed by the court pursuant to subdivision (a), the court in its discretion may permit the use of affidavits, in lieu of personal testimony, as to all or any part of the evidence or proof required or permitted to be offered, received, or heard in those cases. The facts stated in the affidavit or affidavits shall be within the personal knowledge of the affiant and shall be set forth with particularity, and each affidavit shall show affirmatively that the affiant, if sworn as a witness, can testify competently thereto.

(e) If a defendant files a cross-complaint against another defendant or the plaintiff, a default may be entered against that party on that cross-complaint if the plaintiff or that cross-defendant has been served with that cross-complaint and has failed to file an answer, demurrer, notice of motion to strike of the character specified in subdivision (f), notice of motion to transfer pursuant to Section 396b, notice of motion to dismiss pursuant to Article 2 (commencing with Section 583.210) of Chapter 1.5 of Title 8, notice of motion to quash service of summons or to stay or dismiss the action pursuant to Section 418.10, or notice of the filing of a petition for a writ of mandate as provided in Section 418.10 within the time specified in the summons, or within another time period as may be allowed. However, no judgment may separately be entered on that cross-complaint unless a separate judgment may, in fact, be properly awarded on that cross-complaint and the court finds that a separate judgment on that cross-complaint would not substantially delay the final disposition of the action between the parties.

(f) A notice of motion to strike within the meaning of this section is a notice of motion to strike the whole or any part of a pleading filed within the time which the moving party is required otherwise to plead to that pleading. The notice of motion to strike shall specify a hearing date set in accordance with Section 1005. The filing of a notice of motion does not extend the time within which to demur.

(g) This section shall remain in effect only until January 1, 2027, and as of that date is repealed. *(Enacted 1872. Amended Stats.1905, c. 47, § 1; Stats.1907, c. 376, § 4; Stats.1915, c. 553, § 1; Stats.1931, c. 285, § 1; Stats.1933, c. 744, § 92; Stats.1951, c. 1737, § 85; Stats.1955, c. 512, § 1; Stats.1955, c. 1452, § 6; Stats.1961, c. 393, § 1; Stats.1967, c. 135, § 1; Stats.1969, c. 345, § 3; Stats.1969, c. 567, § 1.5; Stats.1969, c. 1611, § 6.7; Stats.1973, c. 312, § 1; Stats.1980, c. 367, § 2; Stats.1982, c. 704, § 6.5; Stats.1986, c. 540, § 9; Stats.1993, c. 456, § 10; Stats.1995, c. 796, § 10; Stats.2007, c. 263, § 6; Stats.2025, c. 563, § 17.)*

§ 585.5. Affidavit Accompanying Application to Enter Default; Motion to Set Aside Default and for Leave to Defend; Procedure

(a) Every application to enter default under subdivision (a) of Section 585 shall include, or be accompanied by, an affidavit stating facts showing that the action is or is not subject to Section 1812.10 or 2984.4 of the Civil Code or subdivision (b) of Section 395.

(b) When a default or default judgment has been entered without full compliance with Section 1812.10 or 2984.4 of the Civil Code, or subdivision (b) of Section 395, the defendant may serve and file a notice of motion to set aside the default or default judgment and for leave to defend the action in the proper court. The notice of motion shall be served and filed within 60 days after the defendant first receives notice of levy under a writ of execution, or notice of any other procedure for enforcing, the default judgment.

(c) A notice of motion to set aside a default or default judgment and for leave to defend the action in the proper court shall designate as the time for making the motion a date prescribed by subdivision (b) of Section 1005, and it shall be accompanied by an affidavit showing under oath that the action was not commenced in the proper court according to Section 1812.10 or 2984.4 of the Civil Code or subdivision (b) of Section 395. The party shall serve and file with the notice a copy of the answer, motion, or other pleading proposed to be filed in the action.

(d) Upon a finding by the court that the motion was made within the period permitted by subdivision (b) and that the action was not commenced in the proper court, it shall set aside the default or default judgment on such terms as may be just and shall allow such a party to defend the action in the proper court.

(e) Unless the plaintiff can show that the plaintiff used reasonable diligence to avoid filing the action in the improper court, upon a finding that the action was commenced in the improper court the court shall award the defendant actual damages and costs, including reasonable attorney's fees. *(Amended by Stats.1982, c. 497, § 36; Stats.1983, c. 142, § 6; Stats.1991, c. 1090, § 3.)*

§ 586. Proceedings and Judgment as if Defendant Had Failed to Answer; Cases Where Applicable

(a) In the following cases the same proceedings shall be had, and judgment shall be rendered in the same manner, as if the defendant had failed to answer:

(1) If the complaint has been amended, and the defendant fails to answer it, as amended, or demur thereto, or file a notice of motion to strike, of the character specified in Section 585, within 30 days after service thereof or within the time allowed by the court.

(2) If the demurrer to the complaint is overruled and a motion to strike, of the character specified in Section 585, is denied, or where only one thereof is filed, if the demurrer is overruled or the motion to strike is denied, and the defendant fails to answer the complaint within the time allowed by the court.

(3) If a motion to strike, of the character specified in Section 585, is granted in whole or in part, and the defendant fails to answer the unstricken portion of the complaint within the time allowed by the court, no demurrer having been sustained or being then pending.

(4) If a motion to quash service of summons or to stay or dismiss the action has been filed, or writ of mandate sought and notice thereof given, as provided in Section 418.10, and upon denial of the motion or writ, the defendant fails to respond to the complaint within the time provided in that section or as otherwise provided by law.

(5) If the demurrer to the answer is sustained and the defendant fails to amend the answer within the time allowed by the court.

(6)(A) If a motion to transfer pursuant to Section 396b is denied and the defendant fails to respond to the complaint within the time allowed by the court pursuant to subdivision (e) of Section 396b or within the time provided in subparagraph (C).

(B) If a motion to transfer pursuant to Section 396b is granted and the defendant fails to respond to the complaint within 30 days of the mailing of notice of the filing and case number by the clerk of the court to which the action or proceeding is transferred or within the time provided in subparagraph (C).

(C) If the order granting or denying a motion to transfer pursuant to Section 396a or 396b is the subject of an appeal pursuant to Section 904.2 in which a stay is granted or of a mandate proceeding pursuant to Section 400, the court having jurisdiction over the trial, upon application or on its own motion after the appeal or mandate proceeding becomes final or upon earlier termination of a stay, shall allow the defendant a reasonable time to respond to the complaint. Notice of the order allowing the defendant further time to respond to the complaint shall be promptly served by the party who obtained the order or by the clerk if the order is made on the court's own motion.

(7) If a motion to strike the answer in whole, of the character specified in Section 585, is granted without leave to amend, or if a motion to strike the answer in whole or in part, of the character specified in Section 585, is granted with leave to amend and the defendant fails to amend the answer within the time allowed by the court.

(8) If a motion to dismiss pursuant to Section 583.250 is denied and the defendant fails to respond within the time allowed by the court.

(b) For the purposes of this section, "respond" means to answer, to demur, or to move to strike. *(Formerly § 872, enacted 1872. Amended by Stats.1921, c. 127, § 1. Renumbered § 586, and amended by Stats.1933, c. 744, § 93; Stats.1955, c. 1452, § 7; Stats.1969, c. 345, § 4; Stats.1969, c. 1611, § 7.5; Stats.1970, c. 587, § 1; Stats.1973, c. 167, § 12; Stats.1982, c. 704, § 7; Stats.1983, c. 1167, § 7; Stats.1991, c. 1090, § 4; Stats.1993, c. 456, § 11; Stats.1995, c. 796, § 11; Stats.2007, c. 43, § 6.)*

Chapter 3. Issues—The Mode of Trial and Postponements

§ 588. Issues Defined; Kinds of Issues

Issues arise upon the pleadings when a fact or a conclusion of law is maintained by the one party and is controverted by the other. They are of two kinds:

1. Of law; and,

2. Of fact. *(Enacted 1872.)*

§ 592. Issue of Fact; Jury Trial; Waiver; Reference; Issues of Law Disposed Of First

In actions for the recovery of specific, real, or personal property, with or without damages, or for money claimed as due upon contract, or as damages for breach of contract, or for injuries, an issue of fact must be tried by a jury, unless a jury trial is waived, or a reference is ordered, as provided in this Code. Where in these cases there are issues both of law and fact, the issue of law must be first disposed of. In other cases, issues of fact must be tried by the Court, subject to its power to order any such issue to be tried by a jury, or to be referred to a referee, as provided in this Code. *(Enacted 1872. Amended by Code Am. 1873–74, c. 383, § 74.)*

§ 598. Precedence of Issues; Motion

The court may, when the convenience of witnesses, the ends of justice, or the economy and efficiency of handling the litigation would be promoted thereby, on motion of a party, after notice and hearing, make an order, no later than the close of pretrial conference in cases in which such pretrial conference is to be held, or, in other cases, no later than 30 days before the trial date, that the trial of any issue or any part thereof shall precede the trial of any other issue or any part thereof in the case, except for special defenses which may be tried first pursuant to Sections 597 and 597.5. The court, on its own motion, may make such an order at any time. Where trial of the issue of liability as to all causes of action precedes the trial of other issues or parts thereof, and the decision of the court, or the verdict of the jury upon such issue so tried is in favor of any party on whom liability is sought to be imposed, judgment in favor of such party shall thereupon be entered and no trial of other issues in the action as against such party shall be had unless such judgment shall be reversed upon appeal or otherwise set aside or vacated.

If the decision of the court, or the verdict of the jury upon the issue of liability so tried shall be against any party on whom liability is sought to be imposed, or if the decision of the court or the verdict of the jury upon any other issue or part thereof so tried does not result in a judgment being entered pursuant to this chapter, then the trial of the other issues or parts thereof shall thereafter be had at such time, and if a jury trial, before the same or other jury, as ordered by the court either upon its own motion or upon the motion of any party, and judgment shall be entered in the same manner and with the same effect as if all the issues in the case had been tried at one time. *(Added by Stats.1963, c. 1205, § 1. Amended by Stats.1977, c. 57, § 1; Stats.1979, c. 216, § 3; Stats.1979, c. 349, § 1.)*

Chapter 4. Trial by Jury

§ 607. Order of Proceedings

When the jury has been sworn, the trial must proceed in the following order, unless the court, for special reasons otherwise directs:

1. The plaintiff may state the issue and his case;

2. The defendant may then state his defense, if he so wishes, or wait until after plaintiff has produced his evidence;

3. The plaintiff must then produce the evidence on his part;

4. The defendant may then open his defense, if he has not done so previously;

5. The defendant may then produce the evidence on his part;

6. The parties may then respectively offer rebutting evidence only, unless the court, for good reason, in furtherance of justice, permit them to offer evidence upon their original case;

7. When the evidence is concluded, unless the case is submitted to the jury on either side or on both sides without argument, the plaintiff must commence and may conclude the argument;

8. If several defendants having separate defenses, appear by different counsel, the court must determine their relative order in the evidence and argument;

9. The court may then charge the jury. *(Enacted 1872. Amended by Stats.1933, c. 744, § 100; Stats.1965, c. 841, § 1.)*

§ 607a. Proposed Jury Instructions

In every case which is being tried before the court with a jury, it shall be the duty of counsel for the respective parties, before the first witness is sworn, to deliver to the judge presiding at the trial and serve upon opposing counsel, all proposed instructions to the jury covering the law as disclosed by the pleadings. Thereafter, and before the commencement of the argument, counsel may deliver to such judge, and serve upon opposing counsel, additional proposed instructions to the jury upon questions of law developed by the evidence and not disclosed by the pleadings. All proposed instructions shall be typewritten, each on a separate sheet of paper. Before the commencement of the argument, the court, on request of counsel, must: (1) decide whether to give, refuse, or modify the proposed instructions; (2) decide which instructions shall be given in addition to those proposed, if any; and (3) advise counsel of all instructions to be given. However, if, during the argument, issues are raised which have not been covered by instructions given or refused, the court may, on request of counsel, give additional instructions on the subject matter thereof. *(Added by Stats.1929, c. 481, § 1. Amended by Stats.1933, c. 744, § 101; Stats.1951, c. 1737, § 89; Stats.1957, c. 1698, § 1.)*

§ 608. Charge to Jury; Written Statement of Points of Law

In charging the jury the Court may state to them all matters of law which it thinks necessary for their information in giving their verdict; and, if it state the testimony of the case, it must inform the jury that they are the exclusive judges of all questions of fact. The Court must furnish to either party, at the time, upon request, a statement in writing of the points of law contained in the charge, or sign, at the time, a statement of such points prepared and submitted by the counsel of either party. (*Enacted 1872.*)

§ 613. Decision in Court; Deliberation; Communications

When the case is finally submitted to the jury, they may decide in court or retire for deliberation. If they retire, they must be kept together in some convenient place, under charge of an officer, until at least three-fourths of them agree upon a verdict or are discharged by the court. Unless by order of the court, the officer having them under his or her charge shall not permit any communication to be made to them, including any form of electronic or wireless communication, or make any himself or herself, except to ask them if they or three-fourths of them are agreed upon a verdict. The officer shall not, before their verdict is rendered, communicate to any person the state of their deliberations, or the verdict agreed upon. *(Enacted 1872. Amended by Code Am.1880, c. 21, § 1; Stats.2011, c. 181, § 2.)*

§ 618. Verdict; Polling Jury

When the jury, or three-fourths of them, have agreed upon a verdict, they must be conducted into court and the verdict rendered by their foreperson. The verdict must be in writing, signed by the foreperson, and must be read to the jury by the clerk, and the inquiry made whether it is their verdict. Either party may require the jury to be polled, which is done by the court or clerk, asking each juror if it is the juror's verdict. If upon inquiry or polling, more than one-fourth of the jurors disagree thereto, the jury must be sent out again, but if no disagreement is expressed, the verdict is complete and the jury discharged from the case. *(Enacted 1872. Amended by Code Am.1880, c. 21, § 3; Stats.1933, c. 744, § 102; Stats.1935, c. 722, § 9; Stats.1978, c. 258, § 1; Stats.2007, c. 263, § 7.)*

§ 624. General and Special Verdicts Defined

The verdict of a jury is either general or special. A general verdict is that by which they pronounce generally upon all or any of the issues, either in favor of the plaintiff or defendant; a special verdict is that by which the jury find the facts only, leaving the judgment to the Court. The special verdict must present the conclusions of fact as established by the evidence, and not the evidence to prove them; and those conclusions of fact must be so presented as that nothing shall remain to the Court but to draw from them conclusions of law. *(Enacted 1872.)*

§ 625. Special Verdict or Findings; Punitive Damages; Filing and Entry Upon Minutes; General Verdict Controlled by Special Findings

In all cases the court may direct the jury to find a special verdict in writing, upon all, or any of the issues, and in all cases may instruct them, if they render a general verdict, to find upon particular questions of fact, to be stated in writing, and may direct a written finding thereon. In all cases in which the issue of punitive damages is presented to the jury the court shall direct the jury to find a special verdict in writing separating punitive damages from compensatory damages. The special verdict or finding must be filed with the clerk and entered upon the minutes. Where a special finding of fact is inconsistent with the general verdict, the former controls the latter, and the court must give judgment accordingly. *(Enacted 1872. Amended by Stats.1905, c. 62, § 1; Stats.1909, c. 121, § 1; Stats.1957, c. 1443, § 1; Stats.1983, c. 176, § 2.)*

§ 629. Judgment Notwithstanding Verdict

(a) The court, before the expiration of its power to rule on a motion for a new trial, either of its own motion, after five days' notice, or on motion of a party against whom a verdict has been rendered, shall render judgment in favor of the aggrieved party notwithstanding the verdict whenever a motion for a directed verdict for the aggrieved party should have been granted had a previous motion been made.

(b) A motion for judgment notwithstanding the verdict shall be made within the period specified by Section 659 for the filing and service of a notice of intention to move for a new trial. The moving, opposing, and reply briefs and any accompanying documents shall be filed and served within the periods specified by Section 659a and the hearing on the motion shall be set in the same manner as the hearing on a motion for new trial under Section 660. The making of a motion for judgment notwithstanding the verdict shall not extend the time within which a party may file and serve notice of intention to move for a new trial. The court shall not rule upon the motion for judgment notwithstanding the verdict until the expiration of the time within which a motion for a new trial must be served and filed, and if a motion for a new trial has been filed with the court by the aggrieved party, the court shall rule upon both motions at the same time. The power of the court to rule on a motion for judgment notwithstanding the verdict shall not extend beyond the last date upon which it has the power to rule on a motion for a new trial. If a motion for judgment notwithstanding the verdict is not determined before that date, the effect shall be a denial of that motion without further order of the court.

(c) If the motion for judgment notwithstanding the verdict is denied and if a new trial is denied, the appellate court shall, if it appears that the motion for judgment notwithstanding the verdict should have been granted, order judgment to be so entered on appeal from the judgment or from the order denying the motion for judgment notwithstanding the verdict.

(d) If a new trial is granted to the party moving for judgment notwithstanding the verdict, and the motion for judgment notwithstanding the verdict is denied, the order denying the motion for judgment notwithstanding the verdict shall nevertheless be reviewable on appeal from that order by the aggrieved party. If the court grants the motion for judgment notwithstanding the verdict or of its own motion directs the entry of judgment notwithstanding the verdict and likewise grants the motion for a new trial, the order granting the new trial shall be effective only if, on appeal, the judgment notwithstanding the verdict is reversed, and the order granting a new trial is not appealed from or, if appealed from, is affirmed. *(Added by Stats.1923, c. 366, § 1. Amended by Stats.1935, c. 722, § 10; Stats.1937, c. 551, § 1; Stats.1951, c. 801, § 1; Stats.1961, c. 604, § 1; Stats.1963, c. 205, § 1; Stats.2014, c. 93, § 1; Stats.2015, c. 303, § 40.)*

§ 630. Motion for Directed Verdict; Granting of Motion for All or Part of Issues Involved; Effect; Ordering Judgment After Discharge of Jury and Failure to Grant Directed Verdict

(a) Unless the court specified an earlier time for making a motion for directed verdict, after all parties have completed the presentation of all of their evidence in a trial by jury, any party may, without waiving his or her right to trial by jury in the event the motion is not granted, move for an order directing entry of a verdict in its favor.

(b) If it appears that the evidence presented supports the granting of the motion as to some, but not all, of the issues involved in the action, the court shall grant the motion as to those issues and the action shall proceed on any remaining issues. Despite the granting of such a motion, no final judgment shall be entered prior to the termination of the action, but the final judgment, in addition to any matter determined in the trial, shall reflect the verdict ordered by the court as determined by the motion for directed verdict.

(c) If the motion is granted, unless the court in its order directing entry of the verdict specifies otherwise, it shall operate as an adjudication upon the merits.

(d) In actions which arise out of an injury to a person or property, when a motion for directed verdict was granted on the basis that a defendant was without fault, no other defendant during trial, over plaintiff's objection, shall attempt to attribute fault to or comment on the absence or involvement of the defendant who was granted the motion.

(e) The order of the court granting the motion for directed verdict is effective without any assent of the jury.

(f) When the jury for any reason has been discharged without having rendered a verdict, the court on its own motion or upon motion of a party, notice of which was given within 10 days after discharge of the jury, may order judgment to be entered in favor of a party whenever a motion for directed verdict for that party should have been granted had a previous motion been made. Except as otherwise provided in Section 12a, the power of the court to act under the provisions of this section shall expire 30 days after the day upon which the jury was discharged, and if judgment has not been ordered within that time the effect shall be the denial of any motion for judgment without further order of the court. *(Added by Stats.1947, c. 984, § 2. Amended by Stats.1967, c. 625, § 1; Stats.1986, c. 540, § 12.)*

Chapter 4.5 Voluntary Expedited Jury Trials

§ 630.01. Definitions

For purposes of this chapter:

(a) "Expedited jury trial" means a consensual, binding jury trial before a reduced jury panel and a judicial officer.

(b) "High/low agreement" means a written agreement entered into by the parties that specifies a minimum amount of damages that a plaintiff is guaranteed to receive from the defendant, and a maximum amount of damages that the defendant will be liable for, regardless of the ultimate verdict returned by the jury. Neither the existence of, nor the amounts contained in, any high/low agreements may be disclosed to the jury.

(c) "Post-trial motions" does not include motions relating to costs and attorney's fees, motions to correct a judgment for a clerical error, and motions to enforce a judgment. *(Added by Stats.2010, c. 674, § 2. Amended by Stats.2011, c. 296, § 37.)*

§ 630.02. Rules and Procedures Applicable to Expedited Jury Trials

The rules and procedures applicable to expedited jury trials are as follows:

(a) The procedures in this chapter and in the implementing rules of court shall apply to expedited jury trials, unless the parties agree otherwise, as permitted under subparagraph (E) of paragraph (1) of subdivision (e) of Section 630.03, and the court so orders.

(b) Any matters not expressly addressed in this chapter, in the implementing rules of court, or in a consent order authorized by this chapter and the implementing rules, are governed by applicable statutes and rules governing civil actions. *(Added by Stats.2010, c. 674, § 2.)*

§ 630.07. Binding Nature of Agreement; Vote of Jurors

(a) The verdict in an expedited jury trial case is binding, subject to any written high/low agreement or other stipulations concerning the amount of the award agreed upon by the parties.

(b) A vote of six of the eight jurors is required for a verdict, unless the parties stipulate otherwise. *(Added by Stats.2010, c. 674, § 2.)*

§ 630.08. Waiver of Motions for Directed Verdicts, to Set Aside Verdict or Judgment Rendered by Jury, or for New Trial Based on Amount of Damages; Limitation of Court's Authority to Direct Verdict, Enter Judgment as a Matter of Law, or Order New Trial

(a) By agreeing to participate in the expedited jury trial process, the parties agree to waive any motions for directed verdict motions to set aside the verdict or any judgment rendered by the jury, or motions for a new trial on the basis of inadequate or excessive damages.

(b) The court shall not set aside any verdict or any judgment, shall not direct that judgment be entered in favor of a party entitled to judgment as a matter of law, and shall not order a new trial, except on the grounds stated in Section 630.09. *(Added by Stats.2010, c. 674, § 2. Amended by Stats.2011, c. 296, § 38.)*

§ 630.09. Waiver of Right to Bring Post-trial Motions or Appeal; Exceptions; Procedures

(a) By agreeing to participate in the expedited jury trial process, the parties agree to waive the right to bring post-trial motions or to appeal from the determination of the matter, except as provided in this section. The only grounds on which a party may move for a new trial or appeal are any of the following:

(1) Judicial misconduct that materially affected the substantial rights of a party.

(2) Misconduct of the jury.

(3) Corruption, fraud, or other undue means employed in the proceedings of the court, jury, or adverse party that prevented a party from having a fair trial.

(b) Within 10 court days of the entry of a jury verdict, a party may file with the clerk and serve on each adverse party a notice of the intention to move for a new trial on any of the grounds specified in subdivision (a). The notice shall be deemed to be a motion for a new trial.

(c) Except as provided in subdivision (b), parties to an expedited jury trial shall not make any post-trial motions except for motions relating to costs and attorney's fees, motions to correct a judgment for clerical error, and motions to enforce a judgment.

(d) Before filing an appeal, a party shall make a motion for a new trial under subdivision (b). If the motion for a new trial is denied, the party may appeal the judgment to the appropriate court with appellate jurisdiction and seek a new trial on any of the grounds specified in subdivision (a). Parties to an expedited jury trial may not appeal on any other ground. *(Added by Stats.2010, c. 674, § 2.)*

§ 630.10. Applicability of Statutes and Rules Governing Attorney's Fees

All statutes and rules governing costs and attorney's fees shall apply in expedited jury trials, unless the parties agree otherwise in the consent order. *(Added by Stats.2010, c. 674, § 2.)*

§ 630.11. Rules and Forms to Establish Uniform Procedures Implementing Chapter

The Judicial Council shall, on or before July 1, 2016, update rules and forms to establish uniform procedures implementing the provisions of this chapter, including, but not limited to, rules for all of the following:

(a) Additional content of proposed consent orders.

(b) Pretrial exchanges and submissions.

(c) Pretrial conferences.

(d) Presentation of evidence and testimony.

(e) Any other procedures necessary to implement the provisions of this chapter. *(Added by Stats.2010, c. 674, § 2. Amended by Stats.2015, c. 330, § 3.)*

Chapter 4.6 Mandatory Expedited Jury Trials in Limited Civil Cases

§ 630.20. Actions or Special Proceedings to Be Conducted as Mandatory Expedited Jury Trials; Opt Out Criteria; Exceptions; Appeal

(a) Except as provided in subdivisions (b) and (c), an action or special proceeding treated as a limited civil case pursuant to Article 1 (commencing with Section 85) of Chapter 5.1 of Title 1 of Part 1, including an action or special proceeding initially filed as a limited civil case or remanded as one thereafter, shall be conducted as a mandatory expedited jury trial pursuant to this chapter.

(b) Either party may opt out of the mandatory expedited jury trial procedures if any of the following criteria is met:

(1) Punitive damages are sought.

(2) Damages in excess of insurance policy limits are sought.

(3) A party's insurer is providing a legal defense subject to a reservation of rights.

(4) The case involves a claim reportable to a governmental entity.

(5) The case involves a claim of moral turpitude that may affect an individual's professional licensing.

(6) The case involves claims of intentional conduct.

(7) The case has been reclassified as unlimited pursuant to Section 403.020.

(8) The complaint contains a demand for attorney's fees, unless those fees are sought pursuant to Section 1717 of the Civil Code.

(9) The judge finds good cause exists for the action not to proceed under the rules of this chapter. Good cause includes, but is not limited to, a showing that a party needs more than five hours to present or defend the action and that the parties have been unable to stipulate to additional time.

(c) This chapter does not apply to a proceeding in forcible entry or forcible or unlawful detainer.

(d) A judgment in a limited civil case conducted as a mandatory expedited jury trial may be appealed to the appellate division of the superior court in which the case was tried. *(Added by Stats.2015, c. 330, § 5, operative July 1, 2016.)*

§ 630.21. Definitions

For purposes of this chapter:

(a) "Mandatory expedited jury trial" means a jury trial before a reduced jury panel and a judge, conducted pursuant to this chapter.

(b) "High/low agreement" means a written agreement entered into by the parties that specifies a minimum amount of damages that a plaintiff is guaranteed to receive from the defendant, and a maximum amount of damages that the defendant will be liable for, regardless of the ultimate verdict returned by the jury. Neither the existence of, nor the amounts contained in, any high/low agreements may be disclosed to the jury. *(Added by Stats.2015, c. 330, § 5, operative July 1, 2016.)*

§ 630.22. Rules and Procedures Applicable to Mandatory Expedited Jury Trials; Matters Not Expressly Addressed

(a) The procedures in this chapter and in the implementing rules of court shall apply to mandatory expedited jury trials conducted in limited civil cases, unless the parties agree otherwise, as permitted under subdivision (d) of Section 630.23, and the court so orders.

(b) Any matters not expressly addressed in this chapter, in the implementing rules of court, or in an agreement authorized by this chapter and the implementing rules, are governed by applicable statutes and rules governing civil actions. *(Added by Stats.2015, c. 330, § 5, operative July 1, 2016.)*

§ 630.23. Rules and Procedures Applicable to Mandatory Expedited Jury Trials; Time Allowed; Jurors; Challenges; Modification

The following rules and procedures apply to mandatory expedited jury trials conducted pursuant to this chapter:

(a) Each side shall have up to five hours in which to complete voir dire and to present its case.

(b) The jury shall be composed of eight jurors and one alternate, unless the parties have agreed to fewer jurors.

(c) Each side shall be limited to four peremptory challenges, unless the court permits an additional challenge in cases with more than two sides. If there are more than two parties in a case and more than two sides, as determined by the court under subdivision (c) of Section 231, the parties may request one additional peremptory challenge each, which is to be granted by the court as the interests of justice may require.

(d) The parties may agree to modify the rules and procedures specified in this chapter and the implementing rules of court, subject to the court's approval. *(Added by Stats.2015, c. 330, § 5, operative July 1, 2016.)*

§ 630.24. Jury Deliberation

Nothing in this chapter is intended to preclude a jury from deliberating as long as needed. *(Added by Stats.2015, c. 330, § 5, operative July 1, 2016.)*

§ 630.25. Applicability of Rules of Evidence; Waiver or Stipulation Not to Affect Privilege; Right to Issue Subpoenas and Notices to Appear

(a) The rules of evidence apply to mandatory expedited jury trials conducted in limited civil cases, unless the parties stipulate otherwise.

(b) Any stipulation by the parties to use relaxed rules of evidence shall not be construed to eliminate, or in any way affect, the right of a witness or party to invoke any applicable privilege or other law protecting confidentiality.

(c) The right to issue subpoenas and notices to appear to secure the attendance of witnesses or the production of documents at trial shall be in accordance with this code. *(Added by Stats.2015, c. 330, § 5, operative July 1, 2016.)*

§ 630.26. Vote of Jurors; Appeal of Verdict

(a) A vote of six of the eight jurors is required for a verdict, unless the parties stipulate otherwise.

(b) The verdict in a limited civil case following a mandatory expedited jury trial case shall be appealable under subdivision (d) of Section 630.20 and subject to any written high/low agreement or other stipulations concerning the amount of the award agreed upon by the parties. *(Added by Stats.2015, c. 330, § 5, operative July 1, 2016.)*

§ 630.27. Applicability of Statutes and Rules Governing Costs and Attorney's Fees

All statutes and rules governing costs and attorney's fees shall apply in limited civil cases that are conducted as mandatory expedited jury trials, unless the parties stipulate otherwise. *(Added by Stats.2015, c. 330, § 5, operative July 1, 2016.)*

§ 630.28. Rules and Forms to Establish Uniform Procedures Implementing Chapter

The Judicial Council shall, on or before July 1, 2016, adopt rules and forms to establish uniform procedures implementing the provisions of this chapter, including, rules for the following:

(a) Pretrial exchanges and submissions.

(b) Pretrial conferences.

(c) Opt-out procedures pursuant to subdivision (b) of Section 630.20.

(d) Presentation of evidence and testimony.

(e) Any other procedures necessary to implement the provisions of this chapter. *(Added by Stats.2015, c. 330, § 5, operative July 1, 2016.)*

§ 630.29. Operative Date

Sections 630.20 to 630.27, inclusive, shall become operative on July 1, 2016. *(Added by Stats.2015, c. 330, § 5.)*

Chapter 5. Trial by Court

§ 631. Waiver of Jury Trial; Manner; Demand for Jury Trial; Exception

(a) The right to a trial by jury as declared by Section 16 of Article I of the California Constitution shall be preserved to the parties inviolate. In civil cases, a jury may only be waived pursuant to subdivision (f).

(b) At least one party demanding a jury on each side of a civil case shall pay a nonrefundable fee of one hundred fifty dollars ($150), unless the fee has been paid by another party on the same side of the case. The fee shall offset the costs to the state of providing juries in civil cases. If there are more than two parties to the case, for purposes of this section only, all plaintiffs shall be considered one side of the case, and all other parties shall be considered the other side of the case. Payment of the fee by a party on one side of the case shall not relieve parties on the other side of the case from waiver pursuant to subdivision (f).

(c) The fee described in subdivision (b) shall be due on or before the date scheduled for the initial case management conference in the action, except as follows:

(1) In unlawful detainer actions, the fees shall be due at least five days before the date set for trial.

(2) If no case management conference is scheduled in a civil action, or the initial case management conference occurred before June 28, 2012, and the initial complaint was filed on or after July 1, 2011, the fee shall be due no later than 365 calendar days after the filing of the initial complaint.

(3) If the initial case management conference occurred before June 28, 2012, and the initial complaint in the case was filed before July 1, 2011, the fee shall be due at least 25 calendar days before the date initially set for trial.

(4) If the party requesting a jury has not appeared before the initial case management conference, or first appeared more than 365 calendar days after the filing of the initial complaint, the fee shall be due at least 25 calendar days before the date initially set for trial.

(d) If a party failed to timely pay the fee described in subdivision (b) that was due between June 27, 2012, and November 30, 2012, the party will be relieved of a jury waiver on that basis only if the party pays the fee on or before December 31, 2012, or 25 calendar days before the date initially set for trial, whichever is earlier.

(e) The parties demanding a jury trial shall deposit with the clerk or judge, at the beginning of the second and each succeeding day's session, a sum equal to that day's fees and mileage of the jury, including the fees and mileage for the trial jury panel if the trial jury has not yet been selected and sworn. If more than one party has demanded a jury, the respective amount to be paid daily by each party demanding a jury shall be determined by stipulation of the parties or by order of the court.

(f) A party waives trial by jury in any of the following ways:

(1) By failing to appear at the trial.

(2) By written consent filed with the clerk or judge.

(3) By oral consent, in open court, entered in the minutes.

(4) By failing to announce that a jury is required, at the time the cause is first set for trial, if it is set upon notice or stipulation, or within five days after notice of setting if it is set without notice or stipulation.

(5) By failing to timely pay the fee described in subdivision (b), unless another party on the same side of the case has paid that fee.

(6) By failing to deposit with the clerk or judge, at the beginning of the second and each succeeding day's session, the sum provided in subdivision (e).

(g) The court may, in its discretion upon just terms, allow a trial by jury although there may have been a waiver of a trial by jury.

(h) The court shall transmit the fee described in subdivision (b) to the State Treasury for deposit in the Trial Court Trust Fund within 45 calendar days after the end of the month in which the fee is paid to the court. *(Added by Stats.1988, c. 10, § 3. Amended by Stats.1988, c. 278, § 1; Stats.1989, c. 15, § 2; Stats.1998, c. 931, § 83; Stats.1999, c. 83, § 24; Stats.2000, c. 127, § 2; Stats.2002, c. 806, § 15; Stats.2012, c. 41, § 3, eff. June 27, 2012; Stats.2012, c. 342, § 1, eff. Sept. 17, 2012.)*

§ 631.2. County Payment of Jury Fees; Reimbursement

(a) Notwithstanding any other provision of law, the superior court may pay jury fees in civil cases from general funds of the court available therefor. Nothing in this section shall be construed to change the requirements for the deposit of jury fees in any civil case by the appropriate party to the litigation at the time and in the manner otherwise provided by law. Nothing in this section shall preclude the right of the superior court to be reimbursed by the party to the litigation liable therefor for any payment of jury fees pursuant to this section. Nothing in this section shall preclude the right of the county to be reimbursed by the party to the litigation liable therefor for any payment of jury fees pursuant to this section as it read in Section 4 of Chapter 10 of the Statutes of 1988, or pursuant to former Section 631.1 as it read in Section 1 of Chapter 144 of the Statutes of 1971.

(b) The party who has demanded trial by jury shall reimburse the Superior Court for the fees and mileage of all jurors appearing for voir dire examination, except those jurors who are excused and subsequently on the same day are called for voir dire examination in another case. *(Added by Stats.1988, c. 10, § 4. Amended by Stats.2012, c. 470, § 6.)*

§ 631.3. Forfeiture of Jury Fees Deposited; Disposition of Fees

(a) Notwithstanding any other law, when a party to the litigation has deposited jury fees with the judge or clerk and that party waives a jury or obtains a continuance of the trial, or the case is settled, none of the deposit shall be refunded if the court finds there has been insufficient time to notify the jurors that the trial would not proceed at the time set. If the jury fees so deposited are not refunded for any of these reasons, or if a refund of jury fees deposited with the judge or clerk has not been requested, in writing, by the depositing party within 20 business days from the date on which the jury is waived or the action is settled, dismissed, or a continuance thereof granted, the fees shall be transmitted to the Controller for deposit into the Trial Court Trust Fund.

(b) All jury fees and mileage fees that may accrue by reason of a juror serving on more than one case in the same day shall be transmitted to the Controller for deposit into the Trial Court Trust Fund. All jury fees that were deposited with the court in advance of trial pursuant to Section 631 prior to January 1, 1999, and that remain on deposit in cases that were settled, dismissed, or otherwise disposed of, and three years have passed since the date the case was settled, dismissed, or otherwise disposed of, shall be transmitted to the Controller for deposit into the Trial Court Trust Fund.

(c) The fee described in subdivision (b) of Section 631 shall be nonrefundable and is not subject to this section. *(Added by Stats.1949, c. 444, § 1. Amended by Stats.1955, c. 511, § 1; Stats.1963, c. 678, § 1; Stats.1998, c. 1003, § 1; Stats.1998, c. 1004, § 1; Stats.2000, c. 447, § 2; Stats.2001, c. 824, § 9; Stats.2012, c. 41, § 4; Stats.2012, c. 342, § 2.)*

§ 631.8. Motion for Judgment; Partial Grant for Motion; Effect

(a) After a party has completed his presentation of evidence in a trial by the court, the other party, without waiving his right to offer evidence in support of his defense or in rebuttal in the event the motion is not granted, may move for a judgment. The court as trier of the facts shall weigh the evidence and may render a judgment in favor of the moving party, in which case the court shall make a statement of decision as provided in Sections 632 and 634, or may decline to render any judgment until the close of all the evidence. The court may consider all evidence received, provided, however, that the party against whom the motion for judgment has been made shall have had an opportunity to present additional evidence to rebut evidence received during the presentation of evidence deemed by the presenting party to have been adverse to him, and to rehabilitate the testimony of a witness whose credibility has been attacked by the moving party. Such motion may also be made and granted as to any cross-complaint.

(b) If it appears that the evidence presented supports the granting of the motion as to some but not all the issues involved in the action, the court shall grant the motion as to those issues and the action shall proceed as to the issues remaining. Despite the granting of such a motion, no final judgment shall be entered prior to the termination of the action, but the final judgment in such action shall, in addition to any matters determined in the trial, award judgment as determined by the motion herein provided for.

(c) If the motion is granted, unless the court in its order for judgment otherwise specifies, such judgment operates as an adjudication upon the merits. *(Added by Stats.1961, c. 692, § 2. Amended by Stats.1971, c. 244, § 53; Stats.1978, c. 372, § 1; Stats.1980, c. 187, § 2; Stats.1986, c. 540, § 13.)*

Chapter 6. Of References and Trials by Referees

§ 638. Appointment of Referee; Agreement of Parties

A referee may be appointed upon the agreement of the parties filed with the clerk, or judge, or entered in the minutes, or upon the motion of a party to a written contract or lease that provides that any controversy arising therefrom shall be heard by a referee if the court finds a reference agreement exists between the parties:

(a) To hear and determine any or all of the issues in an action or proceeding, whether of fact or of law, and to report a statement of decision.

(b) To ascertain a fact necessary to enable the court to determine an action or proceeding.

(c) In any matter in which a referee is appointed pursuant to this section, a copy of the order shall be forwarded to the office of the presiding judge. The Judicial Council shall, by rule, collect information on the use of these referees. The Judicial Council shall also collect information on fees paid by the parties for the use of referees to the extent that information regarding those fees is reported to the court. The Judicial Council shall report thereon to the Legislature by July 1, 2003. This subdivision shall become inoperative on January 1, 2004. *(Enacted 1872. Amended by Stats.1933, c. 744, § 107; Stats.1951, c. 1737, § 93; Stats.1982, c. 440, § 1; Stats.1984, c. 350, § 1; Stats.2000, c. 644, § 1; Stats.2001, c. 44, § 5; Stats.2002, c. 1008, § 4.)*

§ 639. Appointment of Referee

(a) When the parties do not consent, the court may, upon the written motion of any party, or of its own motion, appoint a referee in the following cases pursuant to the provisions of subdivision (b) of Section 640:

(1) When the trial of an issue of fact requires the examination of a long account on either side; in which case the referees may be directed to hear and decide the whole issue, or report upon any specific question of fact involved therein.

(2) When the taking of an account is necessary for the information of the court before judgment, or for carrying a judgment or order into effect.

(3) When a question of fact, other than upon the pleadings, arises upon motion or otherwise, in any stage of the action.

(4) When it is necessary for the information of the court in a special proceeding.

(5) When the court in any pending action determines that it is necessary for the court to appoint a referee to hear and determine any and all discovery motions and disputes relevant to discovery in the action and to report findings and make a recommendation thereon.

(b) In a discovery matter, a motion to disqualify an appointed referee pursuant to Section 170.6 shall be made to the court by a party either:

(A) Within 10 days after notice of the appointment, or if the party has not yet appeared in the action, a motion shall be made within 10 days after the appearance, if a discovery referee has been appointed for all discovery purposes.

(B) At least five days before the date set for hearing, if the referee assigned is known at least 10 days before the date set for hearing and the discovery referee has been assigned only for limited discovery purposes.

(c) When a referee is appointed pursuant to paragraph (5) of subdivision (a), the order shall indicate whether the referee is being appointed for all discovery purposes in the action.

(d) All appointments of referees pursuant to this section shall be by written order and shall include the following:

(1) When the referee is appointed pursuant to paragraph (1), (2), (3), or (4) of subdivision (a), a statement of the reason the referee is being appointed.

(2) When the referee is appointed pursuant to paragraph (5) of subdivision (a), the exceptional circumstances requiring the reference, which must be specific to the circumstances of the particular case.

(3) The subject matter or matters included in the reference.

(4) The name, business address, and telephone number of the referee.

(5) The maximum hourly rate the referee may charge and, at the request of any party, the maximum number of hours for which the referee may charge. Upon the written application of any party or the referee, the court may, for good cause shown, modify the maximum number of hours subject to any findings as set forth in paragraph (6).

(6)(A) Either a finding that no party has established an economic inability to pay a pro rata share of the referee's fee or a finding that one or more parties has established an economic inability to pay a pro rata share of the referee's fees and that another party has agreed voluntarily to pay that additional share of the referee's fee. A court shall not appoint a referee at a cost to the parties if neither of these findings is made.

(B) In determining whether a party has established an inability to pay the referee's fees under subparagraph (A), the court shall consider only the ability of the party, not the party's counsel, to pay these fees. If a party is proceeding in forma pauperis, the party shall be deemed by the court to have an economic inability to pay the referee's fees. However, a determination of economic inability to pay the fees shall not be limited to parties that proceed in forma pauperis. For those parties who are not proceeding in forma pauperis, the court, in determining whether a party has established an inability to pay the fees, shall consider, among other things, the estimated cost of the referral and the impact of the proposed fees on the party's ability to proceed with the litigation.

(e) In any matter in which a referee is appointed pursuant to paragraph (5) of subdivision (a), a copy of the order appointing the referee shall be forwarded to the office of the presiding judge of the court. The Judicial Council shall, by rule, collect information on the use of these references and the reference fees charged to litigants, and shall report thereon to the Legislature by July 1, 2003. This subdivision shall become inoperative on January 1, 2004. *(Enacted 1872. Amended by Stats.1933, c. 744, § 108; Stats.1951, c. 1737, § 94; Stats.1977, c. 1257, § 23; Stats.1981, c. 299, § 1; Stats.2000, c. 644, § 2; Stats.2000, c. 1011, § 1.5; Stats.2001, c. 362, § 1.)*

Chapter 7. Provisions Relating to Trials in General

§ 657. Relief Available on Motion for New Trial; Causes; Specification of Grounds and Reasons; New Trial for Insufficient Evidence; Manner of Making and Entering Order; Appeal

The verdict may be vacated and any other decision may be modified or vacated, in whole or in part, and a new or further trial granted on all or part of the issues, on the application of the party aggrieved, for any of the following causes, materially affecting the substantial rights of such party:

1. Irregularity in the proceedings of the court, jury or adverse party, or any order of the court or abuse of discretion by which either party was prevented from having a fair trial.

2. Misconduct of the jury; and whenever any one or more of the jurors have been induced to assent to any general or special verdict, or to a finding on any question submitted to them by the court, by a resort to the determination of chance, such misconduct may be proved by the affidavit of any one of the jurors.

3. Accident or surprise, which ordinary prudence could not have guarded against.

4. Newly discovered evidence, material for the party making the application, which he could not, with reasonable diligence, have discovered and produced at the trial.

5. Excessive or inadequate damages.

6. Insufficiency of the evidence to justify the verdict or other decision, or the verdict or other decision is against law.

7. Error in law, occurring at the trial and excepted to by the party making the application.

When a new trial is granted, on all or part of the issues, the court shall specify the ground or grounds upon which it is granted and the court's reason or reasons for granting the new trial upon each ground stated.

A new trial shall not be granted upon the ground of insufficiency of the evidence to justify the verdict or other decision, nor upon the ground of excessive or inadequate damages, unless after weighing the evidence the court is convinced from the entire record, including reasonable inferences therefrom, that the court or jury clearly should have reached a different verdict or decision.

The order passing upon and determining the motion must be made and entered as provided in Section 660 and if the motion is granted must state the ground or grounds relied upon by the court, and may contain the specification of reasons. If an order granting such motion does not contain such specification of reasons, the court must, within 10 days after filing such order, prepare, sign and file such specification of reasons in writing with the clerk. The court shall not direct the attorney for a party to prepare either or both said order and said specification of reasons.

On appeal from an order granting a new trial the order shall be affirmed if it should have been granted upon any ground stated in the motion, whether or not specified in the order or specification of reasons, except that (a) the order shall not be affirmed upon the ground of the insufficiency of the evidence to justify the verdict or other decision, or upon the ground of excessive or inadequate damages, unless such ground is stated in the order granting the motion and (b) on appeal from an order granting a new trial upon the ground of the insufficiency of the evidence to justify the verdict or other decision, or upon the ground of excessive or inadequate damages, it shall be conclusively presumed that said order as to such ground was made only for the reasons specified in said order or said specification of reasons, and such order shall be reversed as to such ground only if there is no substantial basis in the record for any of such reasons. *(Enacted 1872. Amended by Stats.**1919**, c. 100, § 1; Stats.**1929**, c. 479, § 2; Stats.**1939**, c. 713, § 1; Stats.**1965**, c. 1749, § 1; Stats.**1967**, c. 72, § 1.)*

§ 659. Notice of Motion; Filing and Service, Time; Contents; Extension of Time

(a) The party intending to move for a new trial shall file with the clerk and serve upon each adverse party a notice of their intention to move for a new trial, designating the grounds upon which the motion will be made and whether the same will be made upon affidavits or the minutes of the court, or both, either:

(1) After the decision is rendered and before the entry of judgment.

(2) Within 15 days of the date of serving notice of entry of judgment by the clerk of the court pursuant to Section 664.5, or service upon them by any party of written notice of entry of judgment, or within 180 days after the entry of judgment, whichever is earliest; provided, that upon the filing of the first notice of intention to move for a new trial by a party, each other party shall have 15 days after the service of that notice upon them to file and serve a notice of intention to move for a new trial.

(b) That notice of intention to move for a new trial shall be deemed to be a motion for a new trial on all the grounds stated in the notice. The times specified in paragraphs (1) and (2) of subdivision (a) shall not be extended by order or stipulation or by those provisions of Section 1013 that extend the time for exercising a right or doing an act where service is by mail. *(Enacted 1872. Amended by Code Am.1873–74, c. 383, § 85; Stats.1907, c. 380, § 2; Stats.1915, c. 107, § 2; Stats.1923, c. 367, § 1; Stats.1929, c. 479, § 3; Stats.1951, c. 801, § 2; Stats.1959, c. 469, § 1; Stats.1961, c. 604, § 2; Stats.1965, c. 1890, § 1.5; Stats.1967, c. 169, § 1; Stats.1970, c. 621, § 1; Stats.2012, c. 83, § 1; Stats.2024, c. 853, § 20.)*

§ 660. Hearing; Reference to Pleadings, Orders, Depositions, Documentary Evidence, Transcript, Recollection of Judge; Attendance of Reporter; Precedence; Time for Ruling; Automatic Denial; Determination; Minute Order

(a) On the hearing of the motion, reference may be had in all cases to the pleadings and orders of the court on file, and when the motion is made on the minutes, reference may also be had to any depositions and documentary evidence offered at the trial and to the report of the proceedings on the trial taken by the phonographic reporter, or to any certified transcript of the report or if there be no such report or certified transcript, to proceedings occurring at the trial that are within the recollection of the judge; when the proceedings at the trial have been phonographically reported, but the reporter's notes have not been transcribed, the reporter shall, upon request of the court or either party, attend the hearing of the motion and read his or her notes, or such parts thereof as the court, or either party, may require.

(b) The hearing and determination of the motion for a new trial shall have precedence over all other matters except criminal cases, probate matters, and cases actually on trial, and it shall be the duty of the court to determine the motion at the earliest possible moment.

(c) Except as otherwise provided in Section 12a of this code, the power of the court to rule on a motion for a new trial shall expire 75 days after the mailing of notice of entry of judgment by the clerk of the court pursuant to Section 664.5 or 75 days after service on the moving party by any party of written notice of entry of judgment, whichever is earlier, or if that notice has not been given, 75 days after the filing of the first notice of intention to move for a new trial. If the motion is not determined within the 75-day period, or within that period as extended, the effect shall be a denial of the motion without further order of the court. A motion for a new trial is not determined within the meaning of this section until an order ruling on the motion is entered in the permanent minutes of the court or signed by the judge and filed with the clerk. The entry of a new trial order in the permanent minutes of the court shall constitute a determination of the motion even though that minute order, as entered, expressly directs that a written order be prepared, signed, and filed. The minute entry shall in all cases show the date on which the order is entered in the permanent minutes, but failure to comply with this direction shall not impair the validity or effectiveness of the order. *(Enacted 1872. Amended by Code Am.1873–74, c. 383, § 86; Stats.1907, c. 380, § 3; Stats.1915, c. 107, § 3; Stats.1917, c. 156, § 1; Stats.1923, c. 105, § 1; Stats.1929, c. 479, § 5; Stats.1933, c. 29, § 5; Stats.1959, c. 468, § 1; Stats.1969, c. 87, § 1; Stats.1970, c. 621, § 2; Stats.2018, c. 317, § 1.)*

§ 662. Cause Tried by Court; Powers of Judge on Motion for New Trial

In ruling on such motion, in a cause tried without a jury, the court may, on such terms as may be just, change or add to the statement of decision, modify the judgment, in whole or in part, vacate the judgment, in whole or in part, and grant a new trial on all or part of the issues, or, in lieu of granting a new trial, may vacate and set aside the statement of decision and judgment and reopen the case for further proceedings and the introduction of additional evidence with the same effect as if the case had been reopened after the submission thereof and before a decision had been filed or judgment rendered. Any judgment thereafter entered shall be subject to the provisions of sections 657 and 659. *(Added by Stats.1929, c. 479, § 7. Amended by Stats.1981, c. 900, § 4.)*

§ 662.5. Inadequate or Excessive Damages as Grounds

(a) In any civil action where after trial by jury an order granting a new trial limited to the issue of damages would be proper, the trial court may in its discretion:

(1) If the ground for granting a new trial is inadequate damages, issue a conditional order granting the new trial unless the party against whom the verdict has been rendered consents to the addition of damages in an amount the court in its independent judgment determines from the evidence to be fair and reasonable.

(2) If the ground for granting a new trial is excessive damages, issue a conditional order granting the new trial unless the party in whose favor the verdict has been rendered consents to the reduction of so much thereof as the court in its independent judgment determines from the evidence to be fair and reasonable.

(b) If a deadline for acceptance or rejection of the addition or reduction of damages is not set forth in the conditional order, the deadline is 30 days from the date the conditional order is served by the clerk of the court. Failure to respond to the order in accordance with this section shall be deemed a rejection of the addition or reduction of damages and a new trial limited to the issue of damages shall be granted automatically.

(c) A party filing and serving an acceptance of a conditionally ordered addition or reduction of damages shall concurrently serve and submit to the court a proposed amended judgment reflecting the modified judgment amount, as well as any other uncontested judgment awards. *(Added by Stats.1967, c. 72, § 2. Amended by Stats.1969, c. 115, § 1; Stats.2011, c. 409, § 2.)*

§ 663. Setting Aside Judgment or Decree; Entry of New Judgment; Grounds

A judgment or decree, when based upon a decision by the court, or the special verdict of a jury, may, upon motion of the party aggrieved, be set aside and vacated by the same court, and another and different judgment entered, for either of the following causes, materially affecting the substantial rights of the party and entitling the party to a different judgment:

1. Incorrect or erroneous legal basis for the decision, not consistent with or not supported by the facts; and in such case when the judgment is set aside, the statement of decision shall be amended and corrected.

2. A judgment or decree not consistent with or not supported by the special verdict. *(Added by Stats.1897, c. 67, § 1. Amended by Stats.1933, c. 744, § 120; Stats.1981, c. 900, § 5.)*

Chapter 8. The Manner of Giving and Entering Judgment

§ 664.6. Entry of Judgment Pursuant to Terms of Stipulation for Settlement; Signed Writing; Exceptions; Entry of Judgment or Dismissal Without Prejudice

(a) If parties to pending litigation stipulate, in a writing signed by the parties outside of the presence of the court or orally before the court, for settlement of the case, or part thereof, the court, upon motion, may enter judgment pursuant to the terms of the settlement. If requested by the parties, the court may retain jurisdiction over the parties to enforce the settlement until performance in full of the terms of the settlement.

(b) For purposes of this section, a writing is signed by a party if it is signed by any of the following:

(1) The party.

(2) An attorney who represents the party.

(3) If an insurer is defending and indemnifying a party to the action, an agent who is authorized in writing by the insurer to sign on the party's behalf. This paragraph does not apply if the party whom the insurer is defending would be liable under the terms of the settlement for any amount above the policy limits.

(c) Paragraphs (2) and (3) of subdivision (b) do not apply in a civil harassment action, an action brought pursuant to the Family Code, an action brought pursuant to the Probate Code, or a matter that is being adjudicated in a juvenile court or a dependency court.

(d) In addition to any available civil remedies, an attorney who signs a writing on behalf of a party pursuant to subdivision (b) without the party's express authorization shall, absent good cause, be subject to professional discipline.

(e)(1) If a plaintiff, cross-complainant, or other party seeking affirmative relief has filed a notice of conditional settlement, the court may, upon its own motion, without stipulation from the parties or their counsel, set an order to show cause as to why the court should not dismiss the entire action without prejudice and retain jurisdiction to enforce the settlement.

(2) This subdivision does not apply to actions brought pursuant to Chapter 5 of Title 3 of Part 2 of the Code of Civil Procedure (commencing with Section 378) and Part 13 of Division 2 of the Labor Code (commencing with Section 2698).

(f) If the Court enters judgment or dismisses the case without prejudice pursuant to this section, the following shall apply:

(1) A party may file a motion or other document pertaining to the settlement, including an application for determination of good faith

settlement, a motion for the reduction or determination of a lien, a petition related to the compromise of the claim of a minor or person with a disability, or, if the terms of a settlement are not performed, a motion based upon such terms. Responsive filings and related documents may also be filed.

(2) The court shall exercise its retained jurisdiction if a party files a notice that a written settlement agreement required of all parties was not signed by all parties.

(3) A party who has paid a first appearance fee shall not be assessed a first appearance fee again for filing a motion, notice or other document pertaining to the settlement after entry of judgment or dismissal without prejudice.

(4) The clerk of the court shall accept any motion, notice, or other document properly filed by a party after entry of judgment or dismissal without prejudice.

(g) Nothing in this section shall preclude a party from filing a request for dismissal with prejudice after the court has dismissed the case without prejudice pursuant to this section.

(h) On or before January 1, 2025, the Judicial Council shall update or develop new forms or Rules of Court as necessary to implement this section.

(i) This section shall become operative on January 1, 2025. *(Added by Stats.2023, c. 478, § 13.)*

TITLE 9. ENFORCEMENT OF JUDGMENTS

Chapter 3. Period for Enforcement and Renewal of Judgments

§ 683.010. Entry of Judgment

Except as otherwise provided by statute or in the judgment, a judgment is enforceable under this title upon entry. *(Added by Stats.1982, c. 1364, § 2.)*

§ 683.020. Period of Enforceability

Except as otherwise provided by statute, upon the expiration of 10 years after the date of entry of a money judgment or a judgment for possession or sale of property:

(a) The judgment may not be enforced.

(b) All enforcement procedures pursuant to the judgment or to a writ or order issued pursuant to the judgment shall cease.

(c) Any lien created by an enforcement procedure pursuant to the judgment is extinguished. *(Added by Stats.1982, c. 1364, § 2.)*

§ 683.120. Application for Renewal; Effect

(a) The judgment creditor may renew a judgment by filing an application for renewal of the judgment with the court in which the judgment was entered.

(b) Except as otherwise provided in this article, the filing of the application renews the judgment in the amount determined under Section 683.150 and extends the period of enforceability of the judgment as renewed for a period of 10 years from the date the application is filed.

(c) Notwithstanding subdivisions (a) and (b), for a judgment identified in subdivision (c) of Section 683.110, a judgment creditor may renew the judgment only once. The filing of the application under this subdivision renews the judgment in the amount determined under Section 683.150 and extends the period of enforceability of the judgment as renewed for a period of five years from the date the application is filed. No application may be filed if the judgment was renewed on or before December 31, 2022.

(d) In the case of a money judgment payable in installments, for the purposes of enforcement and of any later renewal, the amount of the judgment as renewed shall be treated as a lump-sum money judgment entered on the date the application is filed. *(Added by Stats.1982, c. 1364, § 2. Amended by Stats.2022, c. 883, § 3.)*

§ 683.180. Judgment Liens; Effect of Renewal

(a) If a judgment lien on an interest in real property has been created pursuant to a money judgment and the judgment is renewed pursuant to this article, the duration of the judgment lien is extended until 10 years from the date of the filing of the application for renewal if, before the expiration of the judgment lien, a certified copy of the application for renewal is recorded with the county recorder of the county where the real property subject to the judgment lien is located.

(b) A judgment lien on an interest in real property that has been transferred subject to the lien is not extended pursuant to subdivision (a) if the transfer was recorded before the application for renewal was filed unless both of the following requirements are satisfied:

(1) A copy of the application for renewal is personally served on the transferee.

(2) Proof of such service is filed with the court clerk within 90 days after the filing of the application for renewal. *(Added by Stats.1982, c. 1364, § 2. Amended by Stats.1983, c. 155, § 9.5.)*

TITLE 11. CONTRIBUTION AMONG JOINT JUDGMENT DEBTORS

Chapter 1. Releases from and Contribution Among Joint Tortfeasors

§ 877. Release of One or More Joint Tortfeasors or Co-obligors; Effect Upon Liability

Where a release, dismissal with or without prejudice, or a covenant not to sue or not to enforce judgment is given in good faith before verdict or judgment to one or more of a number of tortfeasors claimed to be liable for the same tort, or to one or more other co-obligors mutually subject to contribution rights, it shall have the following effect:

(a) It shall not discharge any other such party from liability unless its terms so provide, but it shall reduce the claims against the others in the amount stipulated by the release, the dismissal or the covenant, or in the amount of the consideration paid for it, whichever is the greater.

(b) It shall discharge the party to whom it is given from all liability for any contribution to any other parties.

(c) This section shall not apply to co-obligors who have expressly agreed in writing to an apportionment of liability for losses or claims among themselves.

(d) This section shall not apply to a release, dismissal with or without prejudice, or a covenant not to sue or not to enforce judgment given to a co-obligor on an alleged contract debt where the contract was made prior to January 1, 1988. *(Added by Stats.1957, c. 1700, § 1. Amended by Stats.1987, c. 677, § 2; Stats.2011, c. 296, § 39.)*

§ 877.5. Sliding Scale Recovery Agreement; Disclosure to Court and Jury; Service of Notice of Intent to Enter

(a) Where an agreement or covenant is made which provides for a sliding scale recovery agreement between one or more, but not all, alleged defendant tortfeasors and the plaintiff or plaintiffs:

(1) The parties entering into any such agreement or covenant shall promptly inform the court in which the action is pending of the existence of the agreement or covenant and its terms and provisions.

(2) If the action is tried before a jury, and a defendant party to the agreement is called as a witness at trial, the court shall, upon motion of a party, disclose to the jury the existence and content of the agreement or covenant, unless the court finds that such disclosure will create substantial danger of undue prejudice, of confusing the issues, or of misleading the jury.

The jury disclosure herein required shall be no more than necessary to inform the jury of the possibility that the agreement may bias the testimony of the witness.

(b) As used in this section, a "sliding scale recovery agreement" means an agreement or covenant between a plaintiff or plaintiffs and one or more, but not all, alleged tortfeasor defendants, which limits the liability of the agreeing tortfeasor defendants to an amount which is dependent upon the amount of recovery which the plaintiff is able to recover from the nonagreeing defendant or defendants. This includes, but is not limited to, agreements within the scope of Section 877, and agreements in the form of a loan from the agreeing tortfeasor defendant or defendants to the plaintiff or plaintiffs which is repayable in whole or in part from the recovery against the nonagreeing tortfeasor defendant or defendants.

(c) No sliding scale recovery agreement is effective unless, at least 72 hours prior to entering into the agreement, a notice of intent to enter into an agreement has been served on all nonsignatory alleged defendant tortfeasors. However, upon a showing of good cause, the court or a judge thereof may allow a shorter time. The failure to comply with the notice requirements of this subdivision shall not constitute good cause to delay commencement of trial. *(Added by Stats.1977, c. 568, § 1. Amended by Stats.1987, c. 1201, § 3; Stats.1987, c. 1202, § 1; Stats.1990, c. 17, § 1.)*

§ 877.6. Determination of Good Faith of Settlement With One or More Tortfeasors or Co-obligors; Review by Writ of Mandate; Tolling of Time Limitations

(a)(1) Any party to an action in which it is alleged that two or more parties are joint tortfeasors or co-obligors on a contract debt shall be entitled to a hearing on the issue of the good faith of a settlement entered into by the plaintiff or other claimant and one or more alleged tortfeasors or co-obligors, upon giving notice in the manner provided in subdivision (b) of Section 1005. Upon a showing of good cause, the court may shorten the time for giving the required notice to permit the determination of the issue to be made before the commencement of the trial of the action, or before the verdict or judgment if settlement is made after the trial has commenced.

(2) In the alternative, a settling party may give notice of settlement to all parties and to the court, together with an application for determination of good faith settlement and a proposed order. The application shall indicate the settling parties, and the basis, terms, and amount of the settlement. The notice, application, and proposed order shall be given by certified mail, return receipt requested, or by personal service. Proof of service shall be filed with the court. Within 25 days of the mailing of the notice, application, and proposed order, or within 20 days of personal service, a nonsettling party may file a notice of motion to contest the good

faith of the settlement. If none of the nonsettling parties files a motion within 25 days of mailing of the notice, application, and proposed order, or within 20 days of personal service, the court may approve the settlement. The notice by a nonsettling party shall be given in the manner provided in subdivision (b) of Section 1005. However, this paragraph shall not apply to settlements in which a confidentiality agreement has been entered into regarding the case or the terms of the settlement.

(b) The issue of the good faith of a settlement may be determined by the court on the basis of affidavits served with the notice of hearing, and any counter affidavits filed in response, or the court may, in its discretion, receive other evidence at the hearing.

(c) A determination by the court that the settlement was made in good faith shall bar any other joint tortfeasor or co-obligor from any further claims against the settling tortfeasor or co-obligor for equitable comparative contribution, or partial or comparative indemnity, based on comparative negligence or comparative fault.

(d) The party asserting the lack of good faith shall have the burden of proof on that issue.

(e) When a determination of the good faith or lack of good faith of a settlement is made, any party aggrieved by the determination may petition the proper court to review the determination by writ of mandate. The petition for writ of mandate shall be filed within 20 days after service of written notice of the determination, or within any additional time not exceeding 20 days as the trial court may allow.

(1) The court shall, within 30 days of the receipt of all materials to be filed by the parties, determine whether or not the court will hear the writ and notify the parties of its determination.

(2) If the court grants a hearing on the writ, the hearing shall be given special precedence over all other civil matters on the calendar of the court except those matters to which equal or greater precedence on the calendar is granted by law.

(3) The running of any period of time after which an action would be subject to dismissal pursuant to the applicable provisions of Chapter 1.5 (commencing with Section 583.110) of Title 8 of Part 2 shall be tolled during the period of review of a determination pursuant to this subdivision. *(Added by Stats.1980, c. 562, § 1. Amended by Stats.1984, c. 311, § 1; Stats.1985, c. 621, § 2; Stats.1987, c. 677, § 3; Stats.1988, c. 128, § 1; Stats.1989, c. 693, § 5; Stats.1992, c. 876, § 6; Stats.1995, c. 796, § 13; Stats.2001, c. 812, § 7; Stats.2017, c. 64, § 1.)*

TITLE 13. APPEALS IN CIVIL ACTIONS

Chapter 1. Appeals in General

§ 901. Review of Judgment or Order; Authority of Judicial Council

A judgment or order in a civil action or proceeding may be reviewed as prescribed in this title. The Judicial Council shall prescribe rules for the practice and procedure on appeal not inconsistent with the provisions of this title. *(Added by Stats.1968, c. 385, § 2.)*

§ 902. Appeal by Party Aggrieved; Appellant and Respondent Defined

Any party aggrieved may appeal in the cases prescribed in this title. A party appealing is known as an appellant, and an adverse party as a respondent. *(Added by Stats.1968, c. 385, p. 812, § 2.)*

§ 904.1. Appealable Judgments and Orders

(a) An appeal may be taken from a superior court in the following cases:

(1) From a judgment, except an interlocutory judgment, other than as provided in paragraphs (8), (9), and (11), or a judgment of contempt that is made final and conclusive by Section 1222.

(2) From an order made after a judgment made appealable by paragraph (1).

(3) From an order granting a motion to quash service of summons or granting a motion to stay the action on the ground of inconvenient forum, or from a written order of dismissal under Section 581d following an order granting a motion to dismiss the action on the ground of inconvenient forum.

(4) From an order granting a new trial or denying a motion for judgment notwithstanding the verdict.

(5) From an order discharging or refusing to discharge an attachment or granting a right to attach order.

(6) From an order granting or dissolving an injunction, or refusing to grant or dissolve an injunction.

(7) From an order appointing a receiver.

(8) From an interlocutory judgment, order, or decree, made or entered in an action to redeem real or personal property from a mortgage thereof, or a lien thereon, determining the right to redeem and directing an accounting.

(9) From an interlocutory judgment in an action for partition determining the rights and interests of the respective parties and directing partition to be made.

(10) From an order or decree made appealable by the Probate Code or the Family Code.

(11) From an interlocutory judgment directing payment of monetary sanctions by a party or an attorney for a party if the amount exceeds five thousand dollars ($5,000).

(12) From an order directing payment of monetary sanctions by a party or an attorney for a party if the amount exceeds five thousand dollars ($5,000).

(13) From an order granting or denying a special motion to strike under Sections 425.16 and 425.19.

(14) From a final order or judgment in a bifurcated proceeding regarding child custody or visitation rights.

(b) Sanction orders or judgments of five thousand dollars ($5,000) or less against a party or an attorney for a party may be reviewed on an appeal by that party after entry of final judgment in the main action, or, at the discretion of the court of appeal, may be reviewed upon petition for an extraordinary writ. *(Added by Stats.1968, c. 385, § 2. Amended by Stats.1969, c. 1611, § 21; Stats.1971, c. 1210, § 8; Stats.1978, c. 395, § 1; Stats.1982, c. 931, § 1; Stats.1982, c. 1198, § 63.2; Stats.1983, c. 1159, § 12; Stats.1984, c. 29, § 2; Stats.1988, c. 1447, § 1; Stats.1989, c. 1416, § 25; Stats.1992, c. 163, § 54; Stats.1993, c. 456, § 12; Stats.1998, c. 931, § 100; Stats.1999, c. 960, § 2; Stats.2006, c. 567, § 8; Stats.2007, c. 43, § 9; Stats.2017, c. 41, § 1; Stats.2023, c. 779, § 2.)*

§ 906. Powers of Reviewing Court; Matters Reviewable

Upon an appeal pursuant to Section 904.1 or 904.2, the reviewing court may review the verdict or decision and any intermediate ruling, proceeding, order or decision which involves the merits or necessarily affects the judgment or order appealed from or which substantially affects the rights of a party, including, on any appeal from the judgment, any order on motion for a new trial, and may affirm, reverse or modify any judgment or order appealed from and may direct the proper judgment or order to be entered, and may, if necessary or proper, direct a new trial or further proceedings to be had. The respondent, or party in whose favor the judgment was given, may, without appealing from such judgment, request the reviewing court to and it may review any of the foregoing matters for the purpose of determining whether or not the appellant was prejudiced by the error or errors upon which he relies for reversal or modification of the judgment from which the appeal is taken. The provisions of this section do not authorize the reviewing court to review any decision or order from which an appeal might have been taken. *(Added by Stats.1968, c. 385, § 2. Amended by Stats.1976, c. 1288, § 16.)*

§ 907. Frivolous Appeal; Appeal for Delay; Damages

When it appears to the reviewing court that the appeal was frivolous or taken solely for delay, it may add to the costs on appeal such damages as may be just. *(Added by Stats.1968, c. 385, § 2.)*

§ 909. Factual Determinations on Appeal; Nonjury Cases; Additional Evidence; Giving or Directing Entry of Judgment or Order; Construction of Section

In all cases where trial by jury is not a matter of right or where trial by jury has been waived, the reviewing court may make factual determinations contrary to or in addition to those made by the trial court. The factual determinations may be based on the evidence adduced before the trial court either with or without the taking of evidence by the reviewing court. The reviewing court may for the purpose of making the factual determinations or for any other purpose in the interests of justice, take additional evidence of or concerning facts occurring at any time prior to the decision of the appeal, and may give or direct the entry of any judgment or order and may make any further or other order as the case may require. This section shall be liberally construed to the end among others that, where feasible, causes may be finally disposed of by a single appeal and without further proceedings in the trial court except where in the interests of justice a new trial is required on some or all of the issues. *(Added by Stats.1968, c. 385, § 2. Amended by Stats.1981, c. 900, § 7.)*

TITLE 14. MISCELLANEOUS PROVISIONS

Chapter 2. Bonds and Undertakings

§ 996.440. Bond in Action or Proceeding; Motion to Enforce; Judgment; Trial; Stay

(a) If a bond is given in an action or proceeding, the liability on the bond may be enforced on motion made in the court without the necessity of an independent action.

(b) The motion shall not be made until after entry of the final judgment in the action or proceeding in which the bond is given and the time for appeal has expired or, if an appeal is taken, until the appeal is finally determined. The motion shall not be made or notice of motion served more than one year after the later of the preceding dates.

(c) Notice of motion shall be served on the principal and sureties at least 30 days before the time set for hearing of the motion. The notice shall state the amount of the claim and shall be supported by affidavits setting forth the facts on which the claim is based. The notice and affidavits shall be served in accordance with any procedure authorized by Chapter 5 (commencing with Section 1010).

(d) Judgment shall be entered against the principal and sureties in accordance with the motion unless the principal or sureties serve and file affidavits in opposition to the motion showing such facts as may be deemed by the judge hearing the motion sufficient to present a triable issue of fact. If such a showing is made, the issues to be tried shall be specified by the court. Trial shall be by the court and shall be set for the earliest date convenient to the court, allowing sufficient time for such discovery proceedings as may be requested.

(e) The principal and sureties shall not obtain a stay of the proceedings pending determination of any conflicting claims among beneficiaries. *(Added by Stats.1982, c. 998, § 1.)*

Chapter 3. Offers by a Party to Compromise

§ 998. Withholding or Augmenting Costs Following Rejection or Acceptance of Offer to Allow Judgment

(a) The costs allowed under Sections 1031 and 1032 shall be withheld or augmented as provided in this section.

(b) Not less than 10 days prior to commencement of trial or arbitration (as provided in Section 1281 or 1295) of a dispute to be resolved by arbitration, any party may serve an offer in writing upon any other party to the action to allow judgment to be taken or an award to be entered in accordance with the terms and conditions stated at that time. The written offer shall include a statement of the offer, containing the terms and conditions of the judgment or award, and a provision that allows the accepting party to indicate acceptance of the offer by signing a statement that the offer is accepted. Any acceptance of the offer, whether made on the document containing the offer or on a separate document of acceptance, shall be in writing and shall be signed by counsel for the accepting party or, if not represented by counsel, by the accepting party.

(1) If the offer is accepted, the offer with proof of acceptance shall be filed and the clerk or the judge shall enter judgment accordingly. In the case of an arbitration, the offer with proof of acceptance shall be filed with the arbitrator or arbitrators who shall promptly render an award accordingly.

(2) If the offer is not accepted prior to trial or arbitration or within 30 days after it is made, whichever occurs first, it shall be deemed withdrawn, and cannot be given in evidence upon the trial or arbitration.

(3) For purposes of this subdivision, a trial or arbitration shall be deemed to be actually commenced at the beginning of the opening statement of the plaintiff or counsel, or, if there is no opening statement, at the time of the administering of the oath or affirmation to the first witness, or the introduction of any evidence.

(c)(1) If an offer made by a defendant is not accepted and the plaintiff fails to obtain a more favorable judgment or award, the plaintiff shall not recover their postoffer costs and shall pay the defendant's costs from the time of the offer. In addition, in any action or proceeding other than an eminent domain action, the court or arbitrator, in its discretion, may require the plaintiff to pay a reasonable sum to cover postoffer costs of the services of expert witnesses, who are not regular employees of any party, actually incurred and reasonably necessary in either, or both, preparation for trial or arbitration, or during trial or arbitration, of the case by the defendant.

(2)(A) In determining whether the plaintiff obtains a more favorable judgment, the court or arbitrator shall exclude the postoffer costs.

(B) It is the intent of the Legislature in enacting subparagraph (A) to supersede the holding in Encinitas Plaza Real v. Knight, 209 Cal.App.3d 996, 257 Cal.Rptr. 646, that attorney's fees awarded to the prevailing party were not costs for purposes of this section but were part of the judgment.

(d) If an offer made by a plaintiff is not accepted and the defendant fails to obtain a more favorable judgment or award in any action or proceeding other than an eminent domain action, the court or arbitrator, in its discretion may require the defendant to pay a reasonable sum to cover postoffer costs of the services of expert witnesses, who are not regular employees of any party, actually incurred and reasonably necessary in either, or both, preparation for trial or arbitration, or during trial or arbitration, of the case by the plaintiff, in addition to plaintiff's costs.

(e) If an offer made by a defendant is not accepted and the plaintiff fails to obtain a more favorable judgment or award, the costs under this section, from the time of the offer, shall be deducted from any damages awarded in favor of the plaintiff. If the costs awarded under this section exceed the amount of the damages awarded to the plaintiff the net amount shall be awarded to the defendant and judgment or award shall be entered accordingly.

(f) Police officers shall be deemed to be expert witnesses for the purposes of this section. For purposes of this section, "plaintiff" includes a cross-complainant and "defendant" includes a cross-defendant. Any judgment or award entered pursuant to this section shall be deemed to be a compromise settlement.

(g) This chapter does not apply to either of the following:

(1) An offer that is made by a plaintiff in an eminent domain action.

(2) Any enforcement action brought in the name of the people of the State of California by the Attorney General, the Insurance Commissioner, a district attorney, or a city attorney, acting as a public prosecutor.

(h) The costs for services of expert witnesses for trial under subdivisions (c) and (d) shall not exceed those specified in Section 68092.5 of the Government Code.

(i) This section shall not apply to labor arbitrations filed pursuant to memoranda of understanding under the Ralph C. Dills Act (Chapter 10.3 (commencing with Section 3512) of Division 4 of Title 1 of the Government Code). *(Added by Stats.1971, c. 1679, § 3. Amended by Stats.1977, c. 458, § 1; Stats.1986, c. 540, § 14; Stats.1987, c. 1080, § 8; Stats.1994, c. 332, § 1; Stats.1997, c. 892, § 1; Stats.1999, c. 353, § 1; Stats.2001, c. 153, § 1; Stats.2005, c. 706, § 13; Stats.2015, c. 345, § 2; Stats.2024, c. 444, § 2.)*

Chapter 3.5 Confidential Settlement Agreements

§ 1001. Prohibition of Provisions in Settlement Agreements that Prevent Disclosure of Factual Information Relating to Certain Claims of Sexual Assault, Sexual Harassment, or Harassment or Discrimination Based on Sex

(a) Notwithstanding any other law, a provision within a settlement agreement that prevents or restricts the disclosure of factual information related to a claim filed in a civil action or a complaint filed in an administrative action, regarding any of the following, is prohibited:

(1) An act of sexual assault that is not governed by subdivision (a) of Section 1002.

(2) An act of sexual harassment, as defined in Section 51.9 of the Civil Code.

(3) An act of workplace harassment or discrimination, failure to prevent an act of workplace harassment or discrimination, or an act of retaliation against a person for reporting or opposing harassment or discrimination, as described in subdivisions (a), (h), (i), (j), and (k) of Section 12940 of the Government Code.

(4) An act of harassment or discrimination, or an act of retaliation against a person for reporting harassment or discrimination by the owner of a housing accommodation, as described in Section 12955 of the Government Code.

(b) Notwithstanding any other law, in a civil matter described in paragraphs (1) to (4), inclusive, of subdivision (a), a court shall not enter, by stipulation or otherwise, an order that restricts the disclosure of information in a manner that conflicts with subdivision (a).

(c) Notwithstanding subdivisions (a) and (b), a provision that shields the identity of the claimant and all facts that could lead to the discovery of the claimant's identity, including pleadings filed in court, may be included within a settlement agreement at the request of the claimant. This subdivision does not apply if a government agency or public official is a party to the settlement agreement.

(d) Except as authorized by subdivision (c), a provision within a settlement agreement that prevents or restricts the disclosure of factual information related to the claim described in subdivision (a) that is entered into on or after January 1, 2019, is void as a matter of law and against public policy.

(e) This section does not prohibit the entry or enforcement of a provision in any agreement that precludes the disclosure of the amount paid in settlement of a claim.

(f) In determining the factual foundation of a cause of action for civil damages under subdivision (a), a court may consider the pleadings and other papers in the record, or any other findings of the court.

(g) The amendments made to paragraphs (3) and (4) of subdivision (a) by Senate Bill 331 of the 2021–22 Regular Session apply only to agreements entered into on or after January 1, 2022. All other amendments made to this section by Senate Bill 331 of the 2021–22 Regular Session shall not be construed as substantive changes, but instead as merely clarifying existing law. *(Added by Stats.2018, c. 953, § 1. Amended by Stats.2021, c. 638, § 1; Stats.2022, c. 28, § 26.)*

§ 1002. Settlement Agreement Provisions or Court Orders Preventing Disclosure of Factual Information Relating to Action; Actions Where Prohibited

(a) Notwithstanding any other law, a provision within a settlement agreement that prevents the disclosure of factual information related to the action is prohibited in any civil action the factual foundation for which establishes a cause of action for civil damages for any of the following:

(1) An act that may be prosecuted as a felony sex offense.

(2) An act of childhood sexual assault, as defined in Section 340.1.

(3) An act of sexual exploitation of a minor, as defined in Section 11165.1 of the Penal Code, or conduct prohibited with respect to a minor pursuant to Section 311.1, 311.5, or 311.6 of the Penal Code.

(4) An act of sexual assault, as defined in paragraphs (1) to (8), inclusive, of subdivision (e) of Section 15610.63 of the Welfare and Institutions Code, against an elder or dependent adult, as defined in Sections 15610.23 and 15610.27 of the Welfare and Institutions Code.

(b) Notwithstanding any other law, in a civil action described in paragraphs (1) to (4), inclusive, of subdivision (a), a court shall not enter, by stipulation or otherwise, an order that restricts the disclosure of information in a manner that conflicts with subdivision (a).

(c) Subdivisions (a) and (b) do not preclude an agreement preventing the disclosure of any medical information or personal identifying information, as defined in subdivision (b) of Section 530.55 of the Penal Code, regarding the victim of the offense listed in subdivision (a) or of any information revealing the nature of the relationship between the victim and the defendant. This subdivision shall not be construed to limit the right of a crime victim to disclose this information.

(d) Except as authorized by subdivision (c), a provision within a settlement agreement that prevents the disclosure of factual information related to the action described in subdivision (a) that is entered into on or after January 1, 2017, is void as a matter of law and against public policy.

(e) An attorney's failure to comply with the requirements of this section by demanding that a provision be included in a settlement agreement that prevents the disclosure of factual information related to the action described in subdivision (a) that is not otherwise authorized by subdivision (c) as a condition of settlement, or advising a client to sign an agreement that includes such a provision, may be grounds for professional discipline and the State Bar of California shall investigate and take appropriate action in any such case brought to its attention. *(Added by Stats.2006, c. 151, § 1. Amended by Stats.2016, c. 876, § 1; Stats.2017, c. 561, § 24; Stats.2019, c. 861, § 2; Stats.2023, c. 131, § 22.)*

Chapter 4. Motions and Orders

§ 1003. Order and Motion Defined

Every direction of a court or judge, made or entered in writing, and not included in a judgment, is denominated an order. An application for an order is a motion. *(Enacted 1872. Amended by Stats.1933, c. 744, § 173; Stats.1951, c. 1737, § 131, operative Jan. 1, 1952.)*

§ 1005. Written Notice for Motions; Service and Filing of Moving and Supporting Papers

(a) Written notice shall be given, as prescribed in subdivisions (b) and (c), for the following motions:

(1) Notice of Application and Hearing for Writ of Attachment under Section 484.040.

(2) Notice of Application and Hearing for Claim and Delivery under Section 512.030.

(3) Notice of Hearing for Claim of Exemption under Section 706.105.

(4) Motion to Quash Summons pursuant to subdivision (b) of Section 418.10.

(5) Motion for Determination of Good Faith Settlement pursuant to Section 877.6.

(6) Hearing for Discovery of Peace Officer Personnel Records in a civil action pursuant to Section 1043 of the Evidence Code.

(7) Notice of Hearing of Third-Party Claim Pursuant to Section 720.320.

(8) Motion for an Order to Attend Deposition more than 150 miles from deponent's residence pursuant to Section 2025.060.

(9) Notice of Hearing of Application for Relief pursuant to Section 946.6 of the Government Code.

(10) Motion to Set Aside Default or Default Judgment and for Leave to Defend Actions pursuant to Section 473.5.

(11) Motion to Expunge Notice of Pendency of Action pursuant to Section 405.30.

(12) Motion to Set Aside Default and for Leave to Amend pursuant to Section 585.5.

(13) Any other proceeding under this code in which notice is required and no other time or method is prescribed by law or by court or judge.

(b) Unless otherwise ordered or specifically provided by law, all moving and supporting papers shall be served and filed at least 16 court days before the hearing. The moving and supporting papers served shall be a copy of the papers filed or to be filed with the court. However, if the notice is served by mail, the required 16-day period of notice before the hearing shall be increased by five calendar days if the place of mailing and the place of address are within the State of California, 10 calendar days if either the place of mailing or the place of address is outside the State of California but within the United States, 12 calendar days if the place of address is the Secretary of State's address confidentiality program (Chapter 3.1 (commencing with Section 6205) of Division 7 of Title 1 of the Government Code), and 20 calendar days if either the place of mailing or the place of address is outside the United States, and if the notice is served by facsimile transmission, express mail, or another method of delivery providing for overnight delivery, the required 16-day period of notice before the hearing shall be increased by two calendar days. Section 1013, which extends the time within which a right may be exercised or an act may be done, does not apply to a notice of motion, papers opposing a motion, or reply papers governed by this section. All papers opposing a motion so noticed shall be filed with the court and a copy served on each party at least nine court days, and all reply papers at least five court days before the hearing.

The court, or a judge thereof, may prescribe a shorter time.

(c) Notwithstanding any other provision of this section, all papers opposing a motion and all reply papers shall be served by personal delivery, facsimile transmission, express mail, or other means consistent with

Sections 1010, 1011, 1012, and 1013, and reasonably calculated to ensure delivery to the other party or parties not later than the close of the next business day after the time the opposing papers or reply papers, as applicable, are filed. This subdivision applies to the service of opposition and reply papers regarding motions for summary judgment or summary adjudication, in addition to the motions listed in subdivision (a).

The court, or a judge thereof, may prescribe a shorter time. *(Amended by Stats.1980, c. 196, § 1; Stats.1981, c. 197, § 1; Stats.1984, c. 352, § 2; Stats.1986, c. 246, § 1; Stats.1989, c. 693, § 6; Stats.1990, c. 1491, § 7; Stats.1991, c. 1090, § 5; Stats.1992, c. 339, § 2; Stats.1993, c. 456, § 14.5; Stats.1997, c. 571, § 1.3; Stats.1998, c. 932, § 18; Stats.1999, c. 43, § 1; Stats.2002, c. 806, § 16; Stats.2004, c. 171, § 3; Stats.2004, c. 182, § 13, operative July 1, 2005; Stats.2005, c. 294, § 3; Stats.2019, c. 585, § 1; Stats.2022, c. 686, § 1.)*

§ 1008. Application to Reconsider and Modify or Revoke Prior Order; Affidavit; Noncompliance; Revocation of Order; Contempt

(a) When an application for an order has been made to a judge, or to a court, and refused in whole or in part, or granted, or granted conditionally, or on terms, any party affected by the order may, within 10 days after service upon the party of written notice of entry of the order and based upon new or different facts, circumstances, or law, make application to the same judge or court that made the order, to reconsider the matter and modify, amend, or revoke the prior order. The party making the application shall state by affidavit what application was made before, when and to what judge, what order or decisions were made, and what new or different facts, circumstances, or law are claimed to be shown.

(b) A party who originally made an application for an order which was refused in whole or part, or granted conditionally or on terms, may make a subsequent application for the same order upon new or different facts, circumstances, or law, in which case it shall be shown by affidavit what application was made before, when and to what judge, what order or decisions were made, and what new or different facts, circumstances, or law are claimed to be shown. For a failure to comply with this subdivision, any order made on a subsequent application may be revoked or set aside on ex parte motion.

(c) If a court at any time determines that there has been a change of law that warrants it to reconsider a prior order it entered, it may do so on its own motion and enter a different order.

(d) A violation of this section may be punished by contempt and with sanctions as allowed by Section 128.7. In addition, an order made contrary to this section may be revoked by the judge or commissioner who made it, or vacated by a judge of the court in which the action or proceeding is pending.

(e) This section specifies the court's jurisdiction with regard to applications for reconsideration of its orders and renewals of previous motions, and applies to all applications to reconsider any order of a judge or court, or for the renewal of a previous motion, whether the order deciding the previous matter or motion is interim or final. No application to reconsider any order or for the renewal of a previous motion may be considered by any judge or court unless made according to this section.

(f) For the purposes of this section, an alleged new or different law shall not include a later enacted statute without a retroactive application.

(g) An order denying a motion for reconsideration made pursuant to subdivision (a) is not separately appealable. However, if the order that was the subject of a motion for reconsideration is appealable, the denial of the motion for reconsideration is reviewable as part of an appeal from that order.

(h) This section applies to all applications for interim orders. *(Added by Stats.1978, c. 631, § 2. Amended by Stats.1992, c. 460, § 4; Stats.1998, c. 200, § 2; Stats.2011, c. 78, § 1.)*

Chapter 5. Notices, and Filing and Service of Papers

§ 1010. Notices; Writing; Contents; Supporting Papers; Service; Defaulting Party

Notices must be in writing, and the notice of a motion, other than for a new trial, must state when, and the grounds upon which it will be made, and the papers, if any, upon which it is to be based. If any such paper has not previously been served upon the party to be notified and was not filed by him, a copy of such paper must accompany the notice. Notices and other papers may be served upon the party or attorney in the manner prescribed in this chapter, when not otherwise provided by this code. No bill of exceptions, notice of appeal, or other notice or paper, other than amendments to the pleadings, or an amended pleading, need be served upon any party whose default has been duly entered or who has not appeared in the action or proceeding. *(Enacted 1872. Amended by Stats.1907, c. 327, § 1; Stats.1935, c. 722, § 28.)*

§ 1010.6. Electronic Service of Documents; Local Rules for Electronic Filing; Uniform Rules

(a) A document may be served electronically in an action filed with the court as provided in this section, in accordance with rules adopted pursuant to subdivision (h).

(1) For purposes of this section:

(A) "Electronic service" means service of a document, on a person, by either electronic transmission or electronic notification. Electronic service may be performed directly by a person, including a party, by a person's agent, including the person's attorney, or through an electronic filing service provider, and by a court.

(B) "Electronic transmission" means the transmission of a document by electronic means to the electronic service address at or through which a person receives electronic service.

(C) "Electronic notification" means the notification of the person that a document is served by sending an electronic message to the electronic address at or through which the person receives electronic service, specifying the exact name of the document served, and providing a hyperlink at which the served document may be viewed and downloaded.

(D) "Electronic filing" means the electronic transmission to a court of a document presented for filing in electronic form. For purposes of this section, this definition of electronic filing concerns the activity of filing and does not include the processing and review of the document and its entry into the court's records, which are necessary for a document to be officially filed.

(2) If a document is required to be served by certified or registered mail, electronic service of the document is not authorized.

(3)(A) If a document may be served by mail, express mail, overnight delivery, or facsimile transmission, electronic service of that document is deemed complete at the time of the electronic transmission of the document or at the time that the electronic notification of service of the document is sent.

(B) Any period of notice, or any right or duty to do any act or make any response within any period or on a date certain after the service of the document, which time period or date is prescribed by statute or rule of court, shall be extended after service by electronic means by two court days, but the extension shall not apply to extend the time for filing any of the following:

(i) A notice of intention to move for new trial.

(ii) A notice of intention to move to vacate judgment under Section 663a.

(iii) A notice of appeal.

(C) This extension applies in the absence of a specific exception provided by any other statute or rule of court.

(4) Any document that is served electronically between 12:00 a.m. and 11:59:59 p.m. on a court day shall be deemed served on that court day. Any document that is served electronically on a noncourt day shall be deemed served on the next court day.

(5) Confidential or sealed records shall be electronically served through encrypted methods to ensure that the documents are not improperly disclosed.

(b)(1) This subdivision applies to mandatory electronic service. The court may order electronic service on a person represented by counsel who has appeared in an action or proceeding.

(2) A person represented by counsel, who has appeared in an action or proceeding, shall accept electronic service of a notice or document that may be served by mail, express mail, overnight delivery, or facsimile transmission.

(3) Before first serving a represented person electronically, the person effecting service shall confirm the appropriate electronic service address for the counsel being served.

(4) A person represented by counsel shall, upon the request of any person who has appeared in an action or proceeding and who provides an electronic service address, electronically serve the requesting person with any notice or document that may be served by mail, express mail, overnight delivery, or facsimile transmission.

(c)(1) This subdivision applies to electronic service by consent of an unrepresented person in a civil action.

(2) An unrepresented party may consent to receive electronic service.

(3) Express consent to electronic service may be given by either of the following:

(i) Serving a notice on all parties and filing the notice with the court.

(ii) Manifesting affirmative consent through electronic means with the court or the court's electronic filing service provider, and concurrently providing the party's electronic address with that consent for the purpose of receiving electronic service. The act of electronic filing shall not be construed as express consent.

(4) A person who has provided express consent to accept service electronically may withdraw consent at any time by completing and filing with the court the appropriate Judicial Council form.

(5) Consent, or the withdrawal of consent, to receive electronic service may only be completed by a person entitled to service.

(d) On and after July 1, 2025, in any action in which a party or other person is subject to mandatory electronic service under subdivision (b) or has consented to electronic service under subdivision (c), the court shall electronically serve, to a person subject to mandatory electronic service or who consented to electronic service, any document issued by the court that the court is required to transmit, deliver, or serve. The electronic service of documents by the court shall have the same legal effect as service by mail, except as provided in paragraph (3) of subdivision (a).

(e) A trial court may adopt local rules permitting electronic filing of documents, subject to rules adopted by the Judicial Council pursuant to subdivision (h) and the following conditions:

(1) A document that is filed electronically shall have the same legal effect as an original paper document.

(2)(A) When a document to be filed requires the signature of any person, not under penalty of perjury, the document shall be deemed to have been signed by that person if filed electronically and if either of the following conditions is satisfied:

(i) The filer is the signer.

(ii) The person has signed the document pursuant to the procedure set forth in the California Rules of Court.

(B) When a document to be filed requires the signature, under penalty of perjury, of any person, the document shall be deemed to have been signed by that person if filed electronically and if either of the following conditions is satisfied:

(i) The person has signed a printed form of the document before, or on the same day as, the date of filing. The attorney or other person filing the document represents, by the act of filing, that the declarant has complied with this section. The attorney or other person filing the document shall maintain the printed form of the document bearing the original signature until final disposition of the case, as defined in subdivision (c) of Section 68151 of the Government Code, and make it available for review and copying upon the request of the court or any party to the action or proceeding in which it is filed.

(ii) The person has signed the document using a computer or other technology pursuant to the procedure set forth in a rule of court adopted by the Judicial Council by January 1, 2019.

(3) Any document received electronically by the court between 12:00 a.m. and 11:59:59 p.m. on a court day shall be deemed filed on that court day. Any document that is received electronically on a noncourt day shall be deemed filed on the next court day.

(4)(A) Whichever of a court, an electronic filing service provider, or an electronic filing manager is the first to receive a document submitted for electronic filing shall promptly send a confirmation of receipt of the document indicating the date and time of receipt to the party or person who submitted the document.

(B) If a document received by the court under subparagraph (A) complies with filing requirements and all required filing fees have been paid, the court shall promptly send confirmation that the document has been filed to the party or person who submitted the document.

(C) If the clerk of the court does not file a document received by the court under subparagraph (A) because the document does not comply with applicable filing requirements or the required filing fee has not been paid, the court shall promptly send notice of the rejection of the document for filing to the party or person who submitted the document. The notice of rejection shall state the reasons that the document was rejected for filing and include the date the clerk of the court sent the notice.

(D) If the court utilizes an electronic filing service provider or electronic filing manager to send the notice of rejection described in subparagraph (C), the electronic filing service provider or electronic filing manager shall promptly send the notice of rejection to the party or person who submitted the document. A notice of rejection sent pursuant to this subparagraph shall include the date the electronic filing service provider or electronic filing manager sent the notice.

(E) If the clerk of the court does not file a complaint or cross complaint because the complaint or cross complaint does not comply with applicable filing requirements or the required filing fee has not been paid, any statute of limitations applicable to the causes of action alleged in the complaint or cross complaint shall be tolled for the period beginning on the date on which the court received the document and as shown on the confirmation of receipt described in subparagraph (A), through the later of either the date on which the clerk of the court sent the notice of rejection described in subparagraph (C) or the date on which the electronic filing service provider or electronic filing manager sent the notice of rejection as described in subparagraph (D), plus one additional day if the complaint or cross complaint is subsequently submitted in a form that corrects the errors which caused the document to be rejected. The party filing the complaint or cross complaint shall not make any change to the complaint or cross complaint other than those required to correct the errors which caused the document to be rejected.

(5) Upon electronic filing of a complaint, petition, or other document that must be served with a summons, a trial court, upon request of the party filing the action, shall issue a summons with the court seal and the case number. The court shall keep the summons in its records and shall electronically transmit a copy of the summons to the requesting party. Personal service of a printed form of the electronic summons shall have the same legal effect as personal service of an original summons.

(6) The court shall permit a party or attorney to file an application for waiver of court fees and costs, in lieu of requiring the payment of the filing fee, as part of the process involving the electronic filing of a document. The court shall consider and determine the application in accordance with Article 6 (commencing with Section 68630) of Chapter 2 of Title 8 of the Government Code and shall not require the party or attorney to submit any documentation other than that set forth in Article 6 (commencing with Section 68630) of Chapter 2 of Title 8 of the Government Code. The court, an electronic filing service provider, or an electronic filing manager shall waive any fees charged to a party or the party's attorney if the party has been granted a waiver of court fees pursuant to Section 68631 of the Government Code or if the party is indigent or being represented by the public defender or court-appointed counsel. The electronic filing manager or electronic filing service provider shall not seek payment from the court of any fee waived by the court. This section does not require the court to waive a filing fee that is not otherwise waivable.

(7) If a party electronically files a filing that is exempt from the payment of filing fees under any other law, including a filing described in Section 212 of the Welfare and Institutions Code or Section 6103.9, subdivision (b) of Section 70617, or Section 70672 of the Government Code, the party shall not be required to pay any court fees associated with the electronic filing. An electronic filing service provider or an electronic filing manager shall not seek payment of these fees from the court.

(8) A fee, if any, charged by the court, an electronic filing service provider, or an electronic filing manager to process a payment for filing fees and other court fees shall not exceed the costs incurred in processing the payment.

(9) The court shall not charge fees for electronic filing and service of documents that are more than the court's actual cost of electronic filing and service of the documents.

(f)(1) Except as provided in paragraph (2), if a trial court adopts rules conforming to subdivision (e), it may provide by order, subject to the requirements and conditions stated in paragraphs (2) to (4), inclusive, of subdivision (g), and the rules adopted by the Judicial Council under subdivision (i), that all parties to an action file documents electronically in a class action, a consolidated action, a group of actions, a coordinated action, or an action that is deemed complex under Judicial Council rules, provided that the trial court's order does not cause undue hardship or significant prejudice to any party in the action.

(2) Unrepresented persons are exempt from any mandatory electronic filing imposed pursuant to this subdivision.

(g) A trial court may, by local rule, require electronic filing in civil actions, subject to the requirements and conditions stated in subdivision (e), the rules adopted by the Judicial Council under subdivision (i), and the following conditions:

(1) The court shall have the ability to maintain the official court record in electronic format for all cases where electronic filing is required.

(2) The court and the parties shall have access to more than one electronic filing service provider capable of electronically filing documents with the court or to electronic filing access directly through the court. Any fees charged by an electronic filing service provider shall be reasonable. An electronic filing manager or an electronic filing service provider shall waive any fees charged if the court deems a waiver appropriate, including in instances where a party has received a fee waiver.

(3) The court shall have a procedure for the filing of nonelectronic documents in order to prevent the program from causing undue hardship or significant prejudice to any party in an action, including, but not limited to, unrepresented parties. The Judicial Council shall make a form available to allow a party to seek an exemption from mandatory electronic filing and service on the grounds provided in this paragraph.

(4) Unrepresented persons are exempt from mandatory electronic filing imposed pursuant to this subdivision.

(5) Until January 1, 2021, a local child support agency, as defined in subdivision (h) of Section 17000 of the Family Code, is exempt from a trial court's mandatory electronic filing and service requirements, unless the Department of Child Support Services and the local child support agency determine it has the capacity and functionality to comply with the trial court's mandatory electronic filing and service requirements.

(h) The Judicial Council shall adopt uniform rules for the electronic filing and service of documents in the trial courts of the state, which shall include statewide policies on vendor contracts, privacy, and access to public records, and rules relating to the integrity of electronic service. These rules shall conform to the conditions set forth in this section, as amended from time to time.

(i) The Judicial Council shall adopt uniform rules to permit the mandatory electronic filing and service of documents for specified civil actions in the trial courts of the state, which shall include statewide policies on vendor contracts, privacy, access to public records, unrepresented parties, parties with fee waivers, hardships, reasonable exceptions to electronic filing, and rules relating to the integrity of electronic service. These rules shall conform to the conditions set forth in this section, as amended from time to time.

(j)(1) Any system for the electronic filing and service of documents, including any information technology applications, internet websites and web-based applications, used by an electronic service provider or any other vendor or contractor that provides an electronic filing and service system to a trial court, regardless of the case management system used by the trial court, shall satisfy both of the following requirements:

(A) The system shall be accessible to individuals with disabilities, including parties and attorneys with disabilities, in accordance with Section 508 of the federal Rehabilitation Act of 1973 (29 U.S.C. Sec. 794d), as amended, the regulations implementing that act set forth in Part 1194 of Title 36 of the Code of Federal Regulations and Appendices A, C, and D of that part, and the federal Americans with Disabilities Act of 1990 (42 U.S.C. Sec. 12101 et seq.).

(B) The system shall comply with the Web Content Accessibility Guidelines 2.0 at a Level AA success criteria.

(2) Commencing on June 27, 2017, the vendor or contractor shall provide an accommodation to an individual with a disability in accordance with subparagraph (D) of paragraph (3).

(3) A trial court that contracts with an entity for the provision of a system for electronic filing and service of documents shall require the entity, in the trial court's contract with the entity, to do all of the following:

(A) Test and verify that the entity's system complies with this subdivision and provide the verification to the Judicial Council no later than June 30, 2019.

(B) Respond to, and resolve, any complaints regarding the accessibility of the system that are brought to the attention of the entity.

(C) Designate a lead individual to whom any complaints concerning accessibility may be addressed and post the individual's name and contact information on the entity's internet website.

(D) Provide to an individual with a disability, upon request, an accommodation to enable the individual to file and serve documents electronically at no additional charge for any time period that the entity is not compliant with paragraph (1). Exempting an individual with a disability from mandatory electronic filing and service of documents shall not be deemed an accommodation unless the person chooses that as an accommodation. The vendor or contractor shall clearly state in its internet website that an individual with a disability may request an accommodation and the process for submitting a request for an accommodation.

(4) A trial court that provides electronic filing and service of documents directly to the public shall comply with this subdivision to the same extent as a vendor or contractor that provides electronic filing and services to a trial court.

(5)(A) The Judicial Council shall submit four reports to the appropriate committees of the Legislature relating to the trial courts that have implemented a system of electronic filing and service of documents. The first report is due by June 30, 2018; the second report is due by December 31, 2019; the third report is due by December 31, 2021; and the fourth report is due by December 31, 2023.

(B) The Judicial Council's reports shall include all of the following information:

(i) The name of each court that has implemented a system of electronic filing and service of documents.

(ii) A description of the system of electronic filing and service.

(iii) The name of the entity or entities providing the system.

(iv) A statement as to whether the system complies with this subdivision and, if the system is not fully compliant, a description of the actions that have been taken to make the system compliant.

(6) An entity that contracts with a trial court to provide a system for electronic filing and service of documents shall cooperate with the Judicial Council by providing all information, and by permitting all testing, necessary for the Judicial Council to prepare its reports to the Legislature in a complete and timely manner. *(Added by Stats.1999, c. 514, § 1. Amended by Stats.2001, c. 824, § 10.5; Stats.2005, c. 300, § 5; Stats.2010, c. 156, § 1; Stats.2011, c. 296, § 40; Stats.2012, c. 320, § 1; Stats.2016, c. 461, § 1; Stats.2017, c. 17, § 5, eff. June 27, 2017; Stats.2017, c. 319, § 2; Stats.2018, c. 504, § 1; Stats.2020, c. 112, § 2, eff. Sept. 18, 2020; Stats.2020, c. 215, § 1.5; Stats.2021, c. 124, § 14; Stats.2021, c. 214, § 7; Stats.2022, c. 215, § 1; Stats.2024, c. 151, § 1, eff. July 18, 2024.)*

§ 1011. Personal Service; Service Upon Attorney; Service at Party's Residence

The service may be personal, by delivery to the party or attorney on whom the service is required to be made, or it may be as follows:

(a) If upon an attorney, service may be made at the attorney's office, by leaving the notice or other papers in an envelope or package clearly labeled to identify the attorney being served, with a receptionist or with a person having charge thereof. If there is no person in the office with whom the notice or papers may be left for purposes of this subdivision at the time service is to be effected, service may be made by leaving them between the hours of 9 a.m. and 5 p.m., in a conspicuous place in the office, or, if the attorney's office is not open so as to admit of that service, then service may be made by leaving the notice or papers at the attorney's residence, with some person of not less than 18 years of age, if the attorney's residence is in the same county with his or her office, and, if the attorney's residence is not known or is not in the same county with his or her office, or being in the same county it is not open, or a person 18 years of age or older cannot be found at the attorney's residence, then service may be made by putting the notice or papers, enclosed in a sealed envelope, into the post office or a mail box, subpost office, substation, or mail chute or other like facility regularly maintained by the Government of the United States directed to the attorney at his or her office, if known and otherwise to the attorney's residence, if known. If neither the attorney's office nor residence is known, service may be made by delivering the notice or papers to the address of the attorney or party of record as designated on the court papers, or by delivering to the clerk of the court, for the attorney.

(b) If upon a party, service shall be made in the manner specifically provided in particular cases, or, if no specific provision is made, service may be made by leaving the notice or other paper at the party's residence with some person 18 years of age or older.

(1) Any attempt of service upon a party at the party's residence shall be made between the hours of 8 a.m. and 8 p.m.

(2) If, at the time of service, as provided in paragraph (1), a person 18 years of age or older cannot be found at the party's residence, the notice or papers may be served by mail.

(3) If the party's residence is not known, any attempt of service pursuant to this subdivision may be made by delivering the notice or papers to the clerk of the court, for that party.

(c) If service is made by electronic service, it shall be made pursuant to Section 1010.6 and applicable rules on electric service in the California Rules of Court. *(Enacted 1872. Amended by Stats.1907, c. 327, § 2; Stats.1919, c. 194, § 1; Stats.1933, c. 744, § 178; Stats.1949, c. 456, § 2; Stats.1951, c. 1737, § 135; Stats.1989, c. 1105, § 8; Stats.1994, c. 467, § 1; Stats.2007, c. 263, § 11; Stats.2017, c. 319, § 3; Stats.2018, c. 212, § 1.)*

§ 1014. Appearance Defined; Right to Notices

A defendant appears in an action when the defendant answers, demurs, files a notice of motion to strike, files a notice of motion to transfer pursuant to Section 396b, moves for reclassification pursuant to Section 403.040, gives the plaintiff written notice of appearance, or when an attorney gives notice of appearance for the defendant. After appearance, a defendant or the defendant's attorney is entitled to notice of all subsequent proceedings of which notice is required to be given. Where a defendant has not appeared, service of notice or papers need not be made upon the defendant. *(Enacted 1872. Amended by Stats.1955, c. 1452, § 8; Stats.1969, c. 345, § 5; Stats.1973, c. 20, § 11; Stats.1998, c. 931, § 106; Stats.1999, c. 344, § 15.)*

Chapter 6. Of Costs

§ 1021. Attorney's Fees; Determination by Agreement; Right to Costs

Except as attorney's fees are specifically provided for by statute, the measure and mode of compensation of attorneys and counselors at law is left to the agreement, express or implied, of the parties; but parties to actions or proceedings are entitled to their costs, as hereinafter provided. *(Enacted 1872. Amended by Stats.1933, c. 744, § 180; Stats.1986, c. 377, § 2.)*

§ 1021.5. Attorney Fees; Enforcement of Important Rights Affecting Public Interest

Upon motion, a court may award attorney's fees to a successful party against one or more opposing parties in any action which has resulted in the enforcement of an important right affecting the public interest if: (a) a significant benefit, whether pecuniary or nonpecuniary, has been conferred on the general public or a large class of persons, (b) the necessity and financial burden of private enforcement, or of enforcement by one public entity against another public entity, are such as to make the award appropriate, and (c) such fees should not in the interest of justice be paid out of the recovery, if any. With respect to actions involving public entities, this section applies to allowances against, but not in favor of, public entities, and no claim shall be required to be filed therefor, unless one or more successful parties and one or more opposing parties are public entities, in which case no claim shall be required to be filed therefor under Part 3 (commencing with Section 900) of Division 3.6 of Title 1 of the Government Code.

Attorney's fees awarded to a public entity pursuant to this section shall not be increased or decreased by a multiplier based upon extrinsic circumstances, as discussed in Serrano v. Priest, 20 Cal.3d 25, 49, 141 Cal.Rptr. 315, 328, 569 P.2d 1303, 1317. *(Added by Stats.1977, c. 1197, § 1. Amended by Stats.1993, c. 645, § 2.)*

§ 1032. Prevailing Party in Any Action or Proceeding; Stipulation to Alternative Procedures

(a) As used in this section, unless the context clearly requires otherwise:

(1) "Complaint" includes a cross-complaint.

(2) "Defendant" includes a cross-defendant, a person against whom a complaint is filed, or a party who files an answer in intervention.

(3) "Plaintiff" includes a cross-complainant or a party who files a complaint in intervention.

(4) "Prevailing party" includes the party with a net monetary recovery, a defendant in whose favor a dismissal is entered, a defendant where neither plaintiff nor defendant obtains any relief, and a defendant as against those plaintiffs who do not recover any relief against that defendant. If any party recovers other than monetary relief and in situations other than as specified, the "prevailing party" shall be as determined by the court, and under those circumstances, the court, in its discretion, may allow costs or not and, if allowed may apportion costs between the parties on the same or adverse sides pursuant to rules adopted under Section 1034.

(b) Except as otherwise expressly provided by statute, a prevailing party is entitled as a matter of right to recover costs in any action or proceeding.

(c) Nothing in this section shall prohibit parties from stipulating to alternative procedures for awarding costs in the litigation pursuant to rules adopted under Section 1034. *(Added by Stats.1986, c. 377, § 6. Amended by Stats.2017, c. 131, § 2.)*

§ 1033.5. Items Allowable

(a) The following items are allowable as costs under Section 1032:

(1) Filing, motion, and jury fees.

(2) Juror food and lodging while they are kept together during trial and after the jury retires for deliberation.

(3)(A) Taking, video recording, and transcribing necessary depositions, including an original and one copy of those taken by the claimant and one copy of depositions taken by the party against whom costs are allowed.

(B) Fees of a certified or registered interpreter for the deposition of a party or witness who does not proficiently speak or understand the English language.

(C) Travel expenses to attend depositions.

(4) Service of process by a public officer, registered process server, or other means, as follows:

(A) When service is by a public officer, the recoverable cost is the fee authorized by law at the time of service.

(B) If service is by a process server registered pursuant to Chapter 16 (commencing with Section 22350) of Division 8 of the Business and Professions Code, the recoverable cost is the amount actually incurred in effecting service, including, but not limited to, a stake out or other means employed in locating the person to be served, unless those charges are successfully challenged by a party to the action.

(C) When service is by publication, the recoverable cost is the sum actually incurred in effecting service.

(D) When service is by a means other than that set forth in subparagraph (A), (B), or (C), the recoverable cost is the lesser of the sum actually incurred, or the amount allowed to a public officer in this state for that service, except that the court may allow the sum actually incurred in effecting service upon application pursuant to paragraph (4) of subdivision (c).

(5) Expenses of attachment including keeper's fees.

(6) Premiums on necessary surety bonds.

(7) Ordinary witness fees pursuant to Section 68093 of the Government Code.

(8) Fees of expert witnesses ordered by the court.

(9) Transcripts of court proceedings ordered by the court.

(10) Attorney's fees, when authorized by any of the following:

(A) Contract.

(B) Statute.

(C) Law.

(11) Court reporter fees as established by statute.

(12) Court interpreter fees for a qualified court interpreter authorized by the court for an indigent person represented by a qualified legal services project, as defined in Section 6213 of the Business and Professions Code or a pro bono attorney as defined in Section 8030.4 of the Business and Professions Code.

(13) Models, the enlargements of exhibits and photocopies of exhibits, and the electronic presentation of exhibits, including costs of rental equipment and electronic formatting, may be allowed if they were reasonably helpful to aid the trier of fact.

(14) Fees for the electronic filing or service of documents through an electronic filing service provider if a court requires or orders electronic filing or service of documents.

(15) Fees for the hosting of electronic documents if a court requires or orders a party to have documents hosted by an electronic filing service provider. This paragraph shall become inoperative on January 1, 2022.

(16) Any other item that is required to be awarded to the prevailing party pursuant to statute as an incident to prevailing in the action at trial or on appeal.

(b) The following items are not allowable as costs, except when expressly authorized by law:

(1) Fees of experts not ordered by the court.

(2) Investigation expenses in preparing the case for trial.

(3) Postage, telephone, and photocopying charges, except for exhibits.

(4) Costs in investigation of jurors or in preparation for voir dire.

(5) Transcripts of court proceedings not ordered by the court.

(c) An award of costs shall be subject to the following:

(1) Costs are allowable if incurred, whether or not paid.

(2) Allowable costs shall be reasonably necessary to the conduct of the litigation rather than merely convenient or beneficial to its preparation.

(3) Allowable costs shall be reasonable in amount.

(4) Items not mentioned in this section and items assessed upon application may be allowed or denied in the court's discretion.

(5)(A) If a statute of this state refers to the award of "costs and attorney's fees," attorney's fees are an item and component of the costs to be awarded and are allowable as costs pursuant to subparagraph (B) of paragraph (10) of subdivision (a). A claim not based upon the court's established schedule of attorney's fees for actions on a contract shall bear the burden of proof. Attorney's fees allowable as costs pursuant to subparagraph (B) of paragraph (10) of subdivision (a) may be fixed as follows: (i) upon a noticed motion, (ii) at the time a statement of decision is rendered, (iii) upon application supported by affidavit made concurrently with a claim for other costs, or (iv) upon entry of default judgment. Attorney's fees allowable as costs pursuant to subparagraph (A) or (C) of paragraph (10) of subdivision (a) shall be fixed either upon a noticed motion or upon entry of a default judgment, unless otherwise provided by stipulation of the parties.

(B) Attorney's fees awarded pursuant to Section 1717 of the Civil Code are allowable costs under Section 1032 as authorized by subparagraph (A) of paragraph (10) of subdivision (a). *(Added by Stats.1986, c. 377, § 13. Amended by Stats.1987, c. 1080, § 8.5; Stats.1989, c. 1416, § 26; Stats.1990, c. 804, § 1; Stats.1993, c. 456, § 15; Stats.2009, c.*

88, § 17; Stats.2011, c. 409, § 3; Stats.2012, c. 758, § 2; Stats.2015, c. 90, § 1; Stats.2016, c. 461, § 2; Stats.2017, c. 583, § 1.)

Chapter 7. General Provisions

§ 1048. Consolidation and Severance of Actions

(a) When actions involving a common question of law or fact are pending before the court, it may order a joint hearing or trial of any or all the matters in issue in the actions; it may order all the actions consolidated and it may make such orders concerning proceedings therein as may tend to avoid unnecessary costs or delay.

(b) The court, in furtherance of convenience or to avoid prejudice, or when separate trials will be conducive to expedition and economy, may order a separate trial of any cause of action, including a cause of action asserted in a cross-complaint, or of any separate issue or of any number of causes of action or issues, preserving the right of trial by jury required by the Constitution or a statute of this state or of the United States. *(Enacted 1872. Amended by Stats.1927, c. 320, § 1; Stats.1971, c. 244, § 58.)*

§ 1049. Pending Action Defined

Actions, when deemed pending. An action is deemed to be pending from the time of its commencement until its final determination upon appeal, or until the time for appeal has passed, unless the judgment is sooner satisfied. *(Enacted 1872.)*

Chapter 8. Declaratory Relief

§ 1060. Right of Action; Actual Controversy; Scope; Effect of Declaration

Any person interested under a written instrument, excluding a will or a trust, or under a contract, or who desires a declaration of his or her rights or duties with respect to another, or in respect to, in, over or upon property, or with respect to the location of the natural channel of a watercourse, may, in cases of actual controversy relating to the legal rights and duties of the respective parties, bring an original action or cross-complaint in the superior court for a declaration of his or her rights and duties in the premises, including a determination of any question of construction or validity arising under the instrument or contract. He or she may ask for a declaration of rights or duties, either alone or with other relief; and the court may make a binding declaration of these rights or duties, whether or not further relief is or could be claimed at the time. The declaration may be either affirmative or negative in form and effect, and the declaration shall have the force of a final judgment. The declaration may be had before there has been any breach of the obligation in respect to which said declaration is sought. *(Added by Stats.1921, c. 463, § 1. Amended by*

Stats.1965, c. 959, § 2; Stats.1976, c. 1288, § 18; Stats.1993, c. 1262, § 6; Stats.1994, c. 806, § 1; Stats.1998, c. 931, § 110; Stats.2002, c. 784, § 73.)

PART 3. OF SPECIAL PROCEEDINGS OF A CIVIL NATURE

TITLE 3. OF SUMMARY PROCEEDINGS

Chapter 2.5 Judicial Arbitration

§ 1141.10. Legislative Findings and Declarations and Intent

(a) The Legislature finds and declares that litigation involving small civil cases can be so costly and complex that efficiently resolving these civil cases is difficult, and that the resulting delays and expenses may deny parties their right to a timely resolution of minor civil disputes. The Legislature further finds and declares that arbitration has proven to be an efficient and equitable method for resolving small civil cases, and that courts should encourage or require the use of arbitration for those actions whenever possible.

(b) It is the intent of the Legislature that:

(1) Arbitration hearings held pursuant to this chapter shall provide parties with a simplified and economical procedure for obtaining prompt and equitable resolution of their disputes.

(2) Arbitration hearings shall be as informal as possible and shall provide the parties themselves maximum opportunity to participate directly in the resolution of their disputes, and shall be held during nonjudicial hours whenever possible.

(3) Members of the State Bar selected to serve as arbitrators should have experience with cases of the type under dispute and are urged to volunteer their services without compensation whenever possible. *(Added by Stats.1978, c. 743, § 2. Amended by Stats.2003, c. 449, § 9.)*

§ 1141.11. Nonexempt Unlimited Civil Cases; Amount in Controversy; Submission to Arbitration; Use of Case Questionnaires

(a) In each superior court with 18 or more judges, all nonexempt unlimited civil cases shall be submitted to arbitration under this chapter if the amount in controversy, in the opinion of the court, will not exceed fifty thousand dollars ($50,000) for each plaintiff.

(b) In each superior court with fewer than 18 judges, the court may provide by local rule, when it determines that it is in the best interests of justice, that all nonexempt, unlimited civil cases shall be submitted to arbitration under this chapter if the amount in controversy, in the opinion of the court, will not exceed fifty thousand dollars ($50,000) for each plaintiff.

(c) Each superior court may provide by local rule, when it is determined to be in the best interests of justice, that all nonexempt, limited civil cases shall be submitted to arbitration under this chapter. This section does not apply to any action in small claims court, or to any action maintained pursuant to Section 1781 of the Civil Code or Section 1161.

(d)(1) In each court that has adopted judicial arbitration pursuant to subdivision (c), all limited civil cases that involve a claim for money damages against a single defendant as a result of a motor vehicle collision, except those heard in the small claims division, shall be submitted to arbitration within 120 days of the filing of the defendant's answer to the complaint (except as may be extended by the court for good cause) before an arbitrator selected by the court.

(2) The court may provide by local rule for the voluntary or mandatory use of case questionnaires, established under Section 93, in any proceeding subject to these provisions. Where local rules provide for the use of case questionnaires, the questionnaires shall be exchanged by the parties upon the defendant's answer and completed and returned within 60 days.

(3) For the purposes of this subdivision, the term "single defendant" means any of the following:

(A) An individual defendant, whether a person or an entity.

(B) Two or more persons covered by the same insurance policy applicable to the motor vehicle collision.

(C) Two or more persons residing in the same household when no insurance policy exists that is applicable to the motor vehicle collision.

(4) The naming of one or more cross-defendants, not a plaintiff, shall constitute a multiple-defendant case not subject to the provisions of this subdivision. *(Added by Stats.1978, c. 743, § 2. Amended by Stats.1979, c. 46, § 1; State.1979, c. 948, § 1; Stats.1979, c. 1146, § 2; Stats.1981, c. 1110, § 1; Stats.1982, c. 31, § 1; Stats.1982, c. 921, § 1; Stats.1982, c. 1522, § 2; Stats.1983, c. 978, § 1; Stats.1985, c. 1383, § 3; Stats.1986, c. 287, § 1; Stats.1987, c. 1201, § 4; Stats.1987, c. 1204, § 1; Stats.1989, c. 894, § 1; Stats.1990, c. 1305, § 9; Stats.1998, c. 931, § 116; Stats.2002, c. 784, § 78; Stats.2003, c. 449, § 10.)*

§ 1141.12. Uniform System of Arbitration; Stipulation; Election by Plaintiff to Award Limit

In all superior courts, the Judicial Council shall provide by rule for a uniform system of arbitration of the following causes:

(a) Any cause, regardless of the amount in controversy, upon stipulation of the parties.

(b) Upon filing of an election by the plaintiff, any cause in which the plaintiff agrees that the arbitration award shall not exceed the amount in controversy as specified in Section 1141.11. *(Added by Stats.1978, c. 743, § 2. Amended by Stats.1981, c. 1110, § 2; Stats.1983, c. 123, § 1; Stats.1998, c. 931, § 117; Stats.2002, c. 784, § 79; Stats.2003, c. 449, § 11.)*

§ 1141.17. Suspension of Running of Limitations; Exception

(a) Submission of an action to arbitration pursuant to this chapter shall not suspend the running of the time periods specified in Chapter 1.5 (commencing with Section 583.110) of Title 8 of Part 2 except as provided in this section.

(b) If an action is or remains submitted to arbitration pursuant to this chapter more than four years and six months after the plaintiff has filed the action, then the time beginning on the date four years and six months after the plaintiff has filed the action and ending on the date on which a request for a de novo trial is filed under Section 1141.20 shall not be included in computing the five-year period specified in Section 583.310. *(Amended by Stats.1983, c. 123, § 3; Stats.1984, c. 1705, § 6.)*

§ 1141.20. Finality of Award; De Novo Trial; Request; Limitation; Calendar

(a) An arbitration award shall be final unless a request for a de novo trial or a request for dismissal in the form required by the Judicial Council is filed within 60 days after the date the arbitrator files the award with the court.

(b) Any party may elect to have a de novo trial, by court or jury, both as to law and facts. Such trial shall be calendared, insofar as possible, so that the trial shall be given the same place on the active list as it had prior to arbitration, or shall receive civil priority on the next setting calendar. *(Added by Stats.1978, c. 743, § 2. Amended by Stats.1984, c. 1249, § 2; Stats.2011, c. 49, § 3.)*

§ 1141.21. Judgment on Trial De Novo Equal to or Less Favorable Than Arbitration Award for Party Electing; Payment of Nonrefundable Costs and Fees

(a)(1) If the judgment upon the trial de novo is not more favorable in either the amount of damages awarded or the type of relief granted for the party electing the trial de novo than the arbitration award, the court shall order that party to pay the following nonrefundable costs and fees, unless the court finds in writing and upon motion that the imposition of these costs and fees would create such a substantial economic hardship as not to be in the interest of justice:

(A) To the court, the compensation actually paid to the arbitrator, less any amount paid pursuant to subparagraph (D).

(B) To the other party or parties, all costs specified in Section 1033.5, and the party electing the trial de novo shall not recover his or her costs.

(C) To the other party or parties, the reasonable costs of the services of expert witnesses, who are not regular employees of any party, actually incurred or reasonably necessary in the preparation or trial of the case.

(D) To the other party or parties, the compensation paid by the other party or parties to the arbitrator, pursuant to subdivision (b) of Section 1141.28.

(2) Those costs and fees, other than the compensation of the arbitrator, shall include only those incurred from the time of election of the trial de novo.

(b) If the party electing the trial de novo has proceeded in the action in forma pauperis and has failed to obtain a more favorable judgment, the costs and fees under subparagraphs (B) and (C) of paragraph (1) of subdivision (a) shall be imposed only as an offset against any damages awarded in favor of that party.

(c) If the party electing the trial de novo has proceeded in the action in forma pauperis and has failed to obtain a more favorable judgment, the costs under subparagraph (A) of paragraph (1) of subdivision (a) shall be imposed only to the extent that there remains a sufficient amount in the judgment after the amount offset under subdivision (b) has been deducted from the judgment. *(Added by Stats.1978, c. 743, § 2, operative July 1, 1979. Amended by Stats.1982, c. 1354, § 4; Stats.1982, c. 1408, § 1; Stats.1986, c. 377, § 20; Stats.2005, c. 706, § 14; Stats.2006, c. 538, § 66.)*

TITLE 5. OF CONTEMPTS

§ 1209. Acts or Omissions Constituting; Stay of Sentence Pending Appeal

(a) The following acts or omissions in respect to a court of justice, or proceedings therein, are contempts of the authority of the court:

(1) Disorderly, contemptuous, or insolent behavior toward the judge while holding the court, tending to interrupt the due course of a trial or other judicial proceeding.

(2) A breach of the peace, boisterous conduct, or violent disturbance, tending to interrupt the due course of a trial or other judicial proceeding.

(3) Misbehavior in office, or other willful neglect or violation of duty by an attorney, counsel, clerk, sheriff, coroner, or other person, appointed or elected to perform a judicial or ministerial service.

(4) Abuse of the process or proceedings of the court, or falsely pretending to act under authority of an order or process of the court.

(5) Disobedience of any lawful judgment, order, or process of the court.

(6) Willful disobedience by a juror of a court admonishment related to the prohibition on any form of communication or research about the case, including all forms of electronic or wireless communication or research.

(7) Rescuing any person or property in the custody of an officer by virtue of an order or process of that court.

(8) Unlawfully detaining a witness or party to an action while going to, remaining at, or returning from the court where the action is on the calendar for trial.

(9) Any other unlawful interference with the process or proceedings of a court.

(10) Disobedience of a subpoena duly served, or refusing to be sworn or answer as a witness.

(11) When summoned as a juror in a court, neglecting to attend or serve as a juror, or improperly conversing with a party to an action to be tried at the court, or with any other person, in relation to the merits of the action, or receiving a communication from a party or other person in respect to the action, without immediately disclosing the communication to the court.

(12) Disobedience by an inferior tribunal or judicial officer of the lawful judgment, order, or process of a superior court, or proceeding in an action or special proceeding contrary to law, after the action or special proceeding is removed from the jurisdiction of the inferior tribunal or judicial officer.

(b) A speech or publication reflecting upon or concerning a court or an officer thereof shall not be treated or punished as a contempt of the court unless made in the immediate presence of the court while in session and in such a manner as to actually interfere with its proceedings.

(c) Notwithstanding Section 1211 or any other law, if an order of contempt is made affecting an attorney, his or her agent, investigator, or any person acting under the attorney's direction, in the preparation and conduct of an action or proceeding, the execution of any sentence shall be stayed pending the filing within three judicial days of a petition for extraordinary relief testing the lawfulness of the court's order, the violation of which is the basis of the contempt, except for conduct proscribed by subdivision (b) of Section 6068 of the Business and Professions Code, relating to an attorney's duty to maintain respect due to the courts and judicial officers.

(d) Notwithstanding Section 1211 or any other law, if an order of contempt is made affecting a public safety employee acting within the scope of employment for reason of the employee's failure to comply with a duly issued subpoena or subpoena duces tecum, the execution of any sentence shall be stayed pending the filing within three judicial days of a petition for extraordinary relief testing the lawfulness of the court's order, a violation of which is the basis for the contempt.

As used in this subdivision, "public safety employee" includes any peace officer, firefighter, paramedic, or any other employee of a public law enforcement agency whose duty is either to maintain official records or to analyze or present evidence for investigative or prosecutorial purposes. *(Enacted 1872. Amended by Stats.1891, c. 9, § 1; Stats.1907, c. 255, § 1; Stats.1939, c. 979, § 1; Stats.1975, c. 836, § 2; Stats.1982, c. 510, § 2; Stats.2011, c. 181, § 3.)*

§ 1209.5. Noncompliance With Order for Care or Support of Child

When a court of competent jurisdiction makes an order compelling a parent to furnish support or necessary food, clothing, shelter, medical attendance, or other remedial care for his or her child, proof that the order was made, filed, and served on the parent or proof that the parent was present in court at the time the order was pronounced and proof that the parent did not comply with the order is prima facie evidence of a contempt of court. *(Added by Stats.1955, c. 1359, § 1. Amended by Stats.1961, c. 1307, § 1; Stats.1992, c. 163, § 57.)*

§ 1211. Summary Punishment; Order; Affidavit or Statement of Facts; Compliance by Filing of Form

(a) When a contempt is committed in the immediate view and presence of the court, or of the judge at chambers, it may be punished summarily; for which an order must be made, reciting the facts as occurring in such immediate view and presence, adjudging that the person proceeded against is thereby guilty of a contempt, and that he or she be punished as therein prescribed. When the contempt is not committed in the immediate view and presence of the court, or of the judge at chambers, an affidavit shall be presented to the court or judge of the facts constituting the contempt, or a statement of the facts by the referees or arbitrators, or other judicial officers.

(b) In family law matters, filing of the Judicial Council form entitled "Order to Show Cause and Affidavit for Contempt (Family Law)" shall constitute compliance with this section. *(Enacted 1872. Amended by Stats.1933, c. 745, § 11; Stats.1951, c. 1737, § 162; Stats.1995, c. 904, § 1; Stats.2001, c. 754, § 1.)*

§ 1218. Determination of Guilt; Punishment; Restriction on Enforcement of Order by Party in Contempt

(a) Upon the answer and evidence taken, the court or judge shall determine whether the person proceeded against is guilty of the contempt charged, and if it be adjudged that the person is guilty of the contempt, a fine may be imposed on the person not exceeding one thousand dollars ($1,000), payable to the court, or the person may be imprisoned not exceeding five days, or both. In addition, a person who is subject to a court order as a party to the action, or any agent of this person, who is adjudged guilty of contempt for violating that court order may be ordered to pay to the party initiating the contempt proceeding the reasonable attorney's fees and costs incurred by this party in connection with the contempt proceeding.

(b) Any party, who is in contempt of a court order or judgment in a dissolution of marriage, dissolution of domestic partnership, or legal separation action, shall not be permitted to enforce such an order or judgment, by way of execution or otherwise, either in the same action or by way of a separate action, against the other party. This restriction shall not affect nor apply to the enforcement of child or spousal support orders.

(c)(1) In any court action in which a party is found in contempt of court for failure to comply with a court order pursuant to the Family Code, the court shall, subject to the sentencing option provided in paragraph (2), order the following:

(A) Upon a first finding of contempt, the court shall order the contemner to perform community service of up to 120 hours, or to be imprisoned up to 120 hours, for each count of contempt.

(B) Upon the second finding of contempt, the court shall order the contemner to perform community service of up to 120 hours, in addition to ordering imprisonment of the contemner up to 120 hours, for each count of contempt.

(C) Upon the third or any subsequent finding of contempt, the court shall order that the contemner serve a term of imprisonment of up to 240 hours and perform community service of up to 240 hours, for each count of contempt. The court shall also order the contemner to pay an administrative fee, not to exceed the actual cost of the contemner's administration and supervision, while assigned to a community service program pursuant to this paragraph.

(D) The court shall take parties' employment schedules into consideration when ordering either community service or imprisonment, or both.

(2) In lieu of an order of imprisonment, community service, or both, as set forth in paragraph (1), the court may grant probation or a conditional

sentence for a period not to exceed one year upon a first finding of contempt, a period not to exceed two years upon a second finding of contempt, and a period not to exceed three years upon a third or any subsequent finding of contempt.

(3) For purposes of this subdivision, "probation" and "conditional sentence" shall have the meanings set forth in subdivision (a) of Section 1203 of the Penal Code.

(d) Pursuant to Section 1211 and this section, a district attorney or city attorney may initiate and pursue a court action for contempt against a party for failing to comply with a court order entered pursuant to the Domestic Violence Protection Act (Division 10 (commencing with Section 6200) of the Family Code). Any attorney's fees and costs ordered by the court pursuant to subdivision (a) against a party who is adjudged guilty of contempt under this subdivision shall be paid to the Office of Emergency Services' account established for the purpose of funding domestic violence shelter service providers pursuant to subdivision (f) of Section 13823.15 of the Penal Code. *(Enacted 1872. Amended by Stats.1933, c. 745, § 17; Stats.1951, c. 1737, § 168, operative Jan. 1, 1952; Stats.1968, c. 938, § 2; Stats.1977, c. 1257, § 39, eff. Jan. 3, 1977; Stats.1983, c. 1092, § 72, eff. Sept. 27, 1983, operative Jan. 1, 1984; Stats.1988, c. 969, § 2; Stats.1993, c. 745, § 1; Stats.1993, c. 746, § 1; Stats.1994, c. 368, § 1; Stats.1994, c. 1269, § 3.3; Stats.1995, c. 576, § 5.5; Stats.2000, c. 808, § 20, eff. Sept. 28, 2000; Stats.2005, c. 75, § 44, eff. July 19, 2005, operative Jan. 1, 2006; Stats.2005, c. 631, § 1; Stats.2010, c. 618, § 3; Stats.2013, c. 352, § 56; Stats.2020, c. 283, § 1.)*

§ 1219. Imprisonment to Compel Performance of Acts; Exemption of Sexual Assault and Domestic Violence Victims Who Refuse to Testify

(a) Except as provided in subdivisions (b) and (c), if the contempt consists of the omission to perform an act which is yet in the power of the person to perform, he or she may be imprisoned until he or she has performed it, and in that case the act shall be specified in the warrant of commitment.

(b) Notwithstanding any other law, a court shall not imprison or otherwise confine or place in custody the victim of a sexual assault or domestic violence crime for contempt if the contempt consists of refusing to testify concerning that sexual assault or domestic violence crime. Before finding a victim of a domestic violence crime in contempt as described in this section, the court may refer the victim for consultation with a domestic violence counselor. All communications between the victim and the domestic violence counselor that occur as a result of that referral shall remain confidential under Section 1037.2 of the Evidence Code.

(c) Notwithstanding any other law, a court shall not imprison, hold in physical confinement, or otherwise confine or place in custody a minor for contempt if the contempt consists of the minor's failure to comply with a court order pursuant to subdivision (b) of Section 601 of, or Section 727 of, the Welfare and Institutions Code, if the minor was adjudged a ward of the court on the ground that he or she is a person described in subdivision (b) of Section 601 of the Welfare and Institutions Code. Upon a finding of contempt of court, the court may issue any other lawful order, as necessary, to secure the minor's attendance at school.

(d) As used in this section, the following terms have the following meanings:

(1) "Sexual assault" means any act made punishable by Section 261, 262, 264.1, 285, 286, 287, 288, or 289 of, or former Section 288a of, the Penal Code.

(2) "Domestic violence" means "domestic violence" as defined in Section 6211 of the Family Code.

(3) "Domestic violence counselor" means "domestic violence counselor" as defined in subdivision (a) of Section 1037.1 of the Evidence Code.

(4) "Physical confinement" has the same meaning as defined in subdivision (d) of Section 726 of the Welfare and Institutions Code. *(Enacted 1872. Amended by Stats.1980, c. 676, § 68; Stats.1984, c. 1644, § 2; Stats.1991, c. 866, § 4; Stats.1992, c. 163, § 58; Stats.1993, c. 219, § 69.7; Stats.2008, c. 49, § 1; Stats.2009, c. 35, § 3; Stats.2012, c. 510, § 1; Stats.2014, c. 70, § 1; Stats.2018, c. 423, § 9.)*

TITLE 9. ARBITRATION

Chapter 2. Enforcement of Arbitration Agreements

§ 1281. Validity, Enforceability and Irrevocability of Agreements

A written agreement to submit to arbitration an existing controversy or a controversy thereafter arising is valid, enforceable and irrevocable, save upon such grounds as exist for the revocation of any contract. *(Added by Stats.1961, c. 461, § 2.)*

§ 1281.2. Order to Arbitrate Controversy; Petition; Determination of Court

On petition of a party to an arbitration agreement alleging the existence of a written agreement to arbitrate a controversy and that a party to the agreement refuses to arbitrate that controversy, the court shall order the petitioner and the respondent to arbitrate the controversy if it determines that an agreement to arbitrate the controversy exists, unless it determines that:

(a) The right to compel arbitration has been waived by the petitioner; or

(b) Grounds exist for rescission of the agreement.

(c) A party to the arbitration agreement is also a party to a pending court action or special proceeding with a third party, arising out of the same transaction or series of related transactions and there is a possibility of conflicting rulings on a common issue of law or fact. For purposes of this section, a pending court action or special proceeding includes an action or proceeding initiated by the party refusing to arbitrate after the petition to compel arbitration has been filed, but on or before the date of the hearing on the petition. This subdivision shall not be applicable to an agreement to arbitrate disputes as to the professional negligence of a health care provider made pursuant to Section 1295.

(d) The petitioner is a state or federally chartered depository institution that, on or after January 1, 2018, is seeking to apply a written agreement to arbitrate, contained in a contract consented to by a respondent consumer, to a purported contractual relationship with that respondent consumer that was created by the petitioner fraudulently without the respondent consumer's consent and by unlawfully using the respondent consumer's personal identifying information, as defined in Section 1798.92 of the Civil Code.

If the court determines that a written agreement to arbitrate a controversy exists, an order to arbitrate that controversy may not be refused on the ground that the petitioner's contentions lack substantive merit.

If the court determines that there are other issues between the petitioner and the respondent which are not subject to arbitration and which are the subject of a pending action or special proceeding between the petitioner and the respondent and that a determination of such issues may make the arbitration unnecessary, the court may delay its order to arbitrate until the determination of such other issues or until such earlier time as the court specifies.

If the court determines that a party to the arbitration is also a party to litigation in a pending court action or special proceeding with a third party as set forth under subdivision (c), the court (1) may refuse to enforce the arbitration agreement and may order intervention or joinder of all parties in a single action or special proceeding; (2) may order intervention or joinder as to all or only certain issues; (3) may order arbitration among the parties who have agreed to arbitration and stay the pending court action or special proceeding pending the outcome of the arbitration proceeding; or (4) may stay arbitration pending the outcome of the court action or special proceeding. *(Added by Stats.1961, c. 461, § 2. Amended by Stats.1978, c. 260, § 1; Stats.2017, c. 480, § 1; Stats.2018, c. 106, § 1.)*

§ 1281.4. Stay of Pending Actions or Proceedings

If a court of competent jurisdiction, whether in this State or not, has ordered arbitration of a controversy which is an issue involved in an action or proceeding pending before a court of this State, the court in which such action or proceeding is pending shall, upon motion of a party to such action or proceeding, stay the action or proceeding until an arbitration is had in accordance with the order to arbitrate or until such earlier time as the court specifies.

If an application has been made to a court of competent jurisdiction, whether in this State or not, for an order to arbitrate a controversy which is an issue involved in an action or proceeding pending before a court of this State and such application is undetermined, the court in which such action or proceeding is pending shall, upon motion of a party to such action or proceeding, stay the action or proceeding until the application for an order to arbitrate is determined and, if arbitration of such controversy is ordered, until an arbitration is had in accordance with the order to arbitrate or until such earlier time as the court specifies.

If the issue which is the controversy subject to arbitration is severable, the stay may be with respect to that issue only. *(Added by Stats.1961, c. 461, § 2.)*

Chapter 5. General Provisions Relating to Judicial Proceedings

§ 1294. Appealable Orders

An aggrieved party may appeal from:

(a) An order dismissing or denying a petition to compel arbitration. Notwithstanding Section 916, the perfecting of such an appeal shall not automatically stay any proceedings in the trial court during the pendency of the appeal.

(b) An order dismissing a petition to confirm, correct or vacate an award.

(c) An order vacating an award unless a rehearing in arbitration is ordered.

(d) A judgment entered pursuant to this title.

(e) A special order after final judgment. *(Added by Stats.1961, c. 461, § 2. Amended by Stats.2023, c. 710, § 1.)*

TITLE 9.3. ARBITRATION AND CONCILIATION OF INTERNATIONAL COMMERCIAL DISPUTES

Chapter 1. Application and Interpretation

§ 1297.13. International Status of Agreement; Requirements

An arbitration or conciliation agreement is international if any of the following applies:

(a) The parties to an arbitration or conciliation agreement have, at the time of the conclusion of that agreement, their places of business in different states.

(b) One of the following places is situated outside the state in which the parties have their places of business:

(i) The place of arbitration or conciliation if determined in, or pursuant to, the arbitration or conciliation agreement.

(ii) Any place where a substantial part of the obligations of the commercial relationship is to be performed.

(iii) The place with which the subject matter of the dispute is most closely connected.

(c) The parties have expressly agreed that the subject matter of the arbitration or conciliation agreement relates to commercial interests in more than one state.

(d) The subject matter of the arbitration or conciliation agreement is otherwise related to commercial interests in more than one state. *(Added by Stats.1988, c. 23, § 1.)*

TITLE 11. MONEY JUDGMENTS OF OTHER JURISDICTIONS

Chapter 1. Sister State Money Judgments

§ 1710.10. Definitions

As used in this chapter:

(a) "Judgment creditor" means the person or persons who can bring an action to enforce a sister state judgment.

(b) "Judgment debtor" means the person or persons against whom an action to enforce a sister state judgment can be brought.

(c) "Sister state judgment" means that part of any judgment, decree, or order of a court of a state of the United States, other than California, which requires the payment of money, but does not include a support order as defined in Section 155 of the Family Code. *(Added by Stats.1974, c. 211, § 3. Amended by Stats.1992, c. 163, § 64.)*

§ 1710.15. Application for Entry; Statement; Contents

(a) A judgment creditor may apply for the entry of a judgment based on a sister state judgment by filing an application pursuant to Section 1710.20.

(b) The application shall be executed under oath and shall include all of the following:

(1) A statement that an action in this state on the sister state judgment is not barred by the applicable statute of limitations.

(2) A statement, based on the applicant's information and belief, that no stay of enforcement of the sister state judgment is currently in effect in the sister state.

(3) A statement of the amount remaining unpaid under the sister state judgment and, if accrued interest on the sister state judgment is to be included in the California judgment, a statement of the amount of interest accrued on the sister state judgment (computed at the rate of interest applicable to the judgment under the law of the sister state), a statement of the rate of interest applicable to the judgment under the law of the sister state, and a citation to the law of the sister state establishing the rate of interest.

(4) A statement that no action based on the sister state judgment is currently pending in any court in this state and that no judgment based on the sister state judgment has previously been entered in any proceeding in this state.

(5) Where the judgment debtor is an individual, a statement setting forth the name and last known residence address of the judgment debtor. Where the judgment debtor is a corporation, a statement of the corporation's name, place of incorporation, and whether the corporation, if foreign, has qualified to do business in this state under the provisions of Chapter 21 (commencing with Section 2100) of Division 1 of Title 1 of the Corporations Code. Where the judgment debtor is a partnership, a statement of the name of the partnership, whether it is a foreign partnership, and, if it is a foreign partnership, whether it has filed a statement pursuant to Section 15800 of the Corporations Code designating an agent for service of process. Except for facts which are matters of public record in this state, the statements required by this paragraph may be made on the basis of the judgment creditor's information and belief.

(6) A statement setting forth the name and address of the judgment creditor.

(c) A properly authenticated copy of the sister state judgment shall be attached to the application. *(Added by Stats.1974, c. 211, § 3. Amended by Stats.1977, c. 232, § 1; Stats.1982, c. 150, § 4; Stats.1984, c. 311, § 2; Stats.1985, c. 106, § 11.)*

§ 1710.25. Entry of Judgment; Accrued Interest

(a) Upon the filing of the application, the clerk shall enter a judgment based upon the application for the total of the following amounts as shown therein:

(1) The amount remaining unpaid under the sister state judgment.

(2) The amount of interest accrued on the sister state judgment (computed at the rate of interest applicable to the judgment under the law of the sister state).

(3) The amount of the fee for filing the application for entry of the sister state judgment.

(b) Entry shall be made in the same manner as entry of an original judgment of the court. From the time of entry, interest shall accrue on the judgment so entered at the rate of interest applicable to a judgment entered in this state. *(Added by Stats.1974, c. 211, § 3. Amended by Stats.1977, c. 232, § 2; Stats.1982, c. 150, § 5; Stats.1984, c. 311, § 4.)*

§ 1710.50. Stay of Enforcement

(a) The court shall grant a stay of enforcement where:

(1) An appeal from the sister state judgment is pending or may be taken in the state which originally rendered the judgment. Under this paragraph, enforcement shall be stayed until the proceedings on appeal have been concluded or the time for appeal has expired.

(2) A stay of enforcement of the sister state judgment has been granted in the sister state. Under this paragraph, enforcement shall be stayed until the sister state stay of enforcement expires or is vacated.

(3) The judgment debtor has made a motion to vacate pursuant to Section 1710.40. Under this paragraph, enforcement shall be stayed until the judgment debtor's motion to vacate is determined.

(4) A money judgment or lien on real property was obtained against a person or entity for exercising a right guaranteed under the United States Constitution or a right guaranteed under the California Constitution, or against a person or entity for aiding and abetting the exercise of said rights. The stay of enforcement shall remain in place until such time as the statute of limitations in Section 1798.303 of the Civil Code has elapsed or an action prosecuted under Section 1798.303 has concluded, whichever is later.

(5) Any other circumstance exists where the interests of justice require a stay of enforcement.

(b) The court may grant a stay of enforcement under this section on its own motion, on ex parte motion, or on noticed motion.

(c) The court shall grant a stay of enforcement under this section on such terms and conditions as are just including but not limited to the following:

(1) The court may require an undertaking in an amount it determines to be just, but the amount of the undertaking shall not exceed double the amount of the judgment creditor's claim.

(2) If a writ of execution has been issued, the court may order that it remain in effect.

(3) If property of the judgment debtor has been levied upon under a writ of execution, the court may order the levying officer to retain possession of the property capable of physical possession and to maintain the levy on other property. *(Added by Stats.1974, c. 211, § 3. Amended by Stats.2023, c. 260, § 9.)*

§ 1710.55. Restrictions on Entry of Judgment

No judgment based on a sister state judgment may be entered pursuant to this chapter in any of the following cases:

(a) A stay of enforcement of the sister state judgment is currently in effect in the sister state.

(b) An action based on the sister state judgment is currently pending in any court in this state.

(c) A judgment based on the sister state judgment has previously been entered in any proceeding in this state. *(Added by Stats.1974, c. 211, § 3.)*

PART 4. MISCELLANEOUS PROVISIONS

TITLE 3. OF THE PRODUCTION OF EVIDENCE

Chapter 2. Means of Production

§ 1985.8. Electronically Stored Information; Form of Production; Undue Burden or Expense; Limits on Discovery

(a)(1) A subpoena in a civil proceeding may require that electronically stored information, as defined in Section 2016.020, be produced and that the party serving the subpoena, or someone acting on the party's request, be permitted to inspect, copy, test, or sample the information.

(2) Any subpoena seeking electronically stored information shall comply with the requirements of this chapter.

(b) A party serving a subpoena requiring production of electronically stored information may specify the form or forms in which each type of information is to be produced.

(c) If a person responding to a subpoena for production of electronically stored information objects to the specified form or forms for producing the information, the subpoenaed person may provide an objection stating the form or forms in which it intends to produce each type of information.

(d) Unless the subpoenaing party and the subpoenaed person otherwise agree or the court otherwise orders, the following shall apply:

(1) If a subpoena requiring production of electronically stored information does not specify a form or forms for producing a type of electronically stored information, the person subpoenaed shall produce the information in the form or forms in which it is ordinarily maintained or in a form that is reasonably usable.

(2) A subpoenaed person need not produce the same electronically stored information in more than one form.

(e) The subpoenaed person opposing the production, inspection, copying, testing, or sampling of electronically stored information on the basis that information is from a source that is not reasonably accessible because of undue burden or expense shall bear the burden of demonstrating that the information is from a source that is not reasonably accessible because of undue burden or expense.

(f) If the person from whom discovery of electronically stored information is subpoenaed establishes that the information is from a source that is not reasonably accessible because of undue burden or expense, the court may nonetheless order discovery if the subpoenaing party shows good cause, subject to any limitations imposed under subdivision (i).

(g) If the court finds good cause for the production of electronically stored information from a source that is not reasonably accessible, the court may set conditions for the discovery of the electronically stored information, including allocation of the expense of discovery.

(h) If necessary, the subpoenaed person, at the reasonable expense of the subpoenaing party, shall, through detection devices, translate any data compilations included in the subpoena into a reasonably usable form.

(i) The court shall limit the frequency or extent of discovery of electronically stored information, even from a source that is reasonably accessible, if the court determines that any of the following conditions exists:

(1) It is possible to obtain the information from some other source that is more convenient, less burdensome, or less expensive.

(2) The discovery sought is unreasonably cumulative or duplicative.

(3) The party seeking discovery has had ample opportunity by discovery in the action to obtain the information sought.

(4) The likely burden or expense of the proposed discovery outweighs the likely benefit, taking into account the amount in controversy, the resources of the parties, the importance of the issues in the litigation, and the importance of the requested discovery in resolving the issues.

(j) If a subpoenaed person notifies the subpoenaing party that electronically stored information produced pursuant to a subpoena is subject to a claim of privilege or of protection as attorney work product, as described in Section 2031.285, the provisions of Section 2031.285 shall apply.

(k) A party serving a subpoena requiring the production of electronically stored information shall take reasonable steps to avoid imposing undue burden or expense on a person subject to the subpoena.

(*l*) An order of the court requiring compliance with a subpoena issued under this section shall protect a person who is neither a party nor a party's officer from undue burden or expense resulting from compliance.

(m)(1) Absent exceptional circumstances, the court shall not impose sanctions on a subpoenaed person or any attorney of a subpoenaed person for failure to provide electronically stored information that has been lost, damaged, altered, or overwritten as the result of the routine, good faith operation of an electronic information system.

(2) This subdivision shall not be construed to alter any obligation to preserve discoverable information. *(Added by Stats.2009, c. 5, § 2, eff. June 29, 2009. Amended by Stats.2012, c. 72, § 4.)*

Chapter 3. Manner of Production

§ 2015.5. Certification or Declaration Under Penalty of Perjury

Whenever, under any law of this state or under any rule, regulation, order or requirement made pursuant to the law of this state, any matter is required or permitted to be supported, evidenced, established, or proved by the sworn statement, declaration, verification, certificate, oath, or affidavit, in writing of the person making the same (other than a deposition, or an oath of office, or an oath required to be taken before a specified official other than a notary public), such matter may with like force and effect be supported, evidenced, established or proved by the unsworn statement, declaration, verification, or certificate, in writing of such person which recites that it is certified or declared by him or her to be true under penalty of perjury, is subscribed by him or her, and (1), if executed within this state, states the date and place of execution, or (2), if executed at any place, within or without this state, states the date of execution and that is so certified or declared under the laws of the State of California. The certification or declaration may be in substantially the following form:

(a) If executed within this state:

"I certify (or declare) under penalty of perjury that the foregoing is true and correct":

______________________	______________________
(Date and Place)	(Signature)

(b) If executed at any place, within or without this state:

"I certify (or declare) under penalty of perjury under the laws of the State of California that the foregoing is true and correct":

______________________	______________________
(Date and Place)	(Signature)

(Added by Stats.1957, c. 1612, § 1. Amended by Stats.1961, c. 495, § 1; Stats.1963, c. 2080, § 1; Stats.1975, c. 666, § 1; Stats.1980, c. 889, § 1.)

TITLE 4. CIVIL DISCOVERY ACT

Chapter 1. General Provisions

§ 2016.010. Short Title

This title may be cited as the "Civil Discovery Act." *(Added by Stats.2004, c. 182, § 23, operative July 1, 2005.)*

§ 2016.020. Definitions

As used in this title:

(a) "Action" includes a civil action and a special proceeding of a civil nature.

(b) "Court" means the trial court in which the action is pending, unless otherwise specified.

(c) "Document" and "writing" mean a writing, as defined in Section 250 of the Evidence Code.

(d) "Electronic" means relating to technology having electrical, digital, magnetic, wireless, optical, electromagnetic, or similar capabilities.

(e) "Electronically stored information" means information that is stored in an electronic medium. *(Added by Stats.2004, c. 182, § 23, operative July 1, 2005. Amended by Stats.2009, c. 5, § 3, eff. June 29, 2009.)*

§ 2016.030. Stipulation to Modify Discovery; Requirements

Unless the court orders otherwise, the parties may by written stipulation modify the procedures provided by this title for any method of discovery permitted under Section 2019.010. *(Added by Stats.2004, c. 182, § 23, operative July 1, 2005.)*

§ 2016.040. Meet and Confer Declaration; Requirements

(a) A meet and confer declaration in support of a motion shall state facts showing a reasonable and good faith attempt, either in person, by telephone, or by videoconference, to informally resolve each issue presented by the motion.

(b) The declaration shall also include whether the moving party has met and conferred, including through an electronic communication, regarding the retention of a certified shorthand reporter to report the hearing on the motion. This subdivision does not prevent the retention of a certified shorthand reporter. *(Added by Stats.2004, c. 182, § 23, operative July 1, 2005. Amended by Stats.2025, c. 64, § 1; Stats.2025, c. 200, § 12.)*

§ 2016.050. Service of Notice or Other Papers; Allowed Methods

Sections 1011 and 1013 apply to any method of discovery or service of a motion provided for in this title. *(Added by Stats.2004, c. 182, § 23, operative July 1, 2005. Amended by Stats.2017, c. 64, § 2.)*

§ 2016.060. Saturday, Sunday or Holiday as Last Day to Act

When the last day to perform or complete any act provided for in this title falls on a Saturday, Sunday, or holiday as specified in Section 10, the time limit is extended until the next court day closer to the trial date. *(Added by Stats.2004, c. 182, § 23.5, operative July 1, 2005.)*

§ 2016.070. Application to Enforcement of Money Judgments

This title applies to discovery in aid of enforcement of a money judgment only to the extent provided in Article 1 (commencing with Section 708.010) of Chapter 6 of Title 9 of Part 2. *(Added by Stats.2004, c. 182, § 23, operative July 1, 2005.)*

§ 2016.090. Initial Disclosures

(a) The following shall apply in a civil action unless modified by stipulation by all parties to the action:

(1) Within 60 days of a demand by any party to the action, each party that has appeared in the action, including the party that made the demand, shall provide to the other parties an initial disclosure that includes all of the following information:

(A) The names, addresses, telephone numbers, and email addresses of all persons likely to have discoverable information, along with the subjects of that information, that the disclosing party may use to support its claims or defenses, or that is relevant to the subject matter of the action or the order on any motion made in that action, unless the use would be solely for impeachment. The disclosure required by this subparagraph is not required to include persons who are expert trial witnesses or are retained as consultants who may later be designated as expert trial witnesses, as that term is described in Chapter 18 (commencing with Section 2034.010) of Title 4 of Part 4.

(B) A copy, or a description by category and location, of all documents, electronically stored information, and tangible things that the disclosing party has in its possession, custody, or control and may use to support its claims or defenses, or that is relevant to the subject matter of the action or the order on any motion made in that action, unless the use would be solely for impeachment.

(C) Any contractual agreement and any insurance policy under which an insurance company may be liable to satisfy, in whole or in part, a judgment entered in the action or to indemnify or reimburse for payments made to satisfy the judgment.

(D) Any and all contractual agreements and any and all insurance policies under which a person, as defined in Section 175 of the Evidence Code, may be liable to satisfy, in whole or in part, a judgment entered in the action or to indemnify or reimburse for payments made to satisfy the judgment. Only those provisions of an agreement that are material to the terms of the insurance, indemnification, or reimbursement are required to be included in the initial disclosure. Material provisions include, but are not limited to, the identities of parties to the agreement, the nature and limits of the coverage, and any and all documents regarding whether any insurance carrier is disputing the agreement's or policy's coverage of the claim involved in the action.

(2) A party shall make its initial disclosures based on the information then reasonably available to it. A party is not excused from making its initial disclosures because it has not fully investigated the case, because it challenges the sufficiency of another party's disclosures, or because another party has not made its disclosures.

(3)(A) A party that has made, or responded to, a demand for an initial disclosure pursuant to paragraph (1) may propound a supplemental demand on any other party to elicit any later-acquired information bearing on all disclosures previously made by any party.

(B) A party may propound a supplemental demand twice before the initial setting of a trial date, and, subject to the time limits on discovery proceedings and motions provided in Chapter 8 (commencing with Section 2024.010) of Title 4 of Part 4, once after the initial setting of a trial date.

(C) Notwithstanding subparagraphs (A) and (B), on motion, for good cause shown, the court may grant leave to a party to propound one additional supplemental demand.

(4) A party's obligations under this section may be enforced by a court on its own motion or the motion of a party to compel disclosure.

(5) A party's disclosures under this section shall be verified either in a written declaration by the party or the party's authorized representative, or signed by the party's counsel.

(b) Notwithstanding subdivision (a), this section does not apply to the following actions:

(1) An unlawful detainer action, as defined in Section 1161.

(2) An action in the small claims division of a court, as defined in Section 116.210.

(3) An action or proceeding commenced in whole or in part under the Family Code.

(4) An action or proceeding commenced in whole or in part under the Probate Code.

(5) An action in which a party has been granted preference pursuant to Section 36.

(c) This section does not apply to any party in the action who is not represented by counsel.

(d) The changes made to this section by the act adding this subdivision apply only to civil actions filed on or after January 1, 2024. *(Added by Stats.2019, c. 836, § 1. Amended by Stats.2023, c. 284, § 1; Stats.2025, c. 50, § 1.)*

Chapter 2. Scope of Discovery

Article 1. General Provisions

§ 2017.010. Persons Entitled to Discovery; Matters Discoverable

Unless otherwise limited by order of the court in accordance with this title, any party may obtain discovery regarding any matter, not privileged, that is relevant to the subject matter involved in the pending action or to the determination of any motion made in that action, if the matter either is itself admissible in evidence or appears reasonably calculated to lead to the discovery of admissible evidence. Discovery may relate to the claim or defense of the party seeking discovery or of any other party to the action. Discovery may be obtained of the identity and location of persons having knowledge of any discoverable matter, as well as of the existence, description, nature, custody, condition, and location of any document, electronically stored information, tangible thing, or land or other property.

(Added by Stats.2004, c. 182, § 23, operative July 1, 2005. Amended by Stats.2012, c. 72, § 8.)

§ 2017.020. Judicial Limits Upon Discovery; Order; Sanctions

(a) The court shall limit the scope of discovery if it determines that the burden, expense, or intrusiveness of that discovery clearly outweighs the likelihood that the information sought will lead to the discovery of admissible evidence. The court may make this determination pursuant to a motion for protective order by a party or other affected person. This motion shall be accompanied by a meet and confer declaration under Section 2016.040.

(b) The court shall impose a monetary sanction under Chapter 7 (commencing with Section 2023.010) against any party, person, or attorney who unsuccessfully makes or opposes a motion for a protective order, unless it finds that the one subject to the sanction acted with substantial justification or that other circumstances make the imposition of the sanction unjust.

(c)(1) Notwithstanding subdivision (b), or any other section of this title, absent exceptional circumstances, the court shall not impose sanctions on a party or any attorney of a party for failure to provide electronically stored information that has been lost, damaged, altered, or overwritten as the result of the routine, good faith operation of an electronic information system.

(2) This subdivision shall not be construed to alter any obligation to preserve discoverable information. *(Added by Stats.2004, c. 182, § 23, operative July 1, 2005. Amended by Stats.2012, c. 72, § 9.)*

Article 2. Scope of Discovery in Specific Contexts

§ 2017.210. Insurance Carriers; Nature, Limits or Disputes Regarding Coverage

A party may obtain discovery of the existence and contents of any agreement under which any insurance carrier may be liable to satisfy in whole or in part a judgment that may be entered in the action or to indemnify or reimburse for payments made to satisfy the judgment. This discovery may include the identity of the carrier and the nature and limits of the coverage. A party may also obtain discovery as to whether that insurance carrier is disputing the agreement's coverage of the claim involved in the action, but not as to the nature and substance of that dispute. Information concerning the insurance agreement is not by reason of disclosure admissible in evidence at trial. *(Added by Stats.2004, c. 182, § 23, operative July 1, 2005.)*

§ 2017.220. Sexual Harassment, Assault or Battery Allegations; Monetary Sanctions

(a) In any civil action alleging conduct that constitutes sexual harassment, sexual assault, or sexual battery, any party seeking discovery concerning the plaintiff's sexual conduct with individuals other than the alleged perpetrator shall establish specific facts showing that there is good cause for that discovery, and that the matter sought to be discovered is relevant to the subject matter of the action and reasonably calculated to lead to the discovery of admissible evidence. This showing shall be made by a noticed motion, accompanied by a meet and confer declaration under Section 2016.040, and shall not be made or considered by the court at an ex parte hearing.

(b) The court shall impose a monetary sanction under Chapter 7 (commencing with Section 2023.010) against any party, person, or attorney who unsuccessfully makes or opposes a motion for discovery under subdivision (a), unless it finds that the one subject to the sanction acted with substantial justification or that other circumstances make the imposition of the sanction unjust. *(Added by Stats.2004, c. 182, § 23, operative July 1, 2005.)*

Article 3. Violation of the Elder Abuse and Dependent Adult Civil Protection Act

§ 2017.310. Confidential Settlement Agreements; Recognition or Enforcement by Court; Sealing or Redacting Defendant's Name; Enforcement of Nondisclosure Provisions

(a) Notwithstanding any other provision of law, it is the policy of the State of California that confidential settlement agreements are disfavored in any civil action the factual foundation for which establishes a cause of action for a violation of the Elder Abuse and Dependent Adult Civil Protection Act (Chapter 11 (commencing with Section 15600) of Part 3 of Division 9 of the Welfare and Institutions Code).

(b) Provisions of a confidential settlement agreement described in subdivision (a) may not be recognized or enforced by the court absent a showing of any of the following:

(1) The information is privileged under existing law.

(2) The information is not evidence of abuse of an elder or dependent adult, as described in Sections 15610.30, 15610.57, and 15610.63 of the Welfare and Institutions Code.

(3) The party seeking to uphold the confidentiality of the information has demonstrated that there is a substantial probability that prejudice will result from the disclosure and that the party's interest in the information cannot be adequately protected through redaction.

(c) Nothing in paragraph (1), (2), or (3) of subdivision (b) permits the sealing or redacting of a defendant's name in any information made available to the public.

(d) Except as expressly provided in this section, nothing in this section is intended to alter, modify, or amend existing law.

(e) Nothing in this section may be deemed to prohibit the entry or enforcement of that part of a confidentiality agreement, settlement agreement, or stipulated agreement between the parties that requires the nondisclosure of the amount of any money paid in a settlement of a claim.

(f) Nothing in this section applies to or affects an action for professional negligence against a health care provider. *(Added by Stats.2004, c. 182, § 23, operative July 1, 2005.)*

§ 2017.320. Evidence Subject to Pre-existing Protective Order; Evidence of Abuse Excluded from Protection; Use in Subsequent Proceedings; Standard of Proof; Judicial Authority to Seal or Redact

(a) In any civil action the factual foundation for which establishes a cause of action for a violation of the Elder Abuse and Dependent Adult Civil Protection Act (Chapter 11 (commencing with Section 15600) of Part 3 of Division 9 of the Welfare and Institutions Code), any information that is acquired through discovery and is protected from disclosure by a stipulated protective order shall remain subject to the protective order, except for information that is evidence of abuse of an elder or dependent adult as described in Sections 15610.30, 15610.57, and 15610.63 of the Welfare and Institutions Code.

(b) In that instance, after redacting information in the document that is not evidence of abuse of an elder or dependent adult as described in Sections 15610.30, 15610.57, and 15610.63 of the Welfare and Institutions Code, a party may file that particularized information with the court. The party proposing to file the information shall offer to meet and confer with the party from whom the information was obtained at least one week prior to filing that information with the court.

(c) The filing party shall give concurrent notice of the filing with the court and its basis to the party from whom the information was obtained.

(d) Any filed information submitted to the court shall remain confidential under any protective order for 30 days after the filing and shall be part of the public court record thereafter, unless an affected party petitions the court and shows good cause for a court protective order.

(e) The burden of showing good cause shall be on the party seeking the court protective order.

(f) A stipulated protective order may not be recognized or enforced by the court to prevent disclosure of information filed with the court pursuant to subdivision (b), absent a showing of any of the following:

(1) The information is privileged under existing law.

(2) The information is not evidence of abuse of an elder or dependent adult as described in Sections 15610.30, 15610.57, and 15610.63 of the Welfare and Institutions Code.

(3) The party seeking to uphold the confidentiality of the information has demonstrated that there is a substantial probability that prejudice will result from the disclosure and that the party's interest in the information cannot be adequately protected through redaction.

(g) If the court denies the petition for a court protective order, it shall redact any part of the filed information it finds is not evidence of abuse of an elder or dependent adult, as described in Sections 15610.30, 15610.57, and 15610.63 of the Welfare and Institutions Code. Nothing in this subdivision or in paragraph (1), (2), or (3) of subdivision (f) permits the sealing or redacting of a defendant's name in any information made available to the public.

(h) Nothing in this section applies to or affects an action for professional negligence against a health care provider. *(Added by Stats.2004, c. 182, § 23, operative July 1, 2005.)*

Chapter 4. Attorney Work Product

§ 2018.010. "Client" Defined

For purposes of this chapter, "client" means a "client" as defined in Section 951 of the Evidence Code. *(Added by Stats.2004, c. 182, § 23, operative July 1, 2005.)*

§ 2018.020. Policy of the State

It is the policy of the state to do both of the following:

(a) Preserve the rights of attorneys to prepare cases for trial with that degree of privacy necessary to encourage them to prepare their cases thoroughly and to investigate not only the favorable but the unfavorable aspects of those cases.

(b) Prevent attorneys from taking undue advantage of their adversary's industry and efforts. *(Added by Stats.2004, c. 182, § 23, operative July 1, 2005.)*

§ 2018.030. Writings and Written Documentation

(a) A writing that reflects an attorney's impressions, conclusions, opinions, or legal research or theories is not discoverable under any circumstances.

(b) The work product of an attorney, other than a writing described in subdivision (a), is not discoverable unless the court determines that denial of discovery will unfairly prejudice the party seeking discovery in preparing that party's claim or defense or will result in an injustice. *(Added by Stats.2004, c. 182, § 23, operative July 1, 2005.)*

§ 2018.040. Restatement of Existing Law

This chapter is intended to be a restatement of existing law relating to protection of work product. It is not intended to expand or reduce the extent to which work product is discoverable under existing law in any action. *(Added by Stats.2004, c. 182, § 23, operative July 1, 2005.)*

§ 2018.050. Participation in Crime or Fraud

Notwithstanding Section 2018.040, when a lawyer is suspected of knowingly participating in a crime or fraud, there is no protection of work product under this chapter in any official investigation by a law enforcement agency or proceeding or action brought by a public prosecutor in the name of the people of the State of California if the services of the lawyer were sought or obtained to enable or aid anyone to commit or plan to commit a crime or fraud. *(Added by Stats.2004, c. 182, § 23, operative July 1, 2005.)*

§ 2018.060. In Camera Hearings

Nothing in this chapter is intended to limit an attorney's ability to request an in camera hearing as provided for in People v. Superior Court (Laff) (2001) 25 Cal.4th 703. *(Added by Stats.2004, c. 182, § 23, operative July 1, 2005.)*

§ 2018.070. Disciplinary Proceedings

(a) The State Bar may discover the work product of an attorney against whom disciplinary charges are pending when it is relevant to issues of breach of duty by the lawyer and requisite client approval has been granted.

(b) Where requested and for good cause, discovery under this section shall be subject to a protective order to ensure the confidentiality of the work product except for its use by the State Bar in disciplinary investigations and its consideration under seal in State Bar Court proceedings.

(c) For purposes of this chapter, whenever a client has initiated a complaint against an attorney, the requisite client approval shall be deemed to have been granted. *(Added by Stats.2004, c. 182, § 23, operative July 1, 2005.)*

§ 2018.080. Breach of Duty; Actions Against Attorney by Client or Former Client

In an action between an attorney and a client or a former client of the attorney, no work product privilege under this chapter exists if the work product is relevant to an issue of breach by the attorney of a duty to the client arising out of the attorney-client relationship. *(Added by Stats.2004, c. 182, § 23, operative July 1, 2005.)*

Chapter 5. Methods and Sequence of Discovery

Article 1. General Provisions

§ 2019.010. Approved Methods

Any party may obtain discovery by one or more of the following methods:

(a) Oral and written depositions.

(b) Interrogatories to a party.

(c) Inspections of documents, things, and places.

(d) Physical and mental examinations.

(e) Requests for admissions.

(f) Simultaneous exchanges of expert trial witness information. *(Added by Stats.2004, c. 182, § 23, operative July 1, 2005.)*

§ 2019.020. Sequence and Timing; Discretion of Parties; Court Order

(a) Except as otherwise provided by a rule of the Judicial Council, a local court rule, or a local uniform written policy, the methods of discovery may be used in any sequence, and the fact that a party is conducting discovery, whether by deposition or another method, shall not operate to delay the discovery of any other party.

(b) Notwithstanding subdivision (a), on motion and for good cause shown, the court may establish the sequence and timing of discovery for the convenience of parties and witnesses and in the interests of justice. *(Added by Stats.2004, c. 182, § 23, operative July 1, 2005.)*

§ 2019.030. Court-Imposed Restrictions; Motion; Monetary Sanction

(a) The court shall restrict the frequency or extent of use of a discovery method provided in Section 2019.010 if it determines either of the following:

(1) The discovery sought is unreasonably cumulative or duplicative, or is obtainable from some other source that is more convenient, less burdensome, or less expensive.

(2) The selected method of discovery is unduly burdensome or expensive, taking into account the needs of the case, the amount in controversy, and the importance of the issues at stake in the litigation.

(b) The court may make these determinations pursuant to a motion for a protective order by a party or other affected person. This motion shall be accompanied by a meet and confer declaration under Section 2016.040.

(c) The court shall impose a monetary sanction under Chapter 7 (commencing with Section 2023.010) against any party, person, or attorney who unsuccessfully makes or opposes a motion for a protective order, unless it finds that the one subject to the sanction acted with substantial justification or that other circumstances make the imposition of the sanction unjust. *(Added by Stats.2004, c. 182, § 23, operative July 1, 2005.)*

§ 2019.040. Application of Discovery Methods and Procedures to Electronically Stored Information

(a) When any method of discovery permits the production, inspection, copying, testing, or sampling of documents or tangible things, that method shall also permit the production, inspection, copying, testing, or sampling of electronically stored information.

(b) All procedures available under this title to compel, prevent, or limit the production, inspection, copying, testing, or sampling of documents or tangible things shall be available to compel, prevent, or limit the production, inspection, copying, testing, or sampling of electronically stored information. *(Added by Stats.2012, c. 72, § 14.)*

Article 2. Methods and Sequence of Discovery in Specific Contexts

§ 2019.210. Misappropriation of Trade Secrets

In any action alleging the misappropriation of a trade secret under the Uniform Trade Secrets Act (Title 5 (commencing with Section 3426) of Part 1 of Division 4 of the Civil Code), before commencing discovery relating to the trade secret, the party alleging the misappropriation shall identify the trade secret with reasonable particularity subject to any orders that may be appropriate under Section 3426.5 of the Civil Code. *(Added by Stats.2004, c. 182, § 23, operative July 1, 2005.)*

Chapter 6. Nonparty Discovery

Article 1. General Provisions

§ 2020.010. Persons Within the State; Approved Methods

(a) Any of the following methods may be used to obtain discovery within the state from a person who is not a party to the action in which the discovery is sought:

(1) An oral deposition under Chapter 9 (commencing with Section 2025.010).

(2) A written deposition under Chapter 11 (commencing with Section 2028.010).

(3) A deposition for production of business records and things under Article 4 (commencing with Section 2020.410) or Article 5 (commencing with Section 2020.510).

(b) Except as provided in subdivision (a) of Section 2025.280, the process by which a nonparty is required to provide discovery is a deposition subpoena. *(Added by Stats.2004, c. 182, § 23, operative July 1, 2005.)*

§ 2020.020. Deposition Subpoena; Scope of Authority

A deposition subpoena may command any of the following:

(a) Only the attendance and the testimony of the deponent, under Article 3 (commencing with Section 2020.310).

(b) Only the production of business records for copying, under Article 4 (commencing with Section 2020.410).

(c) The attendance and the testimony of the deponent, as well as the production of business records, other documents, electronically stored information, and tangible things, under Article 5 (commencing with Section 2020.510). *(Added by Stats.2004, c. 182, § 23, operative July 1, 2005. Amended by Stats.2012, c. 72, § 15.)*

§ 2020.030. Application of Evidence Code Provisions to Deposition Subpoena

Except as modified in this chapter, the provisions of Chapter 2 (commencing with Section 1985) of Title 3 of Part 4 of this code, and of Article 4 (commencing with Section 1560) of Chapter 2 of Division 11 of the Evidence Code, apply to a deposition subpoena. *(Added by Stats.2004, c. 182, § 23, operative July 1, 2005.)*

Article 2. Procedures Applicable to All Types of Deposition Subpoenas

§ 2020.210. Issuance by Court Clerk; Alternative Method of Issuance

(a) The clerk of the court in which the action is pending shall issue a deposition subpoena signed and sealed, but otherwise in blank, to a party requesting it, who shall fill it in before service.

(b) Instead of a court-issued deposition subpoena, an attorney of record for any party may sign and issue a deposition subpoena. A deposition subpoena issued under this subdivision need not be sealed. A copy may be served on the nonparty, and the attorney may retain the original. *(Added by Stats.2004, c. 182, § 23, operative July 1, 2005.)*

§ 2020.220. Service of Documents; Timing; Persons Authorized to Serve; Scope of Subpoena Authority

(a) Subject to subdivision (c) of Section 2020.410, service of a deposition subpoena shall be effected a sufficient time in advance of the deposition to provide the deponent a reasonable opportunity to locate and produce any designated business records, documents, electronically stored information, and tangible things, as described in Article 4 (commencing with Section 2020.410), and, where personal attendance is commanded, a reasonable time to travel to the place of deposition.

(b) Any person may serve the subpoena by personal delivery of a copy of it as follows:

(1) If the deponent is a natural person, to that person.

(2) If the deponent is an organization, to any officer, director, custodian of records, or to any agent or employee authorized by the organization to accept service of a subpoena.

(c) Personal service of any deposition subpoena is effective to require all of the following of any deponent who is a resident of California at the time of service:

(1) Personal attendance and testimony, if the subpoena so specifies.

(2) Any specified production, inspection, testing, and sampling.

(3) The deponent's attendance at a court session to consider any issue arising out of the deponent's refusal to be sworn, or to answer any question, or to produce specified items, or to permit inspection or photocopying, if the subpoena so specifies, or specified testing and sampling of the items produced.

(d) Unless the subpoenaing party and the subpoenaed person otherwise agree or the court otherwise orders, the following shall apply:

(1) If a subpoena requiring production of electronically stored information does not specify a form or forms for producing a type of electronically stored information, the person subpoenaed shall produce the information in the form or forms in which it is ordinarily maintained or in a form that is reasonably usable.

(2) A subpoenaed person need not produce the same electronically stored information in more than one form.

(e) The subpoenaed person opposing the production, inspection, copying, testing, or sampling of electronically stored information on the basis that the information is from a source that is not reasonably accessible because of undue burden or expense shall bear the burden of demonstrating that the information is from a source that is not reasonably accessible because of undue burden or expense.

(f) If the person from whom discovery of electronically stored information is subpoenaed establishes that the information is from a source that is not reasonably accessible because of undue burden or expense, the court may nonetheless order discovery if the subpoenaing party shows good cause, subject to any limitations imposed under subdivision (i).

(g) If the court finds good cause for the production of electronically stored information from a source that is not reasonably accessible, the court may set conditions for the discovery of the electronically stored information, including allocation of the expense of discovery.

(h) If necessary, the subpoenaed person, at the reasonable expense of the subpoenaing party, shall, through detection devices, translate any data compilations included in the subpoena into a reasonably usable form.

(i) The court shall limit the frequency or extent of discovery of electronically stored information, even from a source that is reasonably accessible, if the court determines that any of the following conditions exists:

(1) It is possible to obtain the information from some other source that is more convenient, less burdensome, or less expensive.

(2) The discovery sought is unreasonably cumulative or duplicative.

(3) The party seeking discovery has had ample opportunity by discovery in the action to obtain the information sought.

(4) The likely burden or expense of the proposed discovery outweighs the likely benefit, taking into account the amount in controversy, the resources of the parties, the importance of the issues in the litigation, and the importance of the requested discovery in resolving the issues.

(j) If a subpoenaed person notifies the subpoenaing party that electronically stored information produced pursuant to a subpoena is subject to a claim of privilege or of protection as attorney work product, as described in Section 2031.285, the provisions of Section 2031.285 shall apply.

(k) A party serving a subpoena requiring the production of electronically stored information shall take reasonable steps to avoid imposing undue burden or expense on a person subject to the subpoena.

(*l*) An order of the court requiring compliance with a subpoena issued under this section shall protect a person who is neither a party nor a party's officer from undue burden or expense resulting from compliance.

(m)(1) Absent exceptional circumstances, the court shall not impose sanctions on a subpoenaed person or any attorney of a subpoenaed person for failure to provide electronically stored information that has been lost, damaged, altered, or overwritten as the result of the routine, good faith operation of an electronic information system.

(2) The subdivision shall not be construed to alter any obligation to preserve discoverable information. *(Added by Stats.2004, c. 182, § 23, operative July 1, 2005. Amended by Stats.2012, c. 72, § 16.)*

§ 2020.230. Personal Attendance of Deponent; Witness and Mileage fees; Custodian of Records

(a) If a deposition subpoena requires the personal attendance of the deponent, under Article 3 (commencing with Section 2020.310) or Article 5 (commencing with Section 2020.510), the party noticing the deposition shall pay to the deponent in cash or by check the same witness fee and mileage required by Chapter 1 (commencing with Section 68070) of Title 8 of the Government Code for attendance and testimony before the court in which the action is pending. This payment, whether or not demanded by the deponent, shall be made, at the option of the party noticing the deposition, either at the time of service of the deposition subpoena, or at the time the deponent attends for the taking of testimony.

(b) Service of a deposition subpoena that does not require the personal attendance of a custodian of records or other qualified person, under Article 4 (commencing with Section 2020.410), shall be accompanied, whether or not demanded by the deponent, by a payment in cash or by check of the witness fee required by paragraph (6) of subdivision (b) of Section 1563 of the Evidence Code. *(Added by Stats.2004, c. 182, § 23, operative July 1, 2005.)*

§ 2020.240. Failure to Obey Subpoena; Contempt; Punishment; Compliance

A deponent who disobeys a deposition subpoena in any manner described in subdivision (c) of Section 2020.220 may be punished for contempt under Chapter 7 (commencing with Section 2023.010) without the necessity of a prior order of court directing compliance by the witness. The deponent is also subject to the forfeiture and the payment of damages set forth in Section 1992. *(Added by Stats.2004, c. 182, § 23, operative July 1, 2005.)*

Article 3. Subpoena Commanding Only Attendance and Testimony of the Deponent

§ 2020.310. Contents of Subpoena; Summarization of Enumerated Topics; Recordation at Hearing; Visual Displays; Necessity of Attendance by Agents or Employees of Deponent

The following rules apply to a deposition subpoena that commands only the attendance and the testimony of the deponent:

(a) The subpoena shall specify the time when and the place where the deponent is commanded to attend the deposition.

(b) The subpoena shall set forth a summary of all of the following:

(1) The nature of a deposition.

(2) The rights and duties of the deponent.

(3) The penalties for disobedience of a deposition subpoena, as described in Section 2020.240.

(c) If the deposition will be recorded using audio or video technology by, or at the direction of, the noticing party under Section 2025.340, the subpoena shall state that it will be recorded in that manner.

(d) If the deposition testimony will be conducted using instant visual display, the subpoena shall state that it will be conducted in that manner.

(e) If the deponent is an organization, the subpoena shall describe with reasonable particularity the matters on which examination is requested. The subpoena shall also advise the organization of its duty to make the designation of employees or agents who will attend the deposition, as described in Section 2025.230. *(Added by Stats.2004, c. 182, § 23, operative July 1, 2005.)*

Article 4. Subpoena Commanding Only Production of Business Records for Copying

§ 2020.410. Specificity of Requests; Records for Copying Only; Certification by Custodian; Personal Records Pertaining to Consumers

(a) A deposition subpoena that commands only the production of business records for copying shall designate the business records to be produced either by specifically describing each individual item or by reasonably particularizing each category of item, and shall specify the form in which any electronically stored information is to be produced, if a particular form is desired.

(b) Notwithstanding subdivision (a), specific information identifiable only to the deponent's records system, like a policy number or the date when a consumer interacted with the witness, is not required.

(c) A deposition subpoena that commands only the production of business records for copying need not be accompanied by an affidavit or declaration showing good cause for the production of the business records designated in it. It shall be directed to the custodian of those records or another person qualified to certify the records. It shall command compliance in accordance with Section 2020.430 on a date that is no earlier than 20 days after the issuance, or 15 days after the service, of the deposition subpoena, whichever date is later.

(d) If, under Section 1985.3 or 1985.6, the one to whom the deposition subpoena is directed is a witness, and the business records described in the deposition subpoena are personal records pertaining to a consumer, the service of the deposition subpoena shall be accompanied either by a copy of the proof of service of the notice to the consumer described in subdivision (e) of Section 1985.3, or subdivision (b) of Section 1985.6, as applicable, or by the consumer's written authorization to release personal records described in paragraph (2) of subdivision (c) of Section 1985.3, or paragraph (2) of subdivision (c) of Section 1985.6, as applicable. *(Added by Stats.2004, c. 182, § 23, operative July 1, 2005. Amended by Stats.2012, c. 72, § 17.)*

§ 2020.420. Professional Photocopier Services; Qualifications; Objections

The officer for a deposition seeking discovery only of business records for copying under this article shall be a professional photocopier registered under Chapter 20 (commencing with Section 22450) of Division 8 of the Business and Professions Code, or a person exempted from the registration requirements of that chapter under Section 22451 of the Business and Professions Code. This deposition officer shall not be financially interested in the action, or a relative or employee of any attorney of the parties. Any objection to the qualifications of the deposition officer is waived unless made before the date of production or as soon thereafter as the ground for that objection becomes known or could be discovered by reasonable diligence. *(Added by Stats.2004, c. 182, § 23, operative July 1, 2005.)*

§ 2020.430. Delivery for Copying; Requirements; Time to Deliver; Application of Evidence Code Concerning Inspection of Records

(a) Except as provided in subdivision (e), if a deposition subpoena commands only the production of business records for copying, the custodian of the records or other qualified person shall, in person, by messenger, or by mail, deliver both of the following only to the deposition officer specified in the subpoena:

(1) A true, legible, and durable copy of the records.

(2) An affidavit in compliance with Section 1561 of the Evidence Code.

(b) If the delivery required by subdivision (a) is made to the office of the deposition officer, the records shall be enclosed, sealed, and directed as described in subdivision (c) of Section 1560 of the Evidence Code.

(c) If the delivery required by subdivision (a) is made at the office of the business whose records are the subject of the deposition subpoena, the custodian of those records or other qualified person shall do one of the following:

(1) Permit the deposition officer specified in the deposition subpoena to make a copy of the originals of the designated business records during normal business hours, as defined in subdivision (e) of Section 1560 of the Evidence Code.

(2) Deliver to the deposition officer a true, legible, and durable copy of the records on receipt of payment in cash or by check, by or on behalf of the party serving the deposition subpoena, of the reasonable costs of preparing that copy, together with an itemized statement of the cost of preparation, as determined under subdivision (b) of Section 1563 of the Evidence Code. This copy need not be delivered in a sealed envelope.

(d) Unless the parties, and if the records are those of a consumer as defined in Section 1985.3 or 1985.6, the consumer, stipulate to an earlier date, the custodian of the records shall not deliver to the deposition officer the records that are the subject of the deposition subpoena prior to the date and time specified in the deposition subpoena. The following legend shall appear in boldface type on the deposition subpoena immediately following the date and time specified for production: "Do not release the requested records to the deposition officer prior to the date and time stated above."

(e) This section does not apply if the subpoena directs the deponent to make the records available for inspection or copying by the subpoenaing party's attorney or a representative of that attorney at the witness' business address under subdivision (e) of Section 1560 of the Evidence Code.

(f) The provisions of Section 1562 of the Evidence Code concerning the admissibility of the affidavit of the custodian or other qualified person apply to a deposition subpoena served under this article. *(Added by Stats.2004, c. 182, § 23, operative July 1, 2005.)*

§ 2020.440. Distribution of Copies to Parties; Deposition Officer Duties; Additional Copies

Promptly on or after the deposition date and after the receipt or the making of a copy of business records under this article, the deposition officer shall provide that copy to the party at whose instance the deposition subpoena was served, and a copy of those records to any other party to the action who then or subsequently, within a period of six months following the settlement of the case, notifies the deposition officer that the party desires to purchase a copy of those records. *(Added by Stats.2004, c. 182, § 23, operative July 1, 2005.)*

Article 5. Subpoena Commanding Both Production of Business Records and Attendance and Testimony of the Deponent

§ 2020.510. Contents of Subpoena; Necessity of Affidavit or Declaration Showing Good Cause; Personal Records Pertaining to Consumers; Employment Records Pertaining to Employees

(a) A deposition subpoena that commands the attendance and the testimony of the deponent, as well as the production of business records, documents, electronically stored information, and tangible things, shall:

(1) Comply with the requirements of Section 2020.310.

(2) Designate the business records, documents, electronically stored information, and tangible things to be produced either by specifically describing each individual item or by reasonably particularizing each category of item.

(3) Specify any testing or sampling that is being sought.

(4) Specify the form in which any electronically stored information is to be produced, if a particular form is desired.

(b) A deposition subpoena under subdivision (a) need not be accompanied by an affidavit or declaration showing good cause for the production of the documents and things designated.

(c) If, as described in Section 1985.3, the person to whom the deposition subpoena is directed is a witness, and the business records described in the deposition subpoena are personal records pertaining to a consumer, the service of the deposition subpoena shall be accompanied either by a copy of the proof of service of the notice to the consumer described in subdivision (e) of Section 1985.3, or by the consumer's written authorization to release personal records described in paragraph (2) of subdivision (c) of Section 1985.3.

(d) If, as described in Section 1985.6, the person to whom the deposition subpoena is directed is a witness and the business records described in the deposition subpoena are employment records pertaining to an employee, the service of the deposition subpoena shall be accompanied either by a copy of the proof of service of the notice to the employee described in subdivision (e) of Section 1985.6, or by the employee's written authorization to release personal records described in paragraph (2) of subdivision (c) of Section 1985.6. *(Added by Stats.2004, c. 182, § 23, operative July 1, 2005. Amended by Stats.2007, c. 113, § 4; Stats.2012, c. 72, § 18.)*

Chapter 7. Sanctions

§ 2023.010. Conduct Subject to Sanctions

Misuses of the discovery process include, but are not limited to, the following:

(a) Persisting, over objection and without substantial justification, in an attempt to obtain information or materials that are outside the scope of permissible discovery.

(b) Using a discovery method in a manner that does not comply with its specified procedures.

(c) Employing a discovery method in a manner or to an extent that causes unwarranted annoyance, embarrassment, or oppression, or undue burden and expense.

(d) Failing to respond or to submit to an authorized method of discovery.

(e) Making, without substantial justification, an unmeritorious objection to discovery.

(f) Making an evasive response to discovery.

(g) Disobeying a court order to provide discovery.

(h) Making or opposing, unsuccessfully and without substantial justification, a motion to compel or to limit discovery.

(i) Failing to confer or to attempt to confer, in person, by telephone, or by videoconference with an opposing party or attorney in a reasonable and good faith attempt to resolve informally any dispute concerning discovery, if the section governing a p articular discovery motion requires the filing of a declaration stating facts showing that an attempt at informal resolution has been made. *(Added by Stats.2004, c. 182, § 23, operative July 1, 2005. Amended by Stats.2025, c. 200, § 13.)*

§ 2023.020. Monetary Sanctions for Failure to Confer

Notwithstanding the outcome of the particular discovery motion, the court shall impose a monetary sanction ordering that any party or attorney who fails to confer as required pay the reasonable expenses, including attorney's fees, incurred by anyone as a result of that conduct. *(Added by Stats.2004, c. 182, § 23, operative July 1, 2005.)*

§ 2023.030. Monetary Sanctions; Issue Sanctions; Evidence Sanctions; Terminating Sanctions; Contempt Sanctions; Authority of Court to Impose

To the extent authorized by the chapter governing any particular discovery method or any other provision of this title, the court, after notice to any affected party, person, or attorney, and after opportunity for hearing, may impose the following sanctions against anyone engaging in conduct that is a misuse of the discovery process:

(a) The court may impose a monetary sanction ordering that one engaging in the misuse of the discovery process, or any attorney advising that conduct, or both pay the reasonable expenses, including attorney's fees, incurred by anyone as a result of that conduct. The court may also impose this sanction on one unsuccessfully asserting that another has engaged in the misuse of the discovery process, or on any attorney who advised that assertion, or on both. If a monetary sanction is authorized by any provision of this title, the court shall impose that sanction unless it finds that the one subject to the sanction acted with substantial justification or that other circumstances make the imposition of the sanction unjust.

(b) The court may impose an issue sanction ordering that designated facts shall be taken as established in the action in accordance with the claim of the party adversely affected by the misuse of the discovery process. The court may also impose an issue sanction by an order prohibiting any party engaging in the misuse of the discovery process from supporting or opposing designated claims or defenses.

(c) The court may impose an evidence sanction by an order prohibiting any party engaging in the misuse of the discovery process from introducing designated matters in evidence.

(d) The court may impose a terminating sanction by one of the following orders:

(1) An order striking out the pleadings or parts of the pleadings of any party engaging in the misuse of the discovery process.

(2) An order staying further proceedings by that party until an order for discovery is obeyed.

(3) An order dismissing the action, or any part of the action, of that party.

(4) An order rendering a judgment by default against that party.

(e) The court may impose a contempt sanction by an order treating the misuse of the discovery process as a contempt of court.

(f)(1) Notwithstanding subdivision (a), or any other section of this title, absent exceptional circumstances, the court shall not impose sanctions on a party or any attorney of a party for failure to provide electronically stored information that has been lost, damaged, altered, or overwritten as the result of the routine, good faith operation of an electronic information system.

(2) This subdivision shall not be construed to alter any obligation to preserve discoverable information. *(Added by Stats.2004, c. 182, § 23, operative July 1, 2005. Amended by Stats.2012, c. 72, § 19.)*

§ 2023.040. Requests for Sanctions; Form and Supporting Documents

A request for a sanction shall, in the notice of motion, identify every person, party, and attorney against whom the sanction is sought, and specify the type of sanction sought. The notice of motion shall be supported by a memorandum of points and authorities, and accompanied by a declaration setting forth facts supporting the amount of any monetary sanction sought. *(Added by Stats.2004, c. 182, § 23, operative July 1, 2005.)*

§ 2023.050. Monetary Sanctions; Failure to Respond in Good Faith to Document Request; Production of Requested Documents Within 7 days of Motion to Compel; Failure to Meet and Confer

(a) Notwithstanding any other law, and in addition to any other sanctions imposed pursuant to this chapter, a court shall impose a one-thousand-dollar ($1,000) sanction, payable to the requesting party, upon a party, person, or attorney if, upon reviewing a request for a sanction made pursuant to Section 2023.040, the court finds any of the following:

(1) The party, person, or attorney did not respond in good faith to a request for the production of documents made pursuant to Section 2020.010, 2020.410, 2020.510, or 2025.210, or to an inspection demand made pursuant to Section 2031.010.

(2) The party, person, or attorney produced requested documents within seven days before the court was scheduled to hear a motion to compel production of the records pursuant to Section 2025.450, 2025.480, or 2031.320 that is filed by the requesting party as a result of the other party, person, or attorney's failure to respond in good faith.

(3) The party, person, or attorney failed to confer in person, by telephone, letter, or other means of communication in writing, as defined in Section 250 of the Evidence Code, with the party or attorney requesting the documents in a reasonable and good faith attempt to resolve informally any dispute concerning the request.

(b) Notwithstanding paragraph (3) of subdivision (*o*) of Section 6068 of the Business and Professions Code, the court may, in its discretion, require an attorney who is sanctioned pursuant to subdivision (a) to report the sanction, in writing, to the State Bar within 30 days of the imposition of the sanction.

(c) The court may excuse the imposition of the sanction required by subdivision (a) if the court makes written findings that the one subject to the sanction acted with substantial justification or that other circumstances make the imposition of the sanction unjust.

(d) Sanctions pursuant to this section shall be imposed only after notice to the party, person, or attorney against whom the sanction is proposed to be imposed and opportunity for that party, person, or attorney to be heard.

(e) For purposes of this section, there is a rebuttable presumption that a natural person acted in good faith if that person was not represented by an attorney in the action at the time the conduct that is sanctionable under subdivision (a) occurred. This presumption may only be overcome by clear and convincing evidence. *(Added by Stats.2019, c. 836, § 2. Amended by Stats.2023, c. 284, § 3.)*

Chapter 8. Time for Completion of Discovery

§ 2024.010. Completion Date

As used in this chapter, discovery is considered completed on the day a response is due or on the day a deposition begins. *(Added by Stats.2004, c. 182, § 23, operative July 1, 2005.)*

§ 2024.020. Setting of Trial Date; Rights of Parties; Trial Continuance or Postponement

(a) Except as otherwise provided in this chapter, any party shall be entitled as a matter of right to complete discovery proceedings on or before the 30th day, and to have motions concerning discovery heard on or before the 15th day, before the date initially set for the trial of the action.

(b) Except as provided in Section 2024.050, a continuance or postponement of the trial date does not operate to reopen discovery proceedings. *(Added by Stats.2004, c. 182, § 23, operative July 1, 2005.)*

§ 2024.030. Expert Evaluations in Eminent Domain Proceedings

Any party shall be entitled as a matter of right to complete discovery proceedings pertaining to a witness identified under Chapter 18 (commencing with Section 2034.010) on or before the 15th day, and to have motions concerning that discovery heard on or before the 10th day, before the date initially set for the trial of the action. *(Added by Stats.2004, c. 182, § 23, operative July 1, 2005.)*

§ 2024.040. Application to Arbitration Proceedings; Application to Summary Proceedings to Obtain Possession of Real Property or Eminent Domain

(a) The time limit on completing discovery in an action to be arbitrated under Chapter 2.5 (commencing with Section 1141.10) of Title 3 of Part 3 is subject to Judicial Council Rule. After an award in a case ordered to judicial arbitration, completion of discovery is limited by Section 1141.24.

(b) This chapter does not apply to either of the following:

(1) Summary proceedings for obtaining possession of real property governed by Chapter 4 (commencing with Section 1159) of Title 3 of Part 3. Except as provided in Sections 2024.050 and 2024.060, discovery in these proceedings shall be completed on or before the fifth day before the date set for trial.

(2) Eminent domain proceedings governed by Title 7 (commencing with Section 1230.010) of Part 3. *(Added by Stats.2004, c. 182, § 23, operative July 1, 2005. Amended by Stats.2012, c. 162, § 17.)*

§ 2024.050. Motions to Complete Discovery Closer to Initial Trial Date; Reopening of Discovery; Discretion of Court; Monetary Sanctions

(a) On motion of any party, the court may grant leave to complete discovery proceedings, or to have a motion concerning discovery heard, closer to the initial trial date, or to reopen discovery after a new trial date has been set. This motion shall be accompanied by a meet and confer declaration under Section 2016.040.

(b) In exercising its discretion to grant or deny this motion, the court shall take into consideration any matter relevant to the leave requested, including, but not limited to, the following:

(1) The necessity and the reasons for the discovery.

(2) The diligence or lack of diligence of the party seeking the discovery or the hearing of a discovery motion, and the reasons that the discovery was not completed or that the discovery motion was not heard earlier.

(3) Any likelihood that permitting the discovery or hearing the discovery motion will prevent the case from going to trial on the date set, or otherwise interfere with the trial calendar, or result in prejudice to any other party.

(4) The length of time that has elapsed between any date previously set, and the date presently set, for the trial of the action.

(c) The court shall impose a monetary sanction under Chapter 7 (commencing with Section 2023.010) against any party, person, or attorney who unsuccessfully makes or opposes a motion to extend or to reopen discovery, unless it finds that the one subject to the sanction acted with substantial justification or that other circumstances make the imposition of the sanction unjust. *(Added by Stats.2004, c. 182, § 23, operative July 1, 2005.)*

§ 2024.060. Agreements to Extend Time or Reopen Discovery; Written Agreement

Parties to an action may, with the consent of any party affected by it, enter into an agreement to extend the time for the completion of discovery proceedings or for the hearing of motions concerning discovery, or to reopen discovery after a new date for trial of the action has been set. This agreement may be informal, but it shall be confirmed in a writing that specifies the extended date. In no event shall this agreement require a court to grant a continuance or postponement of the trial of the action. *(Added by Stats.2004, c. 182, § 23, operative July 1, 2005.)*

Chapter 9. Oral Deposition Inside California

Article 1. General Provisions

§ 2025.010. Persons and Entities Within the State Subject to Deposition

Any party may obtain discovery within the scope delimited by Chapter 2 (commencing with Section 2017.010) and subject to the restrictions set forth in Chapter 5 (commencing with Section 2019.010), by taking in California the oral deposition of any person, including any party to the action. The person deposed may be a natural person, an organization such as a public or private corporation, a partnership, an association, or a governmental agency. *(Added by Stats.2004, c. 182, § 23, operative July 1, 2005. Amended by Stats.2016, c. 86, § 41.)*

Article 2. Deposition Notice

§ 2025.210. Service of Notice; Time Allowed

Subject to Sections 2025.270 and 2025.610, an oral deposition may be taken as follows:

(a) The defendant may serve a deposition notice without leave of court at any time after that defendant has been served or has appeared in the action, whichever occurs first.

(b) The plaintiff may serve a deposition notice without leave of court on any date that is 20 days after the service of the summons on, or appearance by, any defendant. On motion with or without notice, the court, for good cause shown, may grant to a plaintiff leave to serve a deposition notice on an earlier date. *(Added by Stats.2004, c. 182, § 23, operative July 1, 2005.)*

§ 2025.220. Contents of Deposition Notice; Copy of Deposition Subpoena as Notice of Deposition

(a) A party desiring to take the oral deposition of any person shall give notice in writing. The deposition notice shall state all of the following, in at least 12-point type:

(1) The address where the deposition will be taken.

(2) The date of the deposition, selected under Section 2025.270, and the time it will commence.

(3) The name of each deponent, and the address and telephone number, if known, of any deponent who is not a party to the action. If the name of the deponent is not known, the deposition notice shall set forth instead a general description sufficient to identify the person or particular class to which the person belongs.

(4) The specification with reasonable particularity of any materials or category of materials, including any electronically stored information, to be produced by the deponent.

(5) Any intention by the party noticing the deposition to record the testimony by audio or video technology, in addition to recording the testimony by the stenographic method as required by Section 2025.330 and any intention to record the testimony by stenographic method through the instant visual display of the testimony. If the deposition will be conducted using instant visual display, a copy of the deposition notice shall also be given to the deposition officer. Any offer to provide the instant visual display of the testimony or to provide rough draft transcripts to any party which is accepted prior to, or offered at, the deposition shall also be made by the deposition officer at the deposition to all parties in attendance. Any party or attorney requesting the provision of the instant visual display of the testimony, or rough draft transcripts, shall pay the reasonable cost of those services, which may be no greater than the costs charged to any other party or attorney.

(6) Any intention to reserve the right to use at trial a video recording of the deposition testimony of a treating or consulting physician or of any expert witness under subdivision (d) of Section 2025.620. In this event, the operator of the video camera shall be a person who is authorized to administer an oath, and shall not be financially interested in the action or be a relative or employee of any attorney of any of the parties.

(7) The form in which any electronically stored information is to be produced, if a particular form is desired.

(8)(A) A statement disclosing the existence of a contract, if any is known to the noticing party, between the noticing party or a third party who is financing all or part of the action and either of the following for any service beyond the noticed deposition:

(i) The deposition officer.

(ii) The entity providing the services of the deposition officer.

(B) A statement disclosing that the party noticing the deposition, or a third party financing all or part of the action, directed his or her attorney to use a particular officer or entity to provide services for the deposition, if applicable.

(b) Notwithstanding subdivision (a), where under Article 4 (commencing with Section 2020.410) only the production by a nonparty of business records for copying is desired, a copy of the deposition subpoena shall serve as the notice of deposition. *(Added by Stats.2004, c. 182, § 23, operative July 1, 2005. Amended by Stats.2012, c. 72, § 20; Stats.2015, c. 346, § 2; Stats.2018, c. 268, § 1.)*

§ 2025.230. Contents of Deposition Notice; Deponent Not a Natural Person

If the deponent named is not a natural person, the deposition notice shall describe with reasonable particularity the matters on which examination is requested. In that event, the deponent shall designate and produce at the deposition those of its officers, directors, managing agents, employees, or agents who are most qualified to testify on its behalf as to those matters to the extent of any information known or reasonably available to the deponent. *(Added by Stats.2004, c. 182, § 23, operative July 1, 2005.)*

§ 2025.240. Notice to Parties to the Action; Subpoenaing Party Duties; Consumer or Employee Records

(a) The party who prepares a notice of deposition shall give the notice to every other party who has appeared in the action. The deposition notice, or the accompanying proof of service, shall list all the parties or attorneys for parties on whom it is served.

(b) If, as defined in subdivision (a) of Section 1985.3 or subdivision (a) of Section 1985.6, the party giving notice of the deposition is a subpoenaing party, and the deponent is a witness commanded by a deposition subpoena to produce personal records of a consumer or employment records of an employee, the subpoenaing party shall serve on that consumer or employee all of the following:

(1) A notice of the deposition.

(2) The notice of privacy rights specified in subdivision (e) of Section 1985.3 or in subdivision (e) of Section 1985.6.

(3) A copy of the deposition subpoena.

(c) If the attendance of the deponent is to be compelled by service of a deposition subpoena under Chapter 6 (commencing with Section 2020.010), an identical copy of that subpoena shall be served with the deposition notice. *(Added by Stats.2004, c. 182, § 23, operative July 1, 2005. Amended by Stats.2007, c. 113, § 5.)*

§ 2025.250. Location of Deposition; Mileage Restrictions

(a) Unless the court orders otherwise under Section 2025.260, the deposition of a natural person, whether or not a party to the action, shall be taken at a place that is, at the option of the party giving notice of the deposition, either within 75 miles of the deponent's residence, or within the county where the action is pending and within 150 miles of the deponent's residence.

(b) The deposition of an organization that is a party to the action shall be taken at a place that is, at the option of the party giving notice of the deposition, either within 75 miles of the organization's principal executive or business office in California, or within the county where the action is pending and within 150 miles of that office.

(c) Unless the organization consents to a more distant place, the deposition of any other organization shall be taken within 75 miles of the organization's principal executive or business office in California.

(d) If the organization has not designated a principal executive or business office in California, the deposition shall be taken at a place that is, at the option of the party giving notice of the deposition, either within the county where the action is pending, or within 75 miles of any executive or business office in California of the organization. *(Added by Stats.2004, c. 182, § 23, operative July 1, 2005; Amended by Stats.2005. c. 294, § 7.)*

§ 2025.260. Location of Deposition; Exemption from Mileage Restrictions; Order of Court

(a) A party desiring to take the deposition of a natural person who is a party to the action or an officer, director, managing agent, or employee of a party may make a motion for an order that the deponent attend for deposition at a place that is more distant than that permitted under Section 2025.250. This motion shall be accompanied by a meet and confer declaration under Section 2016.040.

(b) In exercising its discretion to grant or deny this motion, the court shall take into consideration any factor tending to show whether the interests of justice will be served by requiring the deponent's attendance at that more distant place, including, but not limited to, the following:

(1) Whether the moving party selected the forum.

(2) Whether the deponent will be present to testify at the trial of the action.

(3) The convenience of the deponent.

(4) The feasibility of conducting the deposition by written questions under Chapter 11 (commencing with Section 2028.010), or of using a discovery method other than a deposition.

(5) The number of depositions sought to be taken at a place more distant than that permitted under Section 2025.250.

(6) The expense to the parties of requiring the deposition to be taken within the distance permitted under Section 2025.250.

(7) The whereabouts of the deponent at the time for which the deposition is scheduled.

(c) The order may be conditioned on the advancement by the moving party of the reasonable expenses and costs to the deponent for travel to the place of deposition.

(d) The court shall impose a monetary sanction under Chapter 7 (commencing with Section 2023.010) against any party, person, or attorney who unsuccessfully makes or opposes a motion to increase the travel limits for a party deponent, unless it finds that the one subject to the sanction acted with substantial justification or that other circumstances make the imposition of the sanction unjust. *(Added by Stats.2004, c. 182, § 23, operative July 1, 2005.)*

§ 2025.270. Date of Deposition

(a) An oral deposition shall be scheduled for a date at least 10 days after service of the deposition notice.

(b) Notwithstanding subdivision (a), in an unlawful detainer action or other proceeding under Chapter 4 (commencing with Section 1159) of Title 3 of Part 3, an oral deposition shall be scheduled for a date at least five days after service of the deposition notice, but not later than five days before trial.

(c) Notwithstanding subdivisions (a) and (b), if, as defined in Section 1985.3 or 1985.6, the party giving notice of the deposition is a subpoenaing party, and the deponent is a witness commanded by a deposition subpoena to produce personal records of a consumer or employment records of an employee, the deposition shall be scheduled for a date at least 20 days after issuance of that subpoena.

(d) On motion or ex parte application of any party or deponent, for good cause shown, the court may shorten or extend the time for scheduling a deposition, or may stay its taking until the determination of a motion for a protective order under Section 2025.420. *(Added by Stats.2004, c. 182, § 23, operative July 1, 2005. Amended by Stats.2007, c. 113, § 6.)*

§ 2025.280. Service of Notice Upon Party Deponents; Effectiveness as to Production or Inspection of Documents

(a) The service of a deposition notice under Section 2025.240 is effective to require any deponent who is a party to the action or an officer, director, managing agent, or employee of a party to attend and to testify, as well as to produce any document, electronically stored information, or tangible thing for inspection and copying.

(b) The attendance and testimony of any other deponent, as well as the production by the deponent of any document, electronically stored information, or tangible thing for inspection and copying, requires the service on the deponent of a deposition subpoena under Chapter 6 (commencing with Section 2020.010).

(c) A deponent required by notice or subpoena to produce electronically stored information shall provide a means of gaining direct access to, or a translation into a reasonably usable form of, any electronically stored information that is password protected or otherwise inaccessible. *(Added by Stats.2004, c. 182, § 23, operative July 1, 2005. Amended by Stats.2012, c. 72, § 21; Stats.2016, c. 467, § 2.)*

§ 2025.290. Time Limits of Depositions

(a) Except as provided in subdivision (b), or by any court order, including a case management order, a deposition examination of the witness by all counsel, other than the witness' counsel of record, shall be limited to seven hours of total testimony. The court shall allow additional time, beyond any limits imposed by this section, if needed to fairly examine the deponent or if the deponent, another person, or any other circumstance impedes or delays the examination.

(b) This section shall not apply under any of the following circumstances:

(1) If the parties have stipulated that this section will not apply to a specific deposition or to the entire proceeding.

(2) To any deposition of a witness designated as an expert pursuant to Sections 2034.210 to 2034.310, inclusive.

(3) To any case designated as complex by the court pursuant to Rule 3.400 of the California Rules of Court, unless a licensed physician attests in a declaration served on the parties that the deponent suffers from an illness or condition that raises substantial medical doubt of survival of the deponent beyond six months, in which case the deposition examination of the witness by all counsel, other than the witness' counsel of record, shall be limited to two days of no more than seven hours of total testimony each day, or 14 hours of total testimony.

(4) To any case brought by an employee or applicant for employment against an employer for acts or omissions arising out of or relating to the employment relationship.

(5) To any deposition of a person who is designated as the most qualified person to be deposed under Section 2025.230.

(6) To any party who appeared in the action after the deposition has concluded, in which case the new party may notice another deposition subject to the requirements of this section.

(c) It is the intent of the Legislature that any exclusions made by this section shall not be construed to create any presumption or any substantive change to existing law relating to the appropriate time limit for depositions falling within the exclusion. Nothing in this section shall be construed to affect the existing right of any party to move for a protective order or the court's discretion to make any order that justice requires to limit a deposition in order to protect any party, deponent, or other natural person or organization from unwarranted annoyance, embarrassment, oppression, undue burden, or expense. *(Added by Stats.2012, c. 346, § 1.)*

§ 2025.295. Health of Deponent; Additional Time Allowed

(a) Notwithstanding Section 2025.290, in any civil action for injury or illness that results in mesothelioma or silicosis, a deposition examination of the plaintiff by all counsel, other than the plaintiff's counsel of record, shall be limited to seven hours of total testimony if a licensed physician attests in a declaration served on the parties that the deponent suffers from mesothelioma or silicosis, raising substantial medical doubt of the survival of the deponent beyond six months.

(b) Notwithstanding the presumptive time limit in subdivision (a), upon request by a defendant, a court may, in its discretion, grant one of the following up to:

(1) An additional three hours of deposition testimony for no more than 10 hours of total deposition conducted by the defendants if there are more than 10 defendants appearing at the deposition.

(2) An additional seven hours of deposition testimony for no more than 14 hours of total deposition conducted by the defendants if there are more than 20 defendants appearing at the deposition.

(c) The court may grant the additional time provided for in paragraphs (1) and (2) of subdivision (b) only if it finds that an extension, in the instant case, is in the interest of fairness, which includes consideration of the number of defendants appearing at the deposition, and determines that the health of the deponent does not appear to be endangered by the grant of additional time. *(Added by Stats.2019, c. 212, § 1.)*

Article 3. Conduct of Deposition

§ 2025.310. Attendance via Remote Electronic Means

(a) At the election of the deponent or the deposing party, the deposition officer may attend the deposition at a different location than the deponent via remote means. A deponent is not required to be physically present with the deposition officer when being sworn in at the time of the deposition.

(b) Subject to Section 2025.420, any party or attorney of record may, but is not required to, be physically present at the deposition at the location of the deponent. If a party or attorney of record elects to be physically present at the location of the deponent, all physically present participants in the deposition shall comply with local health and safety ordinances, rules, and orders.

(c) The procedures to implement this section shall be established by court order in the specific action or proceeding or by the California Rules of Court.

(d) An exercise of the authority granted by subdivision (a) or (b) does not waive any other provision of this title, including, but not limited to, provisions regarding the time, place, or manner in which a deposition shall be conducted.

(e) This section does not alter or amend who may lawfully serve as a deposition officer pursuant to this title or who otherwise may administer oaths pursuant to Sections 2093 and 2094 of this code or Section 8201 of the Government Code. *(Added by Stats.2004, c. 182, § 23, operative July 1, 2005. Amended by Stats.2020, c. 112, § 3, operative Sept. 18, 2020; Stats.2022, c. 92, § 1.)*

§ 2025.320. Deposition Officers; Officer Qualifications and Requirements; Conflict of Interest; Objections; Civil Penalty for Violations

Except as provided in Section 2020.420, the deposition shall be conducted under the supervision of an officer who is authorized to administer an oath and is subject to all of the following requirements:

(a) The officer shall not be financially interested in the action and shall not be a relative or employee of any attorney of the parties, or of any of the parties.

(b) Services and products offered or provided by the deposition officer or the entity providing the services of the deposition officer to any party or to any party's attorney or third party who is financing all or part of the action shall be offered to all parties or their attorneys attending the deposition. No service or product may be offered or provided by the deposition officer or by the entity providing the services of the deposition officer to any party or any party's attorney or third party who is financing all or part of the action unless the service or product is offered or provided to all parties or their attorneys attending the deposition. All services and products offered or provided shall be made available at the same time to all parties or their attorneys.

(c) The deposition officer or the entity providing the services of the deposition officer shall not provide to any party or any party's attorney or third party who is financing all or part of the action any service or product consisting of the deposition officer's notations or comments regarding the demeanor of any witness, attorney, or party present at the deposition. The deposition officer or entity providing the services of the deposition officer shall not collect any personal identifying information about the witness as a service or product to be provided to any party or third party who is financing all or part of the action.

(d) Upon the request of any party or any party's attorney attending a deposition, any party or any party's attorney attending the deposition shall enter in the record of the deposition all services and products made available to that party or party's attorney or third party who is financing all or part of the action by the deposition officer or by the entity providing the services of the deposition officer. A party in the action who is not represented by an attorney shall be informed by the noticing party or the party's attorney that the unrepresented party may request this statement.

(e) Any objection to the qualifications of the deposition officer is waived unless made before the deposition begins or as soon thereafter as the ground for that objection becomes known or could be discovered by reasonable diligence.

(f) Violation of this section by any person may result in a civil penalty of up to five thousand dollars ($5,000) imposed by a court of competent jurisdiction. *(Added by Stats.2004, c. 182, § 23, operative July 1, 2005.)*

§ 2025.330. Oath or Affirmation; Stenographic Record; Electronic Recording; Examination Subject to Evidence Code Provisions; Questions Submitted to Deposition Officer for Answer by Deponent in Lieu of Party Participation

(a) The deposition officer shall put the deponent under oath or affirmation.

(b) Unless the parties agree or the court orders otherwise, the testimony, as well as any stated objections, shall be taken stenographically. If taken stenographically, it shall be by a person certified pursuant to Article 3 (commencing with Section 8020) of Chapter 13 of Division 3 of the Business and Professions Code.

(c) The party noticing the deposition may also record the testimony by audio or video technology if the notice of deposition stated an intention also to record the testimony by either of those methods, or if all the parties agree that the testimony may also be recorded by either of those methods. Any other party, at that party's expense, may make a simultaneous audio or video record of the deposition, provided that the other party promptly, and in no event less than three calendar days before the date for which the deposition is scheduled, serves a written notice of this intention to make an audio or video record of the deposition testimony on the party or attorney who noticed the deposition, on all other parties or attorneys on whom the deposition notice was served under Section 2025.240, and on any deponent whose attendance is being compelled by a deposition subpoena under Chapter 6 (commencing with Section 2020.010). If this notice is given three calendar days before the deposition date, it shall be made by personal service under Section 1011.

(d) Examination and cross-examination of the deponent shall proceed as permitted at trial under the provisions of the Evidence Code.

(e) In lieu of participating in the oral examination, parties may transmit written questions in a sealed envelope to the party taking the deposition for delivery to the deposition officer, who shall unseal the envelope and propound them to the deponent after the oral examination has been completed. *(Added by Stats.2004, c. 182, § 23, operative July 1, 2005. Amended by Stats.2005, c. 294, § 8.)*

§ 2025.340. Recordation by Audio or Video Technology; Procedural Requirements; Submission at Hearing with Stenographic Transcript

If a deposition is being recorded by means of audio or video technology by, or at the direction of, any party, the following procedure shall be observed:

(a) The area used for recording the deponent's oral testimony shall be suitably large, adequately lighted, and reasonably quiet.

(b) The operator of the recording equipment shall be competent to set up, operate, and monitor the equipment in the manner prescribed in this section. Except as provided in subdivision (c), the operator may be an employee of the attorney taking the deposition unless the operator is also the deposition officer.

(c) If a video recording of deposition testimony is to be used under subdivision (d) of Section 2025.620, the operator of the recording equipment shall be a person who is authorized to administer an oath, and shall not be financially interested in the action or be a relative or employee of any attorney of any of the parties, unless all parties attending the deposition agree on the record to waive these qualifications and restrictions.

(d) Services and products offered or provided by the deposition officer or the entity providing the services of the deposition officer to any party or to any party's attorney or third party who is financing all or part of the action shall be offered or provided to all parties or their attorneys attending the deposition. No service or product may be offered or provided by the deposition officer or by the entity providing the services of the deposition officer to any party or any party's attorney or third party who is financing all or part of the action unless the service or product is offered or provided to all parties or their attorneys attending the deposition. All services and products offered or provided shall be made available at the same time to all parties or their attorneys.

(e) The deposition officer or the entity providing the services of the deposition officer shall not provide to any party or any other person or entity any service or product consisting of the deposition officer's notations or comments regarding the demeanor of any witness, attorney, or party present at the deposition. The deposition officer or the entity providing the services of the deposition officer shall not collect any personal identifying information about the witness as a service or product to be provided to any party or third party who is financing all or part of the action.

(f) Upon the request of any party or any party's attorney attending a deposition, any party or any party's attorney attending the deposition shall enter in the record of the deposition all services and products made available to that party or party's attorney or third party who is financing all or part of the action by the deposition officer or by the entity providing the services of the deposition officer. A party in the action who is not represented by an attorney shall be informed by the noticing party that the unrepresented party may request this statement.

(g) The operator shall not distort the appearance or the demeanor of participants in the deposition by the use of camera or sound recording techniques.

(h) The deposition shall begin with an oral or written statement on camera or on the audio recording that includes the operator's name and business address, the name and business address of the operator's employer, the date, time, and place of the deposition, the caption of the case, the name of the deponent, a specification of the party on whose behalf the deposition is being taken, and any stipulations by the parties.

(i) Counsel for the parties shall identify themselves on camera or on the audio recording.

(j) The oath shall be administered to the deponent on camera or on the audio recording.

(k) If the length of a deposition requires the use of more than one unit of tape or electronic storage, the end of each unit and the beginning of each succeeding unit shall be announced on camera or on the audio recording.

(*l*) At the conclusion of a deposition, a statement shall be made on camera or on the audio recording that the deposition is ended and shall set forth any stipulations made by counsel concerning the custody of the audio or video recording and the exhibits, or concerning other pertinent matters.

(m) A party intending to offer an audio or video recording of a deposition in evidence under Section 2025.620 shall notify the court and all parties in writing of that intent and of the parts of the deposition to be offered. That notice shall be given within sufficient time for objections to be made and ruled on by the judge to whom the case is assigned for trial or hearing, and for any editing of the recording. Objections to all or part of the deposition shall be made in writing. The court may permit further designations of testimony and objections as justice may require. With respect to those portions of an audio or video record of deposition testimony that are not designated by any party or that are ruled to be objectionable, the court may order that the party offering the recording of the deposition at the trial or hearing suppress those portions, or that an edited version of the deposition recording be prepared for use at the trial or hearing. The original audio or video record of the deposition shall be preserved unaltered. If no stenographic record of the deposition testimony has previously been made, the party offering an audio or video recording of that testimony under Section 2025.620 shall accompany that offer with a stenographic transcript prepared from that recording. *(Added by Stats.2004, c. 182, § 23, operative July 1, 2005.)*

Article 4. Objections, Sanctions, Protective Orders, Motions to Compel, and Suspension of Depositions

§ 2025.410. Defective Notice; Time to Object; Waiver; Motion to Stay; Meet and Confer Declaration; Monetary Sanctions

(a) Any party served with a deposition notice that does not comply with Article 2 (commencing with Section 2025.210) waives any error or irregularity unless that party promptly serves a written objection specifying that error or irregularity at least three calendar days prior to the date for which the deposition is scheduled, on the party seeking to take the deposition and any other attorney or party on whom the deposition notice was served.

(b) If an objection is made three calendar days before the deposition date, the objecting party shall make personal service of that objection pursuant to Section 1011 on the party who gave notice of the deposition. Any deposition taken after the service of a written objection shall not be used against the objecting party under Section 2025.620 if the party did not attend the deposition and if the court determines that the objection was a valid one.

(c) In addition to serving this written objection, a party may also move for an order staying the taking of the deposition and quashing the deposition notice. This motion shall be accompanied by a meet and confer declaration under Section 2016.040. The taking of the deposition is stayed pending the determination of this motion.

(d) The court shall impose a monetary sanction under Chapter 7 (commencing with Section 2023.010) against any party, person, or attorney who unsuccessfully makes or opposes a motion to quash a deposition notice, unless it finds that the one subject to the sanction acted with substantial justification or that other circumstances make the imposition of the sanction unjust.

(e)(1) Notwithstanding subdivision (d), absent exceptional circumstances, the court shall not impose sanctions on any party, person, or attorney for failure to provide electronically stored information that has been lost, damaged, altered, or overwritten as the result of the routine, good faith operation of an electronic information system.

(2) This subdivision shall not be construed to alter any obligation to preserve discoverable information. *(Added by Stats.2004, c. 182, § 23, operative July 1, 2005. Amended by Stats.2012, c. 72, § 22.)*

§ 2025.420. Protective Orders; Time to Petition Court; Persons Authorized to Petition; Authority and Action by Court; Monetary Sanctions

(a) Before, during, or after a deposition, any party, any deponent, or any other affected natural person or organization may promptly move for a protective order. The motion shall be accompanied by a meet and confer declaration under Section 2016.040.

(b) The court, for good cause shown, may make any order that justice requires to protect any party, deponent, or other natural person or organization from unwarranted annoyance, embarrassment, or oppression, or undue burden and expense. This protective order may include, but is not limited to, one or more of the following directions:

(1) That the deposition not be taken at all.

(2) That the deposition be taken at a different time.

(3) That a video recording of the deposition testimony of a treating or consulting physician or of any expert witness, intended for possible use at trial under subdivision (d) of Section 2025.620, be postponed until the moving party has had an adequate opportunity to prepare, by discovery deposition of the deponent, or other means, for cross-examination.

(4) That the deposition be taken at a place other than that specified in the deposition notice, if it is within a distance permitted by Sections 2025.250 and 2025.260.

(5) That the deposition be taken only on certain specified terms and conditions.

(6) That the deponent's testimony be taken by written, instead of oral, examination.

(7) That the method of discovery be interrogatories to a party instead of an oral deposition.

(8) That the testimony be recorded in a manner different from that specified in the deposition notice.

(9) That certain matters not be inquired into.

(10) That the scope of the examination be limited to certain matters.

(11) That all or certain of the writings or tangible things designated in the deposition notice not be produced, inspected, copied, tested, or sampled, or that conditions be set for the production of electronically stored information designated in the deposition notice.

(12) That designated persons, other than the parties to the action and their officers and counsel, be excluded from attending the deposition.

(13) That a trade secret or other confidential research, development, or commercial information not be disclosed or be disclosed only to specified persons or only in a specified way.

(14) That the parties simultaneously file specified documents enclosed in sealed envelopes to be opened as directed by the court.

(15) That the deposition be sealed and thereafter opened only on order of the court.

(16) That examination of the deponent be terminated. If an order terminates the examination, the deposition shall not thereafter be resumed, except on order of the court.

(c) The party, deponent, or any other affected natural person or organization that seeks a protective order regarding the production, inspection, copying, testing, or sampling of electronically stored information on the basis that the information is from a source that is not reasonably accessible because of undue burden or expense shall bear the burden of demonstrating that the information is from a source that is not reasonably accessible because of undue burden or expense.

(d) If the party or affected person from whom discovery of electronically stored information is sought establishes that the information is from a source that is not reasonably accessible because of undue burden or expense, the court may nonetheless order discovery if the demanding party shows good cause, subject to any limitations imposed under subdivision (f).

(e) If the court finds good cause for the production of electronically stored information from a source that is not reasonably accessible, the court may set conditions for the discovery of the electronically stored information, including allocation of the expense of discovery.

(f) The court shall limit the frequency or extent of discovery of electronically stored information, even from a source that is reasonably accessible, if the court determines that any of the following conditions exist:

(1) It is possible to obtain the information from some other source that is more convenient, less burdensome, or less expensive.

(2) The discovery sought is unreasonably cumulative or duplicative.

(3) The party seeking discovery has had ample opportunity by discovery in the action to obtain the information sought.

(4) The likely burden or expense of the proposed discovery outweighs the likely benefit, taking into account the amount in controversy, the resources of the parties, the importance of the issues in the litigation, and the importance of the requested discovery in resolving the issues.

(g) If the motion for a protective order is denied in whole or in part, the court may order that the deponent provide or permit the discovery against which protection was sought on those terms and conditions that are just.

(h) The court shall impose a monetary sanction under Chapter 7 (commencing with Section 2023.010) against any party, person, or attorney who unsuccessfully makes or opposes a motion for a protective order, unless it finds that the one subject to the sanction acted with substantial justification or that other circumstances make the imposition of the sanction unjust.

(i)(1) Notwithstanding subdivision (h), absent exceptional circumstances, the court shall not impose sanctions on any party, deponent, or other affected natural person or organization or any of their attorneys for failure to provide electronically stored information that has been lost, damaged, altered, or overwritten as the result of the routine, good faith operation of an electronic information system.

(2) This subdivision shall not be construed to alter any obligation to preserve discoverable information. *(Added by Stats.2004, c. 182, § 23, operative July 1, 2005. Amended by Stats.2012, c. 72, § 23.)*

§ 2025.430. Failure to Attend by Party Giving Notice; Sanctions; Exceptions

If the party giving notice of a deposition fails to attend or proceed with it, the court shall impose a monetary sanction under Chapter 7 (commencing with Section 2023.010) against that party, or the attorney for that party, or both, and in favor of any party attending in person or by attorney, unless it finds that the one subject to the sanction acted with substantial justification or that other circumstances make the imposition of the sanction unjust. *(Added by Stats.2004, c. 182, § 23, operative July 1, 2005.)*

§ 2025.440. Failure to Attend by Deponent; Defective Service; Monetary Sanctions; Sanction Where Service is Effective; Refusal to Give Oath

(a) If a deponent does not appear for a deposition because the party giving notice of the deposition failed to serve a required deposition subpoena, the court shall impose a monetary sanction under Chapter 7 (commencing with Section 2023.010) against that party, or the attorney for that party, or both, in favor of any other party who, in person or by attorney, attended at the time and place specified in the deposition notice in the expectation that the deponent's testimony would be taken, unless the court finds that the one subject to the sanction acted with substantial justification or that other circumstances make the imposition of the sanction unjust.

(b) If a deponent on whom a deposition subpoena has been served fails to attend a deposition or refuses to be sworn as a witness, the court may impose on the deponent the sanctions described in Section 2020.240. *(Added by Stats.2004, c. 182, § 23, operative July 1, 2005.)*

§ 2025.450. Failure of Party Deponent to Appear or Produce Documents or Items; Motion to Compel Attendance or Production; Contents of Motion; Monetary Sanctions; Exception; Failure to Follow Court Order

(a) If, after service of a deposition notice, a party to the action or an officer, director, managing agent, or employee of a party, or a person designated by an organization that is a party under Section 2025.230, without having served a valid objection under Section 2025.410, fails to appear for examination, or to proceed with it, or to produce for inspection any document, electronically stored information, or tangible thing described in the deposition notice, the party giving the notice may move for an order compelling the deponent's attendance and testimony, and the production for inspection of any document, electronically stored information, or tangible thing described in the deposition notice.

(b) A motion under subdivision (a) shall comply with both of the following:

(1) The motion shall set forth specific facts showing good cause justifying the production for inspection of any document, electronically stored information, or tangible thing described in the deposition notice.

(2) The motion shall be accompanied by a meet and confer declaration under Section 2016.040, or, when the deponent fails to attend the deposition and produce the documents, electronically stored information, or things described in the deposition notice, by a declaration stating that the petitioner has contacted the deponent to inquire about the nonappearance.

(c) In a motion under subdivision (a) relating to the production of electronically stored information, the party or party-affiliated deponent objecting to or opposing the production, inspection, copying, testing, or sampling of electronically stored information on the basis that the information is from a source that is not reasonably accessible because of the undue burden or expense shall bear the burden of demonstrating that the information is from a source that is not reasonably accessible because of undue burden or expense.

(d) If the party or party-affiliated deponent from whom discovery of electronically stored information is sought establishes that the information is from a source that is not reasonably accessible because of the undue burden or expense, the court may nonetheless order discovery if the demanding party shows good cause, subject to any limitations imposed under subdivision (f).

(e) If the court finds good cause for the production of electronically stored information from a source that is not reasonably accessible, the court may set conditions for the discovery of the electronically stored information, including allocation of the expense of discovery.

(f) The court shall limit the frequency or extent of discovery of electronically stored information, even from a source that is reasonably accessible, if the court determines that any of the following conditions exists:

(1) It is possible to obtain the information from some other source that is more convenient, less burdensome, or less expensive.

(2) The discovery sought is unreasonably cumulative or duplicative.

(3) The party seeking discovery has had ample opportunity by discovery in the action to obtain the information sought.

(4) The likely burden or expense of the proposed discovery outweighs the likely benefit, taking into account the amount in controversy, the resources of the parties, the importance of the issues in the litigation, and the importance of the requested discovery in resolving the issues.

(g)(1) If a motion under subdivision (a) is granted, the court shall impose a monetary sanction under Chapter 7 (commencing with Section 2023.010) in favor of the party who noticed the deposition and against the deponent or the party with whom the deponent is affiliated, unless the court finds that the one subject to the sanction acted with substantial justification or that other circumstances make the imposition of the sanction unjust.

(2) On motion of any other party who, in person or by attorney, attended at the time and place specified in the deposition notice in the expectation that the deponent's testimony would be taken, the court shall

impose a monetary sanction under Chapter 7 (commencing with Section 2023.010) in favor of that party and against the deponent or the party with whom the deponent is affiliated, unless the court finds that the one subject to the sanction acted with substantial justification or that other circumstances make the imposition of the sanction unjust.

(h) If that party or party-affiliated deponent then fails to obey an order compelling attendance, testimony, and production, the court may make those orders that are just, including the imposition of an issue sanction, an evidence sanction, or a terminating sanction under Chapter 7 (commencing with Section 2023.010) against that party deponent or against the party with whom the deponent is affiliated. In lieu of, or in addition to, this sanction, the court may impose a monetary sanction under Chapter 7 (commencing with Section 2023.010) against that deponent or against the party with whom that party deponent is affiliated, and in favor of any party who, in person or by attorney, attended in the expectation that the deponent's testimony would be taken pursuant to that order.

(i)(1) Notwithstanding subdivisions (g) and (h), absent exceptional circumstances, the court shall not impose sanctions on a party or any attorney of a party for failure to provide electronically stored information that has been lost, damaged, altered, or overwritten as the result of the routine, good faith operation of an electronic information system.

(2) This subdivision shall not be construed to alter any obligation to preserve discoverable information. *(Added by Stats.2004, c. 182, § 23, operative July 1, 2005. Amended by Stats.2012, c. 72, § 24.)*

§ 2025.460. Privileged or Protected Information; Time to Object; Waiver; Form of Objection; Adjournment

(a) The protection of information from discovery on the ground that it is privileged or that it is a protected work product under Chapter 4 (commencing with Section 2018.010) is waived unless a specific objection to its disclosure is timely made during the deposition.

(b) Errors and irregularities of any kind occurring at the oral examination that might be cured if promptly presented are waived unless a specific objection to them is timely made during the deposition. These errors and irregularities include, but are not limited to, those relating to the manner of taking the deposition, to the oath or affirmation administered, to the conduct of a party, attorney, deponent, or deposition officer, or to the form of any question or answer. Unless the objecting party demands that the taking of the deposition be suspended to permit a motion for a protective order under Sections 2025.420 and 2025.470, the deposition shall proceed subject to the objection.

(c) Objections to the competency of the deponent, or to the relevancy, materiality, or admissibility at trial of the testimony or of the materials produced are unnecessary and are not waived by failure to make them before or during the deposition.

(d) If a deponent objects to the production of electronically stored information on the grounds that it is from a source that is not reasonably accessible because of undue burden or expense and that the deponent will not search the source in the absence of an agreement with the deposing party or court order, the deponent shall identify in its objection the types or categories of sources of electronically stored information that it asserts are not reasonably accessible. By objecting and identifying information of a type or category of source or sources that are not reasonably accessible, the deponent preserves any objections it may have relating to that electronically stored information.

(e) If a deponent fails to answer any question or to produce any document, electronically stored information, or tangible thing under the deponent's control that is specified in the deposition notice or a deposition subpoena, the party seeking that answer or production may adjourn the deposition or complete the examination on other matters without waiving the right at a later time to move for an order compelling that answer or production under Section 2025.480.

(f) Notwithstanding subdivision (a), if a deponent notifies the party that took a deposition that electronically stored information produced pursuant to the deposition notice or subpoena is subject to a claim of privilege or of protection as attorney work product, as described in Section 2031.285, the provisions of Section 2031.285 shall apply. *(Added by Stats.2004, c. 182, § 23, operative July 1, 2005. Amended by Stats.2012, c. 72, § 25.)*

§ 2025.470. Suspension of Testimony; Authority of Deposition Officer

The deposition officer may not suspend the taking of testimony without the stipulation of all parties present unless any party attending the deposition, including the deponent, demands that the deposition officer suspend taking the testimony to enable that party or deponent to move for a protective order under Section 2025.420 on the ground that the examination is being conducted in bad faith or in a manner that unreasonably annoys, embarrasses, or oppresses that deponent or party. *(Added by Stats.2004, c. 182, § 23, operative July 1, 2005.)*

§ 2025.480. Motion to Compel Answers or Produce Documents or Items; Procedural Requirements; Authority and Action of Court; Failure to Obey Court Order

(a) If a deponent fails to answer any question or to produce any document, electronically stored information, or tangible thing under the deponent's control that is specified in the deposition notice or a deposition subpoena, the party seeking discovery may move the court for an order compelling that answer or production.

(b) This motion shall be made no later than 60 days after the completion of the record of the deposition, and shall be accompanied by a meet and confer declaration under Section 2016.040.

(c) Notice of this motion shall be given to all parties and to the deponent either orally at the examination, or by subsequent service in writing. If the notice of the motion is given orally, the deposition officer shall direct the deponent to attend a session of the court at the time specified in the notice.

(d) In a motion under subdivision (a) relating to the production of electronically stored information, the deponent objecting to or opposing the production, inspection, copying, testing, or sampling of electronically stored information on the basis that the information is from a source that is not reasonably accessible because of the undue burden or expense shall bear the burden of demonstrating that the information is from a source that is not reasonably accessible because of undue burden or expense.

(e) If the deponent from whom discovery of electronically stored information is sought establishes that the information is from a source that is not reasonably accessible because of the undue burden or expense, the court may nonetheless order discovery if the deposing party shows good cause, subject to any limitations imposed under subdivision (g).

(f) If the court finds good cause for the production of electronically stored information from a source that is not reasonably accessible, the court may set conditions for the discovery of the electronically stored information, including allocation of the expense of discovery.

(g) The court shall limit the frequency or extent of discovery of electronically stored information, even from a source that is reasonably accessible, if the court determines that any of the following conditions exists:

(1) It is possible to obtain the information from some other source that is more convenient, less burdensome, or less expensive.

(2) The discovery sought is unreasonably cumulative or duplicative.

(3) The party seeking discovery has had ample opportunity by discovery in the action to obtain the information sought.

(4) The likely burden or expense of the proposed discovery outweighs the likely benefit, taking into account the amount in controversy, the resources of the parties, the importance of the issues in the litigation, and the importance of the requested discovery in resolving the issues.

(h) Not less than five days prior to the hearing on this motion, the moving party shall lodge with the court a certified copy of any parts of the stenographic transcript of the deposition that are relevant to the motion. If a deposition is recorded by audio or video technology, the moving party is required to lodge a certified copy of a transcript of any parts of the deposition that are relevant to the motion.

(i) If the court determines that the answer or production sought is subject to discovery, it shall order that the answer be given or the production be made on the resumption of the deposition.

(j) The court shall impose a monetary sanction under Chapter 7 (commencing with Section 2023.010) against any party, person, or attorney who unsuccessfully makes or opposes a motion to compel an answer or production, unless it finds that the one subject to the sanction acted with substantial justification or that other circumstances make the imposition of the sanction unjust.

(k) If a deponent fails to obey an order entered under this section, the failure may be considered a contempt of court. In addition, if the disobedient deponent is a party to the action or an officer, director, managing agent, or employee of a party, the court may make those orders that are just against the disobedient party, or against the party with whom the disobedient deponent is affiliated, including the imposition of an issue sanction, an evidence sanction, or a terminating sanction under Chapter 7 (commencing with Section 2023.010). In lieu of or in addition to this sanction, the court may impose a monetary sanction under Chapter 7 (commencing with Section 2023.010) against that party deponent or against any party with whom the deponent is affiliated.

(*l*)(1) Notwithstanding subdivisions (j) and (k), absent exceptional circumstances, the court shall not impose sanctions on a deponent or any attorney of a deponent for failure to provide electronically stored information that has been lost, damaged, altered, or overwritten as the result of the routine, good faith operation of an electronic information system.

(2) This subdivision shall not be construed to alter any obligation to preserve discoverable information. *(Added by Stats.2004, c. 182, § 23, operative July 1, 2005. Amended by Stats.2005, c. 22, § 21; Stats.2012, c. 72, § 26.)*

Article 5. Transcript or Recording

§ 2025.510. Transcription of Testimony; Payment of Cost; Distribution of Original and Copies; Record Retention; Audio or Video Recordings; Official Record

(a) Unless the parties agree otherwise, the testimony at a deposition recorded by stenographic means shall be transcribed.

(b) The party noticing the deposition shall bear the cost of the transcription, unless the court, on motion and for good cause shown, orders that the cost be borne or shared by another party.

(c) Notwithstanding subdivision (b) of Section 2025.320, any other party or the deponent, at the expense of that party or deponent, may obtain a copy of the transcript.

(d) If the deposition officer receives a request from a party for an original or a copy of the deposition transcript, or any portion thereof, and the full or partial transcript will be available to that party prior to the time the original or copy would be available to any other party, the deposition officer shall immediately notify all other parties attending the deposition of the request, and shall, upon request by any party other than the party making the original request, make that copy of the full or partial deposition transcript available to all parties at the same time.

(e) Stenographic notes of depositions shall be retained by the reporter for a period of not less than eight years from the date of the deposition, where no transcript is produced, and not less than one year from the date on which the transcript is produced. The notes may be either on paper or electronic media, as long as it allows for satisfactory production of a transcript at any time during the periods specified.

(f) At the request of any other party to the action, including a party who did not attend the taking of the deposition testimony, any party who records or causes the recording of that testimony by means of audio or video technology shall promptly do both of the following:

(1) Permit that other party to hear the audio recording or to view the video recording.

(2) Furnish a copy of the audio or video recording to that other party on receipt of payment of the reasonable cost of making that copy of the recording.

(g) If the testimony at the deposition is recorded both stenographically and by audio or video technology, the stenographic transcript shall be the official record of that testimony for the purpose of the trial and any subsequent hearing or appeal.

(h)(1) The requesting attorney or party appearing in propria persona shall timely pay the deposition officer or the entity providing the services of the deposition officer for the transcription or copy of the transcription described in subdivision (b) or (c), and any other deposition product or service that is requested either orally or in writing.

(2) This subdivision shall apply unless responsibility for the payment is otherwise provided by law or unless the deposition officer or entity is

notified in writing at the time the services or products are requested that the party or another identified person will be responsible for payment.

(3) This subdivision does not prohibit or supersede an agreement between an attorney and a party allocating responsibility for the payment of deposition costs to the party.

(4) Nothing in the case of Serrano v. Stefan Merli Plastering Co., Inc. (2008) 162 Cal.App.4th 1014 shall be construed to alter the standards by which a court acquires personal jurisdiction over a nonparty to an action.

(5) The requesting attorney or party appearing in propria persona, upon the written request of a deposition officer who has obtained a final judgment for payment of services provided pursuant to this subdivision, shall provide to the deposition officer an address that can be used to effectuate service for the purpose of Section 708.110 in the manner specified in Section 415.10.

(i) For purposes of this section, "deposition product or service" means any product or service provided in connection with a deposition that qualifies as shorthand reporting, as described in Section 8017 of the Business and Professions Code, and any product or service derived from that shorthand reporting. *(Added by Stats.2004, c. 182, § 23, operative July 1, 2005. Amended by Stats.2007, c. 115, § 1; Stats.2012, c. 125, § 1; Stats.2014, c. 913, § 12.)*

§ 2025.520. Reading and Correction of Transcript; Signed Approval; Change of Form or Substance of an Answer; Waiver; Suppression Motions

(a) If the deposition testimony is stenographically recorded, the deposition officer shall send written notice to the deponent and to all parties attending the deposition when the original transcript of the testimony for each session of the deposition is available for reading, correcting, and signing, unless the deponent and the attending parties agree on the record that the reading, correcting, and signing of the transcript of the testimony will be waived or that the reading, correcting, and signing of a transcript of the testimony will take place after the entire deposition has been concluded or at some other specific time.

(b) For 30 days following each notice under subdivision (a), unless the attending parties and the deponent agree on the record or otherwise in writing to a longer or shorter time period, the deponent may change the form or the substance of the answer to a question, and may either approve the transcript of the deposition by signing it, or refuse to approve the transcript by not signing it.

(c) Alternatively, within this same period, the deponent may change the form or the substance of the answer to any question and may approve or refuse to approve the transcript by means of a letter to the deposition officer signed by the deponent which is mailed by certified or registered mail with return receipt requested. A copy of that letter shall be sent by first-class mail to all parties attending the deposition.

(d) For good cause shown, the court may shorten the 30-day period for making changes, approving, or refusing to approve the transcript.

(e) The deposition officer shall indicate on the original of the transcript, if the deponent has not already done so at the office of the deposition officer, any action taken by the deponent and indicate on the original of the transcript, the deponent's approval of, or failure or refusal to approve, the transcript. The deposition officer shall also notify in writing the parties attending the deposition of any changes which the deponent timely made in person.

(f) If the deponent fails or refuses to approve the transcript within the allotted period, the deposition shall be given the same effect as though it had been approved, subject to any changes timely made by the deponent.

(g) Notwithstanding subdivision (f), on a seasonable motion to suppress the deposition, accompanied by a meet and confer declaration under Section 2016.040, the court may determine that the reasons given for the failure or refusal to approve the transcript require rejection of the deposition in whole or in part.

(h) The court shall impose a monetary sanction under Chapter 7 (commencing with Section 2023.010) against any party, person, or attorney who unsuccessfully makes or opposes a motion to suppress a deposition under this section, unless the court finds that the one subject to the sanction acted with substantial justification or that other circumstances make the imposition of the sanction unjust. *(Added by Stats.2004, c. 182, § 23, operative July 1, 2005.)*

§ 2025.530. Depositions Without Stenographic Transcription; Review of Recording; Change of Form or Substance of an Answer; Signed Approval; Suppression Motions

(a) If there is no stenographic transcription of the deposition, the deposition officer shall send written notice to the deponent and to all parties attending the deposition that the audio or video recording made by, or at the direction of, any party, is available for review, unless the deponent and all these parties agree on the record to waive the hearing or viewing of the audio or video recording of the testimony.

(b) For 30 days following a notice under subdivision (a), the deponent, either in person or by signed letter to the deposition officer, may change the substance of the answer to any question.

(c) The deposition officer shall set forth in a writing to accompany the recording any changes made by the deponent, as well as either the deponent's signature identifying the deposition as the deponent's own, or a statement of the deponent's failure to supply the signature, or to contact the officer within the period prescribed by subdivision (b).

(d) When a deponent fails to contact the officer within the period prescribed by subdivision (b), or expressly refuses by a signature to identify the deposition as the deponent's own, the deposition shall be given the same effect as though signed.

(e) Notwithstanding subdivision (d), on a reasonable motion to suppress the deposition, accompanied by a meet and confer declaration under Section 2016.040, the court may determine that the reasons given for the refusal to sign require rejection of the deposition in whole or in part.

(f) The court shall impose a monetary sanction under Chapter 7 (commencing with Section 2023.010) against any party, person, or attorney who unsuccessfully makes or opposes a motion to suppress a deposition under this section, unless it finds that the one subject to the sanction acted with substantial justification or that other circumstances make the imposition of the sanction unjust. *(Added by Stats.2004, c. 182, § 23, operative July 1, 2005.)*

§ 2025.540. Certification of Deposition Record; Rough Draft Transcripts

(a) The deposition officer shall certify on the transcript of the deposition, or in a writing accompanying an audio or video record of deposition testimony, as described in Section 2025.530, that the deponent was duly sworn and that the transcript or recording is a true record of the testimony given.

(b) When prepared as a rough draft transcript, the transcript of the deposition may not be certified and may not be used, cited, or transcribed as the certified transcript of the deposition proceedings. The rough draft transcript may not be cited or used in any way or at any time to rebut or contradict the certified transcript of deposition proceedings as provided by the deposition officer. *(Added by Stats.2004, c. 182, § 23, operative July 1, 2005.)*

§ 2025.550. Original Certified Transcript; Transmittal and Custody; Record Retention

(a) The certified transcript of a deposition shall not be filed with the court. Instead, the deposition officer shall securely seal that transcript in an envelope or package endorsed with the title of the action and marked: "Deposition of (here insert name of deponent)," and shall promptly transmit it to the attorney for the party who noticed the deposition. This attorney shall store it under conditions that will protect it against loss, destruction, or tampering.

(b) The attorney to whom the transcript of a deposition is transmitted shall retain custody of it until six months after final disposition of the action. At that time, the transcript may be destroyed, unless the court, on motion of any party and for good cause shown, orders that the transcript be preserved for a longer period. *(Added by Stats.2004, c. 182, § 23, operative July 1, 2005.)*

§ 2025.560. Audio or Video Record of Deposition; Transmittal and Custody of Electronic Media; Distribution of Copies; Record Retention

(a) An audio or video recording of deposition testimony made by, or at the direction of, any party, including a certified recording made by an operator qualified under subdivisions (b) to (f), inclusive, of Section 2025.340, shall not be filed with the court. Instead, the operator shall retain custody of that recording and shall store it under conditions that will protect it against loss, destruction, or tampering, and preserve as far as practicable the quality of the recording and the integrity of the testimony and images it contains.

(b) At the request of any party to the action, including a party who did not attend the taking of the deposition testimony, or at the request of the deponent, that operator shall promptly do both of the following:

(1) Permit the one making the request to hear or to view the recording on receipt of payment of a reasonable charge for providing the facilities for hearing or viewing the recording.

(2) Furnish a copy of the audio or video recording to the one making the request on receipt of payment of the reasonable cost of making that copy of the recording.

(c) The attorney or operator who has custody of an audio or video recording of deposition testimony made by, or at the direction of, any party, shall retain custody of it until six months after final disposition of the action. At that time, the audio or video recording may be destroyed or erased, unless the court, on motion of any party and for good cause shown, orders that the recording be preserved for a longer period. *(Added by Stats.2004, c. 182, § 23, operative July 1, 2005. Amended by Stats.2009, c. 88, § 18.)*

§ 2025.570. Third-Party Request Where Original in Possession of Deposition Officer; Availability; Notice to Parties and Deponent; Protective Orders

(a) Notwithstanding subdivision (b) of Section 2025.320, unless the court issues an order to the contrary, a copy of the transcript of the deposition testimony made by, or at the direction of, any party, or an audio or video recording of the deposition testimony, if still in the possession of the deposition officer, shall be made available by the deposition officer to any person requesting a copy, on payment of a reasonable charge set by the deposition officer.

(b) If a copy is requested from the deposition officer, the deposition officer shall mail a notice to all parties attending the deposition and to the deponent at the deponent's last known address advising them of all of the following:

(1) The copy is being sought.

(2) The name of the person requesting the copy.

(3) The right to seek a protective order under Section 2025.420.

(c) If a protective order is not served on the deposition officer within 30 days of the mailing of the notice, the deposition officer shall make the copy available to the person requesting the copy.

(d) This section shall apply only to recorded testimony taken at depositions occurring on or after January 1, 1998. *(Added by Stats.2004, c. 182, § 23, operative July 1, 2005.)*

Article 6. Post-Deposition Procedures

§ 2025.610. Subsequent Deposition of Deponents; Restrictions; Exceptions

(a) Once any party has taken the deposition of any natural person, including that of a party to the action, neither the party who gave, nor any other party who has been served with a deposition notice pursuant to Section 2025.240 may take a subsequent deposition of that deponent.

(b) Notwithstanding subdivision (a), for good cause shown, the court may grant leave to take a subsequent deposition, and the parties, with the consent of any deponent who is not a party, may stipulate that a subsequent deposition be taken.

(c) This section does not preclude taking one subsequent deposition of a natural person who has previously been examined under either or both of the following circumstances:

(1) The person was examined as a result of that person's designation to testify on behalf of an organization under Section 2025.230.

(2) The person was examined pursuant to a court order under Section 485.230, for the limited purpose of discovering pursuant to Section 485.230 the identity, location, and value of property in which the deponent has an interest.

(d) This section does not authorize the taking of more than one subsequent deposition for the limited purpose of Section 485.230. *(Added by Stats.2004, c. 182, § 23, operative July 1, 2005.)*

§ 2025.620. Use of Deposition at Trial or Other Hearings; Procedural Requirements; Permitted Uses; Submission of Total or Partial Testimony

At the trial or any other hearing in the action, any part or all of a deposition may be used against any party who was present or represented at the taking of the deposition, or who had due notice of the deposition and did not serve a valid objection under Section 2025.410, so far as admissible under the rules of evidence applied as though the deponent were then present and testifying as a witness, in accordance with the following provisions:

(a) Any party may use a deposition for the purpose of contradicting or impeaching the testimony of the deponent as a witness, or for any other purpose permitted by the Evidence Code.

(b) An adverse party may use for any purpose, a deposition of a party to the action, or of anyone who at the time of taking the deposition was an officer, director, managing agent, employee, agent, or designee under Section 2025.230 of a party. It is not ground for objection to the use of a deposition of a party under this subdivision by an adverse party that the deponent is available to testify, has testified, or will testify at the trial or other hearing.

(c) Any party may use for any purpose the deposition of any person or organization, including that of any party to the action, if the court finds any of the following:

(1) The deponent resides more than 150 miles from the place of the trial or other hearing.

(2) The deponent, without the procurement or wrongdoing of the proponent of the deposition for the purpose of preventing testimony in open court, is any of the following:

(A) Exempted or precluded on the ground of privilege from testifying concerning the matter to which the deponent's testimony is relevant.

(B) Disqualified from testifying.

(C) Dead or unable to attend or testify because of existing physical or mental illness or infirmity.

(D) Absent from the trial or other hearing and the court is unable to compel the deponent's attendance by its process.

(E) Absent from the trial or other hearing and the proponent of the deposition has exercised reasonable diligence but has been unable to procure the deponent's attendance by the court's process.

(3) Exceptional circumstances exist that make it desirable to allow the use of any deposition in the interests of justice and with due regard to the importance of presenting the testimony of witnesses orally in open court.

(d) Any party may use a video recording of the deposition testimony of a treating or consulting physician or of any expert witness even though the deponent is available to testify if the deposition notice under Section 2025.220 reserved the right to use the deposition at trial, and if that party has complied with subdivision (m) of Section 2025.340.

(e) Subject to the requirements of this chapter, a party may offer in evidence all or any part of a deposition, and if the party introduces only part of the deposition, any other party may introduce any other parts that are relevant to the parts introduced.

(f) Substitution of parties does not affect the right to use depositions previously taken.

(g) When an action has been brought in any court of the United States or of any state, and another action involving the same subject matter is subsequently brought between the same parties or their representatives or successors in interest, all depositions lawfully taken and duly filed in the initial action may be used in the subsequent action as if originally taken in that subsequent action. A deposition previously taken may also be used as permitted by the Evidence Code. *(Added by Stats.2004, c. 182, § 23, operative July 1, 2005.)*

Chapter 10. Oral Deposition Outside California

§ 2026.010. Depositions in Another State of the United States

(a) Any party may obtain discovery by taking an oral deposition, as described in Section 2025.010, in another state of the United States, or in a territory or an insular possession subject to its jurisdiction. Except as modified in this section, the procedures for taking oral depositions in California set forth in Chapter 9 (commencing with Section 2025.010) apply to an oral deposition taken in another state of the United States, or in a territory or an insular possession subject to its jurisdiction.

(b) If a deponent is a party to the action or an officer, director, managing agent, or employee of a party, the service of the deposition notice is effective to compel that deponent to attend and to testify, as well as to produce any document, electronically stored information, or tangible thing for inspection, copying, testing, or sampling. The deposition notice shall specify a place in the state, territory, or insular possession of the United States that is within 75 miles of the residence or a business office of a deponent.

(c) If the deponent is not a party to the action or an officer, director, managing agent, or employee of a party, a party serving a deposition notice under this section shall use any process and procedures required and available under the laws of the state, territory, or insular possession where the deposition is to be taken to compel the deponent to attend and to testify, as well as to produce any document, electronically stored information, or tangible thing for inspection, copying, testing, sampling, and any related activity.

(d) A deposition taken under this section shall be conducted in either of the following ways:

(1) Under the supervision of a person who is authorized to administer oaths by the laws of the United States or those of the place where the examination is to be held, and who is not otherwise disqualified under Section 2025.320 and subdivisions (b) to (f), inclusive, of Section 2025.340.

(2) Before a person appointed by the court.

(e) An appointment under subdivision (d) is effective to authorize that person to administer oaths and to take testimony.

(f) On request, the clerk of the court shall issue a commission authorizing the deposition in another state or place. The commission shall request that process issue in the place where the examination is to be held, requiring attendance and enforcing the obligations of the deponents to produce documents and electronically stored information and answer questions. The commission shall be issued by the clerk to any party in any action pending in its venue without a noticed motion or court order. The commission may contain terms that are required by the foreign jurisdiction to initiate the process. If a court order is required by the foreign jurisdiction, an order for a commission may be obtained by ex parte application. *(Added by Stats.2004, c. 182, § 23, operative July 1, 2005. Amended by Stats.2012, c. 72, § 27.)*

§ 2027.010. Depositions in a Foreign Nation

(a) Any party may obtain discovery by taking an oral deposition, as described in Section 2025.010, in a foreign nation. Except as modified in this section, the procedures for taking oral depositions in California set forth in Chapter 9 (commencing with Section 2025.010) apply to an oral deposition taken in a foreign nation.

(b) If a deponent is a party to the action or an officer, director, managing agent, or employee of a party, the service of the deposition notice is effective to compel the deponent to attend and to testify, as well as to produce any document, electronically stored information, or tangible thing for inspection, copying, testing, or sampling.

(c) If a deponent is not a party to the action or an officer, director, managing agent or employee of a party, a party serving a deposition notice under this section shall use any process and procedures required and available under the laws of the foreign nation where the deposition is to be taken to compel the deponent to attend and to testify, as well as to produce any document, electronically stored information, or tangible thing for inspection, copying, testing, sampling, and any related activity.

(d) A deposition taken under this section shall be conducted under the supervision of any of the following:

(1) A person who is authorized to administer oaths or their equivalent by the laws of the United States or of the foreign nation, and who is not otherwise disqualified under Section 2025.320 and subdivisions (b) to (f), inclusive, of Section 2025.340.

(2) A person or officer appointed by commission or under letters rogatory.

(3) Any person agreed to by all the parties.

(e) On motion of the party seeking to take an oral deposition in a foreign nation, the court in which the action is pending shall issue a commission, letters rogatory, or a letter of request, if it determines that one is necessary or convenient. The commission, letters rogatory, or letter of request may include any terms and directions that are just and appropriate. The deposition officer may be designated by name or by descriptive title in the deposition notice and in the commission. Letters rogatory or a letter of request may be addressed: "To the Appropriate Judicial Authority in [name of foreign nation]." *(Added by Stats.2004, c. 182, § 23, operative July 1, 2005. Amended by Stats.2012, c. 72, § 28.)*

Chapter 11. Deposition by Written Questions

§ 2028.010. Procedures Applicable

Any party may obtain discovery by taking a deposition by written questions instead of by oral examination. Except as modified in this chapter, the procedures for taking oral depositions set forth in Chapters 9 (commencing with Section 2025.010) and 10 (commencing with Section 2026.010) apply to written depositions. *(Added by Stats.2004, c. 182, § 23, operative July 1, 2005.)*

§ 2028.020. Notice Requirements

The notice of a written deposition shall comply with Sections 2025.220 and 2025.230, and with subdivision (c) of Section 2020.240, except as follows:

(a) The name or descriptive title, as well as the address, of the deposition officer shall be stated.

(b) The date, time, and place for commencement of the deposition may be left to future determination by the deposition officer. *(Added by Stats.2004, c. 182, § 23, operative July 1, 2005.)*

§ 2028.030. Attachment of Questions to Notice; Cross Questions; Redirect and Recross Questions

(a) The questions to be propounded to the deponent by direct examination shall accompany the notice of a written deposition.

(b) Within 30 days after the deposition notice and questions are served, a party shall serve any cross questions on all other parties entitled to notice of the deposition.

(c) Within 15 days after being served with cross questions, a party shall serve any redirect questions on all other parties entitled to notice of the deposition.

(d) Within 15 days after being served with redirect questions, a party shall serve any recross questions on all other parties entitled to notice of the deposition.

(e) The court may, for good cause shown, extend or shorten the time periods for the interchange of cross, redirect, and recross questions. *(Added by Stats.2004, c. 182, § 23, operative July 1, 2005.)*

§ 2028.040. Objection to Form of Question; Service; Time to Serve; Meet and Confer Declaration; Court Action

(a) A party who objects to the form of any question shall serve a specific objection to that question on all parties entitled to notice of the deposition within 15 days after service of the question. A party who fails to timely serve an objection to the form of a question waives it.

(b) The objecting party shall promptly move the court to sustain the objection. This motion shall be accompanied by a meet and confer declaration under Section 2016.040. Unless the court has sustained that objection, the deposition officer shall propound to the deponent that question subject to that objection as to its form.

(c) The court shall impose a monetary sanction under Chapter 7 (commencing with Section 2023.010) against any party, person, or attorney who unsuccessfully makes or opposes a motion to sustain an objection, unless it finds that the one subject to the sanction acted with substantial justification or that other circumstances make the imposition of the sanction unjust. *(Added by Stats.2004, c. 182, § 23, operative July 1, 2005.)*

§ 2028.050. Protection of Privileged or Attorney Work Product; Time to Object; Meet and Confer Declaration; Court Action

(a) A party who objects to any question on the ground that it calls for information that is privileged or is protected work product under Chapter

4 (commencing with Section 2018.010) shall serve a specific objection to that question on all parties entitled to notice of the deposition within 15 days after service of the question. A party who fails to timely serve that objection waives it.

(b) The party propounding any question to which an objection is made on those grounds may then move the court for an order overruling that objection. This motion shall be accompanied by a meet and confer declaration under Section 2016.040. The deposition officer shall not propound to the deponent any question to which a written objection on those grounds has been served unless the court has overruled that objection.

(c) The court shall impose a monetary sanction under Chapter 7 (commencing with Section 2023.010) against any party, person, or attorney who unsuccessfully makes or opposes a motion to overrule an objection, unless it finds that the one subject to the sanction acted with substantial justification or that other circumstances make the imposition of the sanction unjust. *(Added by Stats.2004, c. 182, § 23, operative July 1, 2005.)*

§ 2028.060. Questions on Direct Examination; Copy for Prior Study by Deponent

(a) The party taking a written deposition may forward to the deponent a copy of the questions on direct examination for study prior to the deposition.

(b) No party or attorney shall permit the deponent to preview the form or the substance of any cross, redirect, or recross questions. *(Added by Stats.2004, c. 182, § 23, operative July 1, 2005.)*

§ 2028.070. Orders for Protection of Parties and Deponents; Additional Court Remedies

In addition to any appropriate order listed in Section 2025.420, the court may order any of the following:

(a) That the deponent's testimony be taken by oral, instead of written, examination.

(b) That one or more of the parties receiving notice of the written deposition be permitted to attend in person or by attorney and to propound questions to the deponent by oral examination.

(c) That objections under Sections 2028.040 and 2028.050 be sustained or overruled.

(d) That the deposition be taken before an officer other than the one named or described in the deposition notice. *(Added by Stats.2004, c. 182, § 23, operative July 1, 2005.)*

§ 2028.080. Duty of Officer Before Whom Deposition is Taken

The party taking a written deposition shall deliver to the officer designated in the deposition notice a copy of that notice and of all questions served under Section 2028.030. The deposition officer shall proceed promptly to propound the questions and to take and record the testimony of the deponent in response to the questions. *(Added by Stats.2004, c. 182, § 23, operative July 1, 2005.)*

Chapter 12. Deposition in Action Pending Outside California

Article 1. Interstate and International Depositions and Discovery Act

§ 2029.100. Short Title

This article may be cited as the Interstate and International Depositions and Discovery Act. *(Added by Stats.2008, c. 231, § 3, operative Jan. 1, 2010.)*

§ 2029.200. Definitions

In this article:

(a) "Foreign jurisdiction" means either of the following:

(1) A state other than this state.

(2) A foreign nation.

(b) "Foreign penal civil action" means a civil action authorized by the law of a state other than this state in which the sole purpose is to punish an offense against the public justice of that state.

(c) "Foreign subpoena" means a subpoena issued under authority of a court of record of a foreign jurisdiction.

(d) "Person" means an individual, corporation, business trust, estate, trust, partnership, limited liability company, association, joint venture, public corporation, government, or governmental subdivision, agency, or instrumentality, or any other legal or commercial entity.

(e) "State" means a state of the United States, the District of Columbia, Puerto Rico, the Virgin Islands, a federally recognized Indian tribe, or any territory or insular possession subject to the jurisdiction of the United States.

(f) "Subpoena" means a document, however denominated, issued under authority of a court of record requiring a person to do any of the following:

(1) Attend and give testimony at a deposition.

(2) Produce and permit inspection, copying, testing, or sampling of designated books, documents, records, electronically stored information, or tangible things in the possession, custody, or control of the person.

(3) Permit inspection of premises under the control of the person. *(Added by Stats.2008, c. 231, § 3, operative Jan. 1, 2010. Amended by Stats.2012, c. 72, § 29; Stats.2022, c. 628, § 3, eff. Sept. 27, 2022.)*

§ 2029.300. Issuance of Subpoena

(a) To request issuance of a subpoena under this section, a party shall submit the original or a true and correct copy of a foreign subpoena to the clerk of the superior court in the county in which discovery is sought to be conducted in this state. A request for the issuance of a subpoena under this section does not constitute making an appearance in the courts of this state.

(b) In addition to submitting a foreign subpoena under subdivision (a), a party seeking discovery shall do both of the following:

(1) Submit an application requesting that the superior court issue a subpoena with the same terms as the foreign subpoena. The application shall be on a form prescribed by the Judicial Council pursuant to Section 2029.390. No civil case cover sheet is required.

(2) Pay the fee specified in Section 70626 of the Government Code.

(c) When a party submits a foreign subpoena to the clerk of the superior court in accordance with subdivision (a), and satisfies the requirements of subdivision (b), the clerk shall promptly issue a subpoena for service upon the person to which the foreign subpoena is directed.

(d) A subpoena issued under this section shall satisfy all of the following conditions:

(1) It shall incorporate the terms used in the foreign subpoena.

(2) It shall contain or be accompanied by the names, addresses, and telephone numbers of all counsel of record in the proceeding to which the subpoena relates and of any party not represented by counsel.

(3) It shall bear the caption and case number of the out-of-state case to which it relates.

(4) It shall state the name of the court that issues it.

(5) It shall be on a form prescribed by the Judicial Council pursuant to Section 2029.390.

(e) Notwithstanding subdivision (a), a subpoena shall not be issued pursuant to this section in any of the following circumstances:

(1) If the foreign subpoena is based on a violation of another state's laws that interfere with a person's right to seek or obtain gender-affirming

health care or gender-affirming mental health care or to allow a child to receive gender-affirming health care or gender-affirming mental health care. For the purpose of this paragraph, "gender-affirming health care" and "gender-affirming mental health care" shall have the same meanings as provided in Section 16010.2 of the Welfare and Institutions Code.

(2) If the submitted foreign subpoena relates to a foreign penal civil action and would require disclosure of information related to sensitive services. For purposes of this paragraph, "sensitive services" has the same meaning as defined in Section 791.02 of the Insurance Code. *(Added by Stats.2008, c. 231, § 3, operative Jan. 1, 2010. Amended by Stats.2022, c. 628, § 4, eff. Sept. 27, 2022; Stats.2022, c. 810, § 2.5; Stats.2025, c. 764, § 3.)*

§ 2029.350. Foreign Subpoenas; Issuance of Subpoena under this Article

(a) Notwithstanding Sections 1986 and 2029.300, if a party to a proceeding pending in a foreign jurisdiction retains an attorney licensed to practice in this state, who is an active member of the State Bar, and that attorney receives the original or a true and correct copy of a foreign subpoena, the attorney may issue a subpoena under this article.

(b)(1) Notwithstanding subdivision (a), an authorized attorney shall not issue a subpoena pursuant to subdivision (a) if the foreign subpoena is based on a violation of another state's laws that interfere with a person's right to seek or obtain gender-affirming health care or gender-affirming mental health care or to allow a child to receive gender-affirming health care or gender-affirming mental health care.

(2) For the purpose of this subdivision, "gender-affirming health care" and "gender-affirming mental health care" shall have the same meanings as provided in Section 16010.2 of the Welfare and Institutions Code.

(c) Notwithstanding subdivision (a), an attorney shall not issue a subpoena under this article based on a foreign subpoena that relates to a foreign penal civil action and that would require disclosure of information related to sensitive services. For purposes of this subdivision, "sensitive services" has the same meaning as defined in Section 791.02 of the Insurance Code.

(d) A subpoena issued under this section shall satisfy all of the following conditions:

(1) It shall incorporate the terms used in the foreign subpoena.

(2) It shall contain or be accompanied by the names, addresses, and telephone numbers of all counsel of record in the proceeding to which the subpoena relates and of any party not represented by counsel.

(3) It shall bear the caption and case number of the out-of-state case to which it relates.

(4) It shall state the name of the superior court of the county in which the discovery is to be conducted.

(5) It shall be on a form prescribed by the Judicial Council pursuant to Section 2029.390. *(Added by Stats.2008, c. 231, § 3, operative Jan. 1, 2010. Amended by Stats.2022, c. 628, § 5, eff. Sept. 27, 2022; Stats.2022, c. 810, § 3.5; Stats.2025, c. 764, § 4.)*

§ 2029.390. Judicial Council; Development of Forms

On or before January 1, 2010, the Judicial Council shall do all of the following:

(a) Prepare an application form to be used for purposes of Section 2029.300.

(b) Prepare one or more new subpoena forms that include clear instructions for use in issuance of a subpoena under Section 2029.300 or 2029.350. Alternatively, the Judicial Council may modify one or more existing subpoena forms to include clear instructions for use in issuance of a subpoena under Section 2029.300 or 2029.350. *(Added by Stats.2008, c. 231, § 3.)*

§ 2029.400. Service of Subpoena

A subpoena issued under this article shall be personally served in compliance with the law of this state, including, without limitation, Section 1985. *(Added by Stats.2008, c. 231, § 3, operative Jan. 1, 2010.)*

§ 2029.500. Deposition, Production, and Inspection; Applicable Laws and Rules

Titles 3 (commencing with Section 1985) and 4 (commencing with Section 2016.010) of Part 4, and any other law or court rule of this state governing a deposition, a production of documents or other tangible items, or an inspection of premises, including any law or court rule governing payment of court costs or sanctions, apply to discovery under this article. *(Added by Stats.2008, c. 231, § 3, operative Jan. 1, 2010.)*

§ 2029.600. Application to Court

(a) If a dispute arises relating to discovery under this article, any request for a protective order or to enforce, quash, or modify a subpoena, or for other relief may be filed in the superior court in the county in which discovery is to be conducted and, if so filed, shall comply with the applicable rules or statutes of this state.

(b) A request for relief pursuant to this section shall be referred to as a petition notwithstanding any statute under which a request for the same relief would be referred to as a motion or by another term if it was brought in a proceeding pending in this state.

(c) A petition for relief pursuant to this section shall be accompanied by a civil case cover sheet. *(Added by Stats.2008, c. 231, § 3, operative Jan. 1, 2010.)*

§ 2029.610. Fees; Assignment of Case Number; Requirements for Filed Documents

(a) On filing a petition under Section 2029.600, a petitioner who is a party to the out-of-state proceeding shall pay a first appearance fee as specified in Section 70611 of the Government Code. A petitioner who is not a party to the out-of-state proceeding shall pay the fee specified in subdivision (c) of Section 70626 of the Government Code.

(b) The court in which the petition is filed shall assign it a case number.

(c) On responding to a petition under Section 2029.600, a party to the out-of-state proceeding shall pay a first appearance fee as specified in Section 70612 of the Government Code. A person who is not a party to the out-of-state proceeding may file a response without paying a fee.

(d) Any petition, response, or other document filed under this section shall satisfy all of the following conditions:

(1) It shall bear the caption and case number of the out-of-state case to which it relates.

(2) The first page shall state the name of the court in which the document is filed.

(3) The first page shall state the case number assigned by the court under subdivision (b).

(4) The first page shall state whether or not the person filing the document is a party to the out-of-state case. *(Added by Stats.2008, c. 231, § 3, operative Jan. 1, 2010. Amended by Stats.2011, c. 308, § 4.)*

§ 2029.620. Subsequent Petitions

(a) If a petition has been filed under Section 2029.600 and another dispute later arises relating to discovery being conducted in the same county for purposes of the same out-of-state proceeding, the deponent or other disputant may file a petition for appropriate relief in the same superior court as the previous petition.

(b) The first page of the petition shall clearly indicate that it is not the first petition filed in that court that relates to the out-of-state case.

(c)(1) If the petitioner in the new dispute is a party to the out-of-state case who previously paid a first appearance fee under this article, the petitioner shall pay a motion fee as specified in subdivision (a) of Section 70617 of the Government Code. If the petitioner in the new dispute is a party to the out-of-state case but has not previously paid a first appearance fee under this article, the petitioner shall pay a first appearance fee as specified in Section 70611 of the Government Code.

(2) If the petitioner in the new dispute is not a party to the out-of-state case, the petitioner shall pay the fee specified in subdivision (c) of Section 70626 of the Government Code, unless the petitioner previously paid that fee. If the petitioner previously paid the fee specified in subdivision (c) of Section 70626 of the Government Code, the petitioner shall pay a motion fee as specified in subdivision (a) of Section 70617 of the Government Code.

(d) If a person responding to the new petition is not a party to the out-of-state case, or is a party who previously paid a first appearance fee under this article, that person does not have to pay a fee for responding. If a person responding to the new petition is a party to the out-of-state case but has not previously paid a first appearance fee under this article, that person shall pay a first appearance fee as specified in Section 70612 of the Government Code.

(e) Any petition, response, or other document filed under this section shall satisfy all of the following conditions:

(1) It shall bear the caption and case number of the out-of-state case to which it relates.

(2) The first page shall state the name of the court in which the document is filed.

(3) The first page shall state the same case number that the court assigned to the first petition relating to the out-of-state case.

(4) The first page shall state whether or not the person filing the document is a party to the out-of-state case.

(f) A petition for relief pursuant to this section shall be accompanied by a civil case cover sheet. *(Added by Stats.2008, c. 231, § 3, operative Jan. 1, 2010. Amended by Stats.2011, c. 308, § 5.)*

§ 2029.630. Application of Requirements of Code of Civil Procedure § 1005

A petition under Section 2029.600 or Section 2029.620 is subject to the requirements of Section 1005 relating to notice and to filing and service of papers. *(Added by Stats.2008, c. 231, § 3, operative Jan. 1, 2010.)*

§ 2029.640. Witnesses in State; Necessity of Subpoena

If a party to a proceeding pending in a foreign jurisdiction seeks discovery from a witness in this state by properly issued notice or by agreement, it is not necessary for that party to obtain a subpoena under this article to be able to seek relief under Section 2029.600 or 2029.620. The deponent or any other party may also seek relief under Section

2029.600 or 2029.620 in those circumstances, regardless of whether the deponent was subpoenaed under this article. *(Added by Stats.2008, c. 231, § 3, operative Jan. 1, 2010.)*

§ 2029.650. Writ Petition

(a) If a superior court issues an order granting, denying, or otherwise resolving a petition under Section 2029.600 or 2029.620, a person aggrieved by the order may petition the appropriate court of appeal for an extraordinary writ. No order or other action of a court under this article is appealable in this state.

(b) Pending its decision on the writ petition, the court of appeal may stay the order of the superior court, the discovery that is the subject of that order, or both. *(Added by Stats.2008, c. 231, § 3, operative Jan. 1, 2010.)*

§ 2029.700. Uniformity of Application and Construction

(a) Sections 2029.100, 2029.200, 2029.300, 2029.400, 2029.500, 2029.600, 2029.800, 2029.900, and this section, collectively, constitute and may be referred to as the "California version of the Uniform Interstate Depositions and Discovery Act."

(b) In applying and construing this uniform act, consideration shall be given to the need to promote uniformity of the law with respect to its subject matter among the states that enact it. *(Added by Stats.2008, c. 231, § 3, operative Jan. 1, 2010.)*

Chapter 13. Written Interrogatories

Article 1. Propounding Interrogatories

§ 2030.010. Scope of Discovery; Restrictions

(a) Any party may obtain discovery within the scope delimited by Chapter 2 (commencing with Section 2017.010) and subject to the restrictions set forth in Chapter 5 (commencing with Section 2019.010), by propounding to any other party to the action written interrogatories to be answered under oath.

(b) An interrogatory may relate to whether another party is making a certain contention, or to the facts, witnesses, and writings on which a contention is based. An interrogatory is not objectionable because an answer to it involves an opinion or contention that relates to fact or the application of law to fact, or would be based on information obtained or legal theories developed in anticipation of litigation or in preparation for trial. *(Added by Stats.2004, c. 182, § 23, operative July 1, 2005. Amended by Stats.2015, c. 303, § 42.)*

§ 2030.020. Time to Submit Interrogatories; Motion to Submit at Earlier Time

(a) A defendant may propound interrogatories to a party to the action without leave of court at any time.

(b) A plaintiff may propound interrogatories to a party without leave of court at any time that is 10 days after the service of the summons on, or appearance by, that party, whichever occurs first.

(c) Notwithstanding subdivision (b), in an unlawful detainer action or other proceeding under Chapter 4 (commencing with Section 1159) of Title 3 of Part 3, a plaintiff may propound interrogatories to a party without leave of court at any time that is 10 days after service of the summons on, or appearance by, that party, whichever occurs first.

(d) Notwithstanding subdivisions (b) and (c), on motion with or without notice, the court, for good cause shown, may grant leave to a plaintiff to propound interrogatories at an earlier time. *(Added by Stats.2004, c. 182, § 23, operative July 1, 2005. Amended by Stats.2007, c. 113, § 7; Stats.2025, c. 200, § 14.)*

§ 2030.030. Special Interrogatories; Official Form Interrogatories; Restriction on Number Allowed; Numbers in Excess of Amount Allowed

(a) A party may propound to another party either or both of the following:

(1) Thirty-five specially prepared interrogatories that are relevant to the subject matter of the pending action.

(2) Any additional number of official form interrogatories, as described in Chapter 17 (commencing with Section 2033.710), that are relevant to the subject matter of the pending action.

(b) Except as provided in Section 2030.070, no party shall, as a matter of right, propound to any other party more than 35 specially prepared interrogatories. If the initial set of interrogatories does not exhaust this limit, the balance may be propounded in subsequent sets.

(c) Unless a declaration as described in Section 2030.050 has been made, a party need only respond to the first 35 specially prepared interrogatories served, if that party states an objection to the balance, under Section 2030.240, on the ground that the limit has been exceeded. *(Added by Stats.2004, c. 182, § 23, operative July 1, 2005.)*

§ 2030.040. Special Interrogatories with Supporting Declaration; Exception to Number Restrictions; Burden of Proof; Protective Order

(a) Subject to the right of the responding party to seek a protective order under Section 2030.090, any party who attaches a supporting declaration as described in Section 2030.050 may propound a greater number of specially prepared interrogatories to another party if this greater number is warranted because of any of the following:

(1) The complexity or the quantity of the existing and potential issues in the particular case.

(2) The financial burden on a party entailed in conducting the discovery by oral deposition.

(3) The expedience of using this method of discovery to provide to the responding party the opportunity to conduct an inquiry, investigation, or search of files or records to supply the information sought.

(b) If the responding party seeks a protective order on the ground that the number of specially prepared interrogatories is unwarranted, the propounding party shall have the burden of justifying the number of these interrogatories. *(Added by Stats.2004, c. 182, § 23, operative July 1, 2005.)*

§ 2030.050. Special Interrogatories Exceeding Numeric Restriction; Declaration for Additional Discovery; Form and Contents

Any party who is propounding or has propounded more than 35 specially prepared interrogatories to any other party shall attach to each set of those interrogatories a declaration containing substantially the following:

DECLARATION FOR ADDITIONAL DISCOVERY

I, _______, declare:

1. I am (a party to this action or proceeding appearing in propria persona) (presently the attorney for _______, a party to this action or proceeding).

2. I am propounding to _______ the attached set of interrogatories.

3. This set of interrogatories will cause the total number of specially prepared interrogatories propounded to the party to whom they are directed to exceed the number of specially prepared interrogatories permitted by Section 2030.030 of the Code of Civil Procedure.

4. I have previously propounded a total of _______ interrogatories to this party, of which _______ interrogatories were not official form interrogatories.

5. This set of interrogatories contains a total of ______ specially prepared interrogatories.

6. I am familiar with the issues and the previous discovery conducted by all of the parties in the case.

7. I have personally examined each of the questions in this set of interrogatories.

8. This number of questions is warranted under Section 2030.040 of the Code of Civil Procedure because ______. (Here state each factor described in Section 2030.040 that is relied on, as well as the reasons why any factor relied on is applicable to the instant lawsuit.)

9. None of the questions in this set of interrogatories is being propounded for any improper purpose, such as to harass the party, or the attorney for the party, to whom it is directed, or to cause unnecessary delay or needless increase in the cost of litigation.

I declare under penalty of perjury under the laws of California that the foregoing is true and correct, and that this declaration was executed on ______.

____

(Signature)

Attorney for ______________

(Added by Stats.2004, c. 182, § 23, operative July 1, 2005. Amended by Stats.2005, c. 22, § 22.)

§ 2030.060. Form of Interrogatories; Content Requirements

(a) A party propounding interrogatories shall number each set of interrogatories consecutively.

(b) In the first paragraph immediately below the title of the case, there shall appear the identity of the propounding party, the set number, and the identity of the responding party.

(c) Each interrogatory in a set shall be separately set forth and identified by number or letter.

(d) Each interrogatory shall be full and complete in and of itself. No preface or instruction shall be included with a set of interrogatories unless it has been approved under Chapter 17 (commencing with Section 2033.710).

(e) Any term specially defined in a set of interrogatories shall be typed with all letters capitalized wherever that term appears.

(f) No specially prepared interrogatory shall contain subparts, or a compound, conjunctive, or disjunctive question.

(g) An interrogatory may not be made a continuing one so as to impose on the party responding to it a duty to supplement an answer to it that was initially correct and complete with later acquired information. *(Added by Stats.2004, c. 182, § 23, operative July 1, 2005.)*

§ 2030.070. Supplemental Interrogatories; Restriction on Number Permitted; Exception

(a) In addition to the number of interrogatories permitted by Sections 2030.030 and 2030.040, a party may propound a supplemental interrogatory to elicit any later acquired information bearing on all answers previously made by any party in response to interrogatories.

(b) A party may propound a supplemental interrogatory twice before the initial setting of a trial date, and, subject to the time limits on discovery proceedings and motions provided in Chapter 8 (commencing with Section 2024.010), once after the initial setting of a trial date.

(c) Notwithstanding subdivisions (a) and (b), on motion, for good cause shown, the court may grant leave to a party to propound an additional number of supplemental interrogatories. *(Added by Stats.2004, c. 182, § 23, operative July 1, 2005.)*

§ 2030.080. Service of Documents

(a) The party propounding interrogatories shall serve a copy of them on the party to whom the interrogatories are directed.

(b) The propounding party shall also serve a copy of the interrogatories on all other parties who have appeared in the action. On motion, with or without notice, the court may relieve the party from this requirement on its determination that service on all other parties would be unduly expensive or burdensome. *(Added by Stats.2004, c. 182, § 23, operative July 1, 2005.)*

§ 2030.090. Protective Orders; Persons Entitled to Protection; Time to File; Meet and Confer; Authorized Court Action; Monetary Sanctions

(a) When interrogatories have been propounded, the responding party, and any other party or affected natural person or organization may promptly move for a protective order. This motion shall be accompanied by a meet and confer declaration under Section 2016.040.

(b) The court, for good cause shown, may make any order that justice requires to protect any party or other natural person or organization from unwarranted annoyance, embarrassment, or oppression, or undue burden and expense. This protective order may include, but is not limited to, one or more of the following directions:

(1) That the set of interrogatories, or particular interrogatories in the set, need not be answered.

(2) That, contrary to the representations made in a declaration submitted under Section 2030.050, the number of specially prepared interrogatories is unwarranted.

(3) That the time specified in Section 2030.260 to respond to the set of interrogatories, or to particular interrogatories in the set, be extended.

(4) That the response be made only on specified terms and conditions.

(5) That the method of discovery be an oral deposition instead of interrogatories to a party.

(6) That a trade secret or other confidential research, development, or commercial information not be disclosed or be disclosed only in a certain way.

(7) That some or all of the answers to interrogatories be sealed and thereafter opened only on order of the court.

(c) If the motion for a protective order is denied in whole or in part, the court may order that the party provide or permit the discovery against which protection was sought on terms and conditions that are just.

(d) The court shall impose a monetary sanction under Chapter 7 (commencing with Section 2023.010) against any party, person, or attorney who unsuccessfully makes or opposes a motion for a protective order under this section, unless it finds that the one subject to the sanction acted with substantial justification or that other circumstances make the imposition of the sanction unjust. *(Added by Stats.2004, c. 182, § 23, operative July 1, 2005.)*

Article 2. Response to Interrogatories

§ 2030.210. Mode of Response; Required Contents

(a) The party to whom interrogatories have been propounded shall respond in writing under oath separately to each interrogatory by any of the following:

(1) An answer containing the information sought to be discovered.

(2) An exercise of the party's option to produce writings.

(3) An objection to the particular interrogatory.

(b) In the first paragraph of the response immediately below the title of the case, there shall appear the identity of the responding party, the set number, and the identity of the propounding party.

(c) Each answer, exercise of option, or objection in the response shall bear the same identifying number or letter and be in the same sequence as the corresponding interrogatory. The text of that interrogatory need not be repeated, except as provided in paragraph (6) of subdivision (d).

(d) In order to facilitate the discovery process:

(1) Except as provided in paragraph (5), upon request by the responding party, the propounding party shall provide the interrogatories in an electronic format to the responding party within three court days of the request.

(2) Except as provided in paragraph (5), upon request by the propounding party after receipt of the responses to the interrogatories, the responding party shall provide the responses in an electronic format to the propounding party within three court days of the request.

(3) A party may provide the interrogatories or responses to the interrogatories requested pursuant to paragraphs (1) and (2) in any format agreed upon by the parties. If the parties are unable to agree on a format, the interrogatories or responses to interrogatories shall be provided in plain text format.

(4) A party may transmit the interrogatories or responses to the interrogatories requested pursuant to paragraphs (1) and (2) by any method agreed upon by the parties. If the parties are unable to agree on a method of transmission, the interrogatories or responses to interrogatories shall be transmitted by electronic mail to an email address provided by the requesting party.

(5) If the interrogatories or responses to interrogatories were not created in an electronic format, a party is not required to create the interrogatories or response to interrogatories in an electronic format for the purpose of transmission to the requesting party.

(6) A responding party who has requested and received the interrogatories in an electronic format pursuant to paragraph (1) shall include the text of the interrogatory immediately preceding the response. *(Added by Stats.2004, c. 182, § 23, operative July 1, 2005. Amended by Stats.2019, c. 190, § 1.)*

§ 2030.220. Answers in Response; Contents and Form; Obligations of Responding Party

(a) Each answer in a response to interrogatories shall be as complete and straightforward as the information reasonably available to the responding party permits.

(b) If an interrogatory cannot be answered completely, it shall be answered to the extent possible.

(c) If the responding party does not have personal knowledge sufficient to respond fully to an interrogatory, that party shall so state, but shall make a reasonable and good faith effort to obtain the information by inquiry to other natural persons or organizations, except where the information is equally available to the propounding party. *(Added by Stats.2004, c. 182, § 23, operative July 1, 2005.)*

§ 2030.230. Answers Supplemented by Attached Documents; Specificity of References to Attachments; Examination and Inspection by Responding Party

If the answer to an interrogatory would necessitate the preparation or the making of a compilation, abstract, audit, or summary of or from the documents of the party to whom the interrogatory is directed, and if the burden or expense of preparing or making it would be substantially the same for the party propounding the interrogatory as for the responding party, it is a sufficient answer to that interrogatory to refer to this section and to specify the writings from which the answer may be derived or ascertained. This specification shall be in sufficient detail to permit the propounding party to locate and to identify, as readily as the responding party can, the documents from which the answer may be ascertained. The responding party shall then afford to the propounding party a reasonable opportunity to examine, audit, or inspect these documents and to make copies, compilations, abstracts, or summaries of them. *(Added by Stats.2004, c. 182, § 23, operative July 1, 2005.)*

§ 2030.240. Partial Objection to Form of Interrogatory; Response; Statement of Claim of Privilege or Work Product

(a) If only a part of an interrogatory is objectionable, the remainder of the interrogatory shall be answered.

(b) If an objection is made to an interrogatory or to a part of an interrogatory, the specific ground for the objection shall be set forth clearly in the response. If an objection is based on a claim of privilege, the particular privilege invoked shall be clearly stated. If an objection is based on a claim that the information sought is protected work product under Chapter 4 (commencing with Section 2018.010), that claim shall be expressly asserted. *(Added by Stats.2004, c. 182, § 23, operative July 1, 2005.)*

§ 2030.250. Signature Upon Response; Oath; Officers or Agents of an Entity; Responses Containing Objections

(a) The party to whom the interrogatories are directed shall sign the response under oath unless the response contains only objections.

(b) If that party is a public or private corporation, or a partnership, association, or governmental agency, one of its officers or agents shall sign the response under oath on behalf of that party. If the officer or agent signing the response on behalf of that party is an attorney acting in that capacity for the party, that party waives any lawyer-client privilege and any protection for work product under Chapter 4 (commencing with Section 2018.010) during any subsequent discovery from that attorney concerning the identity of the sources of the information contained in the response.

(c) The attorney for the responding party shall sign any responses that contain an objection. *(Added by Stats.2004, c. 182, § 23, operative July 1, 2005.)*

§ 2030.260. Time to Respond; Shortening of Time; Copies to All Parties

(a) Within 30 days after service of interrogatories, the party to whom the interrogatories are propounded shall serve the original of the response to them on the propounding party, unless on motion of the propounding party the court has shortened the time for response, or unless on motion of the responding party the court has extended the time for response.

(b) Notwithstanding subdivision (a), in an unlawful detainer action or other proceeding under Chapter 4 (commencing with Section 1159) of Title 3 of Part 3, the party to whom the interrogatories are propounded shall have five days from the date of service to respond, unless on motion of the propounding party the court has shortened the time for response, or unless on motion of the responding party the court has extended the time for response.

(c) The party to whom the interrogatories are propounded shall also serve a copy of the response on all other parties who have appeared in the action. On motion, with or without notice, the court may relieve the party from this requirement on its determination that service on all other parties would be unduly expensive or burdensome. *(Added by Stats.2004, c. 182, § 23, operative July 1, 2005. Amended by Stats.2007, c. 113, § 8.)*

§ 2030.270. Time to Respond; Extension of Time by Agreement

(a) The party propounding interrogatories and the responding party may agree to extend the time for service of a response to a set of interrogatories, or to particular interrogatories in a set, to a date beyond that provided in Section 2030.260.

(b) This agreement may be informal, but it shall be confirmed in a writing that specifies the extended date for service of a response.

(c) Unless this agreement expressly states otherwise, it is effective to preserve to the responding party the right to respond to any interrogatory to which the agreement applies in any manner specified in Sections 2030.210, 2030.220, 2030.230, and 2030.240. *(Added by Stats.2004, c. 182, § 23, operative July 1, 2005.)*

§ 2030.280. Custody of Interrogatories, Responses and Supporting Documents; Originals; Record Retention

(a) The interrogatories and the response thereto shall not be filed with the court.

(b) The propounding party shall retain both the original of the interrogatories, with the original proof of service affixed to them, and the original of the sworn response until six months after final disposition of the action. At that time, both originals may be destroyed, unless the court on motion of any party and for good cause shown orders that the originals be preserved for a longer period. *(Added by Stats.2004, c. 182, § 23, operative July 1, 2005.)*

§ 2030.290. Untimely Responses; Waiver of Rights; Exception; Motions to Compel; Monetary Sanctions

If a party to whom interrogatories are directed fails to serve a timely response, the following rules apply:

(a) The party to whom the interrogatories are directed waives any right to exercise the option to produce writings under Section 2030.230, as well as any objection to the interrogatories, including one based on privilege or on the protection for work product under Chapter 4 (commencing with Section 2018.010). The court, on motion, may relieve that party from this waiver on its determination that both of the following conditions are satisfied:

(1) The party has subsequently served a response that is in substantial compliance with Sections 2030.210, 2030.220, 2030.230, and 2030.240.

(2) The party's failure to serve a timely response was the result of mistake, inadvertence, or excusable neglect.

(b) The party propounding the interrogatories may move for an order compelling response to the interrogatories.

(c) The court shall impose a monetary sanction under Chapter 7 (commencing with Section 2023.010) against any party, person, or attorney who unsuccessfully makes or opposes a motion to compel a response to interrogatories, unless it finds that the one subject to the sanction acted with substantial justification or that other circumstances make the imposition of the sanction unjust. If a party then fails to obey an order compelling answers, the court may make those orders that are just, including the imposition of an issue sanction, an evidence sanction, or a terminating sanction under Chapter 7 (commencing with Section 2023.010). In lieu of or in addition to that sanction, the court may impose a monetary sanction under Chapter 7 (commencing with Section 2023.010). *(Added by Stats.2004, c. 182, § 23, operative July 1, 2005.)*

§ 2030.300. Motion to Compel Further Response; Meet and Confer Declaration; Time to Serve Motion; Monetary Sanctions; Failure to Obey Court Order

(a) On receipt of a response to interrogatories, the propounding party may move for an order compelling a further response if the propounding party deems that any of the following apply:

(1) An answer to a particular interrogatory is evasive or incomplete.

(2) An exercise of the option to produce documents under Section 2030.230 is unwarranted or the required specification of those documents is inadequate.

(3) An objection to an interrogatory is without merit or too general.

(b)(1) A motion under subdivision (a) shall be accompanied by a meet and confer declaration under Section 2016.040.

(2) In lieu of a separate statement required under the California Rules of Court, the court may allow the moving party to submit a concise outline of the discovery request and each response in dispute.

(c) Unless notice of this motion is given within 45 days of the service of the verified response, or any supplemental verified response, or on or before any specific later date to which the propounding party and the responding party have agreed in writing, the propounding party waives any right to compel a further response to the interrogatories.

(d) The court shall impose a monetary sanction under Chapter 7 (commencing with Section 2023.010) against any party, person, or attorney who unsuccessfully makes or opposes a motion to compel a further response to interrogatories, unless it finds that the one subject to the sanction acted with substantial justification or that other circumstances make the imposition of the sanction unjust.

(e) If a party then fails to obey an order compelling further response to interrogatories, the court may make those orders that are just, including the imposition of an issue sanction, an evidence sanction, or a terminating sanction under Chapter 7 (commencing with Section 2023.010). In lieu of, or in addition to, that sanction, the court may impose a monetary sanction under Chapter 7 (commencing with Section 2023.010). *(Added by Stats.2004, c. 182, § 23, operative July 1, 2005. Amended by Stats.2013, c. 18, § 1; Stats.2018, c. 317, § 3.)*

§ 2030.310. Amended Answers to Interrogatories; Use at Trial; Motion to Bind Original Answer; Meet and Confer; Court Order; Monetary Sanctions

(a) Without leave of court, a party may serve an amended answer to any interrogatory that contains information subsequently discovered, inadvertently omitted, or mistakenly stated in the initial interrogatory. At the trial of the action, the propounding party or any other party may use the initial answer under Section 2030.410, and the responding party may then use the amended answer.

(b) The party who propounded an interrogatory to which an amended answer has been served may move for an order that the initial answer to that interrogatory be deemed binding on the responding party for the purpose of the pending action. This motion shall be accompanied by a meet and confer declaration under Section 2016.040.

(c) The court shall grant a motion under subdivision (b) if it determines that all of the following conditions are satisfied:

(1) The initial failure of the responding party to answer the interrogatory correctly has substantially prejudiced the party who propounded the interrogatory.

(2) The responding party has failed to show substantial justification for the initial answer to that interrogatory.

(3) The prejudice to the propounding party cannot be cured either by a continuance to permit further discovery or by the use of the initial answer under Section 2030.410.

(d) The court shall impose a monetary sanction under Chapter 7 (commencing with Section 2023.010) against any party, person, or attorney who unsuccessfully makes or opposes a motion to deem binding an initial answer to an interrogatory, unless it finds that the one subject to the sanction acted with substantial justification or that other circumstances make the imposition of the sanction unjust. *(Added by Stats.2004, c. 182, § 23, operative July 1, 2005.)*

Article 3. Use of Interrogatory Answer

§ 2030.410. Trial or Hearing in Which Respondent is a Party

At the trial or any other hearing in the action, so far as admissible under the rules of evidence, the propounding party or any party other than the responding party may use any answer or part of an answer to an interrogatory only against the responding party. It is not ground for objection to the use of an answer to an interrogatory that the responding party is available to testify, has testified, or will testify at the trial or other hearing. *(Added by Stats.2004, c. 182, § 23, operative July 1, 2005.)*

Chapter 14. Inspection, Copying, Testing, Sampling, and Production of Documents, Electronically Stored Information, Tangible Things, Land, and Other Property

Article 1. Inspection Demand

§ 2031.010. Persons Subject to Demand; Scope of Demand; Entrance on Land or Property; Electronically Stored Information

(a) Any party may obtain discovery within the scope delimited by Chapter 2 (commencing with Section 2017.010), and subject to the restrictions set forth in Chapter 5 (commencing with Section 2019.010), by inspecting, copying, testing, or sampling documents, tangible things, land or other property, and electronically stored information in the possession, custody, or control of any other party to the action.

(b) A party may demand that any other party produce and permit the party making the demand, or someone acting on the demanding party's behalf, to inspect and to copy a document that is in the possession, custody, or control of the party on whom the demand is made.

(c) A party may demand that any other party produce and permit the party making the demand, or someone acting on the demanding party's behalf, to inspect and to photograph, test, or sample any tangible things that are in the possession, custody, or control of the party on whom the demand is made.

(d) A party may demand that any other party allow the party making the demand, or someone acting on the demanding party's behalf, to enter on any land or other property that is in the possession, custody, or control of the party on whom the demand is made, and to inspect and to measure, survey, photograph, test, or sample the land or other property, or any designated object or operation on it.

(e) A party may demand that any other party produce and permit the party making the demand, or someone acting on the demanding party's behalf, to inspect, copy, test, or sample electronically stored information in the possession, custody, or control of the party on whom demand is made. *(Added by Stats.2004, c. 182, § 23, operative July 1, 2005. Amended by Stats.2009, c. 5, § 4, eff. June 29, 2009; Stats.2016, c. 86, § 42.)*

§ 2031.020. Time to Make Demand; Inspection, Copying, Testing, or Sampling Prior to Time Allowed

(a) A defendant may make a demand for inspection, copying, testing, or sampling without leave of court at any time.

(b) A plaintiff may make a demand for inspection, copying, testing, or sampling without leave of court at any time that is 10 days after the service of the summons on, or appearance by, the party to whom the demand is directed, whichever occurs first.

(c) Notwithstanding subdivision (b), in an unlawful detainer action or other proceeding under Chapter 4 (commencing with Section 1159) of Title 3 of Part 3, a plaintiff may make a demand for inspection, copying, testing, or sampling without leave of court at any time that is 10 days after service of the summons on, or appearance by, the party to whom the demand is directed, whichever occurs first.

(d) Notwithstanding subdivisions (b) and (c), on motion with or without notice, the court, for good cause shown, may grant leave to a plaintiff to make a demand for inspection, copying, testing, or sampling at an earlier time. *(Added by Stats.2004, c. 182, § 23, operative July 1, 2005.*

Amended by Stats.2007, c. 113, § 9; Stats.2009, c. 5, § 5, eff. June 29, 2009; Stats.2025, c. 200, § 15.)

§ 2031.030. Form and Content of Demand

(a)(1) A party demanding inspection, copying, testing, or sampling shall number each set of demands consecutively.

(2) A party demanding inspection, copying, testing, or sampling of electronically stored information may specify the form or forms in which each type of electronically stored information is to be produced.

(b) In the first paragraph immediately below the title of the case, there shall appear the identity of the demanding party, the set number, and the identity of the responding party.

(c) Each demand in a set shall be separately set forth, identified by number or letter, and shall do all of the following:

(1) Designate the documents, tangible things, land or other property, or electronically stored information to be inspected, copied, tested, or sampled either by specifically describing each individual item or by reasonably particularizing each category of item.

(2) Specify a reasonable time for the inspection, copying, testing, or sampling that is at least 30 days after service of the demand, unless the court for good cause shown has granted leave to specify an earlier date. In an unlawful detainer action or other proceeding under Chapter 4 (commencing with Section 1159) of Title 3 of Part 3, the demand shall specify a reasonable time for the inspection, copying, testing, or sampling that is at least five days after service of the demand, unless the court, for good cause shown, has granted leave to specify an earlier date.

(3) Specify a reasonable place for making the inspection, copying, testing, or sampling, and performing any related activity.

(4) Specify any inspection, copying, testing, sampling, or related activity that is being demanded, as well as the manner in which that activity will be performed, and whether that activity will permanently alter or destroy the item involved. *(Added by Stats.2004, c. 182, § 23, operative July 1, 2005. Amended by Stats.2007, c. 113, § 10; Stats.2009, c. 5, § 6, eff. June 29, 2009.)*

§ 2031.040. Service of Documents

The party making a demand for inspection, copying, testing, or sampling shall serve a copy of the demand on the party to whom it is directed and on all other parties who have appeared in the action. *(Added by Stats.2004, c. 182, § 23, operative July 1, 2005. Amended by Stats.2009, c. 5, § 7, eff. June 29, 2009.)*

§ 2031.050. Supplemental Demands; Limitations and Restrictions; Court Order

(a) In addition to the demands for inspection, copying, testing, or sampling permitted by this chapter, a party may propound a supplemental demand to inspect, copy, test, or sample any later acquired or discovered documents, tangible things, land or other property, or electronically stored information in the possession, custody, or control of the party on whom the demand is made.

(b) A party may propound a supplemental demand for inspection, copying, testing, or sampling twice before the initial setting of a trial date, and, subject to the time limits on discovery proceedings and motions provided in Chapter 8 (commencing with Section 2024.010), once after the initial setting of a trial date.

(c) Notwithstanding subdivisions (a) and (b), on motion, for good cause shown, the court may grant leave to a party to propound an additional number of supplemental demands for inspection, copying, testing, or sampling. *(Added by Stats.2004, c. 182, § 23, operative July 1, 2005. Amended by Stats.2009, c. 5, § 8, eff. June 29, 2009.)*

§ 2031.060. Protective Order; Time to Demand; Meet and Confer; Authorized Court Action; Electronically Stored Information; Monetary Sanctions

(a) When an inspection, copying, testing, or sampling of documents, tangible things, places, or electronically stored information has been demanded, the party to whom the demand has been directed, and any other party or affected person, may promptly move for a protective order. This motion shall be accompanied by a meet and confer declaration under Section 2016.040.

(b) The court, for good cause shown, may make any order that justice requires to protect any party or natural person from unwarranted annoyance, embarrassment, or oppression, or undue burden and expense. This protective order may include, but is not limited to, one or more of the following directions:

(1) That all or some of the items or categories of items in the inspection demand need not be produced or made available at all.

(2) That the time specified in Section 2031.260 to respond to the set of demands, or to a particular item or category in the set, be extended.

(3) That the place of production be other than that specified in the demand.

(4) That the inspection, copying, testing, or sampling be made only on specified terms and conditions.

(5) That a trade secret or other confidential research, development, or commercial information not be disclosed, or be disclosed only to specified persons or only in a specified way.

(6) That the items produced be sealed and thereafter opened only on order of the court.

(c) The party or affected person who seeks a protective order regarding the production, inspection, copying, testing, or sampling of electronically stored information on the basis that the information is from a source that is not reasonably accessible because of undue burden or expense shall bear the burden of demonstrating that the information is from a source that is not reasonably accessible because of undue burden or expense.

(d) If the party or affected person from whom discovery of electronically stored information is sought establishes that the information is from a source that is not reasonably accessible because of undue burden or expense, the court may nonetheless order discovery if the demanding party shows good cause, subject to any limitations imposed under subdivision (f).

(e) If the court finds good cause for the production of electronically stored information from a source that is not reasonably accessible, the court may set conditions for the discovery of the electronically stored information, including allocation of the expense of discovery.

(f) The court shall limit the frequency or extent of discovery of electronically stored information, even from a source that is reasonably accessible, if the court determines that any of the following conditions exist:

(1) It is possible to obtain the information from some other source that is more convenient, less burdensome, or less expensive.

(2) The discovery sought is unreasonably cumulative or duplicative.

(3) The party seeking discovery has had ample opportunity by discovery in the action to obtain the information sought.

(4) The likely burden or expense of the proposed discovery outweighs the likely benefit, taking into account the amount in controversy, the resources of the parties, the importance of the issues in the litigation, and the importance of the requested discovery in resolving the issues.

(g) If the motion for a protective order is denied in whole or in part, the court may order that the party to whom the demand was directed provide or permit the discovery against which protection was sought on terms and conditions that are just.

(h) Except as provided in subdivision (i), the court shall impose a monetary sanction under Chapter 7 (commencing with Section 2023.010) against any party, person, or attorney who unsuccessfully makes or opposes a motion for a protective order, unless it finds that the one subject to the sanction acted with substantial justification or that other circumstances make the imposition of the sanction unjust.

(i)(1) Notwithstanding subdivision (h), absent exceptional circumstances, the court shall not impose sanctions on a party or any attorney of a party for failure to provide electronically stored information that has been lost, damaged, altered, or overwritten as the result of the routine, good faith operation of an electronic information system.

(2) This subdivision shall not be construed to alter any obligation to preserve discoverable information. *(Added by Stats.2004, c. 182, § 23, operative July 1, 2005. Amended by Stats.2009, c. 5, § 9, eff. June 29, 2009; Stats.2021, c. 124, § 15.)*

Article 2. Response to Inspection Demand

§ 2031.210. Content and Form of Response

(a) The party to whom a demand for inspection, copying, testing, or sampling has been directed shall respond separately to each item or category of item by any of the following:

(1) A statement that the party will comply with the particular demand for inspection, copying, testing, or sampling by the date set for the inspection, copying, testing, or sampling pursuant to paragraph (2) of subdivision (c) of Section 2031.030 and any related activities.

(2) A representation that the party lacks the ability to comply with the demand for inspection, copying, testing, or sampling of a particular item or category of item.

(3) An objection to the particular demand for inspection, copying, testing, or sampling.

(b) In the first paragraph of the response immediately below the title of the case, there shall appear the identity of the responding party, the set number, and the identity of the demanding party.

(c) Each statement of compliance, each representation, and each objection in the response shall bear the same number and be in the same sequence as the corresponding item or category in the demand, but the text of that item or category need not be repeated.

(d) If a party objects to the discovery of electronically stored information on the grounds that it is from a source that is not reasonably accessible because of undue burden or expense and that the responding party will not search the source in the absence of an agreement with the demanding party or court order, the responding party shall identify in its response the types or categories of sources of electronically stored information that it asserts are not reasonably accessible. By objecting and identifying information of a type or category of source or sources that are not reasonably accessible, the responding party preserves any objections it may have relating to that electronically stored information. *(Added by Stats.2004, c. 182, § 23, operative July 1, 2005. Amended by Stats.2007, c. 738, § 7; Stats.2009, c. 5, § 10, eff. June 29, 2009.)*

§ 2031.220. Statement of Compliance in Full or in Part

A statement that the party to whom a demand for inspection, copying, testing, or sampling has been directed will comply with the particular demand shall state that the production, inspection, copying, testing, or sampling, and related activity demanded, will be allowed either in whole or in part, and that all documents or things in the demanded category that are in the possession, custody, or control of that party and to which no objection is being made will be included in the production. *(Added by Stats.2004, c. 182, § 23, operative July 1, 2005. Amended by Stats.2009, c. 5, § 11, eff. June 29, 2009.)*

§ 2031.230. Statement of Inability to Comply; Contents

A representation of inability to comply with the particular demand for inspection, copying, testing, or sampling shall affirm that a diligent search and a reasonable inquiry has been made in an effort to comply with that demand. This statement shall also specify whether the inability to comply is because the particular item or category has never existed, has been destroyed, has been lost, misplaced, or stolen, or has never been, or is no longer, in the possession, custody, or control of the responding party. The statement shall set forth the name and address of any natural person or organization known or believed by that party to have possession, custody, or control of that item or category of item. *(Added by Stats.2004, c. 182, § 23, operative July 1, 2005. Amended by Stats.2009, c. 5, § 12, eff. June 29, 2009.)*

§ 2031.240. Partial Objection to Demand; Statement of Compliance or Representation of Inability to Comply

(a) If only part of an item or category of item in a demand for inspection, copying, testing, or sampling is objectionable, the response shall contain a statement of compliance, or a representation of inability to comply with respect to the remainder of that item or category.

(b) If the responding party objects to the demand for inspection, copying, testing, or sampling of an item or category of item, the response shall do both of the following:

(1) Identify with particularity any document, tangible thing, land, or electronically stored information falling within any category of item in the demand to which an objection is being made.

(2) Set forth clearly the extent of, and the specific ground for, the objection. If an objection is based on a claim of privilege, the particular

privilege invoked shall be stated. If an objection is based on a claim that the information sought is protected work product under Chapter 4 (commencing with Section 2018.010), that claim shall be expressly asserted.

(c)(1) If an objection is based on a claim of privilege or a claim that the information sought is protected work product, the response shall provide sufficient factual information for other parties to evaluate the merits of that claim, including, if necessary, a privilege log.

(2) It is the intent of the Legislature to codify the concept of a privilege log as that term is used in California case law. Nothing in this subdivision shall be construed to constitute a substantive change in case law. *(Added by Stats.2004, c. 182, § 23, operative July 1, 2005. Amended by Stats.2009, c. 5, § 13, eff. June 29, 2009; Stats.2012, c. 232, § 1.)*

§ 2031.250. Signatures; Oath; Officers or Agents; Responses with Objections

(a) The party to whom the demand for inspection, copying, testing, or sampling is directed shall sign the response under oath unless the response contains only objections.

(b) If that party is a public or private corporation or a partnership or association or governmental agency, one of its officers or agents shall sign the response under oath on behalf of that party. If the officer or agent signing the response on behalf of that party is an attorney acting in that capacity for a party, that party waives any lawyer-client privilege and any protection for work product under Chapter 4 (commencing with Section 2018.010) during any subsequent discovery from that attorney concerning the identity of the sources of the information contained in the response.

(c) The attorney for the responding party shall sign any responses that contain an objection. *(Added by Stats.2004, c. 182, § 23, operative July 1, 2005. Amended by Stats.2009, c. 5, § 14, eff. June 29, 2009.)*

§ 2031.260. Time to Respond

(a) Within 30 days after service of a demand for inspection, copying, testing, or sampling, the party to whom the demand is directed shall serve the original of the response to it on the party making the demand, and a copy of the response on all other parties who have appeared in the action, unless on motion of the party making the demand, the court has shortened the time for response, or unless on motion of the party to whom the demand has been directed, the court has extended the time for response.

(b) Notwithstanding subdivision (a), in an unlawful detainer action or other proceeding under Chapter 4 (commencing with Section 1159) of Title 3 of Part 3, the party to whom a demand for inspection, copying, testing, or sampling is directed shall have at least five days from the date of service of the demand to respond, unless on motion of the party making the demand, the court has shortened the time for the response, or unless on motion of the party to whom the demand has been directed, the court has extended the time for response. *(Added by Stats.2004, c. 182, § 23, operative July 1, 2005. Amended by Stats.2007, c. 113, § 11; Stats.2009, c. 5, § 15, eff. June 29, 2009.)*

§ 2031.270. Extension of Time to Respond; Agreement of the Parties

(a) The party demanding inspection, copying, testing, or sampling and the responding party may agree to extend the date for the inspection, copying, testing, or sampling or the time for service of a response to a set of demands, or to particular items or categories of items in a set, to a date or dates beyond those provided in Sections 2031.030, 2031.210, 2031.260, and 2031.280.

(b) This agreement may be informal, but it shall be confirmed in a writing that specifies the extended date for inspection, copying, testing, or sampling, or for the service of a response.

(c) Unless this agreement expressly states otherwise, it is effective to preserve to the responding party the right to respond to any item or category of item in the demand to which the agreement applies in any manner specified in Sections 2031.210, 2031.220, 2031.230, 2031.240, and 2031.280. *(Added by Stats.2004, c. 182, § 23, operative July 1, 2005. Amended by Stats.2007, c. 738, § 8; Stats.2009, c. 5, § 16, eff. June 29, 2009.)*

§ 2031.280. Production of Documents; Form; Data Translation

(a) Any documents or category of documents produced in response to a demand for inspection, copying, testing, or sampling shall be identified with the specific request number to which the documents respond.

(b) The documents shall be produced on the date specified in the demand pursuant to paragraph (2) of subdivision (c) of Section 2031.030, unless an objection has been made to that date. If the date for inspection has been extended pursuant to Section 2031.270, the documents shall be produced on the date agreed to pursuant to that section.

(c) If a party responding to a demand for production of electronically stored information objects to a specified form for producing the information, or if no form is specified in the demand, the responding party shall state in its response the form in which it intends to produce each type of information.

(d) Unless the parties otherwise agree or the court otherwise orders, the following shall apply:

(1) If a demand for production does not specify a form or forms for producing a type of electronically stored information, the responding party

shall produce the information in the form or forms in which it is ordinarily maintained or in a form that is reasonably usable.

(2) A party need not produce the same electronically stored information in more than one form.

(e) If necessary, the responding party at the reasonable expense of the demanding party shall, through detection devices, translate any data compilations included in the demand into reasonably usable form. *(Added by Stats.2004, c. 182, § 23, operative July 1, 2005. Amended by Stats.2007, c. 738, § 9; Stats.2009, c. 5, § 17, eff. June 29, 2009; Stats.2019, c. 208, § 1.)*

§ 2031.285. Electronically Stored Information; Privileged Information or Attorney Work Product

(a) If electronically stored information produced in discovery is subject to a claim of privilege or of protection as attorney work product, the party making the claim may notify any party that received the information of the claim and the basis for the claim.

(b) After being notified of a claim of privilege or of protection under subdivision (a), a party that received the information shall immediately sequester the information and either return the specified information and any copies that may exist or present the information to the court conditionally under seal for a determination of the claim.

(c)(1) Prior to the resolution of the motion brought under subdivision (d), a party shall be precluded from using or disclosing the specified information until the claim of privilege is resolved.

(2) A party who received and disclosed the information before being notified of a claim of privilege or of protection under subdivision (a) shall, after that notification, immediately take reasonable steps to retrieve the information.

(d)(1) If the receiving party contests the legitimacy of a claim of privilege or protection, he or she may seek a determination of the claim from the court by making a motion within 30 days of receiving the claim and presenting the information to the court conditionally under seal.

(2) Until the legitimacy of the claim of privilege or protection is resolved, the receiving party shall preserve the information and keep it confidential and shall be precluded from using the information in any manner. *(Added by Stats.2009, c. 5, § 18, eff. June 29, 2009.)*

§ 2031.290. Original Demand, Response and Service Documents; Custody of Documents; Record Retention

(a) The demand for inspection, copying, testing, or sampling, and the response to it, shall not be filed with the court.

(b) The party demanding an inspection, copying, testing, or sampling shall retain both the original of the demand, with the original proof of service affixed to it, and the original of the sworn response until six months after final disposition of the action. At that time, both originals may be destroyed, unless the court, on motion of any party and for good cause shown, orders that the originals be preserved for a longer period. *(Added by Stats.2004, c. 182, § 23, operative July 1, 2005. Amended by Stats.2009, c. 5, § 19, eff. June 29, 2009.)*

§ 2031.300. Untimely Responses; Waiver; Motion to Compel Response; Monetary Sanctions

If a party to whom a demand for inspection, copying, testing, or sampling is directed fails to serve a timely response to it, the following rules shall apply:

(a) The party to whom the demand for inspection, copying, testing, or sampling is directed waives any objection to the demand, including one based on privilege or on the protection for work product under Chapter 4 (commencing with Section 2018.010). The court, on motion, may relieve that party from this waiver on its determination that both of the following conditions are satisfied:

(1) The party has subsequently served a response that is in substantial compliance with Sections 2031.210, 2031.220, 2031.230, 2031.240, and 2031.280.

(2) The party's failure to serve a timely response was the result of mistake, inadvertence, or excusable neglect.

(b) The party making the demand may move for an order compelling response to the demand.

(c) Except as provided in subdivision (d), the court shall impose a monetary sanction under Chapter 7 (commencing with Section 2023.010) against any party, person, or attorney who unsuccessfully makes or opposes a motion to compel a response to a demand for inspection, copying, testing, or sampling, unless it finds that the one subject to the sanction acted with substantial justification or that other circumstances make the imposition of the sanction unjust. If a party then fails to obey the order compelling a response, the court may make those orders that are just, including the imposition of an issue sanction, an evidence sanction, or a terminating sanction under Chapter 7 (commencing with Section 2023.010). In lieu of or in addition to this sanction, the court may impose a monetary sanction under Chapter 7 (commencing with Section 2023.010).

(d)(1) Notwithstanding subdivision (c), absent exceptional circumstances, the court shall not impose sanctions on a party or any attorney of a party for failure to provide electronically stored information that has been lost, damaged, altered, or overwritten as a result of the routine, good faith operation of an electronic information system.

(2) This subdivision shall not be construed to alter any obligation to preserve discoverable information. *(Added by Stats.2004, c. 182, § 23, operative July 1, 2005. Amended by Stats.2005, c. 22, § 23; Stats.2009, c. 5, § 20, eff. June 29, 2009.)*

§ 2031.310. Motion to Compel Further Response; Form and Content; Time to Bring Motion; Monetary Sanctions; Failure to Obey Court Order

(a) On receipt of a response to a demand for inspection, copying, testing, or sampling, the demanding party may move for an order compelling further response to the demand if the demanding party deems that any of the following apply:

(1) A statement of compliance with the demand is incomplete.

(2) A representation of inability to comply is inadequate, incomplete, or evasive.

(3) An objection in the response is without merit or too general.

(b) A motion under subdivision (a) shall comply with each of the following:

(1) The motion shall set forth specific facts showing good cause justifying the discovery sought by the demand.

(2) The motion shall be accompanied by a meet and confer declaration under Section 2016.040.

(3) In lieu of a separate statement required under the California Rules of Court, the court may allow the moving party to submit a concise outline of the discovery request and each response in dispute.

(c) Unless notice of this motion is given within 45 days of the service of the verified response, or any supplemental verified response, or on or before any specific later date to which the demanding party and the responding party have agreed in writing, the demanding party waives any right to compel a further response to the demand.

(d) In a motion under subdivision (a) relating to the production of electronically stored information, the party or affected person objecting to or opposing the production, inspection, copying, testing, or sampling of electronically stored information on the basis that the information is from a source that is not reasonably accessible because of the undue burden or expense shall bear the burden of demonstrating that the information is from a source that is not reasonably accessible because of undue burden or expense.

(e) If the party or affected person from whom discovery of electronically stored information is sought establishes that the information is from a source that is not reasonably accessible because of the undue burden or expense, the court may nonetheless order discovery if the demanding party shows good cause, subject to any limitations imposed under subdivision (g).

(f) If the court finds good cause for the production of electronically stored information from a source that is not reasonably accessible, the court may set conditions for the discovery of the electronically stored information, including allocation of the expense of discovery.

(g) The court shall limit the frequency or extent of discovery of electronically stored information, even from a source that is reasonably accessible, if the court determines that any of the following conditions exists:

(1) It is possible to obtain the information from some other source that is more convenient, less burdensome, or less expensive.

(2) The discovery sought is unreasonably cumulative or duplicative.

(3) The party seeking discovery has had ample opportunity by discovery in the action to obtain the information sought.

(4) The likely burden or expense of the proposed discovery outweighs the likely benefit, taking into account the amount in controversy, the resources of the parties, the importance of the issues in the litigation, and the importance of the requested discovery in resolving the issues.

(h) Except as provided in subdivision (j), the court shall impose a monetary sanction under Chapter 7 (commencing with Section 2023.010) against any party, person, or attorney who unsuccessfully makes or opposes a motion to compel further response to a demand, unless it finds that the one subject to the sanction acted with substantial justification or that other circumstances make the imposition of the sanction unjust.

(i) Except as provided in subdivision (j), if a party fails to obey an order compelling further response, the court may make those orders that are just, including the imposition of an issue sanction, an evidence sanction, or a terminating sanction under Chapter 7 (commencing with Section 2023.010). In lieu of, or in addition to, that sanction, the court may impose a monetary sanction under Chapter 7 (commencing with Section 2023.010).

(j)(1) Notwithstanding subdivisions (h) and (i), absent exceptional circumstances, the court shall not impose sanctions on a party or any attorney of a party for failure to provide electronically stored information that has been lost, damaged, altered, or overwritten as the result of the routine, good faith operation of an electronic information system.

(2) This subdivision shall not be construed to alter any obligation to preserve discoverable information. *(Added by Stats.2004, c. 182, § 23, operative July 1, 2005. Amended by Stats.2009, c. 5, § 21, eff. June 29, 2009; Stats.2013, c. 18, § 2; Stats.2018, c. 317, § 4.)*

§ 2031.320. Failure to Produce Items for Inspection, Copying, Testing, or Sampling; Order Compelling Compliance; Monetary Sanctions; Failure to Obey Court Order

(a) If a party filing a response to a demand for inspection, copying, testing, or sampling under Sections 2031.210, 2031.220, 2031.230, 2031.240, and 2031.280 thereafter fails to permit the inspection, copying, testing, or sampling in accordance with that party's statement of compliance, the demanding party may move for an order compelling compliance.

(b) Except as provided in subdivision (d), the court shall impose a monetary sanction under Chapter 7 (commencing with Section 2023.010) against any party, person, or attorney who unsuccessfully makes or opposes a motion to compel compliance with a demand, unless it finds that the one subject to the sanction acted with substantial justification or that other circumstances make the imposition of the sanction unjust.

(c) Except as provided in subdivision (d), if a party then fails to obey an order compelling inspection, copying, testing, or sampling, the court may make those orders that are just, including the imposition of an issue sanction, an evidence sanction, or a terminating sanction under Chapter 7 (commencing with Section 2023.010). In lieu of or in addition to that sanction, the court may impose a monetary sanction under Chapter 7 (commencing with Section 2023.010).

(d)(1) Notwithstanding subdivisions (b) and (c), absent exceptional circumstances, the court shall not impose sanctions on a party or any attorney of a party for failure to provide electronically stored information that has been lost, damaged, altered, or overwritten as the result of the routine, good faith operation of an electronic information system.

(2) This subdivision shall not be construed to alter any obligation to preserve discoverable information. *(Added by Stats.2004, c. 182, § 23, operative July 1, 2005. Amended by Stats.2009, c. 5, § 22, eff. June 29, 2009.)*

Article 3. Inspection and Production of Documents and Other Property in Specific Contexts

§ 2031.510. Land Patented or Granted by the State; Time to Disclose

(a) In any action, regardless of who is the moving party, where the boundary of land patented or otherwise granted by the state is in dispute, or the validity of any state patent or grant dated before 1950 is in dispute, all parties shall have the duty to disclose to all opposing parties all nonprivileged relevant written evidence then known and available, including evidence against interest, relating to the above issues.

(b) This evidence shall be disclosed within 120 days after the filing with the court of proof of service upon all named defendants. Thereafter, the parties shall have the continuing duty to make all subsequently discovered relevant and nonprivileged written evidence available to the opposing parties. *(Added by Stats.2004, c. 182, § 23, operative July 1, 2005.)*

Chapter 15. Physical or Mental Examination

Article 1. General Provisions

§ 2032.010. Application to Paternity Blood Test Statutes; Disclosure of Certifying Experts in Professional Negligence Actions

(a) This chapter does not affect genetic testing under Chapter 2 (commencing with Section 7550) of Part 2 of Division 12 of the Family Code.

(b) This chapter does not require the disclosure of the identity of an expert consulted by an attorney in order to make the certification required in an action for professional negligence under Section 411.35. *(Added by Stats.2004, c. 182, § 23, operative July 1, 2005. Amended by Stats.2018, c. 876, § 2.)*

§ 2032.020. Persons Subject to Discovery; Restrictions; Qualifications of Examining Physicians and Psychologists

(a) Any party may obtain discovery, subject to the restrictions set forth in Chapter 5 (commencing with Section 2019.010), by means of a physical or mental examination of (1) a party to the action, (2) an agent of any party, or (3) a natural person in the custody or under the legal control of a party, in any action in which the mental or physical condition (including the blood group) of that party or other person is in controversy in the action.

(b) A physical examination conducted under this chapter shall be performed only by a licensed physician or other appropriate licensed health care practitioner.

(c)(1) A mental examination conducted under this chapter shall be performed only by a licensed physician, or by a licensed clinical psychologist who holds a doctoral degree in psychology and has had at least five years of postgraduate experience in the diagnosis of emotional and mental disorders.

(2) If an action involves allegations of sexual abuse of a minor, including any act listed in paragraphs (1) to (3), inclusive, of subdivision (a) of Section 1002, and the examinee is less than 15 years of age, the

licensed physician or clinical psychologist shall have expertise in child abuse and trauma. *(Added by Stats.2004, c. 182, § 23, operative July 1, 2005. Amended by Stats.2017, c. 133, § 1.)*

Article 2. Physical Examination of Personal Injury Plaintiff

§ 2032.210. Definitions

As used in this article, "plaintiff" includes a cross-complainant, and "defendant" includes a cross-defendant. *(Added by Stats.2004, c. 182, § 23, operative July 1, 2005.)*

§ 2032.220. Number of Examinations; Conditions Upon Examination; Time to Demand; Form and Content of Demand; Service upon Parties

(a) In any case in which a plaintiff is seeking recovery for personal injuries, any defendant may demand one physical examination of the plaintiff, if both of the following conditions are satisfied:

(1) The examination does not include any diagnostic test or procedure that is painful, protracted, or intrusive.

(2) The examination is conducted at a location within 75 miles of the residence of the examinee.

(b) A defendant may make a demand under this article without leave of court after that defendant has been served or has appeared in the action, whichever occurs first.

(c) A demand under subdivision (a) shall specify the time, place, manner, conditions, scope, and nature of the examination, as well as the identity and the specialty, if any, of the physician who will perform the examination.

(d) A physical examination demanded under subdivision (a) shall be scheduled for a date that is at least 30 days after service of the demand. On motion of the party demanding the examination, the court may shorten this time.

(e) The defendant shall serve a copy of the demand under subdivision (a) on the plaintiff and on all other parties who have appeared in the action. *(Added by Stats.2004, c. 182, § 23, operative July 1, 2005.)*

§ 2032.230. Statement of Compliance, Partial Compliance or Refusal to Comply; Time to Respond; Shortened or Extended Time by Court

(a) The plaintiff to whom a demand for a physical examination under this article is directed shall respond to the demand by a written statement that the examinee will comply with the demand as stated, will comply with the demand as specifically modified by the plaintiff, or will refuse, for reasons specified in the response, to submit to the demanded physical examination.

(b) Within 20 days after service of the demand the plaintiff to whom the demand is directed shall serve the original of the response to it on the defendant making the demand, and a copy of the response on all other parties who have appeared in the action. On motion of the defendant making the demand, the court may shorten the time for response. On motion of the plaintiff to whom the demand is directed, the court may extend the time for response. *(Added by Stats.2004, c. 182, § 23, operative July 1, 2005.)*

§ 2032.240. Untimely Response to Demand; Waiver; Order Compelling Response and Compliance; Monetary Sanctions; Failure to Obey Court Order

(a) If a plaintiff to whom a demand for a physical examination under this article is directed fails to serve a timely response to it, that plaintiff waives any objection to the demand. The court, on motion, may relieve that plaintiff from this waiver on its determination that both of the following conditions are satisfied:

(1) The plaintiff has subsequently served a response that is in substantial compliance with Section 2032.230.

(2) The plaintiff's failure to serve a timely response was the result of mistake, inadvertence, or excusable neglect.

(b) The defendant may move for an order compelling response and compliance with a demand for a physical examination.

(c) The court shall impose a monetary sanction under Chapter 7 (commencing with Section 2023.010) against any party, person, or attorney who unsuccessfully makes or opposes a motion to compel response and compliance with a demand for a physical examination, unless it finds that the one subject to the sanction acted with substantial justification or that other circumstances make the imposition of the sanction unjust.

(d) If a plaintiff then fails to obey the order compelling response and compliance, the court may make those orders that are just, including the imposition of an issue sanction, an evidence sanction, or a terminating sanction under Chapter 7 (commencing with Section 2023.010). In lieu of or in addition to that sanction the court may impose a monetary sanction under Chapter 7 (commencing with Section 2023.010). *(Added by Stats.2004, c. 182, § 23, operative July 1, 2005.)*

§ 2032.250. Motion to Compel Compliance; Meet and Confer Declaration; Monetary Sanctions

(a) If a defendant who has demanded a physical examination under this article, on receipt of the plaintiff's response to that demand, deems that any modification of the demand, or any refusal to submit to the physical examination is unwarranted, that defendant may move for an order compelling compliance with the demand. This motion shall be accompanied by a meet and confer declaration under Section 2016.040.

(b) The court shall impose a monetary sanction under Chapter 7 (commencing with Section 2023.010) against any party, person, or attorney who unsuccessfully makes or opposes a motion to compel compliance with a demand for a physical examination, unless it finds that the one subject to the sanction acted with substantial justification or that other circumstances make the imposition of the sanction unjust. *(Added by Stats.2004, c. 182, § 23, operative July 1, 2005.)*

§ 2032.260. Original Demand, Response and Service Documents; Custody; Record Retention

(a) The demand for a physical examination under this article and the response to it shall not be filed with the court.

(b) The defendant shall retain both the original of the demand, with the original proof of service affixed to it, and the original response until six months after final disposition of the action. At that time, the original may be destroyed, unless the court, on motion of any party and for good cause shown, orders that the originals be preserved for a longer period. *(Added by Stats.2004, c. 182, § 23, operative July 1, 2005.)*

Article 3. Motion for Physical or Mental Examination

§ 2032.310. Other Forms of Examination by Leave of Court; Form and Contents of Notice of Motion; Parties Served

(a) If any party desires to obtain discovery by a physical examination other than that described in Article 2 (commencing with Section 2032.210), or by a mental examination, the party shall obtain leave of court.

(b) A motion for an examination under subdivision (a) shall specify the time, place, manner, conditions, scope, and nature of the examination, as well as the identity and the specialty, if any, of the person or persons who will perform the examination. The motion shall be accompanied by a meet and confer declaration under Section 2016.040.

(c) Notice of the motion shall be served on the person to be examined and on all parties who have appeared in the action. *(Added by Stats.2004, c. 182, § 23, operative July 1, 2005.)*

§ 2032.320. Standard of Proof; Exceptional Circumstances; Stipulation of Parties; Form and Content of Order; Mileage Limitations

(a) The court shall grant a motion for a physical or mental examination under Section 2032.310 only for good cause shown.

(b) If a party stipulates as provided in subdivision (c), the court shall not order a mental examination of a person for whose personal injuries a recovery is being sought except on a showing of exceptional circumstances.

(c) A stipulation by a party under this subdivision shall include both of the following:

(1) A stipulation that no claim is being made for mental and emotional distress over and above that usually associated with the physical injuries claimed.

(2) A stipulation that no expert testimony regarding this usual mental and emotional distress will be presented at trial in support of the claim for damages.

(d) An order granting a physical or mental examination shall specify the person or persons who may perform the examination, as well as the time, place, manner, diagnostic tests and procedures, conditions, scope, and nature of the examination.

(e) If the place of the examination is more than 75 miles from the residence of the person to be examined, an order to submit to it shall be entered only if both of the following conditions are satisfied:

(1) The court determines that there is good cause for the travel involved.

(2) The order is conditioned on the advancement by the moving party of the reasonable expenses and costs to the examinee for travel to the place of examination. *(Added by Stats.2004, c. 182, § 23, operative July 1, 2005.)*

§ 2032.340. Actions Involving Allegations of Sexual Abuse of a Minor; Mental Examination of Child; Duration

(a) If any action involving allegations of sexual abuse of a minor, including any act listed in paragraphs (1) to (3), inclusive, of subdivision (a) of Section 1002, the mental examination of a child less than 15 years of age shall not exceed three hours, inclusive of breaks.

(b) Notwithstanding subdivision (a), the court may grant an extension of the three-hour limit for good cause. *(Added by Stats.2017, c. 133, § 2.)*

Article 4. Failure To Submit To or Produce Another for Physical or Mental Examination

§ 2032.410. Failure of Party to Submit to Examination; Availability of Sanctions

If a party is required to submit to a physical or mental examination under Articles 2 (commencing with Section 2032.210) or 3 (commencing with Section 2032.310), or under Section 2016.030, but fails to do so, the court, on motion of the party entitled to the examination, may make those orders that are just, including the imposition of an issue sanction, an evidence sanction, or a terminating sanction under Chapter 7 (commencing with Section 2023.010). In lieu of or in addition to that sanction, the court may, on motion of the party, impose a monetary sanction under Chapter 7 (commencing with Section 2023.010). *(Added by Stats.2004, c. 182, § 23, operative July 1, 2005.)*

§ 2032.420. Failure of Nonparty to Submit to Examination; Availability of Sanctions

If a party is required to produce another for a physical or mental examination under Articles 2 (commencing with Section 2032.210) or 3 (commencing with Section 2032.310), or under Section 2032.030, but fails to do so, the court, on motion of the party entitled to the examination, may make those orders that are just, including the imposition of an issue sanction, an evidence sanction, or a terminating sanction under Chapter 7 (commencing with Section 2023.010), unless the party failing to comply demonstrates an inability to produce that person for examination. In lieu of or in addition to that sanction, the court may impose a monetary sanction under Chapter 7 (commencing with Section 2023.010). *(Added by Stats.2004, c. 182, § 23, operative July 1, 2005.)*

Article 5. Conduct of Examination

§ 2032.510. Attendance of Attorney or Attorney's Representative at Examination; Use of Stenographic or Audio Technology Recording; Rights of Attendee to Monitor; Authorization of Attorney's Representative; Suspension of Examination; Monetary Sanctions

(a) The attorney for the examinee or for a party producing the examinee, or that attorney's representative, shall be permitted to attend and observe any physical examination conducted for discovery purposes, and to record stenographically or by audio technology any words spoken to or by the examinee during any phase of the examination.

(b) The observer under subdivision (a) may monitor the examination, but shall not participate in or disrupt it.

(c) If an attorney's representative is to serve as the observer, the representative shall be authorized to so act by a writing subscribed by the attorney which identifies the representative.

(d) If in the judgment of the observer the examiner becomes abusive to the examinee or undertakes to engage in unauthorized diagnostic tests and procedures, the observer may suspend it to enable the party being examined or producing the examinee to make a motion for a protective order.

(e) If the observer begins to participate in or disrupt the examination, the person conducting the physical examination may suspend the examination to enable the party at whose instance it is being conducted to move for a protective order.

(f) The court shall impose a monetary sanction under Chapter 7 (commencing with Section 2023.010) against any party, person, or attorney who unsuccessfully makes or opposes a motion for a protective order under this section, unless it finds that the one subject to the sanction acted with substantial justification or that other circumstances make the imposition of the sanction unjust. *(Added by Stats.2004, c. 182, § 23, operative July 1, 2005. Amended by Stats.2005, c. 294, § 10.)*

§ 2032.520. X-ray Examinations

If an examinee submits or authorizes access to X-rays of any area of his or her body for inspection by the examining physician, no additional X-rays of that area may be taken by the examining physician except with consent of the examinee or on order of the court for good cause shown. *(Added by Stats.2004, c. 182, § 23, operative July 1, 2005.)*

§ 2032.530. Recording Mental Examination by Audio Technology

(a) The examiner and examinee shall have the right to record a mental examination by audio technology.

(b) Nothing in this title shall be construed to alter, amend, or affect existing case law with respect to the presence of the attorney for the examinee or other persons during the examination by agreement or court order. *(Added by Stats.2004, c. 182, § 23, operative July 1, 2005. Amended by Stats.2005, c. 294, § 11.)*

Article 6. Reports of Examination

§ 2032.610. Demand for Copy of Examination Records; Right to Demand; Time to Deliver Documents; Waiver of Work Product Protection

(a) If a party submits to, or produces another for, a physical or mental examination in compliance with a demand under Article 2 (commencing with Section 2032.210), an order of court under Article 3 (commencing with Section 2032.310), or an agreement under Section 2016.030, that party has the option of making a written demand that the party at whose instance the examination was made deliver both of the following to the demanding party:

(1) A copy of a detailed written report setting out the history, examinations, findings, including the results of all tests made, diagnoses, prognoses, and conclusions of the examiner.

(2) A copy of reports of all earlier examinations of the same condition of the examinee made by that or any other examiner.

(b) If the option under subdivision (a) is exercised, a copy of the requested reports shall be delivered within 30 days after service of the demand, or within 15 days of trial, whichever is earlier.

(c) In the circumstances described in subdivision (a), the protection for work product under Chapter 4 (commencing with Section 2018.010) is waived, both for the examiner's writings and reports and to the taking of the examiner's testimony. *(Added by Stats.2004, c. 182, § 23, operative July 1, 2005.)*

§ 2032.620. Untimely Delivery of Requested Documents; Motion to Compel; Meet and Confer Declaration; Monetary Sanction; Failure to Obey Court Order

(a) If the party at whose instance an examination was made fails to make a timely delivery of the reports demanded under Section 2032.610, the demanding party may move for an order compelling their delivery. This motion shall be accompanied by a meet and confer declaration under Section 2016.040.

(b) The court shall impose a monetary sanction under Chapter 7 (commencing with Section 2023.010) against any party, person, or attorney who unsuccessfully makes or opposes a motion to compel delivery of medical reports under this section, unless it finds that the one subject to the sanction acted with substantial justification or that other circumstances make the imposition of the sanction unjust.

(c) If a party then fails to obey an order compelling delivery of demanded medical reports, the court may make those orders that are just, including the imposition of an issue sanction, an evidence sanction, or a terminating sanction under Chapter 7 (commencing with Section 2023.010). In lieu of or in addition to those sanctions, the court may impose a monetary sanction under Chapter 7 (commencing with Section 2023.010). The court shall exclude at trial the testimony of any examiner whose report has not been provided by a party. *(Added by Stats.2004, c. 182, § 23, operative July 1, 2005.)*

§ 2032.630. Waiver of Work Product Privilege in Pending and Subsequent Actions

By demanding and obtaining a report of a physical or mental examination under Section 2032.610 or 2032.620, or by taking the deposition of the examiner, other than under Article 3 (commencing with Section 2034.410) of Chapter 18, the party who submitted to, or produced another for, a physical or mental examination waives in the pending action, and in any other action involving the same controversy, any privilege, as well as any protection for work product under Chapter 4 (commencing with Section 2018.010), that the party or other examinee may have regarding reports and writings as well as the testimony of every other physician, psychologist, or licensed health care practitioner who has examined or may thereafter examine the party or other examinee in respect of the same physical or mental condition. *(Added by Stats.2004, c. 182, § 23, operative July 1, 2005.)*

§ 2032.640. Exchange of Documents and Reports Related to Condition; Exchange of Follow-up or Late Reports

A party receiving a demand for a report under Section 2032.610 is entitled at the time of compliance to receive in exchange a copy of any existing written report of any examination of the same condition by any other physician, psychologist, or licensed health care practitioner. In addition, that party is entitled to receive promptly any later report of any previous or subsequent examination of the same condition, by any physician, psychologist, or licensed health care practitioner. *(Added by Stats.2004, c. 182, § 23, operative July 1, 2005.)*

§ 2032.650. Failure to Deliver or Exchange Reports; Motion to Compel Delivery; Meet and Confer; Monetary Sanctions; Failure to Obey Court Order

(a) If a party who has demanded and received delivery of medical reports under Section 2032.610 fails to deliver existing or later reports of previous or subsequent examinations under Section 2032.640, a party who has complied with Section 2032.610 may move for an order compelling delivery of medical reports. This motion shall be accompanied by a meet and confer declaration under Section 2016.040.

(b) The court shall impose a monetary sanction under Chapter 7 (commencing with Section 2023.010) against any party, person, or attorney who unsuccessfully makes or opposes a motion to compel delivery of medical reports under this section, unless it finds that the one subject to the sanction acted with substantial justification or that other circumstances make the imposition of the sanction unjust.

(c) If a party then fails to obey an order compelling delivery of medical reports, the court may make those orders that are just, including the imposition of an issue sanction, an evidence sanction, or a terminating sanction under Chapter 7 (commencing with Section 2023.010). In lieu of or in addition to the sanction, the court may impose a monetary sanction under Chapter 7 (commencing with Section 2023.010). The court shall exclude at trial the testimony of any health care practitioner whose report has not been provided by a party ordered to do so by the court. *(Added by Stats.2004, c. 182, § 23, operative July 1, 2005.)*

Chapter 16. Requests for Admission

Article 1. Requests for Admission

§ 2033.010. Persons Subject to Admission Requests; Restrictions; Scope of Requests

Any party may obtain discovery within the scope delimited by Chapter 2 (commencing with Section 2017.010), and subject to the restrictions set forth in Chapter 5 (commencing with Section 2019.010), by a written request that any other party to the action admit the genuineness of specified documents, or the truth of specified matters of fact, opinion relating to fact, or application of law to fact. A request for admission may relate to a matter that is in controversy between the parties. *(Added by Stats.2004, c. 182, § 23, operative July 1, 2005. Amended by Stats.2016, c. 86, § 43.)*

§ 2033.020. Admissions Without Leave of Court; Time to Request; Earlier Requests with Leave of Court

(a) A defendant may make requests for admission by a party without leave of court at any time.

(b) A plaintiff may make requests for admission by a party without leave of court at any time that is 10 days after the service of the summons on, or appearance by, that party, whichever occurs first.

(c) Notwithstanding subdivision (b), in an unlawful detainer action or other proceeding under Chapter 4 (commencing with Section 1159) of Title 3 of Part 3, a plaintiff may make requests for admission by a party without leave of court at any time that is 10 days after service of the summons on, or appearance by, that party, whichever occurs first.

(d) Notwithstanding subdivisions (b) and (c), on motion with or without notice, the court, for good cause shown, may grant leave to a plaintiff to make requests for admission at an earlier time. *(Added by Stats.2004, c. 182, § 23, operative July 1, 2005. Amended by Stats.2007, c. 113, § 12; Stats.2025, c. 200, § 16.)*

§ 2033.030. Number of Admission Requests; Limitations; Requests Exceeding Numeric Limitation; Exception

(a) No party shall request, as a matter of right, that any other party admit more than 35 matters that do not relate to the genuineness of documents. If the initial set of admission requests does not exhaust this limit, the balance may be requested in subsequent sets.

(b) Unless a declaration as described in Section 2033.050 has been made, a party need only respond to the first 35 admission requests served that do not relate to the genuineness of documents, if that party states an objection to the balance under Section 2033.230 on the ground that the limit has been exceeded.

(c) The number of requests for admission of the genuineness of documents is not limited except as justice requires to protect the responding party from unwarranted annoyance, embarrassment, oppression, or undue burden and expense. *(Added by Stats.2004, c. 182, § 23, operative July 1, 2005.)*

§ 2033.040. Exemption from Numeric Limitations; Nature and Complexity of Issues; Protective Order; Burden of Proof

(a) Subject to the right of the responding party to seek a protective order under Section 2033.080, any party who attaches a supporting declaration as described in Section 2033.050 may request a greater number of admissions by another party if the greater number is warranted by the complexity or the quantity of the existing and potential issues in the particular case.

(b) If the responding party seeks a protective order on the ground that the number of requests for admission is unwarranted, the propounding party shall have the burden of justifying the number of requests for admission. *(Added by Stats.2004, c. 182, § 23, operative July 1, 2005.)*

§ 2033.050. Admissions Exceeding Numeric Restrictions; Declaration for Additional Discovery; Form and Content

Any party who is requesting or who has already requested more than 35 admissions not relating to the genuineness of documents by any other party shall attach to each set of requests for admissions a declaration containing substantially the following words:

DECLARATION FOR ADDITIONAL DISCOVERY

I, _______, declare:

1. I am (a party to this action or proceeding appearing in propria persona) (presently the attorney for _______, a party to this action or proceeding).

2. I am propounding to _______ the attached set of requests for admission.

3. This set of requests for admission will cause the total number of requests propounded to the party to whom they are directed to exceed the number of requests permitted by Section 2033.030 of the Code of Civil Procedure.

4. I have previously propounded a total of _______ requests for admission to this party.

5. This set of requests for admission contains a total of _______ requests.

6. I am familiar with the issues and the previous discovery conducted by all of the parties in this case.

7. I have personally examined each of the requests in this set of requests for admission.

8. This number of requests for admission is warranted under Section 2033.040 of the Code of Civil Procedure because _______. (Here state the reasons why the complexity or the quantity of issues in the instant lawsuit warrant this number of requests for admission.)

9. None of the requests in this set of requests is being propounded for any improper purpose, such as to harass the party, or the attorney for the party, to whom it is directed, or to cause unnecessary delay or needless increase in the cost of litigation.

I declare under penalty of perjury under the laws of California that the foregoing is true and correct, and that this declaration was executed on _______.

____

(Signature)

Attorney for _______________

(Added by Stats.2004, c. 182, § 23, operative July 1, 2005.)

§ 2033.060. Form and Content of Request for Admissions

(a) A party requesting admissions shall number each set of requests consecutively.

(b) In the first paragraph immediately below the title of the case, there shall appear the identity of the party requesting the admissions, the set number, and the identity of the responding party.

(c) Each request for admission in a set shall be separately set forth and identified by letter or number.

(d) Each request for admission shall be full and complete in and of itself. No preface or instruction shall be included with a set of admission requests unless it has been approved under Chapter 17 (commencing with Section 2033.710).

(e) Any term specially defined in a request for admission shall be typed with all letters capitalized whenever the term appears.

(f) No request for admission shall contain subparts, or a compound, conjunctive, or disjunctive request unless it has been approved under Chapter 17 (commencing with Section 2033.710).

(g) A party requesting an admission of the genuineness of any documents shall attach copies of those documents to the requests, and shall make the original of those documents available for inspection on demand by the party to whom the requests for admission are directed.

(h) No party shall combine in a single document requests for admission with any other method of discovery. *(Added by Stats.2004, c. 182, § 23, operative July 1, 2005.)*

§ 2033.070. Service of Documents

The party requesting admissions shall serve a copy of them on the party to whom they are directed and on all other parties who have appeared in the action. *(Added by Stats.2004, c. 182, § 23, operative July 1, 2005.)*

§ 2033.080. Motion for Protective Order; Meet and Confer Declaration; Standard of Proof; Scope of Order; Monetary Sanctions

(a) When requests for admission have been made, the responding party may promptly move for a protective order. This motion shall be accompanied by a meet and confer declaration under Section 2016.040.

(b) The court, for good cause shown, may make any order that justice requires to protect any party from unwarranted annoyance, embarrassment, oppression, or undue burden and expense. This protective order may include, but is not limited to, one or more of the following directions:

(1) That the set of admission requests, or particular requests in the set, need not be answered at all.

(2) That, contrary to the representations made in a declaration submitted under Section 2033.050, the number of admission requests is unwarranted.

(3) That the time specified in Section 2033.250 to respond to the set of admission requests, or to particular requests in the set, be extended.

(4) That a trade secret or other confidential research, development, or commercial information not be admitted or be admitted only in a certain way.

(5) That some or all of the answers to requests for admission be sealed and thereafter opened only on order of the court.

(c) If the motion for a protective order is denied in whole or in part, the court may order that the responding party provide or permit the discovery against which protection was sought on terms and conditions that are just.

(d) The court shall impose a monetary sanction under Chapter 7 (commencing with Section 2023.010) against any party, person, or attorney who unsuccessfully makes or opposes a motion for a protective order under this section, unless it finds that the one subject to the sanction acted with substantial justification or that other circumstances make the imposition of the sanction unjust. *(Added by Stats.2004, c. 182, § 23, operative July 1, 2005.)*

Article 2. Response to Requests for Admission

§ 2033.210. Written Response; Oath; Form and Contents

(a) The party to whom requests for admission have been directed shall respond in writing under oath separately to each request.

(b) Each response shall answer the substance of the requested admission, or set forth an objection to the particular request.

(c) In the first paragraph of the response immediately below the title of the case, there shall appear the identity of the responding party, the set number, and the identity of the requesting party.

(d) Each answer or objection in the response shall bear the same identifying number or letter and be in the same sequence as the corresponding request. The text of that request need not be repeated, except as provided in paragraph (6) of subdivision (e).

(e) In order to facilitate the discovery process:

(1) Except as provided in paragraph (5), upon request by the responding party, the propounding party shall provide the requests for admission in an electronic format to the responding party within three court days of the request.

(2) Except as provided in paragraph (5), upon request by the propounding party after receipt of the responses to the requests for admission, the responding party shall provide the responses in an electronic format to the propounding party within three court days of the request.

(3) A party may provide the requests for admission or responses to the requests for admission requested pursuant to paragraphs (1) and (2) in any format agreed upon by the parties. If the parties are unable to agree on a format, the requests for admission or responses to the requests for admission shall be provided in plain text format.

(4) A party may transmit the requests for admission or responses to the requests for admission requested pursuant to paragraphs (1) and (2) by any method agreed upon by the parties. If the parties are unable to agree on a method of transmission, the requests for admission or responses to the requests for admission shall be transmitted by electronic mail to an email address provided by the requesting party.

(5) If the requests for admission or responses to the requests for admission were not created in an electronic format, a party is not required to create the requests for admission or responses in an electronic format for the purpose of transmission to the requesting party.

(6) A responding party who has requested and received requests for admission in an electronic format pursuant to paragraph (1) shall include the text of the request immediately preceding the response. *(Added by Stats.2004, c. 182, § 23, operative July 1, 2005. Amended by Stats.2019, c. 190, § 2.)*

§ 2033.220. Scope of Response; Statement of Reasonable Inquiry into Matters Where Respondent Lacks Information or Knowledge

(a) Each answer in a response to requests for admission shall be as complete and straightforward as the information reasonably available to the responding party permits.

(b) Each answer shall:

(1) Admit so much of the matter involved in the request as is true, either as expressed in the request itself or as reasonably and clearly qualified by the responding party.

(2) Deny so much of the matter involved in the request as is untrue.

(3) Specify so much of the matter involved in the request as to the truth of which the responding party lacks sufficient information or knowledge.

(c) If a responding party gives lack of information or knowledge as a reason for a failure to admit all or part of a request for admission, that party shall state in the answer that a reasonable inquiry concerning the matter in the particular request has been made, and that the information known or readily obtainable is insufficient to enable that party to admit the matter. *(Added by Stats.2004, c. 182, § 23, operative July 1, 2005. Amended by Stats.2005, c. 22, § 24.)*

§ 2033.230. Partial Objection to Requested Admission; Grounds for Objection

(a) If only a part of a request for admission is objectionable, the remainder of the request shall be answered.

(b) If an objection is made to a request or to a part of a request, the specific ground for the objection shall be set forth clearly in the response. If an objection is based on a claim of privilege, the particular privilege invoked shall be clearly stated. If an objection is based on a claim that the matter as to which an admission is requested is protected work product under Chapter 4 (commencing with Section 2018.010), that claim shall be expressly asserted. *(Added by Stats.2004, c. 182, § 23, operative July 1, 2005.)*

§ 2033.240. Signatures; Oath; Employees or Agents; Responses That Contain Objections

(a) The party to whom the requests for admission are directed shall sign the response under oath, unless the response contains only objections.

(b) If that party is a public or private corporation, or a partnership or association or governmental agency, one of its officers or agents shall sign the response under oath on behalf of that party. If the officer or agent signing the response on behalf of that party is an attorney acting in that capacity for the party, that party waives any lawyer-client privilege and any protection for work product under Chapter 4 (commencing with Section 2018.010) during any subsequent discovery from that attorney concerning the identity of the sources of the information contained in the response.

(c) The attorney for the responding party shall sign any response that contains an objection. *(Added by Stats.2004, c. 182, § 23, operative July 1, 2005.)*

§ 2033.250. Time to Respond

(a) Within 30 days after service of requests for admission, the party to whom the requests are directed shall serve the original of the response to them on the requesting party, and a copy of the response on all other parties who have appeared, unless on motion of the requesting party the court has shortened the time for response, or unless on motion of the responding party the court has extended the time for response.

(b) Notwithstanding subdivision (a), in an unlawful detainer action or other proceeding under Chapter 4 (commencing with Section 1159) of Title 3 of Part 3, the party to whom the request is directed shall have at least five days from the date of service to respond, unless on motion of the requesting party the court has shortened the time for response, or unless on motion of the responding party the court has extended the time for response. *(Added by Stats.2004, c. 182, § 23, operative July 1, 2005. Amended by Stats.2007, c. 113, § 13.)*

§ 2033.260. Extension of Time by Agreement; Writing; Notice to All Parties

(a) The party requesting admissions and the responding party may agree to extend the time for service of a response to a set of admission requests, or to particular requests in a set, to a date beyond that provided in Section 2033.250.

(b) This agreement may be informal, but it shall be confirmed in a writing that specifies the extended date for service of a response.

(c) Unless this agreement expressly states otherwise, it is effective to preserve to the responding party the right to respond to any request for admission to which the agreement applies in any manner specified in Sections 2033.210, 2033.220, and 2033.230.

(d) Notice of this agreement shall be given by the responding party to all other parties who were served with a copy of the request. *(Added by Stats.2004, c. 182, § 23, operative July 1, 2005.)*

§ 2033.270. Original Requests, Admissions and Proof of Service; Custody; Document Retention

(a) The requests for admission and the response to them shall not be filed with the court.

(b) The party requesting admissions shall retain both the original of the requests for admission, with the original proof of service affixed to them, and the original of the sworn response until six months after final disposition of the action. At that time, both originals may be destroyed, unless the court, on motion of any party and for good cause shown, orders that the originals be preserved for a longer period. *(Added by Stats.2004, c. 182, § 23, operative July 1, 2005.)*

§ 2033.280. Untimely Response; Waiver; Relief from Waiver; Motion for Court Order; Monetary Sanctions

If a party to whom requests for admission are directed fails to serve a timely response, the following rules apply:

(a) The party to whom the requests for admission are directed waives any objection to the requests, including one based on privilege or on the protection for work product under Chapter 4 (commencing with Section 2018.010). The court, on motion, may relieve that party from this waiver on its determination that both of the following conditions are satisfied:

(1) The party has subsequently served a response that is in substantial compliance with Sections 2033.210, 2033.220, and 2033.230.

(2) The party's failure to serve a timely response was the result of mistake, inadvertence, or excusable neglect.

(b) The requesting party may move for an order that the genuineness of any documents and the truth of any matters specified in the requests be deemed admitted, as well as for a monetary sanction under Chapter 7 (commencing with Section 2023.010).

(c) The court shall make this order, unless it finds that the party to whom the requests for admission have been directed has served, before the hearing on the motion, a proposed response to the requests for admission that is in substantial compliance with Section 2033.220. It is mandatory that the court impose a monetary sanction under Chapter 7 (commencing with Section 2023.010) on the party or attorney, or both, whose failure to serve a timely response to requests for admission necessitated this motion.

(Added by Stats.2004, c. 182, § 23, operative July 1, 2005. Amended by Stats.2005, c. 294, § 12.)

§ 2033.290. Motion to Compel Further Response; Meet and Confer Declaration; Time to Bring Motion; Monetary Sanctions; Failure to Obey Court Order

(a) On receipt of a response to requests for admissions, the party requesting admissions may move for an order compelling a further response if that party deems that either or both of the following apply:

(1) An answer to a particular request is evasive or incomplete.

(2) An objection to a particular request is without merit or too general.

(b)(1) A motion under subdivision (a) shall be accompanied by a meet and confer declaration under Section 2016.040.

(2) In lieu of a separate statement required under the California Rules of Court, the court may allow the moving party to submit a concise outline of the discovery request and each response in dispute.

(c) Unless notice of this motion is given within 45 days of the service of the verified response, or any supplemental verified response, or any specific later date to which the requesting party and the responding party have agreed in writing, the requesting party waives any right to compel further response to the requests for admission.

(d) The court shall impose a monetary sanction under Chapter 7 (commencing with Section 2023.010) against any party, person, or attorney who unsuccessfully makes or opposes a motion to compel further response, unless it finds that the one subject to the sanction acted with substantial justification or that other circumstances make the imposition of the sanction unjust.

(e) If a party then fails to obey an order compelling further response to requests for admission, the court may order that the matters involved in the requests be deemed admitted. In lieu of, or in addition to, this order, the court may impose a monetary sanction under Chapter 7 (commencing with Section 2023.010). *(Added by Stats.2004, c. 182, § 23, operative July 1, 2005. Amended by Stats.2013, c. 18, § 3; Stats.2018, c. 317, § 5.)*

§ 2033.300. Withdrawal of or Amendment to Admission; Authority and Discretion of Court

(a) A party may withdraw or amend an admission made in response to a request for admission only on leave of court granted after notice to all parties.

(b) The court may permit withdrawal or amendment of an admission only if it determines that the admission was the result of mistake, inadvertence, or excusable neglect, and that the party who obtained the admission will not be substantially prejudiced in maintaining that party's action or defense on the merits.

(c) The court may impose conditions on the granting of the motion that are just, including, but not limited to, the following:

(1) An order that the party who obtained the admission be permitted to pursue additional discovery related to the matter involved in the withdrawn or amended admission.

(2) An order that the costs of any additional discovery be borne in whole or in part by the party withdrawing or amending the admission. *(Added by Stats.2004, c. 182, § 23, operative July 1, 2005.)*

Article 3. Effect of Admission

§ 2033.410. Conclusiveness of Admission; Application to Other Proceedings

(a) Any matter admitted in response to a request for admission is conclusively established against the party making the admission in the pending action, unless the court has permitted withdrawal or amendment of that admission under Section 2033.300.

(b) Notwithstanding subdivision (a), any admission made by a party under this section is binding only on that party and is made for the purpose of the pending action only. It is not an admission by that party for any other purpose, and it shall not be used in any manner against that party in any other proceeding. *(Added by Stats.2004, c. 182, § 23, operative July 1, 2005.)*

§ 2033.420. Failure to Admit Genuineness of Document or Truth of Any Matter; Binding Effect; Reasonable Expenses and Attorney's Fees

(a) If a party fails to admit the genuineness of any document or the truth of any matter when requested to do so under this chapter, and if the party requesting that admission thereafter proves the genuineness of that document or the truth of that matter, the party requesting the admission may move the court for an order requiring the party to whom the request was directed to pay the reasonable expenses incurred in making that proof, including reasonable attorney's fees.

(b) The court shall make this order unless it finds any of the following:

(1) An objection to the request was sustained or a response to it was waived under Section 2033.290.

(2) The admission sought was of no substantial importance.

(3) The party failing to make the admission had reasonable ground to believe that that party would prevail on the matter.

(4) There was other good reason for the failure to admit. *(Added by Stats.2004, c. 182, § 23, operative July 1, 2005.)*

Chapter 17. Form Interrogatories and Requests for Admission

§ 2033.710. Interrogatories and Requests for Admission of the Genuineness of Documents or Truths; Judicial Council Official Forms

The Judicial Council shall develop and approve official form interrogatories and requests for admission of the genuineness of any relevant documents or of the truth of any relevant matters of fact for use in any civil action in a state court based on personal injury, property damage, wrongful death, unlawful detainer, breach of contract, family law, or fraud and for any other civil actions the Judicial Council deems appropriate. *(Added by Stats.2004, c. 182, § 23, operative July 1, 2005.)*

§ 2033.720. Interrogatories for Use by a Victim Who Has Not Received Complete Payment Under Certain Restitution Orders; Judicial Council Official Forms

(a) The Judicial Council shall develop and approve official form interrogatories for use by a victim who has not received complete payment of a restitution order made pursuant to Section 1202.4 of the Penal Code.

(b) Notwithstanding whether a victim initiates or maintains an action to satisfy the unpaid restitution order, a victim may propound the form interrogatories approved pursuant to this section once each calendar year. The defendant subject to the restitution order shall, in responding to the interrogatories propounded, provide current information regarding the nature, extent, and location of any assets, income, and liabilities in which the defendant claims a present or future interest. *(Added by Stats.2004, c. 182, § 23, operative July 1, 2005.)*

§ 2033.730. Advisory Committee to Assist with Form Development; Use of Nontechnical Language

(a) In developing the form interrogatories and requests for admission required by Sections 2033.710 and 2033.720, the Judicial Council shall consult with a representative advisory committee which shall include, but not be limited to, representatives of all of the following:

(1) The plaintiff's bar.

(2) The defense bar.

(3) The public interest bar.

(4) Court administrators.

(5) The public.

(b) The form interrogatories and requests for admission shall be drafted in nontechnical language. *(Added by Stats.2004, c. 182, § 23, operative July 1, 2005.)*

§ 2033.740. Optional Use of Forms; Rules and Regulations

(a) Use of the form interrogatories and requests for admission approved by the Judicial Council shall be optional.

(b) The form interrogatories and requests for admission shall be made available through the office of the clerk of the appropriate trial court.

(c) The Judicial Council shall promulgate any necessary rules to govern the use of the form interrogatories and requests for admission. *(Added by Stats.2004, c. 182, § 23, operative July 1, 2005.)*

Chapter 18. Simultaneous Exchange of Expert Witness Information

Article 1. General Provisions

§ 2034.010. Application to Eminent Domain Proceedings

This chapter does not apply to exchanges of lists of experts and valuation data in eminent domain proceedings under Chapter 7 (commencing with Section 1258.010) of Title 7 of Part 3. *(Added by Stats.2004, c. 182, § 23, operative July 1, 2005.)*

Article 2. Demand for Exchange of Expert Witness Information

§ 2034.210. Simultaneous Exchange of Information; Time to Issue Demand; Discoverable Reports and Writings Supporting Opinion

After the setting of the initial trial date for the action, any party may obtain discovery by demanding that all parties simultaneously exchange information concerning each other's expert trial witnesses to the following extent:

(a) Any party may demand a mutual and simultaneous exchange by all parties of a list containing the name and address of any natural person, including one who is a party, whose oral or deposition testimony in the form of an expert opinion any party expects to offer in evidence at the trial.

(b) If any expert designated by a party under subdivision (a) is a party or an employee of a party, or has been retained by a party for the purpose of forming and expressing an opinion in anticipation of the litigation or in preparation for the trial of the action, the designation of that witness shall include or be accompanied by an expert witness declaration under Section 2034.260.

(c) Any party may also include a demand for the mutual and simultaneous production for inspection and copying of all discoverable reports and writings, if any, made by any expert described in subdivision (b) in the course of preparing that expert's opinion. *(Added by Stats.2004, c. 182, § 23, operative July 1, 2005.)*

§ 2034.220. Persons Authorized to Issue Demand; Time to Make Demand

Any party may make a demand for an exchange of information concerning expert trial witnesses without leave of court. A party shall make this demand no later than the 10th day after the initial trial date has been set, or 70 days before that trial date, whichever is closer to the trial date. *(Added by Stats.2004, c. 182, § 23, operative July 1, 2005.)*

§ 2034.230. Written Demand; Form and Contents of Demand

(a) A demand for an exchange of information concerning expert trial witnesses shall be in writing and shall identify, below the title of the case, the party making the demand. The demand shall state that it is being made under this chapter.

(b) The demand shall specify the date for the exchange of lists of expert trial witnesses, expert witness declarations, and any demanded production of writings. The specified date of exchange shall be 50 days before the initial trial date, or 20 days after service of the demand, whichever is closer to the trial date, unless the court, on motion and a showing of good cause, orders an earlier or later date of exchange. *(Added by Stats.2004, c. 182, § 23, operative July 1, 2005.)*

§ 2034.240. Service of Documents

The party demanding an exchange of information concerning expert trial witnesses shall serve the demand on all parties who have appeared in the action. *(Added by Stats.2004, c. 182, § 23, operative July 1, 2005.)*

§ 2034.250. Protective Orders; Motion; Meet and Confer Declaration; Standard of Proof; Scope of Order; Monetary Sanctions

(a) A party who has been served with a demand to exchange information concerning expert trial witnesses may promptly move for a protective order. This motion shall be accompanied by a meet and confer declaration under Section 2016.040.

(b) The court, for good cause shown, may make any order that justice requires to protect any party from unwarranted annoyance, embarrassment, oppression, or undue burden and expense. The protective order may include, but is not limited to, one or more of the following directions:

(1) That the demand be quashed because it was not timely served.

(2) That the date of exchange be earlier or later than that specified in the demand.

(3) That the exchange be made only on specified terms and conditions.

(4) That the production and exchange of any reports and writings of experts be made at a different place or at a different time than specified in the demand.

(5) That some or all of the parties be divided into sides on the basis of their identity of interest in the issues in the action, and that the designation of any experts as described in subdivision (b) of Section 2034.210 be made by any side so created.

(6) That a party or a side reduce the list of employed or retained experts designated by that party or side under subdivision (b) of Section 2034.210.

(c) If the motion for a protective order is denied in whole or in part, the court may order that the parties against whom the motion is brought, provide or permit the discovery against which the protection was sought on those terms and conditions that are just.

(d) The court shall impose a monetary sanction under Chapter 7 (commencing with Section 2023.010) against any party, person, or attorney who unsuccessfully makes or opposes a motion for a protective order under this section, unless it finds that the one subject to the sanction acted with substantial justification or that other circumstances make the imposition of the sanction unjust. *(Added by Stats.2004, c. 182, § 23, operative July 1, 2005.)*

§ 2034.260. Method of Exchange; Form and Contents; Expert Witness Declaration; Form and Contents

(a) All parties who have appeared in the action shall exchange information concerning expert witnesses in writing on or before the date of exchange specified in the demand. The exchange of information may occur at a meeting of the attorneys for the parties involved or by serving the information on the other party by any method specified in Section 1011 or 1013, on or before the date of exchange.

(b) The exchange of expert witness information shall include either of the following:

(1) A list setting forth the name and address of a person whose expert opinion that party expects to offer in evidence at the trial.

(2) A statement that the party does not presently intend to offer the testimony of an expert witness.

(c) If a witness on the list is an expert as described in subdivision (b) of Section 2034.210, the exchange shall also include or be accompanied by an expert witness declaration signed only by the attorney for the party designating the expert, or by that party if that party has no attorney. This declaration shall be under penalty of perjury and shall contain all of the following:

(1) A brief narrative statement of the qualifications of each expert.

(2) A brief narrative statement of the general substance of the testimony that the expert is expected to give.

(3) A representation that the expert has agreed to testify at the trial.

(4) A representation that the expert will be sufficiently familiar with the pending action to submit to a meaningful oral deposition concerning the specific testimony, including an opinion and its basis, that the expert is expected to give at trial.

(5) A statement of the expert's hourly and daily fee for providing deposition testimony and for consulting with the retaining attorney. *(Added by Stats.2004, c. 182, § 23, operative July 1, 2005. Amended by Stats.2017, c. 64, § 3; Stats.2018, c. 92, § 45.)*

§ 2034.270. Production of Reports and Writings; Time and Place to Exchange

If a demand for an exchange of information concerning expert trial witnesses includes a demand for production of reports and writings as described in subdivision (c) of Section 2034.210, all parties shall produce and exchange, at the place and on the date specified in the demand, all discoverable reports and writings, if any, made by any designated expert described in subdivision (b) of Section 2034.210. *(Added by Stats.2004, c. 182, § 23, operative July 1, 2005.)*

§ 2034.280. Supplemental Expert Witness Lists

(a) Within 20 days after the exchange described in Section 2034.260, any party who engaged in the exchange may submit a supplemental expert witness list containing the name and address of any experts who will express an opinion on a subject to be covered by an expert designated by an adverse party to the exchange, if the party supplementing an expert witness list has not previously retained an expert to testify on that subject.

(b) This supplemental list shall be accompanied by an expert witness declaration under subdivision (c) of Section 2034.260 concerning those additional experts, and by all discoverable reports and writings, if any, made by those additional experts.

(c) The party shall also make those experts available immediately for a deposition under Article 3 (commencing with Section 2034.410), which deposition may be taken even though the time limit for discovery under

Chapter 8 (commencing with Section 2024.010) has expired. *(Added by Stats.2004, c. 182, § 23, operative July 1, 2005.)*

§ 2034.290. Original Demand for Exchange of Information, Responses and Proof of Service; Custody of Documents; Record Retention; Time to File with Court

(a) A demand for an exchange of information concerning expert trial witnesses, and any expert witness lists and declarations exchanged shall not be filed with the court.

(b) The party demanding the exchange shall retain both the original of the demand, with the original proof of service affixed, and the original of all expert witness lists and declarations exchanged in response to the demand until six months after final disposition of the action. At that time, all originals may be destroyed unless the court, on motion of any party and for good cause shown, orders that the originals be preserved for a longer period.

(c) Notwithstanding subdivisions (a) and (b), a demand for exchange of information concerning expert trial witnesses, and all expert witness lists and declarations exchanged in response to it, shall be lodged with the court when their contents become relevant to an issue in any pending matter in the action. *(Added by Stats.2004, c. 182, § 23, operative July 1, 2005.)*

§ 2034.300. Exclusion of Expert Opinions; Failure of Party to Comply with Certain Conditions

Except as provided in Section 2034.310 and in Articles 4 (commencing with Section 2034.610) and 5 (commencing with Section 2034.710), on objection of any party who has made a complete and timely compliance with Section 2034.260, the trial court shall exclude from evidence the expert opinion of any witness that is offered by any party who has unreasonably failed to do any of the following:

(a) List that witness as an expert under Section 2034.260.

(b) Submit an expert witness declaration.

(c) Produce reports and writings of expert witnesses under Section 2034.270.

(d) Make that expert available for a deposition under Article 3 (commencing with Section 2034.410). *(Added by Stats.2004, c. 182, § 23, operative July 1, 2005.)*

§ 2034.310. Experts Not Designated on Party's List; Testimony at Trial; Permissible Conditions

A party may call as a witness at trial an expert not previously designated by that party if either of the following conditions is satisfied:

(a) That expert has been designated by another party and has thereafter been deposed under Article 3 (commencing with Section 2034.410).

(b) That expert is called as a witness to impeach the testimony of an expert witness offered by any other party at the trial. This impeachment may include testimony to the falsity or nonexistence of any fact used as the foundation for any opinion by any other party's expert witness, but may not include testimony that contradicts the opinion. *(Added by Stats.2004, c. 182, § 23, operative July 1, 2005.)*

Article 3. Deposition of Expert Witness

§ 2034.410. Persons Permitted to Depose Experts; Procedural Requirements

On receipt of an expert witness list from a party, any other party may take the deposition of any person on the list. The procedures for taking oral and written depositions set forth in Chapters 9 (commencing with Section 2025.010), 10 (commencing with Section 2026.010), and 11 (commencing with Section 2028.010) apply to a deposition of a listed trial expert witness except as provided in this article. *(Added by Stats.2004, c. 182, § 23, operative July 1, 2005.)*

§ 2034.415. Production of Materials

An expert described in subdivision (b) of Section 2034.210 whose deposition is noticed pursuant to Section 2025.220 shall, no later than three business days before his or her deposition, produce any materials or category of materials, including any electronically stored information, called for by the deposition notice. *(Added by Stats.2016, c. 467, § 3.)*

§ 2034.420. Location of Deposition; Mileage Limitations; Exception

The deposition of any expert described in subdivision (b) of Section 2034.210 shall be taken at a place that is within 75 miles of the courthouse where the action is pending. On motion for a protective order by the party designating an expert witness, and on a showing of exceptional hardship, the court may order that the deposition be taken at a more distant place from the courthouse. *(Added by Stats.2004, c. 182, § 23, operative July 1, 2005. Amended by Stats.2008, c. 303, § 1.)*

§ 2034.430. Application of Section to Certain Designated Experts; Payment of Fees; Fees for Delay Caused by Tardy Counsel; Daily Fee; Application to Certain Worker Compensation Claims

(a) Except as provided in subdivision (f), this section applies to an expert witness, other than a party or an employee of a party, who is any of the following:

(1) An expert described in subdivision (b) of Section 2034.210.

(2) A treating physician and surgeon or other treating health care practitioner who is to be asked during the deposition to express opinion testimony, including opinion or factual testimony regarding the past or present diagnosis or prognosis made by the practitioner or the reasons for a particular treatment decision made by the practitioner, but not including testimony requiring only the reading of words and symbols contained in the relevant medical record or, if those words and symbols are not legible to the deponent, the approximation by the deponent of what those words or symbols are.

(3) An architect, professional engineer, or licensed land surveyor who was involved with the original project design or survey for which that person is asked to express an opinion within the person's expertise and relevant to the action or proceeding.

(b) A party desiring to depose an expert witness described in subdivision (a) shall pay the expert's reasonable and customary hourly or daily fee for any time spent at the deposition from the time noticed in the deposition subpoena, or from the time of the arrival of the expert witness should that time be later than the time noticed in the deposition subpoena, until the time the expert witness is dismissed from the deposition, regardless of whether the expert is actually deposed by any party attending the deposition.

(c) If any counsel representing the expert or a nonnoticing party is late to the deposition, the expert's reasonable and customary hourly or daily fee for the time period determined from the time noticed in the deposition subpoena until the counsel's late arrival, shall be paid by that tardy counsel.

(d) Notwithstanding subdivision (c), the hourly or daily fee charged to the tardy counsel shall not exceed the fee charged to the party who retained the expert, except where the expert donated services to a charitable or other nonprofit organization.

(e) A daily fee shall only be charged for a full day of attendance at a deposition or where the expert was required by the deposing party to be available for a full day and the expert necessarily had to forgo all business that the expert would otherwise have conducted that day but for the request that the expert be available all day for the scheduled deposition.

(f) In a worker's compensation case arising under Division 4 (commencing with Section 3201) or Division 4.5 (commencing with Section 6100) of the Labor Code, a party desiring to depose any expert on another party's expert witness list shall pay the fee under this section. *(Added by Stats.2004, c. 182, § 23, operative July 1, 2005. Amended by Stats.2008, c. 303, § 2.)*

§ 2034.440. Fees for Preparation and Travel

The party designating an expert is responsible for any fee charged by the expert for preparing for a deposition and for traveling to the place of the deposition, as well as for any travel expenses of the expert. *(Added by Stats.2004, c. 182, § 23, operative July 1, 2005.)*

§ 2034.450. Tender of Fees; Deposition Conducted Beyond Anticipated Length of Time; Time to Tender Additional Fee Amount

(a) The party taking the deposition of an expert witness shall either accompany the service of the deposition notice with a tender of the expert's fee based on the anticipated length of the deposition, or tender that fee at the commencement of the deposition.

(b) The expert's fee shall be delivered to the attorney for the party designating the expert.

(c) If the deposition of the expert takes longer than anticipated, the party giving notice of the deposition shall pay the balance of the expert's fee within five days of receipt of an itemized statement from the expert. *(Added by Stats.2004, c. 182, § 23, operative July 1, 2005.)*

§ 2034.460. Production of Expert at Deposition; Proper Service of Notice and Prepayment of Fees; Proper Service Without Tender of Fees

(a) The service of a proper deposition notice accompanied by the tender of the expert witness fee described in Section 2034.430 is effective to require the party employing or retaining the expert to produce the expert for the deposition.

(b) If the party noticing the deposition fails to tender the expert's fee under Section 2034.430, the expert shall not be deposed at that time unless the parties stipulate otherwise. *(Added by Stats.2004, c. 182, § 23, operative July 1, 2005.)*

§ 2034.470. Reasonableness of Expert Fees; Order Setting Compensation of Expert; Service of Notice; Meet and Confer Declaration; Determination by Court; Monetary Sanctions

(a) If a party desiring to take the deposition of an expert witness under this article deems that the hourly or daily fee of that expert for providing deposition testimony is unreasonable, that party may move for an order setting the compensation of that expert. Notice of this motion shall also be given to the expert.

(b) A motion under subdivision (a) shall be accompanied by a meet and confer declaration under Section 2016.040. In any attempt at an informal resolution under Section 2016.040, either the party or the expert shall provide the other with all of the following:

(1) Proof of the ordinary and customary fee actually charged and received by that expert for similar services provided outside the subject litigation.

(2) The total number of times the presently demanded fee has ever been charged and received by that expert.

(3) The frequency and regularity with which the presently demanded fee has been charged and received by that expert within the two-year period preceding the hearing on the motion.

(c) In addition to any other facts or evidence, the expert or the party designating the expert shall provide, and the court's determination as to the reasonableness of the fee shall be based on, proof of the ordinary and customary fee actually charged and received by that expert for similar services provided outside the subject litigation.

(d) In an action filed after January 1, 1994, the expert or the party designating the expert shall also provide, and the court's determination as to the reasonableness of the fee shall also be based on, both of the following:

(1) The total number of times the presently demanded fee has ever been charged and received by that expert.

(2) The frequency and regularity with which the presently demanded fee has been charged and received by that expert within the two-year period preceding the hearing on the motion.

(e) The court may also consider the ordinary and customary fees charged by similar experts for similar services within the relevant community and any other factors the court deems necessary or appropriate to make its determination.

(f) Upon a determination that the fee demanded by that expert is unreasonable, and based upon the evidence and factors considered, the court shall set the fee of the expert providing testimony.

(g) The court shall impose a monetary sanction under Chapter 7 (commencing with Section 2023.010) against any party, person, or attorney who unsuccessfully makes or opposes a motion to set the expert witness fee, unless it finds that the one subject to the sanction acted with substantial justification or that other circumstances make the imposition of the sanction unjust. *(Added by Stats.2004, c. 182, § 23, operative July 1, 2005.)*

Article 4. Motion to Augment or Amend
Expert Witness List or Declaration

§ 2034.610. Scope of Judicial Authority Where Exchange of Information Was Timely; Time to Complete Additional Discovery; Meet and Confer Declaration

(a) On motion of any party who has engaged in a timely exchange of expert witness information, the court may grant leave to do either or both of the following:

(1) Augment that party's expert witness list and declaration by adding the name and address of any expert witness whom that party has subsequently retained.

(2) Amend that party's expert witness declaration with respect to the general substance of the testimony that an expert previously designated is expected to give.

(b) A motion under subdivision (a) shall be made at a sufficient time in advance of the time limit for the completion of discovery under Chapter 8 (commencing with Section 2024.010) to permit the deposition of any expert to whom the motion relates to be taken within that time limit. Under exceptional circumstances, the court may permit the motion to be made at a later time.

(c) The motion shall be accompanied by a meet and confer declaration under Section 2016.040. *(Added by Stats.2004, c. 182, § 23, operative July 1, 2005.)*

§ 2034.620. Expert Witness Lists; Court Authority Upon Satisfaction of Certain Conditions

The court shall grant leave to augment or amend an expert witness list or declaration only if all of the following conditions are satisfied:

(a) The court has taken into account the extent to which the opposing party has relied on the list of expert witnesses.

(b) The court has determined that any party opposing the motion will not be prejudiced in maintaining that party's action or defense on the merits.

(c) The court has determined either of the following:

(1) The moving party would not in the exercise of reasonable diligence have determined to call that expert witness or have decided to offer the different or additional testimony of that expert witness.

(2) The moving party failed to determine to call that expert witness, or to offer the different or additional testimony of that expert witness as a result of mistake, inadvertence, surprise, or excusable neglect, and the moving party has done both of the following:

(A) Sought leave to augment or amend promptly after deciding to call the expert witness or to offer the different or additional testimony.

(B) Promptly thereafter served a copy of the proposed expert witness information concerning the expert or the testimony described in Section 2034.260 on all other parties who have appeared in the action.

(d) Leave to augment or amend is conditioned on the moving party making the expert available immediately for a deposition under Article 3 (commencing with Section 2034.410), and on any other terms as may be just, including, but not limited to, leave to any party opposing the motion to designate additional expert witnesses or to elicit additional opinions from those previously designated, a continuance of the trial for a reasonable period of time, and the awarding of costs and litigation expenses to any party opposing the motion. *(Added by Stats.2004, c. 182, § 23, operative July 1, 2005.)*

§ 2034.630. Monetary Sanctions; Exception

The court shall impose a monetary sanction under Chapter 7 (commencing with Section 2023.010) against any party, person, or attorney who unsuccessfully makes or opposes a motion to augment or amend expert witness information, unless it finds that the one subject to the sanction acted with substantial justification or that other circumstances make the imposition of the sanction unjust. *(Added by Stats.2004, c. 182, § 23, operative July 1, 2005.)*

Article 5. Motion To Submit Tardy Expert Witness Information

§ 2034.710. Untimely Response to Demand for Witness Information; Court Authority to Extend Time; Time to Complete Discovery; Meet and Confer Declaration

(a) On motion of any party who has failed to submit expert witness information on the date specified in a demand for that exchange, the court may grant leave to submit that information on a later date.

(b) A motion under subdivision (a) shall be made a sufficient time in advance of the time limit for the completion of discovery under Chapter 8 (commencing with Section 2024.010) to permit the deposition of any expert to whom the motion relates to be taken within that time limit. Under exceptional circumstances, the court may permit the motion to be made at a later time.

(c) The motion shall be accompanied by a meet and confer declaration under Section 2016.040. *(Added by Stats.2004, c. 182, § 23, operative July 1, 2005.)*

§ 2034.720. Scope of Judicial Authority to Grant Tardy Filing of List; Satisfaction of Certain Conditions

The court shall grant leave to submit tardy expert witness information only if all of the following conditions are satisfied:

(a) The court has taken into account the extent to which the opposing party has relied on the absence of a list of expert witnesses.

(b) The court has determined that any party opposing the motion will not be prejudiced in maintaining that party's action or defense on the merits.

(c) The court has determined that the moving party did all of the following:

(1) Failed to submit the information as the result of mistake, inadvertence, surprise, or excusable neglect.

(2) Sought leave to submit the information promptly after learning of the mistake, inadvertence, surprise, or excusable neglect.

(3) Promptly thereafter served a copy of the proposed expert witness information described in Section 2034.260 on all other parties who have appeared in the action.

(d) The order is conditioned on the moving party making the expert available immediately for a deposition under Article 3 (commencing with Section 2034.410), and on any other terms as may be just, including, but not limited to, leave to any party opposing the motion to designate additional expert witnesses or to elicit additional opinions from those previously designated, a continuance of the trial for a reasonable period of time, and the awarding of costs and litigation expenses to any party opposing the motion. *(Added by Stats.2004, c. 182, § 23, operative July 1, 2005.)*

§ 2034.730. Monetary Sanctions; Exception

The court shall impose a monetary sanction under Chapter 7 (commencing with Section 2023.010) against any party, person, or attorney who unsuccessfully makes or opposes a motion to submit tardy expert witness information, unless it finds that the one subject to the sanction acted with substantial justification or that other circumstances make the imposition of the sanction unjust. *(Added by Stats.2004, c. 182, § 23, operative July 1, 2005.)*

Chapter 19. Perpetuation of Testimony or Preservation of Evidence Before Filing Action

§ 2035.010. Persons Permitted to Obtain Discovery; Restrictions

(a) One who expects to be a party or expects a successor in interest to be a party to an action that may be cognizable in a court of the state, whether as a plaintiff, or as a defendant, or in any other capacity, may obtain discovery within the scope delimited by Chapter 2 (commencing with Section 2017.010), and subject to the restrictions set forth in Chapter 5 (commencing with Section 2019.010), for the purpose of perpetuating that person's own testimony or that of another natural person or organization, or of preserving evidence for use in the event an action is subsequently filed.

(b) One shall not employ the procedures of this chapter for purposes of either ascertaining the possible existence of a cause of action or a defense to it, or of identifying those who might be made parties to an action not yet filed. *(Added by Stats.2004, c. 182, § 23, operative July 1, 2005. Amended by Stats.2005, c. 294, § 13; Stats.2016, c. 86, § 44.)*

§ 2035.020. Methods Available

The methods available for discovery conducted for the purposes set forth in Section 2035.010 are all of the following:

(a) Oral and written depositions.

(b) Inspections of documents, things, and places.

(c) Physical and mental examinations. *(Added by Stats.2004, c. 182, § 23, operative July 1, 2005.)*

§ 2035.030. Filing of Verified Petition; Content and Form of Petition; Court Order

(a) One who desires to perpetuate testimony or preserve evidence for the purposes set forth in Section 2035.010 shall file a verified petition in the superior court of the county of the residence of at least one expected adverse party, or, if no expected adverse party is a resident of the State of California, in the superior court of a county where the action or proceeding may be filed.

(b) The petition shall be titled in the name of the one who desires the perpetuation of testimony or the preservation of evidence. The petition shall set forth all of the following:

(1) The expectation that the petitioner or the petitioner's successor in interest will be a party to an action cognizable in a court of the State of California.

(2) The present inability of the petitioner and, if applicable, the petitioner's successor in interest either to bring that action or to cause it to be brought.

(3) The subject matter of the expected action and the petitioner's involvement. A copy of any written instrument the validity or construction of which may be called into question, or which is connected with the subject matter of the proposed discovery, shall be attached to the petition.

(4) The particular discovery methods described in Section 2035.020 that the petitioner desires to employ.

(5) The facts that the petitioner desires to establish by the proposed discovery.

(6) The reasons for desiring to perpetuate or preserve these facts before an action has been filed.

(7) The name or a description of those whom the petitioner expects to be adverse parties so far as known.

(8) The name and address of those from whom the discovery is to be sought.

(9) The substance of the information expected to be elicited from each of those from whom discovery is being sought.

(c) The petition shall request the court to enter an order authorizing the petitioner to engage in discovery by the described methods for the purpose of perpetuating the described testimony or preserving the described evidence. *(Added by Stats.2004, c. 182, § 23, operative July 1, 2005. Amended by Stats.2005, c. 294, § 14.)*

§ 2035.040. Service of Notice; Form and Contents; Time; Service by Publication; Appointment of Counsel for Absent Party; Payment of Attorney's Fees

(a) The petitioner shall cause service of a notice of the petition under Section 2035.030 to be made on each natural person or organization named in the petition as an expected adverse party. This service shall be made in the same manner provided for the service of a summons.

(b) The service of the notice shall be accompanied by a copy of the petition. The notice shall state that the petitioner will apply to the court at a time and place specified in the notice for the order requested in the petition.

(c) This service shall be effected at least 20 days prior to the date specified in the notice for the hearing on the petition.

(d) If after the exercise of due diligence, the petitioner is unable to cause service to be made on any expected adverse party named in the petition, the court in which the petition is filed shall make an order for service by publication.

(e) If any expected adverse party served by publication does not appear at the hearing, the court shall appoint an attorney to represent that party for all purposes, including the cross-examination of any person whose testimony is taken by deposition. The court shall order that the petitioner pay the reasonable fees and expenses of any attorney so appointed. *(Added by Stats.2004, c. 182, § 23, operative July 1, 2005.)*

§ 2035.050. Authority to Issue Order; Considerations; Contents of Order

(a) If the court determines that all or part of the discovery requested under this chapter may prevent a failure or delay of justice, it shall make an order authorizing that discovery. In determining whether to authorize discovery by a petitioner who expects a successor in interest to be a party to an action, the court shall consider, in addition to other appropriate factors, whether the requested discovery could be conducted by the petitioner's successor in interest, instead of by the petitioner.

(b) The order shall identify any witness whose deposition may be taken, and any documents, things, or places that may be inspected, and any person whose physical or mental condition may be examined.

(c) Any authorized depositions, inspections, and physical or mental examinations shall then be conducted in accordance with the provisions of this title relating to those methods of discovery in actions that have been filed. *(Added by Stats.2004, c. 182, § 23, operative July 1, 2005. Amended by Stats.2005, c. 294, § 15.)*

§ 2035.060. Use of Deposition to Perpetuate Testimony in Subsequent Actions; Requirements

If a deposition to perpetuate testimony has been taken either under the provisions of this chapter, or under comparable provisions of the laws of the state in which it was taken, or the federal courts, or a foreign nation in which it was taken, that deposition may be used, in any action involving the same subject matter that is brought in a court of the State of California, in accordance with Section 2025.620 against any party, or the successor in interest of any party, named in the petition as an expected adverse party. *(Added by Stats.2004, c. 182, § 23, operative July 1, 2005. Amended by Stats.2005, c. 294, § 16.)*

Chapter 20. Perpetuation of Testimony or Preservation of Information Pending Appeal

§ 2036.010. Persons Permitted to Obtain Discovery; Scope of Use

If an appeal has been taken from a judgment entered by a court of the state, or if the time for taking an appeal has not expired, a party may obtain discovery within the scope delimited by Chapter 2 (commencing with Section 2017.010), and subject to the restrictions set forth in Chapter 5 (commencing with Section 2019.010), for purposes of perpetuating testimony or preserving information for use in the event of further proceedings in that court. *(Added by Stats.2004, c. 182, § 23, operative July 1, 2005. Amended by Stats.2016, c. 86, § 45.)*

§ 2036.020. Methods Available

The methods available for discovery for the purpose set forth in Section 2036.010 are all of the following:

(a) Oral and written depositions.

(b) Inspections of documents, things, and places.

(c) Physical and mental examinations. *(Added by Stats.2004, c. 182, § 23, operative July 1, 2005.)*

§ 2036.030. Motion to Obtain Discovery; Notice and Service of Motion; Form and Contents

(a) A party who desires to obtain discovery pending appeal shall obtain leave of the court that entered the judgment. This motion shall be made on the same notice to and service of parties as is required for discovery sought in an action pending in that court.

(b) The motion for leave to conduct discovery pending appeal shall set forth all of the following:

(1) The names and addresses of the natural persons or organizations from whom the discovery is being sought.

(2) The particular discovery methods described in Section 2036.020 for which authorization is being sought.

(3) The reasons for perpetuating testimony or preserving evidence. *(Added by Stats.2004, c. 182, § 23, operative July 1, 2005.)*

§ 2036.040. Determination of Necessity in the Event of Further Proceedings; Order; Contents; Compliance with Discovery Provisions

(a) If the court determines that all or part of the discovery requested under this chapter may prevent a failure or delay of justice in the event of further proceedings in the action in that court, it shall make an order authorizing that discovery.

(b) The order shall identify any witness whose deposition may be taken, and any documents, things, or places that may be inspected, and any person whose physical or mental condition may be examined.

(c) Any authorized depositions, inspections, and physical and mental examinations shall then be conducted in accordance with the provisions of this title relating to these methods of discovery in a pending action. *(Added by Stats.2004, c. 182, § 23, operative July 1, 2005.)*

§ 2036.050. Use of Deposition at Subsequent Proceedings; Scope of Use

If a deposition to perpetuate testimony has been taken under the provisions of this chapter, it may be used in any later proceeding in accordance with Section 2025.620. *(Added by Stats.2004, c. 182, § 23, operative July 1, 2005.)*

SELECTED CALIFORNIA FORMS—PLEADING AND DISCOVERY

■ ■ ■

SUM-100

SUMMONS
(CITACION JUDICIAL)

FOR COURT USE ONLY
(SOLO PARA USO DE LA CORTE)

NOTICE TO DEFENDANT:
(AVISO AL DEMANDADO):

YOU ARE BEING SUED BY PLAINTIFF:
(LO ESTÁ DEMANDANDO EL DEMANDANTE):

NOTICE! You have been sued. The court may decide against you without your being heard unless you respond within 30 days. Read the information below.

You have 30 CALENDAR DAYS after this summons and legal papers are served on you to file a written response at this court and have a copy served on the plaintiff. A letter or phone call will not protect you. Your written response must be in proper legal form if you want the court to hear your case. There may be a court form that you can use for your response. You can find these court forms and more information at the California Courts Online Self-Help Center (*www.courtinfo.ca.gov/selfhelp*), your county law library, or the courthouse nearest you. If you cannot pay the filing fee, ask the court clerk for a fee waiver form. If you do not file your response on time, you may lose the case by default, and your wages, money, and property may be taken without further warning from the court.

There are other legal requirements. You may want to call an attorney right away. If you do not know an attorney, you may want to call an attorney referral service. If you cannot afford an attorney, you may be eligible for free legal services from a nonprofit legal services program. You can locate these nonprofit groups at the California Legal Services Web site (*www.lawhelpcalifornia.org*), the California Courts Online Self-Help Center (*www.courtinfo.ca.gov/selfhelp*), or by contacting your local court or county bar association. **NOTE:** The court has a statutory lien for waived fees and costs on any settlement or arbitration award of $10,000 or more in a civil case. The court's lien must be paid before the court will dismiss the case.

*¡**AVISO!** Lo han demandado. Si no responde dentro de 30 días, la corte puede decidir en su contra sin escuchar su versión. Lea la información a continuación.*

Tiene 30 DÍAS DE CALENDARIO después de que le entreguen esta citación y papeles legales para presentar una respuesta por escrito en esta corte y hacer que se entregue una copia al demandante. Una carta o una llamada telefónica no lo protegen. Su respuesta por escrito tiene que estar en formato legal correcto si desea que procesen su caso en la corte. Es posible que haya un formulario que usted pueda usar para su respuesta. Puede encontrar estos formularios de la corte y más información en el Centro de Ayuda de las Cortes de California (www.sucorte.ca.gov), en la biblioteca de leyes de su condado o en la corte que le quede más cerca. Si no puede pagar la cuota de presentación, pida al secretario de la corte que le dé un formulario de exención de pago de cuotas. Si no presenta su respuesta a tiempo, puede perder el caso por incumplimiento y la corte le podrá quitar su sueldo, dinero y bienes sin más advertencia.

Hay otros requisitos legales. Es recomendable que llame a un abogado inmediatamente. Si no conoce a un abogado, puede llamar a un servicio de remisión a abogados. Si no puede pagar a un abogado, es posible que cumpla con los requisitos para obtener servicios legales gratuitos de un programa de servicios legales sin fines de lucro. Puede encontrar estos grupos sin fines de lucro en el sitio web de California Legal Services, (www.lawhelpcalifornia.org), en el Centro de Ayuda de las Cortes de California, (www.sucorte.ca.gov) o poniéndose en contacto con la corte o el colegio de abogados locales. AVISO: Por ley, la corte tiene derecho a reclamar las cuotas y los costos exentos por imponer un gravamen sobre cualquier recuperación de $10,000 ó más de valor recibida mediante un acuerdo o una concesión de arbitraje en un caso de derecho civil. Tiene que pagar el gravamen de la corte antes de que la corte pueda desechar el caso.

The name and address of the court is:
(El nombre y dirección de la corte es):

CASE NUMBER:
(Número del Caso):

The name, address, and telephone number of plaintiff's attorney, or plaintiff without an attorney, is:
(El nombre, la dirección y el número de teléfono del abogado del demandante, o del demandante que no tiene abogado, es):

DATE: *(Fecha)* Clerk, by *(Secretario)* ____________________, Deputy *(Adjunto)*

(For proof of service of this summons, use Proof of Service of Summons *(form POS-010).)*
(Para prueba de entrega de esta citatión use el formulario Proof of Service of Summons, *(POS-010)).*

[SEAL]

NOTICE TO THE PERSON SERVED: You are served
1. ☐ as an individual defendant.
2. ☐ as the person sued under the fictitious name of *(specify)*:

3. ☐ on behalf of *(specify)*:

under: ☐ CCP 416.10 (corporation) ☐ CCP 416.60 (minor)
☐ CCP 416.20 (defunct corporation) ☐ CCP 416.70 (conservatee)
☐ CCP 416.40 (association or partnership) ☐ CCP 416.90 (authorized person)
☐ other *(specify)*:

4. ☐ by personal delivery on *(date)*:

Page 1 of 1

Form Adopted for Mandatory Use
Judicial Council of California
SUM-100 [Rev. July 1, 2009]

SUMMONS

Code of Civil Procedure §§ 412.20, 465
www.courtinfo.ca.gov

POS-010

ATTORNEY OR PARTY WITHOUT ATTORNEY *(Name, State Bar number, and address)*: TELEPHONE NO.: FAX NO. *(Optional)*: E-MAIL ADDRESS *(Optional)*: ATTORNEY FOR *(Name)*:	***FOR COURT USE ONLY***
SUPERIOR COURT OF CALIFORNIA, COUNTY OF STREET ADDRESS: MAILING ADDRESS: CITY AND ZIP CODE: BRANCH NAME:	
PLAINTIFF/PETITIONER: DEFENDANT/RESPONDENT:	CASE NUMBER:
PROOF OF SERVICE OF SUMMONS	Ref. No. or File No.:

(Separate proof of service is required for each party served.)

1. At the time of service I was at least 18 years of age and not a party to this action.
2. I served copies of:
   a. ☐ summons
   b. ☐ complaint
   c. ☐ Alternative Dispute Resolution (ADR) package
   d. ☐ Civil Case Cover Sheet *(served in complex cases only)*
   e. ☐ cross-complaint
   f. ☐ other *(specify documents)*:
3. a. Party served *(specify name of party as shown on documents served)*:

   b. ☐ Person (other than the party in item 3a) served on behalf of an entity or as an authorized agent (and not a person under item 5b on whom substituted service was made) *(specify name and relationship to the party named in item 3a)*:

4. Address where the party was served:
5. I served the party *(check proper box)*
   a. ☐ **by personal service.** I personally delivered the documents listed in item 2 to the party or person authorized to receive service of process for the party (1) on *(date)*: (2) at *(time)*:
   b. ☐ **by substituted service.** On *(date)*: at *(time)*: I left the documents listed in item 2 with or in the presence of *(name and title or relationship to person indicated in item 3)*:

      (1) ☐ **(business)** a person at least 18 years of age apparently in charge at the office or usual place of business of the person to be served. I informed him or her of the general nature of the papers.

      (2) ☐ **(home)** a competent member of the household (at least 18 years of age) at the dwelling house or usual place of abode of the party. I informed him or her of the general nature of the papers.

      (3) ☐ **(physical address unknown)** a person at least 18 years of age apparently in charge at the usual mailing address of the person to be served, other than a United States Postal Service post office box. I informed him or her of the general nature of the papers.

      (4) ☐ I thereafter mailed (by first-class, postage prepaid) copies of the documents to the person to be served at the place where the copies were left (Code Civ. Proc., § 415.20). I mailed the documents on *(date)*: from *(city)*: **or** ☐ a declaration of mailing is attached.

      (5) ☐ I attach a **declaration of diligence** stating actions taken first to attempt personal service.

PLAINTIFF/PETITIONER:	CASE NUMBER:
DEFENDANT/RESPONDENT:	

5\. c. ☐ **by mail and acknowledgment of receipt of service.** I mailed the documents listed in item 2 to the party, to the address shown in item 4, by first-class mail, postage prepaid,

(1) on *(date)*: (2) from *(city)*:

(3) ☐ with two copies of the *Notice and Acknowledgment of Receipt* and a postage-paid return envelope addressed to me. *(Attach completed* Notice and Acknowledgement of Receipt.*)* (Code Civ. Proc., § 415.30.)

(4) ☐ to an address outside California with return receipt requested. (Code Civ. Proc., § 415.40.)

d. ☐ **by other means** *(specify means of service and authorizing code section)*:

☐ Additional page describing service is attached.

6\. The "Notice to the Person Served" (on the summons) was completed as follows:

a. ☐ as an individual defendant.

b. ☐ as the person sued under the fictitious name of *(specify)*:

c. ☐ as occupant.

d. ☐ On behalf of *(specify)*:

under the following Code of Civil Procedure section:

☐ 416.10 (corporation)
☐ 416.20 (defunct corporation)
☐ 416.30 (joint stock company/association)
☐ 416.40 (association or partnership)
☐ 416.50 (public entity)
☐ 415.95 (business organization, form unknown)
☐ 416.60 (minor)
☐ 416.70 (ward or conservatee)
☐ 416.90 (authorized person)
☐ 415.46 (occupant)
☐ other:

7\. **Person who served papers**

a. Name:

b. Address:

c. Telephone number:

d. **The fee** for service was: **$**

e. I am:

(1) ☐ not a registered California process server.

(2) ☐ exempt from registration under Business and Professions Code section 22350(b).

(3) ☐ a registered California process server:

(i) ☐ owner ☐ employee ☐ independent contractor.

(ii) Registration No.:

(iii) County:

8\. ☐ **I declare** under penalty of perjury under the laws of the State of California that the foregoing is true and correct.

or

9\. ☐ **I am a California sheriff or marshal and** I certify that the foregoing is true and correct.

Date:

(NAME OF PERSON WHO SERVED PAPERS/SHERIFF OR MARSHAL) ▶ (SIGNATURE)

PLD-PI-001

ATTORNEY OR PARTY WITHOUT ATTORNEY STATE BAR NUMBER: NAME: FIRM NAME: STREET ADDRESS: CITY: STATE: ZIP CODE: TELEPHONE NO.: FAX NO.: EMAIL ADDRESS: ATTORNEY FOR *(name)*:	*FOR COURT USE ONLY*
SUPERIOR COURT OF CALIFORNIA, COUNTY OF STREET ADDRESS: MAILING ADDRESS: CITY AND ZIP CODE: BRANCH NAME:	
PLAINTIFF: DEFENDANT: ☐ DOES 1 TO ________	
COMPLAINT—Personal Injury, Property Damage, Wrongful Death ☐ **AMENDED *(Number)*:** **Type *(check all that apply)*:** ☐ **MOTOR VEHICLE** ☐ **OTHER *(specify)*:** ☐ **Property Damage** ☐ **Wrongful Death** ☐ **Personal Injury** ☐ **Other Damages *(specify)*:**	CASE NUMBER:
Jurisdiction *(check all that apply)*: ☐ **ACTION IS A LIMITED CIVIL CASE (does not exceed $35,000)** Amount demanded ☐ does not exceed $10,000 ☐ exceeds $10,000 ☐ **ACTION IS AN UNLIMITED CIVIL CASE (exceeds $35,000)** ☐ **ACTION IS RECLASSIFIED by this amended complaint** ☐ **from limited to unlimited** ☐ **from unlimited to limited**	

1. **Plaintiff** *(name or names)*:
   alleges causes of action against **defendant** *(name or names)*:

2. This pleading, including attachments and exhibits, consists of the following number of pages:
3. Each plaintiff named above is a competent adult
   a. ☐ **except** plaintiff *(name)*:
      (1) ☐ a corporation qualified to do business in California.
      (2) ☐ an unincorporated entity *(describe)*:
      (3) ☐ a public entity *(describe)*:
      (4) ☐ a minor ☐ an adult
         (a) ☐ for whom a guardian or conservator of the estate or a guardian ad litem has been appointed.
         (b) ☐ other *(specify)*:
      (5) ☐ other *(specify)*:
   b. ☐ **except** plaintiff *(name)*:
      (1) ☐ a corporation qualified to do business in California.
      (2) ☐ an unincorporated entity *(describe)*:
      (3) ☐ a public entity *(describe)*:
      (4) ☐ a minor ☐ an adult
         (a) ☐ for whom a guardian or conservator of the estate or a guardian ad litem has been appointed.
         (b) ☐ other *(specify)*:
      (5) ☐ other *(specify)*:

☐ Information about additional plaintiffs who are not competent adults is shown in Attachment 3.

PLD-PI-001

SHORT TITLE:	CASE NUMBER:

4. ☐ Plaintiff *(name):*
is doing business under the fictitious name *(specify):*

and has complied with the fictitious business name laws.

5. Each defendant named above is a natural person

a. ☐ **except** defendant *(name):*
(1) ☐ a business organization, form unknown.
(2) ☐ a corporation.
(3) ☐ an unincorporated entity *(describe):*
(4) ☐ a public entity *(describe):*
(5) ☐ other *(specify):*

b. ☐ **except** defendant *(name):*
(1) ☐ a business organization, form unknown.
(2) ☐ a corporation.
(3) ☐ an unincorporated entity *(describe):*
(4) ☐ a public entity *(describe):*
(5) ☐ other *(specify):*

c. ☐ **except** defendant *(name):*
(1) ☐ a business organization, form unknown.
(2) ☐ a corporation.
(3) ☐ an unincorporated entity *(describe):*
(4) ☐ a public entity *(describe):*
(5) ☐ other *(specify):*

d. ☐ **except** defendant *(name):*
(1) ☐ a business organization, form unknown.
(2) ☐ a corporation.
(3) ☐ an unincorporated entity *(describe):*
(4) ☐ a public entity *(describe):*
(5) ☐ other *(specify):*

☐ Information about additional defendants who are not natural persons is contained in Attachment 5.

6. The true names of defendants sued as Does are unknown to plaintiff.

a. ☐ Doe defendants *(specify Doe numbers):* were the agents or employees of other named defendants and acted within the scope of that agency or employment.

b. ☐ Doe defendants *(specify Doe numbers):* are persons whose capacities are unknown to plaintiff.

7. ☐ Defendants who are joined under Code of Civil Procedure section 382 are *(names):*

8. This court is the proper court because

a. ☐ at least one defendant now resides in its jurisdictional area.
b. ☐ the principal place of business of a defendant corporation or unincorporated association is in its jurisdictional area.
c. ☐ injury to person or damage to personal property occurred in its jurisdictional area.
d. ☐ other *(specify):*

9. ☐ Plaintiff is required to comply with a claims statute, **and**

a. ☐ has complied with applicable claims statutes, **or**
b. ☐ is excused from complying because *(specify):*

PLD-PI-001

SHORT TITLE:	CASE NUMBER:

10. The following causes of action are attached and the statements above apply to each *(each complaint must have one or more causes of action attached)*:
   a. ☐ Motor Vehicle
   b. ☐ General Negligence
   c. ☐ Intentional Tort
   d. ☐ Products Liability
   e. ☐ Premises Liability
   f. ☐ Other *(specify)*:

11. Plaintiff has suffered *(check all that apply)*
   a. ☐ wage loss.
   b. ☐ loss of use of property.
   c. ☐ hospital and medical expenses.
   d. ☐ general damage.
   e. ☐ property damage.
   f. ☐ loss of earning capacity.
   g. ☐ other damage *(specify)*:

12. ☐ The damages claimed for wrongful death and the relationships of plaintiff to the deceased are
   a. ☐ listed in Attachment 12.
   b. ☐ as follows:

13. The relief sought in this complaint is within the jurisdiction of this court.

14. **Plaintiff prays** for judgment for costs of suit; for such relief as is fair, just, and equitable; and for
   a. (1) ☐ compensatory damages.
      (2) ☐ punitive damages.
   b. The amount of damages is *(in cases for personal injury or wrongful death, you must check (1))*:
      (1) ☐ according to proof.
      (2) ☐ in the amount of: $

15. ☐ The paragraphs of this complaint alleged on information and belief are as follows *(specify paragraph numbers)*:

Date:

_______________________________ ▶ _______________________________
(TYPE OR PRINT NAME) (SIGNATURE OF PLAINTIFF OR ATTORNEY)

PLD-PI-001(2)

SHORT TITLE:	CASE NUMBER:

______________ CAUSE OF ACTION—General Negligence Page ______
(number)

ATTACHMENT TO ☐ Complaint ☐ Cross - Complaint

(Use a separate cause of action form for each cause of action.)

GN-1. Plaintiff *(name)*:

alleges that defendant *(name)*:

☐ Does __________ to __________

was the legal (proximate) cause of damages to plaintiff. By the following acts or omissions to act, defendant negligently caused the damage to plaintiff

on *(date)*:

at *(place)*:

(description of reasons for liability):

Form Approved for Optional Use
Judicial Council of California
PLD-PI-001(2) [Rev. January 1, 2007]

CAUSE OF ACTION—General Negligence

Code of Civil Procedure 425.12
www.courtinfo.ca.gov

PLD-PI-001(6)

SHORT TITLE:	CASE NUMBER:

Exemplary Damages Attachment

Page ____________

ATTACHMENT TO ☐ Complaint ☐ Cross - Complaint

EX-1. As additional damages against defendant *(name)*:

Plaintiff alleges defendant was guilty of

☐ malice

☐ fraud

☐ oppression

as defined in Civil Code section 3294, and plaintiff should recover, in addition to actual damages, damages to make an example of and to punish defendant.

EX-2. The facts supporting plaintiff's claim are as follows:

EX-3. The amount of exemplary damages sought is

a. ☐ not shown, pursuant to Code of Civil Procedure section 425.10.

b. ☐ $

Page 1 of 1

Form Approved for Optional Use
Judicial Council of California
PLD-PI-001(6) [Rev. January 1, 2007]

Exemplary Damages Attachment

Code of Civil Procedure, § 425.12
www.courtinfo.ca.gov

PLD-PI-002

ATTORNEY OR PARTY WITHOUT ATTORNEY STATE BAR NUMBER:	FOR COURT USE ONLY
NAME: FIRM NAME: STREET ADDRESS: CITY: STATE: ZIP CODE: TELEPHONE NO.: FAX NO.: EMAIL ADDRESS: ATTORNEY FOR *(name)*:	
NAME OF COURT: STREET ADDRESS: MAILING ADDRESS: CITY AND ZIP CODE: BRANCH NAME:	
SHORT TITLE:	
CROSS-COMPLAINANT: CROSS-DEFENDANT: ☐ DOES 1 TO	
CROSS-COMPLAINT—Personal Injury, Property Damage, Wrongful Death ☐ **AMENDED** ***(Number)*:** **Causes of Action *(check all that apply)*:** ☐ **Apportionment of Fault** ☐ **Declaratory Relief** ☐ **Indemnification** ☐ **Other *(specify)*:**	
Jurisdiction *(check all that apply)*: ☐ **ACTION IS A LIMITED CIVIL CASE ($35,000 or less)** ☐ **ACTION IS AN UNLIMITED CIVIL CASE (exceeds $35,000)** **It ☐ is ☐ is not reclassified as unlimited by this cross-complaint**	CASE NUMBER:

1. CROSS-COMPLAINANT *(name)*:

   alleges causes of action against CROSS-DEFENDANT *(name)*:

2. This pleading, including exhibits and attachments, consists of the following number of pages:
3. Each cross-complainant named above is a competent adult
   ☐ **except** cross-complainant *(name)*:
   a. ☐ a corporation qualified to do business in California.
   b. ☐ an unincorporated entity *(describe)*:
   c. ☐ a public entity *(describe)*:
   d. ☐ a minor ☐ an adult
      (1) ☐ for whom a guardian or conservator of the estate or a guardian ad litem has been appointed.
      (2) ☐ other *(specify)*:
   e. ☐ other *(specify)*:

☐ Information about additional cross-complainants who are not competent adults is contained in Cross-Complaint—Attachment 3.

Form Approved for Optional Use
Judicial Council of California
PLD-PI-002 [Rev. January 1, 2024]

Code of Civil Procedure, § 425.12
www.courts.ca.gov

PLD-PI-002

SHORT TITLE:	CASE NUMBER:

4. Each cross-defendant named above is a natural person

a. ☐ **except** cross-defendant *(name)*:
   (1) ☐ a business organization, form unknown.
   (2) ☐ a corporation.
   (3) ☐ an unincorporated entity *(describe)*:
   (4) ☐ an public entity *(describe)*:
   (5) ☐ other *(specify)*:

b. ☐ **except** cross-defendant *(name)*:
   (1) ☐ a business organization, form unknown.
   (2) ☐ a corporation.
   (3) ☐ an unincorporated entity *(describe)*:
   (4) ☐ an public entity *(describe)*:
   (5) ☐ other *(specify)*:

☐ Information about additional cross-defendants who are not natural persons is contained in Cross-Complaint—Attachment 4.

5. The true names and capacities of cross-defendants sued as Does are unknown to cross-complainant.

6. ☐ Cross-complainant is required to comply with a claims statute, **and**
   a. ☐ has complied with applicable claims statutes, **or**
   b. ☐ is excused from complying because *(specify)*:

7. ☐ ______________________ **Cause of Action—Indemnification**
(NUMBER)

a. Cross-defendants were the agents, employees, co-venturers, partners, or in some manner agents or principals, or both, for each other and were acting within the course and scope of their agency or employment.

b. The principal action alleges, among other things, conduct entitling plaintiff to compensatory damages against me. I contend that I am not liable for events and occurrences described in plaintiff's complaint.

c. If I am found in some manner responsible to plaintiff or to anyone else as a result of the incidents and occurrences described in plaintiff's complaint, my liability would be based solely upon a derivative form of liability not resulting from my conduct, but only from an obligation imposed upon me by law; therefore, I would be entitled to complete indemnity from each cross-defendant.

8. ☐ ______________________ **Cause of Action—Apportionment of Fault**
(NUMBER)

a. Each cross-defendant was responsible, in whole or in part, for the injuries, if any, suffered by plaintiff.

b. If I am judged liable to plaintiff, each cross-defendant should be required: (1) to pay a share of plaintiffs judgment which is in proportion to the comparative negligence of that cross-defendant in causing plaintiff's damages; and (2) to reimburse me for any payments I make to plaintiff in excess of my proportional share of all cross-defendants' negligence.

PLD-PI-002

SHORT TITLE:	CASE NUMBER:

9. ☐ ____________________ Cause of Action—Declaratory Relief
(NUMBER)

An actual controversy exists between the parties concerning their respective rights and duties because cross-complainant contends and cross-defendant disputes ☐ as specified in Cross-Complaint—Attachment 9

☐ as follows:

10. ☐ ____________________ **Cause of Action—*(specify)*:**
(NUMBER)

11. ☐ The following additional causes of action are attached and the statements below apply to each *(in each of the attachments, "plaintiff" means "cross-complainant" and "defendant" means "cross-defendant")*:

a. ☐ Motor Vehicle
b. ☐ General Negligence
c. ☐ Intentional Tort
d. ☐ Products Liability
e. ☐ Premises Liability
f. ☐ Other *(specify)*:

12. **CROSS-COMPLAINANT PRAYS** for judgment for costs of suit; for such relief as is fair, just, and equitable; and for

a. ☐ total and complete indemnity for any judgments rendered against me.
b. ☐ judgment in a proportionate share from each cross-defendant.
c. ☐ a judicial determination that cross-defendants were the legal cause of any injuries and damages sustained by plaintiff and that cross-defendants indemnify me, either completely or partially, for any sums of money which may be recovered against me by plaintiff.
d. ☐ compensatory damages
(1) ☐ (unlimited civil cases) according to proof.
(2) ☐ (limited civil cases) in the amount of: $
e. ☐ other *(specify)*:

13. ☐ The paragraphs of this cross-complaint alleged on information and belief are as follows *(specify paragraph numbers)*:

Date:

____________________________________ ▶ ____________________________________
(TYPE OR PRINT NAME) SIGNATURE OF CROSS-COMPLAINANT OR ATTORNEY

PLD-PI-003

ATTORNEY OR PARTY WITHOUT ATTORNEY *(NAME AND ADDRESS)*: TELEPHONE NO.: ATTORNEY FOR *(NAME)*:	FOR COURT USE ONLY
Insert name of court, judicial district or branch court, if any, and post office and street address:	
PLAINTIFF:	
DEFENDANT:	
ANSWER—Personal Injury, Property Damage, Wrongful Death ☐ **COMPLAINT OF (name):** ☐ **CROSS-COMPLAINT OF *(name)*:**	CASE NUMBER:

1. This pleading, including attachments and exhibits, consists of the following number of pages: ________

DEFENDANT OR CROSS-DEFENDANT *(name)*:

2. ☐ Generally **denies** each allegation of the unverified complaint or cross-complaint.

3. a. ☐ DENIES each allegation of the following numbered paragraphs:

   b. ☐ ADMITS each allegation of the following numbered paragraphs:

   c. ☐ DENIES, ON INFORMATION AND BELIEF, each allegation of the following numbered paragraphs:

   d. ☐ DENIES, BECAUSE OF LACK OF SUFFICIENT INFORMATION OR BELIEF TO ANSWER, each allegation of the following numbered paragraphs:

   e. ☐ ADMITS the following allegations and generally denies all other allegations:

PLD-PI-003

SHORT TITLE:	CASE NUMBER:

ANSWER—Personal Injury, Property Damage, Wrongful Death

f. ☐ DENIES the following allegations and admits all other allegations:

g. ☐ Other *(specify)*:

AFFIRMATIVELY ALLEGES AS A DEFENSE

4. ☐ The comparative fault of plaintiff or cross-complainant *(name)*:
as follows:

5. ☐ The expiration of the Statute of Limitations as follows:

6. ☐ Other *(specify)*:

7. DEFENDANT OR CROSS - DEFENDANT PRAYS
For costs of suit and that plaintiff or cross-complainant take nothing.
☐ Other *(specify)*:

______________________________ ______________________________
(Type or print name) (Signature of party or attorney)

CIV-100

ATTORNEY OR PARTY WITHOUT ATTORNEY: STATE BAR NO:	FOR COURT USE ONLY
NAME:	
FIRM NAME:	
STREET ADDRESS:	
CITY: STATE: ZIP CODE:	
TELEPHONE NO.: FAX NO.:	
E-MAIL ADDRESS:	
ATTORNEY FOR (name):	
SUPERIOR COURT OF CALIFORNIA, COUNTY OF	
STREET ADDRESS:	
MAILING ADDRESS:	
CITY AND ZIP CODE:	
BRANCH NAME:	
Plaintiff/Petitioner:	
Defendant/Respondent:	
REQUEST FOR (Application) ☐ Entry of Default ☐ Clerk's Judgment ☐ Court Judgment	CASE NUMBER:

Not for use in actions under the Fair Debt Buying Practices Act (Civ. Code, § 1788.50 et seq.); (see form CIV-105)

1. TO THE CLERK: On the complaint or cross-complaint filed
   a. on *(date)*:
   b. by *(name)*:
   c. ☐ Enter default of defendant *(names)*:
   d. ☐ I request a court judgment under Code of Civil Procedure sections 585(b), 585(c), 989, etc., against defendant *(names)*:
      (Testimony required. Apply to the clerk for a hearing date, unless the court will enter a judgment on an affidavit under Code Civ. Proc., § 585(d).)
   e. ☐ Enter clerk's judgment
      (1) ☐ for restitution of the premises only and issue a writ of execution on the judgment. Code of Civil Procedure section 1174(c) does not apply. (Code Civ. Proc., § 1169.)
         ☐ Include in the judgment all tenants, subtenants, named claimants, and other occupants of the premises. The *Prejudgment Claim of Right to Possession* was served in compliance with Code of Civil Procedure section 415.46.
      (2) ☐ under Code of Civil Procedure section 585(a). *(Complete the declaration under Code Civ. Proc., § 585.5 on the reverse (item 5).)*
      (3) ☐ for default previously entered on *(date)*:

2. **Judgment to be entered.**

	Amount	Credits acknowledged	Balance
a. Demand of complaint	$	$	$
b. Statement of damages*			
(1) Special	$	$	$
(2) General	$	$	$
c. Interest	$	$	$
d. Costs *(see reverse)*	$	$	$
e. Attorney fees	$	$	$
f. **TOTALS**	$	$	$

   g. **Daily damages** were demanded in complaint at the rate of: $ per day beginning *(date)*:

   (Personal injury or wrongful death actions; Code Civ. Proc., § 425.11.)*

3. ☐ *(Check if filed in an unlawful detainer case.)* **Legal document assistant or unlawful detainer assistant** information is on the reverse *(complete item 4)*.

Date:

(TYPE OR PRINT NAME) ▶ (SIGNATURE OF PLAINTIFF OR ATTORNEY FOR PLAINTIFF)

FOR COURT USE ONLY	(1) ☐ Default entered as requested on *(date)*: (2) ☐ Default NOT entered as requested *(state reason)*: Clerk, by ________, Deputy

Page 1 of 3

Form Adopted for Mandatory Use
Judicial Council of California
CIV-100 [Rev. January 1, 2023]

REQUEST FOR ENTRY OF DEFAULT
(Application to Enter Default)

Code of Civil Procedure, §§ 585–587, 1169
www.courts.ca.gov

CIV-100

Plaintiff/Petitioner: Defendant/Respondent:	CASE NUMBER:

4. **Legal document assistant or unlawful detainer assistant (Bus. & Prof. Code, § 6400 et seq.).** A legal document assistant or unlawful detainer assistant ☐ did ☐ **did not** for compensation give advice or assistance with this form. If declarant has received **any** help or advice for pay from a legal document assistant or unlawful detainer assistant, state:
   a. Assistant's name:
   b. Street address, city, and zip code:
   c. Telephone no.:
   d. County of registration:
   e. Registration no.:
   f. Expires on *(date)*:

5. ☐ **Declaration under Code Civ. Proc., § 585.5** *(for entry of default under Code Civ. Proc., § 585(a))*. This action
   a. ☐ is ☐ is not on a contract or installment sale for goods or services subject to Civ. Code, § 1801 et seq. (Unruh Act).
   b. ☐ is ☐ is not on a conditional sales contract subject to Civ. Code, § 2981 et seq. (Rees-Levering Motor Vehicle Sales and Finance Act).
   c. ☐ is ☐ is not on an obligation for goods, services, loans, or extensions of credit subject to Code Civ. Proc., § 395(b).

6. **Declaration of mailing (Code Civ. Proc., § 587).** A copy of this *Request for Entry of Default* was
   a. ☐ **not mailed** to the following defendants, whose addresses are unknown to plaintiff or plaintiff's attorney *(names)*:
   b. ☐ **mailed** first-class, postage prepaid, in a sealed envelope addressed to each defendant's attorney of record or, if none, to each defendant's last known address as follows:
      (1) Mailed on *(date)*:
      (2) To *(specify names and addresses shown on the envelopes)*:

I declare under penalty of perjury under the laws of the State of California that the foregoing items 4, 5, and 6 are true and correct.

Date:

(TYPE OR PRINT NAME) ▶ (SIGNATURE OF DECLARANT)

7. **Memorandum of costs** *(required if money judgment requested)*. Costs and disbursements are as follows (Code Civ. Proc., § 1033.5):
   a. Clerk's filing fees . . . . $
   b. Process server's fees . . . . $
   c. Other *(specify)*: $
   d. $
   e. TOTAL . . . . $
   f. ☐ Costs and disbursements are waived.
   g. I am the attorney, agent, or party who claims these costs. To the best of my knowledge and belief this memorandum of costs is correct and these costs were necessarily incurred in this case.

I declare under penalty of perjury under the laws of the State of California that the foregoing item 7 is true and correct.

Date:

(TYPE OR PRINT NAME) ▶ (SIGNATURE OF DECLARANT)

CIV-100 [Rev. January 1, 2023]

REQUEST FOR ENTRY OF DEFAULT
(Application to Enter Default)

Page 2 of 3

CIV-100

Plaintiff/Petitioner:	CASE NUMBER:
Defendant/Respondent:	

8. **Declaration of nonmilitary status** *(required for a judgment).*
No defendant/respondent named in item 1c is in the military service of the United States as defined by either the Servicemembers Civil Relief Act (see 50 U.S.C. § 3911(2)) or California Military and Veterans Code sections 400 and 402(f).

I know that no defendant/respondent named in item 1c is in the U.S. military service because *(check all that apply):*

a. ☐ the search results that I received from https://scra.dmdc.osd.mil/ say the defendant/respondent is not in the U.S. military service.

b. ☐ I am in regular communication with the defendant/respondent and know that they are not in the U.S. military service.

c. ☐ I recently contacted the defendant/respondent, and they told me that they are not in the U.S. military service.

d. ☐ I know that the defendant/respondent was discharged from U.S. military service on or about *(date):*

e. ☐ the defendant/respondent is not eligible to serve in the U.S. military because they are:
☐ incarcerated ☐ a business entity

f. ☐ other *(specify):*

Note

- U.S. military status can be checked online at https://scra.dmdc.osd.mil/.
- If the defendant/respondent is in the military service, or their military status is unknown, the defendant/respondent is entitled to certain rights and protections under federal and state law before a default judgment can be entered.
- For more information, see https://selfhelp.courts.ca.gov/military-defaults.

I declare under penalty of perjury under the laws of the State of California that the foregoing item 8 is true and correct.

Date:

(TYPE OR PRINT NAME) ▶ (SIGNATURE OF DECLARANT)

DISC-001

ATTORNEY OR PARTY WITHOUT ATTORNEY STATE BAR NUMBER:
NAME:
FIRM NAME:
STREET ADDRESS:
CITY: STATE: ZIP CODE:
TELEPHONE NO.: FAX NO.:
EMAIL ADDRESS:
ATTORNEY FOR (name):

SUPERIOR COURT OF CALIFORNIA, COUNTY OF

SHORT TITLE OF CASE:

FORM INTERROGATORIES—GENERAL

CASE NUMBER:

Asking Party:

Answering Party:

Set No.:

Sec. 1. Instructions to All Parties

(a) Interrogatories are written questions prepared by a party to an action that are sent to any other party in the action to be answered under oath. The interrogatories below are form interrogatories approved for use in civil cases.

(b) For time limitations, requirements for service on other parties, and other details, see Code of Civil Procedure sections 2030.010–2030.410 and the cases construing those sections.

(c) These form interrogatories do not change existing law relating to interrogatories nor do they affect an answering party's right to assert any privilege or make any objection.

Sec. 2. Instructions to the Asking Party

(a) These interrogatories are designed for optional use by parties in unlimited civil cases where the amount demanded exceeds $35,000. Separate interrogatories, *Form Interrogatories—Limited Civil Cases (Economic Litigation)* (form DISC-004), which have no subparts, are designed for use in limited civil cases where the amount demanded is $35,000 or less; however, those interrogatories may also be used in unlimited civil cases.

(b) Check the box next to each interrogatory that you want the answering party to answer. Use care in choosing those interrogatories that are applicable to the case.

(c) You may insert your own definition of **INCIDENT** in Section 4, but only where the action arises from a course of conduct or a series of events occurring over a period of time.

(d) The interrogatories in section 16.0, Defendant's Contentions–Personal Injury, should not be used until the defendant has had a reasonable opportunity to conduct an investigation or discovery of plaintiff's injuries and damages.

(e) Additional interrogatories may be attached.

Sec. 3. Instructions to the Answering Party

(a) An answer or other appropriate response must be given to each interrogatory checked by the asking party.

(b) As a general rule, within 30 days after you are served with these interrogatories, you must serve your responses on the asking party and serve copies of your responses on all other parties to the action who have appeared. See Code of Civil Procedure sections 2030.260–2030.270 for details.

(c) Each answer must be as complete and straightforward as the information reasonably available to you, including the information possessed by your attorneys or agents, permits. If an interrogatory cannot be answered completely, answer it to the extent possible.

(d) If you do not have enough personal knowledge to fully answer an interrogatory, say so, but make a reasonable and good faith effort to get the information by asking other persons or organizations, unless the information is equally available to the asking party.

(e) Whenever an interrogatory may be answered by referring to a document, the document may be attached as an exhibit to the response and referred to in the response. If the document has more than one page, refer to the page and section where the answer to the interrogatory can be found.

(f) Whenever an address and telephone number for the same person are requested in more than one interrogatory, you are required to furnish them in answering only the first interrogatory asking for that information.

(g) If you are asserting a privilege or making an objection to an interrogatory, you must specifically assert the privilege or state the objection in your written response.

(h) Your answers to these interrogatories must be verified, dated, and signed. You may wish to use the following form at the end of your answers:

I declare under penalty of perjury under the laws of the State of California that the foregoing answers are true and correct.

(Date) ______________________ *(SIGNATURE)*

Sec. 4. Definitions

Words in **BOLDFACE CAPITALS** in these interrogatories are defined as follows:

(a) *(Check one of the following):*

☐ (1) **INCIDENT** includes the circumstances and events surrounding the alleged accident, injury, or other occurrence or breach of contract giving rise to this action or proceeding.

DISC-001

☐ (2) **INCIDENT** means *(insert your definition here or on a separate, attached sheet labeled "Sec. 4(a)(2)"):*

(b) **YOU OR ANYONE ACTING ON YOUR BEHALF** includes you, your agents, your employees, your insurance companies, their agents, their employees, your attorneys, your accountants, your investigators, and anyone else acting on your behalf.

(c) **PERSON** includes a natural person, firm, association, organization, partnership, business, trust, limited liability company, corporation, or public entity.

(d) **DOCUMENT** means a writing, as defined in Evidence Code section 250, and includes the original or a copy of handwriting, typewriting, printing, photostats, photographs, electronically stored information, and every other means of recording upon any tangible thing and form of communicating or representation, including letters, words, pictures, sounds, or symbols, or combinations of them.

(e) **HEALTH CARE PROVIDER** includes any **PERSON** referred to in Code of Civil Procedure section 667.7(e)(3).

(f) **ADDRESS** means the street address, including the city, state, and zip code.

Sec. 5. Interrogatories

The following interrogatories have been approved by the Judicial Council under Code of Civil Procedure section 2033.710:

CONTENTS

1.0 Identity of Persons Answering These Interrogatories

☐ 1.1 State the name, **ADDRESS,** telephone number, and relationship to you of each **PERSON** who prepared or assisted in the preparation of the responses to these interrogatories. (*Do not identify anyone who simply typed or reproduced the responses.)*

2.0 General Background Information individual—

☐ 2.1 State:
(a) your name;
(b) every name you have used in the past; and
(c) the dates you used each name.

☐ 2.2 State the date and place of your birth.

☐ 2.3 At the time of the **INCIDENT,** did you have a driver's license? If so, state:
(a) the state or other issuing entity;
(b) the license number and type;
(c) the date of issuance; and
(d) all restrictions.

☐ 2.4 At the time of the **INCIDENT,** did you have any other permit or license for the operation of a motor vehicle? If so, state:
(a) the state or other issuing entity;
(b) the license number and type;
(c) the date of issuance; and
(d) all restrictions.

☐ 2.5 State:
(a) your present residence **ADDRESS;**
(b) your residence **ADDRESSES** for the past five years; and
(c) the dates you lived at each **ADDRESS.**

☐ 2.6 State:
(a) the name, **ADDRESS,** and telephone number of your present employer or place of self-employment; and
(b) the name, **ADDRESS,** dates of employment, job title, and nature of work for each employer or self-employment you have had from five years before the **INCIDENT** until today.

☐ 2.7 State:
(a) the name and **ADDRESS** of each school or other academic or vocational institution you have attended, beginning with high school;
(b) the dates you attended;
(c) the highest grade level you have completed; and
(d) the degrees received.

☐ 2.8 Have you ever been convicted of a felony? If so, for each conviction state:
(a) the city and state where you were convicted;
(b) the date of conviction;
(c) the offense; and
(d) the court and case number.

☐ 2.9 Can you speak English with ease? If not, what language and dialect do you normally use?

☐ 2.10 Can you read and write English with ease? If not, what language and dialect do you normally use?

DISC-001

☐ 2.11 At the time of the **INCIDENT** were you acting as an agent or employee for any **PERSON?** If so, state:
(a) the name, **ADDRESS**, and telephone number of that **PERSON;** and
(b) a description of your duties.

☐ 2.12 At the time of the **INCIDENT** did you or any other person have any physical, emotional, or mental disability or condition that may have contributed to the occurrence of the **INCIDENT?** If so, for each person state:
(a) the name, **ADDRESS,** and telephone number;
(b) the nature of the disability or condition; and
(c) the manner in which the disability or condition contributed to the occurrence of the **INCIDENT.**

☐ 2.13 Within 24 hours before the **INCIDENT** did you or any person involved in the **INCIDENT** use or take any of the following substances: alcoholic beverage, marijuana, or other drug or medication of any kind (prescription or not)? If so, for each person state:
(a) the name, **ADDRESS,** and telephone number;
(b) the nature or description of each substance;
(c) the quantity of each substance used or taken;
(d) the date and time of day when each substance was used or taken;
(e) the **ADDRESS** where each substance was used or taken;
(f) the name, **ADDRESS,** and telephone number of each person who was present when each substance was used or taken; and
(g) the name, **ADDRESS,** and telephone number of any **HEALTH CARE PROVIDER** who prescribed or furnished the substance and the condition for which it was prescribed or furnished.

3.0 General Background Information—Business Entity

☐ 3.1 Are you a corporation? If so, state:
(a) the name stated in the current articles of incorporation;
(b) all other names used by the corporation during the past 10 years and the dates each was used;
(c) the date and place of incorporation;
(d) the **ADDRESS** of the principal place of business; and
(e) whether you are qualified to do business in California.

☐ 3.2 Are you a partnership? If so, state:
(a) the current partnership name;
(b) all other names used by the partnership during the past 10 years and the dates each was used;
(c) whether you are a limited partnership and, if so, under the laws of what jurisdiction;
(d) the name and **ADDRESS** of each general partner; and
(e) the **ADDRESS** of the principal place of business.

☐ 3.3 Are you a limited liability company? If so, state:
(a) the name stated in the current articles of organization;
(b) all other names used by the company during the past 10 years and the date each was used;
(c) the date and place of filing of the articles of organization;
(d) the **ADDRESS** of the principal place of business; and
(e) whether you are qualified to do business in California.

☐ 3.4 Are you a joint venture? If so, state:
(a) the current joint venture name;
(b) all other names used by the joint venture during the past 10 years and the dates each was used;
(c) the name and **ADDRESS** of each joint venturer; and
(d) the **ADDRESS** of the principal place of business.

☐ 3.5 Are you an unincorporated association? If so, state:
(a) the current unincorporated association name;
(b) all other names used by the unincorporated association during the past 10 years and the dates each was used; and
(c) the **ADDRESS** of the principal place of business.

☐ 3.6 Have you done business under a fictitious name during the past 10 years? If so, for each fictitious name state:
(a) the name;
(b) the dates each was used;
(c) the state and county of each fictitious name filing; and
(d) the **ADDRESS** of the principal place of business.

☐ 3.7 Within the past five years has any public entity registered or licensed your business? If so, for each license or registration:
(a) identify the license or registration;
(b) state the name of the public entity; and
(c) state the dates of issuance and expiration.

4.0 Insurance

☐ 4.1 At the time of the **INCIDENT,** was there in effect any policy of insurance through which you were or might be insured in any manner (for example, primary, pro-rata, or excess liability coverage or medical expense coverage) for the damages, claims, or actions that have arisen out of the **INCIDENT?** If so, for each policy state:
(a) the kind of coverage;
(b) the name and **ADDRESS** of the insurance company;
(c) the name, **ADDRESS,** and telephone number of each named insured;
(d) the policy number;
(e) the limits of coverage for each type of coverage contained in the policy;
(f) whether any reservation of rights or controversy or coverage dispute exists between you and the insurance company; and
(g) the name, **ADDRESS,** and telephone number of the custodian of the policy.

☐ 4.2 Are you self-insured under any statute for the damages, claims, or actions that have arisen out of the **INCIDENT?** If so, specify the statute.

5.0 *[Reserved]*

6.0 Physical, Mental, or Emotional Injuries

☐ 6.1 Do you attribute any physical, mental, or emotional injuries to the **INCIDENT?** *(If your answer is "no," do not answer interrogatories 6.2 through 6.7).*

☐ 6.2 Identify each injury you attribute to the **INCIDENT** and the area of your body affected.

DISC-001

☐ 6.3 Do you still have any complaints that you attribute to the **INCIDENT?** If so, for each complaint state:

(a) a description;

(b) whether the complaint is subsiding, remaining the same, or becoming worse; and

(c) the frequency and duration.

☐ 6.4 Did you receive any consultation or examination (except from expert witnesses covered by Code of Civil Procedure sections 2034.210–2034.310) or treatment from a **HEALTH CARE PROVIDER** for any injury you attribute to the **INCIDENT?** If so, for each **HEALTH CARE PROVIDER** state:

(a) the name, **ADDRESS,** and telephone number;

(b) the type of consultation, examination, or treatment provided;

(c) the dates you received consultation, examination, or treatment; and

(d) the charges to date.

☐ 6.5 Have you taken any medication, prescribed or not, as a result of injuries that you attribute to the **INCIDENT?** If so, for each medication state:

(a) the name;

(b) the **PERSON** who prescribed or furnished it;

(c) the date it was prescribed or furnished;

(d) the dates you began and stopped taking it; and

(e) the cost to date.

☐ 6.6 Are there any other medical services necessitated by the injuries that you attribute to the **INCIDENT** that were not previously listed (for example, ambulance, nursing, prosthetics)? If so, for each service state:

(a) the nature;

(b) the date;

(c) the cost; and

(d) the name, **ADDRESS,** and telephone number of each provider.

☐ 6.7 Has any **HEALTH CARE PROVIDER** advised that you may require future or additional treatment for any injuries that you attribute to the **INCIDENT?** If so, for each injury state:

(a) the name and **ADDRESS** of each **HEALTH CARE PROVIDER;**

(b) the complaints for which the treatment was advised; and

(c) the nature, duration, and estimated cost of the treatment.

7.0 Property Damage

☐ 7.1 Do you attribute any loss of or damage to a vehicle or other property to the **INCIDENT**? If so, for each item of property:

(a) describe the property;

(b) describe the nature and location of the damage to the property;

(c) state the amount of damage you are claiming for each item of property and how the amount was calculated; and

(d) if the property was sold, state the name, **ADDRESS,** and telephone number of the seller, the date of sale, and the sale price.

☐ 7.2 Has a written estimate or evaluation been made for any item of property referred to in your answer to the preceding interrogatory? If so, for each estimate or evaluation state:

(a) the name, **ADDRESS,** and telephone number of the **PERSON** who prepared it and the date prepared;

(b) the name, **ADDRESS,** and telephone number of each **PERSON** who has a copy of it; and

(c) the amount of damage stated.

☐ 7.3 Has any item of property referred to in your answer to interrogatory 7.1 been repaired? If so, for each item state:

(a) the date repaired;

(b) a description of the repair;

(c) the repair cost;

(d) the name, **ADDRESS,** and telephone number of the **PERSON** who repaired it; and

(e) the name, **ADDRESS,** and telephone number of the **PERSON** who paid for the repair.

8.0 Loss of Income or Earning Capacity

☐ 8.1 Do you attribute any loss of income or earning capacity to the **INCIDENT**? *(If your answer is "no," do not answer interrogatories 8.2 through 8.8).*

☐ 8.2 State:

(a) the nature of your work;

(b) your job title at the time of the **INCIDENT**; and

(c) the date your employment began.

☐ 8.3 State the last date before the **INCIDENT** that you worked for compensation.

☐ 8.4 State your monthly income at the time of the **INCIDENT** and how the amount was calculated.

☐ 8.5 State the date you returned to work at each place of employment following the **INCIDENT.**

☐ 8.6 State the dates you did not work and for which you lost income as a result of the **INCIDENT.**

☐ 8.7 State the total income you have lost to date as a result of the **INCIDENT** and how the amount was calculated.

☐ 8.8 Will you lose income in the future as a result of the **INCIDENT?** If so, state:

(a) the facts on which you base this contention;

(b) an estimate of the amount;

(c) an estimate of how long you will be unable to work; and

(d) how the claim for future income is calculated.

DISC-001

9.0 Other Damages

☐ 9.1 Are there any other damages that you attribute to the **INCIDENT?** If so, for each item of damage state:

(a) the nature;

(b) the date it occurred;

(c) the amount; and

(d) the name, **ADDRESS,** and telephone number of each **PERSON** to whom an obligation was incurred.

☐ 9.2 Do any **DOCUMENTS** support the existence or amount of any item of damages claimed in interrogatory 9.1? If so, describe each document and state the name, **ADDRESS,** and telephone number of the **PERSON** who has each **DOCUMENT.**

10.0 Medical History

☐ 10.1 At any time before the **INCIDENT** did you have complaints or injuries that involved the same part of your body claimed to have been injured in the **INCIDENT?** If so, for each state:

(a) a description of the complaint or injury;

(b) the dates it began and ended; and

(c) the name, **ADDRESS,** and telephone number of each **HEALTH CARE PROVIDER** whom you consulted or who examined or treated you.

☐ 10.2 List all physical, mental, and emotional disabilities you had immediately before the **INCIDENT.** *(You may omit mental or emotional disabilities unless you attribute any mental or emotional injury to the **INCIDENT.**)*

☐ 10.3 At any time after the **INCIDENT,** did you sustain injuries of the kind for which you are now claiming damages? If so, for each incident giving rise to an injury state:

(a) the date and the place it occurred;

(b) the name, **ADDRESS,** and telephone number of any other **PERSON** involved;

(c) the nature of any injuries you sustained;

(d) the name, **ADDRESS,** and telephone number of each **HEALTH CARE PROVIDER** who you consulted or who examined or treated you; and

(e) the nature of the treatment and its duration.

11.0 Other Claims and Previous Claims

☐ 11.1 Except for this action, in the past 10 years have you filed an action or made a written claim or demand for compensation for your personal injuries? If so, for each action, claim, or demand state:

(a) the date, time, and place and location (closest street **ADDRESS** or intersection) of the **INCIDENT** giving rise to the action, claim, or demand;

(b) the name, **ADDRESS,** and telephone number of each **PERSON** against whom the claim or demand was made or the action filed;

(c) the court, names of the parties, and case number of any action filed;

(d) the name, **ADDRESS,** and telephone number of any attorney representing you;

(e) whether the claim or action has been resolved or is pending; and

(f) a description of the injury.

☐ 11.2 In the past 10 years have you made a written claim or demand for workers' compensation benefits? If so, for each claim or demand state:

(a) the date, time, and place of the **INCIDENT** giving rise to the claim;

(b) the name, **ADDRESS,** and telephone number of your employer at the time of the injury;

(c) the name, **ADDRESS,** and telephone number of the workers' compensation insurer and the claim number;

(d) the period of time during which you received workers' compensation benefits;

(e) a description of the injury;

(f) the name, **ADDRESS,** and telephone number of any **HEALTH CARE PROVIDER** who provided services; and

(g) the case number at the Workers' Compensation Appeals Board.

12.0 Investigation—General

☐ 12.1 State the name, **ADDRESS,** and telephone number of each individual:

(a) who witnessed the **INCIDENT** or the events occurring immediately before or after the **INCIDENT;**

(b) who made any statement at the scene of the **INCIDENT;**

(c) who heard any statements made about the **INCIDENT** by any individual at the scene; and

(d) who **YOU OR ANYONE ACTING ON YOUR BEHALF** claim has knowledge of the **INCIDENT** (except for expert witnesses covered by Code of Civil Procedure section 2034).

☐ 12.2 Have **YOU OR ANYONE ACTING ON YOUR BEHALF** interviewed any individual concerning the **INCIDENT?** If so, for each individual state:

(a) the name, **ADDRESS,** and telephone number of the individual interviewed;

(b) the date of the interview; and

(c) the name, **ADDRESS,** and telephone number of the **PERSON** who conducted the interview.

☐ 12.3 Have **YOU OR ANYONE ACTING ON YOUR BEHALF** obtained a written or recorded statement from any individual concerning the **INCIDENT?** If so, for each statement state:

(a) the name, **ADDRESS,** and telephone number of the individual from whom the statement was obtained;

(b) the name, **ADDRESS,** and telephone number of the individual who obtained the statement;

(c) the date the statement was obtained; and

(d) the name, **ADDRESS,** and telephone number of each **PERSON** who has the original statement or a copy.

DISC-001

☐ 12.4 Do **YOU OR ANYONE ACTING ON YOUR BEHALF** know of any photographs, films, or videotapes depicting any place, object, or individual concerning the **INCIDENT** or plaintiff's injuries? If so, state:
(a) the number of photographs or feet of film or videotape;
(b) the places, objects, or persons photographed, filmed, or videotaped;
(c) the date the photographs, films, or videotapes were taken;
(d) the name, **ADDRESS**, and telephone number of the individual taking the photographs, films, or videotapes; and
(e) the name, **ADDRESS**, and telephone number of each **PERSON** who has the original or a copy of the photographs, films, or videotapes.

☐ 12.5 Do **YOU OR ANYONE ACTING ON YOUR BEHALF** know of any diagram, reproduction, or model of any place or thing (except for items developed by expert witnesses covered by Code of Civil Procedure sections 2034.210–2034.310) concerning the **INCIDENT**? If so, for each item state:
(a) the type (i.e., diagram, reproduction, or model);
(b) the subject matter; and
(c) the name, **ADDRESS**, and telephone number of each **PERSON** who has it.

☐ 12.6 Was a report made by any **PERSON** concerning the **INCIDENT**? If so, state:
(a) the name, title, identification number, and employer of the **PERSON** who made the report;
(b) the date and type of report made;
(c) the name, **ADDRESS**, and telephone number of the **PERSON** for whom the report was made; and
(d) the name, **ADDRESS**, and telephone number of each **PERSON** who has the original or a copy of the report.

☐ 12.7 Have **YOU OR ANYONE ACTING ON YOUR BEHALF** inspected the scene of the **INCIDENT**? If so, for each inspection state:
(a) the name, **ADDRESS**, and telephone number of the individual making the inspection (except for expert witnesses covered by Code of Civil Procedure sections 2034.210–2034.310); and
(b) the date of the inspection.

13.0 Investigation—Surveillance

☐ 13.1 Have **YOU OR ANYONE ACTING ON YOUR BEHALF** conducted surveillance of any individual involved in the **INCIDENT** or any party to this action? If so, for each surveillance state:
(a) the name, **ADDRESS**, and telephone number of the individual or party;
(b) the time, date, and place of the surveillance;
(c) the name, **ADDRESS**, and telephone number of the individual who conducted the surveillance; and
(d) the name, **ADDRESS**, and telephone number of each **PERSON** who has the original or a copy of any surveillance photograph, film, or videotape.

☐ 13.2 Has a written report been prepared on the surveillance? If so, for each written report state:
(a) the title;
(b) the date;
(c) the name, **ADDRESS**, and telephone number of the individual who prepared the report; and
(d) the name, **ADDRESS**, and telephone number of each **PERSON** who has the original or a copy.

14.0 Statutory or Regulatory Violations

☐ 14.1 Do **YOU OR ANYONE ACTING ON YOUR BEHALF** contend that any **PERSON** involved in the **INCIDENT** violated any statute, ordinance, or regulation and that the violation was a legal (proximate) cause of the **INCIDENT**? If so, identify the name, **ADDRESS**, and telephone number of each **PERSON** and the statute, ordinance, or regulation that was violated.

☐ 14.2 Was any **PERSON** cited or charged with a violation of any statute, ordinance, or regulation as a result of this **INCIDENT**? If so, for each **PERSON** state:
(a) the name, **ADDRESS**, and telephone number of the **PERSON**;
(b) the statute, ordinance, or regulation allegedly violated;
(c) whether the **PERSON** entered a plea in response to the citation or charge and, if so, the plea entered; and
(d) the name and **ADDRESS** of the court or administrative agency, names of the parties, and case number.

15.0 Denials and Special or Affirmative Defenses

☐ 15.1 Identify each denial of a material allegation and each special or affirmative defense in your pleadings, and for each:
(a) state all facts on which you base the denial or special or affirmative defense;
(b) state the names, **ADDRESSES**, and telephone numbers of all **PERSONS** who have knowledge of those facts; and
(c) identify all **DOCUMENTS** and other tangible things that support your denial or special or affirmative defense, and state the name, **ADDRESS**, and telephone number of the **PERSON** who has each **DOCUMENT**.

16.0 Defendant's Contentions—Personal Injury

☐ 16.1 Do you contend that any **PERSON**, other than you or plaintiff, contributed to the occurrence of the **INCIDENT** or the injuries or damages claimed by plaintiff? If so, for each **PERSON**:
(a) state the name, **ADDRESS**, and telephone number of the **PERSON**;
(b) state all facts on which you base your contention;
(c) state the names, **ADDRESSES**, and telephone numbers of all **PERSONS** who have knowledge of the facts; and
(d) identify all **DOCUMENTS** and other tangible things that support your contention and state the name, **ADDRESS**, and telephone number of the **PERSON** who has each **DOCUMENT** or thing.

☐ 16.2 Do you contend that plaintiff was not injured in the **INCIDENT**? If so:
(a) state all facts on which you base your contention;
(b) state the names, **ADDRESSES**, and telephone numbers of all **PERSONS** who have knowledge of the facts; and
(c) identify all **DOCUMENTS** and other tangible things that support your contention and state the name, **ADDRESS**, and telephone number of the **PERSON** who has each **DOCUMENT** or thing.

DISC-001

☐ 16.3 Do you contend that the injuries or the extent of the injuries claimed by plaintiff as disclosed in discovery proceedings thus far in this case were not caused by the **INCIDENT**? If so, for each injury:
(a) identify it;
(b) state all facts on which you base your contention;
(c) state the names, **ADDRESSES,** and telephone numbers of all **PERSONS** who have knowledge of the facts; and
(d) identify all **DOCUMENTS** and other tangible things that support your contention and state the name, **ADDRESS,** and telephone number of the **PERSON** who has each **DOCUMENT** or thing.

☐ 16.4 Do you contend that any of the services furnished by any **HEALTH CARE PROVIDER** claimed by plaintiff in discovery proceedings thus far in this case were not due to the **INCIDENT**? If so:
(a) identify each service;
(b) state all facts on which you base your contention;
(c) state the names, **ADDRESSES,** and telephone numbers of all **PERSONS** who have knowledge of the facts; and
(d) identify all **DOCUMENTS** and other tangible things that support your contention and state the name, **ADDRESS,** and telephone number of the **PERSON** who has each **DOCUMENT** or thing.

☐ 16.5 Do you contend that any of the costs of services furnished by any **HEALTH CARE PROVIDER** claimed as damages by plaintiff in discovery proceedings thus far in this case were not necessary or unreasonable? If so:
(a) identify each cost;
(b) state all facts on which you base your contention;
(c) state the names, **ADDRESSES,** and telephone numbers of all **PERSONS** who have knowledge of the facts; and
(d) identify all **DOCUMENTS** and other tangible things that support your contention and state the name, **ADDRESS,** and telephone number of the **PERSON** who has each **DOCUMENT** or thing.

☐ 16.6 Do you contend that any part of the loss of earnings or income claimed by plaintiff in discovery proceedings thus far in this case was unreasonable or was not caused by the **INCIDENT**? If so:
(a) identify each part of the loss;
(b) state all facts on which you base your contention;
(c) state the names, **ADDRESSES,** and telephone numbers of all **PERSONS** who have knowledge of the facts; and
(d) identify all **DOCUMENTS** and other tangible things that support your contention and state the name, **ADDRESS,** and telephone number of the **PERSON** who has each **DOCUMENT** or thing.

☐ 16.7 Do you contend that any of the property damage claimed by plaintiff in discovery Proceedings thus far in this case was not caused by the **INCIDENT**? If so:
(a) identify each item of property damage;
(b) state all facts on which you base your contention;
(c) state the names, **ADDRESSES,** and telephone numbers of all **PERSONS** who have knowledge of the facts; and
(d) identify all **DOCUMENTS** and other tangible things that support your contention and state the name, **ADDRESS,** and telephone number of the **PERSON** who has each **DOCUMENT** or thing.

☐ 16.8 Do you contend that any of the costs of repairing the property damage claimed by plaintiff in discovery proceedings thus far in this case were unreasonable? If so:
(a) identify each cost item;
(b) state all facts on which you base your contention;
(c) state the names, **ADDRESSES,** and telephone numbers of all **PERSONS** who have knowledge of the facts; and
(d) identify all **DOCUMENTS** and other tangible things that support your contention and state the name, **ADDRESS,** and telephone number of the **PERSON** who has each **DOCUMENT** or thing.

☐ 16.9 Do **YOU OR ANYONE ACTING ON YOUR BEHALF** have any **DOCUMENT** (for example, insurance bureau index reports) concerning claims for personal injuries made before or after the **INCIDENT** by a plaintiff in this case? If so, for each plaintiff state:
(a) the source of each **DOCUMENT;**
(b) the date each claim arose;
(c) the nature of each claim; and
(d) the name, **ADDRESS,** and telephone number of the **PERSON** who has each **DOCUMENT.**

☐ 16.10 Do **YOU OR ANYONE ACTING ON YOUR BEHALF** have any **DOCUMENT** concerning the past or present physical, mental, or emotional condition of any plaintiff in this case from a **HEALTH CARE PROVIDER** not previously identified (except for expert witnesses covered by Code of Civil Procedure sections 2034.210–2034.310)? If so, for each plaintiff state:
(a) the name, **ADDRESS,** and telephone number of each **HEALTH CARE PROVIDER;**
(b) a description of each **DOCUMENT;** and
(c) the name, **ADDRESS,** and telephone number of the **PERSON** who has each **DOCUMENT.**

17.0 Responses to Request for Admissions

☐ 17.1 Is your response to each request for admission served with these interrogatories an unqualified admission? If not, for each response that is not an unqualified admission:
(a) state the number of the request;
(b) state all facts on which you base your response;
(c) state the names, **ADDRESSES,** and telephone numbers of all **PERSONS** who have knowledge of those facts; and
(d) identify all **DOCUMENTS** and other tangible things that support your response and state the name, **ADDRESS,** and telephone number of the **PERSON** who has each **DOCUMENT** or thing.

18.0 *[Reserved]*

19.0 *[Reserved]*

20.0 How the Incident Occurred—Motor Vehicle

☐ 20.1 State the date, time, and place of the **INCIDENT** (closest street **ADDRESS** or intersection).

☐ 20.2 For each vehicle involved in the **INCIDENT,** state:
(a) the year, make, model, and license number;
(b) the name, ADDRESS, and telephone number of the driver;

DISC-001

(c) the name, **ADDRESS,** and telephone number of each occupant other than the driver;

(d) the name, **ADDRESS,** and telephone number of each registered owner;

(e) the name, **ADDRESS,** and telephone number of each lessee;

(f) the name, **ADDRESS,** and telephone number of each owner other than the registered owner or lien holder; and

(g) the name of each owner who gave permission or consent to the driver to operate the vehicle.

☐ 20.3 State the **ADDRESS** and location where your trip began and the **ADDRESS** and location of your destination.

☐ 20.4 Describe the route that you followed from the beginning of your trip to the location of the **INCIDENT**, and state the location of each stop, other than routine traffic stops, during the trip leading up to the **INCIDENT**.

☐ 20.5 State the name of the street or roadway, the lane of travel, and the direction of travel of each vehicle involved in the **INCIDENT** for the 500 feet of travel before the **INCIDENT**.

☐ 20.6 Did the **INCIDENT** occur at an intersection? If so, describe all traffic control devices, signals, or signs at the intersection.

☐ 20.7 Was there a traffic signal facing you at the time of the **INCIDENT**? If so, state:

(a) your location when you first saw it;

(b) the color;

(c) the number of seconds it had been that color; and

(d) whether the color changed between the time you first saw it and the **INCIDENT**.

☐ 20.8 State how the **INCIDENT** occurred, giving the speed, direction, and location of each vehicle involved:

(a) just before the **INCIDENT**;

(b) at the time of the **INCIDENT**; and

(c) just after the **INCIDENT**.

☐ 20.9 Do you have information that a malfunction or defect in a vehicle caused the **INCIDENT**? If so:

(a) identify the vehicle;

(b) identify each malfunction or defect;

(c) state the name, **ADDRESS,** and telephone number of each **PERSON** who is a witness to or has information about each malfunction or defect; and

(d) state the name, **ADDRESS,** and telephone number of each **PERSON** who has custody of each defective part.

☐ 20.10 Do you have information that any malfunction or defect in a vehicle contributed to the injuries sustained in the **INCIDENT**? If so:

(a) identify the vehicle;

(b) identify each malfunction or defect;

(c) state the name, **ADDRESS,** and telephone number of each **PERSON** who is a witness to or has information about each malfunction or defect; and

(d) state the name, **ADDRESS,** and telephone number of each **PERSON** who has custody of each defective part.

☐ 20.11 State the name, **ADDRESS,** and telephone number of each owner and each **PERSON** who has had possession since the **INCIDENT** of each vehicle involved in the **INCIDENT**.

25.0 *[Reserved]*

30.0 *[Reserved]*

40.0 *[Reserved]*

50.0 Contract

☐ 50.1 For each agreement alleged in the pleadings:

(a) identify each **DOCUMENT** that is part of the agreement and for each state the name, **ADDRESS,** and telephone number of each **PERSON** who has the **DOCUMENT**;

(b) state each part of the agreement not in writing, the name, **ADDRESS,** and telephone number of each **PERSON** agreeing to that provision, and the date that part of the agreement was made;

(c) identify all **DOCUMENTS** that evidence any part of the agreement not in writing and for each state the name, **ADDRESS,** and telephone number of each **PERSON** who has the **DOCUMENT**;

(d) identify all **DOCUMENTS** that are part of any modification to the agreement, and for each state the name, **ADDRESS,** and telephone number of each **PERSON** who has the **DOCUMENT**;

(e) state each modification not in writing, the date, and the name, **ADDRESS,** and telephone number of each **PERSON** agreeing to the modification, and the date the modification was made;

(f) identify all **DOCUMENTS** that evidence any modification of the agreement not in writing and for each state the name, **ADDRESS,** and telephone number of each **PERSON** who has the **DOCUMENT**.

☐ 50.2 Was there a breach of any agreement alleged in the pleadings? If so, for each breach describe and give the date of every act or omission that you claim is the breach of the agreement.

☐ 50.3 Was performance of any agreement alleged in the pleadings excused? If so, identify each agreement excused and state why performance was excused.

☐ 50.4 Was any agreement alleged in the pleadings terminated by mutual agreement, release, accord and satisfaction, or novation? If so, identify each agreement terminated, the date of termination, and the basis of the termination.

☐ 50.5 Is any agreement alleged in the pleadings unenforceable? If so, identify each unenforceable agreement and state why it is unenforceable.

☐ 50.6 Is any agreement alleged in the pleadings ambiguous? If so, identify each ambiguous agreement and state why it is ambiguous.

60.0 *[Reserved]*

SELECTED CALIFORNIA RULES OF COURT

■ ■ ■

Including Amendments Effective January 1, 2026

Table of Rules

TITLE 2. TRIAL COURT RULES

DIVISION 1. GENERAL PROVISIONS

Chapter 4. Sanctions

Rule 2.30. Sanctions for Rules Violations in Civil Cases

(a) Application

This sanctions rule applies to the rules in the California Rules of Court relating to general civil cases, unlawful detainer cases, probate proceedings, civil proceedings in the appellate division of the superior court, and small claims cases.

(b) Sanctions

In addition to any other sanctions permitted by law, the court may order a person, after written notice and an opportunity to be heard, to pay reasonable monetary sanctions to the court or an aggrieved person, or both, for failure without good cause to comply with the applicable rules. For the purposes of this rule, "person" means a party, a party's attorney, a witness, and an insurer or any other individual or entity whose consent is necessary for the disposition of the case. If a failure to comply with an applicable rule is the responsibility of counsel and not of the party, any penalty must be imposed on counsel and must not adversely affect the party's cause of action or defense thereto.

(c) Notice and procedure

Sanctions must not be imposed under this rule except on noticed motion by the party seeking sanctions or on the court's own motion after the court has provided notice and an opportunity to be heard. A party's motion for sanctions must (1) state the applicable rule that has been violated, (2) describe the specific conduct that is alleged to have violated the rule, and (3) identify the attorney, law firm, party, witness, or other person against whom sanctions are sought. The court on its own motion may issue an order to show cause that must (1) state the applicable rule that has been violated, (2) describe the specific conduct that appears to have violated the rule, and (3) direct the attorney, law firm, party, witness, or other person to show cause why sanctions should not be imposed against them for violation of the rule.

(d) Award of expenses

In addition to the sanctions awardable under (b), the court may order the person who has violated an applicable rule to pay to the party aggrieved by the violation that party's reasonable expenses, including reasonable attorney's fees and costs, incurred in connection with the motion for sanctions or the order to show cause.

(e) Order

An order imposing sanctions must be in writing and must recite in detail the conduct or circumstances justifying the order.

(As approved, eff. Jan. 1, 2007.)

DIVISION 8. TRIALS

Chapter 1. Jury Service

Rule 2.1008. Excuses From Jury Service

(a) Duty of citizenship

Jury service, unless excused by law, is a responsibility of citizenship. The court and its staff must employ all necessary and appropriate means to ensure that citizens fulfill this important civic responsibility.

(b) Principles

The following principles shall govern the granting of excuses from jury service by the jury commissioner on grounds of undue hardship under Code of Civil Procedure section 204:

(1) No class or category of persons may be automatically excluded from jury duty except as provided by law.

(2) A statutory exemption from jury service must be granted only when the eligible person claims it.

(3) Deferring jury service is preferred to excusing a prospective juror for a temporary or marginal hardship.

(4) Inconvenience to a prospective juror or an employer is not an adequate reason to be excused from jury duty, although it may be considered a ground for deferral.

(c) Requests to be excused from jury service

All requests to be excused from jury service that are granted for undue hardship must be put in writing by the prospective juror, reduced to writing, or placed on the court's record. The prospective juror must support the request with facts specifying the hardship and a statement why the circumstances constituting the undue hardship cannot be avoided by deferring the prospective juror's service.

(d) Reasons for excusing a juror because of undue hardship

An excuse on the ground of undue hardship may be granted for any of the following reasons:

(1) The prospective juror has no reasonably available means of public or private transportation to the court.

(2) The prospective juror must travel an excessive distance. Unless otherwise established by statute or local rule, an excessive distance is reasonable travel time that exceeds one-and-one-half hours from the prospective juror's home to the court.

(3) The prospective juror will bear an extreme financial burden. In determining whether to excuse the prospective juror for this reason, consideration must be given to:

(A) The sources of the prospective juror's household income;

(B) The availability and extent of income reimbursement;

(C) The expected length of service; and

(D) Whether service can reasonably be expected to compromise the prospective juror's ability to support himself or herself or his or her dependents, or so disrupt the economic stability of any individual as to be against the interests of justice.

(4) The prospective juror will bear an undue risk of material injury to or destruction of the prospective juror's property or property entrusted to the prospective juror, and it is not feasible to make alternative arrangements to alleviate the risk. In determining whether to excuse the prospective juror for this reason, consideration must be given to:

(A) The nature of the property;

(B) The source and duration of the risk;

(C) The probability that the risk will be realized;

(D) The reason alternative arrangements to protect the property cannot be made; and

(E) Whether material injury to or destruction of the property will so disrupt the economic stability of any individual as to be against the interests of justice.

(5) The prospective juror has a physical or mental disability or impairment, not affecting that person's competence to act as a juror, that would expose the potential juror to undue risk of mental or physical harm. In any individual case, unless the person is aged 70 years or older, the prospective juror may be required to furnish verification or a method of verification of the disability or impairment, its probable duration, and the particular reasons for the person's inability to serve as a juror.

(6) The prospective juror's services are immediately needed for the protection of the public health and safety, and it is not feasible to make alternative arrangements to relieve the person of those responsibilities during the period of service as a juror without substantially reducing essential public services.

(7) The prospective juror has a personal obligation to provide actual and necessary care to another, including sick, aged, or infirm dependents, or a child who requires the prospective juror's personal care and attention, and no comparable substitute care is either available or practical without imposing an undue economic hardship on the prospective juror or person cared for. If the request to be excused is based on care provided to a sick, disabled, or infirm person, the prospective juror may be required to furnish verification or a method of verification that the person being cared for is in need of regular and personal care.

(e) Excuse based on previous jury service

A prospective juror who has served on a grand or trial jury or was summoned and appeared for jury service in any state or federal court during the previous 12 months must be excused from service on request. The jury commissioner, in his or her discretion, may establish a longer period of repose.

(As approved, eff. Jan. 1, 2007.)

Rule 2.1031. Juror Note-Taking

Jurors must be permitted to take written notes in all civil and criminal trials. At the beginning of a trial, a trial judge must inform jurors that they may take written notes during the trial. The court must provide materials suitable for this purpose.

(As approved, eff. Jan. 1, 2007.)

Rule 2.1032. Juror Notebooks in Complex Civil Cases

A trial judge should encourage counsel in complex civil cases to include key documents, exhibits, and other appropriate materials in notebooks for use by jurors during trial to assist them in performing their duties.

(As approved, eff. Jan. 1, 2007.)

Rule 2.1033. Juror Questions

A trial judge should allow jurors to submit written questions directed to witnesses. An opportunity must be given to counsel to object to such questions out of the presence of the jury.

(As approved, eff. Jan. 1, 2007.)

Rule 2.1035. Preinstruction

Immediately after the jury is sworn, the trial judge may, in his or her discretion, preinstruct the jury concerning the elements of the charges or claims, its duties, its conduct, the order of proceedings, the procedure for submitting written questions for witnesses as set forth in rule 2.1033, if questions are allowed, and the legal principles that will govern the proceeding.

(As approved, eff. Jan. 1, 2007.)

Chapter 4. Jury Instructions

Rule 2.1050. Judicial Council Jury Instructions

(a) Purpose

The California jury instructions approved by the Judicial Council are the official instructions for use in the state of California. The goal of these instructions is to improve the quality of jury decision making by providing standardized instructions that accurately state the law in a way that is understandable to the average juror.

(b) Accuracy

The Judicial Council endorses these instructions for use and makes every effort to ensure that they accurately state existing law. The articulation and interpretation of California law, however, remains within the purview of the Legislature and the courts of review.

(c) Public access

The Judicial Council must provide copies and updates of the approved jury instructions to the public on the California Courts website. The Judicial Council intends that the instructions be freely available for use and reproduction.

(d) Publication

The Judicial Council may contract with an official publisher and other publishers to publish the instructions in both paper and electronic formats. The Judicial Council may take appropriate actions to maintain the integrity of the jury instructions, including, without limitation, ensuring that publishers accurately publish the Judicial Council's instructions, accurately credit the Judicial Council as the source of the instructions, and do not claim copyright in the instructions.

(e) Updating and revisions

The Judicial Council instructions will be regularly updated and maintained through its advisory committees on jury instructions. Revisions to these instructions will be circulated for public comment before publication. Suggestions for revising an instruction or creating new instructions may be submitted in writing, with an explanation of why the change is proposed, to the Judicial Council of California, Legal Services.

(f) Use of instructions

Use of the Judicial Council instructions is strongly encouraged. If the latest edition of the jury instructions approved by the Judicial Council contains an instruction applicable to a case and the trial judge determines that the jury should be instructed on the subject, it is recommended that the judge use the Judicial Council instruction unless the judge finds that a different instruction would more accurately state the law and be understood by jurors. Whenever the latest edition of the Judicial Council jury instructions does not contain an instruction on a subject on which the trial judge determines that the jury should be instructed, or when a Judicial Council instruction cannot be modified to submit the issue properly, the instruction given on that subject should be accurate, brief, understandable, impartial, and free from argument.

(As approved, eff. Jan. 1, 2007. As amended, eff. Jan. 1, 2016; Apr. 1, 2023.)

Rule 2.1055. Proposed Jury Instructions

(a) Application

(1) This rule applies to proposed jury instructions that a party submits to the court, including:

(A) "Approved jury instructions," meaning jury instructions approved by the Judicial Council of California; and

(B) "Special jury instructions," meaning instructions from other sources, those specially prepared by the party, or approved instructions that have been substantially modified by the party.

(2) This rule does not apply to the form or format of the instructions presented to the jury, which is a matter left to the discretion of the court.

(b) Form and format of proposed instructions

(1) All proposed instructions must be submitted to the court in the form and format prescribed for papers in the rules in division 2 of this title.

(2) Each set of proposed jury instructions must have a cover page, containing the caption of the case and stating the name of the party proposing the instructions, and an index listing all the proposed instructions.

(3) In the index, approved jury instructions must be identified by their reference numbers and special jury instructions must be numbered consecutively. The index must contain a checklist that the court may use to indicate whether the instruction was:

(A) Given as proposed;

(B) Given as modified;

(C) Refused; or

(D) Withdrawn.

(4) Each set of proposed jury instructions filed on paper must be bound loosely.

(c) Format of each proposed instruction

Each proposed instruction must:

(1) Be on a separate page or pages;

(2) Contain the instruction number and title of the instruction at the top of the first page of the instruction; and

(3) Be prepared without any blank lines or unused bracketed portions, so that it can be read directly to the jury.

(d) Citation of authorities

For each special instruction, a citation of authorities that support the instruction must be included at the bottom of the page. No citation is required for approved instructions.

(e) Form and format are exclusive

No local court form or rule for the filing or submission of proposed jury instructions may require that the instructions be submitted in any manner other than as prescribed by this rule.

(As approved, eff. Jan. 1, 2007. As amended, eff. Jan. 1, 2016.)

TITLE 3. CIVIL RULES

DIVISION 1. GENERAL PROVISIONS

Chapter 2. Scope of the Civil Rules

Rule 3.20. Preemption of Local Rules

(a) Fields occupied

The Judicial Council has preempted all local rules relating to pleadings, demurrers, ex parte applications, motions, discovery, provisional remedies, and the form and format of papers. No trial court, or any division or branch of a trial court, may enact or enforce any local rule concerning these fields. All local rules concerning these fields are null and void unless otherwise permitted or required by a statute or a rule in the California Rules of Court.

(b) Application

This rule applies to all matters identified in (a) except:

(1) Trial and post-trial proceedings including but not limited to motions in limine (see rule 3.1112(f));

(2) Proceedings under Code of Civil Procedure sections 527.6, 527.7, and 527.8; the Family Code; the Probate Code; the Welfare and

Institutions Code; and the Penal Code and all other criminal proceedings;

(3) Eminent domain proceedings; and

(4) Local court rules adopted under the Trial Court Delay Reduction Act.

(As approved, eff. Jan. 1, 2007. As amended, eff. Jan. 1, 2015.)

DIVISION 7. CIVIL CASE MANAGEMENT

Chapter 2. Differential Case Management

Rule 3.714. Differentiation of Cases to Achieve Goals

(a) Evaluation and assignment

The court must evaluate each case on its own merits as provided in rule 3.715, under procedures adopted by local court rules. After evaluation, the court must:

(1) Assign the case to the case management program for review under the case management rules in chapter 3 of this division for disposition under the case disposition time goals in (b) of this rule;

(2) Exempt the case as an exceptional case under (c) of this rule from the case disposition time goals specified in rule 3.713(b) and monitor it with the goal of disposing of it within three years; or

(3) Assign the case under (d) of this rule to a local case management plan for disposition within six to nine months after filing.

(b) Civil case disposition time goals

Civil cases assigned for review under the case management rules in chapter 3 of this division should be managed so as to achieve the following goals:

(1) *Unlimited civil cases*

The goal of each trial court should be to manage unlimited civil cases from filing so that:

(A) 75 percent are disposed of within 12 months;

(B) 85 percent are disposed of within 18 months; and

(C) 100 percent are disposed of within 24 months.

(2) *Limited civil cases*

The goal of each trial court should be to manage limited civil cases from filing so that:

(A) 90 percent are disposed of within 12 months;

(B) 98 percent are disposed of within 18 months; and

(C) 100 percent are disposed of within 24 months.

(3) *Individualized case management*

The goals in (1) and (2) are guidelines for the court's disposition of all unlimited and limited civil cases filed in that court. In managing individual civil cases, the court must consider each case on its merits. To enable the fair and efficient resolution of civil cases, each case should be set for trial as soon as appropriate for that individual case consistent with rule 3.729.

(c) Exemption of exceptional cases

(1) The court may in the interest of justice exempt a general civil case from the case disposition time goals under rule 3.713(b) if it finds the case involves exceptional circumstances that will prevent the court and the parties from meeting the goals and deadlines imposed by the program. In making the determination, the court is guided by rules 3.715 and 3.400.

(2) If the court exempts the case from the case disposition time goals, the court must establish a case progression plan and monitor the case to ensure timely disposition consistent with the exceptional circumstances, with the goal of disposing of the case within three years.

(d) Local case management plan for expedited case disposition

(1) For expedited case disposition, the court may by local rule adopt a case management plan that establishes a goal for disposing of appropriate cases within six to nine months after filing. The plan must establish a procedure to identify the cases to be assigned to the plan.

(2) The plan must be used only for uncomplicated cases amenable to early disposition that do not need a case management conference or review or similar event to guide the case to early resolution.

(As approved, eff. Jan. 1, 2007.)

Rule 3.715. Case Evaluation Factors

(a) Time estimate

In applying rule 3.714, the court must estimate the maximum time that will reasonably be required to dispose of each case in a just and effective manner. The court must consider the following factors and any other information the court deems relevant, understanding that no one factor or set of factors will be controlling and that cases may have unique characteristics incapable of precise definition:

(1) Type and subject matter of the action;

(2) Number of causes of action or affirmative defenses alleged;

(3) Number of parties with separate interests;

(4) Number of cross-complaints and the subject matter;

(5) Complexity of issues, including issues of first impression;

(6) Difficulty in identifying, locating, and serving parties;

(7) Nature and extent of discovery anticipated;

(8) Number and location of percipient and expert witnesses;

(9) Estimated length of trial;

(10) Whether some or all issues can be arbitrated or resolved through other alternative dispute resolution processes;

(11) Statutory priority for the issues;

(12) Likelihood of review by writ or appeal;

(13) Amount in controversy and the type of remedy sought, including measures of damages;

(14) Pendency of other actions or proceedings that may affect the case;

(15) Nature and extent of law and motion proceedings anticipated;

(16) Nature and extent of the injuries and damages;

(17) Pendency of underinsured claims; and

(18) Any other factor that would affect the time for disposition of the case.

(As approved, eff. Jan. 1, 2007.)

DIVISION 8. ALTERNATIVE DISPUTE RESOLUTION

Chapter 1. General Provisions

Rule 3.800. Definitions

As used in this division:

(1) "Alternative dispute resolution process" or "ADR process" means a process, other than formal litigation, in which a neutral person or persons resolve a dispute or assist parties in resolving their dispute.

(2) "Mediation" means a process in which a neutral person or persons facilitate communication between disputants to assist them in reaching a mutually acceptable agreement. As used in this division, mediation does not include a settlement conference under rule 3.1380 of the California Rules of Court.

(As approved, eff. Jan. 1, 2007.)

Chapter 2. Judicial Arbitration

Rule 3.811. Cases Subject to and Exempt From Arbitration

(a) Cases subject to arbitration

Except as provided in (b), the following cases must be arbitrated:

(1) In each superior court with 18 or more authorized judges, all unlimited civil cases where the amount in controversy does not exceed $50,000 as to any plaintiff;

(2) In each superior court with fewer than 18 authorized judges that so provides by local rule, all unlimited civil cases where the amount in controversy does not exceed $50,000 as to any plaintiff;

(3) All limited civil cases in courts that so provide by local rule;

(4) Upon stipulation, any limited or unlimited civil case in any court, regardless of the amount in controversy; and

(5) Upon filing of an election by all plaintiffs, any limited or unlimited civil case in any court in which each plaintiff agrees that the arbitration award will not exceed $50,000 as to that plaintiff.

(b) Cases exempt from arbitration

The following cases are exempt from arbitration:

(1) Cases that include a prayer for equitable relief that is not frivolous or insubstantial;

(2) Class actions;

(3) Small claims cases or trials de novo on appeal from the small claims court;

(4) Unlawful detainer proceedings;

(5) Family Law Act proceedings except as provided in Family Code section 2554;

(6) Any case otherwise subject to arbitration that is found by the court not to be amenable to arbitration on the ground that arbitration would not reduce the probable time and expense necessary to resolve the litigation;

(7) Any category of cases otherwise subject to arbitration but excluded by local rule as not amenable to arbitration on the ground that, under the circumstances relating to the particular court, arbitration of such cases would not reduce the probable time and expense necessary to resolve the litigation; and

(8) Cases involving multiple causes of action or a cross-complaint if the court determines that the amount in controversy as to any given cause of action or cross-complaint exceeds $50,000.

(As approved, eff. Jan. 1, 2007.)

Rule 3.822. Discovery

(a) Right to discovery

The parties to the arbitration have the right to take depositions and to obtain discovery, and to that end may exercise all of the same rights, remedies, and procedures, and are subject to all of the same duties, liabilities, and obligations as provided in part 4, title 3, chapter 3 of the Code of Civil Procedure, except that as provided in (b).

(b) Completion of discovery

All discovery must be completed not later than 15 days prior to before the date set for the arbitration hearing unless the court, upon a showing of good cause, makes an order granting an extension of the time within which discovery must be completed.

(As approved, eff. Jan. 1, 2007.)

Rule 3.823. Rules of Evidence at Arbitration Hearing

(a) Presence of arbitrator and parties

All evidence must be taken in the presence of the arbitrator and all parties, except where any of the parties has waived the right to be present or is absent after due notice of the hearing.

(b) Application of civil rules of evidence

The rules of evidence governing civil cases apply to the conduct of the arbitration hearing, except:

(1) *Written reports and other documents*

Any party may offer written reports of any expert witness, medical records and bills (including physiotherapy, nursing, and prescription bills), documentary evidence of loss of income, property damage repair bills or estimates, police reports concerning an accident that gave rise to the case, other bills and invoices, purchase orders, checks, written contracts, and similar documents prepared and maintained in the ordinary course of business.

(A) The arbitrator must receive them in evidence if copies have been delivered to all opposing parties at least 20 days before the hearing.

(B) Any other party may subpoena the author or custodian of the document as a witness and examine the witness as if under cross-examination.

(C) Any repair estimate offered as an exhibit, and the copies delivered to opposing parties, must be accompanied by:

(i) A statement indicating whether or not the property was repaired, and, if it was, whether the estimated repairs were made in full or in part; and

(ii) copy of the receipted bill showing the items of repair made and the amount paid.

(D) The arbitrator must not consider any opinion as to ultimate fault expressed in a police report.

(2) *Witness statements*

The written statements of any other witness may be offered and must be received in evidence if:

(A) They are made by declaration under penalty of perjury;

(B) Copies have been delivered to all opposing parties at least 20 days before the hearing; and

(C) No opposing party has, at least 10 days before the hearing, delivered to the proponent of the evidence a written demand that the witness be produced in person to testify at the hearing. The arbitrator must disregard any portion of a statement received under this rule that would be inadmissible if the witness were testifying in person, but the inclusion of inadmissible matter does not render the entire statement inadmissible.

(3) *Depositions*

(A) The deposition of any witness may be offered by any party and must be received in evidence, subject to objections available under Code of Civil Procedure section 2025.410, notwithstanding that the deponent is not "unavailable as a witness" within the meaning of Evidence Code section 240 and no exceptional circumstances exist, if:

(i) The deposition was taken in the manner provided for by law or by stipulation of the parties and within the time provided for in these rules; and

(ii) Not less than 20 days before the hearing the proponent of the deposition delivered to all opposing parties notice of intention to offer the deposition in evidence.

(B) The opposing party, upon receiving the notice, may subpoena the deponent and, at the discretion of the arbitrator, either the deposition may be excluded from evidence or the deposition may be admitted and the deponent may be further cross-examined by the subpoenaing party. These limitations are not applicable to a deposition admissible under the terms of Code of Civil Procedure section 2025.620.

(c) Subpoenas

(1) *Compelling witnesses to appear*

The attendance of witnesses at arbitration hearings may be compelled through the issuance of subpoenas as provided in the Code of Civil Procedure, in section 1985 and elsewhere in part 4, title 3, chapters 2 and 3. It is the duty of the party requesting the subpoena to modify the form of subpoena so as to show that the appearance is before an arbitrator, and to give the time and place set for the arbitration hearing.

(2) *Adjournment or continuances*

At the discretion of the arbitrator, nonappearance of a properly subpoenaed witness may be a ground for an adjournment or continuance of the hearing.

(3) *Contempt*

If any witness properly served with a subpoena fails to appear at the arbitration hearing or, having appeared, refuses to be sworn or to answer, proceedings to compel compliance with the subpoena on penalty of contempt may be had before the superior court as provided in Code of Civil Procedure section 1991 for other instances of refusal to appear and answer before an officer or commissioner out of court.

(d) Delivery of documents

For purposes of this rule, "delivery" of a document or notice may be accomplished manually, by electronic means under Code of Civil Procedure section 1010.6 and rule 2.251, or by mail in the manner provided by Code of Civil Procedure section 1013. If service is by electronic means, the times prescribed in this rule for delivery of documents, notices, and demands are increased as provided by Code of Civil Procedure section 1010.6. If service is in the manner provided by Code of Civil Procedure section 1013, the times prescribed in this rule are increased as provided by that section.

(As approved, eff. Jan. 1, 2007. As amended, eff. Jan. 1, 2016; Jan. 1, 2017.)

Rule 3.826. Trial After Arbitration

(a) Request for trial; deadline

Within 60 days after the arbitration award is filed with the clerk of the court, a party may request a trial by filing with the clerk a request for trial, with proof of service of a copy upon all other parties appearing in the case. A request for trial filed after the parties have been served with a copy of the award by the arbitrator, but before the award has been filed with the clerk, is valid and timely filed. The 60-day period within which to request trial may not be extended.

(b) Prosecution of the case

If a party makes a timely request for a trial, the case must proceed as provided under an applicable case management order. If no pending order provides for the prosecution of the case after a request for a trial after arbitration, the court must promptly schedule a case management conference.

(c) References to arbitration during trial prohibited

The case must be tried as though no arbitration proceedings had occurred. No reference may be made during the trial to the arbitration award, to the fact that there had been arbitration proceedings, to the evidence adduced at the arbitration hearing, or to any other aspect of the arbitration proceedings, and none of the foregoing may be used as affirmative evidence, or by way of impeachment, or for any other purpose at the trial.

(d) Costs after trial

In assessing costs after the trial, the court must apply the standards specified in Code of Civil Procedure section 1141.21.

(As approved, eff. Jan. 1, 2007. As amended, eff. Jan. 1, 2012.)

DIVISION 10. DISCOVERY

Chapter 1. Format of Discovery

Rule 3.1000. Format of Supplemental and Further Discovery

(a) Supplemental interrogatories and responses, etc.

In each set of supplemental interrogatories, supplemental responses to interrogatories, amended answers to interrogatories, and further responses to interrogatories, inspection demands, and admission requests, the following must appear in the first paragraph immediately below the title of the case:

(1) The identity of the propounding, demanding, or requesting party;

(2) The identity of the responding party;

(3) The set number being propounded or responded to; and

(4) The nature of the paper.

(b) Identification of responses

Each supplemental or further response and each amended answer must be identified by the same number or letter and be in the same sequence as the corresponding interrogatory, inspection demand, or admission request, but the text of the interrogatory, demand, or request need not be repeated.

(As approved, eff. Jan. 1, 2007.)

DIVISION 11. LAW AND MOTION

Chapter 2. Format of Motion Papers

Rule 3.1112. Motions and Other Pleadings

(a) Motions—Required papers

Unless otherwise provided by the rules in this division, the papers filed in support of a motion must consist of at least the following:

(1) A notice of hearing on the motion;

(2) The motion itself; and

(3) A memorandum in support of the motion or demurrer.

(b) Other papers

Other papers may be filed in support of a motion, including declarations, exhibits, appendices, and other documents or pleadings.

(c) Form of motion papers

These papers filed under (a) and (b) may either be filed as separate documents or combined in one or more documents if the party filing a combined pleading specifies these items separately in the caption of the combined pleading.

(d) Motion—required elements

A motion must:

(1) Identify the party or parties bringing the motion;

(2) Name the parties to whom it is addressed;

(3) Briefly state the basis for the motion and the relief sought; and

(4) If a pleading is challenged, state the specific portion challenged.

(e) Additional requirements for motions

In addition to the requirements of this rule, a motion relating to the subjects specified in chapter 6 of this division must comply with any additional requirements in that chapter.

(f) Motion in limine

Notwithstanding (a), a motion in limine filed before or during trial need not be accompanied by a notice of hearing. The timing and place of the filing and service of the motion are at the discretion of the trial judge.

(As approved, eff. Jan. 1, 2007. As amended, eff. July 1, 2008.)

Rule 3.1113. Memorandum

(a) Memorandum in support of motion

A party filing a motion, except for a motion listed in rule 3.1114, must serve and file a supporting memorandum. The court may construe the absence of a memorandum as an admission that the motion or special demurrer is not meritorious and cause for its denial and, in the case of a demurrer, as a waiver of all grounds not supported.

(b) Contents of memorandum

The memorandum must contain a statement of facts, a concise statement of the law, evidence and arguments relied on, and a discussion of the statutes, cases, and textbooks cited in support of the position advanced.

(c) Case citation format

A case citation must include the official report volume and page number and year of decision. The court must not require any other form of citation.

(d) Length of memorandum

Except in a summary judgment or summary adjudication motion, no opening or responding memorandum may exceed 15 pages. In a summary judgment or summary adjudication motion, no opening or responding memorandum may exceed 20 pages. No reply or closing memorandum may exceed 10 pages. The page limit does not include the caption page, the notice of motion and motion, exhibits, declarations, attachments, the table of contents, the table of authorities, or the proof of service.

(e) Application to file longer memorandum

A party may apply to the court ex parte but with written notice of the application to the other parties, at least 24 hours before the memorandum is due, for permission to file a longer memorandum. The application must state reasons why the argument cannot be made within the stated limit.

(f) Format of longer memorandum

A memorandum that exceeds 10 pages must include a table of contents and a table of authorities. A memorandum that exceeds 15 pages must also include an opening summary of argument.

(g) Effect of filing an oversized memorandum

A memorandum that exceeds the page limits of these rules must be filed and considered in the same manner as a late-filed paper.

(h) Pagination of memorandum

The pages of a memorandum must be numbered consecutively beginning with the first page and using only Arabic numerals (e.g., 1, 2, 3). The page number may be suppressed and need not appear on the first page.

(i) Copies of authorities

(1) A judge may require that if any authority other than California cases, statutes, constitutional provisions, or state or local rules is cited, a copy of the authority must be lodged with the papers that cite the authority. If in paper form, the authority must be tabbed or separated as required by rule 3.1110(f)(3). If in electronic form, the authority must be electronically bookmarked as required by rule 3.1110(f)(4).

(2) If a California case is cited before the time it is published in the advance sheets of the Official Reports, the party must include the title, case number, date of decision, and, if from the Court of Appeal, district of the Court of Appeal in which the case was decided. A judge may require that a copy of that case must be lodged. If in paper form, the copy must be tabbed or separated as required by rule 3.1110(f)(3). If in electronic form, the copy must be electronically bookmarked as required by rule 3.1110(f)(4).

(3) Upon the request of a party to the action, any party citing any authority other than California cases, statutes, constitutional provisions, or state or local rules must promptly provide a copy of such authority to the requesting party.

(j) Attachments

To the extent practicable, all supporting memorandums and declarations must be attached to the notice of motion.

(k) Exhibit references

All references to exhibits or declarations in supporting or opposing papers must reference the number or letter of the exhibit, the specific page, and, if applicable, the paragraph or line number.

(*l*) Requests for judicial notice

Any request for judicial notice must be made in a separate document listing the specific items for which notice is requested and must comply with rule 3.1306(c).

(m) Proposed orders or judgments

If a proposed order or judgment is submitted, it must be lodged and served with the moving papers but must not be attached to them. The requirements for proposed orders, including the requirements for submitting proposed orders by electronic means, are stated in rule 3.1312.

(As approved, eff. Jan. 1, 2007. As amended, eff. Jan. 1, 2008; July 1, 2011; Jan. 1, 2016; Jan. 1, 2017.)

Chapter 6. Particular Motions

Rule 3.1320. Demurrers

(a) Grounds separately stated

Each ground of demurrer must be in a separate paragraph and must state whether it applies to the entire complaint, cross-complaint, or answer, or to specified causes of action or defenses.

(b) Demurrer not directed to all causes of action

A demurrer to a cause of action may be filed without answering other causes of action.

(c) Notice of hearing

A party filing a demurrer must serve and file therewith a notice of hearing that must specify a hearing date in accordance with the provisions of Code of Civil Procedure section 1005 and, if service is by electronic means, in accordance with the requirements of Code of Civil Procedure section 1010.6(a)(4) and rule 2.251(h)(2).

(d) Date of hearing

Demurrers must be set for hearing not more than 35 days following the filing of the demurrer or on the first date available to the court thereafter. For good cause shown, the court may order the hearing held on an earlier or later day on notice prescribed by the court.

(e) Caption

A demurrer must state, on the first page immediately below the number of the case, the name of the party filing the demurrer and the name of the party whose pleading is the subject of the demurrer.

(f) Failure to appear at hearing

When a demurrer is regularly called for hearing and one of the parties does not appear, the demurrer must be disposed of on the merits at the request of the party appearing unless for good cause the hearing is continued. Failure to appear in support of a special demurrer may be construed by the court as an admission that the demurrer is not meritorious and as a waiver of all grounds thereof. If neither party appears, the demurrer may be disposed of on its merits or dropped from the calendar, to be restored on notice or on terms as the court may deem proper, or the hearing may be continued to such time as the court orders.

(g) Leave to answer or amend

Following a ruling on a demurrer, unless otherwise ordered, leave to answer or amend within 10 days is deemed granted, except for actions in forcible entry, forcible detainer, or unlawful detainer in which case 5 calendar days is deemed granted.

(h) Ex parte application to dismiss following failure to amend

A motion to dismiss the entire action and for entry of judgment after expiration of the time to amend following the sustaining of a demurrer may be made by ex parte application to the court under Code of Civil Procedure section 581(f)(2).

(i) Motion to strike late-filed amended pleading

If an amended pleading is filed after the time allowed, an order striking the amended pleading must be obtained by noticed motion under Code of Civil Procedure section 1010.

(j) Time to respond after demurrer

Unless otherwise ordered, defendant has 10 days to answer or otherwise plead to the complaint or the remaining causes of action following:

(1) The overruling of the demurrer;

(2) The expiration of the time to amend if the demurrer was sustained with leave to amend; or

(3) The sustaining of the demurrer if the demurrer was sustained without leave to amend.

(As approved, eff. Jan. 1, 2007. As amended, eff. Jan. 1, 2009; Jan. 1, 2011; Jan. 1, 2016.)

Rule 3.1340. Motion for Discretionary Dismissal After Two Years for Delay in Prosecution

(a) Discretionary dismissal two years after filing

The court on its own motion or on motion of the defendant may dismiss an action under Code of Civil Procedure sections 583.410–583.430 for delay in prosecution if the action has not been brought to trial or conditionally settled within two years after the action was commenced against the defendant.

(b) Notice of court's intention to dismiss

If the court intends to dismiss an action on its own motion, the clerk must set a hearing on the dismissal and send notice to all parties at least 20 days before the hearing date.

(c) Definition of "conditionally settled"

"Conditionally settled" means:

(1) A settlement agreement conditions dismissal on the satisfactory completion of specified terms that are not to be fully performed within two years after the filing of the case; and

(2) Notice of the settlement is filed with the court as provided in rule 3.1385.

(As approved, eff. Jan. 1, 2007. As amended, eff. Jan. 1, 2016.)

Rule 3.1342. Motion to Dismiss for Delay in Prosecution

(a) Notice of motion

A party seeking dismissal of a case under Code of Civil Procedure sections 583.410–583.430 must serve and file a notice of motion at least 45 days before the date set for hearing of the motion. The party may, with the memorandum, serve and file a declaration stating facts in support of the motion. The filing of the notice of motion must not preclude the opposing party from further prosecution of the case to bring it to trial.

(b) Written opposition

Within 15 days after service of the notice of motion, the opposing party may serve and file a written opposition. The failure of the opposing party to serve and file a written opposition may be construed by the court as an admission that the motion is meritorious, and the court may grant the motion without a hearing on the merits.

(c) Response to opposition

Within 15 days after service of the written opposition, if any, the moving party may serve and file a response.

(d) Reply

Within five days after service of the response, if any, the opposing party may serve and file a reply.

(e) Relevant matters

In ruling on the motion, the court must consider all matters relevant to a proper determination of the motion, including:

(1) The court's file in the case and the declarations and supporting data submitted by the parties and, where applicable, the availability of the moving party and other essential parties for service of process;

(2) The diligence in seeking to effect service of process;

(3) The extent to which the parties engaged in any settlement negotiations or discussions;

(4) The diligence of the parties in pursuing discovery or other pretrial proceedings, including any extraordinary relief sought by either party;

(5) The nature and complexity of the case;

(6) The law applicable to the case, including the pendency of other litigation under a common set of facts or determinative of the legal or factual issues in the case;

Rule 3.1348. Sanctions for Failure to Provide Discovery

(a) Sanctions despite no opposition

The court may award sanctions under the Discovery Act in favor of a party who files a motion to compel discovery, even though no opposition to the motion was filed, or opposition to the motion was withdrawn, or the requested discovery was provided to the moving party after the motion was filed.

(b) Failure to oppose not an admission

The failure to file a written opposition or to appear at a hearing or the voluntary provision of discovery shall not be deemed an admission that the motion was proper or that sanctions should be awarded.

(As approved, eff. Jan. 1, 2007. Renumbered Rule 3.1345, eff. Jan. 1, 2009.)

Rule 3.1350. Motion for Summary Judgment or Summary Adjudication

(a) Definitions

As used in this rule:

(1) "Motion" refers to either a motion for summary judgment or a motion for summary adjudication.

(2) "Material facts" are facts that relate to the cause of action, claim for damages, issue of duty, or affirmative defense that is the subject of the motion and that could make a difference in the disposition of the motion.

(b) Motion for summary adjudication

If made in the alternative, a motion for summary adjudication may make reference to and depend on the same evidence submitted in support of the summary judgment motion. If summary adjudication is sought, whether separately or as an alternative to the motion for summary judgment, the specific cause of action, affirmative defense, claims for damages, or issues of duty must be stated specifically in the notice of motion and be repeated, verbatim, in the separate statement of undisputed material facts.

(c) Documents in support of motion

Except as provided in Code of Civil Procedure section 437c(r) and rule 3.1351, the motion must contain and be supported by the following documents:

(1) Notice of motion by *[moving party]* for summary judgment or summary adjudication or both;

(2) Separate statement of undisputed material facts in support of *[moving party's]* motion for summary judgment or summary adjudication or both;

(3) Memorandum in support of *[moving party's]* motion for summary judgment or summary adjudication or both;

(4) Evidence in support of *[moving party's]* motion for summary judgment or summary adjudication or both; and

(5) Request for judicial notice in support of *[moving party's]* motion for summary judgment or summary adjudication or both (if appropriate).

(d) Separate statement in support of motion

(1) The Separate Statement of Undisputed Material Facts in support of a motion must separately identify:

(A) Each cause of action, claim for damages, issue of duty, or affirmative defense that is the subject of the motion; and

(B) Each supporting material fact claimed to be without dispute with respect to the cause of action, claim for damages, issue of duty, or affirmative defense that is the subject of the motion.

(2) The separate statement should include only material facts and not any facts that are not pertinent to the disposition of the motion.

(3) The separate statement must be in the two-column format specified in (h). The statement must state in numerical sequence the undisputed material facts in the first column followed by the evidence that establishes those undisputed facts in that same column. Citation to the evidence in support of each material fact must include reference to the exhibit, title, page, and line numbers.

(e) Documents in opposition to motion

Except as provided in Code of Civil Procedure section 437c(r) and rule 3.1351, the opposition to a motion must consist of the following separate documents, titled as shown:

(1) *[Opposing party's]* memorandum in opposition to *[moving party's]* motion for summary judgment or summary adjudication or both;

(2) *[Opposing party's]* separate statement in opposition to *[moving party's]* motion for summary judgment or summary adjudication or both;

(3) *[Opposing party's]* evidence in opposition to *[moving party's]* motion for summary judgment or summary adjudication or both (if appropriate); and

(4) *[Opposing party's]* request for judicial notice in opposition to *[moving party's]* motion for summary judgment or summary adjudication or both (if appropriate).

(f) Content of separate statement in opposition to motion

The Separate Statement in Opposition to Motion must be in the two-column format specified in (h).

(1) Each material fact claimed by the moving party to be undisputed must be set out verbatim on the left side of the page, below which must be set out the evidence said by the moving party to establish that fact, complete with the moving party's references to exhibits.

(2) On the right side of the page, directly opposite the recitation of the moving party's statement of material facts and supporting evidence, the response must unequivocally state whether that fact is "disputed" or "undisputed." An opposing party who contends that a fact is disputed must state, on the right side of the page directly opposite the fact in dispute, the nature of the dispute and describe the evidence that supports the position that the fact is controverted. Citation to the evidence in support of the position that a fact is controverted must include reference to the exhibit, title, page, and line numbers.

(3) If the opposing party contends that additional material facts are pertinent to the disposition of the motion, those facts must be set forth in the separate statement. The separate statement should include only material facts and not any facts that are not pertinent to the disposition of the motion. Each fact must be followed by the evidence that establishes the fact. Citation to the evidence in support of each material fact must include reference to the exhibit, title, page, and line numbers.

(g) Documentary evidence

If evidence in support of or in opposition to a motion exceeds 25 pages, the evidence must be in a separately bound volume and must include a table of contents.

(h) Format for separate statements

Supporting and opposing separate statements in a motion for summary judgment must follow this format:

Supporting Statement:

Moving Party's Undisputed Material Facts and Supporting Evidence:	Opposing Party's Response and Supporting Evidence:
1. Plaintiff and defendant entered into a written contract for the sale of widgets. Jackson declaration, 2:17–21; contract, Ex. A to Jackson declaration.	

2. No widgets were ever received. Jackson declaration, 3:7–21.

Opposing statement:

Moving Party's Undisputed Material Facts and Alleged Supporting Evidence:	Opposing Party's Response and Evidence:
1. Plaintiff and defendant entered into a written contract for the sale of widgets. Jackson declaration, 2:17–21; contract, Ex. A to Jackson declaration.	Undisputed.
2. No widgets were ever received. Jackson declaration, 3:7–21.	Disputed. The widgets were received in New Zealand on August 31, 2001. Baygi declaration, 7:2–5.

Supporting and opposing separate statements in a motion for summary adjudication must follow this format:

Supporting statement:

ISSUE 1—THE FIRST CAUSE OF ACTION FOR

NEGLIGENCE IS BARRED BECAUSE PLAINTIFF

EXPRESSLY ASSUMED THE RISK OF INJURY

Moving Party's Undisputed Material Facts and Supporting Evidence:	Opposing Party's Response and Supporting Evidence:
1. Plaintiff was injured while mountain climbing on a trip with Any Company USA. Plaintiff's deposition, 12:3–4.	
2. Before leaving on the mountain climbing trip, plaintiff signed a waiver of liability for acts of negligence. Smith declaration, 5:4–5; waiver of liability, Ex. A to Smith declaration.	

Opposing statement:

ISSUE 1—THE FIRST CAUSE OF ACTION FOR NEGLIGENCE IS BARRED BECAUSE PLAINTIFF EXPRESSLY ASSUMED THE RISK OF INJURY

	Moving Party's Undisputed Material Facts and Alleged Supporting Evidence:	Opposing Party's Response and Evidence:
1.	Plaintiff was injured while mountain climbing on a trip with Any Company USA. Plaintiff's deposition, 12:3–4.	Undisputed.
2.	Before leaving on the mountain climbing trip, plaintiff signed a waiver of liability for acts of negligence. Smith declaration, 5:4–5; waiver of liability, Ex. A to Smith declaration.	Disputed. Plaintiff did not sign the waiver of liability; the signature on the waiver is forged. Jones declaration, 3:6–7.

(i) Request for electronic version of separate statement

On request, a party must within three days provide to any other party or the court an electronic version of its separate statement. The electronic version may be provided in any form on which the parties agree. If the parties are unable to agree on the form, the responding party must provide to the requesting party the electronic version of the separate statement that it used to prepare the document filed with the court. Under this subdivision, a party is not required to create an electronic version or any new version of any document for the purpose of transmission to the requesting party.

(As approved, eff. Jan. 1, 2007. As amended, eff. Jan. 1, 2008; July 1, 2008; Jan. 1, 2009; Jan. 1, 2016.)

DIVISION 12. SETTLEMENT

Rule 3.1380. Mandatory Settlement Conferences

(a) Settlement conference

On the court's own motion or at the request of any party, the court may set one or more mandatory settlement conferences.

(b) Persons attending

Trial counsel, parties, and persons with full authority to settle the case must personally attend the conference, unless excused by the court for good cause. If any consent to settle is required for any reason, the party with that consensual authority must be personally present at the conference.

(c) Settlement conference statement

No later than five court days before the initial date set for the settlement conference, each party must submit to the court and serve on each party a mandatory settlement conference statement containing:

(1) A good faith settlement demand;

(2) An itemization of economic and noneconomic damages by each plaintiff;

(3) A good faith offer of settlement by each defendant; and

(4) A statement identifying and discussing in detail all facts and law pertinent to the issues of liability and damages involved in the case as to that party.

The settlement conference statement must comply with any additional requirement imposed by local rule.

(d) Restrictions on appointments

A court must not:

(1) Appoint a person to conduct a settlement conference under this rule at the same time as that person is serving as a mediator in the same action; or

(2) Appoint a person to conduct a mediation under this rule.

(As approved, eff. Jan. 1, 2007. As amended, eff. Jan. 1, 2008.)

Rule 3.1385. Duty to Notify Court and Others of Settlement of Entire Case

(a) Notice of settlement

(1) *Court and other persons to be notified*

If an entire case is settled or otherwise disposed of, each plaintiff or other party seeking affirmative relief must immediately file written notice of the settlement or other disposition with the court and serve the notice on all parties and any arbitrator or other court-connected alternative dispute resolution (ADR) neutral involved in the case. Each plaintiff or other party seeking affirmative relief must also immediately give oral notice to all of the above if a hearing, conference, or trial is scheduled to take place within 10 days.

(2) *Compensation for failure to provide notice*

If the plaintiff or other party seeking affirmative relief does not notify an arbitrator or other court-connected ADR neutral involved in the case of a settlement at least 2 days before a scheduled hearing or session with that arbitrator or neutral, the court may order the party to compensate the arbitrator or other neutral for the scheduled hearing time. The amount of compensation ordered by the court must not exceed the maximum amount of compensation the arbitrator would be entitled to receive for service as an arbitrator under Code of Civil Procedure section 1141.18(b) or that the neutral would have been entitled to receive for service as a neutral at the scheduled hearing or session.

(b) Dismissal of case

Except as provided in (c) or (d), each plaintiff or other party seeking affirmative relief must serve and file a request for dismissal of the entire case within 45 days after the date of settlement of the case. If the plaintiff or other party required to serve and file the request for dismissal does not do so, the court must dismiss the entire case 45 days after it receives notice of settlement unless good cause is shown why the case should not be dismissed.

(c) Conditional settlement

(1) *Notice*

If the settlement agreement conditions dismissal of the entire case on the satisfactory completion of specified terms that are not to be performed within 45 days of the settlement, including payment in installment payments, the notice of conditional settlement served and filed by each plaintiff or other party seeking affirmative relief must specify the date by which the dismissal is to be filed.

(2) *Dismissal*

If the plaintiff or other party required to serve and file a request for dismissal within 45 days after the dismissal date specified in the notice does not do so, the court must dismiss the entire case unless good cause is shown why the case should not be dismissed.

(3) *Hearings vacated*

(A) Except as provided in (B), on the filing of the notice of conditional settlement, the court must vacate all hearings and other proceedings requiring the appearance of a party and may not set any hearing or other proceeding requiring the appearance of a party earlier than 45 days after the dismissal date specified in the notice, unless requested by a party.

(B) The court need not vacate a hearing on an order to show cause or other proceeding relating to sanctions, or for determination of good faith settlement at the request of a party under Code of Civil Procedure section 877.6.

(4) *Case disposition time*

Under standard 2.2(n)(1)(A), the filing of a notice of conditional settlement removes the case from the computation of time used to determine case disposition time.

(d) Compromise of claims of a minor or disabled person

If the settlement of the case involves the compromise of the claim of a minor or person with a disability, the court must not hold an order to show cause hearing under (b) before the court has held a hearing to approve the settlement, provided the parties have filed appropriate papers to seek court approval of the settlement.

(e) Request for additional time to complete settlement

If a party who has served and filed a notice of settlement under (a) determines that the case cannot be dismissed within the prescribed 45 days, that party must serve and file a notice and a supporting declaration advising the court of that party's inability to dismiss the case within the prescribed time, showing good cause for its inability to do so, and proposing an alternative date for dismissal. The notice and a supporting declaration must be served and filed at least 5 court days before the time for requesting dismissal has elapsed. If good cause is shown, the court must continue the matter to allow additional time to complete the settlement. The court may take such other actions as may be appropriate for the proper management and disposition of the case.

(As approved, eff. Jan. 1, 2007. As amended, eff. Jan. 1, 2009; July 1, 2013.)

DIVISION 15. TRIAL

Chapter 4. Jury Trials

Rule 3.1540. Examination of Prospective Jurors in Civil Cases

(a) Application

This rule applies to all civil jury trials.

(b) Examination of jurors by the trial judge

In examining prospective jurors in civil cases, the judge should consider the policies and recommendations in standard 3.25 of the Standards of Judicial Administration.

(c) Additional questions and examination by counsel

On completion of the initial examination, the trial judge must permit counsel for each party that so requests to submit additional questions that the judge will put to the jurors.

(As approved, eff. Jan. 1, 2007. As amended, eff. Jan. 1, 2013.)

TITLE 8. APPELLATE RULES

DIVISION 1. RULES RELATING TO THE SUPREME COURT AND COURTS OF APPEAL

Chapter 1. General Provisions

Rule 8.10. Definitions and Use of Terms

Unless the context or subject matter requires otherwise, the definitions and use of terms in rule 1.6 apply to these rules. In addition, the following apply:

(1) "Appellant" means the appealing party.

(2) "Respondent" means the adverse party.

(3) "Party" includes any attorney of record for that party.

(4) "Judgment" includes any judgment or order that may be appealed.

(5) "Superior court" means the court from which an appeal is taken.

(6) "Reviewing court" means the Supreme Court or the Court of Appeal to which an appeal is taken, in which an original proceeding is begun, or to which an appeal or original proceeding is transferred.

(7) The word "briefs" includes petitions for rehearing, petitions for review, and answers thereto. It does not include petitions for extraordinary relief in original proceedings.

(8) "Attach" or "attachment" may refer to either physical attachment or electronic attachment, as appropriate.

(9) "Copy" or "copies" may refer to electronic copies, as appropriate.

(10) "Cover" includes the cover page of a document filed electronically.

(11) "Written" and "writing" include electronically created written materials, whether or not those materials are printed on paper.

(As approved, eff. Jan. 1, 2007. As amended, eff. Jan. 1, 2016.)

Rule 8.60. Extending Time

(a) Computing time

The Code of Civil Procedure governs computing and extending the time to do any act required or permitted under these rules.

(b) Extending time

For good cause—or on an exceptional showing of good cause, when required by these rules—and except as these rules provide otherwise, the Chief Justice or presiding justice may extend the time to do any act required or permitted under these rules.

(c) Application for extension

(1) An application to extend time must include a declaration stating facts, not mere conclusions, and must be served on all parties. For good cause, the Chief Justice or presiding justice may excuse advance service.

(2) The application must state:

(A) The due date of the document to be filed;

(B) The length of the extension requested;

(C) Whether any earlier extensions have been granted and, if so, their lengths and whether granted by stipulation or by the court; and

(D) Good cause—or an exceptional good cause, when required by these rules—for granting the extension, consistent with the factors in rule 8.63(b).

(d) Relief from default

For good cause, a reviewing court may relieve a party from default for any failure to comply with these rules except the failure to file a timely notice of appeal or a timely statement of reasonable grounds in support of a certificate of probable cause.

(e) No extension by superior court

Except as these rules provide otherwise, a superior court may not extend the time to do any act to prepare the appellate record.

(f) Notice to party

(1) In a civil case, counsel must deliver to the client a copy of any stipulation or application to extend time that counsel files. Counsel must attach evidence of such delivery to the stipulation or application, or certify in the stipulation or application that the copy has been delivered.

(2) In a class action, the copy required under (1) need be delivered to only one represented party.

(3) The evidence or certification of delivery under (1) need not include the address of the party notified.

(As approved, eff. Jan. 1, 2007. As amended, eff. Jan. 1, 2023.)

Chapter 2. Civil Appeals

Rule 8.104. Time to Appeal

(a) Normal time

(1) Unless a statute, or rules 8.108, 8.702, or 8.712 provide otherwise, a notice of appeal must be filed on or before the earliest of:

(A) 60 days after the superior court clerk serves the party filing the notice of appeal with a document entitled "Notice of Entry" of judgment or a filed endorsed copy of the judgment, showing the date either was served;

(B) 60 days after the party filing the notice of appeal serves or is served by a party with a document entitled "Notice of Entry" of judgment or a filed endorsed copy of the judgment, accompanied by proof of service; or

(C) 180 days after entry of judgment.

(2) Service under (1)(A) and (B) may be by any method permitted by the Code of Civil Procedure, including electronic service when permitted under Code of Civil Procedure section 1010.6 and rules 2.250–2.261.

(3) If the parties stipulated in the trial court under Code of Civil Procedure section 1019.5 to waive notice of the court order being appealed, the time to appeal under (1)(C) applies unless the court or a party serves notice of entry of judgment or a filed endorsed copy of the judgment to start the time period under (1)(A) or (B).

(b) No extension of time; late notice of appeal

Except as provided in rule 8.66, no court may extend the time to file a notice of appeal. If a notice of appeal is filed late, the reviewing court must dismiss the appeal.

(c) What constitutes entry

For purposes of this rule:

(1) The entry date of a judgment is the date the judgment is filed under Code of Civil Procedure section 668.5, or the date it is entered in the judgment book.

(2) The entry date of an appealable order that is entered in the minutes is the date it is entered in the permanent minutes. But if the minute order directs that a written order be prepared, the entry date is the date the signed order is filed; a written order prepared under rule 3.1312 or similar local rule is not such an order prepared by direction of a minute order.

(3) The entry date of an appealable order that is not entered in the minutes is the date the signed order is filed.

(4) The entry date of a decree of distribution in a probate proceeding is the date it is entered at length in the judgment book or other permanent court record.

(5) An order signed electronically has the same effect as an order signed on paper.

(d) Premature notice of appeal

(1) A notice of appeal filed after judgment is rendered but before it is entered is valid and is treated as filed immediately after entry of judgment.

(2) The reviewing court may treat a notice of appeal filed after the superior court has announced its intended ruling, but before it has rendered judgment, as filed immediately after entry of judgment.

(e) Appealable order

As used in (a) and (d), "judgment" includes an appealable order if the appeal is from an appealable order.

(As approved, eff. Jan. 1, 2007. As amended, eff. Jan. 1, 2010; Jan. 1, 2011; July 1, 2011; July 1, 2012; Jan. 1, 2016; Jan. 1, 2017; July 1, 2017.)

Rule 8.108. Extending the Time to Appeal

(a) Extension of time

This rule operates only to extend the time to appeal otherwise prescribed in rule 8.104(a); it does not shorten the time to appeal. If the normal time to appeal stated in rule 8.104(a) is longer than the time provided in this rule, the time to appeal stated in rule 8.104(a) governs.

(b) Motion for new trial

If any party serves and files a valid notice of intention to move for a new trial, the following extensions of time apply:

(1) If the motion for a new trial is denied, the time to appeal from the judgment is extended for all parties until the earliest of:

(A) 30 days after the superior court clerk or a party serves an order denying the motion or a notice of entry of that order;

(B) 30 days after denial of the motion by operation of law; or

(C) 180 days after entry of judgment.

(2) If the trial court makes a finding of excessive or inadequate damages and grants the motion for a new trial subject to the condition that the motion is denied if a party consents to the additur or remittitur of damages, the time to appeal is extended as follows:

(A) If any party serves an acceptance of a the conditionally ordered additur or remittitur of damages pursuant to a trial court finding of excessive or inadequate damages within the time for accepting the additur or remittitur, the time to appeal from the judgment is extended for all parties until 30 days after the date the party serves the acceptance.

(B) If a party serves a rejection of the additur or remittitur within the time for accepting the additur or remittitur or if the time for accepting the additur or remittitur expires, the time to appeal from the new trial order is extended for all parties until the earliest of 30 days after the date the party serves the rejection or 30 days after the date on which the time for accepting the additur or remittitur expired.

(c) Motion to vacate judgment

If, within the time prescribed by rule 8.104 to appeal from the judgment, any party serves and files a valid notice of intention to move—or a valid motion—to vacate the judgment, the time to appeal from the judgment is extended for all parties until the earliest of:

(1) 30 days after the superior court clerk or a party serves an order denying the motion or a notice of entry of that order;

(2) 90 days after the first notice of intention to move—or motion—is filed; or

(3) 180 days after entry of judgment.

(d) Motion for judgment notwithstanding the verdict

(1) If any party serves and files a valid motion for judgment notwithstanding the verdict and the motion is denied, the time to appeal from the judgment is extended for all parties until the earliest of:

(A) 30 days after the superior court clerk or a party serves an order denying the motion or a notice of entry of that order;

(B) 30 days after denial of the motion by operation of law; or

(C) 180 days after entry of judgment.

(2) Unless extended by (g)(2), the time to appeal from an order denying a motion for judgment notwithstanding the verdict is governed by rule 8.104.

(e) Motion to reconsider appealable order

If any party serves and files a valid motion to reconsider an appealable order under Code of Civil Procedure section 1008, subdivision (a), the time to appeal from that order is extended for all parties until the earliest of:

(1) 30 days after the superior court clerk or a party serves an order denying the motion or a notice of entry of that order;

(2) 90 days after the first motion to reconsider is filed; or

(3) 180 days after entry of the appealable order.

(f) Public entity actions under Government Code section 962, 984, or 985

If a public entity defendant serves and files a valid request for a mandatory settlement conference on methods of satisfying a judgment under Government Code section 962, an election to pay a judgment in periodic payments under Government Code section 984 and rule 3.1804, or a motion for a posttrial hearing on reducing a judgment under Government Code section 985, the time to appeal from the judgment is extended for all parties until the earliest of:

(1) 90 days after the superior court clerk serves the party filing the notice of appeal with a document entitled "Notice of Entry" of judgment, or a filed endorsed copy of the judgment, showing the date either was served;

(2) 90 days after the party filing the notice of appeal serves or is served by a party with a document entitled "Notice of Entry" of judgment or a filed endorsed copy of the judgment, accompanied by proof of service; or

(3) 180 days after entry of judgment.

(g) Cross-appeal

(1) If an appellant timely appeals from a judgment or appealable order, the time for any other party to appeal from the same judgment or order is extended until 20 days after the superior court clerk serves notification of the first appeal.

(2) If an appellant timely appeals from an order granting a motion for new trial, an order granting-within 150 days after entry of judgment-a motion to vacate the judgment, or a judgment notwithstanding the verdict, the time for any other party to appeal from the original judgment or from an order denying a motion for judgment notwithstanding the verdict is extended until 20 days after the clerk serves notification of the first appeal.

(h) Service; proof of service

Service under this rule may be by any method permitted by the Code of Civil Procedure, including electronic service when permitted under Code of Civil Procedure section 1010.6 and rules 2.250–2.261. An order or notice that is served must be accompanied by proof of service.

(As approved, eff. Jan. 1, 2007. As amended, eff. Jan. 1, 2008; Jan. 1, 2011; July 1, 2012; Jan. 1, 2015; Jan. 1, 2016.)

Rule 8.244. Settlement, Abandonment, Voluntary Dismissal, and Compromise

(a) Notice of settlement

(1) If a civil case settles after a notice of appeal has been filed, either as a whole or as to any party, the appellant who has settled must immediately serve and file a notice of settlement in the Court of Appeal. If the parties have designated a clerk's or a reporter's transcript and the record has not been filed in the Court of Appeal, the appellant must also immediately serve a copy of the notice on the superior court clerk.

(2) If the case settles after the appellant receives a notice setting oral argument or a prehearing conference, the appellant must also immediately notify the Court of Appeal of the settlement by telephone or other expeditious method.

(3) Within 45 days after filing a notice of settlement—unless the court has ordered a longer time period on a showing of good cause—the appellant who filed the notice of settlement must file either an abandonment under (b), if the record has not yet been filed in the Court of Appeal, or a request to dismiss under (c), if the record has already been filed in the Court of Appeal.

(4) If the appellant does not file an abandonment, a request to dismiss, or a letter stating good cause why the appeal should not be dismissed within the time period specified under (3), the court may dismiss the appeal as to that appellant and order each side to bear its own costs on appeal.

(5) This subdivision does not apply to settlements requiring findings to be made by the Court of Appeal under Code of Civil Procedure section 128(a)(8).

(b) Abandonment

(1) Before the record is filed in the Court of Appeal, the appellant may serve and file in superior court an abandonment of the appeal or a stipulation to abandon the appeal. The filing effects a dismissal of the appeal and restores the superior court's jurisdiction.

(2) The superior court clerk must promptly notify the Court of Appeal and the parties of the abandonment or stipulation.

(c) Request to dismiss

(1) After the record is filed in the Court of Appeal, the appellant may serve and file in that court a request or a stipulation to dismiss the appeal.

(2) On receipt of a request or stipulation to dismiss, the court may dismiss the appeal and direct immediate issuance of the remittitur.

(d) Approval of compromise

If a guardian or conservator seeks approval of a proposed compromise of a pending appeal, the Court of Appeal may, before ruling on the compromise, direct the trial court to determine whether the compromise is in the minor's or the conservatee's best interests and to report its findings.

(As approved, eff. Jan. 1, 2007.)

Rule 8.276. Sanctions

(a) Grounds for sanctions

On motion of a party or its own motion, a Court of Appeal may impose sanctions, including the award or denial of costs under rule 8.278, on a party or an attorney for:

(1) Taking a frivolous appeal or appealing solely to cause delay;

(2) Including in the record any matter not reasonably material to the appeal's determination;

(3) Filing a frivolous motion; or

(4) Committing any other unreasonable violation of these rules.

(b) Motions for sanctions

(1) A party's motion under (a) must include a declaration supporting the amount of any monetary sanction sought and must be served and filed before any order dismissing the appeal but no later than 10 days after the appellant's reply brief is due.

(2) If a party files a motion for sanctions with a motion to dismiss the appeal and the motion to dismiss is not granted, the party may file a new motion for sanctions within 10 days after the appellant's reply brief is due.

(c) Notice

The court must give notice in writing if it is considering imposing sanctions.

(d) Opposition

Within 10 days after the court sends such notice, a party or attorney may serve and file an opposition, but failure to do so will not be deemed consent. An opposition may not be filed unless the court sends such notice.

(e) Oral argument

Unless otherwise ordered, oral argument on the issue of sanctions must be combined with oral argument on the merits of the appeal.

(As approved, eff. Jan. 1, 2007. As amended, eff. Jan. 1, 2008.)

DIVISION 5. PUBLICATION OF APPELLATE OPINIONS

Rule 8.1105. Publication of Appellate Opinions

(a) Supreme Court

All opinions of the Supreme Court are published in the Official Reports.

(b) Courts of Appeal and appellate divisions

Except as provided in (d), an opinion of a Court of Appeal or a superior court appellate division is published in the Official Reports if a majority of the rendering court certifies the opinion for publication before the decision is final in that court.

(c) Standards for certification

An opinion of a Court of Appeal or a superior court appellate division—whether it affirms or reverses a trial court order or judgment—should be certified for publication in the Official Reports if the opinion:

(1) Establishes a new rule of law;

(2) Applies an existing rule of law to a set of facts significantly different from those stated in published opinions;

(3) Modifies, explains, or criticizes with reasons given, an existing rule of law;

(4) Advances a new interpretation, clarification, criticism, or construction of a provision of a constitution, statute, ordinance, or court rule;

(5) Addresses or creates an apparent conflict in the law;

(6) Involves a legal issue of continuing public interest;

(7) Makes a significant contribution to legal literature by reviewing either the development of a common law rule or the legislative or judicial history of a provision of a constitution, statute, or other written law;

(8) Invokes a previously overlooked rule of law, or reaffirms a principle of law not applied in a recently reported decision; or

(9) Is accompanied by a separate opinion concurring or dissenting on a legal issue, and publication of the majority and separate opinions would make a significant contribution to the development of the law.

(d) Factors not to be considered

Factors such as the workload of the court, or the potential embarrassment of a litigant, lawyer, judge, or other person should not affect the determination of whether to publish an opinion.

(e) Changes in publication status

(1) Unless otherwise ordered under (2):

(A) An opinion is no longer considered published if the rendering court grants rehearing.

(B) Grant of review by the Supreme Court of a decision by the Court of Appeal does not affect the appellate court's certification of the opinion for full or partial publication under rule 8.1105(b) or rule

8.1110, but any such Court of Appeal opinion, whether officially published in hard copy or electronically, must be accompanied by a prominent notation advising that review by the Supreme Court has been granted.

(2) The Supreme Court may order that an opinion certified for publication is not to be published or that an opinion not certified is to be published. The Supreme Court may also order depublication of part of an opinion at any time after granting review.

(f) Editing

(1) Computer versions of all opinions of the Supreme Court and Courts of Appeal must be provided to the Reporter of Decisions on the day of filing. Opinions of superior court appellate divisions certified for publication must be provided as prescribed in rule 8.887.

(2) The Reporter of Decisions must edit opinions for publication as directed by the Supreme Court. The Reporter of Decisions must submit edited opinions to the courts for examination, correction, and approval before finalization for the Official Reports.

(As approved, eff. Jan. 1, 2007. As amended, eff. Apr. 1, 2007; July 23, 2008; July 1, 2009; July 1, 2016.)

Rule 8.1110. Partial Publication

(a) Order for partial publication

A majority of the rendering court may certify for publication any part of an opinion meeting a standard for publication under rule 8.1105.

(b) Opinion contents

The published part of the opinion must specify the part or parts not certified for publication. All material, factual and legal, including the disposition, that aids in the application or interpretation of the published part must be published.

(c) Construction

For purposes of rules 8.1105, 8.1115, and 8.1120, the published part of the opinion is treated as a published opinion and the unpublished part as an unpublished opinion.

(As approved, eff. Jan. 1, 2007.)

Rule 8.1115. Citation of Opinions

(a) Unpublished opinion

Except as provided in (b), an opinion of a California Court of Appeal or superior court appellate division that is not certified for publication or ordered published must not be cited or relied on by a court or a party in any other action.

(b) Exceptions

An unpublished opinion may be cited or relied on:

(1) When the opinion is relevant under the doctrines of law of the case, res judicata, or collateral estoppel; or

(2) When the opinion is relevant to a criminal or disciplinary action because it states reasons for a decision affecting the same defendant or respondent in another such action.

(c) Citation procedure

On request of the court or a party, a copy of an opinion citable under (b) must be promptly furnished to the court or the requesting party.

(d) When a published opinion may be cited

A published California opinion may be cited or relied on as soon as it is certified for publication or ordered published.

(e) When review of published opinion has been granted

(1) *While review is pending*

Pending review and filing of the Supreme Court's opinion, unless otherwise ordered by the Supreme Court under (3), a published opinion of a Court of Appeal in the matter has no binding or precedential effect, and may be cited for potentially persuasive value only. Any citation to the Court of Appeal opinion must also note the grant of review and any subsequent action by the Supreme Court.

(2) *After decision on review*

After decision on review by the Supreme Court, unless otherwise ordered by the Supreme Court under (3), a published opinion of a Court of Appeal in the matter, and any published opinion of a Court of Appeal in a matter in which the Supreme Court has ordered review and deferred action pending the decision, is citable and has binding or precedential effect, except to the extent it is inconsistent with the decision of the Supreme Court or is disapproved by that court.

(3) *Supreme Court order*

At any time after granting review or after decision on review, the Supreme Court may order that all or part of an opinion covered by (1) or (2) is not citable or has a binding or precedential effect different from that specified in (1) or (2).

(As approved, eff. Jan. 1, 2007. As amended, eff. July 1, 2016.)

LONG ARM STATUTES OF ILLINOIS AND NEW YORK

■ ■ ■

ILLINOIS CODE OF CIVIL PROCEDURE

735 ILCS § 5/2–209. Act submitting to jurisdiction—Process

(a) Any person, whether or not a citizen or resident of this State, who in person or through an agent does any of the acts hereinafter enumerated, thereby submits such person, and, if an individual, his or her personal representative, to the jurisdiction of the courts of this State as to any cause of action arising from the doing of any of such acts:

(1) The transaction of any business within this State;

(2) The commission of a tortious act within this State;

(3) The ownership, use, or possession of any real estate situated in this State;

(4) Contracting to insure any person, property or risk located within this State at the time of contracting;

(5) With respect to actions of dissolution of marriage, declaration of invalidity of marriage and legal separation, the maintenance in this State of a matrimonial domicile at the time this cause of action arose or the commission in this State of any act giving rise to the cause of action;

(6) With respect to actions brought under the Illinois Parentage Act of 1984, as now or hereafter amended, or under the Illinois Parentage Act of 2015 on and after the effective date of that Act, the performance of an act of sexual intercourse within this State during the possible period of conception;

(7) The making or performance of any contract or promise substantially connected with this State;

(8) The performance of sexual intercourse within this State which is claimed to have resulted in the conception of a child who resides in this State;

(9) The failure to support a child, spouse or former spouse who has continued to reside in this State since the person either formerly resided with them in this State or directed them to reside in this State;

(10) The acquisition of ownership, possession or control of any asset or thing of value present within this State when ownership, possession or control was acquired;

(11) The breach of any fiduciary duty within this State;

(12) The performance of duties as a director or officer of a corporation organized under the laws of this State or having its principal place of business within this State;

(13) The ownership of an interest in any trust administered within this State; or

(14) The exercise of powers granted under the authority of this State as a fiduciary.

(b) A court may exercise general jurisdiction in any action arising within or without this State against any person who:

(1) Is a natural person present within this State when served;

(2) Is a natural person domiciled or resident within this State when the cause of action arose, the action was commenced, or process was served;

(3) Is a corporation organized under the laws of this State or having its principal place of business in this State;

(4) Is a natural person or corporation doing business within this State; or

(5) Is a foreign business corporation that has consented to general jurisdiction in this State in accordance with subsection (b) of Section 13.20 or subsection (c–5) of Section 13.70 of the Business Corporation Act of 1983, but only if (i) the action alleges injury or illness resulting from exposure to a substance defined as toxic under the Uniform Hazardous Substances Act of Illinois, whether the cause of action arises within or without this State, and (ii) jurisdiction is proper as to one or more named co-defendants under subsection (a) of this Section.

(b–5) Foreign defamation judgment. The courts of this State shall have personal jurisdiction over any person who obtains a judgment in a defamation proceeding outside the United States against any person who is a resident of Illinois or, if not a natural person, has its principal place of business in Illinois, for the purposes of rendering declaratory relief with respect to that resident's liability for the judgment, or for the purpose of determining whether said judgment should be deemed non-recognizable pursuant to this Code, to the fullest extent permitted by the United States Constitution, provided:

(1) the publication at issue was published in Illinois, and

(2) that resident (i) has assets in Illinois which might be used to satisfy the foreign defamation judgment, or (ii) may have to take actions in Illinois to comply with the foreign defamation judgment.

The provisions of this subsection shall apply to persons who obtained judgments in defamation proceedings outside the United States prior to, on, or after the effective date of this amendatory Act of the 95th General Assembly.

(c) A court may also exercise jurisdiction on any other basis now or hereafter permitted by the Illinois Constitution and the Constitution of the United States.

(d) Service of process upon any person who is subject to the jurisdiction of the courts of this State, as provided in this Section, may be made by personally serving the summons upon the defendant outside this State, as provided in this Act, with the same force and effect as though summons had been personally served within this State.

(e) Service of process upon any person who resides or whose business address is outside the United States and who is subject to the jurisdiction of the courts of this State, as provided in this Section, in any action based upon product liability may be made by serving a copy of the summons with a copy of the complaint attached upon the Secretary of State. The summons shall be accompanied by a $5 fee payable to the Secretary of State. The plaintiff shall forthwith mail a copy of the summons, upon which the date of service upon the Secretary is clearly shown, together with a copy of the complaint to the defendant at his or her last known place of residence or business address. Plaintiff shall file with the circuit clerk an affidavit of the plaintiff or his or her attorney stating the last known place of residence or the last known business address of the defendant and a certificate of mailing a copy of the summons and complaint to the defendant at such address as required by this subsection (e). The certificate of mailing shall be prima facie evidence that the plaintiff or his or her attorney mailed a copy of the summons and complaint to the defendant as required. Service of the summons shall be deemed to have been made upon the defendant on the date it is served upon the Secretary and shall have the same force and effect as though summons had been personally served upon the defendant within this State.

(f) Only causes of action arising from acts enumerated herein may be asserted against a defendant in an action in which jurisdiction over him or her is based upon subsection (a).

(g) Nothing herein contained limits or affects the right to serve any process in any other manner now or hereafter provided by law.

(P.A. 82–280, § 2–209, eff. July 1, 1982. Amended by P.A. 82–783, Art. III, § 43, eff. July 13, 1982; P.A. 85–907, Art. II, § 1, eff. Nov. 23, 1987; P.A. 85–1156, Art. I, § 7, eff. Jan. 1, 1989; P.A. 86–840, § 1, eff. Sept. 7, 1989; P.A. 95–865, § 5, eff. Aug. 19, 2008; P.A. 99–85, § 964, eff. Jan. 1, 2016; P.A. 104–352, § 5, eff. Aug. 1, 2025.)

NEW YORK CIVIL PRACTICE LAW AND RULES

§ 301. Jurisdiction over persons, property or status

A court may exercise such jurisdiction over persons, property, or status as might have been exercised heretofore.

(L.1962, c. 308.)

§ 302. Personal jurisdiction by acts of non-domiciliaries

(a) Acts which are the basis of jurisdiction. As to a cause of action arising from any of the acts enumerated in this section, a court may exercise personal jurisdiction over any nondomiciliary, or his executor or administrator, who in person or through an agent:

1. transacts any business within the state or contracts anywhere to supply goods or services in the state; or

2. commits a tortious act within the state, except as to a cause of action for defamation of character arising from the act; or

3. commits a tortious act without the state causing injury to person or property within the state, except as to a cause of action for defamation of character arising from the act, if he

   (i) regularly does or solicits business, or engages in any other persistent course of conduct, or derives substantial revenue from goods used or consumed or services rendered, in the state, or

   (ii) expects or should reasonably expect the act to have consequences in the state and derives substantial revenue from interstate or international commerce; or

4. owns, uses or possesses any real property situated within the state.

(b) Personal jurisdiction over non-resident defendant in matrimonial actions or family court proceedings. A court in any matrimonial action or family court proceeding involving a demand for support, alimony, maintenance, distributive awards or special relief in matrimonial actions may exercise personal jurisdiction over the respondent or defendant notwithstanding the fact that he or she no longer is a resident or domiciliary of this state, or over his or her executor or administrator, if the party seeking support is a resident of or domiciled in this state at the time such demand is made, provided that this state was the matrimonial domicile of the parties before their separation, or the defendant abandoned the plaintiff in this state, or the claim for support, alimony, maintenance, distributive awards or special relief in matrimonial actions accrued under the laws of this state or under an agreement executed in this state. The family court may exercise personal jurisdiction over a non-resident respondent to the extent provided in sections one hundred fifty-four and one thousand thirty-six and article five-B of the family court act and article five-A of the domestic relations law.

(c) Effect of appearance. Where personal jurisdiction is based solely upon this section, an appearance does not confer such jurisdiction with respect to causes of action not arising from an act enumerated in this section.

(d) Foreign defamation judgment. The courts of this state shall have personal jurisdiction over any person who obtains a judgment in a defamation proceeding outside the United States against any person who is a resident of New York or is a person or entity amenable to jurisdiction in New York who has assets in New York or may have to take actions in New York to comply with the judgment, for the purposes of rendering declaratory relief with respect to that person's liability for the judgment, and/or for the purpose of determining whether said judgment should be deemed non-recognizable pursuant to section fifty-three hundred four of this chapter, to the fullest extent permitted by the United States constitution, provided:

1. the publication at issue was published in New York, and

2. that resident or person amenable to jurisdiction in New York (i) has assets in New York which might be used to satisfy the foreign defamation judgment, or (ii) may have to take actions in New York to comply with the foreign defamation judgment.

The provisions of this subdivision shall apply to persons who obtained judgments in defamation proceedings outside the United States prior to and/or after the effective date of this subdivision.

(As amended L.1974, c. 859, § 1; L.1979, c. 252, §§ 1, 2; L.1980, c. 281, § 22; L.1982, c. 505, § 1; L.1991, c. 69, § 7; L.1995, c. 441, § 2; L.2006, c. 184, § 5, eff. July 26, 2006; L.2008, c. 66, § 3, eff. Apr. 28, 2008.)

SELECTED CALIFORNIA CASES

■ ■ ■

JURISDICTION OVER THE PERSON

LG CHEM, LTD. V. SUPERIOR COURT

California Court of Appeal, Fourth District, 2022.
80 Cal.App.5th 348, 295 Cal.Rptr.3d 661.

DO, ASSOCIATE JUSTICE.

INTRODUCTION

Ryan Lawhon, a California resident, alleged he was severely injured when an 18650 lithium-ion battery he bought from a San Diego vape shop suddenly exploded in his pants pocket. In addition to the vape shop and vape distributor, he sued LG Chem Ltd. (LG Chem), the South Korean manufacturer of 18650 lithium-ion batteries (18650 batteries), for negligence and product liability. The trial court denied LG Chem's motion to quash service of summons for lack of personal jurisdiction, finding the court's exercise of specific jurisdiction over LG Chem comported with federal due process. LG Chem petitioned this court for writ of mandate directing the trial court to vacate its order denying the motion to quash.

* * *

FACTUAL AND PROCEDURAL BACKGROUND

I. Lawhon's Claims

Lawhon alleged he purchased an 18650 battery at a San Diego vape shop called Vapin' the 619. The battery did not come in a package. The vape shop "simply placed it in a plastic bag." On February 7, 2019, Lawhon put the battery in his pants pocket, along with another identical battery he previously purchased from the same vape shop and his car keys. One of the batteries "suddenly exploded" in his pocket, severely burning his leg and hand. Lawhon spent "nearly a week" in the hospital, and missed "multiple weeks of work" as a result of his injuries.

On September 9, 2019, Lawhon filed an unverified complaint for damages against four named defendants: Vapin America LLC (Vapin America), a Nevada limited liability corporation with its principal place of business in San Diego County; and It Is What It Is-II, LLC, Morija, LLC, and Flame LLC, three California limited liability corporations with their principal places of business in San Diego County that were in "some combination" doing business as Vapin' the 619. He alleged, on information and belief, that Vapin America sold the battery that injured him to the vape shop.

Lawhon also alleged, on information and belief, there were unknown defendants, Does 1 through 50, who were "in some manner responsible" and legally liable to him because they "design[ed], manufactur[ed], or distribut[ed] the defective product." On December 17, 2020, Lawhon substituted LG Chem for Doe 3 with a form amendment to the complaint. Against all defendants, Lawhon asserted a cause of action for negligence and strict liability causes of action for design defect, manufacturing defect, and failure to warn.

II. LG Chem's Motion to Quash Service of Summons

On June 9, 2021, LG Chem specially appeared and moved to quash service of summons for lack of personal jurisdiction. Lawhon * * * conceded the trial court could not assert general jurisdiction over LG Chem but argued LG Chem's contacts with California were sufficient to support specific jurisdiction. The trial court * * * denied LG Chem's motion to quash * * *.

* * *

A. Jurisdictional Evidence

* * *

LG Chem is a South Korean company with headquarters and principal offices in Seoul, South Korea. It had no office or employees in California, nor was it registered to do business in California. It did not own or lease real property in this state. It did not have a registered agent for service of process in California.

LG Chem did not conduct business with Vapin America, the entity alleged to have sold the defective battery to Vapin' the 619. It also did not conduct business with Vapin' the 619, the vape shop that allegedly sold the defective battery to Lawhon, or with the three entities doing business as the vape shop. LG Chem did not authorize any of these entities to advertise, distribute, or sell LG Chem's 18650 batteries for use by individual consumers as standalone, replaceable batteries for any purpose. Indeed, LG Chem did not have any licensed dealers or retailers of 18650 batteries in California, nor did it authorize or advertise consumer repair or replacement services for 18650 batteries in this state.

If the 18650 battery that injured Lawhon was, in fact, an LG Chem battery, it was not designed or manufactured in California. LG Chem manufactured 18650 batteries "for use by sophisticated companies in specific applications, such as power tools, where the cells are encased in a battery pack with protective circuitry." The batteries are sold as "industrial component products" and only to original equipment manufacturers or battery packers.[6] LG Chem never sold 18650 batteries to vape shops or vape distributors. And it did not advertise, market or solicit buyers for its 18650 batteries in California; instead, "the customers seek [LG Chem] out."

LG Chem did not design, manufacture, distribute, advertise, or sell 18650 batteries to be sold to, or used by, individual consumers as standalone, replaceable batteries. Nor did LG Chem authorize any wholesaler, distributor, retailer, or other individual or entity to do so.

In the two-year period leading up to Lawhon's injury on February 7, 2019, LG Chem's sales of 18650 batteries in California were to three companies in the electric vehicle industry, and the 18650 batteries sold to these customers were for use in electric vehicles. LG Chem's records pertaining to these sales showed the batteries were shipped directly from LG Chem in South Korea to the three companies in California. The number

---

[6] Battery packers place battery cells into battery packs or battery modules and then sell the battery packs or modules to original equipment manufacturers. [Ed. The 18650 batteries are not sold to retail customers individually because "the batteries are particularly dangerous when employed outside of a pack to power e-cigarette—or vaping—devices." B.D. v. Samsung Sdi Co., 143 F.4th 757, 763 (7th Cir.2025).]

of shipments was fewer than 100, although the number of batteries sold, and the dollars generated from these sales, were in the millions.

* * *

LG Chem would only sell batteries to customers that signed a declaration of commitment stating the customer "will not sell the battery cells as loose individual cells and [will] always make sure that the cells are placed in a battery pack or battery module together with the relevant safety devices or the battery cells are put into finished products and sold as such." LG Chem started doing that in 2016, after a person "alleged that a battery cell that he put in his E-cigarette caused him harm and because [LG Chem] wanted to prevent anything like that from ever happening again." LG Chem also added warning labels to the outside of its 18650 batteries.

B. Parties' Arguments

LG Chem argued, as a South Korean company headquartered in Seoul, it is not subject to the general jurisdiction of the California courts because it has no continuous and systematic contacts with California such that it may be considered " 'at home' " there. LG Chem further argued it was not subject to the specific jurisdiction of the California courts because it did not purposefully exploit the California consumer market for standalone batteries. Rather, it only sold 18650 batteries to three California companies in the electric vehicle industry as components for use in electric vehicles. Because it never sold to vape shops or vape distributors, LG Chem asserted that Vapin America could only have acquired an LG Chem 18650 battery through the unilateral actions of third parties. Thus, it argued, Lawhon's claims arise not out of LG Chem's contacts but out of the actions of third parties, with no connection to LG Chem, who sold the standalone batteries to Lawhon.

Lawhon conceded the trial court could not assert general jurisdiction over LG Chem but argued it could assert specific jurisdiction. He argued LG Chem had purposefully availed itself of the benefits and protections of the California forum by selling its 18650 batteries "to certain, specific original equipment manufacturers and battery pack manufacturers in California for the purpose of deriving financial benefit." Lawhon argued his injury arose from or was related to LG Chem's contacts with California, because LG Chem sold batteries "into the California battery market" and he was "was injured by a battery he purchased in California." He asserted considerations of fair play and substantial justice supported the exercise of jurisdiction over LG Chem.

LG Chem, in reply, argued the jurisdictional facts showed it did not serve a California market for standalone consumer batteries, and "trying to prevent the sale of a product to consumers in a forum State is the opposite of purposeful availment." * * *

C. Trial Court's Ruling

Following a hearing, the trial court issued a minute order denying LG Chem's motion to quash. * * *

DISCUSSION

I. Standard of Review

* * * [T]he jurisdictional facts are not disputed as both sides rely on the same jurisdictional evidence produced by LG Chem. We therefore review the trial court's decision de novo.

II. Specific Jurisdiction

"The Fourteenth Amendment's Due Process Clause limits a state court's power to exercise jurisdiction over a defendant." (Ford Motor Co. v. Montana Eighth Judicial Dist. Court (2021) 592 U.S. 351, 141 S.Ct. 1017, 1024, 209 L.Ed.2d 225 (*Ford Motor*); accord Bristol-Myers Squibb Co. v. Superior Court (2017) 582 U.S. 255, 137 S.Ct. 1773, 1779, 198 L.Ed.2d 395 (*Bristol-Myers*).) It "protects an individual's liberty interest in not being subject to the binding judgments of a forum with which he has established no meaningful 'contacts, ties, or relations.' By requiring that individuals have 'fair warning that a particular activity may subject [them] to the jurisdiction of a foreign sovereign,' the Due Process Clause 'gives a degree of predictability to the legal system that allows potential defendants to structure their primary conduct with some minimum assurance as to where that conduct will and will not render them liable to suit.' " (Burger King Corp. v. Rudzewicz (1985) 471 U.S. 462, 471–472, 105 S.Ct. 2174, 85 L.Ed.2d 528 (*Burger King*.)

A California court "may exercise personal jurisdiction on any basis consistent with the Constitutions of California and the United States." (see Code Civ. Proc., § 410.10.) * * *

There are "two kinds of personal jurisdiction: general (sometimes called all-purpose) jurisdiction and specific (sometimes called case-linked) jurisdiction." (*Ford Motor*.) "A state court may exercise general jurisdiction only when a defendant is 'essentially at home' in the State," over " 'any and all claims' brought against a defendant." Specific jurisdiction (the only type at issue in this case) "is different" and can be exerted over a defendant only in a particular case.

As the United States Supreme Court recently explained, specific jurisdiction "covers defendants less intimately connected with a State, but only as to a narrower class of claims. The contacts needed for this kind of jurisdiction often go by the name 'purposeful availment.' " (*Ford Motor*.) For a state to assert specific jurisdiction, the defendant "must take 'some act by which [it] purposefully avails itself of the privilege of conducting activities within the forum State.' The contacts must be the defendant's own choice and not 'random, isolated, or fortuitous.' They must show that the defendant deliberately 'reached out beyond' its home—by, for example, 'exploi[ting] a market' in the forum State or entering a contractual relationship centered there. Yet even then—because the defendant is not 'at home'—the forum State may exercise jurisdiction in only certain cases. The plaintiff's claims . . . 'must *arise out of or relate to* the defendant's contacts' with the forum." (Id., italics added.)

"The inquiry whether a forum State may assert specific jurisdiction over a nonresident defendant 'focuses on "the relationship among the defendant, the forum, and the litigation." ' " (Walden v. Fiore (2014) 571 U.S. 277, 283–284, 134 S.Ct. 1115, 188 L.Ed.2d 12.) A court may exercise specific jurisdiction over a nonresident defendant only if: (1) the defendant has purposefully availed itself of forum benefits; (2) the plaintiff's claims are related to or arise out of the defendant's contacts with the forum state; and (3) the forum state's assertion of personal jurisdiction would comport with fair play and substantial justice. (Pavlovich [v. Superior Court (2002) 29 Cal.4th 262, 269, 127 Cal.Rptr.2d 329, 58 P.3d 2 (*Pavlovich*)]; see *Ford Motor*; *Bristol-Myers*.)

On a motion to quash the service of summons on jurisdictional grounds, the plaintiff has the initial burden to prove, by a preponderance of the evidence, that the defendant had sufficient minimum contacts with the forum. "To meet this burden, a plaintiff must do more than make allegations. A plaintiff must support [his] allegations with 'competent evidence of jurisdictional facts. Allegations in an unverified complaint are insufficient to satisfy this burden of proof.' " (Rivelli v. Hemm (2021) 67 Cal.App.5th 380, 393, 282 Cal.Rptr.3d 181 (*Rivelli*).) "If the plaintiff makes this showing . . . on the first two requirements (i.e., that the defendant has purposefully availed itself of the forum and the plaintiff's claims relate to or arise out of the defendant's forum-related contacts), the burden shifts to the defendant to demonstrate that the exercise of jurisdiction would be unreasonable." (Ibid.)

The specific jurisdictional analysis is "intensely fact-specific." (*Rivelli.*) Indeed, both the United States Supreme Court and our high court have cautioned that the " 'minimum contacts' test . . . is not susceptible of mechanical application; rather, the facts of each case must be weighed to determine whether the requisite 'affiliating circumstances' are present." "[T]his determination is one in which few answers will be written 'in black and white. The greys are dominant and even among them the shades are innumerable.' "

III. Purposeful Availment

Lawhon contends, based on the undisputed evidence of LG Chem's direct sales of 18650 batteries to three California businesses for their use in electric vehicles, that LG Chem purposefully availed itself of the benefits of conducting business in California. LG Chem asserts these transactions do not satisfy the purposeful availment requirement, because the market served by these sales was not a consumer market for standalone, replaceable batteries. On this, we agree with Lawhon.

" 'The purposeful availment inquiry . . . focuses on the defendant's intentionality. This prong is only satisfied when the defendant purposefully and voluntarily directs his activities toward the forum so that he should expect, by virtue of the benefit he receives, to be subject to the court's jurisdiction based on' his contacts with the forum." (*Pavlovich.*) In a products liability case, like this one, the California Supreme Court has held that a nonresident manufacturer purposefully avails itself of the benefits of California when it takes actions "designed to consummate a business arrangement in which [it] would profit financially by selling its product for use in California," and both knows and intends that its product will "enter California and . . . be used" in this state. (Secrest Mach. Corp. v. Superior Court (1983) 33 Cal.3d 664, 671, 190 Cal.Rptr. 175, 660 P.2d 399 (*Secrest*).)

Following *Secrest*, California courts have consistently concluded that a foreign corporation purposefully avails itself of the benefits of the California forum when it knowingly sells and ships its products to California businesses for use in California. (See Jayone Foods, Inc. v. Aekyung Industrial Co. Ltd. (2019) 31 Cal.App.5th 543, 556–557, 242 Cal.Rptr.3d 705 (*Jayone Foods*) (South Korean company that "engaged in a number of direct sales transactions with multiple California distributors of its consumer products" purposefully availed itself of the benefits of doing business in California); Luberski, Inc. v. Oleficio F.LLI Amato S.R.L. (2009) 171 Cal.App.4th 409, 419, 89 Cal.Rptr.3d 774 (Italian company that sold olive oil to California businesses and delivered it to California "had the expectation that the goods . . . would be utilized in California" and thus "purposefully availed itself of the California forum").) We have little difficulty reaching the same conclusion here based on the undisputed jurisdictional facts. LG Chem sold and shipped millions of its 18650 batteries over the course of two years to three California companies for their use. These sales were substantially remunerative for LG Chem. As in *Secrest* and *Jayone Foods*, LG Chem purposefully availed itself of the benefits of doing business in California.

LG Chem seeks to refute this conclusion by pointing out that the facts of this case, in its view, compare unfavorably to the facts of *Ford Motor*. It argues that its contacts with California were not as pervasive as the contacts that Ford had with Minnesota and Montana. The difficulty with this argument is that *Ford Motor* is a relatedness case, not a purposeful availment case. In *Ford Motor*, Ford conceded purposeful availment, so the Supreme Court was not called to decide whether Ford's contacts with Minnesota or Montana met the requirements of purposeful availment. LG

Chem's efforts to distinguish its contacts with California from Ford's contacts with Minnesota and Montana in *Ford Motor* are therefore not meaningful.

Taking a different tack, LG Chem emphasizes that the market served by its sales to California was not a consumer market for standalone, replaceable batteries. It argues the evidence developed in the trial court showed it tried to prevent sales of its 18650 batteries to consumers, and that "trying to prevent the sale of a product to consumers in a forum State is the opposite of purposeful availment." This argument conflates the concepts of purposeful availment and relatedness. (See *Jayone Foods* (the connection between a manufacturer's California-directed activities and the claims at issue is a second-prong consideration on relatedness, whereas "the nature and quality of [the manufacturer's] California sales activities may be considered in deciding whether the company purposefully availed itself of the privilege of doing business in the state").) That LG Chem did not serve a consumer market in California does not dispel the conclusion it knowingly sold and shipped its products to California businesses for their use. By doing so, it purposefully availed itself of the benefits of doing business in California.

Finally, LG Chem, pointing out the absence of any demonstrated connection between its sales of batteries to its California customers on the one hand, and Vapin America, the distributor that allegedly supplied the battery that injured Lawhon, on the other, argues "[t]here is no other way" the defective battery could have made its way to Lawhon except "as the result of unilateral actions of third parties unconnected to LG Chem[.]" Relying on *Burger King,* LG Chem argues that a finding of purposeful availment cannot be based on the " 'unilateral activit[ies]' " of such unrelated third parties. As we discuss next, we agree with LG Chem that, under the facts of this case, this evidentiary gap is dispositive, but at the second prong, not the first prong, of the jurisdictional analysis. At this stage, based on the evidence of LG Chem's direct, repeated, and substantially remunerative sales to three California customers, we conclude that it purposefully availed itself of the benefits of the California forum.

IV. Relatedness

The second element of the minimum contacts test requires a connection between the plaintiff's claims and the nonresident defendant's forum activities. "In order for a state court to exercise specific jurisdiction, 'the *suit*' must 'aris[e] out of or relat[e] to the defendant's contacts with the *forum*.' " (*Bristol-Myers,* quoting *Burger King*; accord *Ford Motor*.) Stated another way, " 'specific jurisdiction is confined to adjudication of issues deriving from, or connected with, the very controversy that establishes jurisdiction.' " (*Bristol-Myers*, quoting Goodyear Dunlop Tires Operations,

S.A. v. Brown (2011) 564 U.S. 915, 919, 131 S.Ct. 2846, 180 L.Ed.2d 796 (*Goodyear*).) "When there is no such connection, specific jurisdiction is lacking regardless of the extent of a defendant's unconnected activities in the State." (*Bristol-Myers*.)

It is Lawhon's burden to prove this second prong of the specific jurisdictional analysis, and he must do that with " 'competent evidence of jurisdictional facts.' " (*Rivelli*.) In the trial court, Lawhon sought to dispatch his burden by merely demonstrating that "LG Chem is selling batteries into the California battery market and [he] was injured by a battery he purchased in California." His effort to establish a connection between LG Chem's California activities and his product liability claims ended there. He argued, and the trial court agreed, "[t]hat alone should be sufficient to establish this prong of the [jurisdictional] test."

It is not. As we explain, Lawhon's alleged injury from an 18650 battery purchased at a vape shop, whose supply chain is unknown and unconnected to LG Chem, " 'in no sense arise' " from LG Chem's sales of 18650 batteries to three California companies in the electric vehicle industry for use in electric vehicles. Nor has Lawhon established that those sales are "related enough" to his product liability claims to permit the constitutional exercise of jurisdiction over LG Chem, in *this specific suit*. (*Ford Motor*.)

But, citing *Ford Motor*, Lawhon argues that this is the " 'paradigm case of specific jurisdiction' " because LG Chem " 'serves a market' " for a product in California, "namely, a market for 18650 lithium-ion batteries, 'and the product malfunction[ed] there.' " The Supreme Court did say in *Ford Motor*, that under its precedent, "specific jurisdiction attaches in cases identical to the ones here—when a company like Ford serves a market for a product in the forum State and the product malfunctions there." However, Lawhon's reliance on this isolated quotation overlooks the chasm that exists between his case and *Ford Motor*.

In *Ford Motor*, a driver of a Ford Explorer was killed in Montana when the tread separated from a rear tire, and a passenger in a Crown Victoria suffered serious brain damage when his airbag failed to deploy in a crash that occurred in Minnesota. Each plaintiff sued Ford in the forum where the accident occurred, asserting products liability claims. Ford argued each state's court "had jurisdiction only if the company's conduct in the State had given rise to the plaintiff's claims," and that "causal link" did not exist because Ford did not design, manufacture, or sell in either state "the particular vehicle involved in the accident." Ford designed the models in Michigan, manufactured them in Kentucky and Canada, and had originally sold the cars at issue outside the forum States. It was only through later resales and relocations by consumers that the cars entered Montana and Minnesota.

The Supreme Court rejected "Ford's causation-only approach" as inconsistent with its own precedent, noting that its "most common formulation of the rule demands that the suit 'arise out of *or relate to* the defendant's contacts with the forum.' " The Court explained that it has "never framed the specific jurisdiction inquiry as *always* requiring proof of causation—i.e., proof that the plaintiff's claim came about because of the defendant's in-state conduct.") Rather, "[t]he first half of that standard asks about causation; but the back half, after the 'or,' contemplates that *some* relationships will support jurisdiction without a causal showing.") The high court then found that Ford's was *one* of those relationships that supported jurisdiction without a causal showing.

"To see why Ford is subject to jurisdiction," the Supreme Court first considered "the business that the company regularly conducts in Montana and Minnesota." "By every means imaginable—among them, billboards, TV and radio spots, print ads, and direct mail—Ford urges Montanans and Minnesotans to buy its vehicles," including the models involved in the accidents. Ford also "encourage[s]" and "fosters an active resale market for its old models." Not only did Ford offer those models for sale, "new or used, [at dealerships] throughout the States," it also "work[ed] hard to foster ongoing connections to its cars' owners" by regularly maintaining and repairing them at its local dealerships and distributing replacement parts through dealerships and auto shops in each state. Through its "veritable truckload of contacts," Ford had "encourage[d] Montanans and Minnesotans to become lifelong Ford drivers."

Based on those in-state activities, the Supreme Court concluded Ford had "*systematically* served a market in Montana and Minnesota for the very vehicles that the plaintiffs allege malfunctioned and injured them in those States. So there is a strong 'relationship among the defendant, the forum, and the litigation'—the 'essential foundation' of specific jurisdiction." It is in this context, which Lawhon omits, that the Supreme Court said "specific jurisdiction attaches in cases identical to the ones here—when a company like Ford serves a market for a product in the forum State and the product malfunctions there."

Moreover, although the majority in *Ford Motor* was clear there is not "always" a requirement of a "strict causal relationship between the defendant's in-state activity and the litigation," in response to a contention made by Ford, it went on to suggest that a causal link *might* be found in the case. Ford asserted that since it was consumers who later sold the cars at issue to the States' residents, the plaintiffs' claims would be "just the same" without Ford's contacts with Montana or Minnesota. Addressing this contention, the majority found "that assumption is far from clear. For the owners of these cars might never have bought them, and so these suits might never have arisen, except for Ford's contacts with their home States." The majority observed that the consumer may purchase the car because of Ford's extensive advertisement, in-state activities "designed to make driving a Ford convenient there"—such as, servicing Ford cars, providing parts—and because "Ford fosters an active resale market for its old models." In other words, Ford, by its in-state *conduct*, had fostered the very sort of consumer behavior that undergirded each plaintiff's claim.

We disagree that *Ford Motor* is anything like the case before us. The undisputed facts establish that LG Chem did not advertise, market or solicit buyers—original equipment manufacturers *or* individual consumers—for its 18650 batteries. The business LG Chem regularly conducted in California consisted of sales of 18650 batteries as industrial component parts to three companies in the electric vehicle industry, for use in electric vehicles. More to the point, unlike the Minnesota and Montana markets served by Ford, the market served by LG Chem's California sales was *not* a consumer market. * * * LG Chem took steps to prevent precisely Lawhon's consumer behavior by placing warning labels on its 18650 batteries and requiring its business customers to sign declarations of commitment promising not to resell its batteries to individual consumers. Thus, unlike *Ford Motor*, it cannot be said (nor is it even alleged) that LG Chem cultivated and "systematically served a market" for consumer purchase or use of its 18650 batteries as standalone replacements.

Under *Ford Motor*, it is not enough to satisfy the second prong of the jurisdictional analysis to simply demonstrate that a company " 'serves *a* market' " for a product in California " 'and the product malfunction[ed] there,' " as Lawhon asserts. (Italics added.) "Serves *a* market" does not mean "serves *any* market." Although under *Ford Motor* specific jurisdiction can attach on a lesser, " 'relate to' " showing, the majority cautioned, "[t]hat does not mean anything goes. In the sphere of specific jurisdiction, the phrase 'relate to' incorporates real limits, as it must to adequately protect defendants foreign to a forum." Lawhon, by ignoring the context of the *Ford Motor* quotation he relies on, seeks to lower the bar on the relatedness test, turning it into an "anything goes" approach to specific jurisdiction.

Essentially, Lawhon contends that specific jurisdiction can be exerted over LG Chem wherever it sold its 18650 batteries, even if, as here, it deliberately limited its sales to a narrow range of businesses and tailored these transactions to avoid a consumer market. Under his contention, there would potentially be personal jurisdiction over a company in a consumer's product liability claim in any jurisdiction that is part of the product's distribution chain. That goes too far. "[T]he foreseeability that is critical to [a] due process analysis is not the mere likelihood that a product will find its way into the forum State. Rather, it is that the defendant's conduct and connection with the forum State are such that he should reasonably anticipate being haled into court there." (World-Wide Volkswagen Corp. v. Woodson (1980) 444 U.S. 286, 297, 100 S.Ct. 559, 62 L.Ed.2d 490 (*World-Wide Volkswagen*); *Ford Motor* (the minimum contacts "doctrine ...

provides defendants with 'fair warning'—knowledge that 'a particular activity may subject [it] to the jurisdiction of a foreign sovereign' ").)

Here, the undisputed facts show LG Chem deliberately structured its transactions to prevent 18650 batteries from being used by individual California consumers, like Lawhon, as standalone replacement batteries. "The Due Process Clause . . . 'gives a degree of predictability to the legal system that allows [LG Chem] to structure [its] primary conduct with some minimum assurance as to where *that conduct* will and will not render [it] liable to suit." (*Burger King,* italics added.) On this record, Lawhon fails to establish that LG Chem's contacts with California gave it fair warning of the possibility of being sued in California by an individual consumer claiming injury from a loose 18650 battery purchased in a vape shop.[8]

Lawhon contends it does not matter that LG Chem's sales are only to "authorized businesses" for use as industrial component parts in electric vehicles and that he purchased a loose battery "outside LG Chem's distribution process," or that LG Chem "has no idea how these batteries end up in California vape shops for resale." Because under his reading of *Ford Motor*, "a plaintiff need not prove there is a causal connection between their injuries and a defendant's in-state conduct." In his words, he "need not prove that his battery left an LG Chem manufacturing plant in Korea, jumped on a freightliner, arrived in a California port, and was transported to Vapin' the 619." Lawhon's focus on causation misses the mark. Evidence of what happened downstream in the distribution chain once LG Chem shipped its 18650 batteries to its business customers is relevant to whether Lawhon's claims are related to those sales.

On this point, *Bristol-Myers* is instructive. In *Bristol-Myers*, a group of plaintiffs consisting of California residents and residents of other States sued Bristol-Myers Squibb (BMS), alleging the company's drug Plavix had damaged their health. The nonresident plaintiffs did not allege that they obtained Plavix (which was designed and manufactured outside of California) in California or from any other California source or that they were injured by Plavix in California. Based on these facts, the United States Supreme Court held specific jurisdiction was lacking because there was no connection between California and the nonresident plaintiffs' specific claims. But in what the Court described as "a last ditch contention," the nonresident plaintiffs asserted that BMS's " 'decision to contract with

---

[8] Lawhon contends that LG Chem has previously appeared as a defendant in 18 lawsuits in California involving claims of personal injury from 18650 batteries, but he does not develop this point further. The relevance of this contention is not clear. If it is being suggested that the existence of these other lawsuits gave LG Chem fair warning of the possibility of being sued in California for personal injury claims like Lawhon's, we disagree. (See *Burger King* ("Although it has been argued that foreseeability of causing *injury* in another State should be sufficient to establish such contacts there when policy considerations so require, the United States Supreme Court has consistently held that this kind of foreseeability is not a 'sufficient benchmark' for exercising personal jurisdiction."), quoting *World-Wide Volkswagen.*)

a California company [McKesson] to distribute [Plavix] nationally' provides a sufficient basis for personal jurisdiction." The Court rejected that contention, finding "[t]he bare fact that BMS contracted with a California distributor is not enough to establish personal jurisdiction in the State." It noted that "[i]n this case, it is not alleged that BMS engaged in relevant acts together with McKesson in California . . . . *And the nonresidents 'have adduced no evidence to show how or by whom the Plavix they took was distributed to the pharmacies that dispensed it to them.'* " (Ibid., italics added.)

Here, the jurisdictional facts developed by Lawhon suffer from a similar evidentiary gap. Although Lawhon has established that LG Chem sold 18650 batteries to three companies in California, he has " 'adduced no evidence to show how or by whom the [allegedly defective 18650 battery] was distributed to' " the vape industry wholesaler (Vapin America) and retailer (Vapin' the 619) that ultimately sold it to him. Nor does he show that LG Chem "engaged in relevant acts together with" its three California customers. Indeed, Lawhon concedes his evidence showed "that after LG Chem sells an 18650 lithium-ion battery to a customer in California, the battery's final destination is no longer within LG Chem's control." As in *Bristol-Myers*, the "bare fact" that LG Chem "contracted with" California companies in the electric vehicle industry "is not enough to establish personal jurisdiction in [this] State." That is because, "even regularly occurring sales of a product in a State do not justify the exercise of jurisdiction over a claim *unrelated to those sales*." (*Goodyear*, italics added; accord *Bristol-Myers*.)

Yet, the trial court ruled "it [wa]s sufficient that LG Chem shipped and sold 18650 lithium-ion batteries in California and one such battery allegedly caused [Lawhon] harm." The trial court's reliance on LG Chem's sales of 18650 batteries to three California companies for use in electric vehicles looks like the " 'sliding scale approach' " that the Supreme Court rejected in *Bristol-Myers*. Under that approach, which the high court stated "resembles a loose and spurious form of general jurisdiction," "the strength of the requisite connection between the forum and the specific claims at issue is relaxed if the defendant has extensive forum contacts that are unrelated to those claims." Finding no precedential support for this approach, the Court reiterated: "For specific jurisdiction, a defendant's general connections with the forum are not enough . . . . '[A] corporation's "continuous activity of some sorts within a state . . . is not enough to support the demand that the corporation be amenable to suits unrelated to that activity." ' " (Ibid., quoting *Goodyear*.) Since Lawhon's products liability claims have no demonstrated connection to LG Chem's sales of 18650 batteries in California, specific jurisdiction is lacking.[9]

* * *

Lawhon failed to meet his threshold burden of establishing that the required connection exists between LG Chem's sales of 18650 batteries to three California companies, for use as industrial component parts in electric vehicles, and his injuries from a standalone 18650 battery purchased at a vape shop. As a result, the trial court may not exercise personal jurisdiction over LG Chem in this products liability case consistent with the Constitutions of California and the United States. It erred in denying LG Chem's motion to quash.

* * *

FORUM NON CONVENIENS

GUIMEI V. GENERAL ELECTRIC CO.

California Court of Appeal, Second District, 2009.
172 Cal.App.4th 689, 91 Cal.Rptr.3d 178.

JACKSON, ASSOCIATE JUSTICE.

INTRODUCTION

Plaintiffs Zhang Guimei[a] et al. * * * appeal from an order staying their consolidated actions on the ground of forum non conveniens. The order was made on the motion of defendants General Electric Co., Bombardier, Inc., Bombardier Aerospace Corp. and China Eastern Airlines Co., Ltd. We affirm.

FACTUAL AND PROCEDURAL BACKGROUND

A. The Parties and the Airplane Crash

On November 21, 2004, China Eastern Yunnan Airlines [later named China Eastern Airlines or CEA] flight MU5210, flying from Baotou in Inner Mongolia to Shanghai, crashed into a lake shortly after takeoff. Forty-seven passengers, six crew members and two people on the ground were killed. With the exception of one Indonesian passenger, all of the victims were Chinese citizens. All of the passengers purchased their tickets in China. All of the crew members were licensed by the General Civil Aviation Administration of China.[1]

---

[9] Because Lawhon has not met his threshold burden of demonstrating facts justifying the exercise of jurisdiction, we need not and do not consider whether the exercise of jurisdiction over LG Chem would comport with fair play and substantial justice.

[a] Note that the plaintiff's surname is Zhang, but this opinion is typically, if incorrectly, cited using her given name in the caption.

[1] "China" in this case refers to the People's Republic of China.

[The airline's] hub of operations and repair and maintenance facilities were located at Wu Jia Ba Airport in Kumming, Yunnan China. * * *

The airplane was a Bombardier CRJ 200 LR Regional Jet, designed, manufactured, assembled and tested in Canada by defendant Bombardier, Inc. (Bombardier). Bombardier is a Canadian Corporation with its principal place of business in Montreal, Quebec, Canada. Bombardier does not conduct business in California. It sold the airplane to China Aviation Supplies Import and Export Corporation in Quebec in 2002.

Defendant Bombardier Aerospace Corporation (Bombardier Aerospace) is a Delaware Corporation with its principal place of business in Richardson, Texas. It did not design, manufacture, assemble, sell or service the airplane.

The airplane was powered by two Model CF34 turbojet engines designed and manufactured by defendant General Electric Co. (GE). GE is incorporated in New York and has its principal place of business in Fairfield, Connecticut. The engines were not designed, manufactured, assembled, tested or shipped in California.

B. The Complaints and the Forum Non Conveniens Motion

* * *

[The plaintiffs began to file their suits in California Superior Court in 2005. They were consolidated in February 2006.] On February 24, 2006, [defendants] moved to dismiss, or in the alternative stay, the actions on the ground of forum non conveniens (Motion). [They] claimed California was not a convenient forum for trial of the actions, and China provided an adequate alternative forum for trial. * * *

As part of their Motion, CEA made a commitment that, if the motion were granted, it would (1) not contest liability in the four actions in the Chinese courts; (2) completely compensate the plaintiffs in accordance with Chinese law and not seek to enforce limitations on wrongful death damages; (3) waive any applicable statutes of limitations so long as the actions were refiled in China within six months of the dismissal or stay; (4) be bound by and satisfy any judgment in the Chinese court following any appropriate appeals.

GE, Bombardier and Bombardier Aerospace similarly agreed they would (1) submit to personal jurisdiction in China; (2) waive any applicable statutes of limitations so long as the actions were refiled in China within six months of the dismissal or stay; (3) accept service of process; (4) comply with discovery orders; and (5) satisfy any final judgment in the Chinese court.

* * *

C. The Trial Court's Ruling

The trial court granted defendants' motion and stayed the consolidated actions for the purpose of permitting proceedings in China. It scheduled status conferences every six months in order to monitor the proceedings. The trial court's ruling was conditioned on the agreements set forth above.

The trial court explained that the first issue to be resolved was whether there was a suitable alternative forum in which plaintiffs could obtain a judgment against defendants, one in which defendants are subject to the court's jurisdiction and the cause of action is not barred by the statute of limitations. (Stangvik v. Shiley Inc. (1991) 54 Cal.3d 744, 752, fn. 3, 1 Cal.Rptr.2d 556, 819 P.2d 14.) Here, defendants unquestionably are subject to the jurisdiction of the Chinese courts, and they agreed to waive the statute of limitations. This makes China a suitable forum, even if California law is more favorable to plaintiffs or recovery would be more difficult in China.

An exception to this rule arises if the remedy provided by the alternative forum is so inadequate as to amount to no remedy at all. This exception may arise where the alternative forum is in a foreign country controlled by a totalitarian regime in which there is no independent judiciary or due process of law. (Piper Aircraft Co. v. Reyno (1981) 454 U.S. 235, 254 & fn. 22, 102 S.Ct. 252, 70 L.Ed.2d 419.) The question before the court was whether the exception applies here. Plaintiffs claimed it did, and that they could not get a fair trial in China.

The trial court rejected this claim. It noted that plaintiffs "present evidence from distinguished academics providing anecdotal evidence, or evidence about the Chinese judicial system's record on issues of human rights and political dissidents, and cases involving challenges to governmental actions. Plaintiffs present evidence that CEA is a government-owned entity, the government is seeking to encourage foreign companies like Bombardier and GE to invest, the courts are under Communist Party leadership, cases are often subject to local protectionism, trials are not public in the sense we understand openness, lower courts seek advice or instruction from a higher court without informing the parties, there is corruption among judges, and judges are often uneducated."

The trial court agreed that "[s]ome or all of these factors may be serious problems in the Chinese judicial system." It was not persuaded to the contrary by defendants' evidence "that this case is likely to be filed in Shanghai, a sophisticated jurisdiction with educated judges and numerous lawyers, China follows the rule of law, state-owned enterprises lose many civil suits in China, plaintiffs prevail in 20–40% of administrative claims against the government, litigants in Shanghai often perceive their case to properly turn on facts and law and not improper influences, and local protectionism is a problem that is less likely in Shanghai."

The trial court was not persuaded by the "general evidence" submitted by both sides. The evidence "shows a legal system in the growing stages, not a fully mature legal system endowed with judges and juries who follow the rule of law where ever it leads." But this did not establish that plaintiffs would be unlikely to get basic justice if the case were to be tried in China. Plaintiffs failed to present evidence of a personal injury or wrongful death case against a government owned or controlled entity "that has been the subject of the manipulation and interference they fear. Nor have they presented admissible evidence that they are likely to be mistreated."

* * *

The trial court also noted that CEA had agreed not to contest liability and had already paid $2.8 million to settle claims arising from water contamination caused by the crash. There was no evidence CEA had "exerted any kind of political influence against the Plaintiffs or their representatives." There was "no evidence of any sinister conduct on the part of CEA with respect to this lawsuit or the parties thereto." The court also found no reason to suspect there would be government interference in the litigation against Bombardier, Bombardier Aerospace and GE.

The trial court then considered the second issue before it, a balancing of the private interests of the litigants against the public interest in retaining the litigation in California. It concluded that California had "little or no interest in this case. There are no witnesses or documents in California, whereas there are witnesses and evidence in China. California has no interest in requiring its courts and juries to hear a case having no nexus to it."

DISCUSSION

A. *Standard of Review*

Just as the trial court's determination of a forum non conveniens motion is a two-step process, review of that determination requires two separate steps. First, we determine whether substantial evidence supports the trial court's finding as to whether a suitable alternative forum exists. In making this determination, there is no balancing of interests or exercise of discretion.

Second, we review the trial court's determination on balancing private and public interests for abuse of discretion. * * *

B. *Whether China Is an Adequate Alternative Forum for Litigation of Plaintiffs' Product Liability Claims*

An alternative forum is suitable if it has jurisdiction and the action in that forum will not be barred by the statute of limitations. It bears emphasis that "[i]t is sufficient that the action can be brought, although not necessarily won, in the suitable alternative forum." That the law is less favorable to the plaintiffs in the alternative forum, or that recovery would be more difficult if not impossible, is irrelevant to the determination whether the forum is suitable unless "the alternative forum provides no remedy at all."

The "no remedy at all" exception applies "only in 'rare circumstances,' such as where the alternative forum is a foreign country whose courts are ruled by a dictatorship, so that there is no independent judiciary or due process of law." "This exception has been applied in cases where the proposed alternative forum is in a foreign country that lacks an independent judiciary. For example, in Rasoulzadeh v. Associated Press (S.D.N.Y.1983) 574 F.Supp. 854, 861, the court held that an alternative forum in Iran was not available since the courts there were administered by Iranian mullahs and the plaintiffs were likely to be shot if they returned to Iran. Similarly in Phoenix Canada Oil Co. Ltd. v. Texaco, Inc. (D.Del.1978) 78 F.R.D. 445, 455, the court found that Ecuador was not a suitable forum since it did not have an independent judiciary. Courts controlled by a military junta in Chile were likewise found unsuitable."

However, as cases cited by plaintiffs make clear, in order to defeat a forum non conveniens motion, plaintiffs must show more than general allegations of corruption, lack of due process or other factors making an alternative forum unsuitable. * * *

With respect to Chinese courts, plaintiffs claim that "there is increasing recognition that Chinese courts are sub-par." The cases they cite do not support their claim, much less a claim that the "no remedy at all" exception applies.

In S & D Trading Academy, LLC v. AAFIS, Inc. (S.D.Tex.2007) 494 F.Supp.2d 558, the court found that China was a suitable alternative forum, in that Chinese law recognized plaintiffs causes of action, and defendant agreed to submit to the jurisdiction of the Chinese court. The court did refer to "the current nationwide concern about China's lackadaisical enforcement of intellectual property rights," but this was in the context of the balancing of public and private interests, the court noting that this concern "heightens local interest in cases in which international corporations are accused of wrongfully using and profiting from U.S. intellectual property."

* * *

In other cases, China has been accepted as a suitable alternative forum. In Sinochem Int'l Co. v. Malaysia Int'l Shipping Corp. (2007) 549 U.S. 422, 127 S.Ct. 1184, 167 L.Ed.2d 15, the court found the litigation should be dismissed on forum non conveniens grounds based on the pendency of litigation in China. * * *

The trial court, as trier of fact, has the duty to weigh and interpret the evidence and draw reasonable inferences therefrom. We cannot reweigh the evidence or draw contrary inferences. * * *

In support of their forum non conveniens motion, defendants presented the declarations of Randall Peerenboom (Peerenboom) and Jacques deLisle (deLisle). Peerenboom is a professor of law at UCLA, where he has taught on Chinese law. He has written extensively on Chinese law, has worked with Chinese law firms and has been an expert witness on Chinese law.

Peerenboom opined that "that the Chinese courts available to plaintiffs provide an adequate forum in this case." This opinion was based, in part, on Chinese law which provides procedures for multiparty commercial litigation and a right to appeal. It also was based on plaintiffs' ability to choose the venue for the litigation. The choices included Shanghai, where CEA's headquarters were located, whose intermediate court is experienced in handling cases such as the instant one.

Peerenboom disagreed with plaintiffs' "experts attempt to put the entire Chinese legal system on trial." He pointed out that most of the problems with the Chinese legal system arose in politically sensitive cases as opposed to commercial cases such as the instant one. Additionally, evidence showed corruption in Chinese courts was decreasing and was less than that of courts in other countries with similar levels of per capita income.

Peerenboom also noted substantial monetary awards to airplane crash victims in another case, no basis for concern about local protectionism in Shanghai courts, and the availability of counsel in China able to represent plaintiffs. He concluded that "[t]he problems and issues discussed at length by the Plaintiffs and their experts are either not applicable in this case or not a bar to a fair trial."

DeLisle is a professor at the University of Pennsylvania School of Law, who teaches on Chinese law, has authored numerous publications and has been an expert witness on Chinese law. DeLisle opined that the declarations of plaintiffs' experts "paint a picture of the Chinese judiciary and legal system that is far darker than the relevant reality warrants and rely on examples and interpretations that are misleading or potentially so." * * *

In particular, deLisle pointed to the increase in foreign investment in China, which has created a need for a sophisticated, well-functioning legal system. China now has many large law firms as well as branch offices of foreign law firms. DeLisle noted that while practice in China "has frustrations and disappointments," it is not consistent with plaintiffs' picture of a deeply flawed legal system irreconcilable with the professional norms and experiences of lawyers' trained in the United States and other Western countries.

Like Peerenboom, deLisle pointed out that Shanghai boasts a legal system superior to that in other areas of China. It has a high percentage of large and foreign law firms and lawyers educated at elite universities, as well as judges who are "far better and more professionally educated than their counterparts in most of China." Additionally, courts in Shanghai have experience handling cases involving multiple plaintiffs.

According to deLisle, "[l]ocal protectionism and related phenomena are significant problems in China, but they are not nearly as pervasive as plaintiffs imagine." For a number of reasons, they are not a problem in Shanghai. The courts there serve the entire province and are more professional than in other areas. Additionally, CEA is not a local company but is owned by a holding company which is a central body which holds a vast portfolio of state-owned interests. Further, "defendants are not major components of the local economy—a key factor in local protectionism."

DeLisle also noted that "China long ago abandoned the idea that state-owned enterprises (much less partly state-owned ones) are immune from legal liability in Chinese (or foreign) courts. State-owned or largely state-owned enterprises lose many civil lawsuits in China." The Chinese government "increasingly has emphasized the need for the law and courts to protect consumers and ordinary Chinese against harms caused by illegal, careless or otherwise rights-infringing behavior by enterprises."

Plaintiffs go to great lengths to attack the credibility of Peerenboom and deLisle as compared to that of their own experts, whose declarations painted a completely different picture of the legal system in China. * * *

As stated above, it is the trial court, as trier of fact, which must weigh and interpret the evidence and draw reasonable inferences therefrom. We cannot reweigh the evidence or draw contrary inferences. Neither can we reject evidence accepted by the trial court as true unless it is physically impossible or its falsity is obvious without resort to inference or deduction. The evidence of Peerenboom and deLisle does not fall into this category. We thus must accept it as substantial evidence in support of the trial court's finding that China, indeed, provides a suitable alternative forum for this litigation.

C. Whether the Trial Court Abused Its Discretion in Finding Trial of Plaintiffs' Claims in California Would Be So Inconvenient As to Justify Granting the Motion

Once it is determined that there is a suitable alternative forum, the trial court must weigh the private interests of the parties against the interests of the public in retaining the action in California. "The private interest factors are those that make trial and the enforceability of the ensuing judgment expeditious and relatively inexpensive, such as the ease of access to sources of proof, the cost of obtaining attendance of witnesses, and the availability of compulsory process for attendance of unwilling witnesses. The public interest factors include avoidance of overburdening local courts with congested calendars, protecting the interests of potential jurors so that they are not called upon to decide cases in which the local community has little concern, and weighing the competing interests of California and the alternate jurisdiction in the litigation." The trial court has great flexibility in weighing these factors; no one factor is determinative.

We conclude the trial court did not abuse its discretion in determining that California is a seriously inconvenient forum. The trial court found California has "little or no interest in this case. * * *"

These "private interest factors support the conclusion that China is the more convenient forum. The events that are subject to this action occurred exclusively in China. It is thus reasonable to assume that there will be more Chinese witnesses than United States witnesses (if any). Moreover, the relevant evidence is much more likely to be found in China. Indeed, Chinese [aviation] authorities have already conducted an investigation into the incident; the evidence they gathered is in China, Chinese courts would be able to compel the attendance of witnesses located there, it will be less burdensome for those witnesses to attend proceedings in China. . . . To the extent proximity to the location of the collision will assist the finder-of-fact, that factor naturally supports a conclusion that China is more convenient. Although . . . a number of witnesses and other evidence is located in countries other than China, as between the United States and China, the latter has substantially better access to the sources of proof."

Plaintiffs argue that most or all of Bombardier, Bombardier Aerospace and G.E.'s documents relating to the plane and engines involved in the crash are located in the United States or Canada. "The fact that some evidence concerning the aircraft's design and manufacture may be located elsewhere in the United States does not make [California] a convenient forum."

More importantly, all defendants have committed to participating in trial of the action in China, including submitting to the court's jurisdiction, complying with discovery and paying any judgments against them. These factors, too, weigh in favor of trying the case in China.

That plaintiffs selected California as the forum state is of little consequence. While a resident plaintiff's choice of California as the forum state is afforded substantial weight, a nonresident plaintiff's choice is given less deference. "Although [plaintiffs] claim that they are motivated by the convenience of the place of trial, this court, like others before it, recognizes that an additional motivating factor-and perhaps the major one-relates to the circumstance that trial in California will enhance the possibility of substantial recovery." There can be no other reason; none of the plaintiffs has any connection to California, and defendants' connections are greatly attenuated. To the extent the trial court gave little deference to plaintiffs' choice of California as the forum state, it did not abuse its discretion.

Finally, "[i]t seems unduly burdensome for California residents to be expected to serve as jurors on [what promises to be a long and complicated] case having so little to do with California." Additionally, inasmuch as defendants are not California corporations, California has little interest in keeping the litigation in this state to deter future wrongful conduct. Therefore, public interest factors as well favor trial of the matter in China.

Plaintiffs further contend that the trial court's decision "fails to offer a reasoned basis for finding that trial of plaintiffs' claims in the United States would be so inconvenient as to justify dismissal." First, the trial court did not dismiss the instant actions; it stayed them. In the unlikely event that China proves to be an unsuitable alternative forum, the action here may proceed.

Second, we believe the trial court's decision does offer a reasoned basis for finding that trial of the action in California—which is home to none of the parties and where the airplane crash did not occur—would be so inconvenient as to justify staying the action so that it can proceed in China—where the airplane crash occurred, which is home to the vast majority of the plaintiffs and one of the defendants, and where all defendants have agreed to be bound by the judgment of the court.

* * *

By staying the actions, the trial court retained the power to verify both that plaintiffs are able to bring their actions in China and that defendants live up to their stipulations. That is, the trial court can monitor the progress of the litigation in China at its scheduled six-month status conferences, to ensure that the Chinese courts accept jurisdiction by permitting plaintiffs to file and present their claims, and that defendants submit to the jurisdiction of the Chinese courts, do nothing to thwart plaintiffs' ability to try their cases and satisfy any final judgments against them in the Chinese court. If for any reason defendants do not act in accordance with their stipulations, the trial court can revisit the question whether to try the actions.

We note that the trial court's periodic review of the proceedings in China is limited to the procedural aspects of the proceedings, not their merits. Additionally, if it is plaintiffs rather than defendants who thwart the proceedings, the trial court need not continue to stay the action but may dismiss it.

PLEADING

COMMITTEE ON CHILDREN'S TELEVISION, INC. v. GENERAL FOODS CORP.

Supreme Court of California, In Bank, 1983.
35 Cal.3d 197, 197 Cal.Rptr. 783, 673 P.2d 660.

BROUSSARD, JUSTICE.

Plaintiffs appeal from a judgment of dismissal following a trial court order sustaining demurrers without leave to amend to their fourth amended complaint. The complaint essentially charges defendants—General Foods Corporation, Safeway Stores, and two advertising agencies—with fraudulent, misleading and deceptive advertising in the marketing of sugared breakfast cereals. The trial court found its allegations insufficient because they fail to state with specificity the advertisements containing the alleged misrepresentations. We review the allegations of the complaint and conclude that the trial court erred in sustaining demurrers without leave to amend to plaintiffs' causes of action charging fraud and violation of laws against unfair competition and deceptive advertising.

I. SUMMARY OF THE PLEADINGS AND PROCEDURE

Plaintiffs filed their original complaint on June 30, 1977, as a class action on behalf of "California residents who have been misled or deceived, or are threatened with the likelihood of being deceived or misled," by defendants in connection with the marketing of sugared cereals.[1] The named plaintiffs included five organizations (The Committee on Children's Television, Inc.; the California Society of Dentistry for Children; the American G.I. Forum of California; the Mexican-American Political Association; the League of United Latin American Citizens), individual adults, and individual children.*

The principal defendant is General Foods Corporation, the manufacturer of five "sugared cereals"—Alpha Bits, Honeycomb, Fruity Pebbles, Sugar Crisp, and Cocoa Pebbles—which contain from 38 to 50

---

1 Defendants' demurrers did not attack the description of the class or the suitability of the case as a class action. Questions concerning the certification of the class remain to be resolved in further proceedings.

* [Ed.] At the time *Committee on Children's Television* was decided, California law authorized any person acting for the general public to sue for relief from unfair competition. Because the voters approved Proposition 64 at the November 2, 2004, General Election, a private person or entity now has standing to sue only if he or she "has suffered injury in fact and has lost money or property as a result of such unfair competition." Californians For Disability Rights v. Mervyn's, LLC, 39 Cal.4th 223, 227, 46 Cal.Rptr.3d 57, 59, 138 P.3d 207 (2006).

percent sugar by weight. The other corporate defendants are two advertising agencies—Benton and Bowles, Inc., and Ogilvy & Mather International, Inc.—which handled advertising of these cereals, and Safeway Stores, which sold the products to plaintiffs. Finally, the complaint includes as defendants numerous officers and employees of the corporate defendants.

When the court sustained a demurrer to the third amended complaint, it ruled that no cause of action could be stated on behalf of the organizational plaintiffs. The individual plaintiffs remaining then filed their fourth amended complaint; the validity of this complaint is the principal issue on appeal.

The fourth amended complaint presents seven causes of action: two based upon consumer protection statutes, four sounding in fraud, and one for breach of warranty. The first cause of action is based on Business and Professions Code sections 17200–17208, the unfair competition law. Paragraph 34 alleges that defendants "engaged in a sophisticated advertising and marketing program which is designed to capitalize on the unique susceptibilities of children and preschoolers in order to induce them to consume products which, although promoted and labeled as 'cereals,' are in fact more accurately described as sugar products, or candies." The complaint thereafter refers to sugared cereals as "candy breakfasts."

Paragraph 35 lists some 19 representations allegedly made in television commercials aimed at children. Most of these representations are not explicit but, according to plaintiffs, implicit in the advertising. * * *[3]

---

[3] Paragraph 35 of the complaint reads as follows:

35. The advertising scheme routinely and repeatedly employs and utilizes, in commercials aimed at children, each of the following representations which are conveyed both visually and verbally:

(a) Children and young children who regularly eat candy breakfasts are bigger, stronger, more energetic, happier, more invulnerable, and braver than they would have been if they did not eat candy breakfasts.

(b) Eating candy breakfasts is a "fun" thing for children to do, and is invariably equated with entertainment and adventure.

(c) The sweet taste of a product ensures or correlates with nutritional merit.

(d) Eating candy breakfasts will make children happy.

(e) Bright colors in foods ensure or correlate with nutritional merit.

(f) Candy breakfasts are grain products.

(g) Candy breakfasts are more healthful and nutritious for a child than most other kinds and types of cereals.

(h) Adding small amounts of vitamins and minerals to a product automatically makes it "nutritious".

(i) Candy breakfasts inherently possess and/or impart to those ingesting them magical powers, such as the capacity to cause apes and fantastic creatures to appear or disappear.

(j) Candy breakfasts contain adequate amounts of the essential elements of a growing child's diet, including protein.

Plaintiffs allege that commercials containing these representations are broadcast daily. Although the commercials changed every 60 days, "they retain consistent themes and each convey . . . the representations as set forth." Defendants, but not plaintiffs, know the exact times, dates, and places of broadcasts. Plaintiffs further allege that the same representations appear in other media, and on the cereal packages themselves.

Paragraph 42 asserts that defendants concealed material facts, such as the sugar content of their products, that "[t]here is no honey in Honeycomb, no fruit in Fruity Pebbles," that sugared cereals contribute to tooth decay and can have more serious medical consequences, and that they cost more per serving than breakfast foods of greater nutritional value. Such concealment, plaintiffs allege, when joined with the affirmative misrepresentations listed in paragraph 35, render the advertisements misleading and deceptive.

The complaint asserts at length the special susceptibility of children to defendants' "advertising scheme," and explains how defendants take advantage of this vulnerability. It further asserts that, as defendants know, the desires and beliefs of children influence and often determine the decision of adults to buy certain breakfast foods. Finally, claiming that defendants will continue deceptive practices unless enjoined, the first cause of action seeks injunctive relief, plus restitution of monies paid for "candy breakfasts."

(k) The "premiums" (small toys packaged in with the candy breakfast as an inducement to the child) are very valuable and are offered free as a prize in each box of candy breakfast.

(*l*) Candy breakfasts are the most important part of a "well-balanced breakfast" and are at least as nutritious as milk, toast and juice.

(m) Candy breakfasts calm a child's fears and dispel a child's anxiety. . . .

(n) Candy breakfasts have visual characteristics which they do not in fact possess, such as vivid colors and the capacity to glitter or to enlarge from their actual size to a larger size.

In addition to the foregoing representations specified in Paragraph 35(a) through (n), in each of the commercials for each of the products specified below the advertising scheme repeatedly, uniformly and consistently utilizes and relies upon the following representations with respect to particular products:

(*o*) Cocoa Pebbles are good for a child to eat whenever he or she is hungry, and it is a sound nutritional practice to eat chocolatey tasting foods, such as Cocoa Pebbles, for breakfast.

(p) Honeycomb (i) contains honey and (ii) consists of pieces which are each at least two (2) inches in diameter and (iii) will make a child big and strong.

(q) Alpha-Bits (i) will enable a child to conquer his or her enemies, (ii) can be used by a child easily to spell words in his or her spoon, (iii) are an effective cure for the child's anxieties, and (iv) have magical powers and can impart magical powers to a child. . . .

(r) Fruity Pebbles (i) contain fruit and (ii) emit auras, rainbows or mesmerizing colors.

(s) Super Sugar Crisp (i) should be eaten as a snack food without danger to dental health, (ii) should be eaten as a nutritious snack whenever a child is hungry, (iii) makes a child smart and (iv) is coated with golden sugar and such sugar is very valuable.

* * *

The third through sixth causes of action set out various aspects of the tort of fraud. The third cause of action charges deliberate fraud in violation of Civil Code section 1710, subdivision 1. Incorporating the allegations of the first cause of action, it adds allegations of plaintiffs' reasonable reliance upon defendants' representations, especially in light of defendants' claim to superior knowledge about the nutritional value of foods. The fourth cause of action adds allegations of negligent misrepresentation (Civ.Code, § 1710, subd. 2); the fifth cause of action adds fraudulent concealment (Civ.Code, § 1710, subd. 3). The sixth cause of action is based on common law fraud. Each of these causes of action asserts proximate causation, and claims compensatory damages of $10 million; those counts asserting intentional misrepresentation include a prayer for punitive damages.

The prayer for relief is extensive, and includes some novel requests. In addition to seeking damages, restitution, and injunctive relief, plaintiffs seek warning labels in stores and on packages, creation of funds for research on the health effects of sugar consumption by young children, public interest representatives on defendants' boards of directors, and public access to defendants' research on the health effects of their products.

Defendants demurred to the fourth amended complaint for failure to state a cause of action and for uncertainty. The trial court sustained the demurrers without leave to amend. The trial judge explained the basis for his ruling: "[I]n order to state a cause of action for fraud or for breach of warranty, there must be alleged with specificity the basis for the cause and that is, if there are advertisements which contain fraudulent matters, those advertisements must be set out. [¶] In paragraph 35, which is the heart of the allegations concerning the conveying of the representations, we have just a series of very general allegations to which there is no reference of an advertisement actually made. . . . [¶] Paragraph 38 which makes the allegations concerning media dissemination sets out no television stations, no other media, except for the fact that these ads were run on television stations every day in Southern California for a four-year period. [¶] This gives the defendant practically no kind of information concerning that which the defendant must answer, and it doesn't give the court a sufficient factual basis for its administration of the case."

Appealing from the judgment of dismissal, plaintiffs contend that their fourth amended complaint states, or can be amended to state, a valid cause of action. * * *

II. CAUSES OF ACTION BASED ON CONSUMER PROTECTION STATUTES

* * * [P]laintiffs rely on three statutes—the unfair competition law, the false advertising law, and the Sherman Food, Drug and Cosmetic Law—all

of which in similar language prohibit false, unfair, misleading, or deceptive advertising. * * *

To state a cause of action under these statutes for injunctive relief, it is necessary only to show that "members of the public are likely to be deceived." (Chern v. Bank of America (1976) 15 Cal.3d 866, 876, 127 Cal.Rptr. 110, 544 P.2d 1310.) Allegations of actual deception, reasonable reliance, and damage are unnecessary. The court may also order restitution without individualized proof of deception, reliance, and injury if it "determines that such a remedy is necessary 'to prevent the use or employment' of the unfair practice. . . ." (Fletcher v. Security Pacific National Bank [(1979)] 23 Cal.3d 442, 453, 153 Cal.Rptr. 28, 591 P.2d 51.)

Insofar as plaintiffs seek injunctive relief and restitution under the cited consumer protection statutes, defendants' principal basis for demurrer is the charge that the complaint fails to describe the alleged deceptive practices with sufficient particularity. Defendants assert that plaintiffs should not merely describe the substance of the misrepresentations, but should state the specific deceptive language employed, identify the persons making the misrepresentations and those to whom they were made, and indicate the date, time and place of the deception.

The complaint in a civil action serves a variety of purposes, of which two are relevant here: it serves to frame and limit the issues and to apprise the defendant of the basis upon which the plaintiff is seeking recovery. In fulfilling this function, the complaint should set forth the ultimate facts constituting the cause of action, not the evidence by which plaintiff proposes to prove those facts.[11]

The fourth amended complaint in the present case describes the alleged deceptive scheme in considerable detail. Paragraph 35 alleges some 19 misrepresentations—some general, others relatively specific. Paragraph 42 lists material facts which are not disclosed. Finally, plaintiffs allege that each misrepresentation appears (and every listed material fact is concealed) in every advertisement for the specified product during the period in question.[13] There is thus no doubt as to what advertisements are at issue, nor as to what deceptive practices are called into question.[14] We

---

[11] The requirement that fraud be pleaded with specificity, discussed in part III of this opinion, does not apply to causes of action under the consumer protection statutes.

[13] We are skeptical of plaintiffs' claim that every advertisement includes every misrepresentation. But to require plaintiffs in their complaint to review every advertisement to determine, for example, whether the April 1977 advertisements for Fruity Pebbles implied that they would dispel a child's anxiety, would greatly increase the complexity of the pleading without adding any significant increase in clarity.

[14] Plaintiffs' complaint may be uncertain, however, as to what media, other than television and cereal boxes, were employed to advertise the sugared cereals.

believe these allegations are sufficient to notify the defendants of the claim made against them, and to frame the issues for litigation.

Defendants' objection, as we see it, is not really one of lack of specificity or notice. Basically defendants believe that the allegations of paragraph 35 are not a fair paraphrase of the actual language of the advertisements, and that if plaintiffs could be compelled to state the exact language, it would be clear, for example, that defendants are not really representing that Cocoa Puffs will make children braver or that Alpha Bits impart magical powers.

It is not the ordinary function of a demurrer to test the truth of the plaintiff's allegations or the accuracy with which he describes the defendant's conduct. A demurrer tests only the legal sufficiency of the pleading. It "admits the truth of all material factual allegations in the complaint . . .; the question of plaintiff's ability to prove these allegations, or the possible difficulty in making such proof does not concern the reviewing court." (Alcorn v. Anbro Engineering, Inc. (1970) 2 Cal.3d 493, 496, 86 Cal.Rptr. 88, 468 P.2d 216.) We must therefore assume that defendants did in substance make each of the representations listed in paragraph 35 (and omit to state material facts as described in paragraph 42) in each advertisement within the period described by the complaint. Defendants' contention that the words and images used do not constitute such misrepresentations, and did not conceal material facts, frames an issue for trial, not demurrer.

The unsuitability of a demurrer to test the accuracy of a complaint is particularly marked in the present case. Plaintiffs do not, for the most part, claim that defendants made explicit oral or written representations. Instead, they claim that defendants used language, and presented images, in a form such that a particularly susceptible and naive audience—one composed largely of preschool children—would believe defendants were making those representations. Even if plaintiffs pled the exact language and sequence of visual images making up a television advertisement, it would be difficult for judges unaided by expert testimony to determine how a three-year-old would interpret that advertisement.

Important policy considerations also argue against requiring plaintiffs to set out the specific language of each advertisement. Plaintiffs allege that defendants carried out a large scale program of deceptive advertising in which the specific advertisements change constantly, but all follow a pattern of making, in one form or another, certain misleading and deceptive representations. If such is the case, to require plaintiffs to plead the specifics of each advertisement would render a suit challenging the overall program impractical. The complaint would have to include thousands of pages setting out specifics which are largely within defendants' knowledge. The cost and difficulty of compiling, organizing, and setting down the information would seriously deter the filing of any such complaint. The effect of such a pleading requirement, moreover, would not be limited to discouraging private suits; it would also seriously hamper suits by public officials seeking to enjoin schemes of unfair competition and deceptive advertising.

We conclude that the allegations of plaintiffs' fourth amended complaint are sufficient to overcome a general demurrer and to state causes of action for injunctive relief and restitution under both the unfair competition law and the false advertising law. * * *

III. CAUSES OF ACTION BASED ON FRAUD

Plaintiffs base their third, fourth, fifth and sixth causes of action on the tort of fraud. * * * Defendants, citing the rule that fraud must be pleaded specifically, claim plaintiffs' allegations of misrepresentation, reasonable reliance, and damages are insufficient to comply with that rule.

"Fraud actions . . . are subject to strict requirements of particularity in pleading. The idea seems to be that allegations of fraud involve a serious attack on character, and fairness to the defendant demands that he should receive the fullest possible details of the charge in order to prepare his defense. Accordingly the rule is everywhere followed that fraud must be specifically pleaded. The effect of this rule is twofold: (a) General pleading of the legal conclusion of 'fraud' is insufficient; the facts constituting the fraud must be alleged. (b) Every element of the cause of action for fraud must be alleged in the proper manner (i.e., factually and specifically), and the policy of liberal construction of the pleadings . . . will not ordinarily be invoked to sustain a pleading defective in any material respect." (3 Witkin, Cal.Procedure (2d ed. 1971) Pleading, § 574.)[17]

The specificity requirement serves two purposes. The first is notice to the defendant, to "furnish the defendant with certain definite charges which can be intelligently met." (Lavine v. Jessup [(1958)] 161 Cal.App.2d 59, 69, 326 P.2d 238.) The pleading of fraud, however, is also the last remaining habitat of the common law notion that a complaint should be sufficiently specific that the court can weed out nonmeritorious actions on the basis of the pleadings. Thus the pleading should be sufficient " 'to enable the court to determine whether, on the facts pleaded, there is any foundation, prima facie at least, for the charge of fraud.' " (Scafidi v.

[17] Witkin adds, however, that: "In reading the cases one gains the impression that entirely too much emphasis has been laid upon the requirement of specific pleading. The characterization of some actions as 'disfavored' has little to recommend it . . . and actions based on fraud are so numerous and commonplace that the implications of immoral conduct are seldom considered more serious than those involved in other intentional torts. Hence, while it seems sound to require specific pleading of the facts of fraud rather than general conclusions, the courts should not look askance at the complaint, and seek to absolve the defendant from liability on highly technical requirements of form in pleading. Pleading facts in ordinary and concise language is as permissible in fraud cases as in any others, and liberal construction of the pleading is as much a duty of the court in these as in other cases." (3 Witkin, op. cit. supra, Pleading, § 575, quoted in Lacy v. Laurentide Finance Corp. (1972) 28 Cal.App.3d 251, 258, fn. 2, 104 Cal.Rptr. 547.)

Western Loan and Building Co. [(1946)] 72 Cal.App.2d 550, 553, 165 P.2d 260.)

We observe, however, certain exceptions which mitigate the rigor of the rule requiring specific pleading of fraud. Less specificity is required when "it appears from the nature of the allegations that the defendant must necessarily possess full information concerning the facts of the controversy," (Bradley v. Hartford Acc. & Indem. Co. (1973) 30 Cal.App.3d 818, 825, 106 Cal.Rptr. 718); "[e]ven under the strict rules of common law pleading, one of the canons was that less particularity is required when the facts lie more in the knowledge of the opposite party. . . ." (Turner v. Milstein (1951) 103 Cal.App.2d 651, 658, 230 P.2d 25.)

Additionally, in a case such as the present one, considerations of practicality enter in. A complaint should be kept to reasonable length, and plaintiffs' fourth amended complaint, 64 pages long, strains at that limit. Yet plaintiffs allege thousands of misrepresentations in various media over a span of four years—representations which, while similar in substance, differ in time, place, and detail of language and presentation. A complaint which set out each advertisement verbatim, and specified the time, place, and medium, might seem to represent perfect compliance with the specificity requirement, but as a practical matter, it would provide less effective notice and be less useful in framing the issues than would a shorter, more generalized version.

Defendants object to the allegations of misrepresentation on the ground that the complaint fails to state the time and place of each misrepresentation, to identify the speaker and listener, and to set out the representation verbatim or in close paraphrase. The place and time of the advertisements, however, is fully known to defendant General Foods, but became available to plaintiffs only through discovery. That defendant equally knows the distribution of cereal box advertisements. A lengthy list of the dates and times of cereal ads on California television stations would add nothing of value to the complaint; the same is true for a list of California grocers marketing General Foods cereals. The language of the complaint—all ads for sugared cereals within a given four-year period—is sufficient to define the subject of the complaint and provide notice to defendants.

General Foods also knows the content of each questioned advertisement. Plaintiffs initially lacked such detailed knowledge, and although they have now obtained copies of the television storyboards through discovery, quotation or attachment of such copies to the complaint would consume thousands of pages. Attachment of the storyboards, moreover, would not redress defendants' grievance, which is, as we understand it, not that they lacked knowledge of the content of the commercials but that they do not understand what it is in the images and words that gives rise to the alleged misrepresentations.

For plaintiffs to provide an explanation for every advertisement would be obviously impractical. We believe, however, that the trial court could reasonably require plaintiffs to set out or attach a representative selection of advertisements, to state the misrepresentations made by those advertisements, and to indicate the language or images upon which any implied misrepresentations are based. This is a method of pleading which has been endorsed in other cases involving numerous misrepresentations. It represents a reasonable accommodation between defendants' right to a pleading sufficiently specific "that the court can ascertain for itself if the representations . . . were in fact material, and of an actionable nature" (8 Grossman & Van Alstyne, [Cal.Practice (1981)], § 984 (fns. omitted)), and the importance of avoiding pleading requirements so burdensome as to preclude relief in cases involving multiple misrepresentations.[19]

* * *

We turn finally to the question of damages. In an action for fraud, damage is an essential element of the cause of action; the successful plaintiff recovers damages as a matter of right.

* * * The allegations of the complaint are clearly sufficient to state a cause of action for restitution of the money spent to purchase the sugared cereals. The complaint also seeks additional damages, claiming that plaintiffs and members of their class encountered medical or dental injury from consuming sugared cereals and incurred expenses to treat those injuries. It does not, however, assert that any of the named children sustained any specific injury or that any of the named parents spent money to treat such injury. As a result, the allegations appear sufficient to assert injury to a subclass of parents and children (the class being all parents who purchased and children who consumed, even if no injury was incurred), but does not clearly place any of the individually named plaintiffs within their subclass. In view of the requirement for specific pleading in fraud actions, we believe the trial court could view the complaint as uncertain in its failure to make clear whether the individual child plaintiffs have incurred any specific health injury from the consumption of the sugared cereals, and whether their parents have spent any specific sums to treat those injuries.

In summary, the * * * allegations on behalf of the individual plaintiffs—both parents and children—are insufficiently certain and specific, but those deficiencies can be cured by amendment. We recognize that plaintiffs have already had opportunities to amend, but without the

---

[19] We did not suggest the necessity of plaintiffs pleading a representative selection of advertisements when we discussed their causes of action under the consumer protection laws. The requirement of specificity in pleading does not apply to those causes of action; the use of pleadings as a method by which the court can inquire into the merits of the case is confined to fraud actions.

guidance of this opinion, their failure to make the specific amendments we now require is excusable. * * * The judgment must be reversed to permit plaintiffs to correct any uncertainty or lack of required specificity in their fraud causes of action. * * *

V. CONCLUSION

Although the parties argue primarily the sufficiency and specificity of the pleadings, the underlying controversy is of much greater dimension. Defendants engaged in a nationwide, long-term advertising campaign designed to persuade children to influence their parents to buy sugared cereals. Adapted to its audience, the campaign sought to persuade less by direct representation than by imagery and example. While maintaining a constant theme, the particular advertisements changed frequently. Plaintiffs now contend that these advertisements were deceptive and misleading, and while we do not know the actual truth of those charges, we must assume them true for the purpose of this appeal. Yet, if we apply strict requirements of specificity in pleading as defendants argue, the result would be to eliminate the private lawsuit as a practical remedy to redress such past deception or prevent further deception. By directing their advertisements to children, and changing them frequently, defendants would have obtained practical immunity from statutory and common law remedies designed to protect consumers from misleading advertising.

It can be argued that administrative investigation and rule making would be a better method of regulating advertising of this scope and character. The California Legislature, however, has not established the necessary administrative structure. It has enacted consumer protection statutes and codified common law remedies which in principle apply to all deceptive advertising, regardless of complexity and scale, and, we believe, regardless of whether the advertisement seeks to influence the consumer directly or through his children. Established rules of pleading should not be applied so inflexibly that they bar use of such remedies.

We therefore conclude that plaintiffs' complaint states a cause of action for injunctive relief and restitution under the unfair competition law (Bus. & Prof.Code, § 17200 et seq.) and the false advertising law (Bus. & Prof.Code, § 17500 et seq.) Plaintiffs should be permitted to amend their complaint on behalf of the parent and child plaintiffs under the causes of action for fraud. * * *

BIRD, C.J., concurring and dissenting. [Omitted]

DISCOVERY

VINSON V. SUPERIOR COURT

Supreme Court of California, In Bank, 1987.
43 Cal.3d 833, 239 Cal.Rptr. 292, 740 P.2d 404.

MOSK, JUSTICE.

* * *

Plaintiff is a 59-year-old widow who in 1979 applied for a job in Oakland with a federally funded program, administered at the time by defendant Peralta Community College District, under the direction of codefendant Grant. Plaintiff alleges that Grant, during an interview with her in a private cubicle, commented on how attractive she appeared for a woman of her age. He assertedly made some salacious observations regarding her anatomy and expressed his desires with regard thereto. He allegedly concluded the interview by intimating that acquiring the position was subject to a condition precedent: her acquiescence to his sexual yearnings. Plaintiff claims she declined his advances as unconscionable and left greatly distraught.

Unknown to Grant, plaintiff was later hired by defendant college district as a certification technician. She asserts that once he discovered she was working for the program, he had her transferred to the payroll unit, a position for which he apparently knew she had no training. Soon thereafter he terminated her employment.

Plaintiff filed suit on several causes of action, among them sexual harassment, wrongful discharge, and intentional infliction of emotional distress. Defendants' actions are said to have caused her to suffer continuing emotional distress, loss of sleep, anxiety, mental anguish, humiliation, reduced self-esteem, and other consequences.

Defendants moved for an order compelling her to undergo a medical and a psychological examination. The examinations were meant to test the true extent of her injuries and to measure her ability to function in the workplace. Plaintiff opposed the motion as a violation of her right to privacy. In the alternative, if the court were to permit the examination she requested a protective order shielding her from any probing into her sexual history or practices, and asked that her attorney be allowed to attend in order to assure compliance with the order. The court granted the motion without imposing any of these limitations. Plaintiff petitioned the Court of Appeal for a writ of prohibition and/or mandate to direct the trial court to forbid the examination or to issue appropriate protective orders. The Court of Appeal denied the petition.

* * *

I. THE APPROPRIATENESS OF A MENTAL EXAMINATION

Plaintiff first contends the psychiatric examination should not be permitted because it infringes on her right to privacy. Before we can entertain this constitutional question, we must determine the statutory scope of the discovery laws.[2]

Code of Civil Procedure section [2032.020], subdivision (a), permits the mental examination of a party in any action in which the mental condition of that party is in controversy. Plaintiff disputes that her mental condition is in controversy. She points to Cody v. Marriott Corp. (D.Mass.1984) 103 F.R.D. 421, 422, a case interpreting rule 35(a) of the Federal Rules of Civil Procedure. Like the California rule that was patterned on it, rule 35 requires that physical or mental condition be "in controversy" before an examination is appropriate. *Cody* was an employment discrimination case in which the plaintiffs alleged mental and emotional distress. The court held that the claim of emotional distress did not ipso facto place the plaintiff's mental state in controversy.

The reasoning of *Cody* rested in large part on Schlagenhauf v. Holder (1964) 379 U.S. 104, 85 S.Ct. 234, 13 L.Ed.2d 152, in which the United States Supreme Court examined the "in controversy" requirement. In *Schlagenhauf* the plaintiffs were passengers injured when their bus collided with the rear of a truck. The defendant truck company, in answer to a cross-claim by the codefendant bus company, charged that the bus driver had been unfit to drive and moved to have him undergo a mental and physical examination. The Supreme Court recognized that at times the pleadings may be sufficient to put mental or physical condition in controversy, as when a plaintiff in a negligence action alleges mental or physical injury. But it determined that the driver had not asserted his mental condition in support of or in a defense of a claim, nor did the general charge of negligence put his mental state in controversy. *Schlagenhauf* thus stands for the proposition that one party's unsubstantiated allegation cannot put the mental state of another in controversy.

It is another matter entirely, however, when a party places his *own* mental state in controversy by alleging mental and emotional distress. Unlike the bus driver in *Schlagenhauf,* who had a controversy thrust upon him, a party who chooses to allege that he has mental and emotional difficulties can hardly deny his mental state is in controversy. To the extent

---

[2] Part 4, title 3, chapter 3, article 3, of the Code of Civil Procedure (§§ 2016–2036.5), the applicable legislation on depositions and discovery at the time this action began, has been repealed. The repeal was operative July 1, 1987, on which date a new article 3 (entitled the Civil Discovery Act of 1986) came into effect. The act provides, however, that the use of a discovery method initiated before July 1, 1987, will be governed by the law regulating that method at the time it was initiated. We must therefore apply the superseded discovery procedures to this case. But as we shall show by appropriate references to the new act, many of its relevant provisions are substantially similar.

the decision in *Cody, supra,* 103 F.R.D. 421, is inconsistent with this conclusion, we decline to follow it.

In the case at bar, plaintiff haled defendants into court and accused them of causing her various mental and emotional ailments. Defendants deny her charges. As a result, the existence and extent of her mental injuries is indubitably in dispute. In addition, by asserting a causal link between her mental distress and defendants' conduct, plaintiff implicitly claims it was not caused by a preexisting mental condition, thereby raising the question of alternative sources for the distress. We thus conclude that her mental state is in controversy.

We emphasize that our conclusion is based solely on the allegations of emotional and mental damages in this case. A simple sexual harassment claim asking compensation for having to endure an oppressive work environment or for wages lost following an unjust dismissal would not normally create a controversy regarding the plaintiff's mental state. To hold otherwise would mean that every person who brings such a suit implicitly asserts he or she is mentally unstable, obviously an untenable proposition.

Determining that the mental or physical condition of a party is in controversy is but the first step in our analysis. In contrast to more pedestrian discovery procedures, a mental or physical examination requires the discovering party to obtain a court order. The court may grant the motion only for good cause shown.

* * * The requirement of a court order following a showing of good cause is doubtless designed to protect an examinee's privacy interest by preventing an examination from becoming an annoying fishing expedition. While a plaintiff may place his mental state in controversy by a general allegation of severe emotional distress, the opposing party may not require him to undergo psychiatric testing solely on the basis of speculation that something of interest may surface.

Plaintiff in the case at bar asserts that she continues to suffer diminished self-esteem, reduced motivation, sleeplessness, loss of appetite, fear, lessened ability to help others, loss of social contacts, anxiety, mental anguish, loss of reputation, and severe emotional distress. In their motion defendants pointed to these allegations. Because the truth of these claims is relevant to plaintiff's cause of action and justifying facts have been shown with specificity, good cause as to these assertions has been demonstrated. Subject to limitations necessitated by plaintiff's right to privacy, defendants must be allowed to investigate the continued existence and severity of plaintiff's alleged damages.

II. PRIVACY LIMITATIONS ON THE SCOPE OF A MENTAL EXAMINATION

If we find, as we do, that an examination may be ordered, plaintiff urges us to circumscribe its scope to exclude any probing into her sexual history, habits, or practices. Such probing, she asserts, would intrude impermissibly into her protected sphere of privacy. Furthermore, it would tend to contravene the state's strong interest in eradicating sexual harassment by means of private suits for damages. An examination into a plaintiff's past and present sexual practices would inhibit the bringing of meritorious sexual harassment actions by compelling the plaintiff—whose privacy has already been invaded by the harassment—to suffer another intrusion into her private life.

* * *

Defendants acknowledge plaintiff's right to privacy *in abstracto* but maintain she has waived it for purposes of the present suit. In addition, they urge us to take heed of their right to a fair trial, which they claim depends on a "meaningful" examination of plaintiff. Defendants contend they would not have requested a mental examination if plaintiff had simply brought a sexual harassment suit; but because she claims emotional and mental damage, they should be entitled to present expert testimony on the extent of the injury. Preparing such testimony, they suggest, requires not simply a mental examination, but one without substantial restrictions on its scope.

We cannot agree that the mere initiation of a sexual harassment suit, even with the rather extreme mental and emotional damage plaintiff claims to have suffered, functions to waive all her privacy interests, exposing her persona to the unfettered mental probing of defendants' expert. Plaintiff is not compelled, as a condition to entering the courtroom, to discard entirely her mantle of privacy. At the same time, plaintiff cannot be allowed to make her very serious allegations without affording defendants an opportunity to put their truth to the test.

* * *

Plaintiff's present mental and emotional condition is directly relevant to her claim and essential to a fair resolution of her suit; she has waived her right to privacy in this respect by alleging continuing mental ailments. But she has not, merely by initiating this suit for sexual harassment and emotional distress, implicitly waived her right to privacy in respect to her sexual history and practices. Defendants fail to explain why probing into this area is directly relevant to her claim and essential to its fair resolution. * * *

But even though plaintiff retains certain unwaived privacy rights, these rights are not necessarily absolute. On occasion her privacy interests may have to give way to her opponent's right to a fair trial. Thus courts must balance the right of civil litigants to discover relevant facts against the privacy interests of persons subject to discovery.

Before proceeding, we note the Legislature recently enacted a measure designed to protect the privacy of plaintiffs in cases such as these. Section 2036.1 (operative until July 1, 1987; presently, substantially the same provision is contained in § [2017.220], subdivision [(a)]), provides that in a civil suit alleging conduct that constitutes sexual harassment, sexual assault, or sexual battery, any party seeking discovery concerning the plaintiff's sexual conduct with individuals other than the alleged perpetrator must establish specific facts showing good cause for that discovery, and that the inquiry is relevant to the subject matter and reasonably calculated to lead to the discovery of admissible evidence. We must determine whether the general balancing of interests embodied in this new legislation has obviated the need for us to engage in an individualized balancing of privacy with discovery in the case at bar.

In enacting the measure, the Legislature took pains to declare that "The discovery of sexual aspects of complainant's [sic] lives, as well as those of their past and current friends and acquaintances, has the clear potential to discourage complaints and to annoy and harass litigants . . . without protection against it, individuals whose intimate lives are unjustifiably and offensively intruded upon might face the 'Catch-22' of invoking their remedy only at the risk of enduring further intrusions into the details of their personal lives in discovery. . . . [¶] . . . Absent extraordinary circumstances, inquiry into those areas should not be permitted, either in discovery or at trial." (Stats.1985, ch. 1328, § 1.)[8]

Nowhere do defendants establish specific facts justifying inquiry into plaintiff's zone of sexual privacy or show how such discovery would be relevant. Rather they make only the most sweeping assertions regarding the need for wide latitude in the examination. Because good cause has not been shown, discovery into this area of plaintiff's life must be denied.

Section 2036.1 thus amply protects plaintiff's privacy interests. We anticipate that in the majority of sexual harassment suits, a separate weighing of privacy against discovery will not be necessary. It should normally suffice for the court, in ruling on whether good cause exists for probing into the intimate life of a victim of sexual harassment, sexual

---

[8] Plaintiff suggests that section [2017.220] does not adequately protect her privacy interests because section [2032.320] already requires "good cause" for a mental examination, and nothing is added by again requiring good cause for inquiry into a plaintiff's sexual history and practices. But the above-quoted legislative declaration accompanying section [2017.220], i.e., that inquiry into sexuality should not be permitted absent "extraordinary circumstances," suggests that a stronger showing of good cause must be made to justify inquiry into this topic than is needed for a general examination. Furthermore, section [2032.320] merely requires good cause for the examination as a whole; in emotional distress cases that will often be present. By contrast, a defendant in a sexual harassment case desiring to ask sex-related questions must show specific facts justifying that particular inquiry.

battery, or sexual assault, to evaluate the showing of good cause in light of the legislative purpose in enacting this section and the plaintiff's constitutional right to privacy.

III. PRESENCE OF COUNSEL

In the event a limited psychiatric examination is proper, plaintiff urges us to authorize the attendance of her attorney. She fears that the examiner will stray beyond the permitted area of inquiry. Counsel would monitor the interview and shield her from inappropriate interrogation. And depicting the examination as an "alien and frankly hostile environment," she asserts that she needs her lawyer to provide her with aid and comfort.

Defendants, joined by amici California Psychiatric Association and Northern California Psychiatric Association, counter that a meaningful mental examination cannot be conducted with an attorney interposing objections. And if plaintiff's counsel is present, defense counsel would also seek to attend. Defendants maintain these adversaries would likely convert the examination into a chaotic deposition.

We contemplated whether counsel must be allowed to attend the psychiatric examination of a client in Edwards v. Superior Court (1976) 16 Cal.3d 905, 130 Cal.Rptr. 14, 549 P.2d 846. The plaintiff in *Edwards* alleged that because of the defendant school district's failure to properly instruct and supervise users of school equipment, she sustained physical and emotional injuries. The trial court granted a motion compelling her to undergo a psychiatric examination alone. Holding that the plaintiff could not insist on the presence of her counsel, a majority of this court denied her petition for a peremptory writ.

The plaintiff in *Edwards* raised many of the points urged upon us here. She asserted that her attorney should be present to protect her from improper inquiries. We were skeptical that a lawyer, unschooled in the ways of the mental health profession, would be able to discern the psychiatric relevance of the questions. And the examiner should have the freedom to probe deeply into the plaintiff's psyche without interference by a third party. The plaintiff further suggested counsel should be present to lend her comfort and support in an inimical setting. We responded that an examinee could view almost any examination of this sort, even by her own expert, as somewhat hostile. Whatever comfort her attorney's handholding might afford was substantially outweighed by the distraction and potential disruption caused by the presence of a third person. Finally, we concluded counsel's presence was not necessary to ensure accurate reporting. Verbatim transcription might inhibit the examinee, preventing an effective examination. Furthermore, other procedural devices—pretrial discovery of the examiner's notes or cross-examination, for example—were available for the plaintiff's protection.

* * *

Despite the dissent in *Edwards* 16 Cal.3d 905, 914, 130 Cal.Rptr. 14, 549 P.2d 846 (dis. opn. by Sullivan, J. and Mosk, J.), we conclude that a reconsideration of that decision—which is barely 10 years old—is not justified.[9] We emphasize, however, that *Edwards* should be viewed as standing for the proposition that the presence of an attorney is not *required* during a mental examination. In light of their broad discretion in discovery matters, trial courts retain the power to permit the presence of counsel or to take other prophylactic measures when needed.

Plaintiff makes no showing that the court abused its discretion in excluding her counsel from the examination. Her fears are wholly unfounded at this point; not a shred of evidence has been produced to show that defendants' expert will not respect her legitimate rights to privacy or might disobey any court-imposed restrictions. Plaintiff's apprehension appears to derive less from the reality of the proposed analysis than from the popular image of mental examinations.

Plaintiff's interests can be adequately protected without having her attorney present. In the first place, section [2032.310] requires the court granting a physical or mental examination to specify its conditions and scope. We must assume, absent evidence to the contrary, that the examiner will proceed in an ethical manner, adhering to these constraints. And if plaintiff truly fears that the examiner will probe into impermissible areas, she may record the examination on audio tape. This is an unobtrusive measure that will permit evidence of abuse to be presented to the court in any motion for sanctions.[10]

Plaintiff refers us to the history of psychiatric examinations for victims of sexual assault. Such examinations were widely viewed as inhibiting prosecutions for rape by implicitly placing the victim on trial, leading to a legislative prohibition of examinations to assess credibility. The victim of sexual harassment is analogous to the prosecutrix in a rape case, plaintiff asserts, and she points to legislative findings that discovery of sexual aspects of complainants' lives "has the clear potential to discourage complaints." (Stats.1985, ch. 1328, § 1.) If we conclude on the basis of general considerations that a mental examination is appropriate and that it should occur without the presence of counsel, plaintiff urges us to adopt

---

9 Section [2032.510(a)] now specifically provides for the attendance of an attorney at a *physical* examination. [Section 2032.530(b)] states, however, that nothing in the discovery statutes shall be construed to alter, amend, or affect existing case law with respect to the presence of counsel or other persons during a mental examination by agreement or court order. * * * [I]n the course of that revision the Legislature considered and rejected a provision that would have annulled our decision in *Edwards* by permitting counsel to attend a mental examination.

10 We note that the new discovery act explicitly provides both examiners and examinees the opportunity to perpetuate the interview on audio tape. [Section 2032.530(a).]

a special rule exempting those who bring harassment charges from either or both of these requirements.

We believe that in these circumstances such a special rule is unwarranted. In the first place, we should be guided by the maxim that *entia non sunt multiplicanda praeter necessitatem:* we should carve out exceptions from general rules only when the facts require it. The state admittedly has a strong interest in eradicating the evil of sexual harassment, and the threat of a mental examination could conceivably dampen a plaintiff's resolve to bring suit. But we have seen that those who allege harassment have substantial protection under existing procedural rules. In general it is unlikely that a simple sexual harassment suit will justify a mental examination. Such examinations may ordinarily be considered only in cases in which the alleged mental or emotional distress is said to be ongoing. When an examination is permitted, investigation by a psychiatrist into the private life of a plaintiff is severely constrained, and sanctions are available to guarantee those restrictions are respected.

Finally, the mental examination in this case largely grows out of plaintiff's emotional distress claim. We do not believe the state has a greater interest in preventing emotional distress in sexual harassment victims than it has in preventing such distress in the victims of any other tort.

The judgment of the Court of Appeal is reversed with directions to issue a peremptory writ of mandate compelling respondent court to limit the scope of the mental examination in accordance with the views expressed herein.

COITO V. SUPERIOR COURT

Supreme Court of California, 2012.
54 Cal.4th 480, 142 Cal.Rptr.3d 607, 278 P.3d 860.

LIU, JUSTICE.

In California, an attorney's work product is protected by statute. (Code Civ. Proc., § 2018.010 et seq.) * * *

In this case, we decide what work product protection, if any, should be accorded two items: first, recordings of witness interviews conducted by investigators employed by defendant's counsel, and second, information concerning the identity of witnesses from whom defendant's counsel has obtained statements. Defendant objected to plaintiff's requests for discovery of these items, invoking the work product privilege. The trial court sustained the objection, concluding as a matter of law that the recorded witness interviews were entitled to absolute work product protection and that the other information sought was work product entitled to qualified protection. A divided Court of Appeal reversed, concluding that work product protection does not apply to any of the disputed items. The Court of Appeal issued a writ of mandate directing the trial court to grant the motion to compel discovery.

We conclude that the Court of Appeal erred. * * *

I.

On March 9, 2007, 13-year-old Jeremy Wilson drowned in the Tuolumne River in Modesto, California. His mother, Debra Coito, filed a complaint for wrongful death naming several defendants, including the State of California. The Department of Water Resources (DWR) is the agency defending the action for the state, represented by the Attorney General.

Six other juveniles witnessed what happened. There were allegations that all of the juveniles, including the decedent, were engaged in criminal conduct immediately before the drowning. * * * [C]ounsel for the state sent two investigators, both special agents from the Bureau of Investigation of the Department of Justice, to interview four of the juveniles. The state's counsel provided the investigators with questions he wanted asked. Each interview was audio-recorded and saved on a separate compact disc.

* * * The state's counsel used the content of [one] witness's recorded interview in questioning the witness at [his] deposition.

On February 5, 2009, plaintiff served the state with supplemental interrogatories and document demands. The interrogatories included Judicial Council form interrogatory No. 12.3, which sought the names, addresses, and telephone numbers of individuals from whom written or recorded statements had been obtained. The document demands sought production of the audio recordings of the four witness interviews. The state objected to the requested discovery based on the work product privilege.

Plaintiff filed a motion to compel an answer to form interrogatory No. 12.3 and the production of the recorded interviews. In support of the motion, plaintiff filed declarations from two of the interviewed witnesses asserting that they had not intended their statements to be confidential.* * *

[T]he trial court issued a written order that * * * [denied] plaintiff's motion except as to the recording used by the state * * * during the * * * deposition. As to that recording, the court reasoned that the state had waived the work product privilege by using the interview to examine the witness during the deposition.

Plaintiff petitioned for a writ of mandate that the Court of Appeal granted. The majority * * * concluded that witness interviews and the information sought by form interrogatory No. 12.3 are not entitled as a matter of law to absolute or qualified work product protection. * * *

We granted review. * * *

II.

California's civil work product privilege is codified in section 2018.030. Subdivision (a) provides absolute protection to any "writing that reflects an attorney's impressions, conclusions, opinions, or legal research or theories." Such a writing "is not discoverable under any circumstances." The term "writing" includes any form of recorded information, including audio recordings. Section 2018.030, subdivision (b) provides qualified protection for all other work product. Such material "is not discoverable unless the court determines that denial of discovery will unfairly prejudice the party seeking discovery in preparing that party's claim or defense or will result in an injustice." * * *

The language of section 2018.030 does not otherwise define or describe "work product." Courts have * * * concluded that only derivative or interpretive material—material created by or derived from an attorney's work reflecting the attorney's evaluation of the law or facts—constitutes work product. Examples of such material include "diagrams prepared for trial, audit reports, appraisals, and other expert opinions, developed as a result of the initiative of counsel in preparing for trial." Nonderivative material—material that is only evidentiary in nature—does not constitute work product. Examples of such material include the identity and location of physical evidence or witnesses.

* * *

A.

The idea that an attorney's work product should receive protection from discovery was first recognized by the United States Supreme Court in Hickman v. Taylor (1947) 329 U.S. 495, 67 S.Ct. 385, 91 L.Ed. 451. * * *

At the time *Hickman* was decided, California law protected work product only through the attorney-client privilege. * * *

In 1957, the Legislature took up consideration of the Discovery Act, modeled on provisions of the Federal Rules of Civil Procedure. * * * The text and enactment history * * * left unclear whether California law incorporated *Hickman*'s understanding of protected work product.

Against this statutory backdrop, this court in 1961 concluded that neither the attorney-client privilege nor the work product doctrine protected nonparty witness statements from discovery. * * * "In its essence," the court explained, "the 'work product rule' is a form of federally created privilege. The Legislature expressly refused to extend the concepts of privilege when adopting the discovery procedures. Since privilege is created by statute it should not be extended by judicial fiat. * * *"

In response [in 1963,] the State Bar Committee proposed an amendment the following year with the purpose of codifying a work product privilege. * * * Nearly identical language was ultimately enacted as [what is now section 2018.030.]

* * *

Contemporaneous commentary observed that the 1963 amendments intended to give some work product even greater protection than the qualified protection afforded by *Hickman.*

* * *

B.

In light of the origins and development of the work product privilege in California, we conclude that witness statements obtained as a result of an interview conducted by an attorney, or by an attorney's agent at the attorney's behest, constitute work product protected by section 2018.030.

As mentioned, the Legislature in enacting section 2018.030 did not define "work product" and instead left the term open to judicial interpretation. From the very inception of judicial recognition of the concept, attorney work product has been understood to include witness statements obtained through an interview conducted by an attorney. The high court in *Hickman* specifically referred to "statements" and "interviews" in its nonexclusive enumeration of items comprising the " 'work product of a lawyer.' " * * *

The closest we have come to examining the applicability of section 2018.030 to witness statements is our decision in Rico v. Mitsubishi Motors Corp. (2007) 42 Cal.4th 807, 68 Cal.Rptr.3d 758, 171 P.3d 1092. There, we held that work product "protection extends to an attorney's written notes about a witness's statements" and that "when a witness's statement and the attorney's impressions are inextricably intertwined," the entire document receives absolute protection. The question in *Rico* was not whether a witness's statement is itself protected work product, and the document at issue was not "a verbatim record of the witnesses' statements" but rather a summary prepared at the request of the defendant's attorney. *Rico* thus did not speak to the issue now before us.

Nevertheless, in finding the document protected, *Rico*'s observation that " 'its very existence is owed to the lawyer's thought process' " provides a useful touchstone for our present inquiry. There is no dispute that a statement independently prepared by a witness does not become protected work product simply upon its transmission to an attorney. The issue here is what protection, if any, should be afforded where the witness's statement has been obtained through an attorney-directed interview. "In such situations," the Court of Appeal correctly observed, "it can surely be said that the witness statement is in part the product of the attorney's work."

The witness statement would not exist but for the attorney's initiative, decision, and effort to obtain it. This essential fact informs our analysis of whether absolute or qualified work product privilege applies to such witness statements.

Absolute privilege. It is not difficult to imagine that a recorded witness interview may, in some instances, reveal the "impressions, conclusions, opinions, or legal research and or theories" of the attorney and thus be entitled to absolute protection. This may occur not only when a witness's statements are "inextricably intertwined" with explicit comments or notes by the attorney stating his or her impressions of the witness, the witness's statements, or other issues in the case. It also may occur when the questions that the attorney has chosen to ask (or not ask) provide a window into the attorney's theory of the case or the attorney's evaluation of what issues are most important. Lines of inquiry that an attorney chooses to pursue through follow-up questions may be especially revealing. In such situations, redaction of the attorney's questions may sometimes be appropriate and sufficient to protect privileged material. At other times, however, it may not do to simply redact the questions from the record, as the witness's statements will reveal what questions were asked. Moreover, in some cases, the very fact that the attorney has chosen to interview a particular witness may disclose important tactical or evaluative information, perhaps especially so in cases involving a multitude of witnesses. These are circumstances where absolute work product protection may apply.

We cannot say, however, that witness statements procured by an attorney will always reveal the attorney's thought process. The Court of Appeal below posited a scenario in which an attorney collects statements from witnesses to an accident with no particular foresight, strategy, selectivity, or planning: "What, for example, of the situation in which an attorney sends an investigator to interview all witnesses listed in a police report, and the investigator asks few if any questions while taking the witnesses' statements? Clearly, these statements would reveal nothing significant about the attorney's impressions, conclusions, or opinions about the case." For this reason (and such scenarios do not seem uncommon), we hold that witness statements procured by an attorney are not automatically entitled as a matter of law to absolute work product protection. Instead, the applicability of absolute protection must be determined case by case. An attorney resisting discovery of a witness statement based on absolute privilege must make a preliminary or foundational showing that disclosure would reveal his or her "impressions, conclusions, opinions, or legal research or theories." (§ 2018.030, subd. (a).) Upon an adequate showing, the trial court should then determine, by making an in-camera inspection if necessary, whether absolute work product protection applies to some or all of the material.

Qualified privilege. Although witness statements obtained through an attorney-directed interview may or may not reveal the attorney's thought process, we believe such statements necessarily implicate two other interests that the Legislature sought to protect in enacting the work product privilege. Based on these interests, we conclude that witness statements procured by an attorney are entitled as a matter of law to at least qualified work product protection under section 2018.030, subdivision (b).

First, when an attorney obtains through discovery a witness statement obtained by opposing counsel through his or her own initiative, such discovery undermines the Legislature's policy to "[p]revent attorneys from taking undue advantage of their adversary's industry and efforts." Even when an attorney exercises no selectivity in determining which witnesses to interview, and even when the attorney simply records each witness's answer to a single question ("What happened?"), the attorney has expended time and effort in identifying and locating each witness, securing the witness's willingness to talk, listening to what the witness said, and preserving the witness's statement for possible future use. An attorney who seeks to discover what a witness knows is not without recourse. The attorney is free to interview the witness for himself or herself to find out what information the witness has that is relevant to the litigation. * * * Absent a showing that a witness is no longer available or accessible, or some other showing of unfair prejudice or injustice, the Legislature's declared policy is to prevent an attorney from free-riding on the industry and efforts of opposing counsel.

Second, a default rule authorizing discovery of witness statements procured by an attorney would impede the Legislature's intent "to encourage attorneys to prepare their cases thoroughly and to investigate not only the favorable but the unfavorable aspects of those cases." * * * Accordingly, we hold that a witness statement obtained through an attorney-directed interview is, as a matter of law, entitled to at least qualified work product protection.

C.

The protection afforded by section 2018.030, subdivision (b) to the witness statements in this case is essentially the same protection that the high court afforded to the witness statements in *Hickman.*

* * *

While acknowledging that "an attorney could reveal his or her thoughts about a case by the way in which the attorney conducts a witness interview," the Court of Appeal concluded that "competent counsel will be able to tailor their interviews so as to avoid the problem should they choose to do so." However, * * * [p]lacing the burden on attorneys to tailor witness interviews so as to avoid unwanted discovery is precisely what *Hickman* warned against when it said: "Were such materials open to opposing counsel on mere demand, much of what is now put down in writing would remain unwritten. . . . Inefficiency, unfairness and sharp practices would inevitably develop in the giving of legal advice and in the preparation of cases for trial. The effect on the legal profession would be demoralizing. And the interests of the clients and the cause of justice would be poorly served."

In sum, we * * * hold that a witness statement obtained through an attorney-directed interview is entitled as a matter of law to at least qualified work product protection. A party seeking disclosure has the burden of establishing that denial of disclosure will unfairly prejudice the party in preparing its claim or defense or will result in an injustice. If the party resisting discovery alleges that a witness statement, or portion thereof, is absolutely protected because it "reflects an attorney's impressions, conclusions, opinions, or legal research or theories," that party must make a preliminary or foundational showing in support of its claim. The trial court should then make an in-camera inspection to determine whether absolute work product protection applies to some or all of the material.

* * *

D.

In addition to the witness statements, plaintiff sought to compel defendant to answer form interrogatory No. 12.3, which asked: "Have YOU OR ANYONE ACTING ON YOUR BEHALF obtained a written or recorded statement from any individual concerning the INCIDENT?" For any such statement, the interrogatory requested (among other things) the name, address, and telephone number of the witness and the date the statement was obtained.

The Court of Appeal reasoned that, because the recorded witness statements themselves were not entitled to work product protection, defendant could not refuse to answer form interrogatory No. 12.3. * * *

At the outset, we note that form interrogatory No. 12.3—in asking whether a party or its agent has "obtained" a written or recorded witness statement—appears to include within its compass any statement independently prepared by a witness and subsequently obtained by an attorney. Such statements "neither reflect an attorney's evaluation of the case nor constitute derivative material, and therefore are neither absolute nor qualified work product." It follows that "a list of potential witnesses who turned over to counsel their independently prepared statements would have no tendency to reveal counsel's evaluation of the case" and compelled disclosure of such a list pursuant to form interrogatory No. 12.3 would invade no work product privilege.

The issue here is whether disclosure of a list of witnesses from whom an attorney took recorded statements at his or her own initiative implicates the work product privilege. Parties in litigation typically know the full universe of witnesses, not least because form interrogatory No. 12.1 requires parties to provide a list of all known witnesses. Thus, form interrogatory No. 12.3 specifically aims to reveal which witnesses an attorney for one party saw fit to ask for a recorded statement.

* * * [D]isclosing a list of witnesses from whom an attorney has taken recorded statements may, in some instances, reveal the attorney's impressions of the case. Take, for example, a bus accident involving 50 surviving passengers and an allegation that the driver fell asleep at the wheel. If an attorney for one of the passengers took recorded statements from only 10 individuals, disclosure of the list may well indicate the attorney's evaluation or conclusion as to which witnesses were in the best position to see the cause of the accident. * * * Such information may be entitled to absolute privilege under section 2018.030, subdivision (a). If absolute privilege were inapplicable, such a list may still be entitled to qualified privilege under section 2018.030, subdivision (b) to the extent it reflects the attorney's industry and effort in selecting which witnesses to ask for a recorded statement. * * *

At the same time, however, we cannot say that it will always or even often be the case that a witness list responsive to form interrogatory No. 12.3 reflects counsel's premeditated and carefully considered selectivity as in the scenario above. * * * Although the witness statements themselves reflect the attorney's time and effort in taking the statements and are therefore qualified work product, disclosing the list of such witnesses * * * does not implicate the problem of one attorney free-riding on the work of another, as no significant work or selectivity went into creating the list.

The instant case presents another scenario in which the work product privilege may be inapplicable. Where it appears that an attorney has sought to take recorded statements from all or almost all of the known witnesses to the incident, compelling a response to form interrogatory No. 12.3 is unlikely to violate the work product privilege. * * * "DWR's investigator succeeded in interviewing four eyewitnesses and generated four recorded statements. These facts, had they been disclosed in a response to form interrogatory No. 12.3, would have revealed nothing of consequence regarding DWR's evaluation of the case, one way or the other." Nor would it have implicated any time or effort expended by DWR's attorney in selecting the witnesses to interview, as it does not appear that any meaningful selection occurred.

Because it is not evident that form interrogatory No. 12.3 implicates the policies underlying the work product privilege in all or even most cases, we hold that information responsive to form interrogatory No. 12.3 is not automatically entitled as a matter of law to absolute or qualified work product privilege. Instead, the interrogatory usually must be answered. However, an objecting party may be entitled to protection if it can make a preliminary or foundational showing that answering the interrogatory would reveal the attorney's tactics, impressions, or evaluation of the case, or would result in opposing counsel taking undue advantage of the attorney's industry or efforts. Upon such a showing, the trial court should then determine, by making an in-camera inspection if necessary, whether absolute or qualified work product protection applies to the material in dispute. Of course, a trial court may also have to consider non-party witnesses' privacy concerns.

CONCLUSION

We reverse the judgment of the Court of Appeal and remand the matter for further proceedings, consistent with our opinion, to determine whether the disputed materials should be produced.

SANCTIONS

CITY OF LOS ANGELES V. PRICEWATERHOUSECOOPERS, LLP

Supreme Court of California, 2024.
17 Cal.5th 46, 324 Cal.Rptr.3d 410, 553 P.3d 1194.

KRUGER, JUSTICE.

* * *

I.

A.

In 2010, the City of Los Angeles contracted with PricewaterhouseCoopers (PwC) to modernize the billing system for the City's Department of Water and Power (LADWP). The rollout of the new billing system did not go smoothly. When the system went live in 2013, it sent inaccurate or delayed bills to a significant portion of the City's population.

In March 2015, following the botched rollout, the City filed suit against PwC. In a complaint filed by the City's attorneys and special counsel Paul Paradis, Gina Tufaro, and Paul Kiesel, the City alleged that PwC had fraudulently misrepresented its qualifications to undertake the LADWP billing modernization project. Then, about a month later, in April 2015, attorney Jack Landskroner, representing Los Angeles resident Antwon Jones, filed a putative class action against the City on behalf of overbilled

LADWP customers (*Jones v. City of Los Angeles*). The two lawsuits were assigned to the same trial judge. (City of Los Angeles v. PricewaterhouseCoopers, LLC (2022) 84 Cal.App.5th 466, 477, 300 Cal.Rptr.3d 432 (*City of L.A.*).)

Instead of filing an answer to the *Jones v. City of Los Angeles* complaint, the City quickly entered into negotiations with Landskroner. On August 7, 2015, the parties arrived at a preliminary settlement agreement, which provided that the City would reimburse 1.6 million LADWP customers the full amount by which they were overcharged; that it would implement "remedial and corrective measures" that the City valued at approximately $20 million; and that it would award up to $19 million in attorney's fees to plaintiffs' counsel. In the end, the settlement resulted in a payment of $10.3 million in attorney's fees to Landskroner. The City publicly announced its intent to recover the full cost of the *Jones v. City of Los Angeles* settlement in its lawsuit against PwC.

Meanwhile, over the next five years, pretrial discovery in the PwC case would gradually reveal a more substantial connection between the two lawsuits: Counsel for the City had been behind the *Jones v. City of Los* Angeles lawsuit, and they had sought to engineer the litigation so that the City could definitively settle all of the claims brought by overbilled customers while passing the costs of the settlement in a suit against PwC.

This story, which would ultimately result in federal criminal charges for some of the actors involved, was not immediately—or willingly—revealed.

* * *

[After years of discovery battles, the trial court rejected the City's claim of attorney-client privilege and ordered production of numerous documents.] The City filed a petition for writ of mandate to appeal the court's determination that the attorney-client privilege did not apply. But before the Court of Appeal could review the writ petition, the City voluntarily dismissed with prejudice its case against PwC. As a result of the dismissal, the City did not complete its production of documents responsive to PwC's discovery requests.

After the dismissal, federal prosecutors announced that Paul Paradis, [Chief Assistant City Attorney] Thomas Peters, and two other City officials had pleaded guilty to criminal charges. Paradis and Peters admitted that the City had pursued a collusive litigation strategy wherein Paradis and Kiesel would represent both Jones and the City in parallel lawsuits against PwC. The City later abandoned the parallel litigation strategy and sought outside counsel that would "represent" Jones against the City while remaining amenable to the City's litigation goals. The objective was to use Jones's class action lawsuit in *Jones v. City of Los Angeles* to settle all of the outstanding claims arising out of LADWP billing discrepancies, and to recover the costs of the settlement in a subsequent suit against PwC. Paradis pleaded guilty to a bribery charge and admitted to accepting $2.175 million in kickbacks from Landskroner after Landskroner had been awarded $10.3 million in attorney's fees. Peters pleaded guilty to aiding and abetting extortion by directing Kiesel to make hush money payments to a former employee who had threatened to release documents revealing the fraudulent nature of the *Jones* settlement.

B.

Throughout the pretrial proceedings, PwC had raised the possibility of discovery sanctions, but the trial court had instructed PwC to wait until the close of discovery to move for sanctions so the court could address the motions on a complete record. After the City voluntarily dismissed its suit against PwC and the court declined to order further discovery, PwC proceeded to file a motion for monetary sanctions for the City's discovery misconduct under Code of Civil Procedure sections 2023.010 and 2023.030. In its motion, PwC argued that the City had engaged in [at least 11 significant] misuses of the discovery process.

* * *

After a hearing, the trial court granted PwC's motion for sanctions. The court concluded that "Code of Civil Procedure section 2023.030 authorizes a trial court to direct any party or attorney who has engaged in the misuse of the discovery process to pay the reasonable expenses, including attorneys' fees incurred, as a result of that conduct." "Misuses of the discovery process include, among other things, failing to respond or to submit to an authorized method of discovery, making without substantial justification an unmeritorious objection to discovery, making an evasive response to discovery, disobeying a court order to provide discovery, and making or opposing unsuccessfully and without substantial justification a motion to compel to limit discovery. Code Civ. Proc., section 2023.010." The court also concluded that sanctions could be imposed under its "inherent power to deal with litigation abuse." Finding a "serious abuse of discovery by the City and its counsel," the court awarded PwC $2.5 million in sanctions against the City.

C.

[The Court of Appeal held by a 2–1 vote that the trial court lacked authority to impose the sanctions award under sections 2023.010 and 2023.030.] * * *

The majority concluded that sections 2023.010 and 2023.030 do not independently authorize trial courts to impose monetary sanctions for discovery misuse, but instead supply definitions relevant to other provisions of the Civil Discovery Act (Act) that authorize imposing sanctions for specified abuses of enumerated discovery methods, such as making an unmeritorious motion for a protective order or failing to serve a timely response to a demand for inspection. The court reasoned that while section 2023.030 contains language stating that courts "may impose" various types of sanctions (including monetary sanctions) for discovery misuse, the provision also specifies that courts may impose such sanctions only "[t]o the extent authorized by" other provisions of the Act. The majority acknowledged that several appellate cases had appeared to award sanctions based solely on sections 2023.010 and 2023.030, but it declined to follow them, explaining that none of the cases had carefully considered the meaning of the "[t]o the extent authorized" language in section 2023.030.

The majority considered in the alternative whether the trial court had the inherent authority to impose the sanctions order. It answered no. The majority cited this court's decision in Bauguess v. Paine (1978) 22 Cal.3d 626, 634–638, 150 Cal.Rptr. 461, 586 P.2d 942, which had held that a trial court lacked inherent authority to impose monetary sanctions in lieu of contempt sanctions, in the absence of statutory authority guiding the exercise of the power. The majority concluded that a party seeking monetary sanctions for discovery misuse therefore must rely on the discovery-method-specific sanctions provisions of the Civil Discovery Act alone. It reversed and remanded the sanctions order "to allow the trial court to award PWC's reasonable expenses incurred as a result of sanctionable conduct under provisions of the Discovery Act other than sections 2023.010 and 2023.030."

Justice Grimes dissented. She criticized "the majority's novel conclusion" that sections 2023.010 and 2023.030 do not confer general authority to impose sanctions for discovery abuse. In her view, the majority's reading of the Civil Discovery Act—"that the only way a trial court can deal with an egregious pattern of stonewalling and falsity in discovery responses is by adhering to the procedural prerequisites of each separate discovery statute for each particular discovery violation"—"does not . . . comport with Legislative intent, much less with decades of precedent."

* * *

II.

Sections 2023.010 and 2023.030 were enacted as part of the Civil Discovery Act of 1986 (1986 Act), a " 'comprehensive revision of the statutes governing discovery' " in California courts.[1] Before 1986, discovery in civil cases was governed by the Discovery Act of 1957 (1957 Act), which had

---

1 "Effective July 1, 2005, the Civil Discovery Act of 1986 was repealed and reenacted without substantive changes by the Civil Discovery Act of 2004." * * * Throughout this opinion, we refer to the provisions of the Act as they appear following the 2004 legislation. * * *

been "the California Legislature's first attempt to codify a comprehensive system of discovery procedures in California." To curtail surprises and enhance efficient trial preparation, the 1957 Act provided for new methods of discovery and "liberalized" each method "as to person, scope, and situation." (Greyhound Corp. v. Superior Court (1961) 56 Cal.2d 355, 375, 15 Cal.Rptr. 90, 364 P.2d 266.) But "[t]o protect against the abuses of the liberality thus created, safeguards were provided unknown to the old California procedures."

One such safeguard was found in Code of Civil Procedure section 2034, which for the first time conferred statutory authority on trial courts to impose sanctions for certain abuses of the discovery process. But over time, section 2034 increasingly came under criticism for failing to adequately respond to the problem of discovery abuse. "[C]ase law increasingly was required to fill in the gaps."

In Fairfield v. Superior Court (1966) 246 Cal.App.2d 113, 54 Cal.Rptr. 721, for example, the trial court exercised its inherent power to control the litigation to impose an award of attorney's fees against a party that had refused to obey an order compelling further answers to interrogatories. Although no section of the 1957 Act expressly provided for monetary sanctions in this circumstance, the Court of Appeal held that the court was nonetheless empowered to "impose appropriate sanctions of the nature provided in" the sanctions provision of the 1957 Act. It reasoned that "[e]very court has power 'To compel obedience to its judgments, orders and process' in an action or proceeding pending before it, and to use all necessary means to carry its jurisdiction into effect, even if those means are not specifically pointed out in the code."

After decades of experience under the 1957 Act revealed similar gaps in the statute's coverage, "a Joint Commission on Discovery of the State Bar and Judicial Council began a top-to-bottom reexamination of California's system [of] civil discovery." * * *

The Civil Discovery Act sets out six methods by which litigants can obtain pretrial disclosure of relevant information: (a) depositions; (b) interrogatories; (c) inspections of documents, things, and places; (d) physical and mental examinations; (e) requests for admissions; and (f) exchanges of expert trial witness information. The procedures relevant to discovery under each of these six methods are outlined in different chapters of the Act. * * *

Each chapter authorizes sanctions for certain conduct constituting misuse or abuse of different discovery methods. * * *

Each of the provisions that authorizes a court to impose sanctions states that such sanctions may (or shall) be imposed "under Chapter 7 (commencing with Section 2023.010)."

* * *

Courts have articulated two major guidelines for imposing sanctions under both the current Civil Discovery Act and its predecessor. First, because the very purpose of discovery is to promote the efficient and effective conduct of trial, discovery sanctions are not to be used "to provide a weapon for punishment, forfeiture and the avoidance of a trial on the merits." Second, a more severe sanction is disfavored if a lesser sanction is available.) This means that a court ordinarily must consider monetary sanctions—the form of sanctions ordered here—before it proceeds to consider whether other nonmonetary sanctions are appropriate to address the misconduct at issue.

Much as they had done under the 1957 Act, courts have sometimes invoked their inherent authority to impose discovery sanctions not inconsistent with the current version of the Act. (See, e.g., Stephen Slesinger, Inc. v. Walt Disney Co. (2007) 155 Cal.App.4th 736, 761, 66 Cal.Rptr.3d 268 [imposing terminating sanction]; Peat, Marwick, Mitchell & Co. v. Superior Court (1988) 200 Cal.App.3d 272, 287, fn. 8, 289, 245 Cal.Rptr. 873 [imposing evidentiary sanction].) The existence of such inherent authority is not disputed here. The City contends, however, that courts' inherent authority is limited to nonmonetary sanctions. It argues that the trial court therefore lacked either statutory authority or the inherent authority to impose the monetary sanctions award at issue in this case. Our inquiry begins—and also ends—with the trial court's statutory authority.

III.

Before the Court of Appeal's decision in this case, courts frequently cited sections 2023.010 and 2023.030 as sources of authority to impose sanctions for discovery misuse. * * *

The Court of Appeal in this case acknowledged cases reflecting this prevailing understanding of sections 2023.010 and 2023.030. But as the court correctly noted, none of these cases carefully considered the language of the provisions in their broader statutory context. The primary question before us is whether the Court of Appeal was correct in concluding—contrary to the prevailing understanding—that sections 2023.010 and 2023.030 do not confer any independent authority to impose sanctions for discovery abuses.

This is purely a question of statutory interpretation, and we review it de novo. * * *

A.

Section 2023.010 addresses the general subject of "[m]isuses of the discovery process." Such misuses, it says, "include, but are not limited to," failures to respond or submit to authorized methods of discovery, making unmeritorious objections without substantial justification, and making evasive responses. It is undisputed that the misconduct the trial court found in this case qualifies as discovery misuse within the meaning of section 2023.010. It is also, however, undisputed that section 2023.010 contains no language authorizing action in response to the sorts of discovery misuses it describes.

The focus of the dispute before us thus centers largely on the interaction between section 2023.010 and section 2023.030. The latter section contains language that, on its face, appears to authorize action addressing the sort of discovery misuse described in section 2023.010, including imposition of monetary sanctions: "To the extent authorized by the chapter governing any particular discovery method or any other provision of this title, *the court . . . may impose* the following sanctions against anyone engaging in conduct that is a misuse of the discovery process: [¶] . . . *The court may impose* a monetary sanction." (§ 2023.030 & subd. (a), italics added.) The central question concerns the meaning of the prefatory phrase indicating that a court may impose sanctions "[t]o the extent authorized" by other provisions of the Civil Discovery Act, including, primarily, the provisions governing the six different methods of discovery.

Both parties agree that the prefatory phrase "[t]o the extent authorized" signals a limitation on the court's authority to impose sanctions, but they disagree as to the scope of this limitation. PwC reads this provision to mean simply that when another, more specific provision of the Civil Discovery Act sets conditions or limits on a trial court's authority to sanction particular forms of discovery misuse, a court may not circumvent those limits by relying on the general authority conferred in section 2023.030; sanctions may be ordered under this general provision only "[t]o the extent" they may be ordered under the other, more specific sanctions provision. But when no other provision applies, courts may rely on the general authority conferred in section 2023.030 to impose sanctions for any "[m]isuse[ ] of the discovery process," as that term is defined in section 2023.010.

Although the City had not initially broached the argument, it now adopts the contrary reading laid out in the Court of Appeal majority opinion. Specifically, the City argues that the plain meaning of the prefatory phrase instructs that the sort of sanctions described in section 2023.030 must be authorized by another provision of the Civil Discovery Act. According to the City, sections 2023.010 and 2023.030 confer no sanctions authority of their own; their primary function is to supply the definitions relevant for authority conferred elsewhere. So, for example, a method-specific provision might supply authority for imposing "monetary sanctions" for failing to allow the inspection of an item in discovery (e.g., Code Civ. Proc., § 2031.300), and section 2023.030 then tells us what the term "monetary sanction[s]" means: an "order[ ] that one . . . pay the reasonable expenses, including attorney's fees, incurred by anyone as a result of" a misuse of the discovery process. (§ 2023.030, subd. (a).) But, as the City sees it, if no other sanctions provision of the Civil Discovery Act applies, a court has no authority to impose discovery sanctions under the Act.

To describe this as the "plain meaning" of the relevant statutory language is something of a bold claim, given that for decades commentators and courts—this court included—have read the provision differently. (See, e.g., * * * Levine et al., O'Connor's Cal. Practice (2015 ed.) Civil Pretrial, § 5, p. 1008 ["If the sanctions provisions for the particular discovery method do not address the misconduct . . . the party should then explore the possibility of sanctions under the [Civil Discovery Act's] more general provisions."].) And indeed, consistent with that prevailing understanding, the City did not initially question the trial court's authority to impose sanctions under sections 2023.010 and 2023.030; the Court of Appeal was the first to raise the issue, sua sponte, when it ordered supplemental briefing to address the meaning of these provisions.

Differences in understanding are not, of course, dispositive. And as the Court of Appeal majority rightly noted, none of the cases that have cited sections 2023.010 and 2023.030 as a source of sanctions authority have engaged in a close analysis of the statutory text. But it is not surprising that courts have generally understood the Civil Discovery Act's sanctions provisions as they have. Though the City insists otherwise, its reading of section 2023.030 is far from the only plausible one.

To start, any claim that section 2023.030 is primarily a definitional provision must contend with the fact that section 2023.030 is not written as most definitional provisions are written. The Civil Discovery Act does contain a standard definitional provision: Code of Civil Procedure section 2016.020 (titled "Definitions") says, for instance, that "[a]s used in this title," " 'Document' and 'writing' mean a writing, as defined in Section 250 of the Evidence Code." (Code of Civ. Proc., § 2016.020 & subd. (c).) Had the Legislature intended for section 2023.030 to serve a definitional function, the Legislature presumably could have used similar phrasing. * * * But the Legislature instead used the sort of language conventionally used to convey authority: The court "may impose the following sanctions," including monetary sanctions (§ 2023.030, subd. (a); cf., e.g., In re Richard E. (1978) 21 Cal.3d 349, 354, 146 Cal.Rptr. 604, 579 P.2d 495 ["The ordinary import of 'may' is a grant of discretion."]). It is not unreasonable to think that this choice was deliberate.

The City's view must also contend with the natural inferences to be drawn from the close relationship between section 2023.030 and its neighbor, section 2023.010, which includes a nonexhaustive definition of discovery misuse more encompassing than any of the more specific chapters addressing the misuse of particular discovery methods. (§ 2023.010 ["Misuses of the discovery process include, but are not limited to, the following . . . ."].) This broad definition thus naturally covers forms and patterns of discovery abuse not captured elsewhere in the statute. The scope of the conduct described in section 2023.010 as a "[m]isuse[ ] of the discovery process" suggests a similar scope for section 2023.030, which provides that courts "may impose" appropriate sanctions for "a misuse of the discovery process." If section 2023.030 does not supply any mechanism for addressing the kinds of discovery misuse described in section 2023.010, the effect is to leave section 2023.010's broad definition of misuse without any real significance in the statutory scheme.

To be fair, the use of the introductory phrase "[t]o the extent authorized by . . . any other provision of this title" does raise questions about whether section 2023.030 means to refer the reader to other provisions to look for authority to impose sanctions. But the introductory phrase carries less weight than the City supposes, because when readers look to most of these other provisions, what they will find is language that directs them right back to section 2023.030. One provision of the inspection chapter addressing monetary sanctions, for instance, provides: "[E]xcept as provided in subdivision (d), the court shall impose a monetary sanction *under Chapter 7 (commencing with Section 2023.010)* against any party, person, or attorney who unsuccessfully makes or opposes a motion to compel." (Code Civ. Proc., § 2031.300, subd. (c), italics added.) Other method-specific sanctions provisions are worded more or less identically. * * * The City's argument about the plain language of section 2023.030 thus fails to account not only for the wording of section 2023.030 itself, but also for the wording of the other provisions on which the argument depends.

The City relies on appellate decisions holding that the " '[t]o the extent authorized' " language means that "the statutes governing the particular discovery methods limit the permissible sanctions to those sanctions provided under the applicable governing statutes." These cases have held that, in determining whether and what sort of sanction to order for misuse of a particular discovery method—monetary sanctions, issue sanctions, and so on—a court is ordinarily limited to those sanctions authorized by the relevant method-specific chapter. In [New Albertsons, Inc. v. Superior Court (2008) 168 Cal.App.4th 1403, 1422, 86 Cal.Rptr.3d 457], for instance, the court held that a trial court does not have the statutory authority under section 2023.030 to impose an issue sanction or an evidence sanction for failure to permit inspection of an item when, under the circumstances, the chapter on inspections would not authorize imposing such sanctions. * * *

The City relies on cases like *New Albertsons* to support its argument that the "[t]o the extent" language means that section 2023.030 cannot be read as an independent source of sanctions authority. But these cases stand for a different proposition, one that is undisputed here. As we have noted, PwC agrees that the general sanctions language in section 2023.030 does not permit courts to override the limitations on courts' sanctions authority set forth in applicable method-specific provisions. This follows from the usual interpretive rule that " 'more specific provisions take precedence over more general ones.' "

As PwC rightly notes, it is one thing to read the "[t]o the extent authorized" language to mean that the authority recognized in section 2023.030 cannot extend farther than the authority conferred by other applicable sanctions provisions, assuming other sanctions provisions are applicable. It is something else to say that section 2023.030 confers no sanctions authority at all—even for those relatively uncommon instances that may involve patterns of systemic abuse that transcend any individual instance of misuse, or in situations where the conduct undoubtedly meets section 2023.010's definition of discovery misuse even though there are no other applicable sanctions provisions. The *New Albertsons* line of cases do not speak to this issue, nor do they support the City's argument that the plain language of section 2023.030 marks it as definitional only.

The City is, in short, incorrect that the plain language of section 2023.030 means it confers no independent authority to impose sanctions. On the contrary, section 2023.030 contains language that, on its face, appears to confer such authority. That reading is reinforced, rather than undermined, by the language of other provisions in the Act relating to discovery sanctions.

* * *

C.

This brings us to our final, and ultimately dispositive, consideration, which concerns how the City's proposed interpretation would serve—or, as it happens, disserve—the Legislature's overarching purposes in enacting the sanctions provisions of the Civil Discovery Act.

Again, in the vast majority of cases, the distinction between the parties' proposed interpretations of section 2023.030 makes no practical difference. The method-specific chapters were deliberately designed to cover the most commonly recurring forms of discovery misuse. Whether a court is to look for statutory authority in those chapters, or to section 2023.030, or both, the outcome is the same: The court may impose those sanctions that are authorized by the more specific provision in the chapter governing the relevant discovery method.

But it is not clear that every act of discovery misconduct is covered by the discovery method chapters. As Justice Grimes noted in her dissent in the Court of Appeal, for instance, "the chapters of the Discovery Act governing particular discovery methods do not mention sanctions for spoliation of evidence", even though, as this court has recognized, intentional spoliation "would surely be a misuse of discovery within the meaning" of section 2023.010.

And it is undisputed that no method-specific provision of the Act addresses pervasive patterns of discovery misconduct of the sort that occurred in this case. This pattern of misconduct certainly included various discrete acts of discovery misconduct that would be individually redressable under certain chapters governing discovery methods. * * * But the power to sanction discrete abuses of specific discovery methods—for instance, the City's initial refusal to produce a [Person Most Qualified] witness and the witness's later failure to adequately prepare for the deposition—is not the same thing as the power to sanction a concerted, multi-year campaign to circumvent discovery that would have revealed serious abuses in the initiation and prosecution of the lawsuit.

The issue in this case, at core, concerns courts' power to fill these sorts of gaps in the method-specific discovery chapters to address egregious instances of discovery misconduct. As noted, the City does not dispute that the courts generally do have such powers. It does not dispute, for instance, the holdings of cases that have invoked the courts' inherent authority to impose a variety of serious discovery sanctions, including evidence sanctions, and even terminating sanctions). But the City distinguishes these cases on grounds that they involved sanctions other than monetary sanctions. It reads our decision in *Bauguess* as precluding monetary sanctions unless they have a statutory basis, lest trial courts "be given a power without procedural limits" set by statute.

The implication of the City's approach is that courts could address egregious cases involving patterns of discovery misconduct, or other similarly rarely occurring forms of discovery misuse, only through the exercise of their inherent authority, with no statutory basis for the exercise. And on the City's reading of *Bauguess*, courts would retain the inherent authority to impose only the most serious forms of discovery sanctions, such as evidentiary or terminating sanctions; they could not impose monetary sanctions, which the Act treats as the least serious form of sanctions. Of course, if the party abusing the discovery process dismisses its claims with prejudice, as the City has done here, then an evidentiary or terminating sanction would be futile, and a court would be all but powerless to address the abuse.

* * *

More fundamentally, the City's view of how the system of statutory discovery sanctions works to address egregious discovery abuses is inconsistent with the overarching purposes of the Civil Discovery Act. * * * One of the central purposes of the 1986 Act, * * * was to give courts the tools necessary to respond to those abuses to ensure that civil discovery can serve its central truth-seeking function. * * *

Against this backdrop, we can readily infer that when the Legislature wrote section 2023.030 to provide that a court "may impose" sanctions for discovery misuse, the choice was deliberate. As part of its concerted response to known deficiencies in the prior discovery sanctions statute, the Legislature gave trial courts a statutory basis for exercising authority to address egregious forms of misconduct not addressed elsewhere in the Act. It seems, by contrast, unlikely that a Legislature concerned with stemming the tide of discovery abuse would have consigned courts confronting patterns of egregious abuse to the choice the City's position would offer them: either attempt to fit the component parts of the pattern into individual method-specific sanctions rulings, or else rely purely on their inherent authority to control the litigation, with no statutory guidelines relevant to that exercise.

D.

The City worries that understanding section 2023.030 as an independent source of authority to impose sanctions would undermine the carefully calibrated scheme of escalating sanctions reflected in the individual method-specific chapters, under which courts typically must consider imposing monetary sanctions before turning to more severe sanctions such as issue sanctions or evidence sanctions. The City's professed worry is doubly odd. It is odd, first, because this case concerns only monetary sanctions, which are the least serious form of sanctions authorized under the Act. It is odd, second, because the City acknowledges that courts retain the inherent authority to impose sanctions outside the rubric of the Act (that is, provided the sanctions are nonmonetary sanctions). It is unclear how relegating courts to exercising nonstatutory authority to address discovery abuses would help to shore up the statutory policies underlying the sanctions provisions of the Act.

The straightforward answer to the City's worry, however, is that a court's authority to impose sanctions under section 2023.030 is not limitless. It is already well-established that a court may not rely on section 2023.030 to override the limitations prescribed by any other applicable sanctions provision in the Act. A court may invoke its independent authority to impose sanctions under sections 2023.010 and 2023.030 only when confronted with an unusual form of discovery abuse, or a pattern of abuse, not already addressed by a relevant sanctions provision. And where it invokes that authority, it is constrained by the long-settled rules generally governing the imposition of discovery sanctions under the Act.

Consistent with the practices outlined in the Civil Discovery Act, trial courts must afford any party or person accused of engaging in an abuse of the discovery process "notice" and an "opportunity for hearing," and courts must consider whether the party or person "acted with substantial justification," or whether "other circumstances make the imposition of the sanction unjust." (§ 2023.030 & subd. (a).) Trial courts must also be mindful not to impose sanctions that exceed "the *reasonable* expenses, including attorney's fees, incurred by anyone *as a result* of" the discovery misconduct. (Id., subd. (a), italics added.) These principles of causation and reasonableness ensure fidelity to the well-established principle that " 'the court may not impose sanctions which are designed not to accomplish the objects of discovery but to impose punishment.' "

* * *

Given these long-settled understandings, we see no genuine danger that reading sections 2023.010 and 2023.030 as an independent source of sanctions authority in any way undermines the intended functioning of the statute. Courts have for decades read sections 2023.010 and 2023.030 in just this way. The trial court did not err in relying on those provisions here.

CONCLUSION

We reverse the judgment of the Court of Appeal.

SUMMARY JUDGMENT

AGUILAR V. ATLANTIC RICHFIELD CO.

Supreme Court of California, 2001.
25 Cal.4th 826, 107 Cal.Rptr.2d 841, 24 P.3d 493.

MOSK, JUSTICE.

We granted review in this cause to clarify the law that courts must apply in ruling on motions for summary judgment, both in actions generally and specifically in antitrust actions for unlawful conspiracy.

I

This is an antitrust action arising from a complaint filed by Theresa Aguilar on behalf of herself and all of the other, by her estimate, 24 million retail consumers of California Air Resources Board, or CARB, gasoline—collectively, Aguilar—against Atlantic Richfield Company, Chevron Corporation, Exxon Corporation, Mobil Oil Corporation, Union Oil Company of California (later succeeded by 76 Products Company), Shell Oil Company, Texaco Refining and Marketing, Inc., Tosco Corporation, and Ultramar Inc.—collectively, the petroleum companies.

In conducting our review, we have scrutinized facts that are many and complex. The motions for summary judgment with which we are concerned produced a voluminous record, which fills more than 18,400 pages. They arose out of extensive discovery, which yielded, according to one tally, more than 100 depositions, 1,500 interrogatories, 135 requests for admissions, 900 requests for the production of documents, and 500,000 pages of documents in response to such requests.

But because our review focuses on the law that courts must apply in ruling on motions for summary judgment in all actions including the present, and not on the application of such law in this particular one, we need not state the facts in detail and at length. For our purposes, the following synopsis will suffice.

The Legislature has found and declared that the "petroleum industry is an essential element of the California economy and is therefore of vital importance to the health and welfare of all Californians."

In 1991, the California Air Resources Board adopted regulations requiring the sale in this state of a new, cleaner burning, but more expensive formulation of gasoline—CARB gasoline—beginning in 1996. In 1991, the state's market for gasoline was oligopolistic, that is, it was served by a few large firms, including as major participants the petroleum companies that figure here. Although the gasoline used in the state was not unique, the state itself was relatively isolated. Each of the petroleum companies faced decisions of substantial magnitude and difficulty with respect to CARB gasoline capacity, production, and pricing. In arriving at its own decisions and then following through, each had to make great capital expenditures, from a low of about $100 million to a high of more than $1 billion. In 1996, the state's market for gasoline was even more oligopolistic, being served by even fewer large firms, including as dominant participants the petroleum companies that figure here. The state itself remained relatively isolated. But, now, the gasoline used in the state was unique. The price of CARB gasoline, once introduced, moved generally upward across all of the petroleum companies more or less together, rising quickly and falling slowly. Subsequent state and federal investigations expressly or impliedly attributed the generally upward price movement of CARB gasoline to various market forces, including the higher cost of its production, the higher cost of crude oil from which it was produced, higher demand, lower inventories, unplanned production outages, and higher taxes.

II

On June 7, 1996, on behalf of herself and all other retail consumers of CARB gasoline, Aguilar filed an unverified complaint, with a demand for trial by jury, against the petroleum companies in the Superior Court of San Diego County. In the complaint, as subsequently amended into its operative form, she alleged facts for a primary cause of action for violation of section 1 of the Cartwright Act (Stats.1907, ch. 530, § 1, pp. 984–985, as amended, Bus. & Prof.Code, § 16720 et seq.), which is analogous to section 1 of the Sherman Act (Act of July 2, 1890, ch. 647, § 1, 26 Stat. 209, as amended, 15 U.S.C. § 1), asserting in substance that the petroleum companies had entered into an unlawful conspiracy to restrict the output of CARB gasoline and to raise its price—specifically, a conspiracy among competitors that is unlawful per se without regard to any of its effects. She also alleged facts for a derivative cause of action for violation of the unfair competition law (Bus. & Prof.Code, § 17200 et seq.), asserting in substance that the conspiracy in question, even if not unlawful under the Cartwright Act, was unlawful at least under the unfair competition law itself.

The petroleum companies each answered, denying all of the allegations referred to above.

Later, the petroleum companies each moved the superior court for summary judgment. In support, they each presented evidence including declarations by officers or managers or similar employees with responsibility in the premises, generally stating on personal knowledge how the company made its capacity, production, and pricing decisions about CARB gasoline, asserting that it did so independently, and denying that it did so collusively with any of the others. Aguilar opposed the motions. In support, she presented evidence including the companies' gathering and dissemination of capacity, production, and pricing information, through the independently owned and operated Oil Price Information Service, or OPIS, and otherwise; their use of common consultants; and, perhaps most prominently, their execution of exchange agreements—under which, for example, two companies may trade, with or without a price differential, products of the same type in different geographical areas and/or at different times or products of different types in the same geographical area and/or at the same time—including any consequent activity, or lack of activity, in the spot market, where individual wholesale bulk sales and purchases are transacted. She also presented related evidence in the form of opinion by experts.

After a hearing, the superior court issued an order granting the petroleum companies summary judgment. It caused entry thereof. It specified its reasons at length and in detail, filling 24 pages, to the following effect:

The petroleum companies carried their burden of persuasion to show that there was no triable issue of material fact and that they were entitled to judgment as a matter of law.

Particularly, as to Aguilar's Cartwright Act cause of action, which was primary, the petroleum companies carried an initial burden of production to make a prima facie showing of the absence of any conspiracy through the declarations that they presented from their officers and managers and similar employees in light of Biljac Associates v. First Interstate Bank (1990) 218 Cal.App.3d 1410, 267 Cal.Rptr. 819 (hereafter sometimes *Biljac*), which dealt with the force and effect of similar declarations as to a similar cause of action by certain commercial borrowers against certain banks and bank trade associations. Aguilar did not carry a burden of production, which had shifted onto her shoulders, to make a prima facie showing of her own of the presence of an unlawful conspiracy through any of the evidence that she presented, including that of capacity, production, and pricing information, common consultants, or exchange agreements, or her own experts' opinion. "[T]he *only* logical inference which can be drawn" from Aguilar's evidence, even after it has been "examin[ed] . . . in its entirety and without compartmentalization," is that the "actions" of the petroleum companies "were a pro-competitive response to a regulatory requirement which forced members of an oligopoly to restructure their product mix and incur substantial additional capital expenditures." (Italics added in place of underscoring in original.) Aguilar had "attempted to weave" a "complex, tangled web" of unlawful conspiracy. Her evidence, however, "suggest[ed]" only individual companies "using all available information sources to determine capacity, supply, and pricing decisions which would maximize their own individual profits—without regard to the profits of their competitors"—and did "not support even the inference of" such a conspiracy.

As to Aguilar's unfair competition law cause of action, which was derivative, the petroleum companies, as indicated, carried their initial burden of production to make a prima facie showing of the absence of any conspiracy; Aguilar, as also indicated, did not carry her shifted burden of production to make a prima facie showing of the presence of an unlawful one.

The superior court rendered judgment in accordance with its order granting the petroleum companies summary judgment, and caused entry thereof.

Aguilar moved the superior court for a new trial. In so doing, she challenged its judgment by challenging as erroneous its order granting the petroleum companies summary judgment. Specifically, among her grounds for a new trial was a claim that, in granting summary judgment as to her Cartwright Act cause of action, it made an "error in law" in reading and applying *Biljac* as it did.

After a hearing, the superior court issued an order granting a new trial. In so doing, it recognized that Aguilar had challenged its judgment by challenging as erroneous its order granting the petroleum companies summary judgment. It granted a new trial on the sole ground that, in granting summary judgment as to her Cartwright Act cause of action, it did indeed make an "error in law." In specifying its reasons, it stated that it did in fact misread and misapply *Biljac* to allow the petroleum companies to carry their initial burden of production to make a prima facie showing of the absence of any conspiracy as to her Cartwright Act cause of action by presenting evidence *other than* through declarations by each person responsible within each company for its capacity, production, and pricing decisions about CARB gasoline: it now read and applied *Biljac* to require declarations by each such person. Its order granting a new trial effectively vacated its judgment. Hence, it operated like an order denying summary judgment.

* * *

The Court of Appeal determined that, as to Aguilar's Cartwright Act cause of action, the petroleum companies carried their burden of production to make a prima facie showing of the absence of any conspiracy, but Aguilar did not carry her shifted burden of production to make a prima facie showing of the presence of an unlawful one, her "evidence" often being less than it was claimed to be. The Court of Appeal accepted the superior court's earlier determination that Aguilar's evidence did "not support even the inference of" an unlawful conspiracy, but only individual, "pro-competitive" "actions." But the Court of Appeal rejected the superior court's later determination that it made an error in law in its reading and application of *Biljac,* finding no support therein for any requirement that the petroleum companies had to present evidence in the form of declarations by each person responsible within each company for its capacity, production, and pricing decisions about CARB gasoline.

The Court of Appeal determined that, as to Aguilar's unfair competition law cause of action, the petroleum companies, as indicated, carried their burden of production to make a prima facie showing of the absence of any conspiracy, but Aguilar, as also indicated, did not carry her shifted burden of production to make a prima facie showing of the presence of an unlawful one.

Aguilar petitioned for review. We granted her application. We now affirm.

III

Our task in this cause is to clarify the law that courts must apply in ruling on motions for summary judgment, both in actions generally and specifically in antitrust actions for unlawful conspiracy.

* * *

Under summary judgment law, any party to an action, whether plaintiff or defendant, "may move" the court "for summary judgment" in his favor on a cause of action (i.e., claim) or defense (Code Civ. Proc., § 437c, subd. (a))—a plaintiff "contend[ing] . . . that there is no defense to the action," a defendant "contend[ing] that the action has no merit". The court must "grant[ ]" the "motion" "if all the papers submitted show" that "there is no triable issue as to any material fact" (§ 437c, subd. (c))—that is, there is no issue requiring a trial as to any fact that is necessary under the pleadings and, ultimately, the law—and that the "moving party is entitled to a judgment as a matter of law" (Code Civ. Proc., § 437c, subd. (c)). The moving party must "support[ ]" the "motion" with evidence including "affidavits, declarations, admissions, answers to interrogatories, depositions, and matters of which judicial notice" must or may "be taken." (§ 437c, subd. (b).) Likewise, any adverse party may oppose the motion, and, "where appropriate," must present evidence including "affidavits, declarations, admissions, answers to interrogatories, depositions, and matters of which judicial notice" must or may "be taken." An adverse party who chooses to oppose the motion must be allowed a reasonable opportunity to do so. (§ 437c, subd. (h).) In ruling on the motion, the court must "consider all of the evidence" and "all" of the "inferences" reasonably drawn therefrom (§ 437c, subd. (c)), and must view such evidence and such inferences in the light most favorable to the opposing party.

In 1986, the United States Supreme Court handed down a trio of decisions dealing with the law of summary judgment in the federal courts: Matsushita Elec. Industrial Co. v. Zenith Radio (1986) 475 U.S. 574, 106 S.Ct. 1348, 89 L.Ed.2d 538 (hereafter sometimes *Matsushita*); Anderson v. Liberty Lobby, Inc. (1986) 477 U.S. 242, 106 S.Ct. 2505, 91 L.Ed.2d 202 (hereafter sometimes *Anderson*); and Celotex Corp. v. Catrett (1986) 477 U.S. 317, 106 S.Ct. 2548, 91 L.Ed.2d 265 (hereafter sometimes *Celotex*).

The purpose of federal summary judgment law, which is identical to the purpose of ours, is to provide courts with a mechanism to cut through the parties' pleadings in order to determine whether, despite their allegations, trial is in fact necessary to resolve their dispute.

* * *

In *Celotex*, *Anderson*, and *Matsushita*, the Supreme Court clarified federal summary judgment law, and liberalized the granting of such motions.

Together, *Celotex*, *Anderson*, and *Matsushita* operate generally, to the following effect: From commencement to conclusion, the moving party bears the burden of persuasion that there is no genuine issue of material fact and that he is entitled to judgment as a matter of law.[4] There is a genuine issue of material fact if, and only if, the evidence would allow a reasonable trier of fact to find the underlying fact in favor of the party opposing the motion in accordance with the applicable standard of proof. Initially, the moving party bears a burden of production to make a prima facie showing of the nonexistence of any genuine issue of material fact. If he carries his burden of production, he causes a shift: the opposing party is

[4] On summary judgment, the moving party's burden is more properly labeled as one of persuasion rather than proof. That is because, in order to carry such burden, he must persuade the court that there is no material fact for a reasonable trier of fact to find, and not prove any such fact to the satisfaction of the court itself as though it were sitting as the trier of fact.

then subjected to a burden of production of his own to make a prima facie showing of the existence of a genuine issue of material fact. How each party may carry his burden of persuasion and/or production depends on *which* would bear *what* burden of proof at trial. Thus, if a plaintiff who would bear the burden of proof by a preponderance of evidence at trial moves for summary judgment, he must present evidence that would require a reasonable trier of fact to find any underlying material fact more likely than not. By contrast, if a defendant moves for summary judgment against such a plaintiff, he may present evidence that would require such a trier of fact *not* to find any underlying material fact more likely than not. In the alternative, he may simply point out—he is not required to present evidence (see Fed.Rules Civ.Proc., rule 56(b), 28 U.S.C.)—that the plaintiff does not possess, and cannot reasonably obtain, evidence that would allow such a trier of fact to find any underlying material fact more likely than not.

* * *

At the time of *Celotex*, *Anderson*, and *Matsushita*, summary judgment law in this state differed from its federal counterpart in various particulars, and was more restrictive of the granting of such motions as a result. For example, a plaintiff moving for summary judgment had to disprove any defense asserted by the defendant as well as prove each element of his own cause of action. For his part, a defendant moving for summary judgment had to "conclusively negate"—to quote the potentially misleading phrase—an element of the plaintiff's cause of action. To do so, the defendant had to present evidence, and not simply point out that the plaintiff did not possess, and could not reasonably obtain, needed evidence.

In the wake of *Celotex*, *Anderson*, and *Matsushita*, as we recently noted in Guz v. Bechtel National, Inc. (2000) 24 Cal.4th 317, 335, footnote 7, 100 Cal.Rptr.2d 352, 8 P.3d 1089 (hereafter sometimes *Guz*), summary judgment law has been amended, most significantly in 1992 and 1993 * * *.

* * *

Together, the 1992 and 1993 amendments, which continue in effect to this day, have " 'changed' " summary judgment law " 'dramatically.' " As follows:

In moving for summary judgment, a "plaintiff . . . has met" his "burden of showing that there is no defense to a cause of action if" he "has proved each element of the cause of action entitling" him "to judgment on that cause of action. Once the plaintiff . . . has met that burden, the burden shifts to the defendant . . . to show that a triable issue of one or more material facts exists as to that cause of action or a defense thereto. The defendant . . . may not rely upon the mere allegations or denials" of his "pleadings to show that a triable issue of material fact exists but, instead," must "set forth the specific facts showing that a triable issue of material fact exists as to that cause of action or a defense thereto." (Code Civ. Proc., § 437c, subd. (*o*)(1).)

Similarly, in moving for summary judgment, a "defendant . . . has met" his "burden of showing that a cause of action has no merit if" he "has shown that one or more elements of the cause of action . . . cannot be established, or that there is a complete defense to that cause of action. Once the defendant . . . has met that burden, the burden shifts to the plaintiff . . . to show that a triable issue of one or more material facts exists as to that cause of action or a defense thereto. The plaintiff . . . may not rely upon the mere allegations or denials" of his "pleadings to show that a triable issue of material fact exists but, instead," must "set forth the specific facts showing that a triable issue of material fact exists as to that cause of action or a defense thereto." (Code Civ. Proc., § 437c, subd. (*o*)(2).)

In light of the foregoing, we believe that summary judgment law in this state now conforms, largely but not completely, to its federal counterpart as clarified and liberalized in *Celotex*, *Anderson*, and *Matsushita*. The language added by the 1992 and 1993 amendments, which follows the substance of those decisions, supports our view. The legislative history of the bills that would result in those amendments provides confirmation, making plain that they "follow" their "example."

First, and generally, from commencement to conclusion, the party moving for summary judgment bears the burden of persuasion that there is no triable issue of material fact and that he is entitled to judgment as a matter of law.[11] That is because of the general principle that a party who seeks a court's action in his favor bears the burden of persuasion thereon. There is a triable issue of material fact if, and only if, the evidence would allow a reasonable trier of fact to find the underlying fact in favor of the party opposing the motion in accordance with the applicable standard of proof. In Reader's Digest Assn. v. Superior Court (1984) 37 Cal.3d 244, 252, 208 Cal.Rptr. 137, 690 P.2d 610 (hereafter sometimes *Reader's Digest*), we held to the effect that the placement and quantum of the burden of proof at trial were crucial for purposes of summary judgment, expressly as to the burden's placement and impliedly as to its quantum. There is nothing contrary in the language or legislative history of the 1992 and 1993 amendments. Thus, a plaintiff bears the burden of persuasion that "each element of" the "cause of action" in question has been "proved," and hence that "there is no defense" thereto. (Code Civ. Proc., § 437c, subd. (*o*)(1).) A defendant bears the burden of persuasion that "one or more elements of"

---

[11] Again, on summary judgment, the moving party's burden is more properly one of persuasion rather than of proof, since he must persuade the court that there is no material fact for a reasonable trier of fact to find, and not prove any such fact to the satisfaction of the court itself as though it were sitting as the trier of fact.

the "cause of action" in question "cannot be established," or that "there is a complete defense" thereto. (§ 437c, subd. (*o*)(2).)

Second, and generally, the party moving for summary judgment bears an initial burden of production to make a prima facie showing of the nonexistence of any triable issue of material fact; if he carries his burden of production, he causes a shift, and the opposing party is then subjected to a burden of production of his own to make a prima facie showing of the existence of a triable issue of material fact. Although not expressly, the 1992 and 1993 amendments impliedly provide in this regard for a burden of *production* as opposed to a burden of *persuasion*. A burden of production entails only the presentation of "evidence." A burden of persuasion, however, entails the "establish[ment]" through such evidence of a "requisite degree of belief." It would make little, if any, sense to allow for the shifting of a burden of persuasion. For if the moving party carries a burden of persuasion, the opposing party can do nothing other than concede. Further, although not expressly, the 1992 and 1993 amendments impliedly provide for a burden of production *to make a prima facie showing*. A prima facie showing is one that is sufficient to support the position of the party in question. No more is called for.

Third, and generally, how the parties moving for, and opposing, summary judgment may each carry their burden of persuasion and/or production depends on *which* would bear *what* burden of proof at trial. Again, in *Reader's Digest*, we held to the effect that the placement and quantum of the burden of proof at trial were crucial for purposes of summary judgment. In the legislative history, if not the quoted language, of the 1992 and 1993 amendments, there is support for such a proposition; in neither is there anything contrary. Thus, if a plaintiff who would bear the burden of proof by a preponderance of evidence at trial moves for summary judgment, he must present evidence that would *require* a reasonable trier of fact to find any underlying material fact more likely than not—otherwise, he would not be entitled to judgment *as a matter of law*, but would have to present his evidence to a trier of fact. By contrast, if a defendant moves for summary judgment against such a plaintiff, he must present evidence that would require a reasonable trier of fact *not* to find any underlying material fact more likely than not—otherwise, *he* would not be entitled to judgment *as a matter of law*, but would have to present *his* evidence to a trier of fact.

Fourth, and specifically as to an antitrust action for unlawful conspiracy under provisions including section 1 of the Cartwright Act, which, like its Sherman Act analogue, makes a conspiracy among competitors to restrict output and/or raise prices unlawful per se without regard to any of its effects: On the defendants' motion for summary judgment, in order to carry a burden of production to make a prima facie showing that there is a triable issue of the material fact of the existence of an unlawful conspiracy, a plaintiff, who would bear the burden of proof by a preponderance of evidence at trial, must present evidence that would allow a reasonable trier of fact to find in his favor on the unlawful-conspiracy issue by a preponderance of the evidence, that is, to find an unlawful conspiracy more likely than not. Ambiguous evidence or inferences showing or implying conduct that is as consistent with permissible competition by independent actors as with unlawful conspiracy by colluding ones do not allow such a trier of fact so to find. Antitrust law, including the Cartwright Act, compels the result. Otherwise, it might effectively chill procompetitive conduct in the world at large, the very thing that it is designed to protect, by subjecting it to undue costs in the judicial sphere. Therefore, in addition, the plaintiff must present evidence that tends to exclude, although it need not actually exclude, the possibility that the alleged conspirators acted independently rather than collusively. Insufficient is a mere assertion that a reasonable trier of fact might disbelieve any denial by the defendants of an unlawful conspiracy. "If" the defendants are "otherwise entitled to a summary judgment," as a general rule "summary judgment" may "not be denied on grounds of credibility or for want of cross-examination. . . ." (Code Civ. Proc., § 437c, subd. (e).) We own that, in Corwin v. Los Angeles Newspaper Service Bureau, Inc. (1971) 4 Cal.3d 842, 852, 94 Cal.Rptr. 785, 484 P.2d 953, we expressed a belief that, in such an action, courts should grant motions for summary judgment by defendants "sparingly." But "sparingly" does not mean "seldom if ever." Hence, although such motions should be denied when they should, they must be granted when they must.

It follows that summary judgment law in this state now conforms, largely but not completely, to its federal counterpart as clarified and liberalized in *Celotex*, *Anderson*, and *Matsushita*.

For example, summary judgment law in this state no longer requires a plaintiff moving for summary judgment to disprove any defense asserted by the defendant as well as prove each element of his own cause of action. In this particular, it now accords with federal law. All that the plaintiff need do is to "prove[ ] each element of the cause of action." (Code Civ. Proc., § 437c, subd. (*o*)(1).)

Neither does summary judgment law in this state any longer require a defendant moving for summary judgment to conclusively negate an element of the plaintiff's cause of action. In this particular too, it now accords with federal law. All that the defendant need do is to "show[ ] that one or more elements of the cause of action . . . cannot be established" by the plaintiff. (Code Civ. Proc., § 437c, subd. (*o*)(2).) In other words, all that the defendant need do is to show that the plaintiff cannot establish at least one element of the cause of action—for example, that the plaintiff cannot prove element X. Although he remains free to do so, the defendant need not himself conclusively negate any such element—for example, himself prove *not* X. This is in line with the purpose of the 1992 and 1993 amendments, which was to liberalize the granting of motions for summary judgment. As Justice Chin stated in his concurring opinion in *Guz*, "[g]iven the difficulty of proving a negative, . . . a test" requiring conclusive negation "is often impossibly high." The defendant has shown that the plaintiff cannot establish at least one element of the cause of action by showing that the plaintiff does not possess, and cannot reasonably obtain, needed evidence: The defendant must show that the plaintiff *does not possess* needed evidence, because otherwise the plaintiff might be able to establish the elements of the cause of action; the defendant must also show that the plaintiff *cannot reasonably obtain* needed evidence, because the plaintiff must be allowed a reasonable opportunity to oppose the motion (Code Civ. Proc., § 437c, subd. (h)). * * *

Summary judgment law in this state, however, continues to require a defendant moving for summary judgment to present evidence, and not simply point out that the plaintiff does not possess, and cannot reasonably obtain, needed evidence. In this particular at least, it still diverges from federal law. For the defendant *must* "support [ ]" the "motion" with evidence including "affidavits, declarations, admissions, answers to interrogatories, depositions, and matters of which judicial notice" must or may "be taken." (Code Civ. Proc., § 437c, subd. (b).) The defendant may, but need not, present evidence that conclusively negates an element of the plaintiff's cause of action. The defendant may also present evidence that the plaintiff does not possess, and cannot reasonably obtain, needed evidence—as through admissions by the plaintiff following extensive discovery to the effect that he has discovered nothing. But, as Fairbank v. Wunderman Cato Johnson (9th Cir.2000) 212 F.3d 528 concludes, the defendant *must* indeed present "evidence": Whereas, under federal law, "pointing out through argument" may be sufficient, under state law, it is not.

To speak broadly, all of the foregoing discussion of summary judgment law in this state, like that of its federal counterpart, may be reduced to, and justified by, a single proposition: If a party moving for summary judgment in any action, including an antitrust action for unlawful conspiracy, would prevail at trial without submission of any issue of material fact to a trier of fact for determination, then he should prevail on summary judgment. In such a case, as Justice Chin stated in his concurring opinion in *Guz*, the "court should grant" the motion "and avoid a . . . trial" rendered "useless" by nonsuit or directed verdict or similar device.

Aguilar concedes that, on the defendants' motion for summary judgment in an antitrust action for unlawful conspiracy under provisions including section 1 of the Cartwright Act, a plaintiff must present evidence that tends to exclude the possibility that the defendants acted independently rather than collusively, in order to carry a burden of production to make a prima facie showing that there is a triable issue of the material fact of the existence of an unlawful conspiracy.

Aguilar also concedes that ambiguous evidence or inferences showing or implying conduct that is as consistent with permissible competition by independent actors as with unlawful conspiracy by colluding ones do not allow a reasonable trier of fact to find in the plaintiff's favor on the unlawful-conspiracy issue by a preponderance of the evidence.

But Aguilar claims that the court must consider all of the evidence and all of the inferences drawn therefrom. We agree. (Code Civ. Proc., § 437c, subd. (c).)

Aguilar also claims that the court may not weigh the plaintiff's evidence or inferences against the defendants' as though it were sitting as the trier of fact. We agree here as well. The court may not "grant[ ]" the defendants' motion for summary judgment "based on inferences . . ., if contradicted by other inferences or evidence, which raise a triable issue as to any material fact." (Code Civ. Proc., § 437c, subd. (c).) Neither, apparently, may the court grant their motion based on any evidence from which such inferences are drawn, if so contradicted. That means that, if the court concludes that the plaintiff's evidence or inferences raise a triable issue of material fact, it must conclude its consideration and deny the defendants' motion.

But, even though the court may not weigh the plaintiff's evidence or inferences against the defendants' as though it were sitting as the trier of fact, it must nevertheless determine what any evidence or inference *could show or imply to a reasonable trier of fact*. Aguilar effectively admits as much. In so doing, it does not decide on any finding of its own, but simply decides what finding such a trier of fact could make for itself.

Thus, if the court determines that any evidence or inference presented or drawn by the plaintiff indeed shows or implies unlawful conspiracy *more likely than* permissible competition, it must then deny the defendants' motion for summary judgment, even in the face of contradictory evidence or inference presented or drawn by the defendants, because a reasonable trier of fact could find for the plaintiff. Under such circumstances, the unlawful-conspiracy issue is triable—that is, it must be submitted to a trier of fact for determination in favor of either the plaintiff or the defendants, and may not be taken from the trier of fact and resolved by the court itself in the defendants' favor and against the plaintiff.

But if the court determines that all of the evidence presented by the plaintiff, and all of the inferences drawn therefrom, show and imply unlawful conspiracy *only as likely as* permissible competition *or even less likely*, it must then grant the defendants' motion for summary judgment, even apart from any evidence presented by the defendants or any inferences drawn therefrom, because a reasonable trier of fact could not find for the plaintiff. Under such circumstances, the unlawful-conspiracy issue is not triable—that is, it may not be submitted to a trier of fact for determination in favor of either the plaintiff or the defendants, but must be taken from the trier of fact and resolved by the court itself in the defendants' favor and against the plaintiff.

We acknowledge that a plaintiff like Aguilar must often rely on inference rather than evidence since, usually, unlawful conspiracy is conceived in secrecy and lives its life in the shadows. But, when he does so, he must all the same rely on an inference implying unlawful conspiracy *more likely than* permissible competition, either in itself or together with other inferences or evidence. Aguilar claims that the inference need only be reasonable. True. But, as she herself effectively admits, the inference is reasonable if, and only if, it implies unlawful conspiracy more likely than permissible competition.

IV

* * *

In arriving at our determination, we do not ignore the fact that this is, primarily, a complex antitrust action for unlawful conspiracy under section 1 of the Cartwright Act, indeed, a very complex one. We could not do so even if we would, confronting as we do the Court of Appeal's lengthy and detailed opinion. But neither can we ignore the fact that summary judgment is available, and always remains available, even in complex cases.

To proceed, the superior court's order granting the petroleum companies summary judgment was not erroneous as to Aguilar's primary cause of action, which was for an unlawful conspiracy under section 1 of the Cartwright Act to restrict the output of CARB gasoline and to raise its price.

At trial, Aguilar as plaintiff would have borne the burden of proof by a preponderance of the evidence as to her Cartwright Act cause of action. * * *

The petroleum companies carried their burden of persuasion to show that there was no triable issue of material fact and that they were entitled to judgment as a matter of law as to Aguilar's Cartwright Act cause of action.

At the outset, the petroleum companies carried their initial burden of production to make a prima facie showing of the absence of any conspiracy. Through the declarations by their officers and managers and similar employees—and through material from others including third parties—they presented evidence that would require a reasonable jury *not* to find any conspiracy more likely than not. The declarations in question, it must be emphasized, generally stated on personal knowledge how the companies made their capacity, production, and pricing decisions about CARB gasoline. Hence, they did more than baldly assert that they made them independently, and did more than baldly deny that they made them collusively with each other.

It is impossible to summarize the petroleum companies' evidence within a scope that would be appropriate to this opinion. The Court of Appeal's recounting itself fills 38 pages. With that said, the petroleum companies' evidence showed independence rather than collusion as to their most fundamental strategies with respect to CARB gasoline. For example, at one end of the range, there was Chevron's altogether active plan, which was to "gain an advantage over its competitors by becoming the largest producer of CARB gasoline in the world." At the other end, there was Union Oil's relatively passive stance, which would put it at a disadvantage vis-a-vis its competitors in this regard, and would lead it to exit the market completely.

By contrast, Aguilar did not carry the burden of production shifted onto her shoulders to make a prima facie showing of the presence of an unlawful conspiracy. She did not present evidence that would allow a reasonable jury to find a conspiracy more likely than not—her "evidence," as the Court of Appeal noted, often being less than it was claimed to be.

Specifically, the evidence that Aguilar did present was at best ambiguous, as were the inferences that she drew therefrom, showing or implying conduct that was at least as consistent with permissible competition by the petroleum companies as independent actors, as with unlawful conspiracy by them as colluding ones. Evidence of this sort, however, was insufficient. So too were related inferences.

Therefore, in addition, Aguilar had to present evidence that tended to exclude the possibility that the petroleum companies acted independently rather than collusively. This she did not do.

* * *

We recognize that Aguilar did indeed present evidence that the petroleum companies may have possessed the motive, opportunity, and means to enter into an unlawful conspiracy. But that is all. And that is not enough. Such evidence merely allows speculation about an unlawful conspiracy. Speculation, however, is not evidence. As a result, Aguilar's evidence of the petroleum companies' possible motive, opportunity, and means for entry into an unlawful conspiracy does not amount to evidence showing such a conspiracy more likely than not. Neither does it even support an inference implying as much.

The Court of Appeal rejected the superior court's determination that, in granting the petroleum companies summary judgment as to Aguilar's Cartwright Act cause of action, it made an error in law in its reading and application of *Biljac*. Appropriately so. *Biljac* held *at most* that declarations by each person responsible within each of certain entities for certain decisions were *sufficient* under summary judgment law as it stood prior to the 1992 and 1993 amendments to negate an unlawful conspiracy, presumably conclusively. *Biljac* did *not* hold that declarations by officers and managers and similar employees of the sort that the petroleum companies presented here were *insufficient* under summary judgment law as it stands now even to carry their initial burden of production to make a prima facie showing of the absence of any conspiracy.

To the extent that the superior court may have erred as to Aguilar's Cartwright Act cause of action, Aguilar cannot raise any complaint, for any such error could have benefited her alone. The superior court appears to have concluded that, in order to carry their initial burden of production, the petroleum companies had to present evidence that conclusively negated an unlawful conspiracy.[34] Such a conclusion, however, would be contrary to our analysis. The superior court also appears to have concluded that, in order to carry the burden of production shifted onto her shoulders, Aguilar did *not* have to present evidence that tended to exclude the possibility that the petroleum companies acted independently rather than collusively, but could present no more than ambiguous evidence or inferences showing or implying conduct that was as consistent with permissible competition by independent actors as with unlawful conspiracy by colluding ones. Such a conclusion, however, would also be contrary to our analysis.

Just as the superior court's order granting the petroleum companies summary judgment was not erroneous as to Aguilar's primary cause of action for an unlawful conspiracy under section 1 of the Cartwright Act to restrict the output of CARB gasoline and to raise its price, neither was it erroneous as to her derivative cause of action, which was for an unlawful conspiracy under the unfair competition law for the same purpose.

At trial, Aguilar as plaintiff would have borne the burden of proof by a preponderance of the evidence as to her unfair competition law cause of action. Again, as a general rule, the party desiring relief bears the burden of proof by a preponderance of the evidence. So it is here.

The petroleum companies carried their burden of persuasion to show that there was no triable issue of material fact and that they were entitled to judgment as a matter of law as to Aguilar's unfair competition law cause of action. They did so by doing so as to her Cartwright Act cause of action. Again, they carried their burden of production to make a prima facie showing of the absence of any conspiracy, but she did not carry her shifted

[34] Although it did not criticize the superior court on this score, the Court of Appeal all but expressly concluded that evidence that conclusively negated an unlawful conspiracy was of course sufficient, but not necessary, to carry an initial burden of production to make a prima facie showing of the absence of any conspiracy.

burden of production to make a prima facie showing of the presence of an unlawful one.

It is true, as Aguilar argues, that her unfair competition law cause of action is not based on allegations asserting a conspiracy *unlawful under the Cartwright Act*. But it is indeed based on allegations asserting a *conspiracy*, specifically, one unlawful at least under the unfair competition law itself. As stated, the petroleum companies showed that there was no triable issue of the material fact of conspiracy. Aguilar claims that conspiracy is not an element of an unfair competition law cause of action in the abstract as a matter of law. Correctly so. But she simply cannot deny that conspiracy is indeed a component of the unfair competition law cause of action *in this case as a matter of fact*.

V

For the reasons stated above, we conclude that we must affirm the judgment of the Court of Appeal.

It is so ordered.

JOINDER

DOE V. REGENTS OF UNIVERSITY OF CALIFORNIA

California Court of Appeal, First District, 2022.
80 Cal.App.5th 282, 295 Cal.Rptr.3d 625.

TUCHER, PRESIDING JUSTICE.

John Doe filed a petition for writ of mandate against the Regents of the University of California (the University), seeking to set aside the University's decision to discipline John for sexually assaulting Jane Roe. The trial court granted the petition, finding John was not afforded procedural due process during the University's investigation of Jane's complaint. Jane, who was not a party in John's writ case, moved to vacate the mandate order on the ground that the order is void because she did not receive notice of, and an opportunity to participate in, the writ proceeding. The trial court denied Jane's motion. We acknowledge that Jane's interests were affected by the mandate proceeding, such that she may have been a real party in interest or a necessary party, but she has not established that she was an indispensable party. Nor has she established that the absence of even an indispensable party is grounds to void a judgment. We accordingly affirm.

FACTUAL AND PROCEDURAL BACKGROUND

I. The Incident and University Investigation

At the beginning of September 2015, John and Jane were friends and undergraduate students at the University of California, Santa Barbara

(UCSB). On September 7, they went to a party together and then had a sexual encounter. The next day, a dispute arose about whether the encounter was consensual. Jane filed a police report about the incident, which led to a criminal investigation but no criminal charges.

Thirteen months after the alleged assault, on October 10, 2016, Jane filed a complaint about John with UCSB's Title IX and sexual harassment policy compliance office.

* * *

[Investigator] Quillen interviewed John on May 17, 2017, which was the first time that a UCSB representative interviewed John about the incident. On May 24, after the factfinding phase of UCSB's investigation was almost completed, Quillen met with John for an oral "debriefing" interview. During that meeting, Quillen provided verbal summaries of witness statements and John proposed questions for Quillen to ask Jane. The next day, UCSB Investigator Yahyavi interviewed Jane and asked her John's questions.

On August 9, 2017, Quillen submitted a report to the University's office of judicial affairs (OJA). Quillen's report summarizes evidence collected during the investigation and contains express findings of fact and recommendations. Quillen found that John was aware, or should have been aware, that Jane was incapacitated during their sexual encounter. Quillen also found that John fabricated audio recordings that he represented to be Jane giving consent to the encounter. Quillen recommended that the OJA decide that John sexually assaulted Jane and suspend John for three years.

On August 24, 2017, the OJA issued a decision that adopted Quillen's findings and recommendation. John appealed the OJA's decision to UCSB's interpersonal violence appeal review committee. As grounds for appeal, John alleged procedural errors, findings unsupported by substantial evidence, and a disproportionate punishment.

* * *

On November 13, 2017, the review committee denied John's appeal and upheld his suspension.

II. John's Writ Petition

In January 2018, John filed a petition against the University, seeking a writ of mandate under [CCP § 1085]. John alleged that UCSB's disciplinary action against him was invalid because the University did not grant him a fair hearing, failed to proceed in the manner required by law, and made a decision unsupported by the evidence. Seeking independent review, John alleged he was denied his right under Title IX to continue his education without the stigma of having been found responsible for a sexual assault. John's petition names as respondent only the Regents of the University of California; Jane Roe is described as a "[n]on-party."

In January 2019, the trial court granted John's petition, in a 41-page order directing the University to set aside its decision against John. * * *

John's first claim was that UCSB's process was unconstitutional because it did not afford John the right to question Jane. Recognizing that the precise requirements of due process depend on the context, the court found that in this case, the University was required to provide John an "effective opportunity to present questions to [Jane] in front of the finder of fact" because of "the felony level nature" of the charge against John, the "importance of the relative credibility" of Jane and John, and the "seriousness of the potential consequences" of the University's decision. The procedures followed in this case did not meet that standard, the court found.

* * *

[T]he court [also] found that the University's record of the proceeding contained substantial evidence supportive of Investigator Quillen's findings. Nevertheless, because of the due process violations, the court granted the petition for a writ of mandate directing the University to set aside and vacate the disciplinary decision against John. In directing John to prepare a proposed judgment, the court ordered that "[t]he judgment must not interfere with the discretion of the [University] regarding further proceedings."

On February 22, 2019, the court entered judgment and issued the peremptory writ of mandate. When the judgment was not appealed, it became final.

III. Jane's Motion to Vacate

On June 9, 2020, Jane filed a motion to vacate the order granting the writ of mandate. Jane argued that the mandate order and resulting judgment are void because her statutory rights to notice and the opportunity to participate in the proceeding were violated. Jane argued further that she was an indispensable party in the proceeding because her rights and interests were injured by the mandate order, which failed to "weigh her interests against [John's]."

In a declaration filed in support of her motion, Jane stated that she did not learn about the writ proceeding until after the court granted John's petition. Jane averred that in April 2019, her "CARE Advocate" notified her that the University intended to reopen her Title IX case against John. Jane contacted the University and a UCSB official sent her a copy of the mandate order. * * * With the assistance of counsel, Jane filed her motion to vacate and advised the University that she would not participate in a rehearing of her Title IX complaint until her motion was decided.

Jane's declaration described how UCSB's Title IX investigation had impacted her life, put her reputation at stake, and made her vulnerable to accusations that she lied about what happened. She stated further that her exclusion from John's writ proceeding made her feel that her experiences as a sexual assault victim and survivor were meaningless. Jane also opined that she had a right to present her "side of this story" before the court made its decision.

Opposing Jane's motion to vacate, John argued that Jane did not have a right to notice of his writ proceeding, and if Jane wanted to challenge the Title IX process, her recourse was against the University rather than John. The University filed a "Response" to Jane's motion, in which it declined to take a position as to whether Jane was entitled to relief from the judgment, but disputed Jane's legal theory that the failure to provide her notice of the proceeding deprived the court of jurisdiction to issue the mandate order.

On September 24, 2020, the court denied Jane's motion to vacate the mandate order, outlining its reasons in a written order (the September 2020 order). First, the court rejected Jane's claim that the mandate order and resulting judgment were void for failure to give Jane notice of the proceeding. * * * Second, the court doubted that Jane was a real party in interest because John's request for a determination that his constitutional right to due process had been violated did not directly affect Jane's rights or status as a UCSB student. Third, even if Jane could establish that her interests in this case made her an indispensable party, her absence from the proceeding was not a jurisdictional defect but would only preclude the court from requiring Jane to take some action or depriving her of a substantial right; the order granting John's petition did not violate these rules, the court found. In Jane's absence, the court accorded "complete relief" to the parties to the action—John and the University—by "determining whether [the University's] process for adjudicating complaints of sexual assault complied with the accused's constitutional due process rights." It did not decide the separate issue of whether Jane's evidence would have supported disciplinary action against John under a process that complied with constitutional mandates. * * *

DISCUSSION

* * *

II. Dismissal of the Appeal Is Not Required

* * *

[Before turning to the principal question of whether Jane was "necessary and indispensable" to the writ proceeding, the Court first considered whether Jane even had standing to appeal the mandate order, which requires her to be a "party" to the proceedings who was "aggrieved" by the order she now seeks to challenge. Although Jane was not named as a party to John's writ petition against the University, the Court found that she became a "party" for purposes of appellate standing when she filed her motion to vacate the mandate order. The Court also concluded that Jane was "aggrieved" by the mandate order:]

"One is considered 'aggrieved' whose rights or interests are injuriously affected by the judgment." "An aggrieved person, for this purpose, is one whose rights or interests are injuriously affected by the decision in an immediate and substantial way, and not as a nominal or remote consequence of the decision."

John contends that Jane was not aggrieved by the denial of her motion to vacate because the mandate order does not injuriously affect her rights. According to this argument, the mandate order has no impact on Jane because it is a determination of John's due process rights in the Title IX disciplinary proceeding, and because the trial court did not make any ruling about Jane's rights. * * *

We disagree. * * * [A]lthough the writ proceeding was an adjudication of John's due process rights, the resulting judgment reversed a disciplinary decision that the University made to resolve Jane's sexual assault complaint. Reversal of that decision directly impacts and potentially injures Jane's education-related rights under Title IX.[5]

Moreover, John's reliance on the order denying Jane's motion to vacate as proof that Jane's interests are not injuriously affected affords an independent ground for denying his motion to dismiss the appeal. As a general rule, when the "disposition of a motion to dismiss requires a consideration of the appeal upon its merits, the motion must be denied."

* * *

III. The Mandate Order Is Not Void

* * *

B. Real Parties in Interest and Necessary and Indispensable Parties

Jane contends that she had a right to receive notice and participate in the writ proceeding because she was a real party in interest and, as such, a necessary and indispensable party. According to this argument, John's failure to name Jane as a real party in interest was error, and this alleged error deprived the court of jurisdiction to issue the mandate order.

[5] "A student may bring a Title IX claim against a school for sexual harassment by another student where the harassment 'is so severe, pervasive, and objectively offensive that it effectively bars the victim's access to an educational opportunity or benefit,' and 'the funding recipient acts with deliberate indifference to known acts of harassment in its programs or activities.' Sexual assault 'qualifies as being severe, pervasive, and objectively offensive sexual harassment that could deprive [plaintiff] of access to the educational opportunities provided by her school.' "

1. Whether Jane is a Real Party in Interest is not dispositive

The concept of a real party in interest is not susceptible to a single meaning or fixed consequence. Generally, the term refers to a person or entity that has an actual and substantial interest that is directly affected by a proceeding. Thus, a real party in interest is a "person who possesses the right to sue under the substantive law." * * * In writ proceedings, the real party in interest can be "the other party" in a lawsuit or proceeding involving the petitioner, or the "real adverse party" in whose favor the act complained of by the petitioner was done.

Jane contends that she was a real party in interest in John's court case because the mandate order directly affects her interests as the alleged victim of John's sexual assault. Jane reasons that the policies and procedures the University adopted in order to comply with Title IX and related federal regulations are designed to protect her, and those protections were directly implicated by John's writ petition, which sought to overturn the University's decision to sanction him for assaulting Jane.

Jane is persuasive that her actual and substantial interests were directly affected by John's writ case. She was, after all, the complaining witness in the disciplinary proceeding that resulted in John's suspension from the University, which John successfully petitioned the trial court to set aside. Jane might fairly be described as the "real adverse party" in whose favor the University's disciplinary decision was entered. But the trial court made no finding as to whether Jane was a real party in interest, concluding that issue is not dispositive. We agree.

Whether Jane could have been named a real party in interest is not dispositive because John chose not to identify her as such in his writ petition.

* * *

2. Jane fails to show she was an Indispensable Party

Jane contends that the mandate order is void because she was an indispensable party to the writ proceeding, such that excluding her from the proceeding deprived the court of jurisdiction. We conclude that even if Jane may have been a necessary party, she has not established she was indispensable to adjudication of this writ petition or that excluding her from the writ proceeding was a jurisdictional error.

Section 389, subdivision (a) provides that a person who may be properly joined as a party in an action "shall" be so joined in certain circumstances: "if (1) in his absence complete relief cannot be accorded among those already parties or (2) he claims an interest relating to the subject of the action and is so situated that the disposition of the action in his absence may (i) as a practical matter impair or impede his ability to protect that interest or (ii) leave any of the persons already parties subject to a substantial risk of incurring double, multiple, or otherwise inconsistent obligations by reason of his claimed interest." (§ 389, subd. (a).) "A person meeting these requirements is often referred to as a 'necessary party.' " If a person who qualifies as a necessary party "cannot be made a party" to the action, the court must determine under section 389, subdivision (b) whether "in equity and good conscience the action should proceed among the parties before it, or should be dismissed without prejudice, the absent person being thus regarded as indispensable."

Determining whether a nonparty "is necessary and/or indispensable is a matter of trial court discretion in which the court weighs 'factors of practical realities and other considerations.' A court has the power to proceed with a case even if indispensable parties are not joined. Courts must be careful to avoid converting a discretionary power or rule of fairness into an arbitrary and burdensome requirement that may thwart rather than further justice." If the trial court commits a prejudicial abuse of discretion in deciding a case in the absence of an indispensable party, the judgment is properly reversed on appeal.

In the present case, the trial court rejected Jane's contention that she was an indispensable party under the circumstances presented here. With the benefit of having already ruled on the mandate petition, the court concluded that Jane's absence from the proceeding did not preclude the court from affording complete relief to the parties before it; nor did it impair Jane's ability to pursue her allegation that John assaulted her. The court did not need to exercise jurisdiction over Jane in order to adjudicate a writ petition that sought relief solely from the University on the basis that its disciplinary procedures fell short of due process standards.

Jane contends the trial court abused its discretion by concluding she was not an indispensable party because she had a right to defend the favorable administrative decision that she obtained from the University, and that right was destroyed by her exclusion from John's writ proceeding. Under these circumstances, Jane posits, the trial court had no power to issue the writ. As support for this argument, Jane relies primarily on two cases: Pinto Lake MHP LLC v. County of Santa Cruz (2020) 56 Cal.App.5th 1006, 271 Cal.Rptr.3d 9; and Morrical [v. Rogers (2013) 220 Cal.App.4th 438, 163 Cal.Rptr.3d 156].

In *Pinto Lake*, a county rent board denied a mobilehome park owner's application for a special rent adjustment after holding a hearing where the application was vigorously opposed by park residents and their counsel. The park owner challenged the decision by filing a petition for administrative mandamus and complaint for declaratory relief against the county. The trial court sustained the county's demurrer on the ground that the park owner failed to join park residents as the defendants in the case.

However, the resulting judgment dismissing the park owner's action was reversed on appeal.

The *Pinto Lake* court found no abuse of discretion in the trial court's ruling that the park residents were necessary parties, where the record showed that they participated as respondents in the county's administrative proceeding and that judicial review of the county's decision in their absence would "impede their ability to protect the interests they successfully advanced in the administrative proceeding." But the trial court erred by dismissing the lawsuit without deciding whether the residents were also indispensable parties. Because of the discretionary and equitable nature of the indispensable party inquiry, the *Pinto Lake* court remanded the case for the trial court to determine whether to dismiss the case because the residents were indispensable parties, or to proceed in the residents' absence because they were not.

Pinto Lake may provide some support for Jane's contention that she has a cognizable interest in defending the determination that the University rendered in her favor. In affirming the finding that the park residents were necessary parties in the park owner's court proceedings, the *Pinto Lake* court found that the residents had an "interest in the finality of the hearing officer's decision," which "necessarily include[d] an interest in preventing *any* remand." Although there are differences between Jane's role in the University's case against John and the role of the park residents in the county's formal adversarial proceeding, there is also this point of commonality: Jane, too, has an interest in the finality of the administrative decision. But whether Jane, like the park residents, is a necessary party is not the dispositive question.

Pinto Lake does not support Jane's claim that she was an indispensable party. To the contrary, *Pinto Lake* illustrates that a necessary party might not be an indispensable party, and both inquiries are matters of trial court discretion. The fact that the trial court in *Pinto Lake* did not abuse its discretion by finding that the park residents were necessary parties does not mean that the trial court in this case abused its discretion by concluding that Jane is not an indispensable party, which is a different inquiry. *Pinto Lake* does not address whether park residents were indispensable parties because the trial court failed to conduct that inquiry, unlike the trial court in this case. Here, the dispositive issue in John's writ proceeding was whether his due process rights were violated, and the trial court concluded that it was able to resolve that issue without making any ruling about the validity of Jane's complaint against John. By contrast, in *Pinto Lake* the park owner's prayer for relief included a request that the county be ordered to grant its application for a rent increase, reversing on the merits the application the park residents had opposed.

Jane argues that John sought analogous relief because he challenged the sufficiency of the evidence supporting the University's findings against him. It is true that after concluding that the University's process was unconstitutional, the trial court went on to make a conditional finding that "[i]f the process had provided adequate due process, then the Investigator's findings of fact would have been supported by substantial evidence." But the University did not appeal the judgment against it, nor does Jane take issue with the substance of the trial court's conclusion that the University's process violated John's constitutional rights, so this conditional finding is of no moment. Instead of deciding the merits of the University's decision to discipline John, the trial court was careful to ensure its judgment not interfere with the University's "discretion. . .regarding further proceedings." And the court made these rulings before Jane filed her motion to vacate, so they informed the court's discretionary decision that Jane was not an indispensable party.

Jane also relies on *Morrical*, which involved a dispute among three siblings regarding management of a group of family-owned companies. Sibling Ann filed an action under section 709 of the Corporations Code challenging the validity of a shareholder election that gave control of the companies to Altamont, a private equity firm with connections to Ann's brothers. Ann alleged that her brothers' votes were invalid and disqualified because their financial dealings with Altamont constituted a conflict of interest and breach of fiduciary duty. Altamont moved for judgment on the pleadings on the ground that Ann failed to name her brothers as defendants in the action. The trial court denied the motion without explanation, then found that the election was invalid and entered judgment in favor of Ann. Altamont successfully appealed.

The *Morrical* court found that Ann's brothers were indispensable parties whose joinder in the action was required. Because Ann's claim for relief against Altamont was premised on her brothers' alleged self-dealing and breach of fiduciary duty, the brothers' rights were "necessarily" affected by the judgment notwithstanding the fact that the lower court did not directly set aside the brothers' agreements or dealings with Altamont. Furthermore, the brothers were indispensable parties because excluding them impaired their ability to protect their interests and also subjected Altamont to a substantial risk of incurring inconsistent obligations by reason of the brothers' claimed interests, the appellate court found.

Morrical does not support Jane's contention that she was an indispensable party in John's writ case. John's claim against the University was not premised on allegations that would have required the court to make any findings about Jane, either expressly or implicitly. Nor did the mandate order subject the University to a substantial risk of incurring inconsistent obligations to John and Jane, since the court was careful not to dictate how the University should proceed with Jane's complaint after setting aside the original disciplinary decision.

Jane contends that she is an indispensable party under the reasoning of *Morrical* because, although the mandate order was ostensibly directed at the University, as a practical matter, it impaired her rights. According to this argument, the mandate order impairs Jane's rights by setting aside a decision she obtained from the University. This argument confuses Jane's interests with her rights. Jane has an interest in the finality of the University's decision to discipline John, but she fails to establish that she has a cognizable right to preserve a finding and sanction that were rendered in a proceeding that violated John's constitutional rights. The mandate order does not overturn the University's decision because of anything that Jane did. It does not dictate how the University should handle Jane's complaint going forward. And Jane identifies no risk of inconsistent judgments in this case. These factual circumstances distinguish *Morrical* in ways that support the trial court's determination that Jane was not an indispensable party.

Morrical also fails to support Jane's legal argument that a court order issued in the absence of an indispensable party is void. *Morrical* was a direct appeal by a named defendant, Altamont, that made a trial court motion for judgment on the pleadings due to the failure to join indispensable parties. When that motion was summarily denied, the appellate court reviewed the ruling under an abuse-of-discretion standard. And in concluding that the trial court had abused its discretion, *Morrical* emphasized that evidence of prejudice to the unjoined person was "of critical importance." *Morrical* did not hold or intimate that the failure to join an indispensable party deprived the court of jurisdiction to decide a case. We turn, finally, to cases that address that point explicitly.

3. Failure to join an Indispensable Party is not a jurisdictional defect

Jane's collateral attack of the final judgment in John's writ case is premised on proving that the judgment is void for lack of jurisdiction. Even if Jane could establish that she was an indispensable party in the writ case, that would not mean that the mandate order is void. Contrary to Jane's appellate arguments, the "failure to join 'indispensable' parties does not deprive a court of the power to make a legally binding adjudication between the parties properly before it." To be sure, "[a]n indispensable party is not bound by a judgment in an action in which he was not joined." But failing to join an indispensable party "is not 'a jurisdictional defect' in the fundamental sense."

* * *

[It is settled authority] that the decision whether to dismiss an action for failure to name an indispensable party is a matter of judicial discretion, which may turn on many factors. * * *

"[E]ven in the absence of an 'indispensable' party, the court still has the power to render a decision as to the parties before it which will stand. It is for reasons of equity and convenience, and not because it is without power to proceed, that the court should not proceed with a case where it determines that an 'indispensable' party is absent and cannot be joined." Thus, even if Jane could establish error in the failure to designate her an indispensable party, this would not establish that the mandate order is void. The trial court in this case still had "the power to render a decision as to the parties before it." And that decision "will stand."

* * *

DISPOSITION

The September 2020 order denying Jane Roe's motion to vacate the order granting John Doe's petition for writ of mandate is affirmed.

IN RE BAYCOL CASES I AND II

Supreme Court of California, 2011.
51 Cal.4th 751, 248 P.3d 681, 122 Cal.Rptr.3d 153.

WERDEGAR, JUSTICE.

The right to appeal in California is generally governed by the "one final judgment" rule, under which most interlocutory orders are not appealable. (See Code Civ. Proc., § 904.1.) In Daar v. Yellow Cab Co. (1967) 67 Cal.2d 695, 63 Cal.Rptr. 724, 433 P.2d 732 (*Daar*), however, concerned that orders dismissing all class action claims might in some instances escape review, we adopted a "death knell" doctrine that allowed a party to appeal such orders immediately. Here, we address uncertainty over the scope of the death knell doctrine: does it extend to orders that simultaneously terminate individual claims as well, or does it apply only where, as was the case in *Daar* itself, individual claims survive?

* * *

FACTUAL AND PROCEDURAL BACKGROUND

In 1997, defendant Bayer Corporation (Bayer) gained United States Food and Drug Administration approval for, and shortly thereafter began marketing, the drug Baycol. * * * In 2001, Bayer withdrew Baycol from the market after concerns arose about links between the use of Baycol and several acute, and sometimes fatal, muscle tissue diseases.

Following Bayer's withdrawal of Baycol from the market, thousands of plaintiffs filed suit against Bayer. Plaintiff Douglas Shaw filed this case as a class action, alleging claims for violation of the unfair competition law (UCL) (Bus. & Prof.Code, § 17200 et seq.) and for unjust enrichment. The complaint alleged Bayer had engaged in false and misleading advertising regarding Baycol.

* * * The amended complaint sought to certify a class of "[a]ll persons or entities who purchased or paid for the drug *Baycol* between February 18, 1998 and August 8, 2001 . . ., to be used by California Consumers, and not for resale."

Bayer demurred to both the class allegations and each substantive claim. On April 27, 2007, the trial court sustained the demurrer in its entirety without leave to amend. It thereafter denied Shaw's motion for reconsideration on both class and individual claims and entered a judgment of dismissal. Bayer served a notice of entry of judgment on October 29, 2007, and Shaw filed his notice of appeal on December 20, 2007.

The Court of Appeal reversed dismissal of Shaw's individual UCL claim, concluding he should have been granted leave to amend. However, it declined to consider on the merits the appeal of the class claims dismissal and instead dismissed that portion of the appeal. Relying on cases that have held death knell orders terminating class claims are immediately appealable, the Court of Appeal reasoned that, upon entry of the April 27, 2007, order sustaining Bayer's demurrer, the class claims dismissal, unlike the individual claims dismissal, was appealable. Consequently, the December 20, 2007, notice of appeal was, as to the class claims, untimely.

We granted review to resolve uncertainty over the timing of appeals in cases involving class claims.

DISCUSSION

Under the one final judgment rule, "an appeal may be taken only from the final judgment in an entire action." "The theory [behind the rule] is that piecemeal disposition and multiple appeals in a single action would be oppressive and costly, and that a review of intermediate rulings should await the final disposition of the case." * * *

The one final judgment rule is "a fundamental principle of appellate practice."[2] The Legislature first codified the rule in the Practice Act of 1850, later incorporated it in the original Code of Civil Procedure, and has retained it in the Code of Civil Procedure to this day.[3]

---

[2] In the United States, the one final judgment rule was adopted as part of the Judiciary Act of 1789, and its true origins date to "the dim and remote history of the appellate procedure of the English common law." * * *

[3] Section 904.1 directs that an appeal may be taken "[f]rom a judgment" and in its remaining subdivisions lists various specific additional appealable orders that stand as exceptions to the general rule. None are relevant here.

Given the one final judgment rule's deep common law and statutory roots and the substantial policy considerations underlying it, we are reluctant to depart from its principles and endorse broad exceptions that might entail multiple appeals absent compelling justification. "[E]very exception to the final judgment rule not only forges another weapon for the obstructive litigant but also requires a genuinely aggrieved party to choose between immediate appeal and the permanent loss of possibly meritorious objections." Accordingly, "exceptions to the one final judgment rule should not be allowed unless clearly mandated."

We found compelling justifications for one such exception in *Daar,* embracing what is known in this and other jurisdictions as the "death knell" doctrine.[4] In *Daar,* the plaintiff filed a putative class action. The trial court sustained a demurrer, concluding the plaintiff could neither maintain a class action nor satisfy the jurisdictional minimum amount in controversy for superior court actions * * *. On appeal, we considered as a threshold issue whether such an order, determining the plaintiff could not maintain his claims as a class action but could seek individual relief, was appealable, and we concluded it was. What mattered was not the form of the order or judgment but its impact. Because the order effectively rang the death knell for the class claims, we treated it as in essence a final judgment on those claims, which was appealable immediately.

Two procedural circumstances were critical to our decision in *Daar,* first, that the appealed-from order was the practical equivalent of a final judgment for some parties, and second, that in the absence of our treating the order as a de facto final judgment, any appeal likely would be foreclosed. On the first point, the order "virtually demolished the action as a class action" and was in " 'legal effect' . . . tantamount to a dismissal of the action as to all members of the class other than plaintiff." * * * In cases decided since *Daar,* we and the Courts of Appeal have emphasized that orders that only limit the scope of a class or the number of claims available to it are not similarly tantamount to dismissal and do not qualify for immediate appeal under the death knell doctrine; only an order that entirely terminates class claims is appealable. * * *

Equally important in *Daar* was the circumstance that the order appealed from was essentially a dismissal of everyone "*other* than plaintiff." (*Daar,* italics added.) We emphasized that permitting an appeal was necessary because "[i]f the propriety of a disposition terminating class claims could not now be reviewed, it can never be reviewed," and we were understandably reluctant to recognize a category of orders effectively immunized by circumstance from appellate review. This risk of immunity from review arose precisely, and only, because the individual claims lived

[4] The name is traceable to Eisen v. Carlisle & Jacquelin (2d Cir.1966) 370 F.2d 119, 121 ("Where the effect of a district court's order, if not reviewed, is the death knell of the action, review should be allowed.").

while the class claims died. * * * This concern—that an individual plaintiff may lack incentive to pursue his individual claims to judgment, thereby foreclosing any possible appellate review of class issues—is present in cases such as *Daar,* where individual claims persist but remain unresolved, but is wholly absent in cases where a final judgment resolving all claims will follow as a matter of course without further action by the individual plaintiff. * * *

Thus understood as requiring an order that (1) amounts to a de facto final judgment for absent plaintiffs, under circumstances where (2) the persistence of viable but perhaps de minimis individual plaintiff claims creates a risk no *formal* final judgment will ever be entered, the death knell doctrine fits comfortably within the existing statutory framework. * * *

Here, a single order was entered dismissing both individual and class claims. No divergence between individual and class interests was thereby created. No risk arose that the named plaintiff, lacking incentive to pursue his individual claims, might fail to press on until the entry of an appealable final judgment. No need was present to treat the original order as immediately appealable, so as to prevent the trial court's class determinations from never being reviewable. The scope of the death knell doctrine is coextensive with its rationale. The doctrine does not apply here.

* * *

We readily agree that bright lines are essential in this area, to avoid both inadvertent forfeiture of the right to appeal and excessive protective appeals by parties afraid they might suffer such a forfeiture. Properly understood, however, the principle that appeal lies only from the final judgment when an order terminates *both* class and individual claims is not an ill-defined, ad hoc exception to the death knell doctrine, but an appropriate recognition of the doctrine's limits. * * * The rule that the death knell doctrine applies to render an order foreclosing class claims appealable when, and only when, individual claims survive is, we trust, sufficiently bright to guide future courts and litigants.

Bayer's additional arguments on appeal do not persuade us otherwise. Bayer urges on us a wealth of cases applying the death knell doctrine to render orders dismissing class claims appealable.[8] But none of them addressed the appealability of an order that also terminated individual claims.

* * *

---

[8] California follows a "one shot" rule under which, if an order is appealable, appeal must be taken or the right to appellate review is forfeited. (See § 906 (the powers of a reviewing court do not include the power to "review any decision or order from which an appeal might have been taken" but was not).) * * * If the April 27, 2007, order was appealable, it follows that it had to be timely appealed or the right to challenge its particulars be forever lost.

Finally, Bayer expresses concern that departing from the "rule" that orders terminating class claims are always appealable, no matter the disposition of individual claims, would create uncertainty and confusion, requiring courts on a case-by-case basis to assess the degree of "divergence" between the interests of would-be class members and individual named plaintiffs. But as *Daar* did not declare any such rule, no departure is involved here. In any event, no case-by-case assessment of divergence is needed. If an order terminates class claims, but individual claims persist, the order terminating class claims is immediately appealable under *Daar's* death knell doctrine. If an order terminates class claims and individual claims as well, it is not. Because the order here fell in the latter category, it was nonappealable, and it was error to treat the subsequent appeal from a final judgment as untimely.

RES JUDICATA

BOEKEN V. PHILIP MORRIS USA, INC.

Supreme Court of California, 2010.
48 Cal.4th 788, 108 Cal.Rptr.3d 806, 230 P.3d 342.

KENNARD, JUSTICE.

* * *

I

Judy Boeken, plaintiff in the wrongful death action before us, is the widow of Richard Boeken.

Richard began smoking cigarettes in 1957 and was diagnosed with lung cancer in 1999. In March 2000, Richard sued cigarette manufacturer Philip Morris USA, Inc., asserting that it had wrongfully caused his cancer. A jury awarded Richard $5,539,127 in compensatory damages and $3 billion in punitive damages. [Mr. Boeken died in 2002.] * * * The Court of Appeal ultimately reduced the punitive damages award to $50 million * * *. In satisfaction of this judgment (with interest), [Mr. Boeken's estate] received over $80 million in March 2006.

In October 2000, while her husband was still alive, plaintiff filed a separate common law action against Philip Morris for loss of consortium, seeking compensation for the loss of her husband's companionship and affection. Plaintiff alleged that defendant's wrongful conduct had caused her husband's lung cancer and that as a result of the cancer he was "unable to perform the necessary duties as a spouse" and would "not be able to perform such work, services, and duties in the future." Plaintiff further asserted that she had been "permanently deprived" of her husband's consortium. Specifically, plaintiff alleged that she suffered "the loss of love, affection, society, companionship, sexual relations, and support."

About four months after filing that action, plaintiff dismissed it with prejudice. The record before us does not indicate the reason for the dismissal; for purposes of applying the doctrine of res judicata, however, a dismissal with prejudice is the equivalent of a final judgment on the merits, barring the entire cause of action. * * *

A year after dismissal of plaintiff's common law action for loss of consortium, her husband died from the effects of lung cancer. Plaintiff then filed the present wrongful death action under Code of Civil Procedure section 377.60, again seeking compensation from Philip Morris for the loss of her husband's companionship and affection. This time, plaintiff alleged that she had suffered "loss of love, companionship, comfort, affection, society, solace, and moral support." Philip Morris demurred, arguing that plaintiff's action for wrongful death was barred by the doctrine of res judicata because plaintiff's previous loss of consortium action against Philip Morris had involved the same primary right. The trial court sustained the demurrer without leave to amend, and plaintiff appealed. * * *

We granted plaintiff's petition for review.

II

A

* * *

California's wrongful death statute has long permitted a person whose spouse was wrongfully *killed* to sue for loss of consortium damages, but a person whose spouse was *injured,* but not killed, had no right of action for the same damages, because no statute had supplanted the common law rule barring recovery for the wrongful *injury* of a spouse. This disparity remained even when the spouse's injuries were severely disabling and permanent, and the loss of consortium just as great as it would have been if the spouse had died. The inequity of this rule led this court to abrogate it in Rodriguez v. Bethlehem Steel Corp. (1974) 12 Cal.3d 382, 115 Cal.Rptr. 765, 525 P.2d 669. In that case, we recognized a new common law cause of action for loss of consortium resulting from the wrongful injury of a spouse * * *.

But the common law cause of action we recognized in *Rodriguez* was limited to cases involving wrongfully *injured* spouses; the rule remained that a cause of action for wrongful *death* (and the right to recover loss of consortium damages as part of that action) was purely a creature of statute. * * *

Rodriguez involved a spouse who had *nonfatal* injuries, and our opinion did not discuss the possibility that the injured spouse's life expectancy might have been curtailed in any way by his injuries. Therefore, we did not address in *Rodriguez* whether a plaintiff bringing a common law action for loss of consortium can recover for lost companionship and affection *after* the injured spouse's premature death, or whether the common law recovery is limited to *predeath* damages (with postdeath damages recoverable only by way of a statutory wrongful death cause of action). The answer to this question is central to this case, for it determines whether the [court] correctly concluded that plaintiff is now seeking a second adjudication over postdeath damages, or whether, as plaintiff claims, she is seeking only a first adjudication concerning a category of damages that was simply not available in her previous common law action.

With this background concerning the history and scope of the causes of action at issue here, we turn to the specific res judicata question that defendant raised in its demurrer to plaintiff's wrongful death complaint.

B

"As generally understood, 'the doctrine of *res judicata* gives certain *conclusive effect* to a *former judgment* in subsequent litigation involving the same controversy.' The doctrine 'has a double aspect.' 'In its primary aspect,' commonly known as claim preclusion, it 'operates as a bar to the maintenance of a second suit between the same parties on the same cause of action.' 'In its secondary aspect,' commonly known as collateral estoppel, 'the prior judgment . . . "operates" ' in 'a second suit . . . based on a different cause of action . . . "as an estoppel or conclusive adjudication as to such issues in the second action as were actually litigated and determined in the first action." ' * * *"

Here, we are concerned with the claim preclusion aspect of res judicata. To determine whether two proceedings involve identical causes of action for purposes of claim preclusion, California courts have "consistently applied the 'primary rights' theory." Under this theory, "a cause of action . . . arises out of an antecedent primary right and corresponding duty and the delict or breach of such primary right and duty by the person on whom the duty rests. 'Of these elements, the primary right and duty and the delict or wrong combined constitute the cause of action in the legal sense of the term. . . .' "

"In California the phrase 'cause of action' is often used indiscriminately . . . to mean *counts* which state according to different legal theories the same cause of action. . . ." But for purposes of applying the doctrine of res judicata, the phrase "cause of action" has a more precise meaning: The cause of action is the right to obtain redress for a harm suffered, regardless of the specific remedy sought or the legal theory (common law or statutory) advanced. * * * Thus, under the primary rights theory, the determinative factor is the harm suffered. When two actions involving the same parties seek compensation for the same harm, they generally involve the same primary right.

Here, the complaint in plaintiff's common law action for loss of consortium alleged that Philip Morris's wrongful conduct "permanently deprived" her of her husband's companionship and affection. The *primary right* was the right not to be wrongfully deprived of spousal companionship and affection, and the *corresponding duty* was the duty not to wrongfully deprive a person of spousal companionship and affection. The breach was the conduct of defendant Philip Morris that wrongfully induced plaintiff's husband to smoke defendant's cigarettes. It does not matter what weakness, if any, in plaintiff's previous lawsuit might have led her to dismiss it with prejudice. Once plaintiff did so, the primary right and the breach of duty (together, the cause of action) had been adjudicated in defendant's favor. Therefore, plaintiff could not later allege the same breach of duty in a second lawsuit against defendant, based on a new legal theory (statutory wrongful death).

* * *

Plaintiff contends that in her previous action for loss of consortium, she was legally barred from recovering damages for *postdeath* loss of consortium, and therefore her present wrongful death action does not involve the same primary right as the previous action. She argues that a loss of consortium action is a common law tort action permitting recovery for loss of companionship and affection *during the lifetime* of a wrongfully injured spouse, whereas a wrongful death action is a statutorily created action permitting recovery for (among other things) loss of companionship and affection *after the death* of a wrongfully killed spouse. The latter action is a creature of statute, permitting a type of recovery that—absent the statute—is unavailable because of the common law rule barring recovery for injuries that are based on the death of a person. Therefore, in plaintiff's view, a wrongful death action for loss of consortium involves a primary right that is different from the primary right underlying a common law action for loss of consortium. * * *

[I]n a common law action for loss of consortium, the plaintiff can recover not only for the loss of companionship and affection through the time of the trial but also for any *future* loss of companionship and affection that is sufficiently certain to occur. In *Rodriguez,* we held that when a plaintiff's spouse is permanently disabled as a result of a defendant's wrongdoing, future (posttrial) loss of companionship and affection is sufficiently certain to permit an award of prospective damages. If instead the injured spouse will soon *die* as a result of his or her injuries, the future (posttrial) loss of companionship and affection is no less certain. In short, we see no reason to make an exception here to the general rule permitting an award of prospective damages in civil tort actions. Therefore, under long-standing principles of tort liability, the recovery of prospective damages in a common law action for loss of consortium includes damages for lost companionship and affection resulting from the anticipated (and sufficiently certain) premature death of the injured spouse.

Of course, the plaintiff in a common law action for loss of consortium may not recover for loss during a period in which the companionship and affection of the injured spouse would have been lost anyway, irrespective of the defendant's wrongdoing, and therefore the life expectancy of the plaintiff and the life expectancy of the injured spouse, whichever is shorter, necessarily places an outer limit on damages. In this context, however, when we speak of the life expectancy of the injured spouse, we are referring to the life expectancy that the injured spouse would have had if the injury had never occurred. In other words, in the case of a sudden injury we are referring to the life expectancy that the injured spouse had immediately *before* that injury, and in the case of a cumulative injury like the one at issue here we are referring to the life expectancy that the injured spouse would have had absent the harmful conditions to which the defendant wrongfully exposed that spouse. If the life expectancy of the injured spouse was curtailed as a result of the injury, then the resulting "lost years" are no less a deprivation of companionship and affection to the plaintiff than a permanent disability would be, and they are a proper component of prospective damages under Civil Code section 3283. We conclude therefore that a plaintiff in a common law action for loss of consortium can recover prospective damages for the period *after* the injured spouse's death, based on the life expectancy that the injured spouse would have had if the injury had never occurred.

Here, plaintiff did in fact seek such damages. In her previous common law action for loss of consortium, plaintiff alleged that defendant's wrongful conduct had caused her husband's lung cancer and that as a result of the cancer he was "unable to perform the necessary duties as a spouse" and would "not be able to perform such work, services, and duties *in the future*." Moreover, plaintiff's complaint expressly asserted that she had been "*permanently* deprived" of her husband's consortium. Presumably this latter assertion was based on the debilitating and incurable nature of her husband's illness and the great likelihood that it would lead to premature death.

* * *

In arguing that postdeath damages are not recoverable in a common law action for loss of consortium, plaintiff also relies on a comment in the Restatement Second of Torts (Restatement). * * * [W]e disagree.

The section of the Restatement addressing loss of consortium claims states in its comment: "In case of death resulting to the impaired spouse, the deprived spouse may recover under the rule stated in this Section only for harm to his or her interests and expense *incurred between the injury and death. For any loss sustained as a result of the death of the impaired spouse, the other spouse must recover, if at all, under a wrongful death statute.*" (Rest.2d Torts, § 693, com. f, p. 497, italics added.) As the Court of Appeal here pointed out, this comment refers to situations in which the common law loss of consortium claim is brought *after* the death of the injured spouse and joined with a statutory wrongful death claim. For this reason, the introductory phrase of the comment is not "In case death *is likely to result* to the impaired spouse. . . ." Instead, the comment refers to the death as a completed fact.

When a common law loss of consortium claim is brought *after* the death of the injured spouse and joined with a statutory wrongful death claim, it may be appropriate to limit the common law claim to the lifetime of the injured spouse in order to avoid a double recovery with respect to postdeath damages. But we do not have that situation here. Rather, here plaintiff brought her common law loss of consortium claim *before* her husband's death, in an action separate from the current wrongful death action. To read the Restatement's comment as applicable to a loss of consortium claim brought and resolved before the injured spouse's death, as plaintiff urges, would be inconsistent with our long-standing statutory rule that a tort plaintiff may recover *all prospective damages that are sufficiently certain.* * * *

We also note that to adopt plaintiff's proposed rule—limiting common law loss of consortium claims to the lifetime of the injured spouse—would often lead, in the case of a life-curtailing injury, to multiple proceedings and the possibility of a double recovery or an inadequate recovery. Assuming the plaintiff brings a loss of consortium action before the death of the injured spouse, the jury would be forced—under plaintiff's proposed rule—to speculate about how long the injured spouse will live. If the jury guesses wrong, then the plaintiff will either be over- or undercompensated depending on the injured spouse's actual life span. If, after the injured spouse dies, the plaintiff brings a wrongful death action to recover postdeath damages, the result is a second lawsuit concerning essentially the same issue. The whole problem is largely avoided if the plaintiff in a common law action for loss of consortium can recover damages for the period *after* the death of the injured spouse, as our law permits.

* * *

[W]e reject the assertion * * * that the primary right at issue in a wrongful death action is necessarily defined in terms of the death of the decedent. The death of the decedent is certainly a prerequisite if one relies on the wrongful death statute *as one's legal theory of recovery,* but the *primary right* at issue in a wrongful death case may or may not depend on the decedent's death. Here, for example, the primary right is the right not to be permanently and wrongfully deprived of spousal companionship and affection. The violation of that right could be litigated on a common law theory or on a statutory wrongful death theory, but irrespective of the legal theory employed, there is only one cause of action.

We conclude that the primary right at issue in plaintiff's current wrongful death action for loss of consortium is the same as the primary right at issue in her previous common law action for loss of consortium, and therefore the res judicata doctrine bars the wrongful death action insofar as it concerns loss of consortium. Plaintiff's previous common law action sought compensation not only for the loss of consortium injury that she had suffered and would continue to suffer as a result of her husband's physical and emotional condition while he was still alive, but also for the loss of consortium injury that she anticipated she would continue to suffer as a result of her husband's premature death. Plaintiff's present wrongful death action likewise seeks compensation for the loss of consortium injury that she has suffered and will continue to suffer as a result of her husband's premature death. With respect to postdeath loss of consortium, the two actions concern the same plaintiff seeking the same damages from the same defendant for the same harm, and to that extent they involve the same primary right. Plaintiff dismissed her previous action with prejudice. Because such a dismissal is the equivalent of a final judgment on the merits, plaintiff may not now litigate the same primary right a second time.

III

The judgment * * * is affirmed.

Dissenting opinion by MORENO, JUSTICE.

I disagree with the majority's analysis and conclusion. I conclude rather that a statutory wrongful death action is different from a common law action for loss of consortium and implicates a distinct primary right. * * * I would therefore conclude that defendant has failed to carry its burden of demonstrating that plaintiff's wrongful death claim is barred.

As the majority explains, Boeken voluntarily dismissed with prejudice an action for common law loss of consortium that was alleged to be "permanent." We must determine whether such a voluntary dismissal acted via res judicata to bar plaintiff's subsequent wrongful death action.

As the majority recounts, to determine whether two proceedings involve identical causes of action, such that the latter proceeding would be barred by the claim preclusion aspect of res judicata, California courts have "consistently applied the 'primary rights' theory." * * *

As has been recognized, "[N]o generally approved and adequately defined system of classification of primary rights exists; indeed, primary rights are usually defined in terms of such abstraction and elasticity as to be of little or no predictive significance. The concept of 'cause of action' may thus be enlarged or narrowed in proportion to the breadth of the particular court's concept of 'primary rights'." Applying primary rights doctrine to wrongful death and loss of consortium actions presents a particular challenge because of the overlapping nature of these two actions. Notwithstanding these analytical difficulties, there are compelling reasons to view a statutory wrongful death cause of action and a common law loss of consortium action as different causes of action implicating distinct primary rights.

* * *

The distinction between the two causes of action is made apparent by an examination of their elements. "The elements of the cause of action for wrongful death are the tort (negligence or other wrongful act), the resulting death, and the damages, consisting of the pecuniary loss suffered by the heirs." Those pecuniary losses may include "(1) the loss of the decedent's financial support, services, training and advice, and (2) the pecuniary value of the decedent's society and companionship." The latter form of damages is also called loss of consortium. A wrongful death plaintiff may also recover reasonable funeral expenses.

In contrast, a common law loss of consortium action must allege nonfatal tortious injury that is "sufficiently serious and disabling to raise the inference that the conjugal relationship is more than superficially or temporarily impaired." A common law action for loss of consortium does not include an action for loss of financial support, which is generally recovered in a tort action brought by the injured spouse. Also, the loss of consortium action applies only to spouses (see Borer v. American Airlines (1977) 19 Cal.3d 441, 453, 138 Cal.Rptr. 302, 563 P.2d 858 (rejecting a child's action for loss of parental consortium)), whereas a wrongful death action applies to both the spouse[1] and children of the decedent.

The distinctness of these two causes of action can be seen clearly by considering when they begin to accrue. Were the two actions really a single action, then as soon as a person suffered a loss of consortium from the serious injury of a spouse, the statute of limitations would begin on all loss of consortium claims. A wrongful death claim filed outside the limitations period for bringing the common law loss of consortium claim would be time-barred. * * * But in fact it is indisputable that the statute of limitations for a wrongful death claim does not begin to run until the death of the spouse or other relative at the earliest regardless of the timing of any predeath injuries. Nothing in the majority opinion alters that basic principle. Were that not so, then the common law cause of action would alter the requirements for bringing a statutory wrongful death cause of action and in effect amend the wrongful death statute—something it may not do. Thus, although res judicata precludes a party from raising in subsequent litigation against the same party a " 'matter . . . within the scope of the

[1] The wrongful death statute also applies to domestic partners. (Code Civ. Proc., § 377.60, subd. (a).) For shorthand purposes, I will use the term "spouse" to include "domestic partner."

[previous] action, related to the subject matter and relevant to the issues, so that it *could* have been raised. . . .' " in the present case a wrongful death claim could not have been raised at the time the loss of consortium claim was pleaded and then dismissed, because the former claim had not yet accrued.

Moreover, as noted, funeral expenses are recoverable in wrongful death actions. The majority concludes that plaintiff forfeited her appeal of her claim for funeral expenses in the present case. Be that as it may, the majority does not contest that, but for this forfeiture, plaintiff was not barred from pursuing a wrongful death action in which funeral expenses could be recovered. Moreover, as noted, a loss of consortium action does not include damages for loss of economic support and therefore does not bar a wrongful death claimant from seeking such damages. So, the necessary implication of the majority opinion appears to be that a wrongful death action consists of several separate primary rights: the right to economic support, the right to consortium, the right to funeral expenses, and only the loss of consortium "primary right" is foreclosed by a prior common law loss of consortium action.

But there is no authority for parsing a wrongful death claim in this manner into separate primary rights. * * * [W]rongful death is most properly characterized as consisting of a single primary right, created by statute and arising at the time of decedent's death, to be free of various pecuniary losses that result from tortious conduct leading to a spouse's or child's death. This statutorily created primary right is plainly distinct from the common law cause of action for loss of consortium arising from a nonfatal injury.

Contrary to the majority's principal argument, the distinctness of the primary rights arising from a wrongful death and common law loss of consortium causes of action is not altered by the fact that a plaintiff in a common law loss of consortium action can recover damages for the spouse's reduced life expectancy, in other words, for *some* of the damages that are recoverable in a subsequent wrongful death action. As a leading exponent of primary rights theory, John Norton Pomeroy, stated, "if the facts alleged in the pleading show that the plaintiff is possessed of two or more distinct and separate primary rights, each of which has been invaded . . . it follows . . . that the plaintiff has united two or more causes of action, *although the remedial rights arising from each, and the corresponding reliefs, may be exactly of the same kind and nature.*" Moreover, courts have made clear, particularly in the context of litigation involving both statutory and common law causes of action, that "different primary rights may be violated by the same wrongful conduct." * * *

In sum, a defendant's tortious conduct resulting in personal injury may give rise to two distinct causes of action in that person's spouse: a common law loss of consortium claim if the nonfatal injuries are sufficiently serious to result in that loss, and a later-accruing wrongful death claim if the injuries result in the spouse's death, with a spouse being able to claim various damages for pecuniary loss, including a loss of consortium. This is not to say, however, that litigation of the loss of consortium action may not limit the scope of a subsequent wrongful death action. Inasmuch as that litigation recovers for loss of consortium resulting from a shortened life span, i.e., the same loss of consortium damages as would be recoverable in a wrongful death action, a plaintiff cannot again recover those same damages in a wrongful death action, for such would be an improper double recovery. Nothing in the record here indicates that plaintiff would be double recovering for loss of consortium damages.

* * *

We concur: GEORGE, C.J., and WERDEGAR, J.

ATTORNEYS' FEES AND COSTS

GRAHAM V. DAIMLERCHRYSLER CORP.

Supreme Court of California, 2004.
34 Cal.4th 553, 21 Cal.Rptr.3d 331, 101 P.3d 140.

MORENO, JUSTICE.

In this case defendant offered to repurchase a truck that had been marketed with false statements about its towing capacity. This offer came after a lawsuit plaintiffs filed against defendant seeking this repurchase remedy, but before any kind of court judgment was rendered. Plaintiffs were awarded substantial attorney fees under Code of Civil Procedure section 1021.5. Defendant raises several issues regarding those fees. The first is whether we should reconsider the catalyst theory, recognized by this court in Westside Community for Independent Living, Inc. v. Obledo (1983) 33 Cal.3d 348, 188 Cal.Rptr. 873, 657 P.2d 365 (*Westside Community*). Under the catalyst theory, attorney fees may be awarded even when litigation does not result in a judicial resolution if the defendant changes its behavior substantially because of, and in the manner sought by, the litigation. We conclude the catalyst theory should not be abolished but clarified. In order to be eligible for attorney fees under section 1021.5, a plaintiff must not only be a catalyst to defendant's changed behavior, but the lawsuit must have some merit, as discussed below, and the plaintiff must have engaged in a reasonable attempt to settle its dispute with the defendant prior to litigation. Because these limitations on the catalyst theory are to some degree new and were not addressed by the parties or the trial court, we remand for reconsideration of the trial court's award of attorney fees in this case.

Defendant also contends the trial court erred in concluding that the present lawsuit substantially benefited a large group of people or the general public, as required by section 1021.5. We conclude the trial court did not abuse its discretion in making that conclusion. Finally, defendant, while conceding that a plaintiff could be awarded attorney fees for attorney fee litigation, contends that these fees should not be enhanced beyond the "lodestar" amount. We do not endorse such a categorical rule, but we explain below that fees for fee litigation usually should be enhanced at a significantly lower rate than fees for the underlying litigation, if they are enhanced at all. We therefore will remand the cause to the trial court to recalculate the amount of the fee in light of the principles discussed below, assuming it finds on remand that plaintiffs are eligible for some attorney fees.

I. STATEMENT OF FACTS

The facts, taken largely from the Court of Appeal's opinion, are as follows:

DaimlerChrysler incorrectly marketed its 1998 and 1999 Dakota R/T trucks as having a 6,400-pound towing capacity when they could actually tow only 2,000 pounds. The error occurred because the Dakota R/T was a sporty version of an existing truck model, which could tow 6,400 pounds. However, to obtain a sporty design, DaimlerChrysler lowered the suspension on the Dakota R/T, thus reducing its towing capacity.

The reduced towing capacity was a potential risk factor. The lowered suspension meant that towing more than 2,000 pounds would cause the suspension to bottom out, stressing the frame and increasing fatigue and wear. The DaimlerChrysler response team considered this a potential safety issue.

Buyers who wanted to tow more than 2,000 pounds were told they could do so only if their Dakota R/T was modified with a trailer hitch costing $300. The factory installed some of these hitches, while other buyers who wanted to tow had dealer-installed or after-market hitches attached.

Nationwide, DaimlerChrysler sold or leased fewer than 7,000 of the Dakota R/T's in the two relevant years. Fewer than 1,000 affected R/T's were sold in California during the two years.

By February 1999, DaimlerChrysler set up a response team to address the problem. By June 1999, DaimlerChrysler had taken steps to replace the incorrect marketing materials, owners manuals, and engine and door labels for not-yet-sold Dakota R/T's, although public agency investigation revealed that brochures misrepresenting the trucks' towing capacity were still being distributed as of August 1999. DaimlerChrysler also had notified existing buyers of the error, told them not to attempt to tow more than

2,000 pounds, and provided them with the same modified materials. Simultaneously, DaimlerChrysler began to address remedial measures for customers who had bought or leased their Dakota R/T's under the incorrect marketing program.

Many Dakota R/T buyers never intended to tow more than 2,000 pounds. When informed by DaimlerChrysler of the error, most of those customers were satisfied with DaimlerChrysler's offers of cash and merchandise.

Initially, DaimlerChrysler offered $300 refunds to buyers who had purchased hitches of that amount. By the summer, DaimlerChrysler authorized dealers to repurchase or replace Dakota R/Ts on a case-by-case basis, but only for customers who demanded such a remedy.

On July 29, 1999, the Santa Cruz County District Attorney contacted DaimlerChrysler about the problem, threatened legal action, and requested DaimlerChrysler's input before acting. On August 10, 1999, the California Attorney General notified DaimlerChrysler it had joined the Santa Cruz County District Attorney. The public agencies requested a response by the end of August 1999.

Plaintiffs filed their case on August 23, 1999, in Los Angeles County Superior Court. Plaintiffs alleged they all bought 1999 Dakota R/T's from various DaimlerChrysler dealers. Only Graham lived and bought his truck in California. Plaintiffs alleged DaimlerChrysler marketed, sold, and warranted their 1998 and 1999 Dakota R/T's as capable of towing 6,400 pounds when the trucks actually could tow only 2,000 pounds. Plaintiffs alleged DaimlerChrysler acknowledged the error by letter to all purchasers dated June 16, 1999. Plaintiffs alleged they notified DaimlerChrysler of their 1) trucks' failure to comply with the warranted towing capacity, and 2) revocation of their acceptance of their trucks on July 19, 1999. Plaintiffs sought (but never obtained) class certification for all those who bought Dakota R/T's nationwide. Plaintiffs alleged a single breach of express warranty cause of action. Plaintiffs sought return of their purchase or lease payments, compensatory damages, and attorney fees. Also on August 23, 1999, the Detroit News contacted DaimlerChrysler's legal counsel about plaintiffs' case. DaimlerChrysler's counsel claimed DaimlerChrysler had responded appropriately to the marketing error, including offering buybacks to customers who requested it. Plaintiffs faxed their complaint to DaimlerChrysler the same day. The next day, August 24, 1999, DaimlerChrysler's employee newsletter ran an article on plaintiffs' case.

DaimlerChrysler's response team met throughout August 1999. The team knew about both public agency inquiries and the response deadline. Indeed, DaimlerChrysler wrote the public agencies that its internal approval process prohibited a response by August 31, but promised a response by September 8, 1999. On September 10, 1999, DaimlerChrysler issued its offer to all previous Dakota R/T buyers of repurchase or replacement. In response to later inquiries, response team members conceded they were aware of the class action lawsuit filed in California before DaimlerChrysler's September 10, 1999, letter offering repurchase or replacement to all Dakota R/T buyers.

DaimlerChrysler demurred to the complaint. Plaintiffs filed an amended complaint, acknowledging DaimlerChrysler's offer of, among other remedies, repurchase or replacement of the trucks for all previous buyers. The trial court sustained the demurrer without leave to amend and dismissed the case, finding it was moot because DaimlerChrysler already had offered all purchasers the relief plaintiffs sought. Meanwhile, the public agencies continued to pursue legal action against DaimlerChrysler, pointing to the fact that the erroneous marketing of the Dakota R/T continued as late as September 1999. In late 2000, DaimlerChrysler settled the public agency investigations by paying a $75,000 fine and agreeing to ensure that the marketing error did not reoccur. Nationwide, 2,549 Dakota R/T buyers opted for repurchase or replacement. Another 3,101 buyers opted for service contracts and parts coupons. The total value of these offers exceeded $15 million. Fewer than 1,000 of the R/T buyers were Californians.

Although plaintiffs' case was dismissed, the parties continued to litigate plaintiffs' entitlement to attorney fees. DaimlerChrysler insisted throughout that plaintiffs were not entitled to attorney fees, contending plaintiffs had no effect on DaimlerChrysler's recognition of the problem and decision to offer all buyers repurchase or replacement. For over a year, there were hotly contested discovery and other motions to clarify the facts described above. The court held a lengthy evidentiary hearing on October 18, 2000. DaimlerChrysler contended that the Dakota R/T response team was not even aware of the litigation until after September 10, 1999, when its repurchase offer was made, a position that the trial court found to lack credibility.

The trial court filed its final order awarding attorney fees on July 6, 2001. The court concluded after its review of the declarations and documentary evidence presented that DaimlerChrysler's "position that the lawsuit was not a catalyst was largely a transparent fabrication. . . ." It rejected DaimlerChrysler's argument that plaintiffs' action was unnecessary because of the enforcement action of the Santa Cruz County District Attorney and the California Attorney General. The trial court found that these agencies "had only made an inquiry and had not commenced any proceeding when plaintiffs filed this action. Further [those agencies] were only concerned with DaimlerChrysler's false advertising materials and never sought any remedies on behalf of the consumers who acquired these vehicles while they were being misrepresented."

In addition to finding that plaintiffs were the successful party, the trial court found the other requirements of section 1021.5 had been met. It found that the lawsuit "resulted in the enforcement of an important right affecting the public interest, . . . the protection and enforcement of consumer rights, including highway safety," and that "as a result of the lawsuit, thousands of consumers received pecuniary benefits and enhanced safety. Thousands more are likely to benefit from it if DaimlerChrysler and/or other manufacturers are deterred from similar conduct in the future."

The court also concluded that "DaimlerChrysler should pay plaintiffs' attorneys fees in the interest of justice. Plaintiffs' attorney fees will otherwise go unpaid. Fees cannot be paid out of the benefits conferred upon the consumers because DaimlerChrysler . . . distributed the benefits of [its] offer to the consumers without any discussion with plaintiffs or their attorneys. Justice is served by encouraging lawyers to bring meritorious consumer cases, of which this action is an example."

The trial court found the lodestar fee amount was $329,620 through the October 18, 2000, hearing, with a multiplier of 2.25 for the fees incurred until the October 18, 2000, hearing, including fees for litigating attorney fees, and applied no multiplier for time thereafter. The court awarded no fees for work after April 23, 2001. The total award was $762,830.

The Court of Appeal affirmed. It observed that the United States Supreme Court had recently rejected the catalyst theory as a basis for attorney fee awards under various federal statutes in Buckhannon Board & Care Home, Inc. v. West Virginia Dept. of Health and Human Resources (2001) 532 U.S. 598, 121 S.Ct. 1835, 149 L.Ed.2d 855 (*Buckhannon*). But the court declined to follow the United States Supreme Court's lead, noting that the catalyst theory has been long recognized in California. The court also rejected arguments that the litigation was not in the public interest and that it did not benefit a substantial number of people. Further, the court concluded that the trial court did not abuse its discretion in awarding fees for seeking fees, and in permitting those fees to be enhanced over the basic lodestar amount. We granted review.

II. DISCUSSION

A. *Whether the Catalyst Theory Should Be Abolished*

An important exception to the American rule that litigants are to bear their own attorney fees is found in section 1021.5. As we have stated: "The Legislature adopted section 1021.5 as a codification of the private attorney general doctrine of attorney fees developed in prior judicial decisions. Under this section, the court may award attorney fees to a 'successful party' in any action that 'has resulted in the enforcement of an important right affecting the public interest if: (a) a significant benefit, whether pecuniary or nonpecuniary, has been conferred on the general public or a large class of persons, (b) the necessity and financial burden of private enforcement are such as to make the award appropriate, and (c) such fees should not in the interest of justice be paid out of the recovery, if any.' . . . [T]he private attorney general doctrine 'rests upon the recognition that privately initiated lawsuits are often essential to the effectuation of the fundamental public policies embodied in constitutional or statutory provisions, and that, without some mechanism authorizing the award of attorney fees, private actions to enforce such important public policies will as a practical matter frequently be infeasible.' Thus, the fundamental objective of the doctrine is to encourage suits enforcing important public policies by providing substantial attorney fees to successful litigants in such cases." (Maria P. v. Riles (1987) 43 Cal.3d 1281, 1288–1289, 240 Cal.Rptr. 872, 743 P.2d 932 (*Maria P.*).)

In order to effectuate that policy, we have taken a broad, pragmatic view of what constitutes a "successful party." "Our prior cases uniformly explain that an attorney fee award may be justified even when plaintiff's legal action does not result in a favorable final judgment. * * * The trial court in its discretion 'must realistically assess the litigation and determine, from a practical perspective, whether or not the action served to vindicate an important right so as to justify an attorney fee award' under section 1021.5." (*Maria P.*)

The catalyst theory is an application of the above stated principle that courts look to the practical impact of the public interest litigation in order to determine whether the party was successful, and therefore potentially eligible for attorney fees. We specifically endorsed that theory in *Westside Community*.

* * *

We continue to conclude that the catalyst theory, in concept, is sound. The principle upon which the theory is based—that we look to the "impact of the action, not its manner of resolution"—is fully consistent with the purpose of section 1021.5: to financially reward attorneys who successfully prosecute cases in the public interest, and thereby " 'prevent worthy claimants from being silenced or stifled because of a lack of legal resources.' " We therefore reaffirm our endorsement of the catalyst theory.

DaimlerChrysler argues that we should reevaluate that endorsement in light of the rejection of the catalyst theory by the United States Supreme Court in *Buckhannon*. At the outset we state what hardly needs stating: that United States Supreme Court interpretation of federal statutes does not bind us to similarly interpret similar state statutes. * * * As explained below, we do not find the reasoning of the five-to-four majority in *Buckhannon* persuasive, and decline to apply its holding to section 1021.5.

* * *

A good deal of the *Buckhannon* court's reason for rejecting the catalyst theory turns on the definition of "prevailing party." The *Buckhannon* majority found the term " 'prevailing party' " to be "a legal term of art," defined according to Black's Law Dictionary (7th ed.1999) at page 1145 as "a party in whose favor a judgment is rendered, regardless of the amount of damages awarded <in certain cases, the court will award attorney's fees to the prevailing party>.—Also termed *successful party.*" This definition, together with prior court decisions, led the *Buckhannon* majority to conclude that a "prevailing party" must be a party that has brought about a " material alteration of the legal relationship of the parties,' " which could include both a "judgment on the merits," and a settlement agreement "enforced through a consent decree."

The *Buckhannon* majority concluded that "the 'catalyst theory' falls on the other side of the line from these examples. It allows an award where there is no judicially sanctioned change in the legal relationship of the parties. Even under a limited form of the 'catalyst theory,' a plaintiff could recover attorney's fees if it established that the 'complaint had sufficient merit to withstand a motion to dismiss for lack of jurisdiction or failure to state a claim on which relief may be granted.' This is not the type of legal merit that our prior decisions, based upon plain language and congressional intent, have found necessary. . . . A defendant's voluntary change in conduct, although perhaps accomplishing what the plaintiff sought to achieve by the lawsuit, lacks the necessary judicial *imprimatur* on the change. Our precedents thus counsel against holding that the term 'prevailing party' authorizes an award of attorney's fees *without* a corresponding alteration in the legal relationship of the parties."

We agree with DaimlerChrysler that the terms "prevailing party" and "successful party," as used in section 1021.5, are synonymous. We also agree that in the context of section 1021.5, the term "party" refers to a party to litigation, and therefore precludes an award of attorney fees when no lawsuit has been filed. (See Black's Law Dict. (4th rev. ed.1968) at p. 1278 [" 'Party' is a technical term having a precise meaning in legal parlance; it refers to those by or against whom and lawsuit is brought . . ., the party plaintiff or defendant. . . ."]; * * *.) But we are aware of no judicial construction or legislative usage in California that limits the terms "prevailing party" or "successful party" to the meaning found in the most recent edition of Black's Law Dictionary to the exclusion of other meanings, as DaimlerChrysler, following the *Buckhannon* majority, argues.[4]

---

[4] Moreover, if DaimlerChrysler is arguing that Black's Law Dictionary defines "successful party" as a term of art, identical to "prevailing party," and that the Legislature was aware of the definition, then the definition that should be consulted is not from the most recent edition of the dictionary, but the one current when the Legislature adopted section 1021.5 in 1977. Black's Law Dictionary, 4th ed., employs a number of alternative definitions of "prevailing party." "That one of the parties to a suit who successfully prosecutes the action or successfully defends against it, prevailing on the main issue, even though not to the extent of his original contention. [¶] The one

We therefore turn to the "usual and ordinary meaning" of the statutory language in order to discern legislative intent. The term "successful party," as ordinarily understood, means the party to litigation that achieves its objectives. We agree with the dissenting opinion in *Buckhannon*: "In everyday use, 'prevail' means 'gain victory by virtue of strength or superiority: win mastery: triumph.' Webster's Third New International Dictionary 1797 (1976). * * * A lawsuit's ultimate purpose is to achieve actual relief from an opponent. Favorable judgment may be instrumental in gaining that relief. Generally, however, 'the judicial decree is not the end but the means. At the end of the rainbow lies not a judgment, but some action (or cessation of action) by the defendant. . . .' On this common understanding, if a party reaches the 'sought-after destination,' then the party 'prevails' regardless of the 'route taken.' (*Buckhannon* (dis. opn. of Ginsburg, J.).)

* * *

DaimlerChrysler also makes a number of policy arguments. Like the *Buckhannon* majority, it argues that "[a] request for attorney's fees should not result in a second major litigation," (*Buckhannon*), and that the catalyst theory would require a complex causal determination. "Among other things, a 'catalyst theory' hearing would require analysis of the defendant's subjective motivations in changing its conduct, an analysis that 'will likely depend on a highly factbound inquiry and may turn on reasonable inferences from the nature and timing of the defendant's change in conduct.' " We find persuasive the argument of the *Buckhannon* dissent that although some time may be expended in fact finding under the catalyst theory, it is at least as likely as not that that the catalyst rule " 'saves judicial resources,' [citation] by encouraging 'plaintiffs to discontinue litigation after receiving through the defendant's acquiescence the remedy initially sought.' " (*Buckhannon* (dis opn. of Ginsburg, J.).)

* * *

DaimlerChrysler further argues that overall, the benefits that the catalyst rule are supposed to possess are dwarfed by the harms the rule will engender. It contends the evil to which the catalyst rule is addressed—that meritorious plaintiffs and plaintiffs' attorneys will be deprived of

---

in whose favor the decision or verdict is rendered and judgment entered. The party ultimately prevailing when the matter is finally set at rest. The party prevailing in interest, and not necessarily the prevailing person. To be such does not depend upon the degree of success at different stages of the suit, but whether, at the end of the suit, or other proceeding, the party who has made a claim against the other, has successfully maintained it. Thus, where the court grants defendant a new trial after verdict for plaintiff, defendant is the 'prevailing party' on that trial, and entitled to costs, although the plaintiff again gets verdict on retrial." Only one of the alternate definitions set forth above specifies that a "prevailing party" is the one for whom the verdict or judgment is rendered. The above definitions do not exclude the possibility that a party may be considered to be prevailing "when the matter is finally set at rest" by means other than a judgment or verdict.

attorney fees by a favorable settlement—will be a relatively rare occurrence. It quotes the *Buckhannon* majority that " '[I]t is well settled that a defendant's voluntary cessation of a challenged practice does not deprive a federal court of its power to determine the legality of the practice' unless it is 'absolutely clear that the allegedly wrongful behavior could not reasonably be expected to recur.' " On the other hand, Daimler Chrylser argues the catalyst rule could encourage nuisance suits by unscrupulous attorneys hoping to obtain fees without having the merits of their suit adjudicated. It quotes with approval from Justice Scalia's concurrence in *Buckhannon,* joined by Justice Thomas: "If the [catalyst theory] sometimes rewards the plaintiff with a phony claim (there is no way of knowing), [its absence] sometimes denies fees to the plaintiff with a solid case whose adversary slinks away on the eve of judgment. But it seems to me the evil of the former far outweighs the evil of the latter. There is all the difference in the world between a rule that denies the extraordinary boon of attorney's fees to some plaintiffs who are no less 'deserving' of them than others who receive them, and a rule that causes the law to be the very instrument of wrong—exacting the payment of attorney's fees to the extortionist." (*Buckhannon* (con. opn. of Scalia, J.).)

We, of course, have no way of quantifying the magnitude of the potential and actual abuses by plaintiffs under a catalyst rule or by defendants under its absence. DaimlerChrysler and the *Buckhannon* majority's prediction—that defendants' change of behavior depriving worthy plaintiffs of attorney fees will be relatively rare—is one we cannot verify. But as plaintiffs argue, what is objectionable about elimination of the catalyst theory is not only that in a given case an attorney will be unjustly deprived of fees, but that attorneys will be deterred from accepting public interest litigation if there is the prospect they will be deprived of such fees after successful litigation. As matters stand now, public interest attorneys often take a considerable risk that they will not be paid at all because they will not prevail in the litigation or because they will be deemed ineligible for fees under section 1021.5, as when the suit is adjudged not to be sufficiently in the public interest. Abolition of the catalyst theory will increase an already considerable risk. As plaintiffs' attorney succinctly states: "[I]t defies common sense to think attorneys who take meritorious public interest cases with the expectation that they will be compensated if they obtained favorable results for their clients will not be deterred from doing so if the defendant can litigate tenaciously, then avoid paying their fees by voluntarily providing relief before a court order is entered."

Nor do we believe that avoiding this increased risk of public interest litigation must inevitably come at the expense of rewarding a significant number of extortionate lawsuits. We can adopt sensible limitations on the catalyst theory that discourage the latter without putting a damper on lawsuits that genuinely provide a public benefit. * * * A number of circuits of the United States Court of Appeals, prior to *Buckhannon,* adopted a version of the catalyst theory that required not only a causal connection between the lawsuit and the relief obtained but also a determination that defendant's conduct was required by law. Generally speaking, the "required by law" prong was tantamount to a finding that the lawsuit was "not frivolous, unreasonable, or groundless."

This court has not explicitly adopted the above two-pronged test. We now do so. The trial court must determine that the lawsuit is not "frivolous, unreasonable or groundless", in other words that its result was achieved "by threat of victory, not by dint of nuisance and threat of expense." The determination the trial court must make is not unlike the determination it makes when asked to issue a preliminary injunction, i.e., not a final decision on the merits but a determination at a minimum that " 'the questions of law or fact are grave and difficult.' "

* * *

In addition to some scrutiny of the merits, we conclude that another limitation on the catalyst rule proposed by the Attorney General, appearing as amicus curiae, should be adopted by this court. The Attorney General proposes that a plaintiff seeking attorney fees under a catalyst theory must first reasonably attempt to settle the matter short of litigation. We believe this requirement is fully consistent with the basic objectives behind section 1021.5 and with one of its explicit requirements—the "necessity . . . of private enforcement" of the public interest. Awarding attorney fees for litigation when those rights could have been vindicated by reasonable efforts short of litigation does not advance that objective and encourages lawsuits that are more opportunistic than authentically for the public good. Lengthy prelitigation negotiations are not required, nor is it necessary that the settlement demand be made by counsel, but a plaintiff must at least notify the defendant of its grievances and proposed remedies and give the defendant the opportunity to meet its demands within a reasonable time. What constitutes a "reasonable" time will depend on the context.

Applying the catalyst rule, as discussed above, to the present case, the trial court applied the first prong of the rule to conclude that the lawsuit was in fact a substantial causal factor in DaimlerChrysler's change in policy with respect to its willingness to repurchase or replace the Dakota R/T or to offer consumers substantial discounts. DaimlerChrysler does not contend that the trial court's ruling on that point is unsupported by substantial evidence. But it is unclear whether the trial court considered the merits of the suit, and the trial court did not consider whether plaintiffs attempted to reasonably settle the matter short of litigation. We therefore remand the matter for a determination of whether plaintiffs are eligible for attorney fees under the catalyst rule as articulated above.

B. Trial Court Did Not Abuse Its Discretion in Finding the Substantial Benefit And Public Interest Prongs of Section 1021.5 Were Met

DaimlerChrysler also contends that the attorney fee award must be overturned in its entirety because it failed to confer "a significant benefit . . . on the general public or large class of persons" as required by section 1021.5. This contention need not detain us long. * * *

In the present case, the trial court found that the problem addressed by the lawsuit implicated an issue of public safety, and that the lawsuit benefited thousands of consumers and potentially thousands more by acting as a deterrent to discourage lax responses to known safety hazards. In light of the facts reviewed in the first part of this opinion, we conclude the trial court did not abuse its discretion in finding that the lawsuit met the substantial benefit and public interest requirements of section 1021.5.

C. Whether There Should Be A Multiplier for Attorney Fees for Litigating Attorney Fees

In the present case, a large percentage of the attorney fees were awarded for litigation to obtain fees under section 1021.5. As noted, the lodestar amount calculated by the trial court was $329,620, and that amount was multiplied by an enhancement of 2.25, for a total $762, 830. The trial court based the enhancement on "the contingency nature [of the litigation], the delay in payment and the quality of the result." DaimlerChrysler argues that there should be no enhancement for fees for fee-related litigation, or "fees on fees." Assuming the trial court concludes on remand that plaintiffs are entitled to some attorney fees, we address for its benefit whether it appropriately awarded enhancements for fees on fees. We conclude that, while fees for attorney fee litigation under section 1021.5 may be enhanced under some circumstances, that enhancement should generally be lower than fees awarded in the underlying litigation.

* * *

Courts awarding attorney fees under section 1021.5 * * * may generally differentiate between the contingency risk undertaken during the litigation on the merits and the risk undertaken for litigation on fees. The risk that an attorney takes in the underlying public interest litigation has two components: the risk of not being a "successful party," i.e., of not prevailing on the merits, and the risk of not establishing eligibility for an attorney fee award. * * * Generally speaking, by the time of the commencement of fee litigation in section 1021.5 cases, the first and perhaps most substantial component of risk, that of not being a successful party, has been eliminated. What remains is the second component, that plaintiffs may not be able to establish eligibility for fees, i.e., to establish that the litigation confers "a 'significant benefit' . . . 'on the general public or a large class of persons' " or that there was the " 'necessity and financial burden of private enforcement,' " making the award appropriate. Although in the present case, as in other catalyst theory cases, plaintiffs had not established themselves as the successful party at the beginning of the fee litigation, and some enhancement for that risk may be justified, the achievement of their litigation objective before fee litigation would reduce somewhat the uncertainty over their "successful party" status. The fact that the risk of fee litigation is generally less than the risk of litigation on the merits of the suit justifies a lower attorney fee multiplier for the former, if one is given at all. We do not believe a lower multiplier on fees for less risky fee litigation will deter attorneys from accepting worthwhile public interest cases.

* * *

III. DISPOSITION

The judgment of the Court of Appeal affirming the award of attorney fees in the present case is reversed, and the cause is remanded for proceedings consistent with the views expressed in this opinion.

Dissenting Opinion by CHIN, JUSTICE.

I dissent.

Plaintiffs filed a simple seven-page complaint alleging a single cause of action for breach of warranty after the defendant had already acknowledged its marketing mistake and was taking steps to correct it, and while the Santa Cruz County District Attorney and the California Attorney General were investigating the matter and preparing to take appropriate action. The complaint constituted plaintiffs' entire legal effort regarding the underlying lawsuit. They obtained no judicial ruling of any kind in their favor. Nevertheless, to date, plaintiffs have parlayed this complaint into an award of attorney fees of *$762,830,* most of it for work unrelated to the underlying lawsuit. Now the majority remands the matter for yet more litigation. I disagree for several reasons.

This court has never awarded attorney fees to a party with no judicial ruling in its favor. We should not start now. Relying solely on federal cases that have been overruled and California cases that either *denied* attorney fees or involved a plaintiff with a judicial ruling in its favor, the majority permits an award of attorney fees to the plaintiffs as the "prevailing" or "successful" party. To do so, it adopts the so-called catalyst theory, a theory that was once prevalent in federal courts, but that the United States Supreme Court has now repudiated. We should not resurrect it.

* * *

II. DISCUSSION

A. California Should Not Adopt the Catalyst Theory.

"California follows what is commonly referred to as the American rule, which provides that each party to a lawsuit must ordinarily pay his own attorney fees. The Legislature codified the American rule in 1872 when it enacted Code of Civil Procedure section 1021, which states in pertinent part that 'Except as attorney's fees are specifically provided for by statute, the measure and mode of compensation of attorneys and counselors at law is left to the agreement, express or implied, of the parties. . . .' "

Code of Civil Procedure section 1021.5, enacted in 1977, provides an exception to this American rule. * * *

In *Buckhannon*, the high court relied on the plain meaning of the word "prevailing" to reject the catalyst theory. Here, the language of Code of Civil Procedure section 1021.5 militates much more strongly against the catalyst theory. The federal statutes simply give trial courts discretion to allow the "prevailing party" attorney fees. Code of Civil Procedure section 1021.5, however, permits an award only to a "successful" (which is synonymous with "prevailing") party in an action "which has resulted in the *enforcement* of an important *right* affecting the public interest. . . ." (Italics added.) The italicized words means that the plaintiffs must have *compelled* the defendant's conduct to protect some "right." (See Black's Law Dict., at p. 549 (defining "enforcement" as "[t]he act or process of compelling compliance with a law, mandate, or command").)

But voluntary action is not compelled action. Without some judicially enforceable order, there is no way to know whether the action was voluntary or compelled. Persons and entities act voluntarily in response to a lawsuit for many reasons, some unrelated to the lawsuit's merits: to avoid the expense of litigation or bad publicity, to foster good public relations, to make an improvement or take other useful action not required by law, perhaps simply to put the litigation behind and move on.

The pressure to yield voluntarily to a lawsuit's demands, even if not legally required, is exacerbated by the circumstance that historically attorney fee awards have not gone in both directions. Although the statutes do not prohibit awards to prevailing defendants, the private attorney general doctrine has generally resulted only in attorney fee awards to the prevailing plaintiffs and not also to the prevailing defendants. Thus, unlike the plaintiffs who can hope to be reimbursed for their attorney fees, the defendants generally cannot expect to receive compensation from the plaintiffs for *their* attorney fees. Those defendants who choose to fight a lawsuit lose even when they win; they must pay their attorneys themselves, which can be very expensive even for the victor. This circumstance places the defendants under great pressure to settle a lawsuit, even if unmeritorious, as soon as possible.

A "judicial *imprimatur*" (*Buckhannon*) on a defendant's change in conduct is thus necessary to show that the plaintiff actually enforced a legal right. Merely eliciting a voluntary action is not enforcing a legal right. But the catalyst theory simply *assumes* the defendant's action was required to right a legal wrong; it *assumes* the defendant had acted unlawfully. This assumption is contrary to the requirements of Code of Civil Procedure section 1021.5.

* * *

The first of [the majority's] requirements—causation—can itself be difficult to establish. The mere coincidence of lawsuit followed by action is not enough under the majority's catalyst theory. "[I]n order to justify a fee award, there must be a causal connection between the lawsuit and the relief obtained." This requirement generally forces an inquiry into the motivation behind the defendant's actions, actions often undertaken by public or corporate officials. * * * In this case, for example, to show causation, plaintiff had to establish that DaimlerChrysler adopted its policy, announced on September 10, 1999, due to this lawsuit and not due to the ongoing efforts of the response team it had already created to address the problem or the investigations of the Santa Cruz District Attorney and California Attorney General that had begun before the lawsuit.

The second of these requirements forces a court that has entered *no* judicial ruling in the plaintiff's favor (otherwise the catalyst theory would not come into play) to make some sort of ruling regarding the merits of the underlying lawsuit. It is not clear to me exactly what the majority means in this regard, or how the trial court is supposed to go about making this determination, but here, after more than a year of litigating the catalyst theory, no court has yet made the ruling the majority demands. Future courts will have to struggle mightily to decide how to determine whether a moot lawsuit had merit when filed. Finally, the majority requires the plaintiffs to establish that they attempted to settle the litigation without a lawsuit * * *. This, too, is a factual question of some complexity, as today's remand for yet more litigation demonstrates.

* * *

I can perceive of few things less useful to society than generating great amounts of attorney fees litigating the catalyst theory. * * *

The private attorney general doctrine inherently contains both a risk and a cost. A line must be drawn somewhere to balance this risk and this cost. I would hold that the statute here draws the necessary line by requiring some kind of a judicial imprimatur before a plaintiff can be considered to be a successful or prevailing party that enforced an important public right.

* * *

C. Plaintiffs Should Not Receive a Multiplier for Litigating Fees on Fees.

The majority also holds that a plaintiff may recover, as attorney fees, not only its fees incurred prosecuting the underlying litigation, with a multiplier, and its fees incurred litigating its entitlement to attorney fees (i.e., fees on fees), but also a *multiplier* on fees on fees. I appreciate the majority's attempt to limit the size of such multipliers. The majority's efforts might help reduce the instances of the tail wagging the dog like here, where the fee for litigating fees on fees is nine times greater than the fee for litigating the underlying lawsuit. But I would hold that a multiplier is never appropriate for litigating fees on fees. The majority disagrees with courts from other states that have considered this question and, tellingly, cites no out-of-state cases supporting its conclusion. If, as the majority claims, the private attorney general doctrine is intended to encourage societally useful lawsuits (like the majority finds this one to be), and not merely to swell attorneys' coffers, permitting fees for work expended on the actual lawsuit plus a multiplier, and permitting attorneys to be paid for their efforts in obtaining those fees plus that multiplier, is a sufficient incentive. A multiplier on fees generated litigating fees, which, as here, can make the overall reward truly absurd compared to the effort regarding the underlying litigation, is not necessary.

* * *

III. CONCLUSION

At a time when Californians are increasingly concerned about extortionate lawsuits against businesses, large and small, and worried that the legal climate in California is so unfriendly to businesses that many are leaving the state and others are deterred from coming here in the first place, today's ruling goes in exactly the wrong direction. And it goes further in that direction than this court has ever gone before. We should interpret and apply California's private attorney general statutes sensibly to encourage responsible litigation while also keeping attorney fee judgments within reasonable bounds and maintaining some semblance of balance between the litigation positions of the plaintiffs and the defendants.

* * *

We Concur: BAXTER and BROWN, J.J.

RIGHT TO TRIAL BY JURY

NATIONWIDE BIWEEKLY ADMINISTRATION, INC. V. SUPERIOR COURT

Supreme Court of California, 2020.
9 Cal.5th 279, 261 Cal.Rptr.3d 713, 462 P.3d 461.

CANTIL-SAKAUYE, CHIEF JUSTICE.

Under two of California's most prominent consumer protection statutes—the unfair competition law (UCL[; Bus. & Prof. Code, § 17200 et seq.]) and the false advertising law (FAL[; Bus. & Prof. Code, § 17500 et seq.])—the Attorney General or local prosecuting authorities may bring a civil action against a business that has allegedly engaged in an unfair, unlawful or deceptive business act or practice or false or misleading advertising and may obtain civil penalties as well as injunctive relief and restitution in such an action. In this case we must decide whether, when the government seeks civil penalties as well an injunction or other equitable remedies under those statutes, the causes of action are to be tried by the court (that is, the trial judge) or, instead, by a jury.

For more than 45 years, a uniform line of California Court of Appeal decisions has held that such causes of action under the UCL and FAL are to be tried by the court rather than by a jury. In the current writ proceeding in this case, however, the Court of Appeal, relying primarily on a decision of the United States Supreme Court applying the civil jury trial provision of the Seventh Amendment to the federal Constitution—Tull v. United States (1987) 481 U.S. 412, 107 S.Ct. 1831, 95 L.Ed.2d 365 (*Tull*)—disagreed with the earlier line of decisions and held that the jury trial provision of the California Constitution should be interpreted to require a jury trial in any action brought under the UCL or FAL in which the government seeks civil penalties in addition to injunctive or other equitable relief. We granted review to resolve the conflict in the Court of Appeal decisions.

* * *

I. FACTS AND PROCEEDINGS BELOW

Petitioners Nationwide Biweekly Administration, Inc., Loan Payment Administration LLC, and Daniel S. Lipsky, the alleged alter ego, principal and sole shareholder of both entities (hereafter collectively referred to as Nationwide) operated a debt payment service in California and other states. Nationwide's program claimed to save debtors money through a process in which the debtor would reduce the amount of interest owed over the life of a loan by having the debtor accelerate the repayment of the debt through an extra monthly payment each year. * * *

In May 2015, the district attorneys of four counties, acting on behalf of the People, filed a civil complaint alleging that Nationwide had violated the UCL and FAL by, among other things, employing business practices that: (1) misleadingly implied that Nationwide was affiliated with the consumer's lender; (2) disguised the amount that Nationwide's services actually cost by failing to fully and adequately disclose the amount, payment schedule, and effect of Nationwide's fees; and (3) overstated the amount of savings a consumer could reasonably expect to receive through Nationwide's services. The complaint also stated that Nationwide's practices have been the subject of numerous consumer complaints and regulatory and law enforcement activities around the country, including an action brought by the federal Consumer Financial Protection Bureau (CFPB).

The complaint's prayer for relief requested that the court (1) issue an injunction prohibiting the business practices found to violate the provisions of the UCL or FAL, (2) order restitution of all money wrongfully acquired by Nationwide from California consumers in violation of the UCL and FAL, and (3) impose civil penalties up to $2,500 for each violation of the UCL or FAL found by the court.

In its amended answer to the complaint, Nationwide demanded a jury trial "on all issues so triable," and the People, in response, filed a motion to strike the jury demand "based on well settled law that this is an equity action requiring a court trial." After briefing, the trial court granted the People's motion to strike the jury demand.

Nationwide then filed a petition for writ of mandate in the Court of Appeal, challenging the trial court's ruling striking the jury demand. * * *

After briefing and argument, the Court of Appeal held that under article I, section 16 of the California Constitution—the jury trial provision—Nationwide has a right to a jury trial in this matter and that the trial court erred in striking the jury demand. (Nationwide Biweekly Administration, Inc. v. Superior Court (2018) 24 Cal.App.5th 438, 234 Cal.Rptr.3d 468 (*Nationwide Biweekly*).) The Court of Appeal, relying heavily on the reasoning of the United States Supreme Court's decision in *Tull*, concluded that because the People are seeking civil penalties as well as injunctive relief and restitution, the "gist" of the People's UCL and FAL causes of action against Nationwide should properly be considered legal rather than equitable, "giving rise to a right to a jury trial" under article I, section 16. At the same time, the Court of Appeal, again following the approach adopted by the United States Supreme Court in *Tull*, held that Nationwide's jury trial right is limited to the issue of liability—that is, to whether Nationwide's business practices violated the provisions of the UCL or FAL—and does not extend to the issue of remedy, including the amount of civil penalties to be imposed.

In the course of its opinion, the Court of Appeal rejected the People's contention that there is " 'an unbroken line of appellate decisions finding no right to a jury trial [under the California Constitution] in UCL or FAL actions . . . where the People sought penalties,' " finding instead that most of the cases relied upon by the People held only that such actions under the UCL and FAL were not criminal in nature and thus that the jury trial provision of the Sixth Amendment of the federal Constitution did not apply to such actions. Although the Court of Appeal acknowledged that at least one appellate court decision clearly held that the gist of an action under the UCL is equitable in nature and that there is no right to a jury trial in such an action under the California constitutional jury trial provision, the Court of Appeal disagreed with that decision's analysis and declined to follow its holding. In addition, the Court of Appeal questioned the validity of another appellate court decision relied upon by the People—DiPirro v. Bondo Corp. (2007) 153 Cal.App.4th 150, 62 Cal.Rptr.3d 722—which held that there is no right to a jury trial in an action seeking injunctive relief, restitution, and civil penalties under the Safe Drinking Water and Toxic Enforcement Act of 1986 (Health & Saf. Code, § 25249.5 et seq.) (commonly known as Prop. 65). The Court of Appeal found that the *DiPirro* decision had not adequately analyzed the United States Supreme Court's reasoning in *Tull*.

Accordingly, the Court of Appeal concluded that a writ of mandate should issue, directing the trial court to vacate its order striking Nationwide's request for jury trial and to grant a jury trial on all issues except the amount of any statutory penalties to be awarded.

We granted the People's petition for review to determine whether there is a right to a jury trial in a UCL or FAL action brought by the government when the government seeks civil penalties as well as injunctive relief and restitution.

II. GENERAL PRINCIPLES REGARDING THE RIGHT TO JURY TRIAL IN CIVIL CASES UNDER CALIFORNIA LAW

As this court recently explained in Shaw v. Superior Court (2017) 2 Cal.5th 983, 216 Cal.Rptr.3d 643, 393 P.3d 98 (*Shaw*): "Under California law, the right to a jury trial in a civil action may be afforded either by statute or by the California Constitution. . . . [¶] As a general matter, the California Legislature has authority to grant the parties in a civil action the right to a jury trial by statute, either when the Legislature establishes a new cause of action or with respect to a cause of action that rests on the common law or a constitutional provision. Given the Legislature's broad general legislative authority under the California Constitution and in the absence of any constitutional prohibition, the Legislature may extend the right to a jury trial to instances in which the state constitutional jury trial provision does not itself mandate a right to a jury trial. [¶] . . . But even when the language and legislative history of a statute indicate that the Legislature intended that a cause of action established by the statute is to be tried by the court rather than a jury, if the California constitutional jury trial provision itself guarantees a right to a jury trial in such a cause of action, the Constitution prevails and jury trial cannot be denied."

III. IS THERE A *STATUTORY* RIGHT TO JURY TRIAL UNDER EITHER THE UCL OR FAL WHEN THE GOVERNMENT SEEKS CIVIL PENALTIES AS WELL AS INJUNCTIVE RELIEF?

Neither the UCL nor the FAL explicitly addresses the question whether the causes of action created by the two statutes—both of which authorize the government to seek civil penalties as well as injunctive relief and restitution—are to be tried by the court or by a jury. * * * [H]owever, the legislative history and legislative purpose of both statutes convincingly establish that the Legislature intended that such causes of action under these statutes would be tried by the court, exercising the traditional flexible discretion and judicial expertise of a court of equity, and not by a jury, including when civil penalties as well as injunctive relief and restitution are sought. [Ed: The Court detailed the legislative history and "scores" of state appellate cases to support this conclusion.]

* * *

IV. UNDER THE CALIFORNIA CONSTITUTION, IS THERE A *CONSTITUTIONAL* RIGHT TO JURY TRIAL IN A UCL OR FAL ACTION WHEN THE PEOPLE SEEK BOTH INJUNCTIVE RELIEF AND CIVIL PENALTIES?

As already noted, in our recent decision in *Shaw*, we explained that "even when the language and legislative history of a statute indicate that the Legislature intended that a cause of action established by the statute is to be tried by the court rather than by a jury, if the California constitutional jury trial provision itself guarantees a right to a jury trial in such a cause of action, the Constitution prevails and a jury trial cannot be denied." Thus, we turn to the question whether, notwithstanding the Legislature's intent that such actions be tried by the court rather than a jury, the jury trial provision of the California Constitution itself guarantees a right to jury trial in an action brought by the People under the UCL or FAL that seeks both injunctive relief and civil penalties.

A. *General California Constitutional Jury Trial Principles*

Article I, section 16 of the California Constitution—the jury trial provision—states in relevant part that "[t]rial by jury is an inviolate right and shall be secured to all. . . ." From the outset of our state's history, our courts have explained that this provision was intended *to preserve* the right to a civil jury as it existed at common law in 1850 when the jury trial provision was first incorporated into the California Constitution. As this court observed in People v. One 1941 Chevrolet Coupe (1951) 37 Cal.2d 283, 231 P.2d 832 (*One 1941 Chevrolet Coupe*): " 'The right to trial by jury guaranteed by the Constitution is the right as it existed at common law at the time the Constitution was adopted. . . . It is the right to trial by jury as it existed at common law which is preserved; and what that right is, is a purely historical question, a fact which is to be ascertained like any other social, political or legal fact. The right is the historical right enjoyed at the time it was guaranteed by the Constitution.' " "Our state Constitution essentially *preserves* the right to a jury in those actions in which there was a right to a jury trial at common law at the time the Constitution was first adopted." (Crouchman v. Superior Court (1988) 45 Cal.3d 1167, 1175, 248 Cal.Rptr. 626, 755 P.2d 1075.)

Pursuant to this historical approach, as a general matter the California Constitution affords a right to a jury trial in common law actions at law that were triable by a jury in 1850, but not in suits in equity that were not triable by a jury in 1850. (C & K Engineering Contractors v. Amber Steel Co. (1978) 23 Cal.3d 1, 8–9, 151 Cal.Rptr. 323, 587 P.2d 1136 (*C & K Engineering*).) In applying this test, our cases have explained that the *form* or *title* of a statutory cause of action is not controlling and that if the *substance* of the cause of action is one that would have been triable by a jury at common law, there is a right to a jury trial even if the statute's designation might suggest that it is an equitable proceeding. " 'In determining whether the action was one triable by a jury at common law, the court is not bound by the form of the action but rather by the nature of the rights involved and the facts of the particular case—the gist of the action. A jury trial must be granted where the gist of the action is legal, where the action is in reality cognizable at law.' " In the *One 1941 Chevrolet Coupe* decision, for example, the court held that the gist of the action at issue in that case—a civil lawsuit by the government seeking forfeiture of an automobile that was allegedly used to illegally transport a prohibited drug—was legal because at common law a similar cause of action for forfeiture of otherwise lawful property that was allegedly used for unlawful purposes was triable by a jury in a court of law. The court ruled that the fact that the statutory provision authorizing the cause of action designated the forfeiture action as a " 'special proceeding' " did not change the legal nature of the action.

The court in *One 1941 Chevrolet Coupe* further explained that the fact that the statute under which the forfeiture proceeding in that case was brought was enacted after the adoption of the California Constitution did not in itself bring the statutory cause of action outside the guarantee of the constitutional jury trial provision. The court observed in this regard: " 'The constitutional right of trial by jury is not to be narrowly construed. It is not limited strictly to those cases in which it existed before the adoption of the Constitution but is extended to cases of like nature as may afterwards arise. It embraces cases of the same class thereafter arising." In explaining why the lawsuit at issue was of " 'like nature' " or " 'the same class' " as the common law action at law, the court stated: " 'At common law, prior to the adoption of the Constitution, a party against whom the forfeiture of property used in violation of law (then a carriage, wagon, horse or mule, now usually an automobile), was sought to be enforced was entitled to a trial by jury. Consequently such right exists now.' "

In a case like *One 1941 Chevrolet Coupe* that involves a single cause of action that at common law in 1850 was triable only by a jury, or conversely a case involving a single cause of action that at common law was triable only by the court, the determination whether the gist of the action in question is legal or equitable is relatively straightforward. When a case involves multiple causes of action or multiple issues, some of which are legal in nature and would have been triable by a jury at common law and some of which are equitable in nature and would have been triable by the court at common law, the analysis is somewhat more complex.

B. Cases Involving Severable Legal and Equitable Issues

When the legal and equitable causes of action or issues presented in a case are severable, past California decisions establish that a party retains the right to a jury trial of the severable legal issues and a court trial of the severable equitable issues. (See, e.g., Connell v. Bowes (1942) 19 Cal.2d 870, 871, 123 P.2d 456 ("It is now established in this state . . . that if a complaint states two complete rights of action, one legal and one equitable, a jury trial may be obtained upon the issues raised by the legal cause") * * *.)

At the same time, California decisions have also repeatedly held that when severable legal and equitable causes of action or issues are present in a single proceeding, the trial court generally has authority to determine in what order the matters should be heard, and if the equitable issue is tried by the court first and if the court's resolution of that issue determines a matter that would otherwise be resolved by a jury with regard to the legal claim or issue, the court's resolution of the matter will generally be binding and may leave nothing for a jury to resolve. * * * And although a trial court retains discretion regarding the order in which the issues should be tried, the governing California cases express a preference that the equitable issues be tried first. This general "equity first preference" is a long standing feature of California law and has always been viewed as fully compatible with the right to jury trial embodied in the California Constitution.

C. Cases Involving Nonseverable Legal and Equitable Issues

Unlike proceedings in which multiple legal and equitable causes or issues are severable, when a cause of action involves legal and equitable aspects that are not severable California decisions have relied upon "the gist of the action" standard in determining whether the action should be considered legal or equitable for purposes of the constitutional jury trial issue. (See, e.g., *C & K Engineering* (in action seeking damages for breach of contract ("in form an action at law") but relying solely on "the equitable doctrine of promissory estoppel," court concluded "[t]he 'gist' of such an action is equitable"); * * * Martin v. County of Los Angeles (1996) 51 Cal.App.4th 688, 695–697, 59 Cal.Rptr.2d 303 (although a tort defendant's claim for "equitable indemnity" seeking recovery of money damages for the proportional fault of a cotortfeasor involved application of equitable principles, court concluded the gist of the claim was legal because ascertaining the relative fault of cotortfeasors for equitable indemnity "involves determinations of rights and liabilities traditionally arising in common law suits for negligence").) In our decision in *C & K Engineering*, we noted that "[a]lthough we have said that 'the legal or equitable nature of a cause of action ordinarily is determined by the mode of relief to be afforded . . .,' the prayer for relief in a particular case is not conclusive" and " '[t]he fact that damages is one of a full range of possible remedies does not guarantee . . . the right to a jury.' "

* * *

D. Application of Constitutional Principles to UCL and FAL Actions

As we shall explain, in light of the particular nature of the civil causes of action authorized by the UCL and FAL, we conclude that the gist of a civil action under the UCL and FAL is equitable rather than legal in nature. Such causes of action are equitable either when brought by a private party seeking only an injunction, restitution, or other equitable relief or when brought by the Attorney General, a district attorney, or other governmental official seeking not only injunctive relief and restitution but also civil penalties. Accordingly, we conclude that there is no right to a jury trial in such actions under the California Constitution.

To begin with, the statutory causes of action established by the UCL and FAL are clearly not of like nature or of the same class as any common law right of action. As the leading treatise on California's consumer protection statutes explains, under the common law only a business adversely affected by trademark or trade name infringement by a business competitor could file an action for unfair competition against the competitor and such an action could be brought only as a suit in equity. (See Cal. Practice Guide: Stern, Bus. & Prof. Code § 17200 Practice, § 2:1, p. 2–1.) "At common law, deceived consumers had no claim for unfair competition. This made little sense, since ultimately it is the consumer who is harmed by a business that passes off goods or services as genuine, or as those of another. . . . No matter; consumers were left without a claim or remedy. This was the era of *caveat emptor* (that is, let the buyer beware)."

The UCL and FAL were enacted for the specific purpose of creating new rights and remedies that were not available at common law. * * * The statutes explicitly authorize government officials and injured private individuals to obtain injunctive relief to prevent a business from continuing to use the practice to the detriment of other consumers and to obtain restitution and other clearly equitable relief. Such causes of action for unfair competition that authorize injunctive relief against unfair or deceptive business practices had no close or analogous counterpart at common law.

Furthermore, when the Legislature adopted the civil penalty provisions of the UCL and FAL in 1972 and 1965 respectively, permitting government officials, and government officials alone, to seek civil penalties along with injunctive or other equitable relief in the civil actions such officials bring under the UCL and FAL, the causes of action under the UCL and FAL continued to constitute causes of action that were not of like nature or of the same class as any common law action. Prior to 1850, early English law embodied numerous statutes imposing civil penalties for a variety of specifically delineated impermissible business practices—like using false weights and measures in the sale of a product or failing to pay the appropriate excise taxes due—that were enforced by the government through a civil action in the Court of Exchequer in which a jury was available. We are unaware, however, of any early English statute that defined the business conduct proscribed by the statute in the type of broad and sweeping language adopted in the UCL and FAL, which was specifically intended to reach novel but offensive business practices that were not encompassed by more specific statutory prohibitions. Furthermore, the early English statutes generally set forth a specific amount of civil penalty that was to be imposed for each violation; again, we are aware of no such statute that required the amount of the civil penalty to be determined by a consideration of multiple factors comparable to those set out in the relevant provisions of the UCL and FAL. Finally, and perhaps most significantly, unlike the UCL and FAL, none of the early English statutes authorized a prosecuting official to seek and obtain, *in the same action*, a civil penalty and an injunction that would explicitly restrain the business from committing the prohibited conduct in the future.

Accordingly, in the absence of a comparable common law counterpart, in deciding whether there is a right to a jury trial under the California Constitution, we must look to the statutory scheme as a whole to determine whether the gist of a cause of action under the UCL or the FAL seeking both injunctive relief and civil penalties is legal or equitable.

* * *

All parties before us agree that the legal and equitable aspects of the UCL and FAL actions at issue are nonseverable and that the gist of the action standard applies. The legal and equitable aspects of these actions are nonseverable not only because * * * the determination whether a defendant's alleged conduct constitutes a violation of the statute provides the basis for all of the relief authorized by the statutes, but also because the amount of civil penalties that would be appropriate may well depend on the equitable remedies, including restitution, that are or are not imposed.

With respect to the application of the gist of the action standard, our independent analysis of the UCL and FAL causes of action as a whole convinces us that the gist of the civil causes of action authorized by the UCL and FAL must properly be considered equitable, rather than legal, in nature.

To begin with, the bulk of the remedies provided for in the statutes—injunctive relief, restitution, and other clearly equitable remedies such as the appointment of a receiver—are clearly equitable in nature. As the legislative history of both the UCL and FAL make clear, the primary objective of both statutes is preventive, authorizing the exercise of broad equitable authority to protect consumers from unfair or deceptive business practices and advertising.

Second, although the statutes also authorize in actions brought by the Attorney General, a district attorney, or other government officials (but not private parties), the imposition of civil penalties—a type of remedy that in some contexts is properly considered legal in nature—the UCL and FAL statutes specify that in assessing the amount of the civil penalty to be imposed under these statutes, the court is afforded broad discretion to consider a nonexclusive list of factors that include the relative seriousness of the defendant's conduct and the potential deterrent effect of such penalties, the type of qualitative evaluation and weighing of a variety of factors that is typically undertaken by a court and not a jury. Notably, the civil penalties that may be awarded under the UCL and FAL, unlike the classic legal remedy of damages, are noncompensatory in nature; they require no showing of actual harm to consumers and are not based on the amount of losses incurred by the targets of unfair practices or misleading advertising. * * *

Finally, as discussed above, the expansive and broadly worded substantive standards that are to be applied in determining whether a challenged business practice or advertising is properly considered violative of the UCL or FAL call for the exercise of the flexibility and judicial expertise and experience that was traditionally applied by a court of equity. Particularly in light of the equitable nature of the substantive standards that apply in UCL and FAL actions—both in actions brought by private parties and by government officials—we conclude that the gist of the civil causes of action authorized by the UCL and FAL must properly be considered equitable in nature. Accordingly, we conclude that under the California Constitution, there is no right to a jury trial in a cause of action under the UCL and FAL, including when the action is brought by a government official and seeks both injunctive relief and civil penalties.

* * *

In sum, we conclude that there is no right to a jury trial under the California Constitution in a cause of action under the UCL or FAL, including an action in which civil penalties as well as an injunction or other equitable relief are sought. Because our conclusion rests in significant part on the fact that the substantive standards embodied in the UCL and FAL contemplate the exercise of the type of equitable discretion and judgment traditionally applied by a court of equity, we have no occasion in this case to decide how the California constitutional jury trial provision applies to other statutory causes of action that authorize both injunctive relief and civil penalties.

E. Inapplicability of Tull

As already noted, in reaching a contrary conclusion, the Court of Appeal relied heavily upon the United States Supreme Court's decision in *Tull*. As we explain, for a variety of reasons we conclude that the Court of Appeal's reliance upon *Tull* was unwarranted.

Tull involved a civil action filed by the federal government against a real estate developer, alleging that the developer had dumped fill on wetlands without a permit in violation of the federal Clean Water Act. (33 U.S.C. § 1251 et seq.) As authorized by that act, the government sought both injunctive relief and civil penalties. The court in *Tull* observed, however, that at the time the complaint in that case was filed the developer had sold most of the properties in question to a third party, and "[i]njunctive relief was therefore impractical except with regard to a small portion of the land." After denying the developer's demand for a jury trial, the trial court conducted a 15-day bench trial, concluded that the property on which the defendant had admittedly dumped fill constituted "wetlands" within the meaning of the federal statute, and ultimately imposed injunctive relief and civil penalties on defendant.

On appeal, the United States Supreme Court reversed, concluding that the developer was entitled to a jury trial under the Seventh Amendment to the federal Constitution. The court in *Tull* acknowledged that a proceeding under the Clean Water Act seeking both injunctive relief and civil penalties is analogous to two different common law causes of action—an action to abate a nuisance in which there was no right to a jury trial and an action in debt to impose a civil penalty in which there was a right to a jury trial. However, the court concluded that it need not decide which common law action was the closer historical analog, because prior Supreme Court precedent established that "characterizing the relief sought is '[m]ore important' than finding a precisely analogous common-law cause of action in determining whether the Seventh Amendment guarantees a jury trial."

Thereafter, in discussing the relief sought in the action, the court in *Tull* focused primarily on the civil penalties that had been sought and obtained in the action, emphasizing that "[a] civil penalty was a type of remedy at common law that could only be enforced in courts of law" in which a jury trial was available. Although the government had also sought and obtained injunctive relief in the action, the *Tull* court observed that under the applicable federal statute the government was free to seek an equitable remedy independent of legal relief and further explained that prior federal decisions established that "if a 'legal claim is joined with an equitable claim, the right to jury trial on the legal claim, including all issues common to both claims, remains intact. The right cannot be abridged by characterizing the legal claim as "incidental" to the equitable relief sought' " (See also, e.g., Ross v. Bernhard (1970) 396 U.S. 531, 537–538, 90 S.Ct. 733, 24 L.Ed.2d 729 ("where equitable and legal claims are joined in the same action, there is a right to jury trial on the legal claims which must not be infringed either by trying the legal issues as incidental to the equitable ones or by a court trial of a common issue existing between the claims"); Dairy Queen v. Wood (1962) 369 U.S. 469, 473, 82 S.Ct. 894, 8 L.Ed.2d 44 (requiring "that any legal issues for which a trial by jury is timely and properly demanded be submitted to a jury" "whether the trial judge chooses to characterize the legal issues presented as 'incidental' to equitable issues or not"); Beacon Theatres v. Westover (1959) 359 U.S. 500, 510–511, 79 S.Ct. 948, 3 L.Ed.2d 988 ("only under the most imperative circumstances . . . can the right to a jury trial of legal issues be lost through prior determination of equitable claims").) Thus, because prior federal decisions had interpreted the Seventh Amendment generally to require a jury trial whenever a legal claim is joined with an equitable claim, the court in *Tull* held that, for Seventh Amendment purposes, the fact that the government sought civil penalties in the action before it was itself sufficient to conclude that the developer had "a constitutional right to a jury trial to determine his liability on the legal claims."

For a number of reasons, we conclude that the Court of Appeal erred in relying upon the *Tull* decision. First and most fundamentally, the decision in *Tull* rested exclusively on the United States Supreme Court's interpretation of the right to civil jury trial embodied in the Seventh Amendment to the United States Constitution. The federal civil jury trial provision of the Seventh Amendment applies only to civil trials in *federal court*; federal decisions explicitly hold that the civil jury trial provision of the Seventh Amendment does not apply to *state court proceedings*. Instead, the right to jury trial in state court proceedings is governed by the provisions and judicial interpretation of each state's own constitutional jury trial provision.

In California, the constitutional right to a civil jury trial under the California Constitution is entirely independent of the federal constitutional civil jury trial right under the Seventh Amendment, and past California cases have not hesitated to decline to follow the federal interpretation of the Seventh Amendment when the federal interpretation has been found inconsistent with a proper reading of the California provision. (See, e.g., Jehl v. Southern Pacific Co. (1967) 66 Cal.2d 821, 835 & fn. 17, 59 Cal.Rptr. 276, 427 P.2d 988; Rankin v. Frebank Co. (1975) 47 Cal.App.3d 75, 91–92, 121 Cal.Rptr. 348.) The *Tull* decision rested on several points in which the federal interpretation of the Seventh Amendment departs from California's interpretation of the California jury trial provision.

Initially, unlike actions under the UCL and FAL in which the equitable (injunctive relief) and legal (criminal penalties) nature of the available remedies are unquestionably *nonseverable* features of a single cause of action, in *Tull* the court held that under the applicable Clean Water Act, the equitable (injunctive relief) and legal (criminal penalties) remedies were *severable.* * * * And the *Tull* court went on to rely on the severable nature of the claims at issue in finding that the issue of liability was to be tried by a jury rather than by the court, because federal decisions dictate that in cases involving severable legal and equitable issues, the legal issues should be tried prior to the equitable issues. * * * By contrast, as noted above, the governing California decisions hold that when the legal and equitable aspects are severable, there is a preference for trying the equitable issues first and that if common facts are resolved in a manner that obviates the need to try the legal issue, there is no right under the California Constitution to have the legal issues submitted to the jury. Thus, the conclusion reached in *Tull* under the Seventh Amendment is not necessarily the same result as would follow under California law.

Moreover, the *Tull* court's analysis of the jury trial question also demonstrates a second difference between the interpretation and application of the federal and state constitutional civil jury trial provisions. As we have explained, in cases in which a cause of action contains nonseverable legal and equitable aspects, California cases undertake a qualitative, holistic analysis of the action in its entirety to determine whether the gist of the action is legal or equitable, that is, whether the legal or equitable aspects predominate. In *Tull,* by contrast, the court, in determining that under the Seventh Amendment there is a right to a jury trial for the statutory cause of action for civil penalties at issue in that case, relied primarily on its determination that the civil penalties in question were intended, at least in part, to be punitive in nature, which in the court's view was apparently sufficient to render the action legal in nature and require a jury trial. In reaching this conclusion, however, the *Tull* court did not take into account a number of nonseverable equitable aspects of the action for civil penalties at issue there. Thus, the court does not appear to have thought it at all significant that the civil penalties were also intended in part to further the equitable purpose of restitution. Moreover, and significantly, the court did not consider that, unlike actions for civil penalties at common law that typically provided a specific and fixed penalty for each violation, the civil penalties authorized by the statutory cause of action at issue in that case were to be determined by the equitable weighing and balancing of a number of factors similar to the list of factors set forth in the UCL and FAL—a determination that the *Tull* court itself recognized was more appropriate for a court than a jury. Thus, rather than determining whether the statutory cause of action for civil penalties at issue should be characterized as legal or equitable by considering *all* of the legal and equitable aspects of that cause of action holistically, the *Tull* court somewhat artificially severed the cause of action for civil penalties into two parts—one that the court held is to be decided by a jury and one that is to be decided by the court—creating a novel type of cause of action that, as Justice Scalia's dissent in *Tull* pointed out, was unknown at common law. As *Tull* demonstrates, in applying the Seventh Amendment federal courts generally have not applied the type of holistic gist of the action standard that California decisions have utilized in applying California's constitutional jury trial provision, and thus the *Tull* decision is distinguishable from the case before us on this ground as well.

Finally, in addition to the differences attributable to disparate interpretations of the federal and state constitutional civil jury trial provisions, the decision in *Tull* is distinguishable from the present case in yet another significant respect. Unlike the relevant broadly worded and expansive substantive standards embodied in the UCL and FAL—which, as we have explained, call for the exercise of the type of equitable discretion and judgment traditionally employed by a court of equity—under the statute at issue in *Tull*, the question of liability turned simply on the question whether the defendant had, without a permit, deposited fill into an area constituting "wetlands" within the meaning of the Clean Water Act. The parties in *Tull* apparently did not dispute that the substantive statutory standard of liability at issue in that case involved the type of factual determination that in other contexts has traditionally been made by juries. Accordingly, the court in *Tull* had no occasion to decide whether a jury trial is constitutionally required under the Seventh Amendment *whenever* a statute permits the recovery of civil penalties, even when the applicable substantive statutory standard clearly contemplates the exercise of equitable judicial discretion and judgment. We note in this regard that when the court in *Tull* addressed a substantive standard as to which the exercise of such equitable discretion was contemplated—that is, in assessing the *amount* of civil penalties to be imposed through "highly discretionary calculations that take into account multiple factors . . .

traditionally performed by judges"—the *Tull* court found that the trial court could properly resolve that matter without violating the federal constitutional civil jury trial right.

Because of the significant differences in the manner in which the federal and California constitutional civil jury trial provisions have been interpreted and applied and because the court in *Tull* did not address a statutory standard, like those involved in the UCL and FAL, which contemplates the exercise of the type of equitable discretion typically undertaken by a court of equity, we conclude that the Court of Appeal's reliance upon the *Tull* decision was misplaced.

V. CONCLUSION

For the reasons set forth above, we conclude that in causes of action under the UCL or FAL seeking injunctive relief and civil penalties, the gist of the actions is equitable, and there is no right to a jury trial in such actions under California law either as a statutory or constitutional matter. Given the specific attributes of the UCL and FAL discussed above, we have no occasion to determine whether there is a right to a jury trial in other settings in which the government seeks injunctive relief and civil penalties under other statutes authorizing those remedies.

The judgment of the Court of Appeal, holding that Nationwide has a right to a jury trial under the California Constitution in such actions, is reversed and the matter is remanded to the Court of Appeal for further proceedings consistent with this opinion.

Concurring Opinion by JUSTICE KRUGER.

I concur in the judgment. I agree with the majority that article I, section 16 of the California Constitution does not guarantee a jury trial in this action for equitable relief and civil penalties under the unfair competition law (UCL; Bus. & Prof. Code, § 17200 et seq.) and false advertising law (FAL; Bus. & Prof. Code, § 17500 et seq.). But I arrive at that conclusion by a somewhat different—and narrower—path. [Ed: Justice Kruger agreed that UCL liability could readily be characterized as dependent on equitable considerations, but she disagreed regarding liability under the FAL. In her view, liability under the FAL appeared to rest on factual determinations rather than equitable judgment.]

* * *

But in the end, the equitable facets of this action predominate over the legal ones. The amount of any civil penalties would be determined by the trial court on the basis of equitable principles, allowing the court to all but nullify any jury finding of an FAL violation. What is more, the court could effectively override any jury decision *against* FAL liability by imposing liability for the same conduct under the UCL before the FAL issue is ever tried, then awarding plaintiffs injunctive relief and penalties for that violation. For these reasons, I agree with the majority that the action is predominantly equitable in nature.

We Concur: LIU AND CUÉLLAR, J.J.

WILLIAMS V. SUPERIOR COURT

Supreme Court of California, 1989.
49 Cal.3d 736, 263 Cal.Rptr. 503, 781 P.2d 537.

PANELLI, JUSTICE.

The issue in this case is whether jury selection procedures in Los Angeles County violate a criminal defendant's right to an impartial jury, that is, a jury representative of a cross-section of the community. Specifically, we must decide whether, for purposes of cross-section analysis, "community" is defined as the county, the superior court ("judicial") district, or an area extending 20 miles from the courthouse. As explained hereafter, we conclude that the appropriate definition of community for cross-section analysis is the judicial district.[1]

Edward Williams (defendant) is charged with the first degree murder of Bruce Horton. Defendant is Black; Horton was White. The crime occurred in the West Superior Court District of Los Angeles County (West District); trial was scheduled for that district's superior court, located in Santa Monica.[2]

Defendant moved to quash the venire on the ground that Black persons on jury panels in the West District were unconstitutionally underrepresentative of the Black population of Los Angeles County. Defendant sought transfer of the case to either the Central District in downtown Los Angeles or the South Central District in Compton, where a greater number of Blacks could reasonably be expected to appear in the venire.

At the hearing on the motions, defendant called Raymond Arce, Director of Juror Services for Los Angeles County, who testified that since 1981 the county has used its list of registered voters and the Department of Motor Vehicles list of licensed drivers to compile a master list of eligible jurors for both the superior and municipal courts. Arce testified that Black persons presumptively eligible to serve as jurors comprise 11.4 percent of the total county population; in the West District, 5.6 percent of the total

---

1 We note at the outset that this case presents no issue concerning the requirement of a jury of the vicinage. In a companion case filed on this day (Hernandez v. Municipal Court (1989) 49 Cal.3d 713, 263 Cal.Rptr. 513, 781 P.2d 547) we hold that boundaries of the county define the vicinage.

2 Pursuant to the provisions of Government Code sections 69640–69650, Los Angeles County has been divided into 11 superior court or judicial districts.

population is Blacks presumptively eligible to serve as jurors.[3] A survey of jurors in the Santa Monica courthouse for the three-month period preceding defendant's trial indicated that 4.5 percent appearing for jury duty was Black.

Arce also described the Bullseye System, a computer program used by the county for assigning jurors: Although an eligible juror may be assigned to virtually any superior or municipal court in the county, the program assigns the prospective juror to the court nearest the juror's residence. If that court does not require jurors, the juror is assigned to the next nearest courthouse in need of jurors. If that court is located over 20 miles from his residence, the juror is informed that, under Code of Civil Procedure section 203, he has a right to be excused.[4]

Defendant did not argue that the percentage of Blacks on his jury panels was unfair in relation to the percentage of Blacks within the West District or within a 20-mile radius of its courthouse. He argued only that Blacks were underrepresented on the panels in relation to the percentage of Blacks within the entire county.

The trial court denied defendant's motions. The court found the county's jury selection procedure to be "fair and reasonable" and further stated:

> "It appears . . . that Los Angeles County is making a reasonable and good faith effort to meet the constitutional requirements here.
>
> "In any event, there is no showing of any significant underrepresentation of a cognizable group based on the figures presented here."

Defendant then filed a petition for writ of prohibition and/or mandate in the Court of Appeal. The Court of Appeal denied the petition and agreed with the trial court's finding that defendant had not made the required prima facie showing of systematic underrepresentation. Significantly, however, the Court of Appeal held that a criminal defendant in Los Angeles County, in order to establish systematic underrepresentation of a distinctive group, must show that representation of the group is not fair and reasonable in relation to the percentage of such persons residing within a 20-mile radius of that particular courthouse.

REPRESENTATIVE JURY—CROSS-SECTION OF COMMUNITY

In California, the right to trial by a jury drawn from a representative cross-section of the community is guaranteed equally and independently by the Sixth Amendment to the federal Constitution (Taylor v. Louisiana

---

[3] Arce estimated that Blacks comprise over 11.4 percent of the Central District jurors and approximately 25 percent of the South Central District jurors.

[4] After we granted review in this case, the Legislature repealed former section 203. (Stats.1988, ch. 1245, § 1.)

(1975) 419 U.S. 522, 530, 95 S.Ct. 692, 697, 42 L.Ed.2d 690) and by article I, section 16 of the California Constitution. (People v. Wheeler (1978) 22 Cal.3d 258, 272, 148 Cal.Rptr. 890, 583 P.2d 748.)

* * *

It is well settled that no litigant has the right to a jury that mirrors the demographic composition of the population, or necessarily includes members of his own group, or indeed is composed of any particular individuals. What the representative cross-section requirement does mean, however, is that a litigant "is constitutionally entitled to a petit jury that is as near an approximation of the ideal cross-section of the community as the process of random draw permits."[5]

Defendant argues that his right to a jury panel drawn from a representative cross-section of the community is abridged by the jury selection procedures in Los Angeles County. Defendant cites the testimony of Raymond Arce. Blacks comprise 11.4 percent of the countywide, juror-eligible population. Defendant did not argue that the jurors called in his case were not representative of the juror-eligible Black population of the West District, which Arce testified averaged 5.6 percent in the three months preceding defendant's trial. In fact, Blacks comprised 8.6 percent of the jurors appearing for defendant's case.

Under Duren v. Missouri, [439 U.S. 357, 99 S.Ct. 664, 58 L.Ed.2d 579 (1979),] in order to establish a prima facie violation of the fair cross-section requirement, "the defendant must show (1) that the group alleged to be excluded is a 'distinctive' group in the community; (2) that the representation of this group in venires from which juries are selected is not fair and reasonable in relation to the number of such persons in the community; and (3) that this underrepresentation is due to systematic exclusion of the group in the jury-selection process."

We are not concerned with the first prong of the *Duren* test for the People concede that Blacks are a cognizable, distinctive group for purposes of fair cross-section analysis.

To meet the second prong of the *Duren* test, defendant must show that Blacks were underrepresented in jury venires in relation to the number of such persons in the community. Before this court can evaluate the statistical showing of underrepresentation made by defendant, however, we must first determine what community the jury venire must fairly represent. It is here that we confront the central issue of this case.

---

[5] The fair cross-section principles set forth in *Wheeler* were codified by the Legislature in 1980. As amended in 1988, section 197, subdivision (a), requires in part that jurors be selected "at random, from a source or sources inclusive of a representative cross section of the population of the area served by the court." Section 204 (former section 197.1) prohibits exclusion from jury service "by reason of occupation, race, color, religion, sex, national origin, or economic status, or for any other reason."

Defendant argues that community is defined as the entire county. The People argue that community means the judicial district. As noted, the Court of Appeal rejected both definitions, preferring instead a provocative compromise that defines community as that area within a 20-mile radius of the courthouse.[6] Inasmuch as the basis for the decision of the Court of Appeal has been eliminated, no purpose is served by an extended discussion of the propriety of using the 20-mile-radius community in determining the population for cross-section analysis.[7] We turn, instead, to the arguments of the People and defendant who, respectively, propose the judicial district and county. We conclude that the judicial district best serves the constitutional and statutory considerations at issue in the determination of the appropriate community for cross-section analysis as well as the practical problems posed by a far-flung megapolis—Los Angeles County.

County as Community.[8]

Defendant contends that the relevant community is the county. In O'Hare v. Superior Court (1987) 43 Cal.3d 86, 233 Cal.Rptr. 332, 729 P.2d 766, we addressed the issue whether the Sixth Amendment entitled a defendant to a venire drawn from, and representative of, the entire county. We squarely held that it does not.

O'Hare was to be tried on a felony charge in the North County Branch of the San Diego Superior Court, which drew its jurors from an area limited by the boundaries of the North County Municipal Court Judicial District. O'Hare complained that the limited venire contained a significantly lower percentage of jury-eligible Blacks than did the county as a whole.

We held that "the constitutional cross-section requirement is a procedural and not a substantive requirement" and found no constitutional limitation on the government's power to define the "community" against

---

6 The Court of Appeal found support for its definition of community in the provisions of the Code of Civil Procedure relating to jurors (§ 190 et seq.), especially section 203 which provided that persons listed for service as trial jurors "shall be fairly representative of the population of the area served by the court, and shall be selected upon a random basis. . . . In counties of more than one court location, the rules shall reasonably minimize the distance traveled by jurors. In addition, in the County of Los Angeles no juror shall be required to serve at a distance greater than 20 miles from his or her residence." Section 203 has been repealed in the Trial Jury Selection and Management Act, Stats.1988, ch. 1245.

7 Suffice it to say that the appellate court found evidence of legislative intent to make particular provisions for the jury draw in Los Angeles County in the provision that ". . . no juror shall be required to serve at a distance greater than 20 miles from his or her residence." Given the plain language of the statute, however, we may infer that the 20-mile-radius provision was simply intended to facilitate jury convenience by giving jurors an elective exemption if they resided outside the 20-mile radius.

8 The definition of community (no matter what it is) establishes a standard of comparison, not a method of selection. Jurors, selected from a countywide draw, will serve at various courthouse locations and with varying frequencies depending on where they reside in the county, no matter what method is used to determine the representativeness of the resulting jury venires. Cross-section analysis does not address where the jurors are sent to serve, but rather examines the relevant community for determination of its composition.

which the demographics of the venire is measured. * * * [W]e concluded in *O'Hare* that the Sixth Amendment imposes no limitation on the legislative definition of community for the cross-section requirement: "What the Sixth Amendment does guarantee to every defendant, regardless of his personal characteristics, is a jury drawn from a venire from which no member of the local community was arbitrarily or unnecessarily excluded."

Albeit in another context, in *People v. Harris,* Justice Mosk noted the balkanized nature of Los Angeles County and the "significant deceptiveness" of the use of countywide statistical data. "Our code uses the term 'area served by the court' (CCP § 197), not the county in which the court is situated. It takes only a cursory knowledge of the demography of Southern California to realize that Long Beach courts serve an area completely distinct in population characteristics from the totality of Los Angeles County. . . . Figures for the entire County of Los Angeles are not only irrelevant but in this instance significantly deceptive."

Judicial District as Community.

Having concluded that there is no constitutional limitation on the Legislature to create a relevant community for cross-section purposes, we must determine whether in creating superior court (or "judicial") districts in Los Angeles County, the Legislature intended to define community in that county as the judicial district where the case is tried.

* * *

While the Legislature did not explicitly designate the superior court districts as communities for the purpose of assessing the representativeness of jury panels, the considerations that prompted creation of the districts in the first place—the practical realities of the county's unique demographics, its geographical expanse, and the need for judicial efficiency—convince us that the Legislature intended that the districts serve as the community for determination of jury impartiality. In a sense, the districts were to be microcosms of an entity—the Los Angeles Superior Court—that had become unmanageable and inefficient as a single unit.

* * *

Having defined the community which the jury venires must fairly represent, we return to the second prong of the *Duren* test which the defendant must satisfy to establish a prima facie violation of the fair cross-section requirement. The defendant must show that the representation of the excluded group in venires from which juries are selected is not "fair and reasonable in relation to the number of such persons in the community."

Defendant challenged the jury venires as underrepresentative of the Black population of Los Angeles County. At no time did he argue that the percentage of Blacks on the jury panels in the West District was unfair in relation to the percentage of Blacks in the jury eligible population of the West District. Accordingly, defendant has failed to show that the representation of Blacks in venires from which juries are selected is not fair and reasonable in relation to the number of such persons in the community.

Finally, absent a finding of underrepresentation, we do not reach the third prong of *Duren,* i.e., whether the "underrepresentation is due to systematic exclusion of the group in the jury selection process."

CONCLUSION

The judgment of the Court of Appeal is affirmed. The Court of Appeal is directed to remand the cause to the West Superior Court District for trial.

KAUFMAN, JUSTICE, concurring.

I concur fully in the decision and opinion of the majority authored by Justice Panelli. I write separately to respond to the concurring and dissenting opinion penned by Justice Broussard (hereafter the dissent). Justice Broussard, apparently frustrated at his inability to persuade a majority to his view, implies that a majority of the members of this court are insensitive to problems of racial and ethnic discrimination and in a series of decisions have embarked upon an agenda of diminishing the constitutional rights of minority residents of this state. His frustration may be understandable, but his attack on the motives and integrity of the other members of the court is unjustified, improvident and wholly unworthy of him.

Today's decisions in this case and Hernandez v. Municipal Court (1989) 49 Cal.3d 713, 263 Cal.Rptr. 513, 781 P.2d 547 and the other decisions criticized by the dissent are not and were not based on racial considerations at all, much less racial discrimination. They represent reasoned and reasonable resolutions of procedural problems, adopting rules that will afford trial courts the discretion they require to operate the trial court system and conduct criminal trials in a fair yet expeditious manner. Several of the decisions, basically unrelated, reject arguments based on an unwarranted distrust of the trial judges and public prosecutors of our state that this court should adopt ever more impossibly complex standards of review for appellate courts and procedural rules that would continue to ensnare our criminal courts, trial and appellate, in protracted, resource-consuming proceedings having little to do with guilt or innocence or ultimate justice in the particular case. We should have learned from the experience of the past that justice is not achieved by rules and procedures which sound perfect in theory but are unworkable in practice.

In the specific case of jury selection procedures, this means that while the defendant must be afforded a reasonable opportunity to demonstrate invidious or systematic exclusion of members of a cognizable group, a showing of some underrepresentation at a given time is not enough. Neither the venire nor the jury need mirror the racial, ethnic, or religious composition of the community. Once the jury has been fairly selected the law assumes that its members, whether Black, White, Hispanic, Catholic, Jew, rich or poor, are equally capable of representing the entire community. The right to trial by a jury of one's peers does not mean and has never meant that a Black defendant is entitled to be tried by Blacks or a White defendant by Whites. Nor does the right to trial within the vicinage mean that a defendant who commits a crime in Watts has the right to be tried in Watts or that a crime committed in Beverly Hills must be tried in Beverly Hills.

No member of this court, and no thoughtful person in this country today, can be ignorant of the powerful and corrosive force of racism. Nor is there any disagreement on the goal we all seek: a society in which no advantage or disadvantage results from an individual's race, religion, sex, or ethnic background. There is, however, an emotionally-charged debate raging in this country regarding the best means to reach this common goal. According to some, we should eliminate all forms of racial criteria and use only race-neutral procedures. According to others, past wrongs can be redressed and subtle forms of discrimination rooted out only by the use of racial preferences and a heightened race consciousness, hopefully, benign.

It is my personal view that heightened race consciousness and utilization of criteria preferring one race over another, no matter how well intentioned, will in the long run be counterproductive to the common goal and will tend to perpetuate racial bias and hostility. But as justices it is not our function in judicial decisions to take sides in this acrimonious debate, although from time to time we are presented with cases which impinge on some aspect of it. References to the supposed purposes, beliefs, convictions or intentions of other justices, however, are no more than ad hominem attacks and should play no part in the opinions of any member of the judiciary. Refraining from such tactics has been a cherished tradition of this court; it pains me deeply that Justice Broussard now appears to cast this tradition aside.

This is not a matter merely of etiquette or decorum. Forceful and reasoned dissents are, of course, valuable tools in the shaping of the law. But attacks on the purposes and assumed intent of one's colleagues destroy the collegiality essential to the proper functioning of an appellate court and undermine the public respect and confidence so essential to the rule of law. It would be well remembered that each of us, and indeed every judge of this state, took an oath to uphold the Constitutions of the United States and the State of California and that each of us is as equally devoted to fulfilling that oath as any other.

BROUSSARD, JUSTICE, concurring and dissenting.

* * *

II.

This is the latest of a series of recent decisions in which this court has discussed the right to a representative jury, and thus a suitable time to review those decisions as a whole.

The first to be filed was People v. Johnson (1989) 47 Cal.3d 1194, 255 Cal.Rptr. 569, 767 P.2d 1047, which concerned the prosecution's use of peremptory challenges to remove minority members from the jury. Prosecutors will generally attempt to justify such challenges by pointing to individual characteristics of the challenged jurors. Our prior decisions recognized that the most effective way to test the truth of those statements is to see if the prosecutor also challenged nonminority jurors with similar individual characteristics. (People v. Trevino (1985) 39 Cal.3d 667, 217 Cal.Rptr. 652, 704 P.2d 719.) *Johnson,* however, overruled *Trevino,* depriving the appellate courts of the most effective way to review a trial judge's decision upholding the challenges.

Johnson went on to state in dictum that the poor do not constitute a cognizable class, which in context means that the prosecution may systematically exclude poor persons from a jury. That conclusion seems to be contrary to the United States Supreme Court decision in Thiel v. Southern Pacific Co. (1946) 328 U.S. 217, 66 S.Ct. 984, 90 L.Ed. 1181, which held that the state could not systematically exclude economic groups from jury service. Then, in an astonishing footnote, *Johnson* suggests that although Blacks and Hispanics cannot be excluded from juries, Asians and Jews can. If a prosecutor wants a 17th century jury of Christian freeholders, the Constitution, if interpreted as suggested in *Johnson,* is no barrier.

The next case, People v. Morales (1989) 48 Cal.3d 527, 257 Cal.Rptr. 64, 770 P.2d 244, concerned exclusion of minorities from the jury venire. The majority held that a statistical sample of 3,600 jurors was too small to prove systematic exclusion, even though statistical experts testified without dispute that the sample was sufficient to prove the point with a risk of error of only 1 in 1,000. *Morales* further stated that a defendant could not show a constitutional violation by proving that a facially neutral practice had the effect of excluding a cognizable class. What this means is that the state cannot expressly exclude Blacks, but it can exclude all persons of characteristic "x" (low income, for example), even if "x" so closely correlates with race that the practice results in disproportionate exclusion of Blacks.

People v. Bell (1989) 49 Cal.3d 502, 262 Cal.Rptr. 1, 778 P.2d 129 holds a showing of substantial and continuous underrepresentation of Blacks from a county's juries is insufficient even to put the county to the burden of explaining the underrepresentation. Instead, a defendant must now point to a constitutionally impermissible aspect of the county's jury selection procedure and show that this is the cause of the racial disproportionality. Such a specific showing is beyond the resources of most, if not all, defendants. Moreover, the holding itself assumes that the county, confronted with a showing that something in its method of selecting jurors is having the effect of excluding a cognizable group, has no duty to investigate and correct the system; it may continue to exclude minorities until someone is able to prove the exact cause of the problem.

Bell goes on to speak favorably of the "absolute disparity" test for determining when a defendant has made a prima facie showing of exclusion, and unfavorably of all other tests. (49 Cal.3d at p. 527, fn. 14, 262 Cal.Rptr. at p. 14, fn. 14, 778 P.2d at p. 142, fn. 14.) The absolute-disparity test measures the disparity as a percentage of total population. (I.e., if Blacks constitute 8 percent of county population, and all are excluded, this is "only" an 8 percent, not a 100 percent, exclusion.) It is the most restrictive of the competing tests, and in practical effect will make it impossible for a defendant to present a prima facie showing on behalf of a minority group which comprises less than 10 percent or so of the community.

Finally, Hernandez v. Municipal Court, supra, 49 Cal.3d page 713, 263 Cal.Rptr. 513, 781 P.2d 547, together with the present case, deny a defendant the right to a jury chosen from or representative of the community where the crime was committed; he receives instead a jury representative of such community as the prosecutor or courts select.

This court has an obligation to consider the practical consequences of its decisions. Yet none of these decisions show any awareness of their impact on the right of a defendant to obtain a jury which is in fact representative of the community and the vicinage of the crime. None show any recognition that racial bias, conscious or unconscious, is or ever was a matter of concern in this state. None show any sensitivity for the minority defendant facing trial before a predominately White jury. To the contrary, the decisions simply seem to assume that judges, jurors, jury commissioners and prosecutors lack any feelings of racial bias. They erect procedural barriers to make it difficult or impossible to prove subtle forms of bias. And they dismantle, step by step, the legal doctrines which have been created over the years to make the right to a representative jury an effective and enforceable right. I have dissented to each of these decisions, and now register my dissent to the ongoing process of undermining the right of the defendant and the community to a truly representative jury.

MOSK, JUSTICE. I agree in principle with the views of JUSTICE BROUSSARD.